Prior to retirement, **Marinos Yeroulanos** (1930–), a lifelong enthusiast for classical Greek literature, pursued a career in business and public life. He served as Permanent Secretary of the National Environment Council and was President of the Benaki Museum in Athens. He was among the first recipients of the prestigious United Nations 'Global 500' Roll of Honour.

Oliver Taplin, FBA (1943–), is Emeritus Professor of Classical Languages and Literature at the University of Oxford and Emeritus Fellow in Classics, Magdalen College, Oxford.

'The Greeks not only had a word for it, but, whatever that "it" may be, they probably had a quotable quote about it as well. And the definitive way to check that out is now, incontestably, Marinos Yeroulanos' *A Dictionary of Classical Greek Quotations*. With more than 7,500 entries drawn from some twelve centuries (*c.*700BC–*c.*500AD) and from hundreds of individuals – and a great many by Anon. – this is a labour of love that has been pursued for many years, and its range is no less than monumental. Rigorous in its scope and punctilious in its scholarship, *A Dictionary of Classical Greek Quotations* brings up to date a form of Greek scholarship taken seriously from ancient times. Anyone dipping into this treasure store can pluck out many gems, both familiar and unfamiliar.'

– Oliver Taplin, FBA, Emeritus Professor of Classical Languages and Literature at the University of Oxford and Emeritus Fellow in Classics, Magdalen College, Oxford (from the Foreword)

'This is a splendid resource for specialist and generalist alike. The kind of work that can be consulted for all sorts of reasons and on all sorts of occasions, this book will give its readers years of edification and pleasure. Use it for your essays, articles, blogs, columns and tweets. Marinos Yeroulanos has poured heart and soul into creating a remarkable *Wunderkammer* that is as useful as it is impressive: to open it is to find a collection of treasures, at once endlessly diverting, captivating and memorable.'

– Phiroze Vasunia, Professor of Greek, University College London

A Dictionary of

CLASSICAL GREEK QUOTATIONS

Edited by
Marinos Yeroulanos

Foreword by
Oliver Taplin

Published in 2016 by
I.B.Tauris & Co. Ltd
London • New York
www.ibtauris.com

ISBN: 978 1 78453 492 9
eISBN: 978 1 78672 049 8
ePDF: 978 1 78673 049 7

A full CIP record for this book is available from the British Library
A full CIP record is available from the Library of Congress

Library of Congress Catalog Card Number: available

Typeset in Palatino Linotype by A. & D. Worthington, Newmarket, Suffolk

CONTENTS

To Aimilia

FOREWORD

When I was a child there was a copy of the *Oxford Dictionary of Quotations* on the shelves. I noticed that after the many pages of index in the familiar alphabet, there were two pages more in Greek font. This may even have contributed to my incipient fascination with the familiarity yet strangeness of that rich language. And I began to realize that the Greeks did not only have a word for it, they had a saying for it.

I imagine that most educated readers, if challenged to produce some Greek quotations, would claim to be at a loss. But, if encouraged, they might come up with some. For a start, there is 'Eureka!', attributed to Archimedes and adopted as the name of a whole city in California. Then what about 'know thyself' (Delphi); or 'my name is Noman' (*Odyssey*); or 'pity and fear' (Aristotle)? And once undammed, the flow might increase: 'a possession for ever' (Thucydides); 'the way up and the way down are the same' (Heraclitus); 'call no man happy before he is dead' (Solon, Sophocles); 'those whom the gods love die young' (Menander); 'mankind is a political animal' (Aristotle); 'bitter-sweet Love' (Sappho) …

Or they might be prompted to recall that they have seen Greek quotations inscribed here and there, such as over the Pump Room door in Bath ('water is best', from Pindar of course!), or on Jim Morrison's grave in Paris, or round the sculpture of Prometheus in front of the Rockefeller Center in New York. Or in books: the epigraph to Eliot's *Wasteland,* or the last page of Hardy's *Tess,* or Bobby Kennedy's speech on the assassination of Martin Luther King.

So the Greeks not only had a word for it, but, whatever that 'it' may be, they probably had a quotable quote about it as well. And the definitive way to check that out is now, incontestably, the Keyword Index in Marinos Yeroulanos' *A Dictionary of Classical Greek Quotations*. With more than 7,500 entries drawn from some twelve centuries (*c.*700BC–*c.*500AD) and from hundreds of individuals – and a great many by Anon. – this is a labour of love that has been pursued for many years, and its range is no less than monumental. In ancient Greek a pithy quotable quote was known as a *gnome* (two syllables); in modern times the financial gnomes may congregate in Zurich, but the true gnomologist still resides in Athens.

On first hearing one might condescendingly suppose that this project sounds like a rather charming hobby. I have come to appreciate, however, that it is much more than that, since it is rigorous in its scope and punctilious in its scholarship. It strikes me that Mr Yeroulanos' labours are allied to those of an ancient Greek paroemiographer.

These were scholars who as part of their professional work assembled books full of proverbs and sayings (some are collected in the *Corpus Paroemiographorum*). Aristotle is said to have made the first collection (what did that man not do?), and by Hellenistic times it was already big business. So *A Dictionary of Classical Greek Quotations* brings up to date a form of Greek scholarship taken seriously from ancient times.

Anyone dipping into this treasure store can pluck out many gems, both familiar and unfamiliar. Or perhaps fishing in a river is a better metaphor, because there is something dynamic rather than static about this allusive and elusive collection; and it hovers simultaneously in time present and time past. As the eminently quotable Heraclitus put it, 'everything is flowing'; and, as he might have said, 'you never fish in the same river twice'.

Oliver Taplin, FBA
Emeritus Professor of Classical Languages and Literature
at the University of Oxford and Emeritus Fellow
in Classics, Magdalen College, Oxford

ACKNOWLEDGEMENTS

From my earliest days at school, three teachers, George Phylaktopoulos at Athens College in Greece and my teachers of English and Greek at Parktown Boys' High School in South Africa, taught us both Greek and English by making us learn by heart select passages and quotations, from Chaucer ('The lyf so short, the craft so long to lerne') to Churchill ('We shall fight on the beaches, we shall fight on the landing grounds').

Since then my eye has tended to fall on quotable passages everywhere and there is many a book where these are highlighted, from Homer's *Iliad* to the *Greek Anthology* (5th century AD), and to Nelson Mandela's 'Greece is the mother of democracy and South Africa its youngest daughter'.

At the very beginning I sought encouragement for the project. Professors Christopher Pelling, Oliver Taplin and Ewen Bowie, as well as Dr Maria Stamatopoulou whom I saw at Oxford University, were very enthusiastic about it. Towards the end, I showed the full contents of the book to Professors Angelos Delivorrias, Pavlos Kalligas, Lila Marangou and Platon Mavromoustakos in Athens and Dr Jim Coulton, also of Oxford. I am very grateful for their most complimentary remarks and their useful suggestions.

As years passed and my collection grew larger, many a friend helped with recommendations and additions. However, some were more involved than others: first and foremost my beloved wife Aimilia to whom this *Dictionary of Classical Greek Quotations* is dedicated, who not only helped in selecting quotations but also insisted that I prepare the book for publication rather than keeping it for my own speeches and writings. I want to thank her for her continued love and invaluable support and, last but not least, for her tolerance throughout these years.

My sincere thanks also go to Claire Bradshaw, my co-editor and dedicated assistant. Her contribution was invaluable, both in proposing quotations and choosing translations. For ten years she was present with endless improvements and, of course, many translations of her own. I cannot thank her enough.

Daphne Economou must have spent hundreds of hours reviewing all our manuscripts, making endless suggestions for improvements and also submitting a great number of translations. I am immensely indebted to her.

Marina Yeroulanou, my daughter, has been our constant advisor, from the very beginning to the end. She has helped with various problems, with matters of presentation, fonts, italics and other matters of form and all problems concerning computers and websites. In the final steps, her meticulous attention to detail and her sharp, experienced eye for errors were of the greatest help.

Sincere thanks are also due to Kleio Sassalou; although a latecomer to the team, she painstakingly revised the whole book, making endless suggestions and corrections.

Many more friends have been supportive in many ways. Lena Levidi cooperated in the final selection of quotations and suggested additions; Maria Constantinidi provided some translations of her own; Professor Stefanos Geroulanos lent us his personal collection of medical quotations; Dan Hogg was most helpful with Thucydides and Dionysius of Halicarnassus; Lula Kypraiou checked all Greek texts against relevant scholarly publications; Penelope Matsouka of Anavasi Editions was highly professional in preparing the geographical maps, with unfailing care in including all the place names mentioned in the book; Stratis Stratigis pointed to some of Nietzsche's references to Greek philosophers; Nikos Geroulanos was always ready with comments on plants, flowers, shrubs and trees; Stavros Vlizos helped with finding items, and their reference numbers, exhibited in Greek museums; Patroclos Stavrou interceded with the Archbishopric of Cyprus which provided not-for-sale books; Lieutenant Colonel I. Shepherd, Secretary to the Trustees, Scottish National War Memorial, provided information on the inscription on the War Memorial; Stephen Whitehead helped us with the conversion of our outdated Greek fonts to Unicode.

Many thanks are due to the library of the British School in Athens and the British Library and their staff, always helpful in retrieving out-of-print books.

A special word of thanks is also due to the Department of Classics of the University of California, Irvine, for the free use of their Thesaurus Linguae Graecae (TLG) from which we have copied Greek texts throughout the book.

A final expression of gratitude goes to Professor Oliver Taplin for his Foreword to this *Dictionary of Classical Greek Quotations*, for his initial encouragement when I first met him at Oxford, for his continued interest since then and for his suggestions and additions.

Sincere thanks are due to David and Alison Worthington for their dedicated work in typesetting, a huge task with so complicated and demanding a book.

Last, but certainly not least, to I.B.Tauris, our editors, and especially Alex Wright, the chief editor and his team, for their continuous cooperation, their endless attention and, of course, their magnificent presentation of the book.

NOTE TO THE READER

The *Dictionary* includes passages written in Greek from the earliest days to the 5th century AD, not only referring to Greece and Greeks, and not necessarily written by Greeks. Some of Homer's most memorable quotations are spoken by Trojans; Herodotus has long passages on Persians, Egyptians and other 'nationals'; Plutarch and others have Roman emperors speaking or are quoting them in Greek; Marcus Aurelius and Julian the Apostate wrote in Greek; the New Testament was written in Greek.[1]

Greek Texts

All Greek texts have been copied directly from the Thesaurus Linguae Graecae (TLG) as produced by the Department of Classics of the University of California, Irvine.[2]

We have, however, counterchecked practically all entries against the Loeb editions.[3] Wherever there were differences in the Greek texts we have made the necessary amendments following the Loeb texts.

Greek texts are in the form they appear in the passage referred to.[4] They have not been amended in order to supply a grammatically more correct rendering of the passage as translated. As an example, in introductory secondary phrases, often omitted, such as 'Democritus said that …', the Greek rendering would have been grammatically different if Democritus had been speaking (or writing) directly.

Words or passages omitted within a quotation are indicated by an ellipsis.

Some auxiliary words such as 'δέ', 'γὰρ' and 'καί' have sometimes not been retained in the Greek passage since they usually refer to a previous section of the overall text. Even if they have been retained for some reason (e.g. poetry) they may not have been translated.

Translations

Our policy for entering and acknowledging translations has been as follows:

a. We have usually given preference to those translations which are truest to the Greek original text or best convey the spirit of the original. Brevity and succinctness have also been a criterion. But we have also included many translations considered to be well established or to have literary merit; after all, some of the finest poets of the English-speaking world have given us lovely renderings of Greek texts.

b. We have generally entered only one translation for each passage chosen. In a few cases only, when two valid translations have a completely different meaning, or when we have found another translation with some particular interest, a second translation has been added.
c. Full acknowledgement of the translator is given under each passage entered either verbatim or with only minor amendments. In the case of translations copied from publications which do not mention the translator, the title of the publication is given.
d. If one or two substantial words have been changed, added or removed, the editors accept the responsibility of such change and no translator is mentioned. In all such instances translations have been cross-checked and are in conformity with Liddell & Scott.[5]
e. It is not the same to translate a full text and to translate a two-line excerpt. In view of this, or in cases where we could not find a valid English translation, a great number of entries have been translated by the editors, or retranslated from French,[6] Italian,[7] German[8] and Modern Greek scholarly editions. Needless to say the editors accept full responsibility for them. New translations made by members of our editorial group carry no indication of a translator.
f. Spelling has been retained as used by the chosen translator, even in older translations. Poems have usually been entered as they appear in the publication we have used, including capital letters at the beginning of each line, exclamation marks etc.
g. An effort has been made in many cases to present verse, as far as possible, line by line. Where we have used existing translations of verse in prose we have similarly tried a line-by-line representation. In such cases no capitals are used at the beginning of each line.
h. Translation dates are given in brackets after the translator's name. Usually this is the earliest date known to us, being the year of the first edition as mentioned in the volume we have used. Only if our copy has the indication 'extensively edited and reviewed' have we given preference to the later date. If the exact date could not be verified we have entered the author's birth and death dates.
i. A List of Translators, including the publication from which translations are taken (thus serving also as a bibliography), can be found on p.679.

How to Use this Book

The sequence of entries is alphabetical by author.

Author names are followed by dates of birth and death (where known) and the attributes of each author. Cross-references are then given to other quotations which are relevant to this author, e.g. for Aeschylus: *see also* Aristophanes 82, 85.

Names of authors, dates and attributes conform to *The Oxford Classical Dictionary*,[9] place names to the *Atlas of Classical History*.[10]

Within each author, works are listed in alphabetical order (except orators, see 'References' below), followed by fragments, followed by testimonies referring to the author from other sources.

In cases where scholars have doubted authorship or proved that a work of literature cannot have been written by the author under which it is traditionally listed, we have indicated this with an asterisk at the end of the title of the work in question. In some cases these appear at the end of the author in question, e.g. Plato.

An acknowledgement of the translator is given under each passage entered. The date of first publication of the translation used is given in brackets; where the translation date is not known, life dates are indicated. Entries with no reference to a translator are translations provided by the editors.

Any comments on the passage are entered in italics, as well as cross-references to quotations pertaining to it (thus *Aristides 5* refers to 'Aristides, quotation 5' in this dictionary).

References

The reference given applies to the first line of each passage, e.g. *Iliad* 19.415. Additional line numbers are not generally given unless the original passage is large enough to warrant them.

Standard forms of reference have been used. For poetical works, title and line number, e.g. *Agamemnon* 406; or title, book and line number, e.g. *Iliad* 3.455. For prose works, title (if necessary), book and section, or title, book, chapter and section; thus Herodotus 1.2 stands for Book 1 Section 2, Thucydides 3.4.5 stands for Book 3 Chapter 4 Section 5.

References to the works of Aristotle are given in terms of Immanuel Bekker's edition (1831), that is, by title, then Bekker page, column, and line number (e.g. *Politics* 1252a.10). References to the works of Plato are given in terms of the edition produced by Henri Estienne (known as Henricus Stephanus) in 1578, that is, by title, then Stephanus page and column (e.g. *Republic* 464d). References to Plutarch's *Moralia* are also by Stephanus page and column.

In the case of all orators,[11] orations are identified by the numbers traditionally assigned to them and presented in this order; thus 10.34 stands for Oration 10, Section 34.

Bible references follow the traditional order of books, as in the Authorized Version (1611). As the Old Testament and the Apocrypha are only translations, they are placed after the original entries from the New Testament.

We have generally used references from TLG in which all titles of books and their editors are provided; when necessary, parallel references are also inserted.

In all Fragments the name of the editor of the fragment compilation is given in brackets after the fragment number. If the play or prose work is known from which the fragment is taken, the title is added in italics after the name of the editor, e.g. Aeschylus Fragment 161 (Radt) – *Niobe*; or, translated when necessary, e.g. Aeschylus Fragment 176 (Radt) – *Oplon Crisis – The Adjudgement of Arms.*

Other Points to Note

It is not for us, of course, to enter into scholarly discussions regarding, for example, the amendments of indistinct manuscripts and papyri, or differing views on Greek texts. We have had to choose one rendering from among those of equally respected scholars.

The separation of actual quotations from testimonies is not always self-evident. We have in most cases followed the practice of certain standard textbooks, e.g. H. Diels and W. Kranz, *Die Fragmente der Vorsokratiker* (1903) for all Pre-Socratic philosophers.

In the case of authors such as Herodotus and Thucydides, however, it was difficult to decide if their rendering of speeches (or comments) should go under the historian or the speaker. As our intention was to maintain as much continuity as possible, quotations are mostly recorded under the historian with the objective of preserving the flow of narration; all such cases are fully cross-referenced. Pericles' Funeral Speech, however, is entered under Pericles, as are some other important pronouncements by eponymous speakers.

A special case is Socrates, where it is difficult to decide which pronouncements were actually made by him rather than reflecting the views of Plato, Aristotle, Xenophon or, indeed, Aristophanes. We have therefore entered practically all of these under the relevant authors and included under Socrates only statements directly attributed to him (e.g. in Plato's *Apology* and *Crito*), as well as anecdotal references from other sources.

Notes

1. A separate question was, of course, the Septuagint translation of the Old Testament. Since, however, this is the first ever translation, into any language, of a collection of texts of this magnitude, and since it was widely quoted by the early Christian Fathers and is still used by the Greek Orthodox Church today, we have very sparingly included some passages. After all, 'the Greek translation is free enough to have become a creation in its own right' (*Oxford Classical Dictionary*, article on 'Jewish-Greek Literature' by Tessa Rajak).
2. We have used throughout the compilation of this Dictionary the TLG CD-ROM, version E, as available in the years 2005–11, Compilation © 1999, Property of the Regents of the University of California. In many cases texts have been amended following the newer versions now available on 'Online TLG'.
3. The Loeb Classical Library ® is a registered trademark of and copyright © by the President and Fellows of Harvard University.
4. Capital letters in the Greek texts have been retained only for proper names of persons, places, and personifications and, in some cases, entire poems or first lines in a play. All passages start with lower case letters. No capitals are used after full stops (in conformity with standard practice of most users of quotations and of most Loeb editions, which use capital letters only at the beginning of paragraphs). There are no full stops or other punctuation marks (except question marks) at the end of Greek passages (except in autonomous poems and texts). Capitals have not been retained in the English translations for *god, a god* or *the gods*, even if they thus appear in the translations quoted, with the exception of biblical and ecclesiastical texts.
5. Liddell and Scott, *A Greek–English Lexicon*, compiled by Henry George Liddell and Robert Scott, revised and augmented throughout by Sir Henry Stuart Jones with the assistance of Roderick McKenzie and with the cooperation of many scholars. With a revised Supplement, 1996.
6. Mainly the Collection des Universités de France, publiée sous le patronage de l'Association Guillaume Budé. Greek texts with French translations, commentaries and extensive footnotes. Paris: Les Belles Lettres, various dates.

7. Mainly the *Dizionario delle Sentenze Latine e Greche,* prepared by Renzo Tosi. Latin and Greek entries with Italian translations and extensive commentaries. Biblioteca Universale Rizzoli. Milano: Rizzoli, copyright © 1997 RCS Libri S.p.A., 14th edn, December 2000.
8. Mainly the Reclam collection of Greek texts with German translations and commentaries. Stuttgart: Philipp Reclam Jun., various dates.
9. *The Oxford Classical Dictionary,* 3rd edn revised, ed. Simon Hornblower and Antony Spawforth. Oxford: Oxford University Press, 2003.
10. *Atlas of Classical History,* edited by Richard J.A. Talbert. London: Routledge, 2008. The spelling of place names presents some difficulties: Herodotus of Halicarnassus is the established way of referring to Herodotus, whereas in the *Atlas* preference is given to Halicarnassos; Sóloi is variously spelled as Soli or Soloi in English. We have tried to alleviate such difficulties as much as possible.
11. Aeschines, Andocides, Antiphon, Demades, Dio Chrysostom, Demosthenes, Hyperides, Isaeus, Isocrates, Lysias.

βραχεῖ λόγῳ δὲ πολλὰ πρόσκειται σοφά
There is much wisdom to be found in few words

Sophocles

INTRODUCTION

Samuel Johnson said in 1781 that 'Classical quotation is the *parole* of literary men all over the world.' In his usual style, he could be serious in his pronouncements, as in Homer, *Iliad* 6.208, 'αἰὲν ἀριστεύειν καὶ ὑπείροχον ἔμμεναι ἄλλων', of which he says that it is 'the noblest exhortation comprised in a single line', but also quite flippant when he says with some admiration that 'My old friend, Mrs. Carter, could make a pudding as well as translate Epictetus.'

The Greeks, of course, have been great users of quotations, from earliest times to the present day. Already Homer uses some expressions with the indication 'as people say'. Homer, of course, the Seven Sages, the Pre-Socratic philosophers, are still being quoted today in all major Western languages. And indeed the sayings of Heraclitus, for instance, subject of study courses, philosophical conferences and seminars, books and specialized treatises, are known to us only as quotations, his writings having long been lost.

The compilation of any dictionary of quotations is based on the premise that if a passage has been used before it may well be used again. Indeed, more than four-fifths of all excerpts presented here have been quoted before, often again and again through the centuries. Some have found their way into later languages, starting with Latin, and some are used proverbially in several modern languages to this day.

In this book you will find Greek quotations used (as well as by Greeks) by Julius Caesar and the early Church Fathers, by Nietzsche and Karl Marx, but also, more recently, by Robert and J.F. Kennedy, by Margaret Thatcher and Karolos Papoulias, President of the Greek Republic, either in the original Greek or in translation. And Shakespeare, did he know of Democritus' 'The world is a stage' when he wrote *As You Like It*?

Translating Greek texts has always been a difficult undertaking. Roger Ascham in *The Scholemaster* (1568) says 'which excellentlie said in Greek is thus rudelie in English', referring to his translation of the inscription over the portal to Shrewsbury School; Shelley speaks of 'the vanity of rendering the surpassing graces of Greek poems … presenting an imperfect shadow of the language'.

And then, Malcolm Heath: 'How should I interpret a classical text? However I do it, someone else will do so differently. Disagreement is endemic in the field.'

However, 'Translation it is that openeth a window, to let in the light; that breaketh the shell, that we may eat the kernel' (The Bible, Authorised Version, The Translators to the Reader).

Our choice of about 7,500 entries (from a collection of more than 25,000), a project never before attempted to this extent, covers a wide range of interests. After all, a handbook such as this is also intended for browsing, and many a reader will find that views expressed two millennia ago are as applicable today as they were then.

Of course we are aware that it is not possible to please everyone: to paraphrase Aelian, Aristotelians would surely have liked us to include more Aristotle, Platonists more Plato. And we could not have included all 1,100 fragments of Euripides that someone in the past has considered worth quoting.

On the other hand, some will perhaps say that we have included too many. But then, all users of books of quotations select one or two, here and there, which they prefer. If, of course, one is interested in a particular subject, one can turn to the extensive Keyword Index for help.

A note must be inserted here on the procedure for deciding which quotations to include. All proposals for selecting a quotation were submitted to a group of referees together with two or more translations. The process resulted in rejecting nearly 2,000 quotations originally proposed.

The compilation of this anthology of Greek quotations has been a continuous source of pleasure throughout the last few years. It has been a delight from the beginning to the end – if this is the end, because of course there are still many more memorable sayings to add. We hope that the reader will derive equal enjoyment, and interest, from perusing this book. And some readers might even be induced to pick up and read the whole of Homer or, say, Herodotus!

QUOTATIONS

ADAMANTIUS JUDAEUS

4th–5th century AD
Jewish physician

1 ῥῖνα ὀρθήν, ὀφθαλμοὺς ὑγροὺς χαροποὺς γοργοὺς φῶς πολὺ ἔχοντας ἐν ἑαυτοῖς· εὐοφθαλμότατον γὰρ πάντων τῶν ἐθνῶν τὸ Ἑλληνικόν

The nose straight, the eyes lustrous and expressive: the Greeks have the most beautiful eyes of any people in the world.

Physiognomonica 2.32

AELIAN

c.175–c.235 AD
Roman author and teacher of rhetoric who spoke and wrote in Greek

1 νόμος ἐστὶ Κείων, οἱ πάνυ παρ' αὐτοῖς γεγηρακότες, ὥσπερ ἐπὶ ξένια παρακαλοῦντες ἑαυτοὺς ἢ ἐπί τινα ἑορταστικὴν θυσίαν, συνελθόντες καὶ στεφανωσάμενοι πίνουσι κώνειον, ὅταν ἑαυτοῖς συνειδῶσιν ὅτι πρὸς τὰ ἔργα τὰ τῇ πατρίδι λυσιτελοῦντα ἄχρηστοί εἰσιν, ὑποληρούσης ἤδη τι αὐτοῖς καὶ τῆς γνώμης διὰ τὸν χρόνον

There is a law at Ceos that those who are very old invite each other as if going to a party or to a festival with sacrifices, meet, put on garlands and drink hemlock. This they do when they become aware that they are incapable of performing tasks useful to their country, and that their judgement is by now rather feeble owing to the passing of time.

Translated by N.G. Wilson (1997)

Historical Miscellany 3.37

an early law allowing euthanasia; cf. Menander, Fragment 613 (Kock) – 879 (K-A)

2 καὶ οἱ Πυθαγόρειοι μὲν ὁμιληταὶ Πυθαγόρου ὤνηντο, οἱ Δημοκρίτειοι δὲ συγγενόμενοι Δημοκρίτῳ πολλῶν ἀπήλαυσαν

And the Pythagorean disciples delighted in Pythagoras, while the Democriteans were full of admiration for Democritus.

Historical Miscellany 12.25

cf. 'and Thatcherites were full of admiration for Mrs Thatcher, while Blairites delighted in Mr Blair'

3 πρώτῃ καὶ ὀγδοηκοστῇ Ὀλυμπιάδι φασὶ τὴν Αἴτνην ῥυῆναι, ὅτε καὶ Φιλόνομος καὶ Καλλίας οἱ Καταναῖοι τοὺς ἑαυτῶν πατέρας ἀράμενοι διὰ μέσης τῆς φλογὸς ἐκόμισαν, τῶν ἄλλων κτημάτων καταφρονήσαντες. ἀνθ' ὧν καὶ ἀμοιβῆς ἔτυχον τῆς ἐκ τοῦ θείου· τὸ γάρ τοι πῦρ θεόντων αὐτῶν διέστη καθ' ὃ μέρος ἐκεῖνοι παρεγίνοντο

When in the 81st Olympiad Mount Aetna erupted, Philonomus and Callias carried their fathers from the flames, disregarding the loss of their possessions. The gods rewarded them by diverting the fire wheresoever they went.

Fragment 2 (Hercher)

from Catana – Κατάνη, Lat. Catina, modern Catania

AESCHINES

c.397–*c*.322BC
Athenian orator

1 ὁμολογοῦνται γὰρ τρεῖς εἶναι πολιτεῖαι παρὰ πᾶσιν ἀνθρώποις, τυραννὶς καὶ ὀλιγαρχία καὶ δημοκρατία· διοικοῦνται δ' αἱ μὲν τυραννίδες καὶ ὀλιγαρχίαι τοῖς τρόποις τῶν ἐφεστηκότων, αἱ δὲ πόλεις αἱ δημοκρατούμεναι τοῖς νόμοις τοῖς κειμένοις

Of Constitutions there are three: Tyranny, Oligarchy and Democracy; tyrannies and oligarchies are governed by the whims of rulers, democracies by the rule of law.

Against Timarchus 1.4

cf. Polybius 8

2 τὸν γὰρ τὴν ἰδίαν οἰκίαν κακῶς οἰκήσαντα, καὶ τὰ κοινὰ τῆς πόλεως παραπλησίως ἡγήσατο διαθήσειν

The man who has mismanaged his own household will mismanage the affairs of the city too.

Against Timarchus 1.30

3 τῶν ῥητόρων ἐάν τις λέγῃ ἐν τῇ βουλῇ ἢ ἐν τῷ δήμῳ μὴ περὶ τοῦ εἰσφερομένου ... ἢ λοιδορῆται, ἢ κακῶς ἀγορεύῃ τινά ... κυριευέτωσαν οἱ πρόεδροι μέχρι πεντήκοντα δραχμῶν εἰς ἕκαστον ἀδίκημα

If anyone, speaking in the senate or the assembly, should speak beside the point being discussed, or if he speak abusively or slanderously, the chairmen shall impose a fine not exceeding 50 drachmas for each offence.

Against Timarchus 1.35

4 οὕτω γὰρ χρὴ καθαρὸν εἶναι τὸν βίον τοῦ σώφρονος ἀνδρός, ὥστε μηδ' ἐπιδέχεσθαι δόξαν αἰτίας πονηρᾶς

The life of a virtuous man ought to be so clean that it will not admit even a suspicion of wrong-doing.

Translated by Charles Darwin Adams (1919)

Against Timarchus 1.48

5 τὸ γὰρ ψευδὲς ὄνειδος οὐ περαιτέρω τῆς ἀκοῆς ἀφικνεῖται

A false reproach is no more than an empty sound.

On the Embassy 2.149

6 χρὴ γὰρ ... τὸ αὐτὸ φθέγγεσθαι τὸν ῥήτορα καὶ τὸν νόμον

The orator and the law ought to speak the same language.

Translated by Charles Darwin Adams (1919)

Against Ctesiphon 3.16

7 ἐν γὰρ ταύτῃ τῇ πόλει ... οὐδείς ἐστιν ἀνυπεύθυνος τῶν καὶ ὁπωσοῦν πρὸς τὰ κοινὰ προσεληλυθότων

In this city no man is free from audit who has held any public trust.

Translated by Charles Darwin Adams (1919)

Against Ctesiphon 3.17

i.e. everybody who has held any public office in Athens is accountable to auditors as to his handling of public money

8 τοὺς ἱερέας καὶ τὰς ἱερείας ὑπευθύνους εἶναι κελεύει ὁ νόμος ... τὰς εὐχὰς ὑπὲρ ὑμῶν πρὸς τοὺς θεοὺς εὐχομένους

Even priests and priestesses, whose job it is to pray to the gods for you, are subject to audit according to the law.

Against Ctesiphon 3.18

9 οὐδέ γε ὁ ἰδίᾳ πονηρὸς οὐκ ἂν γένοιτο δημοσίᾳ χρηστός

He who is wicked in his private life will never be trustworthy in public affairs.

Against Ctesiphon 3.78.6

10 οὐδ' ὅστις ἐστὶν οἴκοι φαῦλος, οὐδέποτ' ἦν ἐν Μακεδονίᾳ καλὸς κἀγαθός· οὐ γὰρ τὸν τρόπον, ἀλλὰ τὸν τόπον μετήλλαξεν

The man who is base at home will never be a good and honourable man abroad; for by his journey he only changed his position, not his disposition.

Against Ctesiphon 3.78.7

11 πονηρὰ φύσις, μεγάλης ἐξουσίας ἐπιλαβομένη, δημοσίας ἀπεργάζεται συμφοράς

A wicked person in power will cause public disaster.

Against Ctesiphon 3.147

12 ἐπὶ σαυτὸν καλεῖς, ἐπὶ τοὺς νόμους καλεῖς, ἐπὶ τὴν δημοκρατίαν καλεῖς

Against yourself you summon him,
against the laws you summon him,
against democracy you summon him.

Translated by Doreen C. Innes (1995, based on W. Rhys Roberts)

Against Ctesiphon 3.202

quoted by Demetrius Phalereus to highlight the power of repetition in oratory

AESCHINES SOCRATICUS

4th century BC
Philosopher and devoted follower of Socrates

1 οὐ γὰρ μόνον λέγειν ἔμαθον παρὰ Σωκράτει, ἀλλὰ καὶ σιωπᾶν

From Socrates I learnt not only how to speak, but also when to be silent.

Stobaeus, *Anthology* 3.34.10

AESCHYLUS

*c.*525–456BC
Athenian tragic playwright
see also Aristophanes 82, 85

1 Θεοὺς μὲν αἰτῶ τῶνδ' ἀπαλλαγὴν πόνων,
φρουρᾶς ἐτείας μῆκος, ἣν κοιμώμενος
στέγαις Ἀτρειδῶν ἄγκαθεν, κυνὸς δίκην,
ἄστρων κάτοιδα νυκτέρων ὁμήγυριν,
καὶ τοὺς φέροντας χεῖμα καὶ θέρος βροτοῖς
λαμπροὺς δυνάστας ἐμπρέποντας αἰθέρι
ἀστέρας, ὅταν φθίνωσιν, ἀντολάς τε τῶν

I wish the gods would end my plight
as watchman on the palace roof,
doglike, lying askew on bended arm,
marking the conclave of the stars of night,
heavenly potentates that bring
winter and summer to mankind,
the constellations as they wane and rise.

Agamemnon 1

opening lines; cf. Apollonius of Rhodes 3

2 ὧδε γὰρ κρατεῖ
γυναικὸς ἀνδρόβουλον ἐλπίζον κέαρ

Such is the ruling of a woman's heart, which plans like a man.

Translated by Alan H. Sommerstein (2008)

Agamemnon 10

of Clytemnestra, Agamemnon's wife

3 τὰ δ' ἄλλα σιγῶ· βοῦς ἐπὶ γλώσσηι μέγας βέβηκεν

As to the rest I'm silent: a great ox stands upon my tongue.

Agamemnon 36

used as an epigraph to 'Mycene Lookout' by Seamus Heaney; cf. Theognis 53

4 αἴλινον αἴλινον εἰπέ, τὸ δ' εὖ νικάτω

Cry sorrow, sorrow, but may the good prevail!

Translated by Alan H. Sommerstein (2008)

Agamemnon 121

spoken by the Chorus, repeated in lines 138 and 159

5 Ζεὺς ὅστις ποτ' ἐστίν

Zeus – whoever he may be.

Translated by Alan H. Sommerstein (2008)

Agamemnon 160

6 τὸν πάθει μάθος ...
στάζει δ' ἀνθ' ὕπνου πρὸ καρδίας
μνησιπήμων πόνος· καὶ παρ' ἄ-
κοντας ἦλθε σωφρονεῖν
δαιμόνων δέ που χάρις βίαιος

We learn by suffering; and even, instead of sleep, the memory of pain falls drop by drop upon our heart; and in our own despair, against our will, comes wisdom to us by the awful grace of god.

Agamemnon 177

quoted by Robert F. Kennedy in a speech on the death of Martin Luther King, 4 April 1968

7 τί τῶνδ' ἄνευ κακῶν;

Which of these options is not fraught with evil?

Agamemnon 211

8 δίκα δὲ τοῖς μὲν παθοῦσιν μαθεῖν ἐπιρρέπει

It is our fate that we only learn from our misfortune.

Agamemnon 250

9 ἄγουσά τ' ἀντίφερνον Ἰλίῳ φθορὰν

As her dowry she brought to Ilium destruction.

Agamemnon 406

of Helen

10 δόξαι φέρου-
σαι χάριν ματαίαν

Glory bringing idle joy.

Agamemnon 421

11 οὓς μὲν γάρ τις ἔπεμψεν
οἶδεν, ἀντὶ δὲ φωτῶν
τεύχη καὶ σποδὸς εἰς ἑκάστου δόμους ἀφικνεῖται

Well did they know
the men they sent to battle;
but now, in place of men,
ashes and urns come back
to the homes of the fighters.

Agamemnon 432

spoken by the Chorus

12 βαρεῖα δ' ἀστῶν φάτις ξὺν κότῳ

Grievous is a people's voice when charged with wrath.

Agamemnon 456

13 πολλῶν ῥαγεισῶν ἐλπίδων μιᾶς τυχών

Many a hope hath made shipwreck, only one have I seen fulfilled.

Translated by Herbert Weir Smyth (1926)

Agamemnon 505

14 ἀεὶ γὰρ ἡβᾷ τοῖς γέρουσιν εὐμαθεῖν

Never too old to learn, it keeps me young.

Translated by Robert Fagles (1975)

Agamemnon 584

15 θ' Ἑλέναν; ἐπεὶ πρεπόντως
ἑλέναυς ἕλανδρος ἑλέπτολις

Hell to ships, hell to men, hell to cities.

lit. 'Ship-destroyer, man-destroyer, city-destroyer'

Translated in *The Oxford Dictionary of Quotations* (2004)

Agamemnon 687

of Helen; a play on her name and ἕλω *(from* αἱρέω*) = kill; entrap; the 'Hell' translation tries to mimic this effect*

16 παύροις γὰρ ἀνδρῶν ἐστι συγγενὲς τόδε,
φίλον τὸν εὐτυχοῦντ' ἄνευ φθόνων
σέβειν

How rare, men with the character to praise
a friend's success without a trace of envy.

Translated by Robert Fagles (1975)

Agamemnon 832

17 εἴδωλον σκιᾶς

A shadow of a shade.

Translated by Herbert Weir Smyth (1926)

Agamemnon 839

of man

18 ἐν χρόνῳ δ' ἀποφθίνει
τὸ τάρβος ἀνθρώποισιν

With time, even fear dies away.

Agamemnon 857

19 βροτοῖσι τὸν πεσόντα λακτίσαι πλέον

Men tend to trample the fallen.

Agamemnon 885

cf. the English expression 'kick you when you're down'

20 τερπνὸν δὲ τἀναγκαῖον ἐκφυγεῖν ἅπαν

Sweet is it to be rid of need.

Agamemnon 902

21 φθόνος δ' ἀπέστω

Let envy keep her distance.

Translated by Robert Fagles (1975)

Agamemnon 904

22 τὸ μὴ κακῶς φρονεῖν θεοῦ μέγιστον
δῶρον

God's most lordly gift to man
is decency of mind.

Translated by Richmond Lattimore (1953)

Agamemnon 927

23 ὀλβίσαι δὲ χρὴ
βίον τελευτήσαντ' ἐν εὐεστοῖ φίλῃ

Call that man only blest
who has in sweet tranquillity brought
his life to close.

Translated by Richmond Lattimore (1953)

Agamemnon 928

24 φήμη γε μέντοι δημόθρους μέγα σθένει

The people's voice is a mighty power.

Agamemnon 938

25 οὔτοι γυναικός ἐστιν ἱμείρειν μάχης

Surely 'tis not for a woman to long for battle.

Agamemnon 940

26 τὸν κρατοῦντα μαλθακῶς
θεὸς πρόσωθεν εὐμενῶς προσδέρκεται

God from afar looks graciously upon a gentle master.

Translated by Herbert Weir Smyth (1926)

Agamemnon 951

27 ἔστιν θάλασσα, τίς δέ νιν κατασβέσει;

There is the sea – and who shall drain it dry?

Translated by Herbert Weir Smyth (1926)

Agamemnon 958

28 ῥίζης γὰρ οὔσης φυλλὰς ἵκετ’ εἰς δόμους,
σκιὰν ὑπερτείνασα Σειρίου κυνός

When the root lives on, the new leaves
come back,
spreading a dense shroud of shade
across the house
to thwart the Dog Star's fury.

Translated by Robert Fagles (1975)

Agamemnon 966

the Dog Star is Sirius, the brightest fixed star in the sky, in the constellation of Canis Major

29 ὑγιείας ... νόσος γὰρ
γείτων ὁμότοιχος

Disease and health are neighbours with a common wall.

Agamemnon 1001

30 ἀπὸ δὲ θεσφάτων τίς ἀγαθὰ φάτις
βροτοῖς τέλλεται; κακῶν γὰρ διαὶ
πολυεπεῖς τέχναι
θεσπιῳδῶν φόβον φέρουσιν μαθεῖν

From prophecies what good has ever
come to men? A tangled evil art,
a multiplicity of words,
bring terror to them that hear.

Agamemnon 1132

31 ἥξει γὰρ ἡμῶν ἄλλος αὖ τιμάορος
There will come another to avenge us.

Translated by Robert Fagles (1975)

Agamemnon 1280

32 εὐκλεῶς τοι κατθανεῖν χάρις βροτῷ

Surely to die nobly is a blessing for mortals.

Agamemnon 1304

33 ἰὼ βρότεια πράγματ’· εὐτυχοῦντα μὲν
σκιᾷ τις ἂν πρέψειεν· εἰ δὲ δυστυχῇ,
βολαῖς ὑγρώσσων σπόγγος ὤλεσεν
γραφήν

So much for mortal life! The happy ones
are like a shadow: and as for the
wretched,
the dash of a wet sponge blots out the
picture.

Translated by Oliver Taplin (1978)

Agamemnon 1327

34 ὤμοι, πέπληγμαι καιρίαν πληγὴν ἔσω

Alas, I am struck a mortal blow!

Agamemnon 1343

35 κατθανεῖν κρατεῖ·
πεπαιτέρα γὰρ μοῖρα τῆς τυραννίδος

Better to be killed.
Death is a milder fate by far than
tyranny.

Agamemnon 1364

36 ἰὼ ἰή, διαὶ Διὸς
παναιτίου πανεργέτα·
τί γὰρ βροτοῖς ἄνευ Διὸς τελεῖται;

Woe, woe, by will of Zeus,
the cause of all, all-affecting Zeus;
what is fulfilled for mortal men save by
the will of Zeus?

Agamemnon 1485

37 ὄνειδος ἥκει τόδ’ ἀντ’ ὀνείδους ...
φέρει φέροντ’, ἐκτίνει δ’ ὁ καίνων

Insult comes in return for insult.
The ravager is ravaged, the killer pays.

Translated by Alan H. Sommerstein (2008)

Agamemnon 1560

38 γνώσῃ γέρων ὢν ὡς διδάσκεσθαι βαρὺ
τῷ τηλικούτῳ, σωφρονεῖν εἰρημένον

At your late age it is bitter to be taught
temperance you should already practise.

Agamemnon 1619

39 πρὸς κέντρα μὴ λάκτιζε

Do not kick against the pricks.

Translated in *Bartlett's Familiar Quotations* (1980)

Agamemnon 1624

cf. Pindar 73, Bible 190

40 οἶδ’ ἐγὼ φεύγοντας ἄνδρας ἐλπίδας
σιτουμένους

I know how men in exile feed on
dreams of hope.

Translated in *Bartlett's Familiar Quotations* (1980)

Agamemnon 1668

41 μὴ φόβος σε νικάτω φρένας

Let not fear prevail over your senses.

Eumenides 88

42 ὕπνῳ κρατηθεῖσ' ἄγραν ὤλεσα

O'ercome by sleep I lost my prey.

Eumenides 148

43 χρόνος καθαίρει πάντα γηράσκων ὁμοῦ

Time refines all things that age with time.

Translated by Robert Fagles (1975)

Eumenides 286

44 παρακοπά,
παραφορὰ φρενοδαλὴς ...
δέσμιος φρενῶν, ἀφόρ-
μικτος, αὐονὰ βροτοῖς

Fraught with madness,
fraught with frenzy, crazing the brain,
spell to bind the soul, untuned to the lyre,
withering the life of mortal men.

Translated by Herbert Weir Smyth (1926)

Eumenides 329

the Furies' song

45 τὸ πρᾶγμα μεῖζον ... οὐδὲ μὴν ἐμοὶ θέμις φόνου διαιρεῖν

The affair is too grave; nay, it is not lawful even for me to decide
on cases of murder.

Translated by Herbert Weir Smyth (1926)

Eumenides 470

spoken by Athena

46 μήτ' ἄναρκτον βίον
μήτε δεσποτούμενον
αἰνέσῃς

Approve thou not
a life ungoverned
nor one subjected to a tyrant's sway.

Translated by Herbert Weir Smyth (1926)

Eumenides 526

47 ἐκ δ' ὑγιείας
φρενῶν ὁ πᾶσιν φίλος
καὶ πολύευκτος ὄλβος

From a healthy mind,
springs prosperity, dear to all
and much prayed for.

Translated by Alan H. Sommerstein (2008)

Eumenides 535

48 ὧν ἔχεις αὐτὸς κράτει

Rule what is your own.

Eumenides 574

49 πέδας μὲν ἂν λύσειεν· ἔστι τοῦδ' ἄκος ...
ἀνδρὸς δ' ἐπειδὰν αἷμ' ἀνασπάσῃ κόνις
ἅπαξ θανόντος, οὔτις ἔστ' ἀνάστασις

Shackles might undo; from them there is a remedy.
But when the dust hath drained the blood of man,
once he is slain there is no return to life.

Translated by Herbert Weir Smyth (1926)

Eumenides 645

an argument against capital punishment

50 βορβόρῳ θ' ὕδωρ
λαμπρὸν μιαίνων οὔποθ' εὑρήσεις ποτόν

Pollute clear water and thou shalt never find to drink.

Eumenides 694

51 τὸ μήτ' ἄναρχον μήτε δεσποτούμενον ... σέβειν

Hold neither anarchy nor tyranny in reverence.

Eumenides 696

52 καὶ μὴ τὸ δεινὸν πᾶν πόλεως ἔξω βαλεῖν·
τίς γὰρ δεδοικὼς μηδὲν ἔνδικος βροτῶν;

And from your policy do not wholly banish fear;
For what man living, freed from fear, will still be just?

Translated in *The Oxford Dictionary of Political Quotations* (2006)

Eumenides 698

53 γνώμης ἀπούσης πῆμα γίγνεται μέγα

An error in judgement now can mean disaster.

Translated by Robert Fagles (1975)

Eumenides 750

54 ἀνὴρ ὅδ' ἐκπέφευγεν αἵματος δίκην·
ἴσον γάρ ἐστι τἀρίθμημα τῶν πάλων

The man goes free,
cleared of the charge of blood. The lots are equal.

Translated by Robert Fagles (1975)

Eumenides 752

the trial of Orestes; the best citizens of Athens voting, presided over by Athena

55 γλώσσης ματαίας μὴ 'κβάλῃς ἔπη χθονί

Let not a forward tongue utter threats against the land.

Translated by Herbert Weir Smyth (1926)

Eumenides 830

56 θυραῖος ἔστω πόλεμος, οὐ μόλις παρὼν
ἐν ᾧ τις ἔσται δεινὸς εὐκλείας ἔρως·
ἐνοικίου δ' ὄρνιθος οὐ λέγω μάχην

Let our wars
rage on abroad, with all their force, to satisfy
our powerful lust for fame. But as for the bird
that fights at home – my curse on civil war.

Translated by Robert Fagles (1975)

Eumenides 864

57 τὸ δ' εὐτυχεῖν,
τόδ' ἐν βροτοῖς θεός τε καὶ θεοῦ πλέον

Good fortune is a god among men, and more than a god.

Translated in *Bartlett's Familiar Quotations* (1980)

Libation Bearers 59

58 τὸ μόρσιμον γὰρ τόν τ' ἐλεύθερον μένει
καὶ τὸν πρὸς ἄλλης δεσποτούμενον χερός

Destiny waits alike for the free man
as well as for him enslaved by another's might.

Translated in *Bartlett's Familiar Quotations* (1980)

Libation Bearers 103

59 σμικροῦ γένοιτ' ἂν σπέρματος μέγας πυθμήν

A huge tree can tower
From a tiny seed.

Translated by Ted Hughes (1999)

Libation Bearers 204

60 ἀντὶ δὲ πληγῆς φονίας φονίαν
πληγὴν τινέτω. δράσαντι παθεῖν,
τριγέρων μῦθος τάδε φωνεῖ

For murderous stroke let murderous stroke be paid;
'To him that doeth, it shall be done by,'
so sayeth a thrice old tale.

Libation Bearers 312

61 ἀλλὰ κλύοντες, μάκαρες χθόνιοι,
τῆσδε κατευχῆς πέμπετ' ἀρωγὴν
παισὶν προφρόνως ἐπὶ νίκῃ

Now hear, you blissful powers underground –
answer the call, send help.
Bless the children, give them triumph now.

Translated by Robert Fagles (1975)

Libation Bearers 476

quoted by J.K. Rowling, Harry Potter and the Deathly Hallows *(2007), opening pages*

62 τί γὰρ ξένου ξένοισίν ἐστιν εὐμενέστερον;

What is more pleasant than the bond of host and guest?

Libation Bearers 702

63 μύραινά γ' εἴτ' ἔχιδν' ἔφυ,
σήπειν θιγοῦσ' ἂν ἄλλον οὐ δεδηγμένον,
τόλμης ἕκατι κἀκδίκου φρονήματος; ...
τοιάδ' ἐμοὶ ξύνοικος ἐν δόμοισι μὴ γένοιτ'

Had she been born a sea-snake or a viper,
her touch alone, without her bite, would breed corruption;
such was her shamelessness and wickedness of spirit.
May such a woman never dwell in my house!

Libation Bearers 994

of Agamemnon's wife, Clytemnestra

64 ποῖ δῆτα κρανεῖ, ποῖ καταλήξει
μετακοιμισθὲν μένος ἄτης;

Where will this end? When,
lulled to rest, will the power of ruin cease?

Libation Bearers 1075

closing lines

65 πεπέρακεν μὲν ὁ περσέπτολις ἤδη
βασίλειος στρατὸς εἰς ἀντίπορον γείτονα χώραν,
λινοδέσμῳ σχεδίᾳ πορθμὸν ἀμείψας
Ἀθαμαντίδος Ἕλλας,
πολύγομφον ὅδισμα ζυγὸν ἀμφιβαλὼν αὐχένι πόντου

Long since, the king led his destroying ranks
Over the strait to Europe's neighbour ground;
Crossed Helle's channel with a road that floats,

A ribbon of lashed timbers and nailed planks
Yoking the sea's neck in a bridge of boats.

Translated by Philip Vellacott (1961)

Persians 65

of Xerxes' bridge over the Hellespont; the Persians *is Aeschylus' first surviving play, indeed the first extant Greek tragedy*

66 εὐρυπόροιο θαλάσσας
πολιαινομένας πνεύματι λάβρῳ
ἐσορᾶν πόντιον ἄλσος

Where the storm-wind, howling shrill,
Whips the sea's broad channels white.

Translated by Philip Vellacott (1961)

Persians 109

67 λέκτρα δ' ἀνδρῶν πόθῳ
πίμπλαται δακρύμασιν

Marriage-beds are filled with tears
through longing for their husbands.

Translated by Herbert Weir Smyth (1922)

Persians 133

68 ὁρῶ δὲ φεύγοντ' αἰετὸν πρὸς ἐσχάραν
Φοίβου· φόβῳ δ' ἄφθογγος ἐστάθην, φίλοι·
μεθύστερον δὲ κίρκον εἰσορῶ δρόμῳ
πτεροῖν ἐφορμαίνοντα καὶ χηλαῖς κάρα
τίλλονθ'· ὁ δ' οὐδὲν ἄλλο γ' ἢ πτήξας δέμας
παρεῖχε

I saw an eagle fly for refuge to Apollo's hearth.
I watched, speechless with terror; then a falcon came,
And swooped with rushing wings, and with his talons clawed
The eagle's head; it, unresisting, cowered there,
Offering itself to wounds.

Translated by Philip Vellacott (1961)

Persians 205

Queen Atossa's vision, in anticipation of news of Xerxes' expedition against Greece

69 τῆλε πρὸς δυσμαῖς ἄνακτος Ἡλίου φθινασμάτων

Far hence, where the waning fires of our
Lord the Sun sinks in the west.

Translated by Herbert Weir Smyth (1922)

Persians 232

the Chorus asking where Athens is

70 – οὔτινος δοῦλοι κέκληνται φωτὸς οὐδ' ὑπήκοοι
– πῶς ἂν οὖν μένοιεν ἄνδρας πολεμίους ἐπήλυδας;

Chorus: Master? They are not called servants to any man.
Atossa: And can they, masterless, resist invasion?

Translated by Philip Vellacott (1961)

Persians 242

on how the Athenians fight, not being ruled by kings

71 καὐτὸς δ' ἀέλπτως νόστιμον βλέπω φάος

And I myself, beyond all hope, behold the day of my return.

Translated by Herbert Weir Smyth (1922)

Persians 261

72 ὅμως δ' ἀνάγκη πημονὰς βροτοῖς φέρειν
θεῶν διδόντων

And yet necessity dictates that men should bear
The ills the gods bestow.

Translated by Anthony J. Podlecki (1991)

Persians 293

73 ὦ παῖδες Ἑλλήνων, ἴτε,
ἐλευθεροῦτε πατρίδ', ἐλευθεροῦτε δὲ
παῖδας, γυναῖκας, θεῶν τε πατρῴων ἕδη,
θήκας τε προγόνων· νῦν ὑπὲρ πάντων ἀγών

Forward, you sons of Hellas! Set your country free!
Set free your sons, your wives, tombs of your ancestors,
And temples of your gods. All is at stake now! Fight!

Translated by Philip Vellacott (1961)

Persians 402

a battle cry of the Greeks

74 βροτοῖσιν ὡς ὅταν κλύδων
κακῶν ἐπέλθῃ, πάντα δειμαίνειν φιλεῖ,
ὅταν δ' ὁ δαίμων εὐροῇ, πεποιθέναι
τὸν αὐτὸν αἰὲν ἄνεμον οὐριεῖν τύχης

When waves of trouble burst on us, each new event
Fills us with terror; but when Fortune's winds blow soft
We think to enjoy the same fair weather all our lives.

Translated by Philip Vellacott (1961)

Persians 599

75 ἅπερ νεκροῖσι μειλικτήρια,
βοός τ' ἀφ' ἁγνῆς λευκὸν εὔποτον γάλα,
τῆς τ' ἀνθεμουργοῦ στάγμα, παμφαὲς μέλι,
λιβάσιν ὑδρηλαῖς παρθένου πηγῆς μέτα

Gifts that soothe departed souls:
Bring white milk good to drink, from a cow without blemish;
bright honey, too, the drops the bee in her flowery work distils,
with water that purifies, drawn from a virgin spring.

Translated by Edith Hamilton (1964)

Persians 610

76 ἐξέφθινται τρίσκαλμοι
νᾶες ἄναες ἄναες

Our three-banked ships
are ships no more, no more!

Translated by Philip Vellacott (1961)

Persians 679

77 ἄσμενον μολεῖν γέφυραν γαῖν δυοῖν ζευκτηρίαν

He reached at last, with joy after despair, the bridge
yoking two continents.

Translated by Philip Vellacott (1961)

Persians 736

of Xerxes; cf. Aristides 16

78 οὐχ ὑπέρφευ θνητὸν ὄντα χρὴ φρονεῖν·
ὕβρις γὰρ ἐξανθοῦσ' ἐκάρπωσε στάχυν
ἄτης, ὅθεν πάγκλαυτον ἐξαμᾷ θέρος

Man must learn to curb his pride.
When hubris blossoms, ruin is its fruit,
and tears its bitter harvest.

Persians 820

spoken by Darius' ghost

79 μηδέ τις
ὑπερφρονήσας τὸν παρόντα δαίμονα
ἄλλων ἐρασθεὶς ὄλβον ἐκχέῃ μέγαν

Let no one despise his present fortune and pour away his great prosperity from desiring that of others.

Translated by Christopher Collard (2009)

Persians 824

spoken by Darius' ghost

80 ὡς τοῖς θανοῦσι πλοῦτος οὐδὲν ὠφελεῖ

All wealth is useless to the dead.

Persians 842

spoken by Darius' ghost

81 Χθονὸς μὲν εἰς τηλουρὸν ἥκομεν πέδον,
Σκύθην ἐς οἶμον, ἄβροτον εἰς ἐρημίαν

Here we have reached the remotest region of the earth,
The haunt of Scythians, a wilderness without a footprint.

Translated by Philip Vellacott (1961)

Prometheus Bound 1

opening lines; Prometheus dragged to the Caucasus, his place of punishment for having presented fire to mankind

82 δυσλύτοις χαλκεύμασιν
προσπασσαλεύσω τῷδ' ἀπανθρώπῳ πάγῳ,
ἵν' οὔτε φωνὴν οὔτε του μορφὴν βροτῶν ὄψῃ

I now shall fasten you
In bands of bronze immovable, to this desolate peak,
Where you will hear no voice, nor see a human form.

Translated by Philip Vellacott (1961)

Prometheus Bound 19

83 ἀσμένῳ δέ σοι
ἡ ποικιλείμων νὺξ ἀποκρύψει φάος

Glad will you be to see the night,
with her star-spangled robe, extinguishing the light of day!

Prometheus Bound 23

84 ἅπας δὲ τραχὺς ὅστις ἂν νέον κρατῇ

Every ruler new to power is harsh.

Translated by Christopher Collard (2009)

Prometheus Bound 35

85 τὸ ξυγγενές τοι δεινὸν ἥ θ' ὁμιλία

The ties of birth and comradeship are strangely strong.

Translated by Philip Vellacott (1961)

Prometheus Bound 39

86 τὰ μηδὲν ὠφελοῦντα μὴ πόνει μάτην

For things that bring no benefit labour not in vain.

Prometheus Bound 44

87 ὦ πολλὰ μισηθεῖσα χειρωναξία

Oh handicraft that I have come so much to loathe!

Translated by Herbert Weir Smyth (1922)
Prometheus Bound 45

88 ἅπαντ᾽ ἐπαχθῆ πλὴν θεοῖσι κοιρανεῖν·
ἐλεύθερος γὰρ οὔτις ἐστὶ πλὴν Διός

All tasks are burdensome, except to rule the gods.
No one is free but Zeus.

Translated by Philip Vellacott (1961)
Prometheus Bound 49

89 ὦ δῖος αἰθὴρ καὶ ταχύπτεροι πνοαί,
ποταμῶν τε πηγαί … παμμῆτωρ τε γῆ

O wondrous sky, and swift-winged winds,
the surge of rivers, and earth, mother of all.

Prometheus Bound 88

90 ποντίων τε κυμάτων ἀνήριθμον γέλασμα

The ceaseless twinkling laughter of the waves of the sea.

Prometheus Bound 89

91 τὴν πεπρωμένην δὲ χρὴ
αἶσαν φέρειν ὡς ῥᾷστα, γιγνώσκονθ᾽ ὅτι
τὸ τῆς ἀνάγκης ἔστ᾽ ἀδήριτον σθένος.
ἀλλ᾽ οὔτε σιγᾶν οὔτε μὴ σιγᾶν τύχας
οἷόν τέ μοι τάσδ᾽ ἐστί

It doth behove to bear
Calmly what Fate ordaineth, knowing that
Necessity hath force impugnable.
Yet can I not be silent or unsilent,
Of these my woes.

Translated by Elizabeth Barrett Browning (1833)
Prometheus Bound 103

92 ναρθηκοπλήρωτον δὲ θηρῶμαι πυρὸς
πηγὴν κλοπαίαν, ἣ διδάσκαλος τέχνης
πάσης βροτοῖς πέφηνε καὶ μέγας πόρος.
τοιῶνδε ποινὰς ἀμπλακημάτων τίνω
ὑπαίθριος δεσμοῖς πεπασσαλευμένος

I hunted out and stored within the fennel-stalk the stolen source of fire, which was to be the teacher of all arts to men, and a great pathway to achievement. For such wrongs I pay the penalty, riveted in fetters beneath the open sky.

Prometheus Bound 109

of Prometheus' gift of fire to mankind

93 ἆ ἆ ἔα ἔα·
τίς ἀχώ, τίς ὀδμὰ προσέπτα μ᾽ ἀφεγγής,
θεόσυτος, ἢ βρότειος, ἢ κεκραμένη;

Ah! Who is there?
What sound, what fragrant air
Floats by me; whence, I cannot see.
From god, or man, or blend of both?

Translated by Philip Vellacott (1961)
Prometheus Bound 114

on hearing the Chorus of the daughters of Oceanus

94 νέοι γὰρ οἰακονόμοι κρατοῦσ᾽ Ὀλύμπου·
νεοχμοῖς δὲ δὴ νόμοις Ζεὺς ἀθέτως κρατύνει·
τὰ πρὶν δὲ πελώρια νῦν ἀΐστοῖ

New masters are ruling and guide Olympus' helm;
fresh laws without due base are Zeus' power;
what was mighty before, he now obliterates.

Translated by Christopher Collard (2009)
Prometheus Bound 150

95 νῦν δ᾽ αἰθέριον κίνυγμ᾽ ὁ τάλας

And now I am the miserable sport of every wind.

Translated by Philip Vellacott (1961)
Prometheus Bound 158

96 ἔνεστι γάρ πως τοῦτο τῇ τυραννίδι
νόσημα, τοῖς φίλοισι μὴ πεποιθέναι

Somehow, this is tyranny's disease, to trust no friends.

Translated in *Bartlett's Familiar Quotations* (1980)
Prometheus Bound 224

97 τυφλὰς ἐν αὐτοῖς ἐλπίδας κατῴκισα

Blind hopes I settled firmly in the breasts of men.

Prometheus Bound 250

98 ἐλαφρόν, ὅστις πημάτων ἔξω πόδα
ἔχει, παραινεῖν νουθετεῖν τε τὸν κακῶς πράσσοντ᾽

Oh, it is easy for the one who stands outside
The prison-wall of pain to teach the one who suffers.

Translated by Philip Vellacott (1961)
Prometheus Bound 263

99 ταὐτά τοι πλανωμένη
πρὸς ἄλλοτ' ἄλλον πημονὴ προσιζάνει

Misery, you know, wanders everywhere,
and alights on different persons at
different times.

Translated by Alan H. Sommerstein (2008)

Prometheus Bound 275

100 πολλῷ γ' ἀμείνων τοὺς πέλας φρενοῦν
ἔφυς
ἢ σαυτόν

You are much better at admonishing
others than
you are at admonishing yourself.

Translated by Alan H. Sommerstein (2008)

Prometheus Bound 335

101 ὀργῆς νοσούσης εἰσὶν ἰατροὶ λόγοι

Anger is a disease which words can heal.

Translated by Philip Vellacott (1961)

Prometheus Bound 378

102 ἔα με τῇδε τῇ νόσῳ νοσεῖν, ἐπεὶ
κέρδιστον εὖ φρονοῦντα μὴ φρονεῖν
δοκεῖν

Let me be guilty then of foolishness.
Sometimes a wise man gains his point
by being thought not wise.

Translated by Philip Vellacott (1961)

Prometheus Bound 384

103 οἳ πρῶτα μὲν βλέποντες ἔβλεπον μάτην,
κλύοντες οὐκ ἤκουον, ἀλλ' ὀνειράτων
ἀλίγκιοι μορφαῖσι τὸν μακρὸν βίον
ἔφυρον εἰκῇ πάντα

They had eyes, but knew not what they
saw;
heard sounds, but did not understand.
All their life they passed like shapes in
dreams,
confused and purposeless.

Prometheus Bound 447

of mortals; cf. Bible, Jeremiah *5.21*

104 κοὔτε πλινθυφεῖς
δόμους προσείλους ᾖσαν, οὐ ξυλουργίαν,
κατώρυχες δ' ἔναιον ὥστ' ἀήσυροι
μύρμηκες ἄντρων ἐν μυχοῖς ἀνηλίοις

Of brick-built, sun-warmed houses, or
of carpentry,
They had no notion, living in holes, like
swarms of ants,
Or deep in sunless caverns.

Translated by Philip Vellacott (1961)

Prometheus Bound 450

of mortals before being taught by Prometheus

105 ἦν δ' οὐδὲν αὐτοῖς οὔτε χείματος τέκμαρ
οὔτ' ἀνθεμώδους ἦρος οὔτε καρπίμου
θέρους βέβαιον, ἀλλ' ἄτερ γνώμης τὸ
πᾶν
ἔπρασσον

They knew no certain way
To mark off winter, flowery spring, or
fruitful summer;
Their every act was without knowledge.

Translated by Philip Vellacott (1961)

Prometheus Bound 454

of mortals

106 ἔστε δή σφιν ἀντολὰς ἐγὼ
ἄστρων ἔδειξα τάς τε δυσκρίτους δύσεις.
καὶ μὴν ἀριθμόν, ἔξοχον σοφισμάτων,
ἐξηῦρον αὐτοῖς, γραμμάτων τε
συνθέσεις,
μνήμην ἁπάντων, μουσομήτορ' ἐργάνην

I taught them to determine when stars
rise or set –
A difficult art. Number, the primary
science, I
Invented for them, and how to set down
words in writing –
The all-remembering skill, mother of
many arts.

Translated by Philip Vellacott (1961)

Prometheus Bound 457

Prometheus teaching mortals

107 θαλασσόπλαγκτα δ' οὔτις ἄλλος ἀντ'
ἐμοῦ
λινόπτερ' ηὗρε ναυτίλων ὀχήματα

And none, save I, contrived the linen-
wing'd,
Sea-wand'ring ships, whereon the sailors ride.

Translated by Elizabeth Barrett Browning (1833)

Prometheus Bound 467

of mortals

108 ᾀκὲς πεπονθὼς πῆμ', ἀποσφαλεὶς
φρενῶν
πλανᾷ· κακὸς δ' ἰατρὸς ὥς τις ἐς νόσον
πεσὼν ἀθυμεῖς καὶ σεαυτὸν οὐκ ἔχεις
εὑρεῖν ὁποίοις φαρμάκοις ἰάσιμος

Humiliation follows pain, distraught in
mind

You have lost your way; like a bad doctor fallen ill
You now despair of finding drugs to cure yourself.

Translated by Philip Vellacott (1961)

Prometheus Bound 472

109 γαμψωνύχων τε πτῆσιν οἰωνῶν σκεθρῶς
διώρισ', οἵτινές τε δεξιοί φύσιν
εὐωνύμους τε, καὶ δίαιταν ἥντινα
ἔχουσ' ἕκαστοι, καὶ πρὸς ἀλλήλους τίνες
ἔχθραι τε καὶ στέργηθρα καὶ ξυνεδρίαι

The various flights of crook-clawed vultures I defined
Exactly, those by nature favourable, and those
Sinister; how each species keeps its mode of life;
What feuds, friendships, associations kind with kind
Preserves.

Translated by Philip Vellacott (1961)

Prometheus Bound 488

110 ἔνερθε δὲ χθονὸς
κεκρυμμέν' ἀνθρώποισιν ὠφελήματα,
χαλκόν, σίδηρον, ἄργυρον χρυσόν τε, τίς
φήσειεν ἂν πάροιθεν ἐξευρεῖν ἐμοῦ;

Next, the treasures of the earth,
The bronze, iron, silver, gold hidden deep; who else
But I can claim to have found them first?

Translated by Philip Vellacott (1961)

Prometheus Bound 500

111 πᾶσαι τέχναι βροτοῖσιν ἐκ Προμηθέως

All human skill and science was Prometheus' gift.

Translated by Philip Vellacott (1961)

Prometheus Bound 506

112 τέχνη δ' ἀνάγκης ἀσθενεστέρα μακρῷ

Cunning is feebleness beside Necessity.

Translated by Philip Vellacott (1961)

Prometheus Bound 514

113 ἡδύ τι θαρσαλέαις
τὸν μακρὸν τείνειν βίον ἐλπίσι, φαναῖς
θυμὸν ἀλδαίνουσαν ἐν εὐφροσύναις

It is sweet to draw out one's life
to its length in confident hopes, and nourish
one's spirit in bright cheerfulness.

Translated by Christopher Collard (2009)

Prometheus Bound 536

114 τίς γῆ; τί γένος;

What land is this? What race lives here?

Translated by Philip Vellacott (1961)

Prometheus Bound 561

enter Io

115 πυρί με φλέξον, ἢ χθονὶ κάλυψον, ἢ
ποντίοις δάκεσι δὸς βοράν

Burn me with fire, let the earth swallow me,
throw me as food for monsters of the deep.

Prometheus Bound 582

spoken by Io

116 τὸ μὴ μαθεῖν σοι κρεῖσσον ἢ μαθεῖν τάδε

Why, not to know were better than to know.

Translated by Elizabeth Barrett Browning (1850)

Prometheus Bound 624

Prometheus to Io

117 αἰεὶ γὰρ ὄψεις ἔννυχοι πωλεύμεναι
ἐς παρθενῶνας τοὺς ἐμοὺς παρηγόρουν
λείοισι μύθοις· ὦ μέγ' εὔδαιμον κόρη,
τί παρθενεύῃ δαρόν;

For dreams nocturnal ever 'habiting
Within my virgin chamber, me beguiled
With honey'd words: – 'Oh blessed, blessed maid,
Wherefore so long unwedded?'

Translated by Elizabeth Barrett Browning (1833)

Prometheus Bound 645

118 ἦκον δ' ἀναγγέλλοντες αἰολοστόμους
χρησμοὺς, ἀσήμους δυσκρίτως τ' εἰρημένους

But they returned with reports of oracles,
riddling, obscure, and darkly worded.

Translated by Herbert Weir Smyth (1922)

Prometheus Bound 661

119 νόσημα γὰρ
αἴσχιστον εἶναί φημι συνθέτους λόγους

I count false words the foulest vice of all!

Prometheus Bound 685

120 τοῖς νοσοῦσί τοι γλυκὺ
τὸ λοιπὸν ἄλγος προυξεπίστασθαι τορῶς

It comforts those in pain
To know beforehand all the pain they still must bear.

Translated by Philip Vellacott (1961)

Prometheus Bound 698

121 ὀρῶν ὕψιστον, ἔνθα ποταμὸς ἐκφυσᾷ μένος
κροτάφων ἀπ' αὐτῶν. ἀστρογείτονας δὲ χρὴ
κορυφὰς ... βῆναι

Over its star-neighbouring crests you must pass this loftiest of mountains,
from which the river floods forth its fury.

Prometheus Bound 719

of the Caucasus

122 ἔσται δὲ θνητοῖς εἰσαεὶ λόγος μέγας
τῆς σῆς πορείας

Ages to come shall tell the story of your passage.

Translated by Philip Vellacott (1961)

Prometheus Bound 732

123 ἦ γάρ τι λοιπὸν τῇδε πημάτων ἐρεῖς;
δυσχείμερόν γε πέλαγος ἀτηρᾶς δύης

Have you still more to tell her of distress and pain?
Aye, a stormy sea of deadly misery.

Translated by Philip Vellacott (1961)

Prometheus Bound 745

124 κρεῖσσον γὰρ εἰσάπαξ θανεῖν
ἢ τὰς ἁπάσας ἡμέρας πάσχειν κακῶς

Better to die
Once, than suffer torment all my living days.

Translated by Philip Vellacott (1961)

Prometheus Bound 750

125 σοὶ πρῶτον, Ἰοῖ, πολύδονον πλάνην φράσω,
ἣν ἐγγράφου σὺ μνήμοσιν δέλτοις φρενῶν

First, Io, I will name
The many lands where Fate will toss you in your journey.
Write what I tell you in your book of memory.

Translated by Philip Vellacott (1961)

Prometheus Bound 788

126 ἃς οὐδ' ἥλιος προσδέρκεται
ἀκτῖσιν οὔθ' ἡ νύκτερος μήνη ποτέ

No ray of sun
Ever looks down on them, nor moon at night.

Translated by Philip Vellacott (1961)

Prometheus Bound 796

of the Graeae, three sisters, with only one eye and one tooth between them

127 τέρας τ' ἄπιστον, αἱ προσήγοροι δρύες,
ὑφ' ὧν σὺ λαμπρῶς κοὐδὲν αἰνικτηρίως
προσηγορεύθης ἡ Διὸς κλεινὴ δάμαρ
μέλλουσ' ἔσεσθαι

That marvel past belief, the speaking oaks,
greeting you clearly, and in no riddling terms,
as Zeus's destined bride.

Prometheus Bound 832

of the oracle at Dodona

128 χρόνον δὲ τὸν μέλλοντα πόντιος μυχός,
σαφῶς ἐπίστασ', Ἰόνιος κεκλήσεται,
τῆς σῆς πορείας μνῆμα τοῖς πᾶσιν βροτοῖς

That sea shall for all future time –
Mark this – be called Ionian, to perpetuate
For all mankind the story of Io's wanderings.

Translated by Philip Vellacott (1961)

Prometheus Bound 839

of the Ionian Sea, named after Io

129 κραδία δὲ φόβῳ φρένα λακτίζει

My heart from fear beats hard within my chest.

Prometheus Bound 881

130 ὡς τὸ κηδεῦσαι καθ' ἑαυτὸν ἀριστεύει μακρῷ,
καὶ μήτε τῶν πλούτῳ διαθρυπτομένων
μήτε τῶν γέννᾳ μεγαλυνομένων
ὄντα χερνήταν ἐραστεῦσαι γάμων

The best rule by far is to marry in your own rank;
That a man who works with his hands should never crave
To marry either a woman pampered in wealth
Or one who prides herself on her noble family.

Translated by Philip Vellacott (1961)
Prometheus Bound 890

131 ἀπόλεμος ὅδε γ' ὁ πόλεμος, ἄπορα πόριμος

I have no sword to fight that fight,
no strength to tread that path.

Translated by Elizabeth Barrett Browning (1850)
Prometheus Bound 904

132 τινάσσων τ' ἐν χεροῖν πύρπνουν βέλος

Shaking his fire-breathing thunderbolt.

Prometheus Bound 917
of Zeus

133 ὃς δὴ κεραυνοῦ κρείσσον' εὑρήσει φλόγα
βροντῆς θ' ὑπερβάλλοντα καρτερὸν κτύπον,
θαλασσίαν τε γῆς τινάκτειραν νόσον,
ἣ τρίκροον αἰχμὴν τὴν Ποσειδῶνος σκεδᾷ

One who will find a flame hotter than lightning-strokes,
A crash to overwhelm the thunder; one whose strength
Shall split Poseidon's trident-spear, that dreaded scourge
That shakes both land and sea.

Translated by Philip Vellacott (1961)
Prometheus Bound 922

134 πταίσας δὲ τῷδε πρὸς κακῷ μαθήσεται
ὅσον τό τ' ἄρχειν καὶ τὸ δουλεύειν δίχα

His power shall strike and founder, till he learns how great
A chasm lies between ruling and being ruled.

Translated by Philip Vellacott (1961)
Prometheus Bound 926

135 τῆς σῆς λατρείας τὴν ἐμὴν δυσπραξίαν,
σαφῶς ἐπίστασ', οὐκ ἂν ἀλλάξαιμ' ἐγώ

Know for certain, that I would not exchange
my sufferings for your servitude.

Translated by H.T. Riley (1872)
Prometheus Bound 966

136 χλιδᾶν ἔοικας τοῖς παροῦσι πράγμασιν

It seems you find your present state a luxury.

Translated by Philip Vellacott (1961)
Prometheus Bound 971

137 ἀλλ' ἐκδιδάσκει πάνθ' ὁ γηράσκων χρόνος

Time, as he grows old, teaches us all things.

Prometheus Bound 981

138 πρὸς ταῦτα ῥιπτέσθω μὲν αἰθαλοῦσσα φλόξ,
λευκοπτέρῳ δὲ νιφάδι καὶ βροντήμασι
χθονίοις κυκάτω πάντα καὶ ταρασσέτω·
γνάμψει γὰρ οὐδὲν τῶνδέ μ' ὥστε καὶ φράσαι
πρὸς οὗ χρεών νιν ἐκπεσεῖν τυραννίδος

Let scorching flames be flung from heaven; let the whole earth
With white-winged snowstorms, subterranean thunderings,
Heave and convulse: nothing will force me to reveal
By whose hand Fate shall hurl Zeus from his tyranny.

Translated by Philip Vellacott (1961)
Prometheus Bound 992

139 ὀχλεῖς μάτην με κῦμ' ὅπως παρηγορῶν

Seek to persuade the sea wave not to break.
You'll persuade me no more easily.

Translated by Edith Hamilton (1964)
Prometheus Bound 1001

140 αὐθαδία γὰρ τῷ φρονοῦντι μὴ καλῶς
αὐτὴ κατ' αὑτὴν οὐδενὸς μεῖζον σθένει

Obstinacy in a fool has by itself
No strength at all.

Translated by Philip Vellacott (1961)
Prometheus Bound 1012

141 σκέψαι δ', ἐὰν μὴ τοῖς ἐμοῖς πεισθῇς λόγοις,
οἷός σε χειμὼν καὶ κακῶν τρικυμία
ἔπεισ' ἄφυκτος

Consider, if you will not believe my words,
what tempest and what towering wave of woe
shall break upon you past escape.

Prometheus Bound 1014

142 ψευδηγορεῖν γὰρ οὐκ ἐπίσταται στόμα
τὸ Δῖον, ἀλλὰ πᾶν ἔπος τελεῖ

Zeus knows not how to speak

falsehood,
but will accomplish every word he says.

Prometheus Bound 1032

143 πρὸς ταῦτ' ἐπί μοι ῥιπτείσθω μὲν
πυρὸς ἀμφήκης βόστρυχος, αἰθὴρ δ'
ἐρεθιζέσθω βροντῇ σφακέλῳ τ'
ἀγρίων ἀνέμων, χθόνα δ' ἐκ πυθμένων
αὐταῖς ῥίζαις πνεῦμα κραδαίνοι,
κῦμα δὲ πόντου τραχεῖ ῥοθίῳ
ζυγχώσειεν τῶν οὐρανίων
ἄστρων διόδους

Let lightning strike me, then, and ether
be torn asunder by the raging winds;
let hurricanes assault the earth,
and let enormous waves
confound the courses of the stars.

Prometheus Bound 1043

144 τοὺς προδότας γὰρ μισεῖν ἔμαθον,
κοὐκ ἔστι νόσος
τῆσδ' ἥντιν' ἀπέπτυσα μᾶλλον

I was taught to hate those who desert their friends;
And there is no infamy I more despise.

Translated by Philip Vellacott (1961)

Prometheus Bound 1068

145 εἰς ἀπέραντον δίκτυον ἄτης
ἐμπλεχθήσεσθ' ὑπ' ἀνοίας

Only your own folly will entangle you
In the inextricable net of destruction.

Translated by Philip Vellacott (1961)

Prometheus Bound 1078

146 καὶ μὴν ἔργῳ κοὐκέτι μύθῳ

Now in deed, no more in word alone.

Translated by Alan H. Sommerstein (2008)

Prometheus Bound 1080

147 χθὼν σεσάλευται,
βρυχία δ' ἠχὼ παραμυκᾶται
βροντῆς, ἕλικες δ' ἐκλάμπουσι
στεροπῆς ζάπυροι, στρόμβοι δὲ κόνιν
εἱλίσσουσι, σκιρτᾷ δ' ἀνέμων
πνεύματα πάντων εἰς ἄλληλα
στάσιν ἀντίπνουν ἀποδεικνύμενα,
ξυντετάρακται δ' αἰθὴρ πόντῳ

The earth is shaking and reeling!
From the depths, in accompaniment, there bellows
the sound of thunder; fiery twists
of lightning shine out; the dust
is whirled by whirlwinds; the blasts
of all the winds at once leap at one another
in a raging display of mutual strife,
and sky and sea are blended into one.

Translated by Alan H. Sommerstein (2008)

Prometheus Bound 1081

148 τοιάδ' ἐπ' ἐμοὶ ῥιπὴ Διόθεν
τεύχουσα φόβον στείχει φανερῶς.
ὦ μητρὸς ἐμῆς σέβας, ὦ πάντων
αἰθὴρ κοινὸν φάος εἱλίσσων,
ἐσορᾷθ' ὡς ἔκδικα πάσχω

On me the tempest falls.
It does not make me tremble.
O holy Mother Earth,
O air and sun,
behold me. I am wronged.

Translated by Edith Hamilton (1958)

Prometheus Bound 1089

closing lines, spoken by Prometheus as he disappears amid thunder and lightning

149 Κάδμου πολῖται, χρὴ λέγειν τὰ καίρια
ὅστις φυλάσσει πρᾶγος ἐν πρύμνῃ πόλεως
οἴακα νωμῶν, βλέφαρα μὴ κοιμῶν ὕπνῳ

Citizens, sons of Cadmus! What the hour demands
must now be said by him who guides the State,
who holds the helm with sleepless eyes.

Seven against Thebes 1

opening lines

150 εἰ δ' αὖθ', ὃ μὴ γένοιτο, συμφορὰ τύχοι

If, god forbid, misfortune falls upon us.

Seven against Thebes 5

ὃ μὴ γένοιτο – an expression used verbatim to this day

151 ἀλλ' εἴς τ' ἐπάλξεις καὶ πύλας πυργωμάτων
ὁρμᾶσθε πάντες, σοῦσθε σὺν παντευχίᾳ,
πληροῦτε θωρακεῖα, κἀπὶ σέλμασιν
πύργων στάθητε, καὶ πυλῶν ἐπ' ἐξόδοις
μίμνοντες εὖ θαρσεῖτε, μηδ' ἐπηλύδων
ταρβεῖτ' ἄγαν ὅμιλον

Then, to the walls! Swarm to the battlements and gates;
Forward, full-armed; man parapets, fill every floor
Of every tower; and in the gate's mouth hold your ground
With courage. Never fear this horde of

foreigners!

Translated by Philip Vellacott (1961)

Seven against Thebes 30

152 μέλει γὰρ ἀνδρί, μὴ γυνὴ βουλευέτω, τἄξωθεν

War is for men, and women's views unwelcome.

Seven against Thebes 200

153 γείτονες δὲ καρδίας
μέριμναι ζωπυροῦσι τάρβος

Anxiety, close upon my heart, enkindles fear.

Seven against Thebes 289

154 οὐ γὰρ δοκεῖν ἄριστος ἀλλ' εἶναι θέλει

Do not purport to be the best, be the best.

Seven against Thebes 592

cf. the English proverb 'be what you would seem to be'; and Aristides 5 (with 'δίκαιος' in the place of 'ἄριστος')

155 ἐν παντὶ πράγει δ' ἔσθ' ὁμιλίας κακῆς κάκιον οὐδέν

In every undertaking there is nothing worse than evil company.

Translated by Christopher Collard (2009)

Seven against Thebes 599

156 ἄτης ἄρουρα θάνατον ἐκκαρπίζεται

When mischief ploughs, the crop is death.

Seven against Thebes 601

157 γέροντα τὸν νοῦν, σάρκα δ' ἡβῶσαν φύει

He has an aged mind in a youthful body.

Translated by H.T. Riley (1872)

Seven against Thebes 622

158 θεοῦ δὲ δῶρόν ἐστιν εὐτυχεῖν βροτούς

Mortals' good fortune is the gift of god.

Translated by Alan H. Sommerstein (2008)

Seven against Thebes 625

159 κακῶν δ' ὥσπερ θάλασσα κῦμ' ἄγει,
τὸ μὲν πίτνον, ἄλλο δ' ἀείρει
τρίχαλον

And as a troubled sea drives on its billows,
as one wave sinks, another rears aloft,
in groups of three.

Seven against Thebes 758

160 θάρσει παρέσται μηχανὴ δραστήριος ...
αὐδῶ σε μὴ περισσὰ κηρύσσειν ἐμοί

Courage! For I will find the power to act.
Speak not to stay me.

Translated by Edith Hamilton (1964)

Seven against Thebes 1041

161 Διὸς ἵμερος οὐκ εὐθήρατος ἐτύχθη ...
παντᾷ τοι φλεγέθει
κἀν σκότῳ μελαίνᾳ
ξὺν τύχᾳ μερόπεσσι λαοῖς

The pathways of god's purpose are hard to track.
And yet it shines out through the gloom
on mankind's darkest fortunes.

Suppliant Maidens 87

162 μὴ πρόλεσχος μηδ' ἐφολκὸς ἐν λόγῳ γένῃ

Be neither forward nor reluctant in your speech.

Translated by Philip Vellacott (1961)

Suppliant Maidens 200

163 μέμνησο δ' εἴκειν

Remember to give way.

Suppliant Maidens 202

164 σύ τοι πόλις, σὺ δὲ τὸ δάμιον ...
ἄγος φυλάσσου

You are the state, you are the people,
Guard against guilt.

Translated by Philip Vellacott (1961)

Suppliant Maidens 370

the Chorus to the king

165 οὐκ εὔκριτον τὸ κρῖμα· μή μ' αἱροῦ κριτήν

Do not order me to judge; to judge is not an easy matter.

Suppliant Maidens 397

166 γένοιτο μύθου μῦθος ἂν θελκτήριος

Let soothing speech heal speech.

Suppliant Maidens 447

167 θέλω δ' ἄιδρις μᾶλλον ἢ σοφὸς κακῶν εἶναι

In foretelling ruin – I choose ignorance
Rather than knowledge.

Translated by Philip Vellacott (1961)

Suppliant Maidens 453

168 ἀρχῆς γὰρ φιλαίτιος λεώς

All citizens love to find fault with the government.

Translated by Philip Vellacott (1961)

Suppliant Maidens 485

169 τοῖς ἥσσοσιν γὰρ πᾶς τις εὐνοίας φέρει

Everyone has kindly feelings for the underdog.

Translated by Alan H. Sommerstein (2008)

Suppliant Maidens 489

170 φύλαξαι μὴ θράσος τέκῃ φόβον

Beware lest over-confidence beget dismay.

Translated by Herbert Weir Smyth (1922)

Suppliant Maidens 498

171 τοιγὰρ ὑποσκίων
ἐκ στομάτων ποτάσ-
θω φιλότιμος εὐχά ...
μηδ' ἐπιχωρίοις ἔρις
πτώμασιν αἱματίσαι πέδον γᾶς

Therefore let a prayer of gratitude
be wafted forth from our lips:
May civil war never stain
the soil of this country with
the blood of its own race!

Translated by Kathleen Freeman (1947)

Suppliant Maidens 656

172 φυλάσσοι τ' εὖ τὰ τίμι' ἀστοῖς
τὸ δάμιον, τὸ πτόλιν κρατύνει,
προμαθὶς εὐκοινόμητις ἀρχά·
ξένοισί τ' εὐξυμβόλους,
πρὶν ἐξοπλίζειν Ἄρη,
δίκας ἄτερ πημάτων διδοῖεν

And may the people, who
wield power in the State,
keep their privileges unshaken,
ruling with foresight, counselling
wisely for the common good!

Translated by Kathleen Freeman (1947)

Suppliant Maidens 698

173 τὸ γὰρ τεκόντων σέβας ...
Δίκας γέγραπται μεγιστοτίμου

The law of reverence to parents
is worthy of greatest honour.

Suppliant Maidens 707

174 ὠδῖνα τίκτειν νὺξ κυβερνήτῃ σοφῷ

In a cautious helmsman night begets travail of mind.

Suppliant Maidens 770

175 μέλας γενοίμαν καπνὸς
νέφεσσι γειτονῶν Διός

Would that I become black smoke
to mingle with the clouds, not far from god himself.

Suppliant Maidens 779

cf. Bible 257

176 καὶ πόλλ' ἁμαρτὼν οὐδὲν ὤρθωσας φρενί

Having done wrong in many things you have set nothing straight.

Translated in Liddell & Scott

Suppliant Maidens 915

177 οὐ γὰρ ξενοῦμαι τοὺς θεῶν συλήτορας

He is no friend of mine who violates the altars of the gods.

Suppliant Maidens 927

178 πᾶς τις ἐπειπεῖν
ψόγον ἀλλοθρόοις
εὔτυκος

Everyone's quick to blame the alien.

Translated in *The Oxford Dictionary of Quotations* (2004)

Suppliant Maidens 972

179 φύλαξαι τάσδ' ἐπιστολὰς πατρός,
τὸ σωφρονεῖν τιμῶσα τοῦ βίου πλέον

Honour the behests of your father,
count self-control more precious than your life.

Suppliant Maidens 1012

180 ὅ τί τοι μόρσιμόν ἐστιν, τὸ γένοιτ' ἂν

What will be, will be.

Translated by Philip Vellacott (1961)

Suppliant Maidens 1047

181 πάλιν γὰρ ἵκουσ' ἐκ σκότου τόδ' εἰς φάος

They shall return from darkness into the light.

Fragment 6 (Radt, *TrGF*) – *Aetnaeae* – *Women of Aetna*

182 σοὶ μὲν γαμεῖσθαι μόρσιμον, γαμεῖν δ' ἐμοί

It is thy fate to be my wife; mine to be thy husband.

Translated by Herbert Weir Smyth (1926)

Fragment 13 (Radt, *TrGF*) – *Amymone*

183 τό τοι κακὸν ποδῶκες ἔρχεται βροτοῖς
καὶ τἀμπλάκημα τῷ περῶντι τὴν θέμιν

Evil comes swiftly upon mortals
for offences against what we know is right.

Fragment 22 (Radt, *TrGF*) – *Bacchae*

184 ἀγὼν γὰρ ἄνδρας οὐ μένει λελειμμένους

A contest won't wait for athletes arriving late.

Fragment 37 (Radt, *TrGF*) – *Glaucus of Potniae*

185 ὁ μὲν ... βόμβυκας ἔχων ...
δακτυλόθικτον πίμπλησι μέλος,
μανίας ἐπαρωγὸν ὁμοκλάν,
ὁ δὲ χαλκοδέτοις κοτύλαις ὀτοβεῖ
ψαλμὸς δ' ἀλαλάζει·
ταυρόφθογγοι δ' ὑπομυκῶνταί
ποθεν ἐξ ἀφανοῦς φοβεροὶ μῖμοι·
ἠχὼ τυπάνου δ', ὥσθ' ὑπογαίου
βροντῆς φέρεται βαρυταρβής

The one blows on pipes his fingered tune, a sound that wakes to frenzy;
another, loudest clangs on brass-bound cymbals; ... and shrilling twangs;
and unseen, unknown, bull-voiced mimes bellow fearfully in answer;
and rolls of drums, like subterranean thunder, inspiring mighty terror.

Fragment 57 (Radt, *TrGF*) – *Edonoi – The Edonians*

the 'barbarous dissonance of Bacchus' (cf. Milton, Paradise Lost, *7.32)*

186 βίου πονηροῦ θάνατος εὐκλεέστερος

Death is more glorious than a useless life.

Fragment 90 (Radt, *TrGF*) – *Ixion*

187 τὸ μὴ παρὸν δὲ τέρψιν οὐκ ἔχει φίλοις

To them that love, absence brings no delight.

Fragment 99 (Radt, *TrGF*) – *Cares or Europe – Carians or Europa*

188 ἀλλ' Ἄρης φιλεῖ
ἀεὶ τὰ λῷστα πάντ' ἀπανθίζειν στρατοῦ

But Ares ever loves
to pluck the fairest flowers of an army.

Fragment 100 (Radt, *TrGF*) – *Cares or Europe – Carians or Europa of Ares, the god of war*

189 καὶ μὴν πελάζει καὶ καταψύχει πνοὴ
ἄρκειος ὧς ναύταισιν ἀσκεύοις μολών

And lo, he draws near and his advance fills us with chilling fear,
like a northern blast that falls on sailors unprepared.

Translated by Herbert Weir Smyth (1926)

Fragment 127 (Radt, *TrGF*) – *Memnon*

190 ὦ δυσχάριστε τῶν πυκνῶν φιλημάτων

Oh thou ungrateful for my many kisses!

Translated by Herbert Weir Smyth (1926)

Fragment 135 (Radt, *TrGF*) – *Myrmidons*

191 πληγέντ' ἀτρακτῷ τοξικῷ τὸν αἰετὸν
εἰπεῖν ἰδόντα μηχανὴν πτερώματος·
τάδ' οὐχ ὑπ' ἄλλων, ἀλλὰ τοῖς αὑτῶν πτεροῖς
ἁλισκόμεσθα

That eagle's fate and mine are one,
Which, on the shaft that made him die,
Espy'd a feather of his own,
Wherewith he wont to soar so high.

Translated by Edmund Waller (1606–1687)

Fragment 139 (Radt, *TrGF*) – *Myrmidons*

cf. Aesop 9 and Aristophanes, Birds *808*

192 θεὸς μὲν αἰτίαν φύει βροτοῖς,
ὅταν κακῶσαι δῶμα παμπήδην θέλῃ

A god implants the guilty cause in men
When he would utterly destroy a house.

Translated by Paul Shorey (1930)

Fragment 154a (Radt, *TrGF*) – *Niobe*

193 μόνος θεῶν γὰρ Θάνατος οὐ δώρων ἐρᾷ

Death is the only god whom gifts cannot appease.

Translated by D.S. Baker (1998)

Fragment 161 (Radt, *TrGF*) – *Niobe*

194 ἁπλᾶ γάρ ἐστι τῆς ἀληθείας ἔπη

Simple are the words of truth.

Translated by Herbert Weir Smyth (1926)

Fragment 176 (Radt, *TrGF*) – *Oplon Crisis – The Adjudgement of Arms*

195 τίνος κατέκτας ἕνεκα παῖδ' ἐμὸν βλάβης;

By reason of what injury hast thou slain my son?

Translated by Herbert Weir Smyth (1926)

Fragment 181 (Radt, *TrGF*) – *Palamedes*

196 ποῦ μοι τὰ πολλὰ δῶρα κἀκροθίνια;
ποῦ χρυσότευκτα κἀργυρᾶ σκυφώματα;

Where are my many promised gifts and spoils of war?
Where are my gold and silver cups?

Translated by Herbert Weir Smyth (1926)

Fragment 184 (Radt, *TrGF*) – *Perrhaebides – The Women of Perrhaebia*

197 πολλοῖς γάρ ἐστι κέρδος ἡ σιγὴ βροτῶν

Silence is a great benefit to mankind.

Fragment 188 (Radt, *TrGF*) – *Prometheus*

198 τράγος γένειον ἆρα πενθήσεις σύ γε

Like the goat, you'll mourn for your beard, you will.

Translated by Herbert Weir Smyth (1926)

Fragment 207 (Radt, *TrGF*) – *Prometheus Pyrcaeus – Prometheus the Fire-kindler*

Prometheus to the satyr who wished to kiss fire, seeing it for the first time

199 σιγῶν θ' ὅπου δεῖ καὶ λέγων τὰ καίρια

Silent when necessary and explicit on the essential.

Fragment 208 (Radt, *TrGF*) – *Prometheus Pyrphoros – Prometheus the Fire-bearer*

200 Αἰτναῖός ἐστι κάνθαρος βιᾷ πονῶν

Like a beetle from Mount Etna, toiling powerfully.

Translated by Alan H. Sommerstein (2008)

Fragment 233 (Radt, *TrGF*) – *Sisyphus*

of Sisyphus rolling his stone; Mount Aetna was widely believed to be the home of a race of giant beetles

201 νέας γυναικὸς οὔ με μὴ λάθῃ φλέγων ὀφθαλμός

A young woman's flashing glance never escapes me.

Fragment 243 (Radt, *TrGF*) – *Toxotides – The Archer Women*

202 ἔνθ' οὔτε μίμνειν ἄνεμος οὔτ' ἐκπλεῖν ἐᾷ

Where the wind allows one neither to remain nor to sail out.

Translated by Alan H. Sommerstein (2008)

Fragment 250 (Radt, *TrGF*) – *Philoctetes*

203 ὦ θάνατε παιών, μή μ' ἀτιμάσῃς μολεῖν·
μόνος γὰρ εἶ σὺ τῶν ἀνηκέστων κακῶν
ἰατρός, ἄλγος δ' οὐδὲν ἅπτεται νεκροῦ

Fail me not in coming, oh saviour death;
the incurable only you can heal;
for no pain touches the dead.

Fragment 255 (Radt, *TrGF*) – *Philoctetes*

204 δέδοικα μῶρον κάρτα πυραύστου μόρον

I fear I may suffer the very stupid death of a moth.

Translated by Alan H. Sommerstein (2008)

Fragment 288 (Radt, *TrGF*)

the moth which flies into flames

205 ἀπάτης δικαίας οὐκ ἀποστατεῖ θεός

God does not distance himself from justifiable deceit.

Fragment 301 (Radt, *TrGF*)

206 τῷ πονοῦντι δ' ἐκ θεῶν
ὀφείλεται τέκνωμα τοῦ πόνου κλέος

To those who toil, the gods
owe fame, the child of toil.

Fragment 315 (Radt, *TrGF*)

207 θάρσει· πόνου γὰρ ἄκρον οὐκ ἔχει χρόνον

Take heart; suffering, when it climbs highest, lasts but a little time.

Translated by Edith Hamilton (1964)

Fragment 352 (Radt, *TrGF*)

208 ὡς οὐ δικαίως θάνατον ἔχθουσιν βροτοί·
ὅσπερ μέγιστον ῥῦμα τῶν πολλῶν κακῶν

Men hate death unjustly;
for it is the healer of many ills.

Fragment 353 (Radt, *TrGF*)

209 κοινὸν τύχη, γνώμη δὲ τῶν κεκτημένων

Good luck can belong to anyone, but good judgement belongs only to those who possess it.

Translated by Alan H. Sommerstein (2008)

Fragment 389 (Radt, *TrGF*)

210 ὁ χρήσιμ' εἰδώς, οὐχ ὁ πόλλ' εἰδὼς σοφός

Who knows things useful, not many things, is wise.

Translated by Herbert Weir Smyth (1926)

Fragment 390 (Radt, *TrGF*)

211 ἁμαρτάνει τοι χὠ σοφοῦ σοφώτερος

Even the wisest of the wise can make

mistakes.

Fragment 391 (Radt, *TrGF*)

212 ἦ βαρὺ φόρημ' ἄνθρωπος εὐτυχῶν ἄφρων

What a heavy load a prosperous fool is!

Fragment 392 (Radt, *TrGF*)

213 κάτοπτρον εἴδους χαλκός ἐστ', οἶνος δὲ νοῦ

Bronze mirrors the face, wine the mind.

Fragment 393 (Radt, *TrGF*)

214 οὐκ ἀνδρὸς ὅρκοι πίστις, ἀλλ' ὅρκων ἀνήρ

Oaths do not give credibility to men, but men to oaths.

Translated by Alan H. Sommerstein (2008)

Fragment 394 (Radt, *TrGF*)

215 φιλεῖ δέ ... τῷ κάμνοντι συσπεύδειν θεός

God loves to help him who strives to help himself.

Translated by Herbert Weir Smyth (1926)

Fragment 395 (Radt, *TrGF*)

cf. the English proverb 'God helps them that help themselves'

216 καλὸν δὲ καὶ γέροντα μανθάνειν σοφά

Even an old man benefits from learning.

Fragment 396 (Radt, *TrGF*)

217 πρὸ τῶν τοιούτων χρὴ λόγων δάκνειν στόμα

Before uttering such words you better bite your tongue.

Fragment 397 (Radt, *TrGF*)

218 κακοὶ γὰρ εὖ πράσσοντες οὐκ ἀνασχετοί

Successful rascals are insufferable.

Translated by Herbert Weir Smyth (1926)

Fragment 398 (Radt, *TrGF*)

219 τὸ τοῦ καλοῦ καὶ λαμπροῦ Αἰσχύλου, ὃς τὰς αὑτοῦ τραγῳδίας τεμάχη εἶναι ἔλεγεν τῶν Ὁμήρου μεγάλων δείπνων

The noble and brilliant Aeschylus declared that his plays were but cuts from Homer's mighty dinners.

Athenaeus, *Deipnosophists* 8.347e

220 Αἰσχύλον Εὐφορίωνος Ἀθηναῖον τόδε κεύθει
μνῆμα καταφθίμενον πυροφόροιο Γέλας·
ἀλκὴν δ' εὐδόκιμον Μαραθώνιον ἄλσος ἂν εἴποι,
καὶ βαρυχαιτήεις Μῆδος ἐπιστάμενος.

Aeschylus, the Athenian, Euphorion's son, is dead.
This tomb in Gela's cornlands covers him.
His glorious courage the hallowed field of Marathon could tell,
and the longhaired Mede had knowledge of it.

Translated by Edith Hamilton (1964)

Greek Anthology Appendix, Epigrammata sepulcralia 17

some believe that the epigram was written by Aeschylus himself

AESOP

c.550BC

Writer of fables, with fables attributed to him even before or after his time

see also Aristophanes 23

1 τότε ματαίως ἐμελῴδεις, νυνὶ λοιπὸν ὀρχήσασθαι θέλησον

You were idly singing all summer, so dance now.

The Ant and the Cicada, Syntipas 43 (H-H, *Fabulae Syntipae philosophi*) – Perry 373

said the ant to the cicada who was singing all summer

2 κολοιὸς δὲ ... ἃ τῶν ἄλλων ἐξέπιπτε, ταῦτα οἰκεῖον συνέθηκε κόσμον

But the jackdaw decorated himself with feathers dropped by the other birds.

The Beauty Contest of the Birds, Aphthonius 31 (H-H, *Fabulae Aphthonii rhetoris*) – Perry 101

cf. the expression 'borrowed plumes' and Lucian, Apologia *4.3*

3 παραινεῖν ἕτοιμον ἃ ποιεῖν ἀπορώτερον

It's easy to offer advice for what is difficult to do.

The Deer and His Mother, Aphthonius 17 (H-H, *Fabulae Aphthonii rhetoris*) – Perry 351

4 οἵτινες πλειοτέρων ἐπιθυμοῦσιν καὶ ἃ ἔχουσιν ἀπολοῦσιν

Wishing to grab more you may lose what you have.

The Dog, the Meat and His Reflection, Fable 136 (H-H) – Perry 133

5 τὸ ἐν χειρσὶ μικρὸν τοῦ ἐλπιζομένου μείζονος κρεῖσσον

Better little in hand than hope for more.

The Dog, the Meat and His Reflection, Aphthonius 35 (H-H, *Fabulae Aphthonii rhetoris*) – Perry 133

cf. the English proverb 'a bird in the hand is worth two in the bush'

6 βίος ἀβέβαιος παντὸς ἀνδρὸς ἀπλήστου ἐλπίσι ματαίαις πραγμάτων ἀναλοῦται

Every greedy man's life is insecure, vainly spent in hopes of gain.

Translated by Ben Edwin Perry (1965)

The Dog, the Meat and His Reflection, Babrius 79 (*Mythiambi*) – Perry 133

7 οὐ πάντες πρὸς πάντα πεφύκασιν

Not all men are made for the same things.

Translated by Panos Koronakis-Rohlf and Maria Batzini (2007)

The Donkey and the Pet Dog, Fable 93 (H-H) – Perry 91

8 τὸ ἑκάστῳ πεπρωμένον ἀθεράπευτόν ἐστι

No one can escape his destiny.

Donkeys and Zeus, Fable 196 (H-H) – Perry 185

9 ὁ ἀετὸς καὶ τὸ βέλος ἰδὼν ἐπτερωμένον τοῖς οἰκείοις πτεροῖς ἔφη· τὰ παρ' αὐτοῦ τοῖς πολλοῖς πραγμάτων οἰκείων ἐπιβουλή

Said the eagle seeing that the shaft of the arrow which hit him had been feathered with one of his own plumes: 'We often give our enemies the means of our own destruction.'

The Eagle and the Arrow, Aphthonius 32 (H-H, *Fabulae Aphthonii rhetoris*) – Perry 276

cf. Aeschylus 191

10 ὁ κάματος θησαυρός ἐστι τοῖς ἀνθρώποις

Toil is a treasure for men.

The Farmer and his Sons, Fable 42 (H-H) – Perry 42

11 κρεῖσσον πενία ἄφοβος ἢ πλουσιότης μετὰ ἀναγκῶν καὶ ἐπηρειῶν

Better fearless poverty than wealth with its needs and worries.

The Fir Tree and the Bramble Bush, Fable 263 (H-H) – Perry 304

12 χαρᾶς ... ἀδελφὴ ἐστιν ἡ λύπη

Grief, the sister of joy.

Translated by Laura Gibbs (2002)

The Fisherman and the Stone, Fable 13 (H-H) – Perry 13

13 ὄμφακές εἰσιν

These raisyns be soure.

A fox loked and behelde the reysins that grewe upon a hye vyne whych he moch desired. And whan he saw that he might get none, he turned his soro into joy and saide these raisyns be soure and if I had some I wolde not ete them. And therfore he is wyse not to desyre that thinge which he may nat haue.

Translated by William Caxton (1484)

The Fox and the Grapes, Fable 15a (H-H) – Perry 15

cf. the English expression 'sour grapes'

14 τοῦ σωματικοῦ κάλλους ἀμείνων ἐστὶν ὁ τῆς διανοίας κόσμος

Mental endowments are better than the glamour of good looks.

Translated by Laura Gibbs (2002)

The Fox and the Leopard, Fable 12 (H-H) – Perry 12

15 ἡ συνήθεια ... καταπραΰνει

Familiarity breeds contempt.

Translated in *Bartlett's Familiar Quotations* (1980)

The Fox and the Lion, Fable 10 (H-H) – Perry 10

16 οἵα κεφαλὴ ἐγκέφαλον οὐκ ἔχει

So full of beauty, so lacking in brains!

Translated by Laura Gibbs (2002)

The Fox and the Mask, Fable 27 (H-H) – Perry 27

cf. the Latin 'caput vacuum cerebro' (Erasmus, Adages 3.4.40)

17 ἔχεις, κόραξ, ἅπαντα, νοῦς δέ σοι λείπει

O raven, you do have a voice but no brains to go with it!

Translated by Laura Gibbs (2002)

The Fox and the Raven, Babrius 77 (*Mythiambi*) – Perry 124

18 ἀλλὰ μένε τέως σὺ ἐνταῦθα, ἕως ἂν τοιαύτη γένῃ ὁποία οὖσα εἰσῆλθες

Now stay stuck here until you get slim again.

The Fox with the Swollen Belly, Fable 24 (H-H) – Perry 24

advice given to the fox unable to get out of a hole for eating too much; cf. A.A. Milne, Winnie-the-Pooh, *ch. 2, in which Pooh gets into a tight place*

19 ἃ δρᾷ τις καὶ πείσεται

What you do, you will suffer.

The Goat and the Vine, Aphthonius 37 (H-H, *Fabulae Aphthonii rhetoris*) – Perry 374

20 ὡς ἐλπίδι θησαυροῦ ἐπερειδόμενος, καὶ τοῦ ἐν χερσὶ κέρδους ἐξέπεσον

Chasing hopes of a treasure I lost the profit I held in hand.

Translated by Laura Gibbs (2002)

The Goose that Laid the Golden Eggs, Syntipas 27 (H-H, *Fabulae Syntipae philosophi*) – Perry 87

21 οἱ δυστυχοῦντες ἐξ ἑτέρων χείρονα πασχόντων παραμυθοῦνται

The unfortunate find comfort in the misfortunes of those who suffer more.

The Hares and the Frogs, Fable 143 (H-H) – Perry 138

22 τῶν τροχῶν ἅπτου

Put your shoulder to the wheel.

Translated in *Bartlett's Familiar Quotations* (1980)

Heracles and the Driver, Babrius 20.6 (*Mythiambi*) – Perry 291

23 τοῖς θεοῖς δ' εὔχου
ὅταν τι ποιῇς καὐτός, ἢ μάτην εὔξῃ

Pray to the gods only when making an effort on your own behalf; otherwise your prayers are wasted!

Translated by Laura Gibbs (2002)

Heracles and the Driver, Babrius 20.7 (*Mythiambi*) – Perry 291

cf. the English proverb 'God helps them that help themselves'

24 ἰδοὺ Ῥόδος καὶ πήδημα

Here then is Rhodes, jump!

The Jump at Rhodes, Fable 33 (H-H) – Perry 33

of someone who claimed to have made a huge jump in Rhodes

25 οἱ παρὰ τοῖς εἰδόσιν ἀλαζονευόμενοι εἰκότως γέλωτα ὀφλισκάνουσιν

Braggarts only draw laughter from those who know.

The Lion and the Donkey, Fable 156 (H-H) – Perry 151

26 ὁρᾷς ὅσον ἰσχύος ὁ κώνωψ ἔχει, ὡς καὶ ἐλέφαντα φοβεῖν

Look how strong the mosquito is, striking fear even into an elephant!

Lion, Elephant and Mosquito, Fable 292 (H-H) – Perry 259

of the elephant knowing that a mosquito's bite in his ear may cause death

27 ἑώρων πολλῶν εἰσιόντων ἴχνη, ἐξιόντος δὲ οὐδενός

I see many footprints going in, none coming out.

The Lion, the Fox and the Beasts, Fable 147 (H-H) – Perry 142

said the fox, not entering the lion's den

28 ἐν καιρῶν μεταβολαῖς καὶ οἱ σφόδρα δυνατοὶ τῶν ἀσθενεστέρων ἐνδεεῖς γίνονται

In times of change even the strongest have need of the most weak.

Translated by Panos Koronakis-Rohlf and Maria Batzini (2007)

The Lion and the Mouse, Fable 155 (H-H) – Perry 150

29 ἀλκὴ ἐλάφῳ ἐν τοῖς ποσὶν καὶ λέοντι ἐν τῇ καρδίᾳ

The strength of a stag is in his feet, of the lion in his heart.

The Lion and the Stag, Fable 76 (H-H) – Perry 74

30 ἕνα, ἀλλὰ λέοντα

Yes, one; but a lion!

The Lioness and the Vixen, Fable 167 (H-H) – Perry 257

said the lioness to the vixen who bragged on having three offspring, the lioness only one

31 τὸ καλὸν οὐκ ἐν πλήθει, ἀλλ' ἐν ἀρετῇ

The good lies in quality, not quantity.

The Lioness and the Vixen, Fable 167 (H-H) – Perry 257

32 πολλάκις ἐκ τῶν μικρῶν τὰ μεγάλα καὶ ἐκ τῶν προδήλων τὰ ἄδηλα γνωρίζονται

Often from small things you discover the great, through the manifest you discern the obscure.

The Man and His Ill-Tempered Wife, Fable 97 (H-H) – Perry 95

33 κἂν ὁ χρόνος ἐνέγκῃ τινὰ εἰς δόξαν, τῆς ἑαυτοῦ ἀρχῆς μὴ ἐπιλαθέσθαι

Forget not your origins, even if time brings splendour.

The Mule, Fable 285 (H-H) – Perry 315

34 ἐὰν μὲν ὁμοφρονῆτε, ἀχείρωτοι τοῖς ἐχθροῖς ἔσεσθε· ἐὰν δὲ στασιάζητε, εὐάλωτοι

If you are of the same mind no enemy can harm you; if in discord you will soon succumb.

The Old Man and his Sons, Fable 53 (H-H) – Perry 53

the sons could not break a bundle of sticks; separately they were easily broken; often quoted as 'ἐν τῇ ἑνώσει ἡ ἰσχύς'

35 Φιλαδελφία μέγιστον ἀγαθὸν ἀνθρώποις, ἣ καὶ ταπεινοὺς ὄντας ἦρεν εἰς ὕψος

Brotherly love is mankind's greatest good, even the lowly are exalted by it.

Translated by Laura Gibbs (2002)

The Old Man and his Sons, Babrius 47 (*Mythiambi*) – Perry 53

36 παιδίον που πρόβατα νέμον … ἔλεγε· βοηθεῖτε ὧδε, ἔρχεται λύκος … τοῦτο δὲ ποιήσαντος πολλάκις εὕρισκον ψευδόμενον … τοῦ δὲ λύκου προσελθόντος … οὐκέτι τις πεπίστευκε

The shepherd boy cried, 'Wolf, wolf!' and was found to be lying several times; so when the wolf did come no one believed him.

The Shepherd Boy and the Wolf, Fable 226 (H-H) – Perry 210

cf. the expression 'crying wolf'

37 οἱ ψευδόμενοι τὸ μηδέ ὅταν ἀληθεύωσι πιστεύεσθαι

Even if liars tell the truth, no one believes them.

Translated by Laura Gibbs (2002)

The Shepherd Boy and the Wolf, Fable 226 (H-H) – Perry 210

moral to previous entry; cf. Aristotle 328

38 σὺν Ἀθηνᾷ καὶ σὺ χεῖρα κίνει

Invoke Athena, but why don't you try to swim?

The Shipwrecked Man and Athena, Fable 30 (H-H) – Perry 30

to someone who, drowning, invoked the goddess

39 τῶν οἰκιῶν ὑμῶν ἐμπιπραμένων, αὐτοὶ ᾄδετε

Your house is on fire, and yet you sing!

The Snails in the Fire, Fable 54 (H-H) – Perry 54

40 τῇ μὲν φύσει ἀργοὶ τῇ δὲ προθυμίᾳ σύντονοι τοὺς φύσει ταχεῖς, ῥᾳθύμους δὲ νικῶσιν

The slow and steady win over the fast and frivolous.

The Tortoise and the Hare, Fable 254 (H-H) – Perry 226

cf. the English proverb 'slow and steady wins the race'

41 τὸ λιτῶς διάγειν καὶ ζῆν αταράχως ὑπὲρ τὸ τρυφᾶν ἐν φόβῳ μετ' ὀδύνης

A frugal meal eaten in peace is better than a banquet shared in anxiety and fear.

The Town Mouse and the Country Mouse, Fable 245 (Chambry, *Fabulae dodecasyllabi*) – Perry 352

cf. Shakespeare, Henry IV Part I, *3.1.[160]: 'I had rather live with cheese and garlic in a windmill'*

42 τοὺς γνησίους τῶν φίλων αἱ συμφοραὶ δοκιμάζουσιν

True friends are proven in adversity.

The Travellers and the Bear, Fable 66 (H-H) – Perry 65

43 ἔνθα χειρῶν χρεία ἐστίν, ἡ διὰ λόγων βοήθεια οὐδὲν λυσιτελεῖ

When you need someone to lend a hand, mere words are no help at all.

Translated by Laura Gibbs (2002)

The Water-snake, the Viper and the Frogs, Fable 92 (H-H) – Perry 90

44 πολλοὶ μεγάλα ἐπαγγέλλονται, μηδὲ μικρὰ ποιῆσαι δυνάμενοι

Many promise the greatest things when

they cannot even carry out the smallest.

The Witch, Fable 56 (H-H) – Perry 56

45 οὐ σύ με λοιδορεῖς, ἀλλ' ὁ τόπος

It is your position, not you, that insults me.

The Wolf and the Goat, Fable 100 (H-H) – Perry 98

to the goat who taunts the wolf from a housetop

46 λύκος δορὰν οἰὸς περιβεβλημένος

A wolf in sheep's clothing.

The Wolf in Sheep's Clothing, Fable 1 (H-H, *Fabula Nicephori*) – Perry 451

cf. Bible 35

47 ἦθος τὸ πρᾶον καὶ τὸ προσηνὲς ῥῆμα

Character lies in a mild and gentle word.

Proverb 10 (Perry)

48 εἷς οὐδείς, δύο πολλοί, τρεῖς ὄχλος, τέσσαρες πανήγυρις

One is no one, two is company, three is a crowd, four is a rally.

Proverb 117 (Perry)

cf. the English expression 'two is company, three is a crowd'

49 φίλος βλάπτων οὐ διαφέρει ἐχθροῦ

A friend who does me harm is not unlike an enemy.

Proverb 170 (Perry)

50 φίλος καὶ ἵππος ἐν ἀνάγκῃ δοκιμάζονται

It is under constraint that friend and horse are tested.

Proverb 171 (Perry)

51 γλαυκοῖσιν ὀφθαλμοῖσιν αἰδὼς οὐκ ἔνι

There is no shame in shining eyes.

There is no shame in light blue eyes.

Proverb 195 (Perry)

both translations are valid

52 εὐημερῶν μέμνησο καὶ τοῦ θανάτου

In the good days remember death also.

Proverb 198 (Perry)

53 πῦρ γυνὴ καὶ θάλασσα, δυνατὰ τρία

Fire, woman and ocean, the mighty three.

Sententiae 2 (Perry)

54 Αἴσωπος ἐρωτηθεὶς πότ' ἂν ἔμελλε γενέσθαι τοῖς ἀνθρώποις ταραχὴ μεγίστη, ἔφη εἰ οἱ τελευτήσαντες ἀναστάντες ἀπαιτοῖεν ἕκαστος τὰ ἴδια

Aesop, when asked which upheaval would be greatest among men, answered 'When all risen from the dead will demand each his own.'

Sententiae 4 (Perry)

55 τὰ μὲν ὑψηλὰ ταπεινῶν, τὰ δὲ ταπεινὰ ὑψῶν

Zeus is humbling the proud and exalting the humble.

Translated by R.D. Hicks (1925)

Sententiae 9 (Perry)

in answer to Chilon asking what Zeus is doing

56 Αἴσωπος τότε ἔλεγεν κακῶς ἔσεσθαι πᾶσιν, ὅταν πάντες πάντα ἐπιτηδεύωσιν

Everything will go wrong when all deliberate on everything.

Sententiae 10 (Perry)

57 Αἴσωπος ὁ μυθοποιὸς ἐρωτηθεὶς τί ἰσχυρότατον τῶν ἐν ἀνθρώποις, ὁ λόγος ἀπεκρίνατο

Aesop the fable writer, when asked what is most powerful in men, replied, 'Reasoning'.

Sententiae 11 (Perry)

58 ἐρωτηθεὶς ὑπό τινος τί τῶν ζῴων ἐστὶ σοφώτατον, εἶπεν τῶν μὲν χρησίμων μέλισσα, τῶν δὲ ἀχρήστων ἀράχνης

When asked which animal he considered to be the most ingenious, he replied, 'Of the useful, the bee; of the useless, the spider.'

Sententiae 12 (Perry)

59 Αἴσωπος ἔφη δύο πήρας ἕκαστον ἡμῶν φέρειν, τὴν μὲν ἔμπροσθεν, τὴν δὲ ὄπισθεν· καὶ εἰς μὲν τὴν ἔμπροσθεν ἀποτιθέναι τὰ τῶν ἄλλων ἁμαρτήματα, εἰς δὲ τὴν ὄπισθεν τὰ ἑαυτῶν· διὸ οὐδὲ καθορῶμεν αὐτά

We carry two wallets, one in front with the faults of others, the other behind with our own; which is why we never see our own faults, only those of others.

Sententiae 23 (Perry)

60 ὁμιλεῖν δυνάστῃ ... ὡς ἥκιστα ἢ ὡς ἥδιστα

Speak to a ruler as little as possible, or as pleasantly as possible.

Translated by H.T. Riley (1872)

Diodorus Siculus, *Library of History* 9.28.1

61 εἰς τὸν νοῦν ἀφορᾶν δεῖ, φιλόσοφε, καὶ μὴ εἰς τὴν ὄψιν

We must look to the mind, not to outward appearance.

Translated by H.T. Riley (1872)

Vitae Aesopi, Βίος Αἰσώπου 243 (Eberhard)

62 οἵα γὰρ ἡ μορφή, τοιάδε καὶ ἡ ψυχή

Appearance is a reflection of the soul.

Vitae Aesopi, Vita W 55.6 (Perry)

AGATHIAS

6th century AD

Epigrammatist and historian

1 Εἰμὶ μὲν οὐ φιλόοινος· ὅταν δ' ἐθέλῃς με μεθύσσαι,
πρῶτα σὺ γευομένη πρόσφερε, καὶ δέχομαι.
εἰ γὰρ ἐπιψαύσεις τοῖς χείλεσιν, οὐκέτι νήφειν
εὐμαρὲς οὐδὲ φυγεῖν τὸν γλυκὺν οἰνοχόον·
πορθμεύει γὰρ ἔμοιγε κύλιξ παρὰ σοῦ τὸ φίλημα
καί μοι ἀπαγγέλλει τὴν χάριν, ἣν ἔλαβεν.

I care not for wine, but if thou wouldst make me drunk,
taste the cup first and I will receive it when thou offerst it.
For, once thou wilt touch it with thy lips, it is no longer
easy to abstain or to fly from the sweet cup-bearer.
The cup ferries thy kiss to me,
and tells me what joy it tasted.

Translated by W.R. Paton (1916)

Greek Anthology 5.261

cf. Ben Jonson, To Celia (1616): 'Or leave a kiss but in the cup,/And I'll not look for wine'; cf. Philostratus 1

2 ἀλλ' ἔτι μαρμαίρουσι παρηΐδες, ὄμμα δὲ θέλγειν
οὐ λάθε· τῶν δ' ἐτέων ἡ δεκὰς οὐκ ὀλίγη.
μίμνει καὶ τὸ φρύαγμα τὸ παιδικόν· ἐνθάδε δ' ἔγνων,
ὅττι φύσιν νικᾶν ὁ χρόνος οὐ δύναται

Still her cheeks gleam, and her eyes
do not fail to beguile; yet several decades have passed
and her girlish high spirits do survive;
and by this I am told
that nature will not be subdued by time.

Greek Anthology 5.282

3 Τὸν θάνατον τί φοβεῖσθε, τὸν ἡσυχίης γενετῆρα,
τὸν παύοντα νόσους καὶ πενίης ὀδύνας;

Why fear ye death, the parent of repose,
Who numbs the sense of penury and pain?

Translated by Robert Bland (1813)

Greek Anthology 10.69

AGATHON

*c.*447–*c.*400BC

Athenian tragic playwright

see also Plato 312–315

1 μόνου γὰρ αὐτοῦ καὶ θεὸς στερίσκεται,
ἀγένητα ποιεῖν ἅσσ' ἂν ᾖ πεπραγμένα

The only power denied to god
is to undo the past.

Fragment 5 (Snell, *TrGF*)

quoted by Aristotle, Nicomachean Ethics *1139b; cf. Samuel Butler,* Erewhon Revisited *(1900), ch. 4: 'Though God cannot alter the past, historians will'*

2 τέχνη τύχην ἔστερξε καὶ τύχη τέχνην

Art loves chance and chance loves art.

Translated by W.D. Ross (1925)

Fragment 6 (Snell, *TrGF*)

quoted by Aristotle, Nicomachean Ethics *1140a.19*

3 φαῦλοι βροτῶν γὰρ τοῦ πονεῖν ἡσσώμενοι
θανεῖν ἐρῶσιν

The base among mankind, by toil o'ercome,
Conceive a love of death.

Translated by H. Rackham (1935)

Fragment 7 (Snell, *TrGF*)

quoted by Aristotle, Eudemian Ethics *1230a*

4 τάχ' ἄν τις εἰκὸς αὐτὸ τοῦτ' εἶναι λέγοι,
βροτοῖσι πολλὰ τυγχάνειν οὐκ εἰκότα

One might perchance say this was probable –

That things improbable oft will hap to men.

Translated by W. Rhys Roberts (1858–1929), rev. Jonathan Barnes (1984)

Fragment 9 (Snell, *TrGF*)

quoted by Aristotle, Rhetoric *1402a.11; but cf. Aristotle 187*

5 σοφὸν λέγουσι τὸν χρόνον πεφυκέναι

Time, they say, is naturally wise.

Fragment 19 (Snell, *TrGF*)

6 ἀδικεῖν νομίζων ὄψιν αἰδοῦμαι φίλων

Acknowledging my faults, I am ashamed to face my friends.

Fragment 22 (Snell, *TrGF*)

7 τὸν ἄρχοντα τριῶν δεῖ μεμνῆσθαι· πρῶτον μὲν ὅτι ἀνθρώπων ἄρχει, δεύτερον ὅτι νόμους ἄρχει, τρίτον ὅτι οὐκ ἀεὶ ἄρχει

A ruler should remember three things: first, that he rules people; second, that he must rule within the law; and third, that he won't rule for ever.

Stobaeus, *Anthology* 4.5.24

PSEUDO-AGATHON

dates uncertain
Epigrammatist

1 Ὤφελεν, ὡς ἀφανής, οὕτω φανερώτατος εἶναι
καιρός, ὃς αὐξάνεται πλεῖστον ἀπ' εὐλαβίης

Would that Opportunity, which grows best in the soil of discretion,
were as clear to view as it is obscure!

Translated by J.M. Edmonds (1931)

Epigram 1 (Diehl) – Elegiaca Adespota, *Fragments* (West), 23

AGESILAUS II

*c.*445–359BC
King of Sparta, 398–359BC
see also Xenophon 1–3

1 εἰ δὲ δίκαιοι πάντες γένοιντο, μηδὲν ἀνδρείας δεήσεσθαι

If all men were just, there would be no need of valour.

Translated in *Bartlett's Familiar Quotations* (1980)

Plutarch, *Agesilaus* 23.5

when asked which of the virtues was best, bravery or justice

2 τοῦ γὰρ καλοῦ καιρὸν οἰκεῖον εἶναι καὶ ὥραν, μᾶλλον δὲ ὅλως τὰ καλὰ τῶν αἰσχρῶν τῷ μετρίῳ διαφέρειν

It is circumstance and proper timing that give an action its character and make it either good or bad.

Translated in *Bartlett's Familiar Quotations* (1980)

Plutarch, *Agesilaus* 36.2

3 εἰ γάρ τι καλὸν ἔργον πεποίηκα, τοῦτό μου μνημεῖον ἔσται· εἰ δὲ μηδέν, οὐδ' οἱ πάντες ἀνδριάντες

If I have done any noble deed, that is my memorial; but if none, then not all the statues in the world avail.

Translated by Frank Cole Babbitt (1931)

Plutarch, *Sayings of Kings and Commanders* 191d

on his death bed, asking that no statues be erected in his honour

4 οὐχ οἱ τόποι τοὺς ἄνδρας ἐντίμους, ἀλλ' οἱ ἄνδρες τοὺς τόπους ἐπιδεικνύουσι

It is not position that confers honour on its holder, but the man to the position.

Plutarch, *Sayings of Spartans* 208e

5 καταφρονεῖν τῶν ἡδονῶν

Contempt for pleasures.

Translated by Frank Cole Babbitt (1931)

Plutarch, *Sayings of Spartans* 210a

on being asked what advantage Lycurgus' laws had given Sparta

6 ταῦτά ἐστιν τὰ Λακεδαιμονίων τείχη

These are the walls of Sparta.

Plutarch, *Sayings of Spartans* 210e

pointing to his army when asked why Sparta was without walls

7 τὸν δὲ στρατηγὸν δεῖν ἔφασκε πρὸς μὲν τοὺς ἐναντίους τόλμαν, πρὸς δὲ τοὺς ὑποτεταγμένους εὔνοιαν ἔχειν, πρὸς δὲ τοὺς καιροὺς λογισμόν

A general must possess boldness towards the enemy, kindness towards his men, and reasoning in times of crisis.

Plutarch, *Sayings of Spartans* 213c

8 φεῦ σου, ὦ Ἑλλάς, ὁπότε οἱ νῦν τεθνηκότες ἱκανοὶ ἦσαν ζῶντες νικᾶν μαχόμενοι πάντας τοὺς βαρβάρους

Alas for thee, Hellas! those who now lie dead were enough to defeat all the barbarians in battle had they lived!

Translated by E.C. Marchant (1925)

Xenophon, *Agesilaus* 7.5

on hearing the number of dead after the victorious battle of Spartans against Athenians at Corinth, 394BC

AGIS II

King of Sparta, 427–400BC

1 οὐκ ἔφη δὲ τοὺς Λακεδαιμονίους ἐρωτᾶν πόσοι εἰσὶν οἱ πολέμιοι, ἀλλὰ ποῦ εἰσίν

The Spartans do not ask the number of the enemy, but where they are.

Plutarch, *Sayings of Spartans* 215d

ALCAEUS

*c.*625–*c.*575BC

Lyric poet from Lesbos

see also Sappho or Alcaeus

1 φαρξώμεθ' ὡς ὤκιστα

Let us patch up as quickly as we can.

Fragment 6a.7 (Lobel and Page, *PLF*)

originally of a ship's side when damaged

2 ἐς δ' ἔχυρον λίμενα δρόμωμεν

Let us run into a safe harbour.

Translated by C.A. Trypanis (1971)

Fragment 6a.8 (Lobel and Page, *PLF*)

probably the oldest use of the image of the ship of state

3 νῦν τις ἄνηρ δόκιμος γενέσθω

Let each man now prove himself steadfast.

Translated by C.A. Trypanis (1971)

Fragment 6a.12 (Lobel and Page, *PLF*)

4 οἳ κὰτ εὔρηαν χθόνα καὶ θάλασσαν
παῖσαν ἔρχεσθ' ὠκυπόδων ἐπ' ἴππων …
ἀργαλέᾳ δ' ἐν νύκτι φάος φέροντες
νᾶϊ μελαίνᾳ

You who ride across the wide earth and over the whole sea upon swift horses, bringing light to the black ship in the cruel night.

Translated by C.A. Trypanis (1971)

Fragment 34a (Lobel and Page, *PLF*)

of Castor and Polydeuces

5 πῶνε καὶ μέθυ' ὦ Μελάνιππ' ἄμ' ἔμοι. τί φαῖς,
ὄταμε διννάεντ' Ἀχέροντα μέγαν πόρον
ζάβαις ἀελίω κόθαρον φάος ἄψερον
ὄψεσθ';

Drink, and get drunk with me, Melanippus.
What makes you think that after crossing Acheron's swirling stream
you will ever see sunlight again?

Fragment 38a.1 (Lobel and Page, *PLF*)

6 ἀλλ' ἄγι μὴ μεγάλων ἐπιβάλλεο

Come, do not set your heart on too great things.

Translated by C.A. Trypanis (1971)

Fragment 38a.4 (Lobel and Page, *PLF*)

7 φιλότας δ' ἔθαλε
Πήλεος καὶ Νηρεΐδων ἀρίστας

And Peleus and the fairest of the Nereids made love.

Translated by C.A. Trypanis (1971)

Fragment 42 (Lobel and Page, *PLF*)

8 ἄνδρες γὰρ πόλιος πύργος ἀρεύιος

Men are a city's tower of strength.

Fragment 112 (Lobel and Page, *PLF*)

9 καί κ' οὐδὲν ἐκ δενὸς γένοιτο

And naught would come of aught.

Translated by M.L. West (1994)

Fragment 320 (Lobel and Page, *PLF*)

but cf. Democritus 148

10 ἀσυννέτημμι τὼν ἀνέμων στάσιν,
τὸ μὲν γὰρ ἔνθεν κῦμα κυλίνδεται,
τὸ δ' ἔνθεν

I am baffled by the quarrelling winds,
one wave rolls up on this side, another on that.

Translated by C.A. Trypanis (1971)

Fragment 326 (Lobel and Page, *PLF*)

11 οἶνος γὰρ ἀνθρώπω δίοπτρον

Wine is a means for seeing through a man.

Translated by Denys Page (1955)

Fragment 333 (Lobel and Page, *PLF*)

12 οὐ χρῆ κάκοισι θῦμον ἐπιτρέπην,
προκόψομεν γὰρ οὐδὲν ἀσάμενοι

Do not surrender to your troubles,
for grieving is no help.

Fragment 335 (Lobel and Page, *PLF*)

13 πάμπαν δ' ἐτύφωσ' ἐκ δ' ἔλετο φρένας

A whirlwind carried off his wits completely.

Translated by D.A. Campbell (1982)

Fragment 336 (Lobel and Page, *PLF*)

14 κάββαλλε τὸν χείμων', ἐπὶ μὲν τίθεις
πῦρ, ἐν δὲ κέρναις οἶνον ἀφειδέως
μέλιχρον

Defy the storm, lay on the fire, and mix sweet wine unsparingly.

Translated by C.A. Trypanis (1971)

Fragment 338 (Lobel and Page, *PLF*)

15 αἴ κ' εἴπης τὰ θέλης, καί κεν ἀκούσαις τά κεν οὐ θέλοις

If you say what you like, you may hear what you do not like.

Translated by D.A. Campbell (1982)

Fragment 341 (Lobel and Page, *PLF*)

16 μηδὲν ἄλλο φυτεύσης πρότερον δένδριον ἀμπέλω

Plant no tree earlier than the vine.

Translated by D.A. Campbell (1982)

Fragment 342 (Lobel and Page, *PLF*)

17 οἶνον γὰρ Σεμέλας καὶ Δίος υἶος
λαθικάδεα
ἀνθρώποισιν ἔδωκ'. ἔγχεε κέρναις ἔνα
καὶ δύο
πλήαις κὰκ κεφάλας, ἀ δ' ἀτέρα τὰν
ἀτέραν κύλιξ
ὠθήτω

The son of Semele and Zeus gave men wine to make them forget their sorrows. Mix one part of water to two of wine, pour it in brimful, and let one cup jostle another.

Translated by D.A. Campbell (1982)

Fragment 346 (Lobel and Page, *PLF*)

of Dionysus, son of Semele and Zeus

18 τὸ γὰρ ἄστρον περιτέλλεται,
ἀ δ' ὤρα χαλέπα

For the Dog Star is circling, and the season is harsh.

Fragment 347a (Lobel and Page, *PLF*)

of Sirius

19 πτερύγων δ' ὔπα
κακχέει λιγύραν πύκνον ἀοίδαν, θέρος
ὄπποτα
φλόγιον καθέταν ἐπιπτάμενον καταυδείη

When the earth is
bright with flaming
heat falling straight down

the cricket sets
up a high-pitched
singing in his wings.

Translated by Mary Barnard (1958)

Fragment 347b (Lobel and Page, *PLF*)

sometimes attributed to Sappho but more likely to be by Alcaeus

20 ἀργάλεον Πενία κάκον ἄσχετον, ἂ μέγαν
δάμνα λᾶον Ἀμαχανίᾳ σὺν ἀδελφέᾳ

Poverty is a grievous thing, an ungovernable evil,
who with her sister Helplessness lays low a great people.

Translated by D.A. Campbell (1982)

Fragment 364 (Lobel and Page, *PLF*)

21 οἶνος, ὦ φίλε παῖ, καὶ ἀλάθεα

Wine, dear boy, and truth.

Translated by D.A. Campbell (1982)

Fragment 366 (Lobel and Page, *PLF*)

the earliest form of the proverb 'in vino veritas'

ALCIBIADES

c.450–404BC
Athenian general and politician
see also Plato 325–326; Eupolis 1; Thucydides 138.

1 εὐήθες εἶναι τὸν δίκην ἔχοντα ζητεῖν ἀποφυγεῖν, ἐξὸν φυγεῖν

It is foolish for a man facing indictment to try to be acquitted when he can flee the country.

Plutarch, *Sayings of Kings and Commanders* 186e

when going into hiding rather than staying in Athens to be tried for sacrilege

2 ἐπεὶ δημοκρατίαν ... περὶ ὁμολογουμένης ἀνοίας οὐδὲν ἂν καινὸν λέγοιτο

As for democracy, nothing new can be said of a system which is generally recognized as absurd.

Translated by Rex Warner (1954)

Thucydides, *History of the Peloponnesian War* 6.89.6

speaking to the Lacedaemonians when in exile from Athens

ALCIDAMAS

4th century BC
Sophist and teacher of rhetoric from Elaea in Aeolis

1 ἐλευθέρους ἀφῆκε πάντας θεός· οὐδένα δοῦλον ἡ φύσις πεποίηκεν

God has created all men free; nature has made none a slave.

Translated by J.H. Freese (1926)

Scholiast on Aristotle, *Rhetoric, In Aristotelis artem rhetoricam commentarium* 74.31

ALCIPHRON

2nd or 3rd century AD
Sophist

1 λάβρως κατὰ τοῦ πελάγους ἐπέπνεον ἐκ τῶν ἀκρωτηρίων οἱ βορεῖς, καὶ ἐπεφρίκει μὲν ὁ πόντος μελαινόμενος, τοῦ ὕδατος δὲ ἀφρὸς ἐξηνθήκει, πανταχοῦ τῆς θαλάσσης ἐπ' ἀλλήλων ἐπικλωμένων τῶν κυμάτων τὰ μὲν γὰρ ταῖς πέτραις προσηράσσετο, τὰ δὲ εἴσω ἀνοιδοῦντα ἐρρήγνυτο

The winds blew violently down upon the sea from the headlands, the sea turned black and bristled, foam blossomed out of the sea water, everywhere in the sea waves broke against each other, some of them dashing against the rocks, others swelling up from inside the water and bursting into spray.

Translated by Jason König (2007)

Letters of Fishermen 1.1.1

of a three-day storm

2 μάτην ἡμῖν τὰ πάντα πονεῖται, ὦ Κύρτων, δι' ἡμέρας μὲν ὑπὸ τῆς εἴλης φλεγομένοις νύκτωρ δὲ ὑπὸ λαμπάσι τὸν βυθὸν ἀποξύουσι, καὶ τὸ λεγόμενον δὴ τοῦτο εἰς τὸν τῶν Δαναΐδων τοὺς ἀμφορέας ἐκχέομεν πίθον· οὕτως ἄπρακτα καὶ ἀνήνυτα διαμοχθοῦμεν

All of our work is for nothing, Kyrton. By day we are burnt by the heat of the sun, and at night we scrape at the abyss by torchlight, emptying our amphorae into the jar of the Danaids, as the saying goes. That's how unprofitable and endless our labour is.

Translated by Jason König (2007)

Letters of Fishermen 1.2.1

a fisherman on his trade

3 ἡμῖν δὲ οἷς βίος ἐν ὕδασι, θάνατος ἡ γῆ καθάπερ τοῖς ἰχθύσιν ἥκιστα δυναμένοις ἀναπνεῖν τὸν ἀέρα

For us, who have our livelihood from the water, the land brings death, just as it does to the fish who are entirely unable to breathe air.

Translated by Jason König (2007)

Letters of Fishermen 1.4.2

4 οὐκ ᾔτησά σε ἃ ἔχεις, ἀλλ' ἃ μὴ ἔχεις. ἐπεὶ δὲ οὐ βούλει ἃ μὴ ἔχεις ἕτερον ἔχειν, ἔχε ἃ μὴ ἔχεις

I didn't ask for what you possess, but what you don't possess. Since you don't want another to have what you don't have, keep what you don't have!

Translated by Owen Hodkinson (2007)

Letters of Fishermen 1.19.1

ALCMAEON

5th century BC
Philosopher of Croton

1 περὶ τῶν ἀφανέων … σαφήνειαν μὲν θεοὶ ἔχοντι, ὡς δὲ ἀνθρώποις τεκμαίρεσθαι

Concerning things unseen the gods have certainty, whereas to men conjecture only is possible.

Fragment 1 (D-K)

2 τοὺς ἀνθρώπους φησὶν διὰ τοῦτο ἀπόλλυσθαι, ὅτι οὐ δύνανται τὴν ἀρχὴν τῷ τέλει προσάψαι.

Men perish because they cannot join the beginning to the end.

Translated by Kathleen Freeman (1948)

Fragment 2 (D-K)

3 ἐχθρὸν ἄνδρα ῥᾶον φυλάξασθαι ἢ φίλον

It is easier to guard against an enemy than against a friend.

Translated by Kathleen Freeman (1948)

Fragment 5 (D-K)

ALCMAN

fl. mid – late 7th century BC in Sparta
Laconian (or Lydian) lyric poet

1 ὁ δ' ὄλβιος, ὅστις εὔφρων
ἁμέραν διαπλέκει
ἄκλαυτος

Blessed is the man who in wisdom weaves together his day without tears.

Translated by C.A. Trypanis (1971)

Fragment 1.37 (Page, *PMG*)

2 λυσιμελεῖ τε πόσῳ, τακερώτερα
δ' ὕπνω καὶ θανάτω ποτιδέρκεται

She looks at me with limb-loosening
desire
more meltingly than sleep or death.

Fragment 3.61 (Page, *PMG*)

3 μάργος δ' Ἔρως οἷα παῖς παίσδει

Mischievous Eros plays like a child.

Fragment 58 (Page, *PMG*)

4 εὕδουσι δ' ὀρέων κορυφαί τε καὶ
φάραγγες ...
εὕδουσι δ' οἰωνῶν φῦλα τανυπτερύγων

Asleep are the peaks and watercourses
of the mountains,
asleep are the tribes of the broad-
winged birds.

Translated by C.A. Trypanis (1971)

Fragment 89 (Page, *PMG*)

5 λεπτὰ δ' ἀταρπὸς ἀνηλὴς δ' ἀνάγκα

The path is narrow and great my need.

Fragment 102 (Page, *PMG*)

6 τίς κα, τίς ποκα ῥᾷ ἄλλω νόον ἀνδρὸς ἐνίσποι;

Who can, who could, ever read another man's mind?

Fragment 104 (Page, *PMG*)

7 νικῷ δ' ὁ κάρρων

May the better man win!

Translated by David A. Campbell (1988)

Fragment 105 (Page, *PMG*)

cf. the expression 'may the best man win'

8 Πολλαλέγων ὄνυμ' ἀνδρί, γυναικὶ δὲ Πασιχάρηα

Say-much is the man's name, Happy-with-all the woman's.

Translated by David A. Campbell (1988)

Fragment 107 (Page, *PMG*)

meaning 'let the man say much and the woman be happy with whatever she hears'; regarded by some as part of a wedding-hymn (if so, satirical)

9 πῆρά τοι μαθήσιος ἀρχά

Experience is the beginning of knowledge.

Translated by John Simpson and Jennifer Speake (1982)

Fragment 125 (Page, *PMG*)

cf. the English proverb 'experience is the father of wisdom'

ALEXANDER THE GREAT

356–323BC
King of Macedon, 336–323BC
see also Arrian 6; Isocrates 75; Oracles 22; Palladius 1; Phocion 1; Plutarch 2, 88; Proverbial Expressions 17

1 γονεῦσι δὲ αὐτῶν καὶ παισὶ τῶν τε κατὰ τὴν χώραν ἀτέλειαν ἔδωκε καὶ ὅσαι ἄλλαι ἢ τῷ σώματι λειτουργίαι ἢ κατὰ τὰς κτήσεις ἑκάστων εἰσφοραί

To their parents and children he gave remission of land taxes, of all public duties and of property taxes.

Translated by P.A. Brunt (1976)

Arrian, *Anabasis of Alexander* 1.16.5

of the soldiers who were killed in battle

2 Ἀλέξανδρος Φιλίππου καὶ οἱ Ἕλληνες πλὴν Λακεδαιμονίων ἀπὸ τῶν βαρβάρων τῶν τὴν Ἀσίαν κατοικούντων

Alexander and the Greeks, except the Lacedaemonians, set up these spoils from the barbarians dwelling in Asia.

Translated by P.A. Brunt (1976)

Arrian, *Anabasis of Alexander* 1.16.7

inscription on a dedication to Athena of captured Persian armour

3 ὦ παῖ, ζήτει σεαυτῷ βασιλείαν ἴσην· Μακεδονία γάρ σε οὐ χωρεῖ

My son, seek thee out a kingdom equal to thyself; Macedonia has not room enough for thee.

Translated by Bernadotte Perrin (1919)

Plutarch, *Alexander* 6.8

spoken by Philip to Alexander after breaking in a wild horse

4 τὴν μὲν Ἰλιάδα τῆς πολεμικῆς ἀρετῆς ἐφόδιον νομίζων ... εἶχε δ' ἀεὶ μετὰ τοῦ ἐγχειριδίου κειμένην ὑπὸ τὸ προσκεφάλαιον

He considered the *Iliad* a portable treasure of the military art and always kept it with his dagger under his pillow.

Plutarch, *Alexander* 8.2

5 ὡς διὰ τὸν πατέρα μὲν ζῶν, διὰ τοῦτον δὲ καλῶς ζῶν

He said that his father had given him life, but the other had taught him a noble life.

Translated by Bernadotte Perrin (1919)

Plutarch, *Alexander* 8.4

of Aristotle, his tutor

6 εἰ μὴ Ἀλέξανδρος ἤμην, Διογένης ἂν ἤμην

If I were not Alexander, I would be Diogenes.

Translated by Bernadotte Perrin (1919)

Plutarch, *Alexander* 14.5

cf. Diogenes 22

7 Παρμενίωνος εἰπόντος ἐγὼ μὲν εἰ Ἀλέξανδρος ἤμην, ἔλαβον ἂν ταῦτα, κἀγὼ νὴ Δία εἶπεν ὁ Ἀλέξανδρος, εἰ Παρμενίων

Parmenion said, 'I would take it if I were Alexander.' 'And so indeed would I,' said Alexander, 'if I were Parmenion.'

Translated by Frank Cole Babbitt (1931)

Plutarch, *Alexander* 29.8

on being offered a huge sum and shared rule of Asia by the defeated king of Persia; Parmenion was Alexander's closest friend and trusted general

8 οὐ κλέπτω τὴν νίκην

I will not steal my victory.

Translated by Bernadotte Perrin (1919)

Plutarch, *Alexander* 31.12

when asked to attack at night before the battle of Gaugamela, 331BC

9 μυρίας ἐπιστολὰς ἓν δάκρυον ἀπαλείφει μητρός

One tear of a mother effaces ten thousand letters.

Translated by Bernadotte Perrin (1919)

Plutarch, *Alexander* 39.13

after reading a long letter in denunciation of his mother Olympias

10 Ἀλέξανδρος ... πλείονας παρ' Ἀριστοτέλους τοῦ καθηγητοῦ ἢ παρὰ Φιλίππου τοῦ πατρὸς ἀφορμὰς ἔχων διέβαινεν ἐπὶ Πέρσας

Alexander invaded Persia with greater assistance from Aristotle than from his father Philip.

Translated by John Philips (1878)

Plutarch, *On the Fortune or the Virtue of Alexander* 327e

11 ἔα δὲ κατὰ χώραν τὸν Ἄθω μένειν· ἀρκεῖ γὰρ ἑνὸς βασιλέως ἐνυβρίσαντος εἶναι μνημεῖον

Let Athos alone; it is sufficient that it is the monument of the vanquished folly and presuming pride of one king already.

Translated by John Philips (1878)

Plutarch, *On the Fortune or the Virtue of Alexander* 335e

on being asked to allow a huge statue of himself to be sculpted into Mount Athos; the king referred to is Xerxes who had ordered a canal to be cut for his fleet to pass; cf. Herodotus 7.22–25

12 οὐκ ἄξιον δακρύειν, εἰ κόσμων ὄντων ἀπείρων ἑνὸς οὐδέπω κύριοι γεγόναμεν;

Is it not worthy of tears that, when the number of worlds is infinite, we have not yet become lords of a single one?

Translated by William C. Helmbold (1939)

Plutarch, *On Tranquillity of Mind* 466d

when asked why he wept on hearing from Anaxarchus that there was an infinite number of worlds

13 ἡμέρας μὲν ταράσσων ἔθνη, ἐπιστάσης δὲ νυκτὸς ἐκταρασσόμενος ὑπὸ τῶν λογισμῶν μου

By day I torment the nations, but when night comes on I am tormented by my own reflections.

Translated by Richard Stoneman (2010)

Palladius, *On the Brahmans** 2.33

to Dandamis, a Brahman philosopher

ALEXANDER

1st century BC
Comic poet

1 ταμιεῖον ἀρετῆς ἐστι γενναία γυνή

A treasury of excellence is a noble woman.

Fragment 5 (Kock)

Attributed to Anaxandrides by K-A (Fragment 71)

ALEXIS

*c.*375–*c.*275BC
Middle and New Comedy poet born at Thurii

1 τοῦτ' ἔσθ', ὁρᾷς, Ἑλληνικὸς
πότος, μετρίοισι χρωμένους ποτηρίοις
λαλεῖν τι καὶ ληρεῖν πρὸς αὑτοὺς ἡδέως

This is the Greek way,
to drink in measured cups
leading to pleasant talk.

Fragment 9 (Kock) – 9 (K-A) – *Aisopos – Aesop*

2 τοιοῦτο τὸ ζῆν ἐστιν· ὥσπερ οἱ κύβοι

Such is life; much like a game of dice.

Fragment 34 (Kock) – 34 (K-A) – *Brettia*

3 ποῖος γάρ ἐστι φανός, ὦ πρὸς τῶν θεῶν,
τοιοῦτος οἷος ὁ γλυκύτατος ἥλιος

What light is there, oh gods,
as glorious as the sun.

Fragment 87 (Kock) – 91 (K-A) – *Theophoretos – Possessed by a God*

4 σοῦ δ' ἐγὼ λαλιστέραν
οὐπώποτ' εἶδον οὔτε κερκώπην, γύναι,
οὐ κίτταν, οὐκ ἀηδόν', οὔτε τρυγόν', οὐ
τέττιγα

Woman, I never saw
no cricket, magpie or cicada
no nightingale or turtle dove,
as prattling as you!

Fragment 92 (Kock) – 96 (K-A) – *Thrason*

5 πρῶτον μὲν οὖν ὄστρεια παρὰ Νηρεῖ τινα
ἰδὼν γέροντι φῦκος ἠμφιεσμένα
ἔλαβον ἐχίνους τ'· ἔστι γὰρ προοίμιον
δείπνου χαριέντως ταῦτα
πεπρυτανευμένου

Now first I saw some oysters,
Aged fellows, bearded, dressed in seaweed,
So I bought them, and some sea-urchins,
For the proverb says
they are the jolliest chairmen of the feast!

Translated by Kathleen Freeman (1947)

Fragment 110 (Kock) – 115 (K-A) – *Crateuas or Pharmacopolis – The Pharmacist*

cf. Lewis Carroll, Through the Looking-Glass, *ch. 4, The Walrus and the Carpenter*

6 εἰς τοὺς σοφιστὰς τὸν μάγειρον ἐγγράφω

Among the master artists I inscribe the Cook.

Fragment 149 (Kock) – 153 (K-A) – *Milesia – The Milesian Woman*

7 ἔδει θ' ὑπομεῖναι μικροσιτίαν, ῥύπον,
ῥῖγος, σιωπήν, στυγνότητ', ἀλουσίαν

I had to abide by few provisions: dirt,
cold, silence, gloominess, and lack of baths.

Fragment 196 (Kock) – 201 (K-A) – *Pythagorizousa – Female Disciple of Pythagoras*

of the Pythagoreans; cf. Diogenes Laertius, Lives of Eminent Philosophers *8.38*

8 ὅστις διαπλεῖ θάλατταν, ἢ μελαγχολᾷ,
ἢ πτωχός ἐστιν, ἢ θανατᾷ· τούτων τριῶν
ἑνός τ' ἀποτυχεῖν τοὐλάχιστον οὐκ ἔνι

Whoever takes to sea does it out of melancholy,
or else he is poor, or has a desire to die;
of these three at least one is true.

Fragment 211 (Kock) – 214 (K-A) – *Synapothniskontes – Men Dying Together*

9 ἤδη γὰρ ὁ βίος οὑμὸς ἑσπέραν ἄγει

Forthwith my life is travelling towards nightfall.

Fragment 228 (Kock) – 230 (K-A) – *Titthe – The Wet-Nurse*

10 σοφοῦ γὰρ ἀνδρὸς τὰς τύχας ὀρθῶς φέρειν

It is the mark of a wise man to endure upright the sufferings that fortune brings.

Fragment 252 (Kock) – 254 (K-A) – *Philotragodos – Lover of Tragedies*

11 μεῖζω μητρὸς οὐκ ἔστιν ποτέ.
ὅθεν ὁ πρῶτος οὐκ ἀπαιδεύτως ἔχων
ἱδρύσαθ' ἱερὸν μητρός, ...
ἐάσας δ' ὑπονοεῖν εἰς τοὔνομα

There is nothing more sacred than a mother. Thus the first wise man built a shrine to 'a mother', allowing it to signify every mother.

Fragment 267 (Kock) – 269 (K-A)

12 τὰς ἡδονὰς δεῖ συλλέγειν τὸν σώφρονα.
τρεῖς δ' εἰσὶν αἵ γε τὴν δύναμιν κεκτημέναι
τὴν ὡς ἀληθῶς συντελοῦσαν τῷ βίῳ,
τὸ πιεῖν, τὸ φαγεῖν, τὸ τῆς Ἀφροδίτης τυγχάνειν.
τὰ δ' ἄλλα προσθήκας ἅπαντα χρὴ καλεῖν

The man of sense must gather pleasure's fruits,
And three there are which have the potency
Truly to be of import for this life –
To eat and drink and have one's way in love,
All else must be declared accessory.

Translated by Frank Cole Babbitt (1927)

Fragment 271 (Kock) – 273 (K-A)

quoted by Plutarch, How the Young Man Should Study Poetry *21e, in order to highlight how differently Socrates thought*

13 ἀλλ' ἐπὶ τὸ πλῆθος ἐμφερεῖς τοὺς οἰκέτας
ἔχοντας ὄψει τοὺς τρόπους τοῖς δεσπόταις.
τοῖς ἤθεσιν γὰρ οἷς ὑπηρετοῦσ' ἀεὶ
προσέχουσα τούτοις ἡ φύσις κεράννυται

Servants often have their masters' manners; it is natural to imitate those we serve.

Fragment 278b (Kock) – 53 (K-A)

14 οὐκ ἔστι παιδαγωγὸς ἀνθρώποις ἄρα
ἔρωτος οὐδεὶς ἄλλος ἐπιμελέστερος

There is no teacher more attentive to mankind than Love.

Fragment 289 (Kock) – 290 (K-A)

15 τῶν μετρίων αἱ μείζονες
λῦπαι ποιοῦσι τῶν φρενεῖν μετάστασιν

Grief of too great a measure disturbs one's wits.

Fragment 292 (Kock) – 294 (K-A)

16 λύπη μανίας κοινωνίαν ἔχει τινά

Grief has some sort of association with madness.

Fragment 296 (Kock) – 297 (K-A)

17 ψυχὴν ἔχειν δεῖ πλουσίαν· τὰ δὲ χρήματα
ταῦτ' ἐστὶν ὄψις, παραπέτασμα τοῦ βίου

Have richness of soul; as for wealth,
it is but an idea, a screen, for real life.

Fragment 340 (Kock) – 341 (K-A)

also attributed to Antiphanes and Menander

ALPHEIUS

dates uncertain
Epigrammatist from Mytilene

1 Ἀνδρομάχης ἔτι θρῆνον ἀκούομεν, εἰσέτι Τροίην
δερκόμεθ' ἐκ βάθρων πᾶσαν ἐρειπομένην
καὶ μόθον Αἰάντειον ὑπὸ στεφάνῃ τε πόληος
ἔκδετον ἐξ ἵππων Ἕκτορα συρόμενον.

Andromache's lament is still in our ears; we still
watch Troy struck flat; and Ajax goes on struggling
in his fight for ever; and Hector is tied to the chariot
for ever and dragged round the city walls.

Translated by Edwin Morgan (1973)

Greek Anthology 9.97.1

2 Μαιονίδεω διὰ μοῦσαν, ὃν οὐ μία πατρὶς ἀοιδὸν
κοσμεῖται, γαίης δ' ἀμφοτέρης κλίματα.

Such strange Enchantment dwells in Homer's Song;
Whose Birth could more than one poor Realm adorn,
For all the World is proud that he was born.

Greek Anthology 9.97.5

of Homer; Maeonides is a name given to Homer, either as the son of Maeon, or as born, according to one tradition, in Maeonia

AMEIPSIAS

5th – 4th century BC
Athenian Old Comedy poet

1 οὐ χρὴ πόλλ' ἔχειν θνητὸν ἄνθρωπον,
ἀλλ' ἐρᾶν καὶ κατεσθίειν

Mortal man does not have need of many things, just love and eating well.

Fragment 22 (Kock) – 21 (K-A)

AMMIANUS

2nd century AD
Epigrammatist

1 Ὡς κῆπον τεθυκὼς δεῖπνον παρέθηκεν Ἀπελλῆς
οἰόμενος βόσκειν ἀντὶ φίλων πρόβατα.
ἦν ῥαφανίς, σέρις ἦν, τῆλις, θρίδακες, πράσα, βολβοί,
ὤκιμον, ἡδύοσμον, πήγανον, ἀσπάραγος

Apelles served dinner as if he had slaughtered
his whole garden: feeding sheep, not friends.
He served radish and endive, fennel and lettuce,
leeks, onions, basil, mint, rue, and asparagus.

Translated by Peter Constantine (2010)

Greek Anthology 11.413

of a vegetarian dinner

AMPHIS

4th century BC
Middle Comedy poet

1 οὐκ ἔστιν οὐδὲν ἀτυχίας ἀνθρωπίνης
παραμύθιον γλυκύτερον ἐν βίῳ τέχνης·
ἐπὶ τοῦ μαθήματος γὰρ ἑστηκὼς ὁ νοῦς
αὑτὸν λέληθε παραπλέων τὰς συμφοράς

There is in human misadventure
no solace sweeter than practising your trade;
occupying your mind with your endeavours
is the best way to sail past setbacks.

Fragment 3 (Kock) – 3 (K-A) – *Ampelourgos – The Vine Cultivator*

2 πῖνε, παῖζε· θνητὸς ὁ βίος, ὀλίγος οὑπὶ γῇ χρόνος·
ἀθάνατος ὁ θάνατός ἐστιν, ἂν ἅπαξ τις ἀποθάνῃ

Drink and be merry; life will end, our term is short;
death only is immortal, once one is dead.

Fragment 8 (Kock) – 8 (K-A) – *Gynaecocratia – The Rule of Women*

3 εἶτ' οὐχὶ χρυσοῦν ἐστι πρᾶγμ' ἐρημία;
ὁ πατὴρ γε τοῦ ζῆν ἐστιν ἀνθρώποις ἀγρός,
πενίαν τε συγκρύπτειν ἐπίσταται μόνος,
ἄστυ δὲ θέατρον ἀτυχίας σαφοῦς γέμον

Ah, is not solitude a golden thing?
Father of life to mortals is the Country:
Only the Country helps to hide our penury;
The town's a show-place where
Misfortunes jostle, plain for all to see.

Translated by Kathleen Freeman (1947)

Fragment 17 (Kock) – 17 (K-A) – *Erithoi – The Hired Servants*

4 ἐνῆν ἄρ', ὡς ἔοικε, κἀν οἴνῳ λόγος,
ἔνιοι δ' ὕδωρ πίνοντές εἰσ' ἀβέλτεροι

Some find wisdom in wine;
others stupidity in water.

Fragment 41 (Kock) – 41 (K-A)

ANACHARSIS

*fl. c.*600BC
'Legendary' Scythian prince

1 τῶν ἄλλων ἴσων νομιζομένων ἀρετῇ τὸ βέλτιον ὁρίζεται, καὶ κακίᾳ τὸ χεῖρον

All else being held in equal esteem, what is better is determined by virtue and what is worse by vice.

Translated by Frank Cole Babbitt (1928)

Seven Sages, *Apophthegms* 9.1 (Mullach, *FPG*)

of governments

2 ἐρωτηθείς, τί ἐστιν ἐν ἀνθρώποις ἀγαθόν τε καὶ φαῦλον, ἔφη, Γλῶσσα

When asked what in men is both good and bad, he replied, the tongue.

Seven Sages, *Apophthegms* 10.3 (Mullach, *FPG*)

3 παίζειν δ' ὅπως σπουδάζῃ

Play in order that you may work.

Translated by H. Rackham (1926)

Aristotle, *Nicomachean Ethics* 1176b.33

of leisure; cf. Aristotle 157

4 μαθὼν τέτταρας δακτύλους εἶναι τὸ πάχος τῆς νεώς, τοσοῦτον ἔφη τοῦ θανάτου τοὺς πλέοντας ἀπέχειν

On learning that the sides of a ship were four fingers thick he said that the passengers are just that distance from death.

Diogenes Laertius, *Lives of Eminent Philosophers* 1.103

dactylos, a finger's breadth = about 7/10ths of an inch

5 Ἕλληνας πάντας ἀσχόλους εἶναι ἐς πᾶσαν σοφίην πλὴν Λακεδαιμονίων, τούτοισι δὲ εἶναι μούνοισι σωφρόνως δοῦναί τε καὶ δέξασθαι λόγον

All Greeks are zealous for every kind of learning, save only the Lacedaemonians; but these are the only Greeks who speak and listen with discretion.

Translated by A.D. Godley (1925)

Herodotus, *Histories* 4.77

Anacharsis said this of the Greeks, but Herodotus comments that 'this is a tale vainly invented by the Greeks themselves'

6 γράμμασιν ... μηδὲν τῶν ἀραχνίων διαφέρειν, ἀλλ' ὡς ἐκεῖνα τοὺς μὲν ἀσθενεῖς καὶ λεπτοὺς τῶν ἁλισκομένων καθέξειν, ὑπὸ δὲ τῶν δυνατῶν καὶ πλουσίων διαρραγήσεσθαι

Written laws are like spiders' webs; they will catch the weak and poor, but will easily be broken by the rich and powerful.

Translated in *Bartlett's Familiar Quotations* (1980)

Plutarch, *Solon* 5.4

of Solon's claim that laws would restrain citizens

7 λέγουσι μὲν οἱ σοφοὶ παρ' Ἕλλησι, κρίνουσι δὲ οἱ ἀμαθεῖς

In Greece wise men speak and fools decide.

Translated in *Bartlett's Familiar Quotations* (1980)

Plutarch, *Solon* 5.6

8 ψυχῆς γὰρ ὄργανον τὸ σῶμα, θεοῦ δ' ἡ ψυχή

The body is an instrument of the soul, the soul a gift of god.

Plutarch, *Dinner of the Seven Wise Men* 163e

9 Ἀνάχαρσις ὁ Σκύθης ἐρωτηθεὶς ὑπό τινος, τί ἐστι πολέμιον ἀνθρώποις, αὐτοί ἔφη ἑαυτοῖς

Anacharsis the Scythian when asked what is the enemy of men, answered, 'They themselves.'

Stobaeus, *Anthology* 3.2.42

10 Ἀνάχαρσις ὀνειδιζόμενος ὑπό τινος ὅτι Σκύθης ἐστὶν εἶπε τῷ γένει, ἀλλ' οὐ τῷ τρόπῳ

When Anacharsis was reproached for being a Scythian he said, 'In origin, but not in my way of life.'

Stobaeus, *Anthology* 4.29a.16

ANACREON

*c.*570–*c.*480BC

Lyric poet from Teos in Asia Minor

1 ἄγε δηὖτε μηκέτ' οὕτω
πατάγῳ τε κἀλαλητῷ
Σκυθικὴν πόσιν παρ' οἴνῳ
μελετῶμεν, ἀλλὰ καλοῖς
ὑποπίνοντες ἐν ὕμνοις

Come, let us not think of drinking-bouts with noise and shouts, but let us drink gently with beautiful songs.

Translated by C.A. Trypanis (1971)

Fragment 11b (Page, *PMG*)

2 βάλλων χρυσοκόμης Ἔρως ...
ἡ δ', ἐστὶν γὰρ ἀπ' εὐκτίτου Λέσβου ...
πρὸς ἄλλην τινὰ χάσκει

Golden-haired Love strikes me again;
but she is from beauteous Lesbos
and gapes after another girl.

Fragment 13 (Page, *PMG*)

3 χαῖρε φίλον φῶς

Dearest light, welcome!

Fragment 35 (Page, *PMG*)

4 φέρ' ὕδωρ φέρ' οἶνον ὦ παῖ φέρε δ' ἀνθεμόεντας ἡμὶν
στεφάνους ἔνεικον, ὡς δὴ πρὸς Ἔρωτα πυκταλίζω

Bring water, boy, bring wine! Bring flowering garlands!
Bring them that I may try a bout with love.

Fragment 51 (Page, *PMG*)

this poem was found on a portrait of Anacreon on a 2nd century AD mosaic at Autun (Augustodunum) in central France

5 τί δή με
λοξὸν ὄμμασι βλέπουσα
νηλέως φεύγεις

Why do you look at me askance,
why do you cruelly avoid me?

Translated by C.A. Trypanis (1971)
Fragment 72 (Page, *PMG*)

6 ὤλεσας δ' ἥβην ἀμύνων πατρίδος δουληΐην

You lost your youth to protect your country's freedom.

Fragment 74 (Page, *PMG*)

7 ἐρέω τε δηὖτε κοὐκ ἐρέω
καὶ μαίνομαι κοὐ μαίνομαι

I both love and do not love,
and am mad and am not mad.

Translated in *Bartlett's Familiar Quotations* (1980)
Fragment 83 (Page, *PMG*)

8 Ἄρης δ' οὐκ ἀγαθῶν φείδεται, ἀλλὰ κακῶν

War spares the coward, not the brave.

Translated by Andrew Sinclair (1967)
Greek Anthology 7.160

9 δεῖ φροντίδα μὴ κατέχειν

Do not store up worries.

Greek Anthology 10.70

10 Ἀνακρέων δωρεὰν παρὰ Πολυκράτους λαβὼν πέντε τάλαντα, ὡς ἐφρόντισεν ἐπ' αὐτοῖς δυοῖν νυκτοῖν, ἀπέδωκεν αὐτὰ εἰπὼν οὐ τιμᾶσθαι αὐτὰ τῆς ἐπ' αὐτοῖς φροντίδος

Anacreon received from Polycrates five talents as a gift. After he reflected on them for two nights he returned them saying that they were not worth that amount of reflection.

Stobaeus, *Anthology* 4.31c.78
five talents was a great sum of money

ANACREONTEA

1st century BC or AD to 5th or 6th century AD
A collection of approx. sixty-two poems

1 στέφος πλέκων ποτ' εὗρον
ἐν τοῖς ῥόδοις Ἔρωτα,
καὶ τῶν πτερῶν κατασχὼν
ἐβάπτισ' εἰς τὸν οἶνον,
λαβὼν δ' ἔπινον αὐτόν·
καὶ νῦν ἔσω μελῶν μου
πτεροῖσι γαργαλίζει

Plaiting a garland one day
I came upon Love among the roses.
By the wings I caught him,
In my wine I dunked him,
And gulped him down.
And now, deep within,
His feathers tickle my insides.

Translated by Jonathan Williams and Clive Cheesman (2004)
Fragment 6 (West)

2 εἰ φύλλα πάντα δένδρων
ἐπίστασαι κατειπεῖν,
εἰ κύματ' οἶδας εὑρεῖν
τὰ τῆς ὅλης θαλάσσης,
σὲ τῶν ἐμῶν ἐρώτων
μόνον ποῶ λογιστήν

Can you count me on the trees
Every leaf that woos the breeze?
Can you count each sequent wave
That does ocean's margin lave?
Try your skill, and if you can,
To count my loves you are the man.

Translated by R. Swainson Fisher (1838)
Fragment 14 (West)

3 ἐρασμίη πέλεια,
πόθεν, πόθεν πέτασαι;
πόθεν μύρων τοσούτων
ἐπ' ἠέρος θέουσα
πνέεις τε καὶ ψεκάζεις;
τίς εἶ, τί σοι μέλει δέ;

Pretty pigeon, tell me, pray,
Whither speeding, whence away?
Breathing balmy odours round,
Where thy fluttering pinions sound?
Who despatch'd thee through the air?
What commission dost thou bear?

Translated by Thomas Bourne (1864)
Fragment 15 (West)

4 χαλεπὸν τὸ μὴ φιλῆσαι,
χαλεπὸν δὲ καὶ φιλῆσαι,
χαλεπώτερον δὲ πάντων
ἀποτυγχάνειν φιλοῦντα

It is hard not to fall in love,
it is hard to fall in love;
but hardest of all
is to fail in love.

Translated by D.A. Campbell (1988)
Fragment 29 (West)

5 ἄργυρον ...
διὰ τοῦτον οὐκ ἀδελφός,
διὰ τοῦτον οὐ τοκῆες·
πόλεμοι, φόνοι δι' αὐτόν·
τὸ δὲ χεῖρον· ὀλλύμεσθα

διὰ τοῦτον οἱ φιλοῦντες

Money!
Thanks to it we lose brothers and parents;
thanks to it there are wars and murders;
and, worst of all, thanks to it we lovers are destroyed.

Translated by D.A. Campbell (1988)

Fragment 29a (West)

6 μεσονυκτίοις ποτ' ὥραις, ...
τότ' Ἔρως ἐπισταθείς μευ
θυρέων ἔκοπτ' ὀχῆας.
τίς ἔφην θύρας ἀράσσει,
κατά μευ σχίσας ὀνείρους;

At the midnight hour
Love stood at my door.
'Who,' I said, 'is knocking?
You are shattering my dreams.'

Fragment 33 (West)

7 μακαρίζομέν σε, τέττιξ ...
θέρεος γλυκὺς προφήτης ...
ὀλίγην δρόσον πεπωκώς ...
σοφέ, γηγενής, φίλυμνε ...
σχεδὸν εἶ θεοῖς ὅμοιος

Hail cicada, doubly blessed,
sweet harbinger of summer,
tipsy on a drop of dew,
skilful earth-born songster,
equal, nearly, to the gods are you.

Fragment 34 (West)

8 θανεῖν γὰρ εἰ πέπρωται,
τί χρυσὸς ὠφελεῖ με;

If all shall die
what good is gold to me?

Fragment 36 (West)

9 τί γάρ ἐστί σοι τὸ κέρδος
ὀδυνωμένῳ μερίμναις;

What good is gain
if all it brings is worries?

Fragment 38 (West)

10 ἂν δ' ὁ γέρων χορεύῃ,
τρίχας γέρων μέν ἐστιν,
τὰς δὲ φρένας νεάζει

And if the old man dances,
he may be old to look at
but he is young at heart.

Fragment 39 (West)

11 πρὶν ἐμὲ φθάσῃ τὸ τέλος,
παίξω, γελάσω, χορεύσω

Before death catches up with me,
I shall play and laugh and dance.

Fragment 40 (West)

12 ἦ καλόν ἐστι βαδίζειν
ὅπου λειμῶνες κομῶσιν ...
χὐπὸ τὰ πέταλα δῦναι
ἁπαλὴν παῖδα κατέχων
Κύπριν ὅλην πνέουσαν

What in life gives greater pleasure,
What more calms its careful hours,
Than to stroll in easy leisure
Through luxuriant meads and bowers?
Where the leafy thickets screen us,
To wander with some tender maiden,
Breathing sweetly all of Venus!

Translated by R. Swainson Fisher (1838)

Fragment 41 (West)

13 ὅταν πίνω τὸν οἶνον,
εὕδουσιν αἱ μέριμναι

When I drink wine
my worries go to sleep.

Translated by D.A. Campbell (1988)

Fragment 45 (West)

14 μή με φύγῃς ὁρῶσα
τὰν πολιὰν ἔθειραν·
μηδ', ὅτι σοὶ πάρεστιν
ἄνθος ἀκμαῖον ...
ὅρα, κἀν στεφάνοισιν
ὅπως πρέπει τὰ λευκά
ῥόδοις κρίνα πλακέντα

Don't look at my grey hair and run,
simply because you are in the bloom of youth!
Look how well the white lilies woven in garlands
go with the roses.

Translated by D.A. Campbell (1988)

Fragment 51 (West)

15 ἵν' ἴδῃ γέροντος ἀλκήν
δεδαηκότος μὲν εἰπεῖν,
δεδαηκότος δὲ πίνειν
χαριέντως τε μανῆναι

An old man
who has learned to speak,
has learned to drink,
has learned to go mad gracefully.

Translated by D.A. Campbell (1988)

Fragment 53 (West)

16 Ἔρωτα γὰρ τὸν ἁβρὸν
μέλομαι βρύοντα μίτραις
πολυανθέμοις ἀείδειν.
ὅδε καὶ θεῶν δυνάστης,
ὅδε καὶ βροτοὺς δαμάζει.

I sing of Love
garlanded with flowers,
the tyrant of gods
and the tamer of mortals.

Fragment fav1 (West)

ANANIUS

6th century BC
Iambic poet

1 εἴ τις καθείρξαι χρυσὸν ἐν δόμοις πολὺν
καὶ σῦκα βαιὰ καὶ δύ' ἢ τρεῖς ἀνθρώπους,
γνοίη χ' ὅσῳ τὰ σῦκα τοῦ χρυσοῦ κρέσσω

If you lock up some people with a lot of gold and some figs, you will soon find out how much figs are superior to gold.

Fragment 3 (West, *IEG*)

ANAXAGORAS

*c.*500–428BC
Philosopher from Clazomenae

1 πρὸς ἑαυτὸ δὲ ἕκαστόν ἐστι καὶ μέγα καὶ σμικρόν

In relation to itself each thing is both great and small.

Translated by Jonathan Barnes (1979)
Fragment 3 (D-K)

2 βίην δὲ ἡ ταχυτὴς ποιεῖ

The speed produces the force.

Translated by Jonathan Barnes (1987)
Fragment 9 (D-K)
cf. Einstein's $E=mc^2$*?*

3 ἐν παντὶ παντὸς μοῖρα ἔνεστι πλὴν νοῦ, ἔστιν οἷσι δὲ καὶ νοῦς ἔνι

In everything there is a portion of everything, except Mind, and some things contain Mind also.

Translated by Kathleen Freeman (1948)
Fragment 11 (D-K)

4 νοῦς δέ ἐστιν ἄπειρον καὶ αὐτοκρατὲς

Mind is infinite and absolute, ruled by itself.

Fragment 12.4 (D-K)

5 νοῦς ... ἔστι γὰρ λεπτότατόν τε πάντων χρημάτων καὶ καθαρώτατον, καὶ γνώμην γε περὶ παντὸς πᾶσαν ἴσχει καὶ ἰσχύει μέγιστον

Mind (*nous*) is the most rarefied of things and the purest; it has all the knowledge with respect to everything, and it has the greatest power.

Translated by Karl Popper (1977)
Fragment 12.12 (D-K)

6 πάντων νοῦς κρατεῖ

Mind rules all things.

Fragment 12.15 (D-K)

7 καὶ ὁποῖα ἔμελλεν ἔσεσθαι καὶ ὁποῖα ἦν ... καὶ ὅσα νῦν ἐστι καὶ ὁποῖα ἔσται, πάντα διεκόσμησε νοῦς

And mind arranged everything – what was to be and what was and what now is and what will be.

Translated by Jonathan Barnes (1987)
Fragment 12.20 (D-K)

8 οὐδὲν γὰρ χρῆμα γίνεται οὐδὲ ἀπόλλυται, ἀλλ' ἀπὸ ἐόντων χρημάτων συμμίσγεταί τε καὶ διακρίνεται

Nothing comes into being or perishes completely; all are derived from existing things or dissolved into something new.

Fragment 17 (D-K)

9 ἥλιος ἐντίθησι τῇ σελήνῃ τὸ λαμπρόν

It is the sun that endows the moon with its brilliance.

Translated by Kathleen Freeman (1948)
Fragment 18 (D-K)

10 ὄψις γὰρ τῶν ἀδήλων τὰ φαινόμενα

Phenomena are sightings of what is not apparent.

Fragment 21a (D-K)

11 πάντα χρήματα ἦν ὁμοῦ· εἶτα νοῦς ἐλθὼν αὐτὰ διεκόσμησεν

All things were in confusion until Mind came and set them in order.

Translated by Edith Hamilton (1964)
Testimonies, Fragment 1.3 (D-K)

12 πανταχόθεν ὁμοία ἐστὶν ἡ εἰς ἅιδου κατάβασις

The descent to Hades is the same from

every place.

Translated in *Bartlett's Familiar Quotations* (1980)

Testimonies, Fragment 1.49 (D-K)

13 τοὺς παῖδας ἐν ᾧ ἂν ἀποθάνῃ μηνὶ κατ' ἔτος παίζειν συγχωρεῖν

In whatever month I die, give the children every year a holiday.

Translated by Kathleen Freeman (1947)

Testimonies, Fragment 1.80 (D-K)

14 ὦ Περίκλεις, καὶ οἱ τοῦ λύχνου χρείαν ἔχοντες ἔλαιον ἐπιχέουσιν

Pericles, even those who need a lamp pour oil therein.

Translated by Bernadotte Perrin (1916)

Testimonies, Fragment 32 (D-K)

said when dying while Pericles begged him to live

15 ᾔδειν θνητὸν γεννήσας

I knew my son was mortal.

Translated by R.D. Hicks (1925)

Testimonies, Fragment 33 (D-K)

16 δύο ἔλεγε διδασκαλίας εἶναι θανάτου, τόν τε πρὸ τοῦ γενέσθαι χρόνον καὶ τὸν ὕπνον

Two are the teachers of Death: the period before birth, and sleep.

Testimonies, Fragment 34 (D-K)

17 διὰ τὸ χεῖρας ἔχειν φρονιμώτατον εἶναι τῶν ζῴων ἄνθρωπον· εὔλογον δὲ διὰ τὸ φρονιμώτατον εἶναι χεῖρας λαμβάνειν. αἱ μὲν γὰρ χεῖρες ὄργανόν εἰσιν, ἡ δὲ φύσις ἀεὶ διανέμει ... ἕκαστον τῷ δυναμένῳ χρῆσθαι

Man is the cleverest of animals because he has hands; but it is reasonable to hold that he acquired hands because he is the cleverest; for hands are a tool, and nature always distributes each thing to those who are capable of using it.

Translated by Jonathan Barnes (1979)

ANAXANDRIDES

4th century BC
Middle Comedy poet possibly from Rhodes
see also Alexander 1

1 τὸν γὰρ οἴακα στρέφει
δαίμων ἑκάστῳ

Some god turns the helm for each of us.

Fragment 4 (Kock) – 4 (K-A) – *Anchises*

2 τὸ γὰρ κολακεύειν νῦν ἀρέσκειν ὄνομ' ἔχει

Flattery is now named 'a way to please'.

Fragment 42 (Kock) – 43 (K-A) – *Samia – The Woman from Samos*

3 πένης ὢν τὴν γυναῖκα χρήματα
λαβὼν ἔχει δέσποιναν, οὐ γυναῖκ' ἔτι

A poor man who takes a rich wife has a ruler, not a wife.

Translated by H.T. Riley (1872)

Fragment 52 (Kock) – 53 (K-A)

4 οὔτοι τὸ γῆράς ἐστιν, ὡς οἴει, πάτερ,
τῶν φορτίων μέγιστον, ἀλλ' ὃς ἂν φέρῃ
ἀγνωμόνως αὔθ', οὗτός ἐστιν αἴτιος·
ἂν δ' εὐκόλως, ἐνίοτε κοιμίζειν ποιεῖ,
μεταλαμβάνων ἐπιδέξι' αὐτοῦ τὸν τρόπον,
λύπην τ' ἀφαιρῶν ἡδονήν τε προστιθείς

Age is not the greatest among human burdens,
only he who suffers from it is a fool;
lighten the burden skilfully,
restraining sorrow, adding joy.

Fragment 53 (Kock) – 54 (K-A)

5 ἔρως σοφιστοῦ γίγνεται διδάσκαλος
σκαιοῦ πολὺ κρείττων πρὸς τὸν ἀνθρώπων βίον

Love is a greater teacher of truths
of human life than any dull professor.

Translated by Kathleen Freeman (1947)

Fragment 61 (Kock) – 62 (K-A)

6 τὸ συνεχὲς ἔργου παντὸς εὑρίσκει τέλος

Unceasing work always finds fulfilment.

Fragment 63 (Kock) – 64 (K-A)

7 οὐχὶ παρὰ πολλοῖς ἡ χάρις τίκτει χάριν

Charity seldom breeds gratitude.

Fragment 66 (Kock) – 69 (K-A)

but cf. Sophocles 15 and 229

ANAXARCHUS

mid – late 4th century BC
Democritean philosopher from Abdera

1 πολυμαθίη κάρτα μὲν ὠφελεῖ, κάρτα δὲ βλάπτει τὸν ἔχοντα· ὠφελεῖ μὲν τὸν δεξιὸν ἄνδρα, βλάπτει δὲ τὸν ῥηϊδίως φωνεῦντα πᾶν ἔπος κὴν παντὶ δήμῳ. χρὴ δὲ καιροῦ μέτρα εἰδέναι· σοφίης γὰρ οὗτος ὅρος

Much learning can help much, but also can greatly harm him who has it; it helps the clever man, but harms him who readily utters every word in any company. One must know the measure of the right time, for this is the boundary of wisdom.

Translated by Kathleen Freeman (1948)
Fragment 1 (D-K)

2 χαλεπὸν χρήματα συναγείρασθαι, χαλεπώτερον δὲ φυλακὴν τούτοις περιθεῖναι

It is hard to collect money, but harder still to keep it safe.

Fragment 2 (D-K)

ANAXILAS

4th century BC
Middle Comedy poet

1 πῶς ἔχεις; ὡς ἰσχνὸς εἶ;
ἀπόλλυμαι. τρέφω γὰρ ἐν ἀγρῷ χωρίον

– How are you? Why so thin?
– I am undone; I have to tend this property in the country.

Fragment 16 (Kock) – 16 (K-A)

ANAXIMANDER

died soon after 547BC
Philosopher from Miletus

1 τὸ ἄπειρον … ἐξ ὧν δὲ ἡ γένεσίς ἐστι τοῖς οὖσι, καὶ τὴν φθορὰν εἰς ταῦτα γίνεσθαι κατὰ τὸ χρεών

Apeiron, which, although it gives birth to changing things, does not change into something other than itself.

Translated by Karl Popper (1965)
Fragment 1 (D-K)

'Apeiron' as the 'unlimited', the source from which existing things derive their existence, 'infinity'

2 μέσην τε τὴν γῆν κεῖσθαι κέντρου τάξιν ἐπέχουσαν, οὖσαν σφαιροειδῆ

In the middle is the earth, holding a central position, in the shape of a sphere.

Testimonies, Fragment 1.3 (D-K)
cf. Aristarchus of Samos 1

3 τήν τε σελήνην ψευδοφαῆ καὶ ἀπὸ ἡλίου φωτίζεσθαι

The moon, shining with borrowed light, derives its illumination from the sun.

Translated by R.D. Hicks (1925)
Testimonies, Fragment 1.4 (D-K)

4 βέλτιον οὖν ἡμῖν ᾀστέον διὰ τὰ παιδάρια

To please the children I must improve my singing.

Translated by R.D. Hicks (1925)
Testimonies, Fragment 1.15 (D-K)

5 φησὶ τῶν ὄντων ἀρχὴν εἶναι τὸ ἄπειρον· ἐκ γὰρ τούτου πάντα γίγνεσθαι καὶ εἰς τοῦτο πάντα φθείρεσθαι. διὸ καὶ γεννᾶσθαι ἀπείρους κόσμους καὶ πάλιν φθείρεσθαι εἰς τὸ ἐξ οὗ γίγνεσθαι

All beings originate in infinity; from it all things come into being and in it all perish. Infinite worlds are thus born, and disappear from whence they came.

Testimonies, Fragment 14 (D-K)

ANAXIMENES (1)

fl. 546–525BC
Philosopher from Miletus

1 ἀρχὴν τῶν ὄντων ἀέρα ἀπεφήνατο· ἐκ γὰρ τούτου πάντα γίγνεσθαι καὶ εἰς αὐτὸν πάλιν ἀναλύεσθαι

Air is the first principle of things, since it is the source of everything and everything is dissolved back into it.

Translated by Robin Waterfield (2000)
Fragment 2.1 (D-K)

2 οἷον ἡ ψυχή, φησίν, ἡ ἡμετέρα ἀὴρ οὖσα συγκρατεῖ ἡμᾶς, καὶ ὅλον τὸν κόσμον πνεῦμα καὶ ἀὴρ περιέχει

As our soul, being breath, holds us together, so do wind and air surround the whole universe.

Translated by Kathleen Freeman (1948)
Fragment 2.3 (D-K)

ANAXIMENES (2)

*c.*380–320BC
Historian and rhetorician from Lampsacos

1 οἱ γὰρ μετὰ φθόνου κρίνοντες τὸ πρωτεῖον ἀπονέμουσι τοῖς χειρίστοις, οὐ τοῖς βελτίστοις

Those who make judgements based on envy give first place to the worst and not the best.

Fragment 32 (*FGrH*)

2 τί γάρ ἐστι δικαιότερον ἢ τοὺς γενέσεως καὶ παιδείας αἰτίους ὄντας ἀντευεργετεῖν;

Is there anything more just than returning kindness to those who bore you and educated you?

Fragment 34 (*FGrH*)

3 τοῖς γὰρ ἀστείοις πρεσβύταις ὅσον αἱ κατὰ τὸ σῶμα ἡδοναὶ ἀπομαραίνονται, τοσοῦτον αἱ περὶ τοὺς λόγους ἐπιθυμίαι πάλιν αὔξονται, καὶ τοσούτῳ βεβαιότερον αὐτοῖς παρέχει τὸ λέγειν τί χρήσιμον τοῖς ἄλλοις

As their physical desires fade, civilised old men seek pleasure in cultured conversation, seeking to share what is useful with others.

Fragment 38 (*FGrH*)

4 Θεόκριτος Ἀναξιμένους λέγειν μέλλοντος ἄρχεται εἶπεν λέξεων μὲν ποταμός, νοῦ δὲ σταλαγμός

When Anaximenes starts talking, said Theocritus, there's a river of words and only drops of sense.

Testimonies, Fragment 25 (*FGrH*)

ANAXIPPUS

4th–3rd century BC
New Comedy poet

1 ἀλλὰ τούς γε φιλοσόφους
ἐν τοῖς λόγοις φρονοῦντας εὑρίσκω μόνον,
ἐν τοῖσι δ' ἔργοις ὄντας ἀνοήτους ὁρῶ

Philosophers are, I reckon, only good at words, and foolish at deeds.

Fragment 4 (Kock) – 4 (K-A) – *Keraunos – The Thunderbolt*

ANDOCIDES

*c.*440–*c.*390BC
Athenian orator

1 τὰς δὲ δίκας καὶ τὰς διαίτας κυρίας εἶναι, ὁπόσαι ἐν δημοκρατουμένῃ τῇ πόλει ἐγένοντο

Decisions in lawsuits and arbitrations shall be valid only if given under democratic rule.

On the Mysteries 1.87

2 ἐάν τις δημοκρατίαν καταλύῃ τὴν Ἀθήνησιν ... πολέμιος ἔστω Ἀθηναίων καὶ νηποινεὶ τεθνάτω, καὶ τὰ χρήματα αὐτοῦ δημόσια ἔστω, καὶ τῆς θεοῦ τὸ ἐπιδέκατον· ὁ δὲ ἀποκτείνας τὸν ταῦτα ποιήσαντα καὶ ὁ συμβουλεύσας ὅσιος ἔστω καὶ εὐαγής

If anyone abolishes the Athenian democracy he shall be an enemy of the Athenians, he shall be killed with impunity and his property confiscated by the state; as for the assassin and his abettor, they shall be hallowed and guiltless.

On the Mysteries 1.96

cf. Anonymous (Inscriptions) 141

3 ἔστιν ἐν τῷ κοινῷ πᾶσιν ἀνθρώποις καὶ ἐξαμαρτεῖν τι καὶ κακῶς πρᾶξαι· ὧν ἕνεκα, ὦ Ἀθηναῖοι, εἰ ἀνθρωπίνως περὶ ἐμοῦ γιγνώσκοιτε, εἴητε ἂν ἄνδρες εὐγνωμονέστεροι· οὐ γὰρ φθόνου μᾶλλον ἢ οἴκτου ἄξιά μοί ἐστι τὰ γεγενημένα

It is the common fate of humanity to make mistakes and suffer misfortune. I appeal to you, therefore, to consider this frailty of man, and to show kindness when you pass judgement upon me. Indeed what happened to me is more a case for compassion than for malice against me.

On his Return 2.6

ANONYMOUS

see also Oracles, Proverbial; Proverbial expressions; Songs

1 πουλύποδός μοι, τέκνον, ἔχων νόον, Ἀμφίλοχ' ἥρως,
τοῖσιν ἐφαρμόζειν, τῶν κεν κατὰ δῆμον ἵκηαι,
ἄλλοτε δ' ἀλλοῖος τελέθειν καὶ χροιῇ ἕπεσθαι

Follow the octopus, my son,
adopt his wits when it comes to people;
be changeable, and go along with their hues.

Anonymous Epic Works, Thebaïs, Fragment 4 (Bernabé, *PEG*)

author unknown, sometimes attributed to Homer

2 δῶρα γὰρ ἀνθρώπων νοῦν ἤπαφεν ἠδὲ καὶ ἔργα

The minds and actions of men are deceived by gifts.

Anonymous Epic Works, Nostoi, Fragment 8 (Bernabé, *PEG*)

author unknown

3 ὁ νοῶν νοείτω

Whoever can see, let him see.

History of Alexander the Great, Recensio Epsilon 34.4

falsely attributed to Callisthenes

4 ἔγνω δὲ φώρ τε φῶρα καὶ λύκος λύκον

And thief knows thief and wolf his fellow wolf.

Translated by H. Rackham (1935)

Aristotle, *Eudemian Ethics* 1235a.9

cf. the English proverb 'set a thief to catch a thief'

5 παύροις δ' ἀνθρώπων ἀρετὴ καὶ κάλλος ὀπηδεῖ·
ὄλβιος ὃς τούτων ἀμφοτέρων ἔλαχε

Virtue and beauty seldom come together,
but whoever possesses both is doubly blessed.

Arsenius, *Apophthegms* 14.13b

6 ἐπὶ τοῖς παροῦσι τὸν βίον διάπλεκε

Arrange your life according to present circumstance.

Athenaeus, *Deipnosophists* 10.458b

7 σοφός ἐστιν ὁ φέρων τἀπὸ τῆς τύχης καλῶς

Wise is he who bears the turns of fortune well.

Athenaeus, *Deipnosophists* 10.458c

8 αἰεὶ σφῷν κλέος ἔσσεται κατ' αἶαν ...
ὅτι τὸν τύραννον κτανέτην
ἰσονόμους τ' Ἀθήνας ἐποιησάτην

Their fame shall live on the earth for ever,
because they slew the tyrant and
made Athens a city of just laws.

Translated by C.A. Trypanis (1971)

Athenaeus, *Deipnosophists* 15.695b

of Harmodius and Aristogiton, who killed Hipparchus, were executed for it, and later acclaimed as tyrannicides

9 ὅσα τε χθὼν
πόντου τε βένθη καὶ ἀέρος
ἀμέτρητον εὖρος ἐκτρέφει

All that is nourished by the earth and the depths of the sea
and the measureless breadth of the air.

Translated by David A. Campbell (1993)

Clement of Alexandria, *Paedagogus* 2.1.3.2

10 ψυχαὶ δ' ἀσεβῶν ὑπουράνιοι γαίᾳ πωτῶνται
ἐν ἄλγεσι φονίοις ὑπὸ ζεύγλαις ἀφύκτοις κακῶν,
εὐσεβῶν δὲ ἐπουράνιοι νάουσι,
μολπαῖς μάκαρα μέγαν ἀείδουσ' ἐν ὕμνοις

The souls of the wicked flit about below the skies on earth,
In murderous pains beneath inevitable yokes of evils;
But those of the pious dwell in the heavens,
Praising in songs the Great, the Blessed One.

Translated by Philip Schaff (1819–1893)

Clement of Alexandria, *Stromateis* 4.26.167.3

11 ἀπροσδοκήτως εἰς κλύδωνα πραγμάτων
ἐμπεσὼν

I have suddenly tumbled into a sea of troubles.

Translated by D.L. Page (1941)

Comica Adespota, Adespota novae comoediae, Fragment 255.5 (Austin, *CGFPR*) – 1063 (K-A)

12 πολλάκις τὰ δυσχερῆ
ἀντίκειται πάντα· χειμών, πνεῦμ', ὕδωρ, τρικυμία,
ἀστραπαί, χάλαζα, βρονταί, ναυτίαι, σύναγμα, νύξ

Constantly up against every difficulty!
Storm, gale, rain, mountainous seas,

lightning, hail, thunder, seasickness, darkness!

Translated by D.L. Page (1941)

Comica Adespota, Adespota novae comoediae, Fragment 255.10 (Austin, *CGFPR*) – 1063 (K-A)

13 ἀγκωνισαμένοις ῥῆσιν λέγειν
μακρὰν ὀχληράν, ἐκδιδάσκοντας σαφῶς
κἀκτιθεμένους καθ' ἕκαστον, ὧν εὖ οἶδ' ὅτι
οὐθεὶς μεμάθηκεν οὐθέν

They are bound to make a lengthy, tiresome, speech, to an audience half-asleep, giving the clearest information and setting every detail forth: although not one spectator, I am positive, has learnt anything at all in the end.

Translated by D.L. Page (1941)

Comica Adespota, Adespota novae comoediae, Fragment 14 (Demiańczuk) – 1008 (K-A)

14 ἐρημία μέν ἐστι, κοὐκ ἀκούσεται
οὐδεὶς παρών μου τῶν λόγων ὧν ἂν λέγω

Well, this is solitude; whatever I say, there's nobody here to listen.

Translated by D.L. Page (1941)

Comica Adespota, Fragment 104 (Kock) – 1001 (K-A)

also attributed to Menander, possibly from the lost play Hypobolimaios – The Counterfeit Baby

15 παραπλήσιον πρᾶγμ' ἐστι γῆρας καὶ γάμος.
τυχεῖν γὰρ αὐτῶν ἀμφοτέρων σπουδάζομεν,
ὅταν δὲ τύχωμεν ὕστερον λυπούμεθα

Old age and marriage are quite similar;
we seek them both but suffer when we reach them.

Comica Adespota, Fragment 132 (Kock) – 899 (K-A)

16 ὅταν δὲ νυστάζοντά μ' ἡ λύπη λάβῃ,
ἀπόλλυμ' ὑπὸ τῶν ἐνυπνίων

When grief o'ertakes me as I close my eyes,
I'm murdered by my dreams.

Translated by Frank Cole Babbitt (1928)

Comica Adespota, Fragment 185 (Kock) – 714 (K-A)

17 ἐρημία μεγάλη 'στὶν ἡ Μεγάλη πόλις

A large city is a large wilderness.

Translated by Gavin Betts and Alan Henry (1989)

A great city is a great solitude.

Translated by H.T. Riley (1872)

Comica Adespota, Fragment 211 (Kock) – 913 (K-A)

both translations are valid

18 ληρεῖς ἐν οὐ δέοντι καιρῷ φιλοσοφῶν

Ill-timed philosophy equals silliness.

Comica Adespota, Fragment 248 (Kock) – 893 (K-A)

19 πάντα ταῦτα γὰρ
τύχη δίδωσι καὶ παραιρεῖται πάλιν

In all things,
whatever Fate has given, she takes back.

Comica Adespota, Fragment 406 (Kock)

20 ἐκ τοῦ λαλεῖν ἀεὶ τὸ λαλεῖν περιγίνεται

Prattle begets prattle, always.

Comica Adespota, Fragment 514 (Kock)

cf. Himerius, Oration 74 (Colonna)

21 ἅπαντα τὰ καλὰ τοῦ πονοῦντος γίγνεται

All good things are the result of hard work.

Comica Adespota, Fragment 532 (Kock) – *892 (K-A)

22 καλὸν δὲ τὸ ζῆν, ἄν τις ὡς δεῖ ζῆν μάθῃ

Living is fine, if one learns how to live.

Comica Adespota, Fragment 537 (Kock) – 75 (K-A)

23 ἡ γλῶττ' ἀνέγνωχ', ἡ δὲ φρὴν οὐ μανθάνει

My tongue has read, my mind not understood.

Comica Adespota, Fragment 570 (Kock) – *832 (K-A)

24 οὐ γὰρ τὸ εἰπεῖν καλῶς καλόν, ἀλλὰ τὸ εἰπόντα δρᾶσαι τὰ εἰρημένα

It is not to speak nobly that is noble, but after speaking to perform what has been spoken.

Translated by Doreen C. Innes (1995, based on W. Rhys Roberts)

Demetrius, *On Style* 18

25 λεπταῖς ὑπεσύριζε πίτυς αὔραις

The pine was whistling to the accompaniment of the gentle breezes.

Translated by Doreen C. Innes (1995, based on W. Rhys Roberts)

Demetrius, *On Style* 188

26 ψυχῆς ἰατρεῖον

Healing-place of the Soul.

Translated by C.H. Oldfather (1933)

Diodorus Siculus, *Library of History* 1.49.3

inscribed on the library in Thebes, Egypt

27 τάδ' ἔστ' ὀνείρων νερτέρων φαντάσματα

Phantoms are these of dreams o' the world below.

Translated by R.D. Hicks (1925)

Diogenes Laertius, *Lives of Eminent Philosophers* 6.95

quoted by Metrocles (c.300BC) as he burnt all his compositions

28 γυμνὸς ὡς ἐκ μήτρας

Naked as the day he was born.

Diogenianus, *Proverbs (epitome operis)* 4.2

cf. the similar expression in English

29 ἐσθλοὶ μὲν γὰρ ἁπλῶς, παντοδαπῶς δὲ κακοί

Goodness is simple, badness is manifold.

Translated by H. Rackham (1926)

Elegiaca Adespota, Fragment 3 (West, *IEG*)

cf. Aristotle 95

30 πολλὰς δὴ φιλίας ἀπροσηγορία διέλυσεν

Full many a man finds friendship end
For lack of converse with his friend.

Translated by H. Rackham (1935)

Elegiaca Adespota, Fragment 4 (West, *IEG*)

quoted by Aristotle in Nicomachean Ethics *1157b.13; cf. the English proverb 'out of sight, out of mind'*

31 ἐσθλὸς ἐὼν ἄλλου κρείττονος ἀντέτυχεν

Though great and valiant he met a greater still.

Translated by Evelyn S. Shuckburgh (1962)

Elegiaca Adespota, Fragment 10 (West, *IEG*)

of Hannibal, beaten by Publius Cornelius Scipio Africanus; quoted by Polybius 15.16.6.4

32 οὐκ ἔστιν μείζων βάσανος χρόνου οὐδενὸς ἔργου,
ὃς καὶ ὑπὸ στέρνοις ἀνδρὸς ἔδειξε νόον

Of any action there is no better test than Time
who will reveal man's innermost designs.

Elegiaca Adespota, Fragment 22 (West, *IEG*)

33 ὡς ἀν' ἐχινόποδας καὶ ἀνὰ τρηχεῖαν ὄνωνιν
φύονται μαλακῶν ἄνθεα λευκοΐων

Just as amid thistles and noxious weeds
Flowering snowdrops grow, delicate in their bloom.

Fragmenta Adespota, Fragment 1138 (Lloyd-Jones and Parsons, *SH*)

34 Καὶ πενίη καὶ ἔρως δύο μοι κακά· καὶ τὸ μὲν οἴσω
κούφως, πῦρ δὲ φέρειν Κύπριδος οὐ δύναμαι.

Poverty and Love are my two woes. Poverty I will bear easily,
but the fire of Cypris I cannot.

Translated by W.R. Paton (1916)

Greek Anthology 5.50

Cypris (Aphrodite) as the goddess of love

35 Εἴθ' ἄνεμος γενόμην, σὺ δ' ἐπιστείχουσα παρ' αὐγὰς
στήθεα γυμνώσαις καί με πνέοντα λάβοις.

Oh to be the wind,
and you, by the shore,
bare your breasts and let me
touch them as I blow.

Greek Anthology 5.83

36 Εἴθε ῥόδον γενόμην ὑποπόρφυρον, ὄφρα με χερσὶν
ἀρσαμένη χαρίσῃ στήθεσι χιονέοις.

Would that I were a damask rose for you to pluck
and fasten to your snow-white breasts.

Greek Anthology 5.84

37 τίφθ' ὁπόταν νήφω, μεθύεις σύ μοι, ἢν δὲ μεθυσθῶ,
ἐκνήφεις; ἀδικεῖς συμποτικὴν φιλίην

Why, when I'm sober, are you full of wine,
and why, when I'm loaded, do you turn sober?
That surely violates the friendship code of drinkers.

Translated by Edmund Keeley (2010)

Greek Anthology 5.135

38 Μνᾶμα μὲν Ἑλλὰς ἅπασ' Εὐριπίδου, ὀστέα δ' ἴσχει
γῆ Μακεδών, ᾗ γὰρ δέξατο τέρμα βίου.
πατρὶς δ' Ἑλλάδος Ἑλλάς, Ἀθῆναι.

All Hellas is the monument of Euripides;
Macedonian earth holds his bones, where his life reached its goal,
but his native land was the Hellas of Hellas, Athens.

Translated by J.W. MacKail (1890)

Greek Anthology 7.45

variously attributed to Thucydides and Timotheus, but both seem uncertain

39 Αἰετέ, τίπτε βέβηκας ὑπὲρ τάφον ἢ τίνος, εἰπέ,
ἀστερόεντα θεῶν οἶκον ἀποσκοπέεις;
Ψυχῆς εἰμι Πλάτωνος ἀποπταμένης ἐς Ὄλυμπον
εἰκών· σῶμα δὲ γῆ γηγενὲς Ἀτθὶς ἔχει.

Eagle! why soarest thou above that tomb?
To what sublime and star-ypaven home
Floatest thou? –
I am the image of swift Plato's spirit,
Ascending heaven; Athens doth inherit
His corpse below.

Translated by Percy Bysshe Shelley (written 1818; printed posthumously 1839)

Greek Anthology 7.62

40 Κάτθανον, ἀλλὰ μένω σε· μενεις δέ τε καὶ σύ τιν' ἄλλον·
πάντας ὁμῶς θνητοὺς εἷς Ἀίδης δέχεται.

I died, but I await thee; and thou too shalt await some one else:
one Death receives all mortals alike.

Translated by J.W. MacKail (1890)

Greek Anthology 7.342

41 Βαιὰ φαγὼν καὶ βαιὰ πιὼν καὶ πολλὰ νοσήσας
ὀψὲ μέν, ἀλλ' ἔθανον. ἔρρετε πάντες ὁμοῦ.

Little I ate, a little drank, and I was seldom well.
I lasted long. At last I died
– I wish you all in hell!

Translated by Kathleen Freeman (1947)

Greek Anthology 7.349

attributed to Simonides in some manuscripts

42 μελίσσαις
οἶμον ἐπ' εἰαρινὴν λέξατε νισσομέναις,
ὡς ὁ γέρων Λεύκιππος ... ἔφθιτο χειμερίῃ νυκτὶ ...
σμήνεα δ' οὐκέτι οἱ κομέειν φίλον

When bees come hither in the fair springtide,
Tell them, how on a wintry night Leukippus died;
The hives no more shall feel his fostering skill.

Translated by J.A. Pott (1911)

Greek Anthology 7.717

cf. Mark Twain, Huckleberry Finn, *ch. 8: 'If a man owned a beehive, and that man died, the bees must be told before sun-up next morning, or else the bees die'*

43 πόθεν ἔσχες

Now, where did you get this!

Greek Anthology 9.182

a common expression (cf. Aristophanes, Wealth *881: 'πόθεν θοἰμάτιον': 'where did you get this cloak'), still used today for politicians (not) declaring their possessions as required by law; cf. Herodotus 61*

44 Αὐταί σοι στομάτεσσιν ἀνηρείψαντο μέλισσαι
ποικίλα Μουσάων ἄνθεα δρεψάμεναι

The bees themselves, culling the varied flowers
of the Muses, brought honey to thy lips.

Translated by W.R. Paton (1917)

Greek Anthology 9.187

of Menander

45 Τὴν πόλιν οἱ νέκυες πρότερον ζῶσαν κατέλειψαν,
ἡμεῖς δὲ ζῶντες τὴν πόλιν ἐκφέρομεν.

The dead used to leave the city alive behind them,
but we living now carry the city to her grave.

Translated by W.R. Paton (1917)

Greek Anthology 9.501

of an earthquake

46 Ὦ φίλος, εἰ σοφὸς εἶ, λάβε μ' ἐς χέρας· εἰ δέ γε πάμπαν
νῆϊς ἔφυς Μουσέων, ῥῖψον, ἃ μὴ νοης.
εἰμὶ γὰρ οὐ πάντεσσι βατός· παῦροι δ' ἀγάσαντο
Θουκυδίδην Ὀλόρου, Κεκροπίδην τὸ γένος.

If you have wisdom, friend, take me in hand:
If scant of learning,
Away with what you cannot understand!
Mine is no road for all the world to tread:
Few but discerning
Admire Thucydides, Athenian bred.

Translated by A.J. Butler (1881)

Greek Anthology 9.583

47 Ἐν μικρῷ μεγάλη λουτρῷ χάρις· ἐν δ' ἐλαχίστῳ
νάματι λουομένοις ἡδὺς ἔπεστιν Ἔρως.

There is a great delight in a little bath; Eros looks on when we go bathing, be it in the tiniest stream.

Greek Anthology 9.611

48 Εἰς Ἀίδην ἰθεῖα κατήλυσις, εἴτ' ἀπ' Ἀθηνῶν
στείχοις, εἴτε νέκυς νίσεαι ἐκ Μερόης.
μή σέ γ' ἀνιάτω πάτρης ἀποτῆλε θανόντα·
πάντοθεν εἷς ὁ φέρων εἰς Ἀίδην ἄνεμος.

The way down to Hades is straight, be it from Athens
or, when dead, if you start off from Meroe.
Let it not vex thee to die far from thy country.
One fair wind to Hades blows from all lands.

Greek Anthology 10.3

epitaph, probably for an Athenian who died at Meroe in Nubia on the Upper Nile

49 Πολλὰ μεταξὺ πέλει κύλικος καὶ χείλεος ἄκρου.

There's many a slip
'tween the cup and the lip.

Translated by D.M. Moir (1824)

Greek Anthology 10.32

attributed to Palladas and by some to Homer; cf. the English proverb 'there's many a slip 'twixt cup and lip'

50 Ζεῦ βασιλεῦ, τὰ μὲν ἐσθλὰ καὶ εὐχομένοις καὶ ἀνεύκτοις
ἄμμι δίδου· τὰ δὲ λυγρὰ καὶ εὐχομένων ἀπερύκοις.

Unask'd, what good thou knowest grant,
What ill, though ask'd, deny.

Translated by Alexander Pope (1688–1744)

Greek Anthology 10.108

Pope's 'Universal Prayer'; quoted in Plato, Alcibiades II* *143a*

51 Ὁ φθόνος αὐτὸς ἑαυτὸν ἑοῖς βελέεσσι δαμάζει.

Envy slays itself by its own arrows.

Translated by W.R. Paton (1918)

Greek Anthology 10.111

52 Σώματα πολλὰ τρέφειν καὶ δώματα πόλλ' ἀνεγείρειν
ἀτραπὸς εἰς πενίην ἐστὶν ἑτοιμοτάτη.

To feed many persons and to build many houses
is the readiest way to poverty.

Translated by H.T. Riley (1872)

Greek Anthology 10.119

53 Τὸ ῥόδον ἀκμάζει βαιὸν χρόνον· ἢν δὲ παρέλθῃ,
ζητῶν εὑρήσεις οὐ ῥόδον, ἀλλὰ βάτον.

The rose's bloom is short; and when it goes
You'll seek, and find, a thorn and not a rose.

Translated by R.A. Furness (1931)

Greek Anthology 11.53

54 Πῖνε καὶ εὐφραίνου· τί γὰρ αὔριον ἢ τί τὸ μέλλον,
οὐδεὶς γινώσκει. μὴ τρέχε, μὴ κοπία.

Drink and be merry; for what tomorrow brings, or the future,
no one knows; hasten not and toil not!

Greek Anthology 11.56

sometimes attributed to Palladas

55 οὐ πάντα θεοὶ πᾶσιν ἔδωκαν ἔχειν

The gods don't give everything to everyone.

Greek Anthology 12.96

56 Εἰαρινῷ χειμῶνι πανείκελος, ὦ Διόδωρε,
οὑμὸς ἔρως ἀσαφεῖ κρινόμενος πελάγει·
καὶ ποτὲ μὲν φαίνεις πολὺν ὑετόν, ἄλλοτε δ' αὖτε
εὔδιος, ἁβρὰ γελῶν δ' ὄμμασιν ἐκκέχυσαι.

Winter in spring is my love, Diodorus,
as uncertain as what determines the

seas.
At times you show me dark clouds,
at other times the clear sky of a mild
smile.

Translated by Edmund Keeley (2010)

Greek Anthology 12.156

57 Εἰ λύπης κρατέειν ἐθέλεις,
τήνδε μάκαιραν ἀναπτύσσων
βίβλον ἐπέρχεο ἐνδυκέως,
ἧς ὕπο γνώμην ὀλβίστην
ῥεῖά κεν ὄψεαι ἐσσομένων,
ὄντων τ' ἠδὲ παροιχομένων
τερπωλήν τ' ἀνίην τε λέγων
καπνοῦ μηδὲν ἀρειοτέρην.

If thou woulds't master care and pain,
Unfold this book and read and read
again
Its blessed leaves, whereby thou soon
shalt see
The past, the present, and the days to be
With opened eyes; and all delight, all
grief,
Shall be like smoke, as empty and as
brief.

Translated by C.R. Haines (1916)

Greek Anthology 15.23

on the book of Marcus Aurelius; possibly by Arethas, cf. P. Maas in 'Hermes' 48(1913).295

58 Πᾶν τὸ περιττὸν ἄκαιρον, ἐπεὶ λόγος ἐστὶ
παλαιός,
ὡς καὶ τοῦ μέλιτος τὸ πλέον ἐστὶ χολή.

All that is superfluous is inopportune;
for there is an old saying
that even too much of honey is gall.

Translated by W.R. Paton (1918)

Greek Anthology 16.16

59 τόσσ' ἔχω, ὅσσ' ἔφαγον καὶ ἐφύβρισα καὶ
μετ' ἔρωτος τέρπν' ἐδάην

These I take with me, the joys of food
and drink and love.

Greek Anthology 16.27

a much discussed translation of the epitaph of Sardanapalus, the legendary Assyrian king (669–626BC), said to have been composed by himself; cf. Arrian, Anabasis *2.5.4.5; Aristotle, Fragment 90 (Rose); Diodorus Siculus 2.23.3; et al.*

60 Ὁ πτανὸς τὸν πτανὸν ἴδ' ὡς ἄγνυσι
κεραυνόν,
δεικνὺς ὡς κρεῖσσον πῦρ πυρός ἐστιν,
Ἔρως.

See how the winged god breaks the
winged thunderbolt,
showing that there is a fire stronger
than fire, Eros.

Greek Anthology 16.250

of Eros, the winged god

61 Εἰ θεός ἐστιν Ὅμηρος, ἐν ἀθανάτοισι
σεβέσθω·
εἰ δ' αὖ μὴ θεός ἐστι, νομιζέσθω θεὸς
εἶναι.

If Homer be a god, let him be honoured
as one of the gods;
if again he be not a god, let him be
esteemed as if a god.

Greek Anthology 16.301

used as an inscription in the painting 'L'apothéose d'Homère' by Ingres

62 Τὸν νοῦν διδάσκων αἰθερεμβατεῖν
Πλάτων
τοὺς τῶν ὑπὲρ νοῦν ἐξερεύγεται λόγους.

Plato, teaching the mind to walk in
ether,
expresses ideas beyond comprehension.

Greek Anthology 16.328

63 ΝΙΨΟΝΑΝΟΜΗΜΑΤΑΜΗΜΟΝΑΝΟΨΙΝ
νίψον ἀνομήματα, μὴ μόναν ὄψιν

Wash away your sins, not only your face.

Translated by C.A. Trypanis (1971)

Greek Anthology 16.387c

the longest palindrome in literature, cf. the Guinness Book of Records *(e.g. the 1981 edition, p.91); inscribed on fountains in many ancient churches*

64 Ἔγλυψέν με σίδηρος, ἐποίησαν δέ με
χεῖρες
τέχνῃ πειθόμεναι· εἰμὶ δ' ἄγαλμα Δίκης.

Carved by iron, wrought by hand
complying with art, I am the statue of
Justice.

Greek Anthology Appendix, Epigrammata demonstrativa 148 (Cougny)

written under a statue, Rome, 2nd–3rd century AD; recorded in IG XIV.973

65 Ἁγνὸν χρὴ νηοῖο θυώδεος ἐντὸς ἰόντα
ἔμμεναι· ἁγνείη δ' ἔστι φρονεῖν ὅσια.

He who enters the temple must be holy;
and holiness is to possess a pure mind.

Greek Anthology Appendix, Epigrammata exhortatoria et supplicatoria 18 (Cougny)

66 Ἑλλήνων προμαχοῦντες Ἀθηναῖοι Μαραθῶνι
χρυσοφόρων Μήδων ἐστόρεσαν δύναμιν.

Fighting in the forefront of the Greeks, the Athenians
crushed at Marathon the might of the gold-bearing Medes.

Translated in *Bartlett's Familiar Quotations* (1980)

Greek Anthology Appendix, Epigrammata exhortatoria et supplicatoria 25 (Cougny)

quoted by Lycurgus, Against Leocrates *1.109; an indication by some that this is by Simonides is not confirmed in any ancient authority*

67 ἐν βουλαῖς ἄριστος, ἐν βουλαῖσι κράτιστος

Supreme in counsel, mightiest in will.

Greek Anthology Appendix, Epigrammata Graeca 854 (Kaibel)

68 Χαίρετ' Ἀριστείδου τοῦ ῥήτορος ἑπτὰ μαθηταί,
τέσσαρες οἱ τοῖχοι, καὶ τρία συψέλια

All hail, you seven pupils of Aristides:
four walls and benches three.

Greek Anthology Appendix, Epigrammata irrisoria 31 (Cougny)

written of Aristides, a rhetorician from Smyrna, or possibly a later Aristides

69 ΑΙΘΕΡΜΕΜΦΣΥΧΑΣΥΠΕΔΕΧΣΑΤΟΣΟΜ ...

Αἰθὴρ μὲν ψυχὰς ὑπεδέξατο, σώματα δὲ χθὼν

Heaven received their souls, earth their bodies.

Greek Anthology Appendix, Epigrammata sepulcralia 19 (Cougny)

a stone with this inscription is recorded in IG I.442

70 μηδὲν ἁμαρτεῖν ἐστι θεῶν καὶ πάντα κατορθοῦν

God errs not, fails not; god alone is great.

Translated by C.A. Vince and J.H. Vince (1926)

Greek Anthology Appendix, Epigrammata sepulcralia 52 (Cougny)

71 Ἄνθεα πολλὰ γένοιτο νεοδμήτῳ ἐπὶ τύμβῳ,
μὴ βάτος αὐχμηρή, μὴ κακὸν αἰγίπυρον,
ἀλλ' ἴα, καὶ σάμψυχα καὶ ὑδατίνη νάρκισσος,
Οὐίβιε, καὶ περὶ σοῦ πάντα γένοιτο ῥόδα.

May many flowers blossom on your new-built tomb;
not the dry bramble, not the evil thistle,
but violets and marjoram and soft narcissus,
and roses all around you, Vibius.

Greek Anthology Appendix, Epigrammata sepulcralia 238 (Cougny)

72 Μαρκέλλης τάφος εἰμί. Τίς αὐτὴ γράμματα λέξει,
ἀρτίγαμος κούρη εἴκοσιν οὖσ' ἐτέων.
Αὐτὴ ἡ γεννήσασα καὶ κηδεύσασα ἐπέγραψεν,
ἄχθος ἔχουσα κραδίῃ πένθεος οὐκ ὀλίγου.

This is Marcella's tomb, just married, barely twenty.
Who then will write her epitaph?
I bore her, buried her and write of her,
my heart full of grief, and sorrow overflowing.

Greek Anthology Appendix, Epigrammata sepulcralia 504 (Cougny)

73 Οὐ τὸ θανεῖν ἀλγεινὸν, ἐπεὶ τόδε πᾶσι πέπρωται,
ἀλλὰ πρὶν ἡλικίης καὶ γονέων πρότερον.

Not death is bitter, since that is predestined for us all,
but to die before our time and before our parents.

Translated by J.W. MacKail (1890)

Greek Anthology Appendix, Epigrammata sepulcralia 566 (Cougny)

epitaph on a beautiful boy

74 ἐκ γαίας βλαστὼν γαῖα πάλιν γέγονα

From earth I was brought forth and to earth I return.

Greek Anthology Appendix, Epigrammata sepulcralia 603 (Cougny)

75 ἔλπεσθαι χρὴ πάντ', ἐπεὶ οὐκ ἔστ' οὐδὲν ἄελπτον·
ῥάδια πάντα θεῷ τελέσαι, καὶ ἀνήνυτον οὐδέν

Never lose hope, for nothing is beyond hope;
for god everything is easy and nothing impossible.

Iamblichus, *Life of Pythagoras* 28.139

attributed to Linus (Λίνος), a mythical minstrel; linus (λίνος) is a song lamenting the departing summer, cf. Homer, Iliad *18.570*

76 ἡ δημοκρατία τῶν μεγάλων ἀγαθὴ τιθηνός

Democracy is the kindly nurse of genius.

Translated by W.H. Fyfe (1878-1965), rev. Donald Russell, 1995

'Longinus', *On the Sublime* 44.2

77 ἄλλον τρόπον ἄλλον ἐγείρει
φροντὶς ἀνθρώπων

Men's thinking rouses one in this way, another in that.

Translated by David A. Campbell (1993)

Lyrica Adespota, Fragment 77 (Page, *PMG*)

78 μισέω μνάμονα συμπόταν

I hate the fellow-drinker with a good memory.

Translated by David A. Campbell (1993)

Lyrica Adespota, Fragment 84 (Page, *PMG*)

79 πᾶν ὅττι κεν ἐπ' ἀκαιρίμαν
γλῶσσαν ἴῃ κελαδεῖν

Untimely prattling of whatever comes to your tongue.

Lyrica Adespota, Fragment 102 (Page, *PMG*)

80 ὦ γλυκεῖ' Εἰράνα,
πλουτοδότειρα βροτοῖς

O sweet Peace,
bringing wealth to mortals.

Lyrica Adespota, Fragment 103 (Page, *PMG*)

81 ξουθὰ δὲ λιγύφωνα
ὄρνεα διεφοίτα τ'
ἀν' ἐρῆμον δρίος, ἄκροις τ'
ἐπὶ κλωσὶ πίτυος ἥμεν'
ἐμινύριζ' ἐτιττύβιζεν
κέλαδον παντομιγῆ, καὶ
τὰ μὲν ἄρχετο, τὰ δ' ἔμελλεν,
τὰ δ' ἐσίγα, τὰ δὲ βώστρεῦντ'
ἀν' ὄρη λαλεῦσι φωναῖς,
φιλέρημος δὲ νάπαισιν
λάλος ἀνταμείβετ' ἀχώ

Birds nimble and musical,
flitting through the lonely woodland,
perched on the topmost branches,
chirped and twittered
in loud sweet jargoning;
some beginning, some pausing,
some silent, others loudly singing
they spoke with voices on the hillsides;
and babbling Echo, fond of solitude,
made answer in the glades.

Lyrica Adespota, Fragment 7.1 (Powell, *Coll. Alex*)

from a papyrus dated around 100BC

82 πιθαναὶ δ' ἐργατίδες σιμοπρόσωποι
ξουθόπτεροι μέλισσαι,
θαμιναὶ θέρεος ἔριθοι
λιπόκεντροι βαρυαχεῖς
πηλουργοὶ δυσέρωτες
ἀσκεπεῖς τὸ γλυκὺ νέκταρ
μελιτόρρυτον ἀρύουσιν

On brisk wing, with murmur low,
Ground-bees traffic to and fro,
Born to toil, a snub-faced brood,
Summer's faithful harvesters.
Moulded cells of earth are theirs,
Theirs an austere sisterhood:
Harmless creatures, strange to hiving,
That no carnal love ensue,
But in wells of nectar diving
Draw delicious honey-dew.

Translated by T.F. Higham (1938)

Lyrica Adespota, Fragment 7.12 (Powell, *Coll. Alex*)

ground-bee is a species common in Southern Europe, probably Chalicodoma sicula; *it is mentioned only in this fragment from a papyrus dated around 100BC*

83 ἐρῶντα νουθετοῦντες ἀγνοεῖθ' ὅτι
πῦρ ἀνακαιόμενον ἐλαίῳ θέλετε κοιμίσαι

When you rebuke a lover, you know not that
you seek to quench with oil a blazing fire.

Translated by D.L. Page (1941)

Lyrica Adespota, Fragment 8a (Powell, *Coll. Alex*)

84 μὴ κοπία ζητεῖν πόθεν ἥλιος ἢ πόθεν ὕδωρ,
ἀλλὰ πόθεν τὸ μύρον καὶ τοὺς στεφάνους ἀγοράσῃς.
αὔλει μοι

Do not strive to find out whence the sun comes, or water,
but where you can buy the scent and the garlands.
Pipe for me, piper.

Translated by C.A. Trypanis (1971)

Lyrica Adespota, Fragment 37 (Powell, *Coll. Alex*)

85 περὶ ὧν ἅμιν ἔγραψας, οὔ

Concerning what you wrote, 'No'.

Translated by Frank Cole Babbitt (1931)

Plutarch, *Sayings of Spartans* 235a

the Spartans in answer to Philip of Macedon's written 'orders'

86 ἀλλὰ ναὶ τὼ σιώ ... ἀνδρεῖός γε ὁ ἄνθρωπος· πρὸς οὐδὲν ὑποκείμενον εὖ στροβιλοῖ τὴν γλῶτταν

Egad, but the man has courage; he twists his tongue well about no subject at all.

Translated by Frank Cole Babbitt (1931)

Plutarch, *Sayings of Spartans* 235e

spoken by a Spartan listening to an orator 'rolling off long sentences'

87 ἡ χωρὶς λόγων τράπεζα, φάτνης οὐδὲν διαφέρει

Dinner without discussion! I had rather live in a stable!

Simplicius, *Commentarius in Epicteti enchiridion* 114.45

sometimes attributed to Euripides

88 οὐχ εὕδει Διὸς
ὀφθαλμός, ἐγγὺς δ' ἐστί, καίπερ ὢν πρόσω

The eye of god sleeps not: whatever we do he is near.

Stobaeus, *Anthology* 1.3.9

89 στρατεύματος μὲν γὰρ ἁγεῖται στραταγός, πλωτήρων δὲ κυβερνάτας, τῶ δὲ κόσμω θεός, τᾶς δὲ ψυχᾶς νόος, τᾶς δὲ περὶ τὸν βίον εὐδαιμοσύνας φρόνασις

A general leads his army, a captain his ship, god rules the world, the mind our heart, prudence a happy life.

Stobaeus, *Anthology* 3.1.112.27

90 πολλάκι τοι καὶ μωρὸς ἀνὴρ κατακαίριον εἶπε

Many a time has a fool spoken to the point.

Stobaeus, *Anthology* 3.4.24

later proverbial

91 Οὐ καταισχυνῶ ὅπλα τὰ ἱερά, οὐδ' ἐγκαταλείψω τὸν παραστάτην, ὅτῳ ἀνστοιχήσω, ἀμυνῶ δὲ καὶ ὑπὲρ ἱερῶν καὶ ὑπὲρ ὁσίων καὶ μόνος καὶ μετὰ πολλῶν· τὴν πατρίδα δὲ οὐκ ἐλάσσω παραδώσω, πλείω δὲ καὶ ἀρείω ὅσης ἂν παραδέξωμαι· καὶ εὐηκοήσω τῶν ἀεὶ κρινόντων ἐμφρόνως, καὶ τοῖς θεσμοῖς τοῖς ἱδρυμένοις πείσομαι καὶ οὕς τινας ἂν ἄλλους τὸ πλῆθος ἱδρύσηται ὁμοφρόνως· καὶ ἄν τις ἀναιρῇ τοὺς θεσμοὺς ἢ μὴ πείθηται, οὐκ ἐπιτρέψω, ἀμυνῶ δὲ καὶ μόνος καὶ μετὰ πάντων· καὶ ἱερὰ τὰ πάτρια τιμήσω. ἵστορες θεοὶ τούτων

I will not dishonour my sacred arms, nor abandon the comrade by my side, whoever he may be; I will defend our holy shrines, alone and with many; I will not hand down my fatherland smaller, but greater and better; I will obey the ruling magistrates, and the laws both existing and to be established; if anyone seeks to overturn the laws I will defend them alone and with all to help me; I will honour the religion of my fathers; the gods be my witnesses.

Stobaeus, *Anthology* 4.1.48

Oath of Athenian Ephebes

92 Πέρσαις νόμος ἦν, ὁπότε βασιλεὺς ἀποθάνοι, ἀνομίαν εἶναι πέντε ἡμερῶν, ἵν' αἴσθοιντο ὅσου ἄξιός ἐστιν ὁ βασιλεὺς καὶ ὁ νόμος

The Persians had a law whereby there was a five day period of anarchy after the death of a king, for the citizens to realize the value of kingship and law.

Stobaeus, *Anthology* 4.2.26

93 ἡ Λάκαινα πρός τινα Ἰωνικὴν δείξασαν αὐτῇ τὸν κόσμον ἀντεπέδειξε τὰ τέκνα εἰποῦσα ὁ δὲ ἐμὸς κόσμος τοιοῦτος

A Spartan woman, when shown the jewellery owned by an Ionian woman, pointed to her children and said, 'These are my ornaments.'

Stobaeus, *Anthology* 4.24a.11

94 οὐ μακαριεῖς τὸν γέροντα, καθ' ὅσον γηράσκων τελευτᾷ, ἀλλ' εἰ τοῖς ἀγαθοῖς συμπεπλήρωται· ἕνεκα γὰρ χρόνου πάντες ἐσμὲν ἄωροι

Do not deem happy someone who grows old and dies, unless he has filled his life with good deeds and happiness; our life is short and death is always untimely.

Stobaeus, *Anthology* 4.50b.77

Stobaeus attributes this to Metrodorus

95 οὐ λόγων δεῖται Ἑλλάς, ἀλλ' ἔργων

Greece stands in need of deeds, not words.

Suda, Lexicon Omicron 906

96 κούφη γῆ τοῦτον καλύπτοι

May the earth be light upon you.

Translated by H.T. Riley (1872)

Suda, Lexicon Kappa 2198

a common Greek epitaph, cf. Euripides 12

97 ἐχθρὸς μὲν ἀνήρ, ἀλλὰ τὴν δίκην σέβω

The man may be my enemy, but above all I respect justice.

Tragica Adespota, Fragment 5 (Nauck, *TGF*)

98 πυρὸς δ᾽ ἐξ ὀμμάτων
ἔλαμπεν αἴγλην

His eyes flamed,
glowing in splendour.

Tragica Adespota, Fragment 33 (Nauck, *TGF*)

99 κακοῦ γὰρ ἀνδρός ἐστι τοὺς καινοὺς φίλους
τιμᾶν, ἀτιμάζειν δὲ τοὺς παλαιτέρους

It is a wretched man who honours new friends
and brings dishonour on old ones.

Tragica Adespota, Fragment 37 (Nauck, *TGF*)

100 οἵ τοι πέρα στέρξαντες οἱ δὲ καὶ πέρα μισοῦσιν

They that too deeply loved too deeply hate.

Translated by H. Rackham (1932)

Tragica Adespota, Fragment 78 (Nauck, *TGF*)

101 οὐ κατθανεῖν γὰρ δεινόν, ἀλλ᾽ αἰσχρῶς θανεῖν

It is not death that is dreadful, but a shameful death.

Translated by W.A. Oldfather (1925)

Tragica Adespota, Fragment 88 (Nauck, *TGF*)

quoted by Epictetus, Discourses *2.1.13*

102 πόλλ᾽ ἀπιστία δέδρακεν ἀγαθὰ καὶ πίστις κακά

Suspicion has brought much good,
confidence much harm.

Translated by Panos Koronakis-Rohlf and Maria Batzini (2007)

Tragica Adespota, Fragment 113 (Nauck, *TGF*)

103 ἀρετὴ τῶν ἐν ἀνθρώποις μόνη
οὐκ ἐκ θυραίων τἀπίχειρα λαμβάνει,
αὐτὴ δ᾽ ἑαυτὴν ἆθλα τῶν πόνων ἔχει

Virtue, of all attributes to man,
needs no outside rewards;
the prizes for its labours are within.

Tragica Adespota, Fragment 116 (Nauck, *TGF*)

104 τοῦ λαμβάνειν γὰρ πάντες ἡσσῶνται βροτοί

All mortals yield to gain.

Tragica Adespota, Fragment 172 (Nauck, *TGF*)

105 ἄπολις, ἄοικος, πατρίδος ἐστερημένος,
πτωχός, πλανήτης βίον ἔχων τοὐφ᾽ ἡμέραν

Without a city, without a house, without a fatherland
A beggar, a wanderer with a single day's bread.

Translated by R. Bracht Branham (1994)

Tragica Adespota, Fragment 284 (Nauck, *TGF*)

according to Diogenes Laertius, Lives of Eminent Philosophers *38.3, this was used by Diogenes the Cynic to describe himself*

106 χρυσὸς γάρ ἐστιν ὃς βροτῶν ἔχει κράτη

It is gold that holds power over men.

Tragica Adespota, Fragment 294 (Nauck, *TGF*)

107 ἐγὼ δ᾽ ἐμαυτοῦ καὶ κλύειν ἐπίσταμαι
ἄρχειν θ᾽ ὁμοίως, τἀρετῇ σταθμώμενος τὰ πάντα

I know how to obey myself
and govern myself, measuring all against virtue.

Tragica Adespota, Fragment 327 (Nauck, *TGF*)

108 Ζεὺς γὰρ τὰ μὲν μέγιστα φροντίζει βροτῶν,
τὰ μικρὰ δ᾽ ἄλλοις δαίμοσιν παρεὶς ἐᾷ

Zeus attends to the greater issues of mankind,
The little worries he leaves to lesser gods.

Tragica Adespota, Fragment 353 (Nauck, *TGF*)

109 τόδ᾽ ἐστὶ τὸ ζηλωτὸν ἀνθρώποις, ὅτῳ
τόξον μερίμνης εἰς ὃ βούλεται πέσῃ

Most enviable is the man whose ambition attains his target.

Tragica Adespota, Fragment 354 (Nauck, *TGF*)

110 πρὸς θῆλυ νεύει μᾶλλον ἢ ἐπὶ τἄρσενα;
ὅπου προσῇ τὸ κάλλος, ἀμφιδέξιος

To women more than men is he inclined?
Where there is beauty, either suits him best.

Translated by Frank Cole Babbitt (1927)

Tragica Adespota, Fragment 355 (Nauck, *TGF*)

111 τῆς δειλίας γὰρ αἰσχρὰ γίγνεται τέκνα

Cowardice bears dishonourable children.

Tragica Adespota, Fragment 357 (Nauck, *TGF*)

112 κινοῦσα χορδὰς τὰς ἀκινήτους φρενῶν

Stirring heart-strings never stirred before.

Translated by Frank Cole Babbitt (1927)

Tragica Adespota, Fragment 361 (Nauck, *TGF*)

113 ὅταν δ' ὁ δαίμων ἀνδρὶ πορσύνῃ κακά,
τὸν νοῦν ἔβλαψε πρῶτον ᾧ βουλεύεται

Whom god would destroy he first makes mad.

Tragica Adespota, Fragment 455 (Nauck, *TGF*)

cf. the English proverb 'whom the gods would destroy they first make mad' and the Latin 'quos deus perdere vult, dementat prius'; the phrase used in Modern Greek 'μωραίνει Κύριος ὃν βούλεται ἀπωλέσαι' seems to be a translation of the Latin

114 ἐν τῷ λαλεῖν δεῖ μηδὲ μηκύνειν λόγον

Do not drag out your speeches!

Tragica Adespota, Fragment 457 (Nauck, *TGF*)

115 τολμῶ κατειπεῖν, μήποτ' οὐκ εἰσὶν θεοί·
κακοὶ γὰρ εὐτυχοῦντες ἐκπλήσσουσί με

I dare to state that there may be no gods;
wicked men prospering never fail to astound me.

Tragica Adespota, Fragment 465 (Nauck, *TGF*)

116 θνητοῖσιν ἀνθρώποισι καταφυγὴ θεοί, …
ὅθεν λαβόντες αἱ κακῶς πεπραγότες
σωτηρίαν ἀπῆλθον ἐκ δυσπραξίας

A solace to men are the gods, comforting the unfortunate in their misfortune.

Tragica Adespota, Fragment 481 (Nauck, *TGF*)

117 ὀξὺς θεῶν ὀφθαλμὸς εἰς τὰ πάντ' ἰδεῖν

The gods' sharp eyes see everything.

Tragica Adespota, Fragment 491 (Nauck, *TGF*)

118 δίκας δ' ἐξέλαμψε θεῖον φάος

Justice shines forth under god's bright light.

Tragica Adespota, Fragment 500 (Nauck, *TGF*)

119 ὁσίᾳ δ' Ἀνάγκη πολεμιωτάτη θεός

Divine necessity is the most rancorous goddess.

Tragica Adespota, Fragment 501 (Nauck, *TGF*)

120 οὐδεὶς ἀνάγκης μεῖζον ἰσχύει νόμος

There is no law stronger than Necessity.

Tragica Adespota, Fragment 502 (Nauck, *TGF*)

121 ἐμοῦ θανόντος γαῖα μιχθήτω πυρί

When I am dead, may earth be mingled with fire.

Translated by H.T. Riley (1872)

Tragica Adespota, Fragment 513 (Nauck, *TGF*)

this was spoken to Nero who added: 'immo ἐμοῦ ζῶντος' (and while I am living too, Suetonius, Life of Nero *38); cf. the French expression 'après moi le déluge'*

122 μελέτη χρονισθεῖσ' εἰς φύσιν καθίσταται

Practice becomes nature itself over time.

Tragica Adespota, Fragment 516 (Nauck, *TGF*)

123 ἃ δεῖ παρὼν φρόντιζε, μὴ παρὼν ἀπῇς

Do what you must when present, do not feign absence.

Tragica Adespota, Fragment 517 (Nauck, *TGF*)

124 ἀφροδίσιος γὰρ ὅρκος οὐκ ἐμποίνιμος

The oaths of lovers are not to be trusted.

Tragica Adespota, Fragment 525 (Nauck, *TGF*)

125 ἀδικώτατον πρᾶγμ' ἐστὶ τῶν πάντων φθόνος.

Of all things the most unjust is envy.

Tragica Adespota, Fragment 532 (Nauck, *TGF*)

126 χρὴ δ' ἢ λέγειν τι χρηστὸν ἢ λέγουσιν εὖ μὴ δυσμεναίνειν τῷ φθόνῳ νικώμενον

Speak well yourself and do not from envy hate him whom others praise.

Tragica Adespota, Fragment 535 (Nauck, *TGF*)

127 ἡ δὲ μεσότης ἐν πᾶσιν ἀσφαλεστέρα

The middle course is always the safest.

Translated by D.S. Baker (1998)

Tragica Adespota, Fragment 547 (Nauck, *TGF*)

128 ἐσθλοῦ γὰρ ἀνδρὸς γῆρας εὐπροσήγορον

Good-natured is a good man as he grows old.

Tragica Adespota, Fragment 552 (Nauck, *TGF*)

129 ἐλευθέρα γὰρ γλῶσσα τῶν ἐλευθέρων

Free is the tongue of the free.

Tragica Adespota, Fragment 554 (Nauck, *TGF*)

130 ὅρκων ἐρῶσιν οὐδὲν εὐχερέστερον

For those in love nothing is easier than the giving of oaths.

Tragica Adespota, Fragment 567 (Nauck, *TGF*)

131 οὐδεὶς ἑκὼν πονηρὸς οὐδ' ἄκων μάκαρ

No one is voluntarily wretched nor involuntarily blest.

Tragica Adespota, Fragment 75a (Kannicht and Snell, *TrGF*)

possibly a verse by Solon; cf. Aristotle 102

Inscriptions

In approximate chronological order.
See more under 'Inscriptions' in the Keyword Index

132 ΗΟΣ ΝΥΝ ΟΡΧΕΣΤΩΝ ΠΑΝΤΩΝ ΑΤΑΛΩΤΑΤΑ ΠΑΙΖΕΙ

ἧος νῦν ὀρχεστῶν πάντων ἀταλώτατα παίζει

To him who, of all the dancers, has the lightest step.

on a trefoil oinochoe (an Attic vase from Dipylon); considered the oldest known dedicatory inscription for a victory in a competition (late 8th century), now in the National Archaeological Museum in Athens, Inv. no.192; cf. IG I² *919*

133 ΝΕΣΤΟΡΟΣ: ... ΕΥΠΟΤΟΝ: ΠΟΤΕΡΙΟΝ
ΟΣ Δ' ΑΝ ΤΟΔΕ ΠΙΕΣΙ: ΠΟΤΕΡΙΟ: ΑΥΤΙΚΑ ΚΕΝΟΝ
ΙΜΕΡΟΣ ΑΙΡΕΣΕΙ: ΚΑΛΛΙΣΤΕΦΑΝΟ: ΑΦΡΟΔΙΤΕΣ

The wine from Nestor's cup tastes sweet,
but whoever drinks of it will at once be filled
with a burning desire for fair-wreathed Aphrodite.

Translated by Angeliki Kosmopoulou (2009)

the so-called 'Cup of Nestor', dated to about 730BC, was discovered at Ischia (Pithecusae) and is now in the Museum of Lacco Ameno (Villa Arbusto); cf. IGASMG III *2 and Guarducci p.428ff who believes that the inscription is a reference to Nestor's famous cup, cf. Homer,* Iliad *11.632–7*

134 ὡς λύχνον εἰμί, καὶ φαίνω θεοῖσιν κἀνθρώποισιν

As I am a lamp, I shine on gods and men.

on a clay lamp found in a tomb on the island of Berezan in the Black Sea, dated around the 6th century BC; it is now in the Hermitage Museum; cf. SEG *32:805a and Guarducci p.434*

135 Ἔδοξεν τῷ δήμῳ.
Ἔδοξεν τῇ βουλῇ καὶ τῷ δήμῳ.

It was resolved by the Assembly of the People.
It was resolved by the Senate and the Assembly of the People.

thus started all Athenian laws; cf. Stelae 6798, 13044 in the Athens Epigraphical Museum and IG II² *1 et al.; also Thucydides 4.118.11, Andocides,* De mysteriis *96.3; et al.*

136 ΤΟΝ ΠΑΤΕΡΑ ΤΟΝ ΤΕΚΝΟΝ ...

τὸν πατέρα τῶν τέκνων καὶ τῶν χρημάτων κρατερὸν ἤμην τᾶδ δαίσιος καὶ τὰν ματέρα τῶν σῶν αὐτῆς χρημάτων. ἇς κα δώωντι, μὲ ἐπανάνκον ἤμην δατήθθαι· αἰ δέ τις αταθείη, ἀποδάτταθθαι τῷ ἀταμένῳ, ᾇι ἔγρατται

A father has the right to divide his estate between his children, as does a mother between her children; no distribution of estate is necessary as long as they live; however, if any of the children is in great need his share of the estate may be given earlier, as inscribed.

from the 'Laws of Gortyna Column' in the Doric dialect, dated c.480–460BC; cf. Guarducci p.177ff and IC IV *72; an early indication that mothers had their own property, and that daughters were entitled to inheritance, albeit smaller than sons*

137 ΟΣ ΑΝ ΒΑΛΛΗΙ ΤΑ ΕΚΑΘΑΡΜΑΤΑ ΑΝΟΘΕΝ ΤΗΣ ΟΔΟ ΜΙΑΝ ΚΑΙ ΠΕΝΤΗΚΟΝΤΑ ΔΡΑΧΜΑΣ ΩΦΕΛΕΤΟ

ὃς ἂν βάλλῃ τὰ ἐκκαθάρματα ἄνωθεν τῆς ὁδοῦ μίαν καὶ πεντήκοντα δραχμὰς ὠφέλετο

Whosoever throws refuse into the street shall pay a fine of fifty-one drachmas.

a law of Paros dated to the early 5th century BC, written in the Ionic dialect; cf. Guarducci p.171 and IG XII *5.107*

138 ΤΩΝ ΑΘΗΝΗΘΕΝ ΑΘΛΩΝ

From the Athenian Games.

on a Panathenaic amphora, late 5th century BC, given as a prize to the victor; found in a tomb at Teuchira, Cyrene (mod. Cyrenaica), now in the British Museum; cf. Guarducci p.261, pl.V

139 υἱὸς Γῆς εἰμι καὶ Ὀρανοῦ ἀστερόεντος δίψαι δ' εἰμ' αὖος καὶ ἀπόλλυμαι, ἀλλὰ δότ' ὦκα ψυχρὸν ὕδωρ πιεῖν αὐτῆς Μνημοσύνης ἀπὸ λίμνης ... καὶ δὲ καὶ σὺ πιὼν ὁδὸν ἔρχεαι ἅν τε καὶ ἄλλοι μύσται καὶ βάκχοι ἱερὰν στείχωσι κλεινοὶ

I am the son of the Earth and the starry Heavens, I am dry from thirst and am dying, let me drink from the cool waters of the Lake of Remembrance. After drinking, you too will take the sacred road as other inspired famous men before you.

on a gold Orphic lamella found at Hipponium (now Monteleone, Italy) in the tomb of a woman; dated end of 5th century BC; cf. Guarducci p.379ff and pl.IX, SEG *52:951, Orphica, Fragment 17(D-K)*

140 συμμαχία Κορκυραίων καὶ Ἀθηναίων εἰς τὸν ἀεὶ χρόνον· ἐάν τις ἴῃ ἐπὶ πολέμῳ εἰς τὴγ χώραν τὴγ Κορκυραίων ... βοηθεῖν Ἀθηναίοις παντὶ σθένει ... εὐορκοῦντι μέμ μοι εἴη πολλὰ καὶ ἀγαθά, εἰ δὲ μή τἀναντία

A Treaty between the Corcyraeans and the Athenians, to last for ever; if anyone goes to war against Corcyra, the Athenians will help the Corcyraeans with all their power. If I honour this oath may all good fortune befall me, if not, the opposite.

beginning and end of a treaty between Corfu and Athens; inscribed on a marble column, now in the National Archaeological Museum in Athens, 375/4BC; cf. IG II[2] *97*

141 ἐάν τις ἐπαναστῇ τῷ δήμῳ ἐπὶ τυραννίδι ἢ τὴν τυραννίδα συγκαταστήσῃ ... ἢ τὴν δημοκρατίαν τὴν Ἀθήνησιν καταλύσῃ, ὃς ἂν τῶν τούτων τι ποιήσαντα ἀποκτείνῃ, ὅσιος ἔστω

If anyone rises up against the people intent on establishing a tyranny or cooperates with the insurgents or succeeds in abolishing the Athenian democracy, if anyone then kills him the assassin shall be sinless.

from the 'Law against Tyranny', a *stele found in the Athenian Agora, dated to 337/336BC; cf. Guarducci p.167ff and IG II[3] 1 320 (Agora 16 73); cf. Andocides 2*

142 ἐὰν δέ τις τοῦ δήμου ἢ τῆς δημοκρατίας καταλελυμένων τῶν Ἀθήνησιν ἀνίῃ τῶν βουλευτῶν ... εἰς Ἀρεῖον Πάγον ... ἢ βουλεύῃ περὶ τινος, ἄτιμος ἔστω καὶ αὐτὸς καὶ γένος τὸ ἐξ ἐκείνου καὶ ἡ οὐσία δημοσία ἔστω αὐτοῦ

While Athenian democracy and the rights of citizens remain abolished, if any member of the Council as much as walks up to the Areopagus or offers advice on any subject, he and his kin shall be deprived of civil rights and his property confiscated.

from the 'Law against Tyranny', a stele found in the Athenian Agora, dated to 337/336BC; cf. Guarducci p.167ff and IG II[3] 1 320 (Agora 16 73)

143 τοὺς δὲ θύοντας πρὸς θύησιν χρέεσθαι ἐλαίᾳ, μύρτῳ, κηρίῳ, ὀλοαῖς αἱρολογημέναις, ἀγάλματι, μάκωνσι λευκαῖς, λύχνιοις, θυμιάμασιν, ζμύρναι, ἀρώμασιν

Whosoever wishes to make an offering can do so using olive, myrtle, honeycomb, barley clear of darnel, statues, white poppies, lamps, incense, myrrh and aromatic plants.

from the 'Laws of the Temple of Despoina' at

Lycosura, Arcadia, dated second half of the 3rd century BC, inscribed on a column; cf. Guarducci p.298ff and IG V 2 514

144 ...ΙΕΡΟΥ ΛΙΘΟΥ ΤΟΙΣ ΤΕ ΙΕΡΟΙΣ ΚΑΙ ΕΓΧΩΡΙΟΙΣ ΚΑΙ ΕΛΛΗΝΙΚΟΙΣ ΓΡΑΜΜΑΣΙΝ ΚΑΙ ΣΤΗΣΑΙ ΕΝ ΕΚΑΣΤΩΙ ΤΩΝ ΤΕ ΠΡΩΤΩΝ ΚΑΙ ΔΕΥΤΕΡΩΝ ΤΑΞΕΩΝ ΙΕΡΩΙ ...

[The decree should be written on a stela of] hard stone, in sacred writing, document writing, and Greek writing, and it should be set up in the first-class temples, the second-class temples [and the third-class temples, next to the statue of the King, living forever].

Translated by R.S. Simpson (1996)

from the 'Rosetta Stone', Egypt, 196BC; the Rosetta Stone was the key to the decipherment of hieroglyphs by Jean-François Champollion; the translation of this fragment is completed from the other existing texts; British Museum Inv. no. EA 24

145 ἐπὶ στεφανηφόρου Κλευφῶντος ... Νείκη Μενεκράτου ἀνεκήρυξε τὴν ἰδίαν θρεπτὴν Ἡδονὴν ἐλευθέραν, ἐφ' ᾧ παραμενεῖ αὐτῇ τὸν τῆς ζωῆς αὐτῆς χρόνου

In the presence of the magistrate Cleuphon, Nike Menecratou proclaims the freedom of her slave, Hedone, on condition that she remains with her for all her living years.

from the Temple of Apollo, Calymnos, dated to the first half of the 1st century AD; cf. Guarducci p.419f and Tituli Calymnii *196*

146 ἰχθῦς ἱεροὺς μὴ ἀδικεῖν, μηδὲ σκεῦος τῶν τῆς θεοῦ λυμαίνεσθαι, μηδὲ ἐκφέρειν ἐκ τοῦ ἱεροῦ ἐπὶ κλοπήν ... ἐὰν δέ τις τῶν ἰχθύων ἀποθάνῃ, καρπούσθω αὐθημερὸν ἐπὶ τοῦ βωμοῦ

Do no harm to the sacred fish, nor inflict any ill-treatment to objects belonging to the goddess, nor remove any object from this holy place with a view to theft; if any of the sacred fish dies it must be placed on the same day at the altar as an offering.

a law on sacred fish; found in Smyrna, dated 1st century BC; the name of the goddess is uncertain; cf. Guarducci p.300f and I Smyrna *735*

147 ΧΟΙΡΟΣ Ο ΠΑΣΙ ΦΙΛΟΣ ΤΕΤΡΑΠΟΥΣ ΝΕΟΣ ΕΝΘΑΔΕ ΚΕΙΜΑΙ ΔΑΛΜΑΤΙΗΣ ... ΔΩΡΟΝ ΠΡΟΕΝΕΧΘΕΙΣ ... ΚΑΙ ΠΑΣΑΝ ΓΗΝ ΔΙΕΒΗΝ ΠΟΣΙΝ ... ΑΛΙΠΤΟΣ ΝΥΝ ΔΕ ΤΡΟΧΟΙΣ ΡΙΗΤΟ ΦΑΟΣ ΠΡΟΛΕΛΟΙΠΑ ... ΕΝΘΑΔΕ ΝΥΝ ΚΕΙΜΑΙ ΤΩ ΘΑΝΑΤΩ ΜΗΚΕΤ ΟΦΕΙΛΟΜΕΝΟΣ

Here I lie, a young four-legged pig, friend to all, a gift from Dalmatia, who traversed the whole world on foot and now lost my life under the wheels; here I lie, owing nothing to death any more.

an epitaph for a pig; of an early road accident on the Via Egnatia, probably 3rd century AD, on a stele now in the Edessa Archaeological Museum; cf. F. Petsas, AAA2 (1969).189 and G. Daux, BCH *94.609*

148 πίε, ζήσαις καλῶς ἀεί

Drink, live well forever.

on a glass vessel from Köln, dated 4th century AD; cf. Guarducci p.508 and pl.XII

149 ΠΥΘΑΓΟΡΑΣ ΜΑΝΙΑ ΠΑΙΔΩΝ

Pythagoras, children's wonder.

graffiti on a cave wall on the island of Pholegandros

150 μνημόνευέ μου τῆς φιλίας ὁπούποτε

Remember my friendship wherever you may be.

on a signet ring now in the British Museum; cf. Guarducci p.510 and Walters (1926) no.3694

151 ἀφεῖσθαι τοὺς παῖδας ἀπὸ τῶν μαθημάτων

Release our children from their lessons!

from an honorary decree, Miletos, dated to 3rd or 2nd century BC; cf. Milet I 3, *145*

152 1. Ἀβροχίτων δ' ὁ φύλαξ θηροζυγοκαμψιμέτωπος.

2. Ἀβρὸς δ' ἐν προχοαῖς Κύκλωψ φθογγάζετο μύρμηξ.

Two untranslatable nonsense verses which both contain all the letters of the alphabet. The closest translation for 2 is:

By the river, a fair-looking Cyclops called the ant an ant.

Greek Anthology 9.538 and 539

ANTIGONUS (1)

*c.*382–301BC

Macedonian general (the One-eyed)

1 Ἑρμοδότου δ' αὐτὸν ἐν τοῖς ποιήμασιν Ἡλίου παῖδα γράψαντος, οὐ ταῦτά μοι,

ἔφη, σύνοιδεν ὁ λασανοφόρος

When hailed by Hermodotus as 'Son of the Sun': 'My valet is not aware of this,' he said.

Plutarch, *Sayings of Kings and Commanders* 182c

cf. the English phrase 'no man is a hero to his valet'

2 ἢ δόλῳ, ἠὲ βίηφι· ἢ ἀμφαδὸν, ἠὲ κρυφηδόν

By cunning or by force, openly or in secret.

Zenobius, *Epitome* 1.93

how to defeat an enemy

ANTIGONUS (2)

*c.*320–239BC
King of Macedon, 277/276–239BC

1 οἷος γὰρ ἂν ὁ ἡγούμενος ᾖ, τοιούτους εἰκὸς ὡς ἐπὶ τὸ πολὺ γίγνεσθαι καὶ τοὺς ὑποτεταγμένους

As is the ruler, such for the most part may it be expected the subjects will become.

Translated by R.D. Hicks (1925)

Diogenes Laertius, *Lives of Eminent Philosophers* 7.7

from a letter to Zeno asking for instruction in philosophy

2 ἐμὲ δέ, ἔφη, αὐτὸν παρόντα πρὸς πόσας ἀντιτάττεις;

But how many ships do you reckon *my* presence is worth?

Plutarch, *Sayings of Kings and Commanders* 183d

on being informed that the enemy outnumbered him in ships

ANTIMACHUS

8th century BC
Epic poet from Teos

1 ἐκ γὰρ δώρων πολλὰ κάκ' ἀνθρώποισι πέλονται

From gifts much ill comes to mankind.

Translated by Martin L. West (2003)

Fragment 1 (Kinkel)

ANTIPATER OF SIDON

1st century BC
Author of approx. 75 epigrams in *Greek Anthology*

1 Κερκίδα τὴν φιλαοιδὸν Ἀθηναίῃ θέτο Βιττὼ
ἄνθεμα, λιμηρῆς ἄρμενον ἐργασίης,
εἶπε δέ· Χαῖρε, θεά, καὶ τήνδ' ἔχε· χήρη ἐγὼ γὰρ
τέσσαρας εἰς ἐτέων ἐρχομένη δεκάδας
ἀρνεῦμαι τὰ σὰ δῶρα, τὰ δ' ἔμπαλι Κύπριδος ἔργων
ἅπτομαι· ὥρης γὰρ κρεῖσσον ὁρῶ τὸ θέλειν.

Bitto dedicated her musical loom-comb to Athena,
implement of work that left her hungry,
and she said: 'Hail, goddess, take this. I'm a widow
forty years old. I return your gifts
and go to work for the goddess of love.
I see now that desire is mightier than age.'

Translated by Edmund Keeley (2010)

Greek Anthology 6.47

2 Τὰν μὲν ἀνεγρομέναν μέ ποτ' εἴρια νύκτερος ὄρνις,
ἀνία δ' αὐδάσει δώματος ἁνίοχον·
ἱππαστὴρ δ' ὅδε κημὸς ἀείσεται οὐ πολύμυθον,
οὐ λάλον, ἀλλὰ καλᾶς ἔμπλεον ἁσυχίας.

The bird of night vouches that I rise at night to work,
these reins tell that I hold the reins of my household;
and my horse's muzzle says that I am not fond of many words,
but full of admirable silence.

Greek Anthology 7.424

ANTIPATER OF THESSALONICA

1st century BC – 1st century AD
Author of approx. 80 epigrams in the Garland of Philippus

1 Πᾶσα θάλασσα θάλασσα. τί Κυκλάδας ἢ στενὸν Ἕλλης
κῦμα καὶ Ὀξείας ἠλεὰ μεμφόμεθα; ...
νόστιμον εὐπλοΐην ἀρῳτό τις· ὡς τά γε πόντου
πόντος, ὁ τυμβευθεὶς οἶδεν Ἀρισταγόρης.

Every sea is sea. Why blame the

Cyclades,
or the Hellespont and the Sharp Isles?
Let whoever prays for fair weather
know
what Aristagoras knows, buried here:
that the sea is the sea.

Greek Anthology 7.639

epitaph for a sailor; Oxia is an island off the western coast of mainland Greece

ANTIPATER

Uncertain if Antipater of Sidon or of Thessalonica

1 Λείψανον ἀμφίκλαστον ἁλιπλανέος
σκολοπένδρης
τοῦτο κατ' εὐψαμάθου κείμενον ἠϊόνος,
δισσάκι τετρόργυιον, ἅπαν
πεφορυγμένον ἀφρῷ,
πολλὰ θαλασσαίῃ ξανθὲν ὑπὸ σπιλάδι.

This mutilated body of a sea-wandering
scolopendra
eight fathoms long, all foul with foam
and torn by the rocks,
was found lying on this sandy beach.

Translated by W.R. Paton (1916)

Greek Anthology 6.223

a sea-scolopendra, perhaps of the genus Nereïs

ANTIPHANES

4th century BC
Middle Comedy poet

1 πενθεῖν δὲ μετρίως τοὺς προσήκοντας
φίλους·
οὐ γὰρ τεθνᾶσιν, ἀλλὰ τὴν αὐτὴν ὁδόν,
ἣν πᾶσιν ἐλθεῖν ἔστ' ἀναγκαίως ἔχον,
προεληλύθασιν. εἶτα χἠμεῖς ὕστερον
εἰς ταὐτὸ καταγωγεῖον αὐτοῖς ἥξομεν,
κοινῇ τὸν ἄλλον συνδιατρίψοντες χρόνον

Mourn moderately your own beloved
dead.
They are not dead: They have but gone
before,
Treading the road all travellers must go.
One day, we too shall join them at the
Inn,
There to pass all eternity together.

Translated by Kathleen Freeman (1947)

Fragment 53 (Kock) – 54 (K-A) – *Aphrodisios – The Amorous Man*

2 ὀλίγον ἐστὶ τὸ καλὸν πανταχοῦ καὶ τίμιον

Virtue is rare and always held in honour.

Fragment 58 (Kock) – 59 (K-A) – *Boeotis – The Boeotian Girl*

3 λύπη γὰρ ἀνθρώποισι καὶ τὸ ζῆν κακῶς
ὥσπερ πονηρὼ ζωγράφω τὰ χρώματα
πρώτιστον ἀφανίζουσιν ἐκ τοῦ σώματος

Like two bad painters, sorrow and hard living deprive the body of its colours.

Fragment 98 (Kock) – 98 (K-A) – *Euploia – Fair Voyage*

4 δύστηνος ὅστις ζῇ θαλάττιον βίον·
... στάδια ἑκατὸν
ἐλθεῖν που δὴ κρεῖττον ἢ πλεῦσαι
πλέθρον.
πλεῖς τὴν θάλατταν σχοινίων
πωλουμένων;

Miserable, he who lives the sailor's life;
one hundred stadia
by foot is better than navigating a
stadium by sea.
You weave through oceans when there
are ropes for sale?

Fragment 100 (Kock) – 100 (K-A) – *Ephesia – The Woman of Ephesus or The Ephesian Goddess*

5 ἐν γῇ πένεσθαι μᾶλλον ἢ πλουτοῦντα
πλεῖν

Better be a pauper on land than a Croesus at sea.

Fragment 101 (Kock) – 290 (K-A) – *Ephesia – The Woman of Ephesus or The Ephesian Goddess*

6 ἀνδρὸς διαφέρει τοῦτ' ἀνήρ· ὁ μὲν κακῶς
πράττων τὸ λυποῦν ἤγαγ' εἰς
παράστασιν,
ὁ δ' ἐμφρόνως δεξάμενος ἤνεγκεν καλῶς

Man differs from man in this: some bear their grief in silence, others make a public spectacle of it.

Fragment 104 (Kock) – 103 (K-A) – *Heniochos – The Chariot-driver*

7 ἀσταφίδος, ἁλῶν, σιραίου, σιλφίου,
τυροῦ, θύμου,
σησάμου, νίτρου, κυμίνου, ῥοῦ, μέλιτος,
ὀριγάνου,
βοτανίων, ὄξους, ἐλαῶν, εἰς ἀβυρτάκην
χλόης,
καππάριδος, ᾠῶν, ταρίχους, καρδάμων,
θρίων, ὀποῦ

Raisins, salt, boiled must, silphium, cheese, thyme, sesame-seed, soda, cumin, nuts, honey, marjoram, chopped acorns, vinegar, olives, young greens for sour dressing, capers, eggs, smoked fish, cress, fig-leaves, rennet.

Translated by Charles Burton Gulick (1927)

Fragment 142 (Kock) – 140 (K-A) – *Leucadios – Leucadian*

various seasonings

8 ἐπὶ χρήμασιν … φρονεῖ μέγα,
ὧν ἐστι πάντων ἐνίοτ' ἄνεμος κύριος

He boasts of his wealth which the wind is master of.

Fragment 151 (Kock) – 149 (K-A) – *Melitta*

9 ὁ πλοῦτός ἐστι παρακάλυμμα τῶν κακῶν,
ἡ πενία δὲ περιφανές τε καὶ ταπεινόν

Wealth is a cloak of evil,
while poverty makes one humble, yet proud.

Fragment 167 (Kock) – 165 (K-A) – *Neaniskoi – The Striplings*

10 οἷα δ' ἡ χώρα φέρει
διαφέροντα πάσης … τῆς οἰκουμένης,
τὸ μέλι, τοὺς ἄρτους, τὰ σῦκα …
βοσκήματ', ἔρια, μύρτα, θύμα, πυρούς, ὕδωρ,
ὥστε καὶ γνοίην ἂν εὐθὺς Ἀττικὸν πίνων ὕδωρ

Of natural products our land has no dearth.
Our figs, bread and honey excel the whole earth.
Our flocks with their wool, our thyme and our barley,
Our myrtle, and lastly, without any parley,
Our water: the moment you taste it, you're sure
It's the water of Attica, sparkling and pure!

Translated by Kathleen Freeman (1947)

Fragment 179 (Kock) – 177 (K-A) – *Homonimoi – The Namesakes*

11 οἱ νῦν δὲ κισσόπλεκτα καὶ κρηναῖα καὶ
ἀνθεσιπότατα μέλεα μελέοις ὀνόμασιν
ποιοῦσιν ἐμπλέκοντες ἀλλότρια μέλη

Poets nowadays compose ivy-twined, flower-flitting, wretched songs with wretched words, into which they weave other men's melodies.

Translated by David A. Campbell (1993)

Fragment 209 (Kock) – 207 (K-A) – *Tritagonistes – The Third Actor*

12 μεταλλάξαι διάφορα βρώματα
ἔσθ' ἡδύ, καὶ τῶν πολλάκις θρυλουμένων
διάμεστον ὄντα τὸ παραγεύσασθαί τινος
καινοῦ παρέσχε διπλασίαν τὴν ἡδονήν

Sweet is variety, and change of food;
when one is stuffed with common viands,
the taste of something new redoubles pleasure.

Fragment 246 (Kock) – 240 (K-A)

13 καλῶς πένεσθαι μᾶλλον ἢ πλουτεῖν κακῶς·
τὸ μὲν γὰρ ἔλεον, τὸ δ' ἐπιτίμησιν φέρει

Better poor than becoming rich unjustly;
the first brings compassion, the second censure.

Fragment 258 (Kock) – 258 (K-A)

14 ὁ δὲ πλοῦτος ἡμᾶς, καθάπερ ἰατρὸς κακός,
πάντας βλέποντας παραλαβὼν τυφλοὺς ποιεῖ

Wealth, like a bad physician, renders blind those who could see.

Fragment 259 (Kock) – 259 (K-A)

15 υἱῷ γὰρ ἀγαπητῷ τι πράττων πρὸς χάριν
ἔρανον ἐμαυτῷ τοῦτον οἴομαι φέρειν

Whatever I do for my children
is, I believe, to my own benefit.

Fragment 260 (Kock) – 260 (K-A)

16 μὴ χρώμασιν τὸ σῶμα λαμπρύνειν θέλε,
ἔργοις δὲ καθαροῖς καὶ τρόποις τὴν καρδίαν

Do not seek to adorn your body with bright colours,
but with good works and the ways of the heart.

Fragment 264 (Kock) – 262 (K-A)

17 τὸ μὴ συνειδέναι γὰρ αὑτοῦ τῷ βίῳ
ἀδίκημα μηδὲν ἡδονὴν πολλὴν ἔχει

It is a great satisfaction to know that one has never done anyone an injustice.

Translated by Panos Koronakis-Rohlf and Maria Batzini (2007)

Fragment 269 (Kock) – 267 (K-A)

18 δεῖ γὰρ φαγόντας δαψιλῶς βρέχειν

After dining, water your food well!

Fragment 286 (Kock) – 279 (K-A)

19 ὁ μηδὲν ἀδικῶν οὐδενὸς δεῖται νόμου

He who is never unjust has no need of any law.

Fragment 288 (Kock) – 281 (K-A)

20 τρόπος δίκαιος κτῆμα τιμιώτατον

A righteous character is the most precious possession.

Fragment 291 (Kock) – 284 (K-A)

21 ὡς ἔστι τὸ γαμεῖν ἔσχατον τοῦ δυστυχεῖν

Marriage is indeed the worst misfortune!

Fragment 292 (Kock) – 285 (K-A)

22 εἴ φησι τοὺς ἐρῶντας οὐχὶ νοῦν ἔχειν,
ἦ πού τίς ἐστι τοὺς τρόπους ἀβέλτερος.
εἰ γὰρ ἀφέλοι τις τοῦ βίου τὰς ἡδονάς,
καταλείπετ' οὐδὲν ἕτερον ἢ τεθνηκέναι

If someone says that lovers have no sense,
he is surely out of his mind;
for if you exclude the pleasures of life
there's nothing left but to die.

Fragment 324 (Kock) – 318 (K-A)

ANTIPHILUS

1st century AD
Epigrammatist from Byzantium

1 Χεῦμα μὲν Εὐρώταο Λακωνικόν, ἁ δ' ἀκάλυπτος
Λήδα· χὠ κύκνῳ κρυπτόμενος Κρονίδας.
οἳ δέ με τὸν δυσέρωτα καταίθετε. καὶ τί γένωμαι;
ὄρνεον. εἰ γὰρ Ζεὺς κύκνος, ἐγὼ κόρυδος.

This is the Laconian river Eurotas, and there is naked
Leda, and Zeus transformed into a swan.
But I who am burning with love, what bird shall I be?
If Zeus is a swan, shall I be a lark?

Greek Anthology 5.307

2 Λιτὸς ἐγὼ τὰ τύχης, ὦ δεσπότι, φημὶ δὲ πολλῶν
ὄλβον ὑπερκύπτειν τὸν σὸν ἀπὸ κραδίης.

I've not much of my own, lady, mistress, but I
believe that the man who's yours heart and soul stands
a full head above most men's riches.

Translated by W.S. Merwin (1973)

Greek Anthology 6.250

3 Κλῶνες ἀπηόριοι ταναῆς δρυός, εὔσκιον ὕψος
ἀνδράσιν ἄκρητον καῦμα φυλασσομένοις,
εὐπέταλοι, κεράμων στεγανώτεροι, οἰκία φαττῶν,
οἰκία τεττίγων.

Lofty-hung boughs of the tall oak, in whose shadow
men take shelter from the fierce heat,
of foliage fair, more waterproof than tiles,
house of pigeons, house of crickets.

Greek Anthology 9.71

4 οὐ θνάσκει ζᾶλος ἐλευθερίας

The passion for freedom never dies.

Greek Anthology 9.294

from an epigram for the Spartan king Leonidas

5 κενεὸς πομφολύγων θόρυβος

The empty noise of bubbling.

Translated by C.A. Trypanis (1971)

Greek Anthology 9.546

ANTIPHON ORATOR

c.480–411BC
Attic orator

1 οὐδὲν γὰρ πικρότερον τῆς ἀνάγκης

Nothing is as harsh as Necessity.

The First Tetralogy 2.4

2 ἄρχων γὰρ χειρῶν ἀδίκων ... καὶ ἐμοὶ αἴτιος τοῦ ἐγκλήματος γέγονεν

By striking the first blow unjustly he, to me, also became the perpetrator of this crime.

The Third Tetralogy 4.1

3 τὸ ἀδίκως ἀπολῦσαι ὁσιώτερον ἂν εἴη τοῦ μὴ δικαίως ἀπολέσαι· τὸ μὲν γὰρ ἁμάρτημα μόνον ἐστί, τὸ δὲ ἕτερον καὶ ἀσέβημα

It is better to set free unjustly than to unjustly kill; the first is but a fault, the second an affront to god himself.

On the Murder of Herodes 5.91

of the death penalty

ANTIPHON SOPHIST

5th century BC

Athenian sophist

Scholars are divided as to whether he is identical with the previous Antiphon

1 πᾶσι γὰρ ἀνθρώποις ἡ γνώμη τοῦ σώματος ἡγεῖται καὶ εἰς ὑγίειαν καὶ νόσον καὶ εἰς τὰ ἄλλα πάντα

In all human beings the mind leads the body towards health, disease and all else.

Fragment 2 (D-K)

2 νόημα ἢ μέτρον τὸν χρόνον, οὐχ ὑπόστασιν

Time is a thought or a measure, not a substance.

Translated by Kathleen Freeman (1948)

Fragment 9 (D-K)

3 οὐδενὸς δεῖται οὐδὲ προσδέχεται οὐδενός τι, ἀλλ' ἄπειρος καὶ ἀδέητος

God does not need anything nor does he receive anything from anyone, but he is boundless and lacks nothing.

Translated by Patricia Curd, with S. Marc Cohen, and C.D.C. Reeve (2005)

Fragment 10 (D-K)

4 τὰ μὲν γὰρ τῶν νόμων ἐπίθετα, τὰ δὲ τῆς φύσεως ἀναγκαῖα· καὶ τὰ μὲν τῶν νόμων ὁμολογηθέντα οὐ φύντ' ἐστίν, τὰ δὲ τῆς φύσεως φύντα οὐχ ὁμολογηθέντα

The edicts of the laws are imposed artificially, but those of nature are compulsory. And the edicts of the laws are arrived at by consent, not by natural growth, whereas those of nature are not a matter of consent.

Translated by Kathleen Freeman (1948)

Fragment 44A.1.23 (D-K)

5 τῶν δὲ τῇ φύσει ξυμφύτων ἐάν τι παρὰ τὸ δυνατὸν βιάζηται, ἐάν τε πάντας ἀνθρώπους λάθῃ, οὐδὲν ἔλαττον τὸ κακόν, ἐάν τε πάντες ἴδωσιν, οὐδὲν μεῖζον

If anyone violates any of the things which are innate by nature, the evil is no less if no one notices and no greater if all observe.

Translated by Richard D. McKirahan, Jr (1995)

Fragment 44A.2.10 (D-K)

6 τὸ δ' αὖ ζῆν ἐστι τῆς φύσεως καὶ τὸ ἀποθανεῖν

Life and death belong to Nature.

Fragment 44A.3.25 (D-K)

7 οὔτε βάρβαρος ἀφώρισται ἡμῶν οὐδεὶς οὔτε Ἕλλην· ἀναπνέομεν τε γὰρ εἰς τὸν ἀέρα ἅπαντες κατὰ τὸ στόμα καὶ κατὰ τὰς ῥῖνας

None of us is distinguishable as Barbarian or Greek; we all breathe air through our mouths and nostrils.

Fragment 44B.2.24 (D-K)

cf. Shakespeare, The Merchant of Venice *3.1.[63]: 'Hath not a Jew eyes?'*

8 μέγας ἀγὼν γάμος

Great is the struggle of marriage.

Fragment 49 (D-K)

9 τὸ ζῆν ἔοικε φρουρᾷ ἐφημέρῳ τό τε μῆκος τοῦ βίου ἡμέραι μιᾷ, ὡς ἔπος εἰπεῖν, ᾗ ἀναβλέψαντες πρὸς τὸ φῶς παρεγγυῶμεν τοῖς ἐπιγιγνομένοις ἑτέροις

Life is like a day-long watch, and the length of life is like one day, as it were, on which having seen the light we pass on our trust to the next generation.

Translated by Kathleen Freeman (1948)

Fragment 50 (D-K)

10 εὐκατηγόρητος πᾶς ὁ βίος θαυμαστῶς, ὦ μακάριε, οὐδὲν ἔχων περιττὸν οὐδὲ μέγα καὶ σεμνόν, ἀλλὰ πάντα σμικρὰ καὶ ἀσθενῆ καὶ ὀλιγοχρόνια καὶ ἀναμεμειγμένα λύπαις μεγάλαις

The whole of life is wonderfully open to complaint, my friend; it has nothing remarkable, great or noble, but all is petty, feeble, brief-lasting, and mingled with sorrows.

Translated by Kathleen Freeman (1948)

Fragment 51 (D-K)

11 εἰσί τινες οἳ τὸν παρόντα μὲν βίον οὐ ζῶσιν, ἀλλὰ παρασκευάζονται πολλῇ σπουδῇ ὡς ἕτερόν τινα βίον βιωσόμενοι, οὐ τὸν παρόντα· καὶ ἐν τούτῳ παραλειπόμενος ὁ

χρόνος οἴχεται

There are some who do not live this present life, but prepare themselves with great zeal as if they were to live another; meanwhile this life is neglected, and time flies.

Fragment 53a (D-K)

12 κακὸς δ' ἂν εἴη, εἰ ἐπ' ἀποῦσι μὲν καὶ μέλλουσι τοῖς κινδύνοις τῇ γλώττῃ θρασύνεται καὶ τῷ θέλειν ἐπείγει, τὸ δ' ἔργον ἂν παρῇ, ὀκνεῖ

Cowardly is he who is bold in speech concerning absent and future matters, and hurries on in resolve, but shrinks back when the fact is upon him.

Fragment 56 (D-K)

13 νόσος δειλοῖσιν ἑορτή· οὐ γὰρ ἐκπορεύονται ἐπὶ πρᾶξιν

Illness is a holiday for cowards, for they need not march into action.

Translated by Kathleen Freeman (1948)

Fragment 57 (D-K)

by now proverbial

14 ὅστις δὲ δράσειν μὲν οἴεται τοὺς πέλας κακῶς, πείσεσθαι δ' οὔ, οὐ σωφρονεῖ

Whoever thinks he will ill-treat his neighbours and not suffer himself is unwise.

Translated by Kathleen Freeman (1948)

Fragment 58 (D-K)

15 ὅστις δὲ τῶν αἰσχρῶν ἢ τῶν κακῶν μήτε ἐπεθύμησε μήτε ἥψατο, οὐκ ἔστι σώφρων· οὐ γὰρ ἔσθ' ὅτου κρατήσας αὐτὸς ἑαυτὸν κόσμιον παρέχεται

Whoever has neither desired nor touched the base or the bad is not really chaste; unless he has overcome temptation, he cannot claim to be above it.

Fragment 59 (D-K)

cf. Shakespeare, Hamlet *3.1.[148]: 'Be thou as chaste as ice ... thou shalt not escape calumny'*

16 πρῶτον, οἶμαι, τῶν ἐν ἀνθρώποις ἐστὶ παίδευσις

The first thing, I believe, for mankind is education.

Translated by Kathleen Freeman (1948)

Fragment 60 (D-K)

17 ἀναρχίας δ' οὐδὲν κάκιον ἀνθρώποις

Nothing is worse for mankind than anarchy.

Translated by Kathleen Freeman (1948)

Fragment 61 (D-K)

18 οἵῳ τις ἂν τὸ πλεῖστον τῆς ἡμέρας συνῇ, τοιοῦτον ἀνάγκη γενέσθαι καὶ αὐτὸν τοὺς τρόπους

One's behaviour will inevitably resemble those whom one spends most time with.

Fragment 62 (D-K)

19 καθηδυπαθεῖν τὸ πολυτελέστατον ἀνάλωμα, τὸν χρόνον

Squandering this most expensive luxury, time.

Fragment 77 (D-K)

cf. the English proverb 'time is money'

20 ἐρωτηθείς, τί ἐστι μαντική, εἶπεν· ἀνθρώπου φρονίμου εἰκασμός

When asked what a prophecy is he said 'a sensible man guessing'.

Testimonies, Fragment 9 (D-K)

ANTIPHON TRAGEDIAN

5th – 4th century BC

Tragic playwright

1 τέχνῃ κρατοῦμεν ὧν φύσει νικώμεθα

Our skills prevail where nature would defeat us.

Fragment 4 (Snell, *TrGF*)

ANTISTHENES

mid 5th – mid 4th century BC

Athenian philosopher, associate of Socrates

1 ἀρχὴ παιδεύσεως ἡ τῶν ὀνομάτων ἐπίσκεψις

The beginning of education is the examination of terms.

Translated by W.A. Oldfather (1925)

Fragment 38 (Caizzi)

cf. Bible 344

2 θεὸν οὐδενὶ ἐοικέναι ... διόπερ αὐτὸν οὐδεὶς ἐκμαθεῖν ἐξ εἰκόνος δύναται

God is like no one; wherefore no one can come to the knowledge of him from an image.

Translated by Philip Schaff (1819–1893)

Fragment 40b (Caizzi)

3 αἰσχρὸν τὸ γ' αἰσχρόν, κἂν δοκῇ κἂν μὴ δοκῇ

A disgrace is a disgrace, whether one thinks so or not.

Fragment 60 (Caizzi)

4 δεῖ τοὺς μέλλοντας ἀγαθοὺς ἄνδρας γενήσεσθαι τὸ μὲν σῶμα γυμνασίοις ἀσκεῖν, τὴν δὲ ψυχὴν λόγοις

Those wishing to become capable men should train their bodies in exercise, their soul in reason.

Fragment 64 (Caizzi)

5 οὐκ ἀντιλέγοντα δεῖ τὸν ἀντιλέγοντα παύειν, ἀλλὰ διδάσκειν· οὐδὲ γὰρ τὸν μαινόμενον ἀντιμαινόμενός τις ἰᾶται

You cannot silence the contradicting by contradicting, but only by persuasion; a madman will not be cured by a counter-madman.

Fragment 65 (Caizzi)

6 ἀναφαίρετον ὅπλον ἡ ἀρετή

Virtue is a weapon that cannot be taken away.

Translated by R.D. Hicks (1925)

Fragment 71 (Caizzi)

7 προσέχειν τοῖς ἐχθροῖς· πρῶτοι γὰρ τῶν ἁμαρτημάτων αἰσθάνονται

Pay attention to your enemies; they are the first to discover your faults.

Fragment 76 (Caizzi)

8 ὥσπερ ὑπὸ τοῦ ἰοῦ τὸν σίδηρον, οὕτως τοὺς φθονεροὺς ὑπὸ τοῦ ἰδίου ἤθους κατεσθίεσθαι

As iron is eaten away by rust, so the envious are consumed by their own passion.

Translated by R.D. Hicks (1925)

Fragment 82 (Caizzi)

9 κρεῖττον … εἰς κόρακας ἢ εἰς κόλακας ἐμπεσεῖν

Better to fall in with crows than flatterers.

Translated by R.D. Hicks (1925)

Fragment 84a (Caizzi)

10 Ἀντισθένης ἔλεγεν, ὥσπερ τὰς ἑταίρας τἀγαθὰ πάντα εὔχεσθαι τοῖς ἐρασταῖς παρεῖναι, πλὴν νοῦ καὶ φρονήσεως, οὕτω καὶ τοὺς κόλακας οἷς σύνεισιν

As courtesans wish their partners to have all gifts except intellect and prudence, so do flatterers want their prey.

Fragment 89 (Caizzi)

11 ὁμονοούντων ἀδελφῶν συμβίωσιν παντὸς ἔφη τείχους ἰσχυροτέραν εἶναι

Brothers of the same mind are stronger than a fortress.

Fragment 92 (Caizzi)

12 τότ' ἔφη τὰς πόλεις ἀπόλλυσθαι, ὅταν μὴ δύνωνται τοὺς φαύλους ἀπὸ τῶν σπουδαίων διακρίνειν

States are doomed when they are unable to distinguish good men from bad.

Translated by R.D. Hicks (1925)

Fragment 103 (Caizzi)

13 καὶ ἐπισφαλὲς καὶ ὅμοιον μαινομένῳ δοῦναι μάχαιραν καὶ μοχθηρῷ δύναμιν

It is equally dangerous to give a knife to a madman as it is to give power to a scoundrel.

Fragment 105 (Caizzi)

also attributed to Iamblichus, cf. Stobaeus 3.2.39

14 καὶ μὴν καὶ τὸ ἁβρότατόν γε κτῆμα, τὴν σχολὴν ἀεὶ ὁρᾶτέ μοι παροῦσαν, ὥστε καὶ θεᾶσθαι τὰ ἀξιοθέατα καὶ ἀκούειν τὰ ἀξιάκουστα

Most exquisite possession of all! – you observe that I always have leisure, with the result that I can go and see whatever is worth seeing, and hear whatever is worth hearing.

Translated by O.J. Todd (1923)

Fragment 117.59 (Caizzi)

15 ὅστις δὲ ἑτέρους δέδοικε, δοῦλος ὢν λέληθεν ἑαυτόν

Those who fear others are slaves unawares.

Fragment 119 (Caizzi)

16 ἐρωτηθεὶς τί μακαριώτερον ἐν ἀνθρώποις, ἔφη, τὸ εὐτυχοῦντα ἀποθανεῖν

When asked what was the height of human bliss, he replied, 'To die happy.'

Translated by R.D. Hicks (1925)

Diogenes Laertius, *Lives of Eminent Philosophers* 6.5

17 ἐρωτηθεὶς τί αὐτῷ περιγέγονεν ἐκ φιλοσοφίας, ἔφη, τὸ δύνασθαι ἑαυτῷ ὁμιλεῖν

When asked what advantage he gained from philosophy, he answered, 'The ability to hold converse with myself.'

Diogenes Laertius, *Lives of Eminent Philosophers* 6.6

18 τὸν δίκαιον περὶ πλείονος ποιεῖσθαι τοῦ συγγενοῦς

Esteem an honest man above a kinsman.

Translated by R.D. Hicks (1925)

Diogenes Laertius, *Lives of Eminent Philosophers* 6.12

19 τείχη κατασκευαστέον ἐν τοῖς αὑτῶν ἀναλώτοις λογισμοῖς

Your reasoning must build up impregnable walls of defence.

Diogenes Laertius, *Lives of Eminent Philosophers* 6.13

20 ὅτε καὶ Διογένης εἰσιὼν πρὸς αὐτὸν ἔφη, μήτι χρεία φίλου; καί ποτε παρ' αὐτὸν ξιφίδιον ἔχων εἰσῄει. τοῦ δ' εἰπόντος, τίς ἂν ἀπολύσειέ με τῶν πόνων; δείξας τὸ ξιφίδιον, ἔφη τοῦτο· καὶ ὅς, τῶν πόνων, εἶπον, οὐ τοῦ ζῆν

When the ailing Antisthenes cried out, 'Who will release me from these pains?' Diogenes replied, 'This,' showing him a dagger. Antisthenes responded: 'I said from my pains, not from life.'

Translated by R. Bracht Branham and Marie-Odile Goulet-Cazé (1996)

Diogenes Laertius, *Lives of Eminent Philosophers* 6.18

cf. Nietzsche, Philologica *2.196: 'Eine ganz tiefsinnige Äusserung ... "der kürzeste Weg zum Glück" ist so viel als "Lust am Leben an sich"' (a profound pronouncement ... 'the shortest way to bliss' is as much as 'the joy of life itself')*

21 ἐρωτηθεὶς ὑπό τινος, τί διδάξει τὸν υἱόν, εἶπεν, εἰ μὲν θεοῖς μέλλει συμβιοῦν, φιλόσοφον, εἰ δὲ ἀνθρώποις, ῥήτορα

When someone asked what he ought to teach his son, Antisthenes replied, 'If he is to live with gods, philosophy; if he is to live with men, rhetoric.'

Translated by Marie-Odile Goulet-Cazé (1996), translated into English by Helena Caine-Suarez

Stobaeus, *Anthology* 2.31.76

22 Ἀντισθένης ἐρωτηθείς. πῶς ἄν τις προσέλθοι πολιτείᾳ, εἶπε, καθάπερ πυρί, μήτε λίαν ἐγγύς, ἵνα μὴ καῇς, μήτε πόρρω, ἵνα μὴ ῥιγώσῃς

When asked how one should approach public matters Antisthenes answered: 'As with fire; not too close so as not to be burnt, and not too far so as not to freeze.'

Stobaeus, *Anthology* 4.4.28

ANYTE

active early 3rd century BC
Poet from Tegea

1 Ἕσταθι τεῖδε, κράνεια βροτοκτόνε, μηδ' ἔτι λυγρὸν
χάλκεον ἀμφ' ὄνυχα στάζε φόνον δαΐων·
ἀλλ' ἀνὰ μαρμάρεον δόμον ἡμένα αἰπὺν Ἀθάνας,
ἄγγελλ' ἀνορέαν Κρητὸς Ἐχεκρατίδα.

Rest now, my slayer, relieved at last of battle blood
which falls drop by drop, dark tears, from your bronze claw.
Raise your banner in Athena's towering marble halls;
trumpet the triumphs of Echecratidas from Crete.

Translated by Josephine Balmer (1996)

Greek Anthology 6.123

κράνεια (my slayer) refers to a spear made of the wood of the cornelian cherry tree, Cornus mas, *made to stand on Echecratidas' grave*

2 Ἡνία δή τοι παῖδες ἐνί, τράγε, φοινικόεντα
θέντες καὶ λασίῳ φιμὰ περὶ στόματι,
ἵππια παιδεύουσι θεοῦ περὶ ναὸν ἄεθλα,
ὄφρ' αὐτοὺς ἐφορῇ νήπια τερπομένους.

The children put purple reins on you, billy-goat, and a muzzle on your bearded face, and train you to run like a racehorse round the temple of the god that he may see them happy in their childish games.

Translated by C.A. Trypanis (1971)

Greek Anthology 6.312

3 Ἀκρίδι τᾷ κατ' ἄρουραν ἀηδόνι, καὶ δρυοκοίτᾳ
τέττιγι ξυνὸν τύμβον ἔτευξε Μυρώ,
παρθένιον στάξασα κόρα δάκρυ· δισσὰ γὰρ αὐτᾶς
παίγνι' ὁ δυσπειθὴς ᾤχετ' ἔχων Ἀίδας.

For her cricket, the nightingale of the fields, and for her cicada that lived in the trees, Myro made one grave, shedding the tears of a young girl; for inexorable Hades had borne away both her pets.

Translated by C.A. Trypanis (1971)

Greek Anthology 7.190

4 Μνᾶμα τόδε φθιμένου μενεδαΐου εἴσατο Δᾶμις
ἵππου, ἐπεὶ στέρνον τοῦδε δαφοινὸς Ἄρης
τύψε· μέλαν δέ οἱ αἷμα ταλαυρίνου διὰ χρωτὸς
ζέσσ', ἐπὶ δ' ἀργαλέᾳ βῶλον ἔδευσε φονᾷ.

This tomb Damis built for his brave war-horse,
when bloody Ares pierced it through the breast.
The black blood bubbled through its thick tough hide,
and drenched the earth at its painful death.

Translated by C.A. Trypanis (1971)

Greek Anthology 7.208

APELLES

fl. 325BC
Painter from Colophon

1 μηδὲν ὑπὲρ τὰ καλάποδα

Cobbler, stick to your last.

Appendix proverbiorum 3.90

attributed to Apelles, but also to Myrrichus; proverbial, from Pliny the Elder, Natural History *35.36.85: 'ne supra crepidam sutor iudicaret' (the cobbler should not judge beyond the sandal); cf. the similar English proverb*

2 τήμερον οὐδεμίαν γραμμὴν ἤγαγον

Today I have not drawn a single line!

Arsenius, *Apophthegms* 16.44c (von Leutsch, *CPG*)

cf. the Latin 'nulla dies sine linea' (not a day without a line), mentioned as proverbial

APOLLODORUS

active 407–404BC
Athenian painter

1 οὔ τοῖς ἔργοις ἐπιγέγραπται μωμήσεταί τις μᾶλλον ἢ μιμήσεται

Upon his works he inscribed: Criticize if you wish, but then try to imitate!

Plutarch, *Were the Athenians More Famous in War or in Wisdom?* 346a

a word play on 'momesetai' and 'mimesetai'

APOLLODORUS OF CARYSTUS

4th/3rd century BC
New Comedy poet

1 ἀλλ' οὐδὲ εἷς
τέκτων ὀχυρὰν οὕτως ἐποίησεν θύραν,
δι' ἧς γαλῆ καὶ μοιχὸς οὐκ εἰσέρχεται

For there was never yet a carpenter
who made doors strong enough
to keep out cats – or an adulterer.

Fragment 6 (Kock) – 6 (K-A) – *Diavolos – The Slanderer*

2 ἕκαστός ἐστι παρὰ τὰ πράγματα ἢ σεμνὸς ἢ ταπεινός

Man is arrogant or humble, according to his fortune.

Fragment 11 (Kock) – 11 (K-A) – *Hekyra – The Mother-in-law*

3 ἐγὼ γάρ εἰμι τῶν ἐμῶν ἐμὸς μόνος φίλος

I am the only one of my friends that I can rely on.

Fragment 8 (Meineke) – 25 (K-A) – *Epidikazomenos – The Claimant*

APOLLODORUS OF GELA

4th/3rd century BC
New Comedy poet

1 ἀλλὰ σχεδόν τι τὸ κεφάλαιον τῶν κακῶν εἴρηκας· ἐν φιλαργυρίᾳ γὰρ πάντ' ἔνι

You have mentioned nearly all the vices; for avarice contains them all.

Fragment 4 (Kock) – 3 (K-A) – *Philadelphoi – The Brothers in Love*

APOLLODORUS OF CARYSTUS OR GELA

4th/3rd century BC
New Comedy poet

1 ἐν πιθήκοις ὄντα δεῖ εἶναι πίθηκον

In apes' company – act the ape.

Fragment 1 (Kock) – 1 (K-A) – *Adelphoi – Brothers*

2 τοῖς γὰρ μεριμνῶσίν τε καὶ λυπουμένοις
ἅπασα νὺξ ἔοικε φαίνεσθαι μακρά

For those with many sorrows and concerns
each night seems endless.

Fragment 3 (Kock) – 3 (K-A) – *Galatians*

3 οὐδέποτ' ἀθυμεῖν τὸν κακῶς πράττοντα δεῖ,
ἄνδρες, τὰ βελτίω δὲ προσδοκᾶν ἀεί

Never lose courage in adversity,
there's always hope for something better.

Fragment 9 (Kock) – 9 (K-A) – *Paidion – The Little Child*

4 οὐ δεῖ λέγειν γὰρ μακάριον τὸν χρήματα
ἔχοντα πλεῖστα, τὸν δὲ μὴ λυπούμενον

Call blessed not the wealthiest
but him who has no sorrows.

Fragment 11 (Kock) – 11 (K-A) – *Paralogizomenoi – The Beguiling Men*

APOLLONIDES

3rd/2nd century BC
Tragic playwright

1 γυναικὸς ἀρετὰς ἀξίως ἐπαινέσαι
σοφοῦ τινος γένοιτ' ἂν ἵστορος λόγων

Only one highly skilled in words can do justice to a woman's virtues.

Fragment 2 (Snell, TrGF)

APOLLONIUS OF RHODES

3rd century BC
Epic poet

1 τίπτ' ἐπιμειδιάᾳς, ἄφατον κακόν;

Why do you smile in triumph, you unspeakable rascal?

Translated by C.A. Trypanis (1971)
Argonautica 3.129

Aphrodite to her son, Eros, on cheating at dice

2 πάντη καὶ ὅτις μάλα κύντατος ἀνδρῶν
Ξεινίου αἰδεῖται Ζηνὸς θέμιν ἠδ' ἀλεγίζει

All men everywhere, even the most shameless
honour Zeus, god of hospitality, and obey his law.

Argonautica 3.192

3 νὺξ μὲν ἔπειτ' ἐπὶ γαῖαν ἄγεν κνέφας, οἱ δ' ἐνὶ πόντῳ
ναυτίλοι εἰς Ἑλίκην τε καὶ ἀστέρας Ὠρίωνος
ἔδρακον ἐκ νηῶν, ὕπνοιο δὲ καί τις ὁδίτης

The dark of night fell over the earth;
now the sailors at sea look to the Bear and Orion,
and the traveller and the watchman long for sleep.

Argonautica 3.744
cf. Aeschylus 1

4 πυκνὰ δέ οἱ κραδίη στηθέων ἔντοσθεν ἔθυιεν,
ἠελίου ὥς τίς τε δόμοις ἔνι πάλλεται αἴγλη,
ὕδατος ἐξανιοῦσα

In her breast her heart beat fast, as a
sunbeam quivers on the walls of a house
when it is reflected from water.

Translated by C.A. Trypanis (1971)
Argonautica 3.755

5 ποῖον δ' ἐπὶ μῦθον ἐνίψω;
τίς δὲ δόλος, τίς μῆτις ἐπίκλοπος ἔσσετ' ἀρωγῆς;

What story can I tell them?
What trick, what wily skill is there to succour me?

Argonautica 3.780

6 ἐρρέτω αἰδώς,
ἐρρέτω ἀγλαΐη

Away with modesty, away with my good name!

Translated by C.A. Trypanis (1971)
Argonautica 3.785

7 φωριαμὸν μετεκίαθεν ᾗ ἔνι πολλά
φάρμακά οἱ τὰ μὲν ἐσθλὰ τὰ δὲ ῥαιστήρι' ἔκειτο

She fetched a box in which were many

drugs, some good, others for killing.

Translated by C.A. Trypanis (1971)

Argonautica 3.802

of Medea

8 δεῦε δὲ κόλπους
ἄλληκτον δακρύοισι …
αἰν' ὀλοφυρομένης τὸν ἑὸν μόρον

And she wet her bosom
with endless tears as she wept bitterly for her own fate.

Translated by C.A. Trypanis (1971)

Argonautica 3.804

of Medea

9 ἀμφὶ δὲ πᾶσαι
θυμηδεῖς βιότοιο μεληδόνες ἰνδάλλοντο·
μνήσατο μὲν τερπνῶν ὅσ' ἐνὶ ζωοῖσι πέλονται …
καί τέ οἱ ἠέλιος γλυκίων γένετ' εἰσοράασθαι
ἢ πάρος, εἰ ἐτεόν γε νόῳ ἐπεμαίεθ' ἕκαστα

All the pleasant things
for which she cared in life flashed before her.
She thought of the delights that there are for the living;
and the sun grew sweeter than ever to see,
as her heart truly longed for all these things.

Translated by C.A. Trypanis (1971)

Argonautica 3.811

Medea in fear of Hades, finally deciding not to take poison

10 μνήσαθ' ὁμηλικίης περιγηθέος, οἷά τε κούρη

She thought of her happy friends as a young girl does.

Translated by C.A. Trypanis (1971)

Argonautica 3.814

of Medea in her plight

11 πυκνὰ δ' ἀνὰ κληῖδας ἑῶν λύεσκε θυράων,
αἴγλην σκεπτομένη· τῇ δ' ἀσπάσιον βάλε φέγγος
ἠριγενής, κίνυντο δ' ἀνὰ πτολίεθρον ἕκαστοι

She watched for the first glimmer of day;
and rejoiced when Dawn shed her light,
and people in the town began to stir.

Translated by C.A. Trypanis (1971)

Argonautica 3.822

of Medea

12 ὣς φάτο, κυδαίνων· ἡ δ' ἐγκλιδὸν ὄσσε βαλοῦσα
νεκτάρεον μείδησε, χύθη δέ οἱ ἔνδοθι θυμὸς
αἴνῳ ἀειρομένης

So he spoke, paying court to her; and she cast her eyes down with a nectar-sweet smile; and her heart melted within her.

Translated by C.A. Trypanis (1971)

Argonautica 3.1008

of Jason and Medea

13 ἰαίνετο δὲ φρένας εἴσω
τηκομένη, οἷόν τε περὶ ῥοδέῃσιν ἐέρση
τήκεται ἠῴοισιν ἰαινομένη φαέεσσιν

And her heart grew warm within, melting away as the dew melts round roses when warmed by the morning light.

Translated by C.A. Trypanis (1971)

Argonautica 3.1019

14 ὁτὲ δ' αὖτις ἐπὶ σφίσι βάλλον ὀπωπάς
ἱμερόεν φαιδρῇσιν ὑπ' ὀφρύσι μειδιόωντες

And then again they were casting glances at each other, smiling with the light of love under their radiant brows.

Translated by C.A. Trypanis (1971)

Argonautica 3.1023

15 Ἑλλάδι που τάδε καλά, συνημοσύνας ἀλεγύνειν

One of the proprieties in Greece, no doubt, is that ties of friendship are heeded everywhere.

Argonautica 3.1105

16 σχέτλι' Ἔρως, μέγα πῆμα, μέγα στύγος ἀνθρώποισιν,
ἐκ σέθεν οὐλόμεναί τ' ἔριδες στοναχαί τε γόοι τε,
ἄλγεά τ' ἄλλ' ἐπὶ τοῖσιν ἀπείρονα τετρήχασιν

Damned Eros, great evil, and much ill to men,
from you discord, and sighing, weeping
and sorrow, and many more torments come.

Argonautica 4.445

17 ἔνθα σφιν κοῦραι Νηρηΐδες ἄλλοθεν ἄλλαι
ἤντεον, ἡ δ᾽ ὄπιθε πτέρυγος θίγε πηδαλίοιο
δῖα Θέτις, Πλαγκτῇσιν ἐνὶ σπιλάδεσσιν ἔρυσθαι

The Nereids met them here, swimming in from all sides; and Lady Thetis, coming up astern, laid her hand on the rudder-blade to guide them through the Wandering Rocks.

Translated by C.A. Trypanis (1971)

Argonautica 4.930

the Wandering or Clashing Rocks of Greek legend, apparently off the northern end of the Bosporus (cf. Herodotus 4.85)

18 ὡς δ᾽ ὁπόταν δελφῖνες ὑπὲξ ἁλὸς εὐδιόωντες
σπερχομένην ἀγεληδὸν ἑλίσσωνται περὶ νῆα
ἄλλοτε μὲν προπάροιθεν ὁρώμενοι ἄλλοτ᾽ ὄπισθεν
ἄλλοτε παρβολάδην, ναύτῃσι δὲ χάρμα τέτυκται
ὣς αἱ ὑπεκπροθέουσαι ἐπήτριμοι εἱλίσσοντο

As when in fair weather schools of dolphins come up from the depths of the sea and circle round a fast-sailing ship – seen now ahead, now astern, now abeam her, to the delight of the sailors, so the Nereids darted up on all sides.

Translated by C.A. Trypanis (1971)

Argonautica 4.933

19 αἱ δ᾽, ὥστ᾽ ἠμαθόεντος ἐπισχεδὸν αἰγιαλοῖο
παρθενικαί, δίχα κόλπον ἐπ᾽ ἰξύας εἱλίξασαι,
σφαίρῃ ἀθύρουσιν περιηγέι· αἱ μὲν ἔπειτα
ἄλλη ὑπ᾽ ἐξ ἄλλης δέχεται καὶ ἐς ἠέρα πέμπει
ὕψι μεταχρονίην, ἡ δ᾽ οὔ ποτε πίλναται οὔδει
ὣς αἱ νῆα θέουσαν ἀμοιβαδὶς ἄλλοθεν ἄλλη
πέμπε διηερίην ἐπὶ κύμασιν, αἰὲν ἄπωθεν πετράων

Just as young girls by a sandy beach roll up their skirts to the waist on either side, and play with a ball; catching it, one from the other, throwing it high into the air, so it never touches the ground – thus the Nereids in turn, one after the other, sent the ship into the air and over the waves, always keeping her away from the rocks.

Translated by C.A. Trypanis (1971)

Argonautica 4.948

APOLLONIUS OF TYANA

1st century AD
Neopythagorean holy man

1 οἱ κράτιστοι τῶν ἀνθρώπων βραχυλογώτατοι

The most excellent are those who use the fewest words.

*Letters** 80

2 ψεύδεσθαι ἀνελεύθερον, ἀλήθεια γενναῖον

Lies are for the servile, truth for the noble.

*Letters** 83

3 οἱ πολλοὶ τῶν ἀνθρώπων τῶν μὲν ἰδίων ἁμαρτημάτων συνήγοροι γίνονται, τῶν δὲ ἀλλοτρίων κατήγοροι

Most people become advocates of their own mistakes, but critics of others'.

*Letters** 88

4 τὸ μὴ γενέσθαι οὐδέν, τὸ δὲ γενέσθαι πόνος

Indolence produces nothing; creativity only comes with toil.

*Letters** 90

5 καλόν, πρὶν παθεῖν, διδαχθῆναι, πηλίκον ἐστὶν ἡσυχία

Better to learn, before it is too late, what a boon tranquillity can be.

*Letters** 92

6 οὐ θρηνητέον οἵων φίλων ἐστερήθημεν, ἀλλὰ μνημονευτέον, ὅτι μετὰ τῶν φίλων τὴν καλλίστην βιοτὴν ἐβιοτεύσαμεν

Do not lament over friends lost, but remember that with those friends we had the best of times.

*Letters** 93

7 τὸ λυπούμενον ἀλλοτρίοις κακοῖς παραμυθοῦ

In the calamities of others we find comfort for our own.

*Letters** 94

8 ὁ ὑπὲρ μικρῶν ἁμαρτημάτων ἀνυπερβλήτως ὀργιζόμενος οὐκ ἐᾷ διαγνῶναι τὸν ἁμαρτάνοντα, πότε ἔλαττον καὶ πότε μεῖζον ἠδίκησεν

If inordinately angered over trifles you will not be able to distinguish between small and great wrongdoings.

Letters 96*

ARATUS

*c.*315 – before 240BC

Poet born at Soloi in Cilicia and studied at Athens

1 Ἐκ Διὸς ἀρχώμεσθα, τὸν οὐδέποτ' ἄνδρες ἐῶμεν
ἄρρητον· μεσταὶ δὲ Διὸς πᾶσαι μὲν ἀγυιαί,
πᾶσαι δ' ἀνθρώπων ἀγοραί, μεστὴ δὲ θάλασσα
καὶ λιμένες· πάντη δὲ Διὸς κεχρήμεθα πάντες.
Τοῦ γὰρ καὶ γένος εἰμέν

From Zeus let us begin, whom we mortals never leave unnamed: full of Zeus are all the streets and all the gathering places of men, the seas and harbours. Everywhere we have need of Zeus. For we are also his offspring.

Phaenomena 1

the poem Phaenomena *became the most widely read poem, after the* Iliad *and* Odyssey, *in the ancient world; one of the few Greek poems translated into Arabic; the last part was quoted by St Paul in his address to the Athenians (see Bible 194); but see also Aratus 14*

2 ἄξων αἰὲν ἄρηρεν, ἔχει δ' ἀτάλαντον ἁπάντη
μεσσηγὺς γαῖαν, περὶ δ' οὐρανὸν αὐτὸς ἀγινεῖ.
καί μιν πειραίνουσι δύω πόλοι ἀμφοτέρωθεν·
ἀλλ' ὁ μὲν οὐκ ἐπίοπτος, ὁ δ' ἀντίος ἐκ βορέαο
ὑψόθεν ὠκεανοῖο

The axis shifts not a whit, but unchanging it is for ever fixed, holding the earth in equipoise, wheeling the heavens around; ending in two poles on either side, the one not seen, the other in the north facing us high above the horizon.

Phaenomena 22

of the earth's axis

3 ἄγχι δέ … πᾶσαι Πληιάδες φορέονται … ἀφαυραί·
ἑπτάποροι δὴ ταίγε μετ' ἀνθρώπους ὑδέονται,
ἓξ οἷαί περ ἐοῦσαι ἐπόψιαι ὀφθαλμοῖσιν …
αἱ μὲν ὁμῶς ὀλίγαι καὶ ἀφεγγέες, ἀλλ' ὀνομασταὶ
ἦρι καὶ ἑσπέριαι, Ζεὺς δ' αἴτιος, εἱλίσσονται,
ὅ σφισι καὶ θέρεος καὶ χείματος ἀρχομένοιο
σημαίνειν ἐπένευσεν ἐπερχομένου τ' ἀρότοιο

Close by, the Pleiades; singly they dimly shine.
Seven are they in the songs of men, but six are visible.
Small they may be, and dim, yet widely famed,
wheeling through heaven at morn and eventide;
Zeus bade them tell when Summer comes, and Winter,
and of the coming of ploughing-time.

Phaenomena 255

Hipparchus, On Aratus *1.6.14, says that on a moonless night seven stars can be seen*

4 καὶ Χέλυς ἥδ' ὀλίγη· τὴν ἄρ' ἔτι καὶ παρὰ λίκνῳ
Ἑρμείης ἐτόρησε, Λύρην δέ μιν εἶπε λέγεσθαι …
οὐρανὸν εἰσαγαγών

And then comes tiny Tortoise, now called Lyre at Hermes' wish, who set it into heaven; for he had pierced the shell [and added strings] when still beside his cradle.

Phaenomena 268

on the invention of the lyre by Hermes, cf. Homeric Hymns, *'To Hermes' 39–55*

5 ἤτοι γὰρ καὶ Ζηνὶ παρατρέχει αἰόλος Ὄρνις,
ἄλλα μὲν ἠερόεις, τὰ δέ οἱ ἐπὶ τετρήχυνται
ἀστράσιν οὔτι λίην μεγάλοις, ἀτὰρ οὐ μὲν ἀφαυροῖς.
Αὐτὰρ ὅγ' εὐδιόωντι ποτὴν ὄρνιθι ἐοικὼς
οὔριος εἰς ἑτέρην φέρεται

Verily in heaven there is outspread a glittering Bird. Wreathed in mist is the Bird, but yet the parts above him are rough with stars, not very large, yet not obscure. Like a bird in joyous flight, with fair weather it glides to the west.

Translated by G.R. Mair (1921)

Phaenomena 275

of Cygnus, the Swan

6 λοξὸς μὲν Ταύροιο τομῇ ὑποκέκλιται αὐτὸς
Ὠρίων· μὴ κεῖνον ὅτις καθαρῇ ἐνὶ νυκτὶ
ὑψοῦ πεπτηῶτα παρέρχεται, ἄλλα πεποίθοι
οὐρανὸν εἰσανιδὼν προφερέστερα θηήσεσθαι

Aslant beneath the Bull is set the great Orion; gazing on the heavens on a cloudless night no one shall see another constellation more fair.

Phaenomena 322

7 ταῦτά κε θηήσαιο παρερχομένων ἐνιαυτῶν
ἑξείης παλίνωρα· τὰ γὰρ καὶ πάντα μάλ' αὔτως
οὐρανῷ εὖ ἐνάρηρεν ἀγάλματα νυκτὸς ἰούσης

All these constellations thou canst mark as the seasons pass, each returning at its appointed time: for all are unchangingly and firmly fixed in the heavens to be the ornaments of the passing night.

Translated by G.R. Mair (1921)

Phaenomena 451

8 ἄκρα γε μὲν νυκτῶν κεῖναι δυοκαίδεκα μοῖραι
ἄρκιαι ἐξειπεῖν. Τὰ δέ που μέγαν εἰς ἐνιαυτόν,
ὥρη μέν τ' ἀρόσαι νειούς, ὥρη δὲ φυτεῦσαι

Those twelve signs of the Zodiac are sufficient to tell the limits of the night. But they too mark the great year – the season to plough and sow the fallow field and the season to plant the tree.

Translated by G.R. Mair (1921)

Phaenomena 740

9 ἄλλοτε δὲ τρίτον ἦμαρ ἐπιτρέχει, ἄλλοτε πέμπτον,
ἄλλοτε δ' ἀπρόφατον κακὸν ἵκετο

Sometimes the storm comes on the third day, sometimes on the fifth, but sometimes the evil comes all unforeseen.

Translated by G.R. Mair (1921)

Phaenomena 767

10 πάντα γὰρ οὔπω
ἐκ Διὸς ἄνθρωποι γινώσκομεν, ἀλλ' ἔτι πολλὰ
κέκρυπται, τῶν αἴ κε θέλῃ καὶ ἐσαυτίκα δώσει
Ζεύς

Not yet do we mortals know all from Zeus; much still remains hidden, which he may reveal as he sees fit.

Phaenomena 768

11 σκέπτεο δ' εὔδιος μὲν ἐὼν ἐπὶ χείματι μᾶλλον,
ἐς δὲ γαληναίην χειμωνόθεν

Seek in calm for signs of storms, and in storm for signs of calm.

Translated by G.R. Mair (1921)

Phaenomena 799

12 εἰ δ' ὁ μὲν ἀνέφελος βάπτῃ ῥόου ἑσπερίοιο,
ταὶ δὲ κατερχομένου νεφέλαι καὶ ἔτ' οἰχομένοιο
πλησίαι ἑστήκωσιν ἐρευθέες, οὔ σε μάλα χρὴ
αὔριον οὐδ' ἐπὶ νυκτὶ περιτρομέειν ὑετοῖο

If without a cloud the sun dip in the western ocean, and as he is sinking, or still when he is gone, the clouds stand near blushing red, neither on the morrow nor in the night needest thou be over-fearful of rain.

Translated by G.R. Mair (1921)

Phaenomena 858

cf. the English saying 'red sky at night, shepherd's delight'

13 καὶ χῆνες κλαγγηδὸν ἐπειγόμεναι βρωμοῖο
χειμῶνος μέγα σῆμα, καὶ ἐννεάγηρα κορώνη
νύκτερον ἀείδουσα, καὶ ὀψὲ βοῶντε κολοιοί,
καὶ σπίνος ἠῷα σπίζων, καὶ ὄρνεα πάντα
ἐκ πελάγους φεύγοντα, καὶ ὀρχίλος ἢ καὶ ἐριθεὺς
δύνων ἐς κοίλας ὀχεάς, καὶ φῦλα κολοιῶν
ἐκ νομοῦ ἐρχόμενα τραφεροῦ ἐπὶ ὄψιον αὖλιν

Sure signs of storm are geese hastening with many a cackle to their food, the nine-generation crow cawing at night, the jackdaw chattering late, the chaffinch piping in the dawn, waterfowl all fleeing inward from the sea, the wren or the robin retreating into hollow clefts, and tribes of jackdaws returning late to roost from dry feeding-grounds.

Translated by G.R. Mair (1921)

Phaenomena 1021

14 ἐκ θεοῦ ἀρχώμεσθα, τὸν οὐδέποτ' ἄνδρες ἐῶσιν
ἄρρητον· μεσταὶ δὲ θεοῦ πᾶσαι μὲν ἀγυιαί,
πᾶσαι δ' ἀνθρώπων ἀγοραί, μεστὴ δὲ θάλασσα
καὶ λιμένες, πάντη δὲ θεοῦ κεχρήμεθα πάντες.
τοῦ γὰρ καὶ γένος ἐσμέν

From god let us begin, whom we mortals never leave unnamed: full of god are all the streets and all the gathering-places of men, the seas and harbours. Everywhere we have need of god. For we are also his offspring.

Fragment 2.54 (Denis)

'God' has been transposed in this fragment from 'Zeus', see Aratus 1 above; quoted by St Paul in his address to the Athenians (see Bible 194)

ARCESILAUS

316–242BC

Philosopher from Pitane in Aeolis, head of the Academy from *c.*268BC

1 ὥσπερ ὅπου φάρμακα πολλὰ καὶ ἰατροὶ πολλοί, ἐνταῦθα νόσοι πλεῖσται, οὕτω δὴ καὶ ὅπου νόμοι πλεῖστοι, ἐκεῖ καὶ ἀδικίαν εἶναι μεγίστην

As much medicine and many doctors means much disease, thus more laws just means more injustice.

Stobaeus, *Anthology* 4.1.92

ARCHELAUS (1)

5th century BC

Philosopher of Athenian birth, a pupil of Anaxagoras

1 τὸ δίκαιον εἶναι καὶ τὸ αἰσχρὸν οὐ φύσει, ἀλλὰ νόμῳ

Things are just or base not by nature but by convention.

Testimonies, Fragment 1 (D-K)

ARCHELAUS (2)

Macedonian king, 413–399BC

1 κουρέως ἐρωτήσαντος αὐτόν, πῶς σε κείρω; σιωπῶν ἔφη

'How shall I cut your hair?' asked the barber.
'In silence,' replied the King.

Plutarch, *Sayings of Kings and Commanders* 177a

2 τῶν γὰρ καλῶν τοι καὶ τὸ μετόπωρον καλόν

The noble, even in life's autumn, are noble.

Plutarch, *Sayings of Kings and Commanders* 177b

also attributed to Euripides

ARCHIAS

1st century BC

Greek poet of Antioch, given Roman citizenship with the name Aulus Licinius Archias

1 μόχθων οὐδ' Ἀίδης με κατεύνασεν, ἡνίκα μοῦνος
οὐδὲ θανὼν λείῃ κέκλιμαι ἡσυχίῃ

Not even Hades couches me to rest;
Alone of ghosts I cannot lie at ease.

Translated by William Sinclair Marris (1938)

Greek Anthology 7.278

epigram on a tomb by the sea

2 Εὔφημος γλώσσῃ παραμείβεο τὰν λάλον Ἠχώ
κοὐ λάλον, ἤν τι κλύω, τοῦτ' ἀπαμειβομέναν

I'm voluble; I'm voiceless; I am Echo: I reply
To all I hear; so heed your talk as you are passing by.

Translated by William Sinclair Marris (1938)

Greek Anthology 9.27

ARCHIDAMUS

*c.*490–427BC

King of Sparta, *c.*469–427BC

see also Thucydides 16

1 πόλεμον δὲ ξύμπαντας ἀραμένους ἕνεκα τῶν ἰδίων, ὃν οὐχ ὑπάρχει εἰδέναι καθ' ὅ τι

χωρήσει, οὐ ῥᾴδιον εὐπρεπῶς θέσθαι

A war undertaken by a whole confederacy in pursuit of individual grievances, with the outcome impossible to tell, cannot easily be settled on honourable terms.

Translated by Martin Hammond (2009)

Thucydides, *History of the Peloponnesian War* 1.82.6

2 δίκαιον οὖν ἡμᾶς μήτε τῶν πατέρων χείρους φαίνεσθαι μήτε ἡμῶν αὐτῶν τῆς δόξης ἐνδεεστέρους

We must not, then, fall short of our fathers' standards, nor fail to live up to our own reputation.

Translated by Rex Warner (1954)

Thucydides, *History of the Peloponnesian War* 2.11.2

3 ἄδηλα γὰρ τὰ τῶν πολέμων, καὶ ἐξ ὀλίγου τὰ πολλὰ

No one can foresee the events of war, and small incidents may trigger great calamities.

Thucydides, *History of the Peloponnesian War* 2.11.4.1

4 πολλάκις τε τὸ ἔλασσον πλῆθος δεδιὸς ἄμεινον ἠμύνατο τοὺς πλέονας διὰ τὸ καταφρονοῦντας ἀπαρασκεύους γενέσθαι

Often a smaller force will defend itself better against a larger number which thought slightly of the enemy and was therefore unprepared.

Thucydides, *History of the Peloponnesian War* 2.11.4.2

5 ἐν τῇ πολεμίᾳ τῇ μὲν γνώμῃ θαρσαλέους στρατεύειν, τῷ δ' ἔργῳ δεδιότας παρεσκευάσθαι

When campaigning in enemy's country always be bold in spirit, but in action cautious and therefore well prepared.

Translated by Charles Forster Smith (1919)

Thucydides, *History of the Peloponnesian War* 2.11.5

6 οἱ λογισμῷ ἐλάχιστα χρώμενοι θυμῷ πλεῖστα ἐς ἔργον καθίστανται

Those who use least reasoning do not pause to think but rush into action.

Thucydides, *History of the Peloponnesian War* 2.11.7

7 οἳ ἄρχειν τε τῶν ἄλλων ἀξιοῦσι καὶ ἐπιόντες τὴν τῶν πέλας δῃοῦν

They claim the right to rule over others and to attack and ravage their neighbours' land.

Translated by Charles Forster Smith (1919)

Thucydides, *History of the Peloponnesian War* 2.11.8

of the Athenians

8 ξυγγνώμονες δὲ ἔστε τῆς ἀδικίας κολάζεσθαι τοῖς ὑπάρχουσι προτέροις

See to it that punishment may fall on those who were first to do evil.

Thucydides, *History of the Peloponnesian War* 2.74.2

9 τί ἂν ἔφη οὗτος ὑγιὲς εἴποι, ὃς οὐ μόνον ἐπὶ τῇ ψυχῇ τὸ ψεῦδος, ἀλλὰ καὶ ἐπὶ τῇ κεφαλῇ περιφέρει;

What can honourably be said by someone who carries lies not only in his soul, but also on his head?

Aelian, *Historical Miscellany* 7.20

of a man who dyed his hair

ARCHIDAMUS III

*c.*401–338BC
King of Sparta, *c.*360–338BC

1 ἀντὶ χαρίεντος ἰατροῦ κακὸς ποιητὴς καλεῖσθαι ἐπιθυμεῖς;

You prefer to be called a bad poet rather than an accomplished physician?

Plutarch, *Sayings of Spartans* 218f

to a distinguished physician who wrote wretched verse

2 καταπελτικὸν δ' ἰδὼν βέλος τότε πρῶτον ἐκ Σικελίας κομισθὲν ἀνεβόησεν, Ἡράκλεις, ἀπόλωλεν ἀνδρὸς ἀρετά.

When he saw the missile shot by a catapult, brought then for the first time from Sicily, he exclaimed, 'Great Heavens! man's valour is no more!'

Translated by Frank Cole Babbitt (1931)

Plutarch, *Sayings of Spartans* 219a

ARCHILOCHUS

7th century BC
Iambic and elegiac poet from Paros

1 αὐτὸν δ' ἐξεσάωσα. τί μοι μέλει ἀσπὶς ἐκείνη;
ἐρρέτω· ἐξαῦτις κτήσομαι οὐ κακίω

I have saved myself – what care I for that shield?
Away with it! I'll get another one no worse.

Translated in *Bartlett's Familiar Quotations* (1980)

Fragment 5 (West, *IEG*)

of his shield, abandoned in flight

2 θεοὶ γὰρ ἀνηκέστοισι κακοῖσιν,
ὦ φίλ', ἐπὶ κρατερὴν τλημοσύνην ἔθεσαν φάρμακον

The gods give us steadfast endurance to counter incurable woes.

Fragment 13 (West, *IEG*)

3 δήμου μὲν ἐπίρρησιν μελεδαίνων
οὐδεὶς ἂν μάλα πόλλ' ἱμερόεντα πάθοι

If you worry about other peoples' censure
you will hardly experience many delights.

Fragment 14 (West, *IEG*)

4 πάντα πόνος τεύχει θνητοῖς μελέτη τε βροτείη

Hard work and human effort accomplish everything.

Translated by Douglas E. Gerber (1999)

Fragment 17 (West, *IEG*)

5 ἔχουσα θαλλὸν μυρσίνης ἐτέρπετο
ῥοδῆς τε καλὸν ἄνθος. ἡ δέ οἱ κόμη
ὤμους κατεσκίαζε καὶ μετάφρενα

She took delight in holding a sprig of myrtle
and the lovely flower of the rose bush; and her hair
cast a shade over her shoulders and her back.

Translated by Douglas E. Gerber (1999)

Fragment 30 and 31 (West, *IEG*)

6 ἐσμυριχμένας κόμας
καὶ στῆθος, ὡς ἂν καὶ γέρων ἠράσσατο

With scented hair and breasts, so that even an old man would have been enamoured of her.

Fragment 48 (West, *IEG*)

7 ἑπτὰ γὰρ νεκρῶν πεσόντων, οὓς ἐμάρψαμεν ποσίν,
χείλιοι φονῆές εἰμεν

There were seven dead men trodden under foot, and we were a thousand murderers.

Translated by J.A. Pott (1913)

Fragment 101 (West, *IEG*)

8 Γλαῦχ', ὅρα· βαθὺς γὰρ ἤδη κύμασιν ταράσσεται
πόντος, ἀμφὶ δ' ἄκρα Γυρέων ὀρθὸν ἵσταται νέφος,
σῆμα χειμῶνος, κιχάνει δ' ἐξ ἀελπτίης φόβος

Look Glaucus! Already waves are disturbing the deep sea and a cloud
stands straight round about the heights of Gyrae, a sign of storm; from the
unexpected comes fear.

Translated by Douglas E. Gerber (1999)

Fragment 105 (West, *IEG*)

9 ἐτήτυμον γὰρ ξυνὸς ἀνθρώποις Ἄρης

War is truly even-handed towards men.

Fragment 110 (West, *IEG*)

Ares as god of war

10 σμικρός τις στρατηγὸς εἴη καὶ περὶ κνήμας ἰδεῖν
ῥοικός, ἀσφαλέως βεβηκὼς ποσσί, καρδίης πλέως

Give me a general, be he short and bandy-legged,
but walking firmly, full of courage.

Fragment 114 (West, *IEG*)

11 χρημάτων ἄελπτον οὐδέν ἐστιν οὐδ' ἀπώμοτον
οὐδὲ θαυμάσιον

Nothing is unexpected, or impossible, or strange.

Fragment 122.1 (West, *IEG*)

on the occasion of an eclipse of the sun

12 θαλάσσης ἠχέεντα κύματα
φίλτερ' ἠπείρου γένηται

Preferring the thundering ocean waves to land.

Translated by C.A. Trypanis (1971)

Fragment 122.8 (West, *IEG*)

of dolphins

13 χαρτοῖσίν τε χαῖρε καὶ κακοῖσιν ἀσχάλα
μὴ λίην, γίνωσκε δ' οἷος ῥυσμὸς ἀνθρώπους ἔχει

Enjoy that which brings happiness, be not overly saddened by what does not, learn the rhythm by which man is ruled.

Fragment 128 (West, *IEG*)

14 τῇ μὲν ὕδωρ ἐφόρει
δολοφρονέουσα χειρί, θἠτέρῃ δὲ πῦρ

A cunning woman carries water in one hand, fire in the other.

Fragment 184 (West, *IEG*)

15 τοῖος γὰρ φιλότητος ἔρως ὑπὸ καρδίην ἐλυσθεὶς
πολλὴν κατ' ἀχλὺν ὀμμάτων ἔχευεν,
κλέψας ἐκ στηθέων ἁπαλὰς φρένας

Such desire bound up my heart,
poured heavy mist over my eyes
and stole the wits from my breast.

Fragment 191 (West, *IEG*)

16 ἀλλά μ' ὁ λυσιμελὴς ὦταῖρε δάμναται πόθος

But, my friend, limb-loosening desire overwhelms me.

Translated by Douglas E. Gerber (1999)

Fragment 196 (West, *IEG*)

17 πόλλ' οἶδ' ἀλώπηξ, ἀλλ' ἐχῖνος ἓν μέγα

The fox has many tricks, and the hedgehog only one, but that is the best of all.

Translated in Erasmus 'Adagia' (1500)

Fragment 201 (West, *IEG*)

some have a single central vision, others pursue many ends; the first kind of personality belongs to the hedgehogs, the second to the foxes; cf. Isaiah Berlin, The Hedgehog and the Fox *(1953) sect. I*

18 οὐκ ἂν μύροισι γρηῦς ἐοῦσ' ἠλείφεο

You, an old woman, should not seek to be perfumed.

Fragment 205 (West, *IEG*)

19 εὕδοντι δ' αἱρεῖ κύρτος

The trap does the catching while the fisherman sleeps.

Fragment 307 (West, *IEG*)

ARCHIMEDES

c.287–212 or 211 BC
Mathematician and inventor from Syracuse

1 (a) δός μοι ποῦ στῶ, καὶ κινῶ τὴν γῆν
(b) δός μοί πᾷ στῶ καὶ τὰν γᾶν κινήσω

Give me but one firm spot on which to stand, and I will move the earth.

Translated in *The Oxford Dictionary of Quotations* (2004)

Fragment 15 (Heiberg and Stamatis)

on the power of the lever; the second rendering is in the style used more often today

2 εὕρηκα, εὕρηκα

Eureka! I have discovered it!

Translated by G.J. Toomer (2003)

Plutarch, *That Epicurus Actually Makes a Pleasant Life Impossible* 1094C

jumping out of a public bath as he discovered the laws of displacement

3 μή μου τοὺς κύκλους τάραττε

Do not disturb my circles!

on being accosted by a Roman soldier who thereupon killed him; probably from the Latin 'noli turbare circulos meos!', orally recorded in this form and still used today; cf. Valerius Maximus, Memorable Doings and Sayings, *8.7.ext.7 and Diodorus Siculus,* Library of History *26.18.1*

ARCHIPPUS

5th century BC
Athenian Old Comedy poet

1 ὡς ἡδὺ τὴν θάλατταν ἀπὸ τῆς γῆς ὁρᾶν

How sweet it is to view the sea, from the shore.

Fragment 43 (Kock) – 45 (K-A)

2 ἀμαθὴς σοφός, δίκαιος ἄδικος

Uncultured wisdom, unjust justice.

Fragment 46 (Kock) – 51 (K-A)

ARIPHRON

early 4th century BC
Lyric poet from Sicyon

1 Ὑγίεια βροτοῖσι πρεσβίστα μακάρων, μετὰ σεῦ
ναίοιμι τὸ λειπόμενον βιοτᾶς

Health, best of the Blessed Ones to men,

May I dwell with you for the rest of my days.

Translated by C.M. Bowra (1957)

Fragment 1 (Page, *PMG*)

the paean is preserved on an Athenian stone dated c.200AD (now in Kassel; cf. Inscriptiones Graecae, IG2.2.ii.4533)

ARISTARCHUS

5th century BC

Tragic playwright from Tegea, contemporary of Euripides

1 ἔρωτος ὅστις μὴ πεπείραται βροτῶν,
οὐκ οἶδ' ἀνάγκης θεσμόν

Whoever has no knowledge of love,
knows nothing of the nature of anguish.

Fragment 2 (Snell, *TrGF*)

ARISTARCHUS OF SAMOS

310–*c*.230BC

Astronomer, famous for his heliocentric hypothesis

1 τὰ μὲν ἀπλανέα τῶν ἄστρων καὶ τὸν ἅλιον μένειν ἀκίνητον, τὰν δὲ γᾶν περιφέρεσθαι περὶ τὸν ἅλιον κατὰ κύκλου περιφέρειαν

The fixed stars and sun remain unmoved, whereas the earth circles around the sun.

Archimedes, *Arenarius* 2.135.11

cited by Copernicus, the first astronomer to formulate a scientifically based heliocentric cosmology; Aristarchus' theory was in direct conflict with Aristotle's geocentric assertion, later championed by the church; cf. Anaximander 2

2 μένειν τὸν οὐρανὸν ὑποτιθέμενος ἐξελίττεσθαι δὲ κατὰ λοξοῦ κύκλου τὴν γῆν ἅμα καὶ περὶ τὸν αὑτῆς ἄξονα δινουμένην

Heaven is at rest while the earth is revolving along the ecliptic and at the same time is rotating about its own axis.

Translated by Harold Cherniss (1957)

Plutarch, *The Face on the Moon* 923a

LETTER OF ARISTEAS

probably early or late 2nd century BC

Alexandrian Jewish story of the making of the Greek translation of the Torah

1 τίς ἐστι βασιλεῖ κτῆσις ἀναγκαιοτάτη; τῶν ὑποτεταγμένων φιλανθρωπία καὶ ἀγάπησις, ἀπεκρίνατο· διὰ γὰρ τούτων ἄλυτος εὐνοίας δεσμὸς γίνεται

What is the most necessary possession for a king? The benevolence and love of his subjects, he replied, for it is through this that the bond of goodwill is rendered indissoluble.

Translated by R.H. Charles (1913)

Letter of Aristeas 265

at a banquet given by Ptolemy II Philadelphus, in honour of the 70 (72) translators of the Torah, i.e. the Pentateuch (later, expanded, known as the Septuagint)

2 σὺ βασιλεὺς μέγας ὑπάρχεις, οὐ τοσοῦτον τῇ δόξῃ τῆς ἀρχῆς καὶ πλούτῳ προσχών, ὅσον ἐπιεικείᾳ καὶ φιλανθρωπίᾳ πάντας ἀνθρώπους ὑπερῆρκας τοῦ θεοῦ σοι δεδωρημένου ταῦτα

You are a great king not so much because you excel in the glory of your rule and your wealth but rather because you have surpassed all men in clemency and philanthropy, thanks to god who has endowed you with these qualities.

Translated by R.H. Charles (1913)

Letter of Aristeas 290

the 70 (72) translators of the Torah, i.e. the Pentateuch, to Ptolemy II Philadelphus at a banquet in their honour

ARISTIDES

c.540–468BC

Athenian politician and general

see also Herodotus 157

1 Ἀριστείδης δὲ καθ' αὑτὸν ὥσπερ ὁδὸν ἰδίαν ἐβάδιζε διὰ τῆς πολιτείας, πρῶτον μὲν οὐ βουλόμενος συναδικεῖν τοῖς ἑταίροις ἢ λυπηρὸς εἶναι μὴ χαριζόμενος, ἔπειτα τὴν ἀπὸ τῶν φίλων δύναμιν οὐκ ὀλίγους ὁρῶν ἐπαίρουσαν ἀδικεῖν

Aristides walked the way of statesmanship alone, unwilling to join with any comrades in wrongdoing, or to vex them by withholding favours; besides, he saw that power bestowed by friends encouraged many to such wrongdoing.

Plutarch, *Aristides* 2.6.2

2 μόνῳ τῷ χρηστὰ καὶ δίκαια πράσσειν καὶ λέγειν ἀξιῶν θαρρεῖν τὸν ἀγαθὸν πολίτην

He deemed it right that the good citizen should base his confidence only on proper and just conduct.

Plutarch, *Aristides* 2.6.5

3 μήτε ταῖς τιμαῖς ἐπαιρομένου, πρός τε τὰς δυσημερίας ἀθορύβως καὶ πρᾴως ἔχοντος

He was never uplifted by honours, and faced adversity with gentle calm.

Plutarch, *Aristides* 3.4.5

4 ὁμοίως ἡγουμένου χρῆναι τῇ πατρίδι παρέχειν ἑαυτόν οὐ χρημάτων μόνον, ἀλλὰ καὶ δόξης προῖκα καὶ ἀμισθὶ πολιτευόμενον

In all cases he considered it his duty to give his services to his country freely and without reward, either in money, or, more importantly, in honour.

Plutarch, *Aristides* 3.4.7

5 οὐ γὰρ δοκεῖν δίκαιος, ἀλλ' εἶναι θέλει

He wishes not to seem, but rather to be just.

Translated by Bernadotte Perrin (1914)

Plutarch, *Aristides* 3.5

when this verse by Aeschylus was recited in the theatre all the spectators turned to look at Aristides; Plutarch uses 'δίκαιος' (an attribute given by his contemporaries to Aristides), the original is 'ἄριστος'; cf. Aeschylus 154

6 λέγ', ὦ 'γαθέ, φάναι, μᾶλλον, εἴ τι σὲ κακὸν πεποίηκε· σοὶ γάρ, οὐκ ἐμαυτῷ, δικάζω

Tell me rather, my good friend, whether he has done you wrong; it is not my case but yours that is before the court.

Translated by Bernadotte Perrin (1914)

Plutarch, *Aristides* 4.2

Aristides, being the judge, to a man expecting favours, saying that his opponent had done Aristides much injury

7 οὐδὲ γινώσκω τὸν ἄνθρωπον, ἀλλ' ἐνοχλοῦμαι πανταχοῦ τὸν Δίκαιον ἀκούων

I don't even know the man, but it annoys me to hear him called 'The Just' wherever I go.

Plutarch, *Aristides* 7.7

of Aristides, who was himself asked by an illiterate man to inscribe on a potsherd a vote intended for his own exile; cf. Aristides 18

8 οὐκ ἔστι χρυσοῦ τοσοῦτον πλῆθος οὔθ' ὑπὲρ γῆν οὔθ' ὑπὸ γῆν, ὅσον Ἀθηναῖοι δέξαιντο ἂν πρὸ τῆς τῶν Ἑλλήνων ἐλευθερίας

There is no bulk of gold so large, either above the ground or below, that the Athenians would accept in return for the freedom of the Hellenes.

Plutarch, *Aristides* 10.5

on the Persian king's offer to pay handsomely for aborting their fight against him

9 ἄχρι ἂν ὁ ἥλιος ταύτην πορεύηται τὴν πορείαν, Ἀθηναῖοι πολεμήσουσι Πέρσαις

As long as the sun continues its course, so long will the Athenians fight the Persians.

Plutarch, *Aristides* 10.6

spoken by Aristides to the Persian messengers

10 ἥκομεν γὰρ οὐ τοῖς συμμάχοις στασιάσοντες, ἀλλὰ μαχούμενοι τοῖς πολεμίοις, οὐδ' ἐπαινεσόμενοι τοὺς πατέρας, ἀλλ' αὐτοὺς ἄνδρας ἀγαθοὺς τῇ Ἑλλάδι παρέξοντες

We are come not to quarrel with our allies, but to do battle with our foes; not to heap praises on our fathers, but to show ourselves brave men in the service of Hellas.

Translated by Bernadotte Perrin (1914)

Plutarch, *Aristides* 12.3

11 οὐχ ὅπλοις οὐδὲ ναυσὶν οὐδ' ἵπποις, εὐγνωμοσύνῃ δὲ καὶ πολιτείᾳ τὴν ἡγεμονίαν παρελόμενος

Not by means of arms or ships or horsemen, but by tact and diplomacy he had stripped them of the leadership.

Translated by Bernadotte Perrin (1914)

Plutarch, *Aristides* 23.1

12 προσόδους ὁρίσαι τὸ κατ' ἀξίαν ἑκάστῳ καὶ δύναμιν

Fixing taxes according to each member's worth and ability to pay.

Plutarch, *Aristides* 24.1

13 πένης μὲν ἐξῆλθεν, ἐπανῆλθε δὲ πενέστερος

Poor he was when he went on his mission, and he returned from it poorer still.

Plutarch, *Aristides* 24.2

14 πλούτῳ μὲν γὰρ ἔστι πολλοὺς ἰδεῖν εὖ τε καὶ καλῶς χρωμένους, πενίαν δὲ φέροντι γενναίως οὐ ῥᾴδιον ἐντυχεῖν

Many were to be seen who use wealth well or ill, but it was not easy to find a man who endured poverty with a noble spirit.

Translated by Bernadotte Perrin (1914)

Plutarch, *Aristides* 25.8

15 καὶ μέντοι καὶ τάφος ἐστὶν αὐτοῦ Φαληροῖ δεικνύμενος, ὅν φασι κατασκευάσαι τὴν πόλιν αὐτῷ μηδ' ἐντάφια καταλιπόντι

His tomb is pointed out at Phaleron, and they say the city constructed it for him, since he did not leave even enough to pay for his funeral.

Translated by Bernadotte Perrin (1914)

Plutarch, *Aristides* 27.1

16 οὐ τὴν οὖσαν οὖν, ἔφη, δεῖ γέφυραν ... ἡμᾶς ἀναιρεῖν, ἀλλ' ἑτέραν, εἴπερ οἷόν τε, προσκατασκευάσαντας ἐκβαλεῖν διὰ τάχους τὸν ἄνθρωπον ἐκ τῆς Εὐρώπης

Rather than destroy his bridge we should build yet another so that [Xerxes] can flee from Europe as soon as possible.

Plutarch, *Themistocles* 16.4

said by Aristides to Themistocles; cf. the English proverb 'it is good to make a bridge of gold to a flying enemy'; cf. Aeschylus 77

17 Ἀριστείδης ὁ δίκαιος ἐρωτηθεὶς τί ἐστι τὸ δίκαιον τὸ μὴ ἀλλοτρίων ἐπιθυμεῖν ἔφη

When Aristides the Just was asked what is just, he answered, 'Not desiring others' possessions.'

Stobaeus, *Anthology* 3.9.32

18 ΑΡΙΣΤΕΙΔΕΣ ΛΥΣΙΜΑΧΟΥ

Aristides son of Lysimachos

anonymous potsherd found (among hundreds of others) at the Athenian Kerameikos. Potsherds were inscribed with the name of a person to be exiled (ostracized); cf. Guarducci, pl.VI and Aristides 7

ARISTIDES AELIUS

Publius Aelius Aristides
117 – after 181AD
Sophist orator and man of letters

1 εὖ ἔχειν τὸ σῶμα καὶ τὴν ψυχὴν

Keep a healthy mind in a healthy body.

Translated by D.S. Baker (1998)

Πρὸς Πλάτωνα περὶ ῥητορικῆς 7.12

now usually quoted as 'νοῦς ὑγιὴς ἐν σώματι ὑγιεῖ' after the Latin 'mens sana in corpore sano' (Juvenal, Satires *10.356)*

2 τοῦτ' ἐν ψυχῇ λόγοι, ὅπερ κάλλος ἐν σώματι

Language is to the mind what beauty is to the body.

Translated by H.T. Riley (1872)

Πρὸς Πλάτωνα περὶ ῥητορικῆς 103.8

3 ἀνδρῶν ἡρώων τέκνα πήματα

Sons of heroes are a calamity.

Scholia in Aelium Aristidem, Hypothesis – Epigram 160.1

ARISTIPPUS

c.435–350BC
Philosopher from Cyrene, an associate of Socrates

1 ἐὰν πάντες οἱ νόμοι ἀναιρεθῶσιν, ὁμοίως βιώσομεν

If all laws were abolished we'd go on living just the same.

Diogenes Laertius, *Lives of Eminent Philosophers* 2.68

2 οὐδὲ οἱ πολλὰ ἀλλ' οἱ χρήσιμα ἀναγινώσκοντές εἰσι σπουδαῖοι

It is not wide reading but useful reading that tends to excellence.

Translated by R.D. Hicks (1925)

Diogenes Laertius, *Lives of Eminent Philosophers* 2.71

3 κρατεῖ ἡδονῆς οὐχ ὁ ἀπεχόμενος, ἀλλ' ὁ χρώμενος μέν, μὴ παρεκφερόμενος δέ

The continent man is not he who avoids pleasure, but having tasted it, is not carried to excess.

Stobaeus, *Anthology* 3.17.17

4 τοῦ μὲν λέγειν κακῶς σὺ κύριος εἶ, τοῦ δὲ δικαίως ἀκούειν ἐγώ

It may be your right to slander, but it is my prerogative to hear what is just.

Stobaeus, *Anthology* 3.19.6

5 Ἀρίστιππος ὁ Κυρηναῖος φιλόσοφος

ἐρωτηθεὶς ὑπό τινος εἰ ὁ ἔρως ἕνεκα τῆς συνουσίας γίγνεται, οὔτ', ἔφη, διὰ τοῦτο οὔτ' ἄνευ τούτου

Aristippus the Cyrenaic philosopher, when asked if Eros exists for the sake of having sexual intercourse, replied, 'neither for it nor without it.'

Stobaeus, *Anthology* 4.20a.32

ARISTON

before 100BC

Epigrammatist included in the Garland of Meleager

1 Ὦ μύες, εἰ μὲν ἐπ' ἄρτον ἐληλύθατ', ἐς μυχὸν ἄλλον
στείχετ' (ἐπεὶ λιτὴν οἰκέομεν καλύβην) ...
εἰ δ' ἐν ἐμαῖς βίβλοισι πάλιν καταθήξετ' ὀδόντα,
κλαύσεσθ', οὐκ ἀγαθὸν κῶμον ἐπερχόμενοι.

If you mice are looking for *food*, you'd better look
elsewhere, for mine is a frugal shack.
But if you attempt my *books* with your teeth
once more, you will rue it, mice.

Translated by W.G. Shepherd (1973)

Greek Anthology 6.303

ARISTON OF CEOS

3rd century BC

Peripatetic philosopher, probably head of the Lyceum *c.*225BC

1 Σπαρτιατῶν νόμος τάττει ζημίας τὴν μὲν πρώτην ἀγαμίου, τὴν δευτέραν ὀψιγαμίου, τὴν τρίτην καὶ μεγίστην κακογαμίου

Spartan law assigns fines firstly to those who do not marry, secondly to those who marry late, and thirdly, the greatest fine, to those who have a bad marriage.

Fragment 26 (Wehrli)

ARISTON OF CHIOS

3rd century BC

Stoic philosopher, pupil of Zeno

1 εἶναι γὰρ ὅμοιον τὸν σοφὸν τῷ ἀγαθῷ ὑποκριτῇ, ὃς ἄν τε Θερσίτου ἄν τε Ἀγαμέμνονος πρόσωπον ἀναλάβῃ, ἑκάτερον ὑποκρίνεται προσηκόντως

The wise man is like a good actor, who, if called upon to take the part of Thersites or of an Agamemnon, will impersonate them both becomingly.

Translated by R.D. Hicks (1925)

Fragment 351 (von Arnim, *SVF*)

the material does not matter, only what one does with it

2 τὰ ὑπὲρ ἡμᾶς οὐδὲν πρὸς ἡμᾶς

What is above us is beyond us.

Fragment 352 (von Arnim, *SVF*)

of divine matters; cf. the Latin 'quod supra nos nihil ad nos' (Marcus Minucius Felix, Octavius *13.1 et al.)*

3 οἱ ἐν διαλεκτικῇ βαθύνοντες ἐοίκασι καρκίνους μασωμένοις, οἳ δι' ὀλίγον τρόφιμον περὶ πολλὰ ὀστᾶ ἀσχολοῦνται

Those who engage in dialectics are like those who eat crab; for morsels of food they busy themselves with many bones.

Fragment 392 (von Arnim, *SVF*)

4 ἔλεγεν ἐοικέναι τὴν διαλεκτικὴν τῷ ἐν ταῖς ὁδοῖς πηλῷ· πρὸς οὐδὲν γὰρ οὐδ' ἐκεῖνον χρήσιμον ὄντα καταβάλλειν τοὺς βαδίζοντας

Dialectics is like mud on a road; it is of no particular use, but bespatters those walking through it.

Fragment 393 (von Arnim, *SVF*)

5 ὁ ἐλλέβορος ὁλοσχερέστερος μὲν ληφθεὶς καθαίρει, εἰς δὲ πάνυ σμικρὰ τριφθεὶς πνίγει· οὕτω καὶ ἡ κατὰ φιλοσοφίαν λεπτολογία

Hellebore taken in large pieces purifies, crushed into small pieces causes choking; similar is quibbling in philosophy.

Fragment 394 (von Arnim, *SVF*)

cf. Aristophanes 145

ARISTONYMUS

dates unknown

Writer of maxims, known only from Stobaeus

1 κυβερνήτου μὲν ἔργον ἀγαθοῦ πρὸς τὰς τῶν πνευμάτων μεταβολὰς ἁρμόσασθαι, ἀνδρὸς δὲ σοφοῦ πρὸς τὰς τῆς τύχης

An able captain adapts to the change of winds, a wise man to the turns of fortune.

Stobaeus, *Anthology* 3.1.97

2 ὥσπερ τὸ μέλι τὰ ἡλκωμένα δάκνει, τοῖς δὲ κατὰ φύσιν ἡδύ ἐστιν, οὕτω καὶ οἱ ἐκ φιλοσοφίας λόγοι

As honey hurts an open wound though being sweet by nature, so do philosophers' words.

Stobaeus, *Anthology* 3.13.41

3 ὁ φθόνος, ὥσπερ φαῦλος δημαγωγός, ταῖς καλαῖς ἀντιπολιτεύεται πράξεσιν

Envy, just as a bad demagogue, is against good deeds.

Stobaeus, *Anthology* 3.38.36

4 ἔοικεν ὁ βίος θεάτρῳ· διὸ πολλάκις χείριστοι τὸν κάλλιστον ἐν αὐτῷ κατέχουσι τόπον

Life is like the theatre; which is why many times the worst people occupy the best seats.

Stobaeus, *Anthology* 4.42.14

ARISTOPHANES

*c.*450–385BC
Athenian Old Attic Comedy poet
see also Cratinus 4; Lucian 10; Plato 306–311, 379

1 ἀποβλέπων εἰς τὸν ἀγρόν, εἰρήνης ἐρῶν,
στυγῶν μὲν ἄστυ, τὸν δ' ἐμὸν δῆμον ποθῶν,
ὃς οὐδεπώποτ' εἶπεν, ἄνθρακας πρίω,
οὐκ ὄξος, οὐκ ἔλαιον

I think of my fields, yearn for peace,
curse city life and long for my village;
no one there shouted 'coal for sale'
nor oil or vinegar either.

Acharnians 32

the play won first prize at the Lenaea in 425BC

2 εἰς τὴν προεδρίαν πᾶς ἀνὴρ ὠστίζεται

Pushing and fighting for the front seats.

Acharnians 42

3 τίς ἀγορεύειν βούλεται;

Who wishes to address the house?

Translated in Liddell & Scott

Acharnians 45

the basis of Athenian democracy – anyone wishing to speak could address the Assembly; cf. Euripides 332

4 δεινὸν γὰρ οὕτως ὀμφακίαν πεφυκέναι
τὸν θυμὸν ἀνδρῶν ὥστε βάλλειν καὶ βοᾶν
ἐθέλειν τ' ἀκοῦσαι μηδὲν ἴσον ἴσῳ φέρον

What an irritable nature, like sour wine!
You shout and throw stones, and will not hear my arguments.

Acharnians 352

5 πυκνῇ γὰρ λεπτὰ μηχανᾷ φρενί

Subtle are thy schemes, and intricate the courses of thy mind.

Translated by Alan H. Sommerstein (1973)

Acharnians 445

6 μή μοι φθονήσητ', ἄνδρες οἱ θεώμενοι,
εἰ πτωχὸς ὢν ἔπειτ' ἐν Ἀθηναίοις λέγειν
μέλλω περὶ τῆς πόλεως, τρυγῳδίαν ποιῶν.
Τὸ γὰρ δίκαιον οἶδε καὶ τρυγῳδία

Condemn me not, you in the audience
If, while I am a beggar, among us Athenians
I talk affairs of state in a comedy.
You see, comedy has a sense of duty too.

Translated by M.S. Silk (2000)

Acharnians 497

7 ἐγὼ δὲ λέξω δεινὰ μέν, δίκαια δέ

I shall tell things terrible but just.

Translated by C.A. Trypanis (1971)

Acharnians 501

8 ἐντεῦθεν ὀργῇ Περικλέης οὑλύμπιος
ἤστραπτ', ἐβρόντα, ξυνεκύκα τὴν Ἑλλάδα,
ἐτίθει νόμους ὥσπερ σκόλια γεγραμμένους

For then, in wrath, the Olympian Pericles
Thundered and lightened, and confounded Hellas
Enacting laws which ran like drinking songs.

Translated by Benjamin Bickley Rogers (1924)

Acharnians 530

9 πολλοῦ γε καὶ δεῖ

Far from it!

Translated in Liddell & Scott

Acharnians 543

still in use today

10 οἱ γέροντες οἱ παλαιοὶ μεμφόμεσθα τῇ πόλει·
οὐ γὰρ ἀξίως ἐκείνων ὧν ἐναυμαχήσαμεν
γηροβοσκούμεσθ' ὑφ' ὑμῶν, ἀλλὰ δεινὰ πάσχομεν

We old men, the elderly, have a complaint against the state.
The care we receive from you in our old age is unworthy of
the sea battles we've fought; in fact you treat us terribly.

Translated by Jeffrey Henderson (1998)

Acharnians 676

11 πάγχρηστον ἄγγος ἔσται,
κρατὴρ κακῶν, τριπτὴρ δικῶν,
φαίνειν ὑπευθύνους λυχνοῦ-
χος καὶ κύλιξ
τὰ πράγματ' ἐγκυκᾶσθαι

This pot will serve for many needs:
A bowl, a mortar, or a cup
To mix or pound or stir things up
While bent on shady deeds;
Or you could light a lamp in it
To scan officials' files.

Translated by Alan H. Sommerstein (2002)

Acharnians 936

12 ἰὼ στρατηγοὶ πλείονες ἢ βελτίονες

Ah, the generals, how numerous they are – and good for nothing!

Acharnians 1078

13 οἱ μὲν γὰρ οὖν τέττιγες ἕνα μῆν' ἢ δύο
ἐπὶ τῶν κραδῶν ᾄδουσ', Ἀθηναῖοι δ' ἀεὶ
ἐπὶ τῶν δικῶν ᾄδουσι πάντα τὸν βίον

Cicadas prattle for a month or two
among the fig-trees; Athenians in
the law-courts prattle all their lives.

Birds 39

the play won second prize at the Dionysia in 414BC

14 εἴ τινα πόλιν φράσειας ἡμῖν εὔερον
ὥσπερ σισύραν ἐγκατακλινῆναι μαλθακήν

Perhaps you can tell us where to find a really comfortable city, warm and welcoming, like a soft, warm, fleecy blanket.

Translated by David Barrett (1978)

Birds 121

15 ἐγὼ γὰρ αὐτοὺς βαρβάρους ὄντας πρὸ τοῦ
ἐδίδαξα τὴν φωνὴν ξυνὼν πολὺν χρόνον

A savage tribe I came to teach
Civilised speech.
I won, but flung a life-time in the breach.

Translated by Kathleen Freeman (1947)

Birds 199

a teacher of Greek about his pupils

16 ἐλελιζομένη διεροῖς μέλεσιν …
πρὸς Διὸς ἕδρας, ἵν' ὁ χρυσοκόμας
Φοῖβος ἀκούων τοῖς σοῖς ἐλέγοις
ἀντιψάλλων ἐλεφαντόδετον
φόρμιγγα θεῶν ἵστησι χορούς

Your trills reach up to Zeus's throne
where golden Phoebus hears your elegies,
answering on his ivory-inlaid lyre; and soon
the gods get up and dance.

Birds 213

of the nightingale

17 τοῦ φθέγματος τοὐρνιθίου·
οἷον κατεμελίτωσε τὴν λόχμην ὅλην

What a voice that little bird has!
It makes you feel as if the woods were drenched with honey.

Birds 223

of the nightingale

18 κίττα, τρυγών, κορυδός, ἐλεᾶς, ὑποθυμίς, περιστερά,
νέρτος, ἱέραξ, φάττα, κόκκυξ, ἐρυθρόπους, κεβλήπυρις, πορφυρίς, κερχνῄς,
κολυμβίς, ἀμπελίς, φήνη, δρύοψ …
ἰοὺ ἰού, τῶν ὀρνέων

A jay, a turtledove, a crested lark, reed warbler, wheatear, pigeon, merlin, sparrowhawk, ringdove, cuckoo, stockdove, firecrest, rail, kestrel, dabchick, waxwing, vulture, woodpecker. What a crowd of birds!

Translated by David Barrett (1978)

Birds 302

19 ἀλλ' ἀπ' ἐχθρῶν δῆτα πολλὰ μανθάνουσιν οἱ σοφοί

The wise learn many things from enemies.

Birds 375

20 πυκνότατον κίναδος,
σόφισμα, κύρμα, τρῖμμα, παιπάλημ' ὅλον

He's a real trickster,
All skill, swag, spice, sophistry.

Translated by M.S. Silk (2000)

Birds 429

21 δολερὸν μὲν ἀεὶ κατὰ πάντα δὴ τρόπον
πέφυκεν ἄνθρωπος

Full of wiles, full of guile, at all times, in all ways,
Are the children of Men.

Translated by Benjamin Bickley Rogers (1924)

Birds 451

22 ὃ γὰρ ἂν σὺ τύχῃς μοι
ἀγαθὸν πορίσας, τοῦτο κοινὸν ἔσται

'Tis to your own interest as well as to mine, for if you secure me some advantage, I will surely share it with you.

Translated by Eugene O'Neill, Jr (1938)

Birds 458

23 ἀμαθὴς γὰρ ἔφυς κοὐ πολυπράγμων, οὐδ' Αἴσωπον πεπάτηκας

You must be very unobservant, or very uneducated: you don't even know your Aesop.

Translated by David Barrett (1978)

Birds 471

24 οὐδεὶς οἶδεν τὸν θησαυρὸν τὸν ἐμὸν πλὴν εἴ τις ἄρ' ὄρνις

None but some bird knows where my treasure lies.

Translated by Jeffrey Henderson (2000)

Birds 601

25 ἄνδρες ἀμαυρόβιοι, φύλλων γενεᾷ προσόμοιοι,
ὀλιγοδρανέες, πλάσματα πηλοῦ, σκιοειδέα φῦλ' ἀμενηνά,
ἀπτῆνες ἐφημέριοι, ταλαοὶ βροτοί, ἀνέρες εἰκελόνειροι

Mankind, fleet of life, like tree leaves,
weak creatures of clay, unsubstantial as shadows,
wingless, ephemeral, wretched, mortal and dreamlike.

Translated in *Bartlett's Familiar Quotations* (1980)

Birds 685

26 πρῶτα μὲν ὥρας φαίνομεν ἡμεῖς ἦρος, χειμῶνος, ὀπώρας·
σπείρειν μέν, ὅταν γέρανος κρώζουσ' εἰς τὴν Λιβύην μεταχωρῇ·
καὶ πηδάλιον τότε ναυκλήρῳ φράζει κρεμάσαντι καθεύδειν,
... εἶτα χελιδών,
ὅτε χρὴ χλαῖναν πωλεῖν ἤδη καὶ ληδάριόν τι πρίασθαι

We birds tell the seasons of autumn, of winter, and spring;
it's time to sow when the crane whoops off to Africa;
then, for the captain to hang up his rudder and go to sleep;
and the swallow in spring, to sell your coat and buy a jacket.

Birds 709

27 ὄρνιν τε νομίζετε πάνθ' ὅσαπερ περὶ μαντείας διακρίνει·
φήμη γ' ὑμῖν ὄρνις ἐστί, πταρμόν τ' ὄρνιθα καλεῖτε,
ξύμβολον ὄρνιν, φωνὴν ὄρνιν, θεράποντ' ὄρνιν, ὄνον ὄρνιν.
ἆρ' οὐ φανερῶς ἡμεῖς ὑμῖν ἐσμὲν μαντεῖον;

Birds you use to foretell the future, good luck or bad luck;
an ominous utterance is a bird, a sneeze you call a bird,
any portent is a bird, a sound, a servant, a donkey.
Are we not then your favourite oracle?

Birds 719

28 ἢν οὖν ἡμᾶς νομίσητε θεούς,
ἕξετε χρῆσθαι μάντεσι, μούσαις,
αὔραις, ὥραις, χειμῶνι, θέρει
μετρίῳ, πνίγει· κοὐκ ἀποδράντες
καθεδούμεθ' ἄνω σεμνυνόμενοι
παρὰ ταῖς νεφέλαις ὥσπερ χὠ Ζεύς

Well then, if you treat us as gods
you'll have the benefit of prophets, muses,
breezes, seasons, – winter, mild summer,
stifling heat. And we won't run off
and sit up there affecting a solemn air,
preening among the clouds, like Zeus.

Translated by Jeffrey Henderson (2000)

Birds 723

29 ἐντευθενὶ
ἐκ τῶν νεφελῶν καὶ τῶν μετεώρων

χωρίων
χαῦνόν τι πάνυ.
βούλει Νεφελοκοκκυγίαν;

Somewhere, with all these clouds, and all this air,
There must be a name, somewhere.
How about 'Cloud-Cuckoo-Land'?

Birds 817

naming the capital city of the birds

30 καὶ πῶς ἂν ἔτι γένοιτ' ἂν εὔτακτος πόλις,
ὅπου θεὸς γυνὴ γεγονυῖα πανοπλίαν
ἕστηκ' ἔχουσα, Κλεισθένης δὲ κερκίδα;

And just how can a city remain well disciplined,
where a god, born a woman, stands there wearing full armour,
while Cleisthenes plies a spindle?

Translated by Jeffrey Henderson (2000)

Birds 829

31 γεωμετρῆσαι βούλομαι τὸν ἀέρα
ὑμῖν διελεῖν τε κατὰ γύας

I want to survey the air for you and parcel it into acres.

Translated by Jeffrey Henderson (2000)

Birds 995

32 ὀρθῷ μετρήσω κανόνι προστιθείς, ἵνα
ὁ κύκλος γένηταί σοι τετράγωνος

I'll take a measure laying a straight ruler alongside,
so that you will get a circle squared.

Translated by Jeffrey Henderson (2000)

Birds 1004

33 σῴζω δ' εὐθαλεῖς καρποὺς ...
κτείνω δ' οἳ κήπους εὐώδεις
φθείρουσιν λύμαις ἐχθίσταις,
ἑρπετά τε καὶ δάκετα πάνθ'

We preserve the thriving crops,
We kill the destroyers of sweet-smelling gardens,
The ravishers of plants,
And everything that creeps and stings.

Translated by David Barrett (1978)

Birds 1062

34 εὔδαιμον φῦλον πτηνῶν
οἰωνῶν, οἳ χειμῶνος μὲν
χλαίνας οὐκ ἀμπισχνοῦνται·
οὐδ' αὖ θερμὴ πνίγους ἡμᾶς
ἀκτὶς τηλαυγὴς θάλπει

Happy race of feathered fowls,
Who in winter
Are not muffled up in blankets,
And in summer
Live unscorched by the stifling heat.

Translated by David Barrett (1978)

Birds 1088

35 πρὶν μὲν γὰρ οἰκίσαι σε τήνδε τὴν πόλιν,
ἐλακωνομάνουν ἅπαντες ἄνθρωποι τότε,
ἐκόμων, ἐπείνων, ἐρρύπων, ἐσωκράτων,
σκυτάλι' ἐφόρουν

Why, before you built this city all men were crazy about the Spartans: they wore their hair long, went hungry, never bathed, acted like Socrates, brandished batons.

Translated by Jeffrey Henderson (2000)

Birds 1280

36 οὐκ ἔστιν οὐδὲν τοῦ πέτεσθαι γλυκύτερον

There's nothing sweeter than to fly.

Birds 1342

37 ὑπὸ γὰρ λόγων ὁ νοῦς τε μετεωρίζεται
ἐπαίρεταί τ' ἄνθρωπος

Words give man wings, wings to his spirit, wings to his imagination.

Birds 1447

38 ἀλλὰ πτέρου με ταχέσι καὶ κούφοις πτεροῖς
ἱέρακος ἢ κερχνῆδος

Just fit me out with the nimble wings
of a hawk or a kestrel.

Birds 1453

39 πολλὰ δὴ καὶ καινὰ καὶ θαυ-
μάστ' ἐπεπτόμεσθα καὶ
δεινὰ πράγματ' εἴδομεν

Many things new and strange
have we seen in our flights,
wondrous beyond belief.

Birds 1470

40 τουτὶ λαβών μου τὸ σκιάδειον ὑπέρεχε,
ἄνωθεν ὡς ἂν μή μ' ὁρῶσιν οἱ θεοί

Take this parasol and hold it over me,
so that the gods above can't see me.

Translated by Jeffrey Henderson (2000)

Birds 1508

41 ὦ δημοκρατία, ποῖ προβιβᾷς ἡμᾶς ποτε;

O democracy, where are you leading us!

Birds 1570

42 ἀλκυονίδας τ᾽ ἂν ἤγεθ᾽ ἡμέρας ἀεί
Halcyon days to enjoy year round.

Translated by Jeffrey Henderson (2000)

Birds 1594

43 πανοῦργον ἐγ-
γλωττογαστόρων γένος,
οἳ θερίζουσίν τε καὶ σπείρουσι
καὶ τρυγῶσι ταῖς γλώτταισι ...
πανταχοῦ τῆς Ἀττικῆς ἡ
γλῶττα χωρὶς τέμνεται

The wicked race of Thrive-by-Tongues,
who do their harvesting and sowing
and vintaging by tongue;
all over Attica the tongue is specially excised.

Translated by Jeffrey Henderson (2000)

Birds 1695

of the teachers of rhetoric

44 εἶναι παρ᾽ αὐτοῖς φασιν ἄμφω τὼ λόγω,
τὸν κρείττον᾽, ὅστις ἐστί, καὶ τὸν ἥττονα.
τούτοιν τὸν ἕτερον τοῖν λόγοιν, τὸν ἥττονα,
νικᾶν λέγοντά φασι τἀδικώτερα

They say they have two Arguments in there –
Right and Wrong, they call them –
and one of them, the Wrong,
can always win its case even when justice is against it.

Translated by Alan H. Sommerstein (2002)

Clouds 112

of Socrates and his school; it ridicules Socrates as a corrupt teacher of rhetoric; the play won last prize at the city Dionysia in 423BC

45 ἀνήρετ᾽ ἄρτι ... Σωκράτης
ψύλλαν ὁπόσους ἅλλοιτο ... πόδας

Just now Socrates asked
how many feet a flea could jump.

Translated by Alan H. Sommerstein (1973)

Clouds 145

of Socrates' endless enquiries

46 ἀέναοι Νεφέλαι,
ἀρθῶμεν φανεραὶ δροσερὰν φύσιν εὐάγητον
πατρὸς ἀπ᾽ Ὠκεανοῦ βαρυαχέος ...
τηλεφανεῖς σκοπιὰς ἀφορώμεθα

Rise, my sisters, Clouds eternal,
Shining bright with morning dew,
From the roaring Ocean's bosom
To the sky, the world to view.

Translated by Alan H. Sommerstein (1973)

Clouds 275

chorus of clouds

47 πλείστους αὗται βόσκουσι σοφιστάς ...
ἰατροτέχνας, σφραγιδονυχαργοκομήτας
...
ἄνδρας μετεωροφένακας
οὐδὲν δρῶντας βόσκουσ᾽ ἀργούς

They feed countless sophists,
quack doctors, lazy long-haired fops
with rings and natty nails,
astronomical charlatans,
idle people doing nothing.

Clouds 332

48 ἤδη ποτ᾽ ἀναβλέψας εἶδες νεφέλην κενταύρῳ ὁμοίαν
ἢ παρδάλει ἢ λύκῳ ἢ ταύρῳ;

Have you never seen a cloud looking like a centaur?
Or perhaps a leopard, a wolf, a bull?

Clouds 346

Socrates speaking

49 βρενθύει τ᾽ ἐν ταῖσιν ὁδοῖς καὶ τὠφθαλμὼ παραβάλλεις

With swagg'ring gait and roving eye.

Translated by Alexander Nehamas and Paul Woodruff (1989)

Clouds 362

of Socrates; cf. Plato, Symposium *221b*

50 ὁ Ζεὺς δ᾽ ὑμῖν, φέρε, πρὸς τῆς Γῆς, Οὐλύμπιος οὐ θεός ἐστιν;
ποῖος Ζεύς; οὐ μὴ ληρήσεις. οὐδ᾽ ἐστὶ Ζεύς

– But come, by Earth, is not Jupiter, the Olympian, a god?
– What Jupiter? Do not trifle. There is no Jupiter.

Translated by William James Hickie (1853?)

Clouds 366

as if said by Socrates

51 εἴπερ τὰ χρέα διαφευξοῦμαι
τοῖς τ᾽ ἀνθρώποις εἶναι δόξω
θρασύς, εὔγλωττος, τολμηρός, ἴτης,
βδελυρός, ψευδῶν συγκολλητής,
εὑρησιεπής, περίτριμμα δικῶν

If I can beat my debts
And make men think me

Bold, glib, confident, cavalier,
Shocking, a mint of lies,
A coiner of phrases, a smooth lawyer.

Translated by M.S. Silk (2000)

Clouds 443

52 δυσβουλίαν τῇδε τῇ πόλει προσεῖναι

It is bad policymaking that afflicts this city.

Translated by Jeffrey Henderson (1998)

Clouds 588

53 μή νυν περὶ σαυτὸν εἶλλε τὴν γνώμην ἀεί,
ἀλλ' ἀποχάλα τὴν φροντίδ' εἰς τὸν ἀέρα

Now don't stay wrapped up in your thoughts;
relax, unwind, give up all cares into the open air.

Clouds 761

54 καὶ γνωσθήσει ποτ' Ἀθηναίοις
οἷα διδάσκεις τοὺς ἀνοήτους

And one day the Athenians will realize
what sort of education you've been giving the idiots!

Translated by Jeffrey Henderson (1998)

Clouds 918

of Athenian young men

55 λέξω τοίνυν τὴν ἀρχαίαν παιδείαν ὡς διέκειτο ...
πρῶτον μὲν ἔδει παιδὸς φωνὴν γρύξαντος μηδέν' ἀκοῦσαι

Let me tell you of education in the good old days
when children would be seen and not heard.

Clouds 961

56 ἀλλ' οὖν λιπαρός γε καὶ εὐανθὴς ἐν γυμνασίοις διατρίψεις,
οὐ στωμύλλων κατὰ τὴν ἀγορὰν τριβολεκτράπελ', οἷάπερ οἱ νῦν

Spend your time in the gymnasium, get sleek and healthy, not in the agora chattering about thorny subjects as people do now.

Clouds 1002

57 καί σ' ἀναπείσει τὸ μὲν αἰσχρὸν ἅπαν
καλὸν ἡγεῖσθαι, τὸ καλὸν δ' αἰσχρόν

He will persuade you
to consider all that's foul fair,
and fair foul.

Translated by Jeffrey Henderson (1998)

Clouds 1020

58 κλάετ' ὦ 'βολοστάται,
αὐτοί τε καὶ τἀρχαῖα καὶ τόκοι τόκων

Weep, ye moneylenders, weep,
Yourselves, your capital, and your interest's interest!

Translated by Alan H. Sommerstein (1973)

Clouds 1155

59 ἀμφήκει γλώττῃ λάμπων,
πρόβολος ἐμός, σωτὴρ δόμοις, ἐχθροῖς βλάβη,
λυσανίας πατρῴων μεγάλων κακῶν

The brilliant wielder of a two-edged tongue,
My shield and bulwark, saviour of my house,
Bane of my foes, dispeller of my griefs!

Translated by Alan H. Sommerstein (2002)

Clouds 1160

60 ὡς ἡδὺ καινοῖς πράγμασιν καὶ δεξιοῖς ὁμιλεῖν
καὶ τῶν καθεστώτων νόμων ὑπερφρονεῖν δύνασθαι

Well pleased I am to know new, clever things,
and to be ready to look down upon established laws!

Clouds 1399

61 οὐδ' ἂν τρί' εἰπεῖν ῥήμαθ' οἷός τ' ἦν πρὶν ἐξαμαρτεῖν

He couldn't say three words without a howler.

Translated by M.S. Silk (2000)

Clouds 1402

62 ὡς δὶς παῖδες οἱ γέροντες

Old men are children twice.

Clouds 1417

cf. Shakespeare, Hamlet *2.2.[413] 'They say an old man is twice a child'*

63 οὐδέν σε κωλύσει σεαυτὸν ἐμβαλεῖν
εἰς τὸ βάραθρον

There's nothing to hinder you from
throwing yourself down the Pit.

Clouds 1448

the Pit, where criminals were executed: cf. Herodotus 139

64 τῆς σελήνης ἐσκοπεῖσθε τὴν ἕδραν

Arguing about the back side of the moon.

Translated by Alan H. Sommerstein (1973)

Clouds 1507

65 ἡγεῖσθ' ἔξω· κεχόρευται γὰρ
μετρίως τό γε τήμερον ἡμῖν

Lead the dancers on their way:
we've done enough performing for today.

Translated by Jeffrey Henderson (1998)

Clouds 1511

closing lines

66 ὁρῶ γὰρ αὐτὴν προστάταισι χρωμένην
ἀεὶ πονηροῖς. κἄν τις ἡμέραν μίαν
χρηστὸς γένηται, δέκα πονηρὸς γίγνεται

I perceive that the affairs of state are invariably entrusted to crooks and rascals; and if they spend one day doing good they spend another ten doing irreparable harm.

Ecclesiazusae – Assemblywomen 176

67 τὰ δημόσια γὰρ μισθοφοροῦντες χρήματα
ἰδίᾳ σκοπεῖσθ' ἕκαστος ὅ τι τις κερδανεῖ,
τὸ δὲ κοινὸν … κυλίνδεται

While drawing your civic pay from public funds,
each of you angles for a personal profit,
and meanwhile the public finances flounder.

Translated by Jeffrey Henderson (2002)

Ecclesiazusae – Assemblywomen 206

68 καθήμεναι φρύγουσιν ὥσπερ καὶ πρὸ τοῦ …
τοὺς ἄνδρας ἐπιτρίβουσιν ὥσπερ καὶ πρὸ τοῦ·
μοιχοὺς ἔχουσιν ἔνδον ὥσπερ καὶ πρὸ τοῦ·
αὑταῖς παροψωνοῦσιν ὥσπερ καὶ πρὸ τοῦ

The women settle down to their cooking, as they always have;
they drive their husbands nuts, as they always have;
they hide their lovers in the house, as they always have;
they buy themselves extra treats, as they always have.

Translated by Jeffrey Henderson (2002)

Ecclesiazusae – Assemblywomen 221

69 ἡ δ' Ἀθηναίων πόλις,
εἰ τοῦτο χρηστῶς εἶχεν, οὐκ ἂν ἐσῴζετο,
εἰ μή τι καινὸν γ' ἄλλο περιηργάζετο

If the City had some institution that worked well,
do you think *you'd* try to preserve it? You wouldn't rest,
I tell you, till you'd thought up something different.

Translated by David Barrett (1978)

Ecclesiazusae – Assemblywomen 218

70 χρήματα πορίζειν εὐπορώτατον γυνή,
ἄρχουσά τ' οὐκ ἂν ἐξαπατηθείη ποτέ·
αὐταὶ γάρ εἰσιν ἐξαπατᾶν εἰθισμέναι

In raising money, most ingenious is woman,
never to be deceived in office;
for she knows all the tricks already!

Ecclesiazusae – Assemblywomen 236

71 τὸ πρὸς βίαν δεινότατον

Oh, how I hate compulsion!

Ecclesiazusae – Assemblywomen 471

72 λόγος γέ τοί τις ἔστι τῶν γεραιτέρων,
ὅσ' ἂν ἀνόητ' ἢ καὶ μῶρα βουλευσώμεθα,
ἅπαντ' ἐπὶ τὸ βέλτιον ἡμῖν ξυμφέρειν

Well, there *is* an ancestral saying,
that however brainless or foolish our policies,
all affairs will turn out for the best.

Translated by Jeffrey Henderson (2002)

Ecclesiazusae – Assemblywomen 473

73 ὡς τὸ ταχύνειν χαρίτων μετέχει πλεῖστον παρὰ τοῖσι θεαταῖς

It's quick action that pleases the audience.

Translated by Eugene O'Neill, Jr (1938)

Ecclesiazusae – Assemblywomen 582

74 τὴν γῆν πρώτιστα ποιήσω
κοινὴν πάντων καὶ τἀργύριον καὶ τἄλλ' ὁπόσ' ἐστὶν ἑκάστῳ

My first act will be
to communize all the land, money, and other property that's now individually owned.

Translated by Jeffrey Henderson (2002)

Ecclesiazusae – Assemblywomen 597

75 λοπαδοτεμαχοσελαχογαλεοκρανιολειψα
νοδριμυποτριμματοσιλφιολιπαρομελ
ιτοκατακεχυμενοκιχλεπικοσσυφοφαττοπ
εριστεραλεκτρυονοπτοπιφαλλιδοκιγ
κλοπελειολαγῳοσιραιοβαφητραγανοπτ
ερυγών

Shellfish, slice of shark and ray,
skull of blackbird, flesh of dove,
rind of wort and grease and honey,
roasted cock and thrush and dabchick,
crispy pigeon, he-goat gristle,
hare in boiled-down wine.

Ecclesiazusae – Assemblywomen 1169 (practically closing lines)

longest word ever to appear in world literature (Guinness Book of Records, *1981, p.91)*

76 εἴπω τι τῶν εἰωθότων, ὦ δέσποτα,
ἐφ' οἷς ἀεὶ γελῶσιν οἱ θεώμενοι;

Shall I crack any of those old jokes, master,
At which the audience never fail to laugh?

Translated by Benjamin Bickley Rogers (1924)

Frogs 1

opening lines; Frogs *is a comedy satirizing Euripides; the play won first prize at the Lenaea, a Dionysiac festival held in Athens, in 405BC*

77 ὁ δ' εὔκολος μὲν ἐνθάδ', εὔκολος δ' ἐκεῖ

He was contented here, will be contented there.

Frogs 82

of Sophocles, deceased; here, on earth; there, in Hades

78 βρεκεκεκεξ κοαξ κοαξ

Brekekekex, ko-ax, ko-ax

Translated by Benjamin Bickley Rogers (1924)

Frogs 209 and elsewhere

adopted as a Yale College cheer

79 καὶ πολλὰ μὲν γέλοιά μ' εἰπεῖν, πολλὰ δὲ σπουδαῖα

There's much that's funny I can say,
and much that's serious.

Frogs 389

80 ἐξισῶσαι τοὺς πολίτας κἀφελεῖν τὰ δείματα

Make all men equal and extinguish all fears.

Frogs 688

81 πολλάκις γ' ἡμῖν ἔδοξεν ἡ πόλις πεπονθέναι
ταὐτὸν εἴς τε τῶν πολιτῶν τοὺς καλούς τε κἀγαθοὺς
εἴς τε τἀρχαῖον νόμισμα καὶ τὸ καινὸν χρυσίον.
οὔτε γὰρ τούτοισιν οὖσιν οὐ κεκιβδηλευμένοις,
ἀλλὰ καλλίστοις ἁπάντων, ὡς δοκεῖ, νομισμάτων
καὶ μόνοις ὀρθῶς κοπεῖσι καὶ κεκωδωνισμένοις
ἔν τε τοῖς Ἕλλησι καὶ τοῖς βαρβάροισι πανταχοῦ
χρώμεθ' οὐδέν, ἀλλὰ τούτοις τοῖς πονηροῖς χαλκίοις
χθές τε καὶ πρώην κοπεῖσι τῷ κακίστῳ κόμματι

I'll tell you what I think about the way
This city treats her soundest men today:
By a coincidence more sad than funny,
It's very like the way we treat our money.
The noble silver drachma, that of old
We were so proud of, and the recent gold,
Coins that rang a tune, clean-stamped and worth their weight
Throughout the world, have ceased to circulate.
Instead, the purses of Athenian shoppers
Are full of shoddy silver-plated coppers.

Translated by David Barrett (1964)

Frogs 718

the earliest expression of the economic principle known as Gresham's Law – 'bad money drives out good money from circulation' (Henry Dunning Macleod)

82 ἄνθρωπον ἀγριοποιόν, αὐθαδόστομον,
ἔχοντ' ἀχάλινον, ἀκρατές, ἀπύλωτον στόμα,
ἀπεριλάλητον, κομποφακελορρήμονα

A savage-creating, stubborn-pulling fellow,
Uncurbed, unfettered, uncontrolled of speech,
Unperiphrastic, bombastiloquent.

Translated by Benjamin Bickley Rogers (1924)

Frogs 837

of Aeschylus, ridiculing his long compounds

83 λοιδορεῖσθαι δ' οὐ πρέπει
ἄνδρας ποητὰς ὥσπερ ἀρτοπώλιδας

It does not become poets to abuse one another, like old wives selling cakes.

Frogs 857

84 νοεῖν, ὁρᾶν, ξυνιέναι, στρέφειν ἔδραν, τεχνάζειν,
κάχ' ὑποτοπεῖσθαι, περινοεῖν ἅπαντα

To think, to see, to understand, to love to twist, to connive,
to suspect the worst, to question everything.

Frogs 957

what Euripides taught the Athenians

85 σκέψαι γὰρ ἀπ' ἀρχῆς
ὡς ὠφέλιμοι τῶν ποιητῶν οἱ γενναῖοι γεγένηνται

Just consider how, from earliest times,
how beneficial the noble poets have become.

Frogs 1030

Aeschylus speaking

86 ἀνάγκη
μεγάλων γνωμῶν καὶ διανοιῶν ἴσα καὶ τὰ ῥήματα τίκτειν

It is imperative that
great thoughts and minds beget words of equal import.

Frogs 1058

87 εὐθὺς γὰρ ἡμάρτηκεν οὐράνιον ὅσον

You see, he starts off right away with a preposterous blunder – a mistake of cosmic scale.

Frogs 1135

cf. the Latin 'toto caelo errare' (a mistake as high as heaven)

88 ὦ νυκτὸς κελαινοφαὴς ὄρφνα,
τίνα μοι δύστανον ὄνειρον;

O night's gloom, black-lit,
What is this unhappy apparition?

Translated by M.S. Silk (2000)

Frogs 1331

of Euripides, parodying his style

89 μισῶ πολίτην, ὅστις ὠφελεῖν πάτραν
βραδὺς φανεῖται, μεγάλα δὲ βλάπτειν ταχύς,
καὶ πόριμον αὑτῷ, τῇ πόλει δ' ἀμήχανον

I hate the citizen who, slow to help his country,
is swift to harm it, making a profit on the side;
resourceful for himself and useless to the city.

Frogs 1427

90 τίς δ' οἶδεν εἰ τὸ ζῆν μέν ἐστι κατθανεῖν,
τὸ πνεῖν δὲ δειπνεῖν, τὸ δὲ καθεύδειν κῴδιον;

Who knows if living is dying,
and breathing is eating, and sleeping is a wool blanket?

Frogs 1477

the first line is from the lost play Polyidus, *Euripides 492*

91 μακάριός γ' ἀνὴρ ἔχων
ξύνεσιν ἠκριβωμένην

Blessed the man who possesses a sharp mind.

Frogs 1482

92 καὶ σκαριφησμοῖσι λήρων
διατριβὴν ἀργὸν ποιεῖσθαι

They waste our time with quibbles and quarrels.

Translated by David Barrett (1964)

Frogs 1498

93 καὶ παίδευσον
τοὺς ἀνοήτους· πολλοὶ δ' εἰσίν

Educate the fools – you'll find a good many.

Translated by David Barrett (1964)

Frogs 1502

94 ὁρᾷς, ὅταν πίνωσιν ἄνθρωποι, τότε
πλουτοῦσι, διαπράττουσι, νικῶσιν δίκας,
εὐδαιμονοῦσιν, ὠφελοῦσι τοὺς φίλους.
Ἀλλ' ἐξένεγκέ μοι ταχέως οἴνου χοᾶ,
τὸν νοῦν ἵν' ἄρδω καὶ λέγω τι δεξιόν

You see, when men drink wine,
they grow rich, successful, win lawsuits,
are happy and help their friends;
be quick, bring me some wine
to wet my mind and say something clever.

Knights 92

the play won first prize at the Lenaea in 424BC

95 ἡ δημαγωγία γὰρ οὐ πρὸς μουσικοῦ
ἔτ' ἐστὶν ἀνδρὸς οὐδὲ χρηστοῦ τοὺς

τρόπους,
ἀλλ' εἰς ἀμαθῆ καὶ βδελυρόν

A demagogue must be neither an educated nor an honest man; he has to be an ignoramus and a rogue.

Translated by Eugene O'Neill, Jr (1938)

Knights 191

96 τὸν δῆμον ἀεὶ προσποιοῦ
ὑπογλυκαίνων ῥηματίοις μαγειρικοῖς

Always keep the people on your side,
sweetening them with words they like to hear.

Knights 215

97 φωνὴ μιαρά, γέγονας κακῶς, ἀγοραῖος εἶ
ἔχεις ἅπαντα πρὸς πολιτείαν ἃ δεῖ

You have all the characteristics of a popular politician:
a horrible voice, bad breeding, and a vulgar manner.

Translated in *The Oxford Dictionary of Quotations* (2004)

Knights 218

98 ἐρέτην χρῆναι πρῶτα γενέσθαι πρὶν πηδαλίοις ἐπιχειρεῖν
κᾆτ' ἐντεῦθεν πρῳρατεῦσαι καὶ τοὺς ἀνέμους διαθρῆσαι,
κᾆτα κυβερνᾶν αὐτὸν ἑαυτῷ

Before you take the helm, first ply the oar;
Then for'ard stand, and study weather-lore;
Then you may steer.

Translated by Alan H. Sommerstein (1978)

Knights 542

99 ὁ δὲ δῆμος
ὑπὸ τοῦ πολέμου καὶ τῆς ὁμίχλης ἃ πανουργεῖς μὴ καθορᾷ σου

You're using *war* and *mist* to stop the people
Seeing through your crimes.

Translated by M.S. Silk (2000)

Knights 803

100 καί κε γυνὴ φέροι ἄχθος, ἐπεί κεν ἀνὴρ ἀναθείη

A woman would carry a heavy burden only if a man had laid it upon her.

Knights 1056

cf. the Little Ilias (Ilias Parva), *Fragment 2*

101 ἀλλ' εὐπαράγωγος εἶ,
θωπευόμενός τε χαί-
ρεις κἀξαπατώμενος,
πρὸς τόν τε λέγοντ' ἀεὶ
κέχηνας

But you're easily led astray:
you enjoy being flattered
and thoroughly deceived
and every speechmaker
has you gaping.

Translated by Jeffrey Henderson (1998)

Knights 1115

of the people

102 ὁ νοῦς δέ σου
παρὼν ἀποδημεῖ

Your mind, you being here, is elsewhere.

Knights 1119

103 ἀλλ', ὦ μέλ', ὄψει τοι σφόδρ' αὐτὰς Ἀττικάς,
ἅπαντα δρώσας τοῦ δέοντος ὕστερον

Well, my friend, you'll find they're typical Athenians:
everything they do, they do too late.

Translated by Jeffrey Henderson (2000)

Lysistrata 56

first produced in 411BC; the citizens' wives go on a sex strike in order to compel their menfolk to make peace

104 ἦ πόλλ' ἄελπτ' ἔνεστιν ἐν τῷ μακρῷ βίῳ

How upside-down and wrong-way-round
a long life sees things happen.

Translated by Jack Lindsay (1926)

Lysistrata 256

105 ὦ ξύμμαχοι γυναῖκες, ἐκθεῖτ' ἔνδοθεν,
ὦ σπερμαγοραιολεκιθολαχανοπώλιδες,
ὦ σκοροδοπανδοκευτριαρτοπώλιδες,
οὐχ ἕλξετ', οὐ παιήσετ', οὐκ ἀράξετε

Forward, you spawn of the marketplace,
you soup and vegetable mongers!
Forward, you landladies, you hawkers of garlic and bread!
Tackle them! Hit them! Smash them!

Translated by Jeffrey Henderson (2000)

Lysistrata 456

106 κἂν ὑμῖν γ' εἴ τις ἐνῆν νοῦς,
ἐκ τῶν ἐρίων τῶν ἡμετέρων ἐπολιτεύεσθ' ἂν ἅπαντα

If you had any sense in your heads

you would deal with everything the way we spin wool.

Lysistrata 572

107 πλεῖν ἢ τὸ διπλοῦν αὐτοῦ φέρομεν·
πρώτιστον μέν γε τεκοῦσαι
κἀκπέμψασαι παῖδας ὁπλίτας

We have suffered twice over. First we give birth to our sons, and then we send them off to war.

Lysistrata 589

Lysistrata in answer to what women have done for the war effort

108 τῆς δὲ γυναικὸς μικρὸς ὁ καιρός, κἂν τούτου μὴ 'πιλάβηται,
οὐδεὶς ἐθέλει γῆμαι ταύτην, ὀττευομένη δὲ κάθηται

A woman's time of opportunity is short, and if she doesn't seize it,
no one wants to marry her, and she sits watching for omens.

Translated in *Bartlett's Familiar Quotations* (1980)

Lysistrata 596

109 οὐδέν ἐστι θηρίον γυναικὸς ἀμαχώτερον,
οὐδὲ πῦρ, οὐδ' ὧδ' ἀναιδὴς οὐδεμία πόρδαλις

There is no beast more invincible than a woman,
nor fire, or a wildcat so ruthless.

Lysistrata 1014

110 κἄστ' ἐκεῖνο τοὔπος ὀρθῶς κοὐ κακῶς εἰρημένον,
οὔτε σὺν πανωλέθροισιν οὔτ' ἄνευ πανωλέθρων

The saying's true –
We can't live *with* you, we can't live *without* you!

Translated by Alan H. Sommerstein (1973)

Lysistrata 1038

of women

111 δεῖ δὴ νυνί σε γενέσθαι
δεινὴν μαλακήν, ἀγαθὴν φαύλην, σεμνὴν ἀγανήν, πολύπειρον

Show yourself
Fierce and gentle, noble and mean, strict and mellow,
A woman of the world.

Translated by M.S. Silk (2000)

Lysistrata 1108

112 ἐγὼ γυνὴ μέν εἰμι, νοῦς δ' ἔνεστί μοι·
αὐτὴ δ' ἐμαυτῆς οὐ κακῶς γνώμης ἔχω

I am a woman, but I have a mind.
I am not badly off for brains myself.

Translated by M.S. Silk (2000)

Lysistrata 1124

113 ἀλλ' ὑφ' ἡδονῆς
οὐκ ἐμοῦ κινοῦντος αὐτὼ τὼ σκέλει χορεύετον

I'm not moving my legs, but from sheer joy they're dancing on their own.

Translated by Jeffrey Henderson (1998)

Peace 324

the play won second prize at the city Dionysia in 421BC; it celebrates the conclusion of peace with Sparta

114 ἥδομαι γὰρ καὶ γέγηθα καὶ πέπορδα καὶ γελῶ
μᾶλλον ἢ τὸ γῆρας ἐκδὺς ἐκφυγὼν τὴν ἀσπίδα

I feel I'm young again!
I sing, I laugh, I fart,
Rejoicing that at long, long last
My shield and I can part!

Translated by Alan H. Sommerstein (1978)

Peace 335

115 κεἴ τις δορυξὸς ἢ κάπηλος ἀσπίδων,
ἵν' ἐμπολᾷ βέλτιον, ἐπιθυμεῖ μαχῶν

And if any spear-maker or shield-merchant,
intent on protecting his profits, wishes for more battles.

Translated by Alan H. Sommerstein (1978)

Peace 447

116 ὦ πότνια βοτρυόδωρε, τί προσείπω σ' ἔπος;
πόθεν ἂν λάβοιμι ῥῆμα μυριάμφορον
ὅτῳ προσείπω σ';

Ah! venerated goddess, who givest us our grapes,
where can I find a thousand-gallon word
wherewith to greet thee?

Translated by Eugene O'Neill, Jr (1938)

Peace 520

117 τάς τε συκᾶς ἃς ἐγὼ 'φύτευον ὢν νεώτερος
ἀσπάσασθαι θυμὸς ἡμῖν ἐστι πολλοστῷ χρόνῳ

It is my heart's desire, after many a long season, to embrace the fig trees that I planted myself when I was young.

Translated by Jeffrey Henderson (1998)

Peace 558

118 Περικλέης ... ἐξέφλεξε τὴν πόλιν
ἐμβαλὼν σπινθῆρα μικρὸν Μεγαρικοῦ ψηφίσματος·
κἀξεφύσησεν τοσοῦτον πόλεμον ὥστε τῷ καπνῷ
πάντας Ἕλληνας δακρῦσαι

Pericles threw out that little spark, the Megarian decree,
which set the city aflame, and caused a hurricane of war,
so that the smoke had all the Greeks in tears.

Peace 609

a trade embargo against Megara, viewed as a gross provocation by Sparta

119 μοῦσα, σὺ μὲν πολέμους ἀπωσαμένη μετ' ἐμοῦ
τοῦ φίλου χόρευσον

Lady, I pray, cast out war
And, sweetheart, dance with me instead.

Translated by M.S. Silk (2000)

Peace 774

120 μεῖξον δ' ἡμᾶς τοὺς Ἕλληνας πάλιν ἐξ ἀρχῆς
φιλίας χυλῷ καὶ συγγνώμῃ
τινὶ πρᾳοτέρᾳ κέρασον τὸν νοῦν

Mix us all again, all Greeks, from the beginning,
with a flavour of friendship and forbearance,
temper our thoughts with gentleness.

Peace 996

121 πρίν κεν λύκος οἶν ὑμεναιοῖ

Till that a wolf shall mate with a sheep.

Translated by Alan H. Sommerstein (1978)

Peace 1076a

122 οὔποτε ποιήσεις τὸν καρκίνον ὀρθὰ βαδίζειν

You'll never teach a crab to walk straight.

Peace 1083

123 ἆρα φενακίζων ποτ' Ἀθηναίους ἔτι παύσει;

Will you ever stop bamboozling the people of Athens?

Translated by Jeffrey Henderson (1998)

Peace 1087

124 χἄμα τὴν Θρᾷτταν κυνῶν
τῆς γυναικὸς λουμένης

Kissing the Thracian maid
while the wife's in the bath.

Translated by Jeffrey Henderson (1998)

Peace 1138

125 οὐ γὰρ ἔσθ' ἥδιον ἢ τυχεῖν μὲν ἤδη 'σπαρμένα,
τὸν θεὸν δ' ἐπιψακάζειν, καί τιν' εἰπεῖν γείτονα·
εἰπέ μοι, τί τηνικαῦτα δρῶμεν

Nothing's more delightful than having the seed in the ground,
the god pattering it with rain, and a neighbour saying,
'How shall we pass our time?'

Translated by Jeffrey Henderson (1998)

Peace 1140

126 οἴκοι μὲν λέοντες,
ἐν μάχῃ δ' ἀλώπεκες

Lions at home,
but foxes in battle.

Translated by H.T. Riley (1872)

Peace 1189

127 κρεῖττον γάρ, ὦ τᾶν, ἐστιν ἢ μηδὲν λαβεῖν

Something is better than nothing, my friend.

Peace 1220

128 ὦ Ζεῦ, χελιδὼν ἆρά ποτε φανήσεται;

Ah Zeus, will the spring swallow ever show up?

Translated by Jeffrey Henderson (2000)

Thesmophoriazusae – Women at the Thesmophoria 1

opening lines

129 χρὴ γὰρ ποιητὴν ἄνδρα πρὸς τὰ δράματα
ἃ δεῖ ποεῖν, πρὸς ταῦτα τοὺς τρόπους ἔχειν

A dramatist must tailor his life-style
To the dramatic task in hand.

Translated by M.S. Silk (2000)

Thesmophoriazusae – Women at the Thesmophoria 149

130 τὰς συμφορὰς γὰρ οὐχὶ τοῖς τεχνάσμασιν
φέρειν δίκαιον, ἀλλὰ τοῖς παθήμασιν

Calamities are not meant to be wriggled out of,
they have to be endured.

Translated by David Barrett (1964)

Thesmophoriazusae – Women at the Thesmophoria 198

131 τί γὰρ οὗτος ἡμᾶς οὐκ ἐπισμῇ τῶν κακῶν;
ποῦ δ' οὐχὶ διαβέβληχ', ὅπουπερ ἔμβραχύ
εἰσιν θεαταὶ καὶ τραγῳδοὶ καὶ χοροί,
τὰς μοιχοτρόπους, τὰς ἀνδρεραστρίας καλῶν,
τὰς οἰνοπότιδας, τὰς προδότιδας, τὰς λάλους,
τὰς οὐδὲν ὑγιές, τὰς μέγ' ἀνδράσιν κακόν;

Can you think of any evil
that he has left unsaid? Give him some actors,
a chorus, an audience, and there he goes
proving that women are good-for-nothing, incarnate
wine-jugs, walking sinks of lust, deceivers,
babblers, fly-by-nights, knives in the flesh of honest men.

Translated by Dudley Fitts (1954)

Thesmophoriazusae – Women at the Thesmophoria 389

of Euripides

132 ὑπὸ λίθῳ γὰρ παντί που χρὴ
μὴ δάκῃ ῥήτωρ ἀθρεῖν

Under every stone lurks a politician.

Translated in *The Oxford Dictionary of Quotations* (2004)

Thesmophoriazusae – Women at the Thesmophoria 529

cf. Proverbial 143

133 ἀλλ' οὐ γάρ ἐστι τῶν ἀναισχύντων φύσει γυναικῶν
οὐδὲν κάκιον εἰς ἅπαντα πλὴν ἄρ' εἰ γυναῖκες

There is but one thing in the world worse than a shameless woman, and that's another woman.

Translated by Eugene O'Neill, Jr (1938)

Thesmophoriazusae – Women at the Thesmophoria 531

134 ἀνὴρ ἔοικεν οὐ προδώσειν, ἀλλά μοι
σημεῖον ὑπεδήλωσε Περσεὺς ἐκδραμών,
ὅτι δεῖ με γίγνεσθ' Ἀνδρομέδαν

It seems the man won't give up on me:
He just showed up as Perseus! – it was a sign
For me to become Andromeda.

Thesmophoriazusae – Women at the Thesmophoria 1011

Euripides shows up as Perseus, signalling to the other fellow to be his Andromeda

135 σκαιοῖσι γάρ τοι καινὰ προσφέρων σοφὰ
μάτην ἀναλίσκοις ἄν

Serve wisdom to fools
and you have laboured in vain.

Thesmophoriazusae – Women at the Thesmophoria 1130

136 ἀνόνητον ἄρ' ὦ θυ-
λάκιόν σ' εἶχον ἄγαλμα

Ah shopping bag, it seems you've been
a useless ornament to carry!

Translated by Jeffrey Henderson (1998)

Wasps 314

the play won second prize at the Lenaea in 422BC

137 καὶ παππίζουσ' ἅμα τῇ γλώττῃ τὸ τριώβολον ἐκκαλαμᾶται

And all the while it's 'Daddy, this' and 'Daddy, that',
Her tongue's fishing the coppers out of me.

Translated by M.S. Silk (2000)

Wasps 609

138 ἐρήμας ᾤεθ' οὕτω ῥᾳδίως τρυγήσειν

He thought he'd be picking unwatched vines.

Translated by Jeffrey Henderson (1998)

Wasps 634

later proverbial, of one who is bold where there is nothing to fear

139 ἦ που σοφὸς ἦν ὅστις ἔφασκεν· πρὶν ἂν ἀμφοῖν μῦθον ἀκούσῃς,
οὐκ ἂν δικάσαις

There was a wise man who said: Do not judge anyone before hearing both sides.

Wasps 725

quoting Hesiod 79, probably proverbial by now; cf. Euripides, Children of Heracles *179*

140 τὸ πρᾶγμα φανερόν ἐστιν· αὐτὸ γὰρ βοᾷ

The matter speaks for itself; it howls for itself.

Wasps 921

a dog on trial

141 οὐ γὰρ ἄν ποτε
τρέφειν δύναιτ' ἂν μία λόχμη κλέπτα δύο

One thicket cannot hide two thieves.

Wasps 927

parody of the proverb 'one bush cannot hold two robins'; cf. Proverbial 123

142 τοῦτο δ' ἔστ' ἄλγιστον ἡμῖν, ἥν τις ἀστράτευτος ὢν
ἐκροφῇ τὸν μισθὸν ἡμῶν, τῆσδε τῆς χώρας ὕπερ
μήτε κώπην μήτε λόγχην μήτε φλύκταιναν λαβών

This is what grieves us, that a man who never fought
Should contrive our fees to pilfer, one who for his native land
Never to this day had oar, or lance, or blister on his hand.

Translated by Benjamin Bickley Rogers (1897)

Wasps 1117

143 ἔρδοι τις ἣν ἕκαστος εἰδείη τέχνην

Let each man exercise the skills he knows.

Translated by Benjamin Bickley Rogers (1924)

Wasps 1431

144 οἷ μετέστη
ξηρῶν τρόπων καὶ βιοτῆς.
ἕτερα δὲ νῦν ἀντιμαθὼν
... ἐπὶ τὸ τρυφῶν καὶ μαλακόν

What a turn-around
from his arid habits and lifestyle!
to a life of delicate luxury.

Translated by Jeffrey Henderson (1998)

Wasps 1450

145 πῖθ' ἐλλέβορον

You are mad, go fill yourself with hellebore.

Wasps 1489

Helleborus orientalis, *a plant thought to relieve mental disorders; but also a purgative, cf. Ariston of Chios 5; surely Aristophanes plays on this*

146 ὡς ἀργαλέον πρᾶγμ' ἐστίν, ὦ Ζεῦ καὶ θεοί,
δοῦλον γενέσθαι παραφρονοῦντος δεσπότου

Zeus and you other gods, how hard it is
To be the slave of a demented master.

Translated by M.S. Silk (2000)

Wealth 1

opening lines; first produced in 388BC

147 οἱ γὰρ βλέποντες τοῖς τυφλοῖς ἡγούμεθα

It is for us who see to guide those who don't.

Wealth 15

148 δῆλον ὁτιὴ καὶ τυφλῷ

Even a *blind* man can see that.

Translated by Alan H. Sommerstein (1978)

Wealth 48

149 τέχναι δὲ πᾶσαι διὰ σὲ καὶ σοφίσματα
ἐν τοῖσιν ἀνθρώποισίν ἐσθ' ηὑρημένα

All crafts, all inventions,
originate from you, Wealth.

Wealth 160

of Plutus, as a personification of wealth

150 νὴ τὸν Δί', ἀλλὰ καὶ λέγουσι πάντες ὡς
δειλότατόν ἐσθ' ὁ πλοῦτος

But, by Zeus, everybody says that
wealth equals wretchedness.

Wealth 202

151 ἔστιν δέ μοι τοῦτ' αὐτὸ θαυμάσιον, ὅπως
χρηστόν τι πράττων τοὺς φίλους μεταπέμπεται

I am amazed that anyone who has made a fortune should send for his friends.

Translated in *Bartlett's Familiar Quotations* (1980)

Wealth 340

152 εἰ γὰρ ὁ Πλοῦτος βλέψειε πάλιν διανείμειέν τ' ἴσον αὑτόν,
οὔτε τέχνην ἂν τῶν ἀνθρώπων οὔτ' ἂν σοφίαν μελετῴη
οὐδείς

Let Plutus recover his sight and divide his favours out equally to all, and none will ply either trade or art any longer; all toil would be done away with.

Translated by Eugene O'Neill, Jr (1938)

Wealth 510

Plutus, or Wealth, is usually described as a young boy; as a blind old man only in Aristophanes

153 οὐ γὰρ πείσεις, οὐδ' ἢν πείσῃς

Even if you persuade me, you won't persuade me.

Translated in *Bartlett's Familiar Quotations* (1980)

Wealth 600

154 κἀγὼ μὲν ᾤμην οὓς τέως
εὐεργέτησα δεομένους ἕξειν φίλους
ὄντως βεβαίους, εἰ δεηθείην ποτέ·
οἱ δ' ἐξετρέποντο κοὐκ ἐδόκουν ὁρᾶν μ' ἔτι

I thought I could count, in case of need, upon the friends whom I had helped, but they turned their backs on me and pretended not to see me.

Wealth 834

155 – σύ; τί μαθών;
– βούλομαι

– You! What did you do to qualify for it?
– I just *wanted* the job.

Wealth 906

of qualifications for a public position

156 ἐκεῖνο δ' οὐ βούλοι' ἄν, ἡσυχίαν ἔχων ζῆν ἀργός;
ἀλλὰ προβατίου βίον λέγεις,
εἰ μὴ φανεῖται διατριβή τις τῷ βίῳ

– Would you not prefer to live quietly and free from all care and anxiety?
– To do nothing is to live a sheep's life.

Wealth 921

157 πατρὶς γάρ ἐστι πᾶσ' ἵν' ἂν πράττῃ τις εὖ

A man's homeland is wherever he prospers.

Translated in *Bartlett's Familiar Quotations* (1980)

Wealth 1151

cf. the Latin 'ubi bene, ibi patria'

158 ἐλαφρὸν οἷά τις μόλυβδος

As nimbly as a lump of lead.

Translated by Jeffrey Henderson (2007)

Fragment 63.93 (Austin, *CGFPR*) – 591.93 (K-A)

159 ὦ Ζεῦ, τὸ χρῆμα τῆς νεολαίας ὡς καλόν

O Zeus, how wonderful is this thing called youth!

Fragment 67 (Kock) – 73 (K-A) – *Babylonians*

160 Εἰρήνη βαθύπλουτε καὶ ζευγάριον βοεικόν,
εἰ γὰρ ἐμοὶ παυσαμένῳ τοῦ πολέμου γένοιτο
σκάψαι τ' ἀποκλάσαι τε καὶ λουσαμένῳ διελκύσαι
τῆς τρυγός, ἄρτον λιπαρὸν καὶ ῥάφανον φαγόντι

Oh Peace, so rich in wealth,
And oh, my team of oxen,
Would it were my lot to rest from war,
And dig my garden,
Prune my vines,
And take my bath,
And live the simple life,
Dining on bread and wine and radishes!

Translated by Kathleen Freeman (1947)

Fragment 109 (Kock) – 111 (K-A) – *Georgoi – The Farmers*

cf. Shakespeare, Henry IV Part I, *3.1.[160]: 'I had rather live with cheese and garlic in a windmill'*

161 περὶ τοῦ γὰρ ὑμῖν ὁ πόλεμος
νῦν ἐστι; περὶ ὄνου σκιᾶς

War, for the sake of what?
The shadow of a donkey.

Fragment 192 (Kock) – 199 (K-A) – *Daedalus*

cf. Demosthenes 95; Aristophanes, Wasps *191*

162 ἢν γὰρ ἕν' ἄνδρ' ἄδικον σὺ διώκῃς, ἀντιμαρτυροῦσι
δώδεκα τοῖς ἑτέροις ἐπισίτιοι

If you prosecute one wrongdoer, twelve of his hangers-on, equally bad, will bring a countersuit.

Translated by Jeffrey Henderson (2007)

Fragment 437 (Kock) – 452 (K-A) – *Pelargoi – Storks*

163 ἐπὶ πῦρ δὲ πῦρ ἔοιχ' ἥκειν ἄγων

It seems I'm adding fuel to the fire.

Fragment 453 (Kock) – 469 (K-A) – *Polyidus*

almost certainly an allusion to Euripides 451

164 (A.) ἆρ' οὐ μέγιστον ἀγαθόν, εἴπερ ἔστι δι' ἐνιαυτοῦ
ὅτου τις ἐπιθυμεῖ λαβεῖν;
(B.) κακὸν μὲν οὖν μέγιστον·
εἰ μὴ γὰρ ἦν, οὐκ ἂν ἐπεθύμουν οὐδ' ἂν ἐδαπανῶντο

– Well, isn't it fine indeed if, at any time of the year,
you can get what your heart desires?
– In fact there's nothing worse;
if you can't get it, you'd not want it, and you'd save money.

Fragment 569 (Kock) – 581.8 (K-A) – *Horai – Seasons*

of buying whatever fruit and vegetables you like all year round

165 αἰσχρὸν νέᾳ γυναικὶ πρεσβύτης ἀνήρ

An old man to a young wife suits but ill.

Translated by Philip Schaff (1819–1893)

Fragment 600 (Kock) – 616 (K-A)

166 γαλῆν καταπέπωκεν

He swallowed a cat.

Translated by Jeffrey Henderson (2007)

Fragment 664 (Kock) – 732 (K-A)

of a tongue-tied man; cf. the English phrase 'the cat got your tongue?' and the nursery rhyme 'now fancy that, to swallow a cat!'

167 δύναται γὰρ ἴσον τῷ δρᾶν τὸ νοεῖν

The intellect has as much force as action.

Fragment 691 (Kock) – 711 (K-A)

168 ἄγροικός εἰμι· τὴν σκάφην σκάφην λέγω

Blunt as I am, I call a wash-tub a wash-tub.

Fragment 901b (Kock) – 927f (K-A)

169 οὐ παντὸς ἀνδρὸς ἐς Κόρινθον ἔσθ' ὁ πλοῦς

It is not every man's lot to sail to Corinth.

Fragment 902 (Kock) – 928 (K-A)

because of the high cost of living in Corinth – also the high fees of prostitutes; quoted in Greek by Aulus Gellius, Attic Nights *1.8.4; cf. Demosthenes 102*

ARISTOPHANES OF BYZANTIUM

probably *c.*257–180BC
Head of the Alexandrian library *c.*194BC, scholar of wide learning

1 ἄκουε τοῦ τὰ τέσσαρα ὦτα ἔχοντος

Listen to him who has four ears.

Translated by H.T. Riley (1872)

Proverbs, Fragment 7 (Nauck)

ARISTOPHON

4th century BC
Comic poet

1 σαφὴς ὁ χειμών ἐστι τῆς πενίας λύχνος·
ἅπαντα φαίνει τὰ κακὰ καὶ τὰ δυσχερῆ

Clearly does winter spotlight poverty,
with all its woes and miseries.

Fragment 1 (Kock) – 1 (K-A) – *Babias*

ARISTOTLE

384–322BC
Philosopher from Stagira, founder of the Lyceum in Athens
see also Alexander the Great 5

1 τήν τε φιλαργυρίαν τήν θ' ὑπερηφανίαν

Both love of money and o'erweening pride.

Translated by H. Rackham (1935)

Athenian Constitution 5.3

quoted by Aristotle from an elegy by Solon, implying that this was the cause of the enmity that prevailed in Athens before Solon was invited to rule; cf. Plutarch, Solon *14.3*

2 ὃς ἂν στασιαζούσης τῆς πόλεως μὴ θῆται τὰ ὅπλα μηδὲ μεθ' ἑτέρων ἄτιμον εἶναι καὶ τῆς πόλεως μὴ μετέχειν

When civil strife prevailed, whoever did not join forces with either party was disenfranchised and could not participate in matters of state.

Athenian Constitution 8.5

of a law enacted by Solon

3 οἷον περὶ τοῦ δοῦναι τὰ ἑαυτοῦ ᾧ ἂν ἐθέλῃ κύριον ποιήσαντες καθάπαξ, τὰς δὲ προσούσας δυσκολίας, ἐὰν μὴ μανιῶν ἢ γήρως ἕνεκα ἢ γυναικὶ πιθόμενος, ἀφεῖλον ὅπως μὴ ᾖ τοῖς συκοφάνταις ἔφοδος

In order to make a testator free to leave his property as he pleased, they abolished existing limitations as to insanity, age or a woman's influence, leaving no opening for blackmailers.

Athenian Constitution 35.2

4 νόμος γάρ ἐστιν ὃς κελεύει τοὺς ἐντὸς τριῶν μνῶν κεκτημένους καὶ τὸ σῶμα πεπηρωμένους ὥστε μὴ δύνασθαι μηδὲν ἔργον ἐργάζεσθαι δοκιμάζειν μὲν τὴν βουλήν, διδόναι δὲ δημοσίᾳ τροφὴν δύο

ὀβολοὺς ἑκάστῳ τῆς ἡμέρας

Persons unable to work because of physical incapacity and possessing less than three minae, the law says, are granted two obols a day at public expense after inspection by the Council.

Athenian Constitution 49.4

5 ὅπως τῶν κοπρολόγων μηδεὶς ἐντὸς δέκα σταδίων τοῦ τείχους καταβαλεῖ κόπρον ἐπιμελοῦνται

They see to it that no waste-collector deposits refuse within two kilometres of the city wall.

Athenian Constitution 50.2

of the City Inspectors; ten stadia is approx. 2000 yards

6 τὰς ὁδοὺς κωλύουσι κατοικοδομεῖν καὶ δρυφάκτους ὑπὲρ τῶν ὁδῶν ὑπερτείνειν

They prevent the construction of buildings encroaching on roads or of balconies overhanging roads.

Translated by H. Rackham (1935)

Athenian Constitution 50.2

of the City Inspectors; all public officials were elected by lot

7 ἀγορανόμοι ... τούτοις δὲ ὑπὸ τῶν νόμων προστέτακται τῶν ὠνίων ἐπιμελεῖσθαι πάντων, ὅπως καθαρὰ καὶ ἀκίβδηλα πωλῆται

Market-controllers are assigned by law to inspect all merchandise in order to prevent the sale of adulterated and spurious articles.

Athenian Constitution 51.1

8 μετρονόμοι ... τῶν μέτρων καὶ τῶν σταθμῶν ἐπιμελοῦνται πάντων, ὅπως οἱ πωλοῦντες χρήσωνται δικαίοις

Controllers of Measures inspect all weights and measures so that the ones merchants use are just.

Athenian Constitution 51.2

9 ὁδοποιοὺς ... οἷς προστέτακται δημοσίους ἐργάτας ἔχουσι τὰς ὁδοὺς ἐπισκευάζειν

Road maintenance is carried out by road surveyors using public workmen.

Athenian Constitution 54.1

of the Highway-Constructors (elected by lot)

10 κἂν μέν τινα κλέπτοντ' ἐξελέγξωσι, κλοπὴν οἱ δικασταὶ καταγιγνώσκουσι, καὶ τὸ γνωσθὲν ἀποτίνεται δεκαπλοῦν

If an official is found (by the Auditors) to have embezzled public funds, the Jury convict him of fraud and the fine is ten times the amount of which he is found guilty.

Translated by H. Rackham (1935)

Athenian Constitution 54.2

11 ἐὰν δέ τινα δῶρα λαβόντα ἐπιδείξωσιν καὶ καταγνῶσιν οἱ δικασταί, δώρων τιμῶσιν, ἀποτίνεται δὲ καὶ τοῦτο δεκαπλοῦν

And if they show that a man has taken bribes and the Jury convict, they assess the value of the bribes and in this case also the fine is ten times the amount.

Translated by H. Rackham (1935)

Athenian Constitution 54.2

of the Auditors

12 ἂν δ' ἀδικεῖν καταγνῶσιν, ἀδικίου τιμῶσιν, ἀποτίνεται δὲ τοῦθ' ἁπλοῦν

If a man is found guilty of maladministration, they assess the damage, and the fine paid is that amount only.

Translated by H. Rackham (1935)

Athenian Constitution 54.2

of the Auditors

13 ὁ μὲν ἄρχων ... ἐπιμελεῖται δὲ καὶ τῶν ὀρφανῶν καὶ τῶν ἐπικλήρων, καὶ τῶν γυναικῶν ὅσαι ἂν τελευτήσαντος τοῦ ἀνδρὸς σκήπτωνται κύειν, καὶ κύριός ἐστι τοῖς ἀδικοῦσιν ἐπιβάλλειν ἢ εἰσάγειν εἰς τὸ δικαστήριον

The Archon also supervises orphans and heiresses and women professing to be with child after the husband's death; he has absolute power to fine offenders, or to bring them before the court.

Translated by H. Rackham (1935)

Athenian Constitution 56.7

14 ἡ γὰρ εὐδαιμονία κάλλιστον καὶ ἄριστον ἁπάντων οὖσα ἥδιστόν ἐστιν

Happiness is at once the pleasantest and the fairest and best of all things whatever.

Translated by H. Rackham (1935)

Eudemian Ethics 1214a.7

in disagreement with Theognis 21

15 σκεπτέον ἐν τίνι τὸ εὖ ζῆν καὶ πῶς κτητόν, πότερον φύσει γίγνονται πάντες εὐδαίμονες ... ὥσπερ μεγάλοι καὶ μικροὶ καὶ τὴν χροιὰν διαφέροντες, ἢ διὰ μαθήσεως, ὡς οὔσης ἐπιστήμης τινὸς τῆς εὐδαιμονίας, ἢ διά τινος ἀσκήσεως

We must consider what the good life consists of and how it is to be obtained – whether it is happiness by nature, as in being tall or short or different in complexion, whether by study, which would imply that there is a science of happiness, or whether by training of some form.

Eudemian Ethics 1214a.15

16 οἱ μὲν γὰρ τὴν φρόνησιν μέγιστον εἶναί φασιν ἀγαθόν, οἱ δὲ τὴν ἀρετήν, οἱ δὲ τὴν ἡδονήν

Some people say that wisdom is the greatest good, others excellence, and others pleasure.

Eudemian Ethics 1214a.32

17 τρεῖς ὁρῶμεν καὶ βίους ὄντας, οὓς οἱ ἐξουσίας τυγχάνοντες προαιροῦνται ζῆν ἅπαντες, πολιτικὸν φιλόσοφον ἀπολαυστικόν

There are three ways of life which all those choose who come to be in power: politics, philosophy, or a life devoted to enjoyment.

Eudemian Ethics 1215a.35

18 ὁ μὲν φιλόσοφος βούλεται περὶ φρόνησιν εἶναι καὶ τὴν θεωρίαν τὴν περὶ τὴν ἀλήθειαν, ὁ δὲ πολιτικὸς περὶ τὰς πράξεις τὰς καλάς ... ὁ δ' ἀπολαυστικὸς περὶ τὰς ἡδονὰς τὰς σωματικάς

The philosopher is concerned with the contemplation of truth, the politician with honourable activities and the man of pleasure with sensual enjoyment.

Eudemian Ethics 1215b.1

19 ὁ μὲν γὰρ πολιτικὸς τῶν καλῶν ἐστὶ πράξεων προαιρετικὸς αὐτῶν χάριν, οἱ δὲ πολλοὶ χρημάτων καὶ πλεονεξίας ἕνεκεν ἅπτονται τοῦ ζῆν οὕτως

The 'political' man is one who chooses noble acts for their own sake, while most take up the 'political' life for the sake of money and greed.

Translated by J. Solomon, rev. Jonathan Barnes (1984)

Eudemian Ethics 1216a.25

20 περὶ ἀρετῆς οὐ τὸ εἰδέναι τιμιώτατον τί ἐστιν, ἀλλὰ τὸ γινώσκειν ἐκ τίνων ἐστίν

What is most valuable regarding excellence is not just to know what it is, but to ascertain out of what it arises.

Eudemian Ethics 1216b.20

21 οὐ γὰρ εἰδέναι βουλόμεθα τί ἐστιν ἀνδρεία, ἀλλ' εἶναι ἀνδρεῖοι, οὐδέ τί ἐστι δικαιοσύνη, ἀλλ' εἶναι δίκαιοι

Our aim is not to know what courage is but to be courageous, not to know what justice is but to be just.

Translated by H. Rackham (1935)

Eudemian Ethics 1216b.22

22 φρόνησις γὰρ καὶ ἀρετὴ καὶ ἡδονὴ ἐν ψυχῇ, ὧν ἢ ἔνια ἢ πάντα τέλος εἶναι δοκεῖ πᾶσιν

Wisdom, excellence, and pleasure are in the soul, and some or all of these seem to all to be the end.

Translated by J. Solomon, rev. Jonathan Barnes (1984)

Eudemian Ethics 1218b.34

23 τῶν δὲ ἐν ψυχῇ τὰ μὲν ἕξεις ἢ δυνάμεις εἰσί, τὰ δ' ἐνέργειαι καὶ κινήσεις

Of the contents of the soul some are acquired habits or elementary faculties, others activities and processes.

Eudemian Ethics 1218b.35

24 περὶ ἀρετῆς, ὅτι ἐστὶν ἡ βελτίστη διάθεσις ἢ ἕξις ἢ δύναμις ἑκάστων ὅσων ἐστί τις χρῆσις ἢ ἔργον

Excellence is the best state or condition or faculty of all things that have some use or work.

Translated by J. Solomon, rev. Jonathan Barnes (1984)

Eudemian Ethics 1218b.37

ἀρετή can also be translated as 'virtue' or 'goodness'

25 ἕτερον εὐδαιμονισμὸς καὶ ἔπαινος καὶ ἐγκώμιον· τὸ μὲν γὰρ ἐγκώμιον λόγος τοῦ καθ' ἕκαστον ἔργου, ὁ δ' ἔπαινος τοῦ τοιοῦτον εἶναι καθόλου, ὁ δ' εὐδαιμονισμὸς τέλους

Felicitation, praise and panegyric are different things: panegyric is a recital of a particular exploit, praise a statement of a man's general distinction, felicitation is bestowed on an end achieved.

Translated by H. Rackham (1935)

Eudemian Ethics 1219b.14

26 οὐθὲν βελτίους οἱ σπουδαῖοι τῶν φαύλων τὸν ἥμισυν τοῦ βίου, ὅμοιοι γὰρ καθεύδοντες πάντες

For half their lives the good are no better than the bad, for all are alike when asleep.

Translated by J. Solomon, rev. Jonathan Barnes (1984)

Eudemian Ethics 1219b.17

27 ἀρετῆς δ' εἴδη δύο, ἡ μὲν ἠθικὴ ἡ δὲ διανοητική· ἐπαινοῦμεν γὰρ οὐ μόνον τοὺς δικαίους ἀλλὰ καὶ τοὺς συνετοὺς καὶ τοὺς σοφούς

Goodness has two forms, moral virtue and intellectual excellence; for we praise not only the just but also the intelligent and the wise.

Translated by H. Rackham (1935)

Eudemian Ethics 1220a.5

28 πᾶν τὸ κατ' ἐπιθυμίαν ἑκούσιον ... τὸ γὰρ ἀκούσιον πᾶν δοκεῖ εἶναι βίαιον, τὸ δὲ βίαιον λυπηρόν

Everything that conforms with desire is voluntary; for everything involuntary seems to be forced, and what is forced is painful.

Translated by H. Rackham (1935)

Eudemian Ethics 1223a.28

29 ἡ ἐγκράτεια ἀρετή, ἡ δ' ἀρετὴ δικαιοτέρους ποιεῖ· ἐγκρατεύεται δ' ὅταν πράττῃ παρὰ τὴν ἐπιθυμίαν κατὰ τὸν λογισμόν

Self-control is goodness, and goodness makes men more righteous. A man exercises self-control when he acts against his desire in conformity with rational calculation.

Translated by H. Rackham (1935)

Eudemian Ethics 1223b.12

30 πειθὼ τῇ βίᾳ καὶ ἀνάγκῃ ἀντιτίθεται, ὁ δ' ἐγκρατὴς ἐφ' ἃ πέπεισται ἄγεται, καὶ πορεύεται οὐ βίᾳ, ἀλλ' ἑκών

Persuasion is the opposite of force and necessity; and the self-controlled proceed as persuaded, not under force but voluntarily.

Eudemian Ethics 1224a.39

31 τὸν ἔρωτα πολλοὶ ἀκούσιον τιθέασιν, καὶ θυμοὺς ἐνίους καὶ τὰ φυσικά, ὅτι ἰσχυρὰ καὶ ὑπὲρ τὴν φύσιν

Many reckon even love as involuntary, and some forms of anger, and natural impulses, because their power is even beyond nature.

Translated by H. Rackham (1935)

Eudemian Ethics 1225a.20

32 ἔτι διὰ τὸ μὴ ῥᾴδιον εἶναι ἰδεῖν τὴν προαίρεσιν ὁποία τις, διὰ ταῦτα ἐκ τῶν ἔργων ἀναγκαζόμεθα κρίνειν ὁποῖός τις

It is not easy to see the quality of a man's purpose; we are thus forced to judge his character from his actions.

Translated by H. Rackham (1935)

Eudemian Ethics 1228a.15

33 ὁ μὲν οὖν δειλὸς καὶ ἃ μὴ δεῖ φοβεῖται

A coward fears even things he ought not to fear.

Translated by H. Rackham (1935)

Eudemian Ethics 1229a.4

34 ἔστι δ' εἴδη ἀνδρείας πέντε ... μία μὲν πολιτική· αὕτη δ' ἐστὶν ἡ δι' αἰδῶ οὖσα· δευτέρα ἡ στρατιωτική· αὕτη δὲ δι' ἐμπειρίαν καὶ τὸ εἰδέναι ... τρίτη δ' ἡ δι' ἀπειρίαν καὶ ἄγνοιαν ... ἄλλη δ' ἡ κατ' ἐλπίδα ... ἄλλη δὲ διὰ πάθος ἀλόγιστον, οἷον δι' ἔρωτα καὶ θυμόν

Five are the types of courage: a. civic courage, due to a sense of shame; b. military courage, due to experience and knowledge; c. courage due to inexperience and ignorance; d. courage caused by hope; e. courage due to an irrational emotion, for example love or passion.

Translated by H. Rackham (1935)

Eudemian Ethics 1229a.13

35 ἀήττητον ὁ θυμός

Unconquerable is passion.

Eudemian Ethics 1229a.28

36 μᾶλλον ἂν φροντίσειεν ... τί δοκεῖ ἑνὶ σπουδαίῳ ἢ πολλοῖς τοῖς τυγχάνουσιν

Consider more the views of one virtuous man than that of the many.

Eudemian Ethics 1232b.6

37 ἔστι δ' ἐναντιώτερον τοῖς ἄκροις τὸ μέσον ἢ ἐκεῖνα ἀλλήλοις, διότι τὸ μὲν μετ' οὐδετέρου γίνεται αὐτῶν, τὰ δὲ πολλάκις μετ' ἀλλήλων

The mean is more opposed to the extremes than the extremes to one another, because the mean is found with neither; but the extremes often with one another.

Translated by J. Solomon, rev. Jonathan Barnes (1984)

Eudemian Ethics 1234b.1

38 τῆς τε γὰρ πολιτικῆς ἔργον εἶναι δοκεῖ μάλιστα ποιῆσαι φιλίαν

To promote friendship is the special task of the art of politics.

Eudemian Ethics 1234b.22

39 τῶν μεγίστων ἀγαθῶν τὸν φίλον εἶναι ὑπολαμβάνομεν, τὴν δὲ ἀφιλίαν καὶ τὴν ἐρημίαν δεινότατον

We consider a friend to be one of the greatest goods, and friendlessness and solitude a very terrible thing.

Translated by H. Rackham (1935)

Eudemian Ethics 1234b.32

40 οὐκ ἔστι δ' ἄνευ πίστεως φιλία βέβαιος, ἡ δὲ πίστις οὐκ ἄνευ χρόνου

There is no stable friendship without confidence, and confidence only comes with time.

Translated by H. Rackham (1935)

Eudemian Ethics 1237b.12

41 ἡ δ' ἀτυχία δηλοῖ τοὺς μὴ ὄντως ὄντας φίλους

Misfortune shows those who are not really friends.

Translated by J. Solomon, rev. Jonathan Barnes (1984)

Eudemian Ethics 1238a.19

42 τοὺς ἐμμένοντας τῷ φιλεῖν πρὸς τοὺς τεθνεῶτας ἐπαινοῦμεν· γινώσκουσι γάρ, ἀλλ' οὐ γινώσκονται

We praise those who remain constant in affection towards the dead; for they know, but are not known.

Translated by H. Rackham (1935)

Eudemian Ethics 1239b.1

43 ἐνίοτε ἀνομοίοις χαίρουσιν, οἷον αὐστηροὶ εὐτραπέλοις καὶ ὀξεῖς ῥᾳθύμοις· εἰς τὸ μέσον γὰρ καθίστανται ὑπ' ἀλλήλων

Some delight in what is unlike themselves, the austere in the witty, the energetic in the lazy; for they reduce each other to the mean state.

Translated by J. Solomon, rev. Jonathan Barnes (1984)

Eudemian Ethics 1240a.2

44 ἕκαστος αὐτὸς αὑτῷ φίλος εἶναι

Every man is his own best friend.

Translated by H. Rackham (1935)

Eudemian Ethics 1240a.10

45 δοκεῖ φίλος εἶναι ὁ βουλόμενός τινι τἀγαθά, ἢ οἷα οἴεται ἀγαθά, μὴ δι' αὑτὸν ἀλλ' ἐκείνου ἕνεκα

A friend is one who wishes the best, or what he considers best, not for himself but for the other's sake.

Eudemian Ethics 1240a.24

46 τὸ χαίρειν μὴ δι' ἕτερόν τι, ἀλλὰ δι' ἐκεῖνον, ὅτι χαίρει, φιλικόν

It is characteristic of a friend to rejoice for no other reason than because the other is rejoicing.

Translated by H. Rackham (1935)

Eudemian Ethics 1240a.39

47 αἱ δὲ πολιτεῖαι πᾶσαι ἐν ταῖς οἰκείαις συνυπάρχουσι ... βασιλικὴ μὲν ἡ τοῦ γεννήσαντος, ἀριστοκρατικὴ δ' ἡ ἀνδρὸς καὶ γυναικός, πολιτεία δ' ἡ τῶν ἀδελφῶν

All forms of constitution exist together in the household; paternal authority is royal, the relationship of man and wife aristocratic, that of brothers a republic.

Translated by H. Rackham (1935)

Eudemian Ethics 1241b.27

48 ὁ γὰρ ἄνθρωπος οὐ μόνον πολιτικὸν ἀλλὰ καὶ οἰκονομικὸν ζῷον

Man is not only a political but also a house-holding animal.

Translated by H. Rackham (1935)

Eudemian Ethics 1242a.22

cf. Aristotle 191

49 ἐν οἰκίᾳ πρῶτον ἀρχαὶ καὶ πηγαὶ φιλίας καὶ πολιτείας καὶ δικαίου

In the household are first found the origins of friendship, of political organizations and of justice.

Translated by H. Rackham (1935)

Eudemian Ethics 1242a.40

50 ὁ θεὸς ἀνέχεται κατὰ δύναμιν λαμβάνων τὰς θυσίας

God is content to receive sacrifices according to our ability.

Eudemian Ethics 1243b.12

51 οὐ χρήσεως ἕνεκα ὁ φίλος οὐδ' ὠφελείας, ἀλλὰ ὁ δι' ἀρετὴν φίλος μόνος

A friend is not for the sake of usefulness or benefit; the real friend is loved on account of goodness.

Translated by H. Rackham (1935)

Eudemian Ethics 1244b.15

52 οὐθεὶς φίλος ᾧ πολλοὶ φίλοι

One who has many friends has no friend.

Translated by H. Rackham (1935)

Eudemian Ethics 1245b.21

cf. Dr. Johnson: 'οἱ φίλοι, οὐ φίλος-- he had friends but no friend' (Boswell, The Life of Samuel Johnson, *Everyman Paperback, ch. 'AD 1779', vol. 2, p.274); Jacques Derrida,* Politiques de l'amitié *(1994); et al.*

53 μικραὶ μεταστάσεις μεγάλων αἰτίαι γίγνονται

Small changes are the causes of great ones.

Translated by Arthur Platt (1860–1925), rev. Jonathan Barnes (1984)

Generation of Animals 788a.11

54 ἔχει δ' ἀκριβεστάτην ἄνθρωπος τῶν αἰσθήσεων τὴν ἁφήν, δευτέραν δὲ τὴν γεῦσιν· ἐν δὲ ταῖς ἄλλαις λείπεται πολλῶν

Of man's senses, touch is the most accurate; taste is second; in the others, man is surpassed by a great number of animals.

Translated by d'Arcy Wentworth Thompson (1860–1948), rev. Jonathan Barnes (1984)

History of Animals 494b.16

55 τοῦτο δὲ τὸ σημεῖον πηδᾷ καὶ κινεῖται ὥσπερ ἔμψυχον

This point beats and moves as though endowed with life.

Translated by d'Arcy Wentworth Thompson (1860–1948), rev. Jonathan Barnes (1984)

History of Animals 561a.12

of a speck of blood in a three-day-old bird's egg; cf. the Latin 'punctum saliens' (the salient point)

56 ἐν τούτοις γὰρ τῶν μὲν ὕστερον ἕξεων ἐσομένων ἔστιν ἰδεῖν οἷον ἴχνη καὶ σπέρματα

In children may be observed the traces and seeds of what will one day be settled habits.

Translated by d'Arcy Wentworth Thompson (1860–1948), rev. Jonathan Barnes (1984)

History of Animals 588a.32

57 μεταβαίνει κατὰ μικρὸν ἡ φύσις

Nature proceeds little by little.

Translated by d'Arcy Wentworth Thompson (1860–1948), rev. Jonathan Barnes (1984)

History of Animals 588b.4

cf. the Latin 'natura non facit saltus' (nature makes no jumps)

58 ὁ αἰγοθήλας ... θηλάζει δὲ τὰς αἶγας προσπετόμενος, ὅθεν καὶ τοὔνομ' εἴληφεν

The goat-sucker ... flies up to the she-goat and sucks its milk, from which habit it derives its name.

Translated by d'Arcy Wentworth Thompson (1860–1948), rev. Jonathan Barnes (1984)

History of Animals 618b.11

of the nightjar: even Aristotle made mistakes – and they die hard; this error survived into our days, the scientific name still is Caprimulgus europaeus; *Liddell & Scott also refer to this bird as goatsucker – though it does no such thing*

59 τὰ δὲ δυνάμεις, οἷον ἀρχὴ πλοῦτος ἰσχὺς κάλλος· τούτοις γὰρ καὶ ὁ σπουδαῖος εὖ ἂν δύνηται χρήσασθαι καὶ ὁ φαῦλος κακῶς

These are the powers: authority, wealth, strength, beauty; and these can be used well by the worthy, badly by the base.

Magna Moralia 1183b.28

60 οὗ πλεῖστος νοῦς καὶ λόγος, ἐνταῦθα ἐλαχίστη καὶ τύχη, οὗ δὲ πλείστη τύχη, ἐνταῦθ' ἐλάχιστος νοῦς

Where mind and reason prevail little is left to chance; where chance prevails little is left to reason.

Magna Moralia 1207a.5

61 πάντες ἄνθρωποι τοῦ εἰδέναι ὀρέγονται φύσει

By nature, all mankind yearns for knowledge.

Metaphysics 980a.21

opening lines

62 γίγνεται δ' ἐκ τῆς μνήμης ἐμπειρία τοῖς ἀνθρώποις αἱ γὰρ πολλαὶ μνῆμαι τοῦ αὐτοῦ πράγματος μιᾶς ἐμπειρίας δύναμιν ἀποτελοῦσιν

It is from memory that men acquire experience, because the numerous memories of the same thing eventually produce the effect of a single experience.

Translated by Hugh Tredennick (1933)

Metaphysics 980b.28

63 ἀποβαίνει δ' ἐπιστήμη καὶ τέχνη διὰ τῆς ἐμπειρίας τοῖς ἀνθρώποις

Science and skill are the result of experience.

Metaphysics 981a.3

64 ὀρθῶς δ' ἔχει καὶ τὸ καλεῖσθαι τὴν φιλοσοφίαν ἐπιστήμην τῆς ἀληθείας

Philosophy is rightly called the science of truth.

Metaphysics 993b.19

65 οὐκ ἴσμεν δὲ τὸ ἀληθὲς ἄνευ τῆς αἰτίας

We cannot know the truth without knowing its cause.

Metaphysics 993b.23

66 πάντων γὰρ ὅσα πλείω μέρη ἔχει ... τὸ πᾶν ἔστι τι τὸ ὅλον παρὰ τὰ μόρια

In all things which have a plurality of parts the whole is something beyond the sum of its parts.

Metaphysics 1045a.8

more commonly rendered 'the whole is greater than the sum of its parts'

67 αἱ μεταβολαὶ τέτταρες, ἢ κατὰ τὸ τί ἢ κατὰ τὸ ποιὸν ἢ ποσὸν ἢ πού, καὶ γένεσις μὲν ἡ ἁπλῆ καὶ φθορὰ ἡ κατὰ τὸ τόδε, αὔξησις δὲ καὶ φθίσις ἡ κατὰ τὸ ποσόν, ἀλλοίωσις δὲ ἡ κατὰ τὸ πάθος, φορὰ δὲ ἡ κατὰ τόπον

Change is of four kinds: of substance, quality, quantity, or place; change of substance is generation or destruction, change of quantity is increase or decrease, change of affection is alteration, change of place is motion.

Metaphysics 1069b.9

68 τὸ οὗ ἕνεκα ... κινεῖ δὲ ὡς ἐρώμενον

The final cause then, produces motion as being an object of love.

Metaphysics 1072b.3

cf. the Latin 'movet autem ut amatum'; Lucian 23

69 ἡ γὰρ νοῦ ἐνέργεια ζωή

The actuality of thought is life.

Translated by Hugh Tredennick (1935)

Metaphysics 1072b.27

70 ζωὴ καὶ αἰὼν συνεχὴς καὶ ἀΐδιος ὑπάρχει τῷ θεῷ· τοῦτο γὰρ ὁ θεός

Life and continuous eternal existence belong to god; for that is what god is.

Translated by Hugh Tredennick (1935)

Metaphysics 1072b.29

71 ὅτι μὲν οὖν ἔστιν οὐσία τις ἀΐδιος καὶ ἀκίνητος καὶ κεχωρισμένη τῶν αἰσθητῶν, φανερὸν

Thus it is evident that there is some substance which is eternal and immovable and separate from sensible things.

Translated by Hugh Tredennick (1935)

Metaphysics 1073a.3

72 καὶ τὸ πρῶτον κινοῦν ἀκίνητον εἶναι καθ' αὑτό, καὶ τὴν ἀΐδιον κίνησιν ὑπὸ ἀϊδίου κινεῖσθαι

The first mover must be in itself unmovable, and eternal movement must be produced by something eternal.

Translated by W.D. Ross (1877–1971), rev. Jonathan Barnes (1984)

Metaphysics 1073a.26

cf. St Thomas Aquinas, Summa Theologica *(c.1256) 1.2.3: 'ergo necesse est devenire ad aliquod primum movens, quod a nullo movetur; et hoc omnes intelligunt Deum' (therefore it is necessary to arrive at a first mover, put in motion by no other; and this everyone understands to be God, tr. Fathers of the English Dominican Province); cf. Aristotle 182*

73 ἓν ἄρα ... τὸ πρῶτον κινοῦν ἀκίνητον ὄν· καὶ τὸ κινούμενον ἄρα ἀεὶ καὶ συνεχῶς· εἷς ἄρα οὐρανὸς μόνος

Thus the unmovable first mover is one; therefore also, that which is moved always and continuously is one alone; therefore there is one heaven alone.

Translated by W.D. Ross (1877–1971), rev. Jonathan Barnes (1984)

Metaphysics 1074a.36

74 ὅτι θεοί τέ εἰσιν ... μυθικῶς ἤδη προσῆκται πρὸς τὴν πειθὼ τῶν πολλῶν καὶ πρὸς τὴν εἰς τοὺς νόμους καὶ τὸ συμφέρον χρῆσιν

The myth that there are other gods has been added later in order to prevail upon the multitude, and as a legal and utilitarian expedient.

Metaphysics 1074b.2

75 ἡ νόησις αὑτὸν ἄρα νοεῖ, εἴπερ ἐστὶ τὸ κράτιστον, καὶ ἔστιν ἡ νόησις νοήσεως νόησις

Thought, then, supreme of all things, must be itself that thinks, and its thinking is a thinking on thinking.

Metaphysics 1074b.33

76 καὶ ὁ ἥλιος οὐ μόνον καθάπερ Ἡράκλειτός φησιν, νέος ἐφ' ἡμέρῃ ἐστίν, ἀλλ' ἀεὶ νέος συνεχῶς

The sun is not, as Heraclitus says, new every day, it renews itself incessantly.

Meteorology 355a.13

cf. Heraclitus, Fragment 6 (D-K)

77 πᾶσα τέχνη καὶ πᾶσα μέθοδος, ὁμοίως δὲ πρᾶξίς τε καὶ προαίρεσις, ἀγαθοῦ τινὸς ἐφίεσθαι δοκεῖ· διὸ καλῶς ἀπεφήναντο τἀγαθόν οὗ πάντ' ἐφίεται

Every science and every investigation, and similarly every action and resolve, seems to aim at some good; hence the Good has been rightly defined as 'that at which all things aim'.

Nicomachean Ethics 1094a.1

opening lines

78 τοιαύτη δ' ἡ πολιτική ... τὸ ταύτης τέλος ... ὥστε τοῦτ' ἂν εἴη τἀνθρώπινον ἀγαθόν

The good of man must be the objective of politics.

Translated in *The Oxford Dictionary of Political Quotations* (1996)

Nicomachean Ethics 1094b.6

79 τὸ τέλος ἐστὶν οὐ γνῶσις ἀλλὰ πρᾶξις

The end aimed at is not knowledge but action.

Translated by W.D. Ross (1925)

Nicomachean Ethics 1095a.5

80 διαφέρει δ' οὐδὲν νέος τὴν ἡλικίαν ἢ τὸ ἦθος νεαρός, οὐ γὰρ παρὰ τὸν χρόνον ἡ ἔλλειψις, ἀλλὰ διὰ τὸ κατὰ πάθος ζῆν καὶ διώκειν ἕκαστα

It makes no difference whether they are young in years or immature in character; the defect is not a question of time, it is because their life and its aims are guided by sentiment.

Translated by H. Rackham (1926)

Nicomachean Ethics 1095a.6

of the young, whom Aristotle believed unfit to be students of political science

81 λέγομεν τὴν πολιτικὴν ἐφίεσθαι ... εὐδαιμονίαν ... τὸ δ' εὖ ζῆν καὶ τὸ εὖ πράττειν ταὐτὸν ... τῷ εὐδαιμονεῖν

We consider the aim of politics to be happiness, which means living well and doing well in life.

Nicomachean Ethics 1095a.15

82 περὶ δὲ τῆς εὐδαιμονίας ... πολλάκις δὲ καὶ ὁ αὐτὸς ἕτερον· νοσήσας μὲν γὰρ ὑγίειαν, πενόμενος δὲ πλοῦτον

Concerning happiness, often even the same man identifies it with different things, with health when he is ill, with wealth when he is poor.

Translated by W.D. Ross (1925)

Nicomachean Ethics 1095a.20

83 ὁ πλοῦτος δῆλον ὅτι οὐ τὸ ζητούμενον ἀγαθόν· χρήσιμον γὰρ καὶ ἄλλου χάριν

Wealth is evidently not the good we are seeking; for it is merely useful for something else.

Translated by W.D. Ross (1925)

Nicomachean Ethics 1096a.6

84 ἀμφοῖν γὰρ ὄντοιν φίλοιν ὅσιον προτιμᾶν τὴν ἀλήθειαν

While both are dear, piety requires us to honour truth above our friends.

Translated by W.D. Ross (1925)

Nicomachean Ethics 1096a.16

an allusion to Plato has much later been inferred here, giving rise to the popular misquotation: 'Plato is dear to me, but dearer still is truth'; cf. the Latin 'amicus Plato sed magis amica veritas', quoted e.g. in Cervantes, Don Quixote, *pt. 2, ch. 51*

85 τὸ γὰρ τέλειον ἀγαθὸν αὔταρκες εἶναι δοκεῖ

The final good must be a thing sufficient in itself.

Translated by H. Rackham (1926)

Nicomachean Ethics 1097b.7

86 μία γὰρ χελιδὼν ἔαρ οὐ ποιεῖ, οὐδὲ μία ἡμέρα· οὕτω δὲ οὐδὲ μακάριον καὶ εὐδαίμονα μία ἡμέρα οὐδ' ὀλίγος χρόνος

One swallow does not make spring, nor does one fine day; and similarly one day or a brief period of happiness does not make a man supremely blessed and happy.

Translated by H. Rackham (1926)

Nicomachean Ethics 1098a.18

by now proverbial, cf. Proverbial 21

87 δοκεῖ γὰρ πλεῖον ἢ ἥμισυ παντὸς εἶναι ἡ ἀρχή

The beginning seems to be more than half of the whole.

Translated by H. Rackham (1926)

Nicomachean Ethics 1098b.7

referring to principles and definitions; a play on the word 'αρχη', used for both 'beginning' and 'first principles'

88 πάσας οἰόμεθα τὰς τύχας εὐσχημόνως φέρειν

Bear all kinds of fortune in a seemly way.

Translated by H. Rackham (1926)

Nicomachean Ethics 1101a.1

89 ἡ μὲν διανοητικὴ τὸ πλεῖον ἐκ διδασκαλίας ἔχει καὶ τὴν γένεσιν καὶ τὴν αὔξησιν

Intellectual virtue is for the most part both produced and increased by instruction.

Translated by H. Rackham (1926)

Nicomachean Ethics 1103a.15

90 οὐδεμία τῶν ἠθικῶν ἀρετῶν φύσει ἡμῖν ἐγγίνεται· οὐθὲν γὰρ τῶν φύσει ὄντων ἄλλως ἐθίζεται

None of the moral virtues is engendered in us by nature, for no natural property can be altered by habit.

Translated by H. Rackham (1926)

Nicomachean Ethics 1103a.19

91 ἃ γὰρ δεῖ μαθόντας ποιεῖν, ταῦτα ποιοῦντες μανθάνομεν

What we have to learn to do we learn by the actual doing of it.

Translated by J.A.K. Thomson (1953)

Nicomachean Ethics 1103a.32

cf. the expression 'learning by doing'

92 οἱ γὰρ νομοθέται τοὺς πολίτας ἐθίζοντες ποιοῦσιν ἀγαθούς, καὶ τὸ μὲν βούλημα παντὸς νομοθέτου τοῦτ' ἐστίν ... καὶ διαφέρει τούτῳ πολιτεία πολιτείας ἀγαθὴ φαύλης

Lawgivers make the citizens good by training them in habits of right action; this is the aim of all legislation, and it is what distinguishes a good form of government from a bad one.

Translated by H. Rackham (1926)

Nicomachean Ethics 1103b.3

93 ἡ δ' ἀρετὴ πάσης τέχνης ἀκριβεστέρα καὶ ἀμείνων ἐστὶν, ὥσπερ καὶ ἡ φύσις, τοῦ μέσου ἂν εἴη στοχαστική

If virtue, like nature, is more accurate and better than any art, it follows that virtue has the quality of hitting the mean.

Translated by H. Rackham (1926)

Nicomachean Ethics 1106b.14

94 ἔτι τὸ μὲν ἁμαρτάνειν πολλαχῶς ἔστιν ... τὸ δὲ κατορθοῦν μοναχῶς (διὸ καὶ τὸ μὲν ῥᾴδιον τὸ δὲ χαλεπόν, ῥᾴδιον μὲν τὸ ἀποτυχεῖν τοῦ σκοποῦ, χαλεπὸν δὲ τὸ ἐπιτυχεῖν)

To fail is possible in many ways, to succeed only in one; which is why the one is easy and the other difficult, why it is easy to miss the target and difficult to hit it.

Nicomachean Ethics 1106b.28

95 ἐσθλοὶ μὲν γὰρ ἁπλῶς, παντοδαπῶς δὲ κακοί

For men are bad in countless ways, but good in only one.

Translated by J.A.K. Thomson (1953)

Nicomachean Ethics 1106b.35

quoting a verse from an unknown source; cf. Anonymous 29

96 ἔστιν ἄρα ἡ ἀρετὴ ἕξις προαιρετική, ἐν μεσότητι οὖσα τῇ πρὸς ἡμᾶς, ὡρισμένῃ

λόγῳ καὶ ὡς ἂν ὁ φρόνιμος ὁρίσειεν

Virtue, then, is a state of character concerned with choice, lying at the mean of two extremes determined by a rational principle which a prudent man would use.

Nicomachean Ethics 1106b.36

97 κατὰ τὸν δεύτερον … πλοῦν τὰ ἐλάχιστα ληπτέον τῶν κακῶν

As a second-best course take the least of two evils.

Nicomachean Ethics 1109a.35

cf. the English proverb 'of two evils choose the less'

98 ἐν τούτοις γὰρ καὶ ἔλεος καὶ συγγνώμη· ὁ γὰρ τούτων τι ἀγνοῶν ἀκουσίως πράττει

Pity and forgiveness may apply, if an act is committed in ignorance.

Nicomachean Ethics 1111a.1

99 ἄνθρωπος εἶναι ἀρχὴ τῶν πράξεων

Man is the origin of his actions.

Translated by H. Rackham (1926)

Nicomachean Ethics 1112b.31

100 εἰ δὲ ἀεὶ βουλεύσεται, εἰς ἄπειρον ἥξει

If we are to always deliberate we shall go on forever.

Nicomachean Ethics 1113a.2

101 ἐφ' ἡμῖν δὴ καὶ ἡ ἀρετή, ὁμοίως δὲ καὶ ἡ κακία

Virtue lies in our power, and so does vice.

Nicomachean Ethics 1113b.6

102 τὸ δὲ λέγειν ὡς οὐδεὶς ἑκὼν πονηρὸς οὐδ' ἄκων μακάρ ἔοικε τὸ μὲν ψευδεῖ τὸ δ' ἀληθεῖ· μακάριος μὲν γὰρ οὐδεὶς ἄκων, ἡ δὲ μοχθηρία ἑκούσιον

The saying that 'no one is voluntarily wicked nor involuntarily blessed' seems to be partly false and partly true; for no one is involuntarily blessed, but wickedness *is* voluntary.

Translated by W.D. Ross (1877–1971), rev. J.O. Urmson, ed. Jonathan Barnes (1984)

Nicomachean Ethics 1113b.14

cf. Anonymous 131

103 τὸ γὰρ θαρρεῖν εὐέλπιδος

Confidence is the mark of optimism.

Translated by J.A.K. Thomson (1953)

Nicomachean Ethics 1116a.3

104 τὸ δ' ἀποθνήσκειν φεύγοντα πενίαν ἢ ἔρωτα ἤ τι λυπηρὸν οὐκ ἀνδρείου, ἀλλὰ μᾶλλον δειλοῦ· μαλακία γὰρ τὸ φεύγειν τὰ ἐπίπονα, καὶ οὐχ ὅτι καλὸν ὑπομένει, ἀλλὰ φεύγων κακόν

To die to escape from poverty or love or anything painful is not the mark of a brave man, but rather a coward; for it is softness to fly from what is troublesome, and such a man endures death not because it is noble but to fly from evil.

Translated by W.D. Ross (1925)

Nicomachean Ethics 1116a.12

of suicide

105 ὁ γὰρ ἐν τοῖς φοβεροῖς ἀτάραχος … ἀνδρεῖος

Truly brave is he who is unperturbed in the presence of danger.

Nicomachean Ethics 1117a.30

106 καὶ ἐπιθυμεῖ ὁ σώφρων ὧν δεῖ καὶ ὡς δεῖ καὶ ὅτε

Temperance is to desire only what you need, as you need it and when you need it.

Nicomachean Ethics 1119b.16

107 τῆς ἀρετῆς γὰρ ἆθλον ἡ τιμή, καὶ ἀπονέμεται τοῖς ἀγαθοῖς

Honour is the prize of virtue, and the tribute we pay to the good.

Translated by H. Rackham (1926)

Nicomachean Ethics 1123b.35

108 διὰ τοῦτο χαλεπὸν τῇ ἀληθείᾳ μεγαλόψυχον εἶναι· οὐ γὰρ οἷόν τε ἄνευ καλοκαγαθίας

It is hard to be truly great-souled, for greatness of soul is impossible without moral nobility.

Translated by H. Rackham (1926)

Nicomachean Ethics 1124a.3

an echo of Simonides 22

109 ὁ μὲν οὖν ἐφ' οἷς δεῖ καὶ οἷς δεῖ ὀργιζόμενος, ἔτι δὲ καὶ ὡς δεῖ καὶ ὅτε καὶ ὅσον χρόνον, ἐπαινεῖται

A man is praised when he is angry at the

right things and with the right people, in the right way, at the right time and for the right length of time.

Nicomachean Ethics 1125b.31

110 οὐ γὰρ τιμωρητικὸς ὁ πρᾶος, ἀλλὰ μᾶλλον συγγνωμονικός

The good-tempered man is not revengeful, but rather tends to forgive.

Translated by W.D. Ross (1925), rev. J.O. Urmson, ed. Jonathan Barnes (1984)

Nicomachean Ethics 1126a.2

111 οὐ γὰρ ῥᾴδιον διορίσαι τὸ πῶς καὶ τίσι καὶ ἐπὶ ποίοις καὶ πόσον χρόνον ὀργιστέον, καὶ τὸ μέχρι τίνος ὀρθῶς ποιεῖ τις ἢ ἁμαρτάνει

It is not easy to define how, with whom, at what, and how long one should be angry, and at what point right action ceases and wrong begins.

Translated by W.D. Ross (1925)

Nicomachean Ethics 1126a.32

112 ἐκ τῶν κωμῳδιῶν τῶν παλαιῶν καὶ τῶν καινῶν, τοῖς μὲν γὰρ ἦν γελοῖον ἡ αἰσχρολογία, τοῖς δὲ μᾶλλον ἡ ὑπόνοια· διαφέρει δ' οὐ μικρὸν ταῦτα πρὸς εὐσχημοσύνην

Comparing earlier comedy with new it is to be noted that earlier dramatists found their fun in obscenity, the moderns prefer innuendo; this marks a great advance where decency is concerned.

Nicomachean Ethics 1128a.22

comparing Old and New Comedy

113 δοκεῖ δὲ ἡ ἀνάπαυσις καὶ ἡ παιδιὰ ἐν τῷ βίῳ εἶναι ἀναγκαῖον

Relaxation and amusement seem to be a necessary element in life.

Translated by H. Rackham (1926)

Nicomachean Ethics 1128b.3

114 τὸ μὲν δίκαιον ἄρα τὸ νόμιμον καὶ τὸ ἴσον, τὸ δ' ἄδικον τὸ παράνομον καὶ τὸ ἄνισον

The just, then, is the lawful and the fair, the unjust the unlawful and the unfair.

Translated by W.D. Ross (1925)

Nicomachean Ethics 1129a.34

115 ἀλλ' ἐντεῦθεν αἱ μάχαι καὶ τὰ ἐγκλήματα, ὅταν ἢ ἴσοι μὴ ἴσα ἢ μὴ ἴσοι ἴσα ἔχωσι καὶ νέμωνται

This is the origin of quarrels and complaints: when either equals have or are awarded unequal shares, or unequals equal shares.

Translated by W.D. Ross (1925)

Nicomachean Ethics 1131a.22

116 ἐν μὲν ταῖς κοινωνίαις ταῖς ἀλλακτικαῖς συνέχει τὸ τοιοῦτον δίκαιον, τὸ ἀντιπεπονθὸς κατ' ἀναλογίαν καὶ μὴ κατ' ἰσότητα. τῷ ἀντιποιεῖν γὰρ ἀνάλογον συμμένει ἡ πόλις

In societies where citizens can freely exchange their wares, these exchanges are based not on equality, but on proportionate reciprocity; the very existence of the state depends on this.

Nicomachean Ethics 1132b.31

117 οἷον δ' ὑπάλλαγμα τῆς χρείας τὸ νόμισμα γέγονε κατὰ συνθήκην· καὶ διὰ τοῦτο τοὔνομα ἔχει νόμισμα, ὅτι οὐ φύσει ἀλλὰ νόμῳ ἐστί, καὶ ἐφ' ἡμῖν μεταβαλεῖν καὶ ποιῆσαι ἄχρηστον

Demand has come to be conventionally represented by money; this is why money is called nomisma (legal currency), because it does not exist by nature but by law (nomos), and can be altered and rendered useless at will.

Nicomachean Ethics 1133a.28

118 τὸ νόμισμα οἷον ἐγγυητής ἐσθ' ἡμῖν· δεῖ γὰρ τοῦτο φέροντι εἶναι λαβεῖν. πάσχει μὲν οὖν καὶ τοῦτο τὸ αὐτό, οὐ γὰρ ἀεὶ ἴσον δύναται· ὅμως δὲ βούλεται μένειν μᾶλλον. διὸ δεῖ πάντα τετιμῆσθαι· οὕτω γὰρ ἀεὶ ἔσται ἀλλαγή, εἰ δὲ τοῦτο, κοινωνία

Money acts as a guarantee to the bearer, to be used as needed. Its shortcoming is that its value is not always stable; but it is steadier than others. Set prices are therefore in order, to always assure exchange and, through exchange, sharing.

Nicomachean Ethics 1133b.11

119 οὐκ ἐῶμεν ἄρχειν ἄνθρωπον, ἀλλὰ τὸν νόμον, ὅτι ἑαυτῷ τοῦτο ποιεῖ, καὶ γίνεται τύραννος

We do not permit one man to rule, but the law, because a man rules in his own interest, and becomes a tyrant.

Translated by H. Rackham (1926)

Nicomachean Ethics 1134a.35

120 δοκεῖ δ' ἐνίοις εἶναι πάντα τοιαῦτα, ὅτι τὸ μὲν φύσει ἀκίνητον καὶ πανταχοῦ τὴν αὐτὴν ἔχει δύναμιν, ὥσπερ τὸ πῦρ καὶ ἐνθάδε καὶ ἐν Πέρσαις καίει, τὰ δὲ δίκαια κινούμενα ὁρῶσιν

Some people think that all rules of justice are merely conventional, because whereas a law of nature is immutable and has the same validity everywhere, as fires burn both here and in Persia, rules of justice are seen to vary.

Translated by H. Rackham (1926)

Nicomachean Ethics 1134b.24

121 τὸ ἐπιεικὲς δίκαιον μέν ἐστιν, οὐ τὸ κατὰ νόμον δέ, ἀλλ' ἐπανόρθωμα νομίμου δικαίου

Equity is just, but not what is legally just: it is a rectification of legal justice.

Translated by J.A.K. Thomson (1953)

Nicomachean Ethics 1137b.11

122 δοκεῖ δὴ φρονίμου εἶναι τὸ δύνασθαι καλῶς βουλεύσασθαι περὶ τὰ αὑτῷ ἀγαθὰ καὶ συμφέροντα ... πρὸς τὸ εὖ ζῆν

It is the mark of a prudent man to be able to deliberate well about what is good and advantageous for himself as a means to a good life.

Translated by H. Rackham (1926)

Nicomachean Ethics 1140a.26

123 καὶ δοκεῖ ὁ τὸ περὶ αὑτὸν εἰδὼς καὶ διατρίβων φρόνιμος εἶναι, οἱ δὲ πολιτικοὶ πολυπράγμονες

People think that the man who knows and minds his own business is prudent, and that all politicians are busybodies.

Translated by H. Rackham (1926)

Nicomachean Ethics 1142a.1

cf. Euripides 511

124 διότι γεωμετρικοὶ μὲν νέοι καὶ μαθηματικοὶ γίνονται καὶ σοφοὶ τὰ τοιαῦτα, φρόνιμος δ' οὐ δοκεῖ γίνεσθαι

Although the young develop ability in geometry and mathematics and become wise in such matters, they are not thought to develop prudence.

Translated by J.A.K. Thomson (1953)

Nicomachean Ethics 1142a.12

125 νέος δ' ἔμπειρος οὐκ ἔστιν· πλῆθος γὰρ χρόνου ποιεῖ τὴν ἐμπειρίαν

Youth has no experience; for it is length of years that gives experience.

Translated by H.T. Riley (1872)

Nicomachean Ethics 1142a.15

126 καὶ γὰρ τῶν πρώτων ὅρων καὶ τῶν ἐσχάτων νοῦς ἐστὶ καὶ οὐ λόγος ... διὸ καὶ φυσικὰ δοκεῖ εἶναι ταῦτα, καὶ φύσει σοφὸς μὲν οὐδείς, γνώμην δ' ἔχειν καὶ σύνεσιν καὶ νοῦν ... καὶ ἀρχὴ καὶ τέλος νοῦς

Ultimates as well as primary definitions are grasped by intelligence and not reached by reasoning. This is why it is thought that these qualities are a natural gift, and that a man is considerate, understanding and intelligent by nature, though no one is wise by nature. Intelligence is both a beginning and an end.

Translated by H. Rackham (1926)

Nicomachean Ethics 1143a.36

127 ὥστε δεῖ προσέχειν τῶν ἐμπείρων καὶ πρεσβυτέρων ἢ φρονίμων ταῖς ἀναποδείκτοις φάσεσι καὶ δόξαις οὐχ ἧττον τῶν ἀποδείξεων· διὰ γὰρ τὸ ἔχειν ἐκ τῆς ἐμπειρίας ὄμμα ὁρῶσιν ὀρθῶς

Pay no less attention to the unproved assertions and opinions of experienced and older people than to demonstrations of fact; because they have an insight from their experience which enables them to see correctly.

Translated by J.A.K. Thomson (1953)

Nicomachean Ethics 1143b.11

128 διαστρέφει γὰρ ἡ μοχθηρία καὶ διαψεύδεσθαι ποιεῖ περὶ τὰς πρακτικὰς ἀρχάς

Wickedness distorts the vision and causes serious error about the principles of conduct.

Translated by J.A.K. Thomson (1953)

Nicomachean Ethics 1144a.34

129 πᾶσι γὰρ δοκεῖ ἕκαστα τῶν ἠθῶν ὑπάρχειν φύσει πως· καὶ γὰρ δίκαιοι καὶ σωφρονικοὶ καὶ ἀνδρεῖοι καὶ τἄλλα ἔχομεν εὐθὺς ἐκ γενετῆς

It is universally believed that the various kinds of character are in some sense the gifts of nature – because if we have a disposition towards justice or temperance or courage or the other virtues we have it from the moment of birth.

Translated by J.A.K. Thomson (1953)

Nicomachean Ethics 1144b.4

130 τῶν περὶ τὰ ἤθη φευκτῶν τρία ἐστὶν εἴδη, κακία ἀκρασία θηριότης

Of moral states to be avoided there are three kinds: vice, incontinence, brutishness.

Translated by W.D. Ross (1925)

Nicomachean Ethics 1145a.16

cf. Dante, Inferno *(1300), Canto 11.79: 'Have you forgotten how your* Ethics *reads … / the three conditions that the heavens hate,/malice, incontinence and bestiality? (tr. Mark Musa)*

131 πάντα γὰρ φύσει ἔχει τι θεῖον

Nature has implanted in all things something of the divine.

Translated by H. Rackham (1926)

Nicomachean Ethics 1153b.32

132 ἄνευ γὰρ φίλων οὐδεὶς ἕλοιτ' ἂν ζῆν, ἔχων τὰ λοιπὰ ἀγαθὰ πάντα

Without friends no one would choose to live, though he had all other goods.

Translated by W.D. Ross (1925)

Nicomachean Ethics 1155a.5

133 τελεία δ' ἐστὶν ἡ τῶν ἀγαθῶν φιλία καὶ κατ' ἀρετὴν ὁμοίων

Perfect friendship is the friendship of men who are good, and alike in virtue.

Translated by W.D. Ross (1925)

Nicomachean Ethics 1156b.7

134 βούλησις μὲν γὰρ ταχεῖα φιλίας γίνεται, φιλία δ' οὔ

A wish for a friendship may arise quickly, but friendship does not.

Translated by W.D. Ross (1925)

Nicomachean Ethics 1156b.31

135 οἱ δὲ διὰ τὸ χρήσιμον ὄντες φίλοι ἅμα τῷ συμφέροντι διαλύονται

A friendship based on utility dissolves as soon as its profit ceases.

Translated by H. Rackham (1926)

Nicomachean Ethics 1157a.14

136 μόνη δὲ ἡ τῶν ἀγαθῶν φιλία ἀδιάβλητός ἐστιν

Only friendship between good men is proof against slander.

Nicomachean Ethics 1157a.20

137 μάλιστα γὰρ ἡ φύσις φαίνεται τὸ μὲν λυπηρὸν φεύγειν, ἐφίεσθαι δὲ τοῦ ἡδέος

It seems to be one of the strangest instincts of nature to shun what is painful and seek what is pleasant.

Translated by H. Rackham (1926)

Nicomachean Ethics 1157b.16

138 ἐν δὲ τοῖς στρυφνοῖς καὶ πρεσβυτικοῖς ἧττον γίνεται ἡ φιλία, ὅσῳ δυσκολώτεροί εἰσι καὶ ἧττον ταῖς ὁμιλίαις χαίρουσιν

Morose and elderly people rarely make friends, as they are inclined to be surly and do not take much pleasure in society.

Translated by H. Rackham (1926)

Nicomachean Ethics 1158a.1

139 εἰς ὀλιγαρχίαν … νέμουσι τὰ τῆς πόλεως παρὰ τὴν ἀξίαν, καὶ πάντα ἢ τὰ πλεῖστα τῶν ἀγαθῶν … περὶ πλείστου ποιούμενοι τὸ πλουτεῖν· ὀλίγοι δὴ ἄρχουσι καὶ μοχθηροὶ ἀντὶ τῶν ἐπιεικεστάτων

In oligarchy rulers distribute the resources of the state without regard to merit, keeping all benefits for themselves, bent on acquiring wealth; thus power is held by a few bad men, rather than the best.

Nicomachean Ethics 1160b.12

140 εἰς δημοκρατίαν … πλῆθος γὰρ βούλεται … καὶ ἴσοι πάντες οἱ ἐν τῷ τιμήματι· ἥκιστα δὲ μοχθηρόν ἐστιν ἡ δημοκρατία

In democracy it is government by the mass of the citizens, all with equal qualifications; democracy is the least bad form of government.

Translated by H. Rackham (1926)

Nicomachean Ethics 1160b.16

cf. Plato 268 and Winston Churchill (11 Nov 1947): 'democracy is the worst form of government except all those other forms that have been tried from time to time'

141 ἔστι γὰρ ὁ φίλος ἄλλος αὐτός

A friend is another self.

Translated by H. Rackham (1926)

Nicomachean Ethics 1166a.31

cf. the Latin 'alter ego'

142 οἱ δ' εὐεργέται τοὺς εὐεργετηθέντας δοκοῦσι μᾶλλον φιλεῖν ἢ οἱ εὖ παθόντες τοὺς δράσαντας

Benefactors seem to love those they benefit more than the receivers love the benefactor.

Nicomachean Ethics 1167b.17

143 ἀμνήμονες γὰρ οἱ πολλοί

Most men have short memories.

Translated by H. Rackham (1926)

Nicomachean Ethics 1167b.27

e.g. those who receive some benefit

144 πᾶς γὰρ τὸ οἰκεῖον ἔργον ἀγαπᾷ

Every artist loves his own handiwork.

Translated by H. Rackham (1926)

Nicomachean Ethics 1167b.34

145 τὸ εἶναι πᾶσιν αἱρετὸν καὶ φιλητόν, ἐσμὲν δ' ἐνεργείᾳ, τῷ ζῆν γὰρ καὶ πράττειν

All things desire and love existence; but we exist in activity, since we exist by living and doing.

Translated by H. Rackham (1926)

Nicomachean Ethics 1168a.5

146 ἡδεῖα δ' ἐστὶ τοῦ μὲν παρόντος ἡ ἐνέργεια, τοῦ δὲ μέλλοντος ἡ ἐλπίς, τοῦ δὲ γεγενημένου ἡ μνήμη· ἥδιστον δὲ τὸ κατὰ τὴν ἐνέργειαν

It is the activity of a present action, the expectation of a future one, and the memory of a past one, that gives pleasure; but the greatest pleasure is that which accompanies present activity.

Translated by J.A.K. Thomson (1953)

Nicomachean Ethics 1168a.13

ἐνέργεια is variously translated as 'activity' or 'actuality'

147 ἔστι τοῦ ἀγαθοῦ καὶ τῆς ἀρετῆς τὸ εὐεργετεῖν

Doing good to others is characteristic of virtue and the good man.

Translated by J.A.K. Thomson (1953)

Nicomachean Ethics 1169b.11

148 τὸ δ' ὅτι αἰσθανόμεθα ἢ νοοῦμεν, ὅτι ἐσμέν

To be conscious that we are perceiving or thinking is to be conscious that we exist.

Translated by H. Rackham (1926)

Nicomachean Ethics 1170a.32

cf. René Descartes: 'cogito, ergo sum' (from the 1641 Latin edition of Le Discours de la Méthode, *4.3)*

149 πρὸς τὴν τοῦ ἤθους ἀρετὴν μέγιστον εἶναι τὸ χαίρειν οἷς δεῖ καὶ μισεῖν ἃ δεῖ

To enjoy the things we ought and to hate the things we ought has the greatest bearing on excellence of character.

Translated by W.D. Ross (1925)

Nicomachean Ethics 1172a.21

150 οὐδείς τ' ἂν ἕλοιτο ζῆν παιδίου διάνοιαν ἔχων διὰ βίου, ἡδόμενος ἐφ' οἷς τὰ παιδία ὡς οἷόν τε μάλιστα

Nobody would choose to live out his life with the mentality of a child, even if he continued to take the greatest pleasure in the things that children like.

Translated by J.A.K. Thomson (1953)

Nicomachean Ethics 1174a.1

151 κατὰ πᾶσαν γὰρ αἴσθησίν ἐστιν ἡδονή, ὁμοίως δὲ καὶ διάνοιαν καὶ θεωρίαν, ἡδίστη δ' ἡ τελειοτάτη, τελειοτάτη δ' ἡ τοῦ εὖ ἔχοντος

There is a pleasure corresponding to each of the senses, just as there is to thought and contemplation; and it is most pleasurable when it is most perfect, and most perfect when in a healthy condition.

Translated by J.A.K. Thomson (1953)

Nicomachean Ethics 1174b.20

152 πάντα γὰρ τὰ ἀνθρώπεια ἀδυνατεῖ συνεχῶς ἐνεργεῖν

No human faculty is capable of uninterrupted activity.

Translated by H. Rackham (1926)

Nicomachean Ethics 1175a.4

153 πότερον δὲ διὰ τὴν ἡδονὴν τὸ ζῆν αἱρούμεθα ἢ διὰ τὸ ζῆν τὴν ἡδονήν

The question is whether we desire life for the sake of pleasure or pleasure for the sake of life.

Translated by H. Rackham (1926)

Nicomachean Ethics 1175a.18

154 ἄνευ τε γὰρ ἐνεργείας οὐ γίνεται ἡδονή, πᾶσάν τε ἐνέργειαν τελειοῖ ἡ ἡδονή

There is no pleasure without activity, and also no perfect activity without pleasure.

Translated by H. Rackham (1926)

Nicomachean Ethics 1175a.20

155 μᾶλλον γὰρ ἕκαστα κρίνουσι καὶ ἐξακριβοῦσιν οἱ μεθ' ἡδονῆς ἐνεργοῦντες

Those who work with pleasure always work with more discernment and with greater accuracy.

Translated by H. Rackham (1926)

Nicomachean Ethics 1175a.31

156 πολλαὶ γὰρ φθοραὶ καὶ λῦμαι ἀνθρώπων γίνονται

Men may be ruined and spoilt in many ways.

Translated by W.D. Ross (1925)

Nicomachean Ethics 1176a.20

157 ἀναπαύσει γὰρ ἔοικεν ἡ παιδιά, ἀδυνατοῦντες δὲ συνεχῶς πονεῖν ἀναπαύσεως δέονται

Amusement is a form of rest; and we need rest because we are not able to go on working without a break.

Translated by H. Rackham (1926)

Nicomachean Ethics 1176b.34

cf. Anacharsis 3

158 εἰ δ' ἐστὶν ἡ εὐδαιμονία κατ' ἀρετὴν ἐνέργεια, εὔλογον κατὰ τὴν κρατίστην

If happiness is activity in accordance with virtue, it is reasonable that it should be in accordance with the highest virtue.

Translated by H. Rackham (1926)

Nicomachean Ethics 1177a.12

'ἀρετή' is often translated as 'excellence' by other scholars

159 πολεμοῦμεν ἵν' εἰρήνην ἄγωμεν

We make war that we may live in peace.

Translated by W.D. Ross (1925)

Nicomachean Ethics 1177b.5

cf. *Vegetius,* Epitoma rei militaris *book 3, prologue 'qui desiderat pacem, praeparet bellum' (let him who desires peace prepare for war), usually quoted as 'si vis pacem, para bellum'*

160 ἔστι δὲ καὶ ἡ τοῦ πολιτικοῦ ἄσχολος, καὶ παρ' αὐτὸ τὸ πολιτεύεσθαι περιποιουμένη δυναστείας καὶ τιμὰς ἢ τήν γε εὐδαιμονίαν

Politicians have no leisure, because they are always aiming at something beyond political life itself, power and glory, or happiness.

Translated in *The Oxford Dictionary of Quotations* (2004)

Nicomachean Ethics 1177b.12

161 ἡ δὲ τοῦ νοῦ ἐνέργεια ... τελεία δὴ εὐδαιμονία ... ἂν εἴη ἀνθρώπου

It is the activity of the intellect that constitutes complete human happiness.

Translated by H. Rackham (1926)

Nicomachean Ethics 1177b.19

162 ὁ δὲ τοιοῦτος ἂν εἴη βίος κρείττων ἢ κατ' ἄνθρωπον· οὐ γὰρ ᾗ ἄνθρωπός ἐστιν οὕτω βιώσεται, ἀλλ' ᾗ θεῖόν τι ἐν αὐτῷ ὑπάρχει ... οὐ χρὴ δὲ κατὰ τοὺς παραινοῦντας ἀνθρώπινα φρονεῖν ἄνθρωπον ὄντα ... ἀλλ' ἐφ' ὅσον ἐνδέχεται ἀθανατίζειν καὶ πάντα ποιεῖν πρὸς τὸ ζῆν κατὰ τὸ κράτιστον τῶν ἐν αὐτῷ· εἰ γὰρ καὶ τῷ ὄγκῳ μικρόν ἐστι, δυνάμει καὶ τιμιότητι πολὺ μᾶλλον πάντων ὑπερέχει

There is a life which is higher than the measure of humanity: men will live it not by virtue of their humanity, but by virtue of something in them that is divine. We must not, then, follow those who advise us, being men, to think of human things, but must, as far as we can, aspire to immortality, and strain every nerve to live in accordance with the best in us; for small though it be, in power and worth it is far above the rest.

Nicomachean Ethics 1177b.26

163 οὐδὲ δὴ περὶ ἀρετῆς ἱκανὸν τὸ εἰδέναι, ἀλλ' ἔχειν καὶ χρῆσθαι πειρατέον

To know what virtue is is not enough; we must endeavour to possess and to practise it.

Translated by H. Rackham (1926)

Nicomachean Ethics 1179b.2

164 καὶ τοῖς μὲν ἐλευθεριωτέροις τιμῆς μεταδιδόναι, τοῖς δ' ἐργάταις τροφῆς πλῆθος

A share of honour should be given to those who are doing a freeman's work, and abundant food to workmen.

Translated by G. Cyril Armstrong (1935)

Oeconomica 1344a.30

165 ἐκ τῶν αὐτῶν γὰρ τραγῳδία καὶ κωμῳδία γίνεται γραμμάτων

Tragedy and Comedy are both composed of *the same* letters.

Translated by H.H. Joachim (1868–1938), rev. Jonathan Barnes (1984)

On Generation and Corruption 315b.14

cf. the Latin 'iisdem e litteris comoedia ac tragoedia componitur' (Erasmus, Adages *3.4.93)*

166 μόνον ὡς εἰπεῖν αἰσθάνεται τῶν ζῴων ἄνθρωπος καὶ χαίρει ταῖς τῶν ἀνθῶν καὶ τῶν τοιούτων ὀσμαῖς

Man alone, so to speak, among animals perceives and takes pleasure in the odours of flowers and such things.

Translated by J.I. Beare (d. 1918), rev. Jonathan Barnes (1984)

On Sense and the Sensible 444a.32

167 ὁ δὲ θεὸς καὶ ἡ φύσις οὐδὲν μάτην ποιοῦσιν

God and nature do nothing without reason.

Translated by Gavin Betts and Alan Henry (1989)

On the Heavens 271a.33

168 εἴπερ καὶ τὸ μικρὸν παραβῆναι τῆς ἀληθείας ἀφισταμένοις γίνεται πόρρω μυριοπλάσιον

The least initial deviation from the truth is multiplied later a thousandfold.

Translated by J.L. Stocks (1882–1937), rev. Jonathan Barnes (1984)

On the Heavens 271b.8

169 ὥστ' οὐ μόνον ἐκ τούτων δῆλον περιφερὲς ὂν τὸ σχῆμα τῆς γῆς, ἀλλὰ καὶ σφαίρας οὐ μεγάλης

All of which goes to show not only that the earth is circular in shape, but also that it is a sphere of no great size.

Translated by J.L. Stocks (1882–1937), rev. Jonathan Barnes (1984)

On the Heavens 298a.6

this and the next passage are said to have encouraged Columbus to seek a westward route to India

170 διὸ τοὺς ὑπολαμβάνοντας συνάπτειν τὸν περὶ τὰς Ἡρακλείας στήλας τόπον τῷ περὶ τὴν Ἰνδικήν, καὶ τοῦτον τὸν τρόπον εἶναι τὴν θάλατταν μίαν, μὴ λίαν ὑπολαμβάνειν ἄπιστα δοκεῖν

Hence one should not disbelieve the theory that from the Pillars of Heracles the sea is one as far as the Indian continent.

On the Heavens 298a.9

this and the previous passage are said to have encouraged Columbus to seek a westward route to India

171 τὴν τῶν ὅλων σύστασιν, οὐρανοῦ λέγω καὶ γῆς τοῦ τε σύμπαντος κόσμου … μία διεκόσμησεν ἁρμονία

The Universe, heaven and earth and the whole cosmos, have been organized by a single harmony.

Translated by D.J. Furley (1955)

*On the Universe** 396b.23

172 ὅπερ ἐν νηὶ μὲν κυβερνήτης … τοῦτο θεὸς ἐν κόσμῳ

As the helmsman in his ship, so is god in the universe.

Translated by D.J. Furley (1955)

*On the Universe** 400b.6

173 καματηρὸν τὸ ἄρχειν

To command is wearisome.

Translated by D.J. Furley (1955)

*On the Universe** 400b.9

174 εἷς δὲ ὢν πολυώνυμός ἐστι, κατονομαζόμενος τοῖς πάθεσι πᾶσιν ἅπερ αὐτὸς νεοχμοῖ

Though god is one, he has many names, according to the many conditions he himself creates.

*On the Universe** 401a.12

175 ἐν πᾶσι γὰρ τοῖς φυσικοῖς ἔνεστί τι θαυμαστόν

In all things of nature there is something of the marvellous.

Translated in *Bartlett's Familiar Quotations* (1980)

Parts of Animals 645a.16

176 ὁ μὲν γὰρ ἐγκέφαλος ψυχρότατον τῶν ἐν τῷ σώματι μορίων

Of all the parts of the body there is none so cold as the brain.

Translated by William Ogle (1827–1912), rev. Jonathan Barnes (1984)

Parts of Animals 652a.27

177 ἀεὶ γὰρ ἡ φύσις μηχανᾶται πρὸς τὴν ἑκάστου ὑπερβολὴν βοήθειαν τὴν τοῦ ἐναντίου παρεδρίαν, ἵνα ἀνισάζῃ τὴν θατέρου ὑπερβολὴν θάτερον

Nature contrives to set excess against excess, so that the two may counterbalance each other.

Parts of Animals 652a.31

178 ἡ γὰρ φύσις μεταβαίνει συνεχῶς ἀπὸ τῶν ἀψύχων εἰς τὰ ζῷα διὰ τῶν ζώντων μὲν οὐκ ὄντων δὲ ζῴων, οὕτως ὥστε δοκεῖν πάμπαν μικρὸν διαφέρειν θατέρου θάτερον τῷ σύνεγγυς ἀλλήλοις

Nature passes from the inanimate to animals in unbroken sequence, interposing between them beings, alive and yet not animals, so that scarcely any difference seems to exist between two neighbouring groups owing to their close proximity.

Parts of Animals 681a.12

cf. the Latin 'natura non facit saltus' (nature makes no jumps); and Aristotle, History of Animals *588b*

179 ἄλλῳ γὰρ εἴδει ἄλλη ὕλη

For different forms there is different matter.

Translated by R.P. Hardie (1864–1942) and R.K. Gaye (1877–1909), rev. Jonathan Barnes (1984)

Physics 194b.9

180 ὥστ' εἰ ἐν τῇ τέχνῃ ἔνεστι τὸ ἕνεκά του, καὶ ἐν τῇ φύσει

If, therefore, purpose is present in art, it is present also in nature.

Translated by R.P. Hardie (1864–1942) and R.K. Gaye (1877–1909), rev. Jonathan Barnes (1984)

Physics 199b.29

181 κατατήκει ὁ χρόνος, καὶ γηράσκει πάνθ' ὑπὸ τοῦ χρόνου, καὶ ἐπιλανθάνεται διὰ τὸν χρόνον

Time crumbles things; everything grows old under the power of Time and is forgotten through the lapse of Time.

Translated by Philip H. Wicksteed and Francis Cornford (1929)

Physics 221a.31

182 εἴπερ οὖν ἀΐδιος ἡ κίνησις, ἀΐδιον καὶ τὸ κινοῦν ἔσται πρῶτον, εἰ ἕν

Motion being eternal, the first mover, if there is but one, will be eternal also.

Translated by R.P. Hardie (1864–1942) and R.K. Gaye (1877–1909), rev. Jonathan Barnes (1984)

Physics 259a.6

cf. Aristotle 72

183 ἔστιν οὖν τραγῳδία μίμησις πράξεως σπουδαίας καὶ τελείας μέγεθος ἐχούσης ... δι' ἐλέου καὶ φόβου περαίνουσα τὴν τῶν τοιούτων παθημάτων κάθαρσιν

Tragedy is the imitation of an action of importance and magnitude, complete in itself, with incidents arousing pity and fear, leading to catharsis.

Poetics 1449b.24

the accepted definition of tragedy

184 ὅλον δέ ἐστιν τὸ ἔχον ἀρχὴν καὶ μέσον καὶ τελευτήν

A whole is that which has a beginning, a middle, and an end.

Translated by I. Bywater (1840–1914), rev. Jonathan Barnes (1984)

Poetics 1450b.26

185 ἐπὶ τῶν μύθων ἔχειν μὲν μῆκος, τοῦτο δὲ εὐμνημόνευτον εἶναι

A story or plot must be of some length, but length that can be coherently remembered.

Poetics 1451a.5

186 φιλοσοφώτερον καὶ σπουδαιότερον ποίησις ἱστορίας ἐστίν· ἡ μὲν γὰρ ποίησις μᾶλλον τὰ καθόλου, ἡ δ' ἱστορία τὰ καθ' ἕκαστον λέγει

Poetry is more philosophical and more elevated than history, since poetry relates more of the universal, while history relates particulars.

Translated by Stephen Halliwell (1995)

Poetics 1451b.5

187 προαιρεῖσθαί τε δεῖ ἀδύνατα εἰκότα μᾶλλον ἢ δυνατὰ ἀπίθανα

Probable impossibilities are to be preferred to improbable possibilities.

Translated in *The Oxford Dictionary of Quotations* (2004)

Poetics 1460a.26

188 Σοφοκλῆς ἔφη αὐτὸς μὲν οἵους δεῖ ποιεῖν, Εὐριπίδην δὲ οἷοι εἰσίν

Sophocles said he created characters as they ought to be, Euripides as they really are.

Translated by Stephen Halliwell (1995)

Poetics 1460b.33

189 εἰς πᾶσαν ἡμέραν συνεστηκυῖα κοινωνία κατὰ φύσιν οἶκός ἐστιν

The association put together by nature for everyday purposes is the family.

Politics 1252b.13

190 ἡ δ' ἐκ πλειόνων κωμῶν κοινωνία τέλειος πόλις ... γινομένη μὲν οὖν τοῦ ζῆν ἕνεκεν, οὖσα δὲ τοῦ εὖ ζῆν

The partnership of several villages is the city-state, originating as a necessity of life, but continuing to exist for the sake of the good life.

Politics 1252b.27

191 ἄνθρωπος φύσει πολιτικὸν ζῷον

Man is by nature a political animal.

Translated by H. Rackham (1932)

Politics 1253a.2

192 τοῦτο γὰρ πρὸς τὰ ἄλλα ζῷα τοῖς ἀνθρώποις ἴδιον, τὸ μόνον ἀγαθοῦ καὶ κακοῦ καὶ δικαίου καὶ ἀδίκου

It is a characteristic of man that he alone has any sense of good and evil, of just and unjust.

Translated by Benjamin Jowett (1817–1893), rev. Jonathan Barnes (1984)

Politics 1253a.15

193 ὁ δὲ μὴ δυνάμενος κοινωνεῖν ἢ μηδὲν δεόμενος δι' αὐτάρκειαν οὐθὲν μέρος πόλεως, ὥστε ἢ θηρίον ἢ θεός

He who is unable to live in society, or who has no need because he is sufficient for himself, must be either a beast or a god.

Translated by Benjamin Jowett (1817–1893), rev. Jonathan Barnes (1984)

Politics 1253a.29

cf. Francis Bacon, Essays *(1597–1625), 'Of Friendship': 'whosoever delights in solitude is either a wild beast or a god'*

194 ἡ κτῆσις μέρος τῆς οἰκίας ἐστὶ καὶ ἡ κτητικὴ μέρος τῆς οἰκονομίας

Property is a part of a household and the art of acquiring property a part of household management.

Translated by H. Rackham (1932)

Politics 1253b.23

of the basic beginnings of economical attitudes and management

195 εἰ γὰρ ἠδύνατο ἕκαστον τῶν ὀργάνων κελευσθὲν ἢ προαισθανόμενον ἀποτελεῖν τὸ αὑτοῦ ἔργον ... οὕτως αἱ κερκίδες ἐκέρκιζον αὐταὶ ... οὐδὲν ἂν ἔδει οὔτε τοῖς ἀρχιτέκτοσιν ὑπηρετῶν οὔτε τοῖς δεσπόταις δούλων

If every tool could perform its own work when ordered, or knew what to do in advance, if shuttles wove of themselves, master-craftsmen would have no need of assistants and masters no need of slaves.

Politics 1253b.33

Karl Marx has emphasized the importance of this passage – presaging the advent of machines and the liberation of the workforce

196 τὸ γὰρ ἄρχειν καὶ ἄρχεσθαι οὐ μόνον τῶν ἀναγκαίων ἀλλὰ καὶ τῶν συμφερόντων ἐστί, καὶ εὐθὺς ἐκ γενετῆς ἔνια διέστηκε τὰ μὲν ἐπὶ τὸ ἄρχεσθαι τὰ δ' ἐπὶ τὸ ἄρχειν

That some should rule, and others be ruled, is a thing not only necessary but expedient, for from the hour of their birth, some are marked for subjection, others for rule.

Translated by Benjamin Jowett (1817–1893), rev. Jonathan Barnes (1984)

Politics 1254a.21

197 φανερόν ἐστιν ὅτι κατὰ φύσιν καὶ συμφέρον τὸ ἄρχεσθαι τῷ σώματι ὑπὸ τῆς ψυχῆς, καὶ τῷ παθητικῷ μορίῳ ὑπὸ τοῦ νοῦ

It is manifest that it is natural and expedient for the body to be governed by the soul and for the emotional part to be governed by the intellect.

Translated by H. Rackham (1932)

Politics 1254b.6

198 οὐχ ἡ αὐτὴ ἡ οἰκονομικὴ τῇ χρηματιστικῇ, δῆλον, τῆς μὲν γὰρ τὸ πορίσασθαι, τῆς δὲ τὸ χρήσασθαι

Now it is clear that wealth-getting is not the same art as household management, for the function of the former is to provide and that of the latter to use.

Translated by H. Rackham (1932)

Politics 1256a.10

199 τά τε φυτὰ τῶν ζῴων ἕνεκεν εἶναι καὶ τὰ ἄλλα ζῷα τῶν ἀνθρώπων χάριν

Plants exist for the sake of animals and animals for the good of man.

Politics 1256b.16

200 ἡ φύσις μηθὲν μήτε ἀτελὲς ποιεῖ μήτε μάτην

Nature makes nothing incomplete, and nothing in vain.

Translated by Benjamin Jowett (1817–1893), rev. Jonathan Barnes (1984)

Politics 1256b.20

201 θησαυρισμὸς χρημάτων πρὸς ζωὴν ἀναγκαίων καὶ χρησίμων εἰς κοινωνίαν πόλεως ἢ οἰκίας

Holding essential goods in store, be they for the good of the city or his home.

Politics 1256b.28

the role of the householder/manager

202 τό τε γὰρ ἄρρεν φύσει τοῦ θήλεος ἡγεμονικώτερον

For the male is by nature better fitted to command than the female.

Translated by H. Rackham (1932)

Politics 1259b.1

203 οἰκία μὲν πᾶσα μέρος πόλεως

Every household is part of the state.

Translated by H. Rackham (1932)

Politics 1260b.13

204 πλῆθος γάρ τι τὴν φύσιν ἐστὶν ἡ πόλις … οὐ μόνον δ᾽ ἐκ πλειόνων ἀνθρώπων ἐστὶν ἡ πόλις, ἀλλὰ καὶ ἐξ εἴδει διαφερόντων. οὐ γὰρ γίνεται πόλις ἐξ ὁμοίων

A state essentially consists of a multitude of persons. And not only does it consist of a multitude of human beings, it consists of human beings differing in kind. A collection of persons all alike does not constitute a state.

Translated by H. Rackham (1932)

Politics 1261a.18

on the necessity of plurality

205 ἥκιστα γὰρ ἐπιμελείας τυγχάνει τὸ πλείστων κοινόν

A matter common to most men receives least attention.

Translated by John Simpson and Jennifer Speake (1982)

Politics 1261b.33

cf. the English proverb 'everybody's business is nobody's business'

206 τῶν γὰρ ἰδίων μάλιστα φροντίζουσιν, τῶν δὲ κοινῶν ἧττον … πρὸς γὰρ τοῖς ἄλλοις ὡς ἑτέρου φροντίζοντος

Everyone thinks chiefly of his own, less of the common interest, expecting others to attend to it.

Politics 1261b.34

207 ἀναγκαῖον ἐγκλήματα γίνεσθαι πρὸς τοὺς ἀπολαύοντας μὲν ἢ λαμβάνοντας πολλά, ὀλίγα δὲ πονοῦντας, τοῖς ἐλάττω μὲν λαμβάνουσι, πλείω δὲ πονοῦσιν

Complaints are bound to arise between those who enjoy or take much but work little, and those who receive less but work more.

Translated by H. Rackham (1932)

Politics 1263a.12

208 τὸ συζῆν καὶ κοινωνεῖν τῶν ἀνθρωπικῶν πάντων χαλεπόν

To live together and share all our human affairs is indeed difficult.

Translated by H. Rackham (1932)

Politics 1263a.15

209 μὴ γὰρ οὐ μάτην τὴν πρὸς αὑτὸν αὐτὸς ἔχει φιλίαν ἕκαστος, ἀλλ᾽ ἔστι τοῦτο φυσικόν. τὸ δὲ φίλαυτον εἶναι ψέγεται δικαίως· οὐκ ἔστι δὲ τοῦτο τὸ φιλεῖν ἑαυτόν, ἀλλὰ τὸ μᾶλλον ἢ δεῖ φιλεῖν

Love for oneself is not purposeless, but a natural instinct. Selfishness on the other hand is justly blamed; but this is not to love oneself but to love oneself more than one ought.

Translated by H. Rackham (1932)

Politics 1263a.41

210 ἔτι δὲ δίκαιοιν μὴ μόνον λέγειν ὅσων στερήσονται κακῶν κοινωνήσαντες, ἀλλὰ καὶ ὅσων ἀγαθῶν· φαίνεται δ᾽ εἶναι πάμπαν ἀδύνατος ὁ βίος

One must consider not only what evils

will be eliminated by adopting a policy of joint ownership, but also which benefits one stands to lose; such manner of living we consider to be utterly impossible.

Politics 1263b.27

of communism, in the sense of a policy of common property

211 λέγεται δ' ὡς δεῖ τὸν νομοθέτην πρὸς δύο βλέποντα τιθέναι τοὺς νόμους, πρός τε τὴν χώραν καὶ τοὺς ἀνθρώπους. ἔτι δὲ καλῶς ἔχει προσθεῖναι καὶ πρὸς τοὺς γειτνιῶντας τόπους

It is said that in laying down the laws the legislator must have his attention fixed on two things, the territory and the population. But also it would be well to add that he must take into account the neighbouring regions.

Translated by H. Rackham (1932)

Politics 1265a.18

212 ἡ δὲ πενία στάσιν ἐμποιεῖ καὶ κακουργίαν

Poverty is the parent of revolution and crime.

Translated by Benjamin Jowett (1817–1893), rev. Jonathan Barnes (1984)

Politics 1265b.12

213 μᾶλλον γὰρ δεῖ τὰς ἐπιθυμίας ὁμαλίζειν ἢ τὰς οὐσίας, τοῦτο δ' οὐκ ἔστι μὴ παιδευομένοις ἱκανῶς ὑπὸ τῶν νόμων

It is desires, not properties which need to be equalized, and this can only be done by an adequate system of education enforced by law.

Politics 1266b.29

214 ἀδικουσί γε τὰ μέγιστα διὰ τὰς ὑπερβολάς, ἀλλ' οὐ διὰ τὰ ἀναγκαῖα

The greatest transgressions spring from a desire for luxuries, not for bare necessities.

Politics 1267a.13

215 ἔτι δ' ἡ πονηρία τῶν ἀνθρώπων ἄπληστον, καὶ τὸ πρῶτον μὲν ἱκανὸν διωβολία μόνον, ὅταν δ' ἤδη τοῦτ' ᾖ πάτριον, ἀεὶ δέονται τοῦ πλείονος, ἕως εἰς ἄπειρον ἔλθωσιν

The avarice of mankind is insatiable; at one time two obols was pay enough; but now, when this sum has become customary, men always want more and more without end.

Translated by Benjamin Jowett (1817–1893), rev. Jonathan Barnes (1984)

Politics 1267a.41

216 ζητοῦσι δ' ὅλως οὐ τὸ πάτριον ἀλλὰ τἀγαθὸν πάντες

Men in general desire the good, and not merely what their fathers had.

Translated by Benjamin Jowett (1817–1893), rev. Jonathan Barnes (1984)

Politics 1269a.3

217 πρὸς δὲ τούτοις οὐδὲ τοὺς γεγραμμένους ἐᾶν ἀκινήτους βέλτιον

Even when laws have been written down, they need not always remain unaltered.

Translated by Benjamin Jowett (1817–1893), rev. Jonathan Barnes (1984)

Politics 1269a.8

218 δεῖ γὰρ καὶ βουλόμενον καὶ μὴ βουλόμενον ἄρχειν τὸν ἄξιον τῆς ἀρχῆς

The man worthiest of office ought to be appointed whether he wants to or not.

Politics 1271a.11

219 τῶν ἀδικημάτων τῶν γ' ἑκουσίων τὰ πλεῖστα συμβαίνει σχεδὸν διὰ φιλοτιμίαν καὶ διὰ φιλοχρηματίαν τοῖς ἀνθρώποις

Most conscious wrongdoing is caused by ambition and greed.

Politics 1271a.16

220 σχεδὸν τῶν Ἑλλήνων ἱδρυμένων περὶ τὴν θάλατταν πάντων

Practically all the Greeks are settled around the sea.

Politics 1271b.34

221 διὸ δεῖ τοὺς δυναμένους ἄριστ' ἄρχειν, τούτους ἄρχειν

Those able to rule best should rule.

Politics 1273b.5

222 οὐκ ἔστιν εὖ ἄρξαι μὴ ἀρχθέντα

It is impossible to become a good ruler without having been a subject.

Translated by H. Rackham (1932)

Politics 1277b.12

223 νῦν δὲ διὰ τὰς ὠφελείας τὰς ἀπὸ τῶν κοινῶν καὶ τὰς ἐκ τῆς ἀρχῆς βούλονται

συνεχῶς ἄρχειν

Nowadays owing to the benefits to be acquired from public sources and from holding office people wish to be in office continuously.

Translated by H. Rackham (1932)

Politics 1279a.13

224 ὅσαι μὲν πολιτεῖαι τὸ κοινῇ συμφέρον σκοποῦσιν, αὗται μὲν ὀρθαὶ τυγχάνουσιν οὖσαι κατὰ τὸ ἁπλῶς δίκαιον, ὅσαι δὲ τὸ σφέτερον μόνον τῶν ἀρχόντων, ἡμαρτημέναι πᾶσαι καὶ παρεκβάσεις τῶν ὀρθῶν πολιτειῶν· δεσποτικαὶ γάρ, ἡ δὲ πόλις κοινωνία τῶν ἐλευθέρων ἐστίν

Constitutions that aim at the common advantage are in effect rightly framed in accordance with absolute justice, while those that aim at the rulers' own advantage are faulty and are all deviations from the right constitutions; for they have an element of despotism, whereas a city is a partnership of free men.

Translated by H. Rackham (1932)

Politics 1279a.17

225 ἡ μὲν τυραννίς ἐστι μοναρχία πρὸς τὸ συμφέρον τὸ τοῦ μοναρχοῦντος, ἡ δ' ὀλιγαρχία πρὸς τὸ τῶν εὐπόρων, ἡ δὲ δημοκρατία πρὸς τὸ συμφέρον τὸ τῶν ἀπόρων, πρὸς δὲ τὸ τῷ κοινῷ λυσιτελοῦν οὐδεμία αὐτῶν

Tyranny is monarchy ruling in the interest of the monarch, oligarchy government in the interest of the rich, democracy government in the interest of the poor, and none of these forms governs with regard to the profit of the community as a whole.

Translated by H. Rackham (1932)

Politics 1279b.6

226 σχεδὸν δ' οἱ πλεῖστοι φαῦλοι κριταὶ περὶ τῶν οἰκείων

Most men are bad judges where their own interests are concerned.

Politics 1280a.15

227 μήτε τοῦ ζῆν μόνον ἕνεκεν ἀλλὰ μᾶλλον τοῦ εὖ ζῆν

Not for the sake of life only but rather for the good life.

Translated by H. Rackham (1932)

Politics 1280a.31

228 καὶ ὁ νόμος συνθήκη καί ... ἐγγυητὴς ἀλλήλοις τῶν δικαίων, ἀλλ' οὐχ οἷος ποιεῖν ἀγαθοὺς καὶ δικαίους τοὺς πολίτας

The law is a covenant and a guarantee of men's claims on one another, not necessarily designed to make the citizens virtuous and just.

Politics 1280b.10

229 φανερὸν τοίνυν ὅτι ἡ πόλις οὐκ ἔστι κοινωνία τόπου καὶ τοῦ μὴ ἀδικεῖν σφᾶς αὐτοὺς καὶ τῆς μεταδόσεως χάριν ... τῶν καλῶν ἄρα πράξεων χάριν θετέον εἶναι τὴν πολιτικὴν κοινωνίαν, ἀλλ' οὐ τοῦ συζῆν

It is manifest that a state is not merely the sharing of a common locality for the purpose of preventing mutual injury and exchanging goods; political society must therefore be deemed to exist for the sake of noble actions, not merely for living in common.

Translated by H. Rackham (1932)

Politics 1280b.29 and 1281a.2

230 τοὺς γὰρ πολλούς, ὧν ἕκαστός ἐστιν οὐ σπουδαῖος ἀνήρ, ὅμως ἐνδέχεται συνελθόντας εἶναι βελτίους ἐκείνων οὐχ ὡς ἕκαστον ἀλλ' ὡς σύμπαντας ... διὸ καὶ κρίνουσιν ἄμεινον οἱ πολλοὶ

It is possible that the many, though not individually excellent, when in council may collectively be better; which is why the many are a better judge.

Politics 1281a.42 and 1281b.7

231 πολλῶν γὰρ ὄντων ἕκαστον μόριον ἔχειν ἀρετῆς καὶ φρονήσεως, καὶ γίνεσθαι συνελθόντας, ὥσπερ ἕνα ἄνθρωπον τὸ πλῆθος, πολύποδα καὶ πολύχειρα καὶ πολλὰς ἔχοντ' αἰσθήσεις, οὕτω καὶ περὶ τὰ ἤθη καὶ τὴν διάνοιαν

Where there are many, each individual, has some portion of virtue and wisdom, and, when together, just as the multitude becomes a single man with many feet and many hands and many senses, so also it becomes one personality as regards the moral and intellectual faculties.

Translated by H. Rackham (1932)

Politics 1281b.4

232 ὅταν γὰρ ἄτιμοι πολλοὶ καὶ πένητες ὑπάρχωσι, πολεμίων ἀναγκαῖον εἶναι

πλήρη τὴν πόλιν ταύτην

A state where many are poor and deprived of civil rights is bound to be full of enemies.

Politics 1281b.29

233 οὐ γὰρ ὁ δικαστὴς οὐδ' ὁ βουλευτὴς οὐδ' ὁ ἐκκλησιαστὴς ἄρχων ἐστίν, ἀλλὰ τὸ δικαστήριον καὶ ἡ βουλὴ καὶ ὁ δῆμος

It is not the individual juryman or councillor or member of the assembly in whom authority rests, but the court, the council and the people.

Translated by H. Rackham (1932)

Politics 1282a.34

234 δεῖ τοὺς νόμους εἶναι κυρίους κειμένους ὀρθῶς, τὸν ἄρχοντα δέ, ἄν τε εἷς ἄν τε πλείους ὦσι, περὶ τούτων εἶναι κυρίους περὶ ὅσων ἐξαδυνατοῦσιν οἱ νόμοι λέγειν ἀκριβῶς διὰ τὸ μὴ ῥᾴδιον εἶναι καθόλου δηλῶσαι περὶ πάντων

It is proper for the laws when rightly laid down to be sovereign, while the ruler or rulers in office should have supreme powers over matters where the laws are unable to pronounce with precision because of the difficulty of making a general rule to cover all cases.

Translated by H. Rackham (1932)

Politics 1282b.2

235 δεῖ δὲ τῷ κατὰ τὸ ἔργον ὑπερέχοντι διδόναι καὶ τῶν ὀργάνων τὴν ὑπεροχήν

It is the superior performers who ought to be given the superior instruments.

Translated by H. Rackham (1932)

Politics 1282b.33

236 πολιτείαν ... δὲ τὴν ἀρίστην ὁ δυνάμενος καὶ προαιρούμενος ἄρχεσθαι καὶ ἄρχειν πρὸς τὸν βίον τὸν κατ' ἀρετήν

Under the best form of government a citizen will be governed and will govern in accordance with virtue.

Politics 1284a.2

237 κρίνει ἄμεινον ὄχλος πολλὰ ἢ εἷς ὁστισοῦν .... καθάπερ ὕδωρ τὸ πλεῖον, οὕτω καὶ τὸ πλῆθος τῶν ὀλίγων ἀδιαφθορώτερον

A crowd judges better than any single person; the mass of citizens is less corruptible than the few, just as the larger stream of water is more difficult to pollute.

Politics 1286a.30

238 ὁ θυμὸς ἄρχοντας διαστρέφει καὶ τοὺς ἀρίστους ἄνδρας

Passion perverts the minds of rulers, even when they are the best of men.

Translated by Benjamin Jowett (1817–1893), rev. Jonathan Barnes (1984)

Politics 1287a.31

239 εἴπερ γὰρ ἐλευθερία μάλιστ' ἔστιν ἐν δημοκρατίᾳ ... καὶ ἰσότης, οὕτως ἂν εἴη μάλιστα κοινωνούτων ἁπάντων μάλιστα τῆς πολιτείας ὁμοίως

If liberty and equality are chiefly to be found in democracy, they will be best attained when all persons alike share fully in the government.

Translated by Benjamin Jowett (1817–1893), rev. Jonathan Barnes (1984)

Politics 1291b.34

240 δεῖ γὰρ τὸν μὲν νόμον ἄρχειν πάντων

The law ought to be supreme in all things.

Politics 1292a.32

241 δοκεῖ δὲ ἀριστοκρατία μὲν εἶναι μάλιστα τὸ τὰς τιμὰς νενεμῆσθαι κατ' ἀρετήν· ἀριστοκρατίας μὲν γὰρ ὅρος ἀρετή, ὀλιγαρχίας δὲ πλοῦτος, δήμου δ' ἐλευθερία

Aristocracy in the fullest sense seems to consist in the distribution of honours according to virtue; for virtue is the defining factor of aristocracy, as wealth is of oligarchy, and freedom of democracy.

Translated by H. Rackham (1932)

Politics 1294a.10

242 ἐπεὶ τοίνυν ὁμολογεῖται τὸ μέτριον ἄριστον καὶ τὸ μέσον, φανερὸν ὅτι καὶ τῶν εὐτυχημάτων ἡ κτῆσις ἡ μέση βελτίστη πάντων

Since it is admitted that what is moderate is best, it is manifest that good fortune in moderation is best.

Politics 1295b.3

243 ὑπέρκαλον δὲ ἢ ὑπερίσχυρον ἢ ὑπερευγενῆ ἢ ὑπερπλούσιον, ἢ τἀναντία τούτοις, ὑπέρπτωχον ἢ ὑπερασθενῆ

ἢ σφόδρα ἄτιμον, χαλεπὸν τῷ λόγῳ ἀκολουθεῖν· γίγνονται γὰρ οἱ μὲν ὑβρισταὶ καὶ μεγαλοπόνηροι μᾶλλον, οἱ δὲ κακοῦργοι καὶ μικροπόνηροι λίαν

The exceedingly beautiful or strong or nobly born or rich, or the opposite, exceedingly poor or weak or of mean station, find it difficult to follow reason; the former turn to insolence and wickedness, the latter to malice and petty vice.

Politics 1295b.6

244 ὡς ὅπου οἱ μὲν πολλὰ σφόδρα κέκτηνται οἱ δὲ μηθέν, ἢ δῆμος ἔσχατος γίγνεται ἢ ὀλιγαρχία ἄκρατος, ἢ τυραννὶς δι' ἀμφοτέρας τὰς ὑπερβολάς

Where some people are very wealthy and others have nothing, the result will be either extreme democracy or absolute oligarchy, or despotism will come from either of those excesses.

Translated in *The Oxford Dictionary of Quotations* (2004)

Politics 1296a.1

245 οὐ γὰρ ἀεὶ συμβαίνει χαρίεντας εἶναι τοὺς μετέχοντας τοῦ πολιτεύματος

It does not always happen that those who are in positions of authority are gentlemen.

Politics 1297b.9

246 ἔστι δὴ τρία μόρια τῶν πολιτειῶν πασῶν ... ἓν μὲν τί τὸ βουλευόμενον περὶ τῶν κοινῶν, δεύτερον δὲ τὸ περὶ τὰς ἀρχάς τοῦτο δ' ἐστὶ τίνας δεῖ καὶ τίνων εἶναι κυρίας, καὶ ποίαν τινὰ δεῖ γίνεσθαι τὴν αἵρεσιν αὐτῶν, τρίτον δέ τί τὸ δικάζον

All constitutions have three elements: one is a council or parliament considering common concerns, the second is the executive (its powers and way of election) and, a third, the judiciary.

Politics 1297b.37

247 δῆμος μὲν γὰρ ἐγένετο ἐκ τοῦ ἴσους ὁτιοῦν ὄντας οἴεσθαι ἁπλῶς ἴσους εἶναι· ὅτι γὰρ ἐλεύθεροι πάντες ὁμοίως, ἁπλῶς ἴσοι εἶναι νομίζουσιν

Democracy arises out of the notion that those who are equal in any respect are equal in all respects; because men are equally free, they claim to be absolutely equal.

Translated by Benjamin Jowett (1817–1893), rev. Jonathan Barnes (1984)

Politics 1301a.28

248 πανταχοῦ γὰρ διὰ τὸ ἄνισον ἡ στάσις, οὐ μὴ τοῖς ἀνίσοις ὑπάρχει ἀνάλογον (ἀΐδιος γὰρ βασιλεία ἄνισος, ἐὰν ᾖ ἐν ἴσοις)· ὅλως γὰρ τὸ ἴσον ζητοῦντες στασιάζουσιν

Strife is caused everywhere by inequality, when unequal classes do not receive a proportionate share of power (a perpetual monarchy is unequal among equals); for it is generally the desire for equality that causes factious strife.

Politics 1301b.26

249 ἡ ἐκ τῶν μέσων πολιτεία ... ἀσφαλεστάτη τῶν πολιτειῶν

The most steadfast political community is formed by citizens of the middle class.

Politics 1302a.14

250 ἐλάττους τε γὰρ ὄντες ὅπως ἴσοι ὦσι στασιάζουσι, καὶ ἴσοι ὄντες ὅπως μείζους

Inferiors revolt in order that they may be equal, and equals that they may be superior.

Translated by Benjamin Jowett (1817–1893), rev. Jonathan Barnes (1984)

Politics 1302a.29

251 γίγνονται μὲν οὖν αἱ στάσεις οὐ περὶ μικρῶν ἀλλ' ἐκ μικρῶν, στασιάζουσι δὲ περὶ μεγάλων

In revolutions the occasions may be trifling, but great interests are at stake.

Translated by Benjamin Jowett (1817–1893), rev. Jonathan Barnes (1984)

Politics 1303b.17

252 κινοῦσι δὲ τὰς πολιτείας ὁτὲ μὲν διὰ βίας ὁτὲ δὲ δι' ἀπάτης

There are two ways which can endanger democratic constitutions: the one is force, the other fraud.

Politics 1304b.7

253 τὰς οὐσίας αἱ μικραὶ δαπάναι δαπανῶσι πολλάκις γινόμεναι

A small expenditure recurring often may ruin great estates.

Politics 1307b.33

254 τὸ ἐν ἀρχῇ γινόμενον κακὸν γνῶναι οὐ τοῦ τυχόντος ἀλλὰ πολιτικοῦ ἀνδρός

It needs a statesman to discern evil from the start.

Politics 1308a.33

255 μηδένα ἐγγίγνεσθαι πολὺ ὑπερέχοντα δυνάμει ... εἰ δὲ μή, ἀποδημητικὰς ποιεῖσθαι τὰς παραστάσεις αὐτῶν

No one should arrive at too much power; if so, he better be ostracized.

Politics 1308b.17

256 μέγιστον δὲ πάντων ... πρὸς τὸ διαμένειν τὰς πολιτείας ... τὸ παιδεύεσθαι πρὸς τὰς πολιτείας

Most important, in order to uphold the state, is to educate all according to the principles of the constitution.

Politics 1310a.12

257 ὑπόθεσις μὲν οὖν τῆς δημοκρατικῆς πολιτείας ἐλευθερία

The basis of a democratic state is liberty.

Translated by Benjamin Jowett (1817–1893), rev. Jonathan Barnes (1984)

Politics 1317a.40

258 ἀεὶ γὰρ ζητοῦσι τὸ ἴσον καὶ τὸ δίκαιον οἱ ἥττους, οἱ δὲ κρατοῦντες οὐδὲν φροντίζουσιν

Equality and justice are always sought by the weaker party; those in power pay no heed to either.

Politics 1318b.4

259 οἱ γὰρ πολλοὶ μᾶλλον ὀρέγονται τοῦ κέρδους ἢ τῆς τιμῆς

The many covet gain rather than honour.

Politics 1318b.16

260 ἥδιον γὰρ τοῖς πολλοῖς τὸ ζῆν ἀτάκτως ἢ τὸ σωφρόνως

Most people prefer a disorderly life to one of self-control.

Politics 1319b.31

261 δεῖ τὸν ἀληθινῶς δημοτικὸν ὁρᾶν ὅπως τὸ πλῆθος μὴ λίαν ἄπορον ᾖ

The truly democratic statesman must study how the multitude may be saved from extreme poverty.

Translated by H. Rackham (1932)

Politics 1320a.32

262 τὰ μὲν ἀπὸ τῶν προσόδων γινόμενα συναθροίζοντας ἀθρόα χρὴ διανέμειν τοῖς ἀπόροις, μάλιστα μὲν εἴ τις δύναται τοσοῦτον ἀθροίζων ὅσον εἰς γηδίου κτῆσιν, εἰ δὲ μή, πρὸς ἀφορμὴν ἐμπορίας καὶ γεωργίας

Proceeds of revenues ought to be distributed to the needy, if possible in sums large enough to acquire a small estate, or, failing this, providing incentives for trade or husbandry.

Politics 1320a.36

263 τοὺς ἀπόρους ἀφορμὰς διδόντας τρέπειν ἐπ᾽ ἐργασίας

Supply the poor with capital to start them in business.

Translated by H. Rackham (1932)

Politics 1320b.8

264 ἀδύνατον γὰρ τὸν μηθὲν πράττοντα πράττειν εὖ

It is impossible for the man who does nothing to do well.

Translated by H. Rackham (1932)

Politics 1325a.21

265 δεῖ δ᾽ οὐ μόνον ἀρετὴν ἀλλὰ καὶ δύναμιν ὑπάρχειν καθ᾽ ἣν ἔσται πρακτικός ... κοινῇ πάσης πόλεως ἂν εἴη καὶ καθ᾽ ἕκαστον ἄριστος βίος ὁ πρακτικός

Excellence alone is not enough, a capacity for action is also necessary; an active life is best for the state as a whole, and for each man individually.

Politics 1325b.12

266 ὅ τε γὰρ νόμος τάξις τίς ἐστι, καὶ τὴν εὐνομίαν ἀναγκαῖον εὐταξίαν εἶναι

Law is order, and good law is good order.

Translated by Benjamin Jowett (1817–1893), rev. Jonathan Barnes (1984)

Politics 1326a.29

267 τὸ δὲ τῶν Ἑλλήνων γένος ... καὶ γὰρ ἔνθυμον καὶ διανοητικόν ἐστιν, διόπερ ἐλεύθερόν τε διατελεῖ καὶ βέλτιστα πολιτευόμενον καὶ δυνάμενον ἄρχειν πάντων, μιᾶς τυγχάνον πολιτείας

Greeks are both energetic and intelligent; they are free and well governed; they could rule all mankind if undivided.

Politics 1327b.29

268 πρὸς γὰρ τοὺς συνήθεις καὶ φίλους ὁ θυμὸς αἴρεται μᾶλλον ἢ πρὸς τοὺς ἀγνῶτας, ὀλιγωρεῖσθαι νομίσας

When slighted, one's anger rises up more against friends and associates than against strangers.

Politics 1328a.1

269 ἡ δὲ πόλις κοινωνία τίς ἐστι τῶν ὁμοίων, ἕνεκεν δὲ ζωῆς τῆς ἐνδεχομένης ἀρίστης

The state is a partnership of similar people whose objective is the best life possible.

Politics 1328a.35

270 ἐν μὲν γὰρ ταῖς δημοκρατίαις μετέχουσι πάντες πάντων

Democracies are states in which everyone participates in everything.

Politics 1328b.32

271 εὐδαίμονα δὲ πόλιν οὐκ εἰς μέρος τι βλέψαντας δεῖ λέγειν αὐτῆς ἀλλ' εἰς πάντας τοὺς πολίτας

We should pronounce a state happy having regard not to a particular section but to all its citizens.

Translated by H. Rackham (1932)

Politics 1329a.23

272 οὐ γὰρ χαλεπόν ἐστι τὰ τοιαῦτα νοῆσαι, ἀλλὰ ποιῆσαι μᾶλλον

The difficulty is not so much in the matter of theory but in that of practice.

Translated by H. Rackham (1932)

Politics 1331b.19

273 αἱ δίκαιαι τιμωρίαι καὶ κολάσεις ἀπ' ἀρετῆς μέν εἰσιν, ἀναγκαῖαι δέ, καὶ τὸ καλῶς ἀναγκαίως ἔχουσιν

Just punishments and chastisements do indeed spring from a good principle, but they are good only because we cannot do without them.

Translated by Benjamin Jowett (1817–1893), rev. Jonathan Barnes (1984)

Politics 1332a.12

274 ἀλλὰ μὴν ἀγαθοί γε καὶ σπουδαῖοι γίγνονται διὰ τριῶν· τὰ τρία δὲ ταῦτά ἐστι φύσις ἔθος λόγος

There are three things by which men are made good and virtuous, and these three things are nature, habit and reason.

Translated by H. Rackham (1932)

Politics 1332a.38

275 πόλεμον μὲν εἰρήνης χάριν, ἀσχολίαν δὲ σχολῆς, τὰ δ' ἀναγκαῖα καὶ χρήσιμα τῶν καλῶν ἕνεκεν

War must be for the sake of peace, business for the sake of leisure, things necessary and useful for the purpose of things noble.

Translated by H. Rackham (1932)

Politics 1333a.35

276 ἀπολαύοντα γὰρ φαίνεται τὰ γεννώμενα τῆς ἐχούσης ὥσπερ τὰ φυόμενα τῆς γῆς

Children before birth are evidently affected by the mother just as growing plants are by the earth.

Translated by H. Rackham (1932)

Politics 1335b.18

277 μέχρι πέντε ἐτῶν, ἣν οὔτε πω πρὸς μάθησιν καλῶς ἔχει προσάγειν οὐδεμίαν οὔτε πρὸς ἀναγκαίους πόνους, ὅπως μὴ τὴν αὔξησιν ἐμποδίζωσιν, δεῖ τοσαύτης τυγχάνειν κινήσεως ὥστε διαφεύγειν τὴν ἀργίαν τῶν σωμάτων

Up to the age of five, a period unsuitable for study or work lest growth be impeded, children should be allowed enough movement to avoid bodily inactivity.

Politics 1336a.23

278 πάντα γὰρ δεῖ τὰ τοιαῦτα προοδοποιεῖν πρὸς τὰς ὕστερον διατριβάς· διὸ τὰς παιδιὰς εἶναι δεῖ τὰς πολλὰς μιμήσεις τῶν ὕστερον σπουδαζομένων

All teaching should pave the way for more advanced learning; therefore many children's games should be simulations of the more serious studies in later life.

Politics 1336a.32

279 ἐπεὶ δ' ἓν τὸ τέλος τῇ πόλει πάσῃ, φανερὸν ὅτι καὶ τὴν παιδείαν μίαν καὶ τὴν αὐτὴν ἀναγκαῖον εἶναι πάντων καὶ ταύτης τὴν ἐπιμέλειαν εἶναι κοινὴν καὶ μὴ κατ' ἰδίαν

Since the whole city has one end, it is manifest that education should be one and the same for all, and that it should be public, and not in private.

Translated by Benjamin Jowett (1817–1893), rev. Jonathan Barnes (1984)

Politics 1337a.21

280 ἔκ τε τῆς ἐμποδὼν παιδείας ταραχώδης ἡ σκέψις, καὶ δῆλον οὐδὲν πότερον ἀσκεῖν δεῖ τὰ χρήσιμα πρὸς τὸν βίον ἢ τὰ τείνοντα πρὸς ἀρετὴν ἢ τὰ περιττά· πάντα γὰρ εἴληφε ταῦτα κριτάς τινας

Our present education is based on disordered attitudes; it is not clear at all if our intent is to teach what is useful in life, to aim at moral excellence or to expound the superfluous; for all these have been advocated.

Politics 1337a.39

281 τὸ δὲ ζητεῖν πανταχοῦ τὸ χρήσιμον ἥκιστα ἁρμόττει τοῖς μεγαλοψύχοις καὶ τοῖς ἐλευθερίοις

To search for material advantage in everything is entirely unbefitting to men who are noble-minded and free.

Politics 1338b.2

282 ἐπεὶ δὲ φανερὸν τὸ πρότερον τοῖς ἔθεσιν ἢ τῷ λόγῳ παιδευτέον εἶναι, καὶ περὶ τὸ σῶμα πρότερον ἢ τὴν διάνοιαν

It is plain that education by habit must come before education by reason, and training of the body before education of the mind.

Translated by H. Rackham (1932)

Politics 1338b.4

283 δεῖ δηλον ὅτι μανθάνειν καὶ συνεθίζεσθαι μηθὲν οὕτως ὡς τὸ κρίνειν ὀρθῶς καὶ τὸ χαίρειν τοῖς ἐπιεικέσιν ἤθεσι καὶ ταῖς καλαῖς πράξεσιν

Nothing is more useful than to learn to judge correctly and to delight in fair manners and noble actions.

Politics 1340a.16

284 αὕτη μὲν οὖν ἐστι τοῖς νηπίοις ἁρμόττουσα τῶν παιδίων, ἡ δὲ παιδεία πλαταγὴ τοῖς μείζοσι τῶν νέων

Whereas a rattle is a suitable occupation for infant children, education serves as a rattle for young people when older.

Translated by H. Rackham (1932)

Politics 1340b.29

285 ἄνθρωπος μὲν γὰρ οὐ παντὶ ζῴῳ, ζῷον δὲ παντὶ ἀνθρώπῳ ὑπάρχει

Not every animal is a man; but every man is an animal.

Translated by A.J. Jenkinson (1878–1928)

Prior Analytics 25a.24

286 ὁ δὲ ψευδὴς λόγος γίνεται παρὰ τὸ πρῶτον ψεῦδος

A false conclusion will follow if the original premise is false.

Prior Analytics 66a.16

287 διὰ τί πάντες ὅσοι περιττοὶ γεγόνασιν ἄνδρες ἢ κατὰ φιλοσοφίαν ἢ πολιτικὴν ἢ ποίησιν ἢ τέχνας φαίνονται μελαγχολικοὶ ὄντες

Why is it that all those who have become eminent in philosophy or politics or poetry or the arts are clearly of an atrabilious temperament?

Translated by E.S. Forster (1879–1950), rev. Jonathan Barnes (1984)

Problems 953a.10

cf. Seneca, Moral Essays, *'On Tranquillity of Mind' 17.10, referring to Aristotle: 'nullum magnum ingenium sine mixtura dementiae fuit' (no great genius has ever existed without some touch of madness, tr. John W. Basore, 1932)*

288 μάλιστα μὲν οὖν προσήκει τοὺς ὀρθῶς κειμένους νόμους, ὅσα ἐνδέχεται, πάντα διορίζειν αὐτούς, καὶ ὅτι ἐλάχιστα καταλείπειν ἐπὶ τοῖς κρίνουσι

It is proper that laws, properly enacted, should themselves define the issue of all cases as far as possible, and leave as little as possible to the discretion of the judges.

Translated by J.H. Freese (1926)

Rhetoric 1354a.31

289 τὸ φιλεῖν ἤδη καὶ τὸ μισεῖν καὶ τὸ ἴδιον συμφέρον συνήρτηται πολλάκις, ὥστε μηκέτι δύνασθαι θεωρεῖν ἱκανῶς τὸ ἀληθές, ἀλλ' ἐπισκοτεῖν τῇ κρίσει τὸ ἴδιον ἡδὺ ἢ λυπηρόν

Love, hate, or personal interest is often involved, so that they are no longer capable of discerning the truth adequately, their judgement being obscured by their own pleasure or pain.

Translated by J.H. Freese (1926)

Rhetoric 1354b.8

of the members of the public assembly

290 τό τε γὰρ ἀληθὲς καὶ τὸ ὅμοιον τῷ ἀληθεῖ τῆς αὐτῆς ἐστι δυνάμεως ἰδεῖν

The true and the approximately true are

apprehended by the same faculty.

Translated by W. Rhys Roberts (1858–1929), rev. Jonathan Barnes (1984)

Rhetoric 1355a.14

291 περὶ γὰρ τῶν ἀδυνάτων ἄλλως ἢ γενέσθαι ἢ ἔσεσθαι ἢ ἔχειν οὐδεὶς βουλεύεται οὕτως ὑπολαμβάνων· οὐδὲν γὰρ πλέον

Impossibilities, past, present or future, no one discusses; for nothing is to be gained by it.

Rhetoric 1357a.4

292 σχεδὸν γάρ, περὶ ὧν βουλεύονται πάντες ... τὰ μέγιστα τυγχάνει πέντε τὸν ἀριθμὸν ὄντα· ταῦτα δ' ἐστὶν περί τε πόρων, καὶ πολέμου καὶ εἰρήνης, ἔτι δὲ περὶ φυλακῆς τῆς χώρας, καὶ τῶν εἰσαγομένων καὶ ἐξαγομένων, καὶ νομοθεσίας

The main matters on which all men deliberate are five in number: ways and means, war and peace, national defence, imports and exports, and legislation.

Translated by W. Rhys Roberts (1858–1929), rev. Jonathan Barnes (1984)

Rhetoric 1359b.19

293 οὐ γὰρ μόνον πρὸς τὰ ὑπάρχοντα προστιθέντες πλουσιώτεροι γίγνονται, ἀλλὰ καὶ ἀφαιροῦντες τῶν δαπανημάτων

Men become wealthier, not only by adding to what they already possess, but also by cutting down expenses.

Translated by J.H. Freese (1926)

Rhetoric 1359b.28

294 ἔστω δὴ εὐδαιμονία εὐπραξία μετ' ἀρετῆς, ἢ αὐτάρκεια ζωῆς, ἢ ὁ βίος ὁ μετὰ ἀσφαλείας ἥδιστος, ἢ εὐθενία κτημάτων καὶ σωμάτων μετὰ δυνάμεως φυλακτικῆς τε καὶ πρακτικῆς τούτων· σχεδὸν γὰρ τούτων ἓν ἢ πλείω τὴν εὐδαιμονίαν ὁμολογοῦσιν εἶναι ἅπαντες

Let us then define happiness as well-being combined with virtue, or autarky in life, or a life free from danger, or abundance of possessions with the ability to use and protect them; for nearly all men agree that one or more of these things constitutes happiness.

Rhetoric 1360b.14

295 εἰ δή ἐστιν ἡ εὐδαιμονία τοιοῦτον, ἀνάγκη αὐτῆς εἶναι μέρη εὐγένειαν, πολυφιλίαν, χρηστοφιλίαν, πλοῦτον, εὐτεκνίαν, πολυτεκνίαν, εὐγηρίαν· ἔτι τὰς τοῦ σώματος ἀρετάς (οἷον ὑγίειαν, κάλλος, ἰσχύν, μέγεθος, δύναμιν ἀγωνιστικήν), δόξαν, τιμήν, εὐτυχίαν, ἀρετήν

If, then, such is the nature of happiness, its component parts must necessarily be: noble birth, numerous friends, good friends, wealth, good children, numerous children, a good old age; further, bodily excellences, such as health, beauty, strength, stature, fitness for athletic contests, a good reputation, honour, good luck, virtue.

Translated by J.H. Freese (1926)

Rhetoric 1360b.19

296 ὅλως δὲ τὸ πλουτεῖν ἐστιν ἐν τῷ χρῆσθαι μᾶλλον ἢ ἐν τῷ κεκτῆσθαι

Wealth consists rather in how it is used than in possessing it.

Rhetoric 1361a.23

297 μέρη δὲ ἀρετῆς δικαιοσύνη, ἀνδρεία, σωφροσύνη, μεγαλοπρέπεια, μεγαλοψυχία, ἐλευθεριότης, φρόνησις, σοφία

The components of virtue are justice, courage, self-control, magnificence, magnanimity, liberality, gentleness, prudence, wisdom.

Translated by J.H. Freese (1926)

Rhetoric 1366b.1

298 καλά ... ὅσα τε ὑπὲρ πατρίδος τις ἐποίησεν παριδὼν τὸ αὑτοῦ, ... καὶ ὅσαι εὐπραγίαι περὶ ἄλλους ... καὶ τὰ εὐεργετήματα

Noble are all things which a man has done for the sake of his country, while neglecting his own interests; all acts done for the sake of others; and all acts of kindness.

Translated by J.H. Freese (1926)

Rhetoric 1366b.37

299 πάντα ὅσα πράττουσιν ἀνάγκη πράττειν δι' αἰτίας ἑπτά, διὰ τύχην, διὰ φύσιν, διὰ βίαν, δι' ἔθος, διὰ λογισμόν, διὰ θυμόν, δι' ἐπιθυμίαν

All actions of men must necessarily be referred to seven causes: chance, nature, compulsion, habit, reason, anger, or desire.

Translated by J.H. Freese (1926)

Rhetoric 1369a.5

300 διαφέρει δὲ τιμωρία καὶ κόλασις· ἡ μὲν γὰρ κόλασις τοῦ πάσχοντος ἕνεκά ἐστιν, ἡ δὲ τιμωρία τοῦ ποιοῦντος, ἵνα πληρωθῇ

There is a difference between revenge and punishment; punishment is inflicted in the interest of the sufferer, revenge in the interest of him who inflicts it.

Translated by J.H. Freese (1926)

Rhetoric 1369b.12

301 τὸ εἰθισμένον ὥσπερ πεφυκὸς ἤδη γίγνεται

That which has become habitual becomes as it were natural.

Translated by J.H. Freese (1926)

Rhetoric 1370a.6

302 παρὰ φύσιν γὰρ ἡ βία

Violence is contrary to nature.

Rhetoric 1370a.9

303 τὸ μεταβάλλειν ἡδύ· εἰς φύσιν γὰρ γίγνεται τὸ μεταβάλλειν· τὸ γὰρ αὐτὸ ἀεὶ ὑπερβολὴν ποιεῖ τῆς καθεστώσης ἕξεως

Change is pleasant; it is in the order of nature; repetition only causes the excessive prolongation of a settled condition.

Rhetoric 1371a.25

cf. Euripides 250

304 ἔστι γάρ τι ὃ μαντεύονται πάντες, φύσει κοινὸν δίκαιον καὶ ἄδικον, κἂν μηδεμία κοινωνία πρὸς ἀλλήλους ᾖ μηδὲ συνθήκη, οἷον καὶ ἡ Σοφοκλέους Ἀντιγόνη φαίνεται λέγουσα, ὅτι δίκαιον ἀπειρημένου θάψαι τὸν Πολυνείκη, ὡς φύσει ὂν τοῦτο δίκαιον

There exists a common idea of what is naturally just and unjust, even if there is no previous communication or agreement; this is what Antigone evidently means, when she declares that it is 'naturally' just to bury her brother.

Rhetoric 1373b.6

of unwritten law; cf. Sophocles 81

305 μηδὲ ποῖός τις νῦν, ἀλλὰ ποῖός τις ἦν ἀεὶ

Ask not what a man is now but what he has always been.

Translated by W. Rhys Roberts (1858–1929), rev. Jonathan Barnes (1984)

Rhetoric 1374b.15

306 ὁ γὰρ διαιτητὴς τὸ ἐπιεικὲς ὁρᾷ, ὁ δὲ δικαστὴς τὸν νόμον

The arbitrator looks to equity, the judge to the law.

Translated by H.T. Riley (1872)

Rhetoric 1374b.20

307 οὐδὲν διαφέρει ἢ μὴ κεῖσθαι ἢ μὴ χρῆσθαι τοὺς νόμους

Not to use the laws is as bad as to have no laws at all.

Translated by W. Rhys Roberts (1858–1929), rev. Jonathan Barnes (1984)

Rhetoric 1375b.20

308 οὐδεὶς γὰρ ὃν φοβεῖται φιλεῖ

No one likes one whom he fears.

Translated by J.H. Freese (1926)

Rhetoric 1381b.33

309 τὸ περὶ αὑτοῦ πάντα λέγειν καὶ ἐπαγγέλλεσθαι, καὶ τὸ τἀλλότρια αὑτοῦ φάσκειν· ἀλαζονείας γάρ

Speaking at length about oneself, making false claims, taking the credit for what another has done, these are signs of boastfulness.

Rhetoric 1384a.4

310 ὑπεροχῆς γὰρ ἐπιθυμεῖ ἡ νεότης, ἡ δὲ νίκη ὑπεροχή τις

Youth is eager for superiority over others, and victory is a form of this.

Translated by W. Rhys Roberts (1858–1929), rev. Jonathan Barnes (1984)

Rhetoric 1389a.12

311 τοῦ πιθανωτέρους εἶναι τοὺς ἀπαιδεύτους τῶν πεπαιδευμένων ἐν τοῖς ὄχλοις

Before a crowd the ignorant are more persuasive than the educated.

Rhetoric 1395b.27

312 φανερῶς μὲν τὰ δίκαια καὶ τὰ καλὰ ἐπαινοῦσι μάλιστα, ἰδίᾳ δὲ τὰ συμφέροντα μᾶλλον βούλονται

Openly they praise what is just and noble, and in secret they go for their own advantage.

Rhetoric 1399a.31

313 πάντες γὰρ μεταφοραῖς διαλέγονται καὶ τοῖς οἰκείοις καὶ τοῖς κυρίοις

All use metaphors in conversation, as well as proper and appropriate words.

Translated by J.H. Freese (1926)

Rhetoric 1404b.34

314 τὰ σκληρὰ μαλακῶς λέγηται

To say harsh things with soothing words.

Rhetoric 1408b.10

315 ἀναγκαῖον ... τὰς τῶν προτέρων δόξας συμπαραλαμβάνειν ... ὅπως τὰ μὲν καλῶς εἰρημένα λάβωμεν, εἰ δέ τι μὴ καλῶς, τοῦτ' εὐλαβηθῶμεν

It is essential to consider the views of our predecessors so as to profit by whatever is sound and to avoid their errors.

On the Soul 403b.20

316 λέγουσιν ὥσπερ εἴ τις φαίη τὴν τεκτονικὴν εἰς αὐλοὺς ἐνδύεσθαι· δεῖ γὰρ τὴν μὲν τέχνην χρῆσθαι τοῖς ὀργάνοις, τὴν δὲ ψυχὴν τῷ σώματι

It is absurd to say that the art of carpentry could embody itself in flutes; each art must use its tools, each soul its body.

Translated by J.A. Smith (1863–1939), rev. Jonathan Barnes (1984)

On the Soul 407b.24

refuting the Pythagorean view that any soul can be 'be clothed upon with any body'

317 οὐκ ἔστιν αἴσθησις ἑτέρα παρὰ τὰς πέντε λέγω δὲ ταύτας ὄψιν, ἀκοήν, ὄσφρησιν, γεῦσιν, ἁφήν

There is no sense in addition to the five – sight, hearing, smell, taste, touch.

Translated by J.A. Smith (1863–1939), rev. Jonathan Barnes (1984)

On the Soul 424b.22

318 εἰσὶ δὲ καὶ αὐτῆς τῆς ὑπολήψεως διαφοραί, ἐπιστήμη καὶ δόξα καὶ φρόνησις καὶ τἀναντία τούτων

Within the field of judgement itself we find varieties: knowledge, opinion, understanding and their opposites.

Translated by J.A. Smith (1863–1939), rev. Jonathan Barnes (1984)

On the Soul 427b.24

319 ἡ χεὶρ ὄργανόν ἐστιν ὀργάνων

The hand, most capable of all instruments.

On the Soul 432a.1

320 ὡς ὄψις ἐν ὀφθαλμῷ, νοῦς ἐν ψυχῇ

As sight is to the eyes, reason is to the spirit.

Topics 108a.11

321 τετάχθαι περὶ τὸν βίον ὁμοίως ἔν τε μικροῖς καὶ μεγάλοις

Live an orderly life in small things and great alike.

Translated by H. Rackham (1935)

*Virtues and Vices** 1250b.10

322 ὁ θεὸς ἢ νοῦς ἐστὶν ἢ ἐπέκεινά τι τοῦ νοῦ

God is either reason or something beyond reason.

Fragment 49 (Rose) – *Peri Euches (On Prayer)*

323 εἰ μὲν φιλοσοφητέον φιλοσοφητέον καὶ εἰ μὴ φιλοσοφητέον φιλοσοφητέον· πάντως ἄρα φιλοσοφητέον

You say one must philosophize. Then you must philosophize. You say one should not philosophize. Then (to prove your contention) you must philosophize. In any case you must philosophize.

Translated by Jacques Maritain (2005), translated into English by E.I. Watkin

Fragment 51 (Rose) – *Protrepticus*

a celebrated dilemma of Aristotle

324 ἢ φιλοσοφητέον οὖν ἢ χαίρειν εἰποῦσι τῷ ζῆν ἀπιτέον ἐντεῦθεν, ὡς τὰ ἄλλα γε πάντα φλυαρία τις ἔοικεν εἶναι πολλὴ καὶ λῆρος

Either philosophize, then, or say farewell to life and depart hence, since all else seems to be mere prattle and trash.

Fragment 61 (Rose) – *Protrepticus*

325 τῶν φιλτάτων τὰ φίλτατα

Most beloved of those we love most.

Fragment 553 (Rose)

326 ὥσπερ ὁ καπνὸς ἐπιδάκνων τὰς ὄψεις οὐκ ἐᾷ βλέπειν τὸ κείμενον ἐν τοῖς ποσίν, οὕτως ὁ θυμὸς ἐπαιρόμενος τῷ λογισμῷ ἐπισκοτεῖ καὶ τὸ συμβησόμενον ἐξ αὐτοῦ ἄτοπον οὐκ ἀφίησι τῇ διανοίᾳ προλαβεῖν

Just as smoke stings our eyes and prevents us from seeing what is under our feet, so anger, once aroused, clouds our reason and does not allow our mind to anticipate the absurdity which will result from it.

Translated by Jonathan Barnes and Gavin Lawrence (1984)

Fragment 660 (Rose)

327 ἀρετά, πολύμοχθε γένει βροτείῳ,
θήραμα κάλλιστον βίῳ,
σᾶς πέρι, παρθένε, μορφᾶς

O virtue, toilsome for mortals to achieve,
the fairest prize that life can win,
for thy beauty, O virgin.

Translated by R.D. Hicks (1925)

Fragment 675 (Rose)

328 τοῖς ψευδομένοις, ὅταν, ἔφη, λέγωσιν ἀληθῆ, μὴ πιστεύεσθαι

Liars when they speak the truth are not believed.

Translated by R.D. Hicks (1925)

Diogenes Laertius, *Lives of Eminent Philosophers* 5.17

cf. Aesop 37

329 τί γηράσκει ταχύ; χάρις

What soon grows old? Gratitude.

Translated in *Bartlett's Familiar Quotations* (1980)

Diogenes Laertius, *Lives of Eminent Philosophers* 5.18.2

330 ἐλπίς ἐγρηγορότος ἐνύπνιον

Hope is a waking dream.

Translated by R.D. Hicks (1925)

Diogenes Laertius, *Lives of Eminent Philosophers* 5.18.3

331 τριῶν ἔφη δεῖν παιδείᾳ, φύσεως, μαθήσεως, ἀσκήσεως

Three things he declared to be indispensable for education: natural endowment, study, and constant practice.

Translated by R.D. Hicks (1925)

Diogenes Laertius, *Lives of Eminent Philosophers* 5.18.8

332 τὸ κάλλος παντὸς ἔλεγεν ἐπιστολίου συστατικώτερον

Beauty he declared to be a greater recommendation than any letter of introduction.

Translated by R.D. Hicks (1925)

Diogenes Laertius, *Lives of Eminent Philosophers* 5.19.1

333 αὐτὸν δὲ θεοῦ δῶρον εἰπεῖν εὐμορφίαν

Beauty is the gift of god.

Translated in *Bartlett's Familiar Quotations* (1980)

Diogenes Laertius, *Lives of Eminent Philosophers* 5.19.2

334 τίνι διαφέρουσιν οἱ πεπαιδευμένοι τῶν ἀπαιδεύτων, 'ὅσῳ,' εἶπεν, 'οἱ ζῶντες τῶν τεθνεώτων'

Being asked how the educated differ from the uneducated, 'As much as the living from the dead' he said.

Translated by R.D. Hicks (1925)

Diogenes Laertius, *Lives of Eminent Philosophers* 5.19.6

335 ἐρωτηθεὶς τί ἐστι φίλος, ἔφη, μία ψυχὴ δύο σώμασιν ἐνοικοῦσα

What is a friend? A single soul dwelling in two bodies.

Translated by R.D. Hicks (1925)

Diogenes Laertius, *Lives of Eminent Philosophers* 5.20.1

336 τῶν ἀνθρώπων ἔλεγε τοὺς μὲν οὕτω φείδεσθαι ὡς ἀεὶ ζησομένους, τοὺς δὲ οὕτως ἀναλίσκειν ὡς αὐτίκα τεθνηξομένους

Mankind, he used to say, were divided into those who were thrifty as if they would live for ever, and those who were extravagant as if they were going to die the next day.

Translated by R.D. Hicks (1925)

Diogenes Laertius, *Lives of Eminent Philosophers* 5.20.2

337 τυφλοῦ τὸ ἐρώτημα

That is a blind man's question.

Translated by R.D. Hicks (1925)

Diogenes Laertius, *Lives of Eminent Philosophers* 5.20.4

when asked why he spent so much time with beautiful people

338 ἐρωτηθεὶς τί ποτ' αὐτῷ περιγέγονεν ἐκ φιλοσοφίας, ἔφη, 'τὸ ἀνεπιτάκτως ποιεῖν ἅ τινες διὰ τὸν ἀπὸ τῶν νόμων φόβον ποιοῦσιν'

I have gained by philosophy this: I do without being commanded, what others do only from fear of the law.

Diogenes Laertius, *Lives of Eminent Philosophers* 5.20.5

339 ἐὰν τοὺς προέχοντας διώκοντες τοὺς ὑστεροῦντας μὴ ἀναμένωσι

By pressing hard on those in front and not waiting for those behind.

Translated by R.D. Hicks (1925)

Diogenes Laertius, *Lives of Eminent Philosophers* 5.20.8

on how students can make progress

340 φίλοις προσφεροίμεθα ὡς ἂν εὐξαίμεθα αὐτοὺς ἡμῖν προσφέρεσθαι

We should behave to our friends as we would wish our friends to behave to us.

Translated in *Bartlett's Familiar Quotations* (1980)

Diogenes Laertius, *Lives of Eminent Philosophers* 5.21.4

cf. the proverb 'do as you would be done by'

341 κάλλιστον ἐφόδιον τῷ γήρᾳ τὴν παιδείαν ἔλεγε

Education is the best provision for old age.

Translated by R.D. Hicks (1925)

Diogenes Laertius, *Lives of Eminent Philosophers* 5.21.6

342 Ἀριστοτέλης τοὺς τὰ ἐναργῆ πράγματα πειρωμένους δεικνύναι ὅμοιον ἔφη ποιεῖν τοῖς διὰ λύχνου τὸν ἥλιον φιλοτιμουμένοις δεικνύναι

Aristotle said of those who wished to explain the obvious, that they were equivalent to those who would endeavour to shine a lantern at the sun.

Stobaeus, *Anthology* 3.4.86

343 Ἀριστοτέλης ἐρωτηθεὶς τί δυσκολώτατόν ἐστιν ἐν τῷ βίῳ, εἶπε τὸ σιωπᾶν ἃ μὴ δεῖ λαλεῖν

When asked what the most difficult thing in life was, Aristotle replied, 'Not to say what shouldn't be said.'

Stobaeus, *Anthology* 3.41.8

344 Ἀριστοτέλης τῆς φύσεως γραμματεὺς ἦν, τὸν κάλαμον ἀποβρέχων εἰς νοῦν

He was the interpreter of nature, dipping his pen in his mind.

Translated by H.T. Riley (1872)

Suda, Lexicon Alpha 3930

ARISTOXENUS

born *c.*370BC

Known for musical writings, also philosopher, biographer and historian from Tarentum

1 τοὺς μὲν γὰρ ἄρχοντας ἔφασκον οὐ μόνον ἐπιστήμονας ἀλλὰ καὶ φιλανθρώπους δεῖν εἶναι

A ruler should not only be cultured but should be charitable too.

Fragment 35 (Wehrli)

2 μὴ εἶναι πρὸς πάντας πάντα ῥητά

You cannot tell everybody everything.

Fragment 43 (Wehrli)

of the doctrines of Pythagoras

ARRIAN

Lucius Flavius Arrianus

86–160AD

Philosopher and historian

1 τὴν γὰρ χελιδόνα σύντροφόν τε εἶναι ὄρνιθα καὶ εὔνουν ἀνθρώποις καὶ λάλον μᾶλλον ἢ ἄλλην ὄρνιθα

The swallow is a companion to man, friendly and more talkative than any other bird.

Anabasis of Alexander 1.25.8

2 πέρας δὲ τῶν πόνων γενναίῳ μὲν ἀνδρὶ οὐδὲν δοκῶ ἔγωγε ὅτι μὴ αὐτοὺς τοὺς πόνους, ὅσοι αὐτῶν ἐς καλὰ ἔργα φέρουσιν

I set no limit to toil for a man of noble spirit as long as toil leads to excellence.

Anabasis of Alexander 5.26.1

3 οὐδὲ γὰρ ὁμοίοις ἔτι χρήσῃ ἐς τοὺς κινδύνους, οἷς τὸ ἑκούσιον ἐν τοῖς ἀγῶσιν ἀπέσται

No longer will men meet dangers when it is not by their own choice that they engage in conflicts.

Anabasis of Alexander 5.27.7

4 καλὸν δέ … εἴπερ τι καὶ ἄλλο, καὶ ἡ ἐν τῷ εὐτυχεῖν σωφροσύνη

Nothing is so unquestionably good as a sound mind in good fortune.

Translated by P.A. Brunt (1983)

Anabasis of Alexander 5.27.9

5 τὰ δὲ ἐκ τοῦ δαιμονίου ἀδόκητά τε καὶ ταύτῃ καὶ ἀφύλακτα τοῖς ἀνθρώποις ἐστί

Unexpected are the whims of god, impossible to guard against.

Anabasis of Alexander 5.27.9

6 βασιλεῦ Ἀλέξανδρε, ἄνθρωπος μὲν ἕκαστος τοσόνδε τῆς γῆς κατέχει ὅσονπερ τοῦτό ἐστιν ἐφ' ὅτῳ βεβήκαμεν ... καὶ ὀλίγον ὕστερον ἀποθανὼν τοσοῦτον καθέξεις τῆς γῆς ὅσον ἐξαρκεῖ ἐντεθάφθαι τῷ σώματι

King Alexander, each man possesses no more of this earth than the patch we stand on; and very soon you too will die, and will possess no more of the earth than suffices for the burial of your body.

Translated by P.A. Brunt (1983)

Anabasis of Alexander 7.1.6

Brahman philosophers to Alexander

7 κομόωντές τε καὶ ῥυπόωντες καὶ μεστοὶ ἅλμης καὶ ῥικνοὶ τὰ σώματα καὶ ὠχροὶ ὑπὸ ἀγρυπνίης τε καὶ τῆς ἄλλης ταλαιπωρίης

With long hair, filthy and covered with brine, their bodies shrivelled, their faces ashen from sleeplessness and other hardships.

Indica 34.7

of Nearchus, admiral to Alexander, and his followers on their arrival from their Indian Ocean expedition

8 ὦ βασιλεῦ, ἔφη, καὶ αἱ νέες τοι σῶαί εἰσι καὶ ὁ στρατός· ἡμεῖς δὲ οὗτοι ἄγγελοι τῆς σωτηρίας αὐτῶν ἥκομεν

Sire, he replied, your ships and force are safe; we are come to tell with our own lips of their safety.

Translated by P.A. Brunt (1983)

Indica 35.6

Nearchus to Alexander who feared that his fleet from India had been wrecked

ARTEMIDORUS

mid/late 2nd century AD

Author of a dream-book from Ephesus

1 τὸ δὲ στόμα τάφῳ· ὅσα γὰρ ἂν λάβῃ τὸ στόμα, ταῦτα διαφθείρει καὶ οὐ φυλάττει

The mouth of man is like the tomb: it hides away whatever it receives.

Onirocriticon 1.80

2 τέλη μὲν γὰρ ἀμφότερα τοῖς ἀνθρώποις εἶναι νενόμισται καὶ ὁ γάμος καὶ ὁ θάνατος

Both marriage and death are held to be ending rites for humans.

Translated by Angeliki Kosmopoulou (2009)

Onirocriticon 2.49

ASCLEPIADES

fl. 300–270BC

Epigrammatist from Samos

1 Φείδῃ παρθενίης. καὶ τί πλέον; οὐ γὰρ ἐς Ἅιδην
ἐλθοῦσ' εὑρήσεις τὸν φιλέοντα, κόρη.

Girl, why so miserly
with your virginity?
None will make love to you
in Hades down below.

Translated by Rachel Hadas (2010)

Epigram 5.85

2 Ἡδὺ θέρους διψῶντι χιὼν ποτόν· ἡδὺ δὲ ναύταις
ἐκ χειμῶνος ἰδεῖν εἰαρινὸν ζέφυρον·
ἥδιον δ', ὁπόταν κρύψῃ μία τοὺς φιλέοντας
χλαῖνα καὶ αἰνῆται Κύπρις ὑπ' ἀμφοτέρων.

Sweet is the spring for the sailor, when winter's storm is over,
Sweet for the thirsty in summer is the cool drink of snow;
But sweeter still the time when one cloak shall cover
A pair of lovers who honour the goddess of Love.

Translated by Andrew Sinclair (1967)

Epigram 5.169

3 Τῷ θαλλῷ Διδύμη με συνήρπασεν· ὤ μοι, ἐγὼ δὲ
τήκομαι ὡς κηρὸς πὰρ πυρί, κάλλος ὁρῶν.
εἰ δὲ μέλαινα, τί τοῦτο; καὶ ἄνθρακες· ἀλλ' ὅτε κείνους
θάλψωμεν, λάμπουσ' ὡς ῥόδεαι κάλυκες.

Didyme waved a branch at me.
I melt as wax before her beauty.
What if she is black? so's coal, that glows
When it's alight, more than the rose.

Translated by Andrew Sinclair (1967)

She's black: what then? so are dead coals, but cherish,
And with soft breath them blow,
And you shall see them glow as bright and flourish,
As spring-borne Roses grow.

Translated by Phineas Fletcher (1623)

Epigram 5.210

cf. Bible, The Song of Solomon 1.5: 'μέλαινά εἰμι καὶ καλή' (I am black, but beautiful)

4 οἶνος ἔρωτος ἔλεγχος

Wine is the test of love.

Translated by C.A. Trypanis (1971)

Epigram 12.135

ASTYDAMAS

4th century BC

Two tragic playwrights, father and son

1 οὐ τοῦ δοκεῖν μοι, τῆς δ' ἀληθείας μέλει

Not what seems good to me, it is the truth I care for.

Fragment 1c (Snell, *TrGF*) – *Alcmeon*

ST ATHANASIUS

*c.*295–373AD

Theologian and church leader, bishop of Alexandria from 328

1 καὶ μὴ ζήτει πῶς· ὅπου γὰρ βούλεται Θεός, νικᾶται φύσεως τάξις

And do not enquire how; for wherever God wills, the order of nature is vanquished.

*Sermon on the Nativity**, vol. 28.960.37 (*MPG*)

of the Virgin Mary having been found with child; incorporated in the Acts of the Ephesus Ecumenical Council *1.1.5.67.17* (ACO); *cf. St Ephraem of Syria,* On the Transfiguration *15.8; and Euripides 529*

2 νεφύδριον ... καὶ θᾶττον παρελεύσεται

It is but a cloudlet and will soon pass away.

Sozomen, *Ecclesiastical History* 5.15.3

of an order given by Julian the Apostate for him to step down as bishop of Alexandria; Athanasius was exiled five times during his bishopric

ATHENAEUS

*fl. c.*200AD

Philosopher from Naucratis in Egypt

1 ὅταν ὕδατα μετοπωρινὰ καὶ βρονταὶ γίνωνται σκληραί, τότε γίνεσθαι, καὶ μᾶλλον ὅταν αἱ βρονταί, ὡς ταύτης αἰτιωτέρας οὔσης

They grow when the autumn rains come with severe thunderstorms; the more thundering there is, the more they grow.

Translated by Charles Burton Gulick (1927)

Deipnosophists 2.62b

of a mushroom species growing in Thrace

2 σῦκα φίλ' ὀρνίθεσσι, φυτεύειν δ' οὐκ ἐθέλουσι

Birds love figs, but they will not plant them.

Translated by Charles Burton Gulick (1927)

Deipnosophists 3.80e

entered by Athenaeus as proverbial

3 εἰ μὴ ἰατροὶ ἦσαν, οὐδὲν ἂν ἦν τῶν γραμματικῶν μωρότερον

If doctors did not exist, there would be nothing more dull than scholars.

Deipnosophists 15.666a

ATTICUS

*c.*150–200AD

Platonist philosopher

1 ἀλλὰ κἂν πενία, κἂν νόσος, κἂν ἀδοξία, κἂν βάσανοι, κἂν πίττα καὶ σταυρός, κἂν τὰ ἐκ τῆς τραγῳδίας, ἅμα πάντα ἐπιρρυῇ, ἔτι ὁ δίκαιος εὐδαίμων καὶ μακάριος

But even if poverty, sickness, ill repute, even agony, pitch and cross, and all events of tragedy beat upon him, the just is blessed with a good and happy spirit.

Fragment 4.13 (Baudry)

AUGUSTUS

63BC–14AD

First Roman emperor

1 τοῦ πρωτογόνου θεοῦ

To the firstborn God.

Translated by Michael Wood (2003)

Malalas, *Chronographia* 232.4

inscribed (in Latin) on an altar on the Roman

Capitol by Emperor Augustus after receiving the oracle from Delphi; cf. Oracles 24

2 ἀκούσατε εἶπε νέοι γέροντος, οὗ νέου γέροντες ἤκουον

Young men, listen to an old man to whom old men listened when he was young.

Plutarch, *Sayings of Romans* 207e

spoken when trying to calm a group of youths of high station who would not listen to him

AUTOMEDON
1st century BC
Epigrammatist

1 Εὐδαίμων ... ὁ μηδενὶ μηδὲν ὀφείλων

Happy is he who owes naught to anyone.

Greek Anthology 11.50

B

BACCHYLIDES

*c.*520–450BC

Lyric poet from Iulis in Ceos (Kea) in the Cyclades

1 χορῷ δ' ἔτερπον κέαρ ὑγροῖσιν ἐν ποσίν

On supple feet, they danced to their heart's delight.

Dithyrambs 17.107

2 πάντ' ἐν τῷ δολιχῷ χρόνῳ τελεῖται

All things come to an end in the long course of time.

Translated by David A. Campbell (1992)

Dithyrambs 18.45

3 παῖδα δ' ἔμμεν
πρώθηβον, ἀρηΐων δ' ἀθυρμάτων
μεμνᾶσθαι πολέμου τε καὶ
χαλκεοκτύπου μάχας

In the prime of youth his thoughts are on war and the clashing bronze of battle, the pastimes of Ares.

Dithyrambs 18.56

4 τὸ δὲ πάν-
των εὐμαρεῖν οὐδὲν γλυκὺ
θνατοῖσιν, ἀλλ' αἰεὶ τὰ φεύγοντα δίζηνται κιχεῖν

To have abundance of everything brings no pleasure; we always seek what eludes us.

Victory Odes 1.174

5 ἀρετὰ δ' ἐπίμοχθος
μέν, τελευταθεῖσα δ' ὀρθῶς
ἀνδρὶ καὶ εὖτε θάνῃ λεί-
πει πολυζήλωτον εὐκλείας ἄγαλμα

Virtue is exacting
but, if accomplished,
it leaves a lasting memorial
to honour, after death.

Victory Odes 1.181

6 τυφλὰ δ' ἐκ χειρῶν βέλη
ψυχαῖς ἔπι δυσμενέων φοι-
τᾷ θάνατόν τε φέρει
τοῖσιν ἂν δαίμων θέλῃ

Blind are the missiles from our hands;
they bring death to those
for whom it is god's wish.

Victory Odes 5.132

7 χρὴ δ' ἀλαθείας χάριν
αἰνεῖν, φθόνον ἀμφοτέραισιν
χερσὶν ἀπωσάμενον,
εἴ τις εὖ πράσσοι βροτῶν

For the sake of truth one must thrust envy aside with both hands and praise any mortal who is successful.

Translated by David A. Campbell (1992)

Victory Odes 5.187

8 ματεύει
δ' ἄλλος ἀλλοίαν κέλευθον,
ἅντινα στείχων ἀριγνώτοιο δόξας
τεύξεται· μυρίαι δ' ἀνδρῶν ἐπιστᾶμαι
πέλονται

Different men go different ways seeking glory,
and human knowledge is of countless kinds.

Victory Odes 10.35

9 τὸ μέλλον
δ' ἀκρίτους τίκτει τελευτάς,

πᾶ τύχα βρίσει

There is no predicting how Fortune will tip the scales.

Translated by David A. Campbell (1992)

Victory Odes 10.45

10 τὸ μὲν κάλλιστον, ἐσθλὸν
ἄνδρα πολλῶν ὑπ' ἀνθρώπων
πολυζήλωτον εἶμεν

This is the finest thing, to be a noble man
much envied by many.

Translated by David A. Campbell (1992)

Victory Odes 10.47

11 οἶδα καὶ πλούτου μεγάλαν δύνασιν,
ἃ καὶ τὸν ἀχρεῖον τίθησι
χρηστόν

I know also wealth's great power,
which makes even the useless man
useful.

Translated by David A. Campbell (1992)

Victory Odes 10.49

12 Νίκα γλυκύδωρε

Victory, giver of sweet joy.

Victory Odes 11.1

13 ὅταν θανάτοιο
κυάνεον νέφος καλύψῃ, λείπεται
ἀθάνατον κλέος εὖ ἐρχθέντος

When covered by the dark blue cloud of death
undying fame is left behind for deeds well done.

Victory Odes 13.63

14 ὥστ' ἐν κυανανθέϊ θυμὸν ἀνέρων
πόντῳ Βορέας ὑπὸ κύ-
μασιν δαΐζει,
νυκτὸς ἀντάσας ἀνατελλομένας,
λῆξεν δὲ σὺν φαεσιμβρότῳ
Ἀοῖ, στόρεσεν δέ τε πόντον
οὐρία· Νότου δὲ κόλπωσαν πνοᾷ
ἱστίον ἁρπαλέως τ' ἄ-
ελπτον ἐξίκοντο χέρσον

As on a dark-blossoming sea
Boreas rends men's hearts with the billows,
coming face to face with them as night rises up,
but ceases on the arrival of Dawn
who gives light to mortals, and a gentle breeze
levels the sea, and before the south wind's breath
they belly out their sail and eagerly reach the dry land
which they had despaired of seeing again.

Translated by David A. Campbell (1992)

Victory Odes 13.124

Boreas, the North Wind

15 βροτῶν δὲ μῶμος
πάντεσσι μέν ἐστιν ἐπ' ἔργοις

Fault is found by mortals in all achievements.

Translated by David A. Campbell (1992)

Victory Odes 13.202

16 ἁ δ' ἀλαθεία φιλεῖ
νικᾶν, ὅ τε πανδαμάτωρ
χρόνος τὸ καλῶς
ἐργμένον αἰὲν ἀέξει

Truth is wont to win,
and all-subduing time
exalts what is well done.

Victory Odes 13.204

17 τιμὰν
δ' ἄλλος ἀλλοίαν ἔχει·
μυρίαι δ' ἀνδρῶν ἀρεταί

Honour comes in different ways;
excellence is shown by man in countless forms.

Victory Odes 14.6

18 εὖ ἔρδοντα δὲ καὶ θεὸς ὀρθοῖ

Him that does well god will also succour.

Victory Odes 14.18

19 ὡς δ' ἅπαξ εἰπεῖν, φρένα καὶ πυκινὰν
κέρδος ἀνθρώπων βιᾶται

Said once and for all, profit corrupts the strongest mind.

Fragment 1 – *Victory Odes*

20 τίκτει δέ τε θνατοῖσιν εἰρήνα μεγαλάνορα πλοῦτον
καὶ μελιγλώσσων ἀοιδᾶν ἄνθεα

Peace creates for men
wealth and honey-tongued songs.

Fragment 4.61 – *Paeans*

21 χαλκεᾶν δ' οὐκ ἔστι σαλπίγγων κτύπος,
οὐδὲ συλᾶται μελίφρων
ὕπνος ἀπὸ βλεφάρων

ἀῷος ὃς θάλπει κέαρ

No din of bronze trumpets can disrupt sleep, honey for the mind, still soothing the heart at daybreak.

Fragment 4.75 – *Paeans*

22 συμποσίων δ' ἐρατῶν βρίθοντ' ἀγυιαί,
παιδικοί θ' ὕμνοι φλέγονται

Full are the streets with joyous happenings
and full of fire are the youngsters' songs.

Fragment 4.79 – *Paeans*

23 ἕτερος ἐξ ἑτέρου σοφὸς
τό τε πάλαι τό τε νῦν· οὐδὲ γὰρ ῥᾷστον
ἀρρήτων ἐπέων πύλας
ἐξευρεῖν

One learns his skill from others,
now as in days of old; for 'tis no easy matter
to discover the gates of verse unspoken before.

Translated by David A. Campbell (1992)

Fragment 5 – *Paeans*

of poetic skill; cf. Pindar 47

24 ἄρκτου παρούσης ἴχνη μὴ ζήτει

Don't look for footprints when the bear's nearby.

Fragment 6 – *Paeans*

25 εἷς ὅρος, μία βροτοῖσίν ἐστιν εὐτυχίας ὁδός,
θυμὸν εἴ τις ἔχων ἀπενθῆ δύναται
διατελεῖν βίον· ὃς δὲ μυ-
ρία μὲν ἀμφιπολεῖ φρενί,
τὸ δὲ παρ' ἆμάρ τε καὶ νύκτα μελλόντων
χάριν αἰὲν ἰάπτεται
κέαρ, ἄκαρπον ἔχει πόνον

There is one guideline, one path to happiness for mortals:
to keep an ungrieving spirit throughout life;
whoever busies his mind with a myriad of cares,
anxious day and night about the future,
is out for fruitless suffering.

Fragment 11 – *Prosodia*

prosodia were processional chants

26 πάντεσσι γὰρ θνατοῖσι δαίμων ἐπέταξε πόνους ἄλλοισιν ἄλλους

For all mortals god ordained toils,
these for one, those for another.

Translated by David A. Campbell (1992)

Fragment 13 – *Prosodia*

27 Λυδία μὲν γὰρ λίθος
μανύει χρυσόν, ἀν-
δρῶν δ' ἀρετὰν σοφία τε
παγκρατής τ' ἐλέγχει
ἀλάθεια

The Lydian stone
betrays what's gold,
whereas men's virtue
is brought to proof
by all-powerful truth.

Fragment 14 – *Hyporchemata*

hyporchemata were dance-songs

28 οὐχ ἕδρας ἔργον οὐδ' ἀμβολᾶς

This is no time for sitting or delay.

Translated by David A. Campbell (1992)

Fragment 15 – *Hyporchemata*

29 ὄλβιος δ' οὐδεὶς βροτῶν πάντα χρόνον

No one can be happy all his days.

Fragment 54

authorship uncertain

ST BASIL

*c.*330–379AD (1st January)
Bishop of Caesarea in Cappadocia

1 μέμνησθε τῶν ἐπῶν δηλονότι, ἐν οἷς ἐκεῖνός φησιν ἄριστον μὲν εἶναι τὸν παρ' ἑαυτοῦ τὰ δέοντα συνορῶντα, ἐσθλὸν δὲ κἀκεῖνον τὸν τοῖς παρ' ἑτέρων ὑποδειχθεῖσιν ἑπόμενον, τὸν δὲ πρὸς οὐδέτερον ἐπιτήδειον ἀχρεῖον εἶναι πρὸς ἅπαντα

Remember Hesiod who says that he is best who, of his own accord, sees at a glance what is necessary. But good also is he who follows advice received from others. But he who is fit for neither thing is worthless for everything.

Translated by D.C. Whimster (1934)

Address to Young Men on Greek Literature 1.16

cf. Hesiod 36

2 τὰ φρέατά φασιν ἀντλούμενα βελτίω γίνεσθαι

The more you draw, the sweeter the water.

Letters 151.1.10

of the intellect, improved with use

3 ἄνω σχῶμεν τὰς καρδίας

Lift up your hearts towards heaven.

Liturgy vol. 31.1636.17 *(MPG)*

4 κύριε, ἐλέησον

Kyrie eleison – Lord, have mercy upon us.

Liturgy vol. 31.1649.50 et al. *(MPG)*

an invocation used from the earliest days of the Christian church, still part of the liturgy of several denominations; cf. Bible 331

5 ἵνα μὴ λήθη κλέψῃ τὴν γνῶσιν … τρόπον ἐπενόησε διδασκαλίας ἀθάνατον· ἵνα ἡ μὲν γλῶττα παρέχῃ τὴν γνῶσιν, ἡ δὲ χεὶρ διὰ τῶν γραμμάτων ἐγχαράττῃ τὴν μνήμην

In order that forgetfulness should not cheat knowledge, he devised an immortal way of teaching: as the tongue would provide knowledge, the hand through writing should engrave it on memory.

Sermon 61.368.30 *(MPG)*

of Moses

6 θεοῦ ἄγνοια θάνατός ἐστι ψυχῆς

Ignorance of god is death of the soul.

Homilia exhortatoria ad sanctum baptisma vol. 31.424.36 *(MPG)*

7 ἀνέγνως, ἀλλ' οὐκ ἔγνως· εἰ γὰρ ἔγνως, οὐκ ἂν κατέγνως

You have read, but you have not understood; if you had understood, you would not have condemned.

Epistles 157

in answer to 'I have read, I have understood, I have condemned' (cf. Julian the Apostate 1)

BATON

mid 3rd century BC
New Comedy poet

1 τί τἀργύριον, ἄνθρωπε, τιμιώτερον σαυτοῦ τέθεικας ἢ πέφυκε τῇ φύσει;

Why, my friend, do you consider money more valuable than it is by its own nature?

BIAS

6th century BC
Philosopher from Priene and one of the Seven Sages
see also Menander 280; Seven Sages 39–40

1 τὸ λέγειν δύνασθαι τὰ συμφέροντα τῇ πόλει ψυχῆς ἴδιον καὶ φρονήσεως

To have the courage to speak of what is truly in the interest of one's country is the mark of high spirit and reason.

Seven Sages, *Apophthegms* 6.2 (Mullach, *FPG*)

2 νόσος ψυχῆς τὸ τῶν ἀδυνάτων ἐρᾶν

It is a sickness of the soul to be enamoured of things impossible to attain.

Seven Sages, *Apophthegms* 6.4 (Mullach, *FPG*)

3 οὕτω πειρῶ ζῆν ὡς καὶ ὀλίγον καὶ πολὺν χρόνον βιωσόμενος

Measure life as if you had both a short and a long time to live.

Translated by R.D. Hicks (1925)

Seven Sages, *Apophthegms* 6.6 (Mullach, *FPG*)

4 ἐρωτηθείς, τί γλυκὺ ἀνθρώποις; ἐλπίς, ἔφη

Being asked, 'What is sweet to men,' he answered, 'Hope.'

Translated by R.D. Hicks (1925)

Seven Sages, *Apophthegms* 6.19 (Mullach, *FPG*)

5 θανάτῳ μέλλων καταδικάζειν τινὰ ἐδάκρυσεν· εἰπόντος δέ τινος, τί παθὼν αὐτὸς καταδικάζεις καὶ κλαίεις; εἶπεν, ὅτι ἀναγκαῖόν ἐστι τῇ μὲν φύσει τὸ συμπαθὲς ἀποδοῦναι, τῷ δὲ νόμῳ τὴν ψῆφον

Just before condemning someone Bias let flow a tear. When asked why he both condemned and wept, he said: 'I have to render to nature my feelings, to law my vote.'

Seven Sages, *Apophthegms* 6.21 (Mullach, *FPG*)

6 οἱ πλεῖστοι ἄνθρωποι κακοί

Most people are bad.

Translated by H.T. Riley (1872)

Seven Sages, *Apophthegms* Fragment 6.2 (D-K)

7 βραδέως ἐγχείρει· οὗ δ' ἂν ἄρξῃ, διαβεβαιοῦ

Be slow to set about an enterprise; but once undertaken persevere.

Seven Sages, *Apophthegms* Fragment 6.4 (D-K)

8 μίσει τὸ ταχὺ λαλεῖν, μὴ ἁμάρτῃς· μετάνοια γὰρ ἀκολουθεῖ

Speak not in haste, lest you err; regret will follow.

Seven Sages, *Apophthegms* Fragment 6.4 (D-K)

9 περὶ θεῶν λέγε, ὡς εἰσίν

Admit the existence of the gods.

Translated by R.D. Hicks (1925)

Seven Sages, *Apophthegms* Fragment 6.6 (D-K)

10 ἄκουε πολλά, λάλει καίρια

Listen to many things, speak only at the right time.

Seven Sages, *Apophthegms* Fragment 6.7 (D-K)

11 ἀνάξιον ἄνδρα μὴ ἐπαίνει διὰ πλοῦτον

Praise not a worthless man because of his wealth.

Seven Sages, *Apophthegms* Fragment 6.8 (D-K)

12 πείσας λαβέ, μὴ βιασάμενος

Win by persuasion, not by force.

Translated by D.S. Baker (1998)

Seven Sages, *Apophthegms* Fragment 6.9 (D-K)

13 κτῆσαι ἐν μὲν νεότητι εὐπραξίαν, ἐν δὲ τῷ γήρᾳ σοφίαν

Build a sensible attitude in youth, wisdom in old age.

Seven Sages, *Apophthegms* Fragment 6.10 (D-K)

14 νόει καὶ τότε πρᾶττε

Think and then act.

Seven Sages, *Sententiae* 215.36 (Mullach, *FPG*)

15 φιλοῦσιν ὡς μισήσοντες καὶ μισοῦσιν ὡς φιλήσοντες

They love as though they will some day hate and hate as though they will some day love.

Translated by W. Rhys Roberts (1858–1929), rev. Jonathan Barnes (1984)

Aristotle, *Rhetoric* 1389b.24

16 ἐφόδιον ἀπὸ νεότητος εἰς γῆρας ἀναλάμβανε σοφίαν· βεβαιότερον γὰρ τοῦτο τῶν ἄλλων κτημάτων

Make wisdom your provision for the journey from youth to old age; for it is a more certain support than all other possessions.

Translated by R.D. Hicks (1925)

Diogenes Laertius, *Lives of Eminent Philosophers* 1.88

BIBLE

All entries follow the traditional order of books

see also Pilate 1–5

New Testament – Authorized Version (1611)

1 Ἰακὼβ δὲ ἐγέννησε τὸν Ἰωσὴφ τὸν ἄνδρα Μαρίας, ἐξ ἧς ἐγεννήθη Ἰησοῦς ὁ λεγόμενος Χριστός

And Jacob begat Joseph the husband of Mary, of whom was born Jesus, who is called Christ.

Matthew 1.16

2 πρὶν ἢ συνελθεῖν αὐτοὺς εὑρέθη ἐν γαστρὶ ἔχουσα ἐκ πνεύματος ἁγίου

Before they came together, she was found with child of the Holy Ghost.

Matthew 1.18

3 προσήνεγκαν αὐτῷ δῶρα, χρυσὸν καὶ λίβανον καὶ σμύρναν

They presented unto him gifts; gold, and frankincense, and myrrh.

Matthew 2.11

4 μετανοεῖτε, ἤγγικεν γὰρ ἡ βασιλεία τῶν οὐρανῶν

Repent ye: for the kingdom of heaven is at hand.

Matthew 3.2

5 φωνὴ βοῶντος ἐν τῇ ἐρήμῳ,
ἑτοιμάσατε τὴν ὁδὸν κυρίου,
εὐθείας ποιεῖτε τὰς τρίβους αὐτοῦ

The voice crying in the wilderness,

Prepare ye the way of the Lord, make his paths straight.

Matthew 3.3

cf. Bible 362

6 ἡ δὲ τροφὴ αὐτοῦ ἦν ἀκρίδες καὶ μέλι ἄγριον

His meat was locusts and wild honey.

Matthew 3.4

7 ἤδη δὲ ἡ ἀξίνη πρὸς τὴν ῥίζαν τῶν δένδρων κεῖται· πᾶν οὖν δένδρον μὴ ποιοῦν καρπὸν καλὸν ἐκκόπτεται καὶ εἰς πῦρ βάλλεται

And now also the axe is laid unto the root of the trees: therefore every tree which bringeth not forth good fruit is hewn down, and cast into the fire.

Matthew 3.10

8 οὗτός ἐστιν ὁ υἱός μου ὁ ἀγαπητός, ἐν ᾧ εὐδόκησα

This is my beloved Son, in whom I am well pleased.

Matthew 3.17

9 οὐκ ἐπ' ἄρτῳ μόνῳ ζήσεται ἄνθρωπος

Man shall not live by bread alone.

Matthew 4.4

10 δεῦτε ὀπίσω μου καὶ ποιήσω ὑμᾶς ἁλιεῖς ἀνθρώπων

Follow me, and I will make you fishers of men.

Matthew 4.19

11 καὶ θεραπεύων πᾶσαν νόσον καὶ πᾶσαν μαλακίαν ἐν τῷ λαῷ

And healing all manner of sickness and all manner of disease among the people.

Matthew 4.23

12 μακάριοι οἱ πτωχοὶ τῷ πνεύματι, ὅτι αὐτῶν ἐστιν ἡ βασιλεία τῶν οὐρανῶν. μακάριοι οἱ πενθοῦντες, ὅτι αὐτοὶ παρακληθήσονται. μακάριοι οἱ πραεῖς, ὅτι αὐτοὶ κληρονομήσουσιν τὴν γῆν. μακάριοι οἱ πεινῶντες καὶ διψῶντες τὴν δικαιοσύνην, ὅτι αὐτοὶ χορτασθήσονται. μακάριοι οἱ ἐλεήμονες, ὅτι αὐτοὶ ἐλεηθήσονται. μακάριοι οἱ καθαροὶ τῇ καρδίᾳ, ὅτι αὐτοὶ τὸν θεὸν ὄψονται. μακάριοι οἱ εἰρηνοποιοί, ὅτι αὐτοὶ υἱοὶ θεοῦ κληθήσονται

Blessed are the poor in spirit: for theirs is the kingdom of heaven.
Blessed are they that mourn: for they shall be comforted.
Blessed are the meek: for they shall inherit the earth.
Blessed are they which do hunger and thirst after righteousness: for they shall be filled.
Blessed are the merciful: for they shall obtain mercy.
Blessed are the pure in heart: for they shall see God.
Blessed are the peacemakers: for they shall be called the children of God.

Matthew 5.3

Sermon on the Mount (all of Chs. 5, 6 and 7)

13 ὑμεῖς ἐστε τὸ ἅλας τῆς γῆς

Ye are the salt of the earth.

Matthew 5.13

14 ὑμεῖς ἐστε τὸ φῶς τοῦ κόσμου. οὐ δύναται πόλις κρυβῆναι ἐπάνω ὄρους κειμένη· οὐδὲ καίουσιν λύχνον καὶ τιθέασιν αὐτὸν ὑπὸ τὸν μόδιον ἀλλ' ἐπὶ τὴν λυχνίαν, καὶ λάμπει πᾶσι τοῖς ἐν τῇ οἰκίᾳ

Ye are the light of the world. A city that is set on a hill cannot be hid. Neither do men light a candle and put it under a bushel, but on a candlestick; and it giveth light unto all that are in the house.

Matthew 5.14

15 οὕτως λαμψάτω τὸ φῶς ὑμῶν ἔμπροσθεν τῶν ἀνθρώπων, ὅπως ἴδωσιν ὑμῶν τὰ καλὰ ἔργα

Let your light so shine before men, that they may see your good works.

Matthew 5.16

16 μὴ νομίσητε ὅτι ἦλθον καταλῦσαι τὸν νόμον ἢ τοὺς προφήτας· οὐκ ἦλθον καταλῦσαι ἀλλὰ πληρῶσαι

Think not that I am come to destroy the law, or the prophets: I am not come to destroy, but to fulfil.

Matthew 5.17

17 ἕως ἂν ἀποδῷς τὸν ἔσχατον κοδράντην

Till thou hast paid the uttermost farthing.

Matthew 5.26

18 πᾶς ὁ βλέπων γυναῖκα πρὸς τὸ ἐπιθυμῆσαι αὐτὴν ἤδη ἐμοίχευσεν αὐτὴν ἐν τῇ καρδίᾳ αὐτοῦ

Whosoever looketh on a woman to lust after her hath committed adultery with her already in his heart.

Matthew 5.28

19 ἐγὼ δὲ λέγω ὑμῖν μὴ ὀμόσαι ὅλως· μήτε ἐν τῷ οὐρανῷ, ὅτι θρόνος ἐστὶ τοῦ θεοῦ· μήτε ἐν τῇ γῇ, ὅτι ὑποπόδιόν ἐστι τῶν ποδῶν αὐτοῦ ... ἔστω δὲ ὁ λόγος ὑμῶν ναὶ ναί, οὒ οὔ

I say unto you, swear not at all; neither by heaven; for it is God's throne: Nor by the earth; for it is his footstool. But let your communication be, Yea, yea; Nay, nay.

Matthew 5.34

cf. Bible 276

20 ἠκούσατε ὅτι ἐρρέθη, ὀφθαλμὸν ἀντὶ ὀφθαλμοῦ καὶ ὀδόντα ἀντὶ ὀδόντος· ἐγὼ δὲ λέγω ὑμῖν ... ὅστις σε ῥαπίσει εἰς τὴν δεξιὰν σου σιαγόνα, στρέψον αὐτῷ καὶ τὴν ἄλλην

Ye have heard that it hath been said, an eye for an eye, and a tooth for a tooth. But I say unto you, whosoever shall smite thee on thy right cheek, turn to him the other also.

Matthew 5.39

cf. Bible 324

21 ἠκούσατε ὅτι ἐρρέθη, ἀγαπήσεις τὸν πλησίον σου καὶ μισήσεις τὸν ἐχθρόν σου· ἐγὼ δὲ λέγω ὑμῖν, ἀγαπᾶτε τοὺς ἐχθροὺς ὑμῶν

Ye have heard that it hath been said, Thou shalt love thy neighbour and hate thine enemy. But I say unto you, Love your enemies.

Matthew 5.44

22 τὸν ἥλιον αὐτοῦ ἀνατέλλει ἐπὶ πονηροὺς καὶ ἀγαθοὺς καὶ βρέχει ἐπὶ δικαίους καὶ ἀδίκους

He maketh his sun to rise on the evil and on the good, and sendeth rain on the just and on the unjust.

Matthew 5.45

23 ἔσεσθε οὖν ὑμεῖς τέλειοι ὥσπερ ὁ πατὴρ ὑμῶν ὁ ἐν τοῖς οὐρανοῖς τέλειός ἐστιν

Be ye therefore perfect, even as your Father which is in heaven is perfect.

Matthew 5.48

24 σοῦ δὲ ποιοῦντος ἐλεημοσύνην μὴ γνώτω ἡ ἀριστερά σου τί ποιεῖ ἡ δεξιά σου

When thou doest alms, let not thy left hand know what thy right hand doeth.

Matthew 6.3

Sermon on the Mount (all of Chs. 5, 6 and 7)

25 προσευχόμενοι δὲ μὴ βατταλογήσητε ὥσπερ οἱ ἐθνικοί, δοκοῦσιν γὰρ ὅτι ἐν τῇ πολυλογίᾳ αὐτῶν εἰσακουσθήσονται

Use not vain repetitions, as the heathen do: for they think that they shall be heard for their much speaking.

Matthew 6.7

26 Πάτερ ἡμῶν ὁ ἐν τοῖς οὐρανοῖς,
ἁγιασθήτω τὸ ὄνομά σου, ἐλθέτω ἡ βασιλεία σου,
γενηθήτω τὸ θέλημά σου, ὡς ἐν οὐρανῷ καὶ ἐπὶ γῆς·
τὸν ἄρτον ἡμῶν τὸν ἐπιούσιον δὸς ἡμῖν σήμερον·
καὶ ἄφες ἡμῖν τὰ ὀφειλήματα ἡμῶν,
ὡς καὶ ἡμεῖς ἀφίεμεν τοῖς ὀφειλέταις ἡμῶν·
καὶ μὴ εἰσενέγκῃς ἡμᾶς εἰς πειρασμόν,
ἀλλὰ ῥῦσαι ἡμᾶς ἀπὸ τοῦ πονηροῦ·
ὅτι σοῦ ἐστιν ἡ βασιλεία καὶ ἡ δύναμις καὶ ἡ δόξα εἰς τοὺς αἰῶνας, ἀμήν.

Our Father which art in heaven, Hallowed be thy name.
Thy kingdom come. Thy will be done in earth, as it is in heaven.
Give us this day our daily bread.
And forgive us our debts, as we forgive our debtors.
And lead us not into temptation, but deliver us from evil:
For thine is the kingdom, and the power, and the glory, for ever. Amen.

Matthew 6.9

27 μὴ θησαυρίζετε ὑμῖν θησαυροὺς ἐπὶ τῆς γῆς, ὅπου σὴς καὶ βρῶσις ἀφανίζει, καὶ ὅπου κλέπται διορύσσουσι καὶ κλέπτουσι. θησαυρίζετε δὲ ὑμῖν θησαυροὺς ἐν οὐρανῷ

Lay not up for yourselves treasures upon earth, where moth and rust doth corrupt, and where thieves break through and steal: But lay up for yourselves treasures in heaven.

Matthew 6.19

28 ὅπου γάρ ἐστιν ὁ θησαυρός ὑμῶν, ἐκεῖ ἔσται καὶ ἡ καρδία ὑμῶν

For where your treasure is, there will your heart be also.

Matthew 6.21

29 οὐδεὶς δύναται δυσὶ κυρίοις δουλεύειν … οὐ δύνασθε θεῷ δουλεύειν καὶ μαμωνᾷ

No man can serve two masters. Ye cannot serve God and Mammon.

Matthew 6.24

30 μὴ κρίνετε, ἵνα μὴ κριθῆτε

Judge not, that ye be not judged.

Matthew 7.1

Sermon on the Mount (all of Chs. 5, 6 and 7)

31 μηδὲ βάλητε τοὺς μαργαρίτας ὑμῶν ἔμπροσθεν τῶν χοίρων

Neither cast ye your pearls before swine.

Matthew 7.6

32 αἰτεῖτε, καὶ δοθήσεται ὑμῖν· ζητεῖτε, καὶ εὑρήσετε· κρούετε, καὶ ἀνοιγήσεται ὑμῖν. πᾶς γὰρ ὁ αἰτῶν λαμβάνει καὶ ὁ ζητῶν εὑρίσκει καὶ τῷ κρούοντι ἀνοιγήσεται

Ask, and it shall be given you; seek, and ye shall find; knock, and it shall be opened unto you: For every one that asketh receiveth; and he that seeketh findeth; and to him that knocketh it shall be opened.

Matthew 7.7

33 πάντα οὖν ὅσα ἂν θέλητε ἵνα ποιῶσιν ὑμῖν οἱ ἄνθρωποι, οὕτως καὶ ὑμεῖς ποιεῖτε αὐτοῖς

Therefore all things whatsoever ye would that men should do to you, do ye even so to them.

Matthew 7.12

34 ὅτι πλατεῖα ἡ πύλη καὶ εὐρύχωρος ἡ ὁδὸς ἡ ἀπάγουσα εἰς τὴν ἀπώλειαν, καὶ πολλοί εἰσιν οἱ εἰσερχόμενοι δι᾽ αὐτῆς· τί στενὴ ἡ πύλη καὶ τεθλιμμένη ἡ ὁδὸς ἡ ἀπάγουσα εἰς τὴν ζωήν, καὶ ὀλίγοι εἰσὶν οἱ εὑρίσκοντες αὐτήν

For wide is the gate, and broad is the way, that leadeth to destruction, and many there be which go in thereat: because strait is the gate, and narrow is the way, which leadeth into life, and few there be that find it.

Matthew 7.13

35 προσέχετε ἀπὸ τῶν ψευδοπροφητῶν, οἵτινες ἔρχονται πρὸς ὑμᾶς ἐν ἐνδύμασιν προβάτων, ἔσωθεν δέ εἰσιν λύκοι ἅρπαγες

Beware of false prophets, which come to you in sheep's clothing, but inwardly they are ravening wolves.

Matthew 7.15

cf. Aesop 46

36 μήτι συλλέγουσιν ἀπὸ ἀκανθῶν σταφυλὰς ἢ ἀπὸ τριβόλων σῦκα;

Do men gather grapes of thorns, or figs of thistles?

Matthew 7.16

37 ἐκβληθήσονται εἰς τὸ σκότος τὸ ἐξώτερον· ἐκεῖ ἔσται ὁ κλαυθμὸς καὶ ὁ βρυγμὸς τῶν ὀδόντων

They shall be cast out into outer darkness: there shall be weeping and gnashing of teeth.

Matthew 8.12

38 αἱ ἀλώπεκες φωλεοὺς ἔχουσιν καὶ τὰ πετεινὰ τοῦ οὐρανοῦ κατασκηνώσεις, ὁ δὲ υἱὸς τοῦ ἀνθρώπου οὐκ ἔχει ποῦ τὴν κεφαλὴν κλίνῃ

The foxes have holes, and the birds of the air have nests; but the Son of man hath not where to lay his head.

Matthew 8.20

39 ἄφες τοὺς νεκροὺς θάψαι τοὺς ἑαυτῶν νεκρούς

Let the dead bury their dead.

Matthew 8.22

40 οὐ χρείαν ἔχουσιν οἱ ἰσχύοντες ἰατροῦ, ἀλλ᾽ οἱ κακῶς ἔχοντες

They that be whole need not a physician, but they that are sick.

Matthew 9.12

41 οὐδὲ βάλλουσιν οἶνον νέον εἰς ἀσκοὺς παλαιούς

Neither do men put new wine into old bottles.

Matthew 9.17

42 δωρεὰν ἐλάβετε, δωρεὰν δότε

Freely ye have received, freely give.

Matthew 10.8

43 ἐξερχόμενοι ἔξω τῆς οἰκίας ἢ τῆς πόλεως ἐκείνης ἐκτινάξατε τὸν κονιορτὸν τῶν ποδῶν ὑμῶν

When ye depart out of that house or city, shake off the dust of your feet.

Matthew 10.14

44 ἰδοὺ ἐγὼ ἀποστέλλω ὑμᾶς ὡς πρόβατα ἐν μέσῳ λύκων· γίνεσθε οὖν φρόνιμοι ὡς οἱ ὄφεις καὶ ἀκέραιοι ὡς αἱ περιστεραί

Behold, I send you forth as sheep in the midst of wolves; be ye therefore wise as serpents, and harmless as doves.

Matthew 10.16

45 οὐδὲν γάρ ἐστιν κεκαλυμμένον ὃ οὐκ ἀποκαλυφθήσεται, καὶ κρυπτὸν ὃ οὐ γνωσθήσεται

There is nothing covered, that shall not be revealed; and hid, that shall not be known.

Matthew 10.26

46 μὴ νομίσητε ὅτι ἦλθον βαλεῖν εἰρήνην ἐπὶ τὴν γῆν· οὐκ ἦλθον βαλεῖν εἰρήνην ἀλλὰ μάχαιραν

Think not that I am come to send peace on earth: I came not to send peace, but a sword.

Matthew 10.34

47 τί ἐξήλθατε εἰς τὴν ἔρημον θεάσασθαι; κάλαμον ὑπὸ ἀνέμου σαλευόμενον;

What went ye out into the wilderness to see? A reed shaken with the wind?

Matthew 11.7

48 ὁ μὴ ὢν μετ' ἐμοῦ κατ' ἐμοῦ ἐστί

He that is not with me is against me.

Matthew 12.30

a favourite saying of George W. Bush

49 ἐκ γὰρ τοῦ περισσεύματος τῆς καρδίας τὸ στόμα λαλεῖ

For out of the abundance of the heart the mouth speaketh.

Matthew 12.34

50 πᾶν ῥῆμα ἀργὸν ὃ λαλήσουσιν οἱ ἄνθρωποι ἀποδώσουσι περὶ αὐτοῦ λόγον ἐν ἡμέρᾳ κρίσεως

Every idle word that men shall speak, they shall give account thereof in the day of judgement.

Matthew 12.36

51 δός μοι ὧδε ἐπὶ πίνακι τὴν κεφαλὴν Ἰωάννου τοῦ βαπτιστοῦ

Give me here John Baptist's head in a charger.

Matthew 14.8

'τὴν κεφαλὴν ἐπὶ πίνακι' is a favourite expression in Modern Greek

52 ὀλιγόπιστε, εἰς τί ἐδίστασας;

O thou of little faith, wherefore didst thou doubt?

Matthew 14.31

53 οὐ τὸ εἰσερχόμενον εἰς τὸ στόμα κοινοῖ τὸν ἄνθρωπον, ἀλλὰ τὸ ἐκπορευόμενον ἐκ τοῦ στόματος τοῦτο κοινοῖ τὸν ἄνθρωπον

Not that which goeth into the mouth defileth a man; but that which cometh out of the mouth, this defileth man.

Matthew 15.11

54 ὁδηγοί εἰσι τυφλοί τυφλῶν· τυφλὸς δὲ τυφλὸν ἐὰν ὁδηγῇ, ἀμφότεροι εἰς βόθυνον πεσοῦνται

They be blind leaders of the blind. And if the blind lead the blind, both shall fall into the ditch.

Matthew 15.14

of the Pharisees

55 καὶ γὰρ τὰ κυνάρια ἐσθίει ἀπὸ τῶν ψιχίων τῶν πιπτόντων ἀπὸ τῆς τραπέζης τῶν κυρίων αὐτῶν

Yet the dogs eat of the crumbs which fall from their master's table.

Matthew 15.27

56 τὸ μὲν πρόσωπον τοῦ οὐρανοῦ γινώσκετε διακρίνειν, τὰ δὲ σημεῖα τῶν καιρῶν οὐ δύνασθε;

Ye can discern the face of the sky; but can ye not discern the signs of the times?

Matthew 16.3

57 ὕπαγε ὀπίσω μου, Σατανᾶ

Get thee behind me, Satan.

Matthew 16.23

58 εἴ τις θέλει ὀπίσω μου ἐλθεῖν, ἀπαρνησάσθω ἑαυτὸν καὶ ἀράτω τὸν σταυρὸν αὐτοῦ καὶ ἀκολουθείτω μοι

If any man will come after me, let him deny himself, and take up his cross, and follow me.

Matthew 16.24

59 ἐὰν ἔχητε πίστιν ὡς κόκκον σινάπεως, ἐρεῖτε τῷ ὄρει τούτῳ, μετάβηθι ἔνθεν ἐκεῖ, καὶ μεταβήσεται· καὶ οὐδὲν ἀδυνατήσει ὑμῖν

If ye have faith as a grain of mustard seed, ye shall say unto this mountain, Remove hence to yonder place; and it shall remove; and nothing shall be impossible unto you.

Matthew 17.20

cf. the English proverb 'faith will move mountains'

60 ἀνάγκη γάρ εστιν ἐλθεῖν τὰ σκάνδαλα· πλὴν οὐαὶ τῷ ἀνθρώπῳ δι' οὗ τὸ σκάνδαλον ἔρχεται

It must needs be that offences come; but woe to that man by whom the offence cometh!

Matthew 18.7

61 οὗ γάρ εἰσι δύο ἢ τρεῖς συνηγμένοι εἰς τὸ ἐμὸν ὄνομα, ἐκεῖ εἰμι ἐν μέσῳ αὐτῶν

For where two or three are gathered together in my name, there am I in the midst of them.

Matthew 18.20

62 ὃ οὖν ὁ θεὸς συνέζευξεν, ἄνθρωπος μὴ χωριζέτω

What therefore God hath joined together, let not man put asunder.

Matthew 19.6

of marriage

63 ἄφετε τὰ παιδία ... ἐλθεῖν πρός με, τῶν γὰρ τοιούτων ἐστὶν ἡ βασιλεία τῶν οὐρανῶν

Suffer little children to come unto me: for of such is the kingdom of heaven.

Matthew 19.14

often quoted as 'for theirs is the kingdom of heaven'

64 εἰ θέλεις τέλειος εἶναι, ὕπαγε πώλησόν σου τὰ ὑπάρχοντα καὶ δὸς τοῖς πτωχοῖς, καὶ ἕξεις θησαυρὸν ἐν οὐρανῷ

If thou wilt be perfect, go and sell that thou hast, and give to the poor, and thou shalt have treasure in heaven.

Matthew 19.21

65 εὐκοπώτερόν ἐστιν κάμηλον διὰ τρυπήματος ῥαφίδος διελθεῖν ἢ πλούσιον εἰς τὴν βασιλείαν τοῦ θεοῦ εἰσελθεῖν

It is easier for a camel to go through the eye of a needle, than for a rich man to enter into the kingdom of God.

Matthew 19.24

66 παρὰ ἀνθρώποις τοῦτο ἀδύνατόν ἐστι, παρὰ δὲ θεῷ πάντα δυνατά ἐστι

With men this is impossible; but with God all things are possible.

Matthew 19.26

67 οὕτως ἔσονται οἱ ἔσχατοι πρῶτοι καὶ οἱ πρῶτοι ἔσχατοι· πολλοὶ γάρ εἰσι κλητοί, ὀλίγοι δὲ ἐκλεκτοί

So the last shall be first, and the first last: for many be called, but few chosen.

Matthew 20.16

68 εὐλογημένος ὁ ἐρχόμενος ἐν ὀνόματι κυρίου· ὡσαννὰ ἐν τοῖς ὑψίστοις

Blessed is he that cometh in the name of the Lord; Hosanna in the highest

Matthew 21.9

69 γέγραπται, ὁ οἶκός μου οἶκος προσευχῆς κληθήσεται· ὑμεῖς δὲ αὐτὸν ἐποιήσατε σπήλαιον λῃστῶν

It is written, My house shall be called the house of prayer; but ye have made it a den of thieves.

Matthew 21.13

70 ἀπόδοτε οὖν τὰ Καίσαρος Καίσαρι καὶ τὰ τοῦ Θεοῦ τῷ Θεῷ

Render therefore unto Caesar the things which are Caesar's; and unto God the things that are God's.

Matthew 22.21

71 ἀγαπήσεις τὸν πλησίον σου ὡς σεαυτόν

Thou shalt love thy neighbour as thyself.

Matthew 22.39

cf. Euripides 223

72 πάντα δὲ τὰ ἔργα αὐτῶν ποιοῦσιν πρὸς τὸ θεαθῆναι τοῖς ἀνθρώποις

But all their works they do for to be seen of men.

Matthew 23.5
of the Pharisees

73 οὐαὶ ὑμῖν, γραμματεῖς καὶ Φαρισαῖοι ὑποκριταί, ὅτι ἀποδεκατοῦτε τὸ ἡδύοσμον καὶ τὸ ἄνηθον καὶ τὸ κύμινον, καὶ ἀφήκατε τὰ βαρύτερα τοῦ νόμου, τὴν κρίσιν καὶ τὸ ἔλεος καὶ τὴν πίστιν

Woe unto you, scribes and Pharisees, hypocrites! for ye pay tithe of mint and anise and cummin, and have omitted the weightier matters of the law, judgement, mercy, and faith.

Matthew 23.23

74 ταῦτα ἔδει ποιῆσαι κἀκεῖνα μὴ ἀφιέναι

These ought ye to have done, and not to leave the other undone.

Matthew 23.23

75 ὁδηγοὶ τυφλοί, οἱ διυλίζοντες τὸν κώνωπα τὴν δὲ κάμηλον καταπίνοντες

Ye blind guides, which strain at a gnat, and swallow a camel.

Matthew 23.24
of the Pharisees

76 ἐγερθήσεται γὰρ ἔθνος ἐπὶ ἔθνος καὶ βασιλεία ἐπὶ βασιλείαν, καὶ ἔσονται λιμοὶ καὶ λοιμοὶ καὶ σεισμοὶ

For nation shall rise against nation, and kingdom against kingdom: and there shall be famines, and pestilences, and earthquakes.

Matthew 24.7

77 γρηγορεῖτε οὖν, ὅτι οὐκ οἴδατε ποίᾳ ὥρᾳ ὁ Κύριος ὑμῶν ἔρχεται

Watch therefore: for ye know not what hour your Lord doth come.

Matthew 24.42

78 θερίζων ὅπου οὐκ ἔσπειρας καὶ συνάγων ὅθεν οὐ διεσκόρπισας

Reaping where thou hast not sown, and gathering where thou hast not strawed.

Matthew 25.24

79 ἐπείνασα γὰρ καὶ ἐδώκατέ μοι φαγεῖν, ἐδίψησα καὶ ἐποτίσατέ με, ξένος ἤμην καὶ συνηγάγετέ με, γυμνὸς καὶ περιεβάλετέ με, ἠσθένησα καὶ ἐπεσκέψασθέ με, ἐν φυλακῇ ἤμην καὶ ἤλθατε πρός με

For I was an hungred, and ye gave me meat: I was thirsty, and ye gave me drink: I was a stranger, and ye took me in: naked, and ye clothed me: I was sick, and ye visited me: I was in prison, and ye came unto me.

Matthew 25.35

80 ἐφ' ὅσον ἐποιήσατε ἑνὶ τούτων τῶν ἀδελφῶν μου τῶν ἐλαχίστων, ἐμοὶ ἐποιήσατε

Inasmuch as ye have done it unto one of the least of these my brethren, ye have done it unto me.

Matthew 25.40

81 εἰς τί ἡ ἀπώλεια αὕτη;

To what purpose is this waste?

Matthew 26.8

82 τί θέλετέ μοι δοῦναι κἀγὼ ὑμῖν παραδώσω αὐτόν; οἱ δὲ ἔστησαν αὐτῷ τριάκοντα ἀργύρια

What will ye give me, and I will deliver him unto you? And they covenanted with him for thirty pieces of silver.

Matthew 26.15

83 ἐσθιόντων δὲ αὐτῶν λαβὼν ὁ Ἰησοῦς τὸν ἄρτον καὶ εὐλογήσας ἔκλασεν καὶ ἐδίδου τοῖς μαθηταῖς καὶ εἶπε· λάβετε φάγετε· τοῦτό ἐστι τὸ σῶμά μου

And as they were eating, Jesus took bread, and blessed it, and brake it, and gave it to the disciples, and said, Take, eat; this is my body.

Matthew 26.26

84 καὶ λαβὼν τὸ ποτήριον καὶ εὐχαριστήσας ἔδωκεν αὐτοῖς λέγων· πίετε ἐξ αὐτοῦ πάντες· τοῦτο γάρ ἐστι τὸ αἷμά μου τὸ τῆς καινῆς διαθήκης τὸ περὶ πολλῶν ἐκχυνόμενον εἰς ἄφεσιν ἁμαρτιῶν

And he took the cup, and gave thanks, and gave it to them, saying, Drink ye all of it; For this is my blood of the new testament, which is shed for many for the remission of sins.

Matthew 26.27

85 ἐν ταύτῃ τῇ νυκτὶ πρὶν ἀλέκτορα φωνῆσαι

τρὶς ἀπαρνήσῃ με

This night, before the cock crow, thou shalt deny me thrice.

Matthew 26.34

86 εἰ δυνατόν ἐστι, παρελθέτω ἀπ' ἐμοῦ τὸ ποτήριον τοῦτο

If it be possible, let this cup pass from me.

Matthew 26.39

87 τὸ μὲν πνεῦμα πρόθυμον, ἡ δὲ σὰρξ ἀσθενής

The spirit indeed is willing, but the flesh is weak.

Matthew 26.41

88 ἰδοὺ ἤγγικεν ἡ ὥρα

Behold, the hour is at hand.

Matthew 26.45

89 πάντες γὰρ οἱ λαβόντες μάχαιραν ἐν μαχαίρᾳ ἀπολοῦνται

All they that take the sword shall perish with the sword.

Matthew 26.52

90 τότε ὁ ἀρχιερεὺς διέρρηξε τὰ ἱμάτια αὐτοῦ λέγων ὅτι ἐβλασφήμησε· τί ἔτι χρείαν ἔχομεν μαρτύρων;

Then the high priest rent his clothes, saying, He hath spoken blasphemy; what further need have we of witnesses?

Matthew 26.65

91 καὶ εὐθέως ἀλέκτωρ ἐφώνησε· καὶ ἐμνήσθη ὁ Πέτρος τοῦ ῥήματος Ἰησοῦ εἰρηκότος αὐτῷ ὅτι πρὶν ἀλέκτορα φωνῆσαι τρὶς ἀπαρνήσῃ με· καὶ ἐξελθὼν ἔξω ἔκλαυσε πικρῶς

And immediately the cock crew. And Peter remembered the word of Jesus, which said unto him, Before the cock crow, thou shalt deny me thrice. And he went out, and wept bitterly.

Matthew 26.74

92 τότε ὁ Ἰούδας … μεταμεληθεὶς … ῥίψας τὰ τριάκοντα ἀργύρια ἐν τῷ ναῷ ἀνεχώρησεν, καὶ ἀπελθὼν ἀπήγξατο

Then Judas … repented himself … and cast down the thirty pieces of silver in the temple, and departed, and hanged himself.

Matthew 27.3–5

cf. Epictetus 12

93 ἄλλους ἔσωσεν, ἑαυτὸν οὐ δύναται σῶσαι

He saved others; himself he cannot save.

Matthew 27.42

94 Ἠλὶ Ἠλί, λιμὰ σαβαχθανί; τοῦτ' ἔστι, Θεέ μου θεέ μου, ἱνατί με ἐγκατέλιπες;

Eli, Eli, lama sabachthani? that is to say, My God, my God, why hast thou forsaken me?

Matthew 27.46

95 καὶ ἔσται ἡ ἐσχάτη πλάνη χείρων τῆς πρώτης

The last error shall be worse than the first.

Matthew 27.64

96 πορευθέντες οὖν μαθητεύσατε πάντα τὰ ἔθνη, βαπτίζοντες αὐτοὺς εἰς τὸ ὄνομα τοῦ Πατρὸς καὶ τοῦ Υἱοῦ καὶ τοῦ Ἁγίου Πνεύματος

Go ye therefore, and teach all nations, baptizing them in the name of the Father, and of the Son, and of the Holy Ghost.

Matthew 28.19

97 καὶ ἰδοὺ ἐγὼ μεθ' ὑμῶν εἰμι πάσας τὰς ἡμέρας ἕως τῆς συντελείας τοῦ αἰῶνος· ἀμήν

And, lo, I am with you alway, even unto the end of the world. Amen.

Matthew 28.20

closing lines

98 πῶς δύναται Σατανᾶς Σατανᾶν ἐκβάλλειν;

How can Satan cast out Satan?

Mark 3.23

99 καὶ ἐὰν οἰκία ἐφ' ἑαυτὴν μερισθῇ, οὐ δύναται σταθῆναι ἡ οἰκία ἐκείνη

If a house be divided against itself, that house cannot stand.

Mark 3.25

100 ὁ ἔχων ὦτα ἀκούειν ἀκουέτω

He that hath ears to hear, let him hear.

Mark 4.9

101 οὐ γάρ ἐστι κρυπτὸν ὃ ἐὰν μὴ φανερωθῇ

For there is nothing hid, which shall not

be manifested.

Mark 4.22

102 ἐν ᾧ μέτρῳ μετρεῖτε, μετρηθήσεται ὑμῖν

With what measure ye mete, it shall be measured to you.

Mark 4.24

103 λεγεὼν ὄνομά μοι, ὅτι πολλοί ἐσμεν

My name is Legion: for we are many.

Mark 5.9

104 βλέπω τοὺς ἀνθρώπους, ὅτι ὡς δένδρα ὁρῶ περιπατοῦντας

I see men as trees, walking.

Mark 8.24

105 τί γὰρ ὠφελήσει ἄνθρωπον ἐὰν κερδήσῃ τὸν κόσμον ὅλον καὶ ζημιωθῇ τὴν ψυχὴν αὐτοῦ;

For what shall it profit a man, if he shall gain the whole world, and lose his own soul?

Mark 8.36

106 πιστεύω, κύριε· βοήθει μου τῇ ἀπιστίᾳ

Lord, I believe; help thou mine unbelief.

Mark 9.24

107 καὶ ἐλθοῦσα μία χήρα πτωχὴ ἔβαλε λεπτὰ δύο

And there came a certain poor widow, and she threw in two mites.

Mark 12.42

108 πάντες γὰρ ἐκ τοῦ περισσεύοντος αὐτοῖς ἔβαλον· αὕτη δὲ ἐκ τῆς ὑστερήσεως αὐτῆς πάντα ὅσα εἶχεν ἔβαλεν, ὅλον τὸν βίον αὐτῆς

For all they did cast in of their abundance; but she of her want did cast in all that she had, even all her living.

Mark 12.44

109 καὶ οὐδενὶ οὐδὲν εἶπον· ἐφοβοῦντο γάρ

Neither said they any thing to any man; for they were afraid.

Mark 16.8

110 χαῖρε, κεχαριτωμένη, ὁ κύριος μετὰ σοῦ· εὐλογημένη σὺ ἐν γυναιξίν

Hail, thou that art highly favoured, the Lord is with thee: blessed art thou among women.

Luke 1.28

111 καὶ εἶπεν Μαριάμ, μεγαλύνει ἡ ψυχή μου τὸν κύριον, καὶ ἠγαλλίασε τὸ πνεῦμά μου ἐπὶ τῷ θεῷ τῷ σωτῆρί μου

And Mary said, My soul doth magnify the Lord, And my spirit hath rejoiced in God my Saviour.

Luke 1.46

known as the 'Magnificat'; cf. the Vulgate: 'Magnificat anima mea Dominum'

112 καθεῖλε δυνάστας ἀπὸ θρόνων καὶ ὕψωσε ταπεινούς

He hath put down the mighty from their seats, and exalted them of low degree.

Luke 1.52

from the 'Magnificat'

113 πεινῶντας ἐνέπλησεν ἀγαθῶν καὶ πλουτοῦντας ἐξαπέστειλε κενούς

He hath filled the hungry with good things; and the rich he hath sent empty away.

Luke 1.53

from the 'Magnificat'

114 καὶ ἔτεκε τὸν υἱὸν αὐτῆς τὸν πρωτότοκον· καὶ ἐσπαργάνωσεν αὐτὸν καὶ ἀνέκλινεν αὐτὸν ἐν φάτνῃ, διότι οὐκ ἦν αὐτοῖς τόπος ἐν τῷ καταλύματι

And she brought forth her firstborn son, and wrapped him in swaddling clothes, and laid him in a manger; because there was no room for them in the inn.

Luke 2.7

115 καὶ ἰδοὺ ἄγγελος κυρίου ἐπέστη αὐτοῖς καὶ δόξα κυρίου περιέλαμψεν αὐτούς, καὶ ἐφοβήθησαν φόβον μέγαν

And, lo, the angel of the Lord came upon them, and the glory of the Lord shone round about them: and they were sore afraid.

Luke 2.9

116 ἰδοὺ γὰρ εὐαγγελίζομαι ὑμῖν χαρὰν μεγάλην

Behold, I bring you good tidings of great joy.

Luke 2.10

117 δόξα ἐν ὑψίστοις θεῷ καὶ ἐπὶ γῆς εἰρήνη, ἐν ἀνθρώποις εὐδοκία

Glory to God in the highest, and on earth

peace, good will toward men.

Luke 2.14

118 νῦν ἀπολύεις τὸν δοῦλόν σου, δέσποτα

Lord, now lettest thou thy servant depart in peace.

Luke 2.29

cf. the Vulgate: 'Nunc dimittis servum tuum'

119 ἰατρέ, θεράπευσον σεαυτόν

Physician, heal thyself.

Luke 4.23

120 οὐδεὶς προφήτης δεκτός ἐστιν ἐν τῇ πατρίδι αὐτοῦ

No prophet is accepted in his own country.

Luke 4.24

cf. the Latin 'nemo propheta in patria'

121 οὐαὶ ὑμῖν ὅταν ὑμᾶς καλῶς εἴπωσιν πάντες οἱ ἄνθρωποι

Woe unto you, when all men shall speak well of you!

Luke 6.26

122 δίδοτε, καὶ δοθήσεται ὑμῖν

Give, and it shall be given unto you.

Luke 6.38

123 ἀφέωνται αἱ ἁμαρτίαι αὐτῆς αἱ πολλαί, ὅτι ἠγάπησε πολύ

Her sins, which are many, are forgiven; for she loved much.

Luke 7.47

124 ὁ γὰρ μικρότερος ἐν πᾶσιν ὑμῖν ὑπάρχων, οὗτός ἐστι μέγας

For he that is least among you all, the same shall be great.

Luke 9.48

125 πορεύου καὶ σὺ ποίει ὁμοίως

Go, and do thou likewise.

Luke 10.37

126 Μάρθα Μάρθα, μεριμνᾷς καὶ τυρβάζῃ περὶ πολλά· ἑνὸς δέ ἐστι χρεία· Μαρία δὲ τὴν ἀγαθὴν μερίδα ἐξελέξατο

Martha, Martha, thou art careful and troubled about many things: but one thing is needful: and Mary hath chosen that good part.

Luke 10.41

127 οὐαὶ ὑμῖν τοῖς νομικοῖς, ὅτι ἤρατε τὴν κλεῖδα τῆς γνώσεως· αὐτοὶ οὐκ εἰσήλθατε καὶ τοὺς εἰσερχομένους ἐκωλύσατε

Woe unto you, lawyers! for ye have taken away the key of knowledge: ye entered not in yourselves, and them that were entering in ye hindered.

Luke 11.52

128 ψυχή, ἔχεις πολλὰ ἀγαθὰ κείμενα εἰς ἔτη πολλά· ἀναπαύου, φάγε, πίε, εὐφραίνου

My soul, thou hast much goods laid up for many years; take thine ease, eat, drink, and be merry.

Luke 12.19

129 παντὶ δὲ ᾧ ἐδόθη πολύ, πολὺ ζητηθήσεται παρ' αὐτοῦ, καὶ ᾧ παρέθεντο πολύ, περισσότερον αἰτήσουσιν αὐτόν

For unto whomsoever much is given, of him shall be much required: and to whom men have committed much, of him they will ask the more.

Luke 12.48

130 ὅτι πᾶς ὁ ὑψῶν ἑαυτὸν ταπεινωθήσεται καὶ ὁ ταπεινῶν ἑαυτὸν ὑψωθήσεται

For whosoever exalteth himself shall be abased; and that humbleth himself shall be exalted.

Luke 14.11

131 καὶ ἤρξαντο ἀπὸ μιᾶς πάντες παραιτεῖσθαι· ὁ πρῶτος εἶπεν αὐτῷ, ἀγρὸν ἠγόρασα καὶ ἔχω ἀνάγκην ἐξελθὼν ἰδεῖν αὐτόν· ἐρωτῶ σε, ἔχε με παρῃτημένον

And they all with one consent began to make excuse. The first said unto him, I have bought a piece of ground and I must needs go and see it: I pray thee have me excused.

Luke 14.18

'ἀγρὸν ἠγόρασε' is a favourite quotation in Modern Greek, of someone who does not care

132 φέρετε τὸν μόσχον τὸν σιτευτόν, θύσατε

Bring hither the fatted calf, and kill it.

Luke 15.23

133 ὅτι οὗτος ὁ υἱός μου νεκρὸς ἦν καὶ ἀνέζησε, ἀπολωλὼς ἦν καὶ εὑρέθη

For this my son was dead, and is alive

again; he was lost, and is found.

Luke 15.24

134 ἰδοὺ γὰρ ἡ βασιλεία τοῦ θεοῦ ἐντὸς ὑμῶν ἐστιν

Behold, the kingdom of God is within you.

Luke 17.21

135 ὁ θεός, ἱλάσθητί μοι τῷ ἁμαρτωλῷ

God be merciful to me as a sinner.

Luke 18.13

136 πάτερ, ἄφες αὐτοῖς· οὐ γὰρ οἴδασι τί ποιοῦσι

Father, forgive them: for they know not what they do.

Luke 23.34

137 μνήσθητί μου, κύριε, ὅταν ἔλθῃς ἐν τῇ βασιλείᾳ σου· καὶ εἶπεν αὐτῷ ὁ Ἰησοῦς, ἀμὴν λέγω σοι, σήμερον μετ' ἐμοῦ ἔσῃ ἐν τῷ παραδείσῳ

Lord, remember me when thou comest into thy kingdom. And Jesus said unto him, Verily I say unto thee, To day shalt thou be with me in paradise.

Luke 23.42

138 πάτερ, εἰς χεῖράς σου παρατίθεμαι τὸ πνεῦμά μου

Father, into thy hands I commend my spirit.

Luke 23.46

139 τί ζητεῖτε τὸν ζῶντα μετὰ τῶν νεκρῶν;

Why seek ye the living among the dead?

Luke 24.5

140 μεῖνον μεθ' ἡμῶν, ὅτι πρὸς ἑσπέραν ἐστὶ καὶ κέκλικεν ἤδη ἡ ἡμέρα

Abide with us: for it is toward evening, and the day is far spent.

Luke 24.29

141 εἰρήνη ὑμῖν

Peace be unto you.

Luke 24.36

cf. the Vulgate: 'Pax vobis'

142 Ἐν ἀρχῇ ἦν ὁ λόγος, καὶ ὁ λόγος ἦν πρὸς τὸν θεόν, καὶ θεὸς ἦν ὁ λόγος

In the beginning was the Word, and the Word was with God, and the Word was God.

John 1.1

143 ἐν αὐτῷ ζωὴ ἦν, καὶ ἡ ζωὴ ἦν τὸ φῶς τῶν ἀνθρώπων· καὶ τὸ φῶς ἐν τῇ σκοτίᾳ φαίνει, καὶ ἡ σκοτία αὐτὸ οὐ κατέλαβεν

In him was life; and the life was the light of men. And the light shineth in darkness; and the darkness comprehended it not.

John 1.4

144 καὶ ὁ λόγος σὰρξ ἐγένετο καὶ ἐσκήνωσεν ἐν ἡμῖν, καὶ ἐθεασάμεθα τὴν δόξαν αὐτοῦ, δόξαν ὡς μονογενοῦς παρὰ πατρός, πλήρης χάριτος καὶ ἀληθείας

And the Word was made flesh, and dwelt among us, (and we beheld his glory, the glory as of the only begotten of the Father), full of grace and truth.

John 1.14

145 θεὸν οὐδεὶς ἑώρακε πώποτε

No man hath seen God at any time.

John 1.18

146 ἐγὼ βαπτίζω ἐν ὕδατι· μέσος δὲ ὑμῶν ἕστηκεν ὃν ὑμεῖς οὐκ οἴδατε· αὐτός ἐστιν ὁ ὀπίσω μου ἐρχόμενος, οὗ ἐγὼ οὐκ εἰμὶ ἄξιος ἵνα λύσω αὐτοῦ τὸν ἱμάντα τοῦ ὑποδήματος

I baptize with water: but there standeth one among you, whom ye know not; he it is, who is coming after me, whose shoe's latchet I am not worthy to unloose.

John 1.26

147 ἴδε ὁ ἀμνὸς τοῦ θεοῦ ὁ αἴρων τὴν ἁμαρτίαν τοῦ κόσμου

Behold the Lamb of God, which taketh away the sin of the world.

John 1.29

148 τί ἐμοὶ καὶ σοί, γύναι; οὔπω ἥκει ἡ ὥρα μου

Woman, what have I to do with thee? mine hour is not yet come.

John 2.4

149 πᾶς ἄνθρωπος πρῶτον τὸν καλὸν οἶνον τίθησι, καὶ ὅταν μεθυσθῶσι, τότε τὸν ἐλάσσω· σὺ τετήρηκας τὸν καλὸν οἶνον ἕως ἄρτι

Every man at the beginning doth set forth good wine; and when men have well drunk, then that which is worse: but thou hast kept the good wine until now.

John 2.10

150 οὕτω γὰρ ἠγάπησεν ὁ θεὸς τὸν κόσμον, ὥστε τὸν υἱὸν αὐτοῦ τὸν μονογενῆ ἔδωκεν, ἵνα πᾶς ὁ πιστεύων εἰς αὐτὸν μὴ ἀπόληται ἀλλ' ἔχῃ ζωὴν αἰώνιον

God so loved the world, that he gave his only begotten Son, that whosoever believeth in him should not perish, but have everlasting life.

John 3.16

151 ἠγάπησαν οἱ ἄνθρωποι μᾶλλον τὸ σκότος ἢ τὸ φῶς· ἦν γὰρ πονηρὰ αὐτῶν τὰ ἔργα

Men loved darkness rather than light, because their deeds were evil.

John 3.19

152 πνεῦμα ὁ θεός, καὶ τοὺς προσκυνοῦντας αὐτὸν ἐν πνεύματι καὶ ἀληθείᾳ δεῖ προσκυνεῖν

God is a Spirit: and they that worship him must worship him in spirit and in truth.

John 4.24

153 ἐὰν μὴ σημεῖα καὶ τέρατα ἴδητε, οὐ μὴ πιστεύσητε

Except ye see signs and wonders, ye will not believe.

John 4.48

154 ἔγειρε, ἆρον τὸν κράβαττόν σου καὶ περιπάτει

Rise, take up thy bed, and walk.

John 5.8

155 καὶ ἐκπορεύσονται οἱ τὰ ἀγαθὰ ποιήσαντες εἰς ἀνάστασιν ζωῆς, οἱ δὲ τὰ φαῦλα πράξαντες εἰς ἀνάστασιν κρίσεως

And shall come forth, they that have done good, unto the resurrection of life; and they that have done evil, unto the resurrection of damnation.

John 5.29

156 ἐραυνᾶτε τὰς γραφάς, ὅτι ὑμεῖς δοκεῖτε ἐν αὐταῖς ζωὴν αἰώνιον ἔχειν· καὶ ἐκεῖναί εἰσιν αἱ μαρτυροῦσαι περὶ ἐμοῦ

Search the scriptures; for in them ye think ye have eternal life: and they are they which testify of me.

John 5.39

157 ἔστιν παιδάριον ὧδε, ὃς ἔχει πέντε ἄρτους κριθίνους καὶ δύο ὀψάρια· ἀλλὰ ταῦτα τί ἐστιν εἰς τοσούτους;

There is a lad here, which hath five barley loaves, and two small fishes: but what are they among so many?

John 6.9

the feeding of the five thousand

158 συναγάγετε τὰ περισσεύσαντα κλάσματα, ἵνα μή τι ἀπόληται

Gather up the fragments that remain, that nothing be lost.

John 6.12

159 ἐγώ εἰμι ὁ ἄρτος τῆς ζωῆς· ὁ ἐρχόμενος πρός με οὐ μὴ πεινάσῃ, καὶ ὁ πιστεύων εἰς ἐμὲ οὐ διψήσει πώποτε

I am the bread of life: he that cometh to me shall never hunger; and he that believeth on me shall never thirst.

John 6.35

160 μὴ κρίνετε κατ' ὄψιν, ἀλλὰ τὴν δικαίαν κρίσιν κρίνατε

Judge not according to the appearance, but judge righteous judgement.

John 7.24

161 ὁ ἀναμάρτητος ὑμῶν πρῶτος βαλέτω λίθον ἐπ' αὐτὴν

He that is without sin among you, let him first cast a stone at her.

John 8.7

162 οὐδὲ ἐγώ σε κατακρίνω· πορεύου καὶ ἀπὸ τοῦ νῦν μηκέτι ἁμάρτανε

Neither do I condemn thee: go, and sin no more.

John 8.11

163 καὶ γνώσεσθε τὴν ἀλήθειαν, καὶ ἡ ἀλήθεια ἐλευθερώσει ὑμᾶς

And ye shall know the truth, and the truth shall make you free.

John 8.32

164 ἐγώ εἰμι ὁ ποιμὴν ὁ καλός· ὁ ποιμὴν ὁ καλὸς τὴν ψυχὴν αὐτοῦ τίθησιν ὑπὲρ τῶν προβάτων

I am the good shepherd: the good shepherd giveth his life for the sheep.

John 10.11

165 καὶ ἄλλα πρόβατα ἔχω, ἃ οὐκ ἔστιν ἐκ τῆς αὐλῆς ταύτης· κἀκεῖνα δεῖ με ἀγαγεῖν, καὶ τῆς φωνῆς μου ἀκούσουσιν, καὶ γενήσεται μία ποίμνη, εἷς ποιμήν

And other sheep I have, which are not of this fold: them also I must bring, and they shall hear my voice; and there shall be one fold, and one shepherd.

John 10.16

166 ἐγώ εἰμι ἡ ἀνάστασις καὶ ἡ ζωή

I am the resurrection, and the life.

John 11.25

167 συμφέρει ἡμῖν ἵνα εἷς ἄνθρωπος ἀποθάνῃ ὑπὲρ τοῦ λαοῦ

It is expedient for us, that one man should die for the people.

John 11.50

spoken by Caiaphas

168 ὃ ποιεῖς, ποίησον τάχιον

That thou doest, do quickly.

John 13.27

cf. Shakespeare, Macbeth 1.7.1: *'If it were done when 'tis done, the 'twere well it were done quickly'*

169 ἐντολὴν καινὴν δίδωμι ὑμῖν, ἵνα ἀγαπᾶτε ἀλλήλους

A new commandment I give unto you, That ye love one another.

John 13.34

170 μὴ ταρασσέσθω ὑμῶν ἡ καρδία

Let not your heart be troubled.

John 14.1

171 ἐγώ εἰμι ἡ ὁδὸς καὶ ἡ ἀλήθεια καὶ ἡ ζωή

I am the way, the truth, and the life.

John 14.6

172 μείζονα ταύτης ἀγάπην οὐδεὶς ἔχει, ἵνα τις τὴν ψυχὴν αὐτοῦ θῇ ὑπὲρ τῶν φίλων αὐτοῦ

Greater love hath no man than this, that a man lay down his life for his friends.

John 15.13

173 νῦν δὲ ὑπάγω πρὸς τὸν πέμψαντά με, καὶ οὐδεὶς ἐξ ὑμῶν ἐρωτᾷ με· ποῦ ὑπάγεις;

But now I go my way to him that sent me; and none of you asketh me, Whither goest thou?

John 16.5

cf. the Vulgate: 'Quo vadis?'

174 ἔτι πολλὰ ἔχω λέγειν ὑμῖν, ἀλλ' οὐ δύνασθε βαστάζειν ἄρτι· ὅταν δὲ ἔλθῃ ἐκεῖνος, τὸ πνεῦμα τῆς ἀληθείας, ὁδηγήσει ὑμᾶς εἰς πᾶσαν τὴν ἀλήθειαν

I have yet many things to say unto you, but ye cannot bear them now. Howbeit when he, the Spirit of truth, is come, he will guide you into all truth.

John 16.12

175 μικρὸν καὶ οὐκέτι θεωρεῖτέ με, καὶ πάλιν μικρὸν καὶ ὄψεσθέ με

A little while, and ye shall not see me: and again, a little while, and ye shall see me.

John 16.16

176 ἡ γυνὴ ὅταν τίκτῃ λύπην ἔχει, ὅτι ἦλθεν ἡ ὥρα αὐτῆς· ὅταν δὲ γεννήσῃ τὸ παιδίον, οὐκέτι μνημονεύει τῆς θλίψεως διὰ τὴν χαρὰν ὅτι ἐγεννήθη ἄνθρωπος εἰς τὸν κόσμον

A woman when she is in travail hath sorrow, because her hour is come; but as soon as she is delivered of the child, she remembereth no more the anguish, for joy that a man is born into the world.

John 16.21

177 καὶ τὰ ἐμὰ πάντα σά ἐστι καὶ τὰ σὰ ἐμά

And all mine are thine, and thine are mine.

John 17.10

178 ἡ βασιλεία ἡ ἐμὴ οὐκ ἔστιν ἐκ τοῦ κόσμου τούτου

My kingdom is not of this world.

John 18.36

179 ὁ Ἰησοῦς οὖν ἰδὼν τὴν μητέρα καὶ τὸν μαθητὴν παρεστῶτα ὃν ἠγάπα, λέγει τῇ μητρί αὐτοῦ· γύναι, ἴδε ὁ υἱός σου. εἶτα λέγει τῷ μαθητῇ, ἴδε ἡ μήτηρ σου

When Jesus saw his mother, and the disciple standing by, whom he loved, he saith unto his mother, Woman, behold thy son! Then saith he to the disciple,

Behold thy mother!

John 19.26

180 τετέλεσται· καὶ κλίνας τὴν κεφαλὴν παρέδωκε τὸ πνεῦμα

It is finished: and he bowed the head, and gave up the ghost.

John 19.30

the last of the 'Seven Words' of Jesus on the Cross

181 μή μου ἅπτου

Touch me not.

John 20.17

to Mary Magdalene; cf. the Vulgate: 'Noli me tangere'

182 καὶ τῶν θυρῶν κεκλεισμένων ὅπου ἦσαν οἱ μαθηταὶ συνηγμένοι διὰ τὸν φόβον τῶν Ἰουδαίων, ἦλθεν ὁ Ἰησοῦς καὶ ἔστη εἰς τὸ μέσον καὶ λέγει αὐτοῖς· εἰρήνη ὑμῖν

When the doors were shut where the disciples were assembled for fear of the Jews, came Jesus and stood in the midst, and saith unto them, Peace be unto you.

John 20.19

183 ἐὰν μὴ ἴδω ἐν ταῖς χερσὶν αὐτοῦ τὸν τύπον τῶν ἥλων, καὶ βάλω τὸν δάκτυλόν μου εἰς τὸν τύπον τῶν ἥλων, καὶ βάλω τὴν χεῖρά μου εἰς τὴν πλευρὰν αὐτοῦ, οὐ μὴ πιστεύσω

Except I shall see in his hands the print of the nails, and put my fingers into the print of the nails, and thrust my hand into his side, I shall not believe.

John 20.25

184 μὴ γίνου ἄπιστος ἀλλὰ πιστός

Be not faithless, but believing.

John 20.27

185 ὅτι ἑώρακάς με πεπίστευκας· μακάριοι οἱ μὴ ἰδόντες καὶ πιστεύσαντες

Thomas, because thou hast seen me, thou hast believed: blessed are they that have not seen, and yet have believed.

John 20.29

186 ἔστι δὲ καὶ ἄλλα πολλὰ ἃ ἐποίησεν ὁ Ἰησοῦς, ἅτινα ἐὰν γράφηται καθ' ἕν, οὐδ' αὐτὸν οἶμαι τὸν κόσμον χωρῆσαι τὰ γραφόμενα βιβλία

And there are also many other things which Jesus did, the which, if they should be written every one, I suppose that even the world itself could not contain the books that should be written.

John 21.25

closing lines

187 ἀργύριον καὶ χρυσίον οὐχ ὑπάρχει μοι· ὃ δὲ ἔχω τοῦτό σοι δίδωμι

Silver and gold I have none; but such as I have give I thee.

Acts of the Apostles 3.6

188 Σαῦλος δὲ ἦν συνευδοκῶν τῇ ἀναιρέσει αὐτοῦ

And Saul was consenting unto his death.

Acts of the Apostles 8.1

of Stephen to be stoned to death

189 τὸ ἀργύριόν σου σὺν σοὶ εἴη εἰς ἀπώλειαν, ὅτι τὴν δωρεὰν τοῦ θεοῦ ἐνόμισας διὰ χρημάτων κτᾶσθαι

Thy money perish with thee, because thou hast thought that the gift of God may be purchased with money.

Acts of the Apostles 8.20

190 Σαοὺλ Σαούλ, τί με διώκεις; ... σκληρόν σοι πρὸς κέντρα λακτίζειν

Saul, Saul, why persecutest thou me? it is hard for thee to kick against the pricks.

Acts of the Apostles 9.4

proverbial by now: cf. Aeschylus 39, Pindar 73 and Bible, Acts 26.14

191 οἱ θεοὶ ὁμοιωθέντες ἀνθρώποις κατέβησαν πρὸς ἡμᾶς

The gods are come down to us in the likeness of men.

Acts of the Apostles 14.11

cf. Cleanthes 1 and Bible 317; but cf. Xenophanes 4

192 τί με δεῖ ποιεῖν ἵνα σωθῶ;

What must I do to be saved?

Acts of the Apostles 16.30

193 εὗρον καὶ βωμὸν ἐν ᾧ ἐπεγέγραπτο, Ἀγνώστῳ θεῷ

I found an altar with this inscription, TO THE UNKNOWN GOD

Acts of the Apostles 17.23

in Athens

194 ἐν αὐτῷ γὰρ ζῶμεν καὶ κινούμεθα καὶ ἐσμέν, ὡς καί τινες τῶν καθ' ὑμᾶς ποιητῶν εἰρήκασιν· τοῦ γὰρ καὶ γένος ἐσμέν

For in him (God) we live, and move, and have our being; as certain of your own poets have said, For we are also his offspring.

Acts of the Apostles 17.28

possibly quoting from Aratus 14 and 1 (which however uses 'εἰμέν', not 'εσμέν'); cf. also Cleanthes 2

195 μακάριόν ἐστι μᾶλλον διδόναι ἢ λαμβάνειν

It is more blessed to give than to receive.

Acts of the Apostles 20.35

196 τὰ πολλά σε γράμματα εἰς μανίαν περιτρέπει

Thou art beside thyself; much learning doth make thee mad.

Acts of the Apostles 26.24

197 ἐν ὀλίγῳ με πείθεις Χριστιανὸν γενέσθαι

Almost thou persuadest me to be a Christian.

Acts of the Apostles 26.28

198 ἑαυτοῖς εἰσι νόμος

A law unto themselves.

Romans 2.14

199 οὗ δὲ οὐκ ἔστι νόμος, οὐδὲ παράβασις

For where no law is, there is no transgression.

Romans 4.15

200 ὃς παρ' ἐλπίδα ἐπ' ἐλπίδι ἐπίστευσεν

Who against hope believed in hope.

Romans 4.18

of Abraham

201 καὶ ἡμεῖς ἐν καινότητι ζωῆς περιπατήσωμεν

We also should walk in newness of life.

Romans 6.4

202 εἰ ὁ θεὸς ὑπὲρ ἡμῶν, τίς καθ' ἡμῶν;

If God be for us, who can be against us?

Romans 8.31

203 χαίρειν μετὰ χαιρόντων καὶ κλαίειν μετὰ κλαιόντων

Rejoice with them that do rejoice, and weep with them that weep.

Romans 12.15

204 μὴ νικῶ ὑπὸ τοῦ κακοῦ, ἀλλὰ νίκα ἐν τῷ ἀγαθῷ τὸ κακόν

Be not overcome of evil, but overcome evil with good.

Romans 12.21

205 θέλω δὲ ὑμᾶς σοφοὺς εἶναι εἰς τὸ ἀγαθόν, ἀκεραίους δὲ εἰς τὸ κακόν

I would have you wise unto that which is good, and simple concerning evil.

Romans 16.19

a better translation of 'ἀκέραιος' would be 'inviolate, incorruptible'

206 ποῦ σοφός; ποῦ γραμματεύς; ποῦ συζητητὴς τοῦ αἰῶνος τούτου; οὐχὶ ἐμώρανεν ὁ θεὸς τὴν σοφίαν τοῦ κόσμου τούτου;

Where is the wise? where is the scribe? where is the disputer of this world? hath not God made foolish the wisdom of this world?

I Corinthians 1.20

207 Ἰουδαῖοι σημεῖα αἰτοῦσιν καὶ Ἕλληνες σοφίαν ζητοῦσιν

The Jews require a sign, and the Greeks seek after wisdom.

I Corinthians 1.22

208 τὸ μωρὸν τοῦ θεοῦ σοφώτερον τῶν ἀνθρώπων ἐστί, καὶ τὸ ἀσθενὲς τοῦ θεοῦ ἰσχυρότερον τῶν ἀνθρώπων ἐστί

The foolishness of God is wiser than men; and the weakness of God is stronger than men.

I Corinthians 1.25

209 θέατρον ἐγενήθημεν τῷ κόσμῳ

We are made a spectacle unto the world.

I Corinthians 4.9

210 ἄχρι τῆς ἄρτι ὥρας καὶ πεινῶμεν καὶ διψῶμεν καὶ γυμνητεύομεν ... καὶ κοπιῶμεν ἐργαζόμενοι ταῖς ἰδίαις χερσί· λοιδορούμενοι εὐλογοῦμεν, διωκόμενοι ἀνεχόμεθα, βλασφημούμενοι παρακαλοῦμεν

Even unto this present hour we both hunger, and thirst, and we are naked.

And labour, working with our own hands: being reviled, we bless: being persecuted, we suffer it: Being defamed, we intreat.

I Corinthians 4.11

211 τί θέλετε; ἐν ῥάβδῳ ἔλθω πρὸς ὑμᾶς, ἢ ἐν ἀγάπῃ πνεύματί τε πραότητος;

What will ye? shall I come unto you with a rod, or in love, and in the spirit of meekness?

I Corinthians 4.21

212 ἀπὼν τῷ σώματι, παρὼν δὲ τῷ πνεύματι

Absent in body, but present in spirit.

I Corinthians 5.3

213 μικρὰ ζύμη ὅλον τὸ φύραμα ζυμοῖ

A little leaven leaveneth the whole lump.

I Corinthians 5.6

214 ὥστε ἑορτάζωμεν μὴ ἐν ζύμῃ παλαιᾷ, μηδὲ ἐν ζύμῃ κακίας καὶ πονηρίας, ἀλλ' ἐν ἀζύμοις εἰλικρινείας καὶ ἀληθείας

Let us keep the feast, not with old leaven, neither with the leaven of malice and wickedness; but with the unleavened bread of sincerity and truth.

I Corinthians 5.8

215 τὸ σῶμα ὑμῶν ναὸς τοῦ ἐν ὑμῖν ἁγίου πνεύματός ἐστιν

Your body is the temple of the Holy Ghost.

I Corinthians 6.19

216 ἡ γνῶσις φυσιοῖ, ἡ δὲ ἀγάπη οἰκοδομεῖ

Knowledge puffeth up, but charity edifieth.

I Corinthians 8.1

217 τίς στρατεύεται ἰδίοις ὀψωνίοις ποτέ; τίς φυτεύει ἀμπελῶνα καὶ ἐκ τοῦ καρποῦ αὐτοῦ οὐκ ἐσθίει;

Who goeth a warfare any time at his own charges? who planteth a vineyard, and eateth not of the fruit thereof?

I Corinthians 9.7

218 οὐκ οἴδατε ὅτι οἱ ἐν σταδίῳ τρέχοντες πάντες μὲν τρέχουσιν, εἷς δὲ λαμβάνει τὸ βραβεῖον;

Know ye not that they which run in a race run all, but one receiveth the prize?

I Corinthians 9.24

219 ὁ δοκῶν ἑστάναι βλεπέτω μὴ πέσῃ

Let him that thinketh he standeth take heed lest he fall.

I Corinthians 10.12

220 αὐτὴ ἡ φύσις διδάσκει ὑμᾶς ὅτι ἀνὴρ μὲν ἐὰν κομᾷ ἀτιμία αὐτῷ ἐστι, γυνὴ δὲ ἐὰν κομᾷ δόξα αὐτῇ ἐστιν

Doth not even nature itself teach you, that if a man have long hair, it is a shame unto him? But if a woman have long hair, it is a glory to her.

I Corinthians 11.14

221 ἐὰν ταῖς γλώσσαις τῶν ἀνθρώπων λαλῶ καὶ τῶν ἀγγέλων, ἀγάπην δὲ μὴ ἔχω, γέγονα χαλκὸς ἠχῶν ἢ κύμβαλον ἀλαλάζον. ἔχω προφητείαν καὶ εἰδῶ τὰ μυστήρια πάντα καὶ πᾶσαν τὴν γνῶσιν, καὶ ἐὰν ἔχω πᾶσαν τὴν πίστιν ὥστε ὄρη μεθιστάνειν, ἀγάπην δὲ μὴ ἔχω, οὐδέν εἰμι

Though I speak with the tongues of men and of angels, and have not charity, I am become as sounding brass, or a tinkling cymbal. And though I have the gift of prophecy, and understand all mysteries, and all knowledge; and though I have all faith, so that I could remove mountains; and have not charity, I am nothing.

I Corinthians 13.1

continued in the next five entries; 'love' is preferred to 'charity' by some translators

222 καὶ ἐὰν ψωμίσω πάντα τὰ ὑπάρχοντά μου, καὶ ἐὰν παραδῶ τὸ σῶμά μου ἵνα καυθήσωμαι, ἀγάπην δὲ μὴ ἔχω, οὐδὲν ὠφελοῦμαι

And though I bestow all my goods to feed the poor, and though I give my body to be burned, and have not charity, it profiteth me nothing.

I Corinthians 13.3

223 ἡ ἀγάπη μακροθυμεῖ, χρηστεύεται, ἡ ἀγάπη οὐ ζηλοῖ, ἡ ἀγάπη οὐ περπερεύεται, οὐ φυσιοῦται, οὐκ ἀσχημονεῖ, οὐ ζητεῖ τὰ ἑαυτῆς, οὐ παροξύνεται, οὐ λογίζεται τὸ κακόν, οὐ χαίρει ἐπὶ τῇ ἀδικίᾳ, συγχαίρει δὲ τῇ ἀληθείᾳ· πάντα στέγει, πάντα πιστεύει, πάντα ἐλπίζει, πάντα ὑπομένει

Charity suffereth long, and is kind; charity envieth not; charity vaunteth not itself, is not puffed up, doth not behave itself unseemly, seeketh not her own, is not easily provoked, thinketh not evil; Rejoiceth not in iniquity, but rejoiceth in the truth; Beareth all things, believeth all things, hopeth all things, endureth all things.

I Corinthians 13.4

224 ἡ ἀγάπη οὐδέποτε ἐκπίπτει. εἴτε δὲ προφητεῖαι, καταργηθήσονται· εἴτε γλῶσσαι, παύσονται· εἴτε γνῶσις, καταργηθήσεται. ἐκ μέρους γὰρ γινώσκομεν καὶ ἐκ μέρους προφητεύομεν· ὅταν δὲ ἔλθῃ τὸ τέλειον, τότε τὸ ἐκ μέρους καταργηθήσεται

Charity never faileth: but whether there be prophecies, they shall fail; whether there be tongues, they shall cease; whether there be knowledge, it shall vanish away. For we know in part, and we prophesy in part. But when that which is perfect is come, then that which is in part shall be done away.

I Corinthians 13.8

225 ὅτε ἤμην νήπιος, ὡς νήπιος ἐλάλουν, ὡς νήπιος ἐφρόνουν, ὡς νήπιος ἐλογιζόμην· ὅτε δὲ γέγονα ἀνήρ, κατήργηκα τὰ τοῦ νηπίου

When I was a child, I spake as a child, I understood as a child, I thought as a child: but when I became a man, I put away childish things.

I Corinthians 13.11

226 βλέπομεν γὰρ ἄρτι δι' ἐσόπτρου ἐν αἰνίγματι, τότε δὲ πρόσωπον πρὸς πρόσωπον· ἄρτι γινώσκω ἐκ μέρους, τότε δὲ ἐπιγνώσομαι καθὼς καὶ ἐπεγνώσθην. νυνὶ δὲ μένει πίστις, ἐλπίς, ἀγάπη, τὰ τρία ταῦτα· μείζων δὲ τούτων ἡ ἀγάπη

For now we see through a glass, darkly; but then face to face: now I know in part; but then I shall know even as also I am known. And now abideth faith, hope, charity, these three; but the greatest of these is charity.

I Corinthians 13.12

227 ἐὰν ἄδηλον φωνὴν σάλπιγξ δῷ, τίς παρασκευάσεται εἰς πόλεμον;

If the trumpet give an uncertain sound, who shall prepare himself to the battle?

I Corinthians 14.8

228 πάντα εὐσχημόνως καὶ κατὰ τάξιν γινέσθω

Let all things be done decently and in order.

I Corinthians 14.40

229 ἔσχατος ἐχθρὸς καταργεῖται ὁ θάνατος

The last enemy that shall be destroyed is death.

I Corinthians 15.26

230 φάγωμεν καὶ πίωμεν, αὔριον γὰρ ἀποθνῄσκομεν

Let us eat and drink, for to-morrow we die.

I Corinthians 15.32

warning against a doctrine of disbelief; cf. Bible, Isaiah 22.13

231 μὴ πλανᾶσθε· φθείρουσιν ἤθη χρηστὰ ὁμιλίαι κακαί

Be not deceived: evil communications corrupt good manners.

I Corinthians 15.33

identical in Euripides 538

232 πάντες δὲ ἀλλαγησόμεθα, ἐν ἀτόμῳ, ἐν ῥιπῇ ὀφθαλμοῦ

We shall all be changed, in a moment, in the twinkling of an eye.

I Corinthians 15.51

233 ποῦ σου, θάνατε, τὸ κέντρον; ποῦ σου, ᾅδη, τὸ νῖκος;

O death, where is thy sting? O grave, where is thy victory?

I Corinthians 15.55

234 μηδὲν ἔχοντες καὶ πάντα κατέχοντες

Having nothing, and yet possessing all things.

II Corinthians 6.10

235 ἱλαρὸν γὰρ δότην ἀγαπᾷ ὁ θεός

God loveth a cheerful giver.

II Corinthians 9.7

236 ἡδέως γὰρ ἀνέχεσθε τῶν ἀφρόνων φρόνιμοι ὄντες

For ye suffer fools gladly, seeing ye yourselves are wise.

II Corinthians 11.19

237 τεσσαράκοντα παρὰ μίαν ἔλαβον πεντάκις

Five times received I forty stripes save one.

II Corinthians 11.24

238 ἡ γὰρ δύναμίς μου ἐν ἀσθενείᾳ τελειοῦται

My strength is made perfect in weakness.

II Corinthians 12.9

239 εἴ τις ὑμᾶς εὐαγγελίζεται παρ' ὃ παρελάβετε, ἀνάθεμα ἔστω

If any man preach any other gospel unto you that ye have received, let him be accursed.

Galatians 1.9

cf. the Vulgate: 'Anathema sit!,' the formal words of excommunication in the Catholic Church

240 οὐκ ἔνι Ἰουδαῖος οὐδὲ Ἕλλην, οὐκ ἔνι δοῦλος οὐδὲ ἐλεύθερος, οὐκ ἔνι ἄρσεν καὶ θῆλυ· πάντες γὰρ ὑμεῖς εἷς ἐστε ἐν Χριστῷ Ἰησοῦ

There is neither Jew nor Greek, there is neither bond nor free, there is neither male nor female: for ye are all one in Christ Jesus.

Galatians 3.28

241 ὁ δὲ καρπὸς τοῦ πνεύματός ἐστιν ἀγάπη, χαρά, εἰρήνη, μακροθυμία, χρηστότης, ἀγαθωσύνη, πίστις, πραότης, ἐγκράτεια

But the fruit of the Spirit is love, joy, peace, longsuffering, gentleness, goodness, faith, meekness, temperance.

Galatians 5.22

242 ἀλλήλων τὰ βάρη βαστάζετε

Bear ye one another's burdens.

Galatians 6.2

243 ὃ γὰρ ἐὰν σπείρῃ ἄνθρωπος, τοῦτο καὶ θερίσει

Whatsoever a man soweth, that shall he also reap.

Galatians 6.7

cf. Plato 182

244 ἐσμὲν ἀλλήλων μέλη

We are members one of another.

Ephesians 4.25

245 ὀργίζεσθε καὶ μὴ ἁμαρτάνετε· ὁ ἥλιος μὴ ἐπιδυέτω ἐπὶ τῷ παροργισμῷ ὑμῶν

Be ye angry and sin not: let not the sun go down upon your wrath.

Ephesians 4.26

cf. Pythagoras 17 and the English proverb 'never let the sun go down on your anger'

246 μηδεὶς ὑμᾶς ἀπατάτω κενοῖς λόγοις

Let no man deceive you with vain words.

Ephesians 5.6

247 μετὰ φόβου καὶ τρόμου τὴν ἑαυτῶν σωτηρίαν κατεργάζεσθε

Work out your own salvation with fear and trembling.

Philippians 2.12

248 οὐκ εἰς κενὸν ἔδραμον οὐδὲ εἰς κενὸν ἐκοπίασα

I have not run in vain, neither laboured in vain.

Philippians 2.16

249 ὅσα ἐστὶν ἀληθῆ, ὅσα σεμνά, ὅσα δίκαια, ὅσα ἁγνά, ὅσα προσφιλῆ, ὅσα εὔφημα, εἴ τις ἀρετὴ καὶ εἴ τις ἔπαινος, ταῦτα λογίζεσθε

Whatsoever things are true, whatsoever things are honest, whatsoever things are just, whatsoever things are pure, whatsoever things are lovely, whatsoever things are of good report; if there be any virtue and if there be any praise, think on these things.

Philippians 4.8

250 ἐν αὐτῷ ἐκτίσθη τὰ πάντα, τὰ ἐν τοῖς οὐρανοῖς καὶ τὰ ἐπὶ τῆς γῆς, τὰ ὁρατὰ καὶ τὰ ἀόρατα

By him were all things created, that are in heaven, and that are in earth, visible and invisible.

Colossians 1.16

251 οἱ ἄνδρες, ἀγαπᾶτε τὰς γυναῖκας καὶ μὴ πικραίνεσθε πρὸς αὐτάς

Husbands, love your wives, and be not bitter against them.

Colossians 3.19

252 οἱ πατέρες, μὴ ἐρεθίζετε τὰ τέκνα ὑμῶν

Fathers, provoke not your children to anger.

Colossians 3.21

253 ὁ λόγος ὑμῶν πάντοτε ἐν χάριτι, ἅλατι ἠρτυμένος

Let your speech be alway with grace, seasoned with salt.

Colossians 4.6

254 φιλοτιμεῖσθαι ἡσυχάζειν καὶ πράσσειν τὰ ἴδια καὶ ἐργάζεσθαι ταῖς χερσὶν ὑμῶν

Study to be quiet, do your own business, and work with your own hands.

I Thessalonians 4.11

255 οὐ θέλομεν ὑμᾶς ἀγνοεῖν, ἀδελφοί, περὶ τῶν κεκοιμημένων, ἵνα μὴ λυπῆσθε καθὼς καὶ οἱ λοιποὶ οἱ μὴ ἔχοντες ἐλπίδα

I would not have you to be ignorant, brethren, concerning them which are asleep, that ye sorrow not, even as others which have no hope.

I Thessalonians 4.13

256 εἰ γὰρ πιστεύομεν ὅτι Ἰησοῦς ἀπέθανε καὶ ἀνέστη, οὕτω καὶ ὁ θεὸς τοὺς κοιμηθέντας διὰ τοῦ Ἰησοῦ ἄξει σὺν αὐτῷ

For if we believe that Jesus died and rose again, even so them also which sleep in Jesus will God bring with him.

I Thessalonians 4.14

257 ἔπειτα ἡμεῖς οἱ ζῶντες οἱ περιλειπόμενοι ἁρπαγησόμεθα ἐν νεφέλαις ... καὶ οὕτω πάντοτε σὺν κυρίῳ ἐσόμεθα

Then we which are alive and remain shall be caught up in the clouds; and so shall we ever be with the Lord.

I Thessalonians 4.17

cf. Aeschylus 175

258 πάντα δὲ δοκιμάζετε, τὸ καλὸν κατέχετε

Prove all things; hold fast that which is good.

I Thessalonians 5.21

259 εἴ τις οὐ θέλει ἐργάζεσθαι μηδὲ ἐσθιέτω

If any would not work, neither should he eat.

II Thessalonians 3.10

now often quoted as 'ὁ μὴ ἐργαζόμενος μὴ ἐσθιέτω'; cf. Ignatius, Epistle 3.9.3; St John Chrysostom, Homily *63.94.33; et al.*

260 δεῖ οὖν τὸν ἐπίσκοπον ἀνεπίληπτον εἶναι, μιᾶς γυναικὸς ἄνδρα, νηφάλιον, σώφρονα, κόσμιον, φιλόξενον, διδακτικόν, μὴ πάροινον, μὴ πλήκτην, μὴ αἰσχροκερδῆ, ἀλλ' ἐπιεικῆ, ἄμαχον, ἀφιλάργυρον

A bishop then must be blameless, the husband of one wife, vigilant, sober, of good behaviour, given to hospitality, apt to teach; not given to wine, no striker, not greedy of filthy lucre; but patient, not a brawler, not covetous.

I Timothy 3.2

261 οἴνῳ ὀλίγῳ χρῶ διὰ τὸν στόμαχόν σου καὶ τὰς πυκνάς σου ἀσθενείας

Use a little wine for thy stomach's sake and thine often infirmities.

I Timothy 5.23

262 οὐδὲν γὰρ εἰσηνέγκαμεν εἰς τὸν κόσμον, δῆλον ὅτι οὐδὲ ἐξενεγκεῖν τι δυνάμεθα

For we brought nothing into this world, and it is certain we can carry nothing out.

I Timothy 6.7

263 ῥίζα γὰρ πάντων τῶν κακῶν ἐστιν ἡ φιλαργυρία

The love of money is the root of all evil.

I Timothy 6.10

cf. the English proverb 'money is the root of all evil'; and Sophocles 67

264 ὑποτύπωσιν ἔχε ὑγιαινόντων λόγων

Hold fast the form of sound words.

II Timothy 1.13

265 ἐὰν δὲ καὶ ἀθλῇ τις, οὐ στεφανοῦται ἐὰν μὴ νομίμως ἀθλήσῃ

And if a man also strive masteries, yet is he not crowned, except he strive lawfully.

II Timothy 2.5

in a more modern context: 'And in competition he will not be crowned unless he contends lawfully', a direct warning for doped athletes

266 τὸν ἀγῶνα τὸν καλὸν ἠγώνισμαι, τὸν δρόμον τετέλεκα, τὴν πίστιν τετήρηκα

I have fought the good fight, I have finished my course, I have kept the faith.

II Timothy 4.7

267 πάντα καθαρὰ τοῖς καθαροῖς

Unto the pure all things are pure.

Titus 1.15

268 ἔστιν δὲ πίστις ἐλπιζομένων ὑπόστασις, πραγμάτων ἔλεγχος οὐ βλεπομένων

Faith is the substance of things hoped for, the evidence of things not seen.

Hebrews 11.1

269 καθὼς τὰ ἄστρα τοῦ οὐρανοῦ τῷ πλήθει καὶ ὡς ἡ ἄμμος ἡ παρὰ τὸ χεῖλος τῆς θαλάσσης ἡ ἀναρίθμητος

So many as the stars of the sky in multitude, and as the sand which is by the sea shore innumerable.

Hebrews 11.12

270 τῆς φιλοξενίας μὴ ἐπιλανθάνεσθε· διὰ ταύτης γὰρ ἔλαθόν τινες ξενίσαντες ἀγγέλους

Be not forgetful to entertain strangers: for thereby some have entertained angels unawares.

Hebrews 13.2

cf. Homer 287 and 369

271 ἡ δὲ ὑπομονὴ ἔργον τέλειον ἐχέτω

Let patience have her perfect work.

James 1.4

272 πᾶσα δόσις ἀγαθὴ καὶ πᾶν δώρημα τέλειον ἄνωθέν ἐστι καταβαῖνον ἀπὸ σοῦ τοῦ πατρὸς τῶν φώτων

Every good gift and every perfect gift is from above, and cometh down from the Father of lights.

James 1.17

273 ταχὺς εἰς τὸ ἀκοῦσαι, βραδὺς εἰς τὸ λαλῆσαι, βραδὺς εἰς ὀργήν

Be swift to hear, slow to speak, slow to wrath.

James 1.19

274 γίνεσθε δὲ ποιηταὶ λόγου καὶ μὴ μόνον ἀκροαταὶ

But be ye doers of the word, and not hearers only.

James 1.22

275 ἡ πίστις χωρὶς τῶν ἔργων ἀργή ἐστιν

Faith without works is dead.

James 2.20

276 πρὸ πάντων δέ ... μὴ ὀμνύετε, μήτε τὸν οὐρανὸν μήτε τὴν γῆν μήτε ἄλλον τινὰ ὅρκον· ἤτω δὲ ὑμῶν τὸ ναὶ ναί, καὶ τὸ οὒ οὔ

Above all things, swear not, neither by heaven, neither by earth, neither by any other oath; but let your yea be yea; and your nay, nay.

James 5.12

cf. Bible 19

277 πᾶσα σὰρξ ὡς χόρτος, καὶ πᾶσα δόξα ἀνθρώπου ὡς ἄνθος χόρτου· ἐξηράνθη ὁ χόρτος, καὶ τὸ ἄνθος αὐτοῦ ἐξέπεσεν

All flesh is grass, and all the glory of man as the flower of grass. The grass withereth, and the flower thereof falleth away.

I Peter 1.24

278 ὁ θέλων ζωὴν ἀγαπᾶν καὶ ἰδεῖν ἡμέρας ἀγαθάς ... ἐκκλινάτω ἀπὸ κακοῦ καὶ ποιησάτω ἀγαθόν, ζητησάτω εἰρήνην καὶ διωξάτω αὐτήν

He that will love life and see good days, let him eschew evil and do good; let him seek peace, and ensue it.

I Peter 3.11

279 πάντων δὲ τὸ τέλος ἤγγικε

The end of all things is at hand.

I Peter 4.7

280 ἀγάπη καλύψει πλῆθος ἁμαρτιῶν

Charity shall cover the multitude of sins.

I Peter 4.8

281 ἕως οὗ ἡμέρα διαυγάσῃ καὶ φωσφόρος ἀνατείλῃ ἐν ταῖς καρδίαις ὑμῶν

Until the day dawn, and the day star arise in your hearts.

II Peter 1.19

282 ἐὰν εἴπωμεν ὅτι ἁμαρτίαν οὐκ ἔχομεν, ἑαυτοὺς πλανῶμεν καὶ ἡ ἀλήθεια οὐκ ἔστιν ἐν ἡμῖν

If we say that we have no sin, we deceive ourselves, and the truth is not in us.

I John 1.8

283 φόβος οὐκ ἔστιν ἐν τῇ ἀγάπῃ, ἀλλ' ἡ τελεία ἀγάπη ἔξω βάλλει τὸν φόβον

There is no fear in love; but perfect love casteth out fear.

I John 4.18

284 ἰδοὺ ἔρχεται μετὰ τῶν νεφελῶν, καὶ ὄψεται αὐτὸν πᾶς ὀφθαλμὸς

Behold, he cometh with clouds; and every eye shall see him.

Revelation 1.7

285 ἐγώ εἰμι τὸ Α καὶ τὸ Ω, λέγει κύριος ὁ θεός, ὁ ὢν καὶ ὁ ἦν καὶ ὁ ἐρχόμενος, ὁ παντοκράτωρ

I am Alpha and Omega, the beginning and the ending, saith the Lord, which is and which was and which is to come, the Almighty.

Revelation 1.8

286 ἐγενόμην ἐν πνεύματι ἐν τῇ κυριακῇ ἡμέρᾳ, καὶ ἤκουσα ὀπίσω μου φωνὴν μεγάλην ὡς σάλπιγγος

I was in the Spirit on the Lord's day, and heard behind me a great voice as of a trumpet.

Revelation 1.10

287 ὃ βλέπεις γράψον εἰς βιβλίον

What thou seest, write in a book.

Revelation 1.11

288 ἡ δὲ κεφαλὴ αὐτοῦ καὶ αἱ τρίχες λευκαὶ ὡς ἔριον λευκόν, ὡς χιών· καὶ οἱ ὀφθαλμοὶ αὐτοῦ ὡς φλὸξ πυρός, καὶ οἱ πόδες αὐτοῦ ὅμοιοι χαλκολιβάνῳ, ὡς ἐν καμίνῳ πεπυρωμένοι, καὶ ἡ φωνὴ αὐτοῦ ὡς φωνὴ ὑδάτων πολλῶν, καὶ ἔχων ἐν τῇ δεξιᾷ χειρὶ αὐτοῦ ἀστέρας ἑπτά, καὶ ἐκ τοῦ στόματος αὐτοῦ ῥομφαία δίστομος ὀξεῖα ἐκπορευομένη, καὶ ἡ ὄψις αὐτοῦ ὡς ὁ ἥλιος φαίνει ἐν τῇ δυνάμει αὐτοῦ. καὶ ὅτε εἶδον αὐτόν, ἔπεσα πρὸς τοὺς πόδας αὐτοῦ ὡς νεκρός

His head and his hairs were white as snow; and his eyes were as a flame of fire; And his feet like unto fine brass, as if they burned in a furnace; and his voice as the sound of many waters. And he had in his right hand seven stars: and out of his mouth went a sharp two-edged sword: and his countenance was as the sun shineth in his strength. And when I saw him, I fell at his feet as dead.

Revelation 1.14

289 ἐγώ εἰμι ὁ πρῶτος καὶ ὁ ἔσχατος καὶ ὁ ζῶν, καὶ ἐγενόμην νεκρός, καὶ ἰδοὺ ζῶν εἰμι εἰς τοὺς αἰῶνας τῶν αἰώνων, καὶ ἔχω τὰς κλεῖς τοῦ θανάτου καὶ τοῦ ᾅδου

I am the first and the last: I am he that liveth, and was dead; and, behold, I am alive for evermore, Amen; and have the keys of hell and of death.

Revelation 1.17

290 ἰδοὺ δέδωκα ἐνώπιόν σου θύραν ἀνεῳγμένην, ἣν οὐδεὶς δύναται κλεῖσαι αὐτήν

Behold, I have set before thee an open door, and no man can shut it.

Revelation 3.8

291 ἰδοὺ ἕστηκα ἐπὶ τὴν θύραν καὶ κρούω· ἐάν τις ἀκούσῃ τῆς φωνῆς μου καὶ ἀνοίξῃ τὴν θύραν, εἰσελεύσομαι πρὸς αὐτὸν καὶ δειπνήσω μετ' αὐτοῦ καὶ αὐτὸς μετ' ἐμοῦ

Behold, I stand at the door, and knock: if any man hear my voice, and open the door, I will come into him, and will sup with him, and he with me.

Revelation 3.20

292 ὅτι σὺ ἔκτισας τὰ πάντα, καὶ διὰ τὸ θέλημά σου ἦσαν καὶ ἐκτίσθησαν

Thou hast created all things, and for thy pleasure they are and were created.

Revelation 4.11

293 τίς ἄξιός ἐστιν ἀνοῖξαι τὸ βιβλίον καὶ λῦσαι τὰς σφραγῖδας αὐτοῦ;

Who is worthy to open the book, and to loose the seals thereof?

Revelation 5.2

294 καὶ ἐξῆλθεν νικῶν καὶ ἵνα νικήσῃ

And he went forth conquering, and to conquer.

Revelation 6.2

295 καὶ εἶδον, καὶ ἰδοὺ ἵππος χλωρός, καὶ ὁ καθήμενος ἐπάνω αὐτοῦ, ὄνομα αὐτῷ ὁ θάνατος

And I looked, and behold a pale horse: and his name that sat on him was Death.

Revelation 6.8

296 καὶ σεισμὸς μέγας ἐγένετο, καὶ ὁ ἥλιος μέλας ἐγένετο ... καὶ πᾶν ὄρος καὶ νῆσος ἐκ τῶν τόπων αὐτῶν ἐκινήθησαν

And, lo, there was a great earthquake; and the sun became black ... and every mountain and island were moved out of their places.

Revelation 6.12

297 ὅτι ἦλθεν ἡ ἡμέρα ἡ μεγάλη τῆς ὀργῆς αὐτοῦ, καὶ τίς δύναται σταθῆναι;

For the great day of his wrath is come; and who shall be able to stand?

Revelation 6.17

cf. the Latin 'Dies irae dies illa'

298 καὶ ἰδοὺ ὄχλος πολύς, ὃν ἀριθμῆσαι αὐτὸν οὐδεὶς ἐδύνατο, ἐκ παντὸς ἔθνους καὶ φυλῶν καὶ λαῶν καὶ γλωσσῶν, ἑστῶτες ἐνώπιον τοῦ θρόνου καὶ ἐνώπιον τοῦ ἀρνίου

A great multitude, which no man could number, of all nations, and kindreds, and people, and tongues, stood before the throne, and before the Lamb.

Revelation 7.9

299 καὶ ἐν ταῖς ἡμέραις ἐκείναις ζητήσουσιν οἱ ἄνθρωποι τὸν θάνατον καὶ οὐ μὴ εὑρήσουσιν αὐτόν, καὶ ἐπιθυμήσουσιν ἀποθανεῖν καὶ φεύξεται ὁ θάνατος ἀπ' αὐτῶν

And in those days shall men seek death, and shall not find it; and shall desire to die, and death shall flee from them.

Revelation 9.6

300 ἦν ἐν τῷ στόματί μου ὡς μέλι γλυκύ· καὶ ὅτε ἔφαγον αὐτό, ἐπικράνθη ἡ κοιλία μου

It was in my mouth sweet as honey: and as soon as I had eaten it, my belly was bitter.

Revelation 10.10

301 καὶ σημεῖον μέγα ὤφθη ἐν τῷ οὐρανῷ, γυνὴ περιβεβλημένη τὸν ἥλιον, καὶ ἡ σελήνη ὑποκάτω τῶν ποδῶν αὐτῆς, καὶ ἐπὶ τῆς κεφαλῆς αὐτῆς στέφανος ἀστέρων δώδεκα

And there appeared a great wonder in heaven; a woman clothed with the sun, and the moon under her feet, and upon her head a crown of twelve stars.

Revelation 12.1

302 ὁ ἔχων νοῦν ψηφισάτω τὸν ἀριθμὸν τοῦ θηρίου, ἀριθμὸς γὰρ ἀνθρώπου ἐστί· καὶ ὁ ἀριθμὸς αὐτοῦ ἑξακόσιοι ἑξήκοντα ἕξ

Let him that hath understanding count the number of the beast: for it is the number of a man; and his number is Six hundred threescore and six.

Revelation 13.18

303 καὶ ἤκουσα φωνὴν ἐκ τοῦ οὐρανοῦ ὡς φωνὴν ὑδάτων πολλῶν καὶ ὡς φωνὴν βροντῆς μεγάλης· καὶ ἡ φωνὴ ἣν ἤκουσα ὡς κιθαρῳδῶν κιθαριζόντων ἐν ταῖς κιθάραις αὐτῶν

And I heard a voice from heaven, as the voice of many waters, and as the voice of a great thunder: and I heard the voice of harpers harping with their harps.

Revelation 14.2

304 ἔπεσεν, ἔπεσε Βαβυλὼν ἡ μεγάλη ... ἡ μήτηρ τῶν πορνῶν καὶ τῶν βδελυγμάτων τῆς γῆς ... Βαβυλὼν ἡ πόλις ἡ ἰσχυρά, ὅτι μιᾷ ὥρᾳ ἦλθεν ἡ κρίσις σου

Babylon is fallen, is fallen, that great city ... mother of harlots and abominations of the earth ... Babylon, that mighty city! for in one hour is thy judgement come.

Revelation 14.8 and 17.5 and 18.10

305 μακάριοι οἱ νεκροὶ οἱ ἐν κυρίῳ ἀποθνήσκοντες ἀπ' ἄρτι· ναί, λέγει τὸ πνεῦμα, ἵνα ἀναπαύσονται ἐκ τῶν κόπων αὐτῶν· τὰ δὲ ἔργα αὐτῶν ἀκολουθεῖ μετ' αὐτῶν

Blessed are the dead which die in the Lord from henceforth: Yea, saith the Spirit, that they may rest from their labours; and their works do follow them.

Revelation 14.13

306 μεγάλα καὶ θαυμαστὰ τὰ ἔργα σου, κύριε ὁ θεὸς ὁ παντοκράτωρ· δίκαιαι καὶ ἀληθιναὶ αἱ ὁδοί σου, ὁ βασιλεὺς τῶν ἐθνῶν

Great and marvellous are thy works, Lord God Almighty; just and true are thy ways, thou King of saints.

Revelation 15.3

307 καὶ εἶδον τὸν οὐρανὸν ἀνεῳγμένον, καὶ ἰδοὺ ἵππος λευκός, καὶ ὁ καθήμενος ἐπ' αὐτὸν καλούμενος πιστὸς καὶ ἀληθινός

And I saw heaven opened, and behold a white horse; and he that sat upon him was called Faithful and True.

Revelation 19.11

308 καὶ ἔδωκεν ἡ θάλασσα τοὺς νεκροὺς τοὺς ἐν αὐτῇ, καὶ ὁ θάνατος καὶ ὁ ᾅδης ἔδωκαν τοὺς νεκροὺς τοὺς ἐν αὐτοῖς, καὶ ἐκρίθησαν ἕκαστος κατὰ τὰ ἔργα αὐτῶν

And the sea gave up the dead which were in it; and death and hell delivered up the dead which were in them: and they were judged every man according to their works.

Revelation 20.13

309 καὶ ἐξαλείψει ὁ θεὸς πᾶν δάκρυον ἐκ τῶν ὀφθαλμῶν αὐτῶν, καὶ ὁ θάνατος οὐκ ἔσται ἔτι, οὔτε πένθος οὔτε κραυγὴ οὔτε πόνος οὐκ ἔσται ἔτι

And God shall wipe away all tears from their eyes; and there shall be no more death, neither sorrow, nor crying, neither shall there be any more pain.

Revelation 21.4

310 καὶ εἶπεν ὁ καθήμενος ἐπὶ τῷ θρόνῳ· ἰδοὺ καινὰ ποιῶ πάντα· καὶ λέγει μοι, γράψον, ὅτι οὗτοι οἱ λόγοι πιστοὶ καὶ ἀληθινοί εἰσι

And he that sat upon the throne said, Behold, I make all things new. And he said unto me, Write: for these words are true and faithful.

Revelation 21.5

311 ἐγὼ τῷ διψῶντι δώσω ἐκ τῆς πηγῆς τοῦ ὕδατος τῆς ζωῆς δωρεάν

I will give unto him that is athirst of the fountain of the water of life freely.

Revelation 21.6

312 καὶ ἔδειξέ μοι ποταμὸν ὕδατος ζωῆς λαμπρὸν ὡς κρύσταλλον, ἐκπορευόμενον ἐκ τοῦ θρόνου τοῦ θεοῦ καὶ τοῦ ἀρνίου

And he shewed me a pure river of water of life, clear as crystal, proceeding out of the throne of God and of the Lamb.

Revelation 22.1

313 καὶ τὰ φύλλα τοῦ ξύλου εἰς θεραπείαν τῶν ἐθνῶν

And the leaves of the tree were for the healing of the nations.

Revelation 22.2

314 ναί, ἔρχομαι ταχύ· ἀμήν, ναί ἔρχου, κύριε Ἰησοῦ

Surely I come quickly. Amen. Even so, come, Lord Jesus.

Revelation 22.20

closing lines

Old Testament – Septuagint Version

315 Ἐν ἀρχῇ ἐποίησεν ὁ θεὸς τὸν οὐρανὸν καὶ τὴν γῆν. ἡ δὲ γῆ ἦν ἀόρατος καὶ ἀκατασκεύαστος, καὶ σκότος ἐπάνω τῆς ἀβύσσου, καὶ πνεῦμα θεοῦ ἐπεφέρετο ἐπάνω τοῦ ὕδατος.

In the beginning God created the heaven and the earth. And the earth was without form, and void; and darkness was upon the face of the deep. And the Spirit of God moved upon the face of the waters.

Authorized Version (1611)

Genesis 1.1

316 καὶ εἶπεν ὁ θεός Γενηθήτω φῶς. καὶ ἐγένετο φῶς

And God said, Let there be light; and there was light.

Authorized Version (1611)

Genesis 1.3

317 καὶ εἶπεν ὁ θεός, ποιήσωμεν ἄνθρωπον κατ' εἰκόνα ἡμετέραν καὶ καθ' ὁμοίωσιν

And God said, Let us make man according to our image and likeness.

Septuagint Version as translated by Lancelot C.L. Brenton (1851)

Genesis 1.26

cf. Cleanthes 1; and Bible 191; but cf. Xenophanes 4

318 αὐξάνεσθε καὶ πληθύνεσθε καὶ πληρώσατε τὴν γῆν

Be fruitful, and multiply, and replenish the earth.

Authorized Version (1611)

Genesis 1.28

319 καὶ ἔπλασεν ὁ θεὸς τὸν ἄνθρωπον χοῦν ἀπὸ τῆς γῆς καὶ ἐνεφύσησεν εἰς τὸ πρόσωπον αὐτοῦ πνοὴν ζωῆς, καὶ ἐγένετο ὁ ἄνθρωπος εἰς ψυχὴν ζῶσαν

And God formed man of the dust of the earth, and breathed upon his face the breath of life, and the man became a living soul.

Septuagint Version as translated by Lancelot C.L. Brenton (1851)

Genesis 2.7

320 οὐ καλὸν εἶναι τὸν ἄνθρωπον μόνον

It is not good that the man should be alone.

Authorized Version (1611)

Genesis 2.18

321 ἕνεκεν τούτου καταλείψει ἄνθρωπος τὸν πατέρα αὐτοῦ καὶ τὴν μητέρα αὐτοῦ καὶ προσκολληθήσεται πρὸς τὴν γυναῖκα αὐτοῦ, καὶ ἔσονται οἱ δύο εἰς σάρκα μίαν

Therefore shall a man leave his father and his mother and shall cleave to his wife, and they two shall be one flesh.

Septuagint Version as translated by Lancelot C.L. Brenton (1851)

Genesis 2.24

322 Ἐγώ εἰμι κύριος ὁ θεός σου ... οὐκ ἔσονταί σοι θεοὶ ἕτεροι πλὴν ἐμοῦ.
Οὐ ποιήσεις σεαυτῷ εἴδωλον ...
Οὐ λήψῃ τὸ ὄνομα κυρίου τοῦ θεοῦ σου ἐπὶ ματαίῳ ...
Μνήσθητι τὴν ἡμέραν τῶν σαββάτων ἁγιάζειν αὐτήν ...
Τίμα τὸν πατέρα σου καὶ τὴν μητέρα ...
Οὐ μοιχεύσεις.
Οὐ κλέψεις.
Οὐ φονεύσεις.
Οὐ ψευδομαρτυρήσεις ...
Οὐκ ἐπιθυμήσεις τὴν γυναῖκα τοῦ πλησίον σου ... οὔτε ὅσα τῷ πλησίον σου ἐστί.

I am the Lord thy God, thou shalt have no other gods beside me.
Thou shalt not make to thyself an idol.
Thou shalt not take the name of the Lord thy God in vain.
Remember the sabbath day to keep it holy.
Honour thy father and thy mother.
Thou shalt not commit adultery.
Thou shalt not steal.
Thou shalt not kill.
Thou shalt not bear false witness.
Thou shalt not covet thy neighbour's wife, nor whatever belongs to thy neighbour.

Septuagint Version as translated by Lancelot C.L. Brenton (1851)

Exodus 20.2

The Ten Commandments

323 ἐγὼ γάρ εἰμι κύριος ὁ θεός σου, θεὸς ζηλωτὴς ἀποδιδοὺς ἁμαρτίας πατέρων ἐπὶ τέκνα ἕως τρίτης καὶ τετάρτης γενεᾶς

For I am the Lord thy God, a jealous God, recompensing the sins of the fathers upon the children, to the third and fourth generation.

Septuagint Version as translated by Lancelot C.L. Brenton (1851)

Exodus 20.5

324 ὀφθαλμὸν ἀντὶ ὀφθαλμοῦ, ὀδόντα ἀντὶ ὀδόντος

Eye for eye, tooth for tooth.

Septuagint Version as translated by Lancelot C.L. Brenton (1851)

Exodus 21.24

but cf. Bible 20

325 ἀποθανέτω ἡ ψυχή μου μετὰ τῶν ἀλλοφύλων

Let my life perish with the Philistines.

Septuagint Version as translated by Lancelot C.L. Brenton (1851)

Judges 16.30

326 ἀνέστη πᾶς ὁ λαὸς ὡς ἀνὴρ εἷς

The people rose up as one man.

Septuagint Version as translated by Lancelot C.L. Brenton (1851)

Judges 20.8

327 βροτὸς γὰρ γεννητὸς γυναικὸς ὀλιγόβιος καὶ πλήρης ὀργῆς ἢ ὥσπερ ἄνθος ἀνθῆσαν ἐξέπεσεν, ἀπέδρα δὲ ὥσπερ σκιὰ καὶ οὐ μὴ στῇ

Man that is born of a woman is of few days, and full of trouble. He cometh forth like a flower, and is cut down: he fleeth also as a shadow, and continueth not.

Authorized Version (1611)

Job 14.1

328 τίς ἐστιν ὑετοῦ πατήρ;

Hath the rain a father?

Authorized Version (1611)

Job 38.28

329 ἄρατε πύλας, οἱ ἄρχοντες ὑμῶν, καὶ ἐπάρθητε πύλαι αἰώνιοι, καὶ εἰσελεύσεται ὁ βασιλεὺς τῆς δόξης

Lift up your gates, ye princes, and be ye lifted up, ye everlasting doors; and the king of glory shall come in.

Septuagint Version as translated by Lancelot C.L. Brenton (1851)

Psalms 23 (24).7

330 πρὸς σέ, κύριε, ἦρα τὴν ψυχήν μου. ὁ θεός μου ἐπὶ σοὶ πέποιθα· μὴ καταισχυνθείην

To thee, O Lord, have I lifted up my soul. O my God, I have trusted in thee: let me not be confounded.

Septuagint Version as translated by Lancelot C.L. Brenton (1851)

Psalms 24 (25).1

331 Κύριε, ἐλέησόν με· ἴασαι τὴν ψυχήν μου, ὅτι ἥμαρτόν σοι.

O Lord, have mercy upon me; heal my soul; for I have sinned against thee.

Septuagint Version as translated by Lancelot C.L. Brenton (1851)

Psalms 40 (41).5

cf. St Basil 4

332 ἡ καρδία μου ἐταράχθη ἐν ἐμοί, καὶ δειλία θανάτου ἐπέπεσεν ἐπ' ἐμέ· φόβος καὶ τρόμος ἦλθεν ἐπ' ἐμέ, καὶ ἐκάλυψέν με σκότος. καὶ εἶπα τίς δώσει μοι πτέρυγας ὡσεὶ περιστερᾶς καὶ πετασθήσομαι καὶ καταπαύσω;

My heart was troubled within me; and the fear of death fell upon me. Fear and trembling came upon me, and darkness covered me. And I said, O that I had wings as those of a dove! then would I flee away, and be at rest.

Septuagint Version as translated by Lancelot C.L. Brenton (1851)

Psalms 54 (55).4

333 Κύριε, καταφυγὴ ἐγενήθης ἡμῖν ἐν γενεᾷ καὶ γενεᾷ

Lord, thou hast been our refuge in all generations.

Septuagint Version as translated by Lancelot C.L. Brenton (1851)

Psalms 89 (90).1

334 μὴ σκληρύνητε τὰς καρδίας ὑμῶν ὡς ἐν τῷ παραπικρασμῷ κατὰ τὴν ἡμέραν τοῦ πειρασμοῦ ἐν τῇ ἐρήμῳ

Harden not your heart, as in the provocation, and as in the day of temptation in the wilderness.

Authorized Version (1611)

Psalms 94 (95).8

quoted by St Paul in Bible, Hebrews 3.8

335 ὡμοιώθην πελεκᾶνι ἐρημικῷ, ἐγενήθην ὡσεὶ νυκτικόραξ ἐν οἰκοπέδῳ, ἠγρύπνησα καὶ ἐγενήθην ὡσεὶ στρουθίον μονάζον ἐπὶ δώματι

I have become like a pelican of the wilderness; I have become like an owl in a ruined house; I have watched, and am become as a swallow dwelling alone on a roof.

Septuagint Version as translated by Lancelot C.L. Brenton (1851)

Psalms 101 (102).7

336 μνήσθητι ὅτι χοῦς ἐσμεν

Remember that we are dust.

Septuagint Version as translated by Lancelot C.L. Brenton (1851)

Psalms 102 (103).14

337 ἄνθρωπος, ὡσεὶ χόρτος αἱ ἡμέραι αὐτοῦ· ὡσεὶ ἄνθος τοῦ ἀγροῦ, οὕτως ἐξανθήσει· ὅτι πνεῦμα διῆλθεν ἐν αὐτῷ, καὶ οὐχ ὑπάρξει καὶ οὐκ ἐπιγνώσεται ἔτι τὸν τόπον αὐτοῦ

As for man, his days are as grass: as a flower of the field, so he flourisheth. For the wind passeth over it, and it is gone; and the place thereof shall know it no more.

Authorized Version (1611)

Psalms 102 (103).15

338 Κύριε ὁ θεός μου ... ὁ στεγάζων ἐν ὕδασιν τὰ ὑπερῷα αὐτοῦ, ὁ τιθεὶς νέφη τὴν ἐπίβασιν αὐτοῦ, ὁ περιπατῶν ἐπὶ πτερύγων ἀνέμων· ὁ ποιῶν τοὺς ἀγγέλους αὐτοῦ πνεύματα καὶ τοὺς λειτουργοὺς αὐτοῦ πῦρ φλέγον

O Lord my God, who layeth the beams of his chambers in the waters: who maketh the clouds his chariot: who walketh upon the wings of the wind: who maketh his angels spirits; his ministers a flaming fire.

Authorized Version (1611)

Psalms 103 (104).1 and 4

339 ἀναβαλλόμενος φῶς ὡς ἱμάτιον

Robe thyself with light as with a garment.

Septuagint Version as translated by Lancelot C.L. Brenton (1851)

Psalms 103 (104).2

340 ἀνὰ μέσον τῶν ὀρέων διελεύσονται ὕδατα· ποτιοῦσιν πάντα τὰ θηρία τοῦ ἀγροῦ, προσδέξονται ὄναγροι εἰς δίψαν αὐτῶν· ἐπ' αὐτὰ τὰ πετεινὰ τοῦ οὐρανοῦ κατασκηνώσει, ἐκ μέσου τῶν πετρῶν δώσουσιν φωνήν

Waters shall run between the mountains. They shall give drink to all the wild beasts of the field: the wild asses shall take of them to quench their thirst. By them shall the birds of the sky lodge: they shall utter a voice out of the midst of the rocks.

Septuagint Version as translated by Lancelot C.L. Brenton (1851)

Psalms 103 (104).10

341 ὁ ἐξανατέλλων χόρτον τοῖς κτήνεσι, καὶ χλόην τῇ δουλείᾳ τῶν ἀνθρώπων· τοῦ ἐξαγαγεῖν ἄρτον ἐκ τῆς γῆς, καὶ οἶνος εὐφραίνει καρδίαν ἀνθρώπου· τοῦ ἱλαρῦναι πρόσωπον ἐν ἐλαίῳ, καὶ ἄρτος καρδίαν ἀνθρώπου στηρίζει

He causeth the grass to grow for the cattle, and herb for the service of man: that he may bring forth food out of the earth; And wine that maketh glad the heart of man, and oil to make his face to shine, and bread which strengtheneth man's heart.

Authorized Version (1611)

Psalms 103 (104).14

342 ἐποίησεν σελήνην εἰς καιρούς, ὁ ἥλιος ἔγνω τὴν δύσιν αὐτοῦ. ἔθου σκότος, καὶ ἐγένετο νύξ, ἐν αὐτῇ διελεύσονται πάντα τὰ θηρία τοῦ δρυμοῦ

He appointed the moon for seasons: the sun knows his going down. Thou didst make darkness, and it was night; in it all the wild beasts of the forest will be abroad.

Septuagint Version as translated by Lancelot C.L. Brenton (1851)

Psalms 103 (104).19

343 ὡς ἐμεγαλύνθη τὰ ἔργα σου, κύριε· πάντα ἐν σοφίᾳ ἐποίησας, ἐπληρώθη ἡ γῆ τῆς κτήσεώς σου

How great are thy works, O Lord! in wisdom hast thou wrought them all: the earth is filled with thy creation.

Septuagint Version as translated by Lancelot C.L. Brenton (1851)

Psalms 103 (104).24

344 ἀρχὴ σοφίας φόβος κυρίου

The fear of the Lord is the beginning of wisdom.

Authorized Version (1611)

Psalms 110 (111).10

cf. Antisthenes 1

345 λίθον, ὃν ἀπεδοκίμασαν οἱ οἰκοδομοῦντες, οὗτος ἐγενήθη εἰς κεφαλὴν γωνίας

The stone which the builders refused is become the head stone of the corner.

Authorized Version (1611)

Psalms 117 (118).22

346 ἐκ βαθέων ἐκέκραξά σε, κύριε

Out of the depths have I cried unto thee, O Lord.

Authorized Version (1611)

Psalms 129 (130).1

cf. the Vulgate: 'De profundis'

347 θοῦ, Κύριε, φυλακὴν τῷ στόματί μου

Set a watch, O Lord, on my mouth.

Septuagint Version as translated by Lancelot C.L. Brenton (1851)

Psalms 140 (141).3

i.e. guard against my saying evil things; often quoted by ecclesiastical writers and, generally, until today

348 αἰνεῖτε αὐτὸν ἐν ἤχῳ σάλπιγγος, αἰνεῖτε αὐτὸν ἐν ψαλτηρίῳ καὶ κιθάρᾳ· αἰνεῖτε αὐτὸν ἐν τυμπάνῳ καὶ χορῷ, αἰνεῖτε αὐτὸν ἐν χορδαῖς καὶ ὀργάνῳ ... πᾶσα πνοὴ αἰνεσάτω τὸν κύριον

Praise him with timbrel and dance: praise him with stringed instruments and the organ. Let every thing that has breath praise the Lord.

Septuagint Version as translated by Lancelot C.L. Brenton (1851)

Psalms 150 (151).3 and 6

349 ἐπὶ δὲ σῇ σοφίᾳ μὴ ἐπαίρου

Be not exalted in thine own wisdom.

Septuagint Version as translated by Lancelot C.L. Brenton (1851)

Lean not unto thine own understanding.

Authorized Version (1611)

Proverbs 3.5

350 ὥσπερ ἐνώτιον ἐν ῥινὶ ὑός, οὕτως γυναικὶ κακόφρονι κάλλος

As an ornament in a swine's snout, so is beauty to an ill-minded woman.

Septuagint Version as translated by Lancelot C.L. Brenton (1851)

Proverbs 11.24

cf. Clement of Alexandria 5

351 σοφαὶ γυναῖκες ᾠκοδόμησαν οἴκους, ἡ δὲ ἄφρων κατέσκαψεν ταῖς χερσὶν αὐτῆς

Wise women build houses: but a foolish one digs hers down with her hands.

Septuagint Version as translated by Lancelot C.L. Brenton (1851)

Proverbs 14.1

352 ὀργὴ ἀπόλλυσιν καὶ φρονίμους

Anger slays even wise men.

Septuagint Version as translated by Lancelot C.L. Brenton (1851)

Proverbs 15.1

this line is not translated in the Authorized Version where ch. 15 starts: 'A soft answer turneth away wrath'

353 ὁδοὶ ἀεργῶν ἐστρωμέναι ἀκάνθαις

The way of sluggards are strewn with thorns.

Septuagint Version translated by Lancelot C.L. Brenton (1851)

The way of the slothful man is as an hedge of thorns.

Authorized Version (1611)

Proverbs 15.19

354 ματαιότης ματαιοτήτων, τὰ πάντα ματαιότης

Vanity of vanities; all is vanity.

Authorized Version (1611)

Ecclesiastes 1.2

cf. the Vulgate: 'Vanitas vanitatum, et omnia vanitas'

355 οὐκ ἔστιν πᾶν πρόσφατον ὑπὸ τὸν ἥλιον

There is no new thing under the sun.

Authorized Version (1611)

Ecclesiastes 1.10

cf. the Latin 'nil sub sole novum'

356 καὶ ἐμίσησα ἐγὼ σὺν πάντα μόχθον μου, ὃν ἐγὼ μοχθῶ ὑπὸ τὸν ἥλιον, ὅτι ἀφίω αὐτὸν τῷ ἀνθρώπῳ τῷ γινομένῳ μετ' ἐμέ· καὶ τίς οἶδεν εἰ σοφὸς ἔσται ἢ ἄφρων;

And I hated the whole of my labour which I took under the sun; because I must leave it to the man who will come after me. And who knows whether he will be a wise man or a fool?

Septuagint Version as translated by Lancelot C.L. Brenton (1851)

Ecclesiastes 2.18

357 τοῖς πᾶσιν χρόνος, καὶ καιρὸς τῷ παντὶ πράγματι ὑπὸ τὸν οὐρανόν καὶ καιρὸς τῷ παντὶ πράγματι ὑπὸ τὸν οὐρανόν. καιρὸς τοῦ τεκεῖν καὶ καιρὸς τοῦ ἀποθανεῖν, καιρὸς τοῦ φυτεῦσαι καὶ καιρὸς τοῦ ἐκτῖλαι πεφυτευμένον ... καιρὸς τοῦ βαλεῖν λίθους καὶ καιρὸς τοῦ συναγαγεῖν λίθους, ... καιρὸς τοῦ ζητῆσαι καὶ καιρὸς τοῦ ἀπολέσαι, καιρὸς τοῦ φυλάξαι καὶ καιρὸς τοῦ ἐκβαλεῖν ... καιρὸς τοῦ σιγᾶν καὶ καιρὸς τοῦ λαλεῖν ... καιρὸς πολέμου καὶ καιρὸς εἰρήνης

To all things there is a time, and a season for every matter under heaven. A time of birth, and a time to die; a time to plant, and a time to pluck up what has been planted. A time to throw stones, and a time to gather stones together. A time to seek, and a time to lose; a time to keep and a time to cast away; a time to be silent, and a time to speak; a time of war, and a time of peace.

Septuagint Version as translated by Lancelot C.L. Brenton (1851)

Ecclesiastes 3.1

358 ἀγαθὸν τὸ ἀκοῦσαι ἐπιτίμησιν σοφοῦ ὑπὲρ ἄνδρα ἀκούοντα ᾆσμα ἀφρόνων

It is better to hear a reproof of a wise man, than to hear the song of fools.

Septuagint Version as translated by Lancelot C.L. Brenton (1851)

Ecclesiastes 7.5

359 καὶ γλυκὺ τὸ φῶς καὶ ἀγαθὸν τοῖς ὀφθαλμοῖς τοῦ βλέπειν σὺν τὸν ἥλιον

Truly the light is sweet, and a pleasant thing it is for the eyes to behold the sun.

Authorized Version (1611)

Ecclesiastes 11.7

360 ἐὰν μὴ πιστεύσητε, οὐδὲ μὴ συνῆτε

If ye believe not, neither will ye at all understand.

Septuagint Version as translated by Lancelot C.L. Brenton (1851)

Isaiah 7.9

361 τότε ἀνοιχθήσονται ὀφθαλμοὶ τυφλῶν, καὶ ὦτα κωφῶν ἀκούσονται. τότε ἁλεῖται ὡς ἔλαφος ὁ χωλός, καὶ τρανὴ ἔσται γλῶσσα μογιλάλων

Then shall the eyes of the blind be opened, and the ears of the deaf shall hear. Then shall the lame man leap as an hart, and the tongue of the stammerers shall speak plainly.

Septuagint Version as translated by Lancelot C.L. Brenton (1851)

Isaiah 35.5

quoted in the minutes of the Ephesus Ecumenical Council, 1.1.1.19.7 (ACO)

362 φωνὴ βοῶντος ἐν τῇ ἐρήμῳ, ἑτοιμάσατε τὴν ὁδὸν κυρίου, εὐθείας ποιεῖτε τὰς τρίβους τοῦ θεοῦ ἡμῶν

The voice of one crying in the wilderness, Prepare ye the way of the Lord, make straight the paths of our God.

Septuagint Version as translated by Lancelot C.L. Brenton (1851)

Isaiah 40.3

cf. Bible 5; cf. other texts which have a different punctuation, with quite a different meaning: 'a voice crying: in the wilderness prepare the way of the Lord'

363 λέγε σὺ τὰς ἀνομίας σου πρῶτος, ἵνα δικαιωθῇς

Do thou first confess thy transgressions, that thou mayest be justified.

Septuagint Version as translated by Lancelot C.L. Brenton (1851)

Declare thou, that thou mayest be justified.

Authorized Version (1611)

Isaiah 43.26

364 φωνὴ ... ἠκούσθη θρήνου καὶ κλαυθμοῦ καὶ ὀδυρμοῦ

A voice was heard of lamentation and weeping and wailing.

Septuagint Version as translated by Lancelot C.L. Brenton (1851)

Jeremiah 38.15

cf. Bible, Matthew 2.18; St John Chrysostom, In Joannem *59.87.33; et al.*

365 ἐστάθη ἐν ζυγῷ καὶ εὑρέθη ὑστεροῦσα

Thou art weighed in the balances, and art found wanting.

Authorized Version (1611)

Daniel 5.27

366 ἐμβληθήσεται εἰς τὸν λάκκον τῶν λεόντων

He shall be cast into the den of lions.

Authorized Version (1611)

Daniel 6.7

colloquially used to this day

Apocrypha

367 παρελεύσεται ὁ βίος ἡμῶν ὡς ἴχνη νεφέλης

Our life will blow over like the last vestige of a cloud.

New English Bible translation (1970)

Wisdom of Solomon 2.4

368 εὐλογία γὰρ πατρὸς στηρίζει οἴκους τέκνων, κατάρα δὲ μητρὸς ἐκριζοῖ θεμέλια

A father's blessing strengthens his children's houses, but a mother's curse uproots their foundations.

New English Bible translation (1970)

Ecclesiasticus 3.9

369 πρὸ τελευτῆς μὴ μακάριζε μηδένα

Call no man happy before he dies.

New English Bible translation (1970)

Ecclesiasticus 11.28

cf. Solon 61

370 σοφία κεκρυμμένη καὶ θησαυρὸς ἀφανής, τίς ὠφέλεια ἐν ἀμφοτέροις;

Hidden wisdom and buried treasure, what use is there in either?

New English Bible translation (1970)

Ecclesiasticus 20.30

371 εἰς μέσον ἀσυνέτων συντήρησον καιρόν, εἰς μέσον δὲ διανοουμένων ἐνδελέχιζε

Grudge every minute among fools, but linger among the wise.

Ecclesiasticus 27.12

372 ἀρχὴ παντὸς ἔργου λόγος, καὶ πρὸ πάσης πράξεως βουλή

The beginning of every undertaking

is the word; and before every action, consultation.

Ecclesiasticus 37.16

373 κύριος ἔκτισεν ἐκ γῆς φάρμακα, καὶ ἀνὴρ φρόνιμος οὐ προσοχθιεῖ αὐτοῖς

The Lord has created medicines from the earth, and a sensible man will not disparage them.

New English Bible translation (1970)

Ecclesiasticus 38.4

BION

*c.*335–*c.*245BC

Popular philosopher from Borysthenes (Olbia)

see also Pittacus 11

1 ὅταν τοξοτῶν χρείαν ἔχῃς, οὐκ ἐρωτῶντα τὸ γένος, ἀλλὰ τιθέντα τὸν σκοπὸν τοὺς ἀρίστους τοξευτὰς παραλαμβάνειν· οὕτως οὖν ἐπὶ τῶν φίλων ἐξέταζε οὐ πόθεν εἰσίν, ἀλλὰ τίνες

When choosing archers you check their marksmanship, not their ancestry; with friends, then, ask what they are, not whence they come.

Fragment 2 (Kindstrand)

to King Antigonus who questioned his parentage

2 Βίων ἔλεγε γελοιοτάτους εἶναι τοὺς ἀστρονομοῦντας, οἳ τοὺς πὰρ ποσὶ τοὺς ἐν τοις αἰγιαλοις ἰχθῦς οὐ βλέποντες τοὺς ἐν τῷ οὐρανῷ φάσκουσιν εἰδέναι

Bion said that astronomers are the silliest people, not seeing the fish next to them in the sea they discern Pisces in the heavens.

Fragment 6 (Kindstrand)

3 Βίων ἐρωτηθεὶς τί ἐστιν ἄνοια, εἶπε προκοπῆς ἐμπόδιον

When Bion was asked 'what is folly' he replied 'Hindrance to progress.'

Fragment 19 (Kindstrand)

4 Βίων ἔλεγε καταγελάστους εἶναι τοὺς σπουδάζοντας περὶ πλοῦτον, ὃν τύχη μὲν παρέχει, ἀνελευθερία δὲ φυλάττει, χρηστότης δὲ ἀφαιρεῖται

Bion said that it is absurd to covet wealth which is provided by good fortune but preserved by stinginess and diminished by soft-heartedness.

Fragment 38a (Kindstrand)

5 τὰ χρήματα τοῖς πλουσίοις ἡ τύχη οὐ δεδώρηται, ἀλλὰ δεδάνεικεν

Fortune has only loaned, not given money to the rich.

Fragment 39b (Kindstrand)

6 τὸν ἀγαθὸν ἄρχοντα παυόμενον τῆς ἀρχῆς μὴ πλουσιώτερον ἀλλ' ἐνδοξότερον γεγονέναι

The righteous ruler should leave his position not wealthier but more highly esteemed.

Fragment 43a (Kindstrand)

7 Βίων ὁ σοφιστὴς ἰδών τινα φθονερὸν σφόδρα κεκυφότα εἶπεν ἢ τούτῳ μέγα κακὸν συμβέβηκεν ἢ ἄλλῳ μέγα ἀγαθόν

Bion the sophist, upon seeing a jealous person walking, head hung low, said, 'Either something very bad has happened to him, or something very good to someone else.'

Fragment 47a (Kindstrand)

8 τὸ γῆρας ἔλεγεν ὅρμον εἶναι κακῶν

Old age is the harbour of all ills.

Translated in *Bartlett's Familiar Quotations* (1980)

Diogenes Laertius, *Lives of Eminent Philosophers* 4.48.5

9 τὸν πλοῦτον νεῦρα πραγμάτων

Wealth is the sinews of affairs.

Translated in *Bartlett's Familiar Quotations* (1980)

Diogenes Laertius, *Lives of Eminent Philosophers* 4.48.7

10 εὔκολον ἔφασκε τὴν εἰς ᾅδου ὁδόν

The road to Hades is easy to travel.

Translated by R.D. Hicks (1925)

Diogenes Laertius, *Lives of Eminent Philosophers* 4.49

11 οὐχ οὗτος τὴν οὐσίαν κέκτηται, ἀλλ' ἡ οὐσία τοῦτον

He has not acquired a fortune; the fortune has acquired him.

Translated by R.D. Hicks (1925)

Diogenes Laertius, *Lives of Eminent Philosophers* 4.50

of a wealthy miser

12 τὰ παιδάρια παίζοντα τῶν βατράχων τοῖς λίθοις ἐφίεσθαι, τοὺς δὲ βατράχους μηκέτι παίζοντας ἀλλ' ἀληθῶς ἀποθνήσκειν

Boys throw stones at frogs for fun, but the frogs don't die for 'fun', but in sober earnest.

Translated in *The Oxford Dictionary of Quotations* (2004)

BION OF SMYRNA

late 2nd century BC
Bucolic poet

1 Κύπριδι μὲν καλὸν εἶδος ὅτε ζώεσκεν Ἄδωνις,
κάτθανε δ' ἁ μορφὰ σὺν Ἀδώνιδι. τὰν Κύπριν αἰαῖ
ὤρεα πάντα λέγοντι, καὶ αἱ δρύες αἶ τὸν Ἄδωνιν

Cypris was beautiful, when Adonis was alive, but her beauty died with Adonis. The hills cried, 'Alas for Cypris' and the oak trees, 'Alas for Adonis.'

Lament for Adonis 30

2 δύσποτμε μεῖνον Ἄδωνι, πανύστατον ὥς σε κιχείω,
ὥς σε περιπτύξω καὶ χείλεα χείλεσι μείξω

O stay dear hapless youth! for Venus stay!
Our breasts once more let close embraces join,
And let me press my glowing lips to thine.

Translated by F. Fawkes (2nd edn, 1789)

Lament for Adonis 43

3 ἐκ θαμινᾶς ῥαθάμιγγος, ὅπως λόγος, αἰὲς ἰοίσας
χὰ λίθος ἐς ῥωχμὸν κοιλαίνεται

Incessant drops, the proverbs say,
Will wear the hardest stone away.

Translated by F. Fawkes (2nd edn, 1789)

Fragment 4 (Gow)

4 οὐ καλόν, ὦ φίλε, πάντα λόγον ποτὶ τέκτονα φοιτῆν,
μηδ' ἐπὶ πάντ' ἄλλω χρέος ἰσχέμεν· ἀλλὰ καὶ αὐτός
τεχνᾶσθαι σύριγγα, πέλει δέ τοι εὐμαρὲς ἔργον

Thus to the smith it is not fair,
My friend, for ever to repair,
And still another's aid to ask:
Make your own pipe; 'tis no such arduous task.

Translated by F. Fawkes (2nd edn, 1789)

Fragment 5 (Gow)

5 οὐκ οἶδ', οὐδ' ἐπέοικεν ἃ μὴ μάθομες πονέεσθαι

This I know not, and 'tis not fit to worry for what we do not know.

Fragment 7 (Gow)

6 Ταὶ Μοῖσαι τὸν Ἔρωτα τὸν ἄγριον οὐ φοβέονται
ἐκ θυμῶ δὲ φιλεῦντι καὶ ἐκ ποδὸς αὐτῷ ἕπονται.
κἢν μὲν ἄρα ψυχάν τις ἔχων ἀνέραστον ἀείδῃ,
τῆνον ὑπεκφεύγοντι καὶ οὐκ ἐθέλοντι διδάσκειν·
ἢν δὲ νόον τις Ἔρωτι δονεύμενος ἁδὺ μελίσδῃ,
ἐς τῆνον μάλα πᾶσαι ἐπειγόμεναι προρέοντι

The Muses know no fear of cruel Love;
their hearts befriend him and their footsteps follow.
Sing loveless songs and flee away untaught;
but learn Love's mellow tunes and, lo, how many caught!

Fragment 9 (Gow)

7 ὡς εὗρεν πλαγίαυλον ὁ Πάν, ὡς αὐλὸν Ἀθάνα,
ὡς χέλυν Ἑρμάων, κίθαριν ὡς ἁδὺς Ἀπόλλων

Pan did invent the cross-flute and Athena the flute,
Hermes the lyre and sweet Apollo the harp.

Translated by J.M. Edmonds (1912)

Fragment 10.7 (Gow)

8 ὃ δ' οὐκ ἐμπάζετο μύθων,
ἀλλά μοι αὐτὸς ἄειδεν ἐρωτύλα, καί με δίδασκε
θνατῶν ἀθανάτων τε πόθως

But nay, the child would give no heed to aught I might say;
rather would he sing love-songs of his own, and taught me
of the desires of gods and men.

Translated by J.M. Edmonds (1912)

Fragment 10.9 (Gow)

Aphrodite of Eros

9 κὴγὼν ἐκλαθόμαν μὲν ὅσων τὸν Ἔρωτα δίδασκον,
ὅσσα δ' Ἔρως με δίδαξεν ἐρωτύλα πάντα διδάχθην

All I did teach to Eros I utterly forgot,
but love-songs taught by him, I learnt them all.

Fragment 10.12 (Gow)

10 ὄλβιοι οἱ φιλέοντες ἐπὴν ἴσον ἀντεράωνται

Lovers are well content when love is returned.

Fragment 12 (Gow)

11 μορφὰ θηλυτέραισι πέλει καλόν, ἀνέρι δ' ἀλκά

A woman's glory is her beauty, a man's his strength.

Fragment 15 (Gow)

BITON

3rd or 2nd century BC
Engineer

1 λιθοβόλου ὀργάνου κατασκευὴν ἐπιβέβλημαι γράψαι, ὦ Ἄτταλε βασιλεῦ, καὶ μὴ σκώψῃς

I have to inform you of the construction of a catapult, O King Attalus, and do not scoff at it.

Κατασκευαὶ πολεμικῶν ὀργάνων καὶ καταπαλτικῶν 1

proposal to King Attalus of Pergamum with full details of construction; cf. Archidamus III 2

BRASIDAS

died 422BC
Spartan commander

1 ἦν δὲ οὐδὲ ἀδύνατος, ὡς Λακεδαιμόνιος, εἰπεῖν

Indeed, for a Lacedaemonian, he was not a bad speaker.

Thucydides, *History of the Peloponnesian War* 4.84.2

of Brasidas

2 ἀπάτη γὰρ εὐπρεπεῖ αἴσχιον τοῖς γε ἐν ἀξιώματι πλεονεκτῆσαι ἢ βίᾳ ἐμφανεῖ

For men of honour it is more shameful to gain advantage by deceit than by open force.

Thucydides, *History of the Peloponnesian War* 4.86.6

3 ὅστις δὲ τὰς τοιαύτας ἁμαρτίας τῶν ἐναντίων κάλλιστα ἰδὼν καὶ ἅμα πρὸς τὴν ἑαυτοῦ δύναμιν τὴν ἐπιχείρησιν ποιεῖται μὴ ἀπὸ τοῦ προφανοῦς μᾶλλον καὶ ἀντιπαραταχθέντος ἢ ἐκ τοῦ πρὸς τὸ παρὸν ξυμφέροντος, πλεῖστ' ἂν ὀρθοῖτο

The most successful general is he who discerns mistakes made by the enemy and adapts his attack to the character of his own forces, not necessarily openly and in regular array, but as may be advantageous under present circumstances.

Thucydides, *History of the Peloponnesian War* 5.9.4

4 τὰ κλέμματα ταῦτα καλλίστην δόξαν ἔχει ἃ τὸν πολέμιον μάλιστ' ἄν τις ἀπατήσας τοὺς φίλους μέγιστ' ἂν ὠφελήσειεν

Those stratagems have won the highest credit by which the enemy is most completely deceived.

Translated by Charles Forster Smith (1921)

Thucydides, *History of the Peloponnesian War* 5.9.5

5 ἐλπὶς γὰρ μάλιστα αὐτοὺς οὕτω φοβηθῆναι· τὸ γὰρ ἐπιὸν ὕστερον δεινότερον τοῖς πολεμίοις τοῦ παρόντος καὶ μαχομένου

Reinforcements always appear more formidable to the enemy than the troops with which he is already engaged; this is your best hope of putting him in a panic.

Thucydides, *History of the Peloponnesian War* 5.9.8

6 νομίσατε τρία εἶναι τοῦ καλῶς πολεμεῖν, τὸ ἐθέλειν καὶ τὸ αἰσχύνεσθαι καὶ τὸ τοῖς ἄρχουσι πείθεσθαι

Three are the virtues of a good soldier: readiness, sense of honour, and obedience to leaders.

Thucydides, *History of the Peloponnesian War* 5.9.9

7 οὐδὲν οὕτως μικρόν ἐστιν, ὃ μὴ σῴζεται τολμῶν ἀμύνεσθαι τοὺς ἐπιχειροῦντας

There is nothing so small that will not try to save itself daring to fend off an attacker.

Plutarch, *Sayings of Kings and Commanders* 190b

letting go of a mouse that bit him

8 Βρασίδας μὲν γὰρ ἦν ἀνὴρ ἀγαθός, ἁ δὲ Λακεδαίμων πολλὼς ἔχει τήνω κάρρονας

Brasidas was a good man, but Sparta has many a better man than him.

Plutarch, *Sayings of Kings and Commanders* 190c

said his mother on being told he had died and that there would never be another like him

C

CALLICRATIDAS

died 406BC
Spartan admiral

1 δεδιέναι οὐ χρὴ παραπλέοντας ἡμᾶς ... εἰ θαλασσοκρατοῦμεν

We need not fear to sail if we are masters of the sea.

Translated by Bernadotte Perrin (1916)
Plutarch, *Lysander* 6.2

CALLIMACHUS

c.305–*c*.240BC
Hellenistic poet and scholar from Cyrene in North Africa

1 ἀηδονίδες δ' ὧδε μελιχρότεραι

Poems are sweeter for being short.

Translated by C.A. Trypanis (1958)
Aetia, Fragment 1.16 (Pfeiffer)

2 ἔλλετε Βασκανίης ὀλοὸν γένος· αὖθι δὲ τέχνῃ
κρίνετε, μὴ σχοίνῳ Περσίδι τὴν σοφίην·
μηδ' ἀπ' ἐμεῦ διφᾶτε μέγα ψοφέουσαν ἀοιδὴν
τίκτεσθαι· βροντᾶν οὐκ ἐμόν, ἀλλὰ Διός

'Begone you murderous race of Jealousy! Hereafter judge poetry by the canons of art, and not by the Persian measure, nor seek from me a loudly resounding song. It is not for me to thunder; that is the business of Zeus.'

Translated by C.A. Trypanis (1971)
Aetia, Fragment 1.17 (Pfeiffer)
of his critics

3 ἑτέρων ἴχνια μὴ καθ' ὁμά
δίφρον ἐλᾶν μηδ' οἶμον ἀνὰ πλατύν, ἀλλὰ κελεύθους
ἀτρίπτους, εἰ καὶ στεινοτέρην ἐλάσεις

Avoid the route that takes a wagon's load;
Leave open ways and trodden tracks alone,
And go the road that's narrow, but your own.

Translated by T.F. Higham (1938)
Aetia, Fragment 1.26 (Pfeiffer)
cf. Robert Frost, 'The Road Not Taken' (1915): 'Two roads diverged in a wood, and I – / I took the one less traveled by.'

4 ἐνὶ τοῖς γὰρ ἀείδομεν οἳ λιγὺν ἦχον
τέττιγος, θόρυβον δ' οὐκ ἐφίλησαν ὄνων

We sing among those who love the voice of the cicada, not the clamour of asses.

Translated by C.A. Trypanis (1971)
Aetia, Fragment 1.29 (Pfeiffer)

5 Μοῦσαι γὰρ ὅσους ἴδον ὄθματι παῖδας
μὴ λοξῷ, πολιοὺς οὐκ ἀπέθεντο φίλους

For if the glance
Of Muses does not fall askance
On boyhood, then, when heads are grey
They will not cast their friends away.

Translated by R.A. Furness (1931)
Aetia, Fragment 1.37 (Pfeiffer)

6 ἄρνες τοι, φίλε κοῦρε, συνήλικες, ἄρνες ἑταῖροι
ἔσκον, ἐνιαυθμοὶ δ' αὐλία καὶ βοτάναι

The sheep, dear boy, sheep playmates and sheep friends,

in fold and pasture and abode.

Aetia, Fragment 27 (Pfeiffer)

7 ξανθὰ σὺν εὐόδμοις ἁβρὰ λίπη στεφάνοις,
ἄπνοα πάντ' ἐγένοντο παρὰ χρέος, ὅσσα τ' ὀδόντων
ἔνδοθι νείαιράν τ' εἰς ἀχάριστον ἔδυ,
καὶ τῶν οὐδὲν ἔμεινεν ἐς αὔριον· ὅσσα δ' ἀκουαῖς
εἰσεθέμην, ἔτι μοι μοῦνα πάρεστι τάδε

Ointments and fragrances have lost their scent,
and all I eat remains not for the morrow;
but what I know I keep.

Aetia, Fragment 43.12 (Pfeiffer)

8 χαλεπὸν κακόν, ὅστις ἀκαρτεῖ
γλώσσης· ὡς ἐτεὸν παῖς ὅδε μαῦλιν ἔχει

Grievous it is, not to control your tongue;
you may as well give a child a knife.

Aetia, Fragment 75.8 (Pfeiffer)

9 ἦλθε δὲ νοῦσος,
αἶγας ἐς ἀγριάδας τὴν ἀποπεμπόμεθα,
ψευδόμενοι δ' ἱερὴν φημίζομεν

She was taken by the disease which we exorcize into the wild goats – the one we falsely call the holy disease.

Translated by C.A. Trypanis (1971)

Aetia, Fragment 75.13 (Pfeiffer)

of epilepsy; 'κατ' αἶγας ἀγρίας' was a wish for exorcizing sickness, by charming it away from men to wild animals

10 ἀργύρῳ οὐ μόλιβον ... ἀλλὰ φαεινῷ
ἤλεκτρον χρυσῷ φημί σε μειξέμεναι

You will not be mingling lead with silver,
but amber with shining gold.

Aetia, Fragment 75.30 (Pfeiffer)

on how well Cydippe and Acontius, the two protagonists of the play, are matched

11 ἔνδιος ἦεν ἔτι, θέρμετο δὲ χθών,
τόφρα δ' ἔην ὑάλοιο φαάντερος οὐρανὸς ἦνοψ
οὐδέ ποθι κνηκὶς ὑπεφαίνετο, πέπτατο δ' αἰθὴρ
ἀννέφελος

It was still midday, and the earth was warm, the brilliant sky was clearer than glass, nor was a wisp of vapour to be seen, and cloudless stretched the heavens.

Translated by C.A. Trypanis (1958)

Hecale, Fragment 238.15 (Pfeiffer)

12 ἐπεὶ θεὸς οὐδὲ γελάσσαι
ἀκλαυτὶ μερόπεσσιν ὀιζυροῖσιν ἔδωκεν

God did not give miserable mortals even the possibility of laughing without crying.

Translated by C.A. Trypanis (1958)

Hecale, Fragment 298 (Pfeiffer)

13 ἀείπλανα χείλεα γρηός

The lips of an old woman are never still.

Translated by C.A. Trypanis (1958)

Hecale, Fragment 310 (Pfeiffer)

14 δηναιοὶ δ' οὐ πάμπαν ἀληθέες ἦσαν ἀοιδοί

The old poets did not wholly speak the truth.

Hymn to Zeus 1.60

15 ψευδοίμην ἀίοντος ἅ κεν πεπίθοιεν ἀκουήν

A poet's fiction should at least be plausible.

Translated by Stanley Lombardo and Diane Rayor (1988)

Hymn to Zeus 1.65

16 ἑσπέριος κεῖνός γε τελεῖ τά κεν ἦρι νοήσῃ·
ἑσπέριος τὰ μέγιστα, τὰ μείονα δ', εὖτε νοήσῃ

He accomplishes by dusk what he thinks of at dawn,
the monumental by dusk, the minor in a trice.

Translated by Stanley Lombardo and Diane Rayor (1988)

Hymn to Zeus 1.87

of Ptolemy II Philadelphus, 285–247BC

17 οὔτ' ἀρετῆς ἄτερ ὄλβος ἐπίσταται ἄνδρας ἀέξειν
οὔτ' ἀρετὴ ἀφένοιο

Men do not prosper through virtue without joy,
nor through virtue without wealth.

Hymn to Zeus 1.95

18 ἑκὰς ἑκὰς ὅστις ἀλιτρός

Away, away ye sinners!

Hymn to Apollo 2.2

cf. Virgil, Aeneid *6.258: 'procul, o procul este, profani!'*

19 ὁ γὰρ θεὸς οὐκέτι μακρήν …
ὡπόλλων οὐ παντὶ φαείνεται, ἀλλ' ὅ τις ἐσθλός·
ὅς μιν ἴδῃ, μέγας οὗτος, ὃς οὐκ ἴδε, λιτὸς ἐκεῖνος

No longer is god far away.
Apollo appears not to all, but only to the good;
mighty is he who sees him, worthless he who does not.

Hymn to Apollo 2.7

20 τάνδε σάω πόλιν ἔν θ' ὁμονοίᾳ
ἔν τ' εὐηπελίᾳ, φέρε δ' ἀγρόθι νόστιμα πάντα·
φέρβε βόας, φέρε μᾶλα, φέρε στάχυν, οἶσε θερισμόν,
φέρβε καὶ εἰράναν, ἵν' ὃς ἄροσε τῆνος ἀμάσῃ

Save this city,
Keep it harmonious and prosperous ever,
Bring good things home from the fields,
Feed our cattle, bring us more flocks,
Bring us ears of grain, bring in the harvest!
And nourish peace so that he who plows
May also reap.

Translated by Stanley Lombardo and Diane Rayor (1988)

Hymn to Demeter 6.134

21 ἄκουε δὴ τὸν αἶνον· ἔν κοτε Τμώλῳ
δάφνην ἐλαίῃ νεῖκος οἱ πάλαι Λυδοί
λέγουσι θέσθαι· καὶ γαρ
καλόν τε δένδρεον

Well listen to this tale. On Tmolus,
once upon a time the ancient Lydians say,
the laurel had a quarrel with the olive,
a beautiful tree.

Translated by C.A. Trypanis (1958)

Iambi, Fragment 194.6 (Pfeiffer)

22 ἄριστον ἡ σωπή

Silence is best.

Translated by C.A. Trypanis (1958)

Iambi, Fragment 194.59 (Pfeiffer)

23 ἀλλά μοι δύ' ὄρνιθες
ἐν τοῖσι φύλλοις ταῦτα τινθυρίζουσαι
πάλαι κάθηνται· κωτίλον δὲ τὸ ζεῦγος

But two birds,
perched in my leaves, are muttering;
what a chattering couple!

Iambi, Fragment 194.61 (Pfeiffer)

24 ὦ κακὴ λώβη,
ὡς δὴ μί' ἡμέων καὶ σύ;

You wretched one,
you pass yourself off as one of us?

Iambi, Fragment 194.103 (Pfeiffer)

said by the laurel tree to a thorny bush

25 τίς ἀπώλετο, τίς πολίων ὁλόκαυτος αἴθει;

Which city has perished, which city all on fire sends forth this light?

Translated by C.A. Trypanis (1958)

Lyrica, Fragment 228.49 (Pfeiffer)

this may refer to the chain of fires lit by the cities of Egypt in lament of Queen Arsinoë's death

26 τὰ δ' ᾇ κεν ἴδῃς, μέλαν ἀμφίεσται χθονὸς ἄστεα

Wherever you turn the cities are clad in black.

Lyrica, Fragment 228.74 (Pfeiffer)

of the cities of Egypt lamenting Queen Arsinoë's death

27 Εἶπέ τις, Ἡράκλειτε, τεὸν μόρον, ἐς δέ με δάκρυ
ἤγαγεν· ἐμνήσθην δ' ὁσσάκις ἀμφότεροι
ἥλιον ἐν λέσχῃ κατεδύσαμεν· ἀλλὰ σὺ μέν που,
ξεῖν' Ἁλικαρνησεῦ, τετράπαλαι σποδιή·
αἱ δὲ τεαὶ ζώουσιν ἀηδόνες, ᾗσιν ὁ πάντων
ἁρπακτὴς Ἀΐδης οὐκ ἐπὶ χεῖρα βαλεῖ.

They told me, Heraclitus, they told me you were dead;
They brought me bitter news to hear, and bitter tears to shed.
I wept, as I remembered, how often you and I
Had tired the sun with talking and sent him down the sky.

And now thou art lying, my dear old Carian guest,
A handful of grey ashes, long long ago

at rest,
Still are thy pleasant voices, thy Nightingales, awake,
For Death, he taketh all away, but them he cannot take.

Translated by William Cory (1858)

Epigram 2 (Pfeiffer)

of Heraclitus the elegiac poet of the third century BC; Nightingales *is the title of a book of his poems*

28 Τῇδε Σάων ὁ Δίκωνος Ἀκάνθιος ἱερὸν ὕπνον
κοιμᾶται· θνήσκειν μὴ λέγε τοὺς ἀγαθούς.

Here Saon sleeps the sleep of the just;
of good men don't say 'they are dead':
the righteous never die.

Epigram 9 (Pfeiffer)

29 Εἴπας Ἥλιε χαῖρε Κλεόμβροτος Ὡμβρακιώτης
ἥλατ' ἀφ' ὑψηλοῦ τείχεος εἰς Ἀΐδην,
ἄξιον οὐδὲν ἰδὼν θανάτου κακόν, ἀλλὰ Πλάτωνος
ἓν τὸ περὶ ψυχῆς γράμμ' ἀναλεξάμενος.

Kleombrotos of Ambrakia said 'Farewell, Sun,'
and leaped from a high wall clear into Hell.
He had no serious problems, as far as we know,
But had just finished reading Plato's *Phaedo.*

Translated by Stanley Lombardo and Diane Rayor (1988)

Epigram 23 (Pfeiffer)

Phaedo, *on the soul being immortal*

30 Ὤμοσε Καλλίγνωτος Ἰωνίδι μήποτ' ἐκείνης
ἕξειν μήτε φίλον κρέσσονα μήτε φίλην.
ὤμοσεν· ἀλλὰ λέγουσιν ἀληθέα τοὺς ἐν ἔρωτι
ὅρκους μὴ δύνειν οὔατ' ἐς ἀθανάτων.

Callignotus swore to Ionis that he would never hold man or woman dearer than her. He swore: but what they say is true – that the immortals are deaf to lovers' oaths.

Epigram 25 (Pfeiffer)

cf. Ovid, Art of Love *1.633: 'Iuppiter ex alto periuria ridet amantum'*

31 τό τ' ἄεισμα ... σύμβολον ἀγρυπνίης

Hail Poetry, product of sleepless nights!

Translated in Liddell & Scott

Epigram 27 (Pfeiffer)

cf. Menander 32

32 οὐδὲ κελεύθῳ
χαίρω, τίς πολλοὺς ὧδε καὶ ὧδε φέρει

Nor do I delight in a road that carries many hither and thither.

Translated by J.W. MacKail (1890)

Epigram 28 (Pfeiffer)

33 μὴ λέγε, πρὸς Χαρίτων, τοὐμὸν ὄνειρον ἐμοί

Tell me not, for heaven's sake, my own dreams!

Translated by W.R. Paton (1918)

Epigram 32 (Pfeiffer) and 48.6 (Pfeiffer)

also proverbially with the meaning 'you are telling me what I know already'

34 Βαττιάδεω παρὰ σῆμα φέρεις πόδας εὖ μὲν ἀοιδὴν
εἰδότος, εὖ δ' οἴνῳ καίρια συγγελάσαι.

You're walking by the tomb of Battiades,
Who knew well how to write poetry, and enjoy
Laughter at the right moment, over wine.

Translated by Peter Jay (1973)

Epigram 35 (Pfeiffer)

his own epitaph; Battiades is used for Callimachus who claimed descent from Battus, founder of Cyrene

35 Ἥμισύ μευ ψυχῆς ἔτι τὸ πνέον, ἥμισυ δ' οὐκ οἶδ'
εἴτ' Ἔρος εἴτ' Ἀΐδης ἥρπασε, πλὴν ἀφανές.

Half my soul's still breathing well,
Half's in love or gone to hell,
I can't tell which.

Translated by Stanley Lombardo and Diane Rayor (1988)

Epigram 41 (Pfeiffer)

36 φωρὸς δ' ἴχνια φὼρ ἔμαθον

Thief that I am, I know a thief's footprints.

Translated by Edmund Keeley (2010)

Epigram 43 (Pfeiffer)

cf. the English proverb 'set a thief to catch a thief'

37 οὐ θαρσέω· μή δή με περίπλεκε

My heart's not in it. Don't get me involved.

Translated by Stanley Lombardo and Diane Rayor (1988)

Epigram 44.3 (Pfeiffer)

38 πολλάκι λήθει
τοῖχον ὑποτρώγων ἡσύχιος ποταμός

Unnoticed, a sluggish stream will often eat away the foundations of a mighty wall.

Epigram 44.3 (Pfeiffer)

39 τοῖς μικκοῖς μικκὰ διδοῦσι θεοί

To little men the gods send little things.

Translated by D.S. Baker (1998)

Fragment 475 (Pfeiffer)

40 ἀμάρτυρον οὐδὲν ἀείδω

I sing nothing that is not attested.

Translated by C.A. Trypanis (1958)

Fragment 612 (Pfeiffer)

41 τί δάκρυον εὗδον ἐγείρεις;

Why do you wake up dormant tears?

Translated by C.A. Trypanis (1958)

Fragment 682 (Pfeiffer)

42 δαῖμον, τῇ κόλποισιν ἐπιπτύουσι γυναῖκες

A goddess, for whom the women spit on their bosoms.

Translated by C.A. Trypanis (1958)

Fragment 687 (Pfeiffer)

of Nemesis, goddess of divine retribution

43 ἢ φίλον ἢ ὅτ' ἐς ἄνδρα συνέμπορον ἢ ὅτε κωφαῖς
ἄλγεα μαψαύραις ἔσχατον ἐξερύγῃ

He blurts out his troubles to a friend, or a fellow-traveller, or even to the deaf gusts of wind.

Translated by C.A. Trypanis (1958)

Fragment 714 (Pfeiffer)

44 πολλὰ μάτην κεράεσσιν ἐς ἠέρα θυμήναντα

Vainly butting with his horns the vacant air.

Translated by E.O. Winstedt (1913)

Fragment 732 (Pfeiffer)

quoted in Greek by Cicero, Letters to Atticus *8.5.1*

45 μέγα βιβλίον ἴσον ... μεγάλῳ κακῷ

Big book, big bore.

Translated by Peter Jay (1973)

Athenaeus, *Deipnosophists* 3.72a

possibly referring to the traditional epics or his work at the Library of Alexandria where he produced a catalogue of the library's holdings; cf. the English proverb 'a great book is a great evil'

CALLINUS

mid 7th century BC
Elegiac poet from Ephesus

1 μέχρις τεῦ κατάκεισθε; ...
ἐν εἰρήνῃ δὲ δοκεῖτε
ἧσθαι, ἀτὰρ πόλεμος γαῖαν ἅπασαν ἔχει

How much longer will you be idle?
You think you are resting in peace
But war grips all the land.

Translated by C.A. Trypanis (1971)

Fragment 1.1 (West, *IEG*)

2 τιμῆέν τε γάρ ἐστι καὶ ἀγλαὸν ἀνδρὶ μάχεσθαι
γῆς πέρι καὶ παίδων κουριδίης τ' ἀλόχου

Honour and glory goes to a man who fights
for land and children and his wedded wife.

Fragment 1.6 (West, *IEG*)

3 θάνατος δὲ τότ' ἔσσεται, ὁππότε κεν δὴ
Μοῖραι ἐπικλώσωσ'

Death shall come whenever the Fates spin in their thread.

Translated by C.A. Trypanis (1971)

Fragment 1.8 (West, *IEG*)

4 οὐ γάρ κως θάνατόν γε φυγεῖν εἱμαρμένον ἐστίν

It is decreed that no one, ever, shall escape death.

Fragment 1.12 (West, *IEG*)

5 ἔρδει γὰρ πολλῶν ἄξια μοῦνος ἐών

Single-handed he does the work of many.

Translated by C.A. Trypanis (1971)

Fragment 1.21 (West, *IEG*)

CAPITO
dates unknown

1 Κάλλος ἄνευ χαρίτων τέρπει μόνον, οὐ κατέχει δέ,
ὡς ἄτερ ἀγκίστρου νηχόμενον δέλεαρ.

Beauty without charm only pleases us, but does not hold us;
it's like a bait floating without a hook.

Translated by W.R. Paton (1916)

Greek Anthology 5.67

CARCINUS
4th century BC
Athenian tragic playwright

1 πολλοῖς γὰρ ἀνθρώποισι φάρμακον κακῶν σιγή

Silence is the healer of many ills.

Fragment 7 (Snell, *TrGF*)

2 ἓν δρᾷ μόνον δίκαιον ὧν ποιεῖ φθόνος·
λυπεῖ γὰρ αὐτὸ τὸ κτῆμα τοὺς κεκτημένους

The only effect of envy is that it harms the envious.

Fragment 8 (Snell, *TrGF*)

CARPHYLLIDES
various assumptions on dates between the 3rd century BC and 2nd century AD
Author of two epigrams in *Greek Anthology*

1 Μὴ μέμψῃ παριὼν τὰ μνήματά μου, παροδῖτα·
οὐδὲν ἔχω θρήνων ἄξιον οὐδὲ θανών.
τέκνων τέκνα λέλοιπα· μιῆς ἀπέλαυσα γυναικὸς
συγγήρου· τρισσοῖς παισὶν ἔδωκα γάμους,
ἐξ ὧν πολλάκι παῖδας ἐμοῖς ἐνεκοίμισα κόλποις,
οὐδενὸς οἰμώξας οὐ νόσον, οὐ θάνατον,
οἵ με κατασπείσαντες ἀπήμονα τὸν γλυκὺν ὕπνον
κοιμᾶσθαι χώρην πέμψαν ἐπ' εὐσεβέων.

Mourn not, O traveller, as you pass my tomb;
my death calls not for mourning.
My children's children live. I loved one wife,
who grew old with me. I married my three children,
and lulled many of their children on my lap to sleep,
with never an illness or a death to weep for.
They all sent me off on a painless journey
to sleep the sweet sleep of the pious dead.

Greek Anthology 7.260

CASSIUS DIO
*c.*164–after 229AD
Greek senator (from Nicaea in Bithynia), author of a history of Rome

1 ῥᾷον ... τῆς εὐεξίας τῆς γνώμης ἐπιμεληθῆναί τινι ἢ τῆς τοῦ σώματος

It is easier to maintain vigour of opinion than vigour of body.

Roman History 38.21.2

CATO THE ELDER
Marcus Porcius Cato (Censorius)
234–149BC
Roman statesman, orator and writer
see also Isocrates 80; Plutarch 25

1 εὔχαρις ἅμα καὶ δεινὸς, ἡδὺς καὶ καταπληκτικός, φιλοσκώμμων καὶ αὐστηρός, ἀποφθεγματικὸς καὶ ἀγωνιστικός

Graceful and powerful, charming and compelling, ironic and severe, sententious and belligerent.

Plutarch, *Cato Major* 7.1

of Cato's oratory

2 χαλεπὸν μέν ἐστιν, ὦ πολῖται, πρὸς γαστέρα λέγειν ὦτα οὐκ ἔχουσαν

It is a hard matter, my fellow citizens, to argue with the belly, since it has no ears to hear.

Translated by Bernadotte Perrin (1914)

Plutarch, *Cato Major* 8.1

3 περὶ δὲ τῆς γυναικοκρατίας διαλεγόμενος, πάντες, εἶπεν, ἄνθρωποι τῶν γυναικῶν ἄρχουσιν, ἡμεῖς δὲ πάντων ἀνθρώπων, ἡμῶν δ' αἱ γυναῖκες

Discoursing on the power of women, he said: 'All other men rule their wives; we rule all other men, and our wives rule us.'

Translated by Bernadotte Perrin (1914)

Plutarch, *Cato Major* 8.4

cf. Themistocles 12

4 βούλεσθαι δ' ἔλεγε μᾶλλον εὖ πράξας ἀποστερηθῆναι χάριν ἢ κακῶς μὴ τυχεῖν κολάσεως, καὶ συγγνώμην ἔφη διδόναι πᾶσι τοῖς ἁμαρτάνουσι πλὴν αὑτοῦ

He used to say that he preferred to do right and get no thanks, rather than to do ill and get no punishment; and that he had pardon for everybody's mistakes except his own.

Translated by Bernadotte Perrin (1914)

Plutarch, *Cato Major* 8.16

5 τοὺς δὲ φρονίμους μᾶλλον ὑπὸ τῶν ἀφρόνων ἢ τοὺς ἄφρονας ὑπὸ τῶν φρονίμων ὠφελεῖσθαι· τούτους μὲν γὰρ φυλάττεσθαι τὰς ἐκείνων ἁμαρτίας, ἐκείνους δὲ τὰς τούτων μὴ μιμεῖσθαι κατορθώσεις

Wise men profit more from fools than fools from wise men; for wise men shun the mistakes of fools, but fools can not imitate the successes of the wise.

Translated by Bernadotte Perrin (1914)

Plutarch, *Cato Major* 9.4

6 οἴεσθαι τὰ ῥήματα τοῖς μὲν Ἕλλησιν ἀπὸ χειλέων, τοῖς δὲ Ῥωμαίοις ἀπὸ καρδίας φέρεσθαι

He thought the words of the Greeks were born on their lips, but those of the Romans in their hearts.

Translated by Bernadotte Perrin (1914)

Plutarch, *Cato Major* 12.7

7 τὸ δ' ἔργον ἅρπαγμα δεῖ τάχους γενέσθαι καὶ τόλμης, ᾗ καὶ λέοντες … ἐπὶ τὰ δειλὰ τῶν θηρίων βαδίζουσι

The task demands swiftness and boldness, as lions that leap on their timorous prey.

Plutarch, *Cato Major* 13.5

8 μηδὲν ὀφείλειν Κάτωνα τῷ δήμῳ τοσοῦτον, ὅσον Κάτωνι τὸν δῆμον

Cato owes less to Rome than Rome to Cato.

Translated by Bernadotte Perrin (1914)

Plutarch, *Cato Major* 14.2

Cato's boast after taking Thermopylae

9 χαλεπόν ἐστιν ἐν ἄλλοις βεβιωκότα ἀνθρώποις ἐν ἄλλοις ἀπολογεῖσθαι

It is hard for one who has lived among men of one generation to make his defence before those of another.

Translated by Bernadotte Perrin (1914)

Plutarch, *Cato Major* 15.4

as defendant in his last case, at the age of eighty-six

10 μᾶλλον βούλομαι ζητεῖσθαι, διὰ τί μου ἀνδριὰς οὐ κεῖται ἢ διὰ τί κεῖται

I would much rather have men ask why I have no statue, than why I have one.

Translated in *Bartlett's Familiar Quotations* (1980)

Plutarch, *Cato Major* 19.6

when asked why there were men of no fame that had statues but he had none

11 τὸν δὲ τύπτοντα γαμετὴν ἢ παῖδα τοῖς ἁγιωτάτοις ἔλεγεν ἱεροῖς προσφέρειν τὰς χεῖρας

A man who strikes his wife or child lays hands on what is most sacred.

Plutarch, *Cato Major* 20.3.1

12 Σωκράτους οὐδὲν ἄλλο θαυμάζειν τοῦ παλαιοῦ πλὴν ὅτι γυναικὶ χαλεπῇ καὶ παισὶν ἀποπλήκτοις χρώμενος ἐπιεικῶς καὶ πρᾴως διετέλεσε

There is nothing else to admire in Socrates of old except that he was kind and gentle to his shrewish wife and his stupid sons.

Plutarch, *Cato Major* 20.3.4

13 ἔλεγε τοὺς δυναμένους κωλύειν τοὺς κακῶς ποιοῦντας, ἐὰν μὴ κωλύωσι, κελεύειν

If those who have the power to discourage crime do not discourage it, then they encourage it.

Translated by Frank Cole Babbitt (1931)

Plutarch, *Sayings of Romans* 198e

14 τὸν ἄρχοντα ἢ κριτὴν δεῖν μήτε ὑπὲρ τῶν δικαίων λιπαρεῖσθαι μήτε ὑπὲρ τῶν ἀδίκων ἐκλιπαρεῖσθαι

An official or judge ought neither to be entreated to grant what is right nor to yield to pressure to grant what is wrong.

Plutarch, *Sayings of Romans* 198f

15 βέλτιον εἶναι πολλοὺς ἔχοντας ἀργύριον ἢ ὀλίγους χρυσίον ἀπὸ τῆς στρατείας ἐπανελθεῖν

It is better that many should return from the campaign with silver than a few with gold.

Translated by Frank Cole Babbitt (1931)

Plutarch, *Sayings of Romans* 199d

on giving all his soldiers a pound of silver before leaving on a campaign

CHAEREMON

middle of 4th century BC
Tragic playwright

1 οὐκ ἔστιν οὐδὲν τῶν ἐν ἀνθρώποις ὅ τι οὐκ ἐν χρόνῳ ζητοῦσιν ἐξευρίσκεται

There is nothing in humanity
which in time cannot be found by one who seeks.

Fragment 21 (Snell, *TrGF*)

2 οὐ ζῶσιν οἵ τι μὴ συνιέντες σοφόν

Whoever has not learnt wisdom is not truly alive.

Fragment 24 (Snell, *TrGF*)

3 γένοιτό μοι τὰς χάριτας ἀποδοῦναι πατρί

Grant me to restore to my father what I owe him.

Fragment 33 (Snell, *TrGF*)

4 οὐδεὶς ἐπὶ σμικροῖσι λυπεῖται σοφός

The wise do not fret over trivialities

Fragment 37 (Snell, *TrGF*)

CHARES

early 4th century BC
Writer of Gnomai, of which over fifty lines are preserved

1 γλώσσης μάλιστα πανταχοῦ πειρῶ κρατεῖν,
ὃ καὶ γέροντι καὶ νέῳ τιμὴν φέρει.
ἡ γλῶσσα σιγὴν καιρίαν κεκτημένη

Try in all events to rule your tongue, as silence
bestows honour on old and young alike.

Sententiae 1.22 (Jaekel)

CHILON

born *c.*600BC
Spartan ephor (*c.*556BC) and one of the Seven Sages
see also Seven Sages 39–40

1 μὴ κακολόγει τοὺς πλησίον· εἰ δὲ μή, ἀκούσῃ, ἐφ' οἷς λυπηθήσῃ

Do not abuse your neighbours for you may hear things you will regret.

Seven Sages, *Apophthegms* Fragment 3.3 (D-K)

2 ἐπὶ τὰ δεῖπνα τῶν φίλων βραδέως πορεύου, ἐπὶ δὲ τὰς ἀτυχίας ταχέως

Tarry when attending your friends' dinners, but hasten to their misfortunes.

Seven Sages, *Apophthegms* Fragment 3.4 (D-K)

3 ζημίαν αἱροῦ μᾶλλον ἢ κέρδος αἰσχρόν· τὸ μὲν γὰρ ἅπαξ λυπήσει, τὸ δὲ ἀεί

Prefer loss to dishonest gain; the one will grieve you once, the other always.

Seven Sages, *Apophthegms* Fragment 3.6 (D-K)

4 ἡ γλῶσσά σου μὴ προτρεχέτω τοῦ νοῦ

Think before you speak.

Seven Sages, *Apophthegms* Fragment 3.9 (D-K)

cf. the English proverb 'think first and speak afterwards'

5 μὴ ἐπιθύμει ἀδύνατα

Do not yearn for the impossible.

Seven Sages, *Apophthegms* Fragment 3.10 (D-K)

cf. the Latin 'ad impossibilia nemo tenetur'

6 θυμοῦ κράτει

Control anger.

Translated by R.D. Hicks (1925)

Seven Sages, *Apophthegms* Fragment 3.10 (D-K)

7 χαλεπώτατον τὸ γινώσκειν ἑαυτὸν

What is most difficult is to know thyself.

Seven Sages, *Apophthegms* 3.15 (Mullach, *FPG*)

also attributed to Thales; cf. Solon 64

8 λυπουμένου τινὸς ἐπὶ τοῖς αὐτοῦ κακοῖς, εἶπεν· εἰ τὰ πάντων κατανοήσῃς, ἧττον

ἐπὶ τοῖς σαυτοῦ δυσφορήσεις

If you consider the troubles of others you will be less vexed with your own.

Seven Sages, *Apophthegms* 3.16 (Mullach, *FPG*)

9 τὸν ἄρχοντα χρὴ μηδὲν φρονεῖν θνητόν, ἀλλὰ πάντα ἀθάνατα

A ruler should never think as a mortal, but of all things as being immortal.

Seven Sages, *Apophthegms* 3.17 (Mullach, *FPG*)

10 τὴν μάλιστα νόμων, ἥκιστα δὲ ῥητόρων ἀκούουσαν πολιτείαν ἀρίστην εἶναι

The best state is one where the laws and not the orators are obeyed.

Seven Sages, *Apophthegms* 9.1 (Mullach, *FPG*)

11 χρόνου φείδου

Use time sparingly.

Seven Sages, *Sententiae* 216.31 (Mullach, *FPG*)

12 ταχύτερον ἐπὶ τὰς ἀτυχίας τῶν φίλων ἢ ἐπὶ τὰς εὐτυχίας πορεύεσθαι

Visit your friends more readily in adversity than in prosperity.

Diogenes Laertius, *Lives of Eminent Philosophers* 1.70.2

13 τὸν τεθνηκότα μὴ κακολογεῖν

Speak no evil of the dead.

Translated by John Simpson and Jennifer Speake (1982)

Diogenes Laertius, *Lives of Eminent Philosophers* 1.70.3

cf. the Latin 'de mortuis nil nisi bene' and the English proverb 'never speak ill of the dead'

14 ἰσχυρὸν ὄντα πρᾷον εἶναι, ὅπως οἱ πλησίον αἰδῶνται μᾶλλον ἢ φοβῶνται

When strong, be merciful, if you would have the respect, not the fear, of your neighbours.

Translated by R.D. Hicks (1925)

Diogenes Laertius, *Lives of Eminent Philosophers* 1.70.6

15 λέγοντα μὴ κινεῖν τὴν χεῖρα· μανικὸν γάρ

When speaking do not wave your hands about; it is a sign of madness.

Diogenes Laertius, *Lives of Eminent Philosophers* 1.70.10

CHOERILUS

late 5th century BC
Epic poet from Samos

1 ἆ μάκαρ, ὅστις ἔην κεῖνον χρόνον ἴδρις ἀοιδῆς,
Μουσάων θεράπων, ὅτ' ἀκήρατος ἦν ἔτι λειμών·
νῦν δ' ὅτε πάντα δέδασται, ἔχουσι δὲ πείρατα τέχναι,
ὕστατοι ὥστε δρόμου καταλειπόμεθ', οὐδέ πῃ ἔστι
πάντῃ παπταίνοντα νεοζυγὲς ἅρμα πελάσσαι

Blessed were the poets in the old days
When the field was still wide open. The arts
Are all fenced in now, the field parceled out,
And we, the latecomers, barred from the race
No room to bring up a new-yoked chariot.

Translated by Stanley Lombardo and Diane Rayor (1988)

Fragment 2 (Bernabé, *PEG*) – *Persica*

Choerilus went on to introduce a new element in the deeds of historical heroes, rather than the myths of old

CHRYSIPPUS

*c.*280–207BC
Stoic philosopher from Soli in Cilicia

1 φύσει τε τὸ δίκαιον εἶναι καὶ μὴ θέσει

Justice exists by nature, not by convention.

Translated by R.D. Hicks (1925)

Fragment 308 (von Arnim, *SVF*)

2 τυφλόν ἐστιν ἡ ὀργή

Anger is blind.

Fragment 390 (von Arnim, *SVF*)

3 εἰ μὲν πονηρά τις πολιτεύεται, τοῖς θεοῖς ἀπαρέσει· εἰ δὲ χρηστὰ τοῖς πολίταις

If one acts wickedly, the gods will be displeased; if rightfully, the citizens.

Fragment 694 (von Arnim, *SVF*)

on not being involved in politics

CIMON

*c.*510–449BC
Athenian statesman and admiral
see also Euripides 460

1 ὑπολαμβάνων πρᾴως τοὺς ἀδικουμένους καὶ φιλανθρώπως ἐξομιλῶν ἔλαθεν οὐ δι' ὅπλων τὴν τῆς Ἑλλάδος ἡγεμονίαν, ἀλλὰ λόγῳ καὶ ἤθει παρελόμενος

He received with mildness those who brought their wrongs to him, treated them humanely, and so, before men were aware of it, secured the leadership of Hellas, not by force or arms, but by virtue of his address and character.

Translated by Bernadotte Perrin (1914)

Plutarch, *Cimon* 6.2

2 μάλιστα τοὺς Ἀθηναίους ἐκίνησε, παρακαλῶν μήτε τὴν Ἑλλάδα χωλὴν μήτε τὴν πόλιν ἑτερόζυγα περιϊδεῖν γεγενημένην

He prevailed upon the Athenians to send help, so that Hellas would not be crippled, nor the balance of power lopsided.

Plutarch, *Cimon* 16.10

on a Spartan request for aid after a large earthquake had destroyed Sparta

CLEAENETUS

4th century BC
Athenian tragic playwright

1 λύπη γὰρ ὀργή τ' εἰς ἕνα ψυχῆς τόπον
ἐλθόντα μανία τοῖς ἔχουσι γίγνεται

Sorrow and anger within the same soul is madness.

Fragment 2 (Snell, *TrGF*)

CLEANTHES

331–232BC
Stoic philosopher from Assos

1 ἐκ σοῦ γὰρ γενόμεσθα

For from you we are born.

Translated by C.A. Trypanis (1971)

Fragment 1.4 (Powell, *Coll.Alex*)

cf. Bible 194

2 θεοῦ μίμημα λαχόντες
μοῦνοι, ὅσα ζώει τε καὶ ἕρπει θνήτ' ἐπὶ γαῖαν

We alone are created in god's image
of all mortal things that live and move upon the earth.

Fragment 1.4 (Powell, *Coll.Alex*)

of human beings, made in the image of Zeus; cf. Bible 317 and Bible 191; but cf. Xenophanes 4

3 αὐτοὶ δ' αὖθ' ὁρμῶσιν ἄνοι κακὸν ἄλλος ἐπ' ἄλλο

They senselessly hurry after all kinds of evil.

Translated by C.A. Trypanis (1971)

Fragment 1.26 (Powell, *Coll.Alex*)

4 ὑμνοῦντες τὰ σὰ ἔργα διηνεκές, ὡς ἐπέοικε
θνητὸν ἐόντ', ἐπεὶ οὔτε βροτοῖς γέρας ἄλλο τι μεῖζον
οὔτε θεοῖς, ἢ κοινὸν ἀεὶ νόμον ἐν δίκῃ ὑμνεῖν

We celebrate your works, as is proper for mortals;
for there is no greater prize for men and gods
than justly to praise universal law.

Translated by C.A. Trypanis (1971)

Fragment 1.38 (Powell, *Coll.Alex*)

of Zeus

5 ἄγου δέ μ', ὦ Ζεῦ, καὶ σύ γ' ἡ Πεπρωμένη,
ὅποι ποθ' ὑμῖν εἰμι διατεταγμένος·
ὡς ἕψομαί γ' ἄοκνος· ἢν δέ γε μὴ θέλω,
κακὸς γενόμενος, οὐδὲν ἧττον ἕψομαι

Lead thou me on, O Zeus, and Destiny,
To that goal long ago to me assigned.
I'll follow and not falter; if my will
Prove weak and craven, still I'll follow on.

Translated by W.A. Oldfather (1928)

Fragment 2 (Powell, *Coll.Alex*)

quoted by Epictetus

6 οὐ γὰρ πλῆθος ἔχει συνετὴν κρίσιν, οὔτε δικαίαν
οὔτε καλήν, ὀλίγοις δὲ παρ' ἀνδράσι τοῦτό κεν εὕροις

A crowd possesses neither prudent judgement, nor just,
nor sound; such you will find only in the few.

Fragment 4 (Powell, *Coll.Alex*)

7 κακουργότερον οὐδὲν διαβολῆς ἔστι πω·
λάθρα γὰρ ἀπατήσασα τὸν πεπεισμένον
μῖσος ἀναπλάττει πρὸς τὸν οὐδὲν αἴτιον

There's nothing more harmful than
slander;
for, having deceived whoever believed,
hatred is born where no cause exists.

Fragment 10 (Powell, *Coll.Alex*)

8 Κλεάνθης ἔφη τοὺς ἀπαιδεύτους μόνῃ τῇ μορφῇ τῶν θηρίων διαφέρειν

The uneducated only differ from beasts in appearance.

Fragment 517 (von Arnim, *SVF*)

9 τὴν λύπην ψυχῆς παράλυσιν

Sorrow paralyses the soul.

Fragment 575 (von Arnim, *SVF*)

10 Κλεάνθης, ἐρωτώμενος πῶς ἄν τις εἴη πλούσιος, εἶπεν εἰ τῶν ἐπιθυμιῶν εἴη πένης

Cleanthes, when asked how to become wealthy, replied, 'Only if one is sparing with one's desires.'

Fragment 617 (von Arnim, *SVF*)

Stobaeus also attributes this to Socrates

11 παράδοξα μὲν ἴσως φασὶν οἱ φιλόσοφοι ... οὐ μὴν παράλογα

Philosophers may say what is unexpected, yet certainly not what is beyond reason.

Fragment 619 (von Arnim, *SVF*)

CLEMENT OF ALEXANDRIA

Titus Flavius Clemens

*c.*150–*c.*212AD

Theologian

1 στόμιον πώλων ἀδαῶν,
πτερὸν ὀρνίθων ἀπλανῶν,
οἴαξ νηῶν ἀτρεκής,
ποιμὴν ἀρνῶν βασιλικῶν

Bridle of untamed horses,
Wing of hovering bird,
Helm of steady ship,
O Shepherd of royal lambs.

Translated by Peter Constantine (2010)

A Hymn to Christ the Saviour 1

2 σοφίας πρύτανι,
στήριγμα πόνων ...
ἁλιεῦ μερόπων

Lord of wisdom,
Assuager of pain
Fisher of Men.

Translated by Peter Constantine (2010)

A Hymn to Christ the Saviour 14

3 σὺ γὰρ εἶ κιθάρα καὶ αὐλὸς καὶ ναὸς ἐμοί· κιθάρα διὰ τὴν ἁρμονίαν, αὐλὸς διὰ τὸ πνεῦμα, ναὸς διὰ τὸν λόγον

Thou art my harp and my pipe and my temple; my harp by reason of the music, my pipe by reason of the breath of the Spirit, my temple by reason of the Word.

Translated by G.W. Butterworth (1919)

Exhortation to the Greeks 1.5.3.6

of God; the source of this quotation is unknown, it may be a fragment of an early Christian hymn

4 μηδαμῶς τοίνυν ἐπικαλυπτώμεθα τὸ σκότος, τὸ γὰρ φῶς ἔνοικον ἡμῖν

Then let us not wrap ourselves in darkness; for the light is within us.

Translated by Jonathan Barnes (1987)

Paedagogus 2.10.99.6

5 κωλύει δὲ βιαζομένους τὴν φύσιν ὁ λόγος τοὺς λοβοὺς τῶν ὠτίων τιτρᾶναι· διὰ τί γὰρ οὐχὶ καὶ τὴν ῥῖνα;

It is against nature to pierce the earlobes. Why not the nose as well?

Paedagogus 3.11.57.1

on earrings and jewellery, with direct reference to Bible, Proverbs 11.22; cf. Bible 350

6 δυσάλωτόν τι χρῆμα καὶ δυσθήρατον, ἐξαναχωροῦν ἀεὶ καὶ πόρρω ἀφιστάμενον τοῦ διώκοντος. ὁ δὲ αὐτὸς μακρὰν ὢν ἐγγυτάτω βέβηκεν, θαῦμα ἄρρητον· 'θεὸς ἐγγίζων ἐγώ,' φησὶ κύριος· πόρρω μὲν κατ' οὐσίαν (πῶς γὰρ ἂν συνεγγίσαι ποτὲ τὸ γεννητὸν ἀγεννήτῳ;)

A Being difficult to grasp and apprehend, ever receding and withdrawing from him who pursues. But He who is far off has – oh ineffable marvel! – come very near. 'I am a God that draws near,' says the Lord. He is in essence remote; 'for how is it that what is begotten can have approached the Unbegotten?'

Translated by Philip Schaff (1819–1893)

Stromateis 2.2.5.3

7 ἐθελοντὴν δὲ συνέπεσθαι τῷ συμφέροντι συνέσεως ἀρχή. μεγάλην γοῦν εἰς γνῶσιν ῥοπὴν ἀπερίσπαστος παρέχει προαίρεσις. αὐτίκα ἡ μελέτη τῆς πίστεως ἐπιστήμη γίνεται θεμελίῳ βεβαίῳ ἐπερηρεισμένη

Voluntarily to follow what is useful is the first principle of understanding. Unswerving choice, then, gives considerable momentum in the direction of knowledge. The exercise of faith directly becomes knowledge, reposing on a sure foundation.

Translated by Philip Schaff (1819–1893)

Stromateis 2.2.9.3

8 χοῖρος βορβόρῳ ἥδεται καὶ κόπρῳ

A pig delights in dung and filth.

Stromateis 2.5.68.3

9 ἡ μὲν οὖν πίστις σύντομός ἐστιν, ὡς εἰπεῖν, τῶν κατεπειγόντων γνῶσις, ἡ γνῶσις δὲ ἀπόδειξις τῶν διὰ πίστεως παρειλημμένων ἰσχυρὰ καὶ βέβαιος, διὰ τῆς κυριακῆς διδασκαλίας ἐποικοδομουμένη τῇ πίστει εἰς τὸ ἀμετάπτωτον καὶ μετ᾽ ἐπιστήμης καὶ καταληπτὸν παραπέμπουσα

Faith is then, so to speak, a comprehensive knowledge of the essentials; and knowledge is the strong and sure demonstration of what is received by faith, built upon faith by the Lord's teaching, conveying the soul on to infallibility, science, and comprehension.

Translated by Philip Schaff (1819–1893)

Stromateis 7.10.57.3

10 ἡσυχίαν μὲν λόγοις ἐπιτήδευε, ἡσυχίαν δὲ ἔργοις, ὡσαύτως δὲ ἐν γλώττῃ καὶ βαδίσματι· σφοδρότητα δὲ ἀπόφευγε προπετῆ

Practise quietness in word, quietness in deed, likewise in speech and gait; and avoid reckless violence.

Fragment 44.4 (Stählin)

11 μάνθανε δὲ ἀσμένως, καὶ ἀφθόνως δίδασκε

Learn gladly, and teach ungrudgingly.

Translated by G.W. Butterworth (1919)

Fragment 44.25 (Stählin)

cf. Chaucer, Canterbury Tales, *Prologue, Clerk, last line 'And gladly wolde he lerne, and gladly teche'*

CLEOBULUS

6th century BC

Lyric poet from Lindos and one of the Seven Sages

see also Enigmata and Riddles 5; Homeric Epigrams 1; Seven Sages 39–40

1 ἀμουσία τὸ πλέον μέρος ἐν βροτοῖσιν λόγων τε πλῆθος

Most people are afflicted by a lack of taste
and a surfeit of words.

Fragment 1 (Bergk, *PLG*)

2 μέτρον ἄριστον

Moderation is best.

Translated by R.D. Hicks (1925)

Seven Sages, *Apophthegms* Fragment 1.2 (D-K)

cf. the Latin 'est modus in rebus'

3 φιλήκοον εἶναι καὶ μὴ πολύλαλον

Be listeners rather than talkers.

Translated by R.D. Hicks (1925)

Seven Sages, *Apophthegms* Fragment 1.3 (D-K)

4 ἡδονῆς κρατεῖν

Prevail over pleasure.

Seven Sages, *Apophthegms* Fragment 1.5 (D-K)

5 βίᾳ μηδὲν πράττειν

Do nothing in violence.

Seven Sages, *Apophthegms* Fragment 1.5 (D-K)

6 τὸν τοῦ δήμου ἐχθρὸν πολέμιον νομίζειν

Consider an enemy of the state your enemy.

Seven Sages, *Apophthegms* Fragment 1.6 (D-K)

7 ἔχθραν διαλύειν

Put an end to enmity.

Translated by R.D. Hicks (1925)

Seven Sages, *Apophthegms* Fragment 1.6 (D-K)

8 γυναικὶ μὴ φιλοφρονεῖσθαι, μηδὲ μάχεσθαι, ἀλλοτρίων παρόντων

In front of strangers neither flatter nor quarrel with your wife.

Seven Sages, *Apophthegms* Fragment 1.7 (D-K)

9 γαμεῖν ἐκ τῶν ὁμοίων· ἐὰν γὰρ ἐκ τῶν κρειττόνων, δεσπότας, οὐ συγγενεῖς κτήσῃ

Marry one equal to you, for to marry above your class brings despots rather than relatives.

Seven Sages, *Apophthegms* Fragment 1.9 (D-K)

10 μὴ ἐπιγελᾶν τῷ σκώπτοντι· ἀπεχθὴς γὰρ ἔσῃ τοῖς σκωπτομένοις

Do not laugh at one who is reviled, for he will hate you more.

Seven Sages, *Apophthegms* Fragment 1.10 (D-K)

11 εὐποροῦντα μὴ ὑπερήφανον εἶναι, ἀποροῦντα μὴ ταπεινοῦσθαι

Do not be proud of your riches nor ashamed of your poverty.

Seven Sages, *Apophthegms* Fragment 1.11 (D-K)

12 ἔφη δὲ δεῖν συνοικίζειν τὰς θυγατέρας, παρθένους μὲν τὴν ἡλικίαν τὸ δὲ φρονεῖν γυναῖκας· ὑποδεικνὺς ὅτι δεῖ παιδεύεσθαι καὶ τὰς παρθένους

We ought to give our daughters to their husbands maidens in years but women in wisdom; thus signifying that girls need to be educated as well as boys.

Translated by R.D. Hicks (1925)

Seven Sages, *Apophthegms* 1.2 (Mullach, *FPG*)

13 τὸν φίλον δεῖν εὐεργετεῖν, ὅπως μᾶλλον ᾖ φίλος· τὸν δὲ ἐχθρὸν φίλον ποιεῖν

Render a service to a friend that the more a friend he be; and an enemy becomes a friend if shown kindness.

Seven Sages, *Apophthegms* 1.3 (Mullach, *FPG*)

14 τὰς μεταβολὰς τῆς τύχης γενναίως ἐπίστασο φέρειν

Know how to bear the changes of fortune with nobility.

Translated by R.D. Hicks (1925)

Seven Sages, *Apophthegms* 1.5 (Mullach, *FPG*)

15 εὐποιίας ἧς ἔτυχες μνημόνευε

Remember kindness shown to you.

Seven Sages, *Sententiae* 216.19 (Mullach, *FPG*)

16 ἀγάπα τὰ τοῦ πλησίου σου καὶ τήρει ὡς τὰ σαυτοῦ

Respect your neighbour's belongings as your own.

Seven Sages, *Sententiae* 216.21 (Mullach, *FPG*)

17 φιλομαθῆ μᾶλλον ἢ ἀμαθῆ· γλῶσσαν εὔφημον ἴσχειν

Choose instruction rather than ignorance and refrain from ill-omened words.

Translated by R.D. Hicks (1925)

Diogenes Laertius, *Lives of Eminent Philosophers* 1.92

18 εὐτυχῶν μὴ ἴσθι ὑπερήφανος

Do not be arrogant in prosperity.

Translated by R.D. Hicks (1925)

Diogenes Laertius, *Lives of Eminent Philosophers* 1.93

CLEOMENES

King of Sparta, 520–490BC
see also Herodotus 94–95

1 Κλεομένης ... τὸν μὲν Ὅμηρον Λακεδαιμονίων εἶναι ποιητὴν ἔφη, τὸν δὲ Ἡσίοδον τῶν εἱλώτων· τὸν μὲν γὰρ ὡς χρὴ πολεμεῖν, τὸν δὲ ὡς χρὴ γεωργεῖν παρηγγελκέναι

Cleomenes said that Homer was the poet of the Spartans, and Hesiod of the Helots; for Homer had taught fighting, and Hesiod farming.

Translated by Frank Cole Babbitt (1931)

Plutarch, *Sayings of Spartans* 223a

CLINIAS

4th century BC
Philosopher from Tarentum

1 ὁπότας δὲ ἔξω τὰς αἰτίας ἀναιρεῖν, δι' ἃς ἀδικεῖν πέφυκεν ἄνθρωπος; αὗται δὲ τρεῖς τυγχάνοντι· φιλαδονία μὲν ἐν ταῖς ἀπολαύσεσι ταῖς διὰ σώματος, πλεονεξία δὲ ἐν τῷ κερδαίνειν· φιλοδοξία δὲ ἐν τῷ καθυπερέχειν καὶ ἄρχειν τῶν ἴσων τε καὶ ὁμοίων

Three are the causes of injustice to which man is naturally adapted: lust, greed and the ambition to surpass your peers.

Fragment 108.9 (Thesleff)

CLITOMACHUS

187/186–110/109BC
Academic sceptic from Carthage

1 Κλειτόμαχος εἴκαζε τὴν διαλεκτικὴν τῇ σελήνῃ· καὶ γὰρ ταύτην οὐ παύεσθαι φθίνουσαν καὶ αὐξομένην

Clitomachus compared dialectic to the moon, as it too never stops decreasing and increasing.

Stobaeus, *Anthology* 2.2.21

CONSTANTINE THE GREAT

*c.*288–337AD
Roman emperor from 306AD

1 τούτῳ νίκα

In this sign shalt thou conquer.

Eusebius, *Life of Constantine* 1.28.2

traditional form of Constantine's vision of the Cross (312AD), reported in Greek, usually quoted as 'ἐν τούτῳ νίκα' or, in Latin, 'in hoc signo vinces'

CORINNA

5th or 3rd century BC
Lyric poet from Tanagra
see also Proverbial 81

1 Θέσπια καλλιγένεθλε φιλόξενε μωσοφίλειτε

Thespia, Thespia,
your daughters are fair
your lovers, strangers
and your strangers, loved;
the Muses hold you in their hearts.

Translated by Josephine Balmer (1996)

Fragment 21 (Page, *PMG*)

Thespiae was a city-state in Boeotia

CRANTOR

*c.*335–275BC
Philosopher from Soloi in Cilicia

1 ἐν μὲν εἰρήνῃ παρέχω τὰ τερπνά, ἐν δὲ πολέμοις νεῦρα τῶν πράξεων γίνομαι

In peace I provide delights, in war I am the sinews of action.

Fragment 13.15 (Mullach, *FPG*)

of wealth; cf. the expression 'the sinews of war' and the Latin 'nervus rerum'

CRASSUS

Marcus Licinius Crassus
*c.*114–53BC
Roman statesman and general

1 εἰ δεῖ τι καὶ παθεῖν τοὺς μεγάλων ἐφιεμένους

Those who aim at great deeds must also suffer greatly.

Translated by Bernadotte Perrin (1916)

Plutarch, *Crassus* 26.7

CRATES

5th century BC
Athenian comic poet

1 ἵππῳ γηράσκοντι τὰ μείονα κύκλ' ἐπίβαλλε

Lay lighter burdens on an old horse.

Fragment 30 (Kock) – 33 (K-A) – *Samioi – The Samians*

2 Κράτης πρὸς νέον πλούσιον πολλοὺς κόλακας ἐπισυρόμενον νεανίσκε εἶπεν ἐλεῶ σου τὴν ἐρημίαν

Crates, to a young wealthy man followed by many flatterers said, 'Young man, I pity your loneliness.'

Stobaeus, *Anthology* 3.14.20

not specified which Crates

CRATES OF THEBES

*c.*368/365–288/2885BC
Cynic philosopher and poet

1 ἔρωτα παύει λιμός, εἰ δὲ μή, χρόνος

Hunger destroys love, and so does time.

Fragment 14 (Diehl)

2 οὐκ οἶσθα, πήρα δύναμιν ἡλίκην ἔχει θέρμων τε χοῖνιξ καὶ τὸ μηδενὸς μέλειν

You do not know the force of a beggar's pouch,
A handful of lupin seeds and freedom from care.

Translated by Marie-Odile Goulet-

Cazé (1996) tr. into English by Helena Caine-Suarez

Fragment 18 (Diehl)

CRATINUS

5th century BC
Athenian Old Comedy poet

1 ὕδωρ δὲ πίνων οὐδὲν ἂν τέκοι σοφόν

Drinking water produces nothing wise.

Fragment 199 (Kock) – *203 (K-A) – *Pytine – The Wineflask*

2 ἄκουε, σίγα, πρόσεχε τὸν νοῦν, δεῦρ' ὅρα

Listen, keep your peace, take heed, look ahead.

Fragment 284 (Kock) – 315 (K-A)

3 ὦ μεγίστη γλῶττα τῶν Ἑλληνίδων

Greek women, their tongues go nineteen to the dozen!

Fragment 293 (Kock) – 324 (K-A)

4 ὑπολεπτολόγος, γνωμιδιώκτης, εὐριπιδαριστοφανίζων

Micro-intellectualist, mega-sloganist, Euripid-Aristophanist.

Translated by M.S. Silk (2000)

Fragment 307 (Kock) – 342 (K-A)

mocking Aristophanes for writing in the style of Euripides

5 ἄγουσιν ἑορτὴν οἱ κλέπται

Every day is a holiday for a thief.

Fragment 18 (Demiańczuk) – 356 (K-A)

CRITIAS

*c.*460–403BC
Poet and tragic playwright, one of the Thirty Tyrants at Athens
see also Plato 134

1 Φοίνικες δ' εὗρον γράμματ' ἀλεξίλογα

The Phoenicians invented writing, aid to thought.

Translated by Kathleen Freeman (1948)

Fragment 2 (D-K)

2 εἶτ' ἀπὸ τοιούτων πόσεων γλώσσας τε λύουσιν
εἰς αἰσχροὺς μύθους, σῶμά τ' ἀμαυρότερον
τεύχουσιν· πρὸς δ' ὄμμ' ἀχλὺς ἀμβλωπὸς ἐφίζει,
λῆστις δ' ἐκτήκει μνημοσύνην πραπίδων,
νοῦς δὲ παρέσφαλται

From so much drinking, their loose tongues use base speech, their bodies are enfeebled; a dim cloud settles on the eye, forgetfulness dissolves memory, and the mind reels.

Fragment 6.12 (D-K)

3 οἱ Λακεδαιμονίων δὲ κόροι πίνουσι τοσοῦτον
ὥστε φρέν' εἰς ἱλαρὰν ἐλπίδα πάντας ἄγειν
εἴς τε φιλοφροσύνην γλῶσσαν μέτριόν τε γέλωτα

Young Spartans drink only so much as to give hope to their hearts, kindness to their words and mirth in moderation.

Fragment 6.17 (D-K)

4 τοιαύτη δὲ πόσις σώματί τ' ὠφέλιμος
γνώμῃ τε κτήσει τε· καλῶς δ' εἰς ἔργ' Ἀφροδίτης
πρός θ' ὕπνον ἥρμοσται, τὸν καμάτων λιμένα,
πρὸς τὴν τερπνοτάτην τε θεῶν θνητοῖς Ὑγίειαν,
καὶ τὴν Εὐσεβίης γείτονα Σωφροσύνην

Such drinking advantages alike body, understanding, and estate;
it well befits the works of Aphrodite
and sleep that's our haven after toil,
befits also Health the god most pleasing unto man,
and Piety's neighbour Discretion.

Translated by J.M. Edmonds (1931)

Fragment 6.20 (D-K)

5 οὐκ ἔστ' ἀπότακτος
ἡμέρα οἰνῶσαι σῶμ' ἀμέτροισι πότοις

There's no day appointed for immoderate drinking.

Fragment 6.30 (D-K)

6 ἐκ μελέτης πλείους ἢ φύσεως ἀγαθοί

More men are good through habit than through character.

Translated by Kathleen Freeman (1948)

Fragment 9 (D-K)

7 φεῦ· οὐδὲν δικαιόν ἐστιν ἐν τῷ νῦν γένει

Alas! Nothing is just in the present generation.

Translated by Kathleen Freeman (1948)

Fragment 12 (D-K) – *Tennes*

8 ὡς τοῖσιν εὖ φρονοῦσι συμμαχεῖ τύχη

Good fortune ever fights on the side of prudence.

Translated by H.T. Riley (1872)

Fragment 21 (D-K) – *Peirithous*

9 πρῶτον οἴομαι πεῖσαί τινα
θνητοὺς νομίζειν δαιμόνων εἶναι γένος

First I think someone persuaded
mortals to believe that a tribe of spirits
exists.

Translated by Jonathan Barnes (1979)

Fragment 25.57 (D-K) – *Sisyphus*

of the gods; there is still disagreement on the authorship of this play

10 δεινὸν δ' ὅταν τις μὴ φρονῶν δοκῇ φρονεῖν

It is terrible when one who is not wise thinks himself so.

Translated by Kathleen Freeman (1948)

Fragment 28 (D-K)

11 σοφῆς δὲ πενίας σκαιότητα πλουσίαν
κρεῖσσον σύνοικόν ἐστιν ἐν δόμοις ἔχειν;

Wise poverty or stupid wealth – which is the better household companion?

Translated by Patricia Curd, with S. Marc Cohen, and C.D.C. Reeve (2005)

Fragment 29 (D-K)

12 σωφροσύνη ἂν εἴη τὰ ἑαυτοῦ πράττειν

Self-restraint is to mind one's own business.

Translated by Kathleen Freeman (1948)

Fragment 41a (D-K)

13 βέβαιον μὲν οὐδέν, εἰ μὴ τό τε καταθανεῖν γενομένῳ καὶ ζῶντι μὴ οἷόν τε ἐκτὸς ἄτης βαίνειν

Nothing is certain, except that having been born we shall die, and that in life one cannot steer clear of disaster.

Fragment 49 (D-K)

14 ὁ χρόνος ἁπάσης ἐστὶν ὀργῆς φάρμακον

Time is the healer of all anger.

Fragment 22 (Snell, *TrGF*)

ST CYRIL OF ALEXANDRIA

*c.*370–444AD
Bishop from 412AD

1 τί γάρ, εἰ μὴ ἔχοι φωνὰς ἡ ἀνθρώπου γλῶττα δυναμένας ἀρκέσαι τῇ θείᾳ δόξῃ πρὸς ἐξήγησιν;

If the human voice were soundless who would extol the glory of God?

Commentary on the Gospel of John 2.258.11

2 μὴ οὐχὶ τὸν οὐρανὸν καὶ τὴν γῆν ἐγὼ πληρῶ, λέγει Κύριος

Am I not he who fills the earth and the sky, says the Lord.

Commentary on the Gospel of John 2.258.24

3 φιλελευθέρα γὰρ λίαν ἡ ἀνθρώπου φύσις

It is in the nature of man to be liberal.

Commentary on the Pentateuch 69.389.56 (*MPG*)

D

DARIUS I

550–486BC
King of Persia, 522–486BC
see also Aeschylus 78–80; Herodotus 77–78, 81, 93, 139

1 ἔνθα γάρ τι δεῖ ψεῦδος λέγεσθαι, λεγέσθω

If a lie is useful, use a lie.

Herodotus, *Histories* 3.72

but see Herodotus 36

2 δέσποτα, μέμνεο τῶν Ἀθηναίων

Master, remember the Athenians.

Translated by A.D. Godley (1922)

Herodotus, *Histories* 5.105

Darius ordered a servant to say this three times at dinner lest he forget the defeat at Marathon

3 Ἕλληνες γὰρ ἐπὶ τὸ πλεῖστον ἀνεπιστήμαντοι σοφοῖς ἀνδράσιν ὄντες παρορῶσι τὰ καλῶς ὑπ' αὐτῶν ἐνδεικνύμενα πρὸς σπουδαίαν ἀκοὴν καὶ μάθησιν

The Greeks as a rule are not prone to mark their wise men; nay, they neglect their excellent precepts which make for good hearing and learning.

Translated by R.D. Hicks (1925)

Diogenes Laertius, *Lives of Eminent Philosophers* 9.14

extract of a letter written to Heraclitus

DEMADES

*c.*380–319BC
Athenian statesman and orator

1 Δημάδης ἐρωτηθεὶς τίς αὐτοῦ διδάσκαλος γεγονὼς εἴη, τὸ τῶν Ἀθηναίων, ἔφη, βῆμα, ἐμφαίνων ὅτι ἡ διὰ τῶν πραγμάτων ἐμπειρία κρείττων πάσης σοφιστικῆς διδασκαλίας ἐστίν

When asked who his teacher was, he replied, 'The Athenian public assembly', meaning that experience is better than any tuition.

Fragment 59 (de Falco)

2 ἔλεγε ἔαρ τοῦ δήμου τοὺς ἐφήβους

The young are the spring-time of a community.

Fragment 68 (de Falco)

3 ἐμποδίζει μου τὸν λόγον ὁ φόβος

Fear is a check upon my speech.

Translated by H.T. Riley (1872)

Fragment 87,5.4 (de Falco) – *On the Twelve Years**

DEMETRIUS

Late Hellenistic or Early Roman period
Author of a treatise on style

1 ὥσπερ τὰ θηρία συστρέψαντα ἑαυτὰ μάχεται, τοιαύτη τις ἂν εἴη συστροφὴ καὶ λόγου καθάπερ ἐσπειραμένου πρὸς δεινότητα

Just as a wild beast gathers itself for an attack, so should speech wind up force to increase intensity.

On Style 8

traditionally ascribed to Demetrius Phalereus; this is most unlikely to be right

2 σοφώτερον τὸ ἐν ὀλίγῳ πολλὴν διάνοιαν ἠθροῖσθαι

Skill in rhetoric consists in compressing a lot of meaning within a small compass.

On Style 9

3 θυμὸς γὰρ τέχνης οὐ δεῖται

Anger needs no artifice.

Translated by Doreen C. Innes (1995, based on W. Rhys Roberts)

On Style 27

4 τὰς μακρὰς ὁδοὺς αἱ συνεχεῖς καταγωγαὶ μικρὰς ποιοῦσιν, αἱ δ' ἐρημίαι κἂν ταῖς μικραῖς ὁδοῖς ἔμφασίν τινα ἔχουσι μήκους

Inns at frequent intervals make long journeys shorter, while desolate roads, even when the distances are short, give the impression of length.

Translated by Doreen C. Innes (1995, based on W. Rhys Roberts)

On Style 47

5 ἐν ταῖς ἑστιάσεσι τὰ ὀλίγα διαταχθέντα πως πολλὰ φαίνεται, οὕτω κἂν τοῖς λόγοις

Speech is like a banquet; a few dishes may be arranged to seem many.

Translated by Doreen C. Innes (1995, based on W. Rhys Roberts)

On Style 62

6 ἔστι γὰρ καὶ μεγάλα μικρῶς λέγοντα ἀπρεπὲς ποιεῖν τῷ πράγματι

Talking small on something big does not befit its import.

On Style 75

7 ᾤετο γὰρ καὶ τὴν ὑπόθεσιν αὐτὴν μέρος εἶναι τῆς ζωγραφικῆς τέχνης, ὥσπερ τοὺς μύθους τῶν ποιητῶν

He held that the theme itself was a part of the painter's skill, just as a plot was part of the poet's.

Translated by Doreen C. Innes (1995, based on W. Rhys Roberts)

On Style 76

of Nicias, an Athenian painter of the later 4th century, famed for his paintings of animals

8 ἔνια γὰρ μὴ ῥηθέντα μείζονα φαίνεται καὶ ὑπονοηθέντα μᾶλλον

Some things seem more significant when they are not openly expressed but only implied.

Translated by Doreen C. Innes (1995, based on W. Rhys Roberts)

On Style 103

9 σχεδὸν γὰρ εἰκόνα ἕκαστος τῆς ἑαυτοῦ ψυχῆς γράφει τὴν ἐπιστολήν. καὶ ἔστι μὲν καὶ ἐξ ἄλλου λόγου παντὸς ἰδεῖν τὸ ἦθος τοῦ γράφοντος, ἐξ οὐδενὸς δὲ οὕτως, ὡς ἐπιστολῆς

Everyone writes a letter in the virtual image of his soul. In every form of speech it is possible to see the writer's character, but never so clearly as in a letter.

Translated by Doreen C. Innes (1995, based on W. Rhys Roberts)

On Style 227

10 ὅλως, συνελόντι φράσαι, πᾶν τὸ εἶδος τοῦ Κυνικοῦ λόγου σαίνοντι ἅμα ἔοικέ τῳ καὶ δάκνοντι

The whole character of Cynic sayings suggests a dog that wags its tail as it bites.

On Style 261

DEMETRIUS PHALEREUS

*c.*350–*c.*283BC

Athenian peripatetic philosopher and statesman

1 ὅσον ἐν πολέμῳ δύνασθαι σίδηρον, τοσοῦτον ἐν πολίταις ἰσχύειν λόγον

All that force could achieve in war was won in politics by eloquence.

Translated by R.D. Hicks (1925)

Fragment 120 (Wehrli)

2 ἃ γὰρ οἱ φίλοι τοῖς βασιλεῦσιν οὐ θαρροῦσι παραινεῖν, ταῦτα ἐν τοῖς βιβλίοις γέγραπται

The advice which friends don't dare give to kings is found written in books.

Plutarch, *Sayings of Kings and Commanders* 189d

to King Ptolemy in whose service he died, in disgrace in spite of his outstanding cultural contribution

DEMOCRITUS

*c.*460–*c.*370BC
Philosopher from Abdera
see also Aelian 2; Marcus Aurelius 23

1 φρόνησις ... γίνεται δὲ ἐκ τοῦ φρονεῖν τρία ταῦτα· βουλεύεσθαι καλῶς, λέγειν ἀναμαρτήτως καὶ πράττειν ἃ δεῖ

From wisdom come these three: thinking straight, speaking well and doing what is right.

Fragment 2 (D-K)

2 μὴ πλέω προσάπτεσθαι τῶν δυνατῶν

Do not attempt what is beyond your capability.

Fragment 3 (D-K)

3 ἐτεῇ δὲ ἄτομα καὶ κενόν

In reality, there are but atoms and void.

Fragment 9 (D-K)

4 ἐτεῇ μέν νυν ὅτι οἷον ἕκαστον ἔστιν ἢ οὐκ ἔστιν οὐ συνίεμεν

Now in reality, we do not know what is and what is not.

Fragment 10 (D-K)

5 δύο φησὶν εἶναι γνώσεις· τὴν μὲν διὰ τῶν αἰσθήσεων τὴν δὲ διὰ τῆς διανοίας

There are two forms of knowledge, one through the senses, the other through the intellect.

Fragment 11 (D-K)

6 ποιητὴς δὲ ἅσσα μὲν ἂν γράφῃ μετ' ἐνθουσιασμοῦ καὶ ἱεροῦ πνεύματος, καλὰ κάρτα ἐστίν

Whatever a poet writes with enthusiasm and divine inspiration is sublime.

Fragment 18 (D-K)

7 ἰατρικὴ μὲν σώματος νόσους ἀκέεται, σοφίη δὲ ψυχὴν παθῶν ἀφαιρεῖται

Medicine heals diseases of the body, wisdom frees the soul from passions.

Translated by Kathleen Freeman (1948)

Fragment 31 (D-K)

8 ἡ φύσις καὶ ἡ διδαχὴ παραπλήσιόν ἐστι. καὶ γὰρ ἡ διδαχὴ μεταρυσμοῖ τὸν ἄνθρωπον, μεταρυσμοῦσα δὲ φυσιοποιεῖ

Nature and teaching are similar, for teaching changes a man's shape and nature acts by changing shapes.

Translated by Jonathan Barnes (1987)

Fragment 33 (D-K)

9 τῷ ἀνθρώπῳ μικρῷ κόσμῳ ὄντι

Man is a microcosm, a miniature universe.

Fragment 34 (D-K)

10 ὁ τὰ ψυχῆς ἀγαθὰ αἱρεόμενος τὰ θειότερα αἱρέεται· ὁ δὲ τὰ σκήνεος τὰ ἀνθρωπήϊα

Who chooses the goods of the soul chooses the more divine; who chooses those of the body chooses the more human.

Translated by Karl Popper (1977)

Fragment 37 (D-K)

11 καλὸν μὲν τὸν ἀδικέοντα κωλύειν· εἰ δὲ μή, μὴ ξυναδικέειν

It is noble to prevent the criminal; but if you cannot, do not join in wrongdoing.

Fragment 38 (D-K)

12 οὔτε σώμασιν οὔτε χρήμασιν εὐδαιμονοῦσιν ἄνθρωποι, ἀλλ' ὀρθοσύνῃ καὶ πολυφροσύνῃ

Men don't get happiness from bodies or from money, but by acting right and thinking wide.

Translated by Karl Popper (1977)

Fragment 40 (D-K)

13 μὴ διὰ φόβον, ἀλλὰ διὰ τὸ δέον ἀπέχεσθαι ἁμαρτημάτων

Refrain from evil not out of fear but because it is right.

Fragment 41 (D-K)

14 μέγα τὸ ἐν ξυμφορῇσι φρονεῖν ἃ δεῖ

It is great to think straight in times of trouble.

Fragment 42 (D-K)

15 ἀληθόμυθον χρὴ εἶναι, οὐ πολύλογον

Speak truthfully; no need for many words.

Fragment 44 (D-K)

16 ὁ ἀδικῶν τοῦ ἀδικουμένου κακοδαιμονέστερος

He who commits an act of injustice is more unhappy than he who suffers it.

Translated by Karl Popper (1977)

Fragment 45 (D-K)

17 μεγαλοψυχίη τὸ φέρειν πραέως πλημμέλειαν

Magnanimity is bearing offence calmly.

Fragment 46 (D-K)

18 νόμῳ καὶ ἄρχοντι καὶ τῷ σοφωτέρῳ εἴκειν κόσμιον

Obey the law, yield to the ruler and the wise.

Fragment 47 (D-K)

19 μωμεομένων φλαύρων ὁ ἀγαθὸς οὐ ποιεῖται λόγον

Pay no heed to the censure of the mean.

Fragment 48 (D-K)

20 χαλεπὸν ἄρχεσθαι ὑπὸ χερείονος

It is hard to be ruled by an inferior.

Translated by Jonathan Barnes (1987)

Fragment 49 (D-K)

21 ὁ χρημάτων παντελῶς ἥσσων οὐκ ἄν ποτε εἴη δίκαιος

A man completely enslaved to money will never be just.

Translated by Jonathan Barnes (1987)

Fragment 50 (D-K)

22 ἰσχυρότερος ἐς πειθὼ λόγος πολλαχῇ γίνεται χρυσοῦ

In power of persuasion, reasoning is far stronger than gold.

Translated by Kathleen Freeman (1948)

Fragment 51 (D-K)

23 τὸν οἰόμενον νοῦν ἔχειν ὁ νουθετέων ματαιοπονεῖ

It is lost labour to advise those who 'know it all'.

Fragment 52 (D-K)

24 πολλοὶ δρῶντες τὰ αἴσχιστα λόγους ἀρίστους ἀσκέουσιν

Many perform the foulest deeds and practise the fairest words.

Translated by Jonathan Barnes (1987)

Fragment 53a (D-K)

25 ἔργα καὶ πρήξιας ἀρετῆς, οὐ λόγους, ζηλοῦν χρεών

Envy the deeds and actions of virtue, not the words.

Fragment 55 (D-K)

26 τὰ καλὰ γνωρίζουσι καὶ ζηλοῦσιν οἱ εὐφυέες πρὸς αὐτά

Noble deeds are recognized and emulated by those of natural virtue.

Fragment 56 (D-K)

27 κτηνέων μὲν εὐγένεια ἡ τοῦ σκήνεος εὐσθένεια, ἀνθρώπων δὲ ἡ τοῦ ἤθεος εὐτροπίη

For beasts, good breeding consists in bodily strength; for man, in grace of character.

Translated by Jonathan Barnes (1987)

Fragment 57 (D-K)

28 ἐλπίδες αἱ τῶν ὀρθὰ φρονεόντων ἐφικταί, αἱ δὲ τῶν ἀξυνέτων ἀδύνατοι

The hopes of the wise are attainable, those of the witless vain.

Fragment 58 (D-K)

29 κρέσσον τὰ οἰκήϊα ἐλέγχειν ἁμαρτήματα ἢ τὰ ὀθνεῖα

Rather examine your own faults than those of others.

Fragment 60 (D-K)

30 οἷσιν ὁ τρόπος ἐστὶν εὔτακτος, τούτοισι καὶ ὁ βίος συντέτακται

If your character is orderly your life will be well-ordered too.

Fragment 61 (D-K)

31 ἀγαθὸν οὐ τὸ μὴ ἀδικεῖν, ἀλλὰ τὸ μηδὲ ἐθέλειν

Virtue consists not in avoiding wrong-doing, but in having no desire for it.

Fragment 62 (D-K)

32 εὐλογέειν ἐπὶ καλοῖς ἔργμασι καλόν· τὸ γὰρ ἐπὶ φλαύροισι κιβδήλου καὶ ἀπατεῶνος ἔργον

To praise someone for noble deeds is noble; to praise bad deeds is the mark of a cheat and a deceiver.

Translated by Jonathan Barnes (1987)

Fragment 63 (D-K)

33 πολλοὶ πολυμαθέες νοῦν οὐκ ἔχουσιν

Many, though widely read, possess no sense.

Fragment 64 (D-K)

34 πολυνοΐην, οὐ πολυμαθίην ἀσκέειν

Practise the intellect, not excessive learning.

Fragment 65 (D-K)

35 προβουλεύεσθαι κρεῖσσον πρὸ τῶν πράξεων ἢ μετανοεῖν

It is better to plan before acting than to repent later.

Fragment 66 (D-K)

36 μὴ πᾶσιν, ἀλλὰ τοῖς δοκίμοισι πιστεύειν

Put faith not in the many, only the trustworthy.

Translated in Liddell & Scott

Fragment 67 (D-K)

37 δόκιμος ἀνὴρ καὶ ἀδόκιμος οὐκ ἐξ ὧν πράσσει μόνον, ἀλλὰ καὶ ἐξ ὧν βούλεται

The worthy and unworthy are known not only by their deeds, but also by their desires.

Fragment 68 (D-K)

38 ἀνθρώποις πᾶσι τωὐτὸν ἀγαθὸν καὶ ἀληθές· ἡδὺ δὲ ἄλλῳ ἄλλο

Goodness and truth are the same for all men; but pleasure differs from man to man.

Fragment 69 (D-K)

39 ἡδοναὶ ἄκαιροι τίκτουσιν ἀηδίας

Untimely pleasures produce aversion.

Fragment 71 (D-K)

40 αἱ περί τι σφοδραὶ ὀρέξεις τυφλοῦσιν εἰς τἄλλα τὴν ψυχήν

Violent desire for one thing blinds the soul to everything else.

Fragment 72 (D-K)

41 κρέσσον ἄρχεσθαι τοῖς ἀνοήτοισιν ἢ ἄρχειν

It is better for fools to be ruled than to rule.

Translated by Kathleen Freeman (1948)

Fragment 75 (D-K)

42 νηπίοισιν οὐ λόγος, ἀλλὰ ξυμφορὴ γίνεται διδάσκαλος

For the foolish, not reason but misfortune is the teacher.

Fragment 76 (D-K)

43 αἰσχρὸν τὰ ὀθνεῖα πολυπραγμονέοντα ἀγνοεῖν τὰ οἰκήϊα

It's none of your business to meddle in the affairs of others; rather look after your own.

Fragment 80 (D-K)

44 τὸ ἀεὶ μέλλειν ἀτελέας ποιεῖ τὰς πρήξιας

Constant procrastination leaves the work undone.

Fragment 81 (D-K)

45 κίβδηλοι καὶ ἀγαθοφανέες οἱ λόγῳ μὲν ἅπαντα, ἔργῳ δὲ οὐδὲν ἔρδοντες

Cheats and hypocrites are those who promise everything and do nothing.

Translated by Jonathan Barnes (1987)

Fragment 82 (D-K)

46 ἁμαρτίης αἰτίη ἡ ἀμαθίη τοῦ κρέσσονος

The cause of error is ignorance of what is better.

Translated by Jonathan Barnes (1987)

Fragment 83 (D-K)

47 ἑωυτὸν πρῶτον αἰσχύνεσθαι χρεὼν τὸν αἰσχρὰ ἔρδοντα

One who does shameful deeds should first be ashamed of himself.

Translated by Jonathan Barnes (1987)

Fragment 84 (D-K)

48 πλεονεξίη τὸ πάντα λέγειν, μηδὲν δὲ ἐθέλειν ἀκούειν

It is greed to do all the talking and not be willing to listen.

Translated by Kathleen Freeman (1948)

Fragment 86 (D-K)

49 τὸν φαῦλον παραφυλάττειν δεῖ, μὴ καιροῦ λάβηται

Guard against bad men lest they seize their opportunity.

Fragment 87 (D-K)

50 ὁ φθονέων ἑωυτὸν ὡς ἐχθρὸν λυπέει

The envious man torments himself like

an enemy.

Translated by Kathleen Freeman (1948)

Fragment 88 (D-K)

51 ἡ τῶν συγγενῶν ἔχθρη τῆς τῶν ὀθνείων χαλεπωτέρη μάλα

Enmity among kin is far worse than enmity among strangers.

Translated by Jonathan Barnes (1987)

Fragment 90 (D-K)

52 μὴ ὕποπτος πρὸς ἅπαντας, ἀλλ' εὐλαβὴς γίνου καὶ ἀσφαλής

Be not suspicious towards everyone, be cautious and firm.

Fragment 91 (D-K)

53 μικραὶ χάριτες ἐν καιρῷ μέγισται τοῖς λαμβάνουσι

Small favours at the right time are huge to those who receive them.

Fragment 94 (D-K)

54 χαριστικὸς οὐχ ὁ βλέπων πρὸς τὴν ἀμοιβήν, ἀλλ' ὁ εὖ δρᾶν προῃρημένος

The generous man is he who does not look for a return, but who does good from choice.

Translated by Kathleen Freeman (1948)

Fragment 96 (D-K)

55 πολλοὶ δοκέοντες εἶναι φίλοι οὐκ εἰσί, καὶ οὐ δοκέοντες εἰσίν

Many who seem to be friends are not; whilst many who don't seem so, are.

Fragment 97 (D-K)

56 ἑνὸς φιλίη ξυνετοῦ κρέσσων ἀξυνέτων πάντων

The friendship of one intelligent man is better than that of many fools.

Fragment 98 (D-K)

57 ζῆν οὐκ ἄξιος, ὅτῳ μηδὲ εἷς ἐστι χρηστὸς φίλος

Life is not worth living for the man who has not even one good friend.

Translated by Kathleen Freeman (1948)

Fragment 99 (D-K)

58 ὅτεῳ μὴ διαμένουσιν ἐπὶ πολλὸν οἱ πειραθέντες φίλοι, δύστροπος

A man who stands to lose his well-tried friends must surely be bad-tempered.

Fragment 100 (D-K)

59 καλὸν ἐν παντὶ τὸ ἴσον· ὑπερβολὴ δὲ καὶ ἔλλειψις οὔ μοι δοκέει

Equality is everywhere noble: excess and deficiency do not to me seem so.

Translated by Jonathan Barnes (1987)

Fragment 102 (D-K)

60 οὐδ' ὑφ' ἑνὸς φιλέεσθαι δοκέει μοι ὁ φιλέων μηδένα

The man who loves nobody is, I think, loved by no one.

Translated by Kathleen Freeman (1948)

Fragment 103 (D-K)

61 σώματος κάλλος ζῳῶδες, ἢν μὴ νοῦς ὑπῇ

Physical beauty is an animal attribute if there is no sense behind it.

Fragment 105 (D-K)

62 ἐν εὐτυχίῃ φίλον εὑρεῖν εὔπορον, ἐν δὲ δυστυχίῃ πάντων ἀπορώτατον

It is easy to find a friend in prosperity, but in adversity nothing is harder.

Fragment 106 (D-K)

63 ὑπὸ γυναικὸς ἄρχεσθαι ὕβρις εἴη ἂν ἀνδρὶ ἐσχάτη

To be ruled by a woman is the ultimate outrage for a man.

Translated by Kathleen Freeman (1948)

Fragment 111 (D-K)

64 θείου νοῦ τὸ ἀεί τι διαλογίζεσθαι καλόν

It is the mark of a divine intellect to be always contemplating something noble.

Translated by Kathleen Freeman (1948)

Fragment 112 (D-K)

65 βέλτερον ὑφ' ἑτέρου ἢ ὑφ' ἑαυτοῦ ἐπαινέεσθαι

It is better to be praised by others than by oneself.

Translated by Jonathan Barnes (1987)

Fragment 114 (D-K)

66 ὁ κόσμος σκηνή, ὁ βίος πάροδος· ἦλθες, εἶδες, απῆλθες

The world is a stage, life our passage: you come, you see, and you depart.

Fragment 115.3 (D-K)

cf. Palladas 7 and Julius Caesar 4; cf. also Shakespeare, As You Like It *2.7.139: 'All the world's a stage / and all the men and women merely players'*

67 ὁ κόσμος ἀλλοίωσις, ὁ βίος ὑπόληψις

The universe is change; our life assumptions.

Fragment 115.5 (D-K)

quoted by Marcus Aurelius, Τὰ εἰς ἑαυτόν *4.3*

68 ἐτεῇ δὲ οὐδὲν ἴδμεν· ἐν βυθῷ γὰρ ἡ ἀλήθεια

We know nothing for certain; for truth is hidden in the deep.

Fragment 117 (D-K)

69 Δημόκριτος γοῦν αὐτός, ὥς φασιν, ἔλεγε βούλεσθαι μᾶλλον μίαν εὑρεῖν αἰτιολογίαν ἢ τὴν Περσῶν οἱ βασιλείαν γενέσθαι

Democritus, so they say, used to claim he would rather discover a single causal explanation than become king of the Persians.

Translated by Jonathan Barnes (1987)

Fragment 118 (D-K)

70 ἄνθρωποι τύχης εἴδωλον ἐπλάσαντο πρόφασιν ἰδίης ἀβουλίης

Men fashioned the image of chance as an excuse for their own indecision.

Fragment 119.9 (D-K)

71 τὰ δὲ πλεῖστα ἐν βίῳ εὐξύνετος ὀξυδερκείη κατιθύνει

But quickness of apprehension and clear-sightedness direct most things in life.

Fragment 119.10 (D-K)

72 νόμῳ χροιή, νόμῳ γλυκύ, νόμῳ πικρόν, ἐτεῇ δ' ἄτομα καὶ κενόν

By convention there is colour, by convention sweetness, by convention bitterness; but in reality there are only atoms and void.

Fragment 125 D-K)

73 λόγος γὰρ ἔργου σκιή

Speech is the shadow of action.

Translated by Kathleen Freeman (1948)

Fragment 145 (D-K)

74 ἐν γὰρ ξυνῷ ἰχθύι ἄκανθαι οὐκ ἔνεισιν

In a shared fish there are no bones.

Translated by Kathleen Freeman (1948)

Fragment 151 (D-K)

no offence where the partner shares the fault

75 τήν τε πολιτικὴν τέχνην μεγίστην οὖσαν ἐκδιδάσκεσθαι καὶ τοὺς πόνους διώκειν, ἀφ' ὧν τὰ μεγάλα καὶ λαμπρὰ γίνονται τοῖς ἀνθρώποις

Learn thoroughly the art of statesmanship which is the greatest, and pursue its toils, from which men win great and brilliant prizes.

Translated by Kathleen Freeman (1948)

Fragment 157 (D-K)

76 μὴ πάντα ἐπίστασθαι προθυμέο, μὴ πάντων ἀμαθὴς γένῃ

Do not be eager to know everything lest you become ignorant of everything.

Translated by Jonathan Barnes (1987)

Fragment 169 (D-K)

77 εὐδαιμονίη ψυχῆς καὶ κακοδαιμονίη

Happiness, like unhappiness, is a property of the soul.

Translated by Kathleen Freeman (1948)

Fragment 170 (D-K)

78 εὐδαιμονίη οὐκ ἐν βοσκήμασιν οἰκεῖ οὐδὲ ἐν χρυσῷ

Happiness does not dwell in herds, nor yet in gold.

Translated by Jonathan Barnes (1987)

Fragment 171 (D-K)

79 ὁκόσα κακὰ καὶ βλαβερὰ καὶ ἀνωφελέα ... διὰ νοῦ τυφλότητα καὶ ἀγνωμοσύνην

Men bring upon themselves all that is bad and harmful and useless through their own blindness and folly.

Fragment 175 (D-K)

80 πάντων κάκιστον ἡ εὐπετείη παιδεῦσαι τὴν νεότητα· αὕτη γάρ ἐστιν ἣ τίκτει τὰς ἡδονὰς ταύτας, ἐξ ὧν ἡ κακότης γίνεται

Indulgence is the worst of all things with regard to the education of youth; for it is this which gives birth to the pleasures from which badness originates.

Translated by Jonathan Barnes (1987)

Fragment 178 (D-K)

81 ἡ παιδεία εὐτυχοῦσι μέν ἐστι κόσμος, ἀτυχοῦσι δὲ καταφύγιον

Education is an ornament for the fortunate, a refuge for the unfortunate.

Translated by Jonathan Barnes (1987)

Fragment 180 (D-K)

82 κρείσσων ἐπ' ἀρετὴν φανεῖται προτροπῇ χρώμενος καὶ λόγου πειθοῖ ἤπερ νόμῳ καὶ ἀνάγκῃ

Exhortation and persuasion is a stronger inducement to virtue than law and necessity.

Fragment 181 (D-K)

83 χρόνος γὰρ οὐ διδάσκει φρονεῖν

It is not time that teaches good sense.

Translated by Jonathan Barnes (1987)

Fragment 183 (D-K)

84 φαύλων ὁμιλίη συνεχὴς ἕξιν κακίης συναύξει

Frequent association with the wicked increases a disposition to vice.

Translated by Jonathan Barnes (1987)

Fragment 184 (D-K)

85 ὁμοφροσύνη φιλίην ποιεῖ

Accord of mind and spirit is the basis of friendship.

Fragment 186 (D-K)

86 ψυχῆς τελεότης σκήνεος μοχθηρίην ὀρθοῖ

Perfection of the soul puts right the faults of the body.

Translated by Karl Popper (1977)

Fragment 187.3 (D-K)

87 σκήνεος μοχθηρίην ὀρθοῖ, σκήνεος δὲ ἰσχὺς ἄνευ λογισμοῦ ψυχὴν οὐδέν τι ἀμείνω τίθησιν

Physical strength without intelligence does nothing to improve the mind.

Translated by Kathleen Freeman (1948)

Fragment 187.4 (D-K)

88 φαύλων ἔργων καὶ τοὺς λόγους παραιτητέον

Avoid even speaking of evil deeds.

Translated by Jonathan Barnes (1987)

Fragment 190 (D-K)

89 ἐπὶ τοῖς δυνατοῖς οὖν δεῖ ἔχειν τὴν γνώμην καὶ τοῖς παρεοῦσιν ἀρκέεσθαι τῶν μὲν ζηλουμένων καὶ θαυμαζομένων ὀλίγην μνήμην ἔχοντα

You must set your judgement on the possible and be satisfied with what you have, giving little thought to things that are envied and admired, and not dwelling on them in your mind.

Translated by Jonathan Barnes (1987)

Fragment 191 (D-K)

90 αἱ μεγάλαι τέρψεις ἀπὸ τοῦ θεᾶσθαι τὰ καλὰ τῶν ἔργων γίνονται

Great pleasure comes from contemplating noble deeds.

Fragment 194 (D-K)

91 εἴδωλα ἐσθῆτι καὶ κόσμῳ διαπρεπέα πρὸς θεωρίην, ἀλλὰ καρδίης κενεά

Images conspicuous for their dress and ornament, empty of heart.

Translated by Kathleen Freeman (1948)

Fragment 195 (D-K)

92 λήθη τῶν ἰδίων κακῶν θρασύτητα γεννᾷ

Forgetfulness of one's own ills breeds insolence.

Fragment 196 (D-K)

93 ἀνοήμονες ῥυσμοῦνται τοῖς τῆς τύχης κέρδεσιν, οἱ δὲ τῶν τοιῶνδε δαήμονες τοῖς τῆς σοφίης

Fools are shaped by the gifts of fortune, those with understanding by the gifts of wisdom.

Fragment 197 (D-K)

94 ἀνοήμονες βιοῦσιν οὐ τερπόμενοι βιοτῇ

Fools live with no enjoyment in life.

Fragment 200 (D-K)

95 ἀνοήμονες δηναιότητος ὀρέγονται οὐ τερπόμενοι δηναιότητι

Fools desire longevity but do not enjoy longevity.

Translated by Jonathan Barnes (1987)

Fragment 201 (D-K)

96 ἀνοήμονες τῶν ἀπεόντων ὀρέγονται τὰ δὲ παρεόντα ... ἀμαλδύνουσιν

Fools yearn for what is gone and squander what they have.

Fragment 202 (D-K)

97 ἀνοήμονες ζωῆς ὀρέγονται θάνατον δεδοικότες

Fools long for life because they are in fear of death.

Fragment 205 (D-K)

98 ἡδονὴν οὐ πᾶσαν, ἀλλὰ τὴν ἐπὶ τῷ καλῷ αἱρεῖσθαι χρεών

Do not seek every pleasure; choose only that which leads to beauty.

Fragment 207 (D-K)

99 πατρὸς σωφροσύνη μέγιστον τέκνοις παράγγελμα

A father's prudence is the greatest precept for his children.

Fragment 208 (D-K)

100 ἡμερήσιοι ὕπνοι σώματος ὄχλησιν ἢ ψυχῆς ἀδημοσύνην ἢ ἀργίην ἢ ἀπαιδευσίην σημαίνουσι

Sleeping during the day indicates a distressed body or a troubled mind or idleness or lack of education.

Fragment 212 (D-K)

101 ἀνδρείη τὰς ἄτας μικρὰς ἔρδει

Courage makes misfortunes seem small.

Translated by Jonathan Barnes (1987)

Fragment 213 (D-K)

102 ἔνιοι δὲ πολίων μὲν δεσπόζουσι, γυναιξὶ δὲ δουλεύουσιν

Some men rule cities and are slaves to women.

Translated by Jonathan Barnes (1987)

Fragment 214 (D-K)

103 δίκης κῦδος γνώμης θάρσος καὶ ἀθαμβίη, ἀδικίης δὲ δεῖμα ξυμφορῆς τέρμα

The glory of justice is confidence of judgement and imperturbability; the prize of injustice is fear of disaster.

Translated by Jonathan Barnes (1987)

Fragment 215 (D-K)

104 πλοῦτος ἀπὸ κακῆς ἐργασίης περιγινόμενος ἐπιφανέστερον τὸ ὄνειδος κέκτηται

Riches derived from evil deeds make the disgrace more conspicuous.

Fragment 218 (D-K)

105 μέζονες γὰρ ὀρέξεις μέζονας ἐνδείας ποιεῦσιν

Greater desires create greater needs.

Translated by Jonathan Barnes (1987)

Fragment 219 (D-K)

106 κακὰ κέρδεα ζημίαν ἀρετῆς φέρει

Evil gains bring loss of virtue.

Translated by Jonathan Barnes (1987)

Fragment 220 (D-K)

107 ἐλπὶς κακοῦ κέρδεος ἀρχὴ ζημίης

Hope of evil gain is the beginning of loss.

Translated by Jonathan Barnes (1987)

Fragment 221 (D-K)

108 ἡ τέκνοις ἄγαν χρημάτων συναγωγὴ πρόφασίς ἐστι φιλαργυρίης

Accumulation of wealth 'for your children' is a pretext of avarice.

Fragment 222 (D-K)

109 ἡ τοῦ πλέονος ἐπιθυμίη τὸ παρεὸν ἀπόλλυσι

He who desires more loses what he has.

Fragment 224 (D-K)

110 οἰκήιον ἐλευθερίης παρρησίη

Freedom of speech is the mark of liberty.

Fragment 226 (D-K)

111 οἱ φειδωλοὶ τὸν τῆς μελίσσης οἶτον ἔχουσιν ἐργαζόμενοι ὡς ἀεὶ βιωσόμενοι

Misers have the fate of bees: they work as if they were going to live for ever.

Translated by Kathleen Freeman (1948)

Fragment 227 (D-K)

112 βίος ἀνεόρταστος μακρὴ ὁδὸς ἀπανδόκευτος

A life without holidays is a long road without taverns.

Fragment 230 (D-K)

113 εὐγνώμων ὁ μὴ λυπεόμενος ἐφ' οἷσιν οὐκ ἔχει, ἀλλὰ χαίρων ἐφ' οἷσιν ἔχει

A sensible man does not grieve for what he has not, but enjoys what he has.

Fragment 231 (D-K)

114 τῶν ἡδέων τὰ σπανιώτατα γινόμενα μάλιστα τέρπει

Rarest pleasures give the greatest joy.

Fragment 232 (D-K)

115 εἴ τις ὑπερβάλλοι τὸ μέτριον, τὰ ἐπιτερπέστατα ἀτερπέστατα ἂν γίγνοιτο

If one oversteps the due measure, the most pleasurable things become the most unpleasant.

Translated by Kathleen Freeman (1948)

Fragment 233 (D-K)

116 ὑγιείην εὐχῇσι παρὰ θεῶν αἰτέονται ἄνθρωποι, τὴν δὲ ταύτης δύναμιν ἐν ἑαυτοῖς ἔχοντες οὐκ ἴσασιν· ἀκρασίῃ δὲ τἀναντία πρήσσοντες αὐτοὶ προδόται τῆς ὑγείης τῇσιν ἐπιθυμίῃσιν γίνονται

Men ask for health in their prayers to the gods; they do not realize that the power to achieve it lies in themselves: lacking self-control, they perform contrary actions and betray health to their desires.

Translated by Jonathan Barnes (1987)

Fragment 234 (D-K)

117 θυμῷ μάχεσθαι χαλεπόν

It is hard to resist desire.

Fragment 236 (D-K)

118 οἱ ἑκούσιοι πόνοι τὴν τῶν ἀκουσίων ὑπομονὴν ἐλαφροτέρην παρασκευάζουσι

Labour performed willingly renders endurable what is done unwillingly.

Fragment 240 (D-K)

119 πλέονες ἐξ ἀσκήσιος ἀγαθοὶ γίνονται ἢ ἀπὸ φύσιος

More men become good through practice than by nature.

Translated by Kathleen Freeman (1948)

Fragment 242 (D-K)

120 τῆς ἡσυχίης πάντες οἱ πόνοι ἡδίονες

All labour is better than inactivity.

Fragment 243 (D-K)

121 φθόνος γὰρ στάσιος ἀρχὴν ἀπεργάζεται

Envy creates the beginning of strife.

Translated by Kathleen Freeman (1948)

Fragment 245 (D-K)

122 ξενιτείη βίου αὐτάρκειαν διδάσκει

Life in a foreign land teaches self-sufficiency.

Translated by Kathleen Freeman (1948)

Fragment 246 (D-K)

123 ἀνδρὶ σοφῷ πᾶσα γῆ βατή· ψυχῆς γὰρ ἀγαθῆς πατρὶς ὁ ξύμπας κόσμος

The whole world is home to a wise man with an upright spirit.

Fragment 247 (D-K)

124 ὁ νόμος βούλεται μὲν εὐεργετεῖν βίον ἀνθρώπων, δύναται δέ, ὅταν αὐτοὶ βούλωνται πάσχειν εὖ· τοῖσι γὰρ πειθομένοισι τὴν ἰδίην ἀρετὴν ἐνδείκνυται

The purpose of law is to benefit men's lives; it can do so when they themselves wish to be benefited; for those who obey, it indicates their own virtue.

Fragment 248 (D-K)

125 στάσις ἐμφύλιος ἐς ἑκάτερα κακόν· καὶ γὰρ νικέουσι καὶ ἡσσωμένοις ὁμοίη φθορή

Civil strife is equally harmful to both sides; for the winner and the loser, the destruction is the same.

Fragment 249 (D-K)

126 ἀπὸ ὁμονοίης τὰ μεγάλα ἔργα

From concord come great deeds.

Translated by Jonathan Barnes (1987)

Fragment 250 (D-K)

127 ἡ ἐν δημοκρατίῃ πενίη τῆς παρὰ τοῖς δυνάστῃσι καλεομένης εὐδαιμονίης τοσοῦτόν ἐστι αἱρετωτέρη, ὁκόσον ἐλευθερίη δουλείης

Poverty in democracy is preferable to prosperity under tyranny – as freedom is preferable to slavery.

Fragment 251 (D-K)

128 πόλις γὰρ εὖ ἀγομένη μεγίστη ὄρθωσίς ἐστι

A well-run state is the best agency for prosperity.

Fragment 252 (D-K)

129 οἱ κακοὶ ἰόντες ἐς τὰς τιμὰς ὁκόσῳ ἂν μᾶλλον ἀνάξιοι ἐόντες ἴωσι, τοσούτῳ μᾶλλον ἀνακηδέες γίγνονται καὶ ἀφροσύνης καὶ θράσεος πίμπλανται

When bad men gain office, the more unworthy they are the more heedless they become and the more they are filled with folly and recklessness.

Translated by Jonathan Barnes (1987)

Fragment 254 (D-K)

130 ἀδικουμένοισι τιμωρεῖν κατὰ δύναμιν χρὴ

Succour the ill-treated as best you can.

Fragment 261 (D-K)

131 φόβος κολακείην μὲν ἐργάζεται, εὔνοιαν δὲ οὐκ ἔχει

Fear produces flattery, it does not gain goodwill.

Translated by Jonathan Barnes (1987)

Fragment 268 (D-K)

132 τόλμα πρήξιος ἀρχή, τύχη δὲ τέλεος κυρίη

Boldness is the beginning of action: fortune controls the end.

Translated by Jonathan Barnes (1987)

Fragment 269 (D-K)

133 ὡς γαμβροῦ ὁ μὲν ἐπιτυχὼν εὗρεν υἱόν, ὁ δὲ ἀποτυχὼν ἀπώλεσε καὶ θυγατέρα

One who is lucky in his son-in-law gains a son, one who is unlucky loses a daughter.

Translated by Jonathan Barnes (1987)

Fragment 272 (D-K)

134 κόσμος ὀλιγομυθίη γυναικί

Speaking little is a woman's ornament.

Fragment 274a (D-K)

135 καλὸν δὲ καὶ κόσμου λιτότης

Simplicity in adornment is finest.

Fragment 274b (D-K)

136 τεκνοτροφίη σφαλερόν· τὴν μὲν γὰρ ἐπιτυχίην ἀγῶνος μεστὴν καὶ φροντίδος κέκτηται, τὴν δὲ ἀποτυχίην ἀνυπέρθετον ἑτέρῃ ὀδύνῃ

The rearing of children is full of pitfalls. Success is attended by strife and care, failure means grief beyond all others.

Translated by Kathleen Freeman (1948)

Fragment 275 (D-K)

137 τοῖς παισὶ μάλιστα χρὴ τῶν ἀνυστῶν δατεῖσθαι τὰ χρήματα, καὶ ἅμα ἐπιμέλεσθαι αὐτῶν, μή τι ἀτηρὸν ποιέωσι διὰ χειρὸς ἔχοντες· ἅμα μὲν γὰρ πολλὸν φειδότεροι γίγνονται ἐς τὰ χρήματα καὶ προθυμότεροι κτᾶσθαι, καὶ ἀγωνίζονται ἀλλήλοισιν

Divide your property among your children as far as possible, and ensure that they avoid mischief when they have it in their hands. They thus become more thrifty and more eager to acquire wealth, competing with one another.

Fragment 279 (D-K)

138 ἔξεστιν οὐ πολλὰ τῶν σφετέρων ἀναλώσαντας παιδεῦσαί τε τοὺς παῖδας καὶ τεῖχός τε καὶ σωτηρίην περιβαλέσθαι τοῖς τε χρήμασι καὶ τοῖς σώμασιν αὐτῶν

It is possible, without spending much money, to educate your children and to thus build a wall and a safeguard about their property and their persons.

Fragment 280 (D-K)

139 χρημάτων χρῆσις ξὺν νόῳ μὲν χρήσιμον εἰς τὸ ἐλευθέριον εἶναι καὶ δημωφελέα

Money when used with sense promotes generosity and charity.

Translated by Jonathan Barnes (1987)

Fragment 282 (D-K)

140 ἢν μὴ πολλῶν ἐπιθυμέῃς, τὰ ὀλίγα τοι πολλὰ δόξει· σμικρὰ γὰρ ὄρεξις πενίην ἰσοσθενέα πλούτῳ ποιέει

If your desires are not great, a little will seem much to you; small desires make poverty equal to riches.

Fragment 284 (D-K)

141 εὐτυχὴς ὁ ἐπὶ μετρίοισι χρήμασιν εὐθυμεόμενος, δυστυχὴς δὲ ὁ ἐπὶ πολλοῖσι δυσθυμεόμενος

Happy is he with moderate needs, miserable he with plenty.

Fragment 286 (D-K)

142 ἀπορίη ξυνὴ τῆς ἑκάστου χαλεπωτέρη· οὐ γὰρ ὑπολείπεται ἐλπὶς ἐπικουρίης

Shared poverty is harder than private poverty; for no hope of relief remains.

Translated by Jonathan Barnes (1987)

Fragment 287 (D-K)

143 οὐκ ἔστιν οὕτως ἀσφαλὴς πλούτου πυλεών, ὃν οὐκ ἀνοίγει τύχης καιρός

There is no gate to wealth secure enough to withstand the opening of fate.

Fragment 288 (D-K)

144 λύπην ἀδέσποτον ψυχῆς ναρκώσης λογισμῷ ἔκκρουε

Drive out by reasoning the ungovernable grief of your numbed soul.

Fragment 290 (D-K)

145 πενίην ἐπιεικέως φέρειν σωφρονέοντος

To bear poverty well is the sign of a sensible man.

Translated by Kathleen Freeman (1948)

Fragment 291 (D-K)

146 ἰσχὺς καὶ εὐμορφίη νεότητος ἀγαθά, γήραος δὲ σωφροσύνη ἄνθος

The good things of youth are strength and beauty; moderation is the flower of age.

Fragment 294 (D-K)

147 ἀρχὰς εἶναι τῶν ὅλων ἀτόμους καὶ κενόν

In the beginning there were atoms and void.

Testimonies, Fragment 1.97 (D-K)

148 μηδέν τε ἐκ τοῦ μὴ ὄντος γίνεσθαι μηδὲ εἰς τὸ μὴ ὂν φθείρεσθαι

Nothing comes of nothing and nothing disintegrates into nothing.

Testimonies, Fragment 1.98 (D-K)

cf. the Latin 'ex nihilo nihil'

149 ἀπείρους τε εἶναι κόσμους καὶ γενητοὺς καὶ φθαρτούς

There are countless worlds, both born and perishable.

Testimonies, Fragment 1.98 (D-K)

150 πάντα τε κατ' ἀνάγκην γίνεσθαι, τῆς δίνης αἰτίας οὔσης τῆς γενέσεως πάντων, ἣν ἀνάγκην λέγει

All things happen by virtue of necessity; since the vortex is the cause of the creation of all things, this too he calls necessity.

Testimonies, Fragment 1.105 (D-K)

151 ἔλεγε δὲ ὡς ἀεὶ κινουμένων τῶν ὄντων ἐν τῷ κενῷ· ἀπείρους δὲ εἶναι κόσμους καὶ μεγέθει διαφέροντας. ἐν τισὶ δὲ μὴ εἶναι ἥλιον μηδὲ σελήνην, ἐν τισὶ δὲ μείζω τῶν παρ' ἡμῖν καὶ ἐν τισὶ πλείω

He said that heavenly bodies were continuously moving in the void; that there is an infinite number of worlds, different in size; in some there is no sun or moon, in some these are larger than ours and in some there are more.

Testimonies, Fragment 40 (D-K)

152 οὐσίας ἀπείρους τὸ πλῆθος ἀτόμους τε κἀδιαφόρους ... ἐν τῷ κενῷ φέρεσθαι διεσπαρμένας· ὅταν δὲ πελάσωσιν ἀλλήλαις ἢ συμπέσωσιν ἢ περιπλακῶσι, φαίνεσθαι τῶν ἀθροιζομένων τὸ μὲν ὕδωρ τὸ δὲ πῦρ τὸ δὲ φυτὸν τὸ δ' ἄνθρωπον

Substances infinite in quantity, indivisible and indestructible, are carried about scattered in the void. When they approach one another or collide or are entangled the aggregates appear as water or fire or plants or men.

Translated by Jonathan Barnes (1987)

Testimonies, Fragment 57 (D-K)

153 τοῦ γαλαξίου ἄλλοι δὲ ἐκ μικρῶν πάνυ καὶ πεπυκνωμένων καὶ ἡμῖν δοκούντων ἡνῶσθαι διὰ τὸ διάστημα τὸ ἀπὸ τοῦ οὐρανοῦ ἐπὶ τὴν γῆν ἀστέρων αὐτὸν εἶναί φασιν, ὡς εἴ τις ἅλασι λεπτοῖς καὶ πολλοῖς καταπάσειέ τι

They say that the galaxy is made up of small and closely packed stars which appear to us united because of their great distance from the earth, as an object besprinkled with fine grains of salt.

Testimonies, Fragment 91 (D-K)

DEMOSTHENES

384–322BC

Athenian orator

see also Diogenes Cynic 24; Menander 173; Phocion 6; Pytheas 1

1 καὶ ὅλως ἄπιστον ... ταῖς πολιτείαις ἡ τυραννίς

Despotism, altogether mistrusted by free commonwealths.

Translated in Liddell & Scott

First Olynthiac 1.5

2 πρὸς γὰρ τὸ τελευταῖον ἐκβὰν ἕκαστον τῶν πρὶν ὑπαρξάντων κρίνεται

Everything in the past is judged by the outcome of the last event.

First Olynthiac 1.11

cf. the Latin 'finis coronat opus'

3 καὶ τὸ προΐεσθαι καθ' ἕκαστον ἀεί τι τῶν πραγμάτων ὡς ἀλυσιτελές

What an expensive thing it is to squander your interests one by one.

Translated by J.H. Vince (1930)

First Olynthiac 1.14

4 οἱ δανειζόμενοι ῥᾳδίως ἐπὶ τοῖς μεγάλοις τόκοις μικρὸν εὐπορήσαντες χρόνον ὕστερον καὶ τῶν ἀρχαίων ἀπέστησαν

People who borrow money recklessly at high interest enjoy temporary relief, only to forfeit their estates in the end.

First Olynthiac 1.15

5 δεῖ δὲ χρημάτων, καὶ ἄνευ τούτων οὐδὲν ἔστι γενέσθαι τῶν δεόντων

'Tis money we need; for without money nothing can be done.

First Olynthiac 1.20.6

6 ἕως ἐστὶ καιρός, ἀντιλάβεσθε τῶν πραγμάτων

Grapple with the problem while there is still time.

First Olynthiac 1.20.9

7 πολλάκις δοκεῖ τὸ φυλάξαι τἀγαθὰ τοῦ κτήσασθαι χαλεπώτερον εἶναι

It often seems more difficult to preserve a blessing than to acquire it.

First Olynthiac 1.23

8 ὥσπερ γὰρ οἰκίας, οἶμαι, καὶ πλοίου ... τὰ κάτωθεν ἰσχυρότατ' εἶναι δεῖ, οὕτω καὶ τῶν πράξεων τὰς ἀρχὰς καὶ τὰς ὑποθέσεις ἀληθεῖς καὶ δικαίας εἶναι προσήκει

As a house or a ship depend for their strength on their substructure, so too in affairs of state, the basic principles must be truth and justice.

Second Olynthiac 2.10

9 ὡς ἅπας μὲν λόγος, ἂν ἀπῇ τὰ πράγματα, μάταιόν τι φαίνεται καὶ κενόν

Words without action seem vain and empty.

Second Olynthiac 2.12

10 αἱ γὰρ εὐπραξίαι δειναὶ συγκρύψαι τὰ ὀνείδη

Success is apt to cover a multitude of faults.

Translated by J.H. Vince (1930)

Second Olynthiac 2.20

11 οὐ γὰρ ἔστι πικρῶς ἐξετάσαι τί πέπρακται τοῖς ἄλλοις, ἂν μὴ παρ' ὑμῶν αὐτῶν πρῶτον ὑπάρξῃ τὰ δέοντα

Do not criticize the deeds of others unless you have first done your duty yourself.

Second Olynthiac 2.27

12 ῥᾷστον ἁπάντων ἐστὶν αὑτὸν ἐξαπατῆσαι· ὃ γὰρ βούλεται, τοῦθ' ἕκαστος καὶ οἴεται

Nothing is easier than self-deceit; for what each man wishes, that he also believes to be true.

Translated by J.H. Vince (1930)

Third Olynthiac 3.19

cf. Caesar, De bello gallico *3.18.2: 'Men willingly believe what they wish'*

13 δικαίου πολίτου κρίνω τὴν τῶν πραγμάτων σωτηρίαν ἀντὶ τῆς ἐν τῷ λέγειν χάριτος αἱρεῖσθαι

It is for a good citizen to set the welfare of the state above pretty words.

Third Olynthiac 3.21

14 ἐξ οὗ δ' οἱ διερωτῶντες ὑμᾶς οὗτοι πεφήνασι ῥήτορες 'τί βούλεσθε; τί γράψω; τί ὑμῖν χαρίσωμαι;' προπέποται τῆς παραυτίκα χάριτος τὰ τῆς πόλεως πράγματα, καὶ τοιαυτὶ συμβαίνει, καὶ τὰ μὲν τούτων πάντα καλῶς ἔχει, τὰ δ' ὑμέτερ' αἰσχρῶς

Ever since this breed of orators appeared who ply you with such questions as 'What would you like? What shall I propose? How can I oblige you?' the interests of the state have been frittered away for momentary popularity.

Translated by J.H. Vince (1930)

Third Olynthiac 3.22

15 οὐ γὰρ εἰς περιουσίαν ἐπράττετ' αὐτοῖς τὰ τῆς πόλεως, ἀλλὰ τὸ κοινὸν αὔξειν ἕκαστος ᾤετο δεῖν

Selfish greed had no place in their statesmanship, but each considered it his duty to further the common weal.

Translated by J.H. Vince (1930)

Third Olynthiac 3.26

of former politicians

16 κύριοι μὲν οἱ πολιτευόμενοι τῶν ἀγαθῶν, καὶ διὰ τούτων ἅπαντα πράττεται, ὑμεῖς δ' ὁ δῆμος, ἐκνενευρισμένοι καὶ περιῃρημένοι χρήματα, συμμάχους, ἐν ὑπηρέτου καὶ προσθήκης μέρει γεγένησθε, ἀγαπῶντες ἐὰν μεταδιδῶσι θεωρικῶν ὑμῖν ... καὶ τὸ πάντων ἀνδρειότατον, τῶν ὑμετέρων αὐτῶν χάριν προσοφείλετε

The politicians hold the purse-strings and manage everything, while you, the people, robbed of nerve and sinew, stripped of wealth and of allies, have sunk to the level of lackeys and hangers-on, content if the politicians gratify you with a dole, and your manliness reaches its climax when you add your thanks for what is yours by right.

Translated by J.H. Vince (1930)

Third Olynthiac 3.31

17 ἔστι δ' οὐδέποτ', οἶμαι, μέγα καὶ νεανικὸν φρόνημα λαβεῖν μικρὰ καὶ φαῦλα πράττοντας· ὁποῖ' ἄττα γὰρ ἂν τὰ ἐπιτηδεύματα τῶν ἀνθρώπων ᾖ, τοιοῦτον ἀνάγκη καὶ τὸ φρόνημ' ἔχειν

You cannot have a proud and chivalrous spirit if your conduct is mean and paltry; for whatever a man's actions are, such must be his spirit.

Translated by J.H. Vince (1930)

Third Olynthiac 3.32

18 ὃ γάρ ἐστι χείριστον αὐτῶν ἐκ τοῦ παρεληλυθότος χρόνου, τοῦτο πρὸς τὰ μέλλοντα βέλτιστον ὑπάρχει

The experience of what was worst in the past is the best assurance for the future.

First Philippic 4.2.3

19 οὐδέν, ὦ ἄνδρες Ἀθηναῖοι, τῶν δεόντων ποιούντων ὑμῶν κακῶς τὰ πράγματ' ἔχει

Your affairs are in this evil plight just because you, men of Athens, utterly failed to do your duty.

Translated by J.H. Vince (1930)

First Philippic 4.2.5

20 φύσει δ' ὑπάρχει τοῖς παροῦσι τὰ τῶν ἀπόντων, καὶ τοῖς ἐθέλουσι πονεῖν καὶ κινδυνεύειν τὰ τῶν ἀμελούντων

The property of those who are absent naturally falls to those who are present, and the property of the careless to the diligent and brave.

First Philippic 4.5

21 ἂν ὑμῶν αὐτῶν ἐθελήσητε γενέσθαι καὶ παύσησθ' αὐτὸς μὲν οὐδὲν ἕκαστος ποιήσειν ἐλπίζων, τὸν δὲ πλησίον πάνθ' ὑπὲρ αὐτοῦ πράξειν

If you wish to become your own masters, each man must cease to expect that others will do everything for him, while he does nothing himself.

First Philippic 4.7

22 πότ' οὖν, ὦ ἄνδρες Ἀθηναῖοι, πόθ' ἃ χρὴ πράξετε; ἐπειδὰν τί γένηται;

When, Athenians, will you take the necessary action? What are you waiting for?

Translated by J.H. Vince (1930)

First Philippic 4.10

23 ἐπεὶ νῦν γε γέλως ἔσθ' ὡς χρώμεθα τοῖς πράγμασιν

For at present our system is a mockery.

Translated by J.H. Vince (1930)

First Philippic 4.25

of using mercenaries in the war against Philip

24 ἄτακτα, ἀδιόρθωτα, ἀόρισθ' ἅπαντα

Everything is ill-arranged, ill-managed, ill-defined.

Translated by J.H. Vince (1930)

First Philippic 4.36

25 οἱ δὲ τῶν πραγμάτων οὐ μένουσι καιροὶ τὴν ἡμετέραν βραδυτῆτα καὶ εἰρωνείαν

The opportunities of fortune do not wait for our sluggishness and hesitation.

First Philippic 4.37

26 ὁρῶ μέν, ὦ ἄνδρες Ἀθηναῖοι, τὰ παρόντα πράγματα πολλὴν δυσκολίαν ἔχοντα καὶ ταραχὴν

I perceive, men of Athens, that the present outlook gives rise to much vexation and perplexity.

Translated by J.H. Vince (1930)

On the Peace 5.1.1

27 μηδὲ καθ' ἓν τὸ συμφέρον πάντας ἡγεῖσθαι, ἀλλὰ τοῖς μὲν ὡδί, τοῖς δ' ἑτέρως δοκεῖν

And no one has the same opinion on what is to our advantage, one favouring this policy, another that.

On the Peace 5.1.3

28 πάντες ἄνθρωποι πρὸ τῶν πραγμάτων εἰώθασι χρῆσθαι τῷ βουλεύεσθαι, ὑμεῖς δὲ μετὰ τὰ πράγματα

Other people deliberate before the event, but you after the event.

Translated by J.H. Vince (1930)

On the Peace 5.2

29 ὅταν δ' ἐπὶ θάτερ' ὥσπερ εἰς τρυτάνην ἀργύριον προσενέγκῃς, οἴχεται φέρον καὶ καθείλκυκε τὸν λογισμὸν ἐφ' αὐτό, καὶ οὐκ ἂν ἔτ' ὀρθῶς οὐδ' ὑγιῶς ὁ τοῦτο ποιήσας περὶ οὐδενὸς λογίσαιτο

The instant you throw money into one scale, its weight will influence your judgement; and for him that has once done this, sound calculation becomes utterly impossible.

On the Peace 5.12

30 καί μοι μὴ θορυβήσῃ μηδεὶς πρὶν ἀκοῦσαι

Hear me before you shout me down.

Translated by J.H. Vince (1930)

On the Peace 5.15

31 ἀλλὰ σῶς μὲν εἶναι πάντες ἂν βούλοινθ' ἕνεχ' αὑτῶν, κρατήσαντας δὲ τοὺς ἑτέρους δεσπότας ὑπάρχειν αὑτῶν οὐδὲ εἷς

They would all have us, for their own sakes, alive and well; but no one will accept that one nation should gain supremacy.

On the Peace 5.17

32 οὐκοῦν εὔηθες καὶ κομιδῇ σχέτλιον ... περὶ τῆς ἐν Δελφοῖς σκιᾶς πολεμῆσαι

It is sheer folly and perversity to fight this phantom at Delphi.

Translated by J.H. Vince (1930)

On the Peace 5.25

of Philip, to meet the Amphictyonic Council at Delphi

33 τοῖς λέγουσιν ἅπασι καὶ τοῖς ἀκούουσιν ὑμῖν τὰ βέλτιστα καὶ τὰ σώσοντα τῶν ῥᾴστων καὶ τῶν ἡδίστων προαιρετέον

All who speak and all who listen must choose the best and safest policy instead of the easiest and most agreeable.

Translated by J.H. Vince (1930)

Second Philippic 6.5

34 οὐ γὰρ ἀσφαλεῖς ταῖς πολιτείαις αἱ πρὸς τοὺς τυράννους αὗται λίαν ὁμιλίαι

Excessive dealings with tyrants are a threat to the security of free states.

Second Philippic 6.21

of the Olynthians who supported Philip but later suffered under his rule

35 ἓν δέ τι κοινὸν ἡ φύσις τῶν εὖ φρονούντων ἐν αὑτῇ κέκτηται φυλακτήριον, ὃ πᾶσι μέν ἐστ' ἀγαθὸν καὶ σωτήριον, μάλιστα δὲ τοῖς πλήθεσι πρὸς τοὺς τυράννους· τί οὖν ἐστι τοῦτο; ἀπιστία

There is one safeguard known generally to the wise, which is an advantage and security to all, but especially to democracies against despots – mistrust.

Second Philippic 6.24

36 τὰ πόλλ' ἐνίους οὐκ εἰς τοὺς αἰτίους, ἀλλ' εἰς τοὺς ὑπὸ χεῖρα μάλιστα τὴν ὀργὴν ἀφιέντας

People vent their wrath not on those who are to blame, but chiefly on those who are at hand.

Second Philippic 6.34

37 ἐκ πτωχῶν ἔνιοι ταχὺ πλούσιοι γίγνονται, καὶ ἐξ ἀνωνύμων καὶ ἀδόξων ἔνδοξοι καὶ γνώριμοι, ὑμεῖς δὲ τοὐναντίον ἐκ μὲν ἐνδόξων ἄδοξοι, ἐκ δ' εὐπόρων ἄποροι

Some were poor and suddenly grew rich, some unknown and disreputable are now well known and of high repute; while you have passed from honour to dishonour, from affluence to destitution.

On the Chersonese 8.66.5

38 πόλεως γὰρ ἔγωγε πλοῦτον ἡγοῦμαι συμμάχους, πίστιν, εὔνοιαν

Credit and goodwill are allies for a city's wealth.

On the Chersonese 8.66.8

'credit' can also be interpreted as 'trust'

39 οἱ τῆς παρ' ἡμέραν χάριτος τὰ μέγιστα τῆς πόλεως ἀπολωλεκότες

For a moment's popularity they have made havoc of the chief resources of the state.

Translated by J.H. Vince (1930)

On the Chersonese 8.70

40 τὸ βέλτιστον ἀεί, μὴ τὸ ῥᾷστον ἅπαντας λέγειν

Support the best, not the easiest policy.

On the Chersonese 8.72

41 τὸ δ' εὐσεβὲς καὶ τὸ δίκαιον, ἄν τ' ἐπὶ μικροῦ τις ἄν τ' ἐπὶ μείζονος παραβαίνῃ, τὴν αὐτὴν ἔχει δύναμιν

Violation of religion and justice, whether small or great, is equally serious.

Third Philippic 9.16

42 μέγας ἐκ μικροῦ καὶ ταπεινοῦ

Risen to greatness from small and humble beginnings.

Translated by J.H. Vince (1930)

Third Philippic 9.21

of Philip of Macedon

43 τί τῆς ἐσχάτης ὕβρεως ἀπολείπει;

What else is needed to crown his insolence?

Third Philippic 9.32

of Philip of Macedon

44 ἦν τι τότ', ἦν, ὦ ἄνδρες Ἀθηναῖοι, ἐν ταῖς τῶν πολλῶν διανοίαις, ὃ νῦν οὐκ ἔστιν, ὃ καὶ τοῦ Περσῶν ἐκράτησε πλούτου καὶ ἐλευθέραν ἦγε τὴν Ἑλλάδα … νῦν δ' ἀπολωλὸς ἅπαντα λελύμανται καὶ ἄνω καὶ κάτω πεποίηκε τὰ πράγματα

There was something, men of Athens, something which animated the mass of the Greeks but which is lacking now, something which triumphed over the wealth of Persia, which upheld the liberties of Hellas, something the decay of which has ruined everything and brought our affairs to a state of chaos.

Translated by J.H. Vince (1930)

Third Philippic 9.36

45 τοὺς παρὰ τῶν ἄρχειν βουλομένων ἢ διαφθείρειν τὴν Ἑλλάδα χρήματα λαμβάνοντας ἅπαντες ἐμίσουν, καὶ χαλεπώτατον ἦν τὸ δωροδοκοῦντ' ἐλεγχθῆναι, καὶ τιμωρίᾳ μεγίστῃ τοῦτον ἐκόλαζον, καὶ παραίτησις οὐδεμί' ἦν οὐδὲ συγγνώμη

Everybody hated those who received bribes either from those who wished to rule Greece or to ruin her; and it was most grievous to be convicted of receiving a bribe, it was punished with utmost severity and no intercession or pardon was allowed.

Third Philippic 9.37

46 ἁπάντων … πολλὴν εἰληφότων ἐπίδοσιν, καὶ οὐδὲν ὁμοίων ὄντων τῶν νῦν τοῖς πρότερον

Practically all the arts have made a great advance and we are living today in a very different world from the old one.

Translated by J.H. Vince (1930)

Third Philippic 9.47

47 ἄν περ, ὦ ἄνδρες Ἀθηναῖοι, ποιεῖν ἐθέλωμεν ἃ δεῖ

Provided, men of Athens, we are willing to do what is necessary.

Translated by J.H. Vince (1930)

Third Philippic 9.52

48 οὐκ ἔνεστι τῶν τῆς πόλεως ἐχθρῶν κρατῆσαι, πρὶν ἂν τοὺς ἐν αὐτῇ τῇ πόλει κολάσηθ' ὑπηρετοῦντας ἐκείνοις

It is impossible to defeat the enemies of our city until you have chastised those, who within our very walls, make themselves their servants.

Translated by J.H. Vince (1930)

Third Philippic 9.53

49 ἀλλ' εἰς τοῦτ' ἀφῖχθε μωρίας ἢ παρανοίας … μή τι δαιμόνιον τὰ πράγματ' ἐλαύνῃ

But you have reached such a degree of folly or of madness that some demon is driving you to your doom.

Translated by J.H. Vince (1930)

Third Philippic 9.54

50 ἕως ἂν σῴζηται τὸ σκάφος, ἄν τε μεῖζον ἄν τ' ἔλαττον ᾖ, τότε χρὴ καὶ ναύτην καὶ κυβερνήτην καὶ πάντ' ἄνδρ' ἑξῆς προθύμους εἶναι … ἐπειδὰν δ' ἡ θάλαττα ὑπέρσχῃ, μάταιος ἡ σπουδή

While the vessel is safe, be it large or small, then is the time for the sailor and helmsman and everyone to show his zeal; when the sea has prevailed all effort is vain.

Third Philippic 9.69

51 ἡμῖν γ' ὑπὲρ τῆς ἐλευθερίας ἀγωνιστέον

We must surely fight the battle of liberty.

Translated by J.H. Vince (1930)

Third Philippic 9.70

52 συμπάσης τῆς πόλεως κοινοὺς δεῖ γονέας τοὺς σύμπαντας ἡγεῖσθαι

We must regard all citizens as the common parents of the State.

*Fourth Philippic** 10.41

53 αἱ γὰρ εὐπραξίαι δειναὶ συγκρύψαι καὶ συσκιάσαι τὰς ἁμαρτίας τῶν ἀνθρώπων εἰσίν· εἰ δέ τι πταίσει, τότ' ἀκριβῶς διακαλυφθήσεται ταῦτα πάντα

Success has the strange power of obscuring men's failings; but make a false step and all weaknesses are revealed.

*Answer to Philip's Letter** 11.13

54 δεῖ γὰρ ἐν μὲν τοῖς ὅπλοις φοβερούς, ἐν δὲ τοῖς δικαστηρίοις φιλανθρώπους εἶναι

Be in battle daunting, in courts humane.

On Organization 13.17

55 ταῦτα δὲ καὶ δυνατά ἐστιν ... καὶ πράττειν καλὰ καὶ συμφέροντα

It is possible, then, to act in a way that is both fair and profitable.

On the Navy-Boards 14.28

often used scoffingly even today when the profit part prevails – cf. later liturgical texts 'τα καλά και συμφέροντα (ταις ψυχαίς ημών)', e.g. Epiphanius, Liturgia 3.189

56 καὶ τὰς κρήνας καὶ τὰ φρέατ' ἐπιλείπειν πέφυκεν, ἐάν τις ἀπ' αὐτῶν ἀθρόα πολλὰ λαμβάνῃ

Even springs and wells may fail if one draws from them constantly and lavishly.

Translated by J.H. Vince (1930)

On the Navy-Boards 14.30

57 μὴ μακρὰ λίαν λέγων ἐνοχλῶ

To spare you the tedium of a lengthy speech.

Translated by J.H. Vince (1930)

On the Navy-Boards 14.41

58 ἐγὼ δ' οὐδεπώποθ' ἡγησάμην χαλεπὸν τὸ διδάξαι τὰ βέλτισθ' ὑμᾶς

Personally, I never thought it a difficult task to teach you the best policy.

For the Liberty of the Rhodians 15.1

59 πολλῶν κακῶν ἡ ἄνοι' αἰτία ... γίγνεται

Of many misfortunes folly is the cause.

For the Liberty of the Rhodians 15.16

60 ἐπειδήπερ ἄδηλον τὸ μέλλον ἅπασιν ἀνθρώποις

Inscrutable is the future to all mankind.

For the Liberty of the Rhodians 15.21

61 τὰ τρόπαια ... οὐχ ἵνα θαυμάζητ' αὐτὰ θεωροῦντες, ἀλλ' ἵνα καὶ μιμῆσθε τὰς τῶν ἀναθέντων ἀρετάς

Trophies are not to gaze at in wonder, but that you may imitate the virtues of the men who set them up.

Translated by J.H. Vince (1930)

For the Liberty of the Rhodians 15.35

of victory trophies set up by ancestors

62 χαλεπὸν τὰ βέλτιστα λέγειν

It is difficult to recommend the wisest course.

Translated by J.H. Vince (1930)

For the People of Megalopolis 16.2

63 οὐδὲν οὕτω τοῖς δημοκρατουμένοις πρέπειν ὡς περὶ τὸ ἴσον καὶ τὸ δίκαιον σπουδάζειν

Nothing becomes a democratic people more than zeal for equity and justice.

Translated by J.H. Vince (1930)

*On the Treaty with Alexander** 17.1

64 τῶν μὲν ὡς ἀληθῶς τετυχηκότων οὐδ' ἂν εἷς εἴποι περὶ αὑτοῦ τοιοῦτον οὐδέν, ἀλλὰ κἂν ἑτέρου λέγοντος ἐρυθριάσειε

No truly educated man would use such language about himself, but would rather blush to hear it from others.

Translated by C.A. Vince and J.H. Vince (1926)

On the Crown 18.128

of laudatory words

65 μεγάλ' ὠφελήσεσθε πρὸς ἱστορίαν τῶν κοινῶν

You will profit greatly from an inquiry into our public affairs.

On the Crown 18.144

66 καὶ θορύβου πλήρης ἦν ἡ πόλις

And the city was full of noise and confusion.

On the Crown 18.169

67 τί δὲ μεῖζον ἔχοι τις ἂν εἰπεῖν ἀδίκημα κατ' ἀνδρὸς ῥήτορος ἢ εἰ μὴ ταὐτὰ φρονεῖ

καὶ λέγει;

What worse charge can any one bring against an orator than that his words and his designs don't tally?

On the Crown 18.282

68 ταὐτὰ λυπεῖσθαι καὶ ταὐτὰ χαίρειν τοῖς πολλοῖς

Hoi polloi whine about the same things in which they rejoice.

On the Crown 18.292

69 τῇ γαστρὶ μετροῦντες καὶ τοῖς αἰσχίστοις τὴν εὐδαιμονίαν, τὴν δ' ἐλευθερίαν καὶ τὸ μηδέν' ἔχειν δεσπότην αὑτῶν, ἃ τοῖς προτέροις Ἕλλησιν ὅροι τῶν ἀγαθῶν ἦσαν καὶ κανόνες, ἀνατετροφότες

They measure their happiness by their belly and their baser parts; they have overthrown for ever that freedom and independence which to the Greeks of an earlier age were the very standard and canon of prosperity.

Translated by C.A. Vince and J.H. Vince (1926)

On the Crown 18.296

quoted by 'Longinus', On the Sublime 32

70 καιροὺς … θεραπεύειν

Exploit circumstances.

On the Crown 18.307

cf. the Latin 'tempori serviendum est'

71 ὡς ὁ μὲν δῆμός ἐστιν ἀσταθμητότατον πρᾶγμα τῶν πάντων καὶ ἀσυνθετώτατον

The multitude is the most unstable and witless thing in the world.

On the Embassy 19.136

72 κρεῖττον εὐήθη δοκεῖν ἢ πονηρὸν εἶναι

It is better to be considered simple-minded than unscrupulous.

Against Leptines 20.6

73 εἰ μὲν γάρ τις ἔχει πολλὰ μηδὲν ὑμᾶς ἀδικῶν, οὐχὶ δεῖ δήπου τούτῳ βασκαίνειν· εἰ δ' ὑφῃρημένον φήσουσιν ἢ τιν' ἄλλον οὐχ ὃν προσήκει τρόπον, εἰσὶ νόμοι καθ' οὓς προσήκει κολάζειν

If a rich man does you no wrong do not begrudge him; but if his wealth is stolen or gained in a disreputable way, there are laws by which he can be suitably punished.

Against Leptines 20.24

74 οἱ νόμοι δ' οὐκ ἐῶσι δὶς πρὸς τὸν αὐτὸν περὶ τῶν αὐτῶν οὔτε δίκας οὔτ' εὐθύνας οὔτε διαδικασίαν οὔτ' ἄλλο τοιοῦτ' οὐδὲν εἶναι

The laws forbid the same man to be tried twice on the same issue, be it a civil action, a scrutiny, a contested claim, or anything else of the sort.

Translated by J.H. Vince (1930)

Against Leptines 20.147

75 τὸ μέλλον ἄδηλον πᾶσιν ἀνθρώποις, καὶ μικροὶ καιροὶ μεγάλων πραγμάτων αἴτιοι γίγνονται

The future is hidden from all men, and great events hang on small chances.

Translated by J.H. Vince (1930)

Against Leptines 20.162

76 τὸν ἡγεμόν' ἂν ἀφέλῃ τις, οἴχεται ὁ λοιπὸς χορός

If the leader is withdrawn, the rest of the chorus is done for.

Translated by J.H. Vince (1935)

Against Meidias 21.60

77 οὐδεὶς γάρ ἐστι δίκαιος τυγχάνειν ἐλέου τῶν μηδέν' ἐλεούντων, οὐδὲ συγγνώμης τῶν ἀσυγγνωμόνων

No one deserves pity who shows no pity; no one deserves pardon who grants no pardon.

Translated by J.H. Vince (1935)

Against Meidias 21.100

78 ἐάν τις Ἀθηναίων λαμβάνῃ παρά τινος, ἢ αὐτὸς διδῷ ἑτέρῳ, ἢ διαφθείρῃ τινὰς ἐπαγγελλόμενος, ἐπὶ βλάβῃ τοῦ δήμου ἢ ἰδίᾳ τινὸς τῶν πολιτῶν, τρόπῳ ἢ μηχανῇ ἡτινιοῦν, ἄτιμος ἔστω καὶ παῖδες καὶ τὰ ἐκείνου

If any Athenian accepts a bribe from another, or himself offers it to another, or corrupts anyone by promises, to the detriment of the people in general, or of any individual citizen, by any means or device whatsoever, he shall be disfranchised together with his children, and his property shall be confiscated.

Translated by J.H. Vince (1935)

Against Meidias 21.113

79 πρὸς ἐμαυτὸν κρίνων

I will judge him by the standards I apply to myself.

Against Meidias 21.154

80 ἀλλ' ἔνεστ' ἔλεος, συγγνώμη, πάνθ' ἃ προσήκει τοῖς ἐλευθέροις

In them we find pity, pardon, everything that becomes free citizens.

Translated by J.H. Vince (1935)

Against Androtion 22.57

of Athenian statutes and basic laws

81 οἱ νόμοι ... οὐδὲν γὰρ ὠμὸν οὐδὲ βίαιον οὐδ' ὀλιγαρχικὸν προστάττουσιν, ἀλλὰ τοὐναντίον πάντα φιλανθρώπως καὶ δημοτικῶς φράζουσι πράττειν

There is nothing offensive or violent or oligarchical in the provisions of our laws; they order business to be done in a courteous, democratic spirit.

Translated by J.H. Vince (1935)

Against Timocrates 24.24

82 ἀκροάσομαι τοῦ τε κατηγόρου καὶ τοῦ ἀπολογουμένου ὁμοίως ἀμφοῖν

I will give impartial hearing to prosecutor and defendant alike.

Translated by J.H. Vince (1935)

Against Timocrates 24.151

83 τοὺς ἀσθενεῖς ἐλεεῖν, τοῖς ἰσχυροῖς καὶ δυναμένοις μὴ ἐπιτρέπειν ὑβρίζειν, οὐ τοὺς μὲν πολλοὺς ὠμῶς μεταχειρίζεσθαι, κολακεύειν δὲ τὸν ἀεί τι δύνασθαι δοκοῦντα

To have compassion for the helpless, not to allow excess in the strong and powerful, not to treat the many harshly, not to flatter the self-satisfied.

Against Timocrates 24.171

84 τοὺς νόμους ὡς πραοτάτους καὶ μετριωτάτους εἶναι ὑπὲρ τῶν ἀδυνάτων μάλιστ' ἐστίν

Laws ought to be applied most mercifully and humanely to the frailest members of the community.

Against Timocrates 24.190

85 πᾶς ἐστι νόμος εὕρημα μὲν καὶ δῶρον θεῶν

Every law is a gift and invention of the gods.

Translated by H.T. Riley (1872)

Against Aristogiton I 25.16

86 ταῦτα ... ὑμῶν ἕκαστος ἔχων οἴκοθεν ἔρχεται, ἔλεον, συγγνώμην, φιλανθρωπίαν

And you, as you come from your homes, bring with you pity, pardon, benevolence.

Against Aristogiton I 25.81.4

to members of the jury, considering this a normal attitude to the defendant

87 ὅτι ὃν ἂν αὐτὸς ἕκαστος νόμον τῇ φύσει κατὰ πάντων ἔχῃ, τούτου τυγχάνειν παρ' ἑκάστου δίκαιός ἐστι καὶ αὐτός

Whatever law each man's nature prompts him to apply to his neighbours, that law is only fair that the they should apply to him.

Translated by J.H. Vince (1935)

Against Aristogiton I 25.81.6

88 ὑμεῖς γάρ, ὦ ἄνδρες Ἀθηναῖοι, τῇ τῆς φύσεως πρὸς ἀλλήλους, ὅπερ εἶπον, χρώμενοι φιλανθρωπίᾳ, ὥσπερ αἱ συγγένειαι τὰς ἰδίας οἰκοῦσιν οἰκίας, οὕτω τὴν πόλιν οἰκεῖτε δημοσίᾳ ... ἐκ δὲ τούτων ἡ κοινὴ καὶ πάντων τῶν ἀγαθῶν αἰτία τῇ πόλει μένει καὶ συνέστηκεν ὁμόνοια

For you, Athenians, observing what I have called the natural bond of mutual kindness, live as a corporate body in this city just as families live in their private homes. Hence it is that that general harmony, which is the source of all our blessings, is firmly established in our city.

Translated by J.H. Vince (1935)

Against Aristogiton I 25.87 and 89

89 δεῖ γὰρ τοὺς εὐπόρους χρησίμους αὑτοὺς παρέχειν τοῖς πολίταις

It is the duty of the wealthy to render service to the state.

Translated by A.T. Murray (1939)

*Against Phaenippus** 42.22

90 μᾶλλον ἄξιον ὀργίλως ἔχειν τοῖς μετ' εὐπορίας πονηροῖς ἢ τοῖς μετ' ἐνδείας. τοῖς μὲν γὰρ ἡ τῆς χρείας ἀνάγκη φέρει τινὰ συγγνώμην παρὰ τοῖς ἀνθρωπίνως λογιζομένοις· οἱ δ' ἐκ περιουσίας, ὥσπερ οὗτος, πονηροὶ οὐδεμίαν πρόφασιν

δικαίαν ἔχοιεν

Feel indignation rather toward those who are rascals in wealth than toward those who are such in poverty. In the case of the latter the pressure of their needy state affords them some human sympathy, whereas those who, like this fellow, are rascals while possessing abundance, have no reasonable excuse to offer.

Against Stephanus 1 45.67

91 οὐκ ἦν ἄρ' ... χαλεπώτερον οὐδὲν ἢ γείτονος πονηροῦ καὶ πλεονέκτου τυχεῖν

There is nothing more vexatious than a base and covetous neighbour.

Against Callicles 55.1

92 τὰς μὲν γὰρ ἑταίρας ἡδονῆς ἕνεκ' ἔχομεν, τὰς δὲ παλλακὰς τῆς καθ' ἡμέραν θεραπείας τοῦ σώματος, τὰς δὲ γυναῖκας τοῦ παιδοποιεῖσθαι γνησίως καὶ τῶν ἔνδον φύλακα πιστὴν ἔχειν

Mistresses we keep for the sake of pleasure, concubines for the daily care of our persons, but wives to bear us legitimate children and to be faithful guardians of our households.

Translated by A.T. Murray (1939)

*Against Neaera** 59.122

93 τελευτῆσαι καλῶς μᾶλλον ἠβουλήθησαν ἢ ζῶντες τὴν Ἑλλάδ' ἰδεῖν ἀτυχοῦσαν

They chose rather to die nobly than to live and look upon Greece in misfortune.

Translated by Norman W. DeWitt and Norman J. DeWitt (1949)

Funeral Oration 60.1

for those who died in the battle of Chaeronea, 338BC

94 αἱ δὲ δημοκρατίαι πολλά τ' ἄλλα καὶ καλὰ καὶ δίκαι' ἔχουσιν, ὧν τὸν εὖ φρονοῦντ' ἀντέχεσθαι δεῖ, καὶ τὴν παρρησίαν ἐκ τῆς ἀληθείας ἠρτημένην οὐκ ἔστι τἀληθὲς δηλοῦν ἀποτρέψαι

Democracies, however, possess many other just and noble features, to which right-minded men should hold fast, and in particular it is impossible to deter freedom of speech, which depends upon speaking the truth, from exposing the truth.

Translated by Norman W. DeWitt and Norman J. DeWitt (1949)

Funeral Oration 60.26

95 ὑπὲρ ὄνου σκιᾶς

Arguing over the worth of a donkey's shadow.

Fragment 1 (Baiter and Sauppe, *Orat.Att.*)

Demosthenes making fun of judges elaborating at great length if, having rented a donkey, the man could for the same price sleep in its shade

96 πάντων ἐστὶ δυσχερέστατον τὸ πολλοῖς ἀρέσκειν

Of all things the most difficult is to please the many.

Fragment 24 (Baiter and Sauppe, *Orat.Att.*)

97 πόλεμος ἔνδοξος εἰρήνης αἰσχρᾶς αἱρετώτερος

A plausible war is preferable to a dishonourable peace.

Fragment 26 (Baiter and Sauppe, *Orat.Att.*)

98 Εἴπερ ἴσην ῥώμην γνώμῃ, Δημόσθενες, ἔσχες, οὔ ποτ' ἂν Ἑλλήνων ἦρξεν Ἄρης Μακεδών

If you had had as much power as strength of opinion, Demosthenes, the warring Macedonian would never have ruled over Greece.

Fragment 56 (Baiter and Sauppe, *Orat.Att.*)

later inscribed by the Athenians on his statue

99 Δημοσθένης ἔλεγεν, ὡς πολλάκις ἐπιὸν αὐτῷ εὔξασθαι τοὺς πονηροὺς ἀπολέσθαι φοβοῖτο μὴ ἔρημον ἄρδην ἐκ τῆς εὐχῆς ποιήσῃ τὴν πόλιν

Demosthenes said that he often wished to curse all evil men to destruction, but was afraid that there would be nobody left in the city.

Fragment 57 (Baiter and Sauppe, *Orat.Att.*)

100 Δημοσθένης πρὸς κλέπτην εἰπόντα, οὐκ ᾔδειν ὅτι σόν ἐστιν, ὅτι δέ, ἔφη, σὸν οὐκ ἔστιν ᾔδεις

A thief said to Demosthenes, 'I didn't know it was yours,' to which he replied, 'But, you knew it wasn't yours.'

Fragment 59 (Baiter and Sauppe, *Orat.Att.*)

101 Δημοσθένης λοιδορουμένου τινὸς αὐτῷ· οὐ συγκαταβαίνω, εἶπεν, εἰς ἀγῶνα, ἐν ᾧ ὁ ἡττώμενος τοῦ νικῶντός ἐστι κρείττων

Demosthenes, to someone who ridiculed him, said, 'I will not commit myself to a contest where the defeated is superior to the winner.'

Fragment 60 (Baiter and Sauppe, *Orat.Att.*)

102 οὐκ ὠνοῦμαι μυρίων δραχμῶν μεταμέλειαν

I will not buy regret for ten thousand drachmas.

Translated by John C. Rolfe (1927)

Aulus Gellius, *Attic Nights* 1.8

to the courtesan Lais who demanded an exorbitant amount of money for her favours; quoted in Greek by Aulus Gellius; cf. George Orwell in Appendix 1. Quotations on Greece and Greeks; Aristophanes 169

103 τὸ δ' ὅπως ἕξουσιν οἱ πολλοὶ πρὸς τὸν λόγον ἀφροντιστεῖν ὀλιγαρχικοῦ καὶ βίᾳ μᾶλλον ἢ πειθοῖ προσέχοντος

To pay no heed to the reaction of your audience is a sign of non-democratic intentions, such as use of force rather than persuasion.

Plutarch, *Demosthenes* 8.6

104 οὐχ ὑπὸ συνάγχης, ἀλλ' ἀργυράγχης εἰλῆφθαι νύκτωρ

This is not an ordinary quinsy, he has been seized overnight with the silver quinsy.

Translated by H.T. Riley (1872)

Plutarch, *Demosthenes* 25.6

said an adversary of Demosthenes when he abstained from speaking on the plea of quinsy, insinuating that he had been paid for his silence

105 Δημοσθένης ἐρωτηθεὶς πῶς τῆς ῥητορικῆς περιεγένου; πλέον ἔφη ἔλαιον οἴνου δαπανήσας

Demosthenes, when asked, how to become distinguished in rhetoric, replied, 'By spending more on oil than on wine.'

Stobaeus, *Anthology* 3.29.90

cf. Pytheas 1

DICAEOGENES

4th century BC

Tragic and dithyrambic playwright

1 μακάριος ὅστις αὐτὸς ἰσχύων ἔτι
παῖδας παρασπίζοντας ἀλκίμους ἔχει

How blessed he who in his youth
can father sturdy children!

Fragment 2 (Snell, *TrGF*)

2 αὐτὸς τραφεὶς δὲ τῶν φυτευσάντων ὕπο
καλῶς, τὸν αὐτὸν ἔρανον αὐτοῖσιν νέμεις

It is paying off sweet debt to care for the parents who cared for you.

Fragment 4 (Snell, *TrGF*)

DIDYMUS

1st century AD

Alexandrian grammarian

1 πᾶσαν μὲν γὰρ πρᾶξιν ἐνέργειαν εἶναί τινα ψυχῆς

Every action is some expression of the soul.

DIO CHRYSOSTOM

(Dio Cocceianus)

*c.*40–*c.*120AD

Orator and popular philosopher from Prusa in Bithynia

1 ἦν δὲ καὶ ὅμιλος περὶ ... τὴν Βασιλείαν, Ὠμότης καὶ Ὕβρις καὶ Ἀνομία καὶ Στάσις

There was also a throng in attendance upon Royalty: Cruelty, Insolence, Lawlessness, and Faction

Translated by J.W. Cohoon (1932)

On Kingship 1.82

2 μὴ οὖν πρότερον, ὦ μάταιε, βασιλεύειν ἐπιχείρει πρὶν ἢ φρονῆσαι

Do not try, you fool, to rule before being in your right mind.

On Kingship 4.70

3 πάντα μὲν οὖν τὰ δεινὰ πέφυκε μᾶλλον ἐκπλήττειν τοὺς προσδεχομένους ἢ λυπεῖν τοὺς πειραθέντας ... ὁ δὲ φόβος οὕτω χαλεπός ἐστιν ὥστε πολλοὶ ἤδη προέλαβον τὸ ἔργον

Now all calamities are naturally more alarming in anticipation than they are grievous in experience. Fear of death, however, is so intense that many have anticipated the event.

Translated by J.W. Cohoon (1932)

Diogenes, or On Tyranny 6.41

4 ἡ γὰρ ἀργία καὶ τὸ σχολὴν ἄγειν ἀπόλλυσι πάντων μάλιστα τοὺς ἀνοήτους ἀνθρώπους

Idleness and lack of occupation are the best things in the world to ruin the foolish.

Translated by J.W. Cohoon (1932)

On Servants 10.7

5 τὸ μὲν γὰρ ἀληθὲς πικρόν ἐστι καὶ ἀηδὲς τοῖς ἀνοήτοις, τὸ δὲ ψεῦδος γλυκὺ καὶ προσηνές

The truth is bitter and disagreeable to fools; while falsehood is sweet and soothing.

Translated by H.T. Riley (1872)

Trojan Discourse 11.1

6 οἱ γὰρ πλεῖστοι τῶν ἀνθρώπων οὕτως ἄγαν εἰσὶν ὑπὸ δόξης διεφθαρμένοι τὰς ψυχὰς ὥστε μᾶλλον ἐπιθυμοῦσι περιβόητοι εἶναι ἐπὶ τοῖς μεγίστοις ἀτυχήμασιν ἢ μηδὲν κακὸν ἔχοντες ἀγνοεῖσθαι

Most men are so impressed by popular repute that they would rather be notorious for the greatest calamities than suffer no ill and be unknown.

Trojan Discourse 11.6

7 τὸν δὲ ἀποιχόμενον μνήμῃ τιμᾶτε, μὴ δάκρυσιν

Honour the dead with remembrance, not with tears.

Melancomas I 29.22

8 οὐ γὰρ τὰ ὀνόματα πίστεις τῶν πραγμάτων εἰσί, τὰ δὲ πράγματα καὶ τῶν ὀνομάτων

It is not titles that gain credit for achievements, but achievements for titles.

On Concord with the Nicomedians 38.40

9 ἔστι δὲ ὁ νόμος τοῦ βίου μὲν ἡγεμών, τῶν πόλεων δὲ ἐπιστάτης κοινός, τῶν δὲ πραγμάτων κανὼν δίκαιος … νόμου δὲ χωρὶς οὐκ ἔστιν οὐδεμίαν οἰκεῖσθαι πόλιν

The law is for life a guide, for cities an impartial overseer, and for the conduct of affairs true and just; without law no city can be administered

Translated by H. Lamar Crosby (1951)

On Law 75.1–2

10 χρὴ οὖν δεσπόζειν ἐπιεικῶς καὶ ἀνεθῆναί ποτε βουλομένοις ἐπιτρέπειν· αἱ γὰρ ἀνέσεις παρασκευαστικαὶ πόνων εἰσί, καὶ τόξον καὶ λύρα καὶ ἄνθρωπος ἀκμάζει δι᾽ ἀναπαύσεως

Rule fairly, then, and allow the ruled to relax sometimes; leisure prepares for toil; bow and lyre and man are at their best when rested.

Fragment 5 (von Arnim)

11 ἐγὼ δὲ κοσμεῖσθαι πρόσωπον ὑπὸ δακρύων ἡγοῦμαι μᾶλλον ἢ ὑπὸ γέλωτος· δάκρυσι μὲν γὰρ ὡς ἐπὶ τὸ πλεῖστον σύνεστι καὶ μάθημά που χρηστόν, γέλωτι δὲ ἀκολασία

As for myself, I hold that a face is adorned by tears more than by laughter; for with tears there is as a rule associated some profitable lesson, with laughter licence.

Translated by H. Lamar Crosby (1951)

Fragment 7 (von Arnim)

12 τὸ μὲν τίκτειν ἀνάγκης ἔργον ἐστί, τὸ ἐκτρέφειν δὲ φιλοστοργίας

While the begetting of offspring is an act of necessity, their rearing is an act of love.

Translated by H. Lamar Crosby (1951)

Fragment 9 (von Arnim)

DIODORUS SICULUS

1st century BC

Historian from Agyrium in Sicily

1 τὸν ἆθλον τὸν Ὀλυμπικὸν ἀγῶνα συνεστήσατο, κάλλιστον τῶν τόπων πρὸς τηλικαύτην πανήγυριν προκρίνας τὸ παρὰ τὸν Ἀλφειὸν ποταμὸν πεδίον, ἐν ᾧ τὸν ἀγῶνα τοῦτον τῷ Διὶ τῷ πατρίῳ καθιέρωσε, στεφανίτην δ᾽ αὐτὸν ἐποίησεν

Heracles established the Olympic Games, having selected for so great a festival the most beautiful of places, a plain by the banks of the Alpheios, dedicating them to Zeus the Father, stipulating that only an olive-sprig crown be the prize.

Library of History 4.14.1

2 τῶν γὰρ καθ᾽ ἡμᾶς φιλοσόφων τοὺς πλείστους ἰδεῖν ἔστι λέγοντας μὲν τὰ κάλλιστα, πράττοντας δὲ τὰ χείριστα

Most philosophers of our time are seen uttering the noblest sentiments, but following the basest practices.

Library of History 9.9.1

DIOGENES

*c.*412/403–*c.*324/321BC
Cynic philosopher from Sinope
see also Anonymous 105

1 γῆν ὁρῶ

I see land.

Translated by R.D. Hicks (1925)

Diogenes Laertius, *Lives of Eminent Philosophers* 6.38

when coming to the end of a large and tiresome book, in which he found himself 'quite at sea'

2 Πλάτωνος ὁρισαμένου, ἄνθρωπός ἐστι ζῷον δίπουν ἄπτερον, καὶ εὐδοκιμοῦντος, τίλας ἀλεκτρυόνα εἰσήνεγκεν αὐτὸν εἰς τὴν σχολὴν καί φησιν, οὗτός ἐστιν ὁ Πλάτωνος ἄνθρωπος

Plato having defined man to be a two-legged animal without feathers, Diogenes plucked a cock and brought it into the Academy, and said, 'This is Plato's man.'

Translated in *Bartlett's Familiar Quotations* (1980)

Diogenes Laertius, *Lives of Eminent Philosophers* 6.40.5

cf. Plato 285

3 εἰ μὲν πλούσιος, ὅταν θέλῃ· εἰ δὲ πένης, ὅταν ἔχῃ

If rich, dine when you will; if poor, when you can.

Diogenes Laertius, *Lives of Eminent Philosophers* 6.40.10

when asked what was the proper time for supper

4 ἄνθρωπον ζητῶ

I am searching for an honest man.

Diogenes Laertius, *Lives of Eminent Philosophers* 6.41

going about town with a lantern in broad daylight; 'ανθρωπον ζητώ' still is a proverbial expression; cf. Nietzsche, Menschliches, Allzumenschliches *2.2.18: 'Bevor man den Menschen sucht, muss man die Laterne gefunden haben' (before searching for the man you should have found the lantern); cf. Proverbial 134*

5 ὥσπερ τῶν ἐν γραμματικῇ ἁμαρτημάτων περιρραινόμενος οὐκ ἂν ἀπαλλαγείης, οὕτως οὐδὲ τῶν ἐν τῷ βίῳ

You can no more improve yourself by sacrificing at the altar than you can correct your grammar.

Translated by Guy Davenport (1976)

Diogenes Laertius, *Lives of Eminent Philosophers* 6.42

6 ὡς ὑπὲρ ὧν μὲν πράττουσιν ὕπαρ, οὐκ ἐπιστρέφονται, ὑπὲρ ὧν δὲ καθεύδοντες φαντασιοῦνται, πολυπραγμονοῦσιν

We are more curious about the meaning of dreams than about things we see when awake.

Translated by Guy Davenport (1976)

Diogenes Laertius, *Lives of Eminent Philosophers* 6.43

7 οἱ μεγάλοι κλέπται τὸν μικρὸν ἀπάγουσι

The great thieves are leading away the little thief.

Translated by R.D. Hicks (1925)

Diogenes Laertius, *Lives of Eminent Philosophers* 6.45

of priests taking into custody a poor man who had stolen a saucerful of food from the temple

8 μελετῶ ἀποτυγχάνειν

To get practice in being refused.

Translated in *The Oxford Dictionary of Quotations* (2004)

Diogenes Laertius, *Lives of Eminent Philosophers* 6.49

on being asked why he was begging for alms from a statue

9 μετὰ τὸν πόλεμον ἡ συμμαχία

After the war, alliance.

Diogenes Laertius, *Lives of Eminent Philosophers* 6.50

10 τὸν ἔρωτα σχολαζόντων ἀσχολίαν

Love, a pastime for the idle.

Diogenes Laertius, *Lives of Eminent Philosophers* 6.51.1

11 ἐρωτηθεὶς τί ἄθλιον ἐν βίῳ, ἔφη, γέρων ἄπορος

When asked what is wretched in life he replied, 'An old man destitute.'

Translated by R.D. Hicks (1925)

Diogenes Laertius, *Lives of Eminent Philosophers* 6.51.2

12 πρὸς τὸν εἰπόντα κακὸν εἶναι τὸ ζῆν, οὐ τὸ ζῆν, εἶπεν, ἀλλὰ τὸ κακῶς ζῆν

When someone declared that life is an evil, Diogenes replied, 'Life is not, but a bad life is.'

Diogenes Laertius, *Lives of Eminent Philosophers* 6.55

13 ἄνθρωπε, εἶπεν, εἰς τροφήν σε αἰτῶ, οὐκ εἰς ταφήν

My friend, it's for food that I'm asking, not for funeral expenses.

Translated by R.D. Hicks (1925)

Diogenes Laertius, *Lives of Eminent Philosophers* 6.56

to a miserly man who took his time deciding whether to give him any money

14 ἐρωτηθεὶς πόθεν εἴη, κοσμοπολίτης, ἔφη

I am a citizen of the world.

Translated by R.D. Hicks (1925)

Diogenes Laertius, *Lives of Eminent Philosophers* 6.63.3

on being asked where he was from; if this answer is authentic, it indicates that the term 'cosmopolitan' originated with Diogenes; cf. Epictetus 56

15 καὶ γὰρ ὁ ἥλιος, ἔφη, εἰς τοὺς ἀποπάτους, ἀλλ' οὐ μιαίνεται

The sun shines into dung but is not defiled itself.

Diogenes Laertius, *Lives of Eminent Philosophers* 6.63.11

cf. the English proverb 'the sun loses nothing by shining into a puddle'

16 ἵνα μὴ πληγῶ

In order that I may not be hit.

Translated by Gavin Betts and Alan Henry (1989)

Diogenes Laertius, *Lives of Eminent Philosophers* 6.67

when asked why he sat close to a poor marksman's target

17 τὴν παιδείαν εἶπε τοῖς μὲν νέοις σωφροσύνην, τοῖς δὲ πρεσβυτέροις παραμυθίαν, τοῖς δὲ πένησι πλοῦτον, τοῖς δὲ πλουσίοις κόσμον εἶναι

Education is wisdom to the young, consolation to the old, wealth to the poor, and ornament to the rich.

Translated by R.D. Hicks (1925)

Diogenes Laertius, *Lives of Eminent Philosophers* 6.68

18 ἐρωτηθεὶς τί κάλλιστον ἐν ἀνθρώποις, ἔφη, παρρησία

Being asked what was the most beautiful thing in the world, he replied, 'Freedom of speech.'

Translated by R.D. Hicks (1925)

Diogenes Laertius, *Lives of Eminent Philosophers* 6.69

19 οὐδέν γε μὴν ἔλεγε τὸ παράπαν ἐν τῷ βίῳ χωρὶς ἀσκήσεως κατορθοῦσθαι

Nothing in life has any chance of succeeding without strenuous practice.

Translated by R.D. Hicks (1925)

Diogenes Laertius, *Lives of Eminent Philosophers* 6.71

20 γνώμαις γὰρ ἀνδρῶν εὖ μὲν οἰκοῦνται πόλεις,
εὖ δ' οἶκος, οὐ ψαλμοῖσι καὶ τερετίσμασιν

By men's minds states are governed well,
and households; not by songs and prattle.

Diogenes Laertius, *Lives of Eminent Philosophers* 6.104

spoken by Diogenes to a man who gave him a musical recital; cf. Euripides, Fragment 200 (Nauck)

21 αὐτὸν οὐ γιγνώσκω· οὐ γάρ εἰμι ἔμπειρος αὐτοῦ τῆς διανοίας

The man I know not, for I am not acquainted with his mind.

Translated by J.W. Cohoon (1932)

Dio Chrysostom, *On Kingship* 4.17

22 μικρὸν, εἶπεν, ἀπὸ τοῦ ἡλίου μετάστηθι

'Yes,' he said 'stand out of my sun a little.'

Plutarch, *Alexander* 14.4

when asked by Alexander if he had any favour to ask; cf. Alexander 6

23 εἰπόντος τινὸς πρὸς αὐτόν, οὗτοι σοῦ καταγελῶσιν, ἀλλ' ἐγώ, εἶπεν, οὐ καταγελῶμαι

When told that many people laughed at him, he made answer, 'But I am not laughed down.'

Translated by R.D. Hicks (1925)

Plutarch, *Fabius Maximus* 10.2

24 ὅσῳ ἐνδοτέρω φεύγεις, μᾶλλον ἐν τῷ καπηλείῳ γίγνῃ

The farther you flee inside, the more you are in the tavern.

Translated by Frank Cole Babbitt (1927)

Plutarch, *Progress in Virtue* 82d

i.e. the more you try to escape, the more you get involved; said to the young Demosthenes, cf. Plutarch, Lives of the Ten Orators *847f*

25 πυνθανομένου τινός, πῶς ἄν τις ἑαυτοῦ διδάσκαλος γένοιτο εἰ ὑπὲρ ὧν ἐπιτιμᾷ τοῖς ἄλλοις ἔφη καὶ ἑαυτῷ ἐπιτιμῴη μάλιστα

When someone enquired of Diogenes how to teach yourself, he replied, 'Whatever you censure in others, censure yourself the more.'

Stobaeus, *Anthology* 3.1.55

26 Διογένης παρὰ μὲν τῶν θεῶν φησίν ὑγίειαν εὔχονται· πάντα δὲ οἱ πλεῖστοι τἀναντία τῇ ὑγιείᾳ πράττουσιν

Diogenes said that even though people ask the gods for good health, everything most of them do, is bad for it.

Stobaeus, *Anthology* 3.6.35

27 ὁρῶν Μεγαρέας ὁ Διογένης τὰ μακρὰ τείχη ἱστάντας ὦ μοχθηροί εἶπε μὴ τοῦ μεγέθους προνοεῖτε τῶν τειχῶν, ἀλλὰ τῶν ἐπ' αὐτῶν στησομένων

When Diogenes saw the Megarians building a great wall he said, 'Poor wretches! Do not concern yourselves with the size of the wall, but with those who will defend it!'

Stobaeus, *Anthology* 3.7.46

28 τῆς ἀλαζονείας καθάπερ τῶν κεχρυσωμένων ὅπλων οὐχ ὅμοιά ἐστι τὰ ἐντὸς τοῖς ἐκτός

Boastfulness is as a gilded weapon; the outside bears no relation to what is inside.

Stobaeus, *Anthology* 3.22.40

29 Διογένης τὰς εὐμόρφους τῶν ἑταιρῶν βασιλίσσας ἐκάλει, πολλοὺς γὰρ πράττειν ἃ ἂν προστάττωσι

Diogenes considered pretty concubines as queens, for many obey what they command.

Stobaeus, *Anthology* 4.21a.15

30 τῶν ἀνθρώπων εὐγενέστατοι οἱ καταφρονοῦντες πλούτου, δόξης, ἡδονῆς, ζωῆς, τῶν δ' ἐναντίων ὑπεράνω ὄντες πενίας, ἀδοξίας, πόνου, θανάτου

Noblest are those who scorn riches, fame, pleasures, life itself; being above poverty, obscurity, suffering and death.

Stobaeus, *Anthology* 4.29d.57

31 ἔλεγε δὲ μήτε ἐν πόλει πλουσίᾳ μήτε ἐν οἰκίᾳ ἀρετὴν οἰκεῖν δύνασθαι

Virtue cannot live in a wealthy city or a wealthy house.

Stobaeus, *Anthology* 4.31c.88

32 οὐδένα τυραννοῦντα διὰ πενίαν ἑώρακα· διὰ δὲ πλοῦτον τοὺς πάντας

I've never seen anyone become a tyrant hoping for poverty; they all go for riches.

Stobaeus, *Anthology* 4.33.26

to one who belittled him on his poverty

33 εὐδαιμονία γὰρ μία ἐστὶ τὸ εὐφραίνεσθαι ἀληθινῶς καὶ μηδέποτε λυπεῖσθαι, ἐν ὁποίῳ δ' ἂν τόπῳ ἢ καιρῷ ᾖ τις

Real happiness is to truly be of good cheer and never to sulk, at whatever occasion and whatever time.

Stobaeus, *Anthology* 4.39.20

34 εὐδαιμονίαν δὲ ταύτην εἶναι φαμὲν ἀληθινὴν τὸ τὴν διάνοιαν καὶ τὴν ψυχὴν ἀεὶ ἐν ἡσυχίᾳ καὶ ἱλαρότητι διατρίβειν

True happiness is to always be, in mind and soul, at peace and in cheerfulness.

Stobaeus, *Anthology* 4.39.21

35 θέλω τύχης σταλαγμὸν ἢ φρενῶν πίθον

Better a drop of luck than a jug of wisdom.

Fragment 2 (Snell, *TrGF*) – *Chrysippus*

some doubt that Diogenes wrote any tragedies; also in Menander, One-liners *333 (Jaekel); quoted by St Gregory of Nazianzus in* Carmina Moralia *968*

DIOGENES LAERTIUS

3rd century AD
Author of a biography of philosophers
see also Periander 26; Theophrastus 12

1 Φοῖβος ἔφυσε βροτοῖς Ἀσκληπιὸν ἠδὲ Πλάτωνα,
τὸν μέν, ἵνα ψυχήν, τὸν δ', ἵνα σῶμα σάοι.

Apollo gave mortals both Asclepius and Plato,
the one to save the body, the other the soul.

Greek Anthology 7.109

said to have been inscribed on Plato's tomb

DIOGENES OF APOLLONIA

5th century BC
Philosopher

1 ἄνθρωποι γὰρ καὶ τὰ ἄλλα ζῷα ἀναπνέοντα ζώει τῷ ἀέρι· καὶ τοῦτο αὐτοῖς καὶ ψυχή ἐστι καὶ νόησις, ... καὶ ἐὰν τοῦτο ἀπαλλαχθῇ, ἀποθνήσκει καὶ ἡ νόησις ἐπιλείπει

Man and the other animals that breathe live by air; and this is both soul and thought for them, and if this is taken away they die and thought leaves them.

Translated by Jonathan Barnes (1979)

Fragment 4 (D-K)

DIOGENES OF BABYLON

*c.*240–152BC
Stoic philosopher

1 ἀρεταὶ δὲ λόγου εἰσὶ πέντε· ἑλληνισμός, σαφήνεια, συντομία, πρέπον, κατασκευή

There are five excellences of speech – pure Greek, lucidity, brevity, appropriateness, distinction.

Translated by R.D. Hicks (1925)

Fragment 24.1 (von Arnim, *SVF*)

2 ἑλληνισμὸς μὲν οὖν ἐστι φράσις ἀδιάπτωτος ἐν τῇ τεχνικῇ καὶ μὴ εἰκαίᾳ συνηθείᾳ

By good Greek is meant language grammatically faultless and free from careless vulgarity.

Translated by R.D. Hicks (1925)

Fragment 24.3 (von Arnim, *SVF*)

3 σαφήνεια δέ ἐστι λέξις γνωρίμως παριστᾶσα τὸ νοούμενον· συντομία δέ ἐστι λέξις αὐτὰ τὰ ἀναγκαῖα περιέχουσα πρὸς δήλωσιν τοῦ πράγματος· πρέπον δέ ἐστι λέξις οἰκεία τῷ πράγματι· κατασκευὴ δέ ἐστι λέξις ἐκπεφευγυῖα τὸν ἰδιωτισμόν

Lucidity is a style which presents the thought in a way easily understood; brevity a style that employs no more words than are necessary for setting forth the subject in hand; appropriateness lies in a style akin to the subject; distinction is the avoidance of colloquialism.

Translated by R.D. Hicks (1925)

Fragment 24.5 (von Arnim, *SVF*)

4 ἐννόημα δέ ἐστι φάντασμα διανοίας, οὔτε τὶ ὂν οὔτε ποιόν, ὡσανεὶ δὲ τὶ ὂν καὶ ὡσανεὶ ποιόν· οἷον γίνεται ἀνατύπωμα ἵππου καὶ μὴ παρόντος

A notion or object of thought is a presentation to the intellect which, though not really substance nor attribute, is quasi-substance or quasi-attribute. Thus an image of a horse may rise before the mind, although there is no horse present.

Translated by R.D. Hicks (1925)

Fragment 25 (von Arnim, *SVF*)

cf. Zeno, Fragment 65 (von Arnim, SVF)

5 ὁ μὲν οὖν Διογένης τέλος φησὶ ῥητῶς τὸ εὐλογιστεῖν ἐν τῇ τῶν κατὰ φύσιν ἐκλογῇ

Diogenes expressly declares the end to be to act with good reason in the selection of what is natural.

Translated by R.D. Hicks (1925)

Fragment 45 (von Arnim, *SVF*)

DIOGENES OF OENOANDA

probably 2nd century AD
Author of a Greek inscription presenting the doctrines of Epicureanism

1 καθ' ἑκάστην μὲν γὰρ ἀποτομὴν τῆς γῆς ἄλλων ἄλλη πατρίς ἐστιν, κατὰ δὲ τὴν ὅλην περιοχὴν τοῦδε τοῦ κόσμου μία πάντων πατρίς ἐστιν ἡ πᾶσα γῆ καὶ εἷς ὁ κόσμος οἶκος

While the various segments of the earth give different people a different country, the whole compass of this world gives all people a single country, the entire earth, and a single home, the world.

Translated by Martin Ferguson Smith (1993)

Fragment 30 (Smith)

from a huge inscription carved on a wall at Oenoanda, excavated by Martin Ferguson Smith; the recovered section illuminates Epicurean theory

DIOGENIANUS

2nd century AD
Grammarian from Heraclea Pontica

1 Ἀβυδηνὸν ἐπιφόρημα ... ἔθος γὰρ τοῖς Ἀβυδηνοῖς μετὰ τὸ δεῖπνον καὶ τὰς σπονδὰς προσάγειν τοὺς παῖδας μετὰ τῶν τιτθῶν τοῖς εὐωχημένοις· κεκραγότων δὲ τῶν παίδων καὶ θορύβου γενομένου, ἀηδίαν πολλὴν εἶναι τοῖς δαιτυμόσιν

The dessert of Abydos: the people of Abydos have the custom, when entertaining guests, of sending for the children after dinner, with their nurses. The children howl, a great din arises, and this is very disagreeable for the guests.

Translated by Kathleen Freeman (1947)

Proverbs 1.1

DIONYSIUS I

*c.*430–*c.*367BC
General, orator, diplomat and dramatist, ruler of Syracuse

1 τυραννὶς ἀδικίας μήτηρ

Tyranny is the mother of injustice.

Fragment 4 (Snell, *TrGF*)

his play The Ransom of Hector *won the prize at the Lenaea at Athens in 367BC*

2 ἢ λέγε τι σιγῆς κρεῖσσον ἢ σιγὴν ἔχε

Say something better than silence – or hold your peace.

Fragment 6 (Snell, *TrGF*)

also found in Menander, One-liners *(Jaekel)* 292

3 τοῖς οὐδὲν οὖσιν οὐδὲ εἷς ὅλως φθονεῖ

Nobody is envious of nonentities.

Fragment 7 (Snell, *TrGF*)

also found in Dionysius Comic, Fragment 7 (Kock) – 7 (K-A)

4 αὐτὸς πενόμενος τοῖς ἔχουσι μὴ φθόνει

When poor, do not begrudge the rich.

Fragment 8 (Snell, *TrGF*)

see also Menander, One-liners *(Meineke) 43*

DIONYSIUS II

*c.*396–357BC
Eldest son of Dionysius I, with a passion for philosophy

1 ὁ δὲ νεώτερος Διονύσιος ... ἐκπεσὼν τῆς ἀρχῆς πρὸς τὸν εἰπόντα, τί σε Πλάτων καὶ φιλοσοφία ὠφέλησε; τὸ τηλικαύτην ἔφη τύχης μεταβολὴν ῥᾳδίως ὑπομένειν

The younger Dionysius, when forced to abdicate, was asked what help Plato and philosophy had given him? 'The power to submit to so great a change of fortune without complaint,' he replied.

Plutarch, *Sayings of Kings and Commanders* 176d

DIONYSIUS OF HALICARNASSUS

*fl.*30–7BC
Greek historian, resident in Rome from 30BC

1 ἱστορίας, ἐν αἷς καθιδρῦσθαι τὴν ἀλήθειαν ὑπολαμβάνομεν ἀρχὴν φρονήσεώς τε καὶ σοφίας οὖσαν

History, in which we have the right to assume that truth is enshrined, is the source of both prudence and wisdom.

Translated by Earnest Cary (1937)

Roman Antiquities 1.1.2

2 ἐπιεικῶς γὰρ ἅπαντες νομίζουσιν εἰκόνας εἶναι τῆς ἑκάστου ψυχῆς τοὺς λόγους

We all pretty well believe that a man's words are the images of his soul.

Roman Antiquities 1.1.3

3 μαχητὰς δέ γε καὶ δικαίους ἄνδρας καὶ τὰς ἄλλας ἀρετὰς ἐπιτηδεύοντας τὸ τῆς πολιτείας σχῆμα ποιεῖν τοῖς φρονίμως αὐτὸ καταστησαμένοις

Brave, just and honourable men are the product of a wise form of government.

Roman Antiquities 2.3.5.5

4 μαλθακούς τε αὖ καὶ πλεονέκτας καὶ δούλους αἰσχρῶν ἐπιθυμιῶν τὰ πονηρὰ ἐπιτηδεύματα ἐπιτελεῖν

Men who are cowardly, rapacious, and slaves of base passions are the product of a knavish way of living.

Roman Antiquities 2.3.5.8

5 οὕτως ἐγκρατὴς ὁ βίος ἦν αὐτοῖς ἁπάσης ἡδονῆς καὶ τὸ μακάριον ἀρετῇ μετρῶν, οὐ τύχῃ

Their manner of life was superior to all pleasure; for they measured their happiness by virtue, not by fortune.

Roman Antiquities 2.10.4

of the Romans under Romulus

6 αὐτίκα περὶ γάμων καὶ τῆς πρὸς γυναῖκας ὁμιλίας, ἀφ' ἧς ἄρχεσθαι δεῖ τὸν νομοθέτην

Marriage and intercourse with women should be the law-maker's starting point.

Roman Antiquities 2.24.4

7 περὶ δὲ φυλακῆς γάμων καὶ σωφροσύνης γυναικῶν νομοθετεῖν οὔτε μεῖζον οὔτ' ἔλαττον οὐδὲν ἐπεχείρησαν, ἀλλ' ὡς ἀδυνάτου πράγματος ἀπέστησαν

Regarding the protection of marriage and the honour of women they have never attempted any regulation whatever, abandoning the idea as impossible.

Translated by Dan Hogg (2006)

Roman Antiquities 2.24.5

of the Romans under Romulus

8 ταῦτα δὲ οἱ συγγενεῖς μετὰ τοῦ ἀνδρὸς ἐδίκαζον· ἐν οἷς ἦν φθορὰ σώματος καί, ὃ πάντων ἐλάχιστον ἁμαρτημάτων Ἕλλησι δόξειεν ἂν ὑπάρχειν, εἴ τις οἶνον εὑρεθείη πιοῦσα γυνή

Some offences, however, were judged by a wife's relations with her husband; among them was adultery, or whether she had drunk wine – a thing which the Greeks would look upon as the least of all faults.

Translated by Earnest Cary (1937)

Roman Antiquities 2.25.6

of the Romans under Romulus

9 νῦν δ' οὐχ ὡς ἄμεινον … ὁρίζουσί τινες ἀπὸ τῶν ἀλλοτρίων τὰ οἰκεῖα, ἀλλ' ἔστιν αὐτοῖς ὅρος τῶν κτήσεων οὐχ ὁ νόμος, ἀλλ' ἡ πάντων ἐπιθυμία

Nowadays there are those who determine what is theirs and what is someone else's not in accordance with the law but through their greed to possess everything.

Roman Antiquities 2.74.5

10 ἀλλὰ καὶ βασιλεῖς ἀποδείκνυτε ξένους

Even for your kings you choose foreigners.

Roman Antiquities 3.10.5

of the Romans

11 μάθε καὶ κατὰ τοῦτο ἁμαρτάνων … λέγων ὅτι … τὸ ἡμέτερον εὐγενὲς διέφθαρται ταῖς ἐπιμιξίαις τοῦ ἀλλοφύλου, καὶ οὐκ ἠξίους ἄρχειν τῶν γνησίων τοὺς νόθους οὐδὲ τῶν αὐθιγενῶν τοὺς ἐπήλυδας

You are greatly mistaken asserting that our nobility has been corrupted by interbreeding with foreigners, and demanding that the base-born should not rule over the well-born, nor newcomers over the native-born.

Roman Antiquities 3.11.3

Tullus Hostilius on his policy of equality of citizens, including immigrants

12 κοινὴν ἀναδείξαντες τὴν πόλιν τοῖς βουλομένοις, ὥστε καὶ σεμνυνόμεθα ἐπὶ τούτῳ μάλιστα τῷ ἔργῳ … παρὰ δὲ τῆς Ἀθηναίων πόλεως τὸ παράδειγμα λαβόντες, ἧς μέγιστον κλέος ἐν Ἕλλησίν ἐστι

We have made the privileges of our city free to all who desired them and even take the greatest pride in this policy, having followed the example of Athens, which enjoys the greatest fame among Greeks.

Roman Antiquities 3.11.4

Tullus Hostilius on his policy of incorporating foreigners as fully privileged citizens

13 οὐ γὰρ ἐν ἄλλῳ τινὶ τὴν ἀνθρωπίνην εὐγένειαν ὑπάρχειν νομίζομεν, ἀλλ' ἐν ἀρετῇ

We look upon nobility as consisting of nothing but virtue.

Roman Antiquities 3.11.5

14 ἐν ἰσχύι γὰρ ὅπλων κεῖται τὸ τῶν πόλεων κράτος

The power of states rests in the force of arms.

Roman Antiquities 3.11.6

15 οὔτε … τά γέ τοι παρὰ τῶν θεῶν ὅμοια ἔμελλε ταῖς ἀνθρωπίναις ἀγνοίαις ἔσεσθαι

It is hardly likely, however, that the gods will act with an ignorance resembling that of men.

Roman Antiquities 3.35.5

16 οὐ γὰρ ἂν γένοιτο φρόνημα εὐγενὲς ἐν ἀνδράσιν ἀπορουμένοις τῶν καθ' ἡμέραν ἀναγκαίων

One cannot expect noble thoughts from men who struggle for daily necessities.

Roman Antiquities 4.9.8

17 οἱ δ' ἀνειμένοι τῶν εἰσφορῶν ... εἰ τιμήσασθαι τοὺς βίους ἀναγκασθήσονται καὶ ἀπὸ τῶν τιμημάτων τὰς εἰσφορὰς συνεισφέρειν

Those who have been exempt from taxes resent being compelled to submit a valuation of their property and to pay taxes in proportion to those valuations.

Translated by Earnest Cary (1939)

Roman Antiquities 4.11.2

18 βεβίωται γάρ ἤδη μοι καὶ πρὸς ἀρετὴν καὶ πρὸς εὐδοξίαν

I have already lived long enough both for virtue and for glory.

Translated by Earnest Cary (1939)

Roman Antiquities 4.11.6

cf. Cicero, Pro Marcello *25: 'satis diu vel naturae vixi vel gloriae' (I have lived long enough either for nature or for glory, tr. N.H. Watts, 1931)*

19 μικρὰ καὶ ὀλιγοχρόνια ... ὄψεώς τ' ἀπάτας, οὐκ ἀληθεῖς βίου καὶ πραγμάτων ὠφελείας, ἐξ ὧν μακαρισμοὶ τοῖς κατασκευασαμένοις ἠκολούθουν μόνον

Trivial and ephemeral, beguilement for the eyes, irrelevant to the conduct of life and public affairs, they serve only to enhance the reputation of their builders.

Roman Antiquities 4.25.3

Servius Tullius on public monuments, such as the pyramids at Memphis

20 κἀμοὶ ψοφοδεὴς καὶ οὐδὲν ἔχων ἀνδρὸς ἀνήρ, ὅς με ταπεινὴν ποιεῖ μεγάλων οὖσαν ἀξίαν καὶ καλὴν τὸ σῶμα, μαρανθεῖσαν δ' ὑπ' αὐτοῦ

I have a faint-hearted, unmanly husband, humbling me though I am capable of great achievements; and, although fair of body, I have withered away in his shadow.

Roman Antiquities 4.29.6

Tullia of her husband Arruns

21 βασιλείας γε χάριν οὐ νέμεσις ἅπαντα τολμᾶν

For the sake of a throne one cannot be blamed for daring anything.

Translated by Earnest Cary (1939)

Roman Antiquities 4.29.7

cf. Euripides 293; and 'οὐ νέμεσις' in Homer 53

22 ἅπαντα μέν, ὡς ἔοικεν, ἄνθρωπον ὄντα δεῖ προσδοκᾶν, ὦ βουλή, τὰ παράδοξα καὶ μηδὲν ἡγεῖσθαι ἄπιστον

Anything, it seems, that is unexpected should be expected by man, and nothing should be regarded as incredible.

Translated by Earnest Cary (1939)

Roman Antiquities 4.33.1

23 ἀλλὰ δυεῖν θάτερον ἅπασιν αἱρετέον, ἢ βίον ἐλεύθερον, ἢ θάνατον ἔνδοξον

We must all choose one of two things – life with liberty or death with glory.

Translated by Earnest Cary (1939)

Roman Antiquities 4.82.4

24 αἰσχρόν ... περὶ ... πλεονεξίας πολλοὺς ἀναιρεῖσθαι πολέμους, περὶ δὲ τῆς ἑαυτῶν ἐλευθερίας μηδένα

It is a disgrace to undertake many wars to satisfy ambition, but not one to recover our own liberty.

Roman Antiquities 4.82.5

25 ἔμφυτος ἅπασιν ἀνθρώποις ὁ τῆς ἐλευθερίας πόθος

Desire for liberty is ingrained in all mankind.

Translated by Dan Hogg (2006)

Roman Antiquities 4.83.2

26 λύπαι τε γὰρ ἡδοναῖς ἐκέκραντο ... καὶ θυμοὶ συνεξέπιπτον φόβοις

Pain was mingled with pleasure and anger went hand in hand with fear.

Translated by Earnest Cary (1939)

Roman Antiquities 4.84.1

27 πεφύκασιν ἅπαντες ἀπὸ τῶν ἰδίων παθῶν τὰ περὶ τῶν ἄλλων λεγόμενα κρίνειν

All men naturally judge others by their own experience.

Translated by Dan Hogg (2006)

Roman Antiquities 5.8.1

28 ἐκ μιᾶς τῆς περὶ τὸν θάνατον ἀρετῆς, κἂν τἄλλα φαῦλος γένηταί τις, ἐξετάζειν οἰόμενοι δεῖν τοὺς ἀγαθούς

Determine a man's merit only on the basis of the valour he shows at his death, even if undistinguished in other things.

Roman Antiquities 5.17.5

29 κρεῖττον γάρ ἐστιν ὀψὲ ἄρξασθαι τὰ δέοντα πράττειν ἢ μηδέποτε

Better to start late than not at all.

Roman Antiquities 9.9.2

cf. the English proverb 'better late than never'

30 κρείττων γὰρ ἡ πρόνοια τῆς μεταμελείας

Precaution is better than repentance.

Translated by H.T. Riley (1872)

Roman Antiquities 11.20.6.10

31 τὸ μὴ πιστεύειν τοῖς πονηροῖς σωφρονέστερον τοῦ προπιστεύσαντας κατηγορεῖν

It is more prudent not to trust the wicked at all than to first trust and then censure them.

Roman Antiquities 11.20.6.11

32 παιδεία ἄρα ἐστὶν ἡ ἔντευξις τῶν ἠθῶν

Education is the contact with manners.

*Ars Rhetorica** 11.2.34

33 ἱστορία φιλοσοφία ἐστὶν ἐκ παραδειγμάτων

History is philosophy teaching by examples.

Translated in *The Oxford Dictionary of Quotations* (1975)

*Ars Rhetorica** 11.2.36

34 χαριεντισμὸς γὰρ πᾶς ἐν σπουδῇ καὶ κακοῖς γινόμενος ἄωρον πρᾶγμα καὶ πολεμιώτατον ἐλέῳ

Any show of wit in sorrow or misfortune is untimely and adverse to compassion.

Critical Essays – Isocrates 12.24

criticizing Isocrates' style

35 καὶ μέλος ἔχουσιν αἱ λέξεις καὶ ῥυθμὸν καὶ μεταβολὴν

There's melody in words and rhythm and change.

On Literary Composition 11.67

DIONYSIUS OF SINOPE

5th/4th century BC
Comic poet

1 πρὸς τὸν τελευτήσανθ' ἕκαστος, κἂν σφόδρα
ζῶν ἐχθρὸς ᾖ τις, γίνεται φίλος τότε

Everyone becomes the friend of the deceased,
even if in life he was your worst enemy.

Fragment 6 (Kock) – 6 (K-A) – *Sozousa*

DIOPHANES

dates unknown
Epigrammatist from Myrina (unknown if Myrina in Aeolis or Myrina of Lemnos)

1 Τρὶς λῃστὴς ὁ Ἔρως καλοῖτ' ἂν ὄντως·
ἀγρυπνεῖ, θρασύς ἐστιν, ἐκδιδύσκει.

A thief, and triply so!
I speak of Love,
Who, daring, comes by night,
And strips us bare.

Translated by Edward Lucie-Smith (1933–)

Greek Anthology 5.309

DIOSCORIDES EPIGRAMMATICUS

not earlier than 3rd century BC
Author of forty epigrams in *Greek Anthology*

1 Ἵππον Ἀθήνιον ᾖσεν ἐμοὶ κακόν· ἐν πυρὶ πᾶσα
Ἴλιος ἦν, κἀγὼ κείνῃ ἅμ' ἐφλεγόμαν,
οὐ δείσας Δαναῶν δεκέτη πόνον· ἐν δ' ἑνὶ φέγγει
τῷ τότε καὶ Τρῶες κἀγὼ ἀπωλόμεθα.

Athenion sang 'The Horse,' the evil horse.
All Troy in flames; and burning thus for her am I.
Ten years of Grecian toil, and in one day
all Trojans perished; and so did I.

Greek Anthology 5.138

Athenion, a songstress only mentioned here

DIOTOGENES

between 3rd century BC and 2nd century AD
Nominal author (otherwise unknown)

1 τίς οὖν ἀρχὰ πολιτείας ἁπάσας; νέων τροφά

The foundation of every state is the

education of its youth.

Translated by H.T. Riley (1872)

DIPHILUS

c.360–350BC

New Comedy poet from Sinope

1 ἀπροσδόκητον οὐδὲν ἀνθρώποις πάθος·
ἐφημέρους γὰρ τὰς τύχας κεκτήμεθα

No human sorrow is unexpected; fate is fleeting.

Fragment 45 (Kock) – 44 (K-A) – *Zographos – The Painter*

2 ὅστις γὰρ αὐτὸς αὑτὸν οὐκ αἰσχύνεται
συνειδόθ' αὑτῷ φαῦλα διαπεπραγμένῳ,
πῶς τόν γε μηδὲν εἰδότ' αἰσχυνθήσεται;

If one is not ashamed of one's own shortcomings, how shall another be ashamed of what he does not know?

Fragment 92 (Kock) – 92 (K-A)

3 εἰ μὴ τὸ λαβεῖν ἦν, οὐδὲ εἷς πονηρὸς ἦν

Without gain there would be no cunning.

Fragment 94 (Kock) – 94 (K-A)

4 πρὸς τῷ λαβεῖν γὰρ ὢν ὁ νοῦς τἄλλ' οὐχ ὁρᾷ

Whoever is bent on grabbing is blind to all else.

Fragment 99 (Kock) – 99 (K-A)

5 ἔργον συναγαγεῖν σωρὸν ἐν πολλῷ χρόνῳ,
ἐν ἡμέρᾳ δὲ διαφορῆσαι ῥᾴδιον

It is hard to gather much over many years,
easy to scatter all in a day.

Fragment 100 (Kock) – 100 (K-A)

6 ὅρκος δ' ἑταίρας ταὐτὸ καὶ δημηγόρου·
ἑκάτερος αὐτῶν ὀμνύει πρὸς ὃν λαλεῖ

A politician's oath is as a prostitute's, given to whoever is there.

Fragment 101 (Kock) – 101 (K-A)

7 πένητος ἀνδρὸς οὐδὲν εὐτυχέστερον·
τὴν ἐπὶ τὸ χεῖρον μεταβολὴν οὐ προσδοκᾷ

No one is more content than a poor man;
he does not expect changes for the worst.

Fragment 104 (Kock) – 104 (K-A)

cf. the English proverb 'blessed is he who expects nothing, for he shall never be disappointed'

8 οὐκ ἔστ' ἀναιδοῦς ζῷον εὐθαρσέστερον

There is no animal as bold as a reckless man.

Fragment 111ab (Kock) – 110 (K-A)

9 ὡς μακάριον φρόνησις ἐν χρηστῷ τρόπῳ

How blessed is wisdom within a righteous character.

Fragment 114 (Kock) – 113 (K-A)

10 θνητὸς πεφυκὼς μὴ εὐλαβοῦ τεθνηκέναι

As you were born mortal, be not afraid of death.

Fragment 116 (Kock) – 115 (K-A)

11 λύπης δὲ πάσης γίνετ' ἰατρὸς χρόνος

Time is a doctor who heals all griefs.

Translated by D.S. Baker (1998)

Fragment 117 (Kock) – 116 (K-A)

12 εὐμετάβολός ἐστιν ἀνθρώπων βίος

How changeful is the life of man!

Fragment 118 (Kock) – 117 (K-A)

DISSOI LOGOI

c.400BC

A philosophical treatise of unknown authorship

1 Δισσοὶ λόγοι λέγονται ἐν τᾷ Ἑλλάδι ὑπὸ τῶν φιλοσοφούντων περὶ τῷ ἀγαθῷ καὶ τῷ κακῷ· τοὶ μὲν γὰρ λέγοντι, ὡς ἄλλο μέν ἐστι τὸ ἀγαθόν, ἄλλο δὲ τὸ κακόν· τοὶ δέ, ὡς τὸ αὐτό ἐστι, καὶ τοῖς μὲν ἀγαθὸν εἴη, τοῖς δὲ κακόν, καὶ τῷ αὐτῷ ἀνθρώπῳ τοτὲ μὲν ἀγαθόν, τοτὲ δὲ κακόν

Double arguments are offered in Greece by those who philosophize about the good and the bad. For some say that the good is one thing, the bad another; others that they are the same – good for some, bad for others; and for the same man now good, now bad.

Translated by Jonathan Barnes (1979)

Dialexeis (Double Arguments), Fragment 1.1 (D-K)

2 νόσος τοίνυν τοῖς μὲν ἀσθενεῦντι κακόν, τοῖς δὲ ἰατροῖς ἀγαθόν· ὁ τοίνυν θάνατος τοῖς μὲν ἀποθανοῦσι κακόν, τοῖς δ' ἐνταφιοπώλαις ἀγαθόν

Illness is bad for the sick, good for the doctors. Death is bad for the dead, good for the undertakers.

Translated by Jonathan Barnes (1979)

Dialexeis (Double Arguments), Fragment 1.7 (D-K)

3 κοσμεῖσθαι καὶ ψιμυθίῳ χρίεσθαι καὶ χρυσία περιάπτεσθαι, τῷ μὲν ἀνδρὶ αἰσχρόν, τᾷ δὲ γυναικὶ καλόν

To adorn oneself and wear gold trinkets and powder one's face is fine for women, shameful for men.

Dialexeis (Double Arguments), Fragment 2 (D-K)

E

ECUMENICAL COUNCILS

various dates AD

1 πίστευε τῷ θαύματι καὶ μὴ ἐρεύνα λογισμοῖς

Believe in miracles and do not search for reason.

Acts of Ecumenical Councils, Council of Ephesus (431AD) 1.1.2.89.31 (Schwartz, *ACO*)

usually quoted as 'πίστευε καὶ μὴ ἐρεύνα'; opposite of 'ἐρεύνα καὶ πίστευε', a precept of the earliest Christian Fathers

EMPEDOCLES

*c.*492–432BC

Philosopher and poet from Acragas in Sicily

see also Xenophanes 15

1 ὠκύμοροι καπνοῖο δίκην ἀρθέντες ἀπέπταν

Transient man rises and flies away like smoke.

Fragment 2 (D-K)

2 ἦ γὰρ καὶ πάρος ἔσκε, καὶ ἔσσεται, οὐδέ ποτ', οἴω,
τούτων ἀμφοτέρων κενεώσεται ἄσπετος αἰών

For they are as they were before and as they will be, nor ever, I think,
will boundless eternity be emptied of these two.

Translated by Jonathan Barnes (1987)

Fragment 16 (D-K)

of Love and Strife

3 ᾗ δὲ διαλλάσσοντα διαμπερὲς οὐδαμὰ λήγει,
ταύτῃ δ' αἰὲν ἔασιν ἀκίνητοι κατὰ κύκλον

They never cease their continual change,
they exist forever, motionless in a cyclic process.

Fragment 17.12 (D-K)

of periodic creation and destruction

4 ἄλλοτε μὲν Φιλότητι συνερχόμεν εἰς ἓν ἅπαντα,
ἄλλοτε δ' αὖ δίχ' ἕκαστα φορεύμενα Νείκεος ἔχθει

Now coming together by Love all into one,
now again being carried apart by the hatred of Strife.

Translated by Jonathan Barnes (1987)

Fragment 17.16 (D-K)

of the one and many

5 μάθη γάρ τοι φρένας αὔξει

It is learning that develops the intellect.

Fragment 17.23 (D-K)

6 τὴν σὺ νόῳ δέρκευ, μηδ' ὄμμασιν ἧσο τεθηπώς

Her you must regard with your mind: do not sit staring with your eyes.

Translated by Jonathan Barnes (1987)

Fragment 17.30 (D-K)

7 καὶ δὶς γάρ, ὃ δεῖ, καλόν ἐστιν ἐνισπεῖν

It is good to insist, even twice, on what is right.

Fragment 25 (D-K)

8 ἀλλ' ὅ γε πάντοθεν ἶσος ἑοῖ καὶ πάμπαν ἀπείρων
Σφαῖρος κυκλοτερὴς μονίῃ περιηγέι γαίων

The nature of god is a circle of which the centre is everywhere and the circumference is nowhere.

Translated in *The Oxford Dictionary of Quotations* (2004)

Fragment 28 (D-K)

quoted in the Roman de la Rose, *and by St Bonaventura in* Itinerarius Mentis in Deum, *closing line of ch. 5*

9 ἐν δὲ μέσῃ Φιλότης στροφάλιγγι γένηται,
ἐν τῇ δὴ τάδε πάντα συνέρχεται ἓν μόνον εἶναι

Love is born in the middle of a whirlwind;
in it all come together as one.

Fragment 35.21 (D-K)

10 ἠπιόφρων Φιλότητος ἀμεμφέος ἄμβροτος ὁρμή

The gentle, immortal power of pure love.

Fragment 35.30 (D-K)

11 Ἥλιος ὀξυβελὴς ἠδ' ἱλάειρα Σελήνη

Sharp-arrowed sun and gentle moon.

Translated by Jonathan Barnes (1987)

Fragment 40 (D-K)

12 κυκλοτερὲς περὶ γαῖαν ἑλίσσεται ἀλλότριον φῶς

Circling around the earth, shedding borrowed light.

Fragment 45 (D-K)

of the moon

13 πολλὰ δ' ἔνερθε οὔδεος πυρὰ καίεται

Many fires burn below the surface.

Translated by Kathleen Freeman (1948)

Fragment 52 (D-K)

of the earth

14 γῆς ἱδρῶτα θάλασσαν

Sea, the sweat of the Earth.

Translated by Kathleen Freeman (1948)

Fragment 55 (D-K)

15 μία γίγνεται ἀμφοτέρων ὄψ

From both eyes comes a single vision.

Translated by Jonathan Barnes (1987)

Fragment 88 (D-K)

16 πρὸς παρεὸν γὰρ μῆτις ἀέξεται ἀνθρώποισιν

Men's wisdom grows in relation to what is present.

Translated by Jonathan Barnes (1987)

Fragment 106 (D-K)

17 ὦ φίλοι, οἶδα μὲν οὕνεκ' ἀληθείη πάρα μύθοις

Friends, there's often truth in fairy tales.

Fragment 114 (D-K)

18 θεῶν ψήφισμα παλαιόν,
ἀίδιον, πλατέεσσι κατεσφρηγισμένον ὅρκοις·
εὖτέ τις ἀμπλακίῃσι φόνῳ φίλα γυῖα μιήνῃ ...
τρίς μιν μυρίας ὥρας ἀπὸ μακάρων ἀλάλησθαι

There is an ancient decree of the gods,
an eternal law, sealed by broad oaths,
that whoever errs and defiles himself with murder
shall wander for three myriad years away from the blessed.

Fragment 115.47 (D-K)

19 τῶν καὶ ἐγὼ νῦν εἰμι, φυγὰς θεόθεν καὶ ἀλήτης

Such am I now, a fugitive from the gods and a wanderer.

Fragment 115.59 (D-K)

20 ἤδη γάρ ποτ' ἐγὼ γενόμην κοῦρός τε κόρη τε
θάμνος τ' οἰωνός τε καὶ ἔξαλος ἔλλοπος ἰχθύς

In a boy and a girl,
The same soul can be,
In a shrub and a bird
And a fish of the sea.

Translated by Andrew Sinclair (1967)

Fragment 117 (D-K)

21 κλαῦσά τε καὶ κώκυσα ἰδὼν ἀσυνήθεα χῶρον ...
ἔνθα Φόνος τε Κότος τε καὶ ἄλλων ἔθνεα Κηρῶν

I wept and lamented when I saw this strange place
of Murder and Wrath and a multitude of Plagues.

Fragment 118.8 and 121.15 (D-K)

on being born

22 ὢ πόποι, ὢ δειλὸν θνητῶν γένος, ὢ δυσάνολβον,
τοίων ἔκ τ' ἐρίδων ἔκ τε στοναχῶν ἐγένεσθε

Alas! Poor wretched race of mortal men! Born of discord and grief!

Fragment 124 (D-K)

23 ἦσαν δὲ κτίλα πάντα καὶ ἀνθρώποισι προσηνῆ,
θῆρές τ' οἰωνοί τε, φιλοφροσύνη τε δεδήει

And all creatures, both animals and birds, were tame and gentle towards men, and friendliness glowed between them.

Translated by Kathleen Freeman (1948)

Fragment 130 (D-K)

24 δειλὸς δ', ᾧ σκοτόεσσα θεῶν πέρι δόξα μέμηλεν

Wretched is he whose heart is weighed down by some sinister superstition.

Translated by Karl Popper (1965)

Fragment 132 (D-K)

25 γάρ τοι θεῖον
οὐκ ἔστιν πελάσασθαι ἐν ὀφθαλμοῖσιν ἐφικτόν

It is not possible to look on god.

Fragment 133 (D-K)

26 οὐ παύσεσθε φόνοιο δυσηχέος; οὐκ ἐσορᾶτε
ἀλλήλους δάπτοντες ἀκηδείῃσι νόοιο;

Will you not cease from slaughter? Do you not see that
you tear at one another in the carelessness of your thought?

Translated by Jonathan Barnes (1987)

Fragment 136 (D-K)

against eating meat

27 οἴμοι ὅτι οὐ πρόσθεν με διώλεσε νηλεὲς ἦμαρ,
πρὶν σχέτλι' ἔργα βορᾶς περὶ χείλεσι μητίσασθαι

Alas, that I was not destroyed before the day
that I contrived the terrible deed of eating flesh.

Fragment 139 (D-K)

28 νηστεῦσαι κακότητος

Abstain from evil.

Translated by Jonathan Barnes (1987)

Fragment 144 (D-K)

29 Ἀκραγαντῖνοι τρυφῶσι μὲν ὡς αὔριον ἀποθανούμενοι, οἰκίας δὲ κατασκευάζονται ὡς πάντα τὸν χρόνον βιωσόμενοι

They live merrily as if tomorrow they would die, but build their houses well as if they were to live for ever.

Testimonies, Fragment 1.83 (D-K)

of the inhabitants of Acragas (Agrigentum)

ENIGMATA AND RIDDLES

1 τί δίπους, τί τρίπους, τί τετράπους

What is two-footed, three-footed, four-footed?

Androtion, Fragment 31 (Müller, *FHG*)

the Riddle of the Sphinx: Man, as a baby crawling on hands and knees, then erect on his feet, in old age with a staff; cf. Sophocles 213

2 Εἰμὶ πατρὸς λευκοῖο μέλαν τέκος, ἄπτερος ὄρνις
ἄχρι καὶ οὐρανίων ἱπτάμενος νεφέων·
κούραις δ' ἀντομένῃσιν ἀπενθέα δάκρυα τίκτω·
εὐθὺ δὲ γεννηθεὶς λύομαι εἰς ἀέρα.

I am black, my father white.
I have no wings, yet fly sky-high.
Tears follow me when I go by.
The air and I at birth unite.

Translated by Andrew Sinclair (1967)

Greek Anthology 14.5

Answer: Smoke

3 Μὴ λέγε, καὶ λέξεις ἐμὸν οὔνομα. δεῖ δέ σε λέξαι;
ὧδε πάλιν, μέγα θαῦμα, λέγων ἐμὸν οὔνομα λέξεις.

Speechless, you shall speak my name.
Must you speak? Why then again
In speaking you shall say the same.

Translated by Andrew Sinclair (1967)

Greek Anthology 14.22

Answer: Silence

4 Οὐδὲν ἔσωθεν ἔχω, καὶ πάντα μοι ἔνδοθέν ἐστι,
προῖκα δ' ἐμῆς ἀρετῆς πᾶσι δίδωμι χάριν.

I have nothing inside me and everything is inside me,
and I grant the use of my virtue to all without charge.

Translated by W.R. Paton (1918)

Greek Anthology 14.108

Answer: A mirror

5 εἷς ὁ πατήρ, παῖδες δυοκαίδεκα. τῶν δὲ ἑκάστῳ
παῖδες δὶς τριάκοντα διάνδιχα εἶδος ἔχουσαι·
αἱ μὲν λευκαὶ ἔασιν ἰδεῖν, αἱ δ' αὖτε μέλαιναι·
ἀθάνατοι δέ τ' ἐοῦσαι, ἀποφθινύθουσιν ἅπασαι

One father has twelve sons, and each of these
Has sixty daughters, of two different kinds.
One half are white, the others black, and all
Though always in existence, yet must die.

Translated by Kathleen Freeman (1947)

Diogenes Laertius, *Lives of Eminent Philosophers* 1.91

a riddle by Cleobulus – the answer is 'the year, the months, the days and nights'

EPAMINONDAS

*c.*420–362BC

Theban general, famous for the battles of Leuctra and Mantinea

1 ὦ Ἡράκλεις, πῶς ἐσχόλασεν ἀνὴρ ἀποθανεῖν ἐν τοσούτοις πράγμασι

Great Heavens! How did he find time to die when there was so much going on?

Translated by Frank Cole Babbitt (1928)

Plutarch, *Advice About Keeping Well* 136d

spoken in regard to a man who fell ill and died at the time of the battle of Leuctra, 371BC

2 ἐμοὶ μέν ἀπόδος τὴν ἀσπίδα, σεαυτῷ δὲ πρίω καπηλεῖον

Give me back my shield, and buy yourself a tavern.

Translated by Frank Cole Babbitt (1931)

Plutarch, *Sayings of Kings and Commanders* 194a.3

to his shield-bearer who was given a large amount of money by a captured enemy

3 δύσκριτον ἕως ζῶμεν

As long as we live, it is hard to decide.

Plutarch, *Sayings of Kings and Commanders* 194a.7

when asked who was the better general, himself or Iphicrates

4 μήτε πλείονα γιγνώσκοντι μήτ' ἐλάττονα φθεγγομένῳ ῥᾳδίως ἐντυχεῖν

Not easy to find a man who knew more and spoke less.

Translated by Frank Cole Babbitt (1927)

Plutarch, *On Listening to Lectures* 39b

of Epaminondas

5 ἀρχὴ ἄνδρα δείκνυσιν ἀλλὰ καὶ ἀρχὴν ἀνήρ

Rule shows the man, but also man the rule.

Plutarch, *Precepts of Statecraft* 811b

cf. Seven Sages 38

6 οὐκ ἂν προδοίη ὁ τούτοις ἀρκούμενος

No one will become a traitor who is satisfied with as little as I am.

Stobaeus, *Anthology* 3.5.51

showing his frugal meal when offered a large sum of money

EPHIPPUS

4th century BC

Middle Comedy poet

1 οὐ γινώσκων ψήφων ἀριθμούς

Knowing not
The simplest sums and plainest figures.

Translated by Charles Duke Yonge (1854)

Fragment 19 (Kock) – 19 (K-A) – *Peltastes – The Warrior*

of a blockhead

2 οὐκοῦν μεθύοντάς φασι τἀληθῆ λέγειν

Drunkards speak the truth.

Fragment 25 (Kock) – 25 (K-A)

EPICHARMUS

active 5th century BC
Comic poet from Sicily

1 ὁ μὲν γὰρ αὔξεθ', ὁ δέ γα μὰν φθίνει,
ἐν μεταλλαγᾷ δὲ πάντες ἐντὶ πάντα τὸν χρόνον

As one man grows, the other declines; all are constantly in the process of change.

Fragment 2 (D-K) – 276 (K-A)

2 ἁ κύων κυνὶ
κάλλιστον εἶμεν φαίνεται καὶ βοῦς βοΐ,
ὄνος δ' ὄνῳ κάλλιστον

A dog appears the fairest thing to a dog, an ox to an ox, and an ass to an ass.

Translated by R.D. Hicks (1925)

Fragment 5 (D-K) – 279 (K-A)

3 σάφα ἴσαμι τοῦθ', ὅτι
τῶν ἐμῶν μνάμα ποκ' ἐσσεῖται λόγων τούτων ἔτι

I know full well that some day my words will be remembered.

Translated by R.D. Hicks (1925)

Fragment 6 (D-K) – 280 (K-A)

4 νοῦς ὁρῇ καὶ νοῦς ἀκούει· τἆλλα κωφὰ καὶ τυφλά

Only mind sees, only mind hears: all else is deaf and blind.

Translated by Karl Popper (1977)

Fragment 12 (D-K) – 214 (K-A)

5 νᾶφε καὶ μέμνασ' ἀπιστεῖν· ἄρθρα ταῦτα τᾶν φρενῶν

A cool head and caution are the sinews of wisdom.

Fragment 13 (D-K) – 218 (K-A)

6 εὐσεβὴς νόῳ πεφυκὼς οὐ πάθοις κ' οὐδὲν κακὸν
κατθανών· ἄνω τὸ πνεῦμα διαμενεῖ κατ' οὐρανόν

Endowed with a pious mind, you will not, in dying,
Suffer evil; the spirit will dwell in heaven above.

Translated by Philip Schaff (1819–1893)

Fragment 22 (D-K) – 254 (K-A)

7 οὐδὲν ἐκφεύγει τὸ θεῖον ... αὐτός ἐσθ' ἁμῶν ἐπόπτης

Nothing escapes god; he watches over all we do.

Fragment 23.3 (D-K) – 255 (K-A)

8 ἀδυνατεῖ δ' οὐδὲν θεός

Nothing is impossible to god.

Fragment 23.4 (D-K) – 255 (K-A)

9 ἐγγύα δ' ἄτας γα θυγάτηρ, ἐγγύας δὲ ζαμία

Surety is the daughter of folly, penury the daughter of surety.

Fragment 25 (D-K) – 257 (K-A)

10 καθαρὸν ἂν τὸν νοῦν ἔχῃς, ἅπαν τὸ σῶμα καθαρὸς εἶ

If you have a pure mind, all your body will be pure.

Fragment 26 (D-K) – 258 (K-A)

11 πάντα τὰ σπουδαῖα νυκτὸς μᾶλλον ἐξευρίσκεται

Serious thoughts tend to come at night.

Fragment 28 (D-K) – 259 (K-A)

cf. the Latin proverb 'in nocte consilium', the English proverb 'night brings counsel' and the French 'la nuit porte conseil'

12 οὐ λέγειν τύγ' ἐσσὶ δεινός, ἀλλὰ σιγᾶν ἀδύνατος

Unskilled at speech yet unable to keep silent.

Fragment 29 (D-K) – 184 (K-A)

13 ἁ δὲ χεὶρ τὰν χεῖρα νίζει

One hand washes the other.

Translated by John Simpson and Jennifer Speake (1982)

Fragment 30 (D-K) – 211 (K-A)

cf. the identical English proverb; some editors join this with the next entry

14 δός τι καὶ λάβοις τί

Give and you will receive.

Fragment 30 (D-K) – 211 (K-A)

some editors join this with the previous entry

15 ἁ δὲ μελέτα φύσιος ἀγαθᾶς πλέονα δωρεῖται, φίλοι

Practice is more effective than natural gifts, my friends.

Fragment 33 (D-K) – 265 (K-A)

16 τῶν πόνων πωλοῦσιν ἡμῖν πάντα τἀγάθ' οἱ θεοί

The gods sell all good things at the price of toil.

Translated by Kathleen Freeman (1948)

Fragment 36 (D-K) – 271 (K-A)

17 μὴ τὰ μαλακὰ μῶσο, μὴ τὰ σκλήρ' ἔχῃς

Do not seek ease, lest only what is hard remains.

Fragment 37 (D-K) – 236 (K-A)

18 οὐ μετανοεῖν ἀλλὰ προνοεῖν χρὴ τὸν ἄνδρα τὸν σοφόν

Wise men think before, not after.

Fragment 41 (D-K) – 263 (K-A)

19 μὴ ἐπὶ μικροῖς αὐτὸς αὐτὸν ὀξύθυμον δείκνυε

Don't get upset over unimportant things.

Fragment 42 (D-K) – 264 (K-A)

20 ἐπιπολάζειν οὔ τι χρὴ τὸν θυμόν, ἀλλὰ τὸν νόον

Reason, not emotion should prevail.

Fragment 43 (D-K) – 264 (K-A)

21 οὐδὲ εἷς οὐδὲν μετ' ὀργῆς κατὰ τρόπον βουλεύεται

Anger distorts reason.

Fragment 44 (D-K) – 264 (K-A)

22 βίος ἀνθρώποις λογισμοῦ κἀριθμοῦ δεῖται πάνυ

The life of man needs reasoning power and numbers.

Translated in Liddell & Scott

Fragment 56 (D-K) – 240 (K-A)

23 γει δὲ παντοδαπὰ κογχύλια,
λεπάδας, ἀστάκους, κραβύζους, κικιβάλους, τηθυνάκια,
κτένια, βαλάνους, πορφύρας, ὄστρεια συμμεμυκότα,
τὰ διελεῖν μέν ἐντι χαλεπά, καταφαγῆμεν δ' εὐμαρέα,
μύας ἀναρίτας τε κάρυκάς τε καὶ σκιφύδρια,
τὰ γλυκέα μέν ἐντ' ἐπέσθειν, ἐμπαγῆμεν δ' ὀξέα,
τούς τε μακρογογγύλους σωλῆνας

He brings all sorts of shellfish – limpets, lobsters, crabs, owl-fish, whelks, scallops, barnacles, purple-shells, oysters tight-closed (to open them is no easy matter, but to eat them is easy enough), mussels, snails, periwinkles, and suckers (which are sweet to eat forthwith, but too acrid when preserved), and the long, round razor-fish.

Translated by Charles Burton Gulick (1927)

Fragment 42 (Kaibel, *CGF*) – 40 (K-A) – *Hebas Gamos – The Marriage of Hebe*

24 ἁ δ' Ἀσυχία χαρίεσσα γυνά,
καὶ Σωφροσύνας πλατίον οἰκεῖ

Tranquillity is a woman who lives close to Good Sense.

Fragment 101 (Kaibel) – 100 (K-A)

EPICTETUS

*c.*50–*c.*120AD

Stoic philosopher from Hierapolis in Phrygia

1 τὸ κυριεῦον οἱ θεοὶ μόνον ἐφ' ἡμῖν ἐποίησαν, τὴν χρῆσιν τὴν ὀρθὴν ταῖς φαντασίαις

The best of all faculties given us by god is the wise use of our imagination.

Discourses 1.1.7

2 τὸ σωμάτιον ... τοῦτο οὐκ ἔστιν σόν, ἀλλὰ πηλὸς κομψῶς πεφυραμένος

This body is not thine own, but only clay cunningly compounded.

Translated by W.A. Oldfather (1925)

Discourses 1.1.10

Zeus 'speaking' to Epictetus

3 ἐδώκαμέν σοι μέρος τι ἡμέτερον, τὴν δύναμιν ταύτην τὴν ὁρμητικήν τε καὶ ἀφορμητικὴν καὶ ὀρεκτικήν τε καὶ ἐκκλιτικὴν

We have given thee a certain portion of ourself, this faculty of choice and refusal, of desire and aversion.

Translated by W.A. Oldfather (1925)

Discourses 1.1.12.2

Zeus 'speaking' to Epictetus

4 οὐ στενάξεις, οὐ μέμψῃ, οὐ κολακεύσεις οὐδένα

Thou shalt not groan, shalt not blame, shalt not flatter any man.

Translated by W.A. Oldfather (1925)

Discourses 1.1.12.7

5 πολλοῖς προσδεδεμένοι βαρούμεθα ὑπ' αὐτῶν καὶ καθελκόμεθα

Being attached to too much, or to too many, we are burdened and dragged down by them.

Discourses 1.1.15

6 σὲ γὰρ οὐκ ἐποίησεν ὁ θεὸς ταμίαν τῶν ἀνέμων, ἀλλὰ τὸν Αἴολον

God has not made you steward of the winds, but Aeolus.

Translated by W.A. Oldfather (1925)

Discourses 1.1.16

i.e. make the best of what is under your control, and take the rest as its nature is

7 ἤθελες πάντας τραχηλοκοπηθῆναι, ἵνα σὺ παραμυθίαν ἔχῃς;

Would you then, want everyone to be beheaded for your consolation?

Discourses 1.1.18

8 ἀποθανεῖν με δεῖ· μή τι οὖν καὶ στένοντα; … φυγαδευθῆναι· μή τις οὖν κωλύει γελῶντα καὶ εὐθυμοῦντα καὶ εὐροοῦντα;

If I must die, must I die groaning? If I am exiled, can anyone prevent me from living with a smile, cheerfully serene?

Discourses 1.1.22

9 τὸ σκέλος μου δήσεις, τὴν προαίρεσιν δὲ οὐδ' ὁ Ζεὺς νικῆσαι δύναται· εἰς φυλακήν σε βαλῶ

My leg you may fetter, but my moral purpose not even Zeus himself has the power to overcome.

Translated by W.A. Oldfather (1925)

Discourses 1.1.23

10 ἐγὼ ἐμαυτῷ ἐμπόδιος οὐ γίνομαι

I shall not become a hindrance to my own self.

Discourses 1.1.28

11 τῷ λογικῷ ζῴῳ μόνον ἀφόρητόν ἐστι τὸ ἄλογον

To the rational being only the irrational is unendurable.

Translated by W.A. Oldfather (1925)

Discourses 1.2.1

12 ὅταν γοῦν πάθῃ τις ὅτι εὔλογον, ἀπελθὼν ἀπήγξατο

At all events whenever a man feels that it is rational he goes and hangs himself.

Translated by W.A. Oldfather (1925)

Discourses 1.2.3

cf. Bible 92

13 ἄλλῳ δ' ἄλλο προσπίπτει τὸ εὔλογον καὶ ἄλογον, καθάπερ … καὶ συμφέρον καὶ ἀσύμφορον· διὰ τοῦτο μάλιστα παιδείας δεόμεθα

The rational and the irrational are different for different persons; so is the profitable and the unprofitable. It is for this reason especially that we need education.

Translated by W.A. Oldfather (1925)

Discourses 1.2.5

14 ἡ ἀρετὴ ταύτην ἔχει τὴν ἐπαγγελίαν εὐδαιμονίαν ποιῆσαι καὶ ἀπάθειαν καὶ εὔροιαν

It is virtue that holds out the promise of happiness and calm and serenity.

Translated by W.A. Oldfather (1925)

Discourses 1.4.3

15 μηδέποτε οὖν ἀλλαχοῦ τὸ ἔργον ζητεῖτε, ἀλλαχοῦ τὴν προκοπήν

Never look for your work in one place and your progress in another.

Translated by W.A. Oldfather (1925)

Discourses 1.4.17

16 τί ἐστι θάνατος, τί φυγή, τί δεσμωτήριον, τί κώνειον, ἵνα δύνηται λέγειν … ὦ φίλε Κρίτων, εἰ ταύτῃ τοῖς θεοῖς φίλον, ταύτῃ γινέσθω

What to you is death, exile, prison, hemlock if you can say, 'Dear Crito, if so it pleases god, so be it.'

Discourses 1.4.24

echoing Socrates in prison; cf. Plato, Crito *43d*

17 οὐ τὴν περὶ τὸ ζῆν, ἀλλὰ τὴν πρὸς τὸ εὖ ζῆν

Consider not mere life, but a good life.

Discourses 1.4.31

cf. Plato 26

18 ἄλλο γάρ ἐστι χρῆσις καὶ ἄλλο παρακολούθησις

Use is one thing, and understanding is another.

Translated by W.A. Oldfather (1925)

Discourses 1.6.13

on the difference between humans and animals who only use what is around them

19 ζητοῦμεν γὰρ ἐπὶ πάσης ὕλης πῶς ἂν εὕροι ὁ καλὸς καὶ ἀγαθὸς τὴν διέξοδον

Our aim in every matter of inquiry is to learn how the good and virtuous man may find the appropriate course.

Translated by W.A. Oldfather (1925)

Discourses 1.7.2

20 τἀληθῆ τιθέναι, τὰ ψευδῆ αἴρειν, πρὸς τὰ ἄδηλα ἐπέχειν

To state the true, to eliminate the false, to suspend judgement in doubtful cases.

Translated by W.A. Oldfather (1925)

Discourses 1.7.5

the 'professed object of reasoning'

21 ὃ ἐξ αὑτοῦ τις ἔχει, περισσὸς καὶ μάταιος παρ' ἄλλου λαμβάνων

It is foolish and superfluous to try to obtain from another that which one can get from oneself.

Translated by W.A. Oldfather (1925)

Discourses 1.9.31

22 οὔτε θάνατος οὔτε φυγὴ οὔτε πόνος οὔτε ἄλλο τι τῶν τοιούτων αἴτιόν ἐστι τοῦ πράττειν τι ἢ μὴ πράττειν ἡμᾶς, ἀλλ' ὑπολήψεις καὶ δόγματα

Neither death, nor exile, nor toil, nor any such thing directs what we do or do not do; it is only opinions and decisions.

Discourses 1.11.33

23 ὅτι σχολαστικόν σε δεῖ γενέσθαι … εἴπερ ἄρα θέλεις ἐπίσκεψιν τῶν σαυτοῦ δογμάτων ποιεῖσθαι· τοῦτο δ' ὅτι μιᾶς ὥρας ἢ ἡμέρας οὐκ ἔστιν

Devote your leisure to learning if you truly wish to examine your own judgement; this is not the work of a single hour or day.

Discourses 1.11.39

24 ὅπου δέ τις ἄκων ἐστίν, ἐκεῖνο φυλακὴ αὐτῷ ἐστιν

Being kept where you don't want to be, that is imprisonment.

Discourses 1.12.23

25 συμπαθεῖν τὰ ἐπίγεια τοῖς οὐρανίοις οὐ δοκεῖ σοι;

Is not earth influenced by what is in heaven?

Discourses 1.14.2

26 ὅταν κλείσητε τὰς θύρας καὶ σκότος ἔνδον ποιήσητε, μέμνησθε μηδέποτε λέγειν ὅτι μόνοι ἐστέ· οὐ γὰρ ἐστέ, ἀλλ' ὁ θεὸς ἔνδον ἐστὶ καὶ ὁ ὑμέτερος δαίμων ἐστίν. καὶ τίς τούτοις χρεία φωτὸς εἰς τὸ βλέπειν τί ποιεῖτε;

When you close your doors, and make darkness within, remember never to say that you are alone; nay, god is within, and your genius within. And what need have they of light to see what you are doing?

Translated by W.A. Oldfather (1925)

Discourses 1.14.13

27 οὐδέν, ἔφη, τῶν μεγάλων ἄφνω γίνεται, ὅπου γε οὐδ' ὁ βότρυς οὐδὲ σῦκον. ἄν μοι νῦν λέγῃς ὅτι θέλω σῦκον, ἀποκρινοῦμαί σοι ὅτι χρόνου δεῖ. ἄφες ἀνθήσῃ πρῶτον, εἶτα προβάλῃ τὸν καρπόν, εἶτα πεπανθῇ

No thing is created suddenly, any more than a bunch of grapes or a fig. If you ask for a fig, I say that there must be time. Let is first blossom, then bear fruit, then ripen.

Discourses 1.15.7

28 τοὺς θεοὺς ἓν τῶν γεγονότων ἀπήρκει πρὸς τὸ αἰσθέσθαι τῆς προνοίας

Any one thing in creation is sufficient to prove the existence of divine providence.

Discourses 1.16.7

29 μή τι ἀχρηστότερον τριχῶν τῶν ἐπὶ γενείου; … πῶς δὲ καλὸν τὸ σύμβολον καὶ εὐπρεπὲς καὶ σεμνόν, πόσῳ κάλλιον τοῦ τῶν ἀλεκτρυόνων λόφου, πόσῳ μεγαλοπρεπέστερον τῆς χαίτης τῶν λεόντων

Can anything be more useless than the hairs on a chin? Nay, but how fair and becoming and dignified the sign is! How much more fair than the cock's comb, how much more magnificent than the lion's mane!

Translated by W.A. Oldfather (1925)

Discourses 1.16.10–13

30 εἰ γοῦν ἀηδὼν ἤμην, ἐποίουν τὰ τῆς ἀηδόνος, εἰ κύκνος, τὰ τοῦ κύκνου. νῦν δὲ λογικός εἰμι· ὑμνεῖν με δεῖ τὸν θεόν

If I were I a nightingale, I should be singing as a nightingale; if a swan, as a swan. But as it is, I am a rational being, therefore I must be singing hymns of praise to god.

Translated by W.A. Oldfather (1925)

Discourses 1.16.20

31 πάντας ἄκοντας ἁμαρτάνειν

All men err involuntarily.

Translated by W.A. Oldfather (1925)

Discourses 1.17.14

cf. Plato 206

32 μελετᾶν ἐπὶ τῶν μικρῶν καὶ ἀπ' ἐκείνων ἀρχομένους διαβαίνειν ἐπὶ τὰ μείζω

Test yourself in little ways and starting from them proceed to greater.

Discourses 1.18.18

33 οὐκ οἶδας ὅτι πᾶς ἄνθρωπος ἑαυτὸν θεραπεύει, σὲ δ' οὕτως ὡς τὸν ὄνον;

Do you not know that every man pays attention to himself, and to you just as he does to his donkey?

Translated by W.A. Oldfather (1925)

Discourses 1.19.5

what Epictetus could say to a tyrant

34 αἱ περιστάσεις εἰσὶν αἱ τοὺς ἄνδρας δεικνύουσαι

Difficulties prove the man.

Discourses 1.24.1

35 τὸ δὲ γυμνὸν κρεῖσσόν ἐστι πάσης περιπορφύρου

Nakedness is better than any scarlet robe.

Discourses 1.24.7

36 οὐδείς πολέμιος ἐγγύς ἐστιν· πάντα εἰρήνης γέμει

There is no enemy near, all is full of peace.

Translated by W.A. Oldfather (1925)

Discourses 1.24.9

37 ὅταν μὴ ἀρέσκῃ τὸ πρᾶγμα ... εἰπὼν οὐκέτι παίζω ἀπαλλάσσου, μένων δὲ μὴ θρήνει

If something does not please you, say you're not in the game; but if you stay, stop wailing.

Discourses 1.24.20

38 τὸ ἀγαθὸν τοῦ ἀνθρώπου ἐν προαιρέσει καὶ τὸ κακόν

The good or ill of man lies within his own will.

Discourses 1.25.1

39 ἐνταῦθα γὰρ οὐδέν ἐστι τὸ ἀνθέλκον ὡς πρὸς τὸ ἀκολουθῆσαι τοῖς διδασκομένοις, ἐπὶ δὲ τῶν βιωτικῶν πολλὰ τὰ περισπῶντα

In theory there is nothing to hinder us from following what we are taught; but in life many things draw us aside.

Discourses 1.26.3

40 τετραχῶς αἱ φαντασίαι γίνονται ἡμῖν· ἢ γὰρ ἔστι τινὰ καὶ οὕτως φαίνεται ἢ οὐκ ὄντα οὐδὲ φαίνεται ὅτι ἔστιν ἢ ἔστι καὶ οὐ φαίνεται ἢ οὐκ ἔστι καὶ φαίνεται

Appearances to the mind are of four kinds. Things either are what they appear to be; or they neither are, nor appear to be; or they are, and do not appear to be; or they are not, and yet appear to be.

Discourses 1.27.1

41 οὐ γὰρ θάνατος ἢ πόνος φοβερόν, ἀλλὰ τὸ φοβεῖσθαι πόνον ἢ θάνατον

For it is not death or hardship that is a fearful thing, but the fear of hardship or death.

Translated by W.A. Oldfather (1925)

Discourses 2.1.13

42 μόνοις ἐξεῖναι παιδεύεσθαι τοῖς ἐλευθέροις

The well-educated alone are free.

Translated by Elizabeth Carter (1758)

Discourses 2.1.22

cf. Samuel Johnson in Boswell, The Life of Samuel Johnson *(L.F. Powell's revision of G.B. Hill's edition), vol. i, p.123, n.1738: 'My old friend, Mrs. Carter, could make a pudding as well as translate Epictetus.'*

43 αἱ ὕλαι ἀδιάφοροι, ἡ δὲ χρῆσις αὐτῶν οὐκ ἀδιάφορος

The materials are indifferent, but the use we make of them is not a matter of indifference.

Translated by W.A. Oldfather (1925)

Discourses 2.5.1

44 τὰ ἔξω οὐκ ἐπ' ἐμοί· προαίρεσις ἐπ' ἐμοί. ποῦ ζητήσω τὸ ἀγαθὸν καὶ τὸ κακόν; ἔσω ἐν τοῖς ἐμοῖς

Externals are not under my control; moral choice is under my control. Where am I to look for the good and the evil? Within me, in that which is my own.

Translated by W.A. Oldfather (1925)

Discourses 2.5.5

45 δείξω ὑμῖν νεῦρα φιλοσόφου· ποῖα νεῦρα; ὄρεξιν ἀναπότευκτον, ἔκκλισιν ἀπερίπτωτον, ὁρμὴν καθήκουσαν, πρόθεσιν ἐπιμελῆ, συγκατάθεσιν ἀπρόπτωτον

Shall I show you the sinews of a philosopher? A will unfaltering; evils avoided; power daily exercised; careful resolutions; unerring decisions.

Discourses 2.8.29

46 οὐδεὶς δίχα ἀπωλείας καὶ ζημίας κακός ἐστιν

No one is wicked without loss and penalty.

Discourses 2.10.19

47 τί πρῶτόν ἐστιν ἔργον τοῦ φιλοσοφοῦντος; ἀποβαλεῖν οἴησιν· ἀμήχανον γάρ, ἅ τις εἰδέναι οἴεται, ταῦτα ἄρξασθαι μανθάνειν

What is the first business of one who practises philosophy? To get rid of self-conceit. For it is impossible for any one to begin to learn that which he thinks he already knows.

Translated by W.A. Oldfather (1925)

Discourses 2.17.1

48 καθόλου οὖν εἴ τι ποιεῖν ἐθέλῃς, ἑκτικὸν ποίει αὐτό· εἴ τι μὴ ποιεῖν ἐθέλῃς, μὴ ποίει αὐτό, ἀλλ' ἔθισον ἄλλο τι πράττειν μᾶλλον ἀντ' αὐτοῦ

Practise whatever you would make habitual; otherwise get used to something else.

Discourses 2.18.4

49 δ' ὑπὸ τῆς ὀξύτητος μὴ συναρπασθῇς, ἀλλ' εἰπὲ ἔκδεξαί με μικρόν, φαντασία· ἄφες ἴδω τίς εἶ καὶ περὶ τίνος, ἄφες σε δοκιμάσω

Do not be overwhelmed by first impressions; say, wait awhile, show me what you are, let me put you to the test.

Discourses 2.18.24

50 τῶν περὶ αὑτοὺς κακῶν τὰ μὲν ῥαδίως ὁμολογοῦσιν ἄνθρωποι, τὰ δ' οὐ ῥαδίως

There are some faults which men readily admit, but others not so readily.

Translated by W.A. Oldfather (1925)

Discourses 2.21.1

51 βυθιζομένου δὲ τοῦ πλοίου ... ἐπαίρεις τοὺς σιφάρους

In a sinking ship you hoist the topsails!

Translated by W.A. Oldfather (1928)

Discourses 3.2.18

52 ληστὴς προαιρέσεως οὐ γίνεται

There is no thief who can steal your principles.

Discourses 3.22.105

53 τίς εἶναι θέλεις, σαυτῷ πρῶτον εἰπέ· εἶθ' οὕτως ποίει ἃ ποιεῖς

First tell yourself what you want to be; then go ahead with what you are doing.

Discourses 3.23.1

54 ἰατρεῖόν ἐστιν ... τὸ τοῦ φιλοσόφου σχολεῖον· οὐ δεῖ ἡσθέντας ἐξελθεῖν, ἀλλ' ἀλγήσαντας

The lecture-room of the philosopher is a hospital; you ought not to walk out of it in pleasure, but in pain.

Translated by W.A. Oldfather (1928)

Discourses 3.23.30

55 ὁ κόσμος οὗτος μία πόλις ἐστὶ

This world of ours is but a single state.

Discourses 3.24.10

56 πᾶσα γῆ πατρὶς

The whole world is our fatherland.

Discourses 3.24.66

quoting Diogenes 14

57 τὰ ἀγαθὰ ἔξω μὴ ζητεῖτε, ἐν ἑαυτοῖς ζητεῖτε

Do not look for your blessings outside, look for them within yourselves.

Translated by W.A. Oldfather (1928)

Discourses 3.24.112

cf. Marcus Aurelius 38

58 λέοντας τρέφουσιν ἡμέρους ἐγκλείσαντες καὶ σιτίζουσι ... καὶ τίς ἐρεῖ τοῦτον τὸν λέοντα ἐλεύθερον; ... τίς δ' ἂν λέων αἴσθησιν καὶ λογισμὸν λαβὼν βούλοιτο τούτων τις εἶναι τῶν λεόντων;

Men shut up lions in a cage and bring them up and feed them; who will call such a lion free? What lion, had he sense and reason, would be one of them?

Discourses 4.1.25

of animals, or men, in captivity

59 τὰ δὲ πτηνὰ ταῦτα ὅταν ληφθῇ καὶ ἐγκεκλειμένα τρέφηται, οἷα πάσχει ζητοῦντα ἐκφυγεῖν; ... πέτεσθαι πέφυκα ὅπου θέλω, ὕπαιθρον διάγειν, ᾄδειν ὅταν θέλω

What bird kept in a cage will not make every effort to escape? I wish to fly where I please, live in the fields, sing as I please.

Discourses 4.1.26–28

60 καὶ νῦν Σωκράτους ἀποθανόντος οὐθὲν ἧττον ἢ καὶ πλεῖον ὠφέλιμός ἐστιν ἀνθρώποις ἡ μνήμη ὧν ἔτι ζῶν ἔπραξεν ἢ εἶπεν

Now Socrates is dead the memory of him is no less useful to men, nay, is perhaps even more useful, than what he did or said while he still lived.

Translated by W.A. Oldfather (1928)

Discourses 4.1.169

61 χάριν ἔχω, ὧν ἔδωκας

For what thou hast given me I am grateful.

Translated by W.A. Oldfather (1928)

Discourses 4.10.16

cf. the prayer, 'For what we are about to receive, may the Lord make us truly thankful'

62 ἂν ὑπατεῦσαι θέλῃς, ἀγρυπνῆσαί σε δεῖ, περιδραμεῖν, τὰς χεῖρας καταφιλῆσαι, πρὸς ταῖς ἀλλοτρίαις θύραις κατασαπῆναι, πολλὰ μὲν εἰπεῖν, πολλὰ δὲ πρᾶξαι ἀνελεύθερα, δῶρα πέμψαι πολλοῖς, ξένια καθ' ἡμέραν ἐνίοις

If you pursue office you must keep vigils, run around, kiss hands, rot away at other men's doors, speak and act with servility, send gifts to many, and to some people every day.

Discourses 4.10.20

63 προαιρέσεως ἀλλοτρίας κύριος οὐδείς

No one has sovereignty over another's will.

Discourses 4.12.7

64 ταράσσει τοὺς ἀνθρώπους οὐ τὰ πράγματα, ἀλλὰ τὰ περὶ τῶν πραγμάτων δόγματα· οἷον ὁ θάνατος οὐδὲν δεινόν, ἐπεὶ καὶ Σωκράτει ἂν ἐφαίνετο, ἀλλὰ τὸ δόγμα τὸ περὶ τοῦ θανάτου, διότι δεινόν, ἐκεῖνο τὸ δεινόν ἐστιν. ὅταν οὖν ἐμποδιζώμεθα ἢ ταρασσώμεθα ἢ λυπώμεθα, μηδέποτε ἄλλον αἰτιώμεθα, ἀλλ' ἑαυτούς, τοῦτ' ἔστι τὰ ἑαυτῶν δόγματα

Men are disturbed not by the things themselves, but by the views about them; for example, death is nothing terrible, or else Socrates too would have thought so; it is the opinion that death is terrible which is the terrible thing. When then we are hindered or disturbed or grieved, let us never blame any other but ourselves, that is, our beliefs.

The Encheiridion (or Manual) 5.1

65 μὴ ζήτει τὰ γινόμενα γίνεσθαι ὡς θέλεις, ἀλλὰ θέλε τὰ γινόμενα ὡς γίνεται καὶ εὐροήσεις

Ask not that everything happens as you wish, but accept that events happen as they do, and you will get along well.

The Encheiridion (or Manual) 8.1

66 μηδέποτε ἐπὶ μηδενὸς εἴπῃς ὅτι ἀπώλεσα αὐτό, ἀλλ' ὅτι ἀπέδωκα. τὸ παιδίον ἀπέθανεν; ἀπεδόθη. ἡ γυνὴ ἀπέθανεν; ἀπεδόθη. τὸ χωρίον ἀφῃρέθην. οὐκοῦν καὶ τοῦτο ἀπεδόθη

Never say of anything, 'I have lost it'; but 'I have restored it.' Is your child dead? It is restored. Is your wife dead? She is restored. Is your estate taken away? Well: and is not that likewise restored?

Translated by Elizabeth Carter (1758)

The Encheiridion (or Manual) 11.1

cf. God giveth and God taketh away

67 τοῦτο οὖν ἄσκει, ὃ δύνασαι

Exercise yourself in what lies in your power.

Translated by P.E. Matheson (1916)

The Encheiridion (or Manual) 14.1

68 μέμνησο, ὅτι ὡς ἐν συμποσίῳ σε δεῖ ἀναστρέφεσθαι. περιφερόμενον γέγονέ τι κατὰ σέ· ἐκτείνας τὴν χεῖρα κοσμίως μετάλαβε. Παρέρχεται· μὴ κάτεχε. οὔπω ἥκει· μὴ ἐπίβαλλε πόρρω τὴν ὄρεξιν, ἀλλὰ περίμενε, μέχρις ἂν γένηται κατὰ σέ. οὕτω πρὸς τέκνα, οὕτω πρὸς γυναῖκα, οὕτω πρὸς ἀρχάς, οὕτω πρὸς πλοῦτον

Behave in life as at a banquet: when something comes around, take your share; when it goes, let it be gone; if not yet with you, await your turn. So act towards your children, wife, authorities, wealth.

The Encheiridion (or Manual) 15.1

69 μέμνησο, ὅτι ὑποκριτὴς εἶ δράματος … σὸν γὰρ τοῦτ' ἔστι, τὸ δοθὲν ὑποκρίνασθαι πρόσωπον καλῶς· ἐκλέξασθαι δ' αὐτὸ ἄλλου

Remember that you are an actor in a play; this is your business, to act well the given part; to choose it, belongs to another.

Translated by Thomas Wentworth Higginson (1865)

The Encheiridion (or Manual) 17.1

'another' is god in most of The Encheiridion

70 πόθεν ἡμῖν αὕτη ἡ ὀφρύς;

How do you suppose he has become such a highbrow?

The Encheiridion (or Manual) 22.1

71 ἐὰν ὁ ἑταῖρος ᾖ μεμολυσμένος, καὶ τὸν συνανατριβόμενον αὐτῷ συμμολύνεσθαι ἀνάγκη, κἂν αὐτὸς ὢν τύχῃ καθαρός

If your companion be impure, he who keeps company with him will perforce become impure though he himself happens to be pure.

Translated by George Long (1890)

The Encheiridion (or Manual) 33.6

72 πᾶν πρᾶγμα δύο ἔχει λαβάς, τὴν μὲν φορητήν, τὴν δὲ ἀφόρητον

There are two sides to all things, one bearable, the other unendurable.

The Encheiridion (or Manual) 43.1

73 ὅ τι δ' ἂν ἐρῇ τις περὶ σοῦ, μὴ ἐπιστρέφου· τοῦτο γὰρ οὐκ ἔτ' ἔστι σόν

Whatever any man shall say about you, do not attend to it: for this is no affair of yours.

Translated by George Long (1890)

The Encheiridion (or Manual) 50.1

74 εἰς ποῖον ἔτι χρόνον ἀναβάλλῃ τὸ τῶν βελτίστων ἀξιοῦν σεαυτὸν

How long will you then still defer thinking yourself worthy of the best?

Translated by George Long (1890)

The Encheiridion (or Manual) 51.1

75 τί μοι μέλει, φησί, πότερον ἐξ ἀτόμων ἢ ἐξ ἀμερῶν ἢ ἐκ πυρὸς καὶ γῆς συνέστηκε τὰ ὄντα; οὐ γὰρ ἀρκεῖ μαθεῖν τὴν οὐσίαν τοῦ ἀγαθοῦ καὶ κακοῦ καὶ τὰ μέτρα τῶν ὀρέξεων καὶ ἐκκλίσεων … καὶ τούτοις ὥσπερ κανόσι χρώμενον διοικεῖν τὰ τοῦ βίου, τὰ δ' ὑπὲρ ἡμᾶς ταῦτα χαίρειν ἐᾶν;

What do I care whether things are composed of atoms, or of indivisibles, or of fire and earth? Is it not enough to learn the true nature of good and evil, of desires and denials, and to order our affairs according to such rules, letting be the things that are above and beyond us?

Fragment 1 (Schenkl)

76 πάντα ὑπακούει τῷ κόσμῳ

All things obey and serve the cosmos.

Translated by W.A. Oldfather (1928)

Fragment 3 (Schenkl)

77 ἀνέχου καὶ ἀπέχου

Bear and forbear.

Translated by John Simpson and Jennifer Speake (1982)

Fragment 10 (Schenkl)

cf. the identical English proverb and the Latin 'substine et abstine'

78 τὸ ὅλον οἱ ἄνθρωποι χαίρουσιν ἀπολογίας τοῖς ἑαυτῶν ἁμαρτήμασι πορίζοντες

In general people delight in finding excuses for their own faults.

Translated by W.A. Oldfather (1928)

Fragment 15 (Schenkl)

79 οὐ ῥᾴδιον δόγμα παραγενέσθαι ἀνθρώπῳ, εἰ μὴ καθ' ἑκάστην ἡμέραν τὰ αὐτὰ καὶ λέγοι τις καὶ ἀκούοι καὶ ἅμα χρῷτο πρὸς τὸν βίον

It is not easy to form a proper opinion, unless day by day one states and hears the same principles, and at the same time applies them to his life.

Fragment 16 (Schenkl)

80 ἐν δὲ τῷ κόσμῳ αἰτοῦμεν τοὺς θεούς, ἃ μὴ διδόασι, καὶ ταῦτα πολλῶν ὄντων, ἅ γε ἡμῖν δεδώκασι

In life we ask of the gods whatever we do not already have, despite the fact that they have already given us plenty.

Fragment 17 (Schenkl)

81 ἆρ' οὖν ἀνθρώπου μόνου ἀρετὴ οὐκ ἔστιν, ἀλλὰ δεῖ ἡμᾶς εἰς τὰς τρίχας ἀφορᾶν καὶ τὰ ἱμάτια καὶ τοὺς πάππους;

Can it be that man has no excellence of his own, but must resort to his hair, his clothes, or his ancestors?

Fragment 18 (Schenkl)

82 ψυχάριον εἶ βαστάζον νεκρόν

You are but a little soul, carrying around a corpse.

Translated by W.A. Oldfather (1928)

Fragment 26 (Schenkl)

quoted by Marcus Aurelius, Τὰ εἰς ἑαυτόν *4.41*

83 οὐ περὶ τοῦ τυχόντος οὖν ἐστὶν ὁ ἀγών, ἀλλὰ περὶ τοῦ μαίνεσθαι ἢ μή

It is no ordinary matter that is at stake, but it is a question of either madness or sanity.

Translated by W.A. Oldfather (1928)

Fragment 28 (Schenkl)

84 οὔτε ναῦν ἐξ ἑνὸς ἀγκυρίου οὔτε βίον ἐκ μιᾶς ἐλπίδος ὁρμιστέον

A ship cannot depend on one anchor, nor life on one hope.

Fragment 30 (Schenkl)

85 καὶ τοῖς σκέλεσι καὶ ταῖς ἐλπίσι τὰ δυνατὰ δεῖ διαβαίνειν

We ought to measure both the length of our stride, and the extent of our hope, by what is possible.

Translated by W.A. Oldfather (1928)

Fragment 31 (Schenkl)

86 ὁ τύχῃ βίος συμπεπλεγμένος ἔοικε χειμάρρῳ ποταμῷ· καὶ γὰρ ταραχώδης καὶ ἰλύος ἀνάμεστος καὶ δυσέμβατος καὶ τυραννικὸς καὶ πολύηχος καὶ ὀλιγοχρόνιος

Life and luck are as a torrent: full of agitation, turbid, hard to ford, thunderous and short-lived.

*Gnomologium** 1 (Schenkl)

87 ψυχὴ ὁμιλοῦσα ἀρετῇ ἔοικεν ἀεννάῳ πηγῇ· καὶ γὰρ καθαρὸν καὶ ἀτάραχον καὶ πότιμον καὶ νόστιμον καὶ κοινωνικὸν καὶ πλούσιον καὶ ἀβλαβὲς καὶ ἀνώλεθρον

A soul attended by virtue is as an ever-flowing spring, whose water is pure and undisturbed, fresh and wholesome, liberal and abundant, harmless and indestructible.

*Gnomologium** 2 (Schenkl)

88 κόλαζε τὰ πάθη, ἵνα μὴ ὑπ' αὐτῶν τιμωρῇ

Keep desires in check lest they become punishments.

*Gnomologium** 5 (Schenkl)

89 εἰ θέλεις καλῶς ἀκούειν, μάθε καλῶς λέγειν· μαθὼν δὲ καλῶς λέγειν πειρῶ καλῶς πράττειν καὶ οὕτω καρπώσῃ τὸ καλῶς ἀκούειν

If you wish to hear fair things, learn to say fair things; once you learn to say fair things, try to act in fairness; thus you shall reap the benefits of fair listening.

*Gnomologium** 7 (Schenkl)

90 οὐ πενία λύπην ἐργάζεται, ἀλλὰ ἐπιθυμία· οὐδὲ πλοῦτος φόβου ἀπαλλάττει, ἀλλὰ λογισμός. κτησάμενος τοιγαροῦν τὸν λογισμὸν οὔτε πλούτου ἐπιθυμήσεις οὔτε πενίαν μέμψῃ

It is not poverty which brings sorrow, but desires; wealth cannot release us from fear, reason can. Therefore by possessing reason, wealth is no longer desired nor poverty cause for complaint.

*Gnomologium** 14 (Schenkl)

91 τὸ καλῶς ζῆν τοῦ πολυτελῶς διαφέρει· τὸ μὲν γὰρ ἐκ σωφροσύνης καὶ αὐταρκείας καὶ εὐταξίας καὶ κοσμιότητος καὶ εὐτελείας παραγίνεται, τὸ δὲ ἐξ ἀκολασίας καὶ τρυφῆς καὶ αταξίας καὶ ἀκοσμίας· τέλος δὲ τοῦ μὲν ἔπαινος ἀληθής, τοῦ δὲ ψόγος

To live well is not the same as to live in luxury; the first depends on wisdom and self-sufficiency, order and simplicity, the other on excess, disorder and unseemliness; the first merits true praise, the second dishonour.

*Gnomologium** 16 (Schenkl)

92 μέτρον ἔστω σοι παντὸς σίτου καὶ ποτοῦ ἡ πρώτη τῆς ὀρέξεως ἔμπλησις

Let moderation in food and drink be your first gratification.

*Gnomologium** 17 (Schenkl)

93 αἰσχρὸν τοῖς τῶν μελιττῶν δωρήμασι γλυκάζοντα τὴν κατάποσιν τὸ τῶν θεῶν δῶρον πικράζειν τὸν λόγον τῇ κακίᾳ

Sad, to sweeten our tongue with the gift of bees, honey, and create bitterness with the gift of god, speech.

*Gnomologium** 22 (Schenkl)

94 ἄριστον μέν, εἰ ... κοινωνεῖς τοῖς θεραπεύουσι τῶν παρόντων· εἰ δὲ τὸ τοιόνδε δυσχερὲς τῷ καιρῷ ὑπάρχοι, μέμνησο, ὅτι μὴ κάμνων ὑπὸ καμνόντων ὑπουργῇ, ἐσθίων ὑπὸ μὴ ἐσθιόντων, πίνων ὑπὸ μὴ πινόντων

Lend a hand to those who labour to prepare and serve a meal, or at least remember that, without any effort on your part, you are served by those who labour, you eat while they fast and drink when they thirst.

*Gnomologium** 24 (Schenkl)

95 ἐρίζειν καὶ φιλονεικεῖν πάντῃ μὲν ἀνοίκειον ... οὔτε γὰρ ἂν μεθύων νήφοντα διδάξειέ τις οὔτ' αὖ μεθύων πρὸς νήφοντος πεισθείη. ἔνθα δ' ἂν μὴ παρῇ πειθοῦς τέλος, εἰκῇ σε παρέχεις διατείνεσθαι

To argue and fight at table is unacceptable; nor can a drunkard instruct or convince one who is sober. Where there is no hope to persuade, there is no sense in arguing.

*Gnomologium** 25 (Schenkl)

96 φεύγεις δὲ δουλείαν

Shun bondage.

*Gnomologium** 36 (Schenkl)

97 εἰ βούλει τὰς κρίσεις δικαίας ποιεῖσθαι, μηδένα τῶν δικαζομένων καὶ δικαιολογούντων ἐπιγίγνωσκε, ἀλλ' αὐτὴν τὴν δίκην

If you wish your judgement to be fair, examine not who is being accused or who defends them, but consider the case without prejudice.

*Gnomologium** 51 (Schenkl)

98 ὀρθοῦ οὐδὲν ὀρθότερον

Nothing is more right than righteousness.

*Gnomologium** 56 (Schenkl)

99 ὥσπερ οἱ ἐπὶ τῶν λιμένων πυρσοὶ δι' ὀλίγων φρυγάνων πολλὴν ἀνάψαντες φλόγα ταῖς ἀλωμέναις ἀνὰ τὸ πέλαγος ναυσὶν ἱκανὴν ἐργάζονται βοήθειαν, οὕτω καὶ ἀνὴρ λαμπρὸς ἐν πόλει χειμαζομένῃ αὐτὸς ὀλίγοις ἀρκούμενος μεγάλα τοὺς πολίτας εὐεργετεῖ

As a harbour beacon will guide ships in distress with but a brushwood fire, thus one enlightened person can prove salutary to a city in distress; satisfied with little himself he can offer much to his fellow citizens.

*Gnomologium** 57 (Schenkl)

100 εἰ πρόκειταί σοι τὴν πόλιν ἀναθήμασι κοσμεῖν, σεαυτῷ πρῶτον ἀνάθες τὸ κάλλιστον ἡμερότητος καὶ δικαιοσύνης καὶ εὐποιίας ἀνάθημα

Rather than adorn your city, charge yourself with the best adornments: gentleness and justice and beneficence.

*Gnomologium** 59 (Schenkl)

101 εὖ ποιήσεις σὺ τὰ μέγιστα τὴν πόλιν, εἰ μὴ τοὺς ὀρόφους ὑψώσεις, ἀλλὰ τὰς ψυχὰς αὐξήσεις. ἄμεινον γὰρ ἐν μικροῖς οἰκήμασι μεγάλας οἰκεῖν ψυχὰς ἢ ἐν μεγάλαις οἰκίαις ταπεινὰ φωλεύειν ἀνδράποδα

You will offer more to the city, not by building high buildings, but by lifting up people's souls. For it is better that free spirits should live in simple dwellings, than slaves in grand homes.

*Gnomologium** 60 (Schenkl)

102 καθάπερ οὔτε κλαγγῇ χὴν οὔτε βληχῇ καταπλήσσε ται πρόβατον, οὕτω μηδὲ πλήθους ἀνοήτου σε δεδιττέσθω φωνή

As the goose does not fear the cries of geese, nor the sheep the baying of other sheep, so should you not fear the noise of the stupid mob.

*Gnomologium** 64 (Schenkl)

EPICURUS

341–270BC
Philosopher, born in Samos, died in Athens
see also Plutarch 168

1 ἀσεβὴς δὲ οὐχ ὁ τοὺς τῶν πολλῶν θεοὺς ἀναιρῶν, ἀλλ' ὁ τὰς τῶν πολλῶν δόξας θεοῖς προσάπτων

Impious is not he who repudiates the beliefs of the many, but he who attaches to the gods all expectations demanded by the multitude.

Letter to Menoeceus 123

2 τὸ φρικωδέστατον οὖν τῶν κακῶν ὁ θάνατος οὐθὲν πρὸς ἡμᾶς, ἐπειδή περ ὅταν μὲν ἡμεῖς ὦμεν, ὁ θάνατος οὐ πάρεστιν, ὅταν δὲ ὁ θάνατος παρῇ, τόθ' ἡμεῖς οὐκ ἐσμέν

Death, the most terrifying of ills, means nothing to us since, as long as we exist, death has not yet come; and, when it comes, then we are no more.

Letter to Menoeceus 125

3 τὴν ἡδονὴν ἀρχὴν καὶ τέλος λέγομεν εἶναι τοῦ μακαρίως ζῆν

Pleasure is the alpha and omega of a blessed life.

Translated by R.D. Hicks (1925)
Letter to Menoeceus 128

4 τὴν αὐτάρκειαν δὲ ἀγαθὸν μέγα νομίζομεν, οὐχ ἵνα πάντως τοῖς ὀλίγοις χρώμεθα, ἀλλ' ὅπως, ἐὰν μὴ ἔχωμεν τὰ πολλά, τοῖς ὀλίγοις ἀρκώμεθα

We consider self-sufficiency a great blessing, not so much in order to always use little but, if we do not have much, to be content with little.

Letter to Menoeceus 130

5 οὐκ ἔστιν ἡδέως ζῆν ἄνευ τοῦ φρονίμως καὶ καλῶς καὶ δικαίως, οὐδὲ φρονίμως καὶ καλῶς καὶ δικαίως ἄνευ τοῦ ἡδέως

It is impossible to live a pleasant life without living wisely, well and justly, and it is impossible to live wisely, well and justly without living pleasantly.

Translated by R.D. Hicks (1925)
Letter to Menoeceus 132

6 κόσμος ἐστὶ περιοχή τις οὐρανοῦ, ἄστρα τε καὶ γῆν καὶ πάντα τὰ φαινόμενα περιέχουσα, ἀποτομὴν ἔχουσα ἀπὸ τοῦ ἀπείρου

A world is a portion of the universe, which contains stars and earth and all visible things, a segment of the infinite.

Letter to Pythocles 88
a 'letter' composed of Epicurean texts, probably by a later writer

7 εἰ βούλει πλούσιον ... ποιῆσαι μὴ χρημάτων προστίθει, τῆς δὲ ἐπιθυμίας ἀφαίρει

If you want to make someone rich do not give him money, but help him to control his desires.

Letters, Fragment 53 (Arrighetti)

8 σαρκὸς δὲ φωνὴ μὴ πεινῆν, μὴ διψῆν, μὴ ῥιγοῦν

Voice of the flesh: do not hunger, do not thirst, avoid being cold.

Gnomologium, Fragment 33 (Arrighetti)

9 ἄπληστον οὐ γαστήρ, ὥσπερ οἱ πολλοί φασιν, ἀλλ' ἡ δόξα ψευδὴς ὑπὲρ τοῦ τῆς γαστρὸς ἀορίστου πληρώματος

It is not the stomach that is insatiable, as is generally said, but the false opinion that the stomach needs an unlimited amount to fill it.

Translated by Kathleen Freeman (1947)
Gnomologium, Fragment 59 (Arrighetti)

10 οὐδὲν ἱκανὸν ᾧ ὀλίγον τὸ ἱκανόν

Nothing will content him who is not content with a little.

Translated by H.T. Riley (1872)
Gnomologium, Fragment 68 (Arrighetti)

11 τῆς αὐταρκείας καρπὸς μέγιστος ἐλευθερία

Freedom is the greatest boon of self-sufficiency.

Gnomologium, Fragment 77 (Arrighetti)

12 ὅρος τοῦ μεγέθους τῶν ἡδονῶν ἡ παντὸς τοῦ ἀλγοῦντος ὑπεξαίρεσις

The magnitude of pleasure reaches its limit in the removal of all pain.

Translated by R.D. Hicks (1925)
Principal Doctrines 3 (Arrighetti)

13 ὧν ἡ σοφία παρασκευάζεται εἰς τὴν τοῦ ὅλου βίου μακαριότητα πολὺ μέγιστόν ἐστιν ἡ τῆς φιλίας κτῆσις

Of all blessings acquired in wisdom through a long life, friendship is the greatest.

Principal Doctrines 27 (Arrighetti)

14 οὐκ ἔστιν ἄφοβον εἶναι φοβερὸν φαινόμενον

He who is seen spreading terror is not without fear himself.

Arsenius, *Apophthegms* 13.39r (von Leutsch, *CPG*)

15 ἀρχὴ καὶ ῥίζα παντὸς ἀγαθοῦ ἡ τῆς γαστρὸς ἡδονή

The beginning and root of all bliss is a satisfied stomach.

Athenaeus, *Deipnosophists* 7.280a

16 χάρις τῇ μακαρίᾳ Φύσει, ὅτι τὰ ἀναγκαῖα ἐποίησεν εὐπόριστα, τὰ δὲ δυσπόριστα οὐκ ἀναγκαῖα

Bless Nature: she is generous with necessities, leaving the superfluous harder to obtain.

Stobaeus, *Anthology* 3.17.22

17 λάθε βιώσας

Passing one's life unnoticed.

Themistius, *Ὑπὲρ τοῦ λέγειν* 324a

cf. the treatise by Plutarch 'εἰ καλῶς εἴρητε τὸ λάθε βιώσας' (Is 'To Live Unknown' a Wise Precept?)

EPIMENIDES

late 7th century BC
Philosopher, poet and holy man from Crete
see also Proverbial Expressions 8; Solon 55

1 Κρῆτες ἀεὶ ψεῦσται

All Cretans are liars.

Translated by D.S. Baker (1998)

Fragment 1 (D-K)

All Cretans are liars. But Epimenides was a Cretan. Therefore he too is a liar. So how true is the phrase? Known as the Epimenides Liar Paradox

EPINICUS

3rd century BC
Athenian New Comedy poet

1 οὐδὲν ἐλέφαντος γὰρ διαφέρεις οὐδὲ σύ

You too are no different from an elephant.

Fragment 2 (Kock) – 2 (K-A) – *Hypoballomenai – The Baby-changers*

of the insensitive, of a thick-skinned person

ERASISTRATUS

*c.*315–*c.*240BC
Scientist and physician from Ceos

1 Ἐρασίστρατος ἅπαντα καλῶς τεθῆναί τε καὶ διαπλασθῆναι τὰ μόρια τοῦ σώματος ὑπὸ τῆς φύσεως οἰόμενος

Erasistratus regarded all the parts of the body as having been well and truly placed and shaped by Nature.

Translated by Arthur John Brock (1916)

Fragment 79 (Garofalo)

Erasistratus and Herophilus were the only ancient scientists to perform dissections of human bodies

2 τό τινος ἕνεκα πάντα ποιεῖν τὴν φύσιν καὶ μάτην μηδέν

Nature does everything for some purpose, and nothing in vain.

Translated by Arthur John Brock (1916)

Fragment 81 (Garofalo)

3 πανταχοῦ μὲν γὰρ ἡ φύσις ἀκριβὴς καὶ φιλότεχνος καὶ ἀνελλιπὴς καὶ ἀπέριττος. οὐδέν ... ἔχουσα ῥωπικόν

Nature is everywhere precise and artful, frugal yet lacking nothing; it has no trumpery about her.

Fragment 83 (Garofalo)

4 Ἐρασίστρατος οἶδεν ὁ τὴν τέχνην τῆς φύσεως ὑμνῶν

Erasistratus, the man who sings the artistic skill of Nature!

Translated by Arthur John Brock (1916)

Fragment 149 (Garofalo)

ERATOSTHENES SCHOLASTICUS

5th century AD
Epigrammatist

1 Καλὰ τὰ παρθενίης κειμήλια· παρθενίη δὲ
τὸν βίον ὤλεσσ' ἂν πᾶσι φυλασσομένη.
τοὔνεκεν εὐθέσμως ἄλοχον λάβε, καί τινα κόσμῳ
δὸς βροτὸν ἀντὶ σέθεν· φεῦγε δὲ μαχλοσύνην.

Fair are the treasures of virginity,
but if observed by all it would put an end to life;
therefore live in lawful wedlock, and give
a mortal to the world to replace thee; but shun lechery.

Translated by W.R. Paton (1917)

Greek Anthology 9.444

ERINNA

4th century BC
Poet
see also Leonidas of Tarentum 3

1 Βάσκανός ἐσσ', Ἀΐδα

Thou art envious, O Death.

Translated by J.W. MacKail (1890)

Greek Anthology 7.712

2 τουτόθεν εἰς Ἀίδαν κενεὰ διανήχεται ἀχώ·
σιγὰ δ' ἐν νεκύεσσι, τὸ δὲ σκότος ὄσσε κατέρρει

From here our fading echoes reach out in vain for Hades;
but the dead know only silence, darkness corrodes the rest.

Translated by Josephine Balmer (1996)

Fragment 1a (Diehl)

3 Βαυκὶ φίλα ...
τῷ τυ κατακλαίοισα τά κάδεα νῦν παραλείπω·
οὐ γάρ μοι πόδες ἐντὶ λιπῆν ἄπο δῶμα βέβαλοι,
οὐδ' ἐσιδῆν φάεσσι πρέπει νέκυν οὐδὲ γοᾶσαι
γυμναῖσιν χαίταισιν, ἀτὰρ φοινίκεος αἰδώς
δρύπτει μ' ἀμφι

My lost friend,
here is my lament: I can't bear that dark death-bed,
can't bring myself to step outside my door; won't look
on your stone face, won't cry or cut my hair for shame ...
but Baucis, this crimson grief
is tearing me in two.

Translated by Josephine Balmer (1996)

Fragment 1b (Diehl) – *Elacate – The Distaff*

4 Πομπίλε, ναύταισιν πέμπων πλόον εὔπλοον, ἰχθύ,
πομπεύσαις πρύμναθεν ἐμὰν ἀδεῖαν ἑταίραν

Pilot-fish, who giv'st to sailors pleasant sailing,
Grant my sweet companion escort from astern.

Translated by C.M. Bowra (1938)

Fragment 2 (Diehl)

pompilos is a fish which follows ships, Nautilus ductor L. *(previously* Gasterosteus ductor L.*)*

EUBULIDES

mid 4th century BC
Dialectician from Miletus and author of many puzzles

1 ἄνθρωπός τις ψευδόμενος λέγει ὅτι ψεύδεται· ψεύδεται ἢ οὐ;

Is 'I am lying' simultaneously true and false? Someone who lies and says he lies, is he lying or isn't he?

Fragment (reconstructed)

The Liar Paradox; cf. Cicero, Academica *2.30.96: 'si mentiris, mentiris; mentiris autem; mentiris igitur?' (if you are lying, you are lying; however, you are lying; therefore, are you lying?)*

2 Εὐβουλίδης ὁ Μιλήσιος, ὃς καὶ πολλοὺς ἐν διαλεκτικῇ λόγους ἠρώτησε ... καὶ τὸν διαλανθάνοντα καὶ Ἠλέκτραν καὶ ἐγκεκαλυμμένον

A known person hiding his face is known or not known? Electra meeting her brother before he uncovers his face knows him or does not know him?

Diogenes Laertius, *Lives of Eminent Philosophers* 2.108

The Known-Unknown Paradox; cf. Sophocles, Electra *1222*

3 εἴ τι οὐκ ἀπέβαλες, τοῦτ' ἔχεις· κέρατα δ' οὐκ ἀπέβαλες· κέρατ' ἄρ' ἔχεις

If you never lost something, you have it still; but you never lost horns, ergo you have horns.

Translated by R.D. Hicks (1925)

Diogenes Laertius, *Lives of Eminent Philosophers* 7.187

The Horned Argument 'Have you lost your horns?'; Diogenes Laertius has this under

Chrysippus, but mentions that it is attributed by some to Eubulides

EUBULUS

active *c.*380–*c.*335BC
Middle Comedy poet

1 πάνθ' ὁμοῦ πωλήσεται
ἐν ταῖς Ἀθήναις· σῦκα, κλητῆρες, βότρυς,
γογγυλίδες, ἄπιοι, μῆλα, μάρτυρες, ῥόδα,
μέσπιλα, χόρια, σχαδόνες, ἐρέβινθοι, δίκαι,
πυός, πυριάτη, μύρτα, κληρωτήρια,
ὑάκινθος, ἄρνες, κλεψύδραι, νόμοι, γραφαί

You'll find everything for sale
at Athens: Figs – informers – grapes,
Turnips, pears, apples – snoopers – roses, medlars,
Haggis and honeycombs, chickpeas and – proceedings,
Curds, clotted cream, myrtles – and ballot-urns.
Hyacinths, lambs – and paraphernalia of the law-courts.

Translated by Kathleen Freeman (1947)

Fragment 74 (Kock) – 74 (K-A) – *Olbia – The Happy Girl*

2 τρεῖς γὰρ μόνους κρατῆρας ἐγκεραννύω
τοῖς εὖ φρονοῦσι· τὸν μὲν ὑγιείας ἕνα,
ὃν πρῶτον ἐκπίνουσι, τὸν δὲ δεύτερον
ἔρωτος ἡδονῆς τε, τὸν τρίτον δ' ὕπνου,
ὃν ἐκπιόντες οἱ σοφοὶ κεκλημένοι
οἴκαδε βαδίζουσ'· ὁ δὲ τέταρτος οὐκ ἔτι
ἡμέτερός ἐστ', ἀλλ' ὕβρεος· ὁ δὲ πέμπτος βοῆς·
ἕκτος δὲ κώμων· ἕβδομος δ' ὑπωπίων·
ὁ δ' ὄγδοος κλητῆρος· ὁ δ' ἔνατος χολῆς·
δέκατος δὲ μανίας, ὥστε καὶ βάλλειν ποιεῖ

Three cups of wine a prudent man may take:
The first of them for constitution sake;
The second to the girl he loves the best;
The third and last, to lull him to his rest –
Then home to bed. But if a fourth he pours,
That is the cup of folly, and not ours.
Loud noisy talking on the fifth attends;
The sixth breeds feuds and falling out of friends;
Seven begets blows, and faces stained with gore;
Eight, and the watch patrol breaks ope' the door;
Mad with the ninth, another cup goes round,
And the swilled sot drops senseless on the ground.

Translated by Jennifer Taylor (1989)

Fragment 94 (Kock) – 93 (K-A) – *Semele or Dionysus*

3 ἄτοπον δὲ τὸν μὲν οἶνον εὐδοκιμεῖν ἀεὶ
… ἄνδρα δὲ
μὴ τὸν παλαιόν, ἀλλὰ τὸν νεώτερον

It is strange that in wine the older is more popular,
whereas in men, not the elder but the younger.

Fragment 124–125 (Kock) – 121–122 (K-A)

EUCLID

dates uncertain, between 325 and 250BC
Mathematician; nothing is known of his life

1 γραμμὴ δὲ μῆκος ἀπλατές

A line is length without breadth.

Translated in *The Oxford Dictionary of Quotations* (2004)

Elements 1 Definition 2

2 ἐντὸς … ἐκτὸς καὶ … ἐπὶ τὰ αὐτὰ

Exterior … interior … and opposite.

Translated by Thomas Little Heath (1908)

Elements 1 Definition 28

of two angles, inside and out, formed by a straight line cutting two parallel straight lines; also used to express 'nothing new', when asked 'where have you been? 'what have you been up to?'

3 ἠτήσθω ἀπὸ παντὸς σημείου ἐπὶ πᾶν σημεῖον εὐθεῖαν γραμμὴν ἀγαγεῖν· καὶ πεπερασμένην εὐθεῖαν κατὰ τὸ συνεχὲς ἐπ' εὐθείας ἐκβαλεῖν· καὶ παντὶ κέντρῳ καὶ διαστήματι κύκλον γράφεσθαι· καὶ πάσας τὰς ὀρθὰς γωνίας ἴσας ἀλλήλαις εἶναι

Let the following be postulated: 1. To draw a straight line from any point to any point. 2. To produce a finite straight line continuously in a straight line. 3. To describe a circle with any centre and distance. 4. That all right angles are equal to one another.

Translated by Ivor Thomas (1939)

Elements 1 Postulates 1–4

four of five basic postulates of Euclidean Geometry; for the fifth see next entry

4 καὶ ἐὰν εἰς δύο εὐθείας εὐθεῖα ἐμπίπτουσα τὰς ἐντὸς καὶ ἐπὶ τὰ αὐτὰ μέρη γωνίας δύο ὀρθῶν ἐλάσσονας ποιῇ, ἐκβαλλομένας τὰς δύο εὐθείας ἐπ' ἄπειρον συμπίπτειν, ἐφ' ἃ μέρη εἰσὶν αἱ τῶν δύο ὀρθῶν ἐλάσσονες

That, if a straight line falling on two straight lines make the interior angles on the same side less than two right angles, the two straight lines, if produced indefinitely, meet on that side on which are the angles less than the two right angles.

Translated by Ivor Thomas (1939)

Elements 1 Postulate 5

the fifth basic postulate of Euclidean Geometry; see previous entry

5 ὅπερ ἔδει δεῖξαι

QED: Quod erat demonstrandum: this is what was to be proved.

Elements 1 Proposition 4 et al.

used wherever a theorem has been proved

6 ἐν τοῖς ὀρθογωνίοις τριγώνοις τὸ ἀπὸ τῆς τὴν ὀρθὴν γωνίαν ὑποτεινούσης πλευρᾶς τετράγωνον ἴσον ἐστὶ τοῖς ἀπὸ τῶν τὴν ὀρθὴν γωνίαν περιεχουσῶν πλευρῶν τετραγώνοις

In right-angled triangles the square on the side opposite the right angle equals the sum of the squares on the sides containing the right angle.

Translated in *The Yale Book of Quotations* (2006)

Elements 1 Proposition 47

The Pythagorean Theorem

7 ὁ δὲ ἀπεκρίνατο, μὴ εἶναι βασιλικὴν ἀτραπὸν ἐπὶ γεωμετρίαν

There is no royal short cut to geometry.

Translated by John Simpson and Jennifer Speake (1982)

Proclus, *Commentary on the First Book of Euclid's Elements* 68.16

Euclid's reply when asked by King Ptolemy I if there is no faster way to learn geometry; cf. the English proverb 'there is no royal road to learning'

EUDAMIDAS

King of Sparta, *c.*331–*c.*321 BC

see also Xenocrates 1

1 ἀκούσας δὲ φιλοσόφου διαλεχθέντος ὅτι μόνος ἀγαθὸς στρατηγὸς ὁ σοφός ἐστιν, ὁ μὲν λόγος, ἔφη, θαυμαστός· ὁ δὲ λέγων ἄπιστος· οὐ γὰρ περισεσάλπισται

Hearing a philosopher declaring that the wise man is the only good general, he said, 'The speech is admirable but the speaker not to be trusted; for he has never been amid the blare of trumpets.'

Translated by Frank Cole Babbitt (1931)

Plutarch, *Sayings of Spartans* 220e

2 μέγας ... κηλικτὰς ἐν μικρῷ πράγματι

He has great power to charm in a trifling matter.

Translated by Frank Cole Babbitt (1931)

Plutarch, *Sayings of Spartans* 220f

of a musician who had produced a very popular tune

EUENUS

5th century BC

Rhetorician and sophist from Paros, writer of elegiac and other verse

1 πολλοῖς δ' ἀντιλέγειν μέν ἔθος περὶ παντὸς ὁμοίως,
ὀρθῶς δ' ἀντιλέγειν, οὐκέτι τοῦτ' ἐν ἔθει.
καὶ πρὸς μὲν τούτους ἀρκεῖ λόγος εἷς ὁ παλαιός·
σοὶ μὲν ταῦτα δοκοῦντ' ἔστω, ἐμοὶ δὲ τάδε

Many a man will contradict on all and every matter,
and care not whether his contradiction be just.
For such the old answer is enough,
Let that be your opinion and this mine.

Translated by J.M. Edmonds (1931)

Fragment 1 (West, *IEG*)

2 Βάκχου μέτρον ἄριστον ὃ μὴ πολὺ μηδ' ἐλάχιστον·
ἔστι γὰρ ἢ λύπης αἴτιος ἢ μανίης

Good measure of wine is best, not too much, not too little;
too little may cause grief, too much, madness.

Fragment 2 (West, *IEG*)

3 πολλάκις ἀνθρώπων ὀργὴ νόον ἐξεκάλυψεν
κρυπτόμενον, μανίης πολὺ χειρότερον

Anger often reveals a hidden mind
much worse than madness.

Fragment 5 (West, *IEG*)

4 ὕβρις ... ἥτις κερδαίνουσ' οὐδὲν ὅμως ἀδικεῖ

Hubris that wrongs others e'en when she gaineth nought.

Translated by H. Rackham (1935)

Fragment 7 (West, *IEG*)

as quoted by Aristotle in Virtues and Vices *1251a.36*

5 πᾶν ἀναγκαῖον πρᾶγμ' ἀνιαρὸν ἔφυ

Compulsion breeds distress.

Fragment 8 (West, *IEG*)

6 φημὶ πολυχρόνιην μελέτην ἔμεναι φίλε, καὶ δὴ
ταύτην ἀνθρώποισι τελευτῶσαν φύσιν εἶναι

I say that practice must be long, my friend,
and thus become second nature.

Fragment 9 (West, *IEG*)

EUGENES

dates unknown
Epigrams in *Greek Anthology*

1 ὄμμα δέ μευ Βρομίῳ βεβαρημένον, ἠδ' ἀπὸ κώμων
τερπνὰ φιλαγρύπνων σήματα παννυχίδων

My eyes are heavy with wine, and I bear from my revelling
the pleasant signs of sleepless night festivals.

Translated by W.R. Paton (1918)

Greek Anthology 16.309

EUNAPIUS

*c.*345–*c.*414AD
Sophist and historian born at Sardis

1 ἕτερόν τί ἐστιν τῷ νῷ θεωρεῖν καὶ τοῖς τοῦ σώματος ἀπατηλοῖς ὄμμασιν

Observe with the mind; eyes are apt to deceive.

Lives of the Sophists 6.11.11

EUPHRATES

*c.*30–*c.*118AD
Stoic philosopher

1 ὦ φιλοσοφία, τυραννικά σου τὰ ἐπιτάγματα, λέγεις, φίλει, κἂν ἀποβάλῃ τις λέγεις μὴ λυποῦ

O, philosophy, and your tyrannical commands! You say 'love', and when your love is lost, you say, 'do not grieve.'

Stobaeus, *Anthology* 4.35.34

Euphrates the Syrian, when he lost his wife

EUPOLIS

fl. 425–415BC
Athenian Old Comedy poet

1 λαλεῖν ἄριστος, ἀδυνατώτατος λέγειν

The best of prattlers, unable to speak to the point.

Fragment 95 (Kock) – *116 (K-A) – *Demoi – Demes*

of Alcibiades who spoke with a lisp

2 καὶ πόλλ' ἔμαθον ἐν τοῖσι κουρείοις ἐγὼ
ἀτόπως καθίζων κοὐδὲ γιγνώσκειν δοκῶν

Much have I learnt in the barber's chair,
sitting idly and seeming not to listen.

Fragment 180 (Kock) – 194 (K-A) – *Maricas*

3 ἄσπουδος δ' ἀνὴρ σπουδαρχίδου κακίων

An unambitious man is worse than the office seeker.

Translated by Ian C. Storey (2011)

Fragment 234 (Kock) – 248 (K-A) – *Poleis – Cities*

4 πάντα γὰρ τυχὼν ἄπει

You grabbed it all and ran.

Fragment 246 (Kock) – 265 (K-A) – *Prospaltii – Prospaltians*

Prospalta was an Attic deme

5 μουσικὴ πρᾶγμ' ἐστὶ βαθύ τι καὶ καμπύλον

Music is something deep with varying tones.

Fragment 336 (Kock) – 366 (K-A)

EURIPIDES

c.480–406BC

Athenian tragic playwright

see also Anonymous 38, 87; Archelaus (2) 2; Aristophanes 76, 84, 88, 131; Aristotle 188; Cratinus 4; Hieronymus of Rhodes 1; Philemon 32

1 φίλου γὰρ ἀνδρὸς συμφοραῖς βαρύνομαι

I share the grief of my friend.

Alcestis 42

2 οὔποτε φήσω γάμον εὐφραίνειν
πλέον ἢ λυπεῖν

Never say that marriage brings more joy than pain.

Alcestis 238

3 ψυχῆς γὰρ οὐδέν ἐστι τιμιώτερον

Nothing is more precious than life.

Translated by David Kovacs (1994)

Alcestis 301

4 ἐχθρὰ γὰρ ἡ 'πιοῦσα μητρυιὰ τέκνοις
τοῖς πρόσθ', ἐχίδνης οὐδὲν ἠπιωτέρα

A stepmother is more harmful to children than a viper.

Alcestis 309

5 παῖς μὲν ἄρσην πατέρ' ἔχει πύργον μέγαν

A father is a tower of strength for his son.

Alcestis 311

6 οὐδὲν μητρὸς εὐμενέστερον

Nothing is more precious than a mother's comfort.

Alcestis 319

7 λόγῳ γὰρ ἦσαν οὐκ ἔργῳ φίλοι

They were friends in word, but not in deed.

Alcestis 339

8 ἐν δ' ὀνείρασιν
φοιτῶσά μ' εὐφραίνοις ἄν· ἡδὺ γὰρ φίλους
κἂν νυκτὶ λεύσσειν

To see a beloved face even in dreams
Brings pleasure, for as long as the illusion lasts.

Translated by Philip Vellacott (1953)

Alcestis 354

9 εἰ δ' Ὀρφέως μοι γλῶσσα καὶ μέλος παρῆν,
ὥστ' ἢ κόρην Δήμητρος ἢ κείνης πόσιν
ὕμνοισι κηλήσαντά σ' ἐξ Ἅιδου λαβεῖν,
κατῆλθον ἄν, καί μ' οὔθ' ὁ Πλούτωνος κύων
οὔθ' οὑπὶ κώπῃ ψυχοπομπὸς ἂν Χάρων
ἔσχ' ἄν, πρὶν ἐς φῶς σὸν καταστῆσαι βίον

Oh, if I had the songs that Orpheus had, his voice,
To enchant with music Pluto and Persephone,
I would go down to fetch you; and neither Cerberus
Would stop me, nor Charon's ferry-load of ghosts,
Till I had brought you living to the light of day!

Translated by Philip Vellacott (1953)

Alcestis 357

10 πᾶσιν ἡμῖν κατθανεῖν ὀφείλεται

Death is a debt which every one of us must pay.

Translated by Philip Vellacott (1953)

Alcestis 419

11 πολλά σε μουσοπόλοι
μέλψουσι καθ' ἑπτάτονόν τ' ὀρείαν
χέλυν ἔν τ' ἀλύροις κλέοντες ὕμνοις

Many a song shall poets make,
Singing your praise to the seven-stringed mountain lyre,
Or in unaccompanied chorus.

Translated by Philip Vellacott (1953)

Alcestis 445

12 κούφα σοι
χθὼν ἐπάνωθε πέσοι

Light be the earth upon you, lightly rest.

Translated by Dudley Fitts and Robert Fitzgerald (1936)

Alcestis 464

13 λυπουμένοις ὀχληρός, εἰ μόλοι, ξένος

No guest is welcome on a day of mourning.

Alcestis 540

14 αἰσχρόν γε παρὰ κλαίουσι θοινᾶσθαι ξένους

It is wrong for guests to feast in a house of mourning.

Alcestis 542

15 τἀμὰ δ' οὐκ ἐπίσταται
μέλαθρ' ἀπωθεῖν οὐδ' ἀτιμάζειν ξένους

It is not the custom
of my house to refuse a guest.

Alcestis 566

16 ἐν τοῖς ἀγαθοῖσι δὲ πάντ' ἔνεστιν

All that is good lives in the hearts of the nobly born.

Translated by David Kovacs (1994)

Alcestis 602

17 μάτην ἄρ' οἱ γέροντες εὔχονται θανεῖν,
γῆρας ψέγοντες καὶ μακρὸν χρόνον βίου·
ἢν δ' ἐγγὺς ἔλθῃ θάνατος, οὐδεὶς βούλεται
θνῄσκειν

Falsely, then, do old men pray for death,
cursing old age and their unending life;
when death is near no one wants to die.

Alcestis 669

18 χαίρεις ὁρῶν φῶς· πατέρα δ' οὐ χαίρειν δοκεῖς;

You love the daylight: do you think I don't enjoy it too?

Alcestis 691

19 ἦ μὴν πολύν γε τὸν κάτω λογίζομαι
χρόνον, τὸ δὲ ζῆν σμικρὸν ἀλλ' ὅμως γλυκύ

By my reckoning, I'm going to spend a long time dead
And a short time alive – yes, short, but very sweet.

Translated by Philip Vellacott (1953)

Alcestis 692

20 κακῶς ἀκούειν οὐ μέλει θανόντι μοι

Little I care who speaks ill of me – in my grave.

Translated by Philip Vellacott (1953)

Alcestis 726

21 κοὐκ ἔστι θνητῶν ὅστις ἐξεπίσταται
τὴν αὔριον μέλλουσαν εἰ βιώσεται

No man knows for certain whether
he will still be living on the morrow.

Translated by David Kovacs (1994)

Alcestis 783

22 τὸ τῆς τύχης γὰρ ἀφανὲς οἷ προβήσεται,
κἄστ' οὐ διδακτὸν οὐδ' ἁλίσκεται τέχνῃ

The ways of fortune are unpredictable,
they cannot be taught nor acquired by human skill.

Alcestis 785

23 τὸν καθ' ἡμέραν
βίον λογίζου σόν, τὰ δ' ἄλλα τῆς τύχης

Your life is yours today, the rest is fortune.

Alcestis 788

24 ὄντας δὲ θνητοὺς θνητὰ καὶ φρονεῖν χρεών

As mortals, we should behave as mortals.

Alcestis 799

25 τοῖς γε σεμνοῖς καὶ συνωφρυωμένοις
ἅπασίν ἐστιν, ὥς γ' ἐμοὶ χρῆσθαι κριτῇ,
οὐ βίος ἀληθῶς ὁ βίος ἀλλὰ συμφορά

As for the grave and solemn, with frowning countenance,
their life is not a life worthy of the name but,
as to me, just one long calamity.

Alcestis 800

26 ἦ βαρυδαίμονα μήτηρ μ' ἔτεκεν.
ζηλῶ φθιμένους

It was to an ill fate that my mother bore me.
I envy all the dead.

Translated by David Kovacs (1994)

Alcestis 865

27 τί γὰρ ἀνδρὶ κακὸν μεῖζον ἁμαρτεῖν
πιστῆς ἀλόχου;

What crueller blow can a man suffer
Than the loss of a faithful wife?

Alcestis 879

28 ὦ μακρὰ πένθη λῦπαί τε φίλων
τῶν ὑπὸ γαίας

Oh, how great is the pain and grief for loved ones
who lie beneath the earth!

Translated by David Kovacs (1994)

Alcestis 895

29 παρ' εὐτυχῆ
σοι πότμον ἦλθεν ἀπειροκάκῳ
τόδ' ἄλγος

In good fortune

this grief has come to you,
a stranger to sorrow.

Alcestis 927

30 ἐγὼ καὶ διὰ μούσας
καὶ μετάρσιος ᾖξα, καὶ
πλείστων ἁψάμενος λόγων
κρεῖσσον οὐδὲν Ἀνάγκας
ηὗρον

I have found power in the mysteries of thought,
exaltation in the chanting of the Muses;
I have been versed in the reasonings of men;
but Fate is stronger than anything I have known.

Translated by Dudley Fitts and Robert Fitzgerald (1936)

Alcestis 962

31 οὐ γὰρ ἀνάξεις ποτ᾽ ἔνερθεν
κλαίων τοὺς φθιμένους ἄνω

You cannot bring up the dead from below by weeping.

Translated by David Kovacs (1994)

Alcestis 986

32 φίλον πρὸς ἄνδρα χρὴ λέγειν ἐλευθέρως

Speak frankly to a friend.

Translated by David Kovacs (1994)

Alcestis 1008

33 τὸν ἡβῶνθ᾽... οὐ ῥᾴδιον εἴργειν

It is not easy to rein in a young man in his prime.

Translated by David Kovacs (1994)

Alcestis 1053

34 ῥᾷον παραινεῖν ἢ παθόντα καρτερεῖν

'Tis easier to give advice to others suffering than bear it patiently yourself.

Alcestis 1078

35 τί δ᾽ ἂν προκόπτοις, εἰ θέλεις ἀεὶ στένειν;

What will you gain by endless grieving?

Alcestis 1079

36 χρόνος μαλάξει, νῦν δ᾽ ἔθ᾽ ἡβάσκει, κακόν

Your wound is fresh now; with time the pain will ease.

Translated by Philip Vellacott (1953)

Alcestis 1085

37 πολλαὶ μορφαὶ τῶν δαιμονίων,
πολλὰ δ᾽ ἀέλπτως κραίνουσι θεοί·
καὶ τὰ δοκηθέντ᾽ οὐκ ἐτελέσθη,
τῶν δ᾽ ἀδοκήτων πόρον ηὗρε θεός

Many are the guises of things divine:
Many things the gods achieve in surprising ways.
Things we expect never come to pass,
While the gods find ways to make the unexpected happen.

Translated by Robin Waterfield (2003)

Alcestis 1159

closing lines

38 πολλὰς ἂν εὕροις μηχανάς· γυνὴ γὰρ εἶ

You will find many ruses: you are a woman.

Translated by David Kovacs (1995)

Andromache 85

39 χρὴ δ᾽ οὔποτ᾽ εἰπεῖν οὐδέν᾽ ὄλβιον βροτῶν,
πρὶν ἂν θανόντος τὴν τελευταίαν ἴδῃς
ὅπως περάσας ἡμέραν ἥξει κάτω

Never call anyone fortunate
until you see his final day
and his departure to the world below.

Andromache 100

40 οἱ γὰρ πνέοντες μεγάλα τοὺς κρείσσους λόγους
πικρῶς φέρουσι τῶν ἐλασσόνων ὕπο

Nothing makes arrogant people angrier than being
Worsted in arguments by the weaker party.

Translated by Philip Vellacott (1972)

Andromache 189

41 οὐ τὸ κάλλος, ὦ γύναι,
ἀλλ᾽ ἀρεταὶ τέρπουσι τοὺς ξυνευνέτας

It's not
Beauty, but character that wins a husband's heart.

Translated by Philip Vellacott (1972)

Andromache 207

42 ὦ δόξα δόξα, μυρίοισι δὴ βροτῶν
οὐδὲν γεγῶσι βίοτον ὤγκωσας μέγαν

O Fame, Fame! a myriad nobodies
you have inflated into high renown!

Andromache 319

43 εὔκλεια δ' οἷς μέν ἐστ' ἀληθείας ὕπο
εὐδαιμονίζω

Blessed is the man whose good repute is based on truth.

Andromache 321

44 ἔξωθέν εἰσιν οἱ δοκοῦντες εὖ φρονεῖν
λαμπροί, τὰ δ' ἔνδον πᾶσιν ἀνθρώποις ἴσοι

Outwardly they look splendid, are considered wise;
but within they are just as any other.

Andromache 330

45 ὅτου τις τυγχάνει χρείαν ἔχων,
τοῦτ' ἔσθ' ἑκάστῳ μεῖζον ἢ Τροίαν ἑλεῖν

Whatever a man desires
means to him more than the conquest of Troy.

Andromache 368

46 τὰ μὲν γὰρ ἄλλα δεύτερ' ἂν πάσχῃ γυνή,
ἀνδρὸς δ' ἁμαρτάνουσ' ἁμαρτάνει βίου

Other misfortunes are secondary to a woman,
but if she loses her husband she loses her life.

Andromache 372

47 πᾶσι δ' ἀνθρώποις ἄρ' ἦν
ψυχὴ τέκν'

Children are the very breath of life.

Translated by James Morwood (2001)

Andromache 418

48 μίαν μοι στεργέτω πόσις γάμοις
ἀκοινώνητον ἀνδρὸς εὐνάν

May my husband be content in marriage with a single mate
and a bed unshared!

Translated by David Kovacs (1995)

Andromache 468

49 πνοαὶ δ' ὅταν φέρωσι ναυτίλους θοαί,
κατὰ πηδαλίων διδύμα πραπίδων γνώμα

When a ship flies before a fresh breeze,
The work of steering is not helped by two opinions.

Translated by Philip Vellacott (1972)

Andromache 479

i.e. in marriage a man cannot have two wives

50 τί με προσπίτνεις, ἁλίαν πέτραν
ἢ κῦμα λιταῖς ὡς ἱκετεύων;

It is no use entreating me; you may as well pray to the rocks or waves.

Andromache 537

51 σμικρᾶς ἀπ' ἀρχῆς νεῖκος ἀνθρώποις μέγα
γλῶσσ' ἐκπορίζει

The tongue can turn some trifling cause to flagrant strife.

Andromache 642

52 πολλῶν νέων γὰρ καὶ γέρων εὔψυχος ὢν
κρείσσων· τί γὰρ δεῖ δειλὸν ὄντ' εὐσωματεῖν;

One brave old man is a match for many youths;
why, what's the use of muscle to a coward?

Andromache 764

53 οὔτοι λείψανα τῶν ἀγαθῶν
ἀνδρῶν ἀφαιρεῖται χρόνος· ἁ δ' ἀρετὰ
καὶ θανοῦσι λάμπει

The remembrance of great men
time does not extinguish; their virtue
shines forth beyond the grave.

Andromache 773

54 πολιὰ ξυνωρίς, ἀλλ' ὅμως χορευτέον

We are a pair of greyheads, but still we must dance.

Translated by David Kovacs (2002)

Bacchae 324

55 μαίνῃ γὰρ ὡς ἄλγιστα, κοὔτε φαρμάκοις
ἄκη λάβοις ἂν οὔτ' ἄνευ τούτων νοσεῖς

You are mad and most painfully so; some drug
has caused it, and no drug can cure it.

Translated by David Kovacs (2002)

Bacchae 326

56 ἄνω κάτω τὰ πάντα

Turn the whole place upside down.

Translated by David Kovacs (2002)

Bacchae 349

57 μῶρα γὰρ μῶρος λέγει

Foolishly speak the foolish.

Bacchae 369

58 ἀχαλίνων στομάτων

ἀνόμου τ᾽ ἀφροσύνας
τὸ τέλος δυστυχία

Of unbridled talk
and lawless folly
misfortune is the end.

Bacchae 386

59 ὁ δὲ τᾶς ἡσυχίας
βίοτος καὶ τὸ φρονεῖν
ἀσάλευτόν τε μένει καὶ
συνέχει δώματα

A life of tranquillity
and wisdom
remains unshaken
and holds houses together.

Translated by T.A. Buckley (1850)

Bacchae 389

60 τὸ σοφὸν δ᾽ οὐ σοφία

Wisdom overmuch is no wisdom.

Translated in Liddell & Scott

Bacchae 395

61 τὸ πλῆθος ὅ τι τὸ φαυλότερον ἐνόμισε χρῆ-
ταί τε, τόδ᾽ ἂν δεχοίμαν

What the simple folk believe and practice,
that shall I accept.

Translated by David Kovacs (2002)

Bacchae 430

62 δόξει τις ἀμαθεῖ σοφὰ λέγων οὐκ εὖ φρονεῖν

Talk sense to a fool and he calls you foolish.

Translated in *Bartlett's Familiar Quotations* (1980)

Bacchae 480

63 οὐκ οἶσθ᾽ ὅ τι ζῇς, οὐδ᾽ ὃ δρᾷς, οὐδ᾽ ὅστις εἶ

You know not why you live, or what you do, or who you are.

Bacchae 506

64 πρὸς σοφοῦ γὰρ ἀνδρὸς ἀσκεῖν σώφρον᾽ εὐοργησίαν

It is for a wise man to practice restrained good temper.

Translated by T.A. Buckley (1850)

Bacchae 641

65 οἴνου δὲ μηκέτ᾽ ὄντος οὐκ ἔστιν Κύπρις
οὐδ᾽ ἄλλο τερπνὸν οὐδὲν ἀνθρώποις ἔτι

Without wine there is no longer Love
or any other pleasure.

Bacchae 773

66 ἆρ᾽ ἐν παννυχίοις χοροῖς
θήσω ποτὲ λευκὸν
πόδ᾽ ἀναβακχεύουσα, δέραν
αἰθέρ᾽ ἐς δροσερὸν ῥίπτουσ᾽

O when will I be dancing,
leaping barefoot through the night,
flinging back my head in ecstasy,
in the clear, cold, dew-fresh air.

Translated by Ian Johnston (2008)

Bacchae 862

67 ὡς νεβρὸς χλοεραῖς ἐμπαί-
ζουσα λείμακος ἡδοναῖς,
ἀνίκ᾽ ἂν φοβερὰν φύγῃ
θήραν ἔξω φυλακᾶς
εὐπλέκτων ὑπὲρ ἀρκύων,
θωύσσων δὲ κυναγέτας
συντείνῃ δράμημα κυνῶν

Like a fawn at play in the grassy delights of a meadow,
having escaped the fearful hunt, leaping the nets,
while the hunter calls back his coursing hounds.

Bacchae 866

of dancing

68 μόχθοις δ᾽ ὠκυδρόμοις ἀελ-
λὰς θρῴσκῃ πεδίον
παραποτάμιον, ἡδομένα
βροτῶν ἐρημίαις σκιαρο-
κόμοιό τ᾽ ἔρνεσιν ὕλας

With swift-running zeal, like a whirlwind over the plain
near the river, rejoicing in the solitude, away from men,
and the saplings of the shady forest.

Bacchae 873

of dancing (compared to a fawn who is joyful at escaping the huntsmen)

69 ὅ τι καλὸν φίλον αἰεί

What is noble is forever loved.

Bacchae 881

70 ὁρμᾶται μόλις, ἀλλ᾽ ὅμως
πιστόν τι τὸ θεῖον σθένος

Slow but sure moves the might of the

gods.

Translated in *Bartlett's Familiar Quotations* (1980)

Bacchae 882

71 τί τὸ σοφόν; ἢ τι κάλλιον
παρὰ θεῶν γέρας ἐν βροτοῖς
ἢ χεῖρ' ὑπὲρ κορυφᾶς
τῶν ἐχθρῶν κρείσσω κατέχειν;

What is wisdom? What gift of god
is nobler in the sight of men
than to hold your hand victorious
over the heads of foes?

Bacchae 897

72 εὐδαίμων μὲν ὃς ἐκ θαλάσσας
ἔφυγε χεῖμα, λιμένα δ' ἔκιχεν·
εὐδαίμων δ' ὃς ὕπερθε μόχθων
ἐγένεθ'

Blessed is he who from the sea
escapes the storm and reaches harbour;
blessed is he who truimphs over misfortune.

Bacchae 902

73 ἕτερα δ' ἕτερος ἕτερον
ὄλβῳ καὶ δυνάμει παρῆλθεν,
μυρίαι δ' ἔτι μυρίοις
εἰσὶν ἐλπίδες· αἱ μὲν
τελευτῶσιν ἐν ὄλβῳ
βροτοῖς, αἱ δ' ἀπέβασαν·
τὸ δὲ κατ' ἦμαρ ὅτῳ βίοτος
εὐδαίμων, μακαρίζω

One man surpasses the next in different ways, in wealth or power. Also, countless are the hopes of countless men: some are fulfilled, and others come to nought. But he who lives happily from day to day, him I consider blessed.

Bacchae 905

74 θάνατος ἀπροφάσιστος

Death implacable, admitting no excuse.

Translated in Liddell & Scott

Bacchae 1002

75 τὸ σωφρονεῖν δὲ καὶ σέβειν τὰ τῶν θεῶν
κάλλιστον· οἶμαι δ' αὐτὸ καὶ σοφώτατον
θνητοῖσιν εἶναι κτῆμα τοῖσι χρωμένοις

To keep fair measure and respect the gods,
this is the best option, and the wisest course,
and much the safest possession for mortal men.

Bacchae 1150

76 καλὸν δέ γ' ἔξω πραγμάτων ἔχειν πόδα,
εὐβουλίας τυχόντα τῆς ἀμείνονος

It's a good thing to keep your feet well clear
Of trouble, and when good counsel's given, to follow it.

Translated by Philip Vellacott (1972)

Children of Heracles 109

77 καὶ πῶς δίκαιον τὸν ἱκέτην ἄγειν βίᾳ;

How can it be right or just to arrest a suppliant?

Translated by Philip Vellacott (1972)

Children of Heracles 254

78 μιᾶς γὰρ χειρὸς ἀσθενὴς μάχη

A single man can put up only a weak fight.

Translated by David Kovacs (1995)

Children of Heracles 274

cf. the English proverb 'two to one is odds'

79 οὐκ ἔστι τοῦδε παισὶ κάλλιον γέρας
ἢ πατρὸς ἐσθλοῦ κἀγαθοῦ πεφυκέναι

There is no finer honour for children than this,
to be born of a brave and noble father.

Translated by David Kovacs (1995)

Children of Heracles 297

80 ἕνα γὰρ ἐν πολλοῖς ἴσως
εὕροις ἂν ὅστις ἐστὶ μὴ χείρων πατρός

Only one man out of a great multitude
can be found who is not inferior to his father.

Translated by David Kovacs (1995)

Children of Heracles 327

81 ἁ δ' ἀρετὰ βαίνει διὰ μόχθων

The course of a noble life must pass through pain.

Translated by Philip Vellacott (1972)

Children of Heracles 625

82 ἔστιν δ' ἐν ὄλβῳ καὶ τόδ' οὐκ ὀρθῶς ἔχον,
εὐψυχίας δόκησις· οἰόμεσθα γὰρ
τὸν εὐτυχοῦντα πάντ' ἐπίστασθαι καλῶς

Wealth and position bring this false gain,

Repute for courage; for we attribute every kind
Of knowledge to the successful man.

Translated by Philip Vellacott (1972)

Children of Heracles 745

83 χρὴ ἀψευδὲς εἶναι τοῖσι γενναίοις στόμα

A truthful tongue brings credit to a noble name.

Children of Heracles 890

84 τερπνὸν δέ τι καὶ φίλων
ἄρ' εὐτυχίαν ἰδέσθαι
τῶν πάρος οὐ δοκούντων

Pleasant it is to see,
When, beyond expectation,
Friends at last have found good fortune.

Translated by Philip Vellacott (1972)

Children of Heracles 895

85 μηδαμοῦ γένος ποτὲ
φῦναι γυναικῶν ὤφελ', εἰ μὴ 'μοὶ μόνῳ

O would that the female sex were nowhere to be found – but in my lap!

Translated by David Kovacs (1994)

Cyclops 186

chorus of Satyrs

86 τὰ καινά γ' ἐκ τῶν ἠθάδων, ὦ δέσποτα,
ἡδίον' ἐστίν

Novelty, good master, is all the pleasanter
after the customary everyday chores.

Cyclops 250

87 νόμος δὲ θ νητοῖς …
ἱκέτας δέχεσθαι ποντίους ἐφθαρμένους

There is a law among mortals
that one must receive shipwrecked suppliants.

Translated by David Kovacs (1994)

Cyclops 299

88 ὁ πλοῦτος, ἀνθρωπίσκε, τοῖς σοφοῖς θεός,
τὰ δ' ἄλλα κόμποι καὶ λόγων εὐμορφία

Little man, wealth is the god of the wise,
the rest is show and fancy talk.

Translated by C.A. Trypanis (1971)

Cyclops 316

spoken by Cyclops

89 ἡ γῆ δ' ἀνάγκῃ, κἂν θέλῃ κἂν μὴ θέλῃ,
τίκτουσα ποίαν τἀμὰ πιαίνει βοτά

The earth must willy-nilly
grow grass to feed my sheep.

Cyclops 332

90 ὡς τοὐμπιεῖν γε καὶ φαγεῖν τοὐφ' ἡμέραν,
Ζεὺς οὗτος ἀνθρώποισι τοῖσι σώφροσιν,
λυπεῖν δὲ μηδὲν αὑτόν

Zeus himself instructs the wise,
to eat and drink and not to worry.

Cyclops 336

91 παιδεύσωμεν τὸν ἀπαίδευτον

Let us impart some culture to this lout.

Translated by David Kovacs (1994)

Cyclops 492

92 πέτρας τὸ λῆμα κἀδάμαντος ἕξομεν

Our hearts shall be like rock or adamant!

Translated by David Kovacs (1994)

Cyclops 596

93 μεγάλη δὲ θνητοῖς μοῖρα συμφορᾶς κακῆς
ἰατρὸν εὑρεῖν

It is a great stroke of fortune
to find a healer of misfortune.

Electra 69

94 αἱ δὲ σάρκες αἱ κεναὶ φρενῶν
ἀγάλματ' ἀγορᾶς εἰσιν

Bodies destitute of brains
are as statues in the marketplace.

Electra 387

95 Λοξίου γὰρ ἔμπεδοι
χρησμοί, βροτῶν δὲ μαντικὴν χαίρειν ἐῶ

I disregard the prophesies of mortal men; only Loxias' oracles are unfailing.

Electra 399

Loxias is an epithet of Apollo, referring to the Delphic Oracle

96 σκοπῶ τὰ χρήμαθ' ὡς ἔχει μέγα σθένος
ξένοις τε δοῦναι σῶμά τ' ἐς νόσους πεσὸν
δαπάναισι σῶσαι· τῆς δ' ἐφ' ἡμέραν βορᾶς
ἐς σμικρὸν ἥκει· πᾶς γὰρ ἐμπλησθεὶς ἀνὴρ
ὁ πλούσιός τε χὠ πένης ἴσον φέρει

I care for riches, to make gifts to friends
or lead a sick man back to health with ease and plenty.
Else, small aid is wealth for daily

gladness;
once a man be done with hunger,
rich and poor are all as one.

Translated by Gilbert Murray (1906)

Electra 427

97 χρὴ μηκέθ' ἡγεῖσθαι θεούς,
εἰ τἄδικ' ἔσται τῆς δίκης ὑπέρτερα

We must no longer believe in the gods
if injustice is triumphant over justice.

Translated by David Kovacs (1998)

Electra 583

98 οὔτοι βασιλέα φαῦλον κτανεῖν

'Tis no slight matter to kill a king.

Translated in Liddell & Scott

Electra 760

99 ἡ γὰρ φύσις βέβαιος, οὐ τὰ χρήματα

It is character that is reliable, not money.

Translated by David Kovacs (1998)

Electra 941

100 σχέτλια μὲν ἔπαθες, ἀνόσια δ' εἰργάσω

Cruel may be your punishment, yet unholy were your deeds.

Electra 1170

101 νόμος δ' ἐν ὑμῖν τοῖς τ' ἐλευθέροις ἴσος
καὶ τοῖσι δούλοις

Among you the same law holds good for slave and free alike.

Translated by E.P. Coleridge (1938)

Hecuba 291

of the Greeks

102 ἐν τῷδε γὰρ κάμνουσιν αἱ πολλαὶ πόλεις,
ὅταν τις ἐσθλὸς καὶ πρόθυμος ὢν ἀνὴρ
μηδὲν φέρηται τῶν κακιόνων πλέον

In this many states fail,
when a capable and willing man
wins no greater prize than his inferiors.

Hecuba 306

103 δεινὸς χαρακτὴρ κἀπίσημος ἐν βροτοῖς
ἐσθλῶν γενέσθαι

How strangely unmistakable among mortals
is the stamp of noble birth!

Translated by David Kovacs (1995)

Hecuba 379

Chorus

104 χάλα τοκεῦσιν εἰκότως θυμουμένοις

Make allowance for a parent's anger.

Hecuba 403

105 τοῖς κρατοῦσι μὴ μάχου

Do not challenge authority.

Hecuba 404

106 αὔρα, ποντιὰς αὔρα,
ἅτε ποντοπόρους κομί-
ζεις θοὰς ἀκάτους ἐπ' οἶδμα λίμνας

Breeze, sea-breeze,
you who carry the swift sea-crossing boats
on the swell of the waves.

Translated by C.A. Trypanis (1971)

Hecuba 444

107 ἔνθα πρωτόγονός τε φοῖ-
νιξ δάφνα θ' ἱεροὺς ἀνέ-
σχε πτόρθους

Where the first palm
and the first laurel-tree
lifted their sacred branches.

Translated by C.A. Trypanis (1971)

Hecuba 458

of Delos, where Zeus had a palm-tree grow, for Leto to grasp during her birth pangs, expectant of Apollo

108 οὐ θέλων τε καὶ θέλων

Both willing and reluctant.

Translated by David Kovacs (1995)

Hecuba 566

cf. the Latin 'velit nolit'

109 ἄνθρωποι δ' ἀεὶ
ὁ μὲν πονηρὸς οὐδὲν ἄλλο πλὴν κακός,
ὁ δ' ἐσθλὸς ἐσθλὸς οὐδὲ συμφορᾶς ὕπο
φύσιν διέφθειρ' ἀλλὰ χρηστός ἐστ' ἀεί;
ἆρ' οἱ τεκόντες διαφέρουσιν ἢ τροφαί;
ἔχει γε μέντοι καὶ τὸ θρεφθῆναι καλῶς
δίδαξιν ἐσθλοῦ

Among men, the base will never be anything but base,
the noble is ever noble, even under misfortune's blows,
his nature never changing but always remaining good.
Is then the difference due to birth or bringing up?
Good training doubtless gives lessons in good conduct.

Hecuba 595
the question of nature or nurture

110 ἀναρχία
κρείσσων πυρός

Anarchy, stronger than fire.
Hecuba 607

111 τολμᾶν ἀνάγκη, κἂν τύχω κἂν μὴ τύχω

Dare I must, whether I win or lose.
Hecuba 751

112 ἀλλ' οἱ θεοὶ σθένουσι χὠ κείνων κρατῶν
νόμος· νόμῳ γὰρ τοὺς θεοὺς ἡγούμεθα
καὶ ζῶμεν ἄδικα καὶ δίκαι' ὡρισμένοι

The gods are strong and so is the law that rules over them;
and it is by virtue of law that we believe in the gods
and distinguish right from wrong.
Translated by David Kovacs (1995)
Hecuba 798

113 καὶ μὴ δίκην δώσουσιν οἵτινες ξένους
κτείνουσιν ἢ θεῶν ἱερὰ τολμῶσιν φέρειν,
οὐκ ἔστιν οὐδὲν τῶν ἐν ἀνθρώποισι σῶν

If they are to escape punishment who murder guests
or dare to plunder the temples of the gods,
then all justice is at an end in human matters.
Hecuba 804

114 φεῦ,
οὐκ ἔστι θνητῶν ὅστις ἔστ' ἐλεύθερος·
ἢ χρημάτων γὰρ δοῦλός ἐστιν ἢ τύχης
ἢ πλῆθος αὐτὸν πόλεος ἢ νόμων γραφαὶ
εἴργουσι χρῆσθαι μὴ κατὰ γνώμην τρόποις

Alas!
there is not in the world a single man who is free;
for he is a slave either to money or to fortune,
or else the mob, or fear of law, prevents him
from following the dictates of his heart.
Hecuba 864

115 μηδὲν θρασύνου μηδὲ τοῖς σαυτοῦ κακοῖς
τὸ θῆλυ συνθεὶς ὧδε πᾶν μέμψῃ γένος

Curb your bold tongue, and don't, because of your own woes,
find fault with all the race of women.
Hecuba 1183

116 ἐν τοῖς κακοῖς γὰρ ἁγαθοὶ σαφέστατοι
φίλοι

Good friends are best seen in adversity.
Hecuba 1226
cf. the English proverb 'a friend in need is a friend indeed'

117 ὡς τὰ χρηστὰ πράγματα
χρηστῶν ἀφορμὰς ἐνδίδωσ' ἀεὶ λόγων

How true it is that a good cause
always affords occasion for good words!
Translated by David Kovacs (1995)
Hecuba 1238

118 ἔχεις μὲν ἀλγεῖν', οἶδα· σύμφορον δέ τοι
ὡς ῥᾷστα τἀναγκαῖα τοῦ βίου φέρειν

Your lot is painful I admit. But it is best, you know,
to bear life's harsh necessities as lightly as you can.
Translated by David Kovacs (2002)
Helen 253

119 δεινῆς ἀνάγκης οὐδὲν ἰσχύειν πλέον

Nothing is as strong as stern necessity.
Translated by John Davie (2002)
Helen 514

120 ἐγὼ μὲν εἴην, κεἰ πέφυχ' ὅμως λάτρις,
ἐν τοῖσι γενναίοισιν ἠριθμημένος
δούλοισι, τοὔνομ' οὐκ ἔχων ἐλεύθερον,
τὸν νοῦν δέ

Though I was born a servant,
let me still be numbered among honest slaves;
my mind is free, if not my name.
Translated by E.P. Coleridge (1938)
Helen 728

121 τὸ τολμᾶν δ' ἀδύνατ' ἀνδρὸς οὐ σοφοῦ

To dare the impossible is no mark of wisdom.
Helen 811

122 μισεῖ γὰρ ὁ θεὸς τὴν βίαν, τὰ κτητὰ δὲ
κτᾶσθαι κελεύει πάντας οὐκ ἐς ἁρπαγάς

God hates violence and bids all men
acquire their possessions without stealing.
Helen 903

123 κοινὸς γάρ ἐστιν οὐρανὸς πᾶσιν βροτοῖς

Heaven is common to all mortals.

Translated by E.P. Coleridge (1938)

Helen 906

124 καίτοι λέγουσιν ὡς πρὸς ἀνδρὸς εὐγενοῦς
ἐν ξυμφοραῖσι δάκρυ' ἀπ' ὀφθαλμῶν βαλεῖν

They say that it is fitting for a noble man to let tears fall from his eyes in misfortune.

Translated by E.P. Coleridge (1938)

Helen 950

125 ὅτι θεὸς ἢ μὴ θεὸς ἢ τὸ μέσον
τίς φησ' ἐρευνάσας βροτῶν;

What is god, or what is not god, or what is in between,
who among searching mortals can assert?

Helen 1137

126 τίς μακρότατον πέρας ηὗρεν ὃς τὰ θεῶν ἐσορᾷ
δεῦρο καὶ αὖθις ἐκεῖσε καὶ πάλιν ἀμφιλόγοις
πηδῶντ' ἀνελπίστοις τύχαις

Who understands, exploring farthest limits, when he sees
divine affairs leaping here and there, wavering,
in contradictory and unexpected acts?

Helen 1139

127 ὡς οὐδὲν ἀνθρώποισι τῶν θείων σαφές

How uncertain are the gods' dealings with man!

Translated by E.P. Coleridge (1938)

Heracles 62

128 οὗτος δ' ἀνὴρ ἄριστος ὅστις ἐλπίσιν
πέποιθεν αἰεί· τὸ δ' ἀπορεῖν ἀνδρὸς κακοῦ

The bravest man is he who puts trust in his hopes;
despair is the mark of a coward.

Heracles 105

129 τῷ δ' ἀναγκαίῳ τρόπῳ
ὃς ἀντιτείνει σκαιὸν ἡγοῦμαι βροτῶν

Any man who struggles against the course of fate is a fool.

Translated by David Kovacs (1998)

Heracles 282

130 ὁ δ' ὄλβος ὁ μέγας ἥ τε δόξ' οὐκ οἶδ' ὅτῳ βέβαιός ἐστι

I know no man whose wealth and reputation is assured.

Heracles 511

131 ἄφιλον ... τὸ δυστυχές

Misfortune has no friends.

Translated by David Kovacs (1998)

Heracles 561

132 πάντα τἀνθρώπων ἴσα·
φιλοῦσι παῖδας οἵ τ' ἀμείνονες βροτῶν
οἵ τ' οὐδὲν ὄντες· χρήμασιν δὲ διάφοροι·
ἔχουσιν, οἱ δ' οὔ· πᾶν δὲ φιλότεκνον γένος

Men's lot is everywhere the same.
High and low alike love their children; they differ
in wealth, and some are rich, others poor,
but the whole human race is fond of its offspring.

Translated by David Kovacs (1998)

Heracles 633

133 ἁ νεότας μοι φίλον

Youth is the thing I love.

Translated by David Kovacs (1998)

Heracles 637

134 ἃ καλλίστα μὲν ἐν ὄλβῳ,
καλλίστα δ' ἐν πενίᾳ

Youth is the fairest thing in the midst of riches,
fairest too in poverty.

Translated by David Kovacs (1998)

Heracles 647

135 τὸ δὲ λυγρὸν φόνιόν τε γῆρας μισῶ ... ἀλλὰ κατ' αἰθέρ' αἰεὶ πτεροῖσι φορείσθω

I hate murderous, sad old age; let it be carried away
on wings to the sky for ever.

Translated by C.A. Trypanis (1971)

Heracles 649

136 καὶ τῷδ' ἂν τούς τε κακοὺς ἦν
γνῶναι καὶ τοὺς ἀγαθούς,
ἴσον ἅτ' ἐν νεφέλαισιν ἀ-

στρων ναύταις ἀριθμὸς πέλει

And one could tell
the bad from the good,
just as through the clouds
the sailor sees the throng of stars.

Translated by David Kovacs (1998)

Heracles 665

137 οὐ παύσομαι τὰς Χάριτας
ταῖς Μούσαισιν συγκαταμει-
γνύς, ἡδίσταν συζυγίαν

I shall not cease mingling
the Graces and the Muses,
a union most sweet.

Translated by David Kovacs (1998)

Heracles 673

138 μὴ ζῴην μετ' ἀμουσίας

May I never have to live among uneducated boors.

Heracles 676

139 προσδόκα δὲ δρῶν κακῶς
κακόν τι πράξειν

Expect the worst yourself when harming others.

Heracles 727

140 ὁ χρυσὸς ἅ τ' εὐτυχία
φρενῶν βροτοὺς ἐξάγεται

Gold and good fortune
tempts men out of their senses.

Heracles 774

141 οὐδεὶς ἀλάστωρ τοῖς φίλοις ἐκ τῶν φίλων

No avenging spirit attacks a friend because of those he befriended.

Heracles 1234

142 γέμω κακῶν δὴ κοὐκέτ' ἔσθ' ὅπῃ τεθῇ

I am loaded with woes and have no room for more.

Translated by W.H. Fyfe (1878–1965), rev. Donald Russell (1995)

Heracles 1245

143 ὅταν δὲ κρηπὶς μὴ καταβληθῇ γένους
ὀρθῶς, ἀνάγκη δυστυχεῖν τοὺς ἐκγόνους

When the foundation of a family is wrongly laid,
the descendants are fated to suffer ill fortune.

Heracles 1261

144 οὐδεὶς δὲ θνητῶν ταῖς τύχαις ἀκήρατος

There is not a man alive who has wholly escaped misfortune.

Translated by E.P. Coleridge (1938)

Heracles 1314

145 δεῖται γὰρ ὁ θεός, εἴπερ ἔστ' ὀρθῶς θεός, οὐδενός

A god, if he truly is a god, stands in need of nothing.

Heracles 1345

146 χρὴ δὲ συγγνώμην ἔχειν·
εἴ τίς σ' ὑφ' ἥβης σπλάγχνον ἔντονον φέρων
μάταια βάζει, μὴ δόκει τούτου κλυεῖν

Forgive the thoughtlessness of youth;
if he spoke rashly, pretend you did not hear.

Hippolytus 117

147 οὐδέ σ' ἀρέσκει τὸ παρόν, τὸ δ' ἀπὸν φίλτερον ἡγῇ

You hate what you have, and crave what you have not.

Translated by Philip Vellacott (1953)

Hippolytus 184

148 ῥᾷον δὲ νόσον μετά θ' ἡσυχίας
καὶ γενναίου λήματος οἴσεις

If you are quiet and keep a brave heart
Your illness will be easier to bear.

Translated by Philip Vellacott (1953)

Hippolytus 205

149 τὸ δ' ὑπὲρ δισσῶν μίαν ὠδίνειν
ψυχὴν χαλεπὸν βάρος

It is a cruel burden
For one heart to endure the pain of two.

Hippolytus 258

150 οὕτω τὸ λίαν ἧσσον ἐπαινῶ
τοῦ μηδὲν ἄγαν

I think the best rule is, *A limit to everything.*

Translated by Philip Vellacott (1953)

Hippolytus 264

151 τί τοῦθ' ὃ δὴ λέγουσιν ἀνθρώπους ἐρᾶν;
ἥδιστον, ὦ παῖ, ταὐτὸν ἀλγεινόν θ' ἅμα

What is that which men call Love?
The sweetest thing, my child, but also the most painful.

Hippolytus 347

152 τὰ χρήστ' ἐπιστάμεσθα καὶ γιγνώσκομεν,
οὐκ ἐκπονοῦμεν δ', οἱ μὲν ἀργίας ὕπο,
οἱ δ' ἡδονὴν προθέντες ἀντὶ τοῦ καλοῦ

Though knowledge and judgement tell us what is good,
We don't act out our knowledge; some through indolence,
Others by putting pleasure before virtue.

Hippolytus 380

spoken by Phaedra

153 μισῶ δὲ καὶ τὰς σώφρονας μὲν ἐν λόγοις,
λάθρᾳ δὲ τόλμας οὐ καλὰς κεκτημένας

I hate women who talk of chastity,
but practise recklessness in secret.

Hippolytus 413

spoken by Phaedra

154 δουλοῖ γὰρ ἄνδρα, κἂν θρασύσπλαγχνός τις ᾖ,
ὅταν ξυνειδῇ μητρὸς ἢ πατρὸς κακά

One thing can make the most bold-hearted man a slave:
To learn the secret of a parent's shameful act.

Translated by Philip Vellacott (1953)

Hippolytus 424

155 μόνον δὲ τοῦτό φασ' ἁμιλλᾶσθαι βίῳ,
γνώμην δικαίαν κἀγαθὴν ὅτῳ παρῇ

There is one thing alone
that stands the brunt of life throughout its course:
a quiet conscience.

Translated by David Grene (1942)

Hippolytus 426

spoken by Phaedra

156 αἱ δεύτεραί πως φροντίδες σοφώτεραι

Second thoughts are invariably wiser.

Translated by John Simpson and Jennifer Speake (1982)

Hippolytus 436

cf. the English proverb 'second thoughts are best'

157 φοιτᾷ δ' ἀν' αἰθέρ', ἔστι δ' ἐν θαλασσίῳ
κλύδωνι Κύπρις, πάντα δ' ἐκ ταύτης ἔφυ·
ἥδ' ἐστὶν ἡ σπείρουσα καὶ διδοῦσ' ἔρον,
οὗ πάντες ἐσμὲν οἱ κατὰ χθόν' ἔκγονοι

Love wanders the high heavens; in the swollen sea
You'll find her; the whole universe was born from Love.
She sows all seeds; and that eager desire from which
Each earthly generation springs – this is her gift.

Translated by Philip Vellacott (1953)

Hippolytus 447

158 οὐ γάρ τι τοῖσιν ὠσὶ τερπνὰ χρὴ λέγειν
ἀλλ' ἐξ ὅτου τις εὐκλεὴς γενήσεται

Instead of saying what you think will flatter me,
Give me sound counsel which will keep my honour safe.

Translated by Philip Vellacott (1953)

Hippolytus 488

159 Ἔρως Ἔρως, ὁ κατ' ὀμμάτων
στάζων πόθον, εἰσάγων γλυκεῖαν ψυχᾷ χάριν οὓς ἐπιστρατεύσῃ,
μή μοί ποτε σὺν κακῷ φανεί-
ης μηδ' ἄρρυθμος ἔλθοις.
οὔτε γὰρ πυρὸς οὔτ' ἄστρων ὑπέρτερον βέλος
οἷον τὸ τᾶς Ἀφροδίτας ἵησιν ἐκ χερῶν
Ἔρως ὁ Διὸς παῖς

Eros, Eros, you who distil
The dew of longing upon lovers' eyes,
Eros, you who invade
With gentle joy those hearts you mark for conquest;
Rise not in cruelty, I pray,
Come not in violence!
Neither fire-blast nor star-stroke is more fearful
Than Aphrodite's dart which flies
From the hand of Eros, child of Zeus.

Translated by Philip Vellacott (1953)

Hippolytus 525

160 ἡ γλῶσσ' ὀμώμοχ', ἡ δὲ φρὴν ἀνώμοτος
'Twas but my tongue, 'twas not my soul that swore.

Translated by Gilbert Murray (1902)

Hippolytus 612

Hippolytus on his breaking of an oath

161 ἁμαρτεῖν εἰκὸς ἀνθρώπους

Mistakes are only human.

Hippolytus 615

162 σοφὴν δὲ μισῶ· μὴ γὰρ ἔν γ' ἐμοῖς δόμοις
εἴη φρονοῦσα πλεῖον' ἢ γυναῖκα χρή

I hate learned women. May there be no woman in my house
who knows more than a woman ought to know.

Translated by H.T. Riley (1872)
Hippolytus 640

163 πρὸς τὰς τύχας γὰρ τὰς φρένας κεκτήμεθα

They call it wisdom when we happen to guess right.

Translated by Philip Vellacott (1953)
Hippolytus 701

164 ἵνα με πτεροῦσσαν ὄρ-
νιν θεὸς ... θείη
ἀρθείην δ' ἐπὶ πόντιον
κῦμ' ες τὰς Ἀδριηνὰς
ἀκτάς

Would that god might change me to a winged bird!
O that I could soar aloft to the Adriatic shore.

Hippolytus 733

165 τὸ πολλὰ πράσσειν οὐκ ἐν ἀσφαλεῖ βίου

To meddle in many things is not a safe course in life.

Hippolytus 785

166 δεινὸν σοφιστὴν εἶπας, ὅστις εὖ φρονεῖν
τοὺς μὴ φρονοῦντας δυνατός ἐστ' ἀναγκάσαι

He certainly would be a clever instructor who
Could drive sense into a fool.

Translated by Philip Vellacott (1953)
Hippolytus 921

167 οἱ γὰρ ἐν σοφοῖς
φαῦλοι παρ' ὄχλῳ μουσικώτεροι λέγειν

Those the wise consider fools
Are often better tuned to speak before a crowd.

Hippolytus 988

168 οὐδ' ἔστι μοίρας τοῦ χρεών τ' ἀπαλλαγή

There is no escape from fate and destiny.

Translated by David Kovacs (1995)
Hippolytus 1256

169 ἅρματα μὲν τάδε λαμπρὰ τεθρίππων
Ἥλιος ἤδη λάμπει κατὰ γῆν,
ἄστρα δὲ φεύγει πυρὶ τῷδ' αἰθέρος
ἐς νύχθ' ἱεράν

Already the sun lights over the earth its flashing four-horsed chariot, and,
driven by this fire, the stars flee from the sky into the holy night.

Translated by C.A. Trypanis (1971)
Ion 82

170 ἂν γὰρ βίᾳ σπεύδωμεν ἀκόντων θεῶν,
ἀνόνητα κεκτήμεσθα τἀγάθ', ὦ γύναι·
ἃ δ' ἂν διδῶσ' ἑκόντες, ὠφελούμεθα

When the gods answer our prayers unwillingly,
we win blessings that bring to us no profit, lady;
our benefit lies in those blessings that they freely confer.

Translated by John Davie (2002)
Ion 378

171 τὰ γὰρ γυναικῶν δυσχερῆ πρὸς ἄρσενας,
κἀν ταῖς κακαῖσιν ἀγαθαὶ μεμειγμέναι
μισούμεθ'· οὕτω δυστυχεῖς πεφύκαμεν

Life is harder for women than for men;
they judge us, good and bad together,
and hate us both alike; such is the fate to which women are born.

Ion 398

172 καὶ γὰρ ὅστις ἂν βροτῶν
κακὸς πεφύκη, ζημιοῦσιν οἱ θεοί·
πῶς οὖν δίκαιον τοὺς νόμους ὑμᾶς βροτοῖς
γράψαντας αὐτοὺς ἀνομίαν ὀφλισκάνειν;

If a man is bad the gods punish him.
How can it then be right that you who
prescribe laws for mortals should be guilty of lawlessness yourselves?

Ion 440

173 οὐκέτ' ἀνθρώπους κακοὺς
λέγειν δίκαιον, εἰ τὰ τῶν θεῶν καλὰ
μιμούμεθ'

No longer is it right to call men bad
for imitating what the gods consider good.

Ion 449

174 ἐμοὶ μὲν πλούτου τε πάρος ...
τροφαὶ κήδειοι τεκέων κεδνῶν ...
μετὰ δὲ κτεάνων μετρίων βιοτᾶς

εὔπαιδος ἐχοίμαν

Before wealth give me children to be proud of;
rather would I be moderately rich but blest with children.

Ion 485

175 οὐ φιλῶ φρενοῦν ἀμούσους καὶ μεμηνότας ξένους

I hate to teach uncouth and raging strangers.

Ion 526

176 οὐ ταὐτὸν εἶδος φαίνεται τῶν πραγμάτων
πρόσωθεν ὄντων ἐγγύθεν θ᾽ ὁρωμένων

Matters do not have the same appearance
when viewed from far or near.

Ion 585

177 λυπρὰ γὰρ τὰ κρείσσονα

Men always hate what is superior.

Ion 597

178 τυραννίδος δὲ τῆς μάτην αἰνουμένης
τὸ μὲν πρόσωπον ἡδύ, τἀν δόμοισι δὲ λυπηρά

Kingship is falsely praised;
behind a pleasant face
there's much distress.

Ion 621

179 ἴση γὰρ ἡ χάρις
μεγάλοισι χαίρειν σμικρά θ᾽ ἡδέως ἔχειν

There is as much delight
in great things as in small.

Ion 646

180 σὺν τοῖς φίλοις γὰρ ἡδὺ μὲν πράσσειν καλῶς·
ὃ μὴ γένοιτο δ᾽, εἴ τι τυγχάνοι κακόν,
ἐς ὄμματ᾽ εὔνου φωτὸς ἐμβλέψαι γλυκύ

It is a joy to share good fortune with a friend;
but, heaven forbid, should some disaster happen,
it is a joy no less to meet a friendly face.

Ion 730

181 τὸ τοῦ ποδὸς μὲν βραδύ, τὸ τοῦ δὲ νοῦ ταχύ

His foot is slow, but quick his mind.

Ion 742

182 οἴμοι, κακούργους ἄνδρας ὡς ἀεὶ στυγῶ,
οἳ συντιθέντες τἄδικ᾽ εἶτα μηχαναῖς κοσμοῦσι

Oh, how I hate villains
who commit crimes and then, with clever ruses,
make them look fair!

Ion 832

183 κακῷ γὰρ ἐσθλὸν οὐ συμμείγνυται

Good and bad can never mix.

Ion 1017

but cf. Euripides 362

184 ὁρᾶθ᾽ ὅσοι δυσκελάδοι-
σιν κατὰ μοῦσαν ἰόντες ἀείδεθ᾽ ὕμνοις
ἁμέτερα λέχεα καὶ γάμους
Κύπριδος ἀθέμιτος ἀνοσίους,
ὅσον εὐσεβίᾳ κρατοῦμεν
ἄδικον ἄροτον ἀνδρῶν.
παλίμφαμος ἀοιδὰ
καὶ μοῦσ᾽ εἰς ἄνδρας ἴτω
δυσκέλαδος ἀμφὶ λέκτρων

All you poets, who float down music's stream,
singing in slanderous strains of women's sinful loves
and criminal passions, mark how much we surpass
in virtue the lawless race of men!
Change your song and let your
voices ring out against men's lustful ways!

Translated by John Davie (2002)

Ion 1090

185 ἀλλ᾽, ὦ φίλη μοι μῆτερ, ἐν χεροῖν σέθεν
ὁ κατθανών τε κοὐ θανὼν

Dear mother, fast within your arms,
dead and yet not dead.

Translated by Oliver Taplin (1978)

Ion 1443

186 ἰὼ ἰὼ λαμπρᾶς αἰθέρος ἀμπτυχαί,
τίν᾽ αὐδὰν ἀύσω βοάσω; πόθεν μοι
συνέκυρσ᾽ ἀδόκητος ἡδονά;
πόθεν ἐλάβομεν χαράν;

Oh, oh, radiant expanse of heaven,
what word shall I speak or cry out? From whence,
did this pleasure unlooked for come?
Whence did I receive such joy!

Translated by David Kovacs (1999)

Ion 1445

187 μηδεὶς δοκείτω μηδὲν ἀνθρώπων ποτὲ
ἄελπτον εἶναι πρὸς τὰ τυγχάνοντα νῦν

After this, let no one consider anything unexpected.

Ion 1510

188 οὐκ ἐπὶ πᾶσίν σ' ἐφύτευσ' ἀγαθοῖς,
Ἀγάμεμνον, Ἀτρεύς· δεῖ δέ σε χαίρειν
καὶ λυπεῖσθαι

Not for a life of blessings only did your father beget you, Agamemnon;
you will meet joy as well as grief.

Iphigenia at Aulis 29

189 χρὴ βοηθεῖν τοῖσιν ἠδικημένοις

Help those that have been wronged.

Iphigenia at Aulis 79

190 θνητῶν δ' ὄλβιος
ἐς τέλος οὐδεὶς οὐδ' εὐδαίμων·
οὔπω γὰρ ἔφυ τις ἄλυπος

No mortal man can be
fortunate all his life. Once born
no one is free of pain.

Iphigenia at Aulis 160

191 γλῶσσ' ἐπίφθονον σοφή

A smooth tongue wins no friends.

Iphigenia at Aulis 333

192 ἄνδρα δ' οὐ χρεὼν
τὸν ἀγαθὸν πράσσοντα μεγάλα τοὺς τρόπους μεθιστάναι

A man of principle
should not change character as he grows great.

Translated by Philip Vellacott (1972)

Iphigenia at Aulis 345

193 ἐς κοινὸν ἀλγεῖν τοῖς φίλοισι χρὴ φίλους

Friends should share their friends' distress.

Iphigenia at Aulis 408

194 οἱ δ' εὐδαίμονες
ἐν πᾶσι κλεινοὶ καὶ περίβλεπτοι βροτοῖς

People love to talk about and gaze at those
Fortune has blessed.

Translated by Philip Vellacott (1972)

Iphigenia at Aulis 428

195 ἡ δυσγένεια δ' ὡς ἔχει τι χρήσιμον.
καὶ γὰρ δακρῦσαι ῥᾳδίως αὐτοῖς ἔχει
ἅπαντά τ' εἰπεῖν· τῷ δὲ γενναίῳ φύσιν
ἄνολβα πάντα· προστάτην δὲ τοῦ βίου
τὸν ὄγκον ἔχομεν τῷ τ' ὄχλῳ δουλεύομεν.
ἐγὼ γὰρ ἐκβαλεῖν μὲν αἰδοῦμαι δάκρυ

To be low-born, I see, has its advantages:
A man can weep, and tell his sorrows to the world.
A king endures sorrows no less; but the demand
For dignity governs our life, and we are slaves
To the masses. I am ashamed to weep.

Translated by Philip Vellacott (1972)

Iphigenia at Aulis 446

cf. Shakespeare, Henry V, *4.1.[256]: 'What infinite heart's ease must kings neglect that private men enjoy?'*

196 διάφοροι δὲ φύσεις βροτῶν,
διάφοροι δὲ τρόποι

As men's natures differ,
so do their ways.

Iphigenia at Aulis 558

197 τροφαί θ' αἱ παιδευόμεναι
μέγα φέρουσ' ἐς τὰν ἀρετάν

A childhood nurtured by sound training
Imparts a strong tendency to virtue.

Translated by Philip Vellacott (1972)

Iphigenia at Aulis 561

198 πόλλ' ἀνδρὶ βασιλεῖ καὶ στρατηλάτῃ μέλει

A man has many cares when he is king and general too.

Translated by E.P. Coleridge (1891)

Iphigenia at Aulis 645

199 μήτ' ἐμοὶ μήτ' ἐμοῖσι τέκνων τέκνοις
ἐλπὶς ἅδε ποτ' ἔλθοι

May neither I, nor any child of my child,
face such a prospect, ever!

Iphigenia at Aulis 785

200 δεινὸν τὸ τίκτειν καὶ φέρει φίλτρον μέγα

How marvellous it is to be a mother, what great affection it carries!

Iphigenia at Aulis 917

201 ὑψηλόφρων μοι θυμὸς αἴρεται πρόσω

I feel my proud heart stirred to noble action.

Translated by Philip Vellacott (1972)

Iphigenia at Aulis 919

202 τίς δὲ μάντις ἔστ' ἀνήρ,
ὃς ὀλίγ' ἀληθῆ, πολλὰ δὲ ψευδῆ λέγει
τυχών, ὅταν δὲ μὴ τύχῃ διοίχεται;

What is a seer?
A man who, if he's lucky, tells a little truth
And a lot of lies; and if he's unlucky, disappears.

Translated by Philip Vellacott (1972)

Iphigenia at Aulis 956

203 αἰνούμενοι γὰρ ἀγαθοὶ τρόπον τινὰ
μισοῦσι τοὺς αἰνοῦντας, ἣν αἰνῶσ' ἄγαν

Good men when praised
will hate the praiser if praising beyond measure.

Iphigenia at Aulis 979

204 αὐτὸ δὲ τὸ σιγᾶν ὁμολογοῦντός ἐστί σου

Your very silence is as good as a confession.

Iphigenia at Aulis 1142

cf. the Latin 'qui tacet, consentire videtur'

205 ἡδὺ γὰρ τὸ φῶς βλέπειν

It is sweet to look upon the light.

Translated by E.P. Coleridge (1891)

Iphigenia at Aulis 1218

Iphigenia pleading for her life

206 αἴσθημά τοι
κἀν νηπίοις γε τῶν κακῶν ἐγγίγνεται

Even a child can sense calamity.

Iphigenia at Aulis 1243

spoken by Iphigenia

207 κακῶς ζῆν κρεῖσσον ἢ καλῶς θανεῖν

Better a life of wretchedness than a noble death.

Translated in *The Oxford Dictionary of Quotations* (2004)

Iphigenia at Aulis 1252

Iphigenia pleading for her life

208 τὰ δ' ἀδύναθ' ἡμῖν καρτερεῖν οὐ ῥᾴδιον

It is no easy matter to patiently endure the irresistible.

Iphigenia at Aulis 1370

209 ζηλῶ δὲ σοῦ μὲν Ἑλλάδ', Ἑλλάδος δὲ σέ

Hellas is fortunate in you, and you in Hellas.

Translated by Philip Vellacott (1972)

Iphigenia at Aulis 1406

210 τοὺς πόνους γὰρ ἀγαθοὶ
τολμῶσι, δειλοὶ δ' εἰσὶν οὐδὲν οὐδαμοῦ

The brave will face the toils of war; cowards are nothing nowhere.

Iphigenia in Tauris 114

211 μόχθος γὰρ οὐδεὶς τοῖς νέοις σκῆψιν φέρει

When young, hardship is no excuse.

Iphigenia in Tauris 122

212 φίλα γὰρ ἐλπὶς γένετ' ἐπὶ πήμασι βροτῶν
ἄπληστος ἀνθρώποις

Such hope is sweet to men;
No mortal sorrow can quench it.

Translated by Philip Vellacott (1953)

Iphigenia in Tauris 414

213 φεύγω ... οὐχ ἑκὼν ἑκών

I go willingly, and yet against my will.

Translated by John Davie (2002)

Iphigenia in Tauris 512

cf. the Latin 'velit nolit'

214 κοὐδαμοῦ καὶ πανταχοῦ

Nowhere and everywhere.

Translated by David Kovacs (1999)

Iphigenia in Tauris 568

215 τὸ δ' εὖ μάλιστά γ' οὕτω γίγνεται,
εἰ πᾶσι ταὐτὸν πρᾶγμ' ἀρεσκόντως ἔχει

A good action is especially so,
if the same matter is pleasing to all.

Translated by Robert Potter (1781)

Iphigenia in Tauris 580

216 ἄζηλά τοι φίλοισι, θνησκόντων φίλων

Unenvied it is to friends, to witness death of friends.

Iphigenia in Tauris 650

217 κλεπτῶν γὰρ ἡ νύξ, τῆς δ' ἀληθείας τὸ φῶς

Night is for thieves, truth comes with the light of day.

Iphigenia in Tauris 1026

218 δειναὶ γὰρ αἱ γυναῖκες εὑρίσκειν τέχνας

Women are wonderfully good at devising crafty plans!

Translated by Robert Potter (1781)

Iphigenia in Tauris 1032

219 γυναῖκές ἐσμεν, φιλόφρον ἀλλήλαις γένος,
σῴζειν τε κοινὰ πράγματ' ἀσφαλέσταται

We are women, we feel for one another,
most steadfast in preserving our common cause.

Iphigenia in Tauris 1061

220 ὄρνις ἃ παρὰ πετρίνας
πόντου δειράδας ἀλκυὼν
ἔλεγον οἶτον ἀείδεις,
εὐξύνετον ξυνετοῖς βοάν,
ὅτι πόσιν κελαδεῖς ἀεὶ μολπαῖς

Bird of the sharp sea-cliffs,
Halcyon, chanting your mournful note,
A cry that speaks to the understanding heart,
A ceaseless song to your lost lover.

Translated by Philip Vellacott (1953)

Iphigenia in Tauris 1089

221 θάλασσα κλύζει πάντα τἀνθρώπων κακά

The sea doth wash away all human ills.

Translated by R.D. Hicks (1925)

Iphigenia in Tauris 1193

inscribed on the public sea-water baths (established 1811) in Tenby, Wales; cf. Diogenes Laertius, Lives of Eminent Philosophers *3.6, on being treated with sea-water by Egyptian priests when falling ill*

222 ἥπερ μεγίστη γίγνεται σωτηρία,
ὅταν γυνὴ πρὸς ἄνδρα μὴ διχοστατῇ

This it is that most keeps a life free of trouble,
when a woman is not at variance with her husband.

Translated by David Kovacs (1994)

Medea 14

of Medea

223 πᾶς τις αὑτὸν τοῦ πέλας μᾶλλον φιλεῖ

Everyone loves himself more than his neighbor.

Translated by Rex Warner (1944)

Medea 86

cf. Bible 71

224 τὸ γὰρ εἰθίσθαι ζῆν ἐπ' ἴσοισιν κρεῖσσον

'Tis better to have been trained to live on equal terms.

Translated by E.P. Coleridge (1891)

Medea 122

225 στυγίους δὲ βροτῶν οὐδεὶς λύπας
ηὕρετο μούσῃ καὶ πολυχόρδοις
ᾠδαῖς παύειν, ἐξ ὧν θάνατοι
δειναί τε τύχαι σφάλλουσι δόμους

But n'er the Flute or Lyre apply'd
To cheer despair, or soften pride,
Nor call'd them to the gloomy cells
Where Want repines, and Vengeance swells,
Where Hate sits musing to betray
And Murder meditates his prey.

Translated by Samuel Johnson (1709–1784)

Medea 195

226 ἵνα δ' εὔδειπνοι
δαῖτες, τί μάτην τείνουσι βοήν;
τὸ παρὸν γὰρ ἔχει τέρψιν ἀφ' αὑτοῦ
δαιτὸς πλήρωμα βροτοῖσιν

Ah, little needs the Minstrel's pow'r
To speed the light convivial hour;
The board with varied plenty crown'd
May spare the luxuries of sound.

Translated by Samuel Johnson (1709–1784)

Medea 200

227 λέγουσι δ' ἡμᾶς ὡς ἀκίνδυνον βίον
ζῶμεν κατ' οἴκους, οἱ δὲ μάρνανται δορί,
κακῶς φρονοῦντες· ὡς τρὶς ἂν παρ' ἀσπίδα
στῆναι θέλοιμ' ἂν μᾶλλον ἢ τεκεῖν ἅπαξ

But we, they say, live a safe life at home,
While they, the men, go forth in arms to war.
Fools! Three times would I rather take my stand
With sword and shield than bring to birth one child.

Translated by Gilbert Murray (1906)

Medea 248

this was a familiar quotation to women suffragists

228 ὅταν δ' ἐς εὐνὴν ἠδικημένη κυρῇ,
οὐκ ἔστιν ἄλλη φρὴν μιαιφονωτέρα

But when a woman is injured in love,
no mind is more murderous than hers.

Translated by David Kovacs (1994)

Medea 265

cf. the English proverb 'hell hath no fury like a woman scorned'

229 γυνὴ γὰρ ὀξύθυμος, ὡς δ' αὔτως ἀνήρ,
ῥᾴων φυλάσσειν ἢ σιωπηλὸς σοφή

It is easier to guard against a hot-headed woman, or a man, than against one who is scheming and silent.

Medea 319

230 φεῦ φεῦ, βροτοῖς ἔρωτες ὡς κακὸν μέγα

Oh, what a bane to mortals is love!

Translated by David Kovacs (1994)

Medea 330

231 κράτιστα τὴν εὐθεῖαν, ᾗ πεφύκαμεν
σοφοὶ μάλιστα, φαρμάκοις αὐτοὺς ἑλεῖν

I love the old way best, the simple way
Of poison, where we too are strong as men.

Translated by Gilbert Murray (1906)

Medea 384

232 ἄνω ποταμῶν ἱερῶν χωροῦσι παγαί,
καὶ δίκα καὶ πάντα πάλιν στρέφεται·
ἀνδράσι μὲν δόλιαι βουλαί, θεῶν δ'
οὐκέτι πίστις ἄραρεν

Backward to their sources flow the streams of holy rivers, and the order of all things is reversed; men's thoughts have become deceitful and their oaths by the gods do not hold fast.

Translated by David Kovacs (1994)

Medea 410

cf. Proverbial 3

233 πόλλ' ἐφέλκεται φυγὴ
κακὰ ξὺν αὑτῇ

Exile brings many hardships.

Translated by David Kovacs (1994)

Medea 462

234 δεινή τις ὀργὴ καὶ δυσίατος πέλει,
ὅταν φίλοι φίλοισι συμβάλωσ' ἔριν

Terrible and hard to heal is the wrath that comes
when kin join in conflict with kin.

Translated by David Kovacs (1994)

Medea 520

235 κακοῦ γὰρ ἀνδρὸς δῶρ' ὄνησιν οὐκ ἔχει

There is no benefit in the gifts of a bad man.

Translated by Rex Warner (1944)

Medea 618

236 ἔρωτες ὑπὲρ μὲν ἄγαν ἐλθόντες οὐκ εὐδοξίαν
οὐδ' ἀρετὰν παρέδωκαν ἀνδράσιν

Excess of passion brings no glory
or honour to men.

Medea 627

237 εἰ δ' ἅλις ἔλθοι
Κύπρις, οὐκ ἄλλα θεὸς εὔχαρις οὕτω

If Aphrodite comes in moderation
no other goddess brings more happiness.

Translated by David Kovacs (1994)

Medea 630

Aphrodite as goddess of love

238 μόχθων δ' οὐκ ἄλλος ὕπερ-
θεν ἢ γᾶς πατρίας στέρεσθαι

There is no greater grief
than the loss of one's fatherland.

Medea 652

239 χαῖρε· τοῦδε γὰρ προοίμιον
κάλλιον οὐδεὶς οἶδε προσφωνεῖν φίλους

I wish you joy: no one knows
a better way to address a friend.

Translated by David Kovacs (1994)

Medea 663

240 ἀλλ' εὐτυχοίης καὶ τύχοις ὅσων ἐρᾷς

I wish you good fortune, and all that you desire.

Medea 688

241 τί μοι ζῆν κέρδος; οὔτε μοι πατρὶς
οὔτ' οἶκος ἔστιν οὔτ' ἀποστροφὴ κακῶν

What do I gain from living? I have no country,
no home, no relief from my misfortune.

Medea 798

242 μηδείς με φαύλην κἀσθενῆ νομιζέτω
μηδ' ἡσυχαίαν, ἀλλὰ θατέρου τρόπου,
βαρεῖαν ἐχθροῖς καὶ φίλοισιν εὐμενῆ·
τῶν γὰρ τοιούτων εὐκλεέστατος βίος

Let no one think me weak, contemptible,
untroublesome; no, quite the opposite,
hurtful to foes, kindly to friends;

such persons live a life of greatest glory.

Translated by David Kovacs (1994)

Medea 807

243 γυνὴ δὲ θῆλυ κἀπὶ δακρύοις ἔφυ

A woman is by nature soft and prone to tears.

Translated by David Kovacs (1994)

Medea 928

spoken by Medea

244 πείθειν δῶρα καὶ θεοὺς λόγος

They say gifts win over even the gods.

Translated by David Kovacs (1994)

Medea 964

245 καὶ μανθάνω μὲν οἷα δρᾶν μέλλω κακά,
θυμὸς δὲ κρείσσων τῶν ἐμῶν βουλευμάτων,
ὅσπερ μεγίστων αἴτιος κακῶν βροτοῖς

I know well what evil I intend to do,
but anger overbears my calculation,
anger, cause of worst misery to man.

Medea 1078

Medea about to murder her children

246 θνητῶν γὰρ οὐδείς ἐστιν εὐδαίμων ἀνήρ·
ὄλβου δ' ἐπιρρυέντος εὐτυχέστερος
ἄλλου γένοιτ' ἂν ἄλλος, εὐδαίμων δ' ἂν οὔ

No mortal ever attains to blessedness;
one may be luckier than another
when wealth flows his way, but blessed never.

Translated by David Kovacs (1994)

Medea 1228

247 Οὐκ ἔστιν οὐδὲν δεινὸν ὧδ' εἰπεῖν ἔπος
οὐδὲ πάθος οὐδὲ ξυμφορὰ θεήλατος,
ἧς οὐκ ἂν ἄραιτ' ἄχθος ἀνθρώπου φύσις

There is no fate so terrifying to describe,
No bodily pain or heaven-sent cruelty so sharp,
Which human flesh will not endure.

Translated by Philip Vellacott (1972)

Orestes 1

opening lines

248 ὦ φίλον ὕπνου θέλγητρον, ἐπίκουρον νόσου

O magic charm of sleep, ally against sickness!

Orestes 211

249 ὦ πότνια Λήθη τῶν κακῶν, ὡς εἶ σοφὴ
καὶ τοῖσι δυστυχοῦσιν εὐκταία θεός

O heavenly Lethe, mistress of forgetfulness,
descending in your wisdom on the unfortunate.

Orestes 213

Lethe is one of the rivers that flow through the realm of Hades – the River of Oblivion

250 μεταβολὴ πάντων γλυκύ

In all things change is sweet.

Translated by J.A.K. Thomson (1953)

Orestes 234

cf. the Latin 'delectat varietas' and the English proverb 'variety is the spice of life'

251 κρεῖσσον δὲ τὸ δοκεῖν, κἂν ἀληθείας ἀπῇ

It's good to *feel* well,
even when the feeling's far from true.

Translated by Philip Vellacott (1972)

Orestes 236

252 ἐκ κυμάτων γὰρ αὖθις αὖ γαλήν' ὁρῶ

The storm is past, once more I see the calm.

Orestes 279

253 γυνὴ τί δράσω; πῶς μόνη σωθήσομαι,
ἀνάδελφος ἀπάτωρ ἄφιλος;

Being a woman what can I do,
how can I, alone, escape destruction,
without brother, without father, without friend?

Orestes 309

254 κἂν μὴ νοσῇ γὰρ ἀλλὰ δοξάζῃ νοσεῖν,
κάματος βροτοῖσιν ἀπορία τε γίγνεται

Such sickness, even when more imaginary than real,
Still racks the sufferer with anguish and despair.

Translated by Philip Vellacott (1972)

Orestes 314

255 ὁ μέγας ὄλβος οὐ μόνιμος ἐν βροτοῖς

Great happiness is not lasting among mortals.

Translated by C.A. Trypanis (1971)

Orestes 340

256 – τί χρῆμα πάσχεις; τίς σ' ἀπόλλυσιν νόσος;

– ἡ σύνεσις, ὅτι σύνοιδα δείν' εἰργασμένος

– What agonies? What is the disease that ravages you?
– Conscience. I recognize the horror of what I did.

Translated by Philip Vellacott (1972)

Orestes 395

Orestes, racked with guilt for killing his mother

257 σοφόν τοι τὸ σαφές, οὐ τὸ μὴ σαφές

Wisdom lies in clarity, not vagueness.

Orestes 397

258 δουλεύομεν θεοῖς, ὅ τι ποτ' εἰσὶν οἱ θεοί

We serve the gods, whatever these gods are.

Orestes 418

259 ὦ τάλαινα καρδία ψυχή τ' ἐμή,
ἀπέδωκ' ἀμοιβὰς οὐ καλάς

Ah me! my wretched heart and soul!
Sad recompense I bring for all his kindness!

Orestes 466

of Tyndareus, who had nurtured Orestes as a boy

260 πᾶν τοὐξ ἀνάγκης δοῦλόν ἐστι

Compulsion makes a man a slave.

Translated by Philip Vellacott (1972)

Orestes 488

261 ζηλωτὸς ὅστις ηὐτύχησεν ἐς τέκνα

Enviable, whoever has been fortunate in his children.

Orestes 542

262 ἔστι δ' οὗ σιγὴ λόγου
κρείσσων γένοιτ' ἄν, ἔστι δ' οὗ σιγῆς λόγος

Silence is sometimes
Better than speech; yet sometimes speech is preferable.

Translated by Philip Vellacott (1972)

Orestes 638

263 ὅταν δ' ὁ δαίμων εὖ διδῷ, τί δεῖ φίλων;

When all goes well, what need of friends?

Orestes 667

quoted by Plutarch 148 who disagrees

264 καὶ ναῦς γὰρ ἐνταθεῖσα πρὸς βίαν ποδὶ
ἔβαψεν, ἔστη δ' αὖθις ἢν χαλᾷ πόδα

A ship with mainsheet drawn too taut will find
Her deck awash; but slack the sheet – she rights herself.

Translated by Philip Vellacott (1972)

Orestes 706

265 μισεῖ γὰρ ὁ θεὸς τὰς ἄγαν προθυμίας,
μισοῦσι δ' ἀστοί

God hates excessive eagerness,
and the people likewise.

Orestes 708

266 πιστὸς ἐν κακοῖς ἀνὴρ
κρείσσων γαλήνης ναυτίλοισιν εἰσορᾶν

More welcome than
Calm sea to sailors is a trusty friend in need.

Translated by Philip Vellacott (1972)

Orestes 727

267 δεινὸν οἱ πολλοί, κακούργους ὅταν ἔχωσι προστάτας

The many are dangerous when they have wicked leaders.

Translated by David Kovacs (2002)

Orestes 772

268 ὄκνος γὰρ τοῖς φίλοις κακὸν μέγα

Hesitation is a grave ill among friends.

Translated by E.P. Coleridge (1938)

Orestes 794

269 ἀνήρ τις ἀθυρόγλωσσος, ἰσχύων θράσει
. . .
θορύβῳ τε πίσυνος κἀμαθεῖ παρρησίᾳ

A man with no check on his tongue, strong in his brashness,
relying on noise from the crowd and the obtuse licence of his tongue.

Translated by David Kovacs (2002)

Orestes 903

270 ὅταν γὰρ ἡδύς τις λόγοις φρονῶν κακῶς
πείθῃ τὸ πλῆθος, τῇ πόλει κακὸν μέγα

When a pleasing speaker, of evil principles,
persuades the people, then disaster's on the way.

Orestes 907

271 ὦ τὰς φρένας μὲν ἄρσενας κεκτημένη,

τὸ σῶμα δ' ἐν γυναιξὶ θηλείαις πρέπον

Oh, what a manly spirit and resolve shines out
From your weak woman's body!

Translated by Philip Vellacott (1972)

Orestes 1204

Orestes to Electra

272 πᾶς ἀνήρ, κἂν δοῦλος ᾖ τις, ἥδεται τὸ φῶς ὁρῶν

Everyone, be he a slave, loves the light of day.

Orestes 1523

273 ἰώ, Νέμεσι καὶ βαρύβρομοι βρονταὶ
Διός κεραύνιόν τε φῶς αἰθαλόεν

Come Nemesis,
Come, violent thunders of Zeus,
Come, white-hot lightnings!

Translated by Philip Vellacott (1972)

Phoenician Women 182

274 φιλόψογον δὲ χρῆμα θηλειῶν ἔφυ,
σμικράς τ' ἀφορμὰς ἢν λάβωσι τῶν λόγων
πλείους ἐπεσφέρουσιν· ἡδονὴ δέ τις
γυναιξὶ μηδὲν ὑγιὲς ἀλλήλας λέγειν

Women love
to criticize, it's their nature.
Give them half an excuse
To talk about you, they'll improve it twenty-fold.
In slandering other women they find a strange delight.

Translated by Philip Vellacott (1972)

Phoenician Women 198

275 Ζεφύρου πνοαῖς
ἱππεύσαντος ἐν οὐρανῷ
κάλλιστον κελάδημα

The West wind rides his horses
and the sky resounds with his song.

Phoenician Women 211

276 οὐ γὰρ ἄδικον
εἰς ἀγῶνα τάνδ' ἔνοπλος ὁρμᾷ
ὃς μετέρχεται δόμους

He serves a just cause who fights to recover his home.

Phoenician Women 258

277 δεινὸν γυναιξὶν αἱ δι' ὠδίνων γοναί

Motherhood sets strange forces in motion.

Translated by Philip Vellacott (1972)

Phoenician Women 355

278 ἀλλ' ἀναγκαίως ἔχει
πατρίδος ἐρᾶν ἅπαντας· ὃς δ' ἄλλως λέγει
λόγοισι χαίρει, τὸν δὲ νοῦν ἐκεῖσ' ἔχει

It is for everyone
to love his fatherland; and who says otherwise
says empty words; his mind is still at home.

Phoenician Women 358

279 ὡς δεινὸν ἔχθρα, μῆτερ, οἰκείων φίλων

What a foul, fearful thing, mother, is enmity
Within a family!

Translated by Philip Vellacott (1972)

Phoenician Women 374

280 τί τὸ στέρεσθαι πατρίδος; ἦ κακὸν μέγα;
μέγιστον· ἔργῳ δ' ἐστὶ μεῖζον ἢ λόγῳ

To be an exile is the utmost misery,
Worse in reality than in report

Phoenician Women 388

281 δούλου τόδ' εἶπας, μὴ λέγειν ἅ τις φρονεῖ

Not to speak one's mind, that is a slave's condition.

Phoenician Women 392

282 τὰς τῶν κρατούντων ἀμαθίας φέρειν χρεών

One has to endure the idiocy of those who rule.

Translated by Philip Vellacott (1972)

Phoenician Women 393

283 καὶ τοῦτο λυπρόν, συνασοφεῖν τοῖς μὴ σοφοῖς

That too is painful, to join fools in their folly.

Phoenician Women 394

284 αἱ δ' ἐλπίδες βόσκουσι φυγάδας, ὡς λόγος

Hope, they say, nourishes an exile.

Phoenician Women 396

285 εὖ πρᾶσσε· τὰ φίλων δ' οὐδέν, ἤν τις δυστυχῇ

There is one rule – succeed; friends vanish if you fail.

Translated by Philip Vellacott (1972)

Phoenician Women 403

286 κακὸν τὸ μὴ 'χειν· τὸ γένος οὐκ ἔβοσκέ με

It's a mistake
not to be rich; my royal blood bought me no bread.

Translated by Philip Vellacott (1972)

Phoenician Women 404

287 τὰ χρήματ' ἀνθρώποισι τιμιώτατα
δύναμίν τε πλείστην τῶν ἐν ἀνθρώποις ἔχει

Wealth is most esteemed by men,
and holds the greatest power of all things.

Phoenician Women 439

288 οὔτοι τὸ ταχὺ τὴν δίκην ἔχει,
βραδεῖς δὲ μῦθοι πλεῖστον ἀνύτουσιν σοφόν

Justice does not consort with haste;
Slow speech most often achieves wisdom.

Translated by Philip Vellacott (1972)

Phoenician Women 452

289 ἁπλοῦς ὁ μῦθος τῆς ἀληθείας

Simple is the tale of truth

Phoenician Women 469

290 ὁ δ' ἄδικος λόγος
νοσῶν ἐν αὑτῷ φαρμάκων δεῖται σοφῶν

The unjust cause
is sick in its own essence, and needs devious remedies.

Translated by Philip Vellacott (1972)

Phoenician Women 471

291 εἰ πᾶσι ταὐτὸ καλὸν ἔφυ σοφόν θ' ἅμα,
οὐκ ἦν ἂν ἀμφίλεκτος ἀνθρώποις ἔρις

If men could all agree on what is wise and noble,
there would be no cause for dispute.

Phoenician Women 499

292 πᾶν γὰρ ἐξαιρεῖ λόγος
ὃ καὶ σίδηρος πολεμίων δράσειεν ἄν

Everything that a military attack could gain
May well be achieved by conference.

Translated by Philip Vellacott (1972)

Phoenician Women 516

293 εἴπερ γὰρ ἀδικεῖν χρή, τυραννίδος πέρι
κάλλιστον ἀδικεῖν

If there is to be wrongdoing,
let it be for the throne.

Phoenician Women 524

Julius Caesar loved this passage and used it constantly according to Cicero, De Officiis *3.82: 'nam si violandum est ius, regnandi gratia violandum est'*

294 οὐχ ἅπαντα τῷ γήρᾳ κακά,
Ἐτεόκλεες, πρόσεστιν· ἀλλ' ἡμπειρία
ἔχει τι λέξαι τῶν νέων σοφώτερον

Not everything in old age is wrong;
experience sometimes speaks
more wisely than youth.

Phoenician Women 528

295 τί τῆς κακίστης δαιμόνων ἐφίεσαι
Φιλοτιμίας, παῖ; μὴ σύ γ' ἄδικος ἡ θεός

Why choose Ambition, worst of deities?
Shun her; she is the goddess of injustice.

Phoenician Women 531

296 κεῖνο κάλλιον, τέκνον,
Ἰσότητα τιμᾶν, ἣ φίλους ἀεὶ φίλοις
πόλεις τε πόλεσι συμμάχους τε συμμάχοις
συνδεῖ· τὸ γὰρ ἴσον νόμιμον ἀνθρώποις ἔφυ

There is a nobler course: to honour
Equity, which binds for ever friend to friend, city
To city, ally to ally. Nature gave to men
The law of equal rights.

Translated by Philip Vellacott (1972)

Phoenician Women 535

297 τῷ πλέονι δ' αἰεὶ πολέμιον καθίσταται
τοὔλασσον ἐχθρᾶς θ' ἡμέρας κατάρχεται·
καὶ γὰρ μέτρ' ἀνθρώποισι καὶ μέρη σταθμῶν
Ἰσότης ἔταξε κἀριθμὸν διώρισεν

Want is the inevitable
Enemy of wealth, and works towards war. Equality
Settled for men fair measure and just weight, and fixed
The laws of number.

Translated by Philip Vellacott (1972)

Phoenician Women 539

298 τί τὴν τυραννίδ', ἀδικίαν εὐδαίμονα,
τιμᾷς ὑπέρφευ καὶ μέγ' ἥγησαι τόδε;
περιβλέπεσθαι τίμιον; κενὸν μὲν οὖν

Why overmuch dost thou prize
Tyranny –
Injustice throned! – and count it some
great thing?
Is worship precious? Nay, 'tis vanity.

Translated by A.S. Way (1912)

Phoenician Women 549

299 οὔτοι τὰ χρήματ' ἴδια κέκτηνται βροτοί,
τὰ τῶν θεῶν δ' ἔχοντες ἐπιμελούμεθα·
ὅταν δὲ χρῄζωσ' αὔτ' ἀφαιροῦνται πάλιν

A man's possessions are not his by right;
we hold in trust what is the gods',
who will, in turn, take from us what is
theirs.

Phoenician Women 555

300 ὁ δ' ὄλβος οὐ βέβαιος ἀλλ' ἐφήμερος

Happiness is not steadfast, ephemeral at best.

Phoenician Women 558

301 καὶ μὴν τὸ νικᾶν γ' ἐστι πᾶν εὐβουλίας

Good counsel and foresight are the springs of victory.

Translated by Philip Vellacott (1972)

Phoenician Women 721

302 ἀπόλωλεν ἀλήθει', ἐπεὶ σὺ δυστυχεῖς;

Is truth undone because of your misfortune?

Phoenician Women 922

303 καὶ συγγνωστὰ μὲν
γέροντι, τοὐμὸν δ' οὐχὶ συγγνώμην ἔχει,
προδότην γενέσθαι πατρίδος ἥ μ'
ἐγείνατο

At his old age this is forgivable; but not
In me. How can I betray the city of my
birth?

Translated by Philip Vellacott (1972)

Phoenician Women 994

304 εἰ γὰρ λαβὼν ἕκαστος ὅ τι δύναιτό τις
χρηστὸν διέλθοι τοῦτο κἀς κοινὸν φέροι
πατρίδι, κακῶν ἂν αἱ πόλεις ἐλασσόνων
πειρώμεναι τὸ λοιπὸν εὐτυχοῖεν ἄν

If everybody would offer his country the best he can afford and contribute it to the common good, our cities would suffer less and prosper forever.

Phoenician Women 1015

305 γενοίμεθ' ὧδε ματέρες,
γενοίμεθ' εὔτεκνοι

May we become mothers,
may we have fine children.

Translated by Robin Lane Fox (2008)

Phoenician Women 1060

306 τίνα προσῳδὸν
ἢ τίνα μουσοπόλον στοναχὰν ἐπὶ
δάκρυσι δάκρυσιν, ὦ δόμος, ὦ δόμος,
ἀγκαλέσωμαι

What music, what chorus of tears,
What song of weeping shall I summon
To mourn for you, my home, my home?

Translated by Philip Vellacott (1972)

Phoenician Women 1498

307 τίς ἄρ' ὄρνις δρυὸς ἢ
ἐλάτας ἀκροκόμοις ἀμ πετάλοις
μονομάτορσιν ὀδυρμοῖ-
σιν ἐμοῖς εἷσ' ἄχεσι συνῳδός;

What bird, hidden aloft
In the leafy boughs of oak or pine,
Mourning for a mother dead,
Will sing in tune with my sorrow?

Translated by Philip Vellacott (1972)

Phoenician Women 1515

308 ἄφρονά γε, καὶ σὺ μῶρος ὃς ἐπίθου τάδε

A madman made these laws, and a fool now honours them.

Phoenician Women 1647

309 ἀλλὰ γὰρ τί ταῦτα θρηνῶ καὶ μάτην
ὀδύρομαι;

But why should I lament thus and weep to no purpose?

Translated by David Kovacs (2002)

Phoenician Women 1762

spoken by Oedipus; 'θρηνῶ καὶ ὀδύρομαι' is still very much in use today

310 οὐ γὰρ αὐτὸς πάντ' ἐπίστασθαι βροτῶν
πέφυκεν· ἄλλῳ δ' ἄλλο πρόσκειται
γέρας,
σὲ μὲν μάχεσθαι, τοὺς δὲ βουλεύειν
καλῶς

No man is by nature given everything;
each has his special gift,
yours to excel in battle, others to counsel
wisely.

Rhesus 106

311 μισθὸν φέρεσθαι; παντὶ γὰρ προσκείμενον
κέρδος πρὸς ἔργῳ τὴν χάριν τίκτει διπλῆν

'Tis wise to do good work, but also wise
To pay the worker well. Aye, and fair reward
Makes twofold pleasure.

Translated by Gilbert Murray (1913)

Rhesus 161

312 κακαὶ γεωργεῖν χεῖρες εὖ τεθραμμέναι

A princely hand is skilless at the plough.

Translated by Gilbert Murray (1913)

Rhesus 176

313 ἦ σπάνις αἰεὶ
τῶν ἀγαθῶν, ὅταν ᾖ δυσάλιον ἐν πελάγει
καὶ σαλεύῃ πόλις

There is a scarcity
of honourable men in states in sore distress,
as on an ocean tempest-tossed.

Rhesus 245

an often used parallel of a turbulent sea and a country in distress

314 ἔγνως· λόγου δὲ δὶς τόσου μ' ἐκούφισας

You've understood me, then; 'tis such a waste to have to say things twice.

Rhesus 281

315 ὅρα τὸ μέλλον· πόλλ' ἀναστρέφει θεός

Watch the future; much may be overturned by god.

Rhesus 332

cf. the expression 'what comes around, goes around'

316 μή νυν τὰ πόρσω τἀγγύθεν μεθεὶς σκόπει

Slight not what's near through aiming at what's far.

Translated in *Bartlett's Familiar Quotations* (1980)

Rhesus 482

317 ἡμῖν δ' οὐ βιαστέον τύχην

'Tis not for us to force the will of fortune.

Rhesus 584

318 χρὴ δ' ἄνδρα τάσσειν οὗ μάλιστ' ἂν ὠφελοῖ

Station a man where he may serve best.

Rhesus 626

319 οὐκ ἂν δύναιο τοῦ πεπρωμένου πλέον

You cannot go beyond what fate ordains.

Rhesus 634

320 ἔλεξε γάρ τις ὡς τὰ χείρονα
πλείω βροτοῖσίν ἐστι τῶν ἀμεινόνων

Some say that there is more evil than good in human nature.

Suppliant Women 196

321 τρεῖς γὰρ πολιτῶν μερίδες· οἱ μὲν ὄλβιοι
ἀνωφελεῖς τε πλειόνων τ' ἐρῶσ' ἀεί·
οἱ δ' οὐκ ἔχοντες καὶ σπανίζοντες βίου
δεινοί, νέμοντες τῷ φθόνῳ πλέον μέρος
...
γλώσσαις πονηρῶν προστατῶν φηλούμενοι·
τριῶν δὲ μοιρῶν ἡ 'ν μέσῳ σῴζει πόλεις,
κόσμον φυλάσσουσ' ὅντιν' ἂν τάξῃ πόλις

There are three ranks of citizens: the rich, a useless set, that ever crave for more; the poor and destitute, fearful folk, that cherish envy more than is right, beguiled as they are by the eloquence of vicious leaders; while the class that is midmost of the three preserves cities, observing such order as the state ordains.

Translated by E.P. Coleridge (1891)

Suppliant Women 238

322 ὡς πολλά γ' ἐστὶ κἀπὸ θηλειῶν σοφά

Wisdom is often heard from women's lips.

Translated by Philip Vellacott (1972)

Suppliant Women 294

323 τὸ γάρ τοι συνέχον ἀνθρώπων πόλεις
τοῦτ' ἔσθ', ὅταν τις τοὺς νόμους σῴζῃ καλῶς

It is the strict observance of the laws that holds together human communities.

Translated by David Kovacs (1998)

Suppliant Women 312

324 σὴ πατρὶς ἐν γὰρ τοῖς πόνοισιν αὔξεται

Your country is greatest when in greatest danger.

Translated by Philip Vellacott (1972)

Suppliant Women 323

325 δόξαι δὲ χρῄζω καὶ πόλει πάσῃ τόδε
δόξει δ' ἐμοῦ θέλοντος

I want the city too to ratify this decision, and ratify it they will, since that is what I wish.

Translated by David Kovacs (1998)

Suppliant Women 349

cf. Winston Churchill, The Second World War, *vol. 4, ch. 5: 'All I wanted was compliance with my wishes after reasonable discussion'*

326 οὐ γὰρ ἄρχεται
ἑνὸς πρὸς ἀνδρὸς ἀλλ' ἐλευθέρα πόλις.
δῆμος δ' ἀνάσσει διαδοχαῖσιν ἐν μέρει
ἐνιαυσίαισιν, οὐχὶ τῷ πλούτῳ διδοὺς
τὸ πλεῖστον, ἀλλὰ χὼ πένης ἔχων ἴσον

The city is not ruled by a single man but is free.
The people rule, and offices are held by yearly turns:
they do not assign the highest honours to the rich,
but the poor also have an equal share.

Translated by David Kovacs (1998)

Suppliant Women 404

of Athens

327 ἄλλως τε πῶς ἂν μὴ διορθεύων λόγους
ὀρθῶς δύναιτ' ἂν δῆμος εὐθύνειν πόλιν;

Incapable of plain reasoning, how can he guide
A city in sound policy?

Translated by Philip Vellacott (1972)

Suppliant Women 417

328 γαπόνος δ' ἀνὴρ πένης,
εἰ καὶ γένοιτο μὴ ἀμαθής, ἔργων ὕπο
οὐκ ἂν δύναιτο πρὸς τὰ κοίν' ἀποβλέπειν

Your poor rustic,
Even though he be no fool – how can he turn his mind
From ploughs to politics?

Translated by Philip Vellacott (1972)

Suppliant Women 420

329 ἦ δὴ νοσῶδες τοῦτο τοῖς ἀμείνοσιν,
ὅταν πονηρὸς ἀξίωμ' ἀνὴρ ἔχῃ
γλώσσῃ κατασχὼν δῆμον, οὐδὲν ὢν τὸ πρίν

The worst pestilence of our time,
as every sane man knows, is the unscrupulous upstart,
whose glib tongue brings him fame and popular power.

Translated by Philip Vellacott (1972)

Suppliant Women 423

330 οὐδὲν τυράννου δυσμενέστερον πόλει

Nothing is more hostile to a city than a tyrant.

Translated by David Kovacs (1998)

Suppliant Women 429

331 νικᾷ δ' ὁ μείων τὸν μέγαν δίκαι' ἔχων

The humble man's just cause defeats the great.

Translated by Philip Vellacott (1972)

Suppliant Women 437

332 τοὐλεύθερον δ' ἐκεῖνο· τίς θέλει πόλει
χρηστόν τι βούλευμ' ἐς μέσον φέρειν ἔχων;
καὶ ταῦθ' ὁ χρῄζων λαμπρός ἐσθ', ὁ δ' οὐ θέλων
σιγᾷ. τί τούτων ἔστ' ἰσαίτερον πόλει;

Freedom consists in this: Who has good counsel he would offer to the city? He who desires fame will speak; he who does not, keeps silent. What could be fairer for a city?

Suppliant Women 438

cf. Aristophanes 3

333 καὶ μὴν ὅπου γε δῆμος εὐθυντὴς χθονὸς
ὑποῦσιν ἀστοῖς ἥδεται νεανίαις

The people, vested with authority,
Values its young men as the city's great resource.

Translated by Phillip Vellacott (1972)

Suppliant Women 442

334 πῶς οὖν ἔτ' ἂν γένοιτ' ἂν ἰσχυρὰ πόλις
ὅταν τις ὡς λειμῶνος ἠρινοῦ στάχυν
τόλμας ἀφαιρῇ κἀπολωτίζῃ νέων;

How can a city grow in strength, when all its young
And bold spirits are mown down like fresh stalks in spring?

Translated by Philip Vellacott (1972)

Suppliant Women 447

perhaps an allusion to Herodotus 100

335 ὅταν γὰρ ἔλθῃ πόλεμος ἐς ψῆφον λεώ,
οὐδεὶς ἔφ' αὑτοῦ θάνατον ἐκλογίζεται,
τὸ δυστυχὲς δὲ τοῦτ' ἐς ἄλλον ἐκτρέπει

When war comes to be voted on by the people,

no one reckons on his own death;
others, he thinks, will suffer that
misfortune.

Translated by David Kovacs (1998)

Suppliant Women 481

336 φιλεῖν μὲν οὖν χρὴ τοὺς σοφοὺς πρῶτον τέκνα,
ἔπειτα τοκέας πατρίδα θ', ἣν αὔξειν χρεὼν
καὶ μὴ κατᾶξαι

A wise man's love is owed first to his children, then
To his parents; and to his native land, which he should strive
To build, not to dismember.

Translated by Philip Vellacott (1972)

Suppliant Women 506

337 σφαλερὸν ἡγεμὼν θρασὺς
… ἥσυχος καιρῷ, σοφός·
καὶ τοῦτό τοι τἀνδρεῖον, ἡ προμηθία

A rash leader is a risk; …
timely inaction, wise.
Foresight is part of bravery.

Suppliant Women 508

cf. the English proverb 'discretion is the better part of valour'

338 ἐάσατ' ἤδη γῇ καλυφθῆναι νεκρούς,
ὅθεν δ' ἕκαστον ἐς τὸ φῶς ἀφίκετο
ἐνταῦθ' ἀπελθεῖν, πνεῦμα μὲν πρὸς αἰθέρα,
τὸ σῶμα δ' ἐς γῆν· οὔτι γὰρ κεκτήμεθα
ἡμέτερον αὐτὸ πλὴν ἐνοικῆσαι βίον,
κἄπειτα τὴν θρέψασαν αὐτὸ δεῖ λαβεῖν

Now let the dead be buried in the earth, and let each element return to the place from whence it came into the light of day, the spirit to the upper air, the body to the earth. We do not possess our bodies as our own: we live our lives in them, and thereafter the earth, our nourisher, must take them back.

Translated by David Kovacs (1998)

Suppliant Women 531

339 σκαιόν γε τἀνάλωμα τῆς γλώσσης τόδε,
φόβους πονηροὺς καὶ κενοὺς δεδοικέναι

It is a foolish waste of breath
to give voice to base and idle fears.

Suppliant Women 547

340 παλαίσμαθ' ἡμῶν ὁ βίος

Our life is an unending struggle.

Suppliant Women 550

341 ὦ κενοὶ βροτῶν,
οἳ τόξον ἐντείνοντες τοῦ καιροῦ πέρα

O foolish mortals,
who stretch the bow beyond due measure!

Suppliant Women 744

cf. Lao Tse, 'Stretch a bow to the very full, / And you wish you had stopped in time.' (tr. Lin Yutang, 1948)

342 τοῦτο γὰρ μόνον βροτοῖς
οὐκ ἔστι τἀνάλωμ' ἀναλωθὲν λαβεῖν,
ψυχὴν βροτείαν· χρημάτων δ' εἰσὶν πόροι

For mortals there is only one thing that cannot be regained once it is spent:
a man's life. Money can be recovered.

Translated by David Kovacs (1998)

Suppliant Women 775

343 ἐπεί τοι κοὐδὲν αἰτία πόλις
κακῶς κλύουσα διὰ κυβερνήτην κακόν

A state should not be held to blame
if a bad ruler causes her to be ill spoken of.

Suppliant Women 879

344 οὐδὲν ἥδιον πατρὶ
γέροντι θυγατρός· ἀρσένων δὲ μείζονες
ψυχαί, γλυκεῖαι δ' ἧσσον ἐς θωπεύματα

When a man's old, there's no one dearer than his daughter.
Sons have more strength of character, but no gentle touch.

Translated by Philip Vellacott (1972)

Suppliant Women 1101

345 τί γὰρ ἂν μεῖζον τοῦδ' ἔτι θνητοῖς
πάθος ἐξεύροις ἢ τέκνα θανόντ' ἐσιδέσθαι;

Is there any greater human suffering
than to see your children dead?

Suppliant Women 1120

346 αἱ γὰρ συγγενεῖς ὁμιλίαι
… φίλτρον οὐ σμικρὸν φρενῶν

Family ties work no small magic on the heart.

Translated by James Morwood (2001)

Trojan Women 51

347 μῶρος δὲ θνητῶν ὅστις ἐκπορθεῖ πόλεις
ναούς τε τύμβους θ', ἱερὰ τῶν κεκμηκότων·
ἐρημίᾳ δούς αὐτὸς ὤλεθ' ὕστερον

A fool is he who sacks the towns of men,
with shrines and tombs, the dead man's hallowed home,
for at the last he makes a desert round himself and dies.

Translated by E.P. Coleridge (1891)

Trojan Women 95

348 μεταβαλλομένου δαίμονος ἄνσχου

Though fortune change, endure your lot.

Translated by E.P. Coleridge (1891)

Trojan Women 101

349 πλεῖ κατὰ πορθμόν, πλεῖ κατὰ δαίμονα,
μηδὲ προσίστη πρῷραν βιότου

Sail with the stream, and follow fortune's tack,
don't steer your ship of life against the tide.

Translated by E.P. Coleridge (1891)

Trojan Women 102

350 τὸ κάλλιστον κλέος,
ὑπὲρ πάτρας ἔθνησκον

Their greatest glory, to die for their country.

Trojan Women 386

351 τὸ της ἀνάγκης δεινόν

Necessity's grim law.

Translated by E.P. Coleridge (1891)

Trojan Women 616

352 οὐ ταὐτόν, ὦ παῖ, τῷ βλέπειν τὸ κατθανεῖν·
τὸ μὲν γὰρ οὐδέν, τῷ δ' ἔνεισιν ἐλπίδες

Dying and living are very different things, my child.
The former is nothing, but while there's life, there's hope.

Translated by James Morwood (2001)

Trojan Women 632

353 τὸ μὴ γενέσθαι τῷ θανεῖν ἴσον λέγω,
τοῦ ζῆν δὲ λυπρῶς κρεῖσσόν ἐστι κατθανεῖν

It is all one, never to have been born and to be dead,
and better far is death than life in misery.

Translated by E.P. Coleridge (1891)

Trojan Women 636

354 ναύται γάρ, ἢν μὲν μέτριος ᾖ χειμὼν φέρειν,
προθυμίαν ἔχουσι σωθῆναι πόνων,
ὁ μὲν παρ' οἴαχ', ὁ δ' ἐπὶ λαίφεσιν βεβώς,
ὁ δ' ἄντλον εἴργων ναός· ἢν δ' ὑπερβάλῃ
πολὺς ταραχθεὶς πόντος, ἐνδόντες τύχῃ
παρεῖσαν αὑτοὺς κυμάτων δραμήμασιν

Now sailors, if there comes a storm of moderate force, are all eagerness to save themselves by toil; one stands at the tiller, another sets himself to work the sheets, a third meanwhile is bailing out the ship; but if tempestuous waves arise to overwhelm them, they yield to fortune and commit themselves to the driving billows.

Translated by E.P. Coleridge (1891)

Trojan Women 688

355 ἀλλ' ἐκ λόγου γὰρ ἄλλος ἐκβαίνει λόγος

One word leads to another.

Trojan Women 706

356 ὦ γῆς ὄχημα κἀπὶ γῆς ἔχων ἕδραν,
ὅστις ποτ' εἶ σύ, δυστόπαστος εἰδέναι,
Ζεύς, εἴτ' ἀνάγκη φύσεος εἴτε νοῦς βροτῶν,
προσηυξάμην σε· πάντα γὰρ δι' ἀψόφου
βαίνων κελεύθου κατὰ δίκην τὰ θνήτ' ἄγεις

O you that do support the earth and rest thereupon,
whoever you are, a riddle past our knowledge!
Zeus, whether you are natural necessity, or man's intellect,
to you I pray; for, though you tread over a noiseless path,
all your dealings with mankind are guided by justice.

Translated by E.P. Coleridge (1891)

Trojan Women 884

357 οὐκ ἔστ' ἐραστὴς ὅστις οὐκ ἀεὶ φιλεῖ

The one who loves once, must love always.

Translated by E.P. Coleridge (1891)

Trojan Women 1051

cf. the Latin 'verae amicitiae sempiternae sunt'

(true friendships are eternal)

358 εἰ μὴ καθέξεις γλῶσσαν, ἔσται σοι κακά

If you don't check your tongue, you will have troubles.

Translated by Gavin Betts and Alan Henry (1989)

Fragment 5 (Nauck, *TGF*) – *Aegeus*

359 τί γὰρ πατρῴας ἀνδρὶ φίλτερον χθονός;

What is dearer to a man than his native land?

Translated by Christopher Collard and Martin Cropp (2008)

Fragment 6 (Nauck, *TGF*) – *Aegeus*

360 κρεῖσσον δὲ πλούτου καὶ βαθυσπόρου χθονὸς
ἀνδρῶν δικαίων κἀγαθῶν ὁμιλίαι

The company of just and righteous men is better
than wealth and a rich estate.

Translated by Morris Hicky Morgan (1859–1910)

Fragment 7 (Nauck, *TGF*) – *Aegeus*

361 μὴ πλοῦτον εἴπῃς· οὐχὶ θαυμάζω θεόν,
ὃν χὠ κάκιστος ῥᾳδίως ἐκτήσατο

Speak not of wealth; I can't admire a god
whom even the basest man can get into his hold.

Fragment 20 (Nauck, *TGF*) – *Aeolus*

Plutus as the god of wealth

362 οὐκ ἂν γένοιτο χωρὶς ἐσθλὰ καὶ κακά,
ἀλλ' ἔστι τις σύγκρασις, ὥστ' ἔχειν καλῶς

There cannot be good without evil,
but in their mixture things may turn out well.

Fragment 21 (Nauck, *TGF*) – *Aeolus*

363 ἦ βραχύ τοι σθένος ἀνέρος· ἀλλὰ
ποικιλίᾳ πραπίδων

Slight is the strength of man, but versatile his mind.

Fragment 27 (Nauck, *TGF*) – *Aeolus*

364 σοφοῦ πρὸς ἀνδρός, ὅστις ἐν βραχεῖ
πολλοὺς καλῶς οἷός τε συντέμνειν λόγους

Wise is he who can compress many thoughts into few words.

Translated by Eugene O'Neill, Jr (1938)

Fragment 28 (Nauck, *TGF*) – *Aeolus*

quoted by Aristophanes, Thesmophoriazusae *177*

365 οἰκτρός τις αἰὼν πατρίδος ἐκλιπεῖν ὅρους

Life is miserable when you leave behind the borders of your fatherland.

Fragment 30 (Nauck, *TGF*) – *Aeolus*

366 ὀργῇ γὰρ ὅστις εὐθέως χαρίζεται,
κακῶς τελευτᾷ

Whoever yields to anger suffers a piteous end.

Fragment 31 (Nauck, *TGF*) – *Aeolus*

367 κακῆς ἀπ' ἀρχῆς γίγνεται τέλος κακόν

A bad end comes from a bad beginning.

Translated by Christopher Collard and Martin Cropp (2008)

Fragment 32 (Nauck, *TGF*) – *Aeolus*

368 αἰεὶ τὸ μὲν ζῇ, τὸ δὲ μεθίσταται κακόν,
τὸ δ' ἐκπέφηνεν αὖθις ἐξ ἀρχῆς νέον

One trouble alive and well, another gone,
as all afresh a new one comes our way.

Fragment 35 (Nauck, *TGF*) – *Aeolus*

369 παλαιὰ καινοῖς δακρύοις οὐ χρὴ στένειν

Waste not fresh tears over old griefs.

Translated by Morris Hicky Morgan (1859–1910)

Fragment 43 (Nauck, *TGF*) – *Alexandros*

370 ἀγλωσσίᾳ δὲ πολλάκις ληφθεὶς ἀνὴρ
δίκαια λέξας ἧσσον εὐγλώσσου φέρει

Quite often the ineloquent lose out to the eloquent even though their case be just.

Fragment 56 (Nauck, *TGF*) – *Alexandros*

371 γυναῖκα καὶ ὠφελίαν
καὶ νόσον ἀνδρὶ φέρειν
μεγίσταν

A woman brings both great benefit and great distress to man.

Fragment 78 (Nauck, *TGF*) – *Alcmeon*

372 ἀτρέκεια δ' ἄριστον ἀνδρὸς ἐν πόλει
δικαίου

A just man's honesty is a city's greatest asset.

Translated by Christopher Collard and Martin Cropp (2008)

Fragment 91 (Nauck, *TGF*) – *Alcmene*

373 τὸν γὰρ κάκιστον πλοῦτος εἰς πρώτους ἄγει

Wealth allows the worst to be ranked among the first.

Fragment 95 (Nauck, *TGF*) – *Alcmene*

374 λόγος γὰρ τοὔργον οὐ νικᾷ ποτε

Words never weigh more than action.

Fragment 97 (Nauck, *TGF*) – *Alcmene*

cf. the saying 'action speaks louder than words'

375 εὖ φέρειν χρὴ συμφορὰς τὸν εὐγενῆ

The nobly born must suffer grief with dignity.

Fragment 98 (Nauck, *TGF*) – *Alcmene*

376 τὸν εὐτυχοῦντα χρῆν σοφὸν πεφυκέναι

The nobly born must nobly meet his fate.

Translated by Morris Hicky Morgan (1859–1910)

Fragment 99 (Nauck, *TGF*) – *Alcmene*

377 δεινόν τι τέκνων φίλτρον ἔθηκεν
θεὸς ἀνθρώποις

God has endowed children with formidable charm.

Fragment 103 (Nauck, *TGF*) – *Alcmene*

378 γυνὴ γυναικὶ σύμμαχος πέφυκέ πως

A woman is a woman's natural ally.

Translated by Christopher Collard and Martin Cropp (2008)

Fragment 108 (Nauck, *TGF*) – *Alope*

379 συναλγησον, ὡς ὁ κάμνων
δακρύων μεταδοὺς ἔχει
κουφότητα μόχθων

Cry with me;
for sharing tears with others is relief in hardship.

Fragment 119 (Nauck, *TGF*) – *Andromeda*

380 σιγᾷς; σιωπὴ δ' ἄπορος ἑρμηνεὺς λόγων

You do not speak? But silence is a poor interpreter of words.

Translated by Christopher Collard and Martin Cropp (2008)

Fragment 126 (Nauck, *TGF*) – *Andromeda*

381 τὰς συμφορὰς γὰρ τῶν κακῶς πεπραγότων
οὐ πώποθ' ὕβρισ', αὐτὸς ὀρρωδῶν παθεῖν

I have never treated the troubles of the unfortunate insultingly,
through fear of suffering them myself.

Translated by John Gibert (2004)

Fragment 130 (Nauck, *TGF*) – *Andromeda*

382 ἀλλ' ἡδύ τοι σωθέντα μεμνῆσθαι πόνων

Sweet is the memory of sorrows past.

Translated by H. Rackham (1914)

Fragment 133 (Nauck, *TGF*) – *Andromeda*

quoted by Cicero, De finibus 2.105, *translated by him as 'suavis laborum est praeteritorum memoria' with the comment 'the Greek line is known to you all'*

383 σὺ δ' ὦ θεῶν τύραννε κἀνθρώπων Ἔρως

You, Eros, tyrant over gods and men.

Translated by Christopher Collard and Martin Cropp (2008)

Fragment 136 (Nauck, *TGF*) – *Andromeda*

384 τῶν γὰρ πλούτων ὅδ' ἄριστος
γενναῖον λέχος εὑρεῖν

Of all treasures this is best:
To find a noble-minded wife.

Fragment 137 (Nauck, *TGF*) – *Andromeda*

385 ὀνόματι μεμπτὸν τὸ νόθον, ἡ φύσις δ' ἴση

An illegitimate child, though shamed in word, is by nature equal.

Fragment 168 (Nauck, *TGF*) – *Antigone*

386 οὐκ ἔστι Πειθοῦς ἱερὸν ἄλλο πλὴν λόγος

Persuasion has only one temple, speech.

Fragment 170 (Nauck, *TGF*) – *Antigone*

387 ἐκ παντὸς ἄν τις πράγματος δισσῶν λόγων
ἀγῶνα θεῖτ' ἄν, εἰ λέγειν εἴη σοφός

A clever speaker can speak on any subject, either for or against.

Fragment 189 (Nauck, *TGF*) – *Antiope*

388 ὅστις δὲ πράσσει πολλὰ μὴ πράσσειν παρόν,
μῶρος, παρὸν ζῆν ἡδέως ἀπράγμονα

Whoever is overactive when he could relax
is foolish, for he misses out on a pleasant life.

Fragment 193 (Nauck, *TGF*) – *Antiope*

389 ὁ δ' ἥσυχος φίλοισί τ' ἀσφαλὴς φίλος
πόλει τ' ἄριστος. μὴ τὰ κινδυνεύματα

αἰνεῖτ'· ἐγὼ γὰρ οὔτε ναυτίλον φιλῶ
τολμῶντα λίαν οὔτε προστάτην χθονός

A cautious man is for a friend the surest friend,
and safest for the city. Do not praise risk!
And as for me, neither do I fancy a daring sailor
nor a leader ready for adventure.

Fragment 194 (Nauck, *TGF*) – *Antiope*

390 ἅπαντα τίκτει χθὼν πάλιν τε λαμβάνει

Earth breeds all and takes back all.

Fragment 195 (Nauck, *TGF*) – *Antiope*

391 τοιόσδε θνητῶν τῶν ταλαιπώρων βίος·
οὔτ' εὐτυχεῖ τὸ πάμπαν οὔτε δυστυχεῖ …
τί δῆτ' ἐν ὄλβῳ μὴ σαφεῖ βεβηκότες
οὐ ζῶμεν ὡς ἥδιστα μὴ λυπούμενοι;

Such is the life of wretched mortals;
a man is neither wholly fortunate nor unfortunate;
why then, on entering prosperity which may be insecure,
do we not live as pleasantly as possible, without distress?

Fragment 196 (Nauck, *TGF*) – *Antiope*

392 τὸ δ' ἀσθενές μου καὶ τὸ θῆλυ σώματος
κακῶς ἐμέμφθης· εἰ γὰρ εὖ φρονεῖν ἔχω,
κρεῖσσον τόδ' ἐστὶ καρτεροῦ βραχίονος

You were wrong to censure my weak and effeminate body;
for if I can think soundly, this is stronger than a sturdy arm.

Translated by Christopher Collard (2004)

Fragment 199 (Nauck, *TGF*) – *Antiope*

393 τὸ μὴ εἰδέναι γὰρ ἡδονὴν ἔχει τινὰ

Ignorance is bliss.

Fragment 205 (Nauck, *TGF*) – *Antiope*

394 κόρος δὲ πάντων· καὶ γὰρ ἐκ καλλιόνων
λέκτροις ἐπ' αἰσχροῖς εἶδον ἐκπεπληγμένους,
δαιτὸς δὲ πληρωθείς τις ἄσμενος πάλιν
φαύλῃ διαίτῃ προσβαλὼν ἥσθη στόμα

There is surfeit in everything. I have seen men abandon beautiful women for ugly ones, and someone sated with rich meals return with pleasure to inferior fare.

Fragment 213 (Nauck, *TGF*) – *Antiope or Antigone*

395 πατέρων γὰρ ἐσθλῶν ἐλπίδας δίδως γεγώς

Born of noble ancestors, you engender hope.

Fragment 231 (Nauck, *TGF*) – *Archelaus*

396 ἐν τοῖς τέκνοις γὰρ ἀρετὴ τῶν εὐγενῶν
ἔλαμψε, κρεῖσσόν τ' ἐστὶ πλουσίου γάμου

In children shines forth their parents' virtue,
a much greater asset than marrying into money.

Fragment 232.1 (Nauck, *TGF*) – *Archelaus*

397 πένης γὰρ οὐκ ἐκεῖν' ἀπώλεσεν
τὸ τοῦ πατρὸς γενναῖον

A poor man does not forfeit his father's nobility.

Fragment 232.3 (Nauck, *TGF*) – *Archelaus*

398 τὰς τύχας ἐκ τῶν πόνων θηρᾶν

Seek your fortunes by hard work.

Translated by Christopher Collard and Martin Cropp (2008)

Fragment 233 (Nauck, *TGF*) – *Archelaus*

399 σὺν μυρίοισι τὰ καλὰ γίγνεται πόνοις

Fine things are achieved through endless toil.

Translated by Christopher Collard and Martin Cropp (2008)

Fragment 236 (Nauck, *TGF*) – *Archelaus*

400 νεανίαν γὰρ ἄνδρα χρὴ τολμᾶν ἀεί·
οὐδεὶς γὰρ ὢν ῥᾴθυμος εὐκλεὴς ἀνήρ,
ἀλλ' οἱ πόνοι τίκτουσι τὴν εὐανδρίαν

A young man must on all occasions dare;
no one who is slack gains good repute;
it is hard work that leads to excellence.

Fragment 237 (Nauck, *TGF*) – *Archelaus*

401 τίς δ' ἄμοχθος εὐκλεής;

Who can get glory without striving for it?

Translated by Christopher Collard and Martin Cropp (2008)

Fragment 240 (Nauck, *TGF*) – *Archelaus*

402 ὀλίγον ἄλκιμον δόρυ
κρεῖσσον στρατηγοῦ μυρίου στρατεύματος

A small but valiant fighting force
is worth more to a general than a vast

army.

Translated by John Gibert (2004)

Fragment 243 (Nauck, *TGF*) – *Archelaus*

403 μὴ ἐπὶ δουλείαν ποτὲ
ζῶν ἑκὼν ἔλθῃς παρὸν σοὶ κατθανεῖν ἐλευθέρως

Never willingly accept bonds when you can die free.

Fragment 245 (Nauck, *TGF*) – *Archelaus*

404 νεανίας τε καὶ πένης σοφός θ᾽ ἅμα·
ταῦτ᾽ εἰς ἓν ἐλθόντ᾽ ἄξι᾽ ἐνθυμήσεως

Young, poor and clever at the same time;
these things combined deserve consideration.

Fragment 246 (Nauck, *TGF*) – *Archelaus*

405 τί δ᾽ οὐκ ἂν εἴη χρηστὸς ὄλβιος γεγώς;

Why not give good service once he is wealthy?

Translated by Christopher Collard and Martin Cropp (2008)

Fragment 247 (Nauck, *TGF*) – *Archelaus*

406 κεῖνο δ᾽ ἰσχύει μέγα,
πλοῦτος λαβών τε τοῦτον εὐγενὴς ἀνήρ

There is great strength
in wealth when combined with nobility.

Fragment 249 (Nauck, *TGF*) – *Archelaus*

407 πολλοὺς δ᾽ ὁ θυμὸς ὁ μέγας ὤλεσεν βροτῶν
ἥ τ᾽ ἀξυνεσία, δύο κακὼ τοῖς χρωμένοις

Anger and stupidity, two evils that have destroyed many men.

Fragment 257 (Nauck, *TGF*) – *Archelaus*

408 ὀργῇ δὲ φαύλῃ πόλλ᾽ ἔνεστ᾽ ἀσχήμονα

There is much unseemliness in petty anger.

Translated by John Gibert (2004)

Fragment 259 (Nauck, *TGF*) – *Archelaus*

409 ἔστι τι καὶ παρὰ δάκρυσι κείμενον
ἡδὺ βροτοῖς, ὅταν ἄνδρα φίλον στενάχῃ τις ἐν οἴκῳ

Even in tears there's something sweet
when a dear friend is mourned at home.

Fragment 263 (Nauck, *TGF*) – *Archelaus*

410 Ἔρωτα δ᾽ ὅστις μὴ θεὸν κρίνει μέγαν ...
ἢ σκαιός ἐστιν ἢ καλῶν ἄπειρος

Whoever does not think Eros a great god
is either silly or ignorant of blessings.

Fragment 269 (Nauck, *TGF*) – *Auge*

411 πτηνὰς διώκεις, ὦ τέκνον, τὰς ἐλπίδας

You are chasing fleeting hopes, my child.

Fragment 271 (Nauck, *TGF*) – *Auge*

412 τίς δ᾽ οὐχὶ χαίρει νηπίοις ἀθύρμασιν;

Who does not take pleasure in childish toys?

Translated by Christopher Collard and Martin Cropp (2008)

Fragment 272 (Nauck, *TGF*) – *Auge*

413 τοὐλεύθερον γὰρ ὄνομα παντὸς ἄξιον

Worth above all is a name fit for the free.

Fragment 275 (Nauck, *TGF*) – *Auge*

414 γυναῖκές ἐσμεν· τὰ μὲν ὄκνῳ νικώμεθα,
τὰ δ᾽ οὐκ ἂν ἡμῶν θράσος ὑπερβάλοιτό τις

We are women; sometimes defeated by fear,
sometimes unsurpassed in courage.

Fragment 276 (Nauck, *TGF*) – *Auge*

415 κακῶν γὰρ ὄντων μυρίων καθ᾽ Ἑλλάδα
οὐδὲν κάκιόν ἐστιν ἀθλητῶν γένους

Of all the myriad evil things in Greece
none is more evil than the tribe of athletes.

Fragment 282 (Nauck, *TGF*) – *Autolycus*

416 φησίν τις εἶναι δῆτ᾽ ἐν οὐρανῷ θεούς;
οὐκ εἰσίν, οὐκ εἴσ᾽, εἴ τις ἀνθρώπων θέλει
μὴ τῷ παλαιῷ μῶρος ὢν χρῆσθαι λόγῳ

Doth someone say that there be gods above?
There are not; no, there are not. Let no fool,
Led by the old false fable, thus deceive you.

Translated by John Addington Symonds (1876)

Fragment 286 (Nauck, *TGF*) – *Bellerophon*

417 τοῖς πράγμασιν γὰρ οὐχὶ θυμοῦσθαι χρεών·
μέλει γὰρ αὐτοῖς οὐδέν· ἀλλ᾽ οὑντυγχάνων
τὰ πράγματ᾽ ὀρθῶς ἢν τιθῇ, πράσσει καλῶς

It does no good to rage at circumstance;
Events will take their course with no regard
For us. But he who makes the best of those
Events he lights upon will not fare ill.

Translated by William C. Helmbold (1939)

Fragment 287 (Nauck, *TGF*) – *Bellerophon*

418 δόλοι δὲ καὶ σκοτεινὰ μηχανήματα
χρείας ἄνανδρα φάρμαχ' ηὕρηται βροτοῖς

Tricks and dark schemes are mankind's invention as
cowardly remedies against need.

Translated by Christopher Collard (1997)

Fragment 288 (Nauck, *TGF*) – *Bellerophon*

419 ψεύδεσιν δ' Ἄρης φίλος

War is a friend to lies.

Translated by Christopher Collard and Martin Cropp (2008)

Fragment 289 (Nauck, *TGF*) – *Bellerophon*

420 ἀεὶ γὰρ ἄνδρα σκαιὸν ἰσχυρὸν φύσει
ἧσσον δέδοικα τἀσθενοῦς τε καὶ σοφοῦ

I fear less the powerful but stupid
than the weak and cunning.

Fragment 290 (Nauck, *TGF*) – *Bellerophon*

421 ὁ γὰρ χρόνος δίδαγμα ποικιλώτατον

Time teaches the most subtle lessons.

Translated by Christopher Collard (1997)

Fragment 291 (Nauck, *TGF*) – *Bellerophon*

422 καὶ τὸν ἰατρὸν χρεὼν ...
μὴ ἐπιτὰξ τὰ φάρμακα
διδόντ', ἐὰν μὴ ταῦτα τῇ νόσῳ πρέπῃ

The doctor, too, should not prescribe medicines not suited to the illness.

Fragment 292 (Nauck, *TGF*) – *Bellerophon*

423 οὐ γὰρ ἄξιον λεύσσειν φάος
κακοὺς ὁρῶντας ἐκδίκως τιμωμένους

It is not worth living,
when we see bad men unjustly honoured.

Translated by Christopher Collard (1997)

Fragment 293 (Nauck, *TGF*) – *Bellerophon*

424 εἰς τἀπίσημα δ' ὁ φθόνος πηδᾶν φιλεῖ

Envy usually leaps upon distinction.

Translated by Christopher Collard and Martin Cropp (2008)

Fragment 294 (Nauck, *TGF*) – *Bellerophon*

425 ἤδη γὰρ εἶδον καὶ δίκης παραστάτας
ἐσθλοὺς πονηρῷ τῷ φθόνῳ νικωμένους

Already have I seen some who stand by righteousness
overcome by wickedness and envy.

Fragment 295 (Nauck, *TGF*) – *Bellerophon*

426 ἀνὴρ δὲ χρηστὸς χρηστὸν οὐ μισεῖ ποτε,
κακὸς κακῷ δὲ συντέτηκεν ἡδονῇ

A good man never hates a good man,
but bad happily blends with bad.

Translated by Christopher Collard (1997)

Fragment 296 (Nauck, *TGF*) – *Bellerophon*

427 οἴμοι· τί δ' οἴμοι; θνητά τοι πεπόνθαμεν

Alas! but why alas? I have suffered only
what all mortals suffer.

Translated by Patrick Cruttwell (1986)

Fragment 300 (Nauck, *TGF*) – *Bellerophon*

quoted by Dr. Samuel Johnson in a letter written to Thomas Warton, Nov. 28, 1754 (Boswell, The Life of Samuel Johnson, *Everyman Paperback, vol. I, p.166)*

428 δούλῳ γὰρ οὐχ οἷόν τε τἀληθῆ λέγειν,
εἰ δεσπόταισι μὴ πρέποντα τυγχάνοι

The servant will not tell a truth
if it is not to his master's liking.

Fragment 313 (Nauck, *TGF*) – *Busiris*

429 γύναι, καλὸν μὲν φέγγος ἡλίου τόδε,
καλὸν δὲ πόντου χεῦμ' ἰδεῖν εὐήνεμον,
γῆ τ' ἠρινὸν θάλλουσα πλούσιόν θ' ὕδωρ,
πολλῶν τ' ἔπαινον ἔστι μοι λέξαι καλῶν·
ἀλλ' οὐδὲν οὕτω λαμπρὸν οὐδ' ἰδεῖν καλὸν
ὡς τοῖς ἄπαισι καὶ πόθῳ δεδηγμένοις
παίδων νεογνῶν ἐν δόμοις ἰδεῖν φάος

Woman, how glorious is this sunshine,
how wonderful to watch the tranquil sea,
the earth in spring, the waters flowing,
how many wonders to recount!
Yet none so marvellous or beautiful a feeling
than when to childless, yearning parents
a child is born.

Fragment 316 (Nauck, *TGF*) – *Danae*

430 καὶ νῦν παραινῶ πᾶσι τοῖς νεωτέροις
μὴ ... σχολῇ τεκνοῦσθαι παῖδας ...
ἀλλ' ὡς τάχιστα· καὶ γὰρ ἐκτροφαὶ καλαὶ
καὶ συννεάζων ἡδὺ παῖς νέῳ πατρί

And now I advise all younger men
not to delay fathering children,
but do it as soon as possible; rearing them is wonderful
and sweet to the youngster is a youthful father.

Fragment 317 (Nauck, *TGF*) – *Danae*

431 οὐκ ἔστιν ... δυσφύλακτον οὐδὲν ὡς γυνή

Nothing is harder to guard than a woman.

Fragment 320 (Nauck, *TGF*) – *Danae*

432 ἔρως γὰρ ἀργὸν κἀπὶ τοιούτοις ἔφυ·
φιλεῖ κάτοπτρα καὶ κόμης ξανθίσματα,
φεύγει δὲ μόχθους

Love is idle by nature, ready to associate with the idle;
it regards mirrors with affection and hair dyed blond,
avoiding all distress.

Fragment 322 (Nauck, *TGF*) – *Danae*

433 φεῦ φεῦ, παλαιὸς αἶνος ὡς καλῶς ἔχει·
οὐκ ἂν γένοιτο χρηστὸς ἐκ κακοῦ πατρός

Alas, alas, how well the old saying has it;
a good son will never be born from a bad father.

Translated by Christopher Collard and Martin Cropp (2008)

Fragment 333 (Nauck, *TGF*) – *Dictys*

434 θάρσει· τό τοι δίκαιον ἰσχύει μέγα

Take heart! There is great power in justice, I tell you.

Translated by Christopher Collard and Martin Cropp (2008)

Fragment 343 (Nauck, *TGF*) – *Dictys*

435 ἐγὼ νομίζω πατρὶ φίλτατον τέκνα
παισίν τε τοὺς τεκόντας, οὐδὲ συμμάχους
ἄλλους γενέσθαι φήμ' ἂν ἐνδικωτέρους

Nothing, I think, is more loved by a father than his children,
and nothing's more loved by children than their parents;
nor are there allies more righteous and trustworthy.

Fragment 345 (Nauck, *TGF*) – *Dictys*

436 εἷς γάρ τις ἔστι κοινὸς ἀνθρώποις νόμος
καὶ θεοῖσι ...
θηρσίν τε πᾶσι, τέκν' ἃ τίκτουσιν φιλεῖν

There is one single law common to all, men, gods
and beasts alike, to love the children born to them.

Fragment 346 (Nauck, *TGF*) – *Dictys*

437 ὡς ἕν γ' ἐμοὶ κρίνοιτ' ἂν οὐ καλῶς φρονεῖν
ὅστις πατρῴας γῆς ἀτιμάζων ὅρους
ἄλλην ἐπαινεῖ

No one, to me, can be in his right mind
who, holding his fatherland in no esteem,
is ready to praise others.

Fragment 347 (Nauck, *TGF*) – *Dictys*

438 οὐδεὶς στρατεύσας ἄδικα σῶς ἦλθεν πάλιν

No one who unjustly goes to war returns unscathed.

Translated by Christopher Collard and Martin Cropp (2008)

Fragment 353 (Nauck, *TGF*) – *Erechtheus*

439 οὐκ ἔστι μητρὸς οὐδὲν ἥδιον τέκνοις·
ἐρᾶτε μητρός, παῖδες, ὡς οὐκ ἔστ' ἔρως
τοιοῦτος ἄλλος ὅστις ἡδίων ἐρᾶν

Nothing is sweeter to children than a mother;
love your mother, children, for nowhere
is there a love as sweet as this.

Fragment 358 (Nauck, *TGF*) – *Erechtheus*

440 βραχεῖ δὲ μύθῳ πολλὰ συλλαβὼν ἐρῶ.
πρῶτον φρένας μὲν ἠπίους ἔχειν χρεών·
τῷ πλουσίῳ τε τῷ τε μὴ διδοὺς μέρος
ἴσον σεαυτὸν εὐσεβεῖν πᾶσιν δίδου

In a brief statement I shall sum up much.
First, you should maintain a gentle frame of mind;
give equal weight to rich and poor alike,
and show yourself respectful to everyone.

Translated by Christopher Collard and Martin Cropp (2008)

Fragment 362.5 (Nauck, *TGF*) – *Erechtheus*

441 βραχεῖα τέρψις ἡδονῆς κακῆς

There's brief enjoyment in dishonourable pleasure.

Translated by Christopher Collard and Martin Cropp (2008)

Fragment 362.23 (Nauck, *TGF*) – *Erechtheus*

442 τοὺς πονηροὺς μήποτ' αὔξαν' ἐν πόλει

Never let villains prosper in the city.

Translated by Martin Cropp (1997)

Fragment 362.28 (Nauck, *TGF*) – *Erechtheus*

443 κείσθω δόρυ μοι μίτον ἀμφιπλέκειν ἀράχναις,
μετὰ δ' ἡσυχίας πολιῷ γήρᾳ συνοικῶν

May my spear idle lie, and spiders spin
Their webs about it! May I, oh may I, pass
My hoary age in peace!

Translated by Christopher Wordsworth (1836)

Fragment 369 (Nauck, *TGF*) – *Erechtheus*

444 τὴν μὲν γὰρ εὐγένειαν αἰνοῦσιν βροτοί,
μᾶλλον δὲ κηδεύουσι τοῖς εὐδαίμοσιν

Men pay lip-service to nobility, but they prefer to ally themselves with those who are prospering.

Translated by Christopher Collard and Martin Cropp (2008)

Fragment 395 (Nauck, *TGF*) – *Thyestes*

445 ἀλλ' εἴπερ ἔστιν ἐν βροτοῖς ψευδηγορεῖν
πιθανά, νομίζειν χρή σε καὶ τοὐναντίον,
ἄπιστ' ἀληθῆ πολλὰ συμβαίνειν βροτοῖς

Probable as it is that men believe false words
you should also consider the opposite:
that men often disbelieve what is true.

Fragment 396 (Nauck, *TGF*) – *Thyestes*

Aristotle, Rhetoric *1397a.17, uses these lines to illustrate the rhetorical ploy of 'demonstration from opposites'*

446 θεοῦ θέλοντος κἂν ἐπὶ ῥιπὸς πλέοις

If god wills, you can float on straw.

Fragment 397 (Nauck, *TGF*) – *Thyestes*

quoted by Aristophanes, Peace *698*

447 νόμοι γυναικῶν οὐ καλῶς κεῖνται πέρι·
χρῆν γὰρ τὸν εὐτυχοῦνθ' ὅπως πλείστας ἔχειν …
ὡς τὴν κακὴν μὲν ἐξέβαλλε δωμάτων,
τὴν δ' οὖσαν ἐσθλὴν ἡδέως ἐσῴζετο

There are laws about wives but they are all wrong:
the prosperous should have as many as possible,
so as to dismiss the one who is bad
and keep the one who brings joy to the house.

Fragment 402 (Nauck, *TGF*) – *Ino*

448 ὡς μικρὰ τὰ σφάλλοντα, καὶ μί' ἡμέρα
τὰ μὲν καθεῖλεν ὑψόθεν, τὰ δ' ἦρ' ἄνω

How do small things overcome us! In a single day
What is exalted is brought low and what lies low is glorified.

Fragment 420 (Nauck, *TGF*) – *Ino*

449 τά τοι μέγιστα πάντ' ἀπείργασται βροτοῖς
τόλμ' ὥστε νικᾶν· οὔτε γὰρ τυραννίδες
χωρὶς πόνου γένοιντ' ἂν οὔτ' οἶκος μέγας

The greatest prizes go to men who dare; neither kingships nor stately homes come without enterprise.

Fragment 426 (Nauck, *TGF*) – *Ixion*

450 οἱ γὰρ Κύπριν φεύγοντες ἀνθρώπων ἄγαν
νοσοῦσ' ὁμοίως τοῖς ἄγαν θηρωμένοις

Those of mankind who flee too much from Cypris
are similarly at fault to those who hunt after her too much.

Translated by Christopher Collard and Martin Cropp (2008)

Fragment 428 (Nauck, *TGF*) – *Hippolytus Veiled*

Aphrodite (Cypris) as the goddess of love

451 ἀντὶ πυρὸς γὰρ ἄλλο πῦρ
μεῖζον ἐβλάστομεν γυναῖ-
κες πολὺ δυσμαχώτερον

Over against fire, another fire
was born much greater, woman,
even more unconquerable.

Fragment 429 (Nauck, *TGF*) – *Hippolytus Veiled*

452 ἔχω δὲ τόλμης καὶ θράσους διδάσκαλον
ἐν τοῖς ἀμηχάνοισιν εὐπορώτατον,
Ἔρωτα, πάντων δυσμαχώτατον θεόν

I have a teacher of daring and audacity,
ingenious when I am at a loss,
Eros, the unconquerable god.

Fragment 430 (Nauck, *TGF*) – *Hippolytus Veiled*

453 ὁρῶ δὲ τοῖς πολλοῖσιν ἀνθρώποις ἐγὼ
τίκτουσαν ὕβριν τὴν πάροιθ' εὐπραξίαν

In much of mankind I see
success leading to arrogance.

Fragment 437 (Nauck, *TGF*) – *Hippolytus Veiled*

454 ὕβριν τε τίκτει πλοῦτος

Wealth gives birth to insolence.

Fragment 438 (Nauck, *TGF*) – *Hippolytus Veiled*

455 φεῦ φεῦ, τὸ μὴ τὰ πράγματ' ἀνθρώποις ἔχειν
φωνήν, ἵν' ἦσαν μηδὲν οἱ δεινοὶ λέγειν.
νῦν δ' εὐρόοισι στόμασι τἀληθέστατα
κλέπτουσιν, ὥστε μὴ δοκεῖν ἃ χρὴ δοκεῖν

Alas, alas, that facts would not have voice,
to bring to naught grand speeches!
Now, fluent tongues disguise the truth
making us doubt what should not be doubted.

Fragment 439 (Nauck, *TGF*) – *Hippolytus Veiled*

456 ἐχρῆν γὰρ ἡμᾶς …
τὸν φύντα θρηνεῖν εἰς ὅσ' ἔρχεται κακά,
τὸν δ' αὖ θανόντα καὶ πόνων πεπαυμένον
χαίροντας εὐφημοῦντας ἐκπέμπειν δόμων

Bewail the newborn child for all the ills which come;
but him that's dead, and from his labours rests,
with joy and blessings bear him from the house.

Fragment 449 (Nauck, *TGF*) – *Cresphontes*

457 φιλῶν μάλιστ' ἐμαυτὸν οὐκ αἰσχύνομαι

I feel no shame in loving myself above all.

Fragment 452 (Nauck, *TGF*) – *Cresphontes*

458 Εἰρήνα βαθύπλουτε καὶ
καλλίστα μακάρων θεῶν,
ζῆλός μοι σέθεν ὡς χρονίζεις

O well of infinite riches!
O fairest of beings divine!
O Peace, how alas! thou delayest.

Translated by Evelyn S. Shuckburgh (1889)

Fragment 453 (Nauck, *TGF*) – *Cresphontes*

459 κέρδη τοιαῦτα χρή τινα κτᾶσθαι βροτῶν,
ἐφ' οἷσι μέλλει μήποθ' ὕστερον στένειν

The kind of profits a mortal should acquire
are those he is never going to lament later.

Translated by Martin Cropp (1997)

Fragment 459 (Nauck, *TGF*) – *Cresphontes*

460 φαῦλον ἄκομψον, τὰ μέγιστ' ἀγαθόν

Plain, unadorned, in a great crisis brave and true.

Translated by Bernadotte Perrin (1914)

Fragment 473 (Nauck, *TGF*) – *Licymnius*

Plutarch, Cimon *4.5, uses this line to describe Cimon*

461 πόνος γάρ, ὡς λέγουσιν, εὐκλείας πατήρ

Hard work, so they say, is the father of fame.

Fragment 474 (Nauck, *TGF*) – *Licymnius*

462 τῆς μὲν κακῆς κάκιον οὐδὲν γίγνεται
γυναικός, ἐσθλῆς δ' οὐδὲν εἰς ὑπερβολὴν
πέφυκ' ἄμεινον

Nothing is worse than a truly bad woman
and nothing nobler than a truly good one.

Fragment 494 (Nauck, *TGF*) – *Melanippe*

there are two plays, Melanippe Wise *and* Melanippe Captive, *but not always unmistakably identified*

463 πλὴν τῆς τεκούσης θῆλυ πᾶν μισῶ γένος

Except for my mother I hate all womankind.

Translated by Christopher Collard and Martin Cropp (2008)

Fragment 498 (Nauck, *TGF*) – *Melanippe*

464 ὅστις δ' ἄμεικτον πατέρ' ἔχει νεανίας
στυγνόν τ' ἐν οἴκοις, μεγάλα κέκτηται κακά

Most unfortunate are the young who live with a harsh and sullen father.

Fragment 500 (Nauck, *TGF*) – *Melanippe*

465 δοκεῖτε πηδᾶν τἀδικήματ' εἰς θεοὺς
πτεροῖσι, κἄπειτ' ἐν Διὸς δέλτου πτυχαῖς
γράφειν τιν' αὐτά, Ζῆνα δ' εἰσορῶντά νιν
θνητοῖς δικάζειν; οὐδ' ὁ πᾶς ἂν οὐρανὸς
Διὸς γράφοντος τὰς βροτῶν ἁμαρτίας
ἐξαρκέσειεν

Think you that wrongdoings fly to the gods on wings,
are inscribed on Zeus' writing-tablet, then Zeus reads them
and passes judgement on men? Not the whole sky
would suffice to write down the trespasses of man.

Fragment 506 (Nauck, *TGF*) – *Melanippe*

466 τί τοὺς θανόντας οὐκ ἐᾷς τεθνηκέναι
καὶ τἀκχυθέντα συλλέγεις ἀλγήματα;

Why do you not let those who have died be dead?
Why are you collecting griefs that are already spent?

Translated by Martin Cropp (1997)

Fragment 507 (Nauck, *TGF*) – *Melanippe*

467 παλαιὸς αἶνος· ἔργα μὲν νεωτέρων,
βουλαὶ δ' ἔχουσι τῶν γεραιτέρων κράτος

It's an old saying, that action belongs to the young
but in counsel the elders are masters.

Fragment 508 (Nauck, *TGF*) – *Melanippe*

468 ἀργὸς πολίτης κεῖνος, ὡς κακός γ' ἀνήρ

An idle citizen is a bad citizen.

Fragment 512 (Nauck, *TGF*) – *Melanippe*

469 δειλοὶ γὰρ ἄνδρες οὐκ ἔχουσιν ἐν μάχῃ
ἀριθμόν, ἀλλ' ἄπεισι κἂν παρῶσ' ὅμως

Cowards don't count in battle;
though they be there, they're nowhere.

Fragment 519 (Nauck, *TGF*) – *Meleagros*

470 ἡ γὰρ Κύπρις πέφυκε τῷ σκότῳ φίλη,
τὸ φῶς δ' ἀνάγκην προστίθησι σωφρονεῖν

Cypris is by nature fond of darkness,
for light, by necessity, brings discretion

Fragment 524 (Nauck, *TGF*) – *Meleagros*

Cypris (Aphrodite) as the goddess of love

471 κατθανὼν δὲ πᾶς ἀνὴρ
γῆ καὶ σκιά· τὸ μηδὲν εἰς οὐδὲν ῥέπει

In death all men are earth and shadow;
naught comes to naught.

Fragment 532 (Nauck, *TGF*) – *Meleagros*

472 φεῦ, τὰ τῶν εὐδαιμονούντων ὡς ταχὺ στρέφει θεός

Alas, how quickly god upsets the fortunes of the prosperous!

Translated by Christopher Collard and Martin Cropp (2008)

Fragment 536 (Nauck, *TGF*) – *Meleagros*

473 οὔτοι νόμισμα λευκὸς ἄργυρος μόνον
καὶ χρυσός ἐστιν, ἀλλὰ κἀρετὴ βροτοῖς
νόμισμα κεῖται πᾶσιν, ᾗ χρῆσθαι χρεών

Not only gold and silver be your currency;
Virtue is the hardest currency worldwide,
be not afraid to use it.

Fragment 542 (Nauck, *TGF*) – *Oedipus*

474 νοῦν χρὴ θεᾶσθαι, νοῦν· τί τῆς εὐμορφίας
ὄφελος, ὅταν τις μὴ φρένας καλὰς ἔχῃ;

The mind is what to watch, the mind!
What use is beauty without good sense?

Fragment 548 (Nauck, *TGF*) – *Oedipus*

475 ἦμαρ ἕν τοι μεταβολὰς πολλὰς ἔχει

But one day truly holds many changes.

Translated by Christopher Collard (2004)

Fragment 549 (Nauck, *TGF*) – *Oedipus*

476 ἐκ τῶν ἀέλπτων ἡ χάρις μείζων βροτοῖς

Men's delight is greater from what is unexpected.

Translated by Christopher Collard and Martin Cropp (2008)

Fragment 550 (Nauck, *TGF*) – *Oedipus*

477 ἐκμαρτυρεῖν γὰρ ἄνδρα τὰς αὑτοῦ τύχας
εἰς πάντας ἀμαθές, τὸ δ' ἐπικρύπτεσθαι σοφόν

It is stupid for a man to air his misfortunes
in front of all; concealing them is wise.

Fragment 553 (Nauck, *TGF*) – *Oedipus*

478 ἀλλ' ἡ Δίκη γὰρ καὶ κατὰ σκότον βλέπει

The eye of Justice sees even in the dark.

Fragment 555 (Nauck, *TGF*) – *Oedipus*

479 ὡς οὐδὲν ἀνδρὶ πιστὸν ἄλλο πλὴν τέκνων

A man can trust nothing more than his children.

Fragment 566 (Nauck, *TGF*) – *Oeneus*

480 ἀμηχανῶ δ' ἔγωγε κοὐκ ἔχω μαθεῖν,
εἴτ' οὖν ἄμεινόν ἐστι γίγνεσθαι τέκνα
θνητοῖσιν εἴτ' ἄπαιδα καρποῦσθαι βίον.
ὁρῶ γὰρ οἷς μὲν οὐκ ἔφυσαν, ἀθλίους·

ὅσοισι δ' εἰσίν, οὐδὲν εὐτυχεστέρους·
καὶ γὰρ κακοὶ γεγῶτες ἐχθίστη νόσος,
κἂν αὖ γένωνται σώφρονες – κακὸν μέγα –
λυποῦσι τὸν φύσαντα μὴ πάθωσί τι

I myself am uncertain and cannot be told
whether 'tis better for men to get children,
or rather to enjoy a childless life.
I see that those without children are miserable,
while those who have them are not much happier;
children are a plague if they turn out bad,
and if well behaved – how distressing! –
their parents are terrified that something might befall them.

Fragment 571 (Nauck, *TGF*) – *Oenomaus*

481 τεκμαιρόμεσθα τοῖς παροῦσι τἀφανῆ

From things present we surmise happenings unseen.

Fragment 574 (Nauck, *TGF*) – *Oenomaus*

482 μακρὸς γὰρ αἰὼν μυρίους τίκτει πόνους

A long life brings a sea of troubles.

Fragment 575 (Nauck, *TGF*) – *Oenomaus*

483 ὁ πλεῖστα πράσσων πλεῖσθ' ἁμαρτάνει βροτῶν

The man who tries to do most makes the most mistakes.

Translated by Christopher Collard and Martin Cropp (2008)

Fragment 576 (Nauck, *TGF*) – *Oenomaus*

484 τὰ τῆς γε λήθης φάρμακ' ὀρθώσας μόνος,
ἄφωνα καὶ φωνοῦντα, συλλαβὰς τιθείς,
ἐξηῦρον ἀνθρώποισι γράμματ' εἰδέναι,
ὥστ' οὐ παρόντα ποντίας ὑπὲρ πλακὸς
τἀκεῖ κατ' οἴκους πάντ' ἐπίστασθαι καλῶς,
παισίν τε τὸν θνῄσκοντα χρημάτων μέτρον
γράψαντα λείπειν, τὸν λαβόντα δ' εἰδέναι

Alone I established remedies for forgetfulness;
making consonants, vowels, syllables,
I invented knowledge of writing for men,
so that one absent over the sea's plain
might know well everything back there in his house,
and a dying man might write down and declare the measure of his wealth
for the heir to know.

Translated by Christopher Collard (2004)

Fragment 578.1 (Nauck, *TGF*) – *Palamedes*

Palamedes, claiming invention of writing

485 ἃ δ' εἰς ἔριν πίπτουσιν ἀνθρώποις κακά,
δέλτος διαιρεῖ, κοὐκ ἐᾷ ψευδῆ λέγειν

The troubles which befall men and lead to strife,
a written tablet settles, and allows no falsehood to be said.

Translated by Christopher Collard (2004)

Fragment 578.8 (Nauck, *TGF*) – *Palamedes*

Palamedes was finally destroyed by a forged letter

486 στρατηλάται τἂν μυρίοι γενοίμεθα,
σοφὸς δ' ἂν εἷς τις ἢ δύ' ἐν μακρῷ χρόνῳ

Commanders certainly we might become, many of us;
but wise ones – just one or two perhaps, over a very long time.

Fragment 581 (Nauck, *TGF*) – *Palamedes*

487 εἷς τοι δίκαιος μυρίων οὐκ ἐνδίκων
κρατεῖ, τὸ θεῖον τὴν δίκην τε συλλαβών

One just man overcomes numberless unjust men
when he has the gods and justice on his side.

Translated by Christopher Collard (2004)

Fragment 584 (Nauck, *TGF*) – *Palamedes*

488 τὸ γῆρας, ὦ παῖ, τῶν νεωτέρων φρενῶν
σοφώτερον πέφυκε κἀσφαλέστερον,
ἐμπειρία τε τῆς ἀπειρίας κρατεῖ

Old age, my child, is naturally
wiser than youth, and safer;
experience is master over inexperience.

Fragment 619 (Nauck, *TGF*) – *Peleus*

489 μηδ' ἄνδρα δήμῳ πιστὸν ἐκβάλῃς ποτὲ
μηδ' αὖξε καιροῦ μείζον' ...
κώλυε δ' ἄνδρα παρὰ δίκην τιμώμενον

Never expel a man who is trusted by the people,
but do not let him grow greater than he should be;
and check a man who gains esteem

unjustly.

Translated by Christopher Collard and Martin Cropp (2008)

Fragment 626 (Nauck, *TGF*) – *Pleisthenes*

490 πολλῶν δὲ χρήματ' αἴτι' ἀνθρώποις κακῶν

Wealth is the cause of many human ills.

Fragment 632 (Nauck, *TGF*) – *Pleisthenes*

491 ὅστις νέμει κάλλιστα τὴν αὑτοῦ φύσιν,
οὗτος σοφὸς πέφυκε πρὸς τὸ συμφέρον

He who manages his natural abilities best
is wise to his own advantage.

Fragment 634 (Nauck, *TGF*) – *Polyidus*

492 τίς δ' οἶδεν εἰ τὸ ζῆν μέν ἐστι κατθανεῖν,
τὸ κατθανεῖν δὲ ζῆν κάτω νομίζεται;

Who knows if life is death,
and if in the underworld death is considered life?

Translated by Christopher Collard and Martin Cropp (2008)

Fragment 638 (Nauck, *TGF*) – *Polyidus*

quoted by Aristophanes 90 and Plato, Gorgias *492e*

493 πόλλ' ἐλπίδες ψεύδουσι ἄλογοι βροτούς

Mortals are much deceived by groundless hopes.

Translated by Christopher Collard and Martin Cropp (2008)

Fragment 650 (Nauck, *TGF*) – *Protesilaus*

494 δυοῖν λεγόντοιν, θατέρου θυμουμένου,
ὁ μὴ ἀντιτείνων τοῖς λόγοις σοφώτερος

When of two speakers one is growing wroth,
Wiser is he that yields in argument.

Translated by Frank Cole Babbitt (1927)

Fragment 654 (Nauck, *TGF*) – *Protesilaus*

495 ὅστις δὲ πάσας συντιθεὶς ψέγει λόγῳ
γυναῖκας ἑξῆς, σκαιός ἐστι κοὐ σοφός·
πολλῶν γὰρ οὐσῶν τὴν μὲν εὑρήσεις κακήν,
τὴν δ' ὥσπερ ἥδε λῆμ' ἔχουσαν εὐγενές

Whoever indiscriminately blames
all women is foolish and not wise;
for there are many: one may be bad,
another of noble character.

Fragment 657 (Nauck, *TGF*) – *Protesilaus*

496 οὐκ ἔστιν ὅστις πάντ' ἀνὴρ εὐδαιμονεῖ

There is no man who is fortunate in everything.

Fragment 661 (Nauck, *TGF*) – *Stheneboea*

much cited and repeated throughout antiquity; cf. Aristophanes, Frogs *1217*

497 ποιητὴν ἄρα
Ἔρως διδάσκει, κἂν ἄμουσος ᾖ τὸ πρίν

Love teaches a poet,
even if the Muses had not touched him before.

Fragment 663 (Nauck, *TGF*) – *Stheneboea*

cf. Plato 313 and Aristophanes, Wasps *1074*

498 ἔστι τοι καλὸν
κακοὺς κολάζειν

It is good, mark you,
for the wicked to be punished.

Fragment 678 (Nauck, *TGF*) – *Sciron*

499 μοχθεῖν ἀνάγκη τοὺς θέλοντας εὐτυχεῖν

Hard work is necessary for those who seek success.

Fragment 701 (Nauck, *TGF*) – *Telephus*

500 τόλμα σύ, κἂν τι τραχὺ νείμωσιν θεοί

Bear up, even if treated harshly by the gods.

Fragment 702 (Nauck, *TGF*) – *Telephus*

501 τί γάρ με πλοῦτος ὠφελεῖ νόσον;

What good is wealth in sickness?

Fragment 714 (Nauck, *TGF*) – *Telephus*

cf. the English proverb 'health is above wealth'

502 χρεία διδάσκει, κἂν βραδύς τις ᾖ, σοφόν

Necessity teaches wisdom even to the stupid.

Translated by D.S. Baker (1998)

Fragment 715 (Nauck, *TGF*) – *Telephus*

503 ῥώμη δέ γ' ἀμαθὴς πολλάκις τίκτει βλάβην

Strength without intelligence is often harmful.

Fragment 732 (Nauck, *TGF*) – *Temenidae – Sons of Temenus*

504 ἀρετὴ δὲ κἂν θάνῃ τις οὐκ ἀπόλλυται,
ζῇ δ' οὐκέτ' ὄντος σώματος· κακοῖσι δὲ
ἅπαντα φροῦδα συνθανόνθ' ὑπὸ χθονός

When good men die their goodness

does not perish,
But lives though they are gone. As for the bad,
All that was theirs dies and is buried with them.

Translated by Morris Hicky Morgan (1859–1910)

Fragment 734 (Nauck, *TGF*) – *Temenidae – Sons of Temenus*

505 ἀσύνετος ὅστις ἐν φόβῳ μὲν ἀσθενής,
λαβὼν δὲ μικρὸν τῆς τύχης φρονεῖ μέγα

Witless is he who is weak in the face of fear,
but, on receipt of a little luck, thinks he is great.

Fragment 735 (Nauck, *TGF*) – *Temenidae – Sons of Temenus*

506 κακοῖς τὸ κέρδος τῆς δίκης ὑπέρτερον

Bad people think profit superior to fairness.

Translated by Martin J. Cropp (2004)

Fragment 758 (Nauck, *TGF*) – *Hypsipyle*

507 ἔξω γὰρ ὀργῆς πᾶς ἀνὴρ σοφώτερος

Free from anger every man is wiser.

Fragment 760 (Nauck, *TGF*) – *Hypsipyle*

508 ἄελπτον οὐδέν, πάντα δ' ἐλπίζειν χρεών

Nothing is beyond expectation; there must always be hope.

Fragment 761 (Nauck, *TGF*) – *Hypsipyle*

509 ναῦν τοι μί' ἄγκυρ' οὐχ ὁμῶς σῴζειν φιλεῖ
τῷ τρεῖς

Surely a ship is safer with three anchors than one.

Fragment 774 (Nauck, *TGF*) – *Phaethon*

510 ὡς πανταχοῦ γε πατρὶς ἡ βόσκουσα γῆ

Fatherland is everywhere where there is nourishing earth.

Fragment 777 (Nauck, *TGF*) – *Phaethon*

511 πῶς δ' ἂν φρονοίην, ᾧ παρῆν ἀπραγμόνως
ἐν τοῖσι πολλοῖς ἠριθμημένῳ στρατοῦ

Would that be prudent? when I might have lived
a quiet life, a cipher in the crowd!

Translated by H. Rackham (1926)

Fragment 787 (Nauck, *TGF*) – *Philoctetes*

quoted by Aristotle, Nicomachean Ethics *1142a.3; cf. Aristotle 123*

512 μακάριος ὅστις εὐτυχῶν οἴκοι μένει

Blessed the man who stays happily at home.

Translated by Christopher Collard and Martin Cropp (2008)

Fragment 793 (Nauck, *TGF*) – *Philoctetes*

513 δέσποινα γὰρ γέροντι νυμφίῳ γυνή

An old man weds a tyrant, not a wife.

Translated in *Bartlett's Familiar Quotations* (1980)

Fragment 804 (Nauck, *TGF*) – *Phoenix*

quoted by Aristophanes, Thesmophoriazusae *413*

514 τοιοῦτός ἐστιν οἷσπερ ἥδεται ξυνών

A man is as good as the company he keeps.

Fragment 812 (Nauck, *TGF*) – *Phoenix*

cf. the English proverb 'a man is known by the company he keeps'

515 σὺ δ', ὦ πατρῴα χθὼν ἐμῶν γεννητόρων,
χαῖρ'· ἀνδρὶ γάρ τοι, κἂν ὑπερβάλλῃ κακοῖς,
οὐκ ἔστι τοῦ θρέψαντος ἥδιον πέδον

And you, fatherland of my ancestors, farewell!
Truly, even if a man has trouble to excess,
there is no soil more pleasing than that which reared him.

Translated by Christopher Collard and Martin Cropp (2008)

Fragment 817 (Nauck, *TGF*) – *Phoenix*

516 γυνὴ γὰρ ἐν κακοῖσι καὶ νόσοις πόσει
ἥδιστόν ἐστι δῶματ' ἢν οἰκῇ καλῶς
ὀργήν τε πραΰνουσα καὶ δυσθυμίας
ψυχὴν μεθιστᾶσα

A wife is most pleasing to her husband amid troubles if she manages his house well, both soothing his anger and changing his spirits from gloom.

Translated by Christopher Collard and Martin Cropp (2008)

Fragment 822 (Nauck, *TGF*) – *Phrixus*

517 χρὴ γὰρ εὐναίῳ πόσει
γυναῖκα κοινῇ τὰς τύχας φέρειν ἀεί

A woman must always share burdens with her husband.

Fragment 823 (Nauck, *TGF*) – *Phrixus*

518 δι᾿ ἐλπίδος ζῆ καὶ δι᾿ ἐλπίδων τρέφου

Live in hope and sustain yourself with hopes!

Translated by Christopher Collard and Martin Cropp (2008)

Fragment 826 (Nauck, *TGF*) – *Phrixus*

519 τίς δ᾿ οἶδεν εἰ ζῆν τοῦθ᾿ ὃ κέκληται θανεῖν,
τὸ ζῆν δὲ θνῄσκειν ἐστί;

Who knoweth if the thing that we call death
Be Life, and our Life dying – who knoweth?

Translated by Gilbert Murray (1913)

Fragment 833 (Nauck, *TGF*) – *Phrixus*

520 χωρεῖ δ᾿ ὀπίσω
τὰ μὲν ἐκ γαίας φύντ᾿ εἰς γαῖαν,
τὰ δ᾿ ἀπ᾿ αἰθερίου βλαστόντα γονῆς
εἰς οὐράνιον πάλιν ἦλθε πόλον·
θνῄσκει δ᾿ οὐδὲν τῶν γιγνομένων,
διακρινόμενον δ᾿ ἄλλο πρὸς ἄλλου
μορφὴν ἑτέραν ἀπέδειξεν

Things born from earth return to earth,
and those that grew from ethereal seed
go back to the heavenly region;
nothing that comes into being perishes,
but one is separated from another
and exhibits a different form.

Translated by Christopher Collard and Martin Cropp (2008)

Fragment 839 (Nauck, *TGF*) – *Chrysippus*

widely cited in antiquity for its 'philosophical' ideas

521 αἰαῖ, τόδ᾿ ἤδη θεῖον ἀνθρώποις κακόν,
ὅταν τις εἰδῇ τἀγαθόν, χρῆται δὲ μή

Alas, this evil is a whim of providence
that, knowing what is right, men do it not.

Fragment 841 (Nauck, *TGF*) – *Chrysippus*

522 λόγων δίκαιον μισθὸν ἂν λόγους φέροις,
ἔργον δ᾿ ἐκεῖνος ἔργον ὃς παρέσχετο

The return you can fairly expect for words is words;
action is earned by one who provided action.

Translated by Christopher Collard and Martin Cropp (2008)

Fragment 890 (Nauck, *TGF*)

quoted by Aristotle, Eudemian Ethics *1244a.11, to highlight the difficulty of repaying non-material debts*

523 τὸ δ᾿ ἐρᾶν προλέγω τοῖσι νέοισιν
μήποτε φεύγειν

To the young I say, never flee the experience of love.

Translated by Christopher Collard and Martin Cropp (2008)

Fragment 897 (Nauck, *TGF*)

524 ἐρᾷ ὄμβρου γαῖα

The earth yearns for rain.

Translated by Christopher Collard and Martin Cropp (2008)

Fragment 898 (Nauck, *TGF*)

525 οὐκ ἂν δυναίμην μὴ στέγοντα πιμπλάναι,
σοφοὺς ἐπαντλῶν ἀνδρὶ μὴ σοφῷ λόγους

I could not fill a leaky vessel,
pouring wise words into a man who is not wise.

Translated by Christopher Collard and Martin Cropp (2008)

Fragment 899 (Nauck, *TGF*)

526 μισῶ σοφιστήν, ὅστις οὐχ αὑτῷ σοφός

I hate the wise man who is not wise for himself.

Translated by H.T. Riley (1872)

Fragment 905 (Nauck, *TGF*)

527 ὄλβιος ὅστις τῆς ἱστορίας
ἔσχε μάθησιν ...
ἀθανάτου καθορῶν φύσεως

Happy the man who has gained knowledge through inquiry,
observing eternal nature's ageless order.

Translated by Christopher Collard and Martin Cropp (2008)

Fragment 910 (Nauck, *TGF*) – *Antiope (?)*

528 πρὸς ταῦθ᾿ ὅτι χρῇ καὶ παλαμάσθω
καὶ πᾶν ἐπ᾿ ἐμοὶ τεκταινέσθω·
τὸ γὰρ εὖ μετ᾿ ἐμοῦ
καὶ τὸ δίκαιον ξύμμαχον ἔσται

Let him plot whatever he wants
and contrive anything against me;
Good will be on my side
and Justice my ally.

Translated by Christopher Collard and Martin Cropp (2008)

Fragment 918 (Nauck, *TGF*)

parodied by Aristophanes, Acharnians *659; quoted in Greek by Cicero,* Letters to Atticus *8.8.2*

529 ἡ φύσις ἐβούλεθ', ᾗ νόμων οὐδὲν μέλει

Nature willed it, which cares nothing for convention.

Translated by Christopher Collard and Martin Cropp (2008)

Fragment 920 (Nauck, *TGF*)

cf. Athanasius 1

530 οὐ γὰρ ἀσφαλὲς
περαιτέρω τὸ κάλλος ἢ μέσον λαβεῖν

It is unsafe to have beauty beyond the average.

Translated by Christopher Collard and Martin Cropp (2008)

Fragment 928 (Nauck, *TGF*)

531 ὁρᾷς τὸν ὑψοῦ τόνδ' ἄπειρον αἰθέρα
καὶ γῆν πέριξ ἔχονθ' ὑγραῖς ἐν ἀγκάλαις;

See'st thou this lofty, this boundless ether,
Holding the earth in its moist embrace?

Translated by Philip Schaff (1819–1893)

Fragment 941 (Nauck, *TGF*)

532 ὁ δ' ἄρτι θάλλων σάρκα διοπετὴς ὅπως
ἀστὴρ ἀπέσβη, πνεῦμ' ἀφεὶς ἐς αἰθέρα

Who was ere while and lately in the floure
Of his fresh youth, all sudden in an houre,
Became extinct (as starre which seemes to fall
From skie) and into aire sent breath and all.

Translated by Philemon Holland (1603)

Fragment 971 (Nauck, *TGF*)

533 μάντις δ' ἄριστος ὅστις εἰκάζει καλῶς

The best prophet is he who makes the best guesses.

Translated by H.T. Riley (1872)

Fragment 973 (Nauck, *TGF*)

quoted in Greek by Cicero, Letters to Atticus *7.13.4*

534 τῶν ἄγαν γὰρ ἅπτεται
θεός, τὰ μικρὰ δ' εἰς τύχην ἀφεὶς ἐᾷ

God will intervene in matters grown too great,
But small things he lets pass and leaves to Fate.

Translated by William C. Helmbold (1939)

Fragment 974 (Nauck, *TGF*)

cf. the Latin 'minima non curat praetor'

535 χαλεποὶ πόλεμοι γὰρ ἀδελφῶν

Grievous are fights between brothers.

Fragment 975 (Nauck, *TGF*)

536 ἡ Δίκη ... σῖγα καὶ βραδεῖ ποδὶ
στείχουσα μάρψει τοὺς κακούς, ὅταν τύχῃ

Justice, leisurely and slow-footed,
shall lay hold of the culprits in time.

Fragment 979 (Nauck, *TGF*)

537 τὰ τῶν τεκόντων σφάλματ' εἰς τοὺς ἐκγόνους
οἱ θεοὶ τρέπουσιν

The gods visit the sins of the fathers upon their children.

Translated by Morris Hicky Morgan (1859–1910)

Fragment 980 (Nauck, *TGF*)

538 φθείρουσιν ἤθη χρήσθ' ὁμιλίαι κακαί

Bad company ruins good morals.

Translated by Christopher Collard and Martin Cropp (2008)

Fragment 1024 (Nauck, *TGF*)

identical in Bible 231

539 τὰ πλεῖστα θνητοῖς τῶν κακῶν αὐθαίρετα

Most of men's troubles are incurred by their own choice.

Translated by Christopher Collard and Martin Cropp (2008)

Fragment 1026 (Nauck, *TGF*)

identical in Menander, One-liners *758 (Jaekel)*

540 ὅστις νέος ὢν Μουσῶν ἀμελεῖ,
τόν τε παρελθόντ' ἀπόλωλε χρόνον
καὶ τὸν μέλλοντα τέθνηκεν

Whoever in his youth neglects the Muses
not only forfeits bygone times
but also kills his future.

Fragment 1028 (Nauck, *TGF*)

the reference to the Muses is variously interpreted as 'neglect learning', 'neglect poetry' or 'the poetry of life'

541 τὸ μὴ εἰδέναι σε μηδὲν ὧν ἁμαρτάνεις,
ἔκκαυμα τόλμης ἱκανόν ἐστι καὶ θράσους

Not knowing your shortcomings
may well ignite your recklessness and cheek.

Fragment 1031 (Nauck, *TGF*)

542 τὸ δ' ὠκὺ τοῦτο καὶ τὸ λαιψηρὸν φρενῶν
εἰς συμφορὰν καθῆκε πολλὰ δὴ βροτούς

This swift and hasty thinking
quite often brings disaster.

Fragment 1032 (Nauck, *TGF*)

543 πότερα θέλεις σοι μαλθακὰ ψευδῆ λέγω
ἢ σκλήρ' ἀληθῆ;

Do you wish me to tell you gentle lies
or hard truths?

Translated by Christopher Collard and Martin Cropp (2008)

Fragment 1036 (Nauck, *TGF*)

544 ἀτὰρ σιωπᾶν τά γε δίκαι' οὐ χρή ποτε

Never be silent when what you have to say is just.

Fragment 1037 (Nauck, *TGF*)

545 ἅπαντές ἐσμεν εἰς τὸ νουθετεῖν σοφοί,
αὐτοὶ δ' ὅταν σφαλῶμεν οὐ γιγνώσκομεν

We are all good at offering advice,
but bad at accepting our own faults.

Fragment 1042 (Nauck, *TGF*)

546 οὐδεὶς ἔπαινον ἡδοναῖς ἐκτήσατο

No one has acquired fame through indulging in pleasures.

Translated by Christopher Collard and Martin Cropp (2008)

Fragment 1043 (Nauck, *TGF*)

547 οὔτ' ἐκ χερὸς μεθέντα καρτερὸν λίθον
οἷόν τ' ἐπισχεῖν οὔτ' ἀπὸ γλώσσης λόγον

Neither a stone, once thrown by mighty hand,
Nor word, once said by tongue, can you take back.

Fragment 1044 (Nauck, *TGF*)

548 ἅπας μὲν αἰθὴρ αἰετῷ περάσιμος

The whole heaven is open to an eagle's crossing.

Translated by Christopher Collard and Martin Cropp (2008)

Fragment 1047.1 (Nauck, *TGF*)

549 ἅπασα χθὼν ἀνδρὶ γενναίῳ πατρίς

The whole world is fatherland to the brave.

Fragment 1047.2 (Nauck, *TGF*)

550 οὐκ ἔστιν οὐδὲν τῶν ἐν ἀνθρώποις ἴσον

There is nothing at all that is equitable in human affairs.

Translated by Christopher Collard and Martin Cropp (2008)

Fragment 1048 (Nauck, *TGF*)

551 γυναικὶ δ' ὄλβος, ἢν πόσιν στέργοντ' ἔχῃ

Happy is the woman who has a loving husband.

Fragment 1062 (Nauck, *TGF*)

552 οὔποτ' ἄνδρα χρὴ σοφὸν
λίαν φυλάσσειν ἄλοχον ἐν μυχοῖς δόμων·
ἐρᾷ γὰρ ὄψις τῆς θύραθεν ἡδονῆς ...
δρᾶν τι δὴ δοκῶν σοφὸν
μάταιός ἐστι καὶ φρονῶν οὐδὲν φρονεῖ

It is not for a wise man
to keep his wife locked up at home,
for she loves all outside pleasures;
thinking he is clever he is but silly,
thinking he is prudent he is only foolish

Fragment 1063 (Nauck, *TGF*)

553 σκαιὸν τὸ πλουτεῖν κἄλλο μηδὲν εἰδέναι

'Tis loutish to be rich, and know naught else.

Translated by Frank Cole Babbitt (1927)

Fragment 1069 (Nauck, *TGF*)

554 λῦπαι γὰρ ἀνθρώποισι τίκτουσιν νόσους

Sorrows are the cause of illness in men.

Fragment 1071 (Nauck, *TGF*)

555 οὐκ ἔστι λύπης ἄλλο φάρμακον βροτοῖς
ὡς ἀνδρὸς ἐσθλοῦ καὶ φίλου παραίνεσις

There is no better remedy for sorrow
than the counsel of a faithful friend.

Fragment 1079 (Nauck, *TGF*)

556 ἄλλων ἰατρὸς αὐτὸς ἕλκεσιν βρύων

Healer of others, full of sores himself.

Translated by William C. Helmbold (1939)

Fragment 1086 (Nauck, *TGF*)

557 – θεὸν δὲ ποῖον, εἰπέ μοι, νοητέον;
– τὸν πάνθ' ὁρῶντα καὐτὸν οὐχ ὁρώμενον

– Tell me whom I should consider god?
– Him who sees all, invisible by all.

Fragment 1129 (Nauck, *TGF*)

EURYPHAMUS

3rd century BC
Pythagorean philosopher from Metapontum in southern Italy

1 οὐθὲν γὰρ οὕτω κοσμοπρεπὲς καὶ θεῶν ἄξιον ἔργον ἀνθρώποις πέπρακται, ὡς πόλιος εὐνομουμένας συναρμογὰ καὶ νόμων καὶ πολιτείας διακόσμασις

No work is more befitting, to man or god himself, than a state well appointed, well governed, well regulated by its laws.

Fragment 86.9 (Thesleff)

author of a work Περί Βίου (Concerning Human Life); *a large fragment of this is saved in Stobaeus, the rest is lost*

EUSEBIUS OF MYNDUS

fl. 4th century AD
Neoplatonist philosopher

1 μήκοτε ὑπὸ εὐπρηγίης ἐς ὑπερηφανίην ἄλογον ἀερθείην

In success, never be overwhelmed by senseless arrogance.

Fragment 1.25 (Mullach, *FPG*)

2 οἱ μάταιοι τῶν ἀνθρώπων τοὺς μὲν μεγάλα χρήματα ἔχοντας καὶ φαύλους ἐόντας τιμῶσί τε καὶ τεθωυμάκασι, τῶν δὲ σπουδαίων ἐπειδὰν ἀχρηματίην καταγνῶσι, ὑπερφρονέουσι

The foolish honour and look in wonder at the rich and vulgar, whilst those that are righteous but poor, are despised.

Fragment 7 (Mullach, *FPG*)

3 ἀκολασίη ψυχὴν ὥσπερ νῆα ἄνεμοι ὑπολαβόντες τῆδε καὶ τῆδε φορέοντες συγκλονέουσι καὶ ἀπειθέα ποιέουσι τῷ κυβερνήτῃ

Intemperance confounds the soul as pounding winds render a boat ungovernable.

Fragment 12 (Mullach, *FPG*)

4 μὴ ἐπὶ τῷ σιτέεσθαι νομίζειν γεγονέναι, μηδὲ ἐν τούτῳ τὴν ζωὴν ἡγέεσθαι, μούνου δὲ αὐτοῦ τοῦ ζώειν εἵνεκα ἀνθρώποισι τροφὴν νομίζειν εὑρῆσθαι

I was not born to eat, and food is not the purpose of life, but it does sustain life.

Fragment 25 (Mullach, *FPG*)

cf. Socrates 58, 'eat to live, not live to eat'

5 πόνοι οἱ ἑκούσιοι πόνοισι τοῖσι μετὰ ταῦτα ἀναγκαίοισι, ὥστε αὐτοὺς εὐπετεστέρους παρασκευασθῆναι, προπονέονται

Work tackled voluntarily prepares for necessary toil.

Fragment 32 (Mullach, *FPG*)

6 σῶμα ἀργίη τήκει, ψυχὴν δ' ἀμελετησίη ἀσκήσιος τῶν αὐτὴν ἀειρόντων

The body wastes away with idleness, the soul by not aiming for higher things.

Fragment 33 (Mullach, *FPG*)

7 ἀρχὴν ἔχων μὴ ἀπομνησικάκεε πρὸς τοὺς ἐν διχοστασίῃ σοι πρότερον γεγενημένους· ἐπὶ τὴν ἀρχὴν εἶ ἀραιρημένος ... ὅκως ... φυλάξῃς τοὺς ὑπὸ σοὶ τεταγμένους καὶ τοῦ ὀρθοῦ φύλαξ ἔῃς καὶ θεοῦ δικαιοσύνης ὑπηρέτης τε καὶ ἐξηγητής

Coming to power do not turn against your enemies; assure safety of your subjects, be guardian of the righteous, servant and interpreter of justice.

Fragment 45 (Mullach, *FPG*)

8 οὐδεὶς ὑπὸ τῆς τοῦ πέλας εὐτυχίης τῆς ὀφειλομένης ἑωυτῷ εὐπρηγίης ἀποστερέεται

Your neighbour's happiness in no way diminishes yours.

Fragment 58.15 (Mullach, *FPG*)

EVAGRIUS PONTICUS

345–399AD
Monastic theologian

1 σιγᾶν τὴν ἀλήθειαν χρυσόν ἐστι θάπτειν

Not to speak up for truth is to bury gold.

Aliae sententiae 71

EVODUS

1st century AD
Author of two short epigrams in *Greek Anthology*

1 Ἠχὼ μιμολόγον, φωνῆς τρύγα, ῥήματος οὐρήν

Oh mocking echo, residue of voice, tail end of speech!

Greek Anthology 16.155

F

FABIUS MAXIMUS

Quintus Fabius Maximus Verrucosus
*c.*275–203BC
Roman statesman

1 ἡ δὲ πρὸς δόξαν ἀνθρώπων καὶ διαβολὰς καὶ ψόγους ἔκπληξις οὐκ ἀξίου τηλικαύτης ἀρχῆς ἀνδρός

To be turned from one's course by censure, slander or the opinion of others shows a man unfit for high office.

Plutarch, *Fabius Maximus* 5.8

2 μήτε ὑβρίζεσθαι μήτε ἀτιμοῦσθαι τὸν ἀγαθὸν ἄνδρα καὶ σπουδαῖον

A sincerely good man can neither be insulted nor dishonoured.

Translated by Bernadotte Perrin (1916)
Plutarch, *Fabius Maximus* 10.2

3 τὸ μὲν ἁμαρτεῖν μηδὲν ... μεῖζον ἢ κατ' ἄνθρωπόν ἐστι, τὸ δ' ἁμαρτόντα χρήσασθαι τοῖς πταίσμασι διδάγμασι πρὸς τὸ λοιπὸν ἀνδρὸς ἀγαθοῦ καὶ νοῦν ἔχοντος

To avoid all mistakes is beyond man's powers; but when a mistake is made, to use setbacks as lessons for the future is the part of a brave and sensible man.

Plutarch, *Fabius Maximus* 13.2

FAVORINUS

*c.*85–155AD
Roman sophist, philosopher and man of letters, born in Arles

1 τὸ γῆρας οὐκ ἐπ' ἐξόδῳ τοῦ βίου εἶναι, ἀλλ' ἐπ' ἀρχῇ μακαρίας ζωῆς

Old age is not the end, but the beginning of a blessed life.

Fragment 12 (Barigazzi)

2 φρονήσῃς μὲν οὖν μηδέποτε ἐπὶ σαυτῷ μέγα, ἀλλὰ μηδὲ καταφρονήσῃς σεαυτοῦ

Neither overestimate nor underestimate yourself.

Fragment 96.20.41 (Barigazzi)

3 ἔστι δὲ οὐκ ἀξιόπιστος ἔπαινος, ὃν ἐπαινεῖ τις ἕτερον διὰ τὸ ἑαυτοῦ συμφέρον

Praise given to others in one's own interest is not trustworthy.

Fragment 101 (Barigazzi)

4 ὥσπερ ὁ Ἀκταίων ὑπὸ τῶν τρεφομένων ὑπ' αὐτοῦ κυνῶν ἀπέθανεν, οὕτως οἱ κόλακες τοὺς τρέφοντας κατεσθίουσιν

As Actaeon was killed by the hounds he kept, so do flatterers destroy those who maintain them.

Fragment 102 (Barigazzi)

5 γραῦν τινά φασι μόσχον μικρὸν ἀραμένην καὶ τοῦτο καθ' ἡμέραν ποιοῦσαν λαθεῖν βοῦν φέρουσαν

They say that an old woman carrying a calf every day did not realize that in the end she was carrying a bull.

Fragment 106 (Barigazzi)

G

GAIUS

*c.*110–*c.*180AD
Roman jurist

1 εὐάγωγον δὲ εἰς τὸ ῥᾳδίως τι τολμῆσαι θυμὸς γυναικός

A woman's spirit leads her easily towards rashness.

Stobaeus, *Anthology* 4.22g.201

uncertain which Gaius; probably Gaius Musonius Rufus (1st century AD*), not the jurist Gaius (c.110–180*AD*)*

2 τὸ μὲν ἀδικεῖσθαι καὶ πᾶν ὁτιοῦν δεινόν ἐστι· τὸ δὲ καὶ τῶν τοιούτων τι παθεῖν, ἃ μηδὲ εἰπεῖν ὁ πεπονθὼς δύναται σαφῶς, δυστυχίας ὑπερβολὴν οὐκ ἔχει

To suffer injustice is bad enough; however, to suffer and not be able to voice a complaint is the utmost adversity.

Stobaeus, *Anthology* 4.40.17

against child abuse; uncertain which Gaius; probably Gaius Musonius Rufus (1st century AD*), not the jurist Gaius (c.110–180*AD*)*

GALEN

129–199AD
Physician from Pergamum

1 μεγίστην λέξεως ἀρετὴν σαφήνειαν εἶναι ... καὶ ταύτην εἰδότες ὑπ' οὐδενὸς οὕτως ὡς ὑπὸ τῶν ἀσυνήθων ὀνομάτων διαφθειρομένην

The chief merit of language is clearness, and we know that nothing detracts so much from this as do unfamiliar terms.

Translated by Arthur John Brock (1916)

On the Natural Faculties 2.1.9

2 οὕτως οὐ μόνον ὑγιὲς οὐδὲν ἴσασιν οἱ ταῖς αἱρέσεσι δουλεύοντες, ἀλλ' οὐδὲ μαθεῖν ὑπομένουσι

Those who are enslaved to their sects are not merely devoid of all sound knowledge, but they will not even stop to learn!

Translated by Arthur John Brock (1916)

On the Natural Faculties 2.35.5

3 τὴν τέχνην τῆς φύσεως

Nature's artistic skill.

Translated by Arthur John Brock (1916)

On the Natural Faculties 2.35.10

4 ἀπιστήσαντα τοῖς φαινομένοις πιστεῦσαι τοῖς ἀδήλοις

Mistrust the obvious and believe in the unseen.

On the Natural Faculties 2.39.17

5 ἡ φύσις ... τὸ μὲν ὀστοῦ μέρος ἅπαν ὀστοῦν ἀποτελεῖ, τὸ δὲ σαρκὸς σάρκα, τὸ δὲ πιμελῆς πιμελὴν καὶ τῶν ἄλλων ἕκαστον· οὐδὲν γάρ ἐστιν ἄψαυστον αὐτῇ μέρος οὐδ' ἀνεξέργαστον οὐδ' ἀκόσμητον

Nature adds bone on every part of bone, flesh to every part of flesh, and so with fat and all the rest; there is no part she does not touch, elaborate, embellish.

On the Natural Faculties 2.82.6

of the natural capability of healing

6 αὐξάνεται μὲν γὰρ τὸ ὄν, γίγνεται δὲ τὸ οὐκ ὄν

That which *is* grows, while that which *is*

not becomes.

Translated by Arthur John Brock (1916)

On the Natural Faculties 2.88.8

7 ὅστις οὖν βούλεται τῶν τῆς φύσεως ἔργων γενέσθαι θεατής, οὐ χρὴ τοῦτον ἀνατομικαῖς βίβλοις πιστεύειν, ἀλλὰ τοῖς ἰδίοις ὄμμασιν

If anyone wishes to observe the works of nature, he should put his trust not in books of anatomy but in his own eyes.

Translated in *The Oxford Dictionary of Quotations* (2004)

On the Usefulness of the Parts of the Body 3.98.14

PSEUDO-GALEN

later than 2nd century AD

1 χειρουργία ἐστὶ χειρῶν ἀτρόμων ὀξεῖα κίνησις μετ' ἐμπειρίας

Surgery is the swift movement of steady, experienced hands.

On Diseases and Symptoms 19.358.1

GORGIAS

*c.*485–*c.*380BC

Sophist philosopher from Leontini

see also Lucian 26

1 οὐδὲν ἔστιν ... εἰ γὰρ ἔστι τι, ἤτοι τὸ ὂν ἔστιν ἢ τὸ μὴ ὄν, ἢ καὶ τὸ ὂν ἔστι καὶ τὸ μὴ ὄν· οὔτε δὲ τὸ ὂν ἔστιν, ὡς παραστήσει, οὔτε τὸ μὴ ὄν, ὡς παραμυθήσεται, οὔτε τὸ ὂν καὶ τὸ μὴ ὄν

Nothing exists; if anything exists, it must be either Being or Not-Being, or both Being and Not-Being; but it cannot be Not-Being, as will be shown, nor Being, as will also be supported, nor both Being and Not-Being.

Fragment 3 (D-K)

a good example of a sophist's reasoning; this syllogism is expounded in a long passage, beyond the scope of this book to include in full

2 δυναίμην ἃ βούλομαι ... λαθὼν μὲν τὴν θείαν νέμεσιν, φυγὼν δὲ τὸν ἀνθρώπινον φθόνον

Would that I could express what I wish, avoiding divine wrath, shunning human envy!

Translated by Kathleen Freeman (1948)

Fragment 6.9 (D-K)

3 τὸ δέον ἐν τῷ δέοντι καὶ λέγειν καὶ σιγᾶν καὶ ποιεῖν καὶ ἐᾶν

Say or keep silent, do or not do, the necessary thing at the necessary moment.

Translated by Kathleen Freeman (1948)

Fragment 6.15 (D-K)

from his Funeral Oration

4 θεράποντες μὲν τῶν ἀδίκως δυστυχούντων, κολασταὶ δὲ τῶν ἀδίκως εὐτυχούντων, αὐθάδεις πρὸς τὸ συμφέρον, εὐόργητοι πρὸς τὸ πρέπον

Helpers of those in undeserved adversity, chastisers of those in undeserved prosperity, bold for the common good, quick to feel for the right cause.

Translated by Kathleen Freeman (1948)

Fragment 6.18 (D-K)

from his Funeral Oration

5 κόσμος πόλει μὲν εὐανδρία, σώματι δὲ κάλλος, ψυχῇ δὲ σοφία, πράγματι δὲ ἀρετή, λόγῳ δὲ ἀλήθεια

The glory of a city is courage, of a body, beauty, of a soul, wisdom, of action, virtue, of speech, truth.

Translated by Kathleen Freeman (1948)

Fragment 11.1 (D-K)

from his Encomium on Helen

6 λόγος δυνάστης μέγας ἐστίν, ὃς σμικροτάτῳ σώματι καὶ ἀφανεστάτῳ θειότατα ἔργα ἀποτελεῖ· δύναται γὰρ καὶ φόβον παῦσαι καὶ λύπην ἀφελεῖν καὶ χαρὰν ἐνεργάσασθαι καὶ ἔλεον ἐπαυξῆσαι

Speech is a powerful master, achieving divine works by least visible means, able to put a stop to fear, remove grief, create joy, enhance pity.

Fragment 11.51 (D-K)

7 τὴν μὲν σπουδὴν διαφθείρειν τῶν ἐναντίων γέλωτι, τὸν δὲ γέλωτα σπουδῇ

Destroy the seriousness of an opponent with laughter, his laughter with seriousness.

Fragment 12 (D-K)

8 σὺ δὲ ταῦτα αἰσχρῶς μὲν ἔσπειρας, κακῶς δὲ ἐθέρισας

Foul was the deed you sowed and evil

the harvest you reaped.

Translated by W. Rhys Roberts (1858–1929), rev. Jonathan Barnes (1984)

Fragment 16 (D-K)

quoted by Aristotle, Rhetoric *1406b.9, berating it as exceedingly poetic*

9 ἡ τραγῳδία … πάθεσιν ἀπάτην … ἣν ὅ τ' ἀπατήσας δικαιότερος τοῦ μὴ ἀπατήσαντος καὶ ὁ ἀπατηθεὶς σοφώτερος τοῦ μὴ ἀπατηθέντος

Tragedy creates a deception in which the deceiver is more just than the nondeceiver and the deceived is wiser than the undeceived.

Translated by Patricia Curd, with S. Marc Cohen, and C.D.C. Reeve (2005)

Fragment 23 (D-K)

10 τοὺς φιλοσοφίας μὲν ἀμελοῦντας, περὶ δὲ τὰ ἐγκύκλια μαθήματα γινομένους ὁμοίους εἶναι τοῖς μνηστῆρσιν, οἳ Πηνελόπην θέλοντες ταῖς θεραπαίναις αὐτῆς ἐμίγνυντο

Those who do not care for philosophy, but engage in ordinary studies are like the suitors, who desired Penelope but slept with her hand-maids.

Translated by Patricia Curd, with S. Marc Cohen, and C.D.C. Reeve (2005)

ST GREGORY OF NAZIANZUS

329–389AD

Bishop and philosopher, educated in Athens

1 λαλεῖν εἰς ὦτα μὴ ἀκουόντων

Speaking to ears of those who will not hear.

Apologetics (Oration 2), vol. 35.460.32 (*MPG*)

2 ἡ μεγαλειότης, καὶ τὸ ὕψος … μόλις χωροῦσαι Θεοῦ λαμπρότητα, ὃν ἄβυσσος καλύπτει, οὗ σκότος ἀποκρυφή, φωτὸς ὄντος τοῦ καθαρωτάτου καὶ ἀπροσίτου τοῖς πλείοσιν

The majesty and the height of heaven can scarcely contain the brightness of God whose depth is unfathomed, whose hiding-place is darkness, although he himself is pure light and dwells in light inaccessible.

Translated by Giles E.M. Gasper (2004)

Apologetics (Oration 2), vol. 35.484.9 (*MPG*)

3 μὴ ἐπιλαθώμεθα τῆς ζάλης ἐν τῇ γαλήνῃ, μηδὲ τῆς ἀῤῥωστίας ἐν τῷ καιρῷ τῆς ὑγιείας

Let us not forget the tempest in the calm, nor sickness in time of health.

Against the Emperor Julian 2 (Oration 5), vol. 35.708.14 (*MPG*)

4 εἰ χρόνος ἐστὶν ἐμεῖο παροίτερος, οὐ πρὸ Λόγοιο
ὁ χρόνος, οὗ γενέτης ἔστ' ἄχρονος

Time may be prior to me
but time is not prior to the Word
whose Father is the Timeless One.

Translated by John McGuckin (1995)

Dogmatic Poems – On the Son, vol. 37.403.4 (*MPG*)

5 δεῦρ' ἄγε, πλαξὶ τεαῖς ὀλιγόστιχα ταῦτα χαράξω
γράμματ' ἐμῇ γραφίδι, ἣ μέλαν οὐδὲν ἔχει

Come here to me that I may cut these verses
on the tablet of your heart with a pen that needs no ink.

Translated by John McGuckin (1995)

Dogmatic Poems – On the Incarnation of Christ, vol. 37.471.13 (*MPG*)

6 πῶς λόγος ὑμνήσει σε; σὺ γὰρ λόγῳ οὐδενὶ ῥητόν·
πῶς νόος ἀθρήσει σε; σὺ γὰρ νόῳ οὐδενὶ ληπτός

How can words sing your praise
when no word can speak of you?
How can the mind consider you
when no mind can ever grasp you?

Translated by John McGuckin (1995)

Dogmatic Poems – Hymn to God, vol. 37.507.7 (*MPG*)

7 κρεῖσσον ἄριστον ἐόντα κακὸν γένος, ἠὲ κάκιστον
ἔμμεναι εὐγενέτην

Better to be the best of a lowly family, than the worst of a noble one.

Moral Poems, vol. 37.853.13 (*MPG*)

8 φύλλων λαγωοὺς ἐκφοβοῦσιν οἱ ψόφοι,
ἄνδρας δ' ἀνάνδρους αἱ σκιαὶ τῶν πραγμάτων

A mere sound will frighten hares away from crops,

cowardly men are frightened by a mere shadow.

Moral Poems, vol. 37.920.12 (*MPG*)

9 ἤδη μοι πολιόν τε κάρη, καὶ ἄψεα ῥικνὰ
ἐκλίνθη βιότοιο πρὸς ἕσπερον ἀλγινόεντος

Now my head is white, and my emaciated limbs
incline to the eventide of life that is full of pain.

Translated by C.A. Trypanis (1971)

To Himself, vol. 37.993.4 (*MPG*)

10 οὐδ᾽ ἐσθῆτά τις
οὕτως ἀμείβει ῥᾳδίως, ὡς σὺ τρόπον·
χθὲς ἐν χορευταῖς ἐστρέφου θηλυδρίαις
...
νῦν σωφρονιστὴς παρθένων καὶ συζύγων

No one changes even a shirt as you change manners!
Yesterday you twirled around with dancing girls,
today you come as chastener of wives and virgins.

To Himself, vol. 37.1196.14 (*MPG*)

11 τέθνηκα τῷδε τῷ ταλαιπώρῳ βίῳ,
ὃς φέρετ᾽ ἄνω κάτω τε, Εὐρίπου δίκην,
βέβαιον οὐδὲν, οὐδ᾽ ἐφ᾽ ἡμέραν, ἔχων

At last I have died to this life of pain,
which ebbs and flows like the restless sea,
nothing in it that endures
firm or stable even for a day.

Translated by John McGuckin (1995)

To Himself, vol. 37.1423.12 (*MPG*)

12 Ἑλλὰς ἐμὴ, νεότης τε φίλη, καὶ ὅσσα πέπασμαι,
καὶ δέμας, ὡς Χριστῷ εἴξατε προφρονέως·
... ἀλλά, Μάκαρ,
σοῖς με, Χριστὲ, χοροῖσι δέχου, καὶ κῦδος ὀπάζοις
υἱέϊ Γρηγορίου, σῷ λάτρι Γρηγορίῳ

O my Greece, my youth, my body, all that I possess,
how gladly you gave way to Christ! ...
And may you, blessed Christ,
receive me in your choirs, and grant glory
to your servant Gregory, the son of Gregory.

Translated by C.A. Trypanis (1971)

To Himself, vol. 37.1449.2 (*MPG*)

13 καιροῖο λαβώμεθα, ὃν προσιόντα ἔστιν ἑλεῖν, ζητεῖν δὲ παραθρέξαντα, μάταιον

Seize opportunity while it is here; it is pointless to seek it after it is gone.

On Others, vol. 37.1513.5 (*MPG*)

14 οὐδὲν γὰρ τοῦ πάσχειν εὑρετικώτερον

There is nothing more inventive than adversity.

Epistles 34.3

cf. the English proverb 'necessity is the mother of invention'

15 τὸ γὰρ κακίας ἐλεύθερον, καὶ ὑφορᾶσθαι κακίαν ἀργότερον

He who is free from vice is slower to suspect vice in others.

Epistles 40.2

16 χρυσὸς, ὁ ἀφανὴς τύραννος

Gold, the invisible tyrant.

To Those Having Come to Live in Egypt (Oration 34), vol. 36.244.36 (*MPG*)

17 πονηρῶν σπερμάτων πονηρὰ τὰ γεώργια

From evil seeds come evil harvests.

On the Birth of Christ (Oration 38), vol. 36.316.32 (*MPG*)

18 κἂν γὰρ τοὺς ἄλλους παραλογιζώμεθα, ἡμᾶς γε αὐτοὺς οὐ δυνησόμεθα

Even if we mislead others we may not mislead ourselves.

On Holy Baptism (Oration 40), vol. 36.381.44 (*MPG*)

19 ἕως θερμὸς ὁ σίδηρος, τῷ ψυχρῷ στομωθήτω

Harden the iron while it still is hot.

On Holy Baptism (Oration 40), vol. 36.396.7 (*MPG*)

of action not to be postponed

20 ποιήσωμεν τὴν ἀνάγκην φιλοτιμίαν

Let us turn necessity into a matter of honour.

In Praise of the Maccabeans (Oration 15), vol. 35.924.23 (*MPG*)

pretending it was your choice when in fact you could not do otherwise

H

HADRIAN
Publius Aelius Hadrianus
76–138AD
Roman emperor 117–138AD

1 Ἕκτορ ... κατὰ χθονὸς εἴ που ἀκούεις,
χαῖρε ...
παρίστασο καὶ λέγ' Ἀχιλλεῖ
Θεσσαλίην κεῖσθαι πᾶσαν ὑπ' Αἰνεάδαις

Hector, if thou hearest where'er thou art under ground, be of good cheer!
Go tell Achilles that now all Thessaly is subject to the sons of Aeneas.

Translated by W.R. Paton (1917)

Greek Anthology 9.387

also attributed to Germanicus

HECATAEUS
6th–5th century BC
Early Ionian prose-writer from Miletus

1 τάδε γράφω, ὥς μοι δοκεῖ ἀληθέα εἶναι· οἱ γὰρ Ἑλλήνων λόγοι πολλοί τε καὶ γελοῖοι, ὡς ἐμοὶ φαίνονται, εἰσίν

I write what seems to me to be true; for the Greeks have many tales which, as it appears to me, are absurd.

Translated by Stephanie Roberta West (2003)

Fragment 1a (*FGrH*)

HEDYLE
4th–3rd century BC
Poet, possibly Athenian

1 Γλαῦκον ἐρασθέντα Σκύλλης ... φέροντα
ἢ κόγχους δωρήματ' Ἐρυθραίης ἀπὸ πέτρης
ἢ τοὺς ἀλκυόνων παῖδας ἔτ' ἀπτερύγους
τῇ νύμφῃ δύσπιστος ἀθύρματα

Glaucus being in love with Scylla came to her cave
Bearing a gift of love, a mazy shell,
Fresh from the Erythrean rock, and with it too
The offspring, yet unfledged, of Halcyon,
To win th' obdurate maid. He gave in vain.

Translated by Charles Duke Yonge (1854)

Fragment 1 (Lloyd-Jones and Parsons, *SH*) – *Scylla*

the only surviving fragment of her work

HEDYLUS
fl. 280BC
Author of epigrams from Samos

1 Πίνωμεν· καὶ γάρ τι νέον, καὶ γάρ τι παρ' οἶνον
εὕροιμεν λεπτὸν καί τι μελιχρὸν ἔπος.

Let us drink. For, indeed, over wine we may find some new,
some elegant, some honey-sweet turn of speech.

Translated by C.A. Trypanis (1971)

Greek Anthology Appendix, Epigrammata exhortatoria et supplicatoria 26

HELIODORUS
3rd century AD
Novelist

1 τὰ μεγάλα τῶν πραγμάτων μεγάλων δεῖται κατασκευῶν

Great achievements require great preparations.

Ethiopian Story of Theagenes and Charicleia 9.24.3

HERACLITUS
*c.*540–*c.*480BC
Philosopher from Ephesus
see also Aristotle 76; Darius I 3; Socrates 51

1 τοῦ λόγου δ' ἐόντος ξυνοῦ ζώουσιν οἱ πολλοὶ ὡς ἰδίαν ἔχοντες φρόνησιν

But although the reasoning is common, most men live as though they had an insight of their own.

Fragment 2 (D-K)

2 τὸ ἀντίξουν συμφέρον καὶ ἐκ τῶν διαφερόντων καλλίστην ἁρμονίαν καὶ πάντα κατ' ἔριν γίνεσθαι

Antithesis brings advantage; from things that differ comes the fairest harmony; all things are born through strife.

Fragment 8 (D-K)

quoted by Aristotle, Nicomachean Ethics *1155b.5*

3 φησιν ὄνους σύρματ' ἂν ἑλέσθαι μᾶλλον ἢ χρυσόν

An ass would prefer chaff to gold.

Translated by H. Rackham (1926)

Fragment 9 (D-K)

4 συνάψιες ὅλα καὶ οὐχ ὅλα, συμφερόμενον διαφερόμενον, συνᾷδον διᾷδον, καὶ ἐκ πάντων ἓν καὶ ἐξ ἑνὸς πάντα

Connected are wholes and non-wholes, homogeneity and heterogeneity, unity and duality, all becomes one and one becomes all.

Translated by Karl Popper (1973)

Fragment 10 (D-K)

5 πᾶν γὰρ ἑρπετὸν πληγῇ νέμεται

Every creature is driven afield with blows.

Translated in Liddell & Scott

Fragment 11 (D-K)

6 δὶς ἐς τὸν αὐτὸν ποταμὸν οὐκ ἂν ἐμβαίης ... ἕτερα γὰρ καὶ ἕτερα ὕδατα ἐπιρρεῖ

You cannot step twice into the selfsame stream; for fresh waters are ever flowing in upon you.

Fragment 12.4 and Testimony 6 (D-K)

several 'River' versions of Heraclitus exist; this is a combination of two, from Plato, Cratylus *402a, and Arius Didymus,* Physica; *but see also Heraclitus 22*

7 οὐ γὰρ φρονέουσι τοιαῦτα πολλοί, ὁκόσοι ἐγκυρεῦσιν, οὐδὲ μαθόντες γινώσκουσιν, ἑωυτοῖσι δὲ δοκέουσι

Many people learn nothing from what they see and experience, nor do they understand what they hear explained, but only imagine that they have.

Translated by Guy Davenport (1976)

Fragment 17 (D-K)

8 ἐὰν μὴ ἔλπηται, ἀνέλπιστον οὐκ ἐξευρήσει, ἀνεξερεύνητον ἐὸν καὶ ἄπορον

He who does not expect the unexpected will not detect it; for him it will remain undetectable and unapproachable.

Translated by Karl Popper (1958)

Fragment 18 (D-K)

9 θάνατός ἐστιν ὁκόσα ἐγερθέντες ὁρέομεν, ὁκόσα δὲ εὕδοντες ὕπνος

All that we see when we have wakened is death; all that we see while slumbering is sleep.

Translated by Kathleen Freeman (1948)

Fragment 21 (D-K)

10 ἀρηιφάτους θεοὶ τιμῶσι καὶ ἄνθρωποι

Gods and men honour those slain in battle.

Translated by Jonathan Barnes (1987)

Fragment 24 (D-K)

11 ἄνθρωπος ἐν εὐφρόνῃ φάος ἅπτεται ἑαυτῷ ἀποθανὼν ἀποσβεσθεὶς ὄψεις

Man, like a light in the night, is kindled and put out.

Translated by W.H.S. Jones (1931)

Fragment 26 (D-K)

12 ἀνθρώπους μένει ἀποθανόντας ἅσσα οὐκ ἔλπονται οὐδὲ δοκέουσιν

There awaits men when they die what they do not expect or imagine.

Translated by Jonathan Barnes (1979)

Fragment 27 (D-K)

13 αἱρεῦνται γὰρ ἓν ἀντὶ ἁπάντων οἱ ἄριστοι, κλέος ἀέναον θνητῶν· οἱ δὲ πολλοὶ κεκόρηνται ὅκωσπερ κτήνεα

The virtuous choose only everlasting fame; the many seek to satisfy themselves, like beasts.

Fragment 29 (D-K)

14 κόσμον τόνδε, τὸν αὐτὸν ἁπάντων, οὔτε τις θεῶν οὔτε ἀνθρώπων ἐποίησεν, ἦν ἀεὶ καὶ ἔστιν καὶ ἔσται πῦρ ἀείζωον, ἁπτόμενον μέτρα καὶ ἀποσβεννύμενον μέτρα

This world was not created, but ever was and is and shall be everlasting Fire, kindled in measure and quenched in measure.

Fragment 30 (D-K)

15 ἀξύνετοι ἀκούσαντες κωφοῖσιν ἐοίκασι

Fools though they hear are like the deaf.

Translated by John Burnet (1892)

Fragment 34 (D-K)

16 πολυμαθίη νόον ἔχειν οὐ διδάσκει

Much learning does not teach sense.

Translated by Jonathan Barnes (1987)

Fragment 40 (D-K)

17 ὕβριν χρὴ σβεννύναι μᾶλλον ἢ πυρκαϊήν

Quench hubris rather than a conflagration.

Fragment 43 (D-K)

18 μάχεσθαι χρὴ τὸν δῆμον ὑπὲρ τοῦ νόμου ὅκωσπερ τείχεος

The people must defend their laws just as their city walls.

Fragment 44 (D-K)

19 ψυχῆς πείρατα ἰὼν οὐκ ἂν ἐξεύροιο, πᾶσαν ἐπιπορευόμενος ὁδόν· οὕτω βαθὺν λόγον ἔχει

The limits of the soul you will not discover, not even if you travel every road; for its depth is limitless.

Fragment 45 (D-K)

20 μὴ εἰκῆ περὶ τῶν μεγίστων συμβαλλώμεθα

Do not pass random judgement on serious matters.

Fragment 47 (D-K)

21 εἷς ἐμοὶ μύριοι, ἐὰν ἄριστος ᾖ

One good man is worth ten thousand.

Fragment 49 (D-K)

22 ποταμοῖς τοῖς αὐτοῖς ἐμβαίνομέν τε καὶ οὐκ ἐμβαίνομεν, εἶμέν τε καὶ οὐκ εἶμεν

Into the same rivers we enter and we enter not; we are and we are not.

Fragment 49a (D-K)

for more 'River' fragments see Heraclitus 6

23 οὐκ ἐμοῦ, ἀλλὰ τοῦ λόγου ἀκούσαντας ὁμολογεῖν σοφόν ἐστιν ἓν πάντα εἶναι

It is wise to listen, not to me but to the Word, and to agree that all things are one.

Translated by W.H.S. Jones (1931)

Fragment 50 (D-K)

24 οὐ ξυνιᾶσιν ὅκως διαφερόμενον ἑωυτῷ ὁμολογέει· παλίντροπος ἁρμονίη ὅκωσπερ τόξου καὶ λύρης

That which differs with itself is in agreement; harmony consists of opposing tension, like that of the bow and the lyre.

Translated by Kathleen Freeman (1948)

Fragment 51 (D-K)

25 αἰὼν παῖς ἐστι παίζων, πεσσεύων· παιδὸς ἡ βασιληίη

Eternity is a child at play, playing draughts: the kingdom is a child's.

Translated by Jonathan Barnes (1987)

Fragment 52 (D-K)

26 πόλεμος πάντων μὲν πατήρ ἐστι, πάντων δὲ βασιλεύς

War is father of all, king of all.

Translated by Jonathan Barnes (1987)

Fragment 53 (D-K)

basically reflecting Heraclitus' theory that strife is the source of all progress

27 ἁρμονίη ἀφανὴς φανερῆς κρείττων

Hidden harmony is stronger than the manifest.

Fragment 54 (D-K)

28 ὅσων ὄψις ἀκοὴ μάθησις, ταῦτα ἐγὼ προτιμέω

Vision, hearing, learning – these I honour most.

Fragment 55 (D-K)

29 ἐξηπάτηνται, φησίν, οἱ ἄνθρωποι πρὸς τὴν γνῶσιν τῶν φανερῶν

Men have been deceived as to their knowledge of what is apparent.

Translated by Jonathan Barnes (1987)

Fragment 56 (D-K)

30 ὁδὸς ἄνω κάτω μία καὶ ὡυτή

The road up and the road down is one and the same.

Translated by W.H.S. Jones (1931)

Fragment 60 (D-K)

31 τὰ δὲ πάντα οἰακίζει Κεραυνός

The thunderbolt governs the universe.

Fragment 64 (D-K)

for 'thunderbolt' one may also read 'eternal fire' (after Hippolytus, Philosophoumena *9.10.7), or 'energy'*

32 ὁ θεὸς ἡμέρη εὐφρόνη, χειμὼν θέρος, πόλεμος εἰρήνη, κόρος λιμός

God is day and night, winter and summer, war and peace, satiety and famine.

Translated by Jonathan Barnes (1987)

Fragment 67 (D-K)

33 οὐ δεῖ ὥσπερ καθεύδοντας ποιεῖν καὶ λέγειν

We should not act and speak like those asleep.

Translated by Jonathan Barnes (1987)

Fragment 73 (D-K)

34 ἀνθρώπων ὁ σοφώτατος πρὸς θεὸν πίθηκος φανεῖται καὶ σοφίᾳ καὶ κάλλει καὶ τοῖς ἄλλοις πᾶσιν

The wisest of men, compared to god, seems an ape in wisdom and beauty and all else.

Fragment 83 (D-K)

35 θυμῷ μάχεσθαι χαλεπόν· ὃ γὰρ ἂν θέλῃ, ψυχῆς ὠνεῖται

It is hard to fight against impulse; whatever it wishes, it buys at the expense of the soul.

Translated by Kathleen Freeman (1948)

Fragment 85 (D-K)

36 βλὰξ ἄνθρωπος ἐπὶ παντὶ λόγῳ ἐπτοῆσθαι φιλεῖ

A foolish man is put in a flutter by every word.

Translated by Jonathan Barnes (1987)

Fragment 87 (D-K)

37 ταὐτό τ' ἔνι ζῶν καὶ τεθνηκὸς καὶ [τὸ] ἐγρηγορὸς καὶ καθεῦδον καὶ νέον καὶ γηραιόν· τάδε γὰρ μεταπεσόντα ἐκεῖνά ἐστι κἀκεῖνα πάλιν μεταπεσόντα ταῦτα

They all are the same, the living and the dead, those who are awake and asleep, young and old. For these turn into those and those into these.

Translated by Karl Popper (1969)

Fragment 88 (D-K)

38 φησι τοῖς ἐγρηγορόσιν ἕνα καὶ κοινὸν κόσμον εἶναι, τῶν δὲ κοιμωμένων ἕκαστον εἰς ἴδιον ἀποστρέφεσθαι

Awake we have a common world, asleep each enters a world of his own.

Fragment 89 (D-K)

quoted by Plutarch, On Superstition *166c*

39 πυρός τε ἀνταμοιβὴ τὰ πάντα καὶ πῦρ ἁπάντων ὅκωσπερ χρυσοῦ χρήματα καὶ χρημάτων χρυσός

All things for fire and fire for all things, like goods for gold and gold for goods.

Translated by Kathleen Freeman (1948)

Fragment 90 (D-K)

40 Σίβυλλα δὲ μαινομένῳ στόματι ... ἀγέλαστα καὶ ἀκαλλώπιστα καὶ ἀμύριστα φθεγγομένη χιλίων ἐτῶν ἐξικνεῖται τῇ φωνῇ διὰ τὸν θεόν

There is madness in the Sibyl's voice, her words are gloomy, ugly, and rough, but they are true for a thousand years, because a god speaks through her.

Translated by Guy Davenport (1976)

Fragment 92 (D-K)

41 ἀμαθίην γὰρ ἄμεινον κρύπτειν, ἔργον δὲ ἐν ἀνέσει καὶ παρ' οἶνον

It is better to hide ignorance, but it is hard to do this when we relax over wine.

Translated by W.H.S. Jones (1931)

Fragment 95 (D-K)

42 ἐδιζησάμην ἐμεωυτόν

I searched myself.

Translated by Karl Popper (1965)

Fragment 101 (D-K)

43 ὀφθαλμοὶ γὰρ τῶν ὤτων ἀκριβέστεροι μάρτυρες

Eyes are more accurate witnesses than ears.

Translated by Jonathan Barnes (1987)

Fragment 101a (D-K)

44 τῷ μὲν θεῷ καλὰ πάντα καὶ ἀγαθὰ καὶ δίκαια, ἄνθρωποι δὲ ἃ μὲν ἄδικα ὑπειλήφασιν ἃ δὲ δίκαια

For god all things are beautiful and good and just, but men assume some things to be unjust, and others to be just.

Translated by Karl Popper (1958)

Fragment 102 (D-K)

45 ξυνὸν γὰρ ἀρχὴ καὶ πέρας ἐπὶ κύκλου περιφερείας

Common are beginning and end on the circumference of a circle.

Fragment 103 (D-K)

46 σοφόν ἐστι πάντων κεχωρισμένον

Wisdom is set apart from all things.

Fragment 108 (D-K)

47 ἀνθρώποις γίνεσθαι ὁκόσα θέλουσιν οὐκ ἄμεινον

It is not good for men to get all they want.

Translated by Jonathan Barnes (1987)

Fragment 110 (D-K)

48 σωφρονεῖν ἀρετὴ μεγίστη, καὶ σοφίη ἀληθέα λέγειν καὶ ποιεῖν κατὰ φύσιν ἐπαΐοντας

Moderation is the greatest virtue, and wisdom is to speak the truth and to act according to nature.

Translated by Kathleen Freeman (1948)

Fragment 112 (D-K)

49 ἀνθρώποισι πᾶσι μέτεστι γινώσκειν ἑωυτοὺς καὶ σωφρονεῖν

All men are capable of self knowledge and moderation.

Fragment 116 (D-K)

50 ἦθος ἀνθρώπῳ δαίμων

A man's character is his fate.

Translated by W.H.S. Jones (1931)

Fragment 119 (D-K)

51 φύσις κρύπτεσθαι φιλεῖ

The real nature of things loves to hide itself.

Translated by Karl Popper (1958)

Fragments 123 and 54 (D-K)

52 πολυμαθίην, κακοτεχνίην

Much learning, poor workmanship.

Translated by R.D. Hicks (1925)

Fragment 129 (D-K)

on the writings of Pythagoras

53 τὴν παιδείαν ἕτερον ἥλιον εἶναι τοῖς πεπαιδευμένοις

Education is another sun to those who are educated.

Translated by Kathleen Freeman (1948)

Fragment 134 (D-K)

54 γίνεσθαί τε πάντα κατ' ἐναντιότητα καὶ ῥεῖν τὰ ὅλα ποταμοῦ δίκην

All things come into being by conflict of opposites, and the sum of things flows like a stream.

Translated by R.D. Hicks (1925)

Testimonies, Fragment 1.49 (D-K)

55 εἷς ἐμοὶ ἄνθρωπος τρισμύριοι, οἱ δ' ἀνάριθμοι οὐδείς

One man for me is as thirty thousand; a crowd as no one.

Testimonies, Fragment 1.102 (D-K)

an epigram written on Heraclitus

56 πάντα χωρεῖ καὶ οὐδὲν μένει

Everything is in flux, and nothing is at rest.

Translated by Karl Popper (1958)

Testimonies, Fragment 6 (D-K)

often quoted as πάντα ῥεῖ; quoted by Plato, Cratylus *402a; cf. Žarko Petan (1929–), Slovenian writer, Aphorisms: 'All flows', said the modern day Heraclitus, 'and we cannot find a plumber!'*

57 ἐκέλευε γὰρ αὐτοὺς εἰσιέναι θαρροῦντας· εἶναι γὰρ καὶ ἐνταῦθα θεούς

Heraclitus invited them to enter without fear; for even here the gods exist.

Testimonies, Fragment 9 (D-K)

cf. Aristotle, Parts of Animals *645a 20; used by Lessing as an epigraph to* Nathan der Weise *in the Latin form 'introite, nam et hic dii sunt' (attributing it to Gellius)*

HERMES TRISMEGISTUS

2nd–4th century AD
A later name for the Egyptian god Thoth

1 θεὸν νοῆσαι μὲν χαλεπόν, φράσαι δὲ ἀδύνατον ᾧ καὶ νοῆσαι δυνατόν· τὸ γὰρ ἀσώματον σώματι σημῆναι ἀδύνατον, καὶ τὸ τέλειον τῷ ἀτελεῖ καταλαβέσθαι οὐ δυνατόν, καὶ τὸ αἴδιον τῷ ὀλιγοχρονίῳ συγγενέσθαι δύσκολον

To apprehend god is difficult, to explain him impossible even if one is able to apprehend him; for it is impossible for the corporeal to interpret the incorporeal, for the imperfect to grasp the perfect, for the ephemeral to converse with the eternal.

Corpus Hermeticum, Fragment 1 (Nock and Festugière, *CH*)

the Corpus Hermeticum, *also referred to as* Hermes Trismegistus, *is a collection of texts which was at the time popular with Neoplatonists who associated Thoth with Hermes*

2 δευρό μοι, ὁ ἐκ τῶν δ' ἀνέμων, ὁ παντοκράτωρ, ὁ ἐμφυσήσας πνεῦμα ἀνθρώποις εἰς ζωήν ... οὗ καὶ οἱ δαίμονες ἀκούοντες τὸ ὄνομα πτοῶνται ... σὺ εἶ ὁ ἀγαθὸς δαίμων. σὺ εἶ ὁ ὠκεανός, ὁ γεννῶν ἀγαθὰ καὶ τροφῶν τὴν οἰκουμένην ... ὁ βασιλεύων τῶν οὐρανῶν καὶ τῆς γῆς ... σὺ γὰρ εἶ ἐγὼ καὶ ἐγὼ σύ

Come you out of the winds, the almighty, who breathed the spirit of life into man, by whose very name demons are terrified, you the benevolent god, an ocean giving wealth and food to the world, ruler of heaven and earth. You are I and I am you.

Papyri magicae 13.761 (Preisendanz and Henrichs, *PGM*)

this extract is classed by some scholars under Hermes Trismegistus

HERMIPPUS

5th century BC
Athenian Old Comedy poet

1 τὴν μὲν διάλεκτον καὶ τὸ πρόσωπον ἀμνίου
ἔχειν δοκεῖς, τὰ δ' ἔνδον οὐδὲν διαφέρεις δράκοντος

Lamb-like your countenance and the sounds you make,
But in your heart you're nothing but a snake.

Translated by Kathleen Freeman (1947)

Fragment 3 (Kock) – 3 (K-A) – *Athinas Gonai – Birth of Athena*

HERMOCRATES

died 408BC
Syracusan statesman and general

1 νομίσαι τε στάσιν μάλιστα φθείρειν τὰς πόλεις

Remember that faction is the chief cause of ruin to states.

Translated by Charles Forster Smith (1920)

Thucydides, *History of the Peloponnesian War* 4.61.1

2 οὐ τοῖς ἄρχειν βουλομένοις μέμφομαι, ἀλλὰ τοῖς ὑπακούειν ἑτοιμοτέροις οὖσιν

My complaint is not of those who seek domination, but rather of those who are ready to submit to it.

Translated by Martin Hammond (2009)

Thucydides, *History of the Peloponnesian War* 4.61.5.2

3 πέφυκε γὰρ τὸ ἀνθρώπειον διὰ παντὸς ἄρχειν μὲν τοῦ εἴκοντος, φυλάσσεσθαι δὲ τὸ ἐπιόν

It is an instinct of man's nature always to rule those who yield, but to guard against those who are ready to attack.

Translated by Charles Forster Smith (1920)

Thucydides, *History of the Peloponnesian War* 4.61.5.4

4 εὐπρεπῶς ἄδικοι ἐλθόντες εὐλόγως ἄπρακτοι ἀπίασιν

They came with a false pretext for injustice and it is with good reason that they depart in failure.

Thucydides, *History of the Peloponnesian*

War 4.61.7

of the Athenians

5 τὸ δὲ ἀστάθμητον τοῦ μέλλοντος ὡς ἐπὶ πλεῖστον κρατεῖ

As regards the future, it is uncertainty that for the most part prevails.

Translated by Charles Forster Smith (1920)

Thucydides, *History of the Peloponnesian War* 4.62.4

6 οὐδὲν γὰρ αἰσχρὸν οἰκείους οἰκείων ἡσσᾶσθαι

There is no disgrace in kinsmen giving way to kinsmen.

Translated by Charles Forster Smith (1920)

Thucydides, *History of the Peloponnesian War* 4.64.3

7 οὐ καταφοβηθεὶς ἐπισχήσω κινδυνευούσης τῆς πόλεως

I will not be frightened into holding my tongue when the state is in danger.

Translated by Charles Forster Smith (1921)

Thucydides, *History of the Peloponnesian War* 6.33.1

8 καὶ πρὸς ἄνδρας τολμηρούς ... τοὺς ἀντιτολμῶντας χαλεπωτάτους αὐτοῖς φαίνεσθαι

Those who with daring confront daring men appear most formidable to them.

Translated by Charles Forster Smith (1923)

Thucydides, *History of the Peloponnesian War* 7.21.3

encouraging the Syracusans to attack the Athenian fleet

HERMOLOCHUS

late 4th century BC (?)
Lyric poet

1 ἀτέκμαρτος ὁ πᾶς βίος οὐδὲν ἔχων
πιστὸν πλανᾶται
συντυχίαις

Man's whole life is baffling, without security, sent astray by events.

Translated by David A. Campbell (1993)

Fragment 1 (Page, *PMG*)

also attributed to Hermarchus

2 ἀντιπνεῖ δὲ πολλάκις εὐτυχίᾳ δεινά τις
αὔρα

Often a grim breeze blows in the face of success.

Translated by David A. Campbell (1993)

Fragment 1.5 (Page, *PMG*)

also attributed to Hermarchus

HERODAS

fl. 240BC
Eight comic poems known, all in the mimiambic mode

1 ἅπαντα ταῦτ' ἔπρηξε κοὐκ ἐπηδέσθη
οὔτε νόμον οὔτε προστάτην οὔτ' ἄρχοντα

He did all that without respect
for either law or patron or any magistrate.

Mimiamboi 2.40 (Cunningham)

of a brothel-keeper

2 ἐπίσταται δ' οὐδ' ἄλφα συλλαβὴν γνῶναι

He cannot grasp even the alpha of my train of thought.

Mimiamboi 3.22 (Cunningham)

3 μὴ δή, Κοριττοῖ, τὴν χολὴν ἐπὶ ῥινός
ἔχ' εὐθύς, ἤν τι ῥῆμα μὴ σοφὸν πεύθῃ·
γυναικός ἐστι κρηγύης φέρειν πάντα

Do not make your anger too obvious, my girl,
when an untoward message comes;
good women cope with all adversity.

Mimiamboi 6.37 (Cunningham)

4 τὰ μέλεα πολλοὶ κάρτα, τοὺς ἐμοὺς
μόχθους, τιλεῦσιν

Many will there be, ready to tear to pieces my poems, my travail.

Mimiamboi 8.71 (Cunningham)

of critics

5 ὡς οἰκίην οὐκ ἔστιν εὐμαρέως εὑρεῖν
ἄνευ κακῶν ζώουσαν· ὃς δ' ἔχει μεῖον,
τοῦτόν τι μέζον τοῦ ἑτέρου δόκει
πρήσσειν

It is not easy to find a home
without some misfortune; whoever has less
can be considered the more fortunate.

Mimiamboi 13 (Cunningham)

HERODORUS

fl. late 6th century BC
Historian from Heraclea Pontica

1 τρεῖς ἀρετάς, τὸ μὴ ὀργίζεσθαι, τὸ μὴ φιλαργυρεῖν, τὸ μὴ φιληδονεῖν

Three are the virtues: refrain from anger, refrain from avarice, refrain from the pursuit of pleasure.

Fragment 24b (Müller, *FHG*)

HERODOTUS

*c.*484–*c.*425BC
Historian from Halicarnassus
see also Darius, Lucian 12, Xerxes

1 Ἡροδότου Θουρίου ἱστορίης ἀπόδεξις ἥδε, ὡς μήτε τὰ γενόμενα ἐξ ἀνθρώπων τῷ χρόνῳ ἐξίτηλα γένηται, μήτε ἔργα μεγάλα τε καὶ θωμαστά, τὰ μὲν Ἕλλησι, τὰ δὲ βαρβάροισι ἀποδεχθέντα, ἀκλέα γένηται, τά τε ἄλλα καὶ δι' ἣν αἰτίην ἐπολέμησαν ἀλλήλοισι

Herodotus the Halicarnassian here sets forth what he has learnt by inquiry, in order to preserve in memory the great and marvellous deeds, by Greeks and foreigners alike, and why they waged war against each other.

Histories 1 P

Preamble, first lines; cf. Thucydides 6, Plutarch 81; cf. also Cicero, De legibus *1.1.5 who calls Herodotus 'Pater historiae', the Father of History, as he has been known since*

2 καὶ Ἕλληνες λέγουσι, Ἰοῦν τὴν Ἰνάχου τὴν τοῦ βασιλέος θυγατέρα ... τοὺς Φοίνικας ἁρπασθῆναι ... μετὰ δὲ ταῦτα Ἑλλήνων τινάς ... φασὶ τῆς Φοινίκης ἁρπάσαι ... τοῦ βασιλέος τὴν θυγατέρα Εὐρώπην· εἴησαν δ' ἂν οὗτοι Κρῆτες· ταῦτα μὲν δὴ ἴσα πρὸς ἴσα σφι γενέσθαι

The Greeks say that the Phoenicians carried away Io, king Inachus' daughter; after which some Greeks (Cretans I suppose) carried off the Phoenician king's daughter, Europe. So far, then, they were quits.

Histories 1.1–2

3 δῆλα γὰρ δὴ ὅτι, εἰ μὴ αὐταὶ ἐβούλοντο, οὐκ ἂν ἡρπάζοντο

It is obvious that these women would never have been carried away, had not they themselves been willing.

Histories 1.4.4

4 τὴν γὰρ Ἀσίην καὶ τὰ ἐνοικέοντα ἔθνεα βάρβαρα οἰκηιεῦνται οἱ Πέρσαι, τὴν δὲ Εὐρώπην καὶ τὸ Ἑλληνικὸν ἥγηνται κεχωρίσθαι

The Persians claim Asia and the foreign nations that inhabit it as their own – considering Europe and Greece as something separate.

Histories 1.4.14

5 τὰ γὰρ τὸ πάλαι μεγάλα ἦν, τὰ πολλὰ αὐτῶν σμικρὰ γέγονε· τὰ δὲ ἐπ' ἐμεῦ ἦν μεγάλα, πρότερον ἦν σμικρά. τὴν ἀνθρωπηίην ὦν ἐπιστάμενος εὐδαιμονίην οὐδαμὰ ἐν τὠυτῷ μένουσαν, ἐπιμνήσομαι ἀμφοτέρων ὁμοίως

Many states that were once great have now become small; and those that were great in my time were previously small. Knowing that human prosperity is ever-changing, I will speak of both alike.

Histories 1.5

6 οὗτος δὴ ὦν ἠράσθη τῆς ἑωυτοῦ γυναικός, ἐρασθεὶς δὲ ἐνόμιζέ οἱ εἶναι γυναῖκα πολλὸν πασέων καλλίστην

He fell in love with his own wife, so much that he supposed her to be by far the fairest woman in the world.

Translated by A.D. Godley (1920)

Histories 1.8.1

of Candaules, ruler of Sardis

7 ὦτα γὰρ τυγχάνει ἀνθρώποισι ἐόντα ἀπιστότερα ὀφθαλμῶν· ποίεε ὅκως ἐκείνην θεήσεαι γυμνήν

Men trust their ears less than their eyes; contrive, then, to see her naked.

Histories 1.8.8

the ruler of Sardis admiring the beauty of his wife

8 ἅμα δὲ κιθῶνι ἐκδυομένῳ συνεκδύεται καὶ τὴν αἰδῶ γυνή

A woman takes off her claim to respect along with her garments.

Translated in *Bartlett's Familiar Quotations* (1980)

Histories 1.8.14

9 ἐς τὸ ἔσχατον κακοῦ

To the last extremity of misery.

Translated by A.D. Godley (1920)

Histories 1.22

10 τὸ δὲ Ἑλληνικὸν ... ἀπὸ σμικροῦ τεο τὴν ἀρχὴν ὁρμώμενον αὔξηται ἐς πλῆθος τῶν ἐθνέων

The Hellenic stock has grown from a small beginning to comprise a multitude of nations

Translated by A.D. Godley (1920)

Histories 1.58

11 ἐκ παλαιτέρου τοῦ βαρβάρου ἔθνεος τὸ Ἑλληνικὸν ἐὸν καὶ δεξιώτερον καὶ εὐηθείης ἠλιθίου ἀπηλλαγμένον μᾶλλον

From ancient times the Hellenic stock has been distinguished from the barbarian by its greater intelligence and freedom from foolishness.

Histories 1.60

12 οὐ πολλῷ λόγῳ εἰπεῖν

To cut a long story short.

Translated by Robin Waterfield (1998)

Histories 1.61

13 καὶ μετὰ τὸ ἄριστον μετεξέτεροι αὐτῶν οἱ μὲν πρὸς κύβους, οἱ δὲ πρὸς ὕπνον

And after the midday meal some betook themselves to dicing and some to sleep.

Histories 1.63

14 κακονομώτατοι ἦσαν σχεδὸν πάντων Ἑλλήνων κατά τε σφέας αὐτοὺς καὶ ξείνοισι ἀπρόσμικτοι

They were the worst governed of well nigh all the Greeks, having little intercourse among themselves or with strangers.

Translated by A.D. Godley (1920)

Histories 1.65

of the Lacedaemonians

15 καὶ δή σφι οὐκέτι ἀπέχρα ἡσυχίην ἄγειν

Nor were they satisfied to remain at peace.

Translated by A.D. Godley (1920)

Histories 1.66

of the Lacedaemonians

16 συντυχίῃ χρησάμενος καὶ σοφίῃ

By means of luck and cunning.

Histories 1.68

on finding the tomb of Orestes; cf. Oracles 4

17 προσκαλέομαι φίλος τε θέλων γενέσθαι καὶ σύμμαχος ἄνευ τε δόλου καὶ ἀπάτης

I would fain be your friend and ally, without deceit or guile.

Translated by A.D. Godley (1920)

Histories 1.69

18 τῆς μάχης συνεστεώσης, τὴν ἡμέρην ἐξαπίνης νύκτα γενέσθαι. τὴν δὲ μεταλλαγὴν ταύτην τῆς ἡμέρης Θαλῆς ὁ Μιλήσιος ... προηγόρευσε ἔσεσθαι, οὖρον προθέμενος ἐνιαυτὸν

During the battle day suddenly turned to night. Thales of Miletus had foretold this eclipse, predicting it to within a year.

Histories 1.74.8

between Lydians and Medes, who agreed to peace after the 'miracle'; cf. Archilochus 11

19 ἄνευ γὰρ ἀναγκαίης ἰσχυρῆς συμβάσιες ἰσχυραὶ οὐκ ἐθέλουσι συμμένειν

Treaties will not hold without determined dedication.

Histories 1.74.19

20 ἐς ἀπορίην πολλὴν ἀπιγμένος, ὥς οἱ παρὰ δόξαν ἔσχε τὰ πρήγματα ἢ ὡς αὐτὸς κατεδόκεε

Everything had turned out contrary to expectations, and he was in a great quandary.

Histories 1.79

of Croesus

21 ἐποιήσαντο νόμον τε καὶ κατάρην

They made a law, with a curse added thereto.

Translated by A.D. Godley (1920)

Histories 1.82

22 κατὰ τὸ χρηστήριόν τε καταπαύσαντα τὴν ἑωυτοῦ μεγάλην ἀρχήν

And as the oracle had foretold he had put an end to a great empire – his own.

Translated by Robin Waterfield (1998)

Histories 1.86.3

of Croesus; cf. Oracles 7

23 ἐπιλεξάμενον ὡς οὐδὲν εἴη τῶν ἐν ἀνθρώποισι ἀσφαλέως ἔχον

He reflected on the total lack of certainty in human life.

Translated by Robin Waterfield (1998)

Histories 1.86.36

Cyrus on the fate of Croesus

24 οὐδεὶς γὰρ οὕτω ἀνόητός ἐστι ὅστις πόλεμον πρὸ εἰρήνης αἱρέεται· ἐν μὲν γὰρ τῇ οἱ παῖδες τοὺς πατέρας θάπτουσι, ἐν δὲ τῷ οἱ πατέρες τοὺς παῖδας

No man is so foolish as to desire war more than peace; for in peace sons bury their fathers, but in war fathers bury their sons.

Translated by A.D. Godley (1920)

Histories 1.87

spoken by Croesus

25 εἰ ἐξαπατᾶν τοὺς εὖ ποιεῦντας νόμος ἐστί οἱ

Ask if it be his custom to deceive those who serve him well.

Translated by A.D. Godley (1920)

Histories 1.90

Croesus of Apollo deceiving suppliants to the Oracle at Delphi

26 ἐξευρεθῆναι δὴ ὦν τότε καὶ τῶν κύβων καὶ τῶν ἀστραγάλων καὶ τῆς σφαίρης καὶ τῶν ἀλλέων πασέων παιγνιέων τὰ εἴδεα, πλὴν πεσσῶν· τούτων γὰρ ὦν τὴν ἐξεύρεσιν οὐκ οἰκηιοῦνται Λυδοί

It was then that they invented the games of dice and knuckle-bones and ball, and all other forms of pastime except for draughts, which the Lydians do not claim to have discovered.

Translated by A.D. Godley (1920)

Histories 1.94

the Lydians invented games to distract themselves from their hunger during times of famine

27 ἐρασθεὶς τυραννίδος

A passionate desire for power.

Histories 1.96.4

28 τῷ δικαίῳ τὸ ἄδικον πολέμιόν ἐστι

Injustice is ever the foe of justice.

Translated by A.D. Godley (1920)

Histories 1.96.9

29 κατ' ἀξίην ἑκάστου ἀδικήματος ἐδικαίευ

Punish as befits each offence.

Histories 1.100

30 εἶδόν τε ἐς πόλιν ἐλθὼν καὶ ἤκουσα τὸ μήτε ἰδεῖν ὤφελον

When I came to the city, I saw and heard what I would never have wished to see or hear.

Histories 1.111

31 τὴν μὲν γὰρ προτέρην ἡμέρην πάντα σφι κακὰ ἔχειν, τὴν δὲ τότε παρεοῦσαν πάντα ἀγαθά

Yesterday was naught but evil and today naught but good.

Histories 1.126

32 μεθυσκόμενοι δὲ ἐώθασι βουλεύεσθαι τὰ σπουδαιέστατα τῶν πρηγμάτων

It is their custom to deliberate about the gravest matters when they are drunk.

Translated by A.D. Godley (1920)

Histories 1.133

of the Persians

33 νομίζοντες ἑωυτοὺς εἶναι ἀνθρώπων μακρῷ τὰ πάντα ἀρίστους

They deem themselves to be in all regards by far the best of men.

Translated by A.D. Godley (1920)

Histories 1.134

of the Persians

34 τὸ πολλὸν δ' ἥγηνται ἰσχυρὸν εἶναι

Strength, they hold, lies in numbers.

Histories 1.136

of the Persians

35 αἰνέω δὲ καὶ τόνδε τὸν νόμον, τὸ μὴ μιῆς αἰτίης εἵνεκα μήτε αὐτὸν τὸν βασιλέα μηδένα φονεύειν

I consider this to be a great law, where not even the king can condemn a man to death for only one offence.

Histories 1.137

of a Persian law

36 αἴσχιστον δὲ αὐτοῖσι τὸ ψεύδεσθαι νενόμισται, δεύτερα δὲ τὸ ὀφείλειν χρέος

They hold lying to be the foulest of all offences and, next to that, debt.

Translated by A.D. Godley (1920)

Histories 1.138
of the Persians; but see Darius I 1

37 τοῦ μὲν οὐρανοῦ καὶ τῶν ὡρέων ἐν τῷ καλλίστῳ ἐτύγχανον ἱδρυσάμενοι πόλιας πάντων ἀνθρώπων τῶν ἡμεῖς ἴδμεν

They had built their cities in places more favoured by the climate and the seasons than any country known to us.

Histories 1.142
of the Ionians

38 ἔλαβε πόθος τε καὶ οἶκτος τῆς πόλιος καὶ τῶν ἠθέων τῆς χώρης

Overcome by longing and sorrow for the city and the customs of their native land.

Translated by Robin Waterfield (1998)
Histories 1.165
of the Phocaeans in exile

39 τὴν δουλοσύνην οὐκ ἀνεχόμενοι ἐξέλιπον τὰς πατρίδας

Unable to endure slavery, they left their native lands.

Translated by A.D. Godley (1920)
Histories 1.169
of some Ionian Greeks when subjected by the Persians

40 μίξιν δὲ τούτων τῶν ἀνθρώπων εἶναι ἐμφανέα κατά περ τοῖσι προβάτοισι

Men and women here have intercourse openly, like beasts of the flock.

Translated by A.D. Godley (1920)
Histories 1.203
of the people of the Caucasus

41 τὰ δέ μοι παθήματα ... μαθήματα γέγονε

My sufferings have been my lessons.

Translated in Liddell & Scott
Histories 1.207.6
spoken by Croesus; still verbatim in use today; observe the Greek wordplay 'pathimata – mathimata'

42 ὡς κύκλος τῶν ἀνθρωπηίων ἐστὶ πρηγμάτων, περιφερόμενος δὲ οὐκ ἐᾷ αἰεὶ τοὺς αὐτοὺς εὐτυχέειν

Men's fortunes are as on a wheel, which in its turning suffers not the same man to prosper for ever.

Translated by A.D. Godley (1920)
Histories 1.207.10
spoken by Croesus

43 ἀγαθῶν ἄπειροι καὶ καλῶν μεγάλων ἀπαθέες

Ignorant of the good things in life, insensible to great blessings.

Histories 1.207.25

44 καὶ ἡμῖν τὸ ἐνθεῦτεν λείπεται ἀπόδεξις ἔργων μεγάλων

It will be for us to achieve mighty deeds.

Histories 1.207.34

45 κατιόντος τοῦ οἴνου ἐς τὸ σῶμα ἐπαναπλέειν ὑμῖν ἔπεα κακά

When the wine is in, evil words flow out.

Histories 1.212

46 Ἕλληνες δὲ λέγουσι ἄλλα τε μάταια πολλά

Greeks tell many foolish tales.

Histories 2.2

47 Αἴγυπτος ἐς τὴν Ἕλληνες ναυτίλλονται ἐστὶ Αἰγυπτίοισι ἐπίκτητός τε γῆ καὶ δῶρον τοῦ ποταμοῦ

The Egypt to which the Greeks sail is acquired land, a gift of the river.

Histories 2.5

48 ὡς μέν νυν ἐν ἐλαχίστῳ δηλῶσαι, πᾶν εἴρηται

All has been said that needs to be said.

Histories 2.24

49 ἔρημος γάρ ἐστι ἡ χώρη αὕτη ὑπὸ καύματος

Because of the heat all this country is a desert.

Histories 2.31

50 ψάμμος τε ἐστὶ καὶ ἄνυδρος δεινῶς καὶ ἔρημος πάντων

All is sand, exceeding waterless and wholly desert.

Translated by A.D. Godley (1920)
Histories 2.32
of parts of Libya (northern Africa beyond the Nile delta)

51 περὶ δὲ τῶν τοῦ Νείλου πηγέων οὐδεὶς ἔχει λέγειν

But no one has any information about the sources of the Nile.

Histories 2.34

52 γενομένου γὰρ τέρατος φυλάσσουσι γραφόμενοι τὠποβαῖνον, καὶ ἤν κοτε ὕστερον παραπλήσιον τούτῳ γένηται, κατὰ τὠυτὸ νομίζουσι ἀποβήσεσθαι

When an ominous thing happens they take note of the outcome and write it down; and if something similar happens again they think it will have a like result.

Translated by A.D. Godley (1920)

Histories 2.82

of the Egyptians

53 πολλὸν τῆς ἀληθείης ἀπολελειμμένοι

Being far indeed from the truth.

Translated by A.D. Godley (1920)

Histories 2.106

54 τῶν μεγάλων ἀδικημάτων μεγάλαι εἰσὶ καὶ αἱ τιμωρίαι παρὰ τῶν θεῶν

The gods do greatly punish great wrong-doing.

Translated by A.D. Godley (1920)

Histories 2.120

55 τοῖσι μέν νυν ὑπ' Αἰγυπτίων λεγομένοισι χράσθω ὅτεῳ τὰ τοιαῦτα πιθανά ἐστι· ἐμοὶ δὲ παρὰ πάντα τὸν λόγον ὑπόκειται ὅτι τὰ λεγόμενα ὑπ' ἑκάστων ἀκοῇ γράφω

These Egyptian stories are for the use of whosoever believes such tales; for myself, it is my rule throughout this history that I record whatever is told me as I have heard it.

Translated by A.D. Godley (1920)

Histories 2.123.1

56 Αἰγύπτιοί εἰσι οἱ εἰπόντες, ὡς ἀνθρώπου ψυχὴ ἀθάνατός ἐστι, τοῦ σώματος δὲ καταφθίνοντος ἐς ἄλλο ζῷον αἰεὶ γινόμενον ἐσδύεται

The Egyptians were the first to teach that the soul is immortal, and at the death of the body enters into some other living thing then coming to birth.

Translated by A.D. Godley (1920)

Histories 2.123.9

57 ὅσα ἔς τε συρμαίην καὶ κρόμμυα καὶ σκόροδα ἀναισιμώθη

How much was spent on purge-plants and onions and garlic.

Translated by A.D. Godley (1920)

Histories 2.125

of an inscription in a pyramid

58 καλὸς κἀγαθός

In all respects a good man.

Translated by A.D. Godley (1920)

Histories 2.144

a much used phrase to this day

59 τὰ τόξα οἱ ἐκτημένοι, ἐπεὰν μὲν δέωνται χρᾶσθαι, ἐντανύουσι, ἐπεὰν δὲ χρήσωνται, ἐκλύουσι· εἰ γὰρ δὴ τὸν πάντα χρόνον ἐντεταμένα εἴη, ἐκραγείη ἄν

People with bows string them when they need to use them and unstring them when they've finished with them. If they kept them strung all the time, the bows would break.

Translated by Robin Waterfield (1998)

Histories 2.173.12

60 οὕτω δὴ καὶ ἀνθρώπου κατάστασις· εἰ ἐθέλοι κατεσπουδάσθαι αἰεὶ μηδὲ ἐς παιγνίην τὸ μέρος ἑωυτὸν ἀνιέναι, λάθοι ἂν ἤτοι μανεὶς ἢ ὅ γε ἀπόπληκτος γενόμενος

Such too is the nature of men. Were they to be ever at serious work and not permit themselves a fair share of sport they would go mad or silly ere they knew it.

Translated by A.D. Godley (1920)

Histories 2.173.15

61 ἀποδεικνύναι ἔτεος ἑκάστου τῷ νομάρχῃ πάντα τινὰ ὅθεν βιοῦται ... Σόλων δὲ ... τοῦτον τὸν νόμον ἔθετο· τῷ ἐκεῖνοι ἐς αἰεὶ χρέωνται, ἐόντι ἀμώμῳ νόμῳ

Solon established this law, each to yearly declare his means of livelihood; may they forever keep it! for it is a perfect law.

Translated by A.D. Godley (1920)

Histories 2.177

cf. Anonymous 43

62 οὔτε ἐκεῖνος ἀνήρ ἐστι δίκαιος· εἰ γὰρ ἦν δίκαιος, οὔτ' ἂν ἐπεθύμησε χώρης ἄλλης ἢ τῆς ἑωυτοῦ, οὔτ' ἂν ἐς δουλοσύνην ἀνθρώπους ἦγε ὑπ' ὧν μηδὲν ἠδίκηται

Nor is your king a righteous man; for were he such, he would not have coveted any country other than his own, nor would he now try to enslave men who have done him no wrong.

Translated by A.D. Godley (1921)

Histories 3.21
the Ethiopians speaking of Cambyses

63 οἷα δὲ ἐμμανής τε ἐὼν καὶ οὐ φρενήρης

Mad he was, right out of his mind!

Histories 3.25
of Cambyses

64 ἀγαθόν τοι πρόνοον εἶναι, σοφὸν δὲ ἡ προμηθίη

Prudence is the best policy, just as forethought is the wisest.

Translated by Tom Holland (2013)
Histories 3.36

65 οὐδένα γάρ κω λόγῳ οἶδα ἀκούσας ὅστις ἐς τέλος οὐ κακῶς ἐτελεύτησε πρόρριζος, εὐτυχέων τὰ πάντα

I know of no man whom continual good fortune did not bring in the end to evil, and utter destruction.

Translated by A.D. Godley (1921)
Histories 3.40
Amasis to Polycrates, notorious for his boundless good fortune

66 ὑπεκρίναντο τὰ μὲν πρῶτα λεχθέντα ἐπιλεληθέναι, τὰ δὲ ὕστερα οὐ συνιέναι

They had forgotten the beginning of the speech, they said, and could not understand its end.

Translated by A.D. Godley (1921)
Histories 3.46
Spartans on the Samians' lengthy speech appealing for help

67 φθονέεσθαι κρέσσον ἐστὶ ἢ οἰκτίρεσθαι

Better to be envied than pitied.

Histories 3.52
cf. the identical English proverb

68 ἐπεὶ δὲ τοῦ χρόνου προβαίνοντος … συνεγινώσκετο ἑωυτῷ οὐκέτι εἶναι δυνατὸς τὰ πρήγματα ἐπορᾶν τε καὶ διέπειν

As time went by he realized that he could no longer oversee and direct all his affairs.

Histories 3.53.1
of Periander

69 φιλοτιμίη κτῆμα σκαιόν

Pride is the possession of fools.

Translated by A.D. Godley (1921)
Histories 3.53.13

70 μὴ τῷ κακῷ τὸ κακὸν ἰῶ

Seek not to cure one ill by another.

Translated by A.D. Godley (1921)
Histories 3.53.13

71 τυραννὶς χρῆμα σφαλερόν, πολλοὶ δὲ αὐτῆς ἐρασταί

Despotism is hard to hold, yet many covet it.

Histories 3.53.16

72 ἐποίησα ταχύτερα ἢ σοφώτερα

I acted with more haste than wisdom.

Translated by A.D. Godley (1921)
Histories 3.65

73 κῶς δ' ἂν εἴη χρῆμα κατηρτημένον μουναρχίη, τῇ ἔξεστι ἀνευθύνῳ ποιέειν τὰ βούλεται;

What righteousness is there to be found in monarchy, when the ruler can do what he will and not be held accountable?

Histories 3.80.9

74 φθόνος δὲ ἀρχῆθεν ἐμφύεται ἀνθρώπῳ

Envy is early born in man.

Histories 3.80.14

75 τίθεμαι ὦν γνώμην μετέντας ἡμέας μουναρχίην τὸ πλῆθος ἀέξειν· ἐν γὰρ τῷ πολλῷ ἔνι τὰ πάντα

Therefore I declare my opinion, that we put an end to monarchy and increase the power of the people, as all good lies in the many.

Histories 3.80.29
proposed by one of the Persian magistrates; cf. Herodotus 76

76 ὁμίλου γὰρ ἀχρηίου οὐδέν ἐστι ἀσυνετώτερον οὐδὲ ὑβριστότερον

Nothing is more foolish and violent than a useless mob.

Translated by A.D. Godley (1921)
Histories 3.81
reply by another Persian magistrate; cf. Herodotus 75

77 ἀνδρὸς γὰρ ἑνὸς τοῦ ἀρίστου οὐδὲν ἄμεινον ἂν φανείη· γνώμῃ γὰρ τοιαύτῃ χρεώμενος ἐπιτροπεύοι ἂν ἀμωμήτως τοῦ

πλήθεος, σιγῷτό τε ἂν βουλεύματα ἐπὶ δυσμενέας ἄνδρας οὕτω μάλιστα

Nothing can be found better than the rule of the one best man; his judgement being like to himself, he will govern his people with perfect wisdom, and conceal plans made for the defeat of enemies.

Translated by A.D. Godley (1921)

Histories 3.82

Darius' position in support of the monarchy was carried by four votes to three

78 ἀστραπὴ ἐξ αἰθρίης καὶ βροντὴ

Thunder and lightning out of a clear sky.

Histories 3.86

taken as an omen for Darius, who was thereupon chosen king

79 ἡ Ἑλλὰς τὰς ὥρας πολλόν τι κάλλιστα κεκρημένας ἔλαχε

In Hellas the seasons have by much the most agreeable temperature.

Histories 3.106

80 καί κως τοῦ θείου ἡ προνοίη, ὥσπερ καὶ οἰκός ἐστι, ἐοῦσα σοφή, ὅσα μὲν ψυχήν τε δειλὰ καὶ ἐδώδιμα, ταῦτα μὲν πάντα πολύγονα πεποίηκε, ἵνα μὴ ἐπιλίπῃ κατεσθιόμενα, ὅσα δὲ σχέτλια καὶ ἀνιηρά, ὀλιγόγονα

Divine providence has ordained in its wisdom that creatures that are timid and good to eat proliferate so as not to be reduced, whereas few are born to the cruel and evil.

Histories 3.108

81 ἔνθα γὰρ σοφίης δέει, βίης ἔργον οὐδέν

Force has no place where there is need of skill.

Translated in *Bartlett's Familiar Quotations* (1980)

Histories 3.127

spoken by Darius

82 νῦν γὰρ ἄν τι καὶ ἀποδέξαιο ἔργον, ἕως νέος εἶς ἡλικίην· αὐξομένῳ γὰρ τῷ σώματι συναύξονται καὶ αἱ φρένες, γηράσκοντι δὲ συγγηράσκουσι καὶ ἐς τὰ πρήγματα πάντα ἀπαμβλύνονται

Now is your time for achieving great deeds, while you are still young; for as a man's mind grows with his body's growth, so as the body ages the mind too grows older and duller for all uses.

Translated by A.D. Godley (1921)

Histories 3.134

83 δικαιότατος ἀνδρῶν γίνεται, ὃς λαβεῖν μὲν διδόμενα οὐκ ἐδικαίου

Most righteous is he who will not accept gifts to which he is not entitled.

Histories 3.148

84 ἔργῳ τῷ αἰσχίστῳ οὔνομα τὸ κάλλιστον ἔθευ

You do but give a fair name to a foul deed.

Translated by A.D. Godley (1921)

Histories 3.155

85 τοῦ ἐπιστάμενος τὸ οὔνομα ἑκὼν ἐπιλήθομαι

I know the man's name but purposely fail to recall it.

Histories 4.43

of Sataspes' eunuch who escaped to Samos with a 'great store of wealth' after his master's death

86 οὔτε γὰρ ἔθνος τῶν ἐντὸς τοῦ Πόντου οὐδὲν ἔχομεν προβαλέσθαι σοφίης πέρι οὔτε ἄνδρα λόγιον οἴδαμεν γενόμενον

For we cannot show that any nation within the region of the Pontus has aught of cleverness, nor do we know of any notable man born there.

Translated by A.D. Godley (1921)

Histories 4.46

87 ἴχνος Ἡρακλέος

From the footprint, Heracles

Histories 4.82

cf. the Latin 'ex pede, Herculem'; from Aulus Gellius, Attic Nights *1.1, on how Pythagoras deduced the stature of Heracles from the length of his foot*

88 ἀλλ' ἐπεὶ ἐξέκοψαν τοὺς ἄνδρας, ἐφέροντο κατὰ κῦμα καὶ ἄνεμον

Having slain the men they were now at the mercy of the winds and waves.

Histories 4.110

of Amazons unable to govern ship after killing their abductors

89 ἐγὼ οὐδένα κω ἀνθρώπων δείσας ἔφυγον

I have never fled for fear of any man.

Translated by A.D. Godley (1921)
Histories 4.127

90 ὡς ἄρα ἀνθρώποισι αἱ λίην ἰσχυραὶ τιμωρίαι πρὸς θεῶν ἐπίφθονοι γίνονται

Excessive punishment by humans is offensive even to the gods.

Histories 4.205

91 νῦν ἂν εἴη ὁ χρησμὸς ἐπιτελεόμενος ἡμῖν, νῦν ἡμέτερον τὸ ἔργον

Now this is surely the fulfilment of the prophecy, now it is for us to act.

Histories 5.1
of an oracle given 'by the god of the Paeonians'

92 Τραυσοὶ… τὸν μὲν γενόμενον περιζόμενοι οἱ προσήκοντες ὀλοφύρονται, ὅσα μιν δεῖ ἐπείτε ἐγένετο ἀναπλῆσαι κακά, ἀνηγεόμενοι τὰ ἀνθρωπήια πάντα πάθεα, τὸν δ' ἀπογενόμενον παίζοντές τε καὶ ἡδόμενοι γῇ κρύπτουσι, ἐπιλέγοντες ὅσων κακῶν ἐξαπαλλαχθείς ἐστι ἐν πάσῃ εὐδαιμονίῃ

The Trausi, when a child is born, lament for all the ills it must endure from birth onward, recounting all the sorrows of men; but the dead they bury with jollity and gladness, as he is released from so many ills and now in a state of perfect blessedness.

Histories 5.4
the Trausi were an ethnic group resident in Thrace

93 κτημάτων πάντων ἐστὶ τιμιώτατον ἀνὴρ φίλος συνετός τε καὶ εὔνοος

The most precious of all possessions is a wise and loyal friend.

Translated by A.D. Godley (1922)
Histories 5.24
spoken by Darius

94 ἦν τε οὐ φρενήρης ἀκρομανής τε, ὡς λέγεται

Now, as the story goes, he was not in his right senses, but on the verge of madness.

Histories 5.42
of Cleomenes; his madness was attributed to his addiction to strong drink

95 πάτερ, διαφθερέει σε ὁ ξεῖνος, ἢν μὴ ἀποστὰς ἴῃς

Father, your visitor is going to corrupt you, if you don't get up and leave.

Translated by Robin Waterfield (1998)
Histories 5.51
said by Gorgo, eight or nine years old, daughter of Cleomenes, King of Sparta, on Aristagoras' attempts to bribe her father

96 Ἀθῆναι, ἐοῦσαι καὶ πρὶν μεγάλαι, τότε ἀπαλλαχθεῖσαι τυράννων ἐγίνοντο μέζονες

Athens, when rid of her tyrants, became even greater than she had been before.

Histories 5.66

97 δηλοῖ δὲ οὐ κατ' ἓν μοῦνον ἀλλὰ πανταχῇ ἡ ἰσηγορίη ὡς ἐστὶ χρῆμα σπουδαῖον

Not in one instance only but everywhere it is proved that equal right of speech is paramount.

Histories 5.78.1

98 κατεχόμενοι μὲν ἐθελοκάκεον ὡς δεσπότῃ ἐργαζόμενοι, ἐλευθερωθέντων δὲ αὐτὸς ἕκαστος ἑωυτῷ προεθυμέετο κατεργάζεσθαι

Working for a master they deliberately played foul; but now, freed, each one was eager to achieve for himself.

Histories 5.78.6

99 τυραννίδας … τοῦ οὔτε ἀδικώτερόν ἐστι οὐδὲν κατ' ἀνθρώπους οὔτε μιαιφονώτερον

Despotism, a thing as unrighteous and bloodthirsty as aught on this earth.

Translated by A.D. Godley (1922)
Histories 5.92.α6

100 Θρασύβουλος … ἐσβὰς ἐς ἄρουραν ἐσπαρμένην … καὶ ἐκόλουε αἰεὶ ὅκως τινὰ ἴδοι τῶν ἀσταχύων ὑπερέχοντα … ἐς ὃ τοῦ ληίου τὸ κάλλιστόν τε καὶ βαθύτατον διέφθειρε

Thrasybulus entered into a sown field and cut off the tallest stalks, till by so doing he had destroyed the best and richest of the crop.

Translated by A.D. Godley (1922)
Histories 5.92.ζ9
as a symbolic message to Periander on how best to subdue his subordinates, killing the most prominent; cf. Thrasybulus 1 and Euripides 334

101 ὅσα γὰρ Κύψελος ἀπέλιπε κτείνων τε καὶ διώκων, Περίανδρός σφεα ἀπετέλεσε

Whatever slaughter or banishment Cypselus had left undone Periander finished off.

Histories 5.92.η4

Plutarch considers this speech an invention of Herodotus (in On the Malice of Herodotus *861a)*

102 πολλοὺς γὰρ οἶκε εἶναι εὐπετέστερον διαβάλλειν ἢ ἕνα

It seems that it is easier to deceive many than one.

Translated by A.D. Godley (1922)

Histories 5.97

103 τοῦτο τὸ ὑπόδημα ἔρραψας μὲν σύ, ὑπεδήσατο δὲ Ἀρισταγόρης

It was you that stitched this shoe, and Aristagoras that put it on.

Translated by A.D. Godley (1922)

Histories 6.1

Artaphrenes to Histiaeus of Miletus who pretended not to know why the Ionians revolted against the Persians under Aristagoras; cf. Erasmus, Adages 3.4.42

104 επὶ ξυροῦ γὰρ ἀκμῆς ἔχεται ἡμῖν τὰ πρήγματα, ἄνδρες Ἴωνες, ἢ εἶναι ἐλευθέροισι ἢ δούλοισι

Men of Ionia, our affairs are balanced on a razor's edge; we can remain free or we can become slaves.

Translated by Robin Waterfield (1998)

Histories 6.11

105 Ἀθηναῖοι ... ἐζημίωσάν μιν ὡς ἀναμνήσαντα οἰκήια κακὰ χιλίῃσι δραχμῇσι, καὶ ἐπέταξαν μηκέτι μηδένα χρᾶσθαι τούτῳ τῷ δράματι

The Athenians fined Phrynichus a thousand drachmae for bringing to mind a calamity that touched them so nearly, and forbade for ever the acting of that play.

Translated by A.D. Godley (1922)

Histories 6.21

on staging his play The Fall of Miletus; *the whole theatre wept when it was shown*

106 φιλέει δέ κως προσημαίνειν, εὖτ' ἂν μέλλῃ μεγάλα κακὰ ἢ πόλι ἢ ἔθνεϊ ἔσεσθαι

Some warning is ever given by heaven, when great ills threaten cities or nations.

Translated by A.D. Godley (1922)

Histories 6.27

of previous calamities, 'plain signs' before the fall of Chios

107 σφέας πίτυος τρόπον ἀπείλεε ἐκτρίψειν

I will raze you from the ground like a pine-tree.

Histories 6.37

the pine tree 'being the only tree that when cut down perishes utterly'; cf. Pericles 59

108 στρατευομένων δὲ πρώτους ἰέναι τοὺς βασιλέας, ὑστάτους δὲ ἀπιέναι

When the armies go forth kings shall be first in the advance, and last in the retreat.

Translated by A.D. Godley (1922)

Histories 6.56

a rule of war for Spartan kings

109 κατὰ τὰ πάτρια ἐπιτελέουσι

They ply their craft by right of birth.

Translated by A.D. Godley (1922)

Histories 6.60

of Spartan heralds, flute-players and cooks

110 ἐπισκύθισον

Pour a Scythian Cup!

Translated by A.D. Godley (1922)

Histories 6.84

of Scythian strong wine, said to have caused the Spartan King Cleomenes' madness; cf. Herodotus 94

111 τὸ πειρηθῆναι τοῦ θεοῦ καὶ τὸ ποιῆσαι ἴσον δύνασθαι

To attempt a deed and do it is the same to god.

Histories 6.86.γ55

112 ταῦτα ὦν πάντα ἐς σὲ νῦν τείνει καὶ ἐκ σέο ἤρτηται

All turns to you now; all hangs on you.

Histories 6.109

Miltiades to Callimachus, persuading him to go to battle against the Persians; he fell at Marathon, greatly distinguishing himself

113 μαχομένων δὲ ἐν τῷ Μαραθῶνι χρόνος ἐγίνετο πολλός ... καὶ ἐνίκων Ἀθηναῖοι

For a long time they fought at Marathon

and the Athenians were victorious.

Translated by A.D. Godley (1922)

Histories 6.113

114 ὡς ἡ Εὐρώπη περικαλλὴς εἴη χώρη ... ἀρετήν τε ἄκρη, βασιλέϊ τε μούνῳ θνητῶν ἀξίη ἐκτῆσθαι

Europe is a land of exceeding beauty and excellence, worthy only of the Great King to possess.

Histories 7.5

Mardonius to Xerxes who was unwilling to march against Greece

115 εἰ τούτους ... καταστρεψόμεθα ... τὴν Περσίδα ἀποδέξομεν τῷ Διὸς αἰθέρι ὁμουρέουσαν· οὐ γὰρ δὴ χώρην γε οὐδεμίαν κατόψεται ἥλιος ὁμουρέουσαν τῇ ἡμετέρῃ

If we subdue them the borders of Persia and of the heavens will be the same; the sun will never set on Persian territory.

Histories 7.8

Xerxes on invading Hellas

116 ὦ δέσποτα, οὐ μοῦνον εἶς τῶν γενομένων Περσέων ἄριστος, ἀλλὰ καὶ τῶν ἐσομένων

Sire, you surpass not only all Persians that have been but also all that shall be.

Translated by A.D. Godley (1922)

Histories 7.9.1

Mardonius to Xerxes

117 τί δείσαντες; κοίην πλήθεος συστροφήν; κοίην δὲ χρημάτων δύναμιν;

What is there to fear? Their greater numbers? Or their greater wealth?

Histories 7.9.9

Mardonius, of the Greeks

118 αὐτόματον γὰρ οὐδέν, ἀλλ' ἀπὸ πείρης πάντα ἀνθρώποισι φιλέει γίνεσθαι

Nothing comes automatically, all men's achievements are but the result of experiment.

Histories 7.9.38

119 ὁρᾷς δὲ ὡς ἐς οἰκήματα τὰ μέγιστα αἰεὶ καὶ δένδρεα τὰ τοιαῦτα ἀποσκήπτει τὰ βέλεα· φιλέει γὰρ ὁ θεὸς τὰ ὑπερέχοντα πάντα κολούειν

It is always on the tallest buildings and trees that thunderbolts fall; for it is heaven's way to bring low all things of surpassing greatness.

Translated by A.D. Godley (1922)

Histories 7.10.50

120 οὐ γὰρ ἐᾷ φρονέειν μέγα ὁ θεὸς ἄλλον ἢ ἑωυτόν

God suffers pride in none but himself.

Translated by A.D. Godley (1922)

Histories 7.10.55

121 ἐπειχθῆναι μέν νυν πᾶν πρῆγμα τίκτει σφάλματα

Haste begets errors, in all affairs.

Histories 7.10.56

122 ἀλλὰ ποιέειν ἢ παθεῖν πρόκειται ... τὸ γὰρ μέσον οὐδὲν

The question is to do or not to do; there is no middle way.

Histories 7.11

spoken by Xerxes

123 ἤν περ μὴ αὐτίκα στρατηλατέῃς, τάδε τοι ἐξ αὐτῶν ἀνασχήσει· ὡς καὶ μέγας καὶ πολλὸς ἐγένεο ἐν ὀλίγῳ χρόνῳ, οὕτω καὶ ταπεινὸς ὀπίσω κατὰ τάχος ἔσεαι

If you do not set out at once with your army, then the result will be that though you have risen swiftly to greatness, yet in no less swift a time will you be cast down again.

Translated by Tom Holland (2013)

Histories 7.14

Xerxes' vision warning him against not sending an army to Greece

124 ἴσον ἐκεῖνο, ὦ βασιλεῦ, παρ' ἐμοὶ κέκριται, φρονέειν τε εὖ καὶ τῷ λέγοντι χρηστὰ ἐθέλειν πείθεσθαι

O King, I judge it of equal worth whether a man be wise, or be willing to obey good counsel.

Translated by A.D. Godley (1922)

Histories 7.16.4

125 ὡς κακὸν εἴη διδάσκειν τὴν ψυχὴν πλέον τι δίζησθαι αἰεὶ ἔχειν τοῦ παρεόντος

It is evil to teach the heart to desire more than it has.

Histories 7.16.12

126 πεπλανῆσθαι αὗται μάλιστα ἐώθασι αἱ ὄψιες τῶν ὀνειράτων, τά τις ἡμέρης φροντίζει

Visions wandering through our dreams are, for the most part, the thoughts of the day.

Histories 7.16.19

127 ὡς ἐν τοῖσι ὠσὶ τῶν ἀνθρώπων οἰκέει ὁ θυμός, ὃς χρηστὰ μὲν ἀκούσας τέρψιος ἐμπιπλέει τὸ σῶμα, ὑπεναντία δὲ τούτοισι ἀκούσας ἀνοιδέει

The spirit of a man dwells in his ears; hearing good words fills him with delight, on hearing the opposite he swells with rage.

Histories 7.39

128 ἐν γὰρ οὕτω βραχέϊ βίῳ οὐδεὶς οὕτω ἄνθρωπος ἐὼν εὐδαίμων πέφυκε ... τῷ οὐ παραστήσεται πολλάκις καὶ οὐκὶ ἅπαξ τεθνάναι βούλεσθαι μᾶλλον ἢ ζώειν

Short though our lives are, there is no man so fortunate that he shall not many times wish himself dead rather than alive.

Histories 7.46.11

129 οὕτω ὁ μὲν θάνατος μοχθηρῆς ἐούσης τῆς ζόης καταφυγὴ αἱρετωτάτη τῷ ἀνθρώπῳ γέγονε

When life is so burdensome, death becomes a sought-after refuge for man.

Histories 7.46.16

130 βιοτῆς μέν νυν ἀνθρωπηίης πέρι, ἐούσης τοιαύτης οἵην περ σὺ διαιρέαι εἶναι

Human life is such as you define it.

Translated by A.D. Godley (1922)

Histories 7.47

Xerxes in answer to Artabanus

131 αἱ συμφοραὶ τῶν ἀνθρώπων ἄρχουσι καὶ οὐκὶ ὤνθρωποι τῶν συμφορέων

Men are at the mercy of circumstances, not their master.

Translated in *The New Penguin Dictionary of Quotations* (2006)

Histories 7.49.10

132 γῆ ... τοσούτῳ τοι γίνεται πολεμιωτέρη ὅσῳ ἂν προβαίνῃς ἑκαστέρω

The land is the more your enemy the further you advance into it.

Translated by A.D. Godley (1922)

Histories 7.49.13

133 τοῖσι τοίνυν βουλομένοισι ποιέειν ὡς τὸ ἐπίπαν φιλέει γίνεσθαι τὰ κέρδεα, τοῖσι δὲ ... ὀκνέουσι οὐ μάλα ἐθέλει

The prizes are won by those who act, not by those who hesitate.

Histories 7.50.11

134 μεγάλα γὰρ πρήγματα μεγάλοισι κινδύνοισι ἐθέλει καταιρέεσθαι

Great deeds are only achieved at great risk.

Histories 7.50.19

135 οὔτε γὰρ ἔθνεος ἑκάστου ἐπάξιοι ἦσαν οἱ ἡγεμόνες

Not all countries have the leaders they deserve.

Histories 7.96

cf. Joseph de Maistre (1753–1821) French writer and Diplomat, Lettres et opuscules inédits (1851) *vol. I, letter 53: 'toute nation a le gouvernement qu'elle mérite' (every country has the government it deserves)*

136 βασιλεῦ, κότερα ἀληθείῃ χρήσωμαι πρὸς σὲ ἢ ἡδονῇ;

Do you want a truthful answer, O King, or a pleasing one?

Translated by Tom Holland (2013)

Histories 7.101

Demaratus, the exiled king of Sparta, to Xerxes

137 τῇ Ἑλλάδι πενίη μὲν αἰεί κοτε σύντροφος ἐστί, ἀρετὴ δὲ ἔπακτος ἐστί, ἀπό τε σοφίης κατεργασμένη καὶ νόμου ἰσχυροῦ· τῇ διαχρεωμένη ἡ Ἑλλὰς τήν τε πενίην ἀπαμύνεται καὶ τὴν δεσποσύνην

In Greece poverty is a familiar feature, but excellence is acquired through wisdom and strong law; thus, by constant application, Hellas fends off both poverty and tyranny.

Histories 7.102

Demaratus, the exiled king of Sparta, to Xerxes

138 Λακεδαιμόνιοι κατὰ μὲν ἕνα μαχόμενοι οὐδαμῶν εἰσι κακίονες ἀνδρῶν, ἁλέες δὲ ἄριστοι ἀνδρῶν ἁπάντων· ἐλεύθεροι γὰρ ἐόντες οὐ πάντα ἐλεύθεροι εἰσί· ἔπεστι γάρ σφι δεσπότης νόμος, τὸν ὑποδειμαίνουσι πολλῷ ἔτι μᾶλλον ἢ οἱ σοὶ σέ

The Lacedaemonians fighting singly are as brave as any man living, and together they are the best warriors on earth. Free they are, yet not wholly free; for law is their master, which they fear much more than your men fear you.

Translated by A.D. Godley (1922)

Histories 7.104

Demaratus to Xerxes of Spartans in battle

139 ἐς δὲ Ἀθήνας καὶ Σπάρτην ... οἱ μὲν αὐτῶν τοὺς αἰτέοντας ἐς τὸ βάραθρον, οἵ δ' ἐς φρέαρ ἐμβαλόντες ἐκέλευον γῆν τε καὶ ὕδωρ ἐκ τούτων φέρειν παρὰ βασιλέα

At Athens and Sparta the demanders were cast at the one city into the Pit and at the other into a well, and bidden to carry thence earth and water to the king.

Translated by A.D. Godley (1922)

Histories 7.133

on Darius' sending heralds to demand earth and water, a sign of submission; the Pit was a cleft into which criminals were thrown; cf. Aristophanes 63

140 νῦν δὲ Ἀθηναίους ἄν τις λέγων σωτῆρας γενέσθαι τῆς Ἑλλάδος οὐκ ἂν ἁμαρτάνοι τἀληθέος ... ἑλόμενοι δὲ τὴν Ἑλλάδα περιεῖναι ἐλευθέρην τοῦτο τὸ Ἑλληνικὸν ... αὐτοὶ οὗτοι ἦσαν οἱ ἐπεγείραντες

To say that the Athenians were the saviours of Hellas is not far from the truth, for they set their hearts on Hellas remaining free, and it was they who roused all other Greeks.

Histories 7.139

141 ἐνθαῦτα ἐδόκεε βουλευομένοισι αὐτοῖσι πρῶτον μὲν χρημάτων πάντων καταλλάσσεσθαι τάς τε ἔχθρας καὶ τοὺς κατ' ἀλλήλους ἐόντας πολέμους

They resolved in debate to make an end of all their feuds and their wars against each other.

Translated by A.D. Godley (1922)

Histories 7.145

the Greeks in view of the Persian invasion

142 ἐγὼ δὲ ὀφείλω λέγειν τὰ λεγόμενα, πείθεσθαί γε μὲν οὐ παντάπασι ὀφείλω, καί μοι τοῦτο τὸ ἔπος ἐχέτω ἐς πάντα τὸν λόγον

I am obliged to record the things I am told, but I am certainly not required to believe them – this remark may be taken to apply to the whole of my account.

Translated by Robin Waterfield (1998)

Histories 7.152

143 τῷ δὲ εὖ βουλευθέντι πρήγματι τελευτὴ ὡς τὸ ἐπίπαν χρηστὴ ἐθέλει ἐπιγίνεσθαι

A well-laid plan commonly leads to a happy issue.

Translated by A.D. Godley (1922)

Histories 7.157

144 ἐοίκατε τοὺς μὲν ἄρχοντας ἔχειν, τοὺς δὲ ἀρξομένους οὐκ ἕξειν

It would seem that you have many that lead, but none that will follow.

Translated by A.D. Godley (1922)

Histories 7.162

Gelon of Syracuse to the Athenian envoys

145 ἐξ ἠοῦς ἀρξάμενοι μέχρι δείλης ὀψίης

Starting at dawn until late at night.

Histories 7.167

146 οὐδαμὰ γὰρ ἀδυνασίης ἀνάγκη κρέσσων ἔφυ

No necessity can prevail over lack of ability.

Translated by A.D. Godley (1922)

Histories 7.172

147 ἡμέρας γὰρ δὴ ἐχείμαζε τρεῖς· τέλος δὲ ἔντομά τε ποιεῦντες οἱ μάγοι τῷ ἀνέμῳ ... ἢ ἄλλως κως αὐτὸς ἐθέλων ἐκόπασε

The storm lasted three days, after which the Magi brought it to an end by sacrificial offerings; or, of course, it may have been that the wind just dropped by itself.

Translated by Aubrey de Sélincourt (1954)

Histories 7.191

of the fleet of Xerxes having been destroyed by a great storm

148 πλέω ἀγαθὰ τῶν ἁμαρτημάτων πεποιημένα

His good services were more than his offences.

Translated by A.D. Godley (1922)

Histories 7.194

149 εἶναι δὲ θνητὸν οὐδένα οὐδὲ ἔσεσθαι τῷ κακὸν ἐξ ἀρχῆς γινομένῳ οὐ συνεμίχθη, τοῖσι δὲ μεγίστοισι αὐτῶν μέγιστα

There is no mortal, nor ever shall be, to whom at birth some admixture of misfortune is not allotted; the greater the man, the greater his misfortunes.

Histories 7.203

150 δῆλον δ' ἐποίευν παντί τεῳ καὶ οὐκ ἥκιστα αὐτῷ βασιλέι, ὅτι πολλοὶ μὲν ἄνθρωποι εἶεν, ὀλίγοι δὲ ἄνδρες

It was plain for all to see, and not least to the king himself, that in his host men there were many, real men but few.

Histories 7.210

of the Persian army after the first day at Thermopylae

151 ὡς πάντα σφι ἀγαθὰ ... ὑπὸ σκιῇ ἔσοιτο πρὸς αὐτοὺς ἡ μάχη

So much the better, we shall fight in the shade.

Histories 7.226

attributed to Dieneces of Sparta, on being told that the enemies were so numerous that their arrows when shot would hide the sun

152 Ἕλληνες ... τοῦ τε εὐτυχέειν φθονέουσι καὶ τὸ κρέσσον στυγέουσι

Greeks are jealous of success and hate those that are more powerful.

Histories 7.236

153 ὑπὸ δὲ ἀρετῆς τε καὶ προθυμίης Πλαταιέες, ἄπειροι τῆς ναυτικῆς ἐόντες, συνεπλήρουν τοῖσι Ἀθηναίοισι τὰς νέας

The Plataeans manned these ships with the Athenians, not that they had any knowledge of seamanship, but through valour and zeal.

Translated by A.D. Godley (1925)

Histories 8.1

of the fleet at Salamis

154 στάσις γὰρ ἔμφυλος πολέμου ὁμοφρονέοντος τοσούτῳ κάκιόν ἐστι ὅσῳ πόλεμος εἰρήνης

Civil strife is worse than war as much as war is worse than peace.

Translated by A.D. Godley (1925)

Histories 8.3

155 κοίους ἐπ' ἄνδρας ἤγαγες μαχησομένους ἡμέας, οἳ οὐ περὶ χρημάτων τὸν ἀγῶνα ποιεῦνται ἀλλὰ περὶ ἀρετῆς

What manner of men are these that you have brought us to fight withall? 'tis not for money they contend but for glory of achievement.

Translated by A.D. Godley (1925)

Histories 8.26

a Persian official on hearing that a crown of olive is given to the victor at the Olympic Games

156 οἰκότα μέν νυν βουλευομένοισι ἀνθρώποισι ὡς τὸ ἐπίπαν ἐθέλει γίνεσθαι· μὴ δὲ οἰκότα βουλευομένοισι οὐκ ἐθέλει, οὐδὲ ὁ θεὸς προσχωρέει πρὸς τὰς ἀνθρωπηίας γνώμας

Most often success comes to men when they plan wisely, but not even god can intercede if they do not do so.

Histories 8.60

157 Θεμιστοκλέα ἐόντα μὲν ἑωυτῷ οὐ φίλον, ἐχθρὸν δὲ τὰ μάλιστα· ὑπὸ δὲ μεγάθεος τῶν παρεόντων κακῶν λήθην ἐκείνων ποιεύμενος ἐξεκαλέετο

Themistocles was no friend of his but his foremost enemy; yet in the seriousness of the present danger he put that old feud from his mind.

Histories 8.79

of Aristides

158 οἷα ὑπερλυπεόμενός τε καὶ πάντας αἰτιώμενος

Displeased beyond measure and ready to blame everybody.

Histories 8.90

of Xerxes

159 τοὺς οὔτε νιφετός, οὐκ ὄμβρος, οὐ καῦμα, οὐ νὺξ ἔργει μὴ οὐ κατανύσαι τὸν προκείμενον αὐτῷ δρόμον τὴν ταχίστην

Neither snow, nor rain, nor heat, nor night keeps them from accomplishing their appointed courses with all speed.

Translated in *Bartlett's Familiar Quotations* (1980)

Histories 8.98

of the Persian messengers; an adaptation of this quotation is inscribed on the James Farley Post Office, New York City

160 καὶ θεοὺς δύο ἀχρήστους οὐκ ἐκλείπειν σφέων τὴν νῆσον ἀλλ' αἰεὶ φιλοχωρέειν, Πενίην τε καὶ Ἀμηχανίην

We have two unkind gods in permanent residence on our island, Poverty and

Hardship.

Histories 8.111

the Andrians' reply to Themistocles demanding money, stating that he has two gods with him, Persuasion and Necessity

161 ὅτι μὲν ἔσωσε βασιλέος τὴν ψυχήν, δωρήσασθαι χρυσέῃ στεφάνῃ τὸν κυβερνήτην, ὅτι δὲ Περσέων πολλοὺς ἀπώλεσε, ἀποταμεῖν τὴν κεφαλὴν αὐτοῦ

Xerxes gave a garland of gold to the helmsman, for saving the king's life – and then cut off his head for causing the deaths of so many Persians!

Translated by Robin Waterfield (1998)

Histories 8.118

of Xerxes; Herodotus states that he did not believe this tale

162 ἐνθαῦτα πᾶς τις αὐτῶν ἑωυτῷ ἐτίθετο τὴν ψῆφον, αὐτὸς ἕκαστος δοκέων ἄριστος γενέσθαι

Each voted for himself considering that he had offered the best service.

Histories 8.123

the Greek admirals after Salamis

163 ἦσαν γὰρ τὸ πάλαι καὶ αἱ τυραννίδες τῶν ἀνθρώπων ἀσθενέες χρήμασι, οὐ μοῦνον ὁ δῆμος

In the old days even the ruling houses, not just the common people, lacked wealth.

Histories 8.137

164 δύναμις ὑπὲρ ἄνθρωπον ἡ βασιλέος ἐστὶ καὶ χεὶρ ὑπερμήκης

The king's might is beyond human might, and his arm reaches very far.

Histories 8.140

165 τύραννος γὰρ ἐὼν τυράννῳ συγκατεργάζεται

One tyrant is bound to help another tyrant.

Histories 8.142

166 Ἀθηναῖοι λέγουσι, ἔστ' ἂν ὁ ἥλιος τὴν αὐτὴν ὁδὸν ἴῃ τῇ περ καὶ νῦν ἔρχεται, μήκοτε ὁμολογήσειν ἡμέας Ξέρξῃ

The Athenians say, that as long as the sun holds its present course, they will on no account make an agreement with Xerxes.

Histories 8.143

167 οὔτε χρυσός ἐστι γῆς οὐδαμόθι τοσοῦτος οὔτε χώρη οὕτω κάλλεϊ καὶ ἀρετῇ μέγα ὑπερφέρουσα, τὰ ἡμεῖς δεξάμενοι ἐθέλοιμεν ἂν μηδίσαντες καταδουλῶσαι τὴν Ἑλλάδα

Nowhere on earth is there so much gold, nor territory of surpassing beauty and excellence, that the gift of it would cause us to go over to the Persian side and enslave Hellas.

Histories 8.144.6

Athenians reassuring the Lacedaemonians

168 αὖτις δὲ τὸ Ἑλληνικόν, ἐὸν ὅμαιμόν τε καὶ ὁμόγλωσσον, καὶ θεῶν ἱδρύματά τε κοινὰ καὶ θυσίαι ἤθεά τε ὁμότροπα, τῶν προδότας γενέσθαι Ἀθηναίους οὐκ ἂν εὖ ἔχοι

This kinship of all Greeks in blood and speech, our common shrines and sacrifices, our way of life, Athenians would never betray.

Histories 8.144.14

Athenians reassuring the Lacedaemonians

169 κατὰ μὲν γὰρ τὸ ἰσχυρὸν Ἕλληνας ὁμοφρονέοντας ... χαλεπὰ εἶναι περιγίνεσθαι καὶ ἅπασι ἀνθρώποισι

As long as the Greeks remain in accord, it would be a hard matter even for the whole world to overcome them by force of arms.

Translated by A.D. Godley (1925)

Histories 9.2

170 ὁ ἥλιος ἀμαυρώθη ἐν τῷ οὐρανῷ

The sun was darkened in the heavens.

Translated by A.D. Godley (1925)

Histories 9.10

171 ἐχθίστη δὲ ὀδύνη ἐστὶ τῶν ἐν ἀνθρώποισι αὕτη, πολλὰ φρονέοντα μηδενὸς κρατέειν

The most hateful torment for men is to have knowledge of everything but power over nothing.

Translated in *The Oxford Dictionary of Quotations* (2004)

Histories 9.16

172 ἀλλ' οὐ γάρ τι προέχει τούτων ἐπιμεμνῆσθαι ... παλαιῶν μέν νυν ἔργων ἅλις ἔστω

It is idle to recall these matters; enough of these doings of old time.

Translated by A.D. Godley (1925)

Histories 9.27

173 ἐπιστάμενοι ... ὡς ἄλλα φρονεόντων καὶ ἄλλα λεγόντων

Well aware of thinking one thing while saying quite another.

Translated by Tom Holland (2013)

Histories 9.54

174 ἄριστος ἐγένετο μακρῷ Ἀριστόδημος ... ὃς ἐκ Θερμοπυλέων μοῦνος τῶν τριηκοσίων σωθεὶς εἶχε ὄνειδος καὶ ἀτιμίην

By far the greatest degree of courage was shown, in my opinion, by Aristodemus, who, as the sole survivor of the three hundred at Thermopylae, had met with abuse and disgrace.

Translated by Robin Waterfield (1998)

Histories 9.71

at the battle of Plataeae

175 ἔργον ἔργασταί τοι ὑπερφυὲς μέγαθός τε καὶ κάλλος

You have done a deed of surpassing greatness and glory.

Translated by A.D. Godley (1925)

Histories 9.78

said of Pausanias, leader of the Greeks at Plataeae

176 ἔλεγε πολλά τε καὶ κακά, ἄλλα τε καὶ γυναικὸς κακίω φὰς αὐτὸν εἶναι ... παρὰ δὲ τοῖσι Πέρσῃσι γυναικὸς κακίω ἀκοῦσαι δέννος μέγιστός ἐστι

He said many things, and bitter, and that he was worse than a woman; and it is the greatest of all taunts in Persia to be called worse than a woman.

Histories 9.107

177 φιλέειν γὰρ ἐκ τῶν μαλακῶν χώρων μαλακοὺς ἄνδρας γίνεσθαι· οὐ γάρ τι τῆς αὐτῆς γῆς εἶναι καρπόν τε θωμαστὸν φύειν καὶ ἄνδρας ἀγαθοὺς τὰ πολέμια ... ἄρχειν τε εἵλοντο λυπρὴν οἰκέοντες μᾶλλον ἢ πεδιάδα σπείροντες ἄλλοισι δουλεύειν

Soft lands breed soft men; no soil produces fine fruits and good soldiers too. And they chose rather to be rulers on their barren mountainsides than bondmen tilling fertile valleys.

Histories 9.122

final lines

HEROPHILUS

c.330–260BC

Alexandrian physician

1 σοφίαν φησὶν ἀνεπίδεικτον καὶ τέχνην ἄδηλον καὶ ἰσχὺν ἀναγώνιστον καὶ πλοῦτον ἀχρεῖον καὶ λόγον ἀδύνατον ὑγείας ἀπούσης

Wisdom cannot be shown, skill remains unseen, strength goes unchallenged, wealth is useless, speech is powerless, if health is absent.

Sextus Empiricus, *Against the Ethicists* 11.50

Herophilus and Erasistratus were the only ancient scientists to perform dissections of human bodies

HESIOD

c.750–*c*.700BC

Epic poet from Ascra in Boeotia

see also 'Hesiod' in Keyword Index and Homerica 3–5

1 Μουσάων Ἑλικωνιάδων ἀρχώμεθ' ἀείδειν

Let us begin our song with the Helicon Muses.

Translated by C.A. Trypanis (1971)

Theogony 1

opening line

2 αἵ νύ ποθ' Ἡσίοδον καλὴν ἐδίδαξαν ἀοιδήν,
ἄρνας ποιμαίνονθ' Ἑλικῶνος ὕπο ζαθέοιο

It was they who once taught Hesiod how to sing beautifully, as he was shepherding his lambs under most holy Helicon.

Translated by C.A. Trypanis (1971)

Theogony 22

of the Muses

3 ἴδμεν ψεύδεα πολλὰ λέγειν ἐτύμοισιν ὁμοῖα,
ἴδμεν δ' εὖτ' ἐθέλωμεν ἀληθέα γηρύσασθαι

We know how to tell true-sounding lies, but also to speak the truth if we so wish.

Theogony 27

4 τῷ μὲν ἐπὶ γλώσσῃ γλυκερὴν χείουσιν ἐέρσην,
τοῦ δ' ἔπε' ἐκ στόματος ῥεῖ μείλιχα

They pour sweet dew upon his tongue,
and from his lips flow gracious words.

Translated by Hugh G. Evelyn-White (1914)

Theogony 83

5 ταῦτά μοι ἔσπετε Μοῦσαι, Ὀλύμπια δώματ' ἔχουσαι
ἐξ ἀρχῆς, καὶ εἴπαθ', ὅτι πρῶτον γένετ' αὐτῶν

Tell me these things from the beginning, Olympian-dwelling Muses,
but tell me which of them came first.

Theogony 114

6 πρώτιστα Χάος γένετ'· αὐτὰρ ἔπειτα
Γαῖ' εὐρύστερνος, πάντων ἕδος ἀσφαλὲς αἰεὶ ...
ἠδ' Ἔρος

First Chaos was; next ample-bosomed Earth,
the seat immovable for evermore;
Love, then.

Translated by C.A. Elton (1778–1853)

Theogony 116

quoted by Phaedrus in Plato's Symposium, *Plato 295; and by Aristotle in* Physics *208b.31*

7 Ἔρος, ὃς κάλλιστος ἐν ἀθανάτοισι θεοῖσι,
λυσιμελής, πάντων δὲ θεῶν πάντων τ' ἀνθρώπων
δάμναται ἐν στήθεσσι νόον καὶ ἐπίφρονα βουλήν

And Eros, loveliest of all the Immortals, who
Makes their bodies (and men's bodies) go limp,
Mastering their minds and subduing their wills.

Translated by Stanley Lombardo (1993)

Theogony 120

8 ἐκ Χάεος δ' Ἔρεβός τε μέλαινά τε Νὺξ ἐγένοντο·
Νυκτὸς δ' αὖτ' Αἰθήρ τε καὶ Ἡμέρη ἐξεγένοντο,
οὓς τέκε κυσαμένη Ἐρέβει φιλότητι μιγεῖσα

From Abyss were born Erebos and dark Night;
And Night, pregnant after sweet intercourse
With Erebos, gave birth to Aether and Day.

Translated by Stanley Lombardo (1993)

Theogony 123

9 ἡ δὲ καὶ ἀτρύγετον πέλαγος τέκεν, οἴδματι θυῖον,
Πόντον, ἄτερ φιλότητος ἐφιμέρου· αὐτὰρ ἔπειτα
Οὐρανῷ εὐνηθεῖσα τέκ' Ὠκεανὸν βαθυδίνην

Then, without any sweet intercourse, she gave birth
to the barren, raging Sea; but later she lay with
Heaven and bore deep-swirling Oceanus.

Theogony 131

of Earth

10 αὐτὰρ Ἔρις στυγερὴ τέκε μὲν Πόνον ἀλγινόεντα
Λήθην τε Λιμόν τε καὶ Ἄλγεα δακρυόεντα
Ὑσμίνας τε Μάχας τε Φόνους τ' Ἀνδροκτασίας τε
Νείκεά τε ψευδέας τε Λόγους τ' Ἀμφιλλογίας τε
Δυσνομίην τ' Ἄτην τε

Hateful Strife bore painful Toil,
Neglect, Starvation, tearful Pain,
Battles, Combats, Bloodshed, Slaughter,
Quarrels, Lies, Pretences, Arguments,
Disorder and Disaster.

Translated by M.L. West (1988)

Theogony 226

11 Νηρῆος δ' ἐγένοντο μεγήριτα τέκνα θεάων
πόντῳ ἐν ἀτρυγέτῳ καὶ Δωρίδος ἠυκόμοιο,
κούρης Ὠκεανοῖο ... Γαλήνη ... Κυμοθόη ...
Φέρουσά τε Δυναμένη τε ... Κυματολήγη

And of Nereus and rich-haired Doris, daughter of Ocean, were born
children, passing lovely among goddesses ... Galene ... Cymothoë ...
Pherousa and Dynamene ... Cymatolege ...

Translated by Hugh G. Evelyn-White (1914)

Theogony 240–253

most of the names of the fifty Nereids express qualities of the sea: Galene is Calm, Cymothoë is Wave-swift, Pherousa Ship-speeding, Dynamene Powerful, Cymatolege Wave-stiller; cf. Exegesis in Hesiodem *386.28*

12 ἐκ τῆς γὰρ γένος ἐστὶ γυναικῶν θηλυτεράων …
πῆμα μέγα θνητοῖσι, σὺν ἀνδράσι ναιετάουσαι

From her is the race of womankind, the deadly race and tribe of women, who cause men so much trouble.

Theogony 590

of the likeness of a maiden shaped by Hephaestus to beguile the race of men; cf. John Knox, 'the monstrous tribe of women' (title of a pamphlet, 1558)

13 ἀπὸ βλεφάρων ἔρος εἴβετο δερκομενάων λυσιμελής

Limb-loosening love flowed from their eyes.

Theogony 910

of the three Graces, Aglaea, Euphrosyne and Thalia

14 βροτοὶ ἄνδρες ὁμῶς ἄφατοί τε φατοί τε, ῥητοί τ' ἄρρητοί τε

Of mortal men the nameless and the known,
The famed, th' inglorious.

Translated by C.A. Elton (1778–1853)

Works and Days 3

15 ῥέα μὲν γὰρ βριάει, ῥέα δὲ βριάοντα χαλέπτει

Confounds the mighty, lends the feeble might.

Translated by C.A. Elton (1778–1853)

Works and Days 5

of Zeus

16 ῥεῖα δέ τ' ἰθύνει σκολιὸν καὶ ἀγήνορα κάρφει

He makes the crooked straight, and blasts the strong.

Translated by C.A. Elton (1778–1853)

Works and Days 7

of Zeus

17 οὐκ ἄρα μοῦνον ἔην Ἐρίδων γένος, ἀλλ' ἐπὶ γαῖαν
εἰσὶ δύω· τὴν μέν κεν ἐπαινέσσειε νοήσας,
ἡ δ' ἐπιμωμητή

Of strife there are two kinds, not one:
we all praise healthy rivalry,
but war we all condemn.

Works and Days 11

18 ἀγαθὴ δ' Ἔρις ἥδε βροτοῖσιν

Rivalry is beneficial for mankind.

Works and Days 24

19 καὶ κεραμεὺς κεραμεῖ κοτέει καὶ τέκτονι τέκτων,
καὶ πτωχὸς πτωχῷ φθονέει καὶ ἀοιδὸς ἀοιδῷ

Then potter is potter's enemy, and craftsman is craftsman's rival; tramp is jealous of tramp and singer of singer.

Translated by Richmond Lattimore (1959)

Works and Days 25

cf. ''tis one beggar's woe to see another by the door go'; and the proverb 'two of a trade never agree'

20 νήπιοι, οὐδὲ ἴσασιν ὅσῳ πλέον ἥμισυ παντὸς

Morons, they know not how often the half is better than the whole.

Works and Days 40

cf. the English proverb 'the half is better than the whole', advising economy or restraint, e.g. in conversation

21 τοῖς δ' ἐγὼ ἀντὶ πυρὸς δώσω κακόν, ᾧ κεν ἅπαντες
τέρπωνται κατὰ θυμὸν ἑὸν κακὸν ἀμφαγαπῶντες

As the price for fire, I will give men an evil thing,
so they may rejoice in their own destruction.

Works and Days 57

a woman (of course!)

22 νῦν γὰρ δὴ γένος ἐστὶ σιδήρεον· οὐδέ ποτ' ἦμαρ παύσονται καμάτου καὶ
ὀιζύος, οὐδέ τι νύκτωρ φθειρόμενοι

Without doubt today's is a race of iron: they never rest from labour and suffering by day, nor from destruction by night.

Translated by C.A. Trypanis (1971)

Works and Days 176

23 χαλεπὰς δὲ θεοὶ δώσουσι μερίμνας·

ἀλλ' ἔμπης καὶ τοῖσι μεμείξεται ἐσθλὰ κακοῖσιν

And the gods shall give them painful cares;
yet shall they also have some good mingled with their evils.

Works and Days 178

of humans

24 οὐδὲ πατὴρ παίδεσσιν ὁμοίιος οὐδέ τι παῖδες,
οὐδὲ ξεῖνος ξεινοδόκῳ καὶ ἑταῖρος ἑταίρῳ,
οὐδὲ κασίγνητος φίλος ἔσσεται, ὡς τὸ πάρος περ

And the father will not agree with his children, nor the guest with his host, nor friend with friend, nor will brother love brother as in the past.

Translated by C.A. Trypanis (1971)

Works and Days 182

of Doomsday

25 αἶψα δὲ γηράσκοντας ἀτιμήσουσι τοκῆας·
μέμψονται δ' ἄρα τοὺς χαλεποῖς βάζοντες ἔπεσσι,
σχέτλιοι

To their parents, as they grow old, children will not pay respect, but will reproach them, addressing them with harsh words – the reckless fools!

Translated by C.A. Trypanis (1971)

Works and Days 185

of Doomsday

26 ζῆλος … δυσκέλαδος κακόχαρτος … στυγερώπης

Envy, ugly-voiced, sour-faced, delighting in evil.

Translated by C.A. Trypanis (1971)

Works and Days 195

27 κακοῦ δ' οὐκ ἔσσεται ἀλκή

And there will be no defence against evil.

Translated by C.A. Trypanis (1971)

Works and Days 201

of Doomsday

28 ἄφρων δ', ὅς κ' ἐθέλῃ πρὸς κρείσσονας ἀντιφερίζειν·
νίκης τε στέρεται πρός τ' αἴσχεσιν ἄλγεα πάσχει

A fool is he who sets himself against the stronger;
he cannot win and suffers pain as well as shame.

Works and Days 210

said the hawk to the nightingale; the earliest record of an animal fable in Western literature

29 δίκη δ' ὑπὲρ ὕβριος ἴσχει
ἐς τέλος ἐξελθοῦσα

Justice beats Outrage
when she comes at length to the end of the race.

Translated by Hugh G. Evelyn-White (1914)

Works and Days 217

30 παθὼν δέ τε νήπιος ἔγνω

Even a fool learns from experience.

Works and Days 218

cf. the English proverb 'experience is the mistress of fools'

31 εἰρήνη δ' ἀνὰ γῆν κουροτρόφος

Peace nurtures children, wherever they may be.

Works and Days 228

32 οὐδέ ποτ' ἰθυδίκῃσι μετ' ἀνδράσι λιμὸς ὀπηδεῖ
οὐδ' ἄτη, θαλίῃς δὲ μεμηλότα ἔργα νέμονται·
τοῖσι φέρει μὲν γαῖα πολὺν βίον, οὔρεσι δὲ δρῦς
ἄκρη μέν τε φέρει βαλάνους, μέσση δὲ μελίσσας

Neither famine haunts right-minded men
nor misadventure; in good cheer they tend their fields;
the earth bears plenty, and on the mountains
the oak bears acorns on the top and bees in the midst.

Works and Days 230

33 πολλάκι καὶ ξύμπασα πόλις κακοῦ ἀνδρὸς ἀπηύρα

Often a whole city is punished for one bad man.

Works and Days 240

34 οἷ αὐτῷ κακὰ τεύχει ἀνὴρ ἄλλῳ κακὰ τεύχων,
ἡ δὲ κακὴ βουλὴ τῷ βουλεύσαντι κακίστη

He harms himself who harms another,
an evil plan is most harmful to the planner.

Works and Days 265

35 τὴν μέν τοι κακότητα καὶ ἰλαδὸν ἔστιν ἑλέσθαι
ῥηιδίως· λείη μὲν ὁδός, μάλα δ᾽ ἐγγύθι ναίει·
τῆς δ᾽ ἀρετῆς ... μακρὸς καὶ ὄρθιος οἶμος ἐς αὐτὴν

Evil is in abundance and easily attained:
the road is smooth and close at hand;
but long and steep is the path to excellence.

Works and Days 287

quoted by both Plato, Republic *364c and Xenophon,* Memorabilia *2.1.20; cf. the Latin 'per aspera ad astra'*

36 οὗτος μὲν πανάριστος, ὃς αὐτῷ πάντα νοήσῃ ...
ἐσθλὸς δ᾽ αὖ κἀκεῖνος ὃς εὖ εἰπόντι πίθηται

Altogether best is he who examines all himself,
but he as well who follows good advice.

Translated by Hugh G. Evelyn-White (1914)

Works and Days 293

cf. St Basil 1

37 τῷ δὲ θεοὶ νεμεσῶσι καὶ ἀνέρες ὅς κεν ἀεργὸς
ζώῃ, κηφήνεσσι κοθούροις εἴκελος ὀργήν,
οἵ τε μελισσάων κάματον τρύχουσιν ἀεργοὶ
ἔσθοντες

Both gods and men are angry with a man who lives idly,
for he is like the stingless drones who waste the labour
of the bees, eating without working.

Translated by Hugh G. Evelyn-White (1914)

Works and Days 303

38 ἔργον δ᾽ οὐδὲν ὄνειδος, ἀεργίη δέ τ᾽ ὄνειδος

Work is no disgrace, idleness is.

Works and Days 311

39 πλούτῳ δ᾽ ἀρετὴ καὶ κῦδος ὀπηδεῖ

Fame and glory attend upon wealth.

Works and Days 313

40 αἰδώς, ἥ τ᾽ ἄνδρας μέγα σίνεται ἠδ᾽ ὀνίνησιν

Shame both greatly harms and benefits man.

Works and Days 318

41 εὖτ᾽ ἂν δὴ κέρδος νόον ἐξαπατήσῃ ἀνθρώπων

Gain deceives men's sense.

Translated by Hugh G. Evelyn-White (1914)

Works and Days 323

42 πῆμα κακὸς γείτων, ὅσσον τ᾽ ἀγαθὸς μέγ᾽ ὄνειαρ

A bad neighbour is as great a misfortune
as a good one is a blessing.

Works and Days 346

43 μὴ κακὰ κερδαίνειν· κακὰ κέρδεα ἶσ᾽ ἄτῃσι

Make not evil gains; evil gains are equal
to a loss.

Translated by H.T. Riley (1872)

Works and Days 352

44 τὸν φιλέοντα φιλεῖν, καὶ τῷ προσιόντι προσεῖναι

Be a friend to him who is your friend,
and give your company to him that seeks it.

Translated by M.L. West (1988)

Works and Days 353

45 ὃς μὲν γάρ κεν ἀνὴρ ἐθέλων, ὅ γε καὶ μέγα, δώῃ,
χαίρει τῷ δώρῳ καὶ τέρπεται ὃν κατὰ θυμόν

A willing gift, even if fairly large,
gives joy to him who gives and makes him glad at heart.

Works and Days 357

46 εἰ γάρ κεν καὶ σμικρὸν ἐπὶ σμικρῷ καταθεῖο
καὶ θαμὰ τοῦτ᾽ ἔρδοις, τάχα κεν μέγα καὶ τὸ γένοιτο

By often adding a little to a little,
that little will forthwith grow great.

Works and Days 361

47 οἴκοι βέλτερον εἶναι

There's no place like home.

Translated by John Simpson and Jennifer

Speake (1982)
Works and Days 365
cf. the identical English proverb

48 ἀρχομένου δὲ πίθου καὶ λήγοντος κορέσασθαι,
μεσσόθι φείδεσθαι· δειλὴ δ' ἐν πυθμένι φειδώ

Drink deeply when the flask is full or almost empty,
be sparing when it is half full.

Works and Days 368

49 πίστεις δ' ἄρα ὁμῶς καὶ ἀπιστίαι ὤλεσαν ἄνδρας

Trust and mistrust ruin men, equally.

Works and Days 372

50 πλείων μὲν πλεόνων μελέτη, μείζων δ' ἐπιθήκη

More hands mean more work done and more increase.

Translated by Hugh G. Evelyn-White (1914)
Works and Days 380
cf. the English proverb 'many hands make light work'

51 σοὶ δ' εἰ πλούτου θυμὸς ἐέλδεται ἐν φρεσὶ σῇσιν
ὧδ' ἔρδειν, καὶ ἔργον ἐπ' ἔργῳ ἐργάζεσθαι

If it is wealth your heart desires
work, work and work again.

Works and Days 381

52 μηδ' ἀναβάλλεσθαι ἔς τ' αὔριον ἔς τε ἔνηφιν·
οὐ γὰρ ἐτωσιοεργὸς ἀνὴρ πίμπλησι καλιὴν

Leave not for the morrow what you can do today;
a sluggish worker does not fill the barn.

Works and Days 410
cf. the English proverb 'never put off till tomorrow what you can do today'

53 μελέτη δέ το ἔργον ὀφέλλει·
αἰεὶ δ' ἀμβολιεργὸς ἀνὴρ ἄτῃσι παλαίει

Industry multiplies results, delay leads to ruin.

Works and Days 412

54 φράζεσθαι δ', εὖτ' ἂν γεράνου φωνὴν ἐπακούσῃς
ὑψόθεν ἐκ νεφέων ἐνιαύσια κεκληγυίης,
ἥτ' ἀρότοιό τε σῆμα φέρει καὶ χείματος ὥρην
δεικνύει ὀμβρηροῦ

Mark yearly when among the clouds on high
Thou hears't the shrill crane's migratory cry;
Of ploughing-time the sign and wintry rains.

Translated by C.A. Elton (1778–1853)
Works and Days 448

55 πολλὰ δ' ἀεργὸς ἀνήρ, κενεὴν ἐπὶ ἐλπίδα μίμνων,
χρηίζων βιότοιο, κακὰ προσελέξατο θυμῷ

The idle man who waits on empty hope,
lacking a livelihood, reaps a host of troubles.

Translated by Hugh G. Evelyn-White (1914)
Works and Days 498

56 οὐκ αἰεὶ θέρος ἐσσεῖται, ποιεῖσθε καλιάς

It will not be summer forever: gather the harvest while you may.

Works and Days 503
cf. the English proverb 'make hay while the sun shines'

57 γῆ πάντων μήτηρ

Earth, the mother of all.

Translated by Hugh G. Evelyn-White (1914)
Works and Days 563

58 ἠώς τοι προφέρει μὲν ὁδοῦ, προφέρει δὲ καὶ ἔργου

Dawn speeds a man on his journey, and speeds him on in his work.

Works and Days 579

59 καὶ κύνα καρχαρόδοντα κομεῖν, μὴ φείδεο σίτου,
μή ποτέ σ' ἡμερόκοιτος ἀνὴρ ἀπὸ χρήμαθ' ἕληται

Tend and feed that fierce dog well, lest those
who sleep by day steal your possessions.

Works and Days 604
sleeping by day, epithet of a thief

60 νῆ' ὀλίγην αἰνεῖν, μεγάλῃ δ' ἐνὶ φορτία θέσθαι

Praise a small ship, but put your goods on a big one.

Translated in Liddell & Scott

Works and Days 643

61 χρήματα γὰρ ψυχὴ πέλεται δειλοῖσι βροτοῖσιν

For wealth means life to wretched mortals.

Translated by C.A. Trypanis (1971)

Works and Days 686

62 μέτρα φυλάσσεσθαι· καιρὸς δ' ἐπὶ πᾶσιν ἄριστος

Observe due measure; moderation is best in all things.

Works and Days 694

cf. the English proverb 'moderation in all things'

63 Ὡραῖος δὲ γυναῖκα τεὸν ποτὶ οἶκον ἄγεσθαι,
μήτε τριηκόντων ἐτέων μάλα πόλλ' ἀπολείπων
μήτ' ἐπιθεὶς μάλα πολλά· γάμος δέ τοι ὥριος οὗτος·
ἡ δὲ γυνὴ τέτορ' ἡβώοι, πέμπτῳ δὲ γαμοῖτο

Bring a wife home only when your age is right,
not much less than thirty, but neither much thereafter;
this is the best age for marriage; as for your wife
wait four years after puberty, marry her in the fifth.

Works and Days 695

64 τὴν δὲ μάλιστα γαμεῖν, ἥτις σέθεν ἐγγύθι ναίει

Marry a woman who lives near you, in preference to others.

Translated by H.T. Riley (1872)

Works and Days 700

or 'with whose mind you are acquainted'

65 πάντα μάλ' ἀμφὶς ἰδών, μὴ γείτοσι χάρματα γήμῃς

Look circumspect and long; lest thou be found
The merry mock of all the dwellers round.

Translated by C.A. Elton (1778–1853)

Works and Days 701

66 γλώσσης τοι θησαυρὸς ἐν ἀνθρώποισιν ἄριστος
φειδωλῆς, πλείστη δὲ χάρις κατὰ μέτρον ἰούσης

The tongue's best treasure among men is when it is sparing, and its greatest charm is when it goes in measure.

Translated by M.L. West (1988)

Works and Days 719

67 εἰ δὲ κακὸν εἴποις, τάχα κ' αὐτὸς μεῖζον ἀκούσαις

If you speak evil, you yourself will soon be worse spoken of.

Translated by Hugh G. Evelyn-White (1914)

Works and Days 721

68 ἐκ κοινοῦ πλείστη τε χάρις δαπάνη τ' ὀλιγίστη

When all share, the pleasure is greatest and the expense least.

Translated by M.L. West (1988)

Works and Days 723

of a banquet and an entertaining conversation; later proverbial

69 φήμη γάρ τε κακὴ πέλεται, κούφη μὲν ἀεῖραι
ῥεῖα μάλ', ἀργαλέη δὲ φέρειν, χαλεπὴ δ' ἀποθέσθαι

A bad reputation is easy to come by, painful to bear, and difficult to clear.

Works and Days 761

70 φήμη δ' οὔ τις πάμπαν ἀπόλλυται

Rumour never wholly dies away.

Translated in Liddell & Scott

Works and Days 763

71 ἄλλοτε μητρυιὴ πέλει ἡμέρη, ἄλλοτε μήτηρ

Sometimes a day comes as a stepmother, sometimes as a mother.

Works and Days 825

72 τάων εὐδαίμων τε καὶ ὄλβιος ὃς τάδε πάντα
εἰδὼς ἐργάζηται ἀναίτιος ἀθανάτοισιν,
ὄρνιθας κρίνων καὶ ὑπερβασίας ἀλεείνων

Blessed and happy he
who lives unblamed by the immortals,
interpreting omens and shunning sin.

Works and Days 826

closing lines

73 σχέτλιος· ἦ που πολλὰ μετεστοναχίζετ' ὀπίσσω
ἣν ἄτην ὀχέων

Unhappy he who grieves hereafter for his previous folly.

Shield of Heracles 92

74 νήπιος, ὃς τὰ ἑτοῖμα λιπὼν ἀνέτοιμα διώκει

A fool is he who forsakes certainty to chase uncertainties.

Fragment 61 (Merkelbach and West)

75 ἐκ τοῦ δ' ὅρκον ἔθηκεν ἀποίνιμον ἀνθρώποισι νοσφιδίων ἔργων πέρι Κύπριδος

Since then he attached no penalty for false oaths taken in love.

Fragment 124 (Merkelbach and West)

of Zeus; cf. the English proverb 'Jove but laughs at lovers' perjury'

76 ἔς τε Κεφαλλήνων ἀγερώχων φῦλον ὄρουσαν,
οὓς τέκεν Ἑρμάωνι Καλυψὼ πότνια νύμφη

To the tribe of the lordly Cephallenians they hastened,
whom Calypso, queenly nymph, bore to Hermes.

Translated by Glenn W. Most (2007)

Fragment 150.30 (Merkelbach and West)

from an Oxyrhynchus papyrus

77 εἴ κε πάθοι, τά τ' ἔρεξε, δίκη κ' ἰθεῖα γένοιτο

It is nothing but strict justice if a man suffers from his own deeds.

Translated by H.T. Riley (1872)

Fragment 286 (Merkelbach and West)

quoted by Aristotle in Nicomachean Ethics *1132b.27 as the Rule of Rhadamanthys and 'as the Pythagoreans said (on the Reciprocity in Justice)'*

78 ἔργα νέων, βουλαὶ δὲ μέσων, εὐχαὶ δὲ γερόντων

Action is for the young, counsel for the middle-aged, prayers for the old.

Fragment 321 (Merkelbach and West)

79 μηδὲ δίκην δικάσῃς, πρὶν ἄμφω μῦθον ἀκούσῃς

Do not pass judgement before hearing both sides.

Fragment 338 (Merkelbach and West)

cf. Euripides, Children of Heracles *179; quoted in Aristophanes 139, probably 'proverbial' by then*

80 Ἡσίοδος ... τὴν ἀργίαν ὡς ἀδικίας ἀρχὴν λελοιδόρηκεν

Hesiod abuses idleness as the beginning of wrongdoing.

Plutarch, *Comparison of Aristides and Cato Major* 3.3

HIERAX

2nd/3rd century AD (?)
Thought to be a Platonist, possibly from Egypt

1 πᾶσα δὲ πρᾶξις ἐνέργεια ψυχῆς διὰ σώματος

Every action originates in the soul; the body is the vehicle.

Stobaeus, *Anthology* 3.9.54

HIEROCLES

active 117–138AD
Stoic philosopher, writer of *Elements of Ethics*

1 ἅπαν μὲν γὰρ ἡμῶν τὸ γένος ἔφυ πρὸς κοινωνίαν, πρώτη δὲ καὶ στοιχειωδεστάτη τῶν κοινωνιῶν ἡ κατὰ τὸν γάμον. οὔτε γὰρ πόλεις ἂν ἦσαν μὴ ὄντων οἴκων, οἶκός τε ἡμιτελὴς μὲν τῷ ὄντι ὁ τοῦ ἀγάμου, τέλειος δὲ καὶ πλήρης ὁ τοῦ γεγαμηκότος

Men are created to live in communities and the first and most essential social bond is that of marriage. For there would be no city without families. The home of the unmarried is unfinished, whilst the perfect and complete family is that of a married man.

Stobaeus, *Anthology* 4.22a.21

HIERONYMUS OF RHODES

lived in Athens *c.*290–230BC
Philosopher and historian of literature

1 εἰπόντος Σοφοκλεῖ τινος ὅτι μισογύνης ἐστὶν Εὐριπίδης, ἔφη ὁ Σοφοκλῆς, ἐπεὶ ἐν γε τῇ κλίνῃ φιλογύνης

Someone said to Sophocles that Euripides was a misogynist; to which Sophocles remarked, 'But not, of course, in bed!'

Fragment 36 (Wehrli)

HIPPARCHUS (1)

died 514BC

Younger son of Pisistratus of Athens, patron and lover of the arts

1 στεῖχε δίκαια φρονῶν

Go along, dwell on just thoughts.

Fragment 1 (Diehl)

inscribed as his epitaph

HIPPARCHUS (2)

*fl. c.*260BC

New Comedy poet and (probably) actor

1 πολύ γ' ἐστὶ πάντων κτῆμα τιμιώτατον
ἅπασιν ἀνθρώποισιν εἰς τὸ ζῆν τέχνη·
τὰ μὲν γὰρ ἄλλα καὶ πόλεμος καὶ μεταβολαὶ
τύχης ἀνήλωσ', ἡ τέχνη δὲ σῴζεται

The most precious possession for all mankind is art; other possessions can be lost through war and change, but art lasts for ever.

Fragment 2 (Kock) – 2 (K-A) – *Zographos – The Painter*

HIPPOCLEIDES

6th century BC

Athenian aristocrat

1 οὐ φροντὶς Ἱπποκλείδῃ

Hippocleides couldn't care less!

Herodotus, *Histories* 6.129

when told that he had forfeited the hand of Agarista, daughter of the tyrant of Sicyon, because of misconduct

HIPPOCRATES

*c.*460–*c.*377BC

Physician from the island of Kos

1 καὶ γὰρ νουσήματα εἴωθεν ἀπὸ σμικρῶν προφασίων μεγάλα καὶ πολυχρόνια γίνεσθαι

Ailments are wont to develop from small causes into severe and long-protracted afflictions.

Affections 33

2 αἱ γὰρ μεταβολαί εἰσι ... αἵ τε ἐγείρουσαι τὴν γνώμην τῶν ἀνθρώπων, καὶ οὐκ ἐῶσαι ἀτρεμίζειν

It is change that keeps us alert and prevents us from stagnation.

Airs, Waters, Places 16

3 οὐδὲν ἄνευ φύσιος γίγνεται

Nothing arises without a natural cause.

Airs, Waters, Places 22

4 ἀπὸ μὲν ἡσυχίης καὶ ῥᾳθυμίης ἡ δειλίη αὔξεται, ἀπὸ δὲ τῆς ταλαιπωρίης καὶ τῶν πόνων αἱ ἀνδρεῖαι

Rest and slackness are food for cowardice, endurance and exertion for bravery.

Translated by W.H.S. Jones (1923)

Airs, Waters, Places 23

5 ἰητρικῇ δὲ πάντα πάλαι ὑπάρχει, καὶ ἀρχὴ καὶ ὁδὸς εὑρημένη, καθ' ἣν καὶ τὰ εὑρημένα πολλά τε καὶ καλῶς ἔχοντα εὕρηται ἐν πολλῷ χρόνῳ, καὶ τὰ λοιπὰ εὑρεθήσεται, ἤν τις ἱκανός τε ἐὼν καὶ τὰ εὑρημένα εἰδώς, ἐκ τουτέων ὁρμώμενος ζητέῃ

The science of medicine has always existed, and many ways of healing have been found and proven successful through the years, and many more shall be discovered by persons capable and bent on research, based on what is already known.

Ancient Medicine 2

6 τό γε εὕρημα καὶ μέγα καὶ πολλῆς τέχνης τε καὶ σκέψιος· ἔτι γοῦν καὶ νῦν ... αἰεί τι προσεξευρίσκουσι, κατὰ τὴν αὐτέην ὁδὸν ζητέοντες

Discovery has been the result of much investigation and art. Even now new discoveries are made constantly following the same way of research.

Ancient Medicine 4

7 τὸ δ' ἀκριβὲς ὀλιγάκις ἐστὶ κατιδεῖν

Perfectly exact truth is but rarely to be seen.

Translated by W.H.S. Jones (1923)

Ancient Medicine 9

8 οὐκ ἔνι δυνατὸν ἰητρικὴν εἰδέναι ὅστις μὴ οἶδεν ὅ τί ἐστιν ἄνθρωπος

It is impossible to understand medicine

if you do not know what is man.

Ancient Medicine 20

9 ὁ βίος βραχύς, ἡ δὲ τέχνη μακρή

The lyf so short, the craft so long to lerne.

Translated by Geoffrey Chaucer, *The Parliament of Fowls* (c.1380) line 1

Aphorisms 1.1

this rendering by Chaucer reflects the words of Hippocrates better than 'Art is long and life is short', by now a proverb in many modern languages (τέχνη having now a more restricted meaning); cf. next entry

10 ὁ βίος βραχύς, ἡ δὲ τέχνη μακρή, ὁ δὲ καιρὸς ὀξύς, ἡ δὲ πεῖρα σφαλερή, ἡ δὲ κρίσις χαλεπή

Life is short, the art is long, opportunity fleeting, experience treacherous, judgement difficult.

Translated by W.H.S. Jones (1931)

Aphorisms 1.1

11 ἐς τὸ ἔσχατον λεπτότητος ἀφιγμέναι δίαιται χαλεπαί

A regimen carried to the extreme of restriction is perilous.

Translated by W.H.S. Jones (1931)

Aphorisms 1.4

12 ἐς δὲ τὰ ἔσχατα νουσήματα αἱ ἔσχαται θεραπεῖαι ἐς ἀκριβείην κράτισται

For extreme illnesses extreme treatments are most fitting.

Translated in *Bartlett's Familiar Quotations* (1980)

Aphorisms 1.6

cf. Shakespeare, Hamlet *4.3.9: 'diseases desperate grown by desperate appliance are reliev'd, or not at all'*

13 ὁκόταν δὲ ἀκμάζῃ τὸ νούσημα, τότε λεπτοτάτῃ διαίτῃ ἀναγκαῖον χρέεσθαι

It is when the disease is at its height that it is necessary to use the strictest course of treatment.

Aphorisms 1.8

14 ὕπνος, ἀγρυπνίη, ἀμφότερα τοῦ μετρίου μᾶλλον γενόμενα, κακόν

Sleep or sleeplessness in undue measure are both bad symptoms.

Aphorisms 2.3

15 πᾶν τὸ πολὺ τῇ φύσει πολέμιον

All excess is hostile to nature.

Translated by W.H.S. Jones (1931)

Aphorisms 2.51

16 πάντα κατὰ λόγον ποιέοντι ... μὴ μεταβαίνειν ἐφ' ἕτερον

When acting in all things according to rule, do not change to another course.

Translated by W.H.S. Jones (1931)

Aphorisms 2.52

17 ὁκόσα φάρμακα οὐκ ἰῆται, σίδηρος ἰῆται· ὅσα σίδηρος οὐκ ἰῆται, πῦρ ἰῆται· ὅσα δὲ πῦρ οὐκ ἰῆται, ταῦτα χρὴ νομίζειν ἀνίατα

Those diseases that medicines do not cure are cured by the knife. Those that the knife does not cure are cured by fire. Those that fire does not cure must be considered incurable.

Translated by W.H.S. Jones (1931)

Aphorisms 7.87

a favourite quotation in operating theatres

18 νομίζω ἰητρικὴν εἶναι τὸ δὴ πάμπαν ἀπαλλάσσειν τῶν νοσεόντων τοὺς καμάτους, καὶ τῶν νοσημάτων τὰς σφοδρότητας ἀμβλύνειν, καὶ τὸ μὴ ἐγχειρέειν τοῖσι κεκρατημένοισιν ὑπὸ τῶν νοσημάτων, εἰδότας ὅτι ταῦτα οὐ δύναται ἰητρική

I believe that essential features of the art of medicine are to deliver the ailing from all pain, to lessen the intensity of the disease, and to refuse to treat those who are incurable, realizing that in such cases medicine is powerless.

The Art 3

cf. Hippocrates 51

19 ὅσα γὰρ τὴν τῶν ὀμμάτων ὄψιν ἐκφεύγει, ταῦτα τῇ τῆς γνώμης ὄψει κεκράτηται

What escapes the eyes is mastered by the eye of the mind.

Translated by W.H.S. Jones (1923)

The Art 11

20 μὴ τόλμῃ μᾶλλον ἢ γνώμῃ, καὶ ῥᾳστώνῃ μᾶλλον ἢ βίῃ θεραπεύῃ

When treating a patient use judgement rather than over-boldness, calm rather than haste.

The Art 11

21 τὸ γὰρ ἔθος τῇσι χερσὶ κάλλιστον διδασκάλιον γίνεται

Practice is the best teacher of the hands.

Breaths 1

22 τὰ ἐναντία τῶν ἐναντίων ἐστὶν ἰήματα

Opposites are cures for opposites.

Translated by W.H.S. Jones (1923)

Breaths 1

23 τὰ μὲν ἄλλα πάντα διαλείπουσιν οἱ ἄνθρωποι πρήσσοντες, ὁ γὰρ βίος μεταβολέων πλέως

Life is full of changes; all our activities are intermittent.

Breaths 4

24 τὸ γὰρ σχολάζον καὶ ἄπρηκτον ζητέει ἐς κακίην καὶ ἀφέλκεσθαι

Idleness and lack of occupation tend – nay are dragged – towards evil.

Translated by W.H.S. Jones (1923)

Decorum 1

25 ἡγεμονικώτατον ... ἁπάντων ... ἡ φύσις

The dominant factor is nature.

Translated by W.H.S. Jones (1923)

Decorum 4

discussing healing

26 πᾶν γὰρ τὸ ποιηθὲν τεχνικῶς ἐκ λόγου ἀνηνέχθη

Everything skilfully achieved is the result of reasoning.

Decorum 4

27 τὸ γὰρ οἴεσθαι μὲν, μὴ πρήσσειν δὲ, ἀμαθίης καὶ ἀτεχνίης σημεῖόν ἐστιν

Opinions not proved in action show lack of education and skill.

Decorum 4

28 καὶ περιπατέειν, καὶ γυμνάζεσθαι ὀλίγα· ἢν δὲ ἀσθενέστερος ᾖ ἢ ὥστε γυμνάζεσθαι, ὁδοιπορίῃ χρῆσθαι

Have him take walks, and do a few exercises; and if he is too weak for exercises, then let him take strolls.

Translated by Paul Potter (1988)

Diseases 2.66

Hippocrates has some five dozen admonitions on when and how to walk and exercise, and when not to

29 ἢν δὲ βούληται περιπατεῖν, περιπατείτω ἐν ὁμαλῷ χωρίῳ καὶ λείῳ, πρὸς ἄναντες δὲ μηδὲν, μηδὲ κάταντες

And if she wants to walk, let her walk on even and smooth ground, by no means uphill, nor downhill.

Diseases of Women 11

of expectant mothers

30 λέγειν τὰ προγενόμενα· γιγνώσκειν τὰ παρεόντα· προλέγειν τὰ ἐσόμενα

Declare the past, diagnose the present, foretell the future.

Translated by W.H.S. Jones (1923)

Epidemics 1.2.5

31 ὠφελέειν, ἢ μὴ βλάπτειν

Help, or at least do no harm.

Epidemics 1.2.5

32 ὁ ἰητρὸς, ὑπηρέτης τῆς τέχνης

The physician is the servant of the art.

Translated by W.H.S. Jones (1923)

Epidemics 1.2.5

33 ὑπεναντιοῦσθαι τῷ νουσήματι τὸν νοσεῦντα μετὰ τοῦ ἰητροῦ χρή

The patient must cooperate with the physician in combating the disease.

Translated by W.H.S. Jones (1923)

Epidemics 1.2.5

34 μέγα δὲ μέρος ἡγεῦμαι τῆς τέχνης εἶναι τὸ δύνασθαι κατασκοπέεσθαι περὶ τῶν γεγραμμένων ὀρθῶς

I consider that using medical literature correctly is a most important part of the art of medicine.

Epidemics 3.3.16

35 μηδὲν εἰκῇ, μηδὲν ὑπερορῆν

Nothing happens at random, overlook nothing.

Epidemics 6.2.12

36 αἱ τοῖσι κάμνουσι χάριτες, οἷον τὸ καθαρίως δρῆν ἢ ποτὰ ἢ βρωτὰ ἢ ἃ ἂν ὁρᾷ, μαλακῶς ὅσα ψαύει ... εἴσοδοι, λόγοι, σχῆμα, ἐσθὴς, τῷ νοσέοντι, κουρὴ, ὄνυχες, ὀδμαί

Be gentle towards those who are ill; Observe cleanliness in their food and drink, and in what they see; touch softly;

be mindful of your entrance, of what you say; attend to the patient's position, his clothing, hair, nails, scent.

Epidemics 6.4.7

this description of courtesy to the patient drew much attention from ancient commentators

37 πόνοι σιτίων ἡγείσθωσαν

Exercise before food.

Translated by Wesley D. Smith (1994)

Epidemics 6.4.23

38 νούσων φύσιες ἰητροί

Nature is the first physician.

Epidemics 6.5.1

39 γῆν μεταμείβειν ξύμφορον ἐπὶ τοῖσι μακροῖσι νουσήμασιν

A change of environment is beneficial in a long illness.

Epidemics 6.5.13

40 σιτία, ποτὰ, ὕπνος, ἀφροδίσια, μέτρια

Food, drink, sleep, sex, in moderation.

Epidemics 6.6.2

41 μάλα γὰρ καὶ φύσις φύσιος, καὶ ἡλικίη ἡλικίης διαφέρει

Constitution from constitution, age from age, differ enormously.

Fractures 7

42 ἔχει γὰρ ὧδε ἡ γῆ ἐν ἑωυτῇ δυνάμιας παντοίας καὶ ἀναρίθμους

The earth has inside herself innumerable forces of all kinds.

On Generation, Nature of the Child, Diseases (IV) 34

43 ἀγαθὸν γὰρ φάρμακόν ἐστιν ἐνίοτε καὶ τὸ μηδὲν προσφέρειν

Sometimes it is good to administer no treatment at all.

On Joints 40

44 αἰσχρὸν μέντοι καὶ ἐν πάσῃ τέχνῃ καὶ οὐχ ἥκιστα ἐν ἰητρικῇ πολὺν ὄχλον, καὶ πολλὴν ὄψιν, καὶ πολὺν λόγον παρασχόντα, ἔπειτα μηδὲν ὠφελῆσαι

It is disgraceful in every art, and more especially in medicine, after much trouble, much display, and much talk, to do no good after all.

Translated by Francis Adams (1796–1861)

On Joints 44

45 ἰητρικὴ τεχνέων μὲν πασέων ἐστὶν ἐπιφανεστάτη· διὰ δὲ ἀμαθίην τῶν τε χρεομένων αὐτῇ, καὶ τῶν εἰκῇ τοὺς τοιούσδε κρινόντων, πολύ τι πασέων ἤδη τῶν τεχνέων ἀπολείπεται

Medicine is the most distinguished of all the arts, but through the ignorance of those who practise it, and of those who casually judge such practitioners, it is now of all the arts by far the least esteemed.

Translated by W.H.S. Jones (1923)

Law 1

46 δειλίη μὲν γὰρ ἀδυναμίην σημαίνει· θρασύτης δὲ, ἀτεχνίην

Cowardice indicates powerlessness; rashness indicates want of art.

Translated by W.H.S. Jones (1923)

Law 4.6

47 δύο γὰρ, ἐπιστήμη τε καὶ δόξα, ὧν τὸ μὲν ἐπίστασθαι ποιέει, τὸ δὲ ἀγνοεῖν

There are two things, science and opinion; the former begets knowledge, the latter ignorance.

Translated by W.H.S. Jones (1923)

Law 4.7

48 τὰ δὲ ἱερὰ ἐόντα πρήγματα ἱεροῖσιν ἀνθρώποισι δείκνυται

What is holy is revealed only to the holy.

Law 5

49 αἱ δὲ νοῦσοι γίνονται, αἱ μὲν ἀπὸ τῶν διαιτημάτων, αἱ δὲ ἀπὸ τοῦ πνεύματος, ὃ ἐσαγόμενοι ζῶμεν

Diseases arise in some cases from a bad diet, in other cases from the very air we breathe.

Nature of Man 9

50 Ὄμνυμι Ἀπόλλωνα ἰητρὸν, καὶ Ἀσκληπιὸν, καὶ Ὑγείαν, καὶ Πανάκειαν, καὶ θεοὺς πάντας τε καὶ πάσας, ἵστορας ποιεύμενος, ἐπιτελέα ποιήσειν κατὰ δύναμιν καὶ κρίσιν ἐμὴν ὅρκον τόνδε καὶ ξυγγραφὴν τήνδε

I swear by Apollo Physician, by Asclepius, by Health, by Panacea, and by all the gods and goddesses, making them my witnesses, that I will carry out, according to my ability and judgement, this oath and this indenture.

Translated by W.H.S. Jones (1923)

The Hippocratic Oath 1

51 διαιτήμασί τε χρήσομαι ἐπ' ὠφελείῃ καμνόντων κατὰ δύναμιν καὶ κρίσιν ἐμὴν, ἐπὶ δηλήσει δὲ καὶ ἀδικίῃ εἴρξειν. οὐ δώσω δὲ οὐδὲ φάρμακον οὐδενὶ αἰτηθεὶς θανάσιμον, οὐδὲ ὑφηγήσομαι ξυμβουλίην τοιήνδε· ὁμοίως δὲ οὐδὲ γυναικὶ πεσσὸν φθόριον δώσω. ἁγνῶς δὲ καὶ ὁσίως διατηρήσω βίον τὸν ἐμὸν καὶ τέχνην τὴν ἐμήν

I will use treatment to help the sick according to my ability and judgement, but never with a view to injury and wrongdoing. Neither will I administer a poison to anybody when asked to do so, nor will I suggest such course. Similarly, I will not give to a woman a pessary to cause abortion. But I will keep pure and holy both my life and my art.

Translated by W.H.S. Jones (1923)

The Hippocratic Oath 12

but cf. Hippocrates 18 and Sophocles 160

52 ἐς οἰκίας δὲ ὁκόσας ἂν ἐσίω, ἐσελεύσομαι ἐπ' ὠφελείῃ καμνόντων, ἐκτὸς ἐὼν πάσης ἀδικίης ἑκουσίης καὶ φθορίης ... ἃ δ' ἂν ἐν θεραπείῃ ἢ ἴδω, ἢ ἀκούσω ... σιγήσομαι, ἄῤῥητα ἡγεύμενος εἶναι τὰ τοιαῦτα

Into whatsoever houses I enter, I will enter to help the sick, and I will abstain from all intentional wrong-doing and harm. And whatsoever I shall see or hear in the course of my profession I will never divulge, holding such things to be holy secrets.

Translated by W.H.S. Jones (1923)

The Hippocratic Oath 18

53 ὅρκον μὲν οὖν μοι τόνδε ἐπιτελέα ποιέοντι καὶ μὴ ξυγχέοντι, εἴη ἐπαύρασθαι καὶ βίου καὶ τέχνης δοξαζομένῳ παρὰ πᾶσιν ἀνθρώποις ἐς τὸν αἰεὶ χρόνον· παραβαίνοντι δὲ καὶ ἐπιορκοῦντι, τἀναντία τουτέων.

Now if I carry out this oath, and break it not, may I gain for ever reputation among all men for my life and for my art; but if I transgress it and forswear myself, may the opposite befall me.

Translated by W.H.S. Jones (1923)

The Hippocratic Oath 24

54 ἰητρικὴν οὐ δυνατόν ἐστι ταχὺ μαθεῖν

Medicine is not a profession that can be learned quickly.

Places in Man 41

55 χρόνος ἐστὶν ἐν ᾧ καιρὸς καὶ καιρὸς ἐν ᾧ χρόνος οὐ πολύς

Time is that wherein there is opportunity, and opportunity is that wherein there is no great time.

Translated by W.H.S. Jones (1923)

Precepts 1

56 ἄκεσις χρόνῳ, ἔστι δὲ ἡνίκα καὶ καιρῷ

Healing is a matter of time, but it is sometimes also a matter of opportunity.

Translated by W.H.S. Jones (1923)

Precepts 1

57 τὴν φύσιν ... ἡ δὲ διάνοια παρ' αὐτῆς λαβοῦσα ὕστερον εἰς ἀληθείην ἤγαγεν

The intellect, taking over from nature, leads us to truth.

Precepts 1

58 ὁτὲ δὲ προῖκα ... ἢν δὲ καιρὸς εἴη χορηγίης ξένῳ τε ἐόντι καὶ ἀπορέοντι, μάλιστα ἐπαρκέειν τοῖσι τοιουτέοισιν· ἢν γὰρ παρῇ φιλανθρωπίη, πάρεστι καὶ φιλοτεχνίη

Sometimes give your services for nothing; and if there is an opportunity of serving one who is a stranger in financial straits, give full assistance to all such; for where there is love of man, there is also love of the art.

Translated by W.H.S. Jones (1923)

Precepts 6

59 πάσῃ γὰρ εὐπορίῃ ἀπορίη ἔνεστι

In all abundance distress is also present.

Precepts 8

a play on the words εὐπορία – ἀπορία

60 ἢν δὲ καὶ εἵνεκα ὁμίλου θέλῃς ἀκρόασιν ποιήσασθαι, οὐκ ἀγακλεῶς ἐπιθυμέεις, μὴ μέντοι γε μετὰ μαρτυρίης ποιητικῆς· ἀδυναμίην γὰρ ἐμφαίνει φιλοπονίη

Do not rejoice unduly in a large audience; and at least don't quote poetry, it is only a sign of weakness.

Precepts 12

61 περὶ δὲ ὕπνων, ὥσπερ κατὰ φύσιν ξύνηθες ἡμῖν ἐστι, τὴν μὲν ἡμέρην ἐγρηγορέναι χρή, τὴν δὲ νύκτα καθεύδειν

As for sleep, the patient ought to follow the natural course of being awake during the day and asleep during the night.

Translated by W.H.S. Jones (1923)

Prognostic 10

62 αἱ ψυχαί τε καὶ τὰ σώματα πλεῖστον διαφέρουσιν αἱ τῶν ἀνθρώπων, καὶ δύναμιν ἔχουσι μεγίστην

The minds and the bodies of people differ very greatly, and these differences have great consequences.

Translated by Paul Potter (1995)

Prorrhetic 2.12

63 οὐ δύναται ἐσθίων ὥνθρωπος ὑγιαίνειν, ἢν μὴ καὶ πονέῃ

Eating is not enough to keep a man well; he must also take exercise.

Regimen 2

64 ἀνθρώπου ψυχὴ ἐν ἀνθρώπῳ αὐξάνεται, ἐν ἄλλῳ δὲ οὐδενί

A man's soul grows in a man, and in no other creature.

Translated by W.H.S. Jones (1931)

Regimen 6

65 ὁ μὲν εἰδὼς ἀεὶ ὀρθῶς, ὁ δὲ μὴ εἰδὼς ἄλλοτε ἄλλως

He who knows rightly understands always, he who knows not, sometimes understands rightly, sometimes not.

Regimen 12

66 πουλλοὶ θαυμάζουσιν, ὀλίγοι γινώσκουσιν

Many admire, few know.

Translated by W.H.S. Jones (1931)

Regimen 24

67 ξυνίστασθαι δὲ δύναται καὶ τὸ θῆλυ καὶ τὸ ἄρσεν πρὸς ἄλληλα … διότι ἡ μὲν ψυχὴ τωὐτὸ πᾶσι τοῖσιν ἐμψύχοισι, τὸ δὲ σῶμα διαφέρει ἑκάστου

Male and female have the power to fuse into one because soul is the same in all living creatures, although the body of each is different.

Translated by W.H.S. Jones (1931)

Regimen 28

68 χρὴ προμηθέεσθαι πρὶν ἂν ἐς τὰς νούσους ἀφικνέωνται

Prevention is imperative, before disease strikes.

Regimen 72

cf. the expression 'prevention is better than cure'

69 καὶ τὸ μὲν εὔχεσθαι πρέπον καὶ λίην ἐστὶν ἀγαθόν· δεῖ δὲ καὶ αὐτὸν ξυλλαμβάνοντα τοὺς θεοὺς ἐπικαλέεσθαι

Prayer indeed is good, but while calling on the gods a man should lend a hand himself.

Translated by W.H.S. Jones (1931)

Regimen 87

70 ὁκόσα δὲ δοκέει ὁ ἄνθρωπος θεωρέειν τῶν συνήθων, ψυχῆς ἐπιθυμίην σημαίνει

Whenever a man dreams of familiar objects, it indicates a desire of the soul.

Regimen 93

71 τῆς διαιτητικῆς ἐστι μέγιστον παρατηρέειν καὶ φυλάσσειν

The most important part of the diet is to observe closely and be on guard.

*Regimen in Acute Diseases (Appendix)** 22

72 δεῖ οὖν πρὸς τὴν ἡλικίην καὶ τὴν ὥρην καὶ τὸ ἔθος καὶ τὴν χώρην καὶ τὰ εἴδεα τὰ διαιτήματα ποιέεσθαι

In fixing a diet pay attention to age, season, habit, land and physique.

Translated by W.H.S. Jones (1931)

Regimen in Health 2

73 ἄνδρα δὲ χρή, ὅς ἐστι συνετός, λογισάμενον ὅτι τοῖσιν ἀνθρώποισι πλείστου ἄξιόν ἐστιν ἡ ὑγιείη, ἐπίστασθαι ἐκ τῆς ἑωυτοῦ γνώμης ἐν τῇσι νούσοισιν ὠφελέεσθαι

A wise man should consider that health is the greatest of human blessings, and learn how by his own thought to derive benefit from his illnesses.

Translated by W.H.S. Jones (1931)

Regimen in Health 9

74 τὸν ἐγκέφαλον … τὴν κίνησιν τοῖσι μέλεσι παρέχει … ἐς δὲ τὴν ξύνεσιν ὁ ἐγκέφαλός ἐστιν ὁ διαγγέλλων

The brain tells the limbs how to act, the brain is the messenger to consciousness and tells it what is happening.

Translated by Karl Popper (1977)

On the Sacred Disease 7 and 16

75 οὐχ ὁ θεὸς τὸ σῶμα λυμαίνεται, ἀλλ' ἡ νοῦσος

It is not a god but the disease which injures the body.

Translated by W.H.S. Jones (1923)

On the Sacred Disease 11

of epilepsy

76 νομίζω τὸν ἐγκέφαλον δύναμιν πλείστην ἔχειν ἐν τῷ ἀνθρώπῳ

I hold that the brain is the most powerful organ of the body.

Translated by W.H.S. Jones (1923)

On the Sacred Disease 16

77 ὅτι χρῆσις κρατύνει, ἀργίη δὲ τήκει

Use strengthens, disuse debilitates.

Translated by E.T. Withington (1928)

In the Surgery 20

78 ὁ ἄριστα διαγνοὺς ἄριστα καὶ θεραπεύει

Perfect diagnosis, perfect treatment.

Stephanus, *Scholia to Hippocrates'* Prognosticon 1.1

HIPPONAX

*c.*570–520BC

Iambic poet of Ephesus and Clazomenae

1 χρόνος δὲ φευγέτω σε μηδὲ εἷς ἀργός

Do not allow time to idly slip away.

Fragment 64 (West, *IEG*)

2 δύ' ἡμέραι γυναικός εἰσιν ἥδισται,
ὅταν γαμῇ τις κἀκφέρῃ τεθνηκυῖαν

There are two days when woman is a pleasure: the day one marries her and the day one buries her.

Translated in *Bartlett's Familiar Quotations* (1980)

Fragment 68 (West, *IEG*)

cf. J. Dryden: 'Here lies my wife: here let her lie! / Now she's at rest, and so am I.' (Epitaph Intended for his Wife)

3 γάμος κράτιστός ἐστιν ἀνδρὶ σώφρονι,
τρόπον γυναικὸς χρηστὸν ἔνδον λαμβάνειν·
αὕτη γὰρ ἡ προὶξ οἰκίαν σώζει μόνη

The best marriage for a sensible man is to get a woman's good character as a wedding gift; for this dowry alone preserves the household.

Translated by Douglas E. Gerber (1999)

Fragment 182.1 (West, *IEG*)

4 ὅστις δὲ τρυφερῶς τὴν γυναῖκ' ἄγει λαβὼν
συνεργὸν οὗτος ἀντὶ δεσποίνης ἔχει
εὔνουν, βεβαίαν εἰς ἅπαντα τὸν βίον

Whoever tenderly brings home a wife marries a kindly helpmate, not a tyrant, steadfast for life.

Fragment 182.4 (West, *IEG*)

HIPPOTHOON

dates uncertain

Possibly a tragic playwright

1 φθόνος κάκιστος κἀδικώτατος θεός,
κακοῖς τε χαίρει κἀγαθοῖς ἀλγύνεται

Envy is the worst and the most unjust god, in misfortune happy, in good fortune wretched.

Fragment 2 (Snell, *TrGF*)

2 παίδων κρατεῖν δεῖ τῶν νεωτέρων σοφούς

Children should be guided by enlightened men.

Fragment 4 (Snell, *TrGF*)

HOMER

8th century BC

Epic poet

see also 'Homer' in Keyword Index

1 Μῆνιν ἄειδε, θεά, Πηληϊάδεω Ἀχιλῆος
οὐλομένην, ἣ μυρί' Ἀχαιοῖς ἄλγε' ἔθηκε,
πολλὰς δ' ἰφθίμους ψυχὰς Ἄϊδι προΐαψεν ἡρώων

The wrath of Peleus' Son, O Muse, resound;
Whose dire effects the Grecian Army found:
And many a Heroe, King and hardy Knight,
Were sent, in early Youth, to Shades of Night.

Translated by John Dryden (1700)

Iliad 1.1

opening lines, of the wrath of Achilles (Peleus' Son)

2 βῆ δ' ἀκέων παρὰ θῖνα πολυφλοίσβοιο θαλάσσης

He walked in silence along the loud-resounding sea.

Iliad 1.34

Tennyson was fond of quoting this line for 'its strong-wing'd music'

3 ὃς ἤδη τά τ' ἐόντα τά τ' ἐσσόμενα πρό τ' ἐόντα

He knew all things that were, that were to be, and that had been before.

Iliad 1.70

of Calchas, 'by far the best of diviners'

4 κρείσσων γὰρ βασιλεὺς ὅτε χώσεται ἀνδρὶ χέρηϊ

Bold is the task, when subjects, grown too wise,
Instruct a monarch where his error lies.

Translated by Alexander Pope (1715)

Iliad 1.80

5 εἴ περ γάρ τε χόλον γε καὶ αὐτῆμαρ καταπέψῃ,
ἀλλά τε καὶ μετόπισθεν ἔχει κότον, ὄφρα τελέσσῃ,
ἐν στήθεσσιν ἑοῖσι

For though we deem the short-lived fury past,
'Tis sure the mighty will revenge at last.

Translated by Alexander Pope (1715)

Iliad 1.81

6 τὸν δ' ἀπαμειβόμενος προσέφη

To him in answer spake.

Translated in *The Oxford Dictionary of Quotations* (1975)

Iliad 1.84 et al.

7 μάντι κακῶν, οὐ πώ ποτέ μοι τὸ κρήγυον εἶπας

Fie upon you, you prophet of evil, forever boding ill! Not once have you been able to say an honest word!

Iliad 1.106

of the seer Calchas

8 ἐπεὶ οὔ ἑθέν ἐστι χερείων,
οὐ δέμας οὐδὲ φυήν, οὔτ' ἂρ φρένας οὔτέ τι ἔργα

She is in no way inferior,
either in form, or stature, or mind, or skill.

Iliad 1.114

Agamemnon of Chryseis as compared to his wife

9 βούλομ' ἐγὼ λαὸν σῶν ἔμμεναι ἢ ἀπολέσθαι

I would rather have my people safe than perishing.

Iliad 1.117

10 ἐπεὶ ἦ μάλα πολλὰ μεταξὺ
οὔρεά τε σκιόεντα θάλασσά τε ἠχήεσσα

Great is the distance that divides us,
shadowy mountains and resounding seas.

Iliad 1.156

Achilles, in anger with Agamemnon

11 ὀλίγον τε φίλον τε

Some small thing, yet mine own.

Translated by A.T. Murray (1924)

Iliad 1.167

12 εἰ μάλα καρτερός ἐσσι, θεός που σοὶ τό γ' ἔδωκεν

Know, vain man! thy valour is from god.

Translated by Alexander Pope (1715)

Iliad 1.178

Agamemnon in reply to Achilles

13 ἔπεα πτερόεντα

Winged words.

Translated in *The Oxford Dictionary of Quotations* (2004)

Iliad 1.201 et al.; also in the *Odyssey*

'Geflügelte Worte', the German translation, is now used for all German collections of quotations

14 ὅς κε θεοῖς ἐπιπείθηται μάλα τ' ἔκλυον αὐτοῦ

The gods heed those who obey them.

Iliad 1.218

Achilles in reply to the goddess Athena

15 κυνὸς ὄμματ' ἔχων, κραδίην δ' ἐλάφοιο

Thou with the face of a dog but the heart of a deer.

Translated by A.T. Murray (1924)

Iliad 1.225

16 ἀπὸ γλώσσης μέλιτος γλυκίων ῥέεν αὐδή

Words sweeter than honey flowed from

his tongue.

Iliad 1.249

of Nestor, king of Pylos

17 κάρτιστοι μὲν ἔσαν καὶ καρτίστοις ἐμάχοντο,
φηρσὶν ὀρεσκῴοισι, καὶ ἐκπάγλως ἀπόλεσσαν

Mightiest they were and against the mightiest,
even the centaurs, they prevailed.

Iliad 1.267

18 καὶ μέν μευ βουλέων ξύνιεν πείθοντό τε μύθῳ·
ἀλλὰ πίθεσθε καὶ ὔμμες, ἐπεὶ πείθεσθαι ἄμεινον

They listened and trusted in my counsel;
you too be persuaded, then, and you will not lose by it.

Iliad 1.273

19 ὃς μέγα πᾶσιν
ἕρκος Ἀχαιοῖσιν πέλεται πολέμοιο κακοῖο

The pride of Greece, and bulwark of our host.

Translated by Alexander Pope (1715)

Iliad 1.283

Nestor of Achilles

20 παρὰ θῖν' ἁλὸς ἀτρυγέτοιο

Along the shore of the unresting sea.

Translated by A.T. Murray (1924)

Iliad 1.327

21 οὐδέ τι οἶδε νοῆσαι ἅμα πρόσσω καὶ ὀπίσσω

This man can neither apprehend the past, nor think ahead.

Iliad 1.343

of Agamemnon

22 ἠριγένεια φάνη ῥοδοδάκτυλος Ἠώς

The lady of the light, the rosy-finger'd Morn
Rose from the hills.

Translated by George Chapman (1598)

Iliad 1.477 et al.

most translators prefer 'the rosy-fingered dawn'

23 οὐ γὰρ ἐμὸν παλινάγρετον οὐδ' ἀπατηλὸν
οὐδ' ἀτελεύτητον, ὅ τί κεν κεφαλῇ κατανεύσω

My word is not revocable, nor false,
nor unfulfilled, once I did nod upon it.

Iliad 1.526

spoken by Zeus

24 ἦ καὶ κυανέῃσιν ἐπ' ὀφρύσι νεῦσε Κρονίων·
ἀμβρόσιαι δ' ἄρα χαῖται ἐπερρώσαντο ἄνακτος
κρατὸς ἀπ' ἀθανάτοιο· μέγαν δ' ἐλέλιξεν Ὄλυμπον

He bent his ponderous black brows down, and locks
ambrosial of his immortal head
swung over them, and all Olympus trembled.

Translated by Robert Fitzgerald (1975)

Iliad 1.528

of Zeus

25 ἄσβεστος δ' ἄρ' ἐνῶρτο γέλως μακάρεσσι θεοῖσιν

Laughter unquenchable seized the blessed gods.

Iliad 1.599

as they saw Hephaestus 'puffing through the palace'

26 οὐ χρὴ παννύχιον εὕδειν βουληφόρον ἄνδρα
ᾧ λαοί τ' ἐπιτετράφαται καὶ τόσσα μέμηλε

It is not right that a ruler sleep all night,
with a nation in his charge, and so much on his mind.

Iliad 2.24

Agamemnon's deceiving dream; cf. Shakespeare, Henry IV, Part II, *3.1.31: 'Weary lies the head that wears the crown'*

27 ἠΰτε ἔθνεα εἶσι μελισσάων ἁδινάων,
πέτρης ἐκ γλαφυρῆς αἰεὶ νέον ἐρχομενάων,
βοτρυδὸν δὲ πέτονται ἐπ' ἄνθεσιν εἰαρινοῖσιν·
αἱ μέν τ' ἔνθα ἅλις πεποτήαται, αἱ δέ τε ἔνθα

And so they came, like buzzing swarms of bees
that issue from some crevice in a rock
in clusters pouring forth upon spring flowers,

some right, some left.

Iliad 2.87

of troops leaving a meeting

28 μετὰ δέ σφισιν ὄσσα δεδήει … Διὸς ἄγγελος

Rumour, the Messenger of Zeus, spread through them like wildfire.

Translated by E.V. Rieu (1950)

Iliad 2.93

29 κινήθη δ' ἀγορὴ φὴ κύματα μακρὰ θαλάσσης
πόντου Ἰκαρίοιο, τὰ μέν τ' Εὖρός τε Νότος τε
ὤρορ' ἐπαΐξας πατρὸς Διός

The gathering stirred, as when the South-East wind from Zeus ruffles the long waves of the Icarian Sea.

Iliad 2.144

30 θυμὸς δὲ μέγας ἐστὶ διοτρεφέων βασιλήων

Proud is the heart of kings, fostered of heaven.

Translated by A.T. Murray (1924)

Iliad 2.196

31 οὐκ ἀγαθὸν πολυκοιρανίη· εἷς κοίρανος ἔστω,
εἷς βασιλεύς

A multitude of rulers is not a good thing.
Let there be one ruler, one king.

Translated in *Bartlett's Familiar Quotations* (1980)

Iliad 2.204

32 Θερσίτης δ' ἔτι μοῦνος ἀμετροεπὴς ἐκολῴα,
ὃς ἔπεα φρεσὶν ᾗσιν ἄκοσμά τε πολλά τε

Thersites, with no control over his tongue, poured out endless abuse.

Iliad 2.212

33 οὐ μὲν ἔοικεν
ἀρχὸν ἐόντα κακῶν ἐπιβασκέμεν υἷας Ἀχαιῶν.
ὦ πέπονες, κάκ' ἐλέγχε', Ἀχαιΐδες, οὐκέτ' Ἀχαιοί

Unseemly is the chief who brings his Greeks to shame.
Ye weaklings, men no more! You've become women!

Iliad 2.233

34 Θερσῖτ' ἀκριτόμυθε, λιγύς περ ἐὼν ἀγορητής,
ἴσχεο, μηδ' ἔθελ' οἶος ἐριζέμεναι βασιλεῦσιν

Thersites, eloquent you may be, but enough of it.
Be still! How dare you vie with kings?

Iliad 2.246

35 καὶ γάρ τίς θ' ἕνα μῆνα μένων ἀπὸ ἧς ἀλόχοιο
ἀσχαλάᾳ σὺν νηῒ πολυζύγῳ, ὅν περ ἄελλαι
χειμέριαι εἰλέωσιν ὀρινομένη τε θάλασσα

Even one month is much to be away from home and wife, away in winter blasts and surging seas.

Iliad 2.292

36 τοιοῦτοι δέκα μοι συμφράδμονες εἶεν

Would that I had ten such counsellors!

Translated by A.T. Murray (1924)

Iliad 2.372

Agamemnon of Nestor

37 Ἀργεῖοι δὲ μέγ' ἴαχον ὡς ὅτε κῦμα
ἀκτῇ ἐφ' ὑψηλῇ, ὅτε κινήσῃ Νότος ἐλθών,
προβλῆτι σκοπέλῳ

The Argives roared aloud, as when a wave,
roused by a southern gale, beats on a jutting rock.

Iliad 2.394

38 μηκέτι νῦν δήθ' αὖθι λεγώμεθα, μηδ' ἔτι δηρὸν
ἀμβαλλώμεθα ἔργον

Let us not prolong this meeting further,
nor any more postpone our work.

Iliad 2.435

39 ἠΰτε πῦρ ἀΐδηλον ἐπιφλέγει ἄσπετον ὕλην
οὔρεος ἐν κορυφῇς, ἕκαθεν δέ τε φαίνεται αὐγή

As when devouring flames some forest seize
On the high mountains, and splendid from afar
The blaze appears.

Translated by William Cowper (1791)

Iliad 2.455

of reflections on the bronze armour of the gathering Greek host

40 τῶν δ', ὥς τ' ὀρνίθων πετεηνῶν ἔθνεα πολλά,
χηνῶν ἢ γεράνων ἢ κύκνων δουλιχοδείρων ...
ἔνθα καὶ ἔνθα ποτῶνται ἀγαλλόμενα πτερύγεσσι,
κλαγγηδὸν προκαθιζόντων, σμαραγεῖ δέ τε λειμών

As the many tribes of winged fowl,
wild geese or cranes or long-necked swans
fly this way and that, glorying in their strength of wing,
and with loud cries settle ever onwards,
and the mead resoundeth.

Translated by A.T. Murray (1924)

Iliad 2.459

of the army preparing for battle

41 ἔσταν δ' ἐν λειμῶνι Σκαμανδρίῳ ἀνθεμόεντι
μυρίοι, ὅσσά τε φύλλα καὶ ἄνθεα γίγνεται ὥρῃ

They filled the flowering land beside Skamander,
as countless as the leaves and blades of spring.

Translated by Robert Fitzgerald (1975)

Iliad 2.467

Scamander is the river below Troy

42 πληθὺν δ' οὐκ ἂν ἐγὼ μυθήσομαι οὐδ' ὀνομήνω,
οὐδ' εἴ μοι δέκα μὲν γλῶσσαι, δέκα δὲ στόματ' εἶεν,
φωνὴ δ' ἄρρηκτος, χάλκεον δέ μοι ἦτορ ἐνείη

I could not tell nor name the multitude,
not even if I had ten tongues, ten mouths,
not if I had a voice unwearying and a heart of bronze.

Translated in *Bartlett's Familiar Quotations* (1980)

Iliad 2.488

of the army preparing for battle

43 μένεα πνείοντες

Breathing fury.

Translated by A.T. Murray (1924)

Iliad 2.536

still much used in everyday speech

44 τίς τὰρ τῶν ὄχ' ἄριστος ἔην, σύ μοι ἔννεπε, Μοῦσα

Now tell me, Muse, who was the greatest of them all?

Iliad 2.761

45 φοίτων ἔνθα καὶ ἔνθα

But the men strolled aimlessly about the camp.

Translated by E.V. Rieu (1950)

Iliad 2.779

of Achilles' followers

46 ἀλλ' οὐκ οἰωνοῖσιν ἐρύσατο κῆρα μέλαιναν

Yet all his powers of augury, all his bird-lore, did not save him from the black hand of death.

Iliad 2.859

of Ennomus, an augur, slain in battle

47 ἠΰτε περ κλαγγὴ γεράνων πέλει οὐρανόθι πρό,
αἵ τ' ἐπεὶ οὖν χειμῶνα φύγον καὶ ἀθέσφατον ὄμβρον,
κλαγγῇ ταί γε πέτονται ἐπ' ὠκεανοῖο ῥοάων

As the clamour of cranes ariseth before the face of heaven, when they flee from wintry storms and measureless rain, and with clamour fly toward the streams of Ocean.

Translated by A.T. Murray (1924)

Iliad 3.3

of the advancing Trojans

48 εὖτ' ὄρεος κορυφῇσι Νότος κατέχευεν ὀμίχλην
ποιμέσιν οὔ τι φίλην, κλέπτῃ δέ τε νυκτὸς ἀμείνω

As when the south wind wraps the mountain top
In mist, the shepherd's dread, but to the thief
Than night itself more welcome.

Translated by William Cowper (1791)

Iliad 3.10

49 οὔ τοι ἀπόβλητ' ἐστὶ θεῶν ἐρικυδέα δῶρα

The glorious gifts of the gods are not to be flung aside as worthless.

Iliad 3.65

50 αἰεὶ δ' ὁπλοτέρων ἀνδρῶν φρένες ἠερέθονται·
οἷς δ' ὁ γέρων μετέῃσιν, ἅμα πρόσσω καὶ ὀπίσσω
λεύσσει

Young men's spirits are ever changeable, whereas an older man in charge considers the future as well as the past.

Iliad 3.108

51 οἳ δὴ νῦν ἕαται σιγῇ

Now is the time to stand in silence.

Iliad 3.134

52 τεττίγεσσιν ἐοικότες, οἵ τε καθ' ὕλην
δενδρέῳ ἐφεζόμενοι ὄπα λειριόεσσαν ἱεῖσι·
τοῖοι ἄρα Τρώων ἡγήτορες ἧντ' ἐπὶ πύργῳ

As cicadas in dry summer
that cling on leafy trees and send out voices
rhythmic and long; so the Trojan elders sat
chatting on the tower.

Iliad 3.151

53 οὐ νέμεσις Τρῶας καὶ ἐϋκνήμιδας Ἀχαιοὺς
τοιῇδ' ἀμφὶ γυναικὶ πολὺν χρόνον ἄλγεα πάσχειν.
αἰνῶς ἀθανάτῃσι θεῇς εἰς ὦπα ἔοικεν

What man can blame
The Greekes and the Troyans to endure for so admir'd a Dame
So many miseries, so long? In her sweet countenance shine
Lookes like the Godesses'.

Translated by George Chapman (1609)

Iliad 3.156

Trojan elders speaking of Helen; cf. Psellus, Chronographia *6.61.9, of Σκλήραινα, favourite of Emperor Constantine IX Monomachus*

54 Μενέλαος ἐπιτροχάδην ἀγόρευε,
παῦρα μέν, ἀλλὰ μάλα λιγέως, ἐπεὶ οὐ πολύμυθος
οὐδ' ἀφαμαρτοεπής

Menelaus spoke fluently, not at great length, but very clearly, being a man of few words, keeping to the point.

Translated by E.V. Rieu (1950)

Iliad 3.213

55 ἔπεα νιφάδεσσιν ἐοικότα χειμερίῃσιν

Words came driving in the air as thick and fast as winter snowflakes.

Translated by Robert Fitzgerald (1975)

Iliad 3.222

of Odysseus

56 Ἠέλιός θ', ὃς πάντ' ἐφορᾷς καὶ πάντ' ἐπακούεις

The sun, which sees all things and hears all things.

Translated in *Bartlett's Familiar Quotations* (1980)

Iliad 3.277

57 στήθεά θ' ἱμερόεντα καὶ ὄμματα μαρμαίροντα

Her lovely bosom, and her flashing eyes.

Translated by A.T. Murray (1924)

Iliad 3.397

of Aphrodite

58 ἔχω δ' ἄχε' ἄκριτα θυμῷ

As though I had not pain enough to bear.

Translated by Robert Fitzgerald (1975)

Iliad 3.412

59 σὺ δέ κεν κακὸν οἶτον ὄληαι

Then wouldst thou perish of an evil fate.

Translated by A.T. Murray (1924)

Iliad 3.417

Aphrodite threatening Helen

60 ἶσον γάρ σφιν πᾶσιν ἀπήχθετο κηρὶ μελαίνῃ

They all hated him like death itself.

Iliad 3.454

of Paris

61 τῷ μὲν κλέος, ἄμμι δὲ πένθος

Glory for himself, mourning for us.

Iliad 4.197

of the Trojan who would kill Menelaus

62 οὐδὲ καταπτώσσοντ', οὐδ' οὐκ ἐθέλοντα μάχεσθαι,
ἀλλὰ μάλα σπεύδοντα μάχην ἐς

κυδιάνειραν

There was no sign in him of nervous fears, no hesitation to give battle, nothing but eagerness for the fight and the glory he might win.

Translated by E.V. Rieu (1950)

Iliad 4.224

of Agamemnon

63 ἀλλ' οὔ πως ἅμα πάντα θεοὶ δόσαν ἀνθρώποισιν

The gods never grant us all their favours all at once.

Iliad 4.320

64 Ἀτρεΐδη, ποῖόν σε ἔπος φύγεν ἕρκος ὀδόντων;

Son of Atreus, what words have escaped the barrier of your teeth!

Iliad 4.350

65 πειθόμενοι τεράεσσι θεῶν καὶ Ζηνὸς ἀρωγῇ

Putting our trust in omens and the help of Zeus.

Iliad 4.408

66 ὡς δ' ὅτ' ἐν αἰγιαλῷ πολυηχέϊ κῦμα θαλάσσης
ὄρνυτ' ἐπασσύτερον Ζεφύρου ὕπο κινήσαντος·
πόντῳ μέν τε πρῶτα κορύσσεται, αὐτὰρ ἔπειτα
χέρσῳ ῥηγνύμενον μεγάλα βρέμει, ἀμφὶ δέ τ' ἄκρας
κυρτὸν ἐὸν κορυφοῦται, ἀποπτύει δ' ἁλὸς ἄχνην

As when the Winds, ascending by degrees,
First move the whitening Surface of the Seas,
The Billows float in order to the Shore,
The Wave behind rolls on the Wave before;
Till, with the growing Storm, the Deeps arise,
Foam o'er the Rocks, and thunder to the skies.

Translated by Alexander Pope (1715)

Iliad 4.422

of the Greeks going into battle

67 ὦρσε δὲ τοὺς μὲν Ἄρης, τοὺς δὲ γλαυκῶπις Ἀθήνη
Δεῖμός τ' ἠδὲ Φόβος καὶ Ἔρις ἄμοτον μεμαυῖα,
Ἄρεος ἀνδροφόνοιο κασιγνήτη ἑτάρη τε,
ἥ τ' ὀλίγη μὲν πρῶτα κορύσσεται, αὐτὰρ ἔπειτα
οὐρανῷ ἐστήριξε κάρη καὶ ἐπὶ χθονὶ βαίνει

Ares spurred on the Trojan forces; Athena the Achaeans.
Terror and Panic were at hand. And so was Strife,
the War-god's Sister, who helps him in his bloody work.
Once she begins, she cannot stop; and then
her feet are on the ground, her head in heaven.

Iliad 4.439

68 τῶν δέ τε τηλόσε δοῦπον ἐν οὔρεσιν ἔκλυε ποιμήν

And far away
the shepherd on the mountain hears the sound.

Translated by Alfred, Lord Tennyson (written 1863–1864?, printed posthumously 1969)

Iliad 4.455

of the sound of battle

69 ἐκ κόρυθός τε καὶ ἀσπίδος ἀκάματον πῦρ,
ἀστέρ' ὀπωρινῷ ἐναλίγκιον, ὅς τε μάλιστα
λαμπρὸν παμφαίνησι λελουμένος ὠκεανοῖο

His helmet flashing and his shield ablaze with fire,
just like the summer star, outshining all the others,
rises in heaven, bathed by the Ocean stream.

Iliad 5.4

of Diomedes as he goes into battle

70 Ἄρες Ἄρες βροτολοιγέ, μιαιφόνε, τειχεσιπλῆτα

Ares, bane of all mankind,
crusted with blood, breacher of city walls.

Translated by Robert Fitzgerald (1975)

Iliad 5.31 and 5.455

Ares as the god of war

71 χερσὶν ἐπίστατο δαίδαλα πάντα τεύχειν

His hands were skilled in every craft.

Iliad 5.60

72 θῦνε γὰρ ἂμ πεδίον ποταμῷ πλήθοντι ἐοικὼς
χειμάρρῳ, ὅς τ᾽ ὦκα ῥέων ἐκέδασσε γεφύρας …
ἐλθόντ᾽ ἐξαπίνης ὅτ᾽ ἐπιβρίσῃ Διὸς ὄμβρος·
πολλὰ δ᾽ ὑπ᾽ αὐτοῦ ἔργα κατήριπε κάλ᾽ αἰζηῶν

He coursed along the plain
most like an April torrent fed by snow,
a river in flood that sweeps away his bank,
suddenly at crest when heaven pours down
the rain of Zeus; many a yeoman's field
of beautiful grain is ravaged.

Translated by Robert Fitzgerald (1975)

Iliad 5.87

of Diomedes

73 δὸς δέ τέ μ᾽ ἄνδρα ἑλεῖν καὶ ἐς ὁρμὴν ἔγχεος ἐλθεῖν,
ὅς μ᾽ ἔβαλε φθάμενος καὶ ἐπεύχεται, οὐδέ μέ φησι
δηρὸν ἔτ᾽ ὄψεσθαι λαμπρὸν φάος ἠελίοιο

Let me destroy that man, bring me in range of him,
who hit me by surprise, and glories in it.
He swears I shall be blind to sunlight soon.

Translated by Robert Fitzgerald (1975)

Iliad 5.118

74 εἰ δέ κε νοστήσω καὶ ἐσόψομαι ὀφθαλμοῖσι
πατρίδ᾽ ἐμὴν ἄλοχόν τε καὶ ὑψερεφὲς μέγα δῶμα

If ever I return,
if ever I lay my eyes on land and wife
and my great hall.

Translated by Robert Fitzgerald (1975)

Iliad 5.212

Pandarus, an ally of the Trojans

75 ὅττι μάλ᾽ οὐ δηναιὸς ὃς ἀθανάτοισι μάχηται,
οὐδέ τί μιν παῖδες ποτὶ γούνασι παππάζουσιν
ἐλθόντ᾽ ἐκ πολέμοιο

His days are numbered who would fight the gods!
His children will not sing around his knees
on his return from war.

Iliad 5.407

76 μηδὲ θεοῖσιν
ἶσ᾽ ἔθελε φρονέειν, ἐπεὶ οὔ ποτε φῦλον ὁμοῖον
ἀθανάτων τε θεῶν χαμαὶ ἐρχομένων τ᾽ ἀνθρώπων

Don't ever presume to be equal to the gods; never will their immortal race be the same as earth-bound man.

Iliad 5.440

77 ὡς δ᾽ ἄνεμος ἄχνας φορέει ἱερὰς κατ᾽ ἀλωὰς
ἀνδρῶν λικμώντων, ὅτε τε ξανθὴ Δημήτηρ
κρίνῃ ἐπειγομένων ἀνέμων καρπόν τε καὶ ἄχνας,
αἱ δ᾽ ὑπολευκαίνονται ἀχυρμιαί

As when the wind from off a threshing-floor,
Where men are winnowing, blows the chaff away;
When yellow Ceres with the breeze divides
The corn and chaff, which lies in whitening heaps.

Translated by Edward, Earl of Derby (1864)

Iliad 5.499

78 οἳ δὲ καὶ αὐτοὶ
οὔτε βίας Τρώων ὑπεδείδισαν οὔτε ἰωκάς,
ἀλλ᾽ ἔμενον νεφέλῃσιν ἐοικότες, ἅς τε Κρονίων
νηνεμίης ἔστησεν ἐπ᾽ ἀκροπόλοισιν ὄρεσσιν
ἀτρέμας, ὄφρ᾽ εὕδῃσι μένος Βορέαο

All fearless of attack or Trojan power,
patient in battle, motionless as clouds
that Zeus may station on high mountaintops
in a calm heaven, while the north wind sleeps.

Translated by Robert Fitzgerald (1975)

Iliad 5.520

of the Greeks holding their ground against the Trojans

79 τοίω τὼ χείρεσσιν ὑπ᾽ Αἰνείαο δαμέντε
καππεσέτην, ἐλάτῃσιν ἐοικότες ὑψηλῇσι

By the hands of Aeneas, like tall fir-trees, they both fell.

Iliad 5.559

80 αἰδώς, Ἀργεῖοι, κάκ' ἐλέγχεα, εἶδος ἀγητοί

Shame upon you, Argives, contemptible, fair in semblance only!

Iliad 5.787 et al.

81 μικρὸς μὲν ἔην δέμας, ἀλλὰ μαχητής

Small in stature, but what a fighter!

Iliad 5.801

82 μητρός τοι μένος ἐστὶν ἀάσχετον, οὐκ ἐπιεικτόν

Thou hast the unbearable, unyielding spirit of thy mother.

Translated by A.T. Murray (1924)

Iliad 5.892

Zeus, of Hera, his wife

83 ἀφνειὸς βιότοιο, φίλος δ' ἦν ἀνθρώποισι·
πάντας γὰρ φιλέεσκεν ὁδῷ ἔπι οἰκία ναίων

Friend to the human race.
Fast by the road, his ever-open door
Obliged the wealthy and relieved the poor.

Translated by Alexander Pope (1715)

Iliad 6.14

84 οἵη περ φύλλων γενεή, τοίη δὲ καὶ ἀνδρῶν·
φύλλα τὰ μέν τ' ἄνεμος χαμάδις χέει, ἄλλα δέ θ' ὕλη
τηλεθόωσα φύει, ἔαρος δ' ἐπιγίγνεται ὥρη·
ὣς ἀνδρῶν γενεὴ ἡ μὲν φύει ἡ δ' ἀπολήγει

As the generation of leaves, so is that of men;
the leaves are scattered by the wind, but the forest
brings forth others when the spring is come;
thus of men, one generation grows and another passes away.

Iliad 6.146

keynote of the Opening Ceremony of the 28th Modern Olympiad, Athens 2004

85 σήματα λυγρὰ
γράψας ἐν πίνακι πτυκτῷ θυμοφθόρα πολλά

Portentous characters
inscribed in a folding tablet, many signs and deadly.

Iliad 6.168

the only passage in Homer which suggests knowledge of the art of writing

86 αἰὲν ἀριστεύειν καὶ ὑπείροχον ἔμμεναι ἄλλων

Strive always to be the best, and distinguished above all others.

Iliad 6.208

Dr. Johnson said that these words were 'the noblest exhortation ... comprised in a single line' (Boswell, The Life of Samuel Johnson, *ch. '1770', Everyman Paperback vol. 1, p.395)*

87 χρύσεα χαλκείων

Gold for bronze.

Iliad 6.236

later proverbial for an unequal exchange; but cf. 'bronze by gold' in James Joyce, Ulysses, *episode [Sirens], passim*

88 ἀνδρὶ δὲ κεκμηῶτι μένος μέγα οἶνος ἀέξει

When a man is spent with toil, wine greatly maketh his strength to wax.

Translated by A.T. Murray (1924)

Iliad 6.261

89 μή μοι οἶνον ἄειρε μελίφρονα, πότνια μῆτερ,
μή μ' ἀπογυιώσῃς, μένεος δ' ἀλκῆς τε λάθωμαι

Bring me no wine, dear mother,
or you will rob me of my might and valour.

Iliad 6.264

90 νίκη δ' ἐπαμείβεται ἄνδρας

Victory shifts from man to man.

Translated in *Bartlett's Familiar Quotations* (1980)

Iliad 6.339

91 τούτῳ δ' οὔτ' ἂρ νῦν φρένες ἔμπεδοι οὔτ' ἄρ' ὀπίσσω
ἔσσονται

This man's mind is unsound and always will be.

Iliad 6.352

Helen, of Paris

92 εὖ γὰρ ἐγὼ τόδε οἶδα κατὰ φρένα καὶ κατὰ θυμόν·

ἔσσεται ἦμαρ ὅτ' ἄν ποτ' ὀλώλῃ Ἴλιος ἱρή

Well do I know this in my heart and soul;
the day will come when sacred Ilium shall be no more.

Iliad 6.447

spoken by Hector; quoted by Scipio A. Africanus on seeing Carthage burning in 146BC (Polybius 38.22)

93 ἀλλ' οὔ μοι Τρώων τόσσον μέλει ἄλγος ὀπίσσω …
ὅσσον σεῦ, ὅτε κέν τις Ἀχαιῶν χαλκοχιτώνων
δακρυόεσσαν ἄγηται, ἐλεύθερον ἦμαρ ἀπούρας

I am not so much distressed by what the Trojans will suffer as by the thought of you dragged weeping into slavery by some Achaean warrior.

Iliad 6.450

Hector replying to his wife's request for him not to go back into battle

94 ποτέ τις εἴποι πατρός γ' ὅδε πολλὸν ἀμείνων

May men say, 'He is far greater than his father.'

Translated in *Bartlett's Familiar Quotations* (1980)

Iliad 6.479

Hector of his son

95 δακρυόεν γελάσασα

Smiling through her tears.

Translated in *The Oxford Dictionary of Quotations* (2004)

Iliad 6.484

96 μοῖραν δ' οὔ τινά φημι πεφυγμένον ἔμμεναι ἀνδρῶν,
οὐ κακὸν, οὐδὲ μὲν ἐσθλόν, ἐπὴν τὰ πρῶτα γένηται

No man, whether weak or valiant, can escape his fate.

Iliad 6.488

97 αἳ μὲν ἔτι ζωὸν γόον Ἕκτορα

While yet he lived they made lament for Hector.

Iliad 6.499

98 ὡς δ' ὅτε ἵππος … ὑψοῦ δὲ κάρη ἔχει, ἀμφὶ δὲ χαῖται
ὤμοις ἀΐσσονται· ὁ δ' ἀγλαΐηφι πεποιθώς,
ῥίμφα ἑ γοῦνα φέρει μετά τ' ἤθεα καὶ νομὸν ἵππων

As when a horse holds high his head, and about his shoulders his mane floateth streaming, and as he glorieth in his splendour, his knees nimbly bear him to the haunts and pastures of mares.

Translated by A.T. Murray (1924)

Iliad 6.509

99 ὡς δὲ θεὸς ναύτῃσιν ἐελδομένοισιν ἔδωκεν
οὖρον, ἐπεί κε κάμωσιν ἐϋξέστῃς ἐλάτῃσι
πόντον ἐλαύνοντες, καμάτῳ δ' ὑπὸ γυῖα λέλυνται,
ὣς ἄρα τὼ Τρώεσσιν ἐελδομένοισι φανήτην

And as a god giveth a fair wind to longing seamen when
they are weary of beating the sea with polished oars of fir,
and with weariness are their limbs fordone;
even so appeared these twain to the longing Trojans.

Translated by A.T. Murray (1924)

Iliad 7.4

opening lines of book 7, of Hector and Paris joining the Trojans in battle

100 Αἴας ὦρτο πελώριος, ἕρκος Ἀχαιῶν,
μειδιόων βλοσυροῖσι προσώπασι

Huge Aias, the bulwark of the Achaeans,
with a smile on his grim face.

Translated by A.T. Murray (1924)

Iliad 7.211

going into battle after drawing the lot to fight against Hector

101 οἶσθα καὶ ἄλλον μῦθον ἀμείνονα τοῦδε νοῆσαι·
εἰ δ' ἐτεὸν δὴ τοῦτον ἀπὸ σπουδῆς ἀγορεύεις,
ἐξ ἄρα δή τοι ἔπειτα θεοὶ φρένας ὤλεσαν αὐτοί

You could have thought of better words to say;
but if you mean what you propose,
then the gods have surely robbed you of your wits.

Iliad 7.358

of Paris offering to give Helen back

102 σειρὴν χρυσείην ἐξ οὐρανόθεν κρεμάσαντες
πάντές τ' ἐξάπτεσθε θεοὶ πᾶσαί τε θέαιναι·
ἀλλ' οὐκ ἂν ἐρύσαιτ' ἐξ οὐρανόθεν πεδίον δὲ
Ζῆν' ὕπατον μήστωρ', οὐδ' εἰ μάλα πολλὰ κάμοιτε

Attach a golden chain from heaven,
and all of you hang on, you gods and goddesses;
tug as you will, you could not haul
Zeus from high heaven.

Iliad 8.19

103 ἀνέρες ἔστε, φίλοι, μνήσασθε δὲ θούριδος ἀλκῆς

Be men, my friends; do justice to your valour.

Translated by E.V. Rieu (1950)

Iliad 8.174

104 μήκων δ' ὡς ἑτέρωσε κάρη βάλεν, ἥ τ' ἐνὶ κήπῳ,
καρπῷ βριθομένη νοτίῃσί τε εἰαρινῇσιν,
ὣς ἑτέρωσ' ἤμυσε κάρη πήληκι βαρυνθέν

As a garden poppy, weighed down by its seed and the showers of spring, so his head, weighed down by his helmet, dropped to one side.

Iliad 8.306

105 τοῦ δ' αὖθι λύθη ψυχή τε μένος τε

Forthwith he fell, his spirit and his strength undone.

Iliad 8.315 et al.

106 ὡς δ' ὅτε τίς τε κύων συὸς ἀγρίου ἠὲ λέοντος
ἅπτηται κατόπισθε, ποσὶν ταχέεσσι διώκων,
ἰσχία τε γλουτούς τε, ἑλισσόμενόν τε δοκεύει,
ὣς Ἕκτωρ ὤπαζε κάρη κομόωντας Ἀχαιούς,
αἰὲν ἀποκτείνων τὸν ὀπίστατον· οἳ δὲ φέβοντο

Like a hound in full cry after a lion or a wild boar, snapping at flank or buttock and following every twist and turn, he hung on the heels of the long-haired Achaeans, killing the hindmost as they ran before him.

Translated by E.V. Rieu (1950)

Iliad 8.338

of Hector

107 ἐν δ' ἔπεσ' Ὠκεανῷ λαμπρὸν φάος ἠελίοιο,
ἕλκον νύκτα μέλαιναν ἐπὶ ζείδωρον ἄρουραν.
Τρωσὶν μέν ῥ' ἀέκουσιν ἔδυ φάος, αὐτὰρ Ἀχαιοῖς
ἀσπασίη τρίλλιστος ἐπήλυθε νὺξ ἐρεβεννή

And now the bright lamp of the Sun dropped into Ocean, drawing black night in its train across the fruitful earth. The Trojans had not wished the day to end, but to the Achaeans the dark came as a tardy answer to their prayers.

Translated by E.V. Rieu (1950)

Iliad 8.485

108 ὡς δ' ὅτ' ἐν οὐρανῷ ἄστρα φαεινὴν ἀμφὶ σελήνην
φαίνετ' ἀριπρεπέα, ὅτε τ' ἔπλετο νήνεμος αἰθήρ·
ἔκ τ' ἔφανεν πᾶσαι σκοπιαὶ καὶ πρώονες ἄκροι
καὶ νάπαι· οὐρανόθεν δ' ἄρ' ὑπερράγη ἄσπετος αἰθήρ,
πάντα δὲ εἴδεται ἄστρα, γέγηθε δέ τε φρένα ποιμήν

As when, high up in Heaven, the stars shine sharp and bright
All round the moon in splendour, while windless lies the night,
Each glen, each hill, each mountain-peak shows clear its face,
And far above bursts open the Heaven's infinite space
With all its stars, and the heart of the shepherd fills with joy.

Translated by F.L. Lucas (1950)

Iliad 8.555

of the Trojan fires burning in the night

109 ὡς δ' ἄνεμοι δύο πόντον ὀρίνετον ἰχθυόεντα,
Βορέης καὶ Ζέφυρος, τώ τε Θρῄκηθεν ἄητον,
ἐλθόντ' ἐξαπίνης· ἄμυδις δέ τε κῦμα κελαινὸν
κορθύεται, πολλὸν δὲ παρὲξ ἅλα φῦκος ἔχευεν

Just as two winds stir up the teeming deep,

North wind and West, blowing from Thrace
in sudden gushes, and forthwith the waves wax high,
casting abundant seaweed on the shore.

Iliad 9.4

110 σκήπτρῳ μέν τοι δῶκε τετιμῆσθαι περὶ πάντων,
ἀλκὴν δ' οὔ τοι δῶκεν ... ἔρχεο· πάρ τοι ὁδός

The sceptre hath he granted thee to be honoured above all,
but valour he gave thee not; get thee gone, before thee lies the way.

Translated by A.T. Murray (1924)

Iliad 9.38

Diomedes to Agamemnon ordering retreat

111 ἀφρήτωρ ἀθέμιστος ἀνέστιός ἐστιν ἐκεῖνος
ὃς πολέμου ἔραται ἐπιδημίου ὀκρυόεντος

A clanless, lawless, hearthless man is he who will encourage civil strife.

Iliad 9.63

quoted verbatim by Aristophanes, Peace *1096*

112 πολλῶν δ' ἀγρομένων τῷ πείσεαι ὅς κεν ἀρίστην
βουλὴν βουλεύσῃ

When many are gathered together, follow him who devises the wisest counsel.

Translated by A.T. Murray (1924)

Iliad 9.74

113 Ἀΐδης τοι ἀμείλιχος ἠδ' ἀδάμαστος

Hades, relentless and unyielding.

Iliad 9.158

114 μείζονα δὴ κρητῆρα ... καθίστα,
ζωρότερον δὲ κέραιε, δέπας δ' ἔντυνον ἑκάστῳ·
οἱ γὰρ φίλτατοι ἄνδρες ἐμῷ ὑπέασι μελάθρῳ

Set forth a larger bowl,
mix stronger drink, each man his cup;
for these are men most dear beneath my roof.

Iliad 9.202

115 οὐδέ τι μῆχος
ῥεχθέντος κακοῦ ἔστ' ἄκος εὑρεῖν

No healing can be found for ill once wrought.

Translated by A.T. Murray (1924)

Iliad 9.249

116 σὺ δὲ μεγαλήτορα θυμὸν
ἴσχειν ἐν στήθεσσι· φιλοφροσύνη γὰρ ἀμείνων

Curb your proud spirit; a kind heart is better than pride.

Iliad 9.255

117 ἐχθρὸς γάρ μοι κεῖνος ὁμῶς Ἀΐδαο πύλῃσιν
ὅς χ' ἕτερον μὲν κεύθῃ ἐνὶ φρεσίν, ἄλλο δὲ εἴπῃ

Hateful to me as the gates of hell is he
who conceals one thing in his mind, and utters another.

Translated by H.T. Riley (1872)

Iliad 9.312

118 ὡς δ' ὄρνις ἀπτῆσι νεοσσοῖσι προφέρῃσι
μάστακ', ἐπεί κε λάβῃσι, κακῶς δ' ἄρα οἱ πέλει αὐτῇ

Like a hen-bird who brings home
To the fledglings of the nest what scraps she wins
And evil fares herself.

Translated by Maurice Hewlett (1928)

Iliad 9.323

119 ἐγὼ πολλὰς μὲν ἀΰπνους νύκτας ἴαυον

Many a night I watcht out sleepless.

Translated by Maurice Hewlett (1928)

Iliad 9.325

120 ὅς τις ἀνὴρ ἀγαθὸς καὶ ἐχέφρων
τὴν αὐτοῦ φιλέει καὶ κήδεται

Does not every decent and right-minded man love and cherish his own woman?

Translated by E.V. Rieu (1950)

Iliad 9.341

121 ἐχθρὰ δέ μοι τοῦ δῶρα, τίω δέ μιν ἐν καρὸς αἴσῃ.
οὐδ' εἴ μοι δεκάκις τε καὶ εἰκοσάκις τόσα δοίη ...
οὐδ' εἴ μοι τόσα δοίη ὅσα ψάμαθός τε κόνις τε
οὐδέ κεν ὧς ἔτι θυμὸν ἐμὸν πείσει' Ἀγαμέμνων

Hateful are his gifts, I count them at a hair's worth.

Not though he gave me ten, aye twenty times as many,
not though he gave me gifts as sand or dust in number,
would Agamemnon persuade my soul.

Iliad 9.378

122 εἰ μέν κ' αὖθι μένων ...
ὤλετο μέν μοι νόστος, ἀτὰρ κλέος ἄφθιτον ἔσται

If I stay and fight,
lost is my home-return, but my renown shall be forever.

Iliad 9.412

123 μύθων τε ῥητῆρ' ἔμεναι πρηκτῆρά τε ἔργων

Be both a speaker of words and a doer of deeds.

Translated by A.T. Murray (1924)

Iliad 9.443

124 δήμου θῆκε φάτιν

Be mindful of the voice of the people.

Iliad 9.460

125 οὐδέ ποτ' ἔσβη πῦρ

And the fire was never quenched.

Iliad 9.471

126 καί μ' ἐφίλησ' ὡς εἴ τε πατὴρ ὃν παῖδα φιλήσῃ

He cherished me as a father cherishes his only son.

Iliad 9.481

127 ὡς ἐπὶ σοὶ μάλα πολλὰ πάθον καὶ πολλ' ἐμόγησα

I suffered exceedingly for thee and am in an evil plight.

Iliad 9.492

128 καὶ γάρ τε Λιταί εἰσι Διὸς κοῦραι μεγάλοιο,
χωλαί τε ῥυσαί τε παραβλῶπές τ' ὀφθαλμώ

Prayers are the daughters of mighty Zeus,
lame and wrinkled and slanting-eyed.

Translated in *Bartlett's Familiar Quotations* (1980)

Iliad 9.502

129 ἢ λάθετ' ἢ οὐκ ἐνόησεν

Perhaps he had forgotten her, or else did not take notice.

Iliad 9.537

130 σῦν ἄγριον ἀργιόδοντα,
ὃς κακὰ πόλλ' ἔρδεσκεν ἔθων Οἰνῆος ἀλωήν·
πολλὰ δ' ὅ γε προθέλυμνα χαμαὶ βάλε δένδρεα μακρὰ
αὐτῇσιν ῥίζῃσι καὶ αὐτοῖς ἄνθεσι μήλων

A ravenous wild boar, with flashing tusks, who settled down to ravage the royal lands. He stewed the ground with the tall fruit-trees he brought tumbling down, rooting them up, with the blossom on the twigs.

Translated by E.V. Rieu (1950)

Iliad 9.539

131 χόλος, ὅς τε καὶ ἄλλων
οἰδάνει ἐν στήθεσσι νόον πύκα περ φρονεόντων

Many a sensible man is at times overmastered by bitter anger.

Iliad 9.553

132 καλλισφύρου εἵνεκα νύμφης

For the sake of a fair-ankled maid.

Translated by A.T. Murray (1924)

Iliad 9.560

133 νῦν μὲν κοιμήσασθε τεταρπόμενοι φίλον ἦτορ
σίτου καὶ οἴνοιο· τὸ γὰρ μένος ἐστὶ καὶ ἀλκή

Now do as I advise
and go to rest. Your hearts have been refreshed
with bread and wine, the pith and nerve of men.

Translated by Robert Fitzgerald (1975)

Iliad 9.705

134 Ἄλλοι μὲν παρὰ νηυσὶν ... εὗδον παννύχιοι ...
ἀλλ' οὐκ Ἀτρεΐδην Ἀγαμέμνονα, ποιμένα λαῶν,
ὕπνος ἔχε γλυκερὸς πολλὰ φρεσὶν ὁρμαίνοντα

Now by their ships they slept the whole night through;
but Agamemnon, shepherd of the host,
had too much on his mind for easeful sleep.

Iliad 10.1

135 ὣς δ' αὔτως Μενέλαον ἔχε τρόμος· οὐδὲ γὰρ αὐτῷ
ὕπνος ἐπὶ βλεφάροισιν ἐφίζανε

Menelaos, like his brother, shaken,
lay unsleeping, open-eyed.

Translated by Robert Fitzgerald (1975)

Iliad 10.25

136 ἀμφὶ δ' ἔπειτα δαφοινὸν ἑέσσατο δέρμα λέοντος
αἴθωνος μεγάλοιο ποδηνεκές …
παρδαλέῃ μὲν πρῶτα μετάφρενον εὐρὺ κάλυψε
ποικίλῃ

The one dressed in a lion's tawny skin that reached his feet, the other covered his broad shoulders with a leopard's dappled pelt.

Iliad 10.21 and 29

of Agamemnon and Menelaus

137 χρεὼ βουλῆς ἐμὲ καὶ σέ …
κερδαλέης

You and I must have some plan of action,
and a good one, too.

Translated by Robert Fitzgerald (1975)

Iliad 10.43

138 ἀλλὰ καὶ αὐτοί περ πονεώμεθα· ὧδέ που ἄμμι
Ζεὺς ἐπὶ γιγνομένοισιν ἵει κακότητα βαρεῖαν

We too must labour; indeed Zeus seems to have picked us out for trouble from the moment we were born.

Translated by E.V. Rieu (1950)

Iliad 10.70

139 πολλάκι γὰρ μεθιεῖ τε καὶ οὐκ ἐθέλει πονέεσθαι

For often is he slack and has no will to work.

Iliad 10.121

Agamemnon of his brother

140 νῦν γὰρ δὴ πάντεσσιν ἐπὶ ξυροῦ ἵσταται ἀκμῆς
ἢ μάλα λυγρὸς ὄλεθρος Ἀχαιοῖς ἠὲ βιῶναι

The issue teeters on a razor's edge
for all Achaeans – whether we live or perish.

Translated by Robert Fitzgerald (1975)

Iliad 10.173

141 σύν τε δύ' ἐρχομένω, καί τε πρὸ ὃ τοῦ ἐνόησεν

Two seize advantages that one would miss.

Translated by E.V. Rieu (1950)

Iliad 10.224

142 ἐγγύθι δ' ἠώς,
ἄστρα δὲ δὴ προβέβηκε, παροίχωκεν δὲ πλέων νὺξ

The dawn draws near,
the stars move onwards, the night is in its wane.

Iliad 10.251

143 τοῖσι δὲ δεξιὸν ἧκεν ἐρωδιὸν ἐγγὺς ὁδοῖο
Παλλὰς Ἀθηναίη· τοὶ δ' οὐκ ἴδον ὀφθαλμοῖσι
νύκτα δι' ὀρφναίην, ἀλλὰ κλάγξαντος ἄκουσαν

Off to the right
along their path, Pallas Athena sent
a heron gliding down the night. They could not
see it passing, but they heard its cry.

Translated by Robert Fitzgerald (1975)

Iliad 10.274

a good omen

144 οὐδέ σε λήθω κινύμενος

Nor when I move am I concealed from thee.

Translated by W.A. Oldfather (1925)

Iliad 10.279

of god; quoted by Epictetus, Discourses *1.12.3*

145 ὡς δ' ὅτε καρχαρόδοντε δύω κύνε, εἰδότε θήρης,
ἢ κεμάδ' ἠὲ λαγωὸν ἐπείγετον ἐμμενὲς αἰεὶ
χῶρον ἀν' ὑλήενθ'

As when two sharp-toothed hunting dogs
press hard behind a young buck or a hare
through wooded country.

Iliad 10.360

of Diomedes and Odysseus, pursuing a Trojan spy

146 τοῦ δὴ καλλίστους ἵππους ἴδον ἠδὲ μεγίστους·
λευκότεροι χιόνος, θείειν δ' ἀνέμοισιν ὁμοῖοι·
ἅρμα δέ οἱ χρυσῷ τε καὶ ἀργύρῳ εὖ ἤσκηται·
τεύχεα δὲ χρύσεια πελώρια θαῦμα ἰδέσθαι

The fairest horses that I ever saw, and the greatest,
whiter than snow, and in speed like the winds;
and his chariot cunningly wrought with gold and silver,
and armour of gold, huge of size, a wonder to behold.

Translated by A.T. Murray (1924)

Iliad 10.436

of the Thracian King Rhesus

147 Ἠὼς δ' ἐκ λεχέων …
ὄρνυθ', ἵν' ἀθανάτοισι φόως φέροι ἠδὲ βροτοῖσι

Now dawn rose from her couch
to bring bright daylight to immortals and to mortal men.

Translated by A.T. Murray (1924)

Iliad 11.1

148 οἷος δ' ἐκ νεφέων ἀναφαίνεται οὔλιος ἀστὴρ
παμφαίνων, τοτὲ δ' αὖτις ἔδυ νέφεα σκιόεντα

As from night clouds a baleful summer star
will blaze into the clear, then fade in cloud.

Translated by Robert Fitzgerald (1975)

Iliad 11.62

149 προσαυδήτην …
μειλιχίοις ἐπέεσσιν· ἀμείλικτον δ' ὄπ' ἄκουσαν

Gentle were their words, but all ungentle what they heard.

Iliad 11.136

150 ὡς ὁπότε νέφεα Ζέφυρος στυφελίξῃ
ἀργεστᾶο Νώτοιο, βαθείῃ λαίλαπι τύπτων·
πολλὸν δὲ τρόφι κῦμα κυλίνδεται, ὑψόσε δ' ἄχνη
σκίδναται ἐξ ἀνέμοιο πολυπλάγκτοιο ἰωῆς

Like a full gale when it strikes from the West and scatters the white clouds that the South Wind has marshalled; when the great billows start their march and the foam flies high on the wings of the travelling wind.

Translated by E.V. Rieu (1950)

Iliad 11.305

151 ἤτοι ἐγὼ μενέω καὶ τλήσομαι

I'll stand with you
and take what comes!

Translated by Robert Fitzgerald (1975)

Iliad 11.317

152 οἵ τέ σε πεφρίκασι λέονθ' ὡς μηκάδες αἶγες

Trembling as bleating goats before a lion.

Iliad 11.383

153 τοξότα, λωβητὴρ, κέρᾳ ἀγλαὲ, παρθενοπῖπα

You bow-and-arrow boy, you curly-head,
all eyes for little girls.

Translated by Robert Fitzgerald (1975)

Iliad 11.385

of Paris

154 ἀλλὰ τί ἤ μοι ταῦτα φίλος διελέξατο θυμός; …
ὃς δέ κ' ἀριστεύῃσι μάχῃ ἔνι, τὸν δὲ μάλα χρεὼ
ἑστάμεναι κρατερῶς, ἤ τ' ἔβλητ' ἤ τ' ἔβαλ' ἄλλον

Why do I ask myself?
A leader is in duty bound
to stand unflinching and to kill or die.

Iliad 11.407

Odysseus in monologue

155 ἀΐσσων ᾧ ἔγχει ἀμύνετο νηλεὲς ἦμαρ

Darting forth with his spear he warded off the pitiless day of doom.

Translated by A.T. Murray (1924)

Iliad 11.484

of Odysseus in defence

156 ὡς δ' ὁπότε πλήθων ποταμὸς πεδίονδε κάτεισι
χειμάρρους κατ' ὄρεσφιν, ὀπαζόμενος Διὸς ὄμβρῳ,
πολλὰς δὲ δρῦς ἀζαλέας, πολλὰς δέ τε

πεύκας
ἐσφέρεται, πολλὸν δέ τ' ἀφυσγετὸν εἰς ἅλα βάλλει

As when a flooded river comes down upon the plain,
a mountain torrent driven by the rain of Zeus,
sweeping along many a withered oak, many a pine,
as driftwood to the sea.

Iliad 11.492

of Aias attacking

157 ἰητρὸς γὰρ ἀνὴρ πολλῶν ἀντάξιος ἄλλων

A surgeon is worth an army full of other men.

Translated by Robert Fitzgerald (1975)

Iliad 11.514

158 ἐν φόβον ὦρσε …
τρέσσε δὲ παπτήνας ἐφ' ὁμίλου, θηρὶ ἐοικώς,
ἐντροπαλιζόμενος, ὀλίγον γόνυ γουνὸς ἀμείβων

Panic-fixed he stood,
And, hemm'd by numbers, with an eye askant,
Watchful retreated. As a beast of prey,
Retiring, turns and looks, so he his face
Turn'd oft, retiring slow, and step by step.

Translated by William Cowper (1791)

Iliad 11.544

of Aias retreating before the Trojans

159 τάχα κεν καὶ ἀναίτιον αἰτιόῳτο

Quite capable of finding fault without reason.

Translated by E.V. Rieu (1950)

Iliad 11.654

of Achilles

160 ἀγαθὴ δὲ παραίφασίς ἐστιν ἑταίρου

A friend's advice is often more effective.

Translated by E.V. Rieu (1950)

Iliad 11.793

161 θεῶν δ' ἀέκητι τέτυκτο
ἀθανάτων· τὸ καὶ οὔ τι πολὺν χρόνον ἔμπεδον ἦεν

It was built against the will
of the immortal gods, and so it did not last for long.

Translated in *Bartlett's Familiar Quotations* (1980)

Iliad 12.8

of the wall built by the Achaeans

162 αὐτὸς δ' ἐννοσίγαιος ἔχων χείρεσσι τρίαιναν
ἡγεῖτ', ἐκ δ' ἄρα πάντα θεμείλια κύμασι πέμπε
φιτρῶν καὶ λάων, τὰ θέσαν μογέοντες Ἀχαιοί,
λεῖα δ' ἐποίησεν παρ' ἀγάρροον Ἑλλήσποντον,
αὖτις δ' ἠϊόνα μεγάλην ψαμάθοισι κάλυψε

Trident in hand, the Earthshaker himself directed the torrent,
washed out to sea all the wooden and stone foundations
that with such labour the Achaeans had laid down,
levelled the shore of the fast-flowing Hellespont,
and once more covered the wide beach with sand.

Iliad 12.28

of Poseidon restoring the illegally scarred countryside (see previous entry)

163 ἕστασαν ὡς ὅτε τε δρύες οὔρεσιν ὑψικάρηνοι,
αἵ τ' ἄνεμον μίμνουσι καὶ ὑετὸν ἤματα πάντα,
ῥίζῃσιν μεγάλῃσι διηνεκέεσσ' ἀραρυῖαι

This pair had planted themselves in front of the high gate, like lofty mountain oaks that resist the wind and rain for ever, supported by their long and sturdy roots.

Translated by E.V. Rieu (1950)

Iliad 12.132

of two warriors guarding the gate

164 Ζεῦ πάτερ ἦ ῥά νυ καὶ σὺ φιλοψευδὴς ἐτέτυξο
πάγχυ μάλ'

Father Zeus, are you not also fond of lies!

Iliad 12.164

165 ὥς τε σφῆκες μέσον αἰόλοι ἠὲ μέλισσαι
οἰκία ποιήσωνται ὁδῷ ἔπι παιπαλοέσσῃ,
οὐδ' ἀπολείπουσιν κοῖλον δόμον, ἀλλὰ μένοντες
ἄνδρας θηρητῆρας ἀμύνονται περὶ

τέκνων

Like agile-waisted hornets
or bees who build their hives by a stony road,
hornets that will not leave their homes but wait
for hunters, and in fury defend their young.

Translated by Robert Fitzgerald (1975)

Iliad 12.167

of steadfast Achaean warriors

166 αἰετὸς ὑψιπέτης ἐπ' ἀριστερὰ λαὸν ἐέργων,
φοινήεντα δράκοντα φέρων ὀνύχεσσι πέλωρον
ζωόν· ἄφαρ δ' ἀφέηκε πάρος φίλα οἰκί' ἱκέσθαι,
οὐδ' ἐτέλεσσε φέρων δόμεναι τεκέεσσιν ἑοῖσιν

An eagle, soaring on our left,
bearing in his talons a blood-red, monstrous snake,
yet let it fall before he reached his nest,
not finishing his course to bring it to his young.

Iliad 12.219

cf. Oracles 33

167 τύνη δ' οἰωνοῖσι τανυπτερύγεσσι κελεύεις
πείθεσθαι, τῶν οὔ τι μετατρέπομ' οὐδ' ἀλεγίζω,
εἴτ' ἐπὶ δεξί' ἴωσι πρὸς ἠῶ τ' ἠέλιόν τε,
εἴτ' ἐπ' ἀριστερὰ τοί γε ποτὶ ζόφον ἠερόεντα

You – you would have me put my faith in birds
whose spreading wings I neither track nor care for,
whether to the right hand sunward they fly
or to the left hand, westward into darkness.

Translated by Robert Fitzgerald (1975)

Iliad 12.237

cf. Oracles 33

168 εἷς οἰωνὸς ἄριστος ἀμύνεσθαι περὶ πάτρης

One omen is supreme, to fight for one's country.

Iliad 12.243

cf. Oracles 33 and Homer 166

169 ὅς τ' ἔξοχος ὅς τε μεσήεις
ὅς τε χερειότερος ... νῦν ἔπλετο ἔργον ἅπασι ...
μή τις ὀπίσσω τετράφθω ... ἀλλὰ πρόσω ἵεσθε

Whoso is pre-eminent, whoso holds a middle place,
or whoso is lesser, now is there work for all.
Let no man turn him back, nay, press ye forward!

Translated by A.T. Murray (1925)

Iliad 12.269

170 ὥς τε νιφάδες χιόνος πίπτωσι θαμειαὶ
ἤματι χειμερίῳ ...
κοιμήσας δ' ἀνέμους χέει ἔμπεδον, ὄφρα καλύψῃ
ὑψηλῶν ὀρέων κορυφὰς καὶ πρώονας ἄκρους
καὶ πεδία λωτοῦντα καὶ ἀνδρῶν πίονα ἔργα·
καί τ' ἐφ' ἁλὸς πολιῆς κέχυται λιμέσιν τε καὶ ἀκταῖς,
κῦμα δέ μιν προσπλάζον ἐρύκεται

As thick as snowflakes on a winter day when Zeus has put winds to sleep and snows without ceasing, till he has covered the hill-tops and the bold headlands of the coast and the clover meadows and the farmer's fields; till even the shores and inlets of the grey sea are under snow, and only the breakers fend it off as they come rolling in.

Translated by E.V. Rieu (1950)

Iliad 12.278

of Trojans and Achaeans pelting stones at one another

171 νῦν δ' ἔμπης γὰρ κῆρες ἐφεστᾶσιν θανάτοιο
μυρίαι, ἃς οὐκ ἔστι φυγεῖν βροτὸν οὐδ' ὑπαλύξαι

Death has a thousand pitfalls for our feet; and nobody can save himself and cheat him.

Translated by E.V. Rieu (1950)

Iliad 12.326

172 πλεόνων δέ τι ἔργον ἄμεινον

Many hands make light work.

Translated by D.S. Baker (1998)

Iliad 12.412

cf. the identical English proverb

173 ὥς τε τάλαντα γυνὴ χερνῆτις ἀληθής,
ἥ τε σταθμὸν ἔχουσα καὶ εἴριον ἀμφὶς ἀνέλκει
ἰσάζουσ', ἵνα παισὶν ἀεικέα μισθὸν ἄρηται

As scales in which an honest working-woman balances the wool against the weights to make sure of the meagre pittance she is earning for her children.

Translated by E.V. Rieu (1950)

Iliad 12.433

174 ὁ δ' ἄρ' ἔσθορε φαίδιμος Ἕκτωρ
νυκτὶ θοῇ ἀτάλαντος ὑπώπια

In glory Hector leapt,
his visage dark as nightfall.

Translated by Robert Fitzgerald (1975)

Iliad 12.462

175 τρὶς μὲν ὀρέξατ' ἰών, τὸ δὲ τέτρατον ἵκετο τέκμωρ,
Αἰγάς, ἔνθα δέ οἱ κλυτὰ δώματα βένθεσι λίμνης
χρύσεα μαρμαίροντα τετεύχαται, ἄφθιτα αἰεί

Three strides he made, and with the fourth he reached his goal, Aigae, where his famous palace was built in the depths of the water, glistening and golden, imperishable for ever.

Translated by C.A. Trypanis (1971)

Iliad 13.20

of Poseidon

176 ἄταλλε δὲ κήτε' ὑπ' αὐτοῦ
πάντοθεν ἐκ κευθμῶν, οὐδ' ἠγνοίησεν ἄνακτα·
γηθοσύνη δὲ θάλασσα διίστατο

The sea beasts from the depths gambolled on all sides under him, for they recognised their king; and in pleasure the sea opened a path for him.

Translated by C.A. Trypanis (1971)

Iliad 13.27

of Poseidon

177 ὥς τ' ἴρηξ ὠκύπτερος ὦρτο πέτεσθαι,
ὅς ῥά τ' ἀπ' αἰγίλιπος πέτρης περιμήκεος ἀρθεὶς
ὁρμήσῃ πεδίοιο διώκειν ὄρνεον ἄλλο

As when a falcon from a rocky height,
Her quarry seen, impetuous at the sight,
Forth-springing instant, darts herself from high,
Shoots on the wing, and skims along the sky.

Translated by Alexander Pope (1715)

Iliad 13.62

178 φράξαντες δόρυ δουρί, σάκος σάκεϊ προθελύμνῳ·
ἀσπὶς ἄρ' ἀσπίδ' ἔρειδε, κόρυς κόρυν, ἀνέρα δ' ἀνήρ

An impenetrable hedge of spears and sloping shields, buckler to buckler, helmet to helmet, man to man.

Translated by E.V. Rieu (1950)

Iliad 13.130

179 συμφερτὴ δ' ἀρετὴ πέλει ἀνδρῶν καὶ μάλα λυγρῶν

Even weak men have strength in unity.

Translated by John Simpson and Jennifer Speake (1982)

Iliad 13.237

cf. the English proverb 'union is strength'

180 ἔνθ' ὅ τε δειλὸς ἀνὴρ ὅς τ' ἄλκιμος ἐξεφαάνθη·
τοῦ μὲν γάρ τε κακοῦ τρέπεται χρὼς ἄλλυδις ἄλλῃ ...
τοῦ δ' ἀγαθοῦ οὔτ' ἂρ τρέπεται χρὼς οὔτε τι λίην
ταρβεῖ

No force, no firmness, the pale coward shows;
He shifts his place: his colour comes and goes
Not so the brave – still dauntless, still the same,
Unchanged his colour, and unmoved his frame.

Translated by Alexander Pope (1715)

Iliad 13.278

181 ἀλλ' ἔμεν' ὡς ὅτε τις σῦς οὔρεσιν ἀλκὶ πεποιθώς,
ὅς τε μένει κολοσυρτὸν ἐπερχόμενον πολὺν ἀνδρῶν
χώρῳ ἐν οἰοπόλῳ, φρίσσει δέ τε νῶτον ὕπερθεν·
ὀφθαλμὼ δ' ἄρα οἱ πυρὶ λάμπετον· αὐτὰρ ὀδόντας
θήγει, ἀλέξασθαι μεμαὼς κύνας ἠδὲ καὶ ἄνδρας

Like a boar in the mountains, confident in his strength,

who awaits the onset of a great horde of men
in a lonely spot, and the hair bristle on his back above,
but his eyes blaze with fire; and he whets his tusks,
eager to defend himself against both dogs and men.

Translated by Kathleen Freeman (1947)

Iliad 13.471

of Idomeneus, standing firm

182 πάντων μὲν κόρος ἐστί, καὶ ὕπνου καὶ φιλότητος

Of all things there is satiety, even of sleep, and love.

Translated by A.T. Murray (1925)

Iliad 13.636

183 ἀλλ' οὔ πως ἅμα πάντα δυνήσεαι αὐτὸς ἑλέσθαι.
ἄλλῳ μὲν γὰρ ἔδωκε θεὸς πολεμήϊα ἔργα,
ἄλλῳ δ' ὀρχηστύν, ἑτέρῳ κίθαριν καὶ ἀοιδήν,
ἄλλῳ δ' ἐν στήθεσσι τιθεῖ νόον εὐρύοπα Ζεὺς
ἐσθλόν

Seek not alone to engross the gifts of Heaven.
To some the powers of bloody war belong,
To some sweet music and the charm of song;
To few, and wondrous few, has Jove assign'd
A wise, extensive, all-considering mind.

Translated by Alexander Pope (1715)

Iliad 13.729

184 ἐπεί τοι θυμὸς ἀναίτιον αἰτιάασθαι

Your temper makes you blame those in whom there is no blame.

Iliad 13.775

185 πὰρ δύναμιν δ' οὐκ ἔστι καὶ ἐσσύμενον πολεμίζειν

However much you strive you cannot fight beyond your strength.

Iliad 13.787

186 νῦν δ' εἴη ὃς τῆσδέ γ' ἀμείνονα μῆτιν ἐνίσποι,
ἢ νέος ἠὲ παλαιός· ἐμοὶ δέ κεν ἀσμένῳ εἴη

Now if there were someone who could offer better counsel,
be he young or old, right glad I'd be to hear it.

Iliad 14.107

187 δὸς νῦν μοι φιλότητα καὶ ἵμερον, ᾧ τε σὺ πάντας
δαμνᾷ ἀθανάτους ἠδὲ θνητοὺς ἀνθρώπους

Lend me longing, lend me desire,
by which you bring immortals low
as you do mortal men!

Translated by Robert Fitzgerald (1975)

Iliad 14.198

Hera to Aphrodite

188 ἔνθα τέ οἱ θελκτήρια πάντα τέτυκτο·
ἔνθ' ἔνι μὲν φιλότης, ἐν δ' ἵμερος, ἐν δ' ὀαριστὺς
πάρφασις, ἥ τ' ἔκλεψε νόον πύκα περ φρονεόντων

All her magic resides in it, Love and Desire and the sweet bewitching words that turn a wise man into a fool.

Translated by E.V. Rieu (1950)

Iliad 14.215

of Aphrodite's girdle

189 ἔνθ' Ὕπνῳ ξύμβλητο, κασιγνήτῳ Θανάτοιο

There she met Sleep, the brother of Death.

Translated by A.T. Murray (1925)

Iliad 14.231

cf. Tennyson, In Memoriam A. H. H. (1850) *68, 'Sleep, Death's twin brother'*

190 Ὠκεανοῦ, ὅς περ γένεσις πάντεσσι τέτυκται

Okeanos, the primal source of all that lives.

Translated by Robert Fitzgerald (1975)

Iliad 14.246

191 τοῖσι δ' ὑπὸ χθὼν δῖα φύεν νεοθηλέα ποίην,
λωτόν θ' ἑρσήεντα ἰδὲ κρόκον ἠδ' ὑάκινθον
πυκνὸν καὶ μαλακόν

The divine earth beneath them put forth newly-sprung grass,

and the dewy lotus, the crocus and the hyacinth,
thickly-growing and soft.

Translated by Kathleen Freeman (1947)

Iliad 14.347

of the couch of Zeus and Hera

192 τῷ ἔνι λεξάσθην, ἐπὶ δὲ νεφέλην ἕσσαντο
καλὴν χρυσείην· στιλπναὶ δ' ἀπέπιπτον ἕερσαι

On this bed they lay, and were covered with a lovely golden cloud, from which fell glistening drops of dew.

Iliad 14.350

of Zeus and Hera

193 ὡς δ' ὅτ' ἂν ἀΐξῃ νόος ἀνέρος, ὅς τ' ἐπὶ πολλὴν
γαῖαν ἐληλουθὼς φρεσὶ πευκαλίμῃσι νοήσῃ,
ἔνθ' εἴην ἢ ἔνθα

Quick as thought itself, a much travelled man may recall some place, and wish 'Would I were here, or there.'

Iliad 15.80

194 νόος δ' ἀπόλωλε καὶ αἰδώς

You have lost your wits and self-respect.

Iliad 15.129

195 αἰδώς, Ἀργεῖοι· νῦν ἄρκιον ἢ ἀπολέσθαι
ἠὲ σαωθῆναι καὶ ἀπώσασθαι κακὰ νηῶν.
ἦ ἔλπεσθ', ἢν νῆας ἕλῃ κορυθαίολος Ἕκτωρ,
ἐμβαδὸν ἵξεσθαι ἣν πατρίδα γαῖαν ἕκαστος;

Shame on you, Argives! It is now sure that we either perish
or save ourselves, thrusting back the peril from our ships.
Or do you think that if they are seized by Hector
we shall go back on foot, each to his native land?

Iliad 15.502

196 αἰδομένων δ' ἀνδρῶν πλέονες σόοι ἠὲ πέφανται·
φευγόντων δ' οὔτ' ἂρ κλέος ὄρνυται οὔτέ τις ἀλκή

On valour's side the odds of combat lie;
The brave live glorious, or lamented die;
The wretch that trembles in the field of fame,
Meets death, and worse than death, eternal shame.

Translated by Alexander Pope (1715)

Iliad 15.563

197 τοῦ γένετ' ἐκ πατρὸς πολὺ χείρονος υἱὸς ἀμείνων
παντοίας ἀρετάς

A great improvement on his worthless father, the son is excellent in all respects.

Translated by E.V. Rieu (1950)

Iliad 15.641

198 δάκρυα θερμὰ χέων ὥς τε κρήνη μελάνυδρος,
ἥ τε κατ' αἰγίλιπος πέτρης δνοφερὸν χέει ὕδωρ

Shedding warm tears – like a shaded mountain spring
that makes a rockledge run with dusky water.

Translated by Robert Fitzgerald (1975)

Iliad 16.3

199 ἀλλὰ τὰ μὲν προτετύχθαι ἐάσομεν

These things we will let be, as past and done with.

Translated by A.T. Murray (1925)

Iliad 16.60

200 κακὸν κακῷ ἐστήρικτο

Evil was heaped upon evil.

Translated by A.T. Murray (1925)

Iliad 16.111

201 ὠκέας ἵππους,
Ξάνθον καὶ Βαλίαν, τὼ ἅμα πνοιῇσι πετέσθην

The fleet horses Xanthus and Balius, swift as the winds.

Translated by A.T. Murray (1925)

Iliad 16.148

cf. Homer 223

202 ἐν γὰρ χερσὶ τέλος πολέμου, ἐπέων δ' ἐνὶ βουλῇ·
τὼ οὔ τι χρὴ μῦθον ὀφέλλειν, ἀλλὰ μάχεσθαι

The outcome of war is in our hands, speeches may win in council.

Iliad 16.630

203 τῶ οὔ τι χρὴ μῦθον ὀφέλλειν, ἀλλὰ μάχεσθαι

Enough of words, now is the time to fight.

Iliad 16.631

204 κεῖτο μέγας μεγαλωστί, λελασμένος ἱπποσυνάων

He lay great and greatly fallen, forgetful of his horsemanship.

Translated in *The Oxford Dictionary of Quotations* (2004)

Iliad 16.776

of Hector's charioteer

205 ῥεχθὲν δέ τε νήπιος ἔγνω

Any fool can see a thing already done.

Translated by Robert Fitzgerald (1975)

Iliad 17.32

cf. Plato, Symposium *222b*

206 κακῶν δέ κε φέρτατον εἴη

The most preferable of evils.

Translated in *Bartlett's Familiar Quotations* (1980)

Iliad 17.105

207 οὐδὲ τοκεῦσι
θρέπτρα φίλοις ἀπέδωκε

Nor ever would he repay his parents for their care.

Translated by Robert Fitzgerald (1975)

Iliad 17.301

of Patroclus slain

208 πολλὰ δὲ μειλιχίοισι προσηύδα, πολλὰ δ' ἀρειῇ

In vain with honeyed words, in vain with threats.

Translated by Edward, Earl of Derby (1864)

Iliad 17.431

209 οὐ μὲν γάρ τί πού ἐστιν ὀϊζυρώτερον ἀνδρὸς
πάντων ὅσσά τε γαῖαν ἔπι πνείει τε καὶ ἕρπει

For of all that breathes and moves upon the earth there is nothing more wretched than man.

Translated by C.A. Trypanis (1971)

Iliad 17.446

210 ἀλλ' ἦ τοι μὲν ταῦτα θεῶν ἐν γούνασι κεῖται

It lies in the lap of the gods.

Translated in *The Oxford Dictionary of Quotations* (2004)

Iliad 17.514 et al.

211 ἐν δὲ φάει καὶ ὄλεσσον, ἐπεί νύ τοι εὔαδεν οὕτως

If it be thy will to destroy us – then at least let us die in the light!

Translated by Kathleen Freeman (1947)

Iliad 17.647

Aias praying to Zeus to lift the mist

212 ὥς τε ψαρῶν νέφος ἔρχεται ἠὲ κολοιῶν
οὖλον κεκλήγοντες, ὅτε προΐδωσιν ἰόντα
κίρκον, ὅ τε σμικρῇσι φόνον φέρει ὀρνίθεσσιν

As flies a cloud of starlings or of jackdaws,
shrieking cries of doom, when they see upon them
a falcon that bears death unto small birds.

Translated by A.T. Murray (1925)

Iliad 17.755

of Achaeans in flight before Hector

213 ἐτώσιον ἄχθος ἀρούρης

A useless burden on the earth.

Iliad 18.104

Achilles of himself; quoted by Socrates in his Apology, cf. Plato 28d et al.; a proverbial expression to this day

214 καὶ χόλος ...
ὅς τε πολὺ γλυκίων μέλιτος καταλειβομένοιο

And anger, far sweeter than trickling honey.

Translated by A.T. Murray (1925)

Iliad 18.108

cf. the English proverb 'revenge is sweet'

215 ἀλλὰ τὰ μὲν προτετύχθαι ἐάσομεν ἀχνύμενοί περ

What is done is better left alone, though we resent it still.

Translated by E.V. Rieu (1950)

Iliad 18.112

quoted in Greek by Cicero, Letters to Atticus *7.1; cf. the English expression 'let bygones be bygones'*

216 ἀμφὶ δέ οἱ κεφαλῇ νέφος ἔστεφε δῖα θεάων

χρύσεον, ἐκ δ' αὐτοῦ δαῖε φλόγα παμφανόωσαν

Around his head
The glorious goddess wreath'd a golden cloud,
And from it lighted an all-shining flame.

Translated by Alfred, Lord Tennyson (1877)

Iliad 18.205

Athena covers Achilles; this was one of Tennyson's favourite Homeric passages

217 ὡς δ' ὅτε καπνὸς ἰὼν ἐξ ἄστεος αἰθέρ' ἵκηται,
τηλόθεν ἐκ νήσου, τὴν δήϊοι ἀμφιμάχωνται,
οἵ τε πανημέριοι στυγερῷ κρίνονται Ἄρηϊ
ἄστεος ἐκ σφετέρου· ἅμα δ' ἠελίῳ καταδύντι
πυρσοί τε φλεγέθουσιν ἐπήτριμοι, ὑψόσε δ' αὐγὴ
γίγνεται ἀΐσσουσα περικτιόνεσσιν ἰδέσθαι,
αἴ κέν πως σὺν νηυσὶν ἄρεω ἀλκτῆρες ἵκωνται

As when a smoke from a city goes to heaven
Far off from out an island girt by foes;
All day the men contend in grievous war
From their own city, but with set of sun
Their fires flame thickly, and aloft the glare
Flies streaming, if perchance the neighbours round
May see, and sail to help them in the war.

Translated by Alfred, Lord Tennyson (1877)

Iliad 18.207

218 ἀλλ' οὐ Ζεὺς ἄνδρεσσι νοήματα πάντα τελευτᾷ

But Zeus will not comply with all the schemes of men.

Iliad 18.328

cf. Homer 221

219 ἐν μὲν γαῖαν ἔτευξ', ἐν δ' οὐρανόν, ἐν δὲ θάλασσαν,
ἠέλιόν τ' ἀκάμαντα σελήνην τε πλήθουσαν,
ἐν δὲ τὰ τείρεα πάντα, τά τ' οὐρανὸς ἐστεφάνωται

He wrought thereon the earth and the sky and the sea
and the unwearying sun and the full moon
and all the stars with which the sky is crowned.

Translated by C.A. Trypanis (1971)

Iliad 18.482

of the shield of Achilles, wrought by Hephaestus

220 Πληϊάδας θ' Ὑάδας τε τό τε σθένος Ὠρίωνος
Ἄρκτόν θ'... ἥ τ' αὐτοῦ στρέφεται ...
οἴη δ' ἄμμορός ἐστι λοετρῶν Ὠκεανοῖο

The Pleiades and the Hyades and mighty Orion
and the Bear, which turns in her place,
and is the only one which does not dip in the Ocean.

Translated by C.A. Trypanis (1971)

Iliad 18.486

all these names of constellation are still in use today

221 θεὸς διὰ πάντα τελευτᾷ

It is god that bringeth all things to their issue.

Translated by A.T. Murray (1925)

Iliad 19.90

cf. Homer 218

222 αὐτίκ' ἔπειθ' ἅμα μῦθος ἔην, τετέλεστο δὲ ἔργον

No sooner was the work assigned than done.

Translated by Robert Fitzgerald (1975)

Iliad 19.242

223 νῶϊ δὲ καί κεν ἅμα πνοιῇ Ζεφύροιο θέοιμεν,
ἥν περ ἐλαφροτάτην φάσ' ἔμμεναι· ἀλλὰ σοὶ αὐτῷ
μόρσιμόν ἐστι θεῷ τε καὶ ἀνέρι ἶφι δαμῆναι.
ὣς ἄρα φωνήσαντος Ἐρινύες ἔσχεθον αὐδήν

We vie in speed with the breath of the of the West-Wind,
Which, men say, is the fleetest of winds; 'tis thou who art fated
To lie low in death, by the hand of a god and a mortal.
Thus far he; and here his voice was stopped by the Furies.

Translated by Matthew Arnold (1861)

Iliad 19.415

Xanthus, one of his two steeds, speaks to Achilles heralding his death, having been given a human voice by Hera

224 στρεπτὴ δὲ γλῶσσ' ἐστὶ βροτῶν, πολέες δ' ἔνι μῦθοι
παντοῖοι, ἐπέων δὲ πολὺς νομὸς ἔνθα καὶ ἔνθα.
ὁπποῖόν κ' εἴπῃσθα ἔπος, τοῖόν κ' ἐπακούσαις

Glib is the tongue of mortals, and words there be therein many and manifold, and of speech the range is wide on this side and on that. Whatever word thou speakest, the like shalt thou also hear.

Translated by A.T. Murray (1925)

Iliad 20.248

the last line is used verbatim in Greek Anthology *9.382, 'He who first heard Echo'*

225 οὐδ' Ἀχιλεὺς πάντεσσι τέλος μύθοις ἐπιθήσει

Even Achilles cannot accomplish all he says.

Iliad 20.369

Hector about to face Achilles

226 ποταμός περ ἐΰρροος ἀργυροδίνης

The fair-flowing river with its silver eddies.

Translated by A.T. Murray (1925)

Iliad 21.130

227 καίοντο πτελέαι τε καὶ ἰτέαι ἠδὲ μυρῖκαι,
καίετο δὲ λωτός τε ἰδὲ θρύον ἠδὲ κύπειρον

Burned were the elms, the willows and the tamarisks,
burned the lotus, the rushes and the galingale.

Translated by A.T. Murray (1925)

Iliad 21.350

228 βροτῶν ἕνεκα πτολεμίξω
δειλῶν, οἳ φύλλοισιν ἐοικότες ἄλλοτε μέν τε
ζαφλεγέες τελέθουσιν, ἀρούρης καρπὸν ἔδοντες,
ἄλλοτε δὲ φθινύθουσιν ἀκήριοι

Pitiful mortals,
ephemeral as leaves,
flourish on the bounty of the earth,
and then waste and die.

Iliad 21.463

229 τότε δὴ χρύσεια πατὴρ ἐτίταινε τάλαντα,
ἐν δ' ἐτίθει δύο κῆρε τανηλεγέος θανάτοιο

The Father lifted on high his golden scales,
and set therein two fates of grievous death.

Translated by A.T. Murray (1925)

Iliad 22.209

Zeus deciding the fate of Hector and Achilles

230 ὡς οὐκ ἔστι λέουσι καὶ ἀνδράσιν ὅρκια πιστά,
οὐδὲ λύκοι τε καὶ ἄρνες ὁμόφρονα θυμὸν ἔχουσιν

Between men and lions there are no oaths of faith,
as between wolves and lambs there is no concord.

Iliad 22.262

231 νῦν αὖτέ με μοῖρα κιχάνει·
μὴ μὰν ἀσπουδί γε καὶ ἀκλειῶς ἀπολοίμην,
ἀλλὰ μέγα ῥέξας τι καὶ ἐσσομένοισι πυθέσθαι

But now my doom is come upon me;
may I not die ingloriously and without struggle,
but by great deeds, worthy to be heard by those to come.

Iliad 22.303

Hector in battle against Achilles

232 μεγάροιο διέσσυτο μαινάδι ἴση,
παλλομένη κραδίην

She hasted through the hall with throbbing heart as one beside herself.

Translated by A.T. Murray (1925)

Iliad 22.460

of Andromache, Hector's wife

233 ὢ πόποι, ἦ ῥά τί ἐστι καὶ εἰν Ἀΐδαο δόμοισι
ψυχὴ καὶ εἴδωλον, ἀτὰρ φρένες οὐκ ἔνι πάμπαν

Ah then, 'tis true that we survive in Hades,
our soul and phantom, but no intellect withal.

Iliad 23.103

Achilles of the ghost of Patroclus eluding his embrace

234 πολλὰ δ' ἄναντα κάταντα πάραντά τε δόχμιά τ' ἦλθον

O'er hills, o'er dales, o'er crags, o'er rocks they go.

Translated by Alexander Pope (1715)

Iliad 23.116

of men collecting wood for the funeral pyre of Patroclus

235 μήτι τοι δρυτόμος μέγ' ἀμείνων ἠὲ βίηφι·
μήτι δ' αὖτε κυβερνήτης ἐνὶ οἴνοπι πόντῳ
νῆα θοὴν ἰθύνει ἐρεχθομένην ἀνέμοισι·
μήτι δ' ἡνίοχος περιγίγνεται ἡνιόχοιο

It is skill, not might, that makes a woodman better;
by skill a helmsman on the wine-dark deep
expertly guides a ship when roughed by winds;
and skill proves charioteer better than charioteer.

Iliad 23.315

236 οὐδ' ἄρα πως ἦν
ἐν πάντεσσ' ἔργοισι δαήμονα φῶτα γενέσθαι

No man can be in everything a master.

Iliad 23.670

237 οὐδέ μιν ὕπνος
ᾕρει πανδαμάτωρ, ἀλλ' ἐστρέφετ' ἔνθα καὶ ἔνθα

All-conquering sleep
refused to visit him, and he tossed from side to side.

Translated by E.V. Rieu (1950)

Iliad 24.4

238 τλητὸν γὰρ Μοῖραι θυμὸν θέσαν ἀνθρώποισιν

The fates have given man a soul steadfast in suffering.

Translated in Liddell & Scott

Iliad 24.49

239 Πρίαμος μέγας, …
χερσὶν Ἀχιλλῆος λάβε γούνατα καὶ κύσε χεῖρας
δεινὰς ἀνδροφόνους, αἵ οἱ πολέας κτάνον υἷας

Great Priam
clasped in his hands Achilles' knees, and kissed his hands,
the terrible, man-slaying hands that had slain his many sons.

Translated by A.T. Murray (1925)

Iliad 24.477

240 ὡς γὰρ ἐπεκλώσαντο θεοὶ δειλοῖσι βροτοῖσι,
ζώειν ἀχνυμένους· αὐτοὶ δέ τ' ἀκηδέες εἰσί.
δοιοὶ γάρ τε πίθοι κατακείαται ἐν Διὸς οὔδει
δώρων οἷα δίδωσι, κακῶν, ἕτερος δὲ ἑάων

This is the way
the gods ordained the destiny of men,
to bear such burdens in our lives, while they
feel no affliction. At the door of Zeus
are those two urns of good and evil gifts
that he may choose for us.

Translated by Robert Fitzgerald (1975)

Iliad 24.525

241 ἄνσχεο, μὴ δ' ἀλίαστον ὀδύρεο σὸν κατὰ θυμόν·
οὐ γάρ τι πρήξεις ἀκαχήμενος υἷος ἑοῖο,
οὐδέ μιν ἀνστήσεις, πρὶν καὶ κακὸν ἄλλο πάθησθα

Mourne not inevitable things; thy teares can spring no deeds
To helpe thee, nor recall thy sonne; impacience ever breeds
Ill upon ill, makes worst things worse.

Translated by George Chapman (1611)

Iliad 24.549

Achilles to Priam

242 Ἄνδρα μοι ἔννεπε, Μοῦσα, πολύτροπον, ὃς μάλα πολλὰ
πλάγχθη, ἐπεὶ Τροίης ἱερὸν πτολίεθρον ἔπερσεν·
πολλῶν δ' ἀνθρώπων ἴδεν ἄστεα καὶ νόον ἔγνω,
πολλὰ δ' ὅ γ' ἐν πόντῳ πάθεν ἄλγεα ὃν κατὰ θυμόν,
ἀρνύμενος ἥν τε ψυχὴν καὶ νόστον ἑταίρων.

Sing to me of the man, Muse, the man of twists and turns
driven time and again off course, once he had plundered
the hallowed heights of Troy.

Many cities of men he saw and learned their minds,
many pains he suffered, heartsick on the open sea,
fighting to save his life and bring his comrades home.

Translated by Robert Fagles (1996)

Odyssey 1.1

opening lines, of Odysseus

243 αὐτῶν γὰρ σφετέρῃσιν ἀτασθαλίῃσιν ὄλοντο,
νήπιοι

Their own recklessness destroyed them all,
the heedless fools.

Odyssey 1.7

of Odysseus' comrades

244 νόστιμον ἦμαρ

The day of their returning.

Translated by A.T. Murray (1919)

Odyssey 1.9 et al.

245 ὢ πόποι, οἷον δή νυ θεοὺς βροτοὶ αἰτιόωνται·
ἐξ ἡμέων γάρ φασι κάκ' ἔμμεναι· οἱ δὲ καὶ αὐτοὶ
σφῇσιν ἀτασθαλίῃσιν ὑπὲρ μόρον ἄλγε' ἔχουσιν

Look now how mortals are blaming the gods as the source of their troubles, rather than blame themselves for their own foolish actions.

Odyssey 1.32

Zeus to the other gods

246 νῦν δ' ἀθρόα πάντ' ἀπέτεισεν

Now he has paid the full price of all

Translated by A.T. Murray (1919)

Odyssey 1.43

of Aegisthus who killed Agamemnon – and was killed by Agamemnon's son, Orestes

247 ὡς ἀπόλοιτο καὶ ἄλλος ὅτις τοιαῦτά γε ῥέζοι

May all thus perish who do the like again.

Odyssey 1.47

of Aegisthus, for killing Agamemnon

248 ὅς τε θαλάσσης
πάσης βένθεα οἶδεν, ἔχει δέ τε κίονας αὐτὸς
μακράς, αἳ γαῖάν τε καὶ οὐρανὸν ἀμφὶς ἔχουσιν

Atlas, who knows the depths of every sea, and himself holds the tall pillars which keep earth and heaven apart.

Translated by A.T. Murray (1919)

Odyssey 1.52

249 μαλακοῖσι καὶ αἱμυλίοισι λόγοισιν θέλγει

Deceiving with soft, persuasive words.

Translated by E.V. Rieu (1946)

Odyssey 1.56

of Calypso keeping Odysseus' mind away from thoughts of Ithaca

250 πέδιλα … τά μιν φέρον ἠμὲν ἐφ' ὑγρὴν
ἠδ' ἐπ' ἀπείρονα γαῖαν ἅμα πνοιῇς ἀνέμοιο

Sandals which carried her over water
and boundless land, swift as the wind.

Odyssey 1.96

of Athena, as she prepares to go to Ithaca

251 χαῖρε, ξεῖνε, παρ' ἄμμι φιλήσεαι

Hail, stranger; welcome shalt thou be in our house.

Translated in Liddell & Scott

Odyssey 1.123

inscribed over the entrance of the rather rustic Hotel 'Belle Hélène' at Mycenae; all Greek and foreign archaeologists lived there while excavating the Mycenaean citadel

252 πλέων ἐπὶ οἴνοπα πόντον ἐπ' ἀλλοθρόους ἀνθρώπους,
ἐς Τεμέσην μετὰ χαλκόν, ἄγω δ' αἴθωνα σίδηρον

Sailing the winedark sea for ports to call
on alien shores – to Témesê, for copper,
bringing bright bars of iron in exchange.

Translated by Robert Fitzgerald (1961)

Odyssey 1.183

Temese: identified by some as Tamassos in Cyprus, others as Temesa in Bruttium

253 οὐ γάρ πώ τις ἑὸν γόνον αὐτὸς ἀνέγνω

Who, on his own,
has ever really known who gave him life?

Translated by Robert Fagles (1996)

Odyssey 1.216

254 οἴχετ' ἄϊστος ἄπυστος

He is gone out of sight, out of hearing.

Translated by A.T. Murray (1919)

Odyssey 1.242

of Odysseus

255 οὐδέ τί σε χρὴ
νηπιάας ὀχέειν, ἐπεὶ οὐκέτι τηλίκος ἐσσί

You are a child no more,
you must put away your childish ways.

Odyssey 1.296

256 ἀγορεύεις
ὥς τε πατὴρ ᾧ παιδί, καὶ οὔ ποτε λήσομαι αὐτῶν

You speak
like a father to his son, and I shall never forget your words.

Odyssey 1.307

257 οὔτ' οὖν ἀγγελίῃ ἔτι πείθομαι, εἴ ποθεν ἔλθοι

No longer do I put trust in tidings, whencesoever they may come.

Translated by A.T. Murray (1919)

Odyssey 1.414

Telemachus on rumours of his father's death

258 πολλὰ φρεσὶ μερμηρίζων

Pondering many things in his mind.

Translated by A.T. Murray (1919)

Odyssey 1.427

259 οὔ πως ἔστι δόμων ἀέκουσαν ἀπῶσαι
ἥ μ' ἔτεχ', ἥ μ' ἔθρεψε

Can I banish against her will,
the mother who bore me and took care of me?

Translated by Robert Fitzgerald (1961)

Odyssey 2.130

260 παῦροι γάρ τοι παῖδες ὁμοῖοι πατρὶ πέλονται,
οἱ πλέονες κακίους, παῦροι δέ τε πατρὸς ἀρείους

Few sons, indeed, are like their fathers; generally they are worse; but just a few are better.

Translated by E.V. Rieu (1946)

Odyssey 2.276

261 τοῖσιν δ' ἴκμενον οὖρον ἵει γλαυκῶπις Ἀθήνη,
ἀκραῆ Ζέφυρον, κελάδοντ' ἐπὶ οἴνοπα πόντον

And bright-eyed Athena sent a favourable breeze,
A hearty western wind, whistling over the dark blue sea.

Odyssey 2.420

262 Ἠέλιος δ' ἀνόρουσε, λιπὼν περικαλλέα λίμνην,
οὐρανὸν ἐς πολύχαλκον, ἵν' ἀθανάτοισι φαείνοι
καὶ θνητοῖσι βροτοῖσιν ἐπὶ ζείδωρον ἄρουραν

The sun sprang up, leaving brilliant waters in its wake,
climbing the bronze sky to shower light on immortal gods
and mortal men across the plowlands ripe with grain.

Translated by Robert Fagles (1996)

Odyssey 3.1

263 αἰδὼς δ' αὖ νέον ἄνδρα γεραίτερον ἐξερέεσθαι

It is not for a young man to question an older one.

Odyssey 3.24

264 πάντες δὲ θεῶν χατέουσ' ἄνθρωποι

All men have need of the gods.

Translated by A.T. Murray (1919)

Odyssey 3.48

265 οὐ γάρ τ' αἶψα θεῶν τρέπεται νόος αἰὲν ἐόντων

It is not easy to divert the immortal gods from their purpose.

Translated by E.V. Rieu (1946)

Odyssey 3.147

266 λίην γὰρ μέγα εἶπες· ἄγη μ' ἔχει

Too great is what thou sayest; amazement holds me.

Translated by A.T. Murray (1919)

Odyssey 3.227

267 τὴν δ' ἐθέλων ἐθέλουσαν ἀνήγαγεν ὅνδε δόμονδε

And, willing as she was willing, he led her to his house.

Translated by A.T. Murray (1919)

Odyssey 3.272

268 ἐκτελέσας μέγα ἔργον, ὃ οὔ ποτε ἔλπετο θυμῷ

He accomplished a mighty deed, beyond his wildest dreams.

Odyssey 3.275

269 μικρὸς δὲ λίθος μέγα κῦμ' ἀποέργει

A small rock wards off a mighty wave.

Odyssey 3.296

270 ψεῦδος δ' οὐκ ἐρέει· μάλα γὰρ πεπνυμένος ἐστίν

A man as wise as he will never lie.

Odyssey 3.328

271 οὐ μὲν νήπιος ἦσθα …
τὸ πρίν· ἀτὰρ μὲν νῦν γε πάις ὣς νήπια βάζεις

You were not a fool
but now you are talking nonsense like a child.

Odyssey 4.31

272 νεμεσσῶμαί γε μὲν οὐδὲν
κλαίειν, ὅς κε θάνῃσι βροτῶν καὶ πότμον ἐπίσπῃ·
τοῦτό νυ καὶ γέρας οἶον ὀιζυροῖσι βροτοῖσιν,
κείρασθαί τε κόμην βαλέειν τ' ἀπὸ δάκρυ παρειῶν

Not that I think it wrong to shed a tear for any man who meets his fate and dies. Indeed, what other tribute can one pay to wretched man than a lock of hair, a tear on the cheek?

Translated by E.V. Rieu (1946)

Odyssey 4.195

273 αὐτίκ' ἄρ' εἰς οἶνον βάλε φάρμακον, ἔνθεν ἔπινον,
νηπενθές τ' ἄχολόν τε, κακῶν ἐπίληθον ἁπάντων

Into their wine she slipped a drug, a remedy
for pain and anger, banishing all memories of woe.

Odyssey 4.220

274 γέρων ἅλιος

The old man of the sea.

Translated by A.T. Murray (1919)

Odyssey 4.349

275 θεοὶ δέ τε πάντα ἴσασιν

The gods know all things.

Translated by A.T. Murray (1919)

Odyssey 4.379

276 ἀλλά σ' ἐς Ἠλύσιον πεδίον … ἀθάνατοι πέμψουσιν, …
οὐ νιφετός, οὔτ' ἂρ χειμὼν πολὺς οὔτε ποτ' ὄμβρος,
ἀλλ' αἰεὶ Ζεφύροιο λιγὺ πνείοντος ἀήτας
Ὠκεανὸς ἀνίησιν ἀναψύχειν ἀνθρώπους

The gods will send you off to the Elysian Fields;
no snow, no winter there, no rain; but at all times
the Ocean sends up winds, sweet Western winds,
bearing refreshment for the souls of men.

Odyssey 4.563

277 κακὸν δ' ἀνεμώλια βάζειν

It does no good to utter empty words.

Odyssey 4.837 et al.

278 λάρῳ ὄρνιθι ἐοικώς,
ὅς τε κατὰ δεινοὺς κόλπους ἁλὸς ἀτρυγέτοιο
ἰχθῦς ἀγρώσσων πυκινὰ πτερὰ δεύεται ἅλμῃ

So wat'ry fowl, that seek their fishy food,
With wings expanded o'er the foaming flood,
Now sailing smooth the level surface sweep,
Now dip their pinions in the briny deep.

Translated by Alexander Pope (1725)

Odyssey 5.51

of Hermes, messenger of the gods

279 οὐδέ μοι αὐτῇ
θυμὸς ἐνὶ στήθεσσι σιδήρεος, ἀλλ' ἐλεήμων

My heart is not made of iron; I know what pity is.

Translated by E.V. Rieu (1946)

Odyssey 5.190

280 ἐθέλω καὶ ἐέλδομαι ἤματα πάντα
οἴκαδέ τ' ἐλθέμεναι καὶ νόστιμον ἦμαρ ἰδέσθαι

All my days I wish and long
to reach my home, to see the day of my return.

Odyssey 5.219

spoken by Odysseus to Calypso who has agreed to set him free

281 τλήσομαι ἐν στήθεσσιν ἔχων ταλαπενθέα θυμόν·
ἤδη γὰρ μάλα πολλὰ πάθον

My soul
Shall bear that also; for, by practice taught,
I have learn'd patience, having much endured.

Translated by William Cowper (1791)

Odyssey 5.222

282 σύναγεν νεφέλας, ἐτάραξε δὲ πόντον
χερσὶ τρίαιναν ἑλών· πάσας δ' ὀρόθυνεν ἀέλλας
παντοίων ἀνέμων, σὺν δὲ νεφέεσσι κάλυψε
γαῖαν ὁμοῦ καὶ πόντον· ὀρώρει δ' οὐρανόθεν νύξ

Brewing high thunderheads, he churned the deep
with both hands on his trident – called up wind
from every quarter, and sent a wall of rain
to blot out land and sea in torrential night.

Translated by Robert Fitzgerald (1961)

Odyssey 5.291

of Poseidon

283 μέγα κῦμα Ποσειδάων ἐνοσίχθων,
δεινόν τ' ἀργαλέον τε, κατηρεφές, ἤλασε δ' αὐτόν·
ὡς δ' ἄνεμος ζαὴς ἠίων θημῶνα τινάξῃ
καρφαλέων· τὰ μὲν ἄρ τε διεσκέδασ' ἄλλυδις ἄλλῃ

Neptune raisd
A huge, a high, and horrid wave, that seisd
Him and his ship and tost them through the Lake.
As when the violent winds together take
Heapes of drie chaffe and hurle them every way.

Translated by George Chapman (1615)

Odyssey 5.366

284 ὁ δ' ἄρ' ἄπνευστος καὶ ἄναυδος
κεῖτ' ὀλιγηπελέων

So he lay breathless and speechless, with scarce strength to move.

Translated by A.T. Murray (1919)

Odyssey 5.456

of Odysseus washed ashore, exhausted

285 Οὔλυμπόνδ' ὅθι φασὶ θεῶν ἕδος ἀσφαλὲς αἰεὶ
ἔμμεναι· οὔτ' ἀνέμοισι τινάσσεται οὔτε ποτ' ὄμβρῳ
δεύεται οὔτε χιὼν ἐπιπίλναται, ἀλλὰ μάλ' αἴθρη
πέπταται ἀνέφελος, λευκὴ δ' ἐπιδέδρομεν αἴγλη

Olympus, eternal dwelling of the gods, unmoved,
not rocked by winds, not drenched by rains,
not touched by snow; where the clear sky,
without a cloud, exudes a splendid radiance.

Odyssey 6.42

286 σοὶ δὲ θεοὶ τόσα δοῖεν, ὅσα φρεσὶ σῇσι μενοινᾷς,
ἄνδρα τε καὶ οἶκον, καὶ ὁμοφροσύνην ὀπάσειαν
ἐσθλήν· οὐ μὲν γὰρ τοῦ γε κρεῖσσον καὶ ἄρειον,
ἢ ὅθ' ὁμοφρονέοντε νοήμασιν οἶκον ἔχητον
ἀνὴρ ἠδὲ γυνή· πόλλ' ἄλγεα δυσμενέεσσι,
χάρματα δ' εὐμενέτῃσι· μάλιστα δέ τ' ἔκλυον αὐτοί

And may the good gods give you all your heart desires:
husband, and a house, and lasting harmony too.
No finer, greater gift in the world than that …
when man and woman possess their home, two minds,
two hearts and work as one. Despair to their enemies,
a joy to their friends. Their own best claim to glory.

Translated by Robert Fagles (1996)

Odyssey 6.180

287 πρὸς γὰρ Διός εἰσιν ἅπαντες
ξεῖνοί τε πτωχοί τε, δόσις δ' ὀλίγη τε φίλη τε

All strangers and beggars come from Zeus,
and whatever gift we give, though small, is precious.

Odyssey 6.207

288 τῶν νέες ὠκεῖαι ὡς εἰ πτερὸν ἠὲ νόημα

Their ships are swift as a bird or a thought.

Translated in *Bartlett's Familiar Quotations* (1980)

Odyssey 7.36

289 οὐ γάρ τι στυγερῇ ἐπὶ γαστέρι κύντερον ἄλλο

There's nothing more demanding than one's stomach!

Odyssey 7.216

290 ἀλλ' ἐμὸν οὔ ποτε θυμὸν ἐνὶ στήθεσσιν ἔπειθεν

But never for a moment did she sway the spirit in my breast.

Odyssey 7.258

Odysseus of Calypso; quoted in Greek by Cicero, Letters to Atticus *7.1*

291 δύσζηλοι γάρ τ' εἰμὲν ἐπὶ χθονὶ φῦλ' ἀνθρώπων

We're all prone to jealousy, we men on earth.

Odyssey 7.307

292 οὕτως οὐ πάντεσσι θεοὶ χαρίεντα διδοῦσιν
ἀνδράσιν, οὔτε φυὴν οὔτ' ἂρ φρένας οὔτ' ἀγορητύν

The gods do not give gifts to all alike,
neither good looks nor intellect nor eloquence.

Odyssey 8.167

293 οὐκ ἀρετᾷ κακὰ ἔργα· κιχάνει τοι βραδὺς ὠκύν

Ill deeds thrive not; and slow outstrips the swift.

Odyssey 8.329

294 ὑμεῖς δ' εἰσορόῳτε θεοὶ πᾶσαί τε θέαιναι,
αὐτὰρ ἐγὼν εὕδοιμι παρὰ χρυσέῃ Ἀφροδίτῃ

Though all you gods and goddesses were looking on, yet would I be glad to sleep by golden Aphrodite's side.

Translated by E.V. Rieu (1946)

Odyssey 8.341

Hermes in reply to Apollo

295 πᾶσι γὰρ ἀνθρώποισιν ἐπιχθονίοισιν ἀοιδοὶ
τιμῆς ἔμμοροί εἰσι καὶ αἰδοῦς, οὕνεκ' ἄρα σφέας
οἴμας μοῦσ' ἐδίδαξε, φίλησε δὲ φῦλον ἀοιδῶν

Singers of songs, among all men on earth,
deserve respect and honour; taught poems by the Muse,
the tribe of minstrels are her favourites.

Odyssey 8.479

296 ἀντὶ κασιγνήτου ξεῖνός θ' ἱκέτης τε τέτυκται
ἀνέρι, ὅς τ' ὀλίγον περ ἐπιψαύῃ πραπίδεσσι

Treat your guest and suppliant like a brother;
anyone with a touch of sense knows that.

Translated by Robert Fagles (1996)

Odyssey 8.546

297 οὐ μὲν γάρ τις πάμπαν ἀνώνυμός ἐστ' ἀνθρώπων,
οὐ κακὸς οὐδὲ μὲν ἐσθλός

No man is nameless, be he base or noble

Translated by A.T. Murray (1919)

Odyssey 8.552

298 ἐπεὶ οὐ μέν τι κασιγνήτοιο χερείων
γίγνεται, ὅς κεν ἑταῖρος ἐὼν πεπνυμένα εἰδῇ

No less dear than a brother
is a comrade who shares our inmost thoughts.

Translated by Robert Fagles (1996)

Odyssey 8.585

299 τί πρῶτόν τοι ἔπειτα, τί δ' ὑστάτιον καταλέξω;

What, then, shall I tell thee first, what last?

Translated by A.T. Murray (1919)

Odyssey 9.14

the beginning of Odysseus' long tale to Alcinous, king of the Phaeacians (to the end of book 12)

300 ὡς οὐδὲν γλύκιον ἧς πατρίδος οὐδὲ τοκήων
γίνεται, εἴ περ καί τις ἀπόπροθι πίονα οἶκον
γαίῃ ἐν ἀλλοδαπῇ ναίει

Nothing is as sweet as a man's own country,
his own parents, even though he's settled down
in some luxurious house, off in a foreign land
and far from those who bore him.

Translated by Robert Fagles (1996)

Odyssey 9.34

301 ἔνθεν δ' ἐννῆμαρ φερόμην ὀλοοῖς ἀνέμοισι
πόντον ἐπ' ἰχθυόεντα

Nine long days was I driv'n by ruinous winds
O'er the fish-teeming deep.

Translated by S.O. Andrew (1948)

Odyssey 9.83

302 ἤ τι ὀισάμενος, ἦ καὶ θεὸς ὣς ἐκέλευσεν

Either from some foreboding, or because a god bade him so.

Translated by A.T. Murray (1919)

Odyssey 9.339

cf. Plutarch 29

303 τρὶς μὲν ἔδωκα φέρων, τρὶς δ' ἔκπιεν ἀφραδίῃσιν.
αὐτὰρ ἐπεὶ Κύκλωπα περὶ φρένας ἤλυθεν οἶνος

Nor could the foole abstaine,
But drunke often. And soon the noble Juyce
Had wrought upon his spirit.

Translated by George Chapman (1615)

Odyssey 9.361

of Cyclops drinking wine given by Odysseus

304 Οὖτις ἐμοί γ' ὄνομα ...
ὦ φίλοι, Οὖτίς με κτείνει

Odysseus: 'Nobody', that's my name.
Cyclops: My friends! Nobody's killing me!

Translated by Robert Fagles (1996)

Odyssey 9.366 and 408

305 τίς, πόθεν εἰς ἀνδρῶν; πόθι τοι πόλις ἠδὲ τοκῆες;

Who art thou? what thy parents? city? whence?

Translated by William Sotheby (1834)

Odyssey 10.325

Circe to Odysseus who is not affected by her potion

306 ἐσθέμεναι δ' ἐκέλευεν· ἐμῷ δ' οὐχ ἥνδανε θυμῷ,
ἀλλ' ἥμην ἀλλοφρονέων, κακὰ δ' ὄσσετο θυμός

She bade me eat; but I had no mind for eating;
elsewhere were my thoughts, full of grim forebodings.

Odyssey 10.373

307 οἴῳ πεπνῦσθαι, τοὶ δὲ σκιαὶ ἀίσσουσιν

Only he has wits, the rest are but fluttering shadows.

Translated by Bernadotte Perrin (1914)

Odyssey 10.495

quoted verbatim by Cato the Elder on hearing of Scipio's daring at Carthage (the elder Cornelius Scipio Africanus); in Plutarch, Cato the Elder *27.6*

308 οὐδέ νύ μοι κῆρ
ἤθελ' ἔτι ζώειν καὶ ὁρᾶν φάος ἠελίοιο

Nor had my heart
any longer the desire to live and behold the light of the sun.

Translated by A.T. Murray (1919)

Odyssey 10.497

309 τὴν δ' ἄνεμός τε κυβερνήτης τ' ἴθυνε·
τῆς δὲ πανημερίης τέταθ' ἱστία ποντοπορούσης·
δύσετό τ' ἠέλιος σκιόωντό τε πᾶσαι ἀγυιαί

Then sat we amidships, wind jamming the tiller,
Thus with stretched sail, we went over sea till day's end.
Sun to his slumber, shadows o'er all the ocean.

Translated by Ezra Pound (1933)

Odyssey 11.10

310 ἡ δ' ἐς πείραθ' ἵκανε βαθυρρόου Ὠκεανοῖο·
ἔνθα δὲ Κιμμερίων ἀνδρῶν δῆμός τε πόλις τε,

ἠέρι καὶ νεφέλῃ κεκαλυμμένοι· οὐδέ ποτ' αὐτοὺς
Ἠέλιος φαέθων καταδέρκεται ἀκτίνεσσιν

Our ship ran onward toward the Ocean's bourne,
the realm and region of the Men of Winter,
hidden in mist and cloud. Never the flaming
eye of Helios lights on those men.

Translated by Robert Fitzgerald (1961)

Odyssey 11.13

of the Cimmerians, a 'mythical' people dwelling at the Ocean's limits

311 σῆμά τέ μοι χεῦαι πολιῆς ἐπὶ θινὶ θαλάσσης,
ἀνδρὸς δυστήνοιο, καὶ ἐσσομένοισι πυθέσθαι·
ταῦτά τέ μοι τελέσαι πῆξαί τ' ἐπὶ τύμβῳ ἐρετμόν,
τῷ καὶ ζωὸς ἔρεσσον ἐὼν μετ' ἐμοῖσ' ἑτάροισιν

And heap my grave-mound where the grey waves break;
A sign for generations yet to be
Of my unhappy fate: do this for me,
And plant on it the oar I rowed with once,
While yet I lived, among your company.

Translated by J.W. MacKail (1903)

Odyssey 11.75

Elpenor, one of his crew, asking Odysseus to bury him

312 ὣς ἔφατ'...
τρὶς μὲν ἐφωρμήθην, ἑλέειν τέ με θυμὸς ἀνώγει,
τρὶς δέ μοι ἐκ χειρῶν σκιῇ εἴκελον ἢ καὶ ὀνείρῳ
ἔπτατ'

Thus she spoke, and thrice I tried to embrace her spirit.
Thrice, like a shadow, or a dream, it slipped through my hands.

Odyssey 11.206

Odysseus in Hades, meeting his mother's ghost

313 ψυχὴ δ' ἠύτ' ὄνειρος ἀποπταμένη πεπότηται

The spirit, like a dream, flits away, and hovers to and fro.

Translated by A.T. Murray (1919)

Odyssey 11.222

314 Ὄσσαν ἐπ' Οὐλύμπῳ μέμασαν θέμεν, αὐτὰρ ἐπ' Ὄσσῃ Πήλιον
εἰνοσίφυλλον, ἵν' οὐρανὸς ἀμβατὸς εἴη

Eager they were to pile Mount Ossa on Olympus; and then
forested Pelion on Ossa, to make a stairway up to heaven.

Odyssey 11.315

of the twins of Iphimedeia, wishing to fight the gods

315 ὥρη μὲν πολέων μύθων, ὥρη δὲ καὶ ὕπνου

There is a time for many tales, a time for sleep as well.

Odyssey 11.379

316 ὣς οὐκ αἰνότερον καὶ κύντερον ἄλλο γυναικός,
ἥ τις δὴ τοιαῦτα μετὰ φρεσὶν ἔργα βάληται·
οἷον δὴ καὶ κείνη ἐμήσατο ἔργον ἀεικές,
κουριδίῳ τεύξασα πόσει φόνον

Nothing is more horrible or fearful than a woman
who contemplates and carries out such deeds,
such monstrous deeds, as murdering her husband.

Odyssey 11.427

Agamemnon in Hades, telling the tale of his death

317 καὶ σὺ γυναικί ...
μηδ' οἱ μῦθον ἅπαντα πιφαυσκέμεν, ὅν κ' εὖ εἰδῇς,
ἀλλὰ τὸ μὲν φάσθαι, τὸ δὲ καὶ κεκρυμμένον εἶναι

Don't tell your wife everything you know,
tell her some things and keep some others hidden.

Odyssey 11.441

318 ἐπεὶ οὐκέτι πιστὰ γυναιξίν

There is no more trusting in women.

Translated in *Bartlett's Familiar Quotations* (1980)

Odyssey 11.456

319 βροτῶν εἴδωλα καμόντων

The phantoms of men outworn.

Translated by A.T. Murray (1919)

Odyssey 11.476

of the dead in Hades

320 βουλοίμην κ' ἐπάρουρος ἐὼν θητευέμεν ἄλλῳ,
ἀνδρὶ παρ' ἀκλήρῳ, ᾧ μὴ βίοτος πολὺς εἴη,
ἢ πᾶσιν νεκύεσσι καταφθιμένοισιν ἀνάσσειν

I would rather work the soil as a serf on hire to some landless impoverished peasant than be King of all these lifeless dead.

Translated by E.V. Rieu (1946)

Odyssey 11.489

321 κατὰ γῆρας ἔχει χεῖράς τε πόδας τε

Now feete and hands are in the hold of Age.

Translated by George Chapman (1615)

Odyssey 11.497

322 ψυχὴ …
φοίτα μακρὰ βιβᾶσα κατ' ἀσφοδελὸν λειμῶνα

The spirit
departed with long strides over the field of asphodel.

Translated by A.T. Murray (1919)

Odyssey 11.538

cf. Tennyson, 'The Lotos-Eaters': 'in Elysian valleys … on beds of asphodel'

323 ὄγχναι καὶ ῥοιαὶ καὶ μηλέαι ἀγλαόκαρποι
συκέαι τε γλυκεραὶ καὶ ἐλαῖαι τηλεθόωσαι

Pear trees, pomegranates, brilliant apples,
luscious figs, and olives ripe and dark.

Translated by Robert Fitzgerald (1961)

Odyssey 11.589

324 ἀλλ' ὅτε μέλλοι
ἄκρον ὑπερβαλέειν, τότ' ἀποστρέψασκε κραταιίς·
αὖτις ἔπειτα πέδονδε κυλίνδετο λᾶας ἀναιδής

But soon as he attains the Mountain's Crown,
It with a Vengeance hurri'd tumbles down.

Translated by John Ogilby (1665)

Odyssey 11.596

of Sisyphus' suffering in Hades, carrying to the mountaintop a huge stone which plunged down as soon as he arrived

325 ἄρκτοι τ' ἀγρότεροί τε σύες χαροποί τε λέοντες,
ὑσμῖναί τε μάχαι τε φόνοι τ' ἀνδροκτασίαι τε·
μὴ τεχνησάμενος μηδ' ἄλλο τι τεχνήσαιτο,
ὃς κεῖνον τελαμῶνα ἑῇ ἐγκάτθετο τέχνῃ

There sullen lions sternly seem to roar,
The bear to growl, to foam the tusky boar:
There war and havoc and destruction stood,
And vengeful murther red with human blood.
Thus teribly adorn'd the figures shine,
Inimitably wrought with skill divine.

Translated by William Broome (with Pope, 1720)

Odyssey 11.611

of Heracles' golden breastplate or belt in Hades

326 ἀλλὰ πρὶν ἐπὶ ἔθνε' ἀγείρετο μυρία νεκρῶν
ἠχῇ θεσπεσίῃ· ἐμὲ δὲ χλωρὸν δέος ᾕρει

But first came shades in thousands, rustling
in a pandemonium of whispers, blown together,
and the horror took me.

Translated by Robert Fitzgerald (1961)

Odyssey 11.632

Odysseus in Hades

327 ἄνεμος μὲν ἐπαύσατο ἠδὲ γαλήνη
ἔπλετο νηνεμίη, κοίμησε δὲ κύματα δαίμων

Sunk were at once the winds; the air above,
And waves below, at once forgot to move;
Some demon calm'd the air and smooth'd the deep,
Hush'd the loud winds, and charm'd the waves to sleep.

Translated by Alexander Pope (1725)

Odyssey 12.168

a sign to Odysseus approaching the Sirens

328 οὐ γάρ πώ τις τῇδε παρήλασε νηὶ μελαίνῃ,

πρίν γ' ἡμέων μελίγηρυν ἀπὸ στομάτων ὄπ' ἀκοῦσαι,
ἀλλ' ὅ γε τερψάμενος νεῖται καὶ πλείονα εἰδώς

Never has any man rowed past our isle in his black ship
and left unheard the sweet-voiced music from our lips;
first he enjoys, then goes his way a wiser man.

Odyssey 12.186

the Sirens' song

329 ὦ φίλοι, οὐ γάρ πώ τι κακῶν ἀδαήμονές εἰμεν·
οὐ μὲν δὴ τόδε μεῖζον ἔπι κακόν

My friends, we're hardly strangers to danger;
and no greater evil threatens us now.

Odyssey 12.208

Odysseus to his crew when expecting rough seas ahead; the second line is quoted in Greek by Cicero, Letters to Atticus *7.6*

330 λιμῷ δ' οἴκτιστον θανέειν

To die of hunger is the most pitiful.

Translated by A.T. Murray (1919)

Odyssey 12.342

331 ἐχθρὸν δέ μοί ἐστιν
αὖτις ἀριζήλως εἰρημένα μυθολογεύειν

I hate repeating tales already plainly told.

Odyssey 12.452

332 εἰς ὅ κε γῆρας
ἔλθῃ καὶ θάνατος, τά τ' ἐπ' ἀνθρώποισι πέλονται

Man's common lot, old age and death.

Translated by E.V. Rieu (1946)

Odyssey 13.59

333 νήδυμος ὕπνος ἐπὶ βλεφάροισιν ἔπιπτε,
νήγρετος, ἥδιστος, θανάτῳ ἄγχιστα ἐοικώς

Sweet sleep fell upon his eyelids,
an unawakening sleep, most sweet, and most alike to death.

Translated by A.T. Murray (1919)

Odyssey 13.79

334 οὐδέ κεν ἴρηξ
κίρκος ὁμαρτήσειεν, ἐλαφρότατος πετεηνῶν

Not even the circling hawk, the swiftest of winged things, could keep pace with her.

Translated by A.T. Murray (1919)

Odyssey 13.86

of the ship carrying Odysseus home

335 τίς γῆ, τίς δῆμος, τίνες ἀνέρες ἐγγεγάασιν;

What is this land and realm, who are the people?

Translated by Robert Fitzgerald (1961)

Odyssey 13.233

Odysseus landing on Ithaca

336 Ὀδυσσεὺς
χαίρων ᾗ γαίῃ, κύσε δὲ ζείδωρον ἄρουραν

Odysseus, overjoyed at the sight of his own land, kissed the fertile soil.

Translated by E.V. Rieu (1946)

Odyssey 13.354

on realizing he was back in Ithaca

337 κακὰ φύτευεν

Sowing the seeds of evil.

Translated by A.T. Murray (1919)

Odyssey 14.110

338 ἔργον δέ μοι οὐ φίλον ἔσκεν
οὐδ' οἰκωφελίη, ἥ τε τρέφει ἀγλαὰ τέκνα,
ἀλλά μοι αἰεὶ νῆες ἐπήρετμοι φίλαι ἦσαν
καὶ πόλεμοι καὶ ἄκοντες ἐΰξεστοι καὶ ὀϊστοί

Labour I never liked,
Nor household thrift, which breeds good children.
But ships equipped with oars were ever my delight,
Battles and polished javelins and arrows.

Translated by Bernadotte Perrin (1916)

Odyssey 14.222

339 ἄλλος γάρ τ' ἄλλοισιν ἀνὴρ ἐπιτέρπεται ἔργοις

For different men take joy in different works.

Translated by A.T. Murray (1919)

Odyssey 14.228

340 τί σε χρὴ … μαψιδίως ψεύδεσθαι;

Why must you lie and all for nothing?

Translated by Robert Fitzgerald (1961)
Odyssey 14.365

341 θεὸς δὲ τὸ μὲν δώσει, τὸ δ' ἐάσει,
… δύναται γὰρ ἅπαντα

God will give one thing and withhold another,
for he can do all things.

Translated by A.T. Murray (1919)
Odyssey 14.444

342 νὺξ δ' ἄρ' ἐπῆλθε κακὴ σκοτομήνιος

Now night came on, foul and without a moon.

Translated by A.T. Murray (1919)
Odyssey 14.457

343 οἶνος γὰρ ἀνώγει
ἠλεός, ὅς τ' ἐφέηκε πολύφρονά περ μάλ' ἀεῖσαι
καί θ' ἁπαλὸν γελάσαι, καί τ' ὀρχήσασθαι ἀνῆκε,
καί τι ἔπος προέηκεν ὅ περ τ' ἄρρητον ἄμεινον

Befooling wine
sets even the wise to singing
and laughing stupidly and dancing,
and saying what was better left unsaid.

Odyssey 14.463

344 τοῦ γάρ τε ξεῖνος μιμνήσκεται ἤματα πάντα
ἀνδρὸς ξεινοδόκου, ὅς κεν φιλότητα παράσχῃ

All his life a guest remembers the host who has treated him kindly.

Translated by E.V. Rieu (1946)
Odyssey 15.54

345 ἶσόν τοι κακόν ἐσθ', ὅς τ' οὐκ ἐθέλοντα νέεσθαι
ξεῖνον ἐποτρύνῃ καὶ ὃς ἐσσύμενον κατερύκῃ

It is equally wrong to send off a guest who wishes to stay,
and to keep back the one who is eager to go.

Odyssey 15.72

cf. Alexander Pope, Imitations of Horace *2.2.159: 'For I, who hold sage Homer's rule the best, / Welcome the coming, speed the going guest'*

346 πλαγκτοσύνης δ' οὐκ ἔστι κακώτερον ἄλλο βροτοῖσιν

Surely to be a vagrant is the worst possible fate for man.

Translated by E.V. Rieu (1946)
Odyssey 15.343

347 ἀνίη καὶ πολὺς ὕπνος

There is weariness even in too much sleep

Translated by A.T. Murray (1919)
Odyssey 15.394

348 μετὰ γάρ τε καὶ ἄλγεσι τέρπεται ἀνήρ,
ὅς τις δὴ μάλα πολλὰ πάθῃ καὶ πόλλ' ἐπαληθῇ

After some time a man finds joy even in old woes,
when he has suffered much, and travelled far.

Odyssey 15.400

349 Ὀδυσσῆος δέ που εὐνὴ
χήτει ἐνευναίων κάκ' ἀράχνια κεῖται ἔχουσα

Odysseus' bed, empty
and hung with dusty spider-webs.

Translated by E.V. Rieu (1946)
Odyssey 16.34

350 οὐ γάρ πω πάντεσσι θεοὶ φαίνονται ἐναργεῖς

Not to everyone the gods reveal themselves.

Odyssey 16.161

351 ἦ καὶ χρυσείῃ ῥάβδῳ ἐπεμάσσατ' Ἀθήνη
… δέμας δ' ὤφελλε καὶ ἥβην·
ἂψ δὲ μελαγχροιὴς γένετο, γναθμοὶ δὲ τάνυσθεν,
κυάνεαι δ' ἐγένοντο γενειάδες ἀμφὶ γένειον

Athene touched him with her golden wand,
made him more tall and young and lithe;
his skin grew bronzed again, his cheeks filled out;
the beard about his chin showed dark once more.

Translated by Walter Shewring (1980)
Odyssey 16.172

352 ὣς ἄρα φωνήσας υἱὸν κύσε, κὰδ δὲ παρειῶν

δάκρυον ἧκε χαμᾶζε· πάρος δ' ἔχε νωλεμὲς αἰεί

He kiss'd his son, while from his cheeks
Tears trickled, tears till then restrained.

Translated by William Cowper (1791)

Odyssey 16.190

353 ῥηΐδιον δὲ θεοῖσι, τοὶ οὐρανὸν εὐρὺν ἔχουσιν,
ἠμὲν κυδῆναι θνητὸν βροτὸν ἠδὲ κακῶσαι

It is no hard thing for the gods of heaven
to glorify a man or bring him low.

Translated by Robert Fitzgerald (1961)

Odyssey 16.211

354 κλαῖον δὲ λιγέως, ἁδινώτερον ἤ τ' οἰωνοί,
φῆναι ἢ αἰγυπιοὶ γαμψώνυχες, οἷσί τε τέκνα
ἀγρόται ἐξείλοντο πάρος πετεηνὰ γενέσθαι

Cries burst from them as loud as those of birds,
eagles or crooked-taloned vultures, whose nestlings
farmers take before they fledged.

Odyssey 16.216

355 αὐτὸς γὰρ ἐφέλκεται ἄνδρα σίδηρος

A weapon in itself tempts men to use it.

Translated in Liddell & Scott

Odyssey 16.294

on carrying arms; quoted by Demetrius, On Style *107*

356 οὐκ ἔσθ' οὗτος ἀνὴρ οὐδ' ἔσσεται

There never was such a man nor ever shall be.

Odyssey 16.437

357 τί δὴ κλέος ἔστ' ἀνὰ ἄστυ;

What news from the city?

Translated by A.T. Murray (1919)

Odyssey 16.461

358 κοίτου τε μνήσαντο καὶ ὕπνου δῶρον ἕλοντο

Ready to rest, they took the gift of sleep.

Odyssey 16.481

closing lines of book 16

359 ἔσθλ' ἀγορεύοντες, κακὰ δὲ φρεσὶ βυσσοδόμευον

Speaking fair, but pondering evil in their hearts.

Translated by A.T. Murray (1919)

Odyssey 17.66

360 ὡς αἰεὶ τὸν ὁμοῖον ἄγει θεὸς ὡς τὸν ὁμοῖον

How god always draws like to like!

Odyssey 17.218

cf. the English proverbs 'like will to like' and 'birds of a feather flock together'

361 μῆλα κακοὶ φθείρουσι νομῆες

It is the bad herdsmen who ruin the flock.

Odyssey 17.246

Eumeaus to Melanthius in reply to his insults

362 ἂν δὲ κύων κεφαλήν τε καὶ οὔατα κείμενος ἔσχεν,
Ἄργος, Ὀδυσσῆος ταλασίφρονος, ὅν ῥά ποτ' αὐτὸς
θρέψε μέν, οὐδ' ἀπόνητο, πάρος δ' εἰς Ἴλιον ἱρὴν
ᾤχετο

A dog lying there lifted head and pricked his ears.
This was Argos whom Odysseus had bred but never worked,
because he left for Ilium too soon.

Translated by T.E. Shaw (T.E. Lawrence) (1932)

Odyssey 17.291

363 Ἄργος … ὡς ἐνόησεν Ὀδυσσέα ἐγγὺς ἐόντα,
οὐρῇ μέν ῥ' ὅ γ' ἔσηνε καὶ οὔατα κάββαλεν ἄμφω,
ἇσσον δ' οὐκέτ' ἔπειτα δυνήσατο οἷο ἄνακτος
ἐλθέμεν· αὐτὰρ ὁ νόσφιν ἰδὼν ἀπομόρξατο δάκρυ

The instant Odysseus approached, the dog knew him.
He thumped his tail and drooped his ears forward,
but lacked the power to drag himself ever so little towards his master;
but Odysseus saw him and brushed away a tear.

Translated by T.E. Shaw (T.E. Lawrence) (1932)

Odyssey 17.300

364 ἢ αὔτως οἷοί τε τραπεζῆες κύνες ἀνδρῶν γίγνοντ', ἀγλαΐης δ' ἕνεκεν κομέουσιν ἄνακτες

Not as lapdogs are, which their masters keep for show.

Translated by A.T. Murray (1919)

Odyssey 17.309

365 Ἄργον δ' αὖ κατὰ μοῖρ' ἔλαβεν μέλανος θανάτοιο,
αὐτίκ' ἰδόντ' Ὀδυσῆα ἐεικοστῷ ἐνιαυτῷ

But black death closed down on Argos straightway, when he saw Odysseus, after twenty years.

Odyssey 17.326

366 αὐτὸς γὰρ φαγέμεν πολὺ βούλεαι ἢ δόμεν ἄλλῳ

You would rather eat the food yourself than give any of it away!

Odyssey 17.404

to Antinous, one of Penelope's suitors

367 ὢ πόποι, οὐκ ἄρα σοί γ' ἐπὶ εἴδεϊ καὶ φρένες ἦσαν

Lo, now, it seems thou hast no wits to match thy beauty.

Translated by A.T. Murray (1919)

Odyssey 17.454

368 οὐ σύ γ' ἂν... οὐδ' ἅλα δοίης
... τὰ δὲ πολλὰ πάρεστιν

You would not give away a grain of salt and yet you own so much.

Odyssey 17.455

369 καί τε θεοὶ ξείνοισιν ἐοικότες ἀλλοδαποῖσι,
παντοῖοι τελέθοντες, ἐπιστρωφῶσι πόληας,
ἀνθρώπων ὕβριν τε καὶ εὐνομίην ἐφορῶντες

Gods do disguise themselves as strangers from abroad, and move from town to town in every shape, observing the deeds of the just and the unjust.

Translated by E.V. Rieu (1946)

Odyssey 17.485

370 οὐδέ τί σε χρὴ ἀλλοτρίων φθονέειν

Do not bear a grudge for another's good fortune.

Odyssey 18.17

371 οὐδὲν ἀκιδνότερον γαῖα τρέφει ἀνθρώποιο,
πάντων ὅσσα τε γαῖαν ἔπι πνείει τε καὶ ἕρπει

Of all the creatures that breathe and creep about on Mother Earth there is none so helpless as man.

Translated by E.V. Rieu (1946)

Odyssey 18.130

372 ἀλλ' ὅ γε σιγῇ δῶρα θεῶν ἔχοι, ὅττι διδοῖεν

Quietly enjoy whatever gifts the gods may give.

Translated by E.V. Rieu (1946)

Odyssey 18.142

373 κάκιον πενθήμεναι ἄκριτον αἰεί

It makes things worse, this grieving on and on.

Translated by Robert Fagles (1996)

Odyssey 18.174

374 σίγα καὶ κατὰ σὸν νόον ἴσχανε μηδ' ἐρέεινε

Hush, check thy thought, and ask no questions.

Translated by A.T. Murray (1919)

Odyssey 19.42

375 ἔνθα καὶ ἠματίη μὲν ὑφαίνεσκον μέγαν ἱστόν,
νύκτας δ' ἀλλύεσκον, ἐπὴν δαΐδας παραθείμην

Every day I wove on the great loom,
but every night by torchlight I unwove it.

Translated by Robert Fitzgerald (1961)

Odyssey 19.149

of Penelope

376 ἴσκε ψεύδεα πολλὰ λέγων ἐτύμοισιν ὁμοῖα

He made the many lies seem similar to the truth.

Translated by Karl Popper (1964)

Odyssey 19.203

of Odysseus

377 ῥέε δάκρυα, τήκετο δὲ χρώς·
ὡς δὲ χιὼν κατατήκετ' ἐν ἀκροπόλοισιν ὄρεσσιν,
ἥν τ' Εὖρος κατέτηξεν, ἐπὴν Ζέφυρος

καταχεύῃ,
τηκομένης δ' ἄρα τῆς ποταμοὶ πλήθουσι ῥέοντες

Her tears flowed and her face melted,
as the snow melts on the lofty mountains,
which the East Wind thaws when the West Wind has strewn it,
and as it melts the streams of the rivers flow full.

Translated by A.T. Murray (1919)

Odyssey 19.204

of Penelope on hearing news of Odysseus

378 ἄνθρωποι δὲ μινυνθάδιοι τελέθουσιν

Our lives are much too brief.

Translated by Robert Fagles (1996)

Odyssey 19.328

379 αἶψα γὰρ ἐν κακότητι βροτοὶ καταγηράσκουσιν

Hardship can age a person overnight.

Translated by Robert Fagles (1996)

Odyssey 19.360

380 τὴν δ' ἅμα χάρμα καὶ ἄλγος ἕλε φρένα, τὼ δέ οἱ ὄσσε
δακρυόφι πλῆσθεν, θαλερὴ δέ οἱ ἔσχετο φωνή
ἁψαμένη δὲ γενείου Ὀδυσσῆα προσέειπεν·
ἦ μάλ' Ὀδυσσεύς ἐσσι, φίλον τέκος

Smiles dew'd with tears the pleasing strife exprest
Of grief, and joy, alternate in her breast.
Her flutt'ring words in melting murmurs dy'd;
At length abrupt – my son! – my King! – she cry'd.

Translated by Elijah Fenton (with Pope, 1720)

Odyssey 19.471

Eurycleia, his nursemaid, recognizing Odysseus

381 αὐτὰρ ἐπὴν νὺξ ἔλθῃ, ἕλῃσί τε κοῖτος ἅπαντας,
κεῖμαι ἐνὶ λέκτρῳ, πυκιναὶ δέ μοι ἀμφ' ἀδινὸν κῆρ
ὀξεῖαι μελεδῶνες ὀδυρομένην ἐρέθουσιν

When night comes and all the world's abed
I lie in mine alone, my heart thudding,
while bitter thoughts and fears crowd
on my grief.

Translated by Robert Fitzgerald (1961)

Odyssey 19.515

spoken by Penelope

382 χλωρηῒς ἀηδών,
καλὸν ἀείδῃσιν ἔαρος νέον ἱσταμένοιο,
δενδρέων ἐν πετάλοισι καθεζομένη πυκινοῖσιν,
ἥ τε θαμὰ τρωπῶσα χέει πολυηχέα φωνήν

Even as the nightingale
sings sweetly when spring is newly come,
perched amid the thick leafage of the trees,
and with many trilling notes her voice pours forth.

Translated by A.T. Murray (1919)

Odyssey 19.518

383 δίχα θυμὸς ὀρώρεται ἔνθα καὶ ἔνθα

My heart sways to and fro in doubt.

Translated by A.T. Murray (1919)

Odyssey 19.524

384 οὐκ ὄναρ, ἀλλ' ὕπαρ ἐσθλόν, ὅ τοι τετελεσμένον ἔσται

Not a dream, but a vision of reality soon to be fulfilled.

Odyssey 19.547

385 ἦ τοι μὲν ὄνειροι ἀμήχανοι ἀκριτόμυθοι
γίνοντ', οὐδέ τι πάντα τελείεται ἀνθρώποισι
δοιαὶ γάρ τε πύλαι ἀμενηνῶν εἰσὶν ὀνείρων·
αἱ μὲν γὰρ κεράεσσι τετεύχαται, αἱ δ' ἐλέφαντι·
τῶν οἳ μέν κ' ἔλθωσι διὰ πριστοῦ ἐλέφαντος,
οἵ ῥ' ἐλεφαίρονται, ἔπε' ἀκράαντα φέροντες·
οἱ δὲ διὰ ξεστῶν κεράων ἔλθωσι θύραζε,
οἵ ῥ' ἔτυμα κραίνουσι, βροτῶν ὅτε κέν τις ἴδηται

Dreams are hard to unravel, wayward, drifting things –
not all we glimpse in them will come to pass …
Two gates there are for our evanescent dreams,
one is made of ivory, the other made of

horn.
Those that pass through the ivory cleanly carved
are will-o'-the-wisps, their message bears no fruit.
The dreams that pass through the gates of polished horn
are fraught with truth, for the dreamer who can see them.

Translated by Robert Fagles (1996)

Odyssey 19.560

the wordplay on 'κέρας', 'horn' and 'κραίνω', 'fulfil' and on 'ἐλέφας', 'ivory' and 'ἐλεφαίρομαι', 'deceive' cannot be preserved in English

386 τέτλαθι δή, κραδίη· καὶ κύντερον ἄλλο ποτ' ἔτλης

Bear up, old heart! You have borne worse, far worse.

Translated by Robert Fagles (1996)

Odyssey 20.18

387 νήπιοι ἀγροιῶται, ἐφημέρια φρονέοντες

Foolish boors, caring only for things ephemeral!

Odyssey 21.85

388 ὡς ὅτ' ἀνὴρ φόρμιγγος ἐπιστάμενος καὶ ἀοιδῆς
ῥηϊδίως ἐτάνυσσε νέῳ περὶ κόλλοπι χορδήν

As one of skill
In song and of the Harpe doth at his will,
In tuning of his Instrument ... and lend
To every wel-wreath'd string his perfect sound.

Translated by George Chapman (1615)

Odyssey 21.406

of Odysseus taking up the bow no one but he could stretch

389 νῦν ὕμιν καὶ πᾶσιν ὀλέθρου πείρατ' ἐφῆπται

Now, for you one and all, the day of doom is set.

Odyssey 22.41

390 ὡς οὐκ ἔστι χάρις μετόπισθ' εὐεργέων

There is no gratitude in aftertime for good deeds done.

Translated by A.T. Murray (1919)

Odyssey 22.319

391 θάρσει ...
ὡς κακοεργίης εὐεργεσίη μέγ' ἀμείνων

Dismiss your fears, doing right is a much better policy than doing wrong.

Translated by E.V. Rieu (1946)

Odyssey 22.372

392 δι' ἀτασθαλίας ἔπαθον κακόν

Through their own wanton folly they have come to harm.

Translated by A.T. Murray (1919)

Odyssey 23.67

of the suitors

393 σοὶ δ' αἰεὶ κραδίη στερεωτέρη ἐστὶ λίθοιο

Your heart still is – and always was – as hard as stone.

Odyssey 23.103

394 θυμός μοι ἐνὶ στήθεσσι τέθηπεν,
οὐδέ τι προσφάσθαι δύναμαι ἔπος οὐδ' ἐρέεσθαι
οὐδ' εἰς ὦπα ἰδέσθαι ἐναντίον

The heart in my breast is lost in wonder,
I have no power to speak at all, nor ask a question,
nor look him in the face.

Translated by A.T. Murray (1919)

Odyssey 23.105

Penelope on Odysseus' return

395 ἔστι γὰρ ἡμῖν
σήμαθ', ἃ δὴ καὶ νῶϊ κεκρυμμένα ἴδμεν ἀπ' ἄλλων

We two have secret signs,
known to us both but hidden from the world.

Translated by Robert Fagles (1996)

Odyssey 23.109

Penelope to Odysseus

396 θεὰ γλαυκῶπις Ἀθήνη
νύκτα μὲν ἐν περάτῃ δολιχὴν σχέθεν, Ἠῶ δ' αὖτε
ῥύσατ' ἐπ' Ὠκεανῷ χρυσόθρονον

Grey-eyed Athena slowed the night
when night was most profound, and held the Dawn
under the Ocean of the East.

Translated by Robert Fitzgerald (1961)

Odyssey 23.242

in order to prolong Penelope's first night with Odysseus

397 ἐν χείρεσσιν ἔχοντ' εὐῆρες ἐρετμόν,
εἰς ὅ κε τοὺς ἀφίκωμαι, οἳ οὐκ ἴσασι θάλασσαν
ἀνέρες οὐδέ θ' ἅλεσσι μεμιγμένον εἶδαρ ἔδουσιν

I was will'd to take
A navall Oare in hand, and with it make
My passage forth till such strange men I met
As knew no Sea, nor ever salt did eat.

Translated by George Chapman (1615)

Odyssey 23.268

398 ὅτε οἱ γλυκὺς ὕπνος
λυσιμελὴς ἐπόρουσε, λύων μελεδήματα θυμοῦ

Sweet sleep came suddenly upon him, relaxing all his limbs, and banishing his cares.

Translated by E.V. Rieu (1946)

Odyssey 23.342

399 ὡς δ' ὅτε νυκτερίδες μυχῷ ἄντρου θεσπεσίοιο
τρίζουσαι ποτέονται, ἐπεί κέ τις ἀποπέσησιν
ὁρμαθοῦ ἐκ πέτρης, ἀνά τ' ἀλλήλῃσιν ἔχονται

As when the bats within some hallow'd cave
Flit squeaking all around, for if but one
Fall from the rock, the rest all follow him,
In such connexion mutual they adhere.

Translated by William Cowper (1791)

Odyssey 24.6

of the suitors' spirits being led 'downward gibbering' to Hades

400 τῷ οἱ κλέος οὔ ποτ' ὀλεῖται
ἧς ἀρετῆς, τεύξουσι δ' ἐπιχθονίοισιν ἀοιδὴν
ἀθάνατοι χαρίεσσαν ἐχέφρονι Πηνελοπείῃ

The glory of her virtue will not fade;
the gods themselves will make a lovely song
for all mankind to praise faithful Penelope.

Odyssey 24.196

401 τοὶ δ' ἀλλήλους φιλεόντων
ὡς τὸ πάρος, πλοῦτος δὲ καὶ εἰρήνη ἅλις ἔστω

And let them love each other as before,
and may their wealth and peace abound.

Odyssey 24.485

HOMERIC EPIGRAMS

dates unknown

Various epigrams attributed to Homer

1 ἔστ' ἂν ὕδωρ τε νάῃ καὶ δένδρεα μακρὰ τεθήλῃ,
ἠέλιός τ' ἀνιὼν λάμπῃ, λαμπρά τε σελήνη,
καὶ ποταμοί γε ῥέωσιν, ἀνακλύζῃ δὲ θάλασσα

So long as water shall flow and tall trees grow,
and the sun shall rise and shine, and the bright moon,
and rivers shall run and the sea wash the shore.

Translated by R.D. Hicks (1925)

Epigram 3.2

the inscription from the tomb of Midas, also attributed to Cleobulus

2 οὐδὲν ἀφραστότερον πέλεται νόου ἀνθρώποισιν

There is nothing more marvellous than the mind of man.

Epigram 5.2

3 πρῶτον μὲν κυσὶ δεῖπνον ἐπ' αὐλείῃσι θύρῃσι δοῦναι. τὼς γὰρ ἄμεινον· ὁ γὰρ καὶ πρόσθεν ἀκούει ἀνδρὸς ἐπερχομένου καὶ ἐς ἕρκεα θηρὸς ἰόντος

First feed the dogs at your gate; for they first will hear man or beast that enters your yard.

Epigram 11.2

HOMERIC HYMNS

8th–6th century BC

Hexameter compositions

1 οὐδέ τις ἀθανάτων οὐδὲ θνητῶν ἀνθρώπων
ἤκουσεν φωνῆς, οὐδ' ἀγλαόκαρποι ἐλαῖαι

No god nor mortal heard her cry,

nor did the bright-berried olives.

Translated by C.A. Trypanis (1971)

Hymn to Demeter 2.22

of Persephone being abducted to the Underworld

2 ὄφρα μὲν οὖν γαῖάν τε καὶ οὐρανὸν ἀστερόεντα
λεῦσσε θεὰ καὶ πόντον ἀγάρροον ἰχθυόεντα
αὐγάς τ' ἠελίου, ἔτι δ' ἤλπετο μητέρα κεδνὴν
ὄψεσθαι καὶ φῦλα θεῶν αἰειγενετάων,
τόφρα οἱ ἐλπὶς ἔθελγε μέγαν νόον ἀχνυμένης περ

As long as she could see the earth and the starry sky
and the violent fish-teeming sea and the light of the sun,
as long as there was hope to see her dear mother
and the race of gods who live for ever,
this hope filled her heart in spite of her grief.

Hymn to Demeter 2.33

of Persephone having been abducted by Hades

3 ὀξὺ δέ μιν κραδίην ἄχος ἔλλαβεν …
σεύατο δ' ὥστ' οἰωνὸς ἐπὶ τραφερήν τε καὶ ὑγρὴν
μαιομένη

Bitter pain seized her heart,
and she sped, like a bird, over the firm land and yielding sea,
seeking her child.

Translated by Hugh G. Evelyn-White (1914)

Hymn to Demeter 2.40

of Demeter searching for Persephone

4 νήιδες ἄνθρωποι καὶ ἀφράδμονες οὔτ' ἀγαθοῖο
αἶσαν ἐπερχομένου προγνώμεναι οὔτε κακοῖο

Men are too foolish to guess ahead of time
the measure of good and evil which is yet to come.

Translated by Apostolos N. Athanassakis (1976)

Hymn to Demeter 2.256

5 περί τ' ἀμφί τε κάλλος ἄητο·
ὀδμὴ δ' ἱμερόεσσα θυηέντων ἀπὸ πέπλων
σκίδνατο, τῆλε δὲ φέγγος ἀπὸ χροὸς ἀθανάτοιο
λάμπε θεᾶς, ξανθαὶ δὲ κόμαι κατενήνοθεν ὤμους

Beauty breathed all around her
and a lovely fragrance drifted from her perfumed robes
and from the immortal skin of the goddess a brightness
shone far away from her and her golden hair streamed down
over her shoulders.

Translated by Jules Cashford (2003)

Hymn to Demeter 2.276

of Demeter

6 μίγδα κρόκον τ' ἀγανὸν καὶ ἀγαλλίδας ἠδ' ὑάκινθον
καὶ ῥοδέας κάλυκας καὶ λείρια, θαῦμα ἰδέσθαι,
νάρκισσόν θ', ὃν ἔφυσ' ὥς περ κρόκον εὐρεῖα χθών

Soft crocus mingled with irises
and hyacinths and rosebuds
and lilies – wondrous to see –
and a narcissus which the wide earth grew,
yellow as a crocus.

Translated by Jules Cashford (2003)

Hymn to Demeter 2.426

7 ὦ κοῦραι, τίς δ' ὔμμιν ἀνὴρ ἥδιστος ἀοιδῶν
ἐνθάδε πωλεῖται, καὶ τέῳ τέρπεσθε μάλιστα; …
τυφλὸς ἀνήρ, οἰκεῖ δὲ Χίῳ ἔνι παιπαλοέσσῃ,
τοῦ πᾶσαι μετόπισθεν ἀριστεύουσιν ἀοιδαί

Girls, who is the sweetest man of all the singers
who comes here to you,
who is it most delights you?
The blind man who lives in rocky Chios,
all his songs will be the best, now
and in all time to come.

Translated by Jules Cashford (2003)

Hymn to Apollo 3.169

8 νήπιοι ἄνθρωποι δυστλήμονες, οἳ μελεδῶνας
βούλεσθ' ἀργαλέους τε πόνους καὶ στείνεα θυμῷ

Foolish men and poor wretches you are for preferring
cares and toilsome hardships and straits for your hearts.

Translated by Apostolos N. Athanassakis (1976)

Hymn to Apollo 3.532

9 πολύτροπον, αἱμυλομήτην,
λῃστῆρ', ἐλατῆρα βοῶν, ἡγήτορ' ὀνείρων,
νυκτὸς ὀπωπητῆρα, πυληδόκον

Versatile and full of tricks,
a thief, a cattle-rustler, a bringer of dreams,
a spy by night, a watcher at the gate.

Translated by Jules Cashford (2003)

Hymn to Hermes 4.13

of Hermes

10 καί τε ἰδὼν μὴ ἰδὼν εἶναι καὶ κωφὸς ἀκούσας,
καὶ σιγᾶν

You didn't see what you just saw,
you didn't hear what you just heard,
so just keep quiet.

Translated by Jules Cashford (2003)

Hymn to Hermes 4.92

Hermes to someone who saw him steal Apollo's cattle

11 πολλοὶ γὰρ ὁδὸν πρήσσουσιν ὁδῖται,
τῶν οἳ μὲν κακὰ πολλὰ μεμαότες, οἳ δὲ μάλ' ἐσθλὰ
φοιτῶσιν· χαλεπὸν δὲ δαήμεναί ἐστιν ἕκαστον

Many wayfarers pass to and fro this way,
some bent on much evil, and some on good:
it is difficult to know each one.

Translated by Hugh G. Evelyn-White (1914)

Hymn to Hermes 4.203

12 ἠΰτε πολλὴν
πρέμνων ἀνθρακιὴν ὕλης σποδὸς ἀμφικαλύπτει

As among fire-brands lies a burning spark
Covered, beneath the ashes cold and dark.

Translated by Percy Bysshe Shelley (written 1820; published posthumously 1824)

Hymn to Hermes 4.237

of Hermes hiding from Apollo

13 ἐν δ' ὀλίγῳ συνέλασσε κάρη χεῖράς τε πόδας τε
φή ῥα νεόλλουτος προκαλεύμενος ἥδυμον ὕπνον,
ἐγρήσσων ἐτεόν γε

There, like an infant who had sucked his fill
And now was newly washed and put to bed,
Awake, but courting sleep with weary will,
And gathered in a lump, hands, feet, and head,
He lay.

Translated by Percy Bysshe Shelley (written 1820; published posthumously 1824)

Hymn to Hermes 4.240

of Hermes hiding from Apollo

14 τίς τέχνη, τίς μοῦσα ἀμηχανέων μελεδώνων,
τίς τρίβος; ἀτρεκέως γὰρ ἅμα τρία πάντα πάρεστιν
εὐφροσύνην καὶ ἔρωτα καὶ ἥδυμον ὕπνον ἑλέσθαι

What Muse, what skill, what unimagined use,
What exercise of subtlest art, has given
Thy songs such power? – for those who hear may choose
From three, the choicest gifts of Heaven,
Delight, and love, and sleep – sweet sleep.

Translated by Percy Bysshe Shelley (written 1820; published posthumously 1824)

Hymn to Hermes 4.447

15 τῶν δ' ἄλλων οὔ πέρ τι πεφυγμένον ἔστ' Ἀφροδίτην οὔτε θεῶν μακάρων
οὔτε θνητῶν ἀνθρώπων

But no one else, none of the blessed gods
or human beings, can ever escape Aphrodite.

Translated by Jules Cashford (2003)

Hymn to Aphrodite 5.34

Aphrodite personifying sexual pleasure

16 τῇσι δ' ἅμ' ἢ ἐλάται ἠὲ δρύες ὑψικάρηνοι
γεινομένῃσιν ἔφυσαν ἐπὶ χθονὶ βωτιανείρῃ

καλαὶ τηλεθάουσαι ἐν οὔρεσιν
ὑψηλοῖσιν.
ἑστᾶσ' ἠλίβατοι, τεμένη δέ ἑ
κικλήσκουσιν
ἀθανάτων· τὰς δ' οὔ τι βροτοὶ κείρουσι
σιδήρῳ

Silver fir and high-topped oaks spring
up on fruitful earth;
beautiful, flourishing trees, towering
high on lofty mountains;
precincts dedicated to the gods, never
touched by axe.

Hymn to Aphrodite 5.264

of a nymph's birthplace

17 σὺ θάρσος
δὸς μάκαρ, εἰρήνης τε μένειν ἐν ἀπήμοσι
θεσμοῖς
δυσμενέων προφυγόντα μόθον κῆράς τε
βιαίους

Blessed god, give me the courage
to stand my ground within the laws of
peace,
shunning hostility and hatred
and the fate of a violent death.

Translated by Jules Cashford (2003)

Hymn to Ares 8.15

last lines

18 ἐκ γὰρ Μουσάων καὶ ἑκηβόλου
Ἀπόλλωνος
ἄνδρες ἀοιδοὶ ἔασιν ἐπὶ χθονὶ καὶ
κιθαρισταί

It is because
of the Muses
and the archer Apollo
that there exist on the earth
people who sing songs
and play the lyre.

Translated by Jules Cashford (2003)

Hymn to The Muses and Apollo 25.2

19 ὁ δ' ὄλβιος ὅν τινα Μοῦσαι
φίλωνται· γλυκερή οἱ ἀπὸ στόματος ῥέει
αὐδή

Happy is he whom the Muses love;
sweet flows speech from his lips.

Translated by Hugh G. Evelyn-White (1914)

Hymn to The Muses and Apollo 25.4

20 Γαῖαν παμμήτειραν ἀείσομαι ἠϋθέμεθλον
πρεσβίστην, ἣ φέρβει ἐπὶ χθονὶ πάνθ'
ὁπόσ' ἐστίν·
ἠμὲν ὅσα χθόνα δῖαν ἐπέρχεται ἠδ' ὅσα
πόντον
ἠδ' ὅσα πωτῶνται, τάδε φέρβεται ἐκ
σέθεν ὄλβου

Eldest of things, Great Earth, I sing of
thee!
All shapes that have their dwelling in
the sea,
All things that fly, or on the ground
divine
Live, move, and there are nourished –
these are thine;
These from thy wealth thou dost
sustain.

Translated by Percy Bysshe Shelley (written 1818; published posthumously 1839)

Hymn to Earth the Mother of All 30.1

HOMERICA

1 πάσης δ' ἡμάρτανε τέχνης·
πόλλ' ἠπίστατο ἔργα, κακῶς δ' ἠπίστατο
πάντα

He meddled in all arts and crafts;
he knew of many occupations, and was
no good at any.

Homer, *Margites* Fragment 2 (West, *IEG*)

a humorous poem attributed to Homer

2 ἦλθον δ' ἐξαίφνης νωτάκμονες,
ἀγκυλοχεῖλαι,
λοξοβάται, στρεβλοί, ψαλιδόστομοι,
ὀστρακόδερμοι,
ὀστοφυεῖς, πλατύνωτοι, ἀποστίλβοντες
ἐν ὤμοις,
βλαισοί, χειλοτένοντες, ἀπὸ στέρνων
ἐσορῶντες

And suddenly they came, anvil-backed,
curve-clawed,
sideways-walking, squint-eyed, pincer-
mouthed, shell-clad,
bony-bodied, wide-backed, shiny-
armoured,
bandy-kneed, curvy-lipped, staring at
you from their chest.

Batrachomyomachia, *Battle of the Frogs and Mice* 294

of the crabs who won the battle for the frogs

3 – τί θνητοῖς κάλλιστον ὀίεαι ἐν φρεσὶν
εἶναι,Ὅμηρε;
– ὁππότ' ἂν εὐφροσύνη μὲν ἔχῃ κατὰ
δῆμον ἅπαντα

Hesiod: What, Homer, do mortals prize
most?

Homer: Good cheer to prevail in the whole country.

Anonymous, *Contest of Homer and Hesiod* 80

4 κάλλιστον μὲν τῶν ἀγαθῶν ἔσται μέτρον εἶναι
αὐτὸν ἑαυτῷ, τῶν δὲ κακῶν ἔχθιστον ἁπάντων

For a good man to be a measure to himself is most
excellent, for the bad man it is the worst of all things.

Anonymous, *Contest of Homer and Hesiod* 158

5 ἐν δ' ἐλαχίστῳ ἄριστον ἔχεις ὅ τι φύεται εἰπεῖν;
ὡς μὲν ἐμῇ γνώμῃ φρένες ἐσθλαὶ σώμασιν ἀνδρῶν

Hesiod: In a few words, can you tell what is best of all?
Homer: A good mind in a strong man.

Anonymous, *Contest of Homer and Hesiod* 166

HYPERIDES

389–322BC
Athenian orator

1 τοῦ μὲν γὰρ βουλεύεσθαι καλῶς ὁ στρατηγὸς αἴτιος, τοῦ δὲ νικᾶν μαχομένους οἱ κινδυνεύειν ἐθέλοντες τοῖς σώμασιν

Though sound strategy depends upon the leader, success in battle is ensured by those who are prepared to risk their lives.

Translated by J.O. Burtt

Funeral Oration 6.15

2 τότε μὲν γὰρ παῖδες ὄντες ἄφρονες ἦσαν, νῦν δ' ἄνδρες ἀγαθοὶ γεγόνασιν … γνωρίμους πᾶσι καὶ μνημονευτοὺς διὰ ἀνδραγαθίαν

Mere children then, they had no understanding, but now they have become men, known to all, to be remembered for their valour.

Funeral Oration 6.28

3 εἰ δ' ἔστιν αἴσθησις ἐν Ἅιδου καὶ ἐπιμέλεια παρὰ τοῦ δαιμονίου, ὥσπερ ὑπολαμβάνομεν, εἰκὸς τοὺς … πλείστης ἐπιμελείας καὶ κηδεμονίας ὑπὸ τοῦ δαιμονίου τυγχάνειν

If in Hades we are conscious still and cared for by some god, as we are led to think, then surely these men must receive from him the greatest care of all.

Translated by J.O. Burtt

Funeral Oration 6.43

of the men who died in battle

4 ἀρχομένων δεῖ τῶν ἀδικημάτων ἐμφράττειν τὰς ὁδούς· ὅταν δ' ἅπαξ ῥιζωθῇ κακία καὶ παλαιὰ γένηται καθάπερ σύντροφος ἀρρωστία, χαλεπὸν αὐτὴν κατασβέσαι

Stamp out misdeeds at their origin; once they strike root and settle they are difficult to curb, much like a lasting illness.

Fragment 204 (Jensen)

5 δεῖ τὴν ἐκ τῆς οἰκίας ἐκπορευομένην ἐν τοιαύτῃ καταστάσει εἶναι τῆς ἡλικίας, ὥστε τοὺς ἀπαντῶντας πυνθάνεσθαι, μὴ τίνος ἐστὶ γυνή, ἀλλὰ τίνος μήτηρ

A woman who walks forth from home should be at such an age that people will ask whose mother and not whose wife she is.

Fragment 205 (Jensen)

6 διὰ δύο προφάσεις τῶν ἀδικημάτων ἄνθρωποι ἀπέχονται, ἢ διὰ φόβον ἢ διὰ αἰσχύνην

There are two things which restrain men from crime, fear and shame.

Translated by J.O. Burtt (1954)

Fragment 210 (Jensen)

I

IAMBLICHUS

*c.*245–*c.*325AD

Neoplatonist philosopher from Chalcis in Coele Syria

1 πίστις μὲν πρώτη ἐγγίγνεται ἐκ τῆς εὐνομίας μεγάλα ὠφελοῦσα τοὺς ἀνθρώπους τοὺς σύμπαντας, καὶ τῶν μεγάλων ἀγαθῶν τοῦτό ἐστι· κοινὰ γὰρ τὰ χρήματα γίγνεται ἐξ αὐτῆς, καὶ οὕτω μὲν ἐὰν καὶ ὀλίγα ᾖ ἐξαρκεῖ ὅμως κυκλούμενα, ἄνευ δὲ ταύτης οὐδ' ἂν πολλὰ ᾖ ἐξαρκεῖ

The first and greatest benefit of good order is trust; with trust, money circulates freely and thus become generally available; without trust, even a large amount of money hidden away is of no avail.

Protrepticus 101.17

IBYCUS

6th century BC

Lyric poet from Rhegium in southern Italy

1 ἐμοὶ δ' ἔρος
οὐδεμίαν κατάκοιτος ὥραν

As for me, love sleeps in no season.

Translated by C.A. Trypanis (1971)

Fragment 5 (Page, *PMG*)

2 Ἔρος αὖτέ με κυανέοισιν ὑπὸ
βλεφάροις τακέρ' ὄμμασι δερκόμενος
κηλήμασι παντοδαποῖς ἐς ἄπειρα δίκτυα Κύπριδος ἐσβάλλει

Once again Love gazes at me
from under his dark lashes, melting me
with his eyes.
With his assorted lures
He coaxes me into Aphrodite's endless
snares.

Translated by Jonathan Williams and Clive Cheesman (2004)

Fragment 6 (Page, *PMG*)

3 ἆμος ἄυπνος κλυτὸς ὄρθρος ἐγείρησιν
ἀηδόνας

When wakeful glorious dawn arouses
nightingales.

Fragment 22b (Page, *PMG*)

4 οὐκ ἔστιν ἀποφθιμένοις ζωᾶς ἔτι
φάρμακον εὑρεῖν

There is no medicine to be found for a
life which has fled.

Translated in *Bartlett's Familiar Quotations* (1980)

Fragment 32 (Page, *PMG*)

5 μύρτα τε καὶ ἴα καὶ ἑλίχρυσος
μᾶλά τε καὶ ῥόδα καὶ τέρεινα δάφνα

Myrtle and violets and golden-tufts,
Apples and roses and tender bay.

Translated by Kathleen Freeman (1947)

Fragment 34 (Page, *PMG*)

Helichrysum siculum = *gold-flowers, or golden-tufts; also:* Helichrysum stoechas

6 κύματος ἔξοθεν ἄκρου
πᾶσα κάλως ἀσινής

When waves are at their highest
and every halyard safely bound.

Fragment 49 (Page, *PMG*)

ST IGNATIUS THEOPHORUS
*fl. c.*100AD
Bishop of Antioch

1 περὶ ἀγάπης οὐ μέλει αὐτοῖς, οὐ περὶ χήρας, οὐ περὶ ὀρφανοῦ, οὐ περὶ θλιβομένου, οὐ περὶ δεδεμένου ἢ λελυμένου, οὐ περὶ πεινῶντος ἢ διψῶντος

They care not for love, for widow or orphan, nor for the oppressed, the bound or the free, the hungry or thirsty.

Epistle to the Smyrnaeans 6.6.2

of non-believers

2 στῆθι ἑδραῖος ὡς ἄκμων τυπτόμενος

Stand firm as an anvil when beaten upon.

Epistle to Polycarp 7.3.1

3 μήτηρ γὰρ τῆς ἐνδείας ἡ ἀργία

Idleness is the mother of want.

Translated by D.S. Baker (1998)

*Epistle to the Tarsians** 4.9.2

ION
*c.*480–*c.*420BC
Poet and prose writer from Chios

1 τῶν δ' ἀγαθῶν βασιλεὺς οἶνος ἔδειξε φύσιν

King Wine reveals the nature of what is good.

Fragment 26 (West, *IEG*)

2 ὅντινα δ' εὐειδὴς μίμνει θήλεια πάρευνος,
κεῖνος τῶν ἄλλων κυδρότερον πίεται

Whosoever has a fair bedfellow awaiting him,
let him drink more bravely than the rest.

Translated by J.M. Edmonds (1931)

Fragment 27 (West, *IEG*)

IPHICRATES
4th century BC
Athenian general, famous for his victory at Corinth (390BC)
see also Epaminondas 3

1 ἐν φιλίᾳ καὶ συμμάχῳ χώρᾳ στρατοπεδεύων καὶ χάρακα βαλλόμενος καὶ τάφρον ὀρύττων ἐπιμελῶς πρὸς τὸν εἰπόντα τί γὰρ φοβούμεθα; χειρίστην ἔφησε στρατηγοῦ φωνὴν εἶναι τὴν οὐκ ἂν προσεδόκησα

Encamping in a friendly, allied country, Iphicrates put up a palisade and dug a ditch with care; to the man who asked, 'What have we to fear?' he replied that the worst words a general could utter were 'I never expected that.'

Plutarch, *Sayings of Kings and Commanders* 187a

2 τὸ μὲν ἐμὸν ἀπ' ἐμοῦ γένος ἄρχεται, τὸ δὲ σὸν ἐν σοὶ παύεται

My family history begins with me, but yours ends with you.

Translated by Frank Cole Babbitt (1931)

Plutarch, *Sayings of Kings and Commanders* 187b

Iphicrates, a shoemaker's son, to Harmodius, of prominent ancestry, when reviled for his mean birth

3 Ἰφικράτης τὸ στράτευμα οὕτως ἔφασκε δεῖν συντετάχθαι ὡς ἓν σῶμα, θώρακα μὲν ἔχον τὴν φάλαγγα, χεῖρας δὲ τοὺς ψιλούς, πόδας δὲ τοὺς ἱππέας, κεφαλὴν δὲ τὸν στρατηγόν

An army should be organized as a body, the thorax being the heavy infantry, the arms as the light troops, the legs as cavalry, the head as the general.

Stobaeus, *Anthology* 4.13.62

ST IRENAEUS
*c.*130–*c.*202AD
Theologian, bishop of Lyons from *c.*178

1 ὥσπερ οἱ βλέποντες τὸ φῶς ἐντός εἰσι τοῦ φωτὸς καὶ τῆς λαμπρότητος αὐτοῦ μετέχουσιν, οὕτως οἱ βλέποντες τὸν Θεὸν ἐντός εἰσι τοῦ Θεοῦ, μετέχοντες αὐτοῦ τῆς λαμπρότητος· ζωῆς οὖν μετέξουσιν οἱ ὁρῶντες Θεόν

Just as those who see the light are within the light, and receive its brilliancy; so too those who see God are within God, and receive his brilliancy. But the brilliancy of God vivifies them; those, therefore, who see God, receive life.

Translated by Giles E.M. Gasper (2004)

Against Heresies Fragment 10

ISAEUS

c.420–340s BC
Athenian speech-writer

1 ἡγοῦμαι μεγίστην εἶναι τῶν λῃτουργιῶν τὸν καθ' ἡμέραν βίον κόσμιον καὶ σώφρονα παρέχειν

The greatest of public services is to daily practise a life of propriety and prudence.

Oration 13 Fragment 4 (Roussel)

cf. Plato 25

2 χρὴ τοὺς νόμους μὲν τίθεσθαι σφοδρῶς, πρᾳοτέρως δὲ κολάζειν ἢ ὡς ἐκεῖνοι κελεύουσιν

Impose stringent laws, be lenient in their application.

Oration 13 Fragment 6.1 (Roussel)

ISOCRATES

436–338BC
Athenian orator
see also Dionysius of Halicarnassus 34

1 οἱ μὲν γὰρ τοὺς φίλους παρόντας μόνον τιμῶσιν, οἱ δὲ καὶ μακρὰν ἀπόντας ἀγαπῶσι ... τὰς δὲ τῶν σπουδαίων φιλίας οὐδ' ἂν ὁ πᾶς αἰὼν ἐξαλείψειεν

The base honour their friends only when present; the good cherish theirs even when far away; and the friendship of great men no eternity will obliterate.

To Demonicus 1.1

2 ῥώμη δὲ μετὰ μὲν φρονήσεως ὠφέλησεν, ἄνευ δὲ ταύτης πλείω τοὺς ἔχοντας ἔβλαψε καὶ τὰ μὲν σώματα τῶν ἀσκούντων ἐκόσμησε, ταῖς δὲ τῆς ψυχῆς ἐπιμελείαις ἐπεσκότησεν

Strength accompanied by wisdom is an asset, but strength without wisdom harms more than helps its possessors; and while it embellishes the bodies of those who exercise, yet it overshadows the care of the soul.

To Demonicus 1.6

3 ἡ δὲ τῆς ἀρετῆς κτῆσις, οἷς ἂν ἀκιβδήλως ταῖς διανοίαις συναυξηθῇ, μόνη μὲν συγγηράσκει, πλούτου δὲ κρείττων, χρησιμωτέρα δ' εὐγενείας ἐστί, τὰ μὲν τοῖς ἄλλοις ἀδύνατα δυνατὰ καθιστᾶσα, τὰ δὲ τῷ πλήθει φοβερὰ θαρσαλέως ὑπομένουσα, καὶ τὸν μὲν ὄκνον ψόγον, τὸν δὲ πόνον ἔπαινον ἡγουμένη

Virtue, when it grows up unadulterated within our hearts, is the one possession which abides with us in old age; it is better than riches and more serviceable than high birth; it makes possible what is for others impossible; it supports with fortitude that which is fearful to the multitude; and it considers sloth a disgrace and toil an honour.

Translated by George Norlin (1928)

To Demonicus 1.7

4 τοιοῦτος γίγνου περὶ τοὺς γονεῖς, οἵους ἂν εὔξαιο περὶ σεαυτὸν γενέσθαι τοὺς σεαυτοῦ παῖδας

Treat your parents as you would wish to be treated by your own children.

To Demonicus 1.14

5 μήτε γέλωτα προπετῆ στέργε

Be not fond of reckless laughter.

To Demonicus 1.15

6 μηδέποτε μηδὲν αἰσχρὸν ποιήσας ἔλπιζε λήσειν· καὶ γὰρ ἂν τοὺς ἄλλους λάθῃς, σεαυτῷ σηνειδήσεις

Never hope to escape when you have done anything shameful; for even if you conceal it from others, your own heart will know.

To Demonicus 1.16

7 εὐλαβοῦ τὰς διαβολάς, κἂν ψευδεῖς ὦσιν

Beware of accusations even if false.

To Demonicus 1.17

8 ἐὰν ᾖς φιλομαθής, ἔσει πολυμαθής

If thou lovest lerning, thou shalt attayne to moch learning (which excellentlie said in *Greeke*, is thus rudelie in Englishe).

Translated by Roger Ascham in his *The Scholemaster* (1568)

To Demonicus 1.18

inscribed at the entry of Isocrates' school; also, in gold letters, over the portal to Shrewsbury School

9 ἡγοῦ τῶν ἀκουσμάτων πολλὰ πολλῶν εἶναι χρημάτων κρείττω· τὰ μὲν γὰρ ταχέως ἀπολείπει, τὰ δὲ πάντα τὸν χρόνον παραμένει· σοφία γὰρ μόνον τῶν κτημάτων ἀθάνατον

Believe that many precepts are better

than much wealth; for wealth quickly fails us, but precepts abide through all time; for wisdom alone of all possessions is imperishable.

Translated by George Norlin (1928)

To Demonicus 1.19.1

10 μὴ κατόκνει μακρὰν ὁδὸν πορεύεσθαι πρὸς τοὺς διδάσκειν τι χρήσιμον ἐπαγγελλομένους· αἰσχρὸν γὰρ τοὺς μὲν ἐμπόρους τηλικαῦτα πελάγη διαπερᾶν ἕνεκα τοῦ πλείω ποιῆσαι τὴν ὑπάρχουσαν οὐσίαν, τοὺς δὲ νεωτέρους μηδὲ τὰς κατὰ γῆν πορείας ὑπομένειν ἐπὶ τῷ βελτίω καταστῆσαι τὴν αὑτῶν διάνοιαν

Do not hesitate to travel a long road to those who can offer some useful instruction; for it were a shame, when merchants cross vast seas in order to increase their wealth, that the young should not endure even journeys by land to improve their understanding.

Translated by George Norlin (1928)

To Demonicus 1.19.4

11 ἡδέως μὲν ἔχε πρὸς ἅπαντας, χρῶ δὲ τοῖς βελτίστοις

Be pleasant to all, but associate with the best.

To Demonicus 1.20

12 ὑφ' ὧν κρατεῖσθαι τὴν ψυχὴν αἰσχρὸν, τούτων ἐγκράτειαν ἄσκει πάντων, κέρδους, ὀργῆς, ἡδονῆς, λύπης

Control all things that would shamefully affect the soul: gain, temper, pleasure and pain.

To Demonicus 1.21

13 ὅρκον ἐπακτὸν προσδέχου διὰ δύο προφάσεις, ἢ σαυτὸν αἰτίας αἰσχρᾶς ἀπολύων, ἢ φίλους ἐκ μεγάλων κινδύνων διασῴζων

Never allow yourself to be put under oath save for two reasons: in order to clear yourself of disgraceful charges or to save your friends from great dangers.

Translated by George Norlin (1928)

To Demonicus 1.23

14 εἶναι βούλου τὰ περὶ τὴν ἐσθῆτα φιλόκαλος, ἀλλὰ μὴ καλλωπιστής· ἔστι δὲ φιλοκάλου μὲν τὸ μεγαλοπρεπὲς, καλλωπιστοῦ δὲ τὸ περίεργον

In matters of dress, resolve to be a man of taste, but not a fop. The man of taste is marked by elegance, the fop by excess.

Translated by George Norlin (1928)

To Demonicus 1.27.1

15 ἀγάπα τῶν ὑπαρχόντων ἀγαθῶν μὴ τὴν ὑπερβάλλουσαν κτῆσιν ἀλλὰ τὴν μετρίαν ἀπόλαυσιν

Set not your heart on the excessive acquisition of goods, but on a moderate enjoyment of what you have.

Translated by George Norlin (1928)

To Demonicus 1.27.4

16 πειρῶ τὸν πλοῦτον χρήματα καὶ κτήματα κατασκευάζειν· ἔστι δὲ χρήματα μὲν τοῖς ἀπολαύειν ἐπισταμένοις, κτήματα δὲ τοῖς κτᾶσθαι δυναμένοις

Try to make of money a thing to use as well as to possess; it is a thing of use to those who understand how to enjoy it, a mere possession to those who are able only to acquire it.

Translated by George Norlin (1928)

To Demonicus 1.28.1

17 τίμα τὴν ὑπάρχουσαν οὐσίαν δυοῖν ἕνεκεν, τοῦ τε ζημίαν μεγάλην ἐκτῖσαι δύνασθαι, καὶ τοῦ φίλῳ σπουδαίῳ δυστυχοῦντι βοηθῆσαι· πρὸς δὲ τὸν ἄλλον βίον μηδὲν ὑπερβαλλόντως ἀλλὰ μετρίως αὐτὴν ἀγάπα

Prize your possessions for two reasons: to meet a heavy loss and to help a worthy friend in distress; as for your life in general, cherish them not in excess but in moderation.

To Demonicus 1.28.4

18 κοινὴ γὰρ ἡ τύχη καὶ τὸ μέλλον ἀόρατον

Fate is common to all, and the future unknown.

To Demonicus 1.29

19 μίσει τοὺς κολακεύοντας ὥσπερ τοὺς ἐξαπατῶντας· ἀμφότεροι γὰρ πιστευθέντες τοὺς πιστεύσαντας ἀδικοῦσιν

Abhor flatterers as you would deceivers; for both, if trusted, injure those who trust them.

Translated by George Norlin (1928)

To Demonicus 1.30

20 μηδὲ παρὰ τὰ γελοῖα σπουδάζων, μηδὲ παρὰ τὰ σπουδαῖα τοῖς γελοίοις χαίρων

Be not grim in times of mirth nor frivolous in times of sorrow.

To Demonicus 1.31.5

21 τὸ γὰρ ἄκαιρον πανταχοῦ λυπηρόν

Ill-timed, ill-received.

To Demonicus 1.31.7

22 ἥ τε ψυχὴ πολλὰ σφάλλεται διαφθαρείσης τῆς διανοίας

The soul stumbles again and again when the intellect is impaired.

Translated by George Norlin (1928)

To Demonicus 1.32

of the effects of wine

23 βουλευόμενος παραδείγματα ποιοῦ τὰ παρεληλυθότα τῶν μελλόντων

In your deliberations, let the past be an exemplar for the future.

Translated by George Norlin (1928)

To Demonicus 1.34.1

24 βουλεύου μὲν βραδέως, ἐπιτέλει δὲ ταχέως τὰ δόξαντα

Be slow in deliberation, prompt to carry out your resolves.

Translated by George Norlin (1928)

To Demonicus 1.34.3

25 εἰς ἀρχὴν κατασταθεὶς μηδενὶ χρῶ πονηρῷ πρὸς τὰς διοικήσεις· ὧν γὰρ ἂν ἐκεῖνος ἁμάρτῃ, σοὶ τὰς αἰτίας ἀναθήσουσιν

When you are placed in authority, do not employ any unworthy person in your administration; for people will blame you for any mistakes which he may make.

Translated by George Norlin (1928)

To Demonicus 1.37.1

26 ἐκ τῶν κοινῶν ἐπιμελειῶν ἀπαλλάττου μὴ πλουσιώτερος ἀλλ' ἐνδοξότερος· πολλῶν γὰρ χρημάτων κρείττων ὁ παρὰ τοῦ πλήθους ἔπαινος

Retire from your public duties, not more wealthy, but more highly esteemed; for public esteem is better than many possessions.

To Demonicus 1.37.3

27 πολλοῖς γὰρ ἡ γλῶττα προτρέχει τῆς διανοίας

In many the tongue outruns their judgement.

To Demonicus 1.41.2

28 δύο ποιοῦ καιροὺς τοῦ λέγειν, ἢ περὶ ὧν οἶσθα σαφῶς, ἢ περὶ ὧν ἀναγκαῖον εἰπεῖν· ἐν τούτοις γὰρ μόνοις ὁ λόγος τῆς σιγῆς κρείττων

There are but two occasions for speech: when you thoroughly know your subject or when the matter makes it imperative to speak; only then is speech better than silence.

To Demonicus 1.41.4

29 νόμιζε μηδὲν εἶναι τῶν ἀνθρωπίνων βέβαιον

Consider that nothing in human life is certain.

Translated by George Norlin (1928)

To Demonicus 1.42

30 τὸ μὲν γὰρ τελευτῆσαι πάντων ἡ πεπρωμένη κατέκρινε, τὸ δὲ καλῶς ἀποθανεῖν ἴδιον τοῖς σπουδαίοις ἀπένειμεν

To die is appointed by providence to all; to die nobly is reserved for the excellent.

To Demonicus 1.43

31 οἴκει τὴν πόλιν ὁμοίως ὥσπερ τὸν πατρῷον οἶκον

Manage the state as you would your father's homestead.

To Nicocles 2.19

32 διὰ παντὸς τοῦ χρόνου τὴν ἀλήθειαν οὕτω φαίνου προτιμῶν, ὥστε πιστοτέρους εἶναι τοὺς σοὺς λόγους μᾶλλον ἢ τοὺς τῶν ἄλλων ὅρκους

Throughout all your life show that you value truth so highly that your word is more to be trusted than the oaths of other men.

Translated by George Norlin (1928)

To Nicocles 2.22

33 ποίει μὲν μηδὲν μετ' ὀργῆς, δόκει δὲ τοῖς ἄλλοις ὅταν σοι καιρὸς ᾖ

Do nothing in anger, but simulate anger when the occasion demands it.

Translated by George Norlin (1928)

To Nicocles 2.23

34 φίλους κτῶ μὴ πάντας τοὺς βουλομένους, ἀλλὰ τοὺς τῆς σῆς φύσεως ἀξίους ὄντας, μηδὲ μεθ' ὧν ἥδιστα συνδιατρίψεις, ἀλλὰ μεθ' ὧν ἄριστα τὴν πόλιν διοικήσεις

Do not give your friendship to everyone who desires it, but only to those who are worthy of you; not to those whose society you will most enjoy, but to those with whose help you will best govern the state.

Translated by George Norlin (1928)

To Nicocles 2.27

35 δίδου παρρησίαν τοῖς εὖ φρονοῦσιν, ἵνα περὶ ὧν ἂν ἀμφιγνοῇς, ἔχῃς τοὺς συνδοκιμάσοντας

Allow outspokenness to those with good judgement so that when in doubt they will help you to decide.

To Nicocles 2.28.3

36 ἄκουε τοὺς λόγους τοὺς περὶ ἀλλήλων, καὶ πειρῶ γνωρίζειν ἅμα τούς τε λέγοντας, ὁποῖοί τινές εἰσι, καὶ περὶ ὧν ἂν λέγωσιν

Listen to what men say about each other and try to discern at the same time the character of those who speak and of those about whom they speak.

Translated by George Norlin (1928)

To Nicocles 2.28.7

37 ἄρχε σαυτοῦ μηδὲν ἧττον ἢ τῶν ἄλλων

Govern yourself no less than your subjects.

Translated by George Norlin (1928)

To Nicocles 2.29

38 τὸ τῆς πόλεως ὅλης ἦθος ὁμοιοῦται τοῖς ἄρχουσιν

The manners of the whole state are copied from its rulers.

Translated by George Norlin (1928)

To Nicocles 2.31

39 περὶ πλείονος ποιοῦ δόξαν καλὴν ἢ πλοῦτον μέγαν τοῖς παισὶ καταλιπεῖν· ὁ μὲν γὰρ θνητός, ἡ δ' ἀθάνατος

Consider it more important to leave to your children a good name than great riches; for riches endure for a day, a good name for all time.

Translated by George Norlin (1928)

To Nicocles 2.32.1

40 δόξα δὲ χρημάτων οὐκ ὠνητὴ

Wealth cannot buy a good name.

Translated by George Norlin (1928)

To Nicocles 2.32.3

41 ἂν τὰ παρεληλυθότα μνημονεύῃς, ἄμεινον περὶ τῶν μελλόντων βουλεύσει

If you are mindful of the past you will plan better for the future.

Translated by George Norlin (1928)

To Nicocles 2.35

42 βούλου τὰς εἰκόνας τῆς ἀρετῆς ὑπόμνημα μᾶλλον ἢ τοῦ σώματος καταλιπεῖν

Prefer to leave behind you as a memorial images of your character rather than of your body.

Translated by George Norlin (1928)

To Nicocles 2.36

43 ἃ τοῖς αὑτοῦ παισὶν ἂν συμβουλεύσειας, τούτοις αὐτὸς ἐμμένειν ἀξίου

Whatever advice you would give to your children, follow it yourself.

Translated by George Norlin (1928)

To Nicocles 2.38

44 σοφοὺς νόμιζε ... τοὺς καλῶς καὶ μετρίως καὶ τὰς συμφορὰς καὶ τὰς εὐτυχίας φέρειν ἐπισταμένους

Consider wise those who know how to bravely and moderately meet both disaster and success.

To Nicocles 2.39

cf. Kipling 'If you can meet both triumph and disaster'

45 οἶμαι γὰρ ἐγὼ πάντας ἂν ὁμολογῆσαι πλείστου τῶν ἀρετῶν ἀξίας εἶναι τήν τε σωφροσύνην καὶ τὴν δικαιοσύνην

I think you would all agree that the most sovereign of the virtues are temperance and justice.

Translated by George Norlin (1928)

Nicocles or The Cyprians 3.29

46 φιλεῖ τὸ πλῆθος ἐν τούτοις τοῖς ἐπιτηδεύμασι τὸν βίον διάγειν, ἐν οἷς ἂν τοὺς ἄρχοντας τοὺς αὑτῶν ὁρῶσι διατρίβοντας

The multitude are likely to copy the practices of their rulers.

Nicocles or The Cyprians 3.37

47 μὴ φθονεῖτε τοῖς παρ' ἐμοὶ πρωτεύουσιν, ἀλλ' ἁμιλλᾶσθε, καὶ πειρᾶσθε ... ἐξισοῦσθαι τοῖς προέχουσιν

Don't envy the best but strive to be their equals.

Nicocles or The Cyprians 3.60

48 ἃ πάσχοντες ὑφ' ἑτέρων ὀργίζεσθε, ταῦτα τοὺς ἄλλους μὴ ποιεῖτε

Do not do unto others what angers you when done to you.

Nicocles or The Cyprians 3.61

49 τὴν πόλιν ἡμῶν ἀρχαιοτάτην εἶναι καὶ μεγίστην καὶ παρὰ πᾶσιν ἀνθρώποις ὀνομαστοτάτην

Our city is the oldest and the greatest in the world and in the eyes of all men the most renowned

Translated by George Norlin (1928)

Panegyricus 4.23

of Athens

50 τὸ τῶν Ἑλλήνων ὄνομα πεποίηκε μηκέτι τοῦ γένους ἀλλὰ τῆς διανοίας δοκεῖν εἶναι

The word 'Greek' has come to mean not a nation but a way of life.

Panegyricus 4.50.4

51 Ἕλληνες καλοῦνται οἱ τῆς παιδεύσεως τῆς ἡμετέρας μετέχοντες

Hellenes are all those who share our common culture.

Panegyricus 4.50.6

inscribed on the Gennadius Library in Athens

52 δεινὸν ἡγούμενοι τοὺς πολλοὺς ὑπὸ τοῖς ὀλίγοις εἶναι, καὶ τοὺς ταῖς οὐσίαις ἐνδεεστέρους τὰ δ' ἄλλα μηδὲν χείρους ὄντας ἀπελαύνεσθαι τῶν ἀρχῶν, ἔτι δὲ κοινῆς τῆς πατρίδος οὔσης τοὺς μὲν τυραννεῖν τοὺς δὲ μετοικεῖν, καὶ φύσει πολίτας ὄντας νόμῳ τῆς πολιτείας ἀποστερεῖσθαι

It is an outrage that the many should be subject to the few, that those who are poorer but not inferior in other respects should be excluded from the offices; that in a common fatherland some should hold the place of masters, others of aliens and that these, though natural inhabitants, should be deprived of their civil rights by law.

Panegyricus 4.105

53 ὡς καλόν ἐστιν ἐντάφιον ἡ τυραννὶς

Royalty is a glorious shroud.

Translated by George Norlin (1928)

Archidamus 6.45

spoken to Dionysius I of Syracuse about to flee the enemy; quoted by the Empress Theodora to Justinian about to abandon Constantinople to insurgents (cf. Procopius 1.24.37)

54 δεῖ καρτερεῖν ἐπὶ τοῖς παροῦσι καὶ θαρρεῖν περὶ τῶν μελλόντων

Endure the present, face the future with courage.

Archidamus 6.48

55 πεποιήκατε τοὺς ῥήτορας μελετᾶν καὶ φιλοσοφεῖν οὐ τὰ μέλλοντα τῇ πόλει συνοίσειν, ἀλλ' ὅπως ἀρέσκοντας ὑμῖν λόγους ἐροῦσιν

You have caused the orators to practice and study, not what will be advantageous to the state, but how they may discourse in a manner pleasing to you.

Translated by George Norlin (1929)

On the Peace 8.5

56 ἆρ' οὖν ἂν ἐξαρκέσειεν ἡμῖν, εἰ τήν τε πόλιν ἀσφαλῶς οἰκοῖμεν καὶ τὰ περὶ τὸν βίον εὐπορώτεροι γιγνοίμεθα καὶ τά τε πρὸς ἡμᾶς αὐτοὺς ὁμονοοῖμεν; ... ὁ μὲν τοίνυν πόλεμος ἁπάντων ἡμᾶς τῶν εἰρημένων ἀπεστέρηκεν

Should we not be well satisfied if we could dwell secure from danger, if we are provided abundantly with the necessities of life, if we could be of one mind amongst ourselves? Because the war has deprived us of all this.

On the Peace 8.19

57 τῶν μὲν περὶ τὸ σῶμα νοσημάτων πολλαὶ θεραπεῖαι καὶ παντοδαπαὶ τοῖς ἰατροῖς εὕρηνται, ταῖς δὲ ψυχαῖς ταῖς ἀγνοούσαις καὶ γεμούσαις πονηρῶν ἐπιθυμιῶν οὐδέν ἐστιν ἄλλο φάρμακον πλὴν λόγος ὁ τολμῶν τοῖς ἁμαρτανομένοις ἐπιπλήττειν

All kinds of treatment have been discovered by physicians for ills of the body, yet there exists no remedy for ignorant souls filled with base desires, except the word which dares to chastise those who do wrong.

On the Peace 8.39

58 ἐπιλίποι δ᾽ ἄν με τὸ λοιπὸν μέρος τῆς ἡμέρας, εἰ πάσας τὰς πλημμελείας τὰς ἐν τοῖς πράγμασιν ἐγγεγενημένας ἐξετάζειν ἐπιχειροίην

The remainder of the day would not suffice if I should attempt to review all the errors which have crept into our conduct of affairs.

Translated by George Norlin (1929)

On the Peace 8.56

59 δυναστείας ὑπὸ πάντων ἐρωμένης καὶ περιμαχήτου γεγενημένης

Imperial power which all the world lusts for and has waged many wars to obtain.

Translated by George Norlin (1929)

On the Peace 8.65

60 τῶν μὲν γὰρ ἀρχόντων ἔργον ἐστὶν τοὺς ἀρχομένους ταῖς αὑτῶν ἐπιμελείαις ποιεῖν εὐδαιμονεστέρους

It is a habit of those who dominate to provide pleasures for themselves through the labours and hardships of others.

Translated by George Norlin (1929)

On the Peace 8.91

61 ἐκεῖνο καταμαθόντες ὅτι μιᾶς μὲν ἑκάστης τῶν πόλεων κρείττους ἐσμέν, ἁπασῶν δ᾽ ἥττους

We have learned the lesson that, while we are stronger than any state taken singly, we are weaker than all of them joined together.

On the Peace 8.134

62 φθόνος … μέγιστον κακὸν τοῖς ἔχουσίν ἐστιν

Envy, most hurtful to those who are prone to it.

Evagoras 9.6

63 τὰς ἐπιδόσεις ἴσμεν γιγνομένας καὶ τῶν τεχνῶν καὶ τῶν ἄλλων ἁπάντων οὐ διὰ τοὺς ἐμμένοντας τοῖς καθεστῶσιν, ἀλλὰ διὰ τοὺς ἐπανορθοῦντας καὶ τολμῶντας ἀεί τι κινεῖν τῶν μὴ καλῶς ἐχόντων

Progress in every activity is made not by those who adhere to established practices, but by those who venture to change all which fares poorly.

Evagoras 9.7

64 τοῦ μὲν ἐπίπονον καὶ φιλοκίνδυνον τὸν βίον κατέστησε, τῆς δὲ περίβλεπτον καὶ περιμάχητον τὴν φύσιν ἐποίησεν

The man's life he created for labours and dangers, the woman's beauty for admiration and strife.

Translated by Doreen C. Innes (1995, based on W. Rhys Roberts)

Helen 10.17

of Heracles and Helen; quoted by Demetrius, On Style *23*

65 τί γάρ ἐστιν ἄλγιον ἢ ζῆν ἀεὶ δεδιότα;

For what, pray, is more grievous than to live in constant fear?

Translated by LaRue Van Hook (1945)

Helen 10.34

66 οὕτω γὰρ νομίμως καὶ καλῶς διῴκει τὴν πόλιν ὥστ᾽ ἔτι καὶ νῦν ἴχνος τῆς ἐκείνου πρᾳότητος ἐν τοῖς ἤθεσιν ἡμῶν καταλελεῖφθαι

So equitably and so well did he administer the city that even to this day traces of his gentleness may be seen remaining in our institutions.

Translated by LaRue Van Hook (1945)

Helen 10.37

of Theseus

67 εἰ πάντες ἤθελον οἱ παιδεύειν ἐπιχειροῦντες ἀληθῆ λέγειν, καὶ μὴ μείζους ποιεῖσθαι τὰς ὑποσχέσεις ὧν ἔμελλον ἐπιτελεῖν, οὐκ ἂν κακῶς ἤκουον ὑπὸ τῶν ἰδιωτῶν

If all who are engaged in the profession of education were willing to state the facts instead of making greater promises than they can possibly fulfil, they would not be in such bad repute with the lay-public.

Translated by George Norlin (1929)

Against the Sophists 13.1

68 οὐδεμίαν ἡγοῦμαι τοιαύτην εἶναι τέχνην, ἥτις τοῖς κακῶς πεφυκόσι πρὸς ἀρετὴν σωφροσύνην ἂν καὶ δικαιοσύνην ἐμποιήσειεν

No art exists which can implant prudence and justice in depraved natures.

Against the Sophists 13.21

69 πάντων ἡγοῦμαι πονηροτάτους εἶναι καὶ μεγίστης ζημίας ἀξίους, οἵτινες οἷς αὐτοὶ

τυγχάνουσιν ὄντες ἔνοχοι, ταῦτα τῶν ἄλλων τολμῶσι κατηγορεῖν

There are none so deserving of the severest punishment as those charging others with offences of which they themselves are guilty.

Antidosis 15.14

70 ὅτε μὲν γὰρ ἐγὼ παῖς ἦν, οὕτως ἐνομίζετο τὸ πλουτεῖν ἀσφαλὲς εἶναι καὶ σεμνὸν ὥστ᾽ ὀλίγου δεῖν πάντες προσεποιοῦντο πλείω κεκτῆσθαι τὴν οὐσίαν ἧς ἔχοντες ἐτύγχανον … νῦν δ᾽ ὑπὲρ τοῦ μὴ πλουτεῖν ὥσπερ τῶν μεγίστων ἀδικημάτων ἀπολογίαν δεῖ παρασκευάζεσθαι

When I was a boy, wealth was regarded as a thing so secure as well as admirable that almost every one affected to own more property than he actually possessed; now, on the other hand, a man has to be ready to defend himself against being rich as if it were the worst of crimes.

Translated by George Norlin (1929)

Antidosis 15.159

71 ἐγὼ μὲν οὖν ἡδονῆς ἢ κέρδους ἢ τιμῆς ἕνεκά φημὶ πάντας πάντα πράττειν

It is either for pleasure or gain or honour that everyone does everything.

Antidosis 15.217

72 τῶν προγόνων ἐπιμνησθεὶς

Having bethought himself of our ancestors.

On the Team of Horses 16.24

engraved on the sword of Pierre Amandry when made a member of the Académie Française in 1975

73 οἶδα μὲν οὖν ὅτι τοῖς συμβουλεύειν ἐπιχειροῦσι πολὺ διαφέρει μὴ διὰ γραμμάτων ποιεῖσθαι τὴν συνουσίαν ἀλλ᾽ αὐτοὺς πλησιάσαντας

I know, to be sure, that it makes a great difference for those trying to give advice that they do not do so by letter, but go in person.

Translated by Owen Hodkinson (2007)

Letter to Dionysius 1.2

74 ἀκούω δέ … ὡς φιλάνθρωπος εἶ καὶ φιλαθήναιος καὶ φιλόσοφος

I hear that you are humane, an admirer of Athens and a lover of wisdom.

Letter to Alexander 5.2

75 τῆς παιδείας τὴν μὲν ῥίζαν εἶναι πικράν, τὸν δὲ καρπὸν γλυκύν

The roots of education are bitter, but the fruit is sweet.

Translated by R.D. Hicks (1925)

Fragment 19 (Mathieu and Brémond)

Diogenes Laertius attributes this to Aristotle, Stobaeus to Demosthenes

76 Ἰσοκράτης εἶπεν ὅτι τὸν χρηστὸν καὶ ἀγαθὸν ἄνδρα δεῖ τῶν μὲν προγεγενημένων μεμνῆσθαι, τὰ δὲ ἐνεστῶτα πράττειν, περὶ δὲ τῶν μελλόντων φυλάττεσθαι

A worthy man should remember the past, be prepared for the present and ready to face the future.

Fragment 23 (Mathieu and Brémond)

77 εὖ σοι τὸ μέλλον ἕξει ἂν τὸ παρὸν εὖ τιθῇς

Put the present in order and your future will go well.

Fragment 36 (Mathieu and Brémond)

78 ὕδωρ θολερὸν καὶ ἀπαίδευτον ψυχὴν οὐ δεῖ ταράττειν

Do not disturb murky water or the mind of an uneducated man.

Fragment 38 (Mathieu and Brémond)

79 ἔλεγεν κάκιστον ἄρχοντα εἶναι τὸν ἄρχειν ἑαυτοῦ μὴ δυνάμενον

The worst ruler is one who cannot rule himself.

Translated by Frank Cole Babbitt (1931)

Fragment 40 (Mathieu and Brémond)

Plutarch, Sayings of Romans *198f, has the selfsame words as having been spoken by Cato the Elder*

J

ST JOHN CHRYSOSTOM

*c.*354–407AD

Bishop of Constantinople and Church Father

1 μέγιστον γάρ ἐστιν εἰς διόρθωσιν τῶν ἡμαρτημένων ἡ ὁμολογία

Admission is the greatest step in the redemption of error.

On the Beginning of Lent (with references to Genesis) 53.168.53 (*MPG*)

2 αἱ μὲν γὰρ ἐμπεπλησμέναι γαστέρες ... τὰς πεινώσας ἀγνοοῦσιν

Full stomachs are unaware of hungry ones.

On the Beginning of Lent (with references to Genesis) 54.603.3 (*MPG*)

3 δίδου μοι τὴν σήμερον, καὶ λάμβανε τὴν αὔριον. Ὦ ὑπερβολὴ ἀνοίας

Give me today, and take tomorrow; what enormous folly!

On the Gospel according to St Matthew 57.214.51 (*MPG*)

condemning this statement

4 διὰ ταῦτα αἰσχύνομαι ὅτι Ἕλληνες τοιαῦτα φιλοσοφοῦσιν, ἡμεῖς δὲ ἀσχημονοῦμεν

I am ashamed that whereas the Greeks took a philosophical view, our behaviour is undignified.

On the Gospel according to St John 59.347.24 (*MPG*)

5 τί τοίνυν παίζεις ἐν οὐ παικτοῖς; τί ἀπατᾷς σαυτὸν καὶ παραλογίζῃ τὴν ψυχήν σου;

Why play you with things not to be played at? Why do you fool yourself and mislead your soul?

On St Paul's Epistle to the Romans 60.674.55 (*MPG*)

6 ὅταν γὰρ ἐξ ἁπάντων συνεισφέρηται, ἑκάστῳ κοῦφον γίνεται τὸ ἐπίταγμα

When all pay their share, the burden to each is light.

Translated by D.S. Baker (1998)

On St Paul's First Epistle to the Corinthians 61.367.50 (*MPG*)

7 κατέλαβε νὺξ, ὁ λιμὴν τῶν ἡμετέρων κακῶν, τὸ παραμύθιον τῶν ἡμετέρων συμφορῶν, τὸ φάρμακον τῶν τραυμάτων

Night came on, harbour of our ills, consolation of our misfortunes, healer of our wounds.

On St Paul's Epistle to the Philippians 62.195.29 (*MPG*)

8 τὸ κοινωνοὺς εἶναι τῶν συμφορῶν φέρειν παραμυθίαν

Misfortunes are more bearable when shared with others.

On St Paul's First Epistle to Timothy 62.552.26 (*MPG*)

9 μηδὲ εἰς τὴν αὔριον ἀναβάλλου· ἡ γὰρ αὔριον οὐδέποτε λαμβάνει τέλος

Put not off until tomorrow; for the morrow admits no fulfilment.

Translated by H.T. Riley (1872)

To the People of Antioch 49.211.5 (*MPG*)

cf. the expression 'for tomorrow never comes'

10 νηστευέτωσαν ὀφθαλμοί, παιδευόμενοι μηδέποτε ὄψεσιν εὐμόρφοις ἐπιπηδᾶν, μηδὲ ἀλλότρια περιεργάζεσθαι κάλλη

Eyes should fast too and not rush to look at fair faces, nor be busy about the beauty of others.

To the People of Antioch 49.53.22 (*MPG*)

11 σὺ δὲ τὸν νόμον τὸν κωλύοντα ὀμνύναι, τοῦτον ὅρκον ποιεῖς; ὢ τῆς ὕβρεως, ὢ τῆς παροινίας

When the Law forbids swearing, you take an oath?
Oh, what contempt! Oh, what outrage!

Translated by W.R.W. Stephens (1886)

To the People of Antioch 49.160.50 (*MPG*)

cf. Bible 19 and 276

12 νηστεύσαντες καὶ μὴ νηστεύσαντες εὐφράνθητε σήμερον

All who kept the fast, and those who did not, be of good cheer today.

*Catechetical Sermon on Holy Easter** 59.722.54 (*MPG*)

13 μηδεὶς φοβείσθω τὸν θάνατον· ἠλευθέρωσε γὰρ ἡμᾶς ὁ τοῦ Σωτῆρος θάνατος

Do not fear death: we are redeemed by our Saviour's death.

*Catechetical Sermon on Holy Easter** 59.723.1 (*MPG*)

14 σκιρτᾷ μὲν ὡς ταῦρος, λακτίζῃ δὲ ὡς ὄνος, μνησικακῇ δὲ ὡς κάμηλος, καὶ γαστριμαργῇ μὲν ὡς ἄρκτος, ἁρπάζῃ δὲ ὡς λύκος, πλήττῃ δὲ ὡς σκορπίος, ὕπουλος δὲ ᾖ ὡς ἀλώπηξ, χρεμετίζῃ δὲ ἐπὶ γυναιξὶν ὡς ἵππος θηλυμανὴς

Unruly as a bull, kicking like a donkey, malicious as a camel, gluttonous as a bear, rapacious as a wolf, poisonous as a scorpion, wily as a fox, lusting after women as a stallion.

*On the Narrow Gate** 51.44.38 (*MPG*)

how can such a man appeal to God?

15 ἵνα πάντα τὰ ἔθνη ἐν ἑνὶ στόματι καὶ μιᾷ καρδίᾳ δοξάσωμεν τὸν ποιητὴν καὶ Σωτῆρα ἡμῶν

Let all nations, with one voice and a common purpose, give praise to our creator and saviour.

*Interpretation of the Paternoster** 59.627.36 (*MPG*)

16 ἄνθρωπος ... ὡς ἄνθος ὡραΐζεται, καὶ ὡς χόρτος ξηραίνεται· ὡς νέφος ὑπεραπλοῦται, καὶ ὡς σταγὼν ἀπομειοῦται· ὡς πομφόλυξ ὀγκοῦται, καὶ ὡς σπινθὴρ ἀποσβέννυται

As a flower man blooms in youthful beauty and as grass he withers away; as a cloud he spreads over the sky and as a drop of water he dries up; as a bubble he is swollen and as a spark he is extinguished.

*On Being Agitated in Vain** 55.559.24 (*MPG*)

JULIAN THE APOSTATE

Iulianus Flavius Claudius
331–363AD
Roman emperor, 361–363AD
see also Oracles 25

1 ἀνέγνων, ἔγνων, κατέγνων

I have read, I have understood, I have condemned.

Epistles 157

handwritten addition to an apocryphal letter to St Basil, for whose answer see St Basil 7; according to another manuscript the remark was included in a letter 'To the bishops', opposing Christian postulations

2 ἐγὼ ᾤμην τὴν παιδιὰν ἄνεσίν τε εἶναι ψυχῆς καὶ ἀπαλλαγὴν τῶν φροντίδων

I considered play to be a holiday for the mind, a relaxation from thought.

Translated by H.T. Riley (1872)

Συμπόσιον 1

3 νενίκηκάς με Ναζωραῖε

You have won, Galilean.

Translated in *The Oxford Dictionary of Quotations* (2004)

Theodoret, *Church History* 205

supposed dying words

JULIUS CAESAR

Gaius Iulius Caesar
100–44BC
Roman general and statesman
see also Plutarch 5, 17

1 τὴν ἐμὴν ἠξίουν μηδὲ ὑπονοηθῆναι

I had the right to expect my wife to be above suspicion.

Plutarch, *Caesar* 10.9

spoken by Julius Caesar divorcing his wife Pompeia after unfounded allegations were made against her; today usually quoted as 'ἠξίουν εἶναι ὑπεράνω ὑποψίας'; cf. the English proverb 'Caesar's wife must be above suspicion'

2 ἐγὼ μὲν ἐβουλόμην παρὰ τούτοις εἶναι μᾶλλον πρῶτος ἢ παρὰ Ῥωμαίοις δεύτερος

I should rather be first among these people than second at Rome.

Translated in *The Oxford Dictionary of Quotations* (2004)

Plutarch, *Caesar* 11.4

3 Καίσαρα φέρεις καὶ τὴν Καίσαρος τύχην συμπλέουσαν

Thou hast Caesar and his fortune with thee.

Translated by Thomas North (1579)

Plutarch, *Caesar* 38.5

4 ἦλθον, εἶδον, ἐνίκησα

I came, I saw, I conquered.

Translated in *The Oxford Dictionary of Quotations* (2004)

Plutarch, *Caesar* 50.3

Plutarch, recording the saying in Greek, points to the striking rendering in Latin 'veni, vidi, vici', cf. Suetonius, Lives of the Caesars, *'Julius' 37.2; also cf. Democritus 66*

5 αἱ μὲν δὴ Μάρτιαι Εἰδοὶ πάρεισιν

The Ides of March have come.

Translated in *Bartlett's Familiar Quotations* (1980)

Plutarch, *Caesar* 63.6

6 ἐμπεσόντος δὲ λόγου, ποῖος ἄρα τῶν θανάτων ἄριστος ... ἐξεβόησεν· ὁ ἀπροσδόκητος

In answer to a question as to what sort of death was the best he cried out: A sudden, unexpected death.

Plutarch, *Caesar* 63.7

7 ὄψει δέ με περὶ Φιλίππους

Meet me at Philippi.

Plutarch, *Caesar* 69.11

spoken by a ghost said to have been seen by Brutus

8 ἀνερρίφθω κύβος

Let the die be cast.

Translated by Kathleen Freeman (1947)

Plutarch, *Pompey* 60.2

spoken in Greek on crossing the river Rubicon; in Latin 'alea iacta est' (the die is cast); cf. Menander, Fragment 65 (Kock) – 168 (K-A)

9 φιλεῖν μὲν προδοσίαν, προδότην δὲ μισεῖν

He loved treason but hated the traitor.

The 'Translation called Dryden's', rev. A.H. Clough (1859)

Plutarch, *Romulus* 17.3

of the Thracian Rhoemetalces

10 καὶ σύ, τέκνον;

You too, my son?

Cassius Dio, *Roman History* 44.19.5

cf. Suetonius, Lives of the Caesars *'Julius' 82, where the same words are also recorded in Greek; cf. Shakespeare,* Julius Caesar *3.1.77: 'Et tu, Brute?'*

L

LACYDES

*fl. c.*241BC

Philosopher from Cyrene, Head of the Middle Academy in 241/240BC

1 ὀψὲ δὲ αὐτῷ γεωμετροῦντι λέγει τις, εἶτα νῦν καιρός; καὶ ὅς εἶτα μηδὲ νῦν;

When asked late in life why he was studying geometry he answered, 'If I should not be learning now, when should I be?'

Diogenes Laertius, *Lives of Eminent Philosophers* 4.60

LAMACHUS

died 414BC

Athenian general

1 οὐκ ἔστιν ἐν πολέμῳ δὶς ἁμαρτεῖν

In war there is no room for two mistakes.

Translated by Frank Cole Babbitt (1931)

Plutarch, *Sayings of Kings and Commanders* 186f

when one of his captains vowed he would never make the same mistake again

LASUS

6th century BC

Composer of hymns and dithyrambs from Hermione

1 Λᾶσος ὁ Ἑρμιονεὺς ἐρωτηθεὶς τί εἴη σοφώτατον, ἡ πεῖρα ἔφη

Lasus of Hermione, when asked what was the wisest of all things, answered, 'Experience'.

Stobaeus, *Anthology* 3.29.70

LEONIDAS

King of Sparta, 490–480BC

see also Antiphilus of Byzantium 4

1 ἀγαθοῖς γαμεῖσθαι καὶ ἀγαθὰ τίκτειν

May you marry good men and bear good children.

Plutarch, *Sayings of Spartans* 225a

to his wife Gorgo who asked for his wishes on leaving for Thermopylae

2 εἰ τὰ καλὰ τοῦ βίου ἐγίγνωσκες, ἀπέστης ἂν τῆς τῶν ἀλλοτρίων ἐπιθυμίας· ἐμοὶ δὲ κρείττων ὁ ὑπὲρ τῆς Ἑλλάδος θάνατος τοῦ μοναρχεῖν τῶν ὁμοφύλων

If you had knowledge of the noble things of life, you would refrain from coveting others' possessions; but for me to die for Greece is better than to be the sole ruler over the people of my race.

Translated by Frank Cole Babbitt (1931)

Plutarch, *Sayings of Spartans* 225c.7

to Xerxes who proposed to make him sole leader of Greece if he would ally himself with him

3 μολὼν λαβέ

Come get!

Plutarch, *Sayings of Spartans* 225c.11

when asked at Thermopylae to surrender his arms

4 τὸ μὲν τῆς φύσεως ἴδιον, τὸ δὲ αὐτῶν εἶναι νομίζουσιν

Life is Nature's gift; a glorious death is the choice of the best of men.

Plutarch, *Sayings of Spartans* 225d

LEONIDAS OF ALEXANDRIA

1st century AD
Epigrammatist working at Rome and inventor of isopsephic poems

1 Πέμματα τίς λιπόωντα, τίς Ἀρεϊ τῷ πτολιπόρθῳ
βότρυς, τίς δὲ ῥόδων θῆκεν ἐμοὶ κάλυκας;
Νύμφαις ταῦτα φέροι τις ἀναιμάκτους δὲ θυηλὰς
οὐ δέχομαι βωμοῖς ὁ θρασύμητις Ἄρης.

Who offered to me, Ares the sacker of cities,
rich cakes, and grapes, and roses?
Let them offer these to the Nymphs, but I, bold Ares,
accept not bloodless sacrifices on my altars.

Translated by W.R. Paton (1916)

Greek Anthology 6.324

an isopsephic poem – the sum of the letters taken as numerical signs is the same in each couplet

LEONIDAS OF TARENTUM

*c.*290–*c.*220BC
Poet

1 Οὐκ ἀδικέω τὸν Ἔρωτα· γλυκύς, μαρτύρομαι αὐτὴν
Κύπριν· βέβλημαι δ' ἐκ δολίου κέραος
καὶ πᾶς τεφροῦμαι.

I haven't wronged Eros. Aphrodite is my witness: I'm a gentle lover.
Yet his deceitful bow has done me in, burning me to ashes.

Translated by Edmund Keeley (2010)

Greek Anthology 5.188

2 Εὐκαπὲς ἄγκιστρον καὶ δούρατα δουλιχόεντα
χὠρμιήν, καὶ τὰς ἰχθυδόκους σπυρίδας,
καὶ τοῦτον νηκτοῖσιν ἐπ' ἰχθύσι τεχνασθέντα
κύρτον, ἁλιπλάγκτων εὕρεμα δικτυβόλων,
τρηχύν τε τριόδοντα, Ποσειδαώνιον ἔγχος,
καὶ τοὺς ἐξ ἀκάτων διχθαδίους ἐρέτας,
ὁ γριπεὺς Διόφαντος ἀνάκτορι θήκατο τέχνας,
ὡς θέμις, ἀρχαίας λείψανα τεχνοσύνας.

As is customary and right, the fisherman Diophantus dedicates to the patron of his art these relics of his ancient craft: the easily swallowed hook, the slender poles, the line, the creels to hold the fish, this wicker-pot devised to trap the swimming fish, an invention of sea-roaming fishermen, his rough trident, a weapon of Poseidon, and the two oars of his boat.

Translated by C.A. Trypanis (1971)

Greek Anthology 6.4

to Poseidon as patron of the fishermen

3 Παρθενικὰν νεάοιδον ἐν ὑμνοπόλοισι μέλισσαν
Ἤρινναν, Μουσῶν ἄνθεα δρεπτομέναν,
Ἅιδας εἰς ὑμέναιον ἀνάρπασεν. ἦ ῥα τόδ' ἔμφρων
εἶπ' ἐτύμως ἁ παῖς· Βάσκανός ἐσσ', Ἀίδα.

The young maiden singer Erinna, bee among poets,
who sipped the flowers of the Muses,
Hades snatched away to be his bride; truly indeed
said the girl in her wisdom, 'Thou art envious, O Death.'

Translated by J.W. MacKail (1890)

Greek Anthology 7.13

also attributed to Meleager

4 Αὐτόμαται δείλῃ ποτὶ ταὔλιον αἱ βόες ἦλθον
ἐξ ὄρεος, πολλῇ νιφόμεναι χιόνι·
αἰαῖ, Θηρίμαχος δὲ παρὰ δρυῒ τὸν μακρὸν εὕδει
ὕπνον, ἐκοιμήθη δ' ἐκ πυρὸς οὐρανίου.

The cattle came home from the hill at dusk
by themselves, through deep snow.
The cowherd Therimachos sleeps an endless sleep under the oak tree
where the sky's fire struck him down.

Translated by Edmund Keeley (2010)

Greek Anthology 7.173

also attributed to Diotimus

5 Μυρίος ἦν, ἄνθρωπε, χρόνος προτοῦ, ἄχρι πρὸς ἠῶ
ἦλθες, χὠ λοιπὸς μυρίος εἰς Ἀΐδην.
τίς μοῖρα ζωῆς ὑπολείπεται, ἢ ὅσον ὅσσον
στιγμὴ καὶ στιγμῆς εἴ τι χαμηλότερον;

Measureless time or ever thy years, O man, were reckon'd;
Measureless time shall run over thee

low in the ground.
And thy life between is – what? The flick of a flying second,
A flash, a point – or less, if a lesser thing can be found.

Translated by Edwyn Bevan (1931)

Greek Anthology 7.472

6 Πολλὸν ἀπ' Ἰταλίης κεῖμαι χθονὸς, ἔκ τε Τάραντος
πάτρης· τοῦτο δέ μοι πικρότερον θανάτου.
τοιοῦτος πλανίων ἄβιος βίος· ἀλλά με Μοῦσαι
ἔστερξαν, λυγρῶν δ' ἀντὶ μελιχρὸν ἔχω.
οὔνομα δ' οὐκ ἤμυσε Λεωνίδου· αὐτά με δῶρα
κηρύσσει Μουσέων πάντας ἐπ' ἠελίους.

Far from Italy, far from my native Tarentum
I lie; and this is the worst of it – worse than death.
An exile's life is no life. But the Muses loved me.
For my suffering they gave me a honeyed gift:
My name survives me. Thanks to the sweet Muses
Leonidas will echo throughout all time.

Translated by Fleur Adcock (1934–)

Greek Anthology 7.715

7 Ὁ πλόος ὡραῖος· καὶ γὰρ λαλαγεῦσα χελιδὼν
ἤδη μέμβλωκεν χὼ χαρίεις ζέφυρος·
λειμῶνες δ' ἀνθεῦσι, σεσίγηκεν δὲ θάλασσα
κύμασι καὶ τρηχεῖ πνεύματι βρασσομένη.
ἀγκύρας ἀνέλοιο καὶ ἐκλύσαιο γύαια,
ναυτίλε, καὶ πλώοις πᾶσαν ἐφεὶς ὀθόνην.

Now is the season of sailing; for already the chattering swallow is come and the gentle West wind; the meadows flower, and the sea, tossed up with waves and rough blasts, has sunk to silence. Weigh thine anchors and unloose thine hawsers, O mariner, and sail with all thy canvas set.

Translated by J.W. MacKail (1890)

Greek Anthology 10.1

LEONTIUS SCHOLASTICUS

dates unknown
Epigrammatist

1 Θῆλυς ἐν ὀρχηθμοῖς κρατέει φύσις· εἴξατε, κοῦροι

Women excel in dancing: give way, young men!

Greek Anthology 16.286

LEUCIPPUS

5th century BC
Philosopher, originator of the atomic theory, born in Elea or Abdera or Miletus

1 οὐδὲν χρῆμα μάτην γίνεται, ἀλλὰ πάντα ἐκ λόγου τε καὶ ὑπ' ἀνάγκης

Nothing happens by chance, but everything for a reason and by necessity.

Fragment 2 (D-K)

LIBANIUS

314–393AD
Rhetorician and man of letters from Antioch

1 παῦσαι μεγάλα περὶ μικρῶν λέγων

Stop using big words on small issues.

Epistulae 688.1

cf. Dr. Johnson: 'Don't, Sir, accustom yourself to use big words for little matters' (Boswell, The Life of Samuel Johnson, *ch. '1763', Everyman Paperback, vol. 1, p.292)*

2 νῦν γὰρ ὡς ἀληθῶς ἔστι ζῆν, ὅτ' εὐδαιμονίας αὖραι τὴν γῆν ἐπιπνέουσιν

Now is the time to truly live, when the breezes of happiness blow fairly upon the earth.

Orations 13.14

'LONGINUS'

1st century AD

1 ἐκ τοῦ φοβεροῦ κατ' ὀλίγον ὑπονοστεῖ πρὸς τὸ εὐκαταφρόνητον

In a moment, we go from the sublime to the ridiculous.

Translated by D.S. Baker (1998)

On the Sublime 3

this manuscript has been ascribed to 'Dionysius Longinus' and 'Dionysius or Longinus'; until the early 19th century it was believed to be by 'Cassius Longinus', but this has now been refuted; the quotation above may refer to a passage of Aeschylus

2 μεγάλων ἀπολισθαίνειν ὅμως εὐγενὲς ἁμάρτημα

In great attempts even failure is glorious.

On the Sublime 3

3 πλὴν ἀλλοτρίων μὲν ἐλεγκτικώτατος ἁμαρτημάτων, ἀνεπαίσθητος δὲ ἰδίων

While keenly critical of others' faults, he is blind and deaf to his own.

Translated by W.H. Fyfe (1878–1965), rev. Donald Russell (1995)

On the Sublime 4

4 ἐν πρώτοις καθαρὰν τοῦ κατ' ἀλήθειαν ὕψους ἐπιστήμην καὶ ἐπίκρισιν, καίτοι τὸ πρᾶγμα δύσληπτον· ἡ γὰρ τῶν λόγων κρίσις πολλῆς ἐστι πείρας τελευταῖον ἐπιγέννημα

Obtain a clear knowledge of what is sublime, though this is not an easy thing to grasp; judgement in literature is the ultimate fruit of ripe experience.

Translated by W.H. Fyfe (1878–1965), rev. Donald Russell (1995)

On the Sublime 6

5 πλοῦτοι τιμαὶ δόξαι τυραννίδες καὶ ὅσα δὴ ἄλλα ἔχει πολὺ τὸ ἔξωθεν προστραγῳδούμενον οὐκ ἂν τῷ γε φρονίμῳ δόξειεν ἀγαθὰ ὑπερβάλλοντα

Riches, honours, reputation, sovereignty, and all the other things which possess in marked degree the external trappings of showy splendour, would not seem to a sensible man to be great blessings.

Translated by T.S. Dorsch (1965)

On the Sublime 7

6 τοῦτο γὰρ τῷ ὄντι μέγα, οὗ πολλὴ μὲν ἡ ἀναθεώρησις, δύσκολος δὲ, μᾶλλον δ' ἀδύνατος ἡ κατεξανάστασις, ἰσχυρὰ δὲ ἡ μνήμη καὶ δυσεξάλειπτος

What is truly great can be submitted to repeated consideration, but it is difficult, nay, impossible to resist its effect; and the memory of it is strong and indelible.

On the Sublime 7

7 ὕψος μεγαλοφροσύνης ἀπήχημα

Sublimity is the echo of a noble mind.

Translated by W.H. Fyfe (1878–1965), rev. Donald Russell (1995)

On the Sublime 9

8 μεγάλης φύσεως ὑποφερομένης ἤδη ἴδιόν ἐστιν ἐν γήρᾳ τὸ φιλόμυθον

As genius ebbs, it is the love of storytelling that characterizes old age.

Translated by W.H. Fyfe (1878–1965), rev. Donald Russell (1995)

On the Sublime 9

9 εἰς λῆρον ἐνίοτε ῥᾷστον κατὰ τὴν ἀπακμὴν τὰ μεγαλοφυῆ παρατρέπεται

Great genius with the decline of vigour often lapses very easily into nonsense.

Translated by W.H. Fyfe (1878–1965), rev. Donald Russell (1995)

On the Sublime 9

10 τῆς δὲ ῥητορικῆς φαντασίας κάλλιστον ἀεὶ τὸ ἔμπρακτον καὶ ἐνάληθες

The most perfect effect of visualization in oratory is always one of reality and truth.

Translated by W.H. Fyfe (1878–1965), rev. Donald Russell (1995)

On the Sublime 15

11 τότε γὰρ ἡ τέχνη τέλειος ἡνίκ' ἂν φύσις εἶναι δοκῇ

Art is only perfect when it looks like nature.

Translated by W.H. Fyfe (1878–1965), rev. Donald Russell (1995)

On the Sublime 22

12 φῶς γὰρ τῷ ὄντι ἴδιον τοῦ νοῦ τὰ καλὰ ὀνόματα

Truly, beautiful words are the very light of thought.

Translated by W.H. Fyfe (1878–1965), rev. Donald Russell (1995)

On the Sublime 30

13 ἐπεὶ τοῖς μικροῖς πραγματίοις περιτιθέναι μεγάλα καὶ σεμνὰ ὀνόματα ταὐτὸν ἂν φαίνοιτο ὡς εἴ τις τραγικὸν προσωπεῖον μέγα παιδὶ περιθείη νηπίῳ

To attach great and stately words to trivial things would be like fastening a great tragic mask on a little child.

Translated by W.H. Fyfe (1878–1965), rev. Donald Russell (1995)

On the Sublime 30

14 τῶν μὲν ἁμαρτημάτων ἀνεξάλειπτος ἡ μνήμη παραμένει, τῶν καλῶν δὲ ταχέως ἀπορρεῖ

Faults leave an ineradicable impression, but beauties soon slip from our memory.

Translated by W.H. Fyfe (1878–1965), rev. Donald Russell (1995)

On the Sublime 33

15 τῇ θεωρίᾳ καὶ διανοίᾳ τῆς ἀνθρωπίνης ἐπιβολῆς οὐδ' ὁ σύμπας κόσμος ἀρκεῖ, ἀλλὰ καὶ τοὺς τοῦ περιέχοντος πολλάκις ὅρους ἐκβαίνουσιν αἱ ἐπίνοιαι

The whole universe is not enough to satisfy the speculative intelligence of human thought; our ideas often pass beyond the limits that confine us.

Translated by W.H. Fyfe (1878–1965), rev. Donald Russell (1995)

On the Sublime 35

16 καλλίστου καὶ γονιμωτάτου λόγων νάματος, τὴν ἐλευθερίαν

The fairest and most fertile source of eloquence is freedom.

Translated by W.H. Fyfe (1878–1965), rev. Donald Russell (1995)

On the Sublime 44

17 ἅπασαν δουλείαν, κἂν ᾖ δικαιοτάτη, ψυχῆς γλωττόκομον καὶ κοινὸν ἄν τις ἀποφήναιτο δεσμωτήριον

All slavery, however equitable, might well be described as a cage for the soul, a common prison.

Translated by W.H. Fyfe (1878–1965), rev. Donald Russell (1995)

On the Sublime 44

18 ἡ γὰρ φιλοχρηματία, πρὸς ἣν ἅπαντες ἀπλήστως ἤδη νοσοῦμεν, καὶ ἡ φιληδονία δουλαγωγοῦσι

It is the love of money, that insatiable sickness from which we all now suffer, and the love of pleasure, that enslave us.

Translated by W.H. Fyfe (1878–1965), rev. Donald Russell (1995)

On the Sublime 44

LONGUS

2nd–early 3rd century AD
Greek novelist

1 πάντως γὰρ οὐδεὶς ἔρωτα ἔφυγεν ἢ φεύξεται, μέχρις ἂν κάλλος ᾖ καὶ ὀφθαλμοὶ βλέπωσιν

As long as beauty lives and eyes can see no one will ever escape love.

Daphnis and Chloe Preface.1.4

cf. Ravel's ballet of the same name (1912) and paintings by various illustrators, among them Corot, Maillol and Chagall

2 ἔστι πένης ὡς μηδὲ κύνα τρέφειν

Too poor to even keep a dog.

Daphnis and Chloe 1.16.2

LUCIAN

2nd century AD
Sophist and satirist from Samosata by the Euphrates

1 καθεζόμενος αὐτὸς ἐν μέσοις τοῖς θεαταῖς βλέποις ἀρετὰς ἀνδρῶν καὶ κάλλη σωμάτων καὶ εὐεξίας θαυμαστὰς καὶ ἐμπειρίας δεινὰς καὶ ἰσχὺν ἄμαχον καὶ τόλμαν καὶ φιλοτιμίαν καὶ γνώμας ἀηττήτους καὶ σπουδὴν ἄλεκτον ὑπὲρ τῆς νίκης

Sit in the midst of spectators, look at the men's courage and physical beauty, their marvellous vigour, their skill and invincible strength, their hardihood, their ambition, their unconquerable spirit, and their unwearied pursuit of victory.

Anacharsis (or Athletics) 12

of athletes at the Olympic Games

2 ὕπτιον καταβαλὼν ἑαυτὸν ἐς τὴν ὀροφὴν ἀνέβλεπεν

Stretched on his back he went on staring at the ceiling.

Translated by M.D. Macleod (1961)

Dialogues of Courtesans 3.3

3 Πυθιὰς ὁ ἐν χρῷ κεκαρμένος; εἶτα δι' ἕκτης
ἡμέρας ἀνεκόμησε τοσαύτην κόμην;

Pythias, shorn to the roots?
How then, in six days,
has he grown so much hair?

Dialogues of Courtesans 12.5

4 οὐκ ἂν λάβοις παρὰ τοῦ μὴ ἔχοντος

You cannot get something from him who has nothing.

Dialogues of the Dead 2.1

5 ἔστι δέ τις ὀβολὸν μὴ ἔχων;

Is there anyone who hasn't a single penny?

Translated by M.D. Macleod (1961)

Dialogues of the Dead 2.1

spoken by the boatman Charon who collected an obolos from souls he ferried into Hades

6 ἤκουσα, ὦ Χείρων, ὡς θεὸς ὢν ἐπεθύμησας ἀποθανεῖν

I heard, Chiron, that though you were a god, you wanted to die.

Translated by M.D. Macleod (1961)

Dialogues of the Dead 8.1

spoken by Menippus

7 πρᾶγμα ἱερὸν καὶ θεῶν παίδευμα καὶ ἀνθρώπων σοφῶν ἐπιτήδευμα

This sacred occupation, taught straight from Heaven, and pursued by the wisest of men.

Translated by H.W. Fowler and F.G. Fowler (1905)

Disowned 23

of the medical profession

8 ἀφωνότερος ἔσομαι τῶν ἰχθύων

More mute than a fish.

Translated by A.M. Harmon (1915)

The Dream, or The Cock 1.23

9 παιδεία μὲν καὶ πόνου πολλοῦ καὶ χρόνου μακροῦ καὶ δαπάνης οὐ μικρᾶς καὶ τύχης δεῖσθαι λαμπρᾶς

Education needs a lot of toil and time, no small expense, and glaring good luck.

The Dream or Lucian's Career 1

10 φύσει γὰρ τοιοῦτόν ἐστιν ὁ πολὺς λεώς, χαίρουσι τοῖς ἀποσκώπτουσιν καὶ λοιδορουμένοις, καὶ μάλισθ' ὅταν τὰ σεμνότατα εἶναι δοκοῦντα διασύρηται

Such is the multitude, enjoying those who revile and jeer, and mostly so when the most revered are ridiculed.

The Fisherman 25.22

of Aristophanes, ridiculing Socrates in Clouds

11 οὐδὲν γὰρ ὄφελος ... ἀφανοῦς τῆς μουσικῆς

What good is music if it is not heard!

Harmonides 1.32

cf. Wordsworth, 'The Solitary Reaper': 'The music in my heart I bore, / Long after it was heard no more'

12 καὶ εἴ πού γε φανείη μόνον, ἐδείκνυτο ἂν τῷ δακτύλῳ, Οὗτος ἐκεῖνος Ἡρόδοτός ἐστιν

Wherever he appeared people would point at him: This is the famous Herodotus.

Herodotus 2

on how respected Herodotus was many years later

13 ἀληθὲς ἄρ' ἦν ἐκεῖνο τό Πόλεμος ἁπάντων πατήρ, εἴ γε καὶ συγγραφέας τοσούτους ἀνέφυσεν ὑπὸ μιᾷ τῇ ὁρμῇ

Very true, it seems, is the saying that 'War is the father of all things' since at one stroke it has begotten so many historians.

Translated by K. Kilburn (1959)

How to Write History 2.11

quoting Heraclitus 26

14 οὐ γὰρ πρὸς ἡμᾶς γε τολμήσειεν ἄν τις, ἁπάντων ἤδη κεχειρωμένων

No one would dare to fight us – we've beaten everybody already.

Translated by K. Kilburn (1959)

How to Write History 5.21

mockingly of over-eulogizing historians

15 διττοῦ δὲ ὄντος τοῦ τῆς συμβουλῆς ἔργου, τὰ μὲν γὰρ αἱρεῖσθαι, τὰ δὲ φεύγειν διδάσκει, φέρε πρῶτα εἴπωμεν ἅτινα φευκτέον τῷ ἱστορίαν συγγράφοντι

Advice works in two ways: it teaches us to choose this and avoid that. So first let us say what the writer of history has to avoid.

Translated by K. Kilburn (1959)

How to Write History 6.1

16 ὡς οὐ στενῷ τῷ ἰσθμῷ διώρισται καὶ διατετείχισται ἡ ἱστορία πρὸς τὸ ἐγκώμιον, ἀλλά τι μέγα τεῖχος ἐν μέσῳ ἐστὶν αὐτῶν

The dividing line and frontier between history and panegyric is not a narrow isthmus but rather a mighty wall.

Translated by K. Kilburn (1959)

How to Write History 7.12

17 ἡ δὲ οὐκ ἄν τι ψεῦδος ἐμπεσὸν ἡ ἱστορία, οὐδὲ ἀκαριαῖον ἀνάσχοιτο, οὐ μᾶλλον ἢ τὴν ἀρτηρίαν ἰατρῶν παῖδές φασι τὴν τραχεῖαν παραδέξασθαι ἄν τι ἐς αὐτὴν καταποθέν

History cannot admit a lie, even a tiny one, any more than the windpipe, as sons of doctors say, can tolerate anything entering it in swallowing.

Translated by K. Kilburn (1959)

How to Write History 7.20

18 ἓν γὰρ ἔργον ἱστορίας καὶ τέλος, τὸ χρήσιμον, ὅπερ ἐκ τοῦ ἀληθοῦς μόνου συνάγεται

History has one task and one end – what is useful – and that comes from truth alone.

Translated by K. Kilburn (1959)

How to Write History 9.12

cf. Polybius 2

19 ἄριστα ἱστορίαν συγγράφοντα δύο μὲν ταῦτα κορυφαιότατα οἴκοθεν ἔχοντα ἥκειν, σύνεσίν τε πολιτικὴν καὶ δύναμιν ἑρμηνευτικήν

The best writer of history comes ready equipped with these two supreme qualities: political understanding and power of expression.

Translated by K. Kilburn (1959)

How to Write History 34.1

20 τοιοῦτος οὖν μοι ὁ συγγραφεὺς ἔστω – ἄφοβος, ἀδέκαστος, ἐλεύθερος, παρρησίας καὶ ἀληθείας φίλος, ὡς ὁ κωμικός φησι, τὰ σῦκα σῦκα, τὴν σκάφην δὲ σκάφην ὀνομάσων, οὐ μίσει οὐδὲ φιλίᾳ τι νέμων οὐδὲ φειδόμενος ἢ ἐλεῶν ἢ αἰσχυνόμενος ἢ δυσωπούμενος, ἴσος δικαστής

The sort of man the historian should be: fearless, incorruptible, free, a friend of free expression and the truth, intent, as the comic poet says, on calling a fig a fig and a trough a trough, giving nothing to hatred or to friendship, sparing no one, showing neither pity nor shame nor obsequiousness, an impartial judge.

Translated by K. Kilburn (1959)

How to Write History 41.1

quoting Aristophanes 168

21 χρὴ τοίνυν καὶ τὴν ἱστορίαν οὕτω γράφεσθαι σὺν τῷ ἀληθεῖ μᾶλλον πρὸς τὴν μέλλουσαν ἐλπίδα ἤπερ σὺν κολακείᾳ πρὸς τὸ ἡδὺ τοῖς νῦν ἐπαινουμένοις

History should be written in truthfulness and with an eye to the future, rather than flattering those presently commended.

How to Write History 63.1

22 τὸ τῆς κυνὸς ποιεῖς τῆς ἐν τῇ φάτνῃ κατακειμένης, ἣ οὔτε αὐτὴ τῶν κριθῶν ἐσθίει οὔτε τῷ ἵππῳ δυναμένῳ φαγεῖν ἐπιτρέπει

You act like the dog in the manger, who neither eats the grain herself nor lets the horse eat it.

Translated by A.M. Harmon (1921)

The Ignorant Book-Collector 30.4

cf. Proverbial 7

23 ὁ τῶν ἰδιωτῶν ἄριστος βίος, καὶ σωφρονέστερος παυσάμενος τοῦ μετεωρολογεῖν καὶ τέλη καὶ ἀρχὰς ἐπισκοπεῖν … καὶ τὰ τοιαῦτα λῆρον ἡγησάμενος … γελῶν τὰ πολλὰ καὶ περὶ μηδὲν ἐσπουδακώς

The life of the ordinary man is best, and you will act more wisely if you stop speculating about heavenly bodies and final causes and first causes, counting all these things idle talk, laughing a great deal and taking nothing seriously.

Menippus or The Descent Into Hades 21.14

spoken by the seer Teiresias whom Menippus met in the Underworld; cf. Aristotle 68

24 μήτ' ἀναβάλλεσθαι τὸ ἀγαθόν, ὅπερ τοὺς πολλοὺς ποιεῖν προθεσμίας ὁριζομένους … ἑορτὰς ἢ πανηγύρεις, ὡς ἀπ' ἐκείνων ἀρξομένους τοῦ τὰ δέοντα ποιῆσαι … ἀμέλλητον εἶναι τὴν πρὸς τὸ καλὸν ὁρμήν

Do not postpone being good, as most people do, setting a date, a holiday or festival, to start doing what they ought to do; there must be no delay for good intentions.

Nigrinus 27

25 κατὰ πᾶσαν γῆν καὶ κατὰ πάντα ἀέρα μακρόβιοι γεγόνασιν ἄνδρες οἱ γυμνασίοις τοῖς προσήκουσιν καὶ διαίτῃ τῇ ἐπιτηδειοτάτῃ πρὸς ὑγίειαν χρώμενοι

In every country and in every clime men who observe the proper exercise and a healthy diet are those who live longest.

Octogenarians 6

26 Γοργίας ... ἐρωτηθέντα τὴν αἰτίαν τοῦ μακροῦ γήρως καὶ ὑγιεινοῦ ἐν πάσαις ταῖς αἰσθήσεσιν εἰπεῖν, διὰ τὸ μηδέποτε συμπεριενεχθῆναι ταῖς ἄλλων εὐωχίαις

Gorgias when asked the reason for his great age, sound in all his faculties, replied that he had never accepted other people's invitations to dinner!

Translated by A.M. Harmon (1913)

Octogenarians 23

27 ἐπὶ τὸ ψεῦδος ἐτραπόμην πολὺ τῶν ἄλλων εὐγνωμονέστερον· κἂν ἓν γὰρ δὴ τοῦτο ἀληθεύσω λέγων ὅτι ψεύδομαι

My lying is far more honest than theirs, for though I tell the truth in nothing else, I shall at least be truthful in saying that I am a liar.

Translated by A.M. Harmon (1913)

A True Story 1.4

comparing himself to Homer and other famous authors

PSEUDO-LUCIAN
2nd century AD

1 Παῖδά με πενταέτηρον, ἀκηδέα θυμὸν ἔχοντα,
νηλειὴς Ἀΐδης ἥρπασε Καλλίμαχον.
ἀλλά με μὴ κλαίοις· καὶ γὰρ βιότοιο μετέσχον
παύρου καὶ παύρων τῶν βιότοιο κακῶν.

The frowning fates have taken hence
Callimachus, a childe
Five years of age: ah well is he
From cruell care exilde.
What though he lived but little tyme,
Waile nought for that at all:
For as his yeres not many were,
So were his troubles small.

Translated by Timothe Kendall (1577)

Epigrams 7.308 (*AG*)

2 Ὡς τεθνηξόμενος τῶν σῶν ἀγαθῶν ἀπόλαυε,
ὡς δὲ βιωσόμενος φείδεο σῶν κτεάνων.
ἔστι δ' ἀνὴρ σοφὸς οὗτος, ὃς ἄμφω ταῦτα νοήσας
φειδοῖ καὶ δαπάνῃ μέτρον ἐφηρμόσατο.

Use up thy store, for thou must die;
Thou hast to live, therefore put by.
Herein lies wisdom's rule, to pair
Expense and thrift in balance fair.

Translated by Walter Leaf (1922)

Epigrams 10.26 (*AG*)

3 φείδεο σῶν κτεάνων

Husband thy resources.

Translated by H.T. Riley (1872)

Epigrams 10.26.2 (*AG*)

4 Θνητὰ τὰ τῶν θνητῶν, καὶ πάντα παρέρχεται ἡμᾶς·
ἢν δὲ μή, ἀλλ' ἡμεῖς αὐτὰ παρερχόμεθα.

The world is fleeting; all things pass away;
Or it is we that pass, and they that stay.

Translated by Walter Leaf (1922)

Epigrams 10.31 (*AG*)

5 πλοῦτος ὁ τῆς ψυχῆς πλοῦτος μόνος ἐστὶν ἀληθής

The wealth of the soul is the only true wealth.

Translated by W.R. Paton (1918)

Epigrams 10.41 (*AG*)

6 Ἀρρήτων ἐπέων γλώσσῃ σφραγὶς ἐπικείσθω·
κρείσσων γὰρ μύθων ἢ κτεάνων φυλακή.

Seal your tongue to avoid words that better be unspoken;
watch your language rather than your possessions.

Epigrams 10.42 (*AG*)

LUCILLIUS
1st century AD

Greek epigrammatist under Nero, author of more than 100 satirical epigrams

1 Τέθνηκ' Εὐτυχίδης ὁ μελογράφος· οἱ κατὰ γαῖαν,
φεύγετ'· ἔχων ᾠδὰς ἔρχεται Εὐτυχίδης·
... ποῦ τις ἀπέλθῃ
λοιπόν, ἐπεὶ χᾴδην Εὐτυχίδης κατέχει;

Eutychides is dead, and what's worse
(fly wretched shades!) he's coming with his verse.
But what I want to know
is where in Hell, now he's in Hell, to go.

Translated by Humbert Wolfe (1927)

Greek Anthology 11.133

2 Ἠγόρασας πλοκάμους, φῦκος, μέλι, κηρόν, ὀδόντας·
τῆς αὐτῆς δαπάνης ὄψιν ἂν ἠγόρασας.

You bought hair, rouge, cream, teeth and paste.
It would cost the same to buy a face.

Translated by Andrew Sinclair (1967)

Greek Anthology 11.310

LYCOPHRON

early 3rd century BC
Tragic playwright and author of satyr-plays from Chalcis

1 ἀλλ' ἡνίκ' ἂν μὲν ᾖ πρόσω τὸ κατθανεῖν,
Ἅιδης ποθεῖται τοῖς δεδυστυχηκόσιν·
ὅταν δ' ἐφέρπῃ κῦμα λοίσθιον βίου,
τὸ ζῆν ποθοῦμεν· οὐ γὰρ ἔστ' αὐτοῦ κόρος

While death is far away
Sad hearts are fain to die;
But when the latest wave
Of life draws nigh,
We fain would live, for life
Knows no satiety.

Translated by A.W. Mair (1921)

Fragment 5 (Snell, *TrGF*) – *Pelopidae – The Children of Pelops*

2 πυκνῇ διοίχνει δυσφάτους αἰνιγμάτων
οἴμας τυλίσσων, ᾗπερ εὐμαθὴς τρίβος
ὀρθῇ κελεύθῳ τὰν σκότῳ ποδηγετεῖ

Pursue the obscure paths of her riddles,
whereso a clear track guides by a straight way
through things wrapped in darkness.

Translated by A.W. Mair (1921)

Alexandra 9

of the prophecies given in riddles by Cassandra

3 ᾧ γέλως ἀπέχθεται
καὶ δάκρυ, νῆις δ' ἐστὶ καὶ τητώμενος
ἀμφοῖν

He to whom laughter and tears are alike abhorred and who is ignorant and bereft of both.

Translated by A.W. Mair (1921)

Alexandra 116

4 τοιαῖσδ' ἐχῖνος μηχαναῖς οἰκοφθορῶν
παραιολίξει τὰς ἀλεκτόρων πικρὰς
στεγανόμους ὄρνιθας

With such craft shall the hedgehog ruin their homes
and mislead the house-keeping hens
embittered against the cocks.

Translated by A.W. Mair (1921)

Alexandra 1093

of the proverbial craftiness of the hedgehog, in this case inducing wives, by lies, to be faithless; cf. Archilochus 17

LYCURGUS

Legendary lawgiver of Sparta
see also Agesilaus II 5; Oracles 2; Xenophon 18

1 μετέστησε τὰ νόμιμα πάντα καὶ ἐφύλαξε ταῦτα μὴ παραβαίνειν

He changed all the laws of the country and made sure that none should transgress his ordinances.

Herodotus, *Histories* 1.65

of Sparta

2 τὰ τρυφῶντα καὶ ὕπουλα καὶ φλεγμαίνοντα τοῦ πλούτου περιελών, ὅπως εὐπορήσωσι τῶν ἀναγκαίων καὶ χρησίμων ἅπαντες

He thus removed the feverish wantonness of wealth, and provided that all alike might have the abundance of the necessary and useful things of life.

Translated by Bernadotte Perrin (1914)

Plutarch, *Comparison of Aristides and Cato Major* 3.1.9

on introducing iron as the currency of Sparta, banishing gold and silver

3 τὸν ἄπορον καὶ ἀνέστιον καὶ πένητα σύνοικον ἐπὶ κοινωνίᾳ πολιτείας μᾶλλον τοῦ πλουσίου καὶ ὑπερόγκου φοβηθείς

He foresaw that the helpless, homeless, and poverty-stricken citizen was a greater menace to the commonwealth than one who was rich and ostentatious.

Translated by Bernadotte Perrin (1914)

Plutarch, *Comparison of Aristides and Cato Major* 3.1.12

4 συνέπεισε τὴν χώραν ἅπασαν εἰς μέσον θέντας ἐξ ἀρχῆς ἀναδάσασθαι, καὶ ζῆν μετ' ἀλλήλων ἅπαντας ὁμαλεῖς καὶ ἰσοκλήρους τοῖς βίοις γενομένους, τὸ δὲ πρωτεῖον ἀρετῇ μετιόντας

He persuaded his fellow-citizens to

make one parcel of all their territory and divide it up anew, and to live with one another on a basis of entire uniformity and equality, seeking pre-eminence through virtue alone.

Translated by Bernadotte Perrin (1914)

Plutarch, *Lycurgus* 8.2

5 τῆς δὲ παιδείας, ἣν μέγιστον ἡγεῖτο τοῦ νομοθέτου καὶ κάλλιστον ἔργον εἶναι

Education he regarded as the greatest and noblest task of the lawgiver.

Translated by Bernadotte Perrin (1914)

Plutarch, *Lycurgus* 14.1

6 Λυκοῦργος ... κατειργάσατο τὸ μέγιστον εἰς σωτηρίαν πόλεως καὶ ὁμόνοιαν, μηδένα πένητα μηδὲ πλούσιον εἶναι τῶν πολιτῶν

He most effectually guaranteed the safety and unanimity of the city by making all its citizens neither rich nor poor.

Translated by Bernadotte Perrin (1914)

Plutarch, *Solon* 16.2

7 ποιητικωτέρα τῆς φύσεως ἡ ἄσκησις πρὸς τὰ καλὰ τυγχάνει

Exercise is of greater benefit than the gifts of nature.

Plutarch, *Sayings of Spartans* 226a

8 τοῦτον μέν τοι λαβὼν ... παρ' ὑμῶν ὑβριστὴν καὶ βίαιον, ἀποδίδωμι ὑμῖν ἐπιεικῆ καὶ δημοτικόν

I took him from you insolent and violent and returned him a modest and sociable man.

Stobaeus, *Anthology* 3.19.13

of a youngster whom he turned from mischief

LYCURGUS ORATOR

*c.*390–*c.*325BC
Athenian statesman and orator

1 ἁπλοῦν τὸ δίκαιον, ῥᾴδιον τὸ ἀληθές, βραχὺς ὁ ἔλεγχος

Justice is plain, truth easy, my argument of disproof brief.

Against Leocrates 1.33

2 οὐ ποιήσομαι περὶ πλείονος τὸ ζῆν τῆς ἐλευθερίας

I will not hold life dearer than liberty.

Translated by C.H. Oldfather (1946)

Against Leocrates 1.81

part of an oath sworn before going into battle

3 ὅταν γυνὴ ὁμονοίας τῆς πρὸς ἄνδρα στερηθῇ, ἀβίωτος ὁ καταλειπόμενος γίγνεται βίος

When a woman is not in harmony with her husband, the life that is left to them is unbearable.

Against Lycophron I and II Orations 10–11, Fragment 3 (Conomis)

4 ἐφ' οἷς καυχᾷ, οἱ ἄλλοι αἰσχύνονται

You take pride in what causes shame to others.

Translated by J.O. Burtt (1954)

On the Oracles Oration 13, Fragment 1a (Conomis)

LYSANDER

died 395BC
Spartan naval commander

1 ὅπου γὰρ ἡ λεοντῆ μὴ ἐφικνεῖται, προσραπτέον ἐκεῖ τὴν ἀλωπεκῆν

Where the lion's skin will not reach, it must be patched out with the fox's.

Translated by Bernadotte Perrin (1916)

Plutarch, *Lysander* 7.4

when accused of profiting by deception; cf. 'what force cannot achieve, the fox's cunning may'; cf. Machiavelli, The Prince *18.3: 'The prince must be a lion, but he must also know how to play the fox' (1532)*

2 τοὺς μὲν παῖδας ἀστραγάλοις, τοὺς δὲ ἄνδρας ὅρκοις ἐξαπατᾶν

Deceive boys with toys, and men with oaths.

Translated in *The Oxford Dictionary of Quotations* (2004)

Plutarch, *Lysander* 8.4

quoted by Francis Bacon, Advancement of Learning *2.23.45 (1605)*

LYSIAS

*c.*450–*c.*380BC
Athenian orator

1 προσήκειν νόμῳ μὲν ὁρίσαι τὸ δίκαιον, λόγῳ δὲ πεῖσαι, ἔργῳ δὲ τούτοις ὑπηρετεῖν,

ὑπὸ νόμου μὲν βασιλευομένους, ὑπὸ λόγου δὲ διδασκομένους

Delimit justice by law, convince by reason; and observe these by submitting to the sovereignty of the law and the commands of reason.

*Funeral Oration** 2.19

2 τὸν εὐκλεᾶ θάνατον ἀθάνατον περὶ τῶν ἀγαθῶν καταλείπειν λόγον

A glorious death commits to eternity an account of deeds well done.

*Funeral Oration** 2.23

3 τῶν αὐτῶν ἐστιν αὐτούς τε πάντα τὰ κακὰ ἐργάζεσθαι καὶ τοὺς τοιούτους ἐπαινεῖν

It is natural for those who commit all sorts of offences to praise others like them.

Translated by Stephen Charles Todd (2000)

Against Eratosthenes 12.41

4 ἀκηκόατε, ἑοράκατε, πεπόνθατε, ἔχετε· δικάζετε

You have heard, you have seen, you have suffered; you have them: give judgement.

Translated by W.R.M. Lamb (1930)

Against Eratosthenes 12.100

closing lines

5 πολίτου χρηστοῦ καὶ δικαστοῦ δικαίου ἔργον εἶναι ταύτῃ τοὺς νόμους διαλαμβάνειν, ὅπῃ εἰς τὸν λοιπὸν χρόνον μέλλει συνοίσειν τῇ πόλει

It is the duty alike of a loyal citizen and of a just juror to handle laws in such a way as to benefit the city in the future.

Against Alcibiades 1 14.4

6 οὐ περὶ πολιτείας εἰσὶν αἱ πρὸς ἀλλήλους διαφοραί, ἀλλὰ περὶ τῶν ἰδίᾳ συμφερόντων ἑκάστῳ

The questions dividing men are concerned, not with politics, but with their personal advantage.

Translated by W.R.M. Lamb (1930)

Subverting the Democracy 25.10

7 μήτηρ, ἣ πέφυκε καὶ ἀδικουμένη ὑπὸ τῶν ἑαυτῆς παίδων μάλιστα ἀνέχεσθαι

A mother is willing to accept an injury even at the hands of her own children.

Against Philon 31.22

8 ψεύδεσθαι προχειρότατον τοῖς πολλάκις ἁμαρτάνουσιν

Lying comes readily to repetitive wrongdoers.

Fragment 423 (Carey)

9 τὴν αὐτὴν γνώμην ἔχειν δικάζοντας ἄξιον, ἥνπερ νομοθετοῦντας

It is imperative that judges and lawmakers think alike.

Fragment 424 (Carey)

M

MARCUS ARGENTARIUS

1st century AD

Epigrammatist included in the *Garland of Philippus*

1 Ποιεῖς πάντα, Μέλισσα, φιλανθέος ἔργα μελίσσης …
καὶ μέλι μὲν στάζεις ὑπὸ χείλεσιν ἡδὺ φιλεῦσα,
ἢν δ' αἰτῇς, κέντρῳ τύμμα φέρεις ἄδικον.

As your name has it, Melissa, you do as the bee
Honey drips from your lips when you kiss,
but when you ask me to pay for it,
the sting is as unjust as a hornet's.

Translated by Edmund Keeley (2010)

Greek Anthology 5.32

'melissa' is the Greek word for bee

MARCUS AURELIUS

121–180AD

Roman emperor, 161–180AD

see also Anonymous 57

1 ὅ τί ποτε τοῦτό εἰμι, σαρκία ἐστὶ καὶ πνευμάτιον καὶ τὸ ἡγεμονικόν

This being of mine, whatever it really is, consists of a little flesh, a little breath, and reason.

Translated by Morris Hicky Morgan (1859–1910)

Τὰ εἰς ἑαυτόν 2.2

ἡγεμονικὸν is the part which governs, or 'reason' in Stoic philosophy

2 μέμνησο ἐκ πόσου ταῦτα ἀναβάλλῃ καὶ ὁποσάκις προθεσμίας λαβὼν παρὰ τῶν θεῶν οὐ χρᾷ αὐταῖς

Remember how often you have postponed minding your interest, and let slip those opportunities the gods have given you.

Translated in *The New Penguin Dictionary of Quotations* (2006)

Τὰ εἰς ἑαυτόν 2.4

3 δεῖ δὲ ἤδη ποτὲ αἰσθέσθαι … ὅτι ὅρος ἐστί σοι περιγεγραμμένος τοῦ χρόνου, ᾧ ἐὰν εἰς τὸ ἀπαιθριάσαι μὴ χρήσῃ, οἰχήσεται καὶ οἰχήσῃ καὶ αὖθις οὐκ ἔξεσται

It is now high time to consider that you have a set period assigned you to act in, and unless you improve it to brighten and compose your thoughts, it will quickly run off with you, and be lost beyond recovery.

Translated in *The New Penguin Dictionary of Quotations* (2006)

Τὰ εἰς ἑαυτόν 2.4

4 ἂν ὡς ἐσχάτην τοῦ βίου ἑκάστην πρᾶξιν ἐνεργῇς

Perform every act in life as if it were your last.

Τὰ εἰς ἑαυτόν 2.5

5 μέμνησο ὅτι οὐδεὶς ἄλλον ἀποβάλλει βίον ἢ τοῦτον ὃν ζῇ, οὐδὲ ἄλλον ζῇ ἢ ὃν ἀποβάλλει

Remember that no man loses another life than that which he lives, nor lives another than that which he loses.

Translated by Morris Hicky Morgan (1859–1910)

Τὰ εἰς ἑαυτόν 2.14

6 πάντα ἐξ ἀιδίου ὁμοειδῆ καὶ ἀνακυκλούμενα

All things, from time everlasting, are cast in the same mould and are repeated cycle after cycle.

Τὰ εἰς ἑαυτόν 2.14

7 ὁ πολυχρονιώτατος καὶ ὁ τάχιστα τεθνηξόμενος τὸ ἴσον ἀποβάλλει

The longest-lived and the shortest-lived man, when they come to die, lose one and the same thing.

Translated by Morris Hicky Morgan (1859–1910)

Τὰ εἰς ἑαυτόν 2.14

8 ὁ δὲ βίος πόλεμος καὶ ξένου ἐπιδημία, ἡ δὲ ὑστεροφημία λήθη

As for life, it is a battle and a sojourning in a strange land; but the fame after death is oblivion.

Τὰ εἰς ἑαυτόν 2.17

9 ὀρθὸν οὖν εἶναι χρή, οὐχὶ ὀρθούμενον

A man should be upright, not be kept upright.

Translated by Morris Hicky Morgan (1859–1910)

Τὰ εἰς ἑαυτόν 3.5

10 μὴ τιμήσῃς ποτὲ ὡς συμφέρον σεαυτοῦ, ὃ ἀναγκάσει σέ ποτε τὴν πίστιν παραβῆναι, τὴν αἰδῶ ἐγκαταλιπεῖν

Never consider anything to your advantage if it makes you break your word or lose your self-respect.

Τὰ εἰς ἑαυτόν 3.7

11 ὥσπερ οἱ ἰατροὶ ἀεὶ τὰ ὄργανα καὶ σιδήρια πρόχειρα ἔχουσι πρὸς τὰ αἰφνίδια τῶν θεραπευμάτων, οὕτω τὰ δόγματα σὺ ἕτοιμα ἔχε

As surgeons always have their implements and instruments at hand for an operation or an emergency, so must you have your precepts in readiness.

Translated by H.T. Riley (1872)

Τὰ εἰς ἑαυτόν 3.13

12 οὐδαμοῦ γὰρ οὔτε ἡσυχιώτερον οὔτε ἀπραγμονέστερον ἄνθρωπος ἀναχωρεῖ ἢ εἰς τὴν ἑαυτοῦ ψυχήν

Nowhere can man find a quieter or more untroubled retreat than in his own soul.

Translated by Maxwell Staniforth (1964)

Τὰ εἰς ἑαυτόν 4.3

13 τὴν δὲ εὐμάρειαν οὐδὲν ἄλλο λέγω ἢ εὐκοσμίαν

By a tranquil mind I mean nothing else than a mind well ordered.

Translated by Morris Hicky Morgan (1859–1910)

Τὰ εἰς ἑαυτόν 4.3

14 ὁ κόσμος ὡσανεὶ πόλις ἐστί· τίνος γὰρ ἄλλου φήσει τις τὸ τῶν ἀνθρώπων πᾶν γένος κοινοῦ πολιτεύματος μετέχειν; ἐκεῖθεν δέ, ἐκ τῆς κοινῆς ταύτης πόλεως

The world is as a city. How else could the whole of mankind participate in such a common state, in such a world-city?

Τὰ εἰς ἑαυτόν 4.4

15 οὐδὲν γὰρ ἐκ τοῦ μηδενὸς ἔρχεται

Nothing comes of nothing.

Τὰ εἰς ἑαυτόν 4.4

16 ὁ θάνατος τοιοῦτον, οἷον γένεσις, φύσεως μυστήριον

Death, like birth, is one of the mysteries of nature.

Τὰ εἰς ἑαυτόν 4.5

17 πᾶν τὸ συμβαῖνον δικαίως συμβαίνει· ὃ ἐὰν ἀκριβῶς παραφυλάσσῃς, εὑρήσεις

Whatever happens, happens justly; you will find this true if you watch closely.

Τὰ εἰς ἑαυτόν 4.10

cf. John Dryden, Oedipus, *Act III: 'Whatever is, is in its cause just'*

18 μὴ ὡς μύρια μέλλων ἔτη ζῆν· τὸ χρεὼν ἐπήρτηται· ἕως ζῇς, ἕως ἔξεστιν, ἀγαθὸς γενοῦ

Do not act as if thou wert to live ten thousand years; death hangs over thee; while thou livest, while it is in thy power, be good.

Translated by George Long (1800–1879)

Τὰ εἰς ἑαυτόν 4.17

19 ὅσην εὐσχολίαν κερδαίνει ὁ μὴ βλέπων τί ὁ πλησίον εἶπεν ἢ ἔπραξεν ἢ διενοήθη, ἀλλὰ μόνον τί αὐτὸς ποιεῖ, ἵνα αὐτὸ τοῦτο δίκαιον ᾖ καὶ ὅσιον

How much time he gains who does not look to see what his neighbour says or does or thinks, but only at what he does himself, to make it just and holy.

Translated by Morris Hicky Morgan (1859–1910)

Τὰ εἰς ἑαυτόν 4.18

20 πᾶν τὸ καὶ ὁπωσοῦν καλὸν ἐξ ἑαυτοῦ καλόν ἐστι καὶ ἐφ' ἑαυτὸ καταλήγει

Whatever is in any way beautiful hath its source of beauty in itself, and is complete in itself.

Translated by Morris Hicky Morgan (1859–1910)

Τὰ εἰς ἑαυτόν 4.20

21 πᾶν μοι συναρμόζει ὃ σοὶ εὐάρμοστόν ἐστιν, ὦ κόσμε· οὐδέν μοι πρόωρον οὐδὲ ὄψιμον ὃ σοὶ εὔκαιρον

All that is harmony for you, my Universe, is in harmony with me as well. Nothing that comes at the right time for you is not too late for me.

Translated by Morris Hicky Morgan (1859–1910)

Τὰ εἰς ἑαυτόν 4.23

22 πᾶν μοι καρπὸς ὃ φέρουσιν αἱ σαὶ ὧραι, ὦ φύσις· ἐκ σοῦ πάντα, ἐν σοὶ πάντα, εἰς σὲ πάντα

Everything is fruit to me that your seasons, Nature, bring. All things come of you, have their being in you, and return to you.

Translated by Morris Hicky Morgan (1859–1910)

Τὰ εἰς ἑαυτόν 4.23

23 ὀλίγα πρῆσσε, φησίν, εἰ μέλλεις εὐθυμήσειν

Let your occupations be few, says the sage, if you would be of good cheer.

Τὰ εἰς ἑαυτόν 4.24

quoting Democritus, Fragment 3 (D-K)

24 τὸ τεχνίον ὃ ἔμαθες φίλει, τούτῳ προσαναπαύου

Love the trade which you have learned, and be content with it.

Translated by Morris Hicky Morgan (1859–1910)

Τὰ εἰς ἑαυτόν 4.31

25 ἡ ἐπιστροφὴ καθ' ἑκάστην πρᾶξιν ἰδίαν ἀξίαν ἔχει καὶ συμμετρίαν

There is a proper dignity and proportion to be observed in the performance of every act of life.

Translated by Morris Hicky Morgan (1859–1910)

Τὰ εἰς ἑαυτόν 4.32

26 πᾶν ἐφήμερον, καὶ τὸ μνημονεῦον καὶ τὸ μνημονευόμενον

All is ephemeral – fame and the famous as well.

Translated by Morris Hicky Morgan (1859–1910)

Τὰ εἰς σεαυτόν 4.35

27 τὰ ἡγεμονικὰ αὐτῶν διάβλεπε καὶ τοὺς φρονίμους, οἷα μὲν φεύγουσιν, οἷα δὲ διώκουσιν

Perceive men's governing principles, and consider the wise, what they shun and what they cleave to.

Translated by Morris Hicky Morgan (1859–1910)

Τὰ εἰς ἑαυτόν 4.38

28 ποταμός τίς ἐστι τῶν γινομένων καὶ ῥεῦμα βίαιον ὁ αἰών· ἅμα τε γὰρ ὤφθη ἕκαστον, καὶ παρενήνεκται καὶ ἄλλο παραφέρεται, τὸ δὲ ἐνεχθήσεται

Time is a sort of river of passing events, and strong is its current; no sooner is a thing brought to sight than it is swept by and another takes its place, and this too will be swept away.

Translated by Morris Hicky Morgan (1859–1910)

Τὰ εἰς ἑαυτόν 4.43

29 πᾶν τὸ συμβαῖνον οὕτως σύνηθες καὶ γνώριμον ὡς τὸ ῥόδον ἐν τῷ ἔαρι καὶ ὀπώρα ἐν τῷ θέρει

Whatever happens is as usual and familiar, as the rose in spring and the harvest in summer.

Τὰ εἰς ἑαυτόν 4.44

30 τὸ γὰρ ὅλον, κατιδεῖν ἀεὶ τὰ ἀνθρώπινα ὡς ἐφήμερα καὶ εὐτελῆ καὶ ἐχθὲς μὲν μυξάριον, αὔριον δὲ τάριχος ἢ τέφρα· τὸ

ἀκαριαῖον οὖν τοῦτο τοῦ χρόνου κατὰ φύσιν διελθεῖν καὶ ἵλεων καταλῦσαι, ὡς ἂν εἰ ἐλαία πέπειρος γενομένη ἔπιπτεν, εὐφημοῦσα τὴν ἐνεγκοῦσαν καὶ χάριν εἰδυῖα τῷ φύσαντι δένδρῳ

Mark how fleeting and paltry is the estate of man, yesterday in infancy, tomorrow embalmed or in ashes. For the hairsbreadth of time assigned to thee, live rationally, and part with life gracefully, as a ripe olive falls, blessing the season that bore it and thanking the tree that gave it life.

Τὰ εἰς ἑαυτόν 4.48

31 ὅμοιον εἶναι τῇ ἄκρᾳ, ᾗ διηνεκῶς τὰ κύματα προσρήσσεται· ἡ δὲ ἕστηκε καὶ περὶ αὐτὴν κοιμίζεται τὰ φλεγμήναντα τοῦ ὕδατος

Be like a headland of rock on which the waves break incessantly; but it stands fast and around it the seething of the waters sinks to rest.

Translated by C.R. Haines (1916)

Τὰ εἰς ἑαυτόν 4.49

32 ὄρθρου, ὅταν δυσόκνως ἐξεγείρῃ, πρόχειρον ἔστω ὅτι ἐπὶ ἀνθρώπου ἔργον ἐγείρομαι

In the morning, when you are sluggish about getting up, let this thought be present: 'I am rising to a man's work.'

Translated by Morris Hicky Morgan (1859–1910)

Τὰ εἰς ἑαυτόν 5.1

33 ἄνθρωπος δ' εὖ ποιήσας οὐκ ἐπιβοᾶται, ἀλλὰ μεταβαίνει ἐφ' ἕτερον, ὡς ἄμπελος ἐπὶ τὸ πάλιν ἐν τῇ ὥρᾳ τὸν βότρυν ἐνεγκεῖν

A man does not proclaim a good deed, but proceeds to another, as a vine bears grapes again in season.

Τὰ εἰς ἑαυτόν 5.6

34 μὴ σικχαίνειν μηδὲ ἀπαυδᾶν μηδὲ ἀποδυσπετεῖν, εἰ μὴ καταπυκνοῦταί σοι τὸ ἀπὸ δογμάτων ὀρθῶν ἕκαστα πράσσειν· ἀλλὰ ἐκκρουσθέντα πάλιν ἐπανιέναι καὶ ἀσμενίζειν, εἰ τὰ πλείω ἀνθρωπικώτερα, καὶ φιλεῖν τοῦτο, ἐφ' ὃ ἐπανέρχῃ

Be not disgusted, nor discouraged, nor dissatisfied, if you do not succeed in doing everything according to right principles; but when you have failed, return back again, and be content if the greater part of what you do is consistent with man's nature, and love this to which you return.

Translated by George Long (1800–1879)

Τὰ εἰς ἑαυτόν 5.9

35 τὸ ἄρα ἀγαθὸν τοῦ λογικοῦ ζῴου κοινωνία

A logical animal can only be a social animal.

Τὰ εἰς ἑαυτόν 5.16

36 οὐδὲν οὐδενὶ συμβαίνει ὃ οὐχὶ πέφυκε φέρειν

Nothing befalls anyone that he is not fitted by nature to bear.

Translated by C.R. Haines (1916)

Τὰ εἰς ἑαυτόν 5.18

37 συζῆν θεοῖς

Walk with the gods.

Translated by C.R. Haines (1916)

Τὰ εἰς ἑαυτόν 5.27

38 ἔσω βλέπε· μηδενὸς πράγματος μήτε ἡ ἰδία ποιότης μήτε ἡ ἀξία παρατρεχέτω σε

Look within; let neither quality nor value go by unnoticed

Τὰ εἰς ἑαυτόν 6.3

39 ὁ διοικῶν λόγος οἶδε πῶς διακείμενος καὶ τί ποιεῖ καὶ ἐπὶ τίνος ὕλης

Controlling reason knows its own disposition, what it does, and on what material it works.

Τὰ εἰς ἑαυτόν 6.5

40 κατὰ τὴν συνουσίαν ἐντερίου παράτριψις καὶ μετά τινος σπασμοῦ μυξαρίου ἔκκρισις

Sexual intercourse is merely internal attrition and the spasmodic excretion of mucus.

Translated by C.R. Haines (1916)

Τὰ εἰς ἑαυτόν 6.13

41 μή, εἴ τι αὐτῷ σοὶ δυσκαταπόνητον, τοῦτο ἀνθρώπῳ ἀδύνατον ὑπολαμβάνειν· ἀλλ' εἴ τι ἀνθρώπῳ δυνατὸν καὶ οἰκεῖον, τοῦτο καὶ σεαυτῷ ἐφικτὸν νόμιζε

Do not consider impossible what is merely difficult; whatever is humanly possible is within your reach.

Τὰ εἰς ἑαυτόν 6.19

42 ὅρα μὴ ἀποκαισαρωθῇς, μὴ βαφῇς

Beware of being Caesarified, be not stained by desire for power.

Τὰ εἰς ἑαυτόν 6.30

43 τήρησον οὖν σεαυτὸν ἁπλοῦν, ἀγαθόν, ἀκέραιον, σεμνόν, ἄκομψον, τοῦ δικαίου φίλον, θεοσεβῆ, εὐμενῆ, φιλόστοργον, ἐρρωμένον πρὸς τὰ πρέποντα ἔργα

Keep yourself simple, gentle, pure, unassuming, unadorned, loving justice, fearing god, kindly and affectionate, steady in your duties.

Τὰ εἰς ἑαυτόν 6.30

44 πᾶν πέλαγος σταγὼν τοῦ κόσμου

Every ocean is but a drop in the universe

Τὰ εἰς ἑαυτόν 6.36

45 πᾶν τὸ ἐνεστὼς τοῦ χρόνου στιγμὴ τοῦ αἰῶνος· πάντα μικρά, εὔτρεπτα, ἐναφανιζόμενα

Every instant of time is a tiny portion of eternity; all things are petty, easily changed, vanishing away.

Τὰ εἰς ἑαυτόν 6.36

46 ὁ τὰ νῦν ἰδὼν πάντα ἑώρακεν, ὅσα τε ἐξ ἀιδίου ἐγένετο καὶ ὅσα εἰς τὸ ἄπειρον ἔσται

He who sees what is now has seen all things, whatever comes from time everlasting and whatever shall be unto everlasting time.

Τὰ εἰς ἑαυτόν 6.37

47 πάντες εἰς ἓν ἀποτέλεσμα συνεργοῦμεν, οἱ μὲν εἰδότως καὶ παρακολουθητικῶς, οἱ δὲ ἀνεπιστάτως ... λοιπὸν οὖν σύνες εἰς τίνας ἑαυτὸν κατατάσσεις

We combine our efforts towards a common cause, some consciously, some randomly; decide where you classify yourself.

Τὰ εἰς ἑαυτόν 6.42

48 τὸ τῷ σμήνει μὴ συμφέρον οὐδὲ τῇ μελίσσῃ συμφέρει

What does not benefit the hive does not benefit the bee.

Translated by R.B. Rutherford (2003)

Τὰ εἰς ἑαυτόν 6.54

49 τοσούτου ἄξιος ἕκαστός ἐστιν, ὅσου ἄξιά ἐστι ταῦτα περὶ ἃ ἐσπούδακεν

Each man is as worthy as his endeavours are worthy.

Τὰ εἰς ἑαυτόν 7.3

50 κόσμος τε γὰρ εἷς ἐξ ἁπάντων καὶ θεὸς εἷς δι' ἁπάντων καὶ οὐσία μία καὶ νόμος εἷς, λόγος κοινὸς πάντων τῶν νοερῶν ζῴων, καὶ ἀλήθεια μία

There is one universe made up of all that is; and one god in it all, and one principle of being, and one law, one reason shared by all thinking creatures, and one truth.

Translated by Morris Hicky Morgan (1859–1910)

Τὰ εἰς ἑαυτόν 7.9

51 ἐγγὺς μὲν ἡ σὴ περὶ πάντων λήθη· ἐγγὺς δὲ ἡ πάντων περὶ σοῦ λήθη

Near is thy forgetfulness of all things; and near the forgetfulness of thee by all.

Translated by George Long (1800–1879)

Τὰ εἰς ἑαυτόν 7.21

52 ἴδιον ἀνθρώπου φιλεῖν καὶ τοὺς πταίοντας

It is peculiar to man to love even those who do wrong.

Translated by George Long (1800–1879)

Τὰ εἰς ἑαυτόν 7.22

53 ἔνδον σκάπτε, ἔνδον ἡ πηγὴ τοῦ ἀγαθοῦ καὶ ἀεὶ ἀναβλύειν δυναμένη, ἐὰν ἀεὶ σκάπτῃς

Search inside yourself; inside you is the fountain of goodness, and it continues to surge as long as you search.

Τὰ εἰς ἑαυτόν 7.59

54 ἐν ὀλιγίστοις κεῖται τὸ εὐδαιμόνως βιῶσαι

Very little is needed to make a happy life.

Translated by Morris Hicky Morgan (1859–1910)

Τὰ εἰς ἑαυτόν 7.67

55 τὸ μετατίθεσθαι καὶ ἕπεσθαι τῷ διορθοῦντι ὁμοίως ἐλεύθερόν ἐστι

To change your opinion and to follow him who corrects your error is equally consistent with freedom as it is to persist in your error.

Τὰ εἰς ἑαυτόν 8.16

56 ἔξω τοῦ κόσμου τὸ ἀποθανὸν οὐ πίπτει

Whatever dies is not lost to the universe.

Τὰ εἰς ἑαυτόν 8.18

57 πρόσεχε τῷ ὑποκειμένῳ ἢ τῇ ἐνεργείᾳ ἢ τῷ δόγματι ἢ τῷ σημαινομένῳ

Look to the essence of a thing, whether it be a point of doctrine, of practice, or of interpretation.

Translated by Morris Hicky Morgan (1859–1910)

Τὰ εἰς ἑαυτόν 8.22

58 μήτε ἐν ταῖς πράξεσιν ἐπισύρειν μήτε ἐν ταῖς ὁμιλίαις φύρειν μήτε ἐν ταῖς φαντασίαις ἀλᾶσθαι

Be not careless in deeds, nor confused in words, nor rambling in thought.

Translated by Morris Hicky Morgan (1859–1910)

Τὰ εἰς ἑαυτόν 8.51

59 οἱ ἄνθρωποι γεγόνασιν ἀλλήλων ἕνεκεν· ἢ δίδασκε οὖν ἢ φέρε

Men were created for one another; either teach them, or endure them.

Τὰ εἰς ἑαυτόν 8.59

60 μὴ καταφρόνει θανάτου, ἀλλὰ εὐαρέστει αὐτῷ, ὡς καὶ τούτου ἑνὸς ὄντος ὧν ἡ φύσις ἐθέλει

Do not despise death, but accept it willingly; look upon it as part of nature.

Translated in *The New Penguin Dictionary of Quotations* (2006)

Τὰ εἰς ἑαυτόν 9.3

61 ἀδικεῖ πολλάκις ὁ μὴ ποιῶν τι, οὐ μόνον ὁ ποιῶν τι

One may often injure by omission, not only by action.

Τὰ εἰς ἑαυτόν 9.5

62 ἐξαλεῖψαι φαντασίαν· στῆσαι ὁρμήν· σβέσαι ὄρεξιν· ἐφ' ἑαυτῷ ἔχειν τὸ ἡγεμονικόν

Blot out vain pomp; check impulse; quench appetite; keep reason under its own control.

Translated by Morris Hicky Morgan (1859–1910)

Τὰ εἰς ἑαυτόν 9.7

63 πάντα ταὐτά· συνήθη μὲν τῇ πείρᾳ, ἐφήμερα δὲ τῷ χρόνῳ, ῥυπαρὰ δὲ τῇ ὕλῃ· πάντα νῦν οἷα ἐπ' ἐκείνων οὓς κατεθάψαμεν

All things are the same; familiar in experience, ephemeral in time, coarse in substance. All things now are as they were in the day of those whom we have buried.

Τὰ εἰς ἑαυτόν 9.14

64 μέτιθι νῦν ἐπὶ ἡλικίαν, οἷον τὴν παιδικήν, τὴν τοῦ μειρακίου, τὴν νεότητα, τὸ γῆρας· καὶ γὰρ τούτων πᾶσα μεταβολή, θάνατος· μήτι δεινόν;

Look back at the phases of your own life: childhood, boyhood, youth, age: each change itself a kind of death. Was this so frightening?

Translated by Maxwell Staniforth (1964)

Τὰ εἰς ἑαυτόν 9.21

65 δόγμα γὰρ αὐτῶν τίς μεταβαλεῖ;

Who will change men's convictions?

Translated by R.B. Rutherford (2003)

Τὰ εἰς ἑαυτόν 9.29

66 ὅταν τινὸς ἀναισχυντίᾳ προσκόπτῃς, εὐθὺς πυνθάνου σεαυτοῦ· δύνανται οὖν ἐν τῷ κόσμῳ ἀναίσχυντοι μὴ εἶναι; οὐ δύνανται· μὴ οὖν ἀπαίτει τὸ ἀδύνατον

When affronted by the shamelessness of others, ask yourself whether a world could exist without shameless men; do not expect, then, what is impossible.

Τὰ εἰς ἑαυτόν 9.42

67 ὅ τι ἄν σοι συμβαίνῃ, τοῦτό σοι ἐξ αἰῶνος προκατεσκευάζετο· καὶ ἡ ἐπιπλοκὴ τῶν αἰτίων συνέκλωθε τὴν σὴν ὑπόστασιν ἐξ ἀιδίου

Whatever may befall you was preordained, and the thread of causes was spinning for you from time everlasting.

Τὰ εἰς ἑαυτόν 10.5

68 ᾧ μὴ εἷς καὶ ὁ αὐτός ἐστιν ἀεὶ τοῦ βίου σκοπός, οὗτος εἷς καὶ ὁ αὐτὸς δι' ὅλου τοῦ βίου εἶναι οὐ δύναται

He who does not keep one and the same object in view through life, cannot be one and the same person throughout life.

Translated by H.T. Riley (1872)

Τὰ εἰς ἑαυτόν 11.21

69 ἡ συγγένεια ἀνθρώπου πρὸς πᾶν τὸ ἀνθρώπειον γένος, οὐ γὰρ αἱματίου ἢ σπερματίου, ἀλλὰ νοῦ κοινωνία

Man is related to all mankind, not through blood and sperm, but through the spirit.

Τὰ εἰς ἑαυτόν 12.26

70 ἄνθρωπε, ἐπολιτεύσω ἐν τῇ μεγάλῃ ταύτῃ πόλει· τί σοι διαφέρει, εἰ πέντε ἔτεσιν ἢ πεντήκοντα;

Man, you have been a citizen in this world city; what does it matter whether for five years or fifty?

Translated in *The Oxford Dictionary of Quotations* (2004)

Τὰ εἰς ἑαυτόν 12.36

MAXIMUS

2nd century AD

Philosopher from Tyre

1 καὶ ἐστὶν καὶ ὁ ἄρχων πόλεως μέρος, καὶ οἱ ἀρχόμενοι παραπλησίως

The ruler is as much a part of the state as those who are ruled.

Translated by H.T. Riley (1872)

Lectures 7.2a

MELEAGER

fl. 100BC

Greek poet and philosopher from Gadara in Syria

1 Ἰξὸν ἔχεις τὸ φίλημα, τὰ δ᾽ ὄμματα, Τιμάριον, πῦρ·
ἢν ἐσίδῃς, καίεις· ἢν δὲ θίγῃς, δέδεκας.

Birdlime is your kiss, Timarion, your eyes are fire;
look at me and it burns, touch me and you've caught me fast.

Greek Anthology 5.96

2 Ὁ στέφανος περὶ κρατὶ μαραίνεται Ἡλιοδώρας·
αὐτὴ δ᾽ ἐκλάμπει τοῦ στεφάνου στέφανος.

The garland withers round Heliodora's head;
but she shines out, the garland of the garland.

Translated by J.W. MacKail (1890)

Greek Anthology 5.143

3 Ἤδη λευκόϊον θάλλει, θάλλει δὲ φίλομβρος
νάρκισσος, θάλλει δ᾽ οὐρεσίφοιτα κρίνα·
ἤδη δ᾽ ἡ φιλέραστος, ἐν ἄνθεσιν ὥριμον ἄνθος,
Ζηνοφίλα Πειθοῦς ἡδὺ τέθηλε ῥόδον.

The white violet is in flower now, and lover-of-rain narcissus, and the hillside lilies; so is Zenophila in bloom now, lovers' darling, rose of inducement, flower of the flowers of spring.

Greek Anthology 5.144

4 Ὀξυβόαι κώνωπες, ἀναιδέες αἵματος ἀνδρῶν
σίφωνες, νυκτὸς κνώδαλα διπτέρυγα

Ye shrill-voiced mosquitoes, ye shameless pack,
suckers of men's blood, night's winged beasts of prey.

Translated by W.R. Paton (1916)

Greek Anthology 5.151

5 Κῦμα τὸ πικρὸν Ἔρωτος, ἀκοίμητοί τε πνέοντες
ζῆλοι, καὶ κώμων χειμέριον πέλαγος,
ποῖ φέρομαι; πάντῃ δὲ φρενῶν οἴακες ἀφεῖνται.

Bitter waves of love, sleepless nights of jealousy,
and this winter sea of reveling,
where are you taking me? My rudder is totally out of control.

Translated by Edmund Keeley (2010)

Greek Anthology 5.190

6 Ἐντὸς ἐμῆς κραδίης τὴν εὔλαλον Ἡλιοδώραν
ψυχὴν τῆς ψυχῆς αὐτὸς ἔπλασεν Ἔρως.

Within my heart is sweet-spoken Heliodora,
soul of my soul, moulded by Eros himself.

Greek Anthology 5.155

7 Ἁ φίλερως χαροποῖς Ἀσκληπιὰς οἷα γαλήνης
ὄμμασι συμπείθει πάντας ἐρωτοπλοεῖν.

Asclepias loves to love. With looks that please
She charms all comers to sail on her love's tranquil seas.

Translated by Jonathan Williams and Clive Cheesman (2004)

Greek Anthology 5.156

8 Αἰεί μοι δινεῖ μὲν ἐν οὔασιν ἦχος Ἔρωτος,
ὄμμα δὲ σῖγα Πόθοις τὸ γλυκὺ δάκρυ φέρει·
οὐδ' ἡ νύξ, οὐ φέγγος ἐκοίμισεν, ἀλλ' ὑπὸ φίλτρων
ἤδη που κραδίᾳ γνωστὸς ἔνεστι τύπος.
ὦ πτανοί, μὴ καί ποτ' ἐφίπτασθαι μέν, Ἔρωτες,
οἴδατ', ἀποπτῆναι δ' οὐδ' ὅσον ἰσχύετε;

The sound of Love is ever in my ears,
and my eye carries in silence a sweet tear to Desire.
Neither night nor day is love at rest, and the spell
has already set its well-known imprint on my heart.
O winged Loves, how is it that you fly towards me,
but have no whit of strength to fly away?

Greek Anthology 5.212

9 ὄφρα ... μεσημβρινὸν ὕπνον ἀγρεύσω

So that I may snatch a midday siesta!

Greek Anthology 7.196

10 εἰ δὲ Σύρος, τί τὸ θαῦμα; μίαν, ξένε, πατρίδα κόσμον
ναίομεν, ἓν θνατοὺς πάντας ἔτικτε Χάος

So what if I am Syrian! Stranger, marvel not!
One is our country, one our world, all of us born of Chaos.

Greek Anthology 7.417

11 Ματρὸς ἔτ' ἐν κόλποισιν ὁ νήπιος ὀρθρινὰ παίζων
ἀστραγάλοις τοὐμὸν πνεῦμ' ἐκύβευσεν Ἔρως.

Eros, a mere child in his mother's lap,
played away my soul this morning, cheating at dice.

Greek Anthology 12.47

12 Ἢν ἐνίδω Θήρωνα, τὰ πάνθ' ὁρῶ· ἢν δὲ τὰ πάντα
βλέψω, τόνδε δὲ μή, τἄμπαλιν οὐδὲν ὁρῶ.

If I see Thero, I see everything; yet if everything
is in my sight but Thero, there's nothing for me to see.

Greek Anthology 12.60

13 Ἠοῦς ἄγγελε, χαῖρε, Φαεσφόρε, καὶ ταχὺς ἔλθοις
Ἕσπερος, ἣν ἀπάγεις, λάθριος αὖθις ἄγων.

Farewell, Morning Star, herald of dawn,
and quickly return as the Evening Star,
bringing again in secret her whom thou
takest away.

Translated by J.W. MacKail (1890)
Greek Anthology 12.114

14 Κύπρις ἐμοὶ ναύκληρος, Ἔρως δ' οἴακα φυλάσσει
ἄκρον ἔχων ψυχῆς ἐν χερὶ πηδάλιον

Cypris is my skipper and Eros keeps the tiller,
holding in his hands the rudder of my soul.

Greek Anthology 12.157
Aphrodite (Cypris) as the goddess of love

15 Ἐν σοὶ τἀμά ... βίου πρυμνήσι' ἀνῆπται·
ἐν σοὶ καὶ ψυχῆς πνεῦμα τὸ λειφθὲν ἔτι.
ναὶ γὰρ δὴ τὰ σά, κοῦρε, τὰ καὶ κωφοῖσι λαλεῦντα
ὄμματα, ναὶ μὰ τὸ σὸν φαιδρὸν ἐπισκύνιον,
ἤν μοι συννεφὲς ὄμμα βάλῃς ποτέ, χεῖμα δέδορκα·
ἢν δ' ἱλαρὸν βλέψῃς, ἡδὺ τέθηλεν ἔαρ.

On thee the cables of my life are fastened;
in thee is the very breath of my soul, what is left of it.
For by thine eyes, O boy, that speak even to the deaf,
and by thy shining brow, if thou ever dost cast
a clouded glance on me, I gaze on winter;
but if thy look is merry, sweet spring bursts into bloom.

Translated by J.W. MacKail (1890)
Greek Anthology 12.159

MELISSUS

5th century BC
Admiral and philosopher from Samos, defeated the Athenians in 441BC

1 ἀεὶ ἦν ὅ τι ἦν καὶ ἀεὶ ἔσται· εἰ γὰρ ἐγένετο, ἀναγκαῖόν ἐστι πρὶν γενέσθαι εἶναι μηδέν· εἰ τοίνυν μηδὲν ἦν, οὐδαμὰ ἂν γένοιτο οὐδὲν ἐκ μηδενός

That which was, was always and always

will be. For if it had come into being, it necessarily follows that before it came into being nothing existed. If nothing existed, in no way could anything come into being out of nothing.

Translated by Kathleen Freeman (1948)

Fragment 1 (D-K)

2 τοῦ γὰρ ἐόντος ἀληθινοῦ κρεῖσσον οὐδέν

Nothing is stronger than what is true.

Translated by Jonathan Barnes (1987)

Fragment 8.30 (D-K)

MENANDER

c.342–*c*.292BC

Athenian New Comedy poet

see also Anonymous 44

1 Κνήμων, ἀπάνθρωπός τις ἄνθρωπος σφόδρα
καὶ δύσκολος πρὸς ἅπαντας, οὐ χαίρων τ' ὄχλῳ

Cnemon, an old man
Who prefers his own to anyone else's company;
Surly-tempered to everybody, detesting crowds.

Translated by Philip Vellacott (1960)

Dyskolos – The Peevish Fellow, or The Bad-Tempered Man 6

2 τὸ μὲν βραδύνειν γὰρ τὸν ἔρωτ' αὔξει πολύ,
ἐν τῷ ταχέως δ' ἔνεστι παύσασθαι ταχύ

The longer he waits, you see, the more he falls in love;
While if he enjoys her soon he soon gets over it.

Translated by Philip Vellacott (1960)

Dyskolos – The Peevish Fellow, or The Bad-Tempered Man 62

3 ἐρημίας οὐκ ἔστιν οὐδαμοῦ τυχεῖν,
οὐδ' ἂν ἀπάγξασθαί τις ἐπιθυμῶν τύχῃ

Nowhere can a man find privacy,
Not even if he wants to hang himself!

Dyskolos – The Peevish Fellow, or The Bad-Tempered Man 169

4 οὐδὲ εἷς
μάγειρον ἀδικήσας ἀθῷος διέφυγεν

No one can wrong
A cook and get away scot-free.

Translated by Maurice Balme (2001)

Dyskolos – The Peevish Fellow, or The Bad-Tempered Man 644

5 περὶ χρημάτων λαλεῖς, ἀβεβαίου πράγματος

You babble about money, a matter insecure.

Translated by Francis G. Allinson (1921)

Dyskolos – The Peevish Fellow, or The Bad-Tempered Man 797

6 πολλῷ δὲ κρεῖττόν ἐστιν ἐμφανὴς φίλος
ἢ πλοῦτος ἀφανής, ὃν σὺ κατορύξας ἔχεις

A friend for everyone to see is worth far more
than wealth which you keep buried out of sight.

Dyskolos – The Peevish Fellow, or The Bad-Tempered Man 811

a play on ἐμφανὴς and ἀφανής, a distinction in Athenian law between 'visible' and 'invisible' property

7 ἁλωτὰ γίνετ' ἐπιμελείᾳ καὶ πόνῳ ἅπαντα

Everything is achieved by diligence and toil.

Dyskolos – The Peevish Fellow, or The Bad-Tempered Man 862

8 οὐθεὶς ἐπλούτησεν ταχέως δίκαιος ὤν

No one made money fast by honest means.

Translated by W.G. Arnott (1996)

Kolax – The Fawner 43

9 οὐθὲν γένος γένους γὰρ οἶμαι διαφέρειν

No race, I believe, differs from another.

Samia – The Woman from Samos 140

10 ταὐτόματόν ἐστιν ὡς ἔοικέ που θεὸς
σῴζει τε πολλὰ τῶν ἀοράτων πραγμάτων

The accidental is a god, methinks,
that saves many unknown situations.

Samia – The Woman from Samos 163

11 τὸ γὰρ τρέφον με τοῦτ' ἐγὼ κρίνω θεόν

That which maintains me I regard as god.

Translated by H.T. Riley (1872)

Fragment 13 (Kock) – *Adelphoi – Brothers*

12 χαλεπόν γε θυγάτηρ κτῆμα καὶ δυσδιάθετον

A daughter is a hard-to-deal-with possession.

Fragment 18 (Kock) – *Alieis – The Fishermen*

13 δύναται τὸ πλουτεῖν καὶ φιλανθρώπους ποιεῖν

Wealth may sometimes lead to philanthropy.

Fragment 19 (Kock) – *Alieis – The Fishermen*

14 ζῶμεν γὰρ οὐχ ὡς θέλομεν, ἀλλ' ὡς δυνάμεθα

We live, not as we wish to, but as best we can.

Translated by Francis G. Allinson (1921)

Fragment 50 (Kock) – *Andria – The Lady of Andros*

15 τὸ γὰρ σύνηθες οὐδαμοῦ παροπτέον

Do not overlook what is customary.

Fragment 53 (Kock) – *Androgynos or Cris*

16 εὐδαιμονία τοῦτ' ἐστὶν υἱὸς νοῦν ἔχων

A son with sense – that's happiness.

Translated by Francis G. Allinson (1921)

Fragment 60 (Kock) – *Anepsioi – The Cousins*

17 τὰ κακῶς τρέφοντα χωρί' ἀνδρείους ποιεῖ

Heroes are bred by lands where livelihood comes hard.

Translated by Francis G. Allinson (1921)

Fragment 63 (Kock) – *Anepsioi – The Cousins*

18 τὰ πατρῷα μὲν ποιεῖ καιρός ποτε
ἀλλότρια, σῴζει δ' αὐτά που τὰ σώματα·
βίου δ' ἔνεστιν ἀσφάλει' ἐν ταῖς τέχναις

Inheritance may be lost in time, though you may stay alive; it is only workmanship that safeguards livelihood.

Fragment 68 (Kock) – *Arrephoros or Aulitris – The Peplos Bearer or The Flute Girl*

19 τυφλὸν ὁ πλοῦτος, καὶ τυφλοὺς
τοὺς ἐμβλέποντας εἰς ἑαυτὸν δεικνύει

Wealth is blind, and rendered blind
are those who yearn for it with longing.

Fragment 83 (Kock) – *Auton Penthon – Grieving for Him*

20 πολλὰ δύσκολα
εὕροις ἂν ἐν τοῖς πᾶσιν· ἀλλ' εἰ πλείονα
τὰ συμφέροντ' ἔνεστι, τοῦτο δεῖ σκοπεῖν

Difficulties there are in everything;
it is advantages that you must look for.

Fragment 89 (Kock) – *Boeotis – The Boeotian Girl*

21 πλοῦτος δὲ πολλῶν ἐπικάλυμμ' ἐστὶν κακῶν

Riches conceal a multitude of woes.

Fragment 90 (Kock) – *Boeotis – The Boeotian Girl*

22 εὐκαταφρόνητόν ἐστι, Γοργία, πένης,
κἂν πάνυ λέγῃ δίκαια· τούτου γὰρ λέγειν
ἕνεκα μόνου νομίζεθ' οὗτος, τοῦ λαβεῖν

A poor man, Gorgias, however sensibly
He talks, always invites contempt; for people think
His talk has one sole object: gain.

Translated by Philip Vellacott (1967)

Fragment 93 (Kock) – Line 129 (Austin) – *Georgos – The Farmer*

23 τὸ τῆς τύχης γὰρ ῥεῦμα μεταπίπτει ταχύ

The tide of fortune quickly turns.

Fragment 94 (Kock) – 1 (Austin) – *Georgos – The Farmer*

24 οὗτος κράτιστός ἐστ' ἀνήρ, ὦ Γοργία,
ὅστις ἀδικεῖσθαι πλεῖστ' ἐπίστατ' ἐγκρατῶς

He is most excellent
who suffers much injustice patiently.

Fragment 95.1 (Kock) – 3.1 (Austin) – *Georgos – The Farmer*

25 τὸ δ' ὀξύθυμον τοῦτο καὶ λίαν πικρὸν
δεῖγμ' ἐστὶν εὐθὺς πᾶσι μικροψυχίας

This anger, this deep bitterness,
betrays to all a pettiness of spirit.

Fragment 95.3 (Kock) – 3.3 (Austin) – *Georgos – The Farmer*

26 ὃν οἱ θεοὶ φιλοῦσιν ἀποθνήσκει νέος

Whom the gods love die young.

Translated by John Simpson and Jennifer Speake (1982)

Fragment 125 (Kock) – 3 (Austin) – *Dis Exapaton – Twice a Swindler*

quoted by Lord Byron, Don Juan *(1819–1824) 4.12; cf. the identical English proverb*

27 ἀνδρὸς χαρακτὴρ ἐκ λόγου γνωρίζεται

A man's character is revealed by his speech.

Translated by Francis G. Allinson (1921)

Fragment 143 (Kock) – *Auton Timoroumenos – The Self-Tormentor*

28 οἴκοι μένειν χρὴ καὶ μένειν ἐλεύθερον

Stay in your native land and remain free.

Fragment 145 (Kock) – *Auton Timoroumenos – The Self-Tormentor*

29 τρία γάρ ἐστι, δέσποτα,
δι' ὧν ἅπαντα γίνετ', ἢ κατὰ τοὺς νόμους,
ἢ ταῖς ἀνάγκαις, ἢ τὸ τρίτον ἔθει τινί

From three things, master,
all things have their beginning; from law
or necessity or thirdly, from custom.

Fragment 155 (Kock) – *Empimpramene – The Woman Set on Fire*

30 ἐφ' ᾧ φρονεῖς μέγιστον ἀπολεῖ τοῦτό σε,
τὸ δοκεῖν τιν' εἶναι· καὶ γὰρ ἄλλους μυρίους

The pride you have in thinking you're special
will ruin you, as it has ruined a myriad others.

Fragment 156 (Kock) – *Empimpramene – The Woman Set on Fire*

31 ὡς ἀγαθὸν τὸ πρᾶγμα τὸ γενέσθαι τινὸς πατέρα

How great a boon, to be a father.

Fragment 157 (Kock) – *Empimpramene – The Woman Set on Fire*

32 ἆρ' ἐστὶ πάντων ἀγρυπνία λαλίστατον

Of all things the most loquacious are sleepless nights.

Fragment 164 (Kock) – *Epicleros – The Heiress*

cf. Callimachus 31

33 ἐν παντὶ δεῖ
καιρῷ τὸ δίκαιον ἐπικρατεῖν ἁπανταχοῦ

On all occasions justice *should* prevail
The whole world over.

Translated by W.G. Arnott (1979)

Fragment 173 (Kock) – *Epitrepontes – Men at Arbitration*

34 οὐθὲν πέπονθας δεινόν, ἂν μὴ προσποιῇ

You will have suffered nothing unless you pretend the contrary.

Fragment 179 (Kock) – *Epitrepontes – Men at Arbitration*

35 οὗτός ἐστι γαλεώτης γέρων

A shrewd old fox this!

Translated by H.T. Riley (1872)

Fragment 188 (Kock) – *Eunouchos – The Eunuch*

36 μί' ἐστὶν ἀρετὴ τὸν ἄτοπον φεύγειν ἀεί

There is one virtue, always to shun the eccentric.

Translated by Francis G. Allinson (1921)

Fragment 203c (Kock) – *Heniochos – The Charioteer*

37 ἔρωτος οὐδὲν ἰσχύει πλέον,
οὐδ' αὐτὸς ὁ κρατῶν τῶν ἐν οὐρανῷ θεῶν
Ζεύς, ἀλλ' ἐκείνῳ πάντ' ἀναγκασθεὶς ποεῖ

There's nothing in this world more powerful than Love;
why, even Zeus, who rules the gods in heaven
yields in all things to Love.

Fragment 209 (Kock) – 1 (Austin) – *Heros – The Guardian Spirit*

38 τὸν ἐλεύθερον δὲ πανταχοῦ φρονεῖν μέγα

High-spirited are the free.

Fragment 210 (Kock) – 2 (Austin) – *Heros – The Guardian Spirit*

39 ὄνον γενέσθαι κρεῖττον ἢ τοὺς χείρονας
ὁρᾶν ἑαυτοῦ ζῶντας ἐπιφανέστερον

Better to be born a jackass than to see worse men living in greater splendour.

Fragment 223 (Kock) – 1 (Austin) – *Theophoroumene – The Woman Possessed with a Divinity*

40 ὁ πλεῖστον νοῦν ἔχων
μάντις τ' ἄριστος ἐστι σύμβουλός θ' ἅμα

He who has the most common sense
is at once the best prophet and adviser.

Translated by Francis G. Allinson (1921)

Fragment 225 (Kock) – 2 (Austin) – *Theophoroumene – The Woman Possessed with a Divinity*

41 ἀπὸ μηχανῆς θεὸς ἐπεφάνης

You appeared to me as a 'deus ex machina'.

Fragment 227 (Kock) – 6 (Austin) – *Theophoroumene – The Woman Possessed with a*

Divinity

the Latin 'deus ex machina' is now used in English for an unexpected power or event saving a seemingly hopeless situation; cf. Plato, Cratylus *425d*

42 μικρά γε πρόφασίς ἐστι τοῦ πρᾶξαι κακῶς

A slight pretence suffices for doing evil.

Translated by H.T. Riley (1872)

Fragment 230 (Kock) – *Thettale*

43 κατὰ πόλλ' ἄρ' ἐστὶν οὐ καλῶς εἰρημένον
τὸ γνῶθι σαυτόν· χρησιμώτερον γὰρ ἦν
τὸ γνῶθι τοὺς ἄλλους

For many reasons 'Know Thyself' is wrongly said;
it is more useful to know everyone else.

Fragment 240 (Kock) – *Thrasyleon*

44 τὸ κρατοῦν γὰρ νῦν νομίζεται θεός

Nowadays whatever holds sway is deemed a god.

Fragment 257 (Kock) – *Carine – The Carian Wailing-Woman*

e.g. money

45 χρεία διδάσκει, κἂν ἄμουσος ᾖ

Practice is a teacher even to the unrefined.

Fragment 263 (Kock) – 3 (Austin) – *Karchedonios – The Man from Carthage*

46 τὸ καλῶς ἔχον που κρεῖττόν ἐστι καὶ νόμου

What is right and fair is better even than the law.

Fragment 265 (Kock) – 5 (Austin) – *Karchedonios – The Man from Carthage*

47 ἆρ' ἐστὶ συγγενές τι λύπη καὶ βίος·
τρυφερῷ βίῳ σύνεστιν, ἐνδόξῳ βίῳ
πάρεστιν, ἀπόρῳ συγκαταγηράσκει βίῳ

Grief and life are in a certain way akin: grief coexists with a life of luxury, is omnipresent in a life of glory, grows old along with poverty.

Fragment 281 (Kock) – 1 (Austin) – *Kitharistes – The Lyre Player*

48 τὸ μηθὲν ἀδικεῖν ἐκμαθεῖν γάρ, ὦ Λάχης,
ἀστεῖον ἐπιτήδευμα κρίνω τῷ βίῳ

Make a habit for life to never do wrong.

Fragment 284 (Kock) – 4 (Austin) – *Kitharistes – The Lyre Player*

49 τὸ 'γνῶθι σαυτὸν' ἔστιν, ἂν τὰ πράγματα
εἰδῇς τὰ σαυτοῦ καὶ τί σοι ποιητέον

'Know Thyself' means to know
what you can do, and what you have to do.

Fragment 307 (Kock) – 1 (Austin) – *Koneiazomenai – The Women Who Would Drink Hemlock*

50 οὕτω μαθεῖν δεῖ πάντα καὶ πλοῦτον φέρειν·
ἀσχημοσύνης γὰρ γίνετ' ἐνίοις αἴτιος

Learn how to deal with wealth;
it can become the cause of many an ugly deed.

Fragment 323 (Kock) – *Menagyrites*

51 ἂν δ' ἐκλέγῃ
ἀεὶ τὸ λυποῦν, μηδὲν ἀντιπαρατιθεὶς
τῶν προσδοκωμένων, ὀδυνήσει διὰ τέλους

If you only consider your troubles, and do not weigh possible blessings in the balance, your whole life will be nothing but sorrow.

Fragment 325 (Kock) – *Misogynes – The Misogynist*

52 παιδισκάριόν με καταδεδούλωκ' εὐτελές,
ὃν οὐδὲ εἷς τῶν πολεμίων οὐπώποτε

A worthless little wench has enslaved me,
me, whom no enemy ever could.

Fragment 338 (Kock) – *Misoumenos – The Hated Man*

53 χρηστοὺς νομιζομένους ἐφόδιον ἀσφαλὲς
εἰς πάντα καιρὸν καὶ τύχης πᾶσαν ῥοπήν

Virtue is a safeguard in any circumstance and in any change of fortune.

Fragment 360 (Kock) – *Homopatrioi – The Brothers*

54 πᾶς ἐρυθριῶν χρηστὸς εἶναί μοι δοκεῖ

A blushing man seems to me to be an honest man.

Fragment 361 (Kock) – *Homopatrioi – The Brothers*

55 τὸν πλησίον γὰρ οἴεται μᾶλλον φρονεῖν
ὁ τοῖς λογισμοῖς τοῖς ἰδίοις πταίων ἀεί

One always considers his neighbour to be at fault
when his own reasoning is wrong.

Fragment 380 (Kock) – *Parakatathiki – The Deposit*

56 οὐπώποτ' ἐζήλωσα πολυτελῆ νεκρόν·
εἰς τὸν ἴσον ὄγκον τῷ σφόδρ' ἔρχετ' εὐτελεῖ

I have never envied a costly funeral;
a cheap one will take you to the same place!

Fragment 394 (Kock) – 3 (Austin) – *Perinthia – The Girl from Perinthus*

57 οὐκ ἔστιν ἀγαθὸν τῷ βίῳ
φυόμενον ὥσπερ δένδρον ἐκ ῥίζης μιᾶς,
ἀλλ' ἐγγὺς ἀγαθοῦ παραπέφυκε καὶ κακόν,
ἐκ τοῦ κακοῦ τ' ἤνεγκεν ἀγαθὸν ἡ φύσις

There is no blessing in life
that springs like tree from single root,
but near to blessing grows up evil too;
and nature from this evil brings forth good.

Translated by Francis G. Allinson (1921)

Fragment 407 (Kock) – *Plocion – The Necklace*

58 ἆρ' ἐστὶν ἀρετῆς καὶ βίου διδάσκαλος
ἐλευθέρου τοῖς πᾶσιν ἀνθρώποις ἀγρός

The open country is for all men the best
teacher of virtue and free thought.

Fragment 408 (Kock) – *Plocion – The Necklace*

59 ἀεὶ τὸ λυποῦν ἀποδίωκε τοῦ βίου·
μικρόν τι τὸ βίου καὶ στενὸν ζῶμεν χρόνον

Chase sorrows from your life
for it is short and time is scant.

Fragment 410 (Kock) – *Plocion – The Necklace*

60 οὐκ ἔστιν εὑρεῖν βίον ἄλυπον οὐδενός

There is no life that's free of grief.

Fragment 411 (Kock) – *Plocion – The Necklace*

61 οἷον τὸ γενέσθαι πατέρα παίδων ἦν·
λύπη, φόβος, φροντίς, πέρας ἐστὶν οὐδὲ ἕν

Such is a father's life:
fear, care, grief without end.

Fragment 418 (Kock) – *Proengalon – The Accuser*

62 οὐ πανταχοῦ τὸ φρόνιμον ἁρμόττει παρόν,
καὶ συμμανῆναι δ' ἔνια δεῖ

At times discretion should be thrown aside,
and with the foolish we should play the fool.

Translated in *Bartlett's Familiar Quotations* (1980)

Fragment 421 (Kock) – *Poloumenoi – Those Offered For Sale*

63 ἀτύχημα κἀδίκημα διαφορὰν ἔχει·
τὸ μὲν διὰ τύχην γίνεται, τὸ δ' αἱρέσει

Misfortune and injury differ:
the one arises from chance, the other from choice.

Translated by Francis G. Allinson (1921)

Fragment 426 (Kock) – *Rapizomene – The Girl Who Gets Flogged*

64 ἔρχεται τἀληθὲς εἰς φῶς ἐνίοτ' οὐ ζητούμενον

The truth is sometimes revealed without
being sought.

Fragment 433 (Kock) – *Rapizomene – The Girl Who Gets Flogged*

65 οὐδεὶς ξύνοιδεν ἐξαμαρτάνων πόσον
ἁμαρτάνει τὸ μέγεθος, ὕστερον δ' ὁρᾷ

Whilst in the act, no one is conscious
of his sin's magnitude – he sees it later.

Fragment 448 (Kock) – *Stratiotae – The Soldiers*

66 αὐτόματα γὰρ τὰ πράγματ' ἐπὶ τὸ συμφέρον
ῥεῖ κἂν καθεύδῃς ἢ πάλιν τοὐναντίον

Even in sleep things happen of themselves,
moving towards fortune or misfortune.

Fragment 460 (Kock) – *Tithe – The Wet-Nurse*

67 ὡς ἡδὺ τῷ μισοῦντι τοὺς φαύλους τρόπους ἐρημία

How sweet is solitude to the man who
hates vulgar ways.

Fragment 466 (Kock) – *Hydria – The Urn*

68 τρόπος ἔσθ' ὁ πείθων τοῦ λέγοντος, οὐ λόγος

'Tis character, not speech, that persuades.

Fragment 472 (Kock) – *Hymnis*

69 τοῦτο μόνον ἐπισκοτεῖ
καὶ δυσγενείᾳ καὶ τρόπου πονηρίᾳ
καὶ πᾶσιν οἷς ἔσχηκεν ἄνθρωπος κακοῖς,
τὸ πολλὰ κεκτῆσθαι

Wealth casts a veil
over both ignoble birth and wicked character
and all the ills that man is heir to.

Translated by Francis G. Allinson (1921)

Fragment 485 (Kock) – *Hypobolimaios or Agroicos – The Counterfeit Baby or The Rustic*

70 ἀεὶ κράτιστόν ἐστι τἀληθῆ λέγειν·
ἐν παντὶ καιρῷ τοῦτ᾽ ἐγὼ παρεγγυῶ
εἰς ἀσφάλειαν τῷ βίῳ

Truth is always best;
at all times I recommend this
for safety throughout life.

Fragment 487 (Kock) – *Hypobolimaios or Agroicos – The Counterfeit Baby or The Rustic*

71 οἷα δὴ φιλοῦσιν ἰατροὶ λέγειν
τὰ φαῦλα μείζω καὶ τὰ δείν᾽ ὑπέρφοβα,
πυργοῦντες αὑτούς

Doctors adore exaggerating the unimportant,
overstating tribulations, magnifying themselves.

Fragment 497 (Kock) – *Phanion – Phanium*

also spuriously (according to M.L. West) attributed to Mimnermus

72 ἄνθρωπος ὢν ἥμαρτον· οὐ θαυμαστέον

I am human, I erred; nothing to wonder at.

Fragment 499 (Kock) – *Phanion – Phanium*

cf. the Latin 'errare humanum est' and the English proverb 'to err is human'

73 τοῦτ᾽ ἔστι τὸ ζῆν, οὐχ ἑαυτῷ ζῆν μόνον

This is life, not to live for oneself alone.

Fragment 507 (Kock) – *Philadelphoi – The Brothers in Love*

74 οἷς ἂν τῇ φύσει
ἀγαθὸν ὑπάρχῃ μηδὲν οἰκεῖον προσόν,
ἐκεῖσε καταφεύγουσιν, εἰς τὰ μνήματα
καὶ τὸ γένος, ἀριθμοῦσίν τε τοὺς πάππους ὅσοι·
οὐδὲν δ᾽ ἔχουσι πλεῖον

People who
Haven't a single good quality to call their own –
They are the ones who talk like that of family,
Or titles, or decorations; reel off grandfathers
One after the other, and that's all
they've got.

Translated by Philip Vellacott (1967)

Fragment 533.2 (Kock)

75 ὃς ἂν εὖ γεγονὼς ᾖ τῇ φύσει πρὸς τἀγαθά,
κἂν Αἰθίοψ ᾖ … ἐστὶν εὐγενής

If a man, by his nature, has a noble bent,
he, be he black, is nobly born.

Fragment 533.11 (Kock)

76 ἅπαντα τὰ ζῷ᾽ ἐστὶ μακαριώτατα
καὶ νοῦν ἔχοντα μᾶλλον ἀνθρώπου πολύ

All animals are heavenly blessed,
possessing much more sense than man.

Fragment 534.1 (Kock)

77 ἂν εἴπῃ κακῶς
ὀργιζόμεθ᾽, ἂν ἴδῃ τις ἐνύπνιον σφόδρα
φοβούμεθ᾽, ἂν γλαῦξ ἀνακράγῃ δεδοίκαμεν.
ἀγωνίαι, δόξαι, φιλοτιμίαι, νόμοι,
ἅπαντα ταῦτ᾽ ἐπίθετα τῇ φύσει κακά

Speak badly of us
and we are vexed, see a bad dream and we are greatly
frightened; an owl hoots and we are filled with fear.
Anxieties, ambitions, fancies, silly customs:
all these curses men have added to Nature's ills.

Fragment 534.9 (Kock)

78 ὅταν εἰδέναι θέλῃς σεαυτὸν ὅστις εἶ,
ἔμβλεψον εἰς τὰ μνήμαθ᾽ ὡς ὁδοιπορεῖς.
ἐνταῦθ᾽ ἔνεστ᾽ ὀστᾶ τε καὶ κούφη κόνις
ἀνδρῶν βασιλέων καὶ τυράννων καὶ σοφῶν
καὶ μέγα φρονούντων ἐπὶ γένει καὶ χρήμασιν
αὑτῶν τε δόξῃ κἀπὶ κάλλει σωμάτων.
κᾆτ᾽ οὐδὲν αὐτοῖς τῶνδ᾽ ἐπήρκεσεν χρόνος.
κοινὸν τὸν ᾅδην ἔσχον οἱ πάντες βροτοί.
πρὸς ταῦθ᾽ ὁρῶν γίνωσκε σαυτὸν ὅστις εἶ

When you're moved to find out who you are,
study the graves you encounter as you pass by.
Inside rest the bones and weightless dust
of men once kings and tyrants, wise men, and those
who took pride in their noble birth or

wealth,
their fame, or their beautiful bodies.
Yet what good was any of that against time?
All mortals come to know Hades in the end.
Look toward these to know who you are.

Translated by Edmund Keeley (2010)

Fragment 538 (Kock)

79 μειράκιον, οὔ μοι κατανοεῖν δοκεῖς ὅτι
ὑπὸ τῆς ἰδίας ἕκαστα κακίας σήπεται,
καὶ πᾶν τὸ λυμαινόμενόν ἐστιν ἔνδοθεν.
οἷον ὁ μὲν ἰός, ἂν σκοπῇς, τὸ σιδήριον,
τὸ δ᾽ ἱμάτιον οἱ σῆτες, ὁ δὲ θρὶψ τὸ ξύλον.
ὃ δὲ τὸ κάκιστον τῶν κακῶν πάντων, φθόνος
φθισικὸν πεποίηκε καὶ ποιήσει καὶ ποιεῖ

My boy, you do not seem to understand
that all things that decay do so of their own corruption,
and all that destroys comes from within;
thus, you see, rust will destroy the iron,
moths the woollen cloak, and worm the wood.
But of all evils envy is the worst;
it has consumed you in the past, it does so now, and will forever.

Fragment 540 (Kock)

80 ἅπαντι δαίμων ἀνδρὶ συμπαρίσταται
εὐθὺς γενομένῳ, μυσταγωγὸς τοῦ βίου
ἀγαθός

A guardian spirit stands by us,
from birth, to lead us on life's way.

Fragment 550 (Kock)

81 κἂν σφόδρα σαφῶς εἰδῇς τι, τὸν κρύπτοντά σε
μηδέποτ᾽ ἐλέγξῃς· δύσκολον πρᾶγμ᾽ ἐστὶ γὰρ
ἃ λανθάνειν τις βούλεται ταῦτ᾽ εἰδέναι

Though you know something well, never disgrace
the man who tries to conceal it; it is often hard
to admit something one would rather keep hidden.

Fragment 570 (Kock)

82 ὅταν ἕτερός σοι μηδὲ ἓν τέλεον διδῷ,
δέξαι τὸ μόριον· τοῦ λαβεῖν γὰρ μηδὲ ἕν
τὸ λαβεῖν ἔλαττον πλεῖον ἔσται σοι πολύ

If someone gives you less
accept this little; rather than wait for more
less will be better than nothing.

Fragment 571 (Kock)

83 τόλμῃ δικαίᾳ καὶ θεὸς συλλαμβάνει

God himself lends a hand to a bold and honest cause.

Fragment 572 (Kock)

84 ἡ νῦν ὑπό τινων χρηστότης καλουμένη
μεθῆκε τὸν ὅλον εἰς πονηρίαν βίον·
οὐδεὶς γὰρ ἀδικῶν τυγχάνει τιμωρίας

This so-called kindness
has cast the whole world into lawlessness;
for no wrongdoer is ever punished.

Fragment 579 (Kock)

85 αἰσχύνομαι τὸν πατέρα … μόνον·
ἀντιβλέπειν ἐκεῖνον οὐ δυνήσομαι
ἀδικῶν

I feel shame before my father only
and cannot look him in the face if I do wrong.

Fragment 586 (Kock)

86 ἀεὶ δ᾽ ὁ σωθεὶς ἐστιν ἀχάριστον φύσει
ἅμ᾽ ἠλέηται καὶ τέθνηκεν ἡ χάρις

Anyone saved is thankless by nature;
as soon as pity is shown gratitude dies.

Fragment 595 (Kock)

87 ἄνθρωπε, μὴ στέναζε, μὴ λυποῦ μάτην …
ἅ σοι τύχη κέχρηκε, ταῦτ᾽ ἀφείλετο

Fellow, stop moaning and do not grieve in vain;
what fortune lent you she has taken back.

Fragment 598 (Kock)

88 οὐδείς ἐστί μοι
ἀλλότριος, ἂν ᾖ χρηστός· ἡ φύσις μία
πάντων, τὸ δ᾽ οἰκεῖον συνίστησιν τρόπος

For me none is a foreigner
If he be good. One nature is in all
And it is character that makes the tie of kin.

Translated by Francis G. Allinson (1921)

Fragment 602 (Kock)

89 οὐκ ἔστι μείζων ἡδονὴ ταύτης πατρί,
ἢ σωφρονοῦντα καὶ φρονοῦντ᾽ ἰδεῖν τινα
τῶν ἐξ ἑαυτοῦ

A father can have no greater joy than to see some of his children both temperate and wise.

Fragment 603 (Kock)

90 πολλοὺς δι' ἀνάγκην γὰρ πονηροὺς οἶδ' ἐγὼ
ὅταν ἀτυχήσωσιν γεγονότας, οὐ φύσει
ὄντας τοιούτους

I know of many men who have perforce turned criminals through misfortune although they were not such by nature.

Translated by Francis G. Allinson (1921)

Fragment 604 (Kock)

91 τὴν γυναῖκα γὰρ
τὴν σώφρον' οὐ δεῖ τὰς τρίχας ξανθὰς ποιεῖν

No sensible woman should dye her hair blond.

Fragment 610 (Kock)

92 πλούσιος
καλοῦμ' ὑπὸ πάντων, μακάριος δ' ὑπ' οὐδενός

I am called rich by all, by none am I called blest.

Fragment 612 (Kock)

93 χαλεπόν γε τοιαῦτ' ἐστὶν ἐξαμαρτάνειν,
ἃ καὶ λέγειν ὀκνοῦμεν οἱ πεπραχότες

Grievous indeed is an offence
you'd dare not even mention.

Fragment 619 (Kock)

94 εὐηθία μοι φαίνεται, Φιλουμένη,
τὸ νοεῖν μὲν ὅσα δεῖ, μὴ φυλάττεσθαι δ' ἃ δεῖ

It seems silly to me, my dear,
to know what you know and not to guard against it.

Fragment 620 (Kock)

95 τἀπίθανον ἰσχὺν τῆς ἀληθείας ἔχει
ἐνίοτε μείζω καὶ πιθανωτέραν ὄχλῳ

For the mob, what is incredible has greater power
and sometimes is more credible than truth.

Fragment 622 (Kock)

96 οὐπώποτ' ἐζήλωσα πλουτοῦντα σφόδρα
ἄνθρωπον, ἀπολαύοντα μηδὲν ὧν ἔχει

I have never envied anyone who has great wealth
who enjoys nothing of what he has.

Fragment 624 (Kock)

also attributed to Antiphanes

97 οὐ γὰρ τὸ πλῆθος, ἂν σκοπῇ τις, τοῦ ποτοῦ
ποιεῖ παροινεῖν, τοῦ πιόντος δ' ἡ φύσις

If you observe, it's not the number of cups that makes
A man drunk, but the character of the man who drinks.

Translated by Philip Vellacott (1967)

Fragment 627 (Kock)

98 χαλεπὸν ὅταν τις ὧν πίῃ πλέον λαλῇ,
μηδὲν κατειδώς, ἀλλὰ προσποιούμενος

It's grievous when anyone talks more when he drinks,
without real knowledge, just making pretence.

Translated by Francis G. Allinson (1921)

Fragment 628 (Kock)

99 οὐκ ἔστιν ὀργῆς, ὡς ἔοικε, φάρμακον
ἀλλ' ἢ λόγος σπουδαῖος ἀνθρώπου φίλου

It seems there is no medicine for anger,
except the earnest counsel of a friend.

Fragment 630 (Kock)

100 ὁ συνιστορῶν αὑτῷ τι, κἂν ᾖ θρασύτατος,
ἡ σύνεσις αὐτὸν δειλότατον εἶναι ποιεῖ

A guilty conscience turns the boldest man into a perfect coward.

Fragment 632 (Kock)

101 ὁ φθονερὸς αὑτῷ πολέμιος καθίσταται·
αὐθαιρέτοις γὰρ συνέχεται λύπαις ἀεί

The jealous man is his own enemy;
he is forever tyrannized by self-imposed distress.

Fragment 634 (Kock)

102 ὁ προκαταγινώσκων δὲ πρὶν ἀκοῦσαι σαφῶς
αὐτὸς πονηρός ἐστι πιστεύσας κακῶς

He who condemns before listening carefully
is criminal himself, having been wickedly credulous.

Fragment 636 (Kock)

103 καλόν γε βασιλεὺς τῇ μὲν ἀνδρείᾳ κρατῶν,
τὰ δὲ τοῦ βίου δίκαια διατηρῶν κρίσει

It were well that a king prevail by fearlessness,
and maintain sound judgement in all traits of life.

Fragment 637 (Kock)

104 μὴ τοῦτο βλέψῃς εἰ νεώτερος λέγω,
ἀλλ' εἰ φρονοῦντος τοὺς λόγους ἀνδρὸς ἐρῶ

I'm rather young; but when I speak, don't think of that;
Just notice if I'm speaking like a man of sense.

Translated by Philip Vellacott (1967)

Fragment 638 (Kock)

105 οὐχ αἱ τρίχες ποιοῦσιν αἱ λευκαὶ φρονεῖν

White hair is proof of age, not of wisdom.

Translated by H.T. Riley (1872)

Fragment 639 (Kock)

106 ὅστις στρατηγεῖ μὴ στρατιώτης γενόμενος,
οὗτος ἑκατόμβην ἐξάγει τοῖς πολεμίοις

A general who never was a soldier
leads out a hecatomb to offer to the foe.

Fragment 640 (Kock)

107 ὅταν ἀτυχῇ τις, εὐνοοῦντος οἰκέτου
οὐκ ἔστιν οὐδὲν κτῆμα κάλλιον βίῳ

For anyone meets who misfortune
there is no fairer asset than a loyal servant.

Fragment 644 (Kock)

108 ὅταν φύσει τὸ κάλλος ἐπικοσμῇ τρόπος
χρηστός, διπλασίως ὁ προσιὼν ἁλίσκεται

When beauty is adorned with virtue,
whoever meets it is doubly won.

Fragment 645 (Kock)

109 ἕν ἐστ' ἀληθὲς φίλτρον, εὐγνώμων τρόπος·
τούτῳ κατακρατεῖν ἀνδρὸς εἴωθεν γυνή

One is the true love-charm, a kindly manner;
by this a woman is apt to sway her man.

Fragment 646 (Kock)

110 οἰκεῖον οὕτως οὐδέν ἐστιν … ὡς ἀνήρ τε καὶ γυνή

Nothing is as closely bonded as man and wife.

Fragment 647 (Kock)

111 τὸ γαμεῖν, ἐάν τις τὴν ἀλήθειαν σκοπῇ,
κακὸν μέν ἐστιν, ἀλλ' ἀναγκαῖον κακόν

Marriage, if one will face the truth,
is an evil, but a necessary evil.

Translated by Francis G. Allinson (1921)

Fragment 651 (Kock)

112 ὀδυνηρόν ἐστιν εὐτυχοῦντα τῷ βίῳ
ἔχειν ἔρημον διαδόχου τὴν οἰκίαν

Happiness turns to grief in life
without an heir about the house.

Fragment 655 (Kock)

113 οὐκ ἔστ' ἄκουσμ' ἥδιον ἢ ῥηθεὶς λόγος
πατρὸς πρὸς υἱὸν περιέχων ἐγκώμιον

Nothing is so sweet to hear,
than a father's praise of his son.

Fragment 660 (Kock)

114 πάντων ἰατρὸς τῶν ἀναγκαίων κακῶν χρόνος ἐστίν

Time is the healer of all necessary evils.

Translated by John Simpson and Jennifer Speake (1982)

Fragment 677 (Kock)

cf. the English proverb 'time is a great healer'

115 ἔξεστι τοῖς σοφοῖς βροτῶν
χρόνῳ σκοπεῖσθαι τῆς ἀληθείας πέρι

Men who are wise will, in time, discover truth.

Fragment 678 (Kock)

116 εἰ πάντες ἐβοηθοῦμεν ἀλλήλοις ἀεί,
οὐδεὶς ἂν ὢν ἄνθρωπος ἐδεήθη τύχης

If each of us offered help to another,
good fortune would never be lacking.

Fragment 679 (Kock)

117 μυστήριόν σου μὴ κατείπῃς τῷ φίλῳ,
κοὐ μὴ φοβηθῇς αὐτὸν ἐχθρὸν γενόμενον

Don't tell your secret to your friend
and you'll not fear him when he turns into an enemy.

Translated by Francis G. Allinson (1921)

Fragment 695 (Kock)

118 ὁ γὰρ ἀδίκως τι καθ' ἑτέρου ζητῶν κακὸν
αὐτὸς προπάσχει τοῦ κακοῦ τὴν ἔκβασιν

He who acts unjustly against another
will soon have a taste of injustice
himself.

Fragment 696 (Kock)

119 μὴ πάσχε πρῶτον τὸν νόμον καὶ μάνθανε·
πρὸ τοῦ παθεῖν δὲ τῷ φόβῳ προλαμβάνου

Don't suffer first under the law, and then learn;
anticipate its consequence in fear.

Fragment 701 (Kock)

120 ὅταν τι μέλλῃς τὸν πέλας κακηγορεῖν,
αὐτὸς τὰ σαυτοῦ πρῶτον ἐπισκέπτου κακά

Before you abuse your neighbour
consider first your own defects.

Fragment 710 (Kock)

121 μηδέποτε πειρῶ στρεβλὸν ὀρθῶσαι κλάδον,
οὐκ ἦν ἐνεγκεῖν ὅπου φύσις βιάζεται

Never try to straighten a crooked branch;
it is impossible to overpower nature.

Fragment 711 (Kock)

122 ἐπὰν ἐκ μεταβολῆς ἐπὶ κρεῖττον γένῃ,
ὅτ' εὐτυχεῖς μέμνησο τῆς προτέρας τύχης

When by some change you better your position,
remember in prosperity your former lot.

Fragment 712 (Kock)

123 εἰρήνη γεωργὸν κἀν πέτραις
τρέφει καλῶς, πόλεμος δὲ κἀν πεδίῳ κακῶς

Peace maintains the farmer well, even on stony ground;
but war bodes ill, even upon the plain.

Translated by Francis G. Allinson (1921)
Fragment 719 (Kock)

124 οὐ λυποῦντα δεῖ
παιδάριον ὀρθοῦν, ἀλλὰ καὶ πείθοντά τι

Correct a child by persuasion, not by punishment.

Fragment 730 (Kock)

125 πᾶς ὁ μὴ φρονῶν
ἀλαζονείᾳ καὶ ψόφοις ἁλίσκεται

Every fool is caught by boastfulness and idle talk.

Fragment 737 (Kock)

126 τὸν τῇ φύσει
οἰκεῖον οὐδεὶς καιρὸς ἀλλότριον ποιεῖ

No circumstance can turn a kinsman to a stranger.

Fragment 742 (Kock)

127 ὡς ἡδὺ πρᾷος καὶ νεάζων τῷ τρόπῳ πατήρ

How charming is a youthful and gentle father.

Fragment 749 (Kock)

128 ὄνειδος αἰσχρὸς βίος ὅμως κἂν ἡδὺς ᾖ

A shameful life is a disgrace, though it be pleasant.

Fragment 756 (Kock)

129 εἷς ἐστι δοῦλος οἰκίας ὁ δεσπότης

The real slave of the household is its master.

Fragment 760 (Kock)

130 ὡς χαρίεν ἔστ' ἄνθρωπος, ὅταν ἄνθρωπος ᾖ

How charming is man, when he is a true man.

Fragment 761 (Kock)

131 ἀνδρὸς τὰ προσπίπτοντα γενναίως φέρειν

It is for man to bear misfortune valiantly.

Fragment 771 (Kock)

132 ὁ πολὺς ἄκρατος ὀλίγ' ἀναγκάζει φρονεῖν

Too much unmixed wine leads to unwise thoughts.

Fragment 779 (Kock)

133 οὐκ ἔστι τόλμης ἐφόδιον μεῖζον βίου

There is no greater asset in life than courage.

Fragment 792 (Kock)

134 ἔχει τι τὸ πικρὸν τῆς γεωργίας γλυκύ

Farming has something of the bittersweet.

Fragment 795 (Kock)

135 ὀργὴ φιλούντων ὀλίγον ἰσχύει χρόνον

Anger towards a loved one lasts but a short time.

Fragment 797 (Kock)

136 νόμος γονεῦσιν ἰσοθέους τιμὰς νέμειν

The law requires that we honour our parents as we do the gods.

Fragment 805 (Kock)

cf. Bible 322

137 ἡδὺς πατὴρ φρόνησιν ἀντ' ὀργῆς ἔχων

Nice to have a father with good sense rather than anger.

Fragment 807 (Kock)

138 ἡδύ γ' ἐν ἀδελφοῖς ἐστιν ὁμονοίας ἔρως

Sweet is the concord of siblings.

Fragment 809 (Kock)

139 ἄνθρωπος ἀτυχῶν σῴζεθ' ὑπὸ τῆς ἐλπίδος

In adversity a man is saved by hope.

Translated by Francis G. Allinson (1921)

Fragment 813 (Kock)

140 ἡδύ γε φίλου λόγος ἐστὶ τοῖς λυπουμένοις

Welcome in sorrow are the words of a friend.

Fragment 814 (Kock)

141 ἀδύνατον ὡς ἔοικε τἀληθὲς λαθεῖν

It is impossible, it seems, for the truth to remain hidden.

Fragment 823 (Kock)

142 μὴ τὸ κέρδος ἐν πᾶσιν σκόπει

Look not for gain in all things.

Fragment 854 (Kock)

143 ὅταν τις ἡμῶν ἀμέριμνον ἔχῃ βίον,
οὐκ ἐπικαλεῖται τὴν τύχην εὐδαιμονῶν·
ὅταν δὲ λύπαις περιπέσῃ καὶ πράγμασιν,
εὐθὺς προσάπτει τῇ τύχῃ τὴν αἰτίαν

When life is carefree no one thinks of his good fortune;
it is when sorrows come that fortune stands accused.

Fragment 1083 (Kock)

144 ἐπὰν ἐν ἀγαθοῖς εὐνοούμενός τις ὢν
ζητῇ τι κρεῖττον ὧν ἔχει, ζητεῖ κακά

A prosperous man does wrong to ask for more.

Fragment 1087 (Kock)

145 ἅπανθ' ὅσ' ὀργιζόμενος ἄνθρωπος ποιεῖ,
ταῦθ' ὕστερον λάβοις ἂν ἡμαρτημένα

Anything a person does in anger
you'll find out later was all wrong.

Fragment 1089 (Kock)

146 οὐχ ὁ λόγος αὔξει τὴν τέχνην περισσὸς ὤν,
ἀλλ' αὐτὰ κοσμεῖ τὴν τέχνην τὰ πράγματα

Not by excessive praise is art improved;
Art is adornment in itself.

Fragment 1095 (Kock)

147 κἂν μυρίων γῆς κυριεύῃς πήχεων,
θανὼν γενήσει τάχα τριῶν ἢ τεττάρων

Though you may conquer a myriad ells of land,
when dead you'll need but three or four.

Fragment 1099 (Kock)

cf. Shakespeare, Henry IV Part I, *5.4.(91), 'but now two paces of the vilest earth is room enough'*

148 ἂν καλὸν ἔχῃ τις σῶμα καὶ ψυχὴν κακήν,
καλὴν ἔχει ναῦν καὶ κυβερνήτην κακόν

If you are fair in body and in spirit wicked,
you possess a fine ship and a worthless captain.

Fragment 1100 (Kock)

149 τύχην ἔχεις, ἄνθρωπε, μὴ μάτην τρέχε·
εἰ δ' οὐκ ἔχεις, κάθευδε, μὴ κενῶς πόνει

If you are in luck, good man, waste no more energy;
if out of it, go off to sleep, all effort is in vain.

Fragment 1101 (Kock)

150 γῆρας λέοντος κρεῖσσον ἀκμαίων νεβρῶν

The lion's old age is better than the fawn's prime.

Translated by Kathleen Freeman (1947)

Fragment 1108 (Kock)

151 ταμιεῖον ἀρετῆς ἐστιν ἡ σώφρων γυνή

A treasury of excellence is a wise woman.

Fragment 1109 (Kock)

152 ὁ γὰρ θεὸς πᾶσι, τοῖς τ' ἐλευθέροις καὶ τοῖσι δούλοις ἐστίν ἴσος

God is the same to free and bond.

Translated by Philip Schaff (1819–1893)

Fragment 681 (Körte and Thierfelder)

153 ὁ γὰρ θεὸς βλέπει σε πλησίον παρών, ὅς ἔργοις δικαίοις ἥδεται κοὐκ ἀδίκοις

God who beholds you from near at hand
is pleased with just, not unjust deeds.

Fragment 683 (Körte and Thierfelder)

Μονόστιχοι (or One-liners)

154 ἀναφαίρετον κτῆμ' ἐστὶ παιδεία βροτοῖς

Learning is a possession of which no one can be deprived.

Sententiae 2 (Jaekel)

155 ἀθάνατον ἔχθραν μὴ φύλαττε θνητὸς ὤν

Do not keep everlasting enemies as you are but mortal.

Sententiae 5 (Jaekel)

156 ἃ ψέγομεν ἡμεῖς, ταῦτα μὴ μιμώμεθα

What we criticize we should not imitate.

Sententiae 7 (Jaekel)

157 ἅπαντα καιρῷ χάριν ἔχει τρυγώμενα

In its proper time, everything is a delight.

Sententiae 9 (Jaekel)

158 ἄνθρωπος ὤν μέμνησο τῆς κοινῆς τύχης

Remember you are but human, sharing a common fate.

Sententiae 10 (Jaekel)

159 ἄδικον τὸ λυπεῖν τοὺς φίλους ἑκουσίως

It is unjust to willingly cause grief to friends.

Sententiae 11 (Jaekel)

160 ἀχάριστος, ὅστις εὖ παθὼν ἀμνημονεῖ

Ungrateful he who having received benefits forgets.

Sententiae 12 (Jaekel)

161 ἄγει δὲ πρὸς φῶς τὴν ἀλήθειαν χρόνος

Time brings the truth to light.

Translated by John Simpson and Jennifer Speake (1982)

Sententiae 13 (Jaekel)

cf. the English proverb 'time will tell'

162 ἀβουλίᾳ γὰρ πολλὰ βλάπτονται βροτοί

Indecision is the cause of many human woes.

Sententiae 17 (Jaekel)

163 ἀνεξέταστον μὴ κόλαζε μηδένα

Punish no one without first ascertaining their guilt.

Sententiae 19 (Jaekel)

164 ἅπαντας αὑτῶν κρείσσονας ἀνάγκη ποιεῖ

We all surpass ourselves in necessity.

Sententiae 23 (Jaekel)

165 ἀνδρῶν δὲ φαύλων ὅρκον εἰς ὕδωρ γράφε

Write the oaths of corrupt men in water.

Sententiae 26 (Jaekel)

166 ἀνδρὸς δικαίου καρπὸς οὐκ ἀπόλλυται

The fruit of the righteous is never lost.

Sententiae 28 (Jaekel)

167 ἀνδρὸς πονηροῦ σπλάγχνον οὐ μαλάσσεται

The heart of the malicious will never soften.

Sententiae 33 (Jaekel)

168 ἀλαζονείας οὔτις ἐκφεύγει δίκην

Arrogance never goes unpunished.

Sententiae 35 (Jaekel)

169 ἀνελεύθεροι γάρ εἰσιν οἱ φιλάργυροι

Lovers of money become its slaves.

Sententiae 45 (Jaekel)

170 ἃ μὴ προσήκει μήτ' ἄκουε μήθ' ὅρα

What does not concern you neither hear nor see.

Sententiae 48 (Jaekel)

171 ἅπαντας ἡ παίδευσις ἡμέρους τελεῖ

Education civilizes us all.

Sententiae 50 (Jaekel)

172 ἀρχῆς τετευχὼς ἴσθι ταύτης ἄξιος

If to rule is thy lot, be worthy of it.

Sententiae 55 (Jaekel)

173 ἀνὴρ ὁ φεύγων καὶ πάλιν μαχήσεται

He who fights and runs away may live to

fight another day.

Translated by John Simpson and Jennifer Speake (1982)

Sententiae 56 (Jaekel)

cf. the identical English proverb; thought to have been said by or of Demosthenes, who ran away at the battle of Chaeronea

174 ἀνὴρ ἄβουλος εἰς κενὸν μοχθεῖ τρέχων

An irresolute man toils in vain.

Sententiae 61 (Jaekel)

175 ἄνευ δὲ λύπης οὐδὲ εἷς βροτῶν βίος

There is no life without sorrow.

Sententiae 65 (Jaekel)

176 ἀρχῆς ἁπάσης ἡγεμὼν ἔστω λόγος

Let reason rule.

Sententiae 68 (Jaekel)

177 ἀρετῆς ἁπάσης σεμνὸς ἡγεῖται λόγος

Humility leads the way to virtue.

Sententiae 69 (Jaekel)

178 ἄξεις ἀλύπως τὸν βίον χωρὶς γάμου

The unmarried state is a life without sorrow.

Sententiae 72 (Jaekel)

179 ἀβέβαιός ἐστι πλοῦτος, ἐάν τις εὖ φρονῇ

The sensible know that wealth may be unstable.

Sententiae 73 (Jaekel)

180 ἀνάπαυσις ὕπνος ἐστὶ πάντων τῶν κακῶν

Relaxation is where all evils slumber.

Sententiae 76 (Jaekel)

181 ἅπασιν ἡμῖν ἡ συνείδησις θεός

For us all, god is our conscience.

Sententiae 81 (Jaekel)

182 ἀπῆλθεν οὐδεὶς τῶν βροτῶν πλοῦτον φέρων

No one has left this world carrying away his riches.

Sententiae 87 (Jaekel)

183 ἀεὶ κράτιστόν ἐστι τἀσφαλέστατον

Best is always safest.

Sententiae 93 (Jaekel)

184 βιοῦν ἀλύπως θνητὸν ὄντ' οὐ ῥᾴδιον

Being mortal, it is difficult to live without sorrow.

Sententiae 97 (Jaekel)

185 βέβαιος ἴσθι καὶ βεβαίοις χρῶ φίλοις

Be trustworthy and your friends will be trustworthy too.

Sententiae 100 (Jaekel)

186 βίου δικαίου γίγνεται τέλος καλόν

Honourable is the end of the just.

Sententiae 108 (Jaekel)

187 βουλῆς γὰρ ὀρθῆς οὐδὲν ἀσφαλέστερον

There is nothing safer than honest counsel.

Sententiae 109 (Jaekel)

188 βοηθὸς ἴσθι τοῖς καλῶς εἰργασμένοις

Support a worthy cause.

Sententiae 114 (Jaekel)

189 βέλτιόν ἐστι σῶμά γ' ἢ ψυχὴν νοσεῖν

Bodily sickness is preferable to sickness of the soul.

Sententiae 116 (Jaekel)

190 βραβεῖον ἀρετῆς ἐστιν εὐπαιδευσία

A good education is a prize for excellence.

Sententiae 124 (Jaekel)

191 γυναιξὶ πάσαις κόσμον ἡ σιγὴ φέρει

Women have grace in silence.

Sententiae 139 (Jaekel)

192 γυνὴ γὰρ οὐδὲν οἶδε πλὴν ὃ βούλεται

A woman only knows what she wants to know.

Sententiae 143 (Jaekel)

193 γέλως ἄκαιρος κλαυθμάτων παραίτιος

Ill-timed laughter leads to woe.

Sententiae 144 (Jaekel)

194 γῆ πάντα τίκτει καὶ πάλιν κομίζεται

Earth brings forth all and takes back all.

Sententiae 145 (Jaekel)

195 γράμματα μαθεῖν δεῖ καὶ μαθόντα νοῦν ἔχειν

Study first and, after learning, use your

brain.

Sententiae 152 (Jaekel)

196 γυνὴ τὸ σύνολόν ἐστι δαπανηρὸν φύσει

All in all, women are extravagant by nature.

Sententiae 153 (Jaekel)

197 γάμει δὲ μὴ τὴν προῖκα, τὴν γυναῖκα δέ

Marry the woman, not the dowry.

Sententiae 154 (Jaekel)

198 γυνὴ δὲ χρηστὴ πηδάλιόν ἐστ' οἰκίας

A good woman steers the home.

Sententiae 155 (Jaekel)

199 γάμος γὰρ ἀνθρώποισιν εὐκταῖον κακόν

Marriage is an evil that most men welcome.

Translated by D.S. Baker (1998)

Sententiae 159 (Jaekel)

200 γύμναζε παῖδας· ἄνδρας οὐ γὰρ γυμνάσεις

Train your children; men will not be trained.

Sententiae 161 (Jaekel)

201 γονεῖς δὲ τίμα καὶ φίλους εὐεργέτει

Honour your parents, show kindness to your friends.

Sententiae 162 (Jaekel)

202 γελᾷ δ' ὁ μῶρος, κἄν τι μὴ γελοῖον ᾖ

Fools laugh even when there is nothing to laugh at.

Sententiae 165 (Jaekel)

203 δίκαιος εἶναι μᾶλλον ἢ χρηστὸς θέλε

Be just rather than kindly.

Sententiae 174 (Jaekel)

204 δεῖ τοὺς φιλοῦντας πίστιν, οὐ λόγους ἔχειν

Offer trust, not words to those you love.

Sententiae 175 (Jaekel)

205 διπλῶς ὁρῶσιν οἱ μαθόντες γράμματα

Doubly perceptive are the educated.

Sententiae 180 (Jaekel)

inscribed over the entrance of Adam House (Examination Halls of the University of Edinburgh)

206 δὶς ἐξαμαρτεῖν ταὐτὸν οὐκ ἀνδρὸς σοφοῦ

Unwise he who makes twice the same mistake.

Sententiae 183 (Jaekel)

still used proverbially today

207 δειναὶ γὰρ αἱ γυναῖκες εὑρίσκειν τέχνας

Wondrous are women in devising wiles.

Sententiae 194 (Jaekel)

208 διὰ τῆς σιωπῆς πικρότερον κατηγόρει

With your silence you voice even more bitter accusations.

Sententiae 201 (Jaekel)

209 δίκαιος ἀδικεῖν οὐκ ἐπίσταται τρόπος

A righteous character knows not unrighteousness.

Sententiae 206 (Jaekel)

210 δίκαιος ἴσθι καὶ φίλοισι καὶ ξένοις

Be fair with both friends and strangers.

Sententiae 208 (Jaekel)

211 ἐν ταῖς ἀνάγκαις χρημάτων κρείττων φίλος

In times of need a friend is better than wealth.

Sententiae 214 (Jaekel)

212 ἐπ' ἀνδρὶ δυστυχοῦντι μὴ πλάσῃς κακόν

Cause no harm or ill to the unfortunate.

Sententiae 216 (Jaekel)

213 εὐχῆς δικαίας οὐκ ἀνήκοος θεός

God is not deaf to an honest prayer.

Sententiae 217 (Jaekel)

214 ἔργων πονηρῶν χεῖρ' ἐλευθέραν ἔχε

Keep your hands free from wicked deeds.

Translated by Gavin Betts and Alan Henry (1989)

Sententiae 220 (Jaekel)

215 ἐν νυκτὶ βουλὴ τοῖς σοφοῖσι γίγνεται

Night brings counsel to the wise.

Sententiae 222 (Jaekel)

cf. the saying 'let us sleep on it.'; and the French 'la nuit porte conseil'

216 ἔστιν Δίκης ὀφθαλμὸς ὃς τὰ πάνθ' ὁρᾷ

There is an eye of Justice, perceiving

everything.

Sententiae 225 (Jaekel)

217 ἐφόδιον εἰς τὸ γῆρας αἰεὶ κατατίθου

Lay up provisions for your old age.

Sententiae 227 (Jaekel)

218 ἔρωτα παύει λιμὸς ἢ χαλκοῦ σπάνις

Hunger and penury kill love.

Sententiae 228 (Jaekel)

219 ἐλευθέρου γάρ ἐστι τἀληθῆ λέγειν

To speak the truth is the privilege of the free.

Sententiae 234 (Jaekel)

220 εἰ μὴ φυλάσσεις μίκρ', ἀπολεῖς τὰ μείζονα

By not preserving what is small, you lose what is great.

Sententiae 245 (Jaekel)

221 ἔργοις φιλόπονος ἴσθι, μὴ λόγοις μόνον

Be industrious in deeds, not only in words.

Sententiae 256 (Jaekel)

222 ἐνίοις τὸ σιγᾶν κρεῖττόν ἐστι τοῦ λαλεῖν

Children should be seen and not heard.

Translated by D.S. Baker (1998)

Sententiae 258 (Jaekel)

223 ζήσεις βίον κράτιστον, ἣν θυμοῦ κρατῇς

You'll live a better life if you control your anger.

Sententiae 269 (Jaekel)

224 ἡ γλῶσσα πολλοὺς εἰς ὄλεθρον ἤγαγεν

Many a man has been ruined by his tongue.

Sententiae 289 (Jaekel)

225 ἡ γλῶσσ' ἁμαρτάνουσα τἀληθῆ λέγει

It is the tongue that errs which speaks the truth.

Sententiae 294 (Jaekel)

226 ἡ φύσις ἁπάντων τῶν διδαγμάτων κρατεῖ

Nature prevails over all instruction.

Sententiae 298 (Jaekel)

227 ἤθους δικαίου φαῦλος οὐ ψαύει λόγος

A virtuous character is untouched by wicked words.

Sententiae 299 (Jaekel)

228 ἡ κοιλία καὶ πολλὰ χωρεῖ κὠλίγα

The stomach can take both a lot and a little.

Sententiae 311 (Jaekel)

229 ἤθη τὰ πάντων ἐν χρόνῳ πειράζεται

Our characters are constantly tested by time.

Sententiae 320 (Jaekel)

230 θάλασσα καὶ πῦρ καὶ γυνὴ τρίτον κακόν

Sea and fire and woman, the third evil.

Sententiae 323 (Jaekel)

231 θεὸς πέφυκεν, ὅστις οὐδὲν δρᾷ κακόν

Whoever does no evil is by nature a god.

Sententiae 327 (Jaekel)

232 θεὸς συνεργὸς πάντα ποιεῖ ῥᾳδίως

Everything is easier when god lends a hand.

Sententiae 330 (Jaekel)

233 θυμῷ χαρίζου μηδὲν ἄνπερ νοῦν ἔχῃς

Do not give way to anger if you have sense.

Sententiae 339 (Jaekel)

234 θανάτου μόνον οὐκ ἔστιν ἐπανόρθωμα

Only death cannot be rectified.

Sententiae 353 (Jaekel)

235 ἴσος ἴσθι κρίνων καὶ φίλους καὶ μὴ φίλους

Be impartial, judging either friend or foe.

Sententiae 373 (Jaekel)

236 ἰατρὸς ἀδόλεσχος ἐπὶ τῇ νόσῳ νόσος

A chattering doctor is yet another illness for the sick.

Sententiae 379 (Jaekel)

237 καιρὸς γάρ ἐστι τῶν νόμων κρείττων πολύ

Time is stronger than any laws of man.

Sententiae 382 (Jaekel)

238 κακοῖς ὁμιλῶν καὐτὸς ἐκβήσῃ κακός

By associating with the wicked you too become wicked.

Sententiae 383 (Jaekel)

239 κρίνει φίλους ὁ καιρός, ὡς χρυσὸν τὸ πῦρ

Time tests friends, as fire tests gold.

Sententiae 385 (Jaekel)

240 καιροὶ δὲ καταλύουσι τὰς τυραννίδας

The turning of time will break up tyrannies.

Sententiae 387 (Jaekel)

241 κάλλιστον ἐν κήποισι φύεται ῥόδον

The rose is the queen of the garden.

Sententiae 403 (Jaekel)

242 κατηγορεῖν οὐκ ἔστι καὶ κρίνειν ὁμοῦ

You cannot be both accuser and judge.

Sententiae 404 (Jaekel)

243 καλῶς ἀκούειν μᾶλλον ἢ πλουτεῖν θέλε

Choose a good reputation rather than wealth.

Translated by Gavin Betts and Alan Henry (1989)

Sententiae 406 (Jaekel)

244 κενῆς δὲ δόξης οὐδὲν ἀθλιώτερον

Nothing is worse than empty glory.

Sententiae 408 (Jaekel)

245 κακὸν φέρουσι καρπὸν οἱ κακοὶ φίλοι

Wicked friends bear wicked fruit.

Translated by Gavin Betts and Alan Henry (1989)

Sententiae 412 (Jaekel)

246 καὶ ζῶν ὁ φαῦλος καὶ θανὼν κολάζεται

In death, as in life, wickedness is censured.

Sententiae 413 (Jaekel)

247 καλόν γε γαστρὸς κἀπιθυμίας κρατεῖν

It is good to control your stomach and your cravings.

Sententiae 425 (Jaekel)

248 κόλαζε κρίνων ἀλλὰ μὴ θυμούμενος

Sit in judgement without ill temper.

Sententiae 429 (Jaekel)

also attributed to Demonax, Fragment 2 (Snell, *TrGF*)

249 λιμὴν ἀτυχίας ἐστὶν ἀνθρώποις τέχνη

Art is a haven in man's misfortune.

Sententiae 430 (Jaekel)

250 λίαν φιλῶν σεαυτὸν οὐχ ἕξεις φίλον

Too much self-love will win no friends.

Sententiae 431 (Jaekel)

251 λόγῳ μ' ἔπεισας φαρμάκῳ σοφωτάτῳ

Your words, wiser than medicine, have convinced me.

Sententiae 437 (Jaekel)

252 λογισμός ἐστι φάρμακον λύπης μόνος

Reason is the only remedy for sorrow.

Sententiae 439 (Jaekel)

253 λαλεῖν μὲν οἶδας, τί δὲ λαλεῖς οὐκ αἰσθάνῃ

You know how to babble, not knowing what you're saying.

Sententiae 441 (Jaekel)

254 λιμὴν νεὼς ὅρμος, βίου δ' ἀλυπία

Ships seek a harbour, life freedom from grief.

Sententiae 444 (Jaekel)

255 λιμῷ γὰρ οὐδέν ἐστιν ἀντειπεῖν ἔπος

Words are no relief from hunger.

Sententiae 447 (Jaekel)

256 λάλει τὰ μέτρια, μὴ λάλει δ', ἃ μή σε δεῖ

Speak in moderation, and not of what you shouldn't.

Sententiae 455 (Jaekel)

257 λύπης ἰατρός ἐστιν ὁ χρηστὸς φίλος

A good friend is a physician for sorrow.

Sententiae 456 (Jaekel)

258 μὴ κρῖν' ὁρῶν τὸ κάλλος, ἀλλὰ τὸν τρόπον

Do not judge by looks but by virtue.

Sententiae 458 (Jaekel)

259 μηδέποτε σαυτὸν δυστυχῶν ἀπελπίσῃς

If misfortune finds you, do not lose hope.

Sententiae 469 (Jaekel)

260 μέγιστον ὀργῆς ἐστι φάρμακον λόγος

Reasoning is the best remedy for anger.

Sententiae 476 (Jaekel)

261 μετὰ τὴν δόσιν τάχιστα γηράσκει χάρις

Gratitude ages fast after the gift is given.

Sententiae 477 (Jaekel)

262 μέμνησο πλουτῶν τοὺς πένητας ὠφελεῖν

Remember in wealth to succour the poor.

Sententiae 478 (Jaekel)

263 μή μοι γένοιθ' ἃ βούλομ', ἀλλ' ἃ συμφέρει

May things come not as I wish, but as they shall be of benefit to me.

Sententiae 481 (Jaekel)

264 μὴ σπεῦδε πλουτῶν, μὴ ταχὺς πένης γένῃ

Hurry not in gaining wealth lest you be hurried into poverty.

Sententiae 487 (Jaekel)

265 μήτηρ άπάντων γαῖα καὶ κοινὴ τροφός

Earth is the mother and provider of everything.

Sententiae 511 (Jaekel)

266 νικᾷ λογισμὸς τὴν παροῦσαν συμφοράν

Power of thought will overcome our present adversity.

Sententiae 515 (Jaekel)

267 νόμιζ' ἀδελφοὺς τοὺς ἀληθινοὺς φίλους

Look at true friends as brothers.

Sententiae 523 (Jaekel)

268 νίκησον ὀργὴν τῷ λογίζεσθαι καλῶς

Win over anger with positive thinking.

Sententiae 528 (Jaekel)

269 Νόμιζε πλουτεῖν, ἂν φίλους πολλοὺς ἔχῃς

Consider yourself wealthy if you have many friends.

Sententiae 541 (Jaekel)

270 ξένους πένητας μὴ παραδράμῃς ἰδών

Look not aside when seeing a beggar, be he a stranger.

Sententiae 542 (Jaekel)

271 ξένοισι πιστοῖς πιστὸς ὢν γίνου φίλος

Be a trusting friend to a trusting foreigner.

Sententiae 543 (Jaekel)

272 ξένος ὢν ἀκολούθει τοῖς ἐπιχωρίοις νόμοις

Being a foreigner, equally abide by the laws of the land.

Sententiae 547 (Jaekel)

273 ξένον προτιμᾶν μᾶλλον ἀνθρώποις ἔθος

People tend to value a foreigner more.

Sententiae 553 (Jaekel)

274 ξένους ξένιζε, μήποτε ξένος γένῃ

Be hospitable to foreigners, you too may be one some day.

Sententiae 554 (Jaekel)

275 οὐκ ἔστιν αἰσχρὸν ἀγνοοῦντα μανθάνειν

It is not shameful to learn what you are ignorant of.

Sententiae 561 (Jaekel)

276 οὐκ ἔσθ' ὑγιείας κρεῖττον οὐδὲν ἐν βίῳ

Nothing in life is more important than health.

Sententiae 562 (Jaekel)

277 οὐδεὶς μετ' ὀργῆς ἀσφαλῶς βουλεύεται

Proper decisions are not taken in anger.

Sententiae 564 (Jaekel)

278 οὐκ ἔστι σοφίας κτῆμα τιμιώτερον

No possession is more valuable than wisdom.

Sententiae 565 (Jaekel)

279 ὀργῆς χάριν τὰ κρυπτὰ μὴ ἐκφάνῃς φίλου

Even in anger do not reveal the secrets of friends.

Sententiae 567 (Jaekel)

280 ὁ σοφὸς ἐν αὑτῷ περιφέρει τὴν οὐσίαν

The wise man carries his wealth with him.

Sententiae 569 (Jaekel)

cf. Cicero, Paradoxa Stoicorum *1.1.8, 'omnia mea mecum porto', of Bias*

281 ὁ μὴ δαρεὶς ἄνθρωπος οὐ παιδεύεται

A boy not beaten will never learn.

Sententiae 573 (Jaekel)

cf. 'spare the rod and spoil the child'

282 ὁ μηδὲν εἰδὼς οὐδὲν ἐξαμαρτάνει

Who knows nothing errs in nothing.

Sententiae 579 (Jaekel)

283 ὅτ' εὐτυχεῖς μάλιστα, μὴ φρόνει μέγα

Do not boast of your present good fortune.

Sententiae 581 (Jaekel)

284 ὅμοια πόρνη δάκρυα καὶ ῥήτωρ ἔχει

The prostitute and the orator weep the same tears.

Sententiae 584 (Jaekel)

285 ὁ λόγος ἰατρὸς ἐστι τοῦ κατὰ ψυχὴν πάθους

Speech, physician for a suffering soul.

Sententiae 587 (Jaekel)

286 οὐ χρὴ φέρειν τὰ πρόσθεν ἐν μνήμῃ κακά

Better not to dwell on past misfortunes.

Sententiae 589 (Jaekel)

287 ὀχληρός ἐστ' ἄνθρωπος ἐν νέοις γέρων

An old man is irksome when among the young.

Sententiae 593 (Jaekel)

288 ὅπου βία πάρεστιν, οὐ σθένει νόμος

Where violence is in attendance law will not prevail.

Sententiae 595 (Jaekel)

289 οὐκ ἔστιν, ὅστις τὴν τύχην οὐ μέμφεται

There is no one who does not blame fortune.

Sententiae 611 (Jaekel)

290 οὐκ ἔστιν οὐδὲν ἀγριώτερον φθόνου

There is nothing more savage than envy.

Sententiae 616 (Jaekel)

291 πανήγυριν νόμιζε τόνδε τὸν βίον

Look at this life as a celebration.

Sententiae 627 (Jaekel)

292 πράττων τὰ σαυτοῦ, μὴ τὰ τῶν ἄλλων σκόπει

Manage your own affairs, ignore what others do.

Sententiae 629 (Jaekel)

293 προπέτεια πολλοῖς ἐστιν αἰτία κακῶν

Rashness is the cause of misfortune to many.

Sententiae 631 (Jaekel)

294 πολλοὶ τραπέζης, οὐκ ἀληθείας φίλοι

Many are friends of your table, not true friends.

Sententiae 641 (Jaekel)

295 πλάνη βίον τίθησι σωφρονέστερον

Travel sharpens the wits.

Translated by D.S. Baker (1998)

Sententiae 644 (Jaekel)

296 πολλοὺς ὁ καιρὸς ἄνδρας οὐκ ὄντας ποιεῖ

Circumstances often promote unworthy men.

Sententiae 646 (Jaekel)

297 πολλοὶ μαθηταὶ κρείττονες διδασκάλων

Many pupils are wiser than their teachers.

Translated by H.T. Riley (1872)

Sententiae 651 (Jaekel)

298 πολλοὺς κακῶς πράσσοντας ὤρθωσεν τύχη

Many a downtrodden fellow is restored by good fortune.

Sententiae 652 (Jaekel)

299 πολυπραγμονεῖν τἀλλότρια μὴ βούλου κακά

Do not busy yourself with other people's problems.

Sententiae 653 (Jaekel)

300 πενίαν φέρειν καὶ γῆράς ἐστι δύσκολον

It is hard to suffer poverty and old age.

Sententiae 656 (Jaekel)

301 πολλῶν ἰατρῶν εἴσοδός μ' ἀπώλεσεν

The visits of many physicians have destroyed me.

Translated by H.T. Riley (1872)

Sententiae 659 (Jaekel)

302 πάντως γὰρ ὁ σοφὸς εὐτελείας ἀνέχεται

A wise man bears poverty best.

Sententiae 662 (Jaekel)

303 πολλοῖς κακοῖσιν ἡ τύχη παρίσταται

Many an unworthy person is favoured by fortune.

Sententiae 663 (Jaekel)

304 ῥῆμα παρὰ καιρὸν ῥηθὲν ἀνατρέπει βίον

An untimely word can destroy the course of a lifetime.

Sententiae 690 (Jaekel)

305 ῥέγχει παρούσης τῆς τύχης τὰ πράγματα

Affairs can sleep soundly when fortune is present.

Translated by H.T. Riley (1872)

Sententiae 691 (Jaekel)

306 ῥίψας λόγον τις οὐκ ἀναιρεῖται πάλιν

Once a word is said there's no taking it back.

Sententiae 692 (Jaekel)

307 ῥήτωρ πονηρὸς τοὺς νόμους λυμαίνεται

A knavish orator corrupts the law.

Sententiae 694 (Jaekel)

308 ῥᾷον βίον ζῇς, ἢν γυναῖκα μὴ τρέφῃς

You will pass your life more easily if you don't have to maintain a wife.

Translated by H.T. Riley (1872)

Sententiae 700 (Jaekel)

309 στρέφει δὲ πάντα τὰν βίῳ μικρὰ τύχη

A small turn of fortune may change a whole life.

Sententiae 708 (Jaekel)

310 σύμβουλος οὐδείς ἐστι βελτίων χρόνου

There is no better counsellor than time.

Translated by H.T. Riley (1872)

Sententiae 714 (Jaekel)

311 σοφοὶ δὲ συγκρύπτουσιν οἰκείας βλάβας

The wise keep their personal misfortunes to themselves.

Sententiae 719 (Jaekel)

312 τὸ μηδὲν εἰκῇ πανταχοῦ 'στι χρήσιμον

The admonition, 'nothing rashly', is useful everywhere.

Translated by H.T. Riley (1872)

Sententiae 736 (Jaekel)

an expression often used, cf. Hippocrates 35

313 ταὐτόματον ἡμῶν καλλίω βουλεύεται

Chance often contrives better than we ourselves.

Translated by H.T. Riley (1872)

Sententiae 738 (Jaekel)

314 τύχη τέχνην ὤρθωσεν, οὐ τέχνη τύχην

Chance sometimes improves on art, not art on chance.

Sententiae 740 (Jaekel)

315 τῶν εὐτυχούντων πάντες εἰσὶ συγγενεῖς

Everyone claims kinship to the fortunate.

Sententiae 748 (Jaekel)

316 τῶν γὰρ πενήτων εἰσὶν οἱ λόγοι κενοί

Poor men's words bear little weight.

Translated by H.T. Riley (1872)

Sententiae 752 (Jaekel)

317 τὰ δάνεια δούλους τοὺς ἐλευθέρους ποιεῖ

Debts turn free men into slaves.

Translated by H.T. Riley (1872)

Sententiae 759 (Jaekel)

318 ὑφ' ἡδονῆς ὁ φρόνιμος οὐχ ἁλίσκεται

A sensible man is not enslaved by passion.

Sententiae 777 (Jaekel)

319 ὑγίεια καὶ νοῦς ἀγαθὰ τῷ βίῳ δύο

Health and intellect are the two blessings of life.

Sententiae 779 (Jaekel)

320 ὕπνος δὲ πάσης ἐστὶν ὑγίεια νόσου

Sleep is beneficial in every distress or anguish.

Sententiae 783 (Jaekel)

321 υἱῷ μέγιστον ἀγαθόν ἐστ' ἔμφρων πατήρ

A prudent father is a great blessing for his son.

Sententiae 788 (Jaekel)

322 ὑπὲρ σεαυτοῦ καὶ φίλου μάχου πάνυ

Fight hard for yourself and your friend.

Sententiae 791 (Jaekel)

323 ὑπὲρ γυναικὸς καὶ φίλου πονητέον

It is our duty to strive for wife and friend.

Sententiae 796 (Jaekel)

324 ὕπουλος ἀνὴρ δίκτυον κεκρυμμένον

The cunning man is a hidden snare.

Translated by Panos Koronakis-Rohlf and Maria Batzini (2007)

Sententiae 797 (Jaekel)

325 φύσιν πονηρὰν μεταβαλεῖν οὐ ῥᾴδιον

It is difficult to transform inborn

wickedness.

Sententiae 801 (Jaekel)

326 φίλων τρόπους γίνωσκε, μὴ μίσει δ' ὅλως

Be accommodating with your friends' ways, never really hate them.

Sententiae 804 (Jaekel)

327 φίλους ἔχων νόμιζε θησαυροὺς ἔχειν

Friends are like possessing treasure.

Sententiae 810 (Jaekel)

328 φιλεῖ δ' ἑαυτοῦ πλεῖον οὐδεὶς οὐδένα

No one loves anyone as much as himself.

Sententiae 814 (Jaekel)

329 χάριν φίλοις εὔκαιρον ἀπόδος ἐμ μέρει

Render a timely service back to your friends in turn.

Translated by D.L. Page (1941)

Sententiae 824 (Jaekel)

330 χρυσὸς δ' ἀνοίγει πάντα καὶ χαλκᾶς πύλας

Gold can open everything, even bronze gates.

Sententiae 826 (Jaekel)

331 χάριν λαβὼν μέμνησο καὶ δοὺς ἐπιλαθοῦ

Remember favours received, forget favours given.

Sententiae 827 (Jaekel)

332 ψυχῆς νοσούσης ἐστὶ φάρμακον λόγος

Words, consolation to an ailing soul.

Sententiae 840 (Jaekel)

333 ψευδόμενος οὐδεὶς λανθάνει πολὺν χρόνον

Liars do not escape notice for long.

Sententiae 841 (Jaekel)

334 ψυχῆς μέγας χαλινὸς ἀνθρώποις ὁ νοῦς

Mind, a mighty bridle for the soul.

Sententiae 844 (Jaekel)

335 ὡς ἡδὺ τὸ ζῆν μὴ φθονούσης τῆς τύχης

How sweet is life if not begrudged by fortune.

Sententiae 855 (Jaekel)

336 ὡς ἡδὺ κάλλος, ὅταν ἔχῃ νοῦν σώφρονα

How welcome beauty is when accompanied by sense.

Sententiae 857 (Jaekel)

337 ὡς εὐκόλως πίπτουσιν αἱ λαμπραὶ τύχαι

How easily great fortunes fall!

Sententiae 862 (Jaekel)

338 ὡς μέγα τὸ μικρόν ἐστιν ἐν καιρῷ δοθέν

How great is a small gift given at the right time.

Sententiae 872 (Jaekel)

339 ὡς ποικίλον πρᾶγμ' ἐστὶ καὶ πλάνον τύχη

How diverse and fickle luck can be!

Sententiae 874 (Jaekel)

340 ἀρχὴ μεγίστη τοῦ φρονεῖν τὰ γράμματα

Letters are the first and foremost guide to understanding.

Translated by D.L. Page (1941)

Sententiae e papyris 2.1 (Jaekel)

341 γέροντα τίμα

Honour old age.

Sententiae e papyris 2.3 (Jaekel)

342 ὁ νοῦς ἐν ἡμῖν μαντικώτατος θεός

Our mind is the greatest god of divination

Translated by D.L. Page (1941)

Sententiae e papyris 2.15 (Jaekel)

343 σῶσον σεαυτὸν ἐκ πονηρῶν πραγμάτων

Save yourself from affairs of the baser sort.

Sententiae e papyris 2.18 (Jaekel)

344 ὦ τῶν ἁπάντων χρημάτων πλείστη χάρις

O gratitude, greatest of all riches!

Sententiae e papyris 2.24 (Jaekel)

345 ὡς εὐάλωτος πρὸς τὸ κέρδος ἔσθ' ἅπας

How easily human nature yields to profit!

Translated by D.L. Page (1941)

Sententiae e papyris 3.5 (Jaekel)

346 ὡς ἡδὺ γονέων καὶ τέκνων ὁμιλία

How sweet is harmony of child and parent!

Translated by D.L. Page (1941)

Sententiae e papyris 3.9 (Jaekel)

347 ἔγωγε πεποίηκα τὴν κωμῳδίαν· ᾠκονόμηται γὰρ ἡ διάθεσις· δεῖ δ' αὐτῇ τὰ στιχίδια ἐπᾷσαι

Oh yes, I've written the play, the plot's worked out – all I have to do is put the lines in.

Translated by M.S. Silk (2000)

Plutarch, *Were the Athenians More Famous in War or in Wisdom* 347e

METAGENES

5th century BC
Athenian Old Comedy poet

1 ὥσπερ ἐπειδὰν δειπνῶμέν που, τότε πλεῖστα λαλοῦμεν ἅπαντες

It's just like when we go to dinner, we all start talking the most.

Translated by Ian C. Storey (2011)

Fragment 3 (Kock) – 3 (K-A) – *Aurae – Breezes*

the same words also appear in the Aristagoras play Mammacythos, *possibly a revision of* Aurae

METRODORUS

4th century BC
Philosopher from Chios

1 πάντα ἐστίν, ὃ ἄν τις νοῆσαι

Everything exists, if it can be perceived by the mind.

Fragment 2 (D-K) – *On Nature*

MILTIADES

*c.*550–489BC
Athenian general, won the battle of Marathon in 490BC
see also Themistocles 18; Herodotus 112

1 Μιλτιάδες ἀνέθεκεν τῷ Διί

Miltiades dedicates this to Zeus.

dedication inscribed on the Helmet of Miltiades, now held at the Olympia Archaeological Museum, Inv. no. B2600

MIMNERMUS

fl. 632–629BC
Elegiac poet from Smyrna

1 τίς δὲ βίος, τί δὲ τερπνὸν ἄτερ χρυσῆς Ἀφροδίτης;

What would life be, what pleasure, without golden Aphrodite?

Translated by C.A. Trypanis (1971)

Fragment 1.1 (West, *IEG*)

Aphrodite as the goddess of love

2 ἥβης ἄνθεα γίνεται ἁρπαλέα
ἀνδράσιν ἠδὲ γυναιξίν

Flowers of youth, delightful to men and women.

Translated by C.A. Trypanis (1971)

Fragment 1.4 (West, *IEG*)

of secret love

3 μίνυνθα δὲ γίνεται ἥβης
καρπός, ὅσον τ' ἐπὶ γῆν κίδναται ἠέλιος

The harvest of youth is as quickly gone
as the rising sun spreads his light abroad.

Translated by J.M. Edmonds (1931)

Fragment 2.7 (West, *IEG*)

4 αὐτὰρ ἐπὴν δὴ τοῦτο τέλος παραμείψεται ὥρης,
αὐτίκα δὴ τεθνάναι βέλτιον ἢ βίοτος

But when the time of maturity is past,
then to be dead is better than to live.

Translated by J.M. Edmonds (1931)

Fragment 2.9 (West, *IEG*)

5 Τιθωνῷ μὲν ἔδωκεν ἔχειν κακὸν ἄφθιτον
γῆρας, ὃ καὶ θανάτου ῥίγιον ἀργαλέου

Zeus gave Tithonus the evil gift of unending old age,
worse even than woeful Death.

Fragment 4 (West, *IEG*)

6 ἀλλ' ὀλιγοχρόνιος γίνεται ὥσπερ ὄναρ
ἥβη τιμήεσσα

But precious youth is short-lived as a dream.

Translated by J.M. Edmonds (1931)

Fragment 5 (West, *IEG*)

7 αἲ γὰρ ἄτερ νούσων τε καὶ ἀργαλέων μελεδωνέων
ἑξηκονταέτη μοῖρα κίχοι θανάτου

Would that by no disease, no cares oppress,
I in my sixtieth year were laid to rest.

Translated by R.D. Hicks (1925)

Fragment 6 (West, *IEG*)

8 ἀληθείη δὲ παρέστω
σοὶ καὶ ἐμοί, πάντων χρῆμα δικαιότατον

Betwixt thee and me let there be truth,
the most righteous of all things.

Translated by J.M. Edmonds (1931)

Fragment 8 (West, *IEG*)

9 δεινοὶ γὰρ ἀνδρὶ πάντες ἐσμὲν εὐκλεεῖ
ζῶντι φθονῆσαι, κατθανόντα δ' αἰνέσαι

We are prone to resent the famous when alive,
and ready to praise them once they're dead.

Fragment 25 (West, *IEG*)

ascribed to Mimnermus Tragedian by Nauck (TGF), Fragment 1; entered under Tragica Adespota *by Kannicht and Snell (*TrGF*), Fragment 6b*

MOSCHION

3rd century BC
Athenian tragic playwright

1 καὶ γὰρ ἐν νάπαις βραχεῖ
πολὺς σιδήρῳ κείρεται πεύκης κλάδος,
καὶ βαιὸς ὄχλος μυρίας λόγχης κρατεῖ

As in a forest
a small axe can fell the largest tree,
so a small army can ward off a myriad spears.

Fragment 1 (Snell, *TrGF*) – *Themistocles*

2 μόνον σὺ θυμοῦ χωρὶς ἔνδεξαι λόγους
οὕς σοι κομίζω· τὸν κλύοντα γὰρ λαβὼν
ὁ μῦθος εὔνουν οὐ μάτην λεχθήσεται

Hear my words without passion;
words that fall on willing ears
are never spoken in vain.

Fragment 5 (Snell, *TrGF*)

3 ὁ δ' ἀσθενὴς ἦν τῶν ἀμεινόνων βορά

The weak are the prey of the powerful.

Fragment 6 (Snell, *TrGF*)

MOSCHUS

mid 2nd century BC
Bucolic poet from Syracuse

1 ταὶ μαλάχαι μέν, ἐπὰν κατὰ κᾶπον ὄλωνται,
ἠδὲ τὰ χλωρὰ σέλινα τό τ' εὐθαλὲς οὖλον ἄνηθον
ὕστερον αὖ ζώοντι καὶ εἰς ἔτος ἄλλο φύοντι·
ἄμμες δ' οἱ μεγάλοι καὶ καρτεροί, οἱ σοφοὶ ἄνδρες,
ὁππότε πρᾶτα θάνωμες, ἀνάκοοι ἐν χθονὶ κοίλᾳ
εὕδομες εὖ μάλα μακρὸν ἀτέρμονα νήγρετον ὕπνον

Ah! when the mallow in the croft dies down,
Or the pale parsley or the crisped anise,
Again they grow, another year they flourish;
But we, the great, the valiant, and the wise,
Once covered over in the hollow earth,
Sleep a long, dreamless, unawakening sleep.

Translated by Walter Savage Landor (1842)

Lament for Bion 99

2 τὰν ἅλα τὰν γλαυκὰν ὅταν ὥνεμος ἀτρέμα βάλλῃ,
τὰν φρένα τὰν δειλὰν ἐρεθίζομαι, οὐδ' ἔτι μοι γᾶ
ἐντὶ φίλα, ποθίει δὲ πολὺ πλέον ἁ μεγάλα μ' ἅλς.
ἀλλ' ὅταν ἀχήσῃ πολιὸς βυθὸς ἁ δὲ θάλασσα
κυρτὸν ἐπαφρίζῃ τὰ δὲ κύματα μακρὰ μεμήνῃ,
ἐς χθόνα παπταίνω καὶ δένδρεα τὰν δ' ἅλα φεύγω

When winds that move not its calm surface sweep
The azure sea, I love the land no more;
The smiles of the serene and tranquil deep
Tempt my unquiet mind. – But when the roar
Of ocean's grey abyss resounds, and foam
Gathers upon the sea, and vast waves burst,
I turn from the drear aspect to the home
Of earth and its deep woods, where interspersed,
When winds blow loud, pines make sweet melody.

Translated by Percy Bysshe Shelley (1816)

Fragment 1.1 (Gow)

3 ἦ κακὸν ὁ γριπεὺς ζώει βίον, ᾧ δόμος ἁ ναῦς,
καὶ πόνος ἐντὶ θάλασσα, καὶ ἰχθύες ἁ πλάνος ἄγρα

A wretched life a fisherman's must be,
His home a ship, his labour in the sea,
And fish, the slippery object of his gain.

Translated by Leigh Hunt (1816)

Fragment 1.9 (Gow)

4 αὐτὰρ ἐμοὶ γλυκὺς ὕπνος ὑπὸ πλατάνῳ βαθυφύλλῳ

I love a sleep under a leafy plane.

Translated by Leigh Hunt (1816)

Fragment 1.11 (Gow)

5 παγᾶς φιλέοιμι τὸν ἐγγύθεν ἆχον ἀκούειν
ἃ τέρπει ψοφέοισα τὸν ἄγρυπνον, οὐχὶ ταράσσει

The brook's murmuring
Moves the calm spirit, but disturbs it not.

Translated by Percy Bysshe Shelley (1816)

Fragment 1.12 (Gow)

MUSAEUS (1)

dates uncertain

A mythical singer, closely connected with Orpheus

1 ὡς δ' αὔτως καὶ φύλλα φύει ζείδωρος ἄρουρα·
ἄλλα μὲν ἐν μελίῃσιν ἀποφθίνει, ἄλλα δὲ φύει·
ὣς δὲ καὶ ἀνθρώπων γενεὴ καὶ φῦλον ἑλίσσει

As life-giving earth sends up the leaves,
some it withers away, others it brings forth;
so the generations of man circle round.

Fragment 5 (D-K)

echoing Homer 84

MUSAEUS (2)

5th/6th century AD

Epic poet, learned Christian and/or Neoplatonist

1 παρθένον οὐκ ἐπέοικεν ὑποδρήσσειν Ἀφροδίτῃ,
παρθενικαῖς οὐ Κύπρις ἰαίνεται

It is not fitting a virgin attend on Aphrodite;
Cypris takes no pleasure in virgins.

Translated by Thomas Gelzer and Cedric H. Whitman (1958)

Hero and Leander 143

cf. Christopher Marlowe, Hero and Leander *(1598)*

2 ἐν δὲ σιωπῇ
ἔργον ὅ περ τελέει τις, ἐνὶ τριόδοισιν ἀκούει

That same deed
that a man does in silence, he hears of at the crossroads.

Translated by Thomas Gelzer and Cedric H. Whitman (1958)

Hero and Leander 183

the τρίοδοι (crossroads) were frequented by fortune-tellers and loungers

3 δεινὸς Ἔρως, καὶ πόντος ἀμείλιχος· ἀλλὰ θαλάσσης
ἐστὶν ὕδωρ, τὸ δ' Ἔρωτος ἐμὲ φλέγει ἐνδόμυχον πῦρ

Fearful is love, and the sea unsparing; yet the sea
keeps its water, while I inwardly burn with the fire of Eros.

Hero and Leander 245

4 νὺξ ἦν· εὖτε μάλιστα βαρυπνείοντες ἀῆται
χειμερίαις πνοιῇσιν ἀκοντίζοντες ἰωὰς
ἀθρόον ἐμπίπτουσιν ἐπὶ ῥηγμῖνι θαλάσσης

Night came down, and violent winds
in stormy blasts, with shrieking sounds,
fell in full force upon the shore.

Hero and Leander 309

of the night Leander drowned

5 ἤδη κύματι κῦμα κυλίνδετο, σύγχυτο δ' ὕδωρ,
αἰθέρι μίσγετο πόντος, ἀνέγρετο πάντοθεν ἠχὴ
μαρναμένων ἀνέμων

Now wave wallowed on wave, the water was all turmoiled,
Sea mingled with upper air, and everywhere rose the sound
Of warring winds.

Translated by Thomas Gelzer and Cedric H. Whitman (1958)

Hero and Leander 314

6 Ἔρως δ' οὐκ ἤρκεσε Μοίρας

Eros could not hold back the Fates.

Translated by C.A. Trypanis (1971)

Hero and Leander 323

7 ἤλυθεν ἠριγένεια, καὶ οὐκ ἴδε νυμφίον Ἡρώ

Dawn came, but Hero did not see her lover.

Translated by C.A. Trypanis (1971)

Hero and Leander 335

8 ῥοιζηδὸν προκάρηνος ἀπ' ἠλιβάτου πέσε πύργου·
κὰδ δ' Ἡρὼ τέθνηκε σὺν ὀλλυμένῳ παρακοίτῃ,
ἀλλήλων δ' ἀπόναντο καὶ ἐν πυμάτῳ περ ὀλέθρῳ

Sweeping headlong down she fell from the lofty tower;
And Hero lay in death beside her dead husband,
And they had joy of each other even in their doom.

Translated by Thomas Gelzer and Cedric H. Whitman (1958)

Hero and Leander 341

closing lines

MUSONIUS

Gaius Musonius Rufus
1st century AD
Roman Stoic philosopher

1 τὸν γὰρ γαμοῦντα καὶ τὴν γαμουμένην ἐπὶ τούτῳ συνιέναι χρὴ ἑκάτερον θατέρῳ, ὥσθ' ἅμα μὲν ἀλλήλοις βιοῦν, ἅμα δὲ παιδοποιεῖσθαι, καὶ κοινὰ δὲ ἡγεῖσθαι πάντα καὶ μηδὲν ἴδιον, μηδ' αὐτὸ τὸ σῶμα· μεγάλη μὲν γὰρ γένεσις ἀνθρώπου, ἣν ἀποτελεῖ τοῦτο τὸ ζεῦγος

Husband and wife should come together for a life in common and for procreating children, regarding all things to belong to both and nothing private to one or the other, not even their own bodies; marvellous will be the children from such a union.

What is the Chief End of Marriage 13A.1

2 δεῖ δὲ ἐν γάμῳ πάντως συμβίωσίν τε εἶναι καὶ κηδεμονίαν ἀνδρὸς καὶ γυναικὸς περὶ ἀλλήλους, καὶ ἐρρωμένους καὶ νοσοῦντας καὶ ἐν παντὶ καιρῷ

In marriage there must be above all perfect companionship and mutual love of husband and wife, both in health and in sickness and always.

What is the Chief End of Marriage 13A.8

3 ὅπου μὲν οὖν ἡ κηδεμονία αὕτη τέλειός ἐστι, καὶ τελέως αὐτὴν οἱ συνόντες ἀλλήλοις παρέχονται, ἁμιλλώμενοι νικᾶν ὁ ἕτερος τὸν ἕτερον, οὗτος μὲν οὖν ὁ γάμος ᾗ προσήκει ἔχει καὶ ἀξιοζήλωτός ἐστι

When love is perfect and both share it completely, each striving to outdo the other in devotion, the marriage is ideal and enviable.

What is the Chief End of Marriage 13A.11

4 τὸν ἄνθρωπον εἶναι δίκαιον, χρηστόν, εὐεργετικόν, σώφρονα, μεγαλόφρονα, κρείττω πόνων, κρείττω ἡδονῶν, φθόνου παντὸς καὶ ἐπιβουλῆς ἁπάσης καθαρόν

Man must be just, good, beneficent, sound, high-minded, a master of toil, a master of pleasures, free of evil and any deceitful schemes.

What is the Chief End of Marriage 16.18

5 τί προβαλλόμεθα τοὺς τυράννους μακρῷ χείρονες αὐτῶν καθεστῶτες; τὰς γὰρ ὁμοίας αὐτοῖς ἔχομεν ὁρμὰς ἐν ταῖς οὐχ ὁμοίαις τύχαις

Why accuse tyrants when we are worse ourselves? We have the same impulses, just not the means to apply them.

Fragment 23 (Lutz)

6 ἀρχὴ τοῦ μὴ κατοκνεῖν τὰ ἀσχήμονα πράττειν τὸ μὴ κατοκνεῖν τὰ ἀσχήμονα λέγειν

Refraining from indecorous speech is the first step to refraining from indecorous action.

Fragment 26 (Lutz)

7 αἰδοῦς παρὰ πᾶσιν ἄξιος ἔσῃ, ἐὰν πρῶτον ἄρξῃ σαυτὸν αἰδεῖσθαι

To be worthy of respect from all you must first respect yourself.

Fragment 30 (Lutz)

8 μὴ θέλε ἐπιτάσσειν τὰ καθήκοντα τοῖς συγγιγνώσκουσί σοι τὰ μὴ καθήκοντα πράττοντι

Don't expect others to do their duty when they know you neglect to do yours.

Fragment 32 (Lutz)

9 τί ἔτι ἀργοὶ καὶ ῥᾴθυμοι καὶ νωθροί ἐσμεν καὶ προφάσεις ζητοῦμεν;

How is it that we are still slow and indifferent and looking for excuses?

Fragment 44 (Lutz)

quoted by Epictetus, Discourses 1.7.30

10 εἰ εὐσχολεῖτε ἐπαινέσαι με, ἐγὼ δ' οὐδὲν λέγω

If you have nothing better to do than to praise me, then I am speaking to no purpose.

Translated by W.A. Oldfather (1928)

Fragment 48 (Lutz)

quoted by Epictetus, Discourses 3.23.29

11 ἄν τι ποιήσῃς αἰσχρὸν μετὰ ἡδονῆς, τὸ μὲν ἡδὺ οἴχεται, τὸ δὲ αἰσχρὸν μένει

If you do evil with pleasure, the pleasure soon goes but the evil remains.

Fragment 51 (Lutz)

MYSON

7th/6th century BC

Philosopher thought to be one of the Seven Sages

1 μὴ ἐκ τῶν λόγων τὰ πράγματα, ἀλλ' ἐκ τῶν πραγμάτων τοὺς λόγους ζήτει· οὐ γὰρ ἕνεκα τῶν λόγων τὰ πράγματα συντελεῖται, ἀλλ' ἕνεκα τῶν πραγμάτων οἱ λόγοι

Do not search for theory in facts, but use facts to question theory; for facts are not caused by theory, but theory is established in view of facts.

Seven Sages, *Apophthegms* 11.1 (Mullach, *FPG*)

counted among the Seven Sages by Plato; cf. Seven Sages 40

N

NERO

Nero Claudius Caesar
37–68AD
Roman emperor 54–68AD
see also Anonymous 121

1 ὁ Νέρων ... τοὺς μύκητας θεῶν βρῶμα ἔλεγεν εἶναι

Nero declared mushrooms to be the food of the gods.

Translated by H.T. Riley (1872)

Cassius Dio, *Roman History* 61.35.4

jokingly referring to Claudius who died eating mushrooms and was then declared a god by the Senate

NICARCHUS

dates unknown
Author of forty satirical epigrams in *Greek Anthology*

1 Τοῦ λιθίνου Διὸς ἐχθὲς ὁ κλινικὸς ἥψατο Μάρκος·
καὶ λίθος ὢν καὶ Ζεύς, σήμερον ἐκφέρεται.

Doctor Marcus touched yesterday the marble statue of Zeus;
though marble, and though Zeus, his funeral is today.

Translated by J.W. MacKail (1890)

Greek Anthology 11.113

2 Νυκτικόραξ ᾄδει θανατηφόρον· ἀλλ' ὅταν ᾄσῃ
Δημόφιλος, θνήσκει καὐτὸς ὁ νυκτικόραξ.

An owl's song bodes death; but when
Demophilus sings, the owl itself drops dead.

Greek Anthology 11.186

νυκτικόραξ is the long-eared owl

NICENE CREED

325 and 381AD
A profession of faith

1 Πιστεύω εἰς ἕνα θεὸν πατέρα παντοκράτορα, ποιητὴν οὐρανοῦ καὶ γῆς ὁρατῶν τε πάντων καὶ ἀοράτων· καὶ εἰς ἕνα κύριον Ἰησοῦν Χριστὸν τὸν υἱὸν τοῦ θεοῦ τὸν μονογενῆ, τὸν ἐκ τοῦ πατρὸς γεννηθέντα πρὸ πάντων τῶν αἰώνων, φῶς ἐκ φωτός, θεὸν ἀληθινὸν ἐκ θεοῦ ἀληθινοῦ, γεννηθέντα οὐ ποιηθέντα, ὁμοούσιον τῷ πατρί, δι' οὗ τὰ πάντα ἐγένετο, τὸν δι' ἡμᾶς τοὺς ἀνθρώπους καὶ διὰ τὴν ἡμετέραν σωτηρίαν κατελθόντα ἐκ τῶν οὐρανῶν καὶ σαρκωθέντα ἐκ πνεύματος ἁγίου καὶ Μαρίας τῆς παρθένου καὶ ἐνανθρωπήσαντα σταυρωθέντα τε ὑπὲρ ἡμῶν ἐπὶ Ποντίου Πιλάτου καὶ παθόντα καὶ ταφέντα καὶ ἀναστάντα τῃ τρίτῃ ἡμέρᾳ κατὰ τὰς γραφὰς καὶ ἀνελθόντα εἰς τοὺς οὐρανοὺς καὶ καθεζόμενον ἐν δεξιᾷ τοῦ πατρὸς καὶ πάλιν ἐρχόμενον μετὰ δόξης κρῖναι ζῶντας καὶ νεκρούς, οὗ τῆς βασιλείας οὐκ ἔσται τέλος· καὶ εἰς τὸ πνεῦμα τὸ ἅγιον, τὸ κύριον καὶ ζωοποιόν, τὸ ἐκ τοῦ πατρὸς ἐκπορευόμενον, τὸ σὺν πατρὶ καὶ υἱῷ συμπροσκυνούμενον καὶ συνδοξαζόμενον, τὸ λαλῆσαν διὰ τῶν προφητῶν· εἰς μίαν ἁγίαν καθολικὴν καὶ ἀποστολικὴν ἐκκλησίαν· ὁμολογῶ ἓν βάπτισμα εἰς ἄφεσιν ἁμαρτιῶν· προσδοκῶ ἀνάστασιν νεκρῶν καὶ ζωὴν τοῦ μέλλοντος αἰῶνος. ἀμήν.

I believe in one God, Father Almighty, Creator of heaven and earth, and of all things visible and invisible; and in one Lord Jesus Christ, the only-begotten Son of God, begotten of the Father before all time; Light of Light, true God of true God, begotten, not created, of one substance with the Father by whom all things were made; who for us men and for our salvation came down from heaven and was incarnate of the Holy Spirit and the Virgin Mary and became man; he was crucified for us under Pontius Pilate, and suffered and was buried; and rose on the third day, according to the scriptures; and ascended into heaven and is seated on the right hand of the Father; and will come again in glory to judge the living and dead; his kingdom shall have no end; and in the Holy Spirit, the Lord and creator of life, who proceeds from the Father, who together with the Father and the Son is worshipped and glorified, who spoke through the prophets; in one, holy, catholic and apostolic Church, I confess one baptism for the forgiveness of sins; I look for the resurrection of the dead and the life of the age to come. Amen.

Acts of Ecumenical Councils 2.1.2.80.1 (Schwartz, *ACO*)

this is the final version of the Nicene Creed of 325 as adopted at the Ecumenical Council of Constantinople in 381; the liturgical version above (with 'πιστεύω – I believe' for the original plurals 'πιστεύομεν – we believe' etc.) is widely used in churches throughout the Christian world; the later addition of 'filioque – and of the Son' by Western churches as to the Holy Spirit proceeding from both Father and Son is controversial to this day

NICIAS

*c.*470–413BC
Athenian politician and general
see also Thucydides 133–137, 139, 150–151

1 ὅτι δὲ μέλλετε ... μὴ ἐς ἀναβολὰς πράσσετε

Whatever you intend to do, do it without delay.

Thucydides, *History of the Peloponnesian War* 7.15.2

cf. Shakespeare, Macbeth *1.7.1: 'If it were done when 'tis done, then 'twere well it were done quickly'*

2 ἄνδρες γὰρ πόλις, καὶ οὐ τείχη οὐδὲ νῆες ἀνδρῶν κεναί

Men make the city, and not walls or ships empty of men.

Thucydides, *History of the Peloponnesian War* 7.77.7

to the Athenian army at Syracuse, 413BC

3 ὁ μὲν τοιαύτῃ ... αἰτίᾳ ἐτεθνήκει, ἥκιστα δὴ ἄξιος ὢν τῶν γε ἐπ' ἐμοῦ Ἑλλήνων ἐς τοῦτο δυστυχίας ἀφικέσθαι διὰ τὴν πᾶσαν ἐς ἀρετὴν νενομισμένην ἐπιτήδευσιν

This was the cause of the death of a man who, of all the Greeks in my time, least deserved such a fate, for all his life had been devoted to the practice of virtue.

Thucydides, *History of the Peloponnesian War* 7.86.5

of Nicias, put to death in Sicily after the failed expedition

NICOLAUS OF DAMASCUS

*c.*64BC
Historian and versatile author, friend of Herod the Great

1 τέτταρας φάλαγγας ἐν ταῖς μάχαις ποιοῦνται, τὴν πρώτην τῶν ἀσθενῶν, τὴν ἐχομένην τῶν κρατίστων, τὴν τρίτην τῶν ἱππέων, τελευταίαν τὴν τῶν γυναικῶν, αἳ αὐτοὺς εἰς φυγὴν τρεπομένους κωλύουσι βλασφημοῦσαι

They have four lines of battle, first the weak, next the strongest, third the cavalry, lastly the women who hinder deserters with disparaging howls.

Fragment 118 (Müller, *FHG*)

of the Triballi, a people on the borders of Thrace

NICOMACHUS

mid 3rd century BC
New Comedy poet

1 ἐργῶδές ἐστιν ἐν βίῳ βεβιωκότα
τοὺς τῶν φθονούντων πάντας
ὀφθαλμοὺς λαθεῖν

It is hard to live an active life
and fail to attract envy.

Fragment 2 (Kock) – 2 (K-A) – *Naumachia – The Sea-battle*

NICOPHON
5th–4th century BC
Athenian Old Comedy poet

1 μεμβραδοπώλαις, ἀνθρακοπώλαις,
ἰσχαδοπώλαις, διφθεροπώλαις,
ἀλφιτοπώλαις, μυστριοπώλαις,
βιβλιοπώλαις, κοσκινοπώλαις,
ἐγκριδοπώλαις, σπερματοπώλαις

Sardine sellers, charcoal sellers, fig sellers, leather sellers, barley-groat sellers, spoon sellers, booksellers, sieve sellers, cake sellers, seed sellers.

Translated by Ian C. Storey (2011)

Fragment 19 (Kock) – 10 (K-A) – *Encheirogastores – Hands-to-Mouth*

of the Athenian agora

NICOSTRATUS
4th century BC
Comic poet

1 ὁ κάπηλος γὰρ οὐκ τῶν γειτόνων
ἄν τ' οἶνον ἄν τε φανὸν ἀποδῶταί τινι
ἄν τ' ὄξος, ἀπέπεμψ' ὁ κατάρατος δοὺς ὕδωρ

The wretched grocer in our neighbourhood,
Whether he's selling wine or vinegar,
Sends off his customer with only water.

Translated by Kathleen Freeman (1947)

Fragment 22 (Kock) – 22 (K-A) – *Patriotae – The Patriots*

2 εἰ τὸ συνεχῶς καὶ πολλὰ καὶ ταχέως λαλεῖν
ἦν τοῦ φρονεῖν παράσημον, αἱ χελιδόνες
ἐλέγοντ' ἂν ἡμῶν σωφρονέστεραι πολύ

If talking all the time and much and fast
is considered wisdom, then swallows
ought to be thought wiser than us all.

Fragment 27 (Kock) – 28 (K-A)

O

OLYMPIAS

married *c.*357; died 316BC
Wife of Philip II of Macedon
see also Alexander the Great 9

1 σὺ ἐν σεαυτῇ τὰ φάρμακα ἔχεις

You carry your magic in yourself!

Translated by Kathleen Freeman (1947)

Plutarch, *Advice to Bride and Groom* 141C

on seeing a striking woman who had been accused of using magic potions to win Philip's love

ORACLES AND OMENS

Entries are in approximate chronological order
see also Aeschylus 30, 68, 109, 118, 127; Aristophanes 27; Euripides 95; Herodotus 78, 91, 123; Thucydides 36, 125; Triphiodorus 1; Zeno of Citium 1

1 λέγων, ὡς μητρὶ μὲν χρείη με μειχθῆναι, γένος δ'
ἄτλητον ἀνθρώποισι δηλώσοιμ' ὁρᾶν,
φονεὺς δ' ἐσοίμην τοῦ φυτεύσαντος πατρός

Doomed to sleep with my own mother,
doomed to raise seed too loathsome to behold,
doomed to slay my father from whose loins I sprang.

Sophocles, *Oedipus the King* 790

Oedipus recounting the terrible prophecy received; but cf. Sophocles 201

2 ᾧ θεοφιλῆ μὲν αὐτὸν ἡ Πυθία προσεῖπε καὶ θεὸν μᾶλλον ἢ ἄνθρωπον

The Pythian priestess addressed him as 'beloved of the gods, and rather god than man'.

Translated by Bernadotte Perrin (1914)

Plutarch, *Lycurgus* 5.3

of Lycurgus

3 ἧσο μέσην κατὰ νῆα κυβερνητήριον ἔργον
εὐθύνων· πολλοί τοι Ἀθηναίων ἐπίκουροι

Take thy seat amidships, the pilot's task is thine;
Grasp the helm; many in Athens are thine allies.

Plutarch, *Solon* 14.6

oracle to Solon

4 καὶ τύπος ἀντίτυπος, καὶ πῆμ' ἐπὶ πήματι κεῖται

Blow is answered by counter-blow,
and anguish laid upon anguish.

Herodotus, *Histories* 1.67

part of an oracle, leading to hammer and anvil and the lost tomb of Orestes; cf. Herodotus 16

5 αἰ τὺ ἐμεῦ Λιβύην μηλοτρόφον οἶδας ἄμεινον,
μὴ ἐλθὼν ἐλθόντος, ἄγαν ἄγαμαι σοφίην σεῦ

I am most impressed with your knowledge, if you know
sheep-breeding Libya
Better than I, when you have not been there and I have.

Translated by Robin Waterfield (1998)

Herodotus, *Histories* 4.157

leading to the foundation of Cyrene in Libya

6 οἶδα δ' ἐγὼ ψάμμου τ' ἀριθμὸν καὶ μέτρα θαλάσσης,
καὶ κωφοῦ συνίημι καὶ οὐ φωνεῦντος ἀκούω

I know the number of the grains of sand and the vastness of the ocean,
I interpret the dumb and listen to the voiceless.

Herodotus, *Histories* 1.47

to Croesus putting the Delphic Oracle to the test

7 προλέγουσαι Κροίσῳ, ἢν στρατεύηται ἐπὶ Πέρσας, μεγάλην ἀρχήν μιν καταλύσειν

If Croesus invades Persia he will destroy a great empire.

Herodotus, *Histories* 1.53

leaving it open as to whose empire; it was Croesus himself who was defeated; cf. Herodotus 22

8 ἀλλ' ὅταν ἡμίονος βασιλεὺς Μήδοισι γένηται,
καὶ τότε … φεύγειν μηδὲ μένειν

Lydian, beware of the day when a mule is lord of the Medians;
then flee for thy life.

Translated by A.D. Godley (1920)

Herodotus, *Histories* 1.55

only many years later Croesus realized that 'mule' was meant to be a half-breed; Cyrus, his conqueror, had parents of different nationality

9 Ἀρκαδίην μ' αἰτεῖς; μέγα μ' αἰτεῖς·
οὔ τοι δώσω …
δώσω τοι Τεγέην … διαμετρήσασθαι

Askest Arcadia from me? 'Tis a boon too great to be given;
I'll give thee Tegean lands to divide among yourselves.

Herodotus, *Histories* 1.66

after this oracle the Spartans turned against Tegea, were badly beaten and made to measure Tegean lands (διαμετρέω having the double meaning of 'divide amongst' and 'measure')

10 τὴν πεπρωμένην μοῖραν ἀδύνατα ἐστὶ ἀποφυγεῖν καὶ θεῷ

None may escape his destined lot, not even a god.

Translated by A.D. Godley (1920)

Herodotus, *Histories* 1.91

in reply to Croesus' complaint that the gods had deceived him

11 ἐπεὶ θάνατός γε καὶ εὔορκον μένει ἄνδρα

Death waits for the just no less than the unjust.

Translated by A.D. Godley (1922)

Herodotus, *Histories* 6.86.γ49

12 ἢ μέγα ἄστυ ἐρικυδὲς πέρθεται, ἢ τὸ μὲν οὐχί, … πενθήσει βασιλῆ φθίμενον Λακεδαίμονος

Either your city shall fall or, if that should not be, you must mourn the death of a Spartan king.

Herodotus, *Histories* 7.220

the oracle before Thermopylae

13 ὦ μέλεοι, τί κάθησθε; λιπὼν φεῦγ' ἐς ἔσχατα γαίης
δώματα καὶ πόλιος τροχοειδέος ἄκρα κάρηνα

Wretches, why tarry ye thus? Nay, flee from your homes and city,
Flee to the ends of the earth from the circular fortress of Athens!

Herodotus, *Histories* 7.140

an oracle given to the Athenians in view of the Persian invasion; the Athenians asked for a more favourable oracle, see below

14 τεῖχος Τριτογενεῖ ξύλινον διδοῖ εὐρύοπα Ζεὺς
μοῦνον ἀπόρθητον τελέθειν, τὸ σὲ τέκνα τ' ὀνήσει

Yet Zeus the all-seeing grants to Athene's prayer
That the wooden wall only shall not fall, but help you and your children.

Translated in *The Oxford Dictionary of Quotations* (2004)

Herodotus, *Histories* 7.141

the second oracle given to the Athenians, the 'wooden wall' interpreted by Themistocles to mean ships; cf. Themistocles 7

15 λύσω γάρ, εἰ καὶ τῶν τριῶν ἓν οἴσομαι

Yet shall I open the seal, even if I were to lose any one of three.

Sophocles, Fragment 908 (Radt, *TrGF*)

an arm, an eye or his tongue – if, before a prescribed date, the seeker of the oracle broke the seal and read it

16 ἀργυρέᾳ εὐλάκᾳ εὐλαξεῖν

Plough with a silver ploughshare.

Translated by Charles Forster Smith (1921)

Thucydides, *History of the Peloponnesian War* 5.16.3

a Delphic oracle to the Lacedaemonians, intimating that there would be a scarcity of food, corn being worth its weight in silver

17 ἀνδρῶν ἁπάντων Σωκράτης σοφώτατος

Of all men Socrates is the wisest.

Diogenes Laertius, *Lives of Eminent Philosophers* 2.37

18 ἐν σοὶ γάρ ἐστι τοῦτο, ὃ ἔχεις, ἢ νεκρὸν εἶναι ἢ ἔμψυχον

You can show it either dead or alive, for each is in your power.

Translated by Michael Wood (2003)

Aesop, The Man and the Sparrow, Fable 36 (H-H)

refusing to answer when asked, taunting the oracle, whether the sparrow the questioner was holding was alive, since he could easily squeeze it to death

19 ΗΞΕΙΣ ΑΦΗΞΕΙΣ ΟΥΚ ΕΝ ΠΟΛΕΜΩ ΘΝΗΞΕΙΣ
ἥξεις ἀφήξεις, οὐκ ἐν πολέμῳ θνήξεις
ἥξεις ἀφήξεις οὐ, ἐν πολέμῳ θνήξεις

You will go, you will return, you will not die in battle.
You will go, not return, you will die in battle.

as oracles were given orally this could be taken to mean either that you were going to die or you weren't, depending on where you thought the sentence broke (after or before the word οὐκ); used even today to indicate an ambiguous meaning; not found in written texts

20 σμῆνα μελισσάων τάχα τοι καὶ σφῆκες ἔσονται

Soon shall your swarms of honey-bees turn out to be hornets.

Translated by Frank Cole Babbitt (1928)

Plutarch, *On Having Many Friends* 96b

foretelling friends turning to enemies

21 Ἀργυρέαις λόγχῃσι μάχου, καὶ πάντα νικήσεις.

Fight with silver spears, and you will conquer all.

Greek Anthology Appendix, Oracles Epigram 89

to Philip of Macedon, taken to mean that by bribery he could get further than by the use of arms; cf. Plutarch 4

22 ἀνίκητος εἶ, ὦ παῖ

Thou art invincible, my son!

Translated by Bernadotte Perrin (1919)

Plutarch, *Alexander* 14.7

of Alexander the Great

23 τοῖς δὲ κακῶς ῥέξασι δίκης τέλος οὐχὶ χρονιστόν

Justice is not long in overtaking those who do ill.

Translated by H.T. Riley (1872)

Greek Anthology Appendix, Oracles Epigram 56

spoken by the Pythia to the Sybarites after they murdered a lutenist; the oracle was soon fulfilled

24 Παῖς Ἑβραῖος κέλεταί με θεοῖς μακάρεσσιν ἀνάσσων
τόνδε δόμον προλιπεῖν καὶ Ἄϊδος αὖθις ἱκέσθαι.
Λοιπὸν ἄπιθε σιγῶν ἐκ βωμῶν ἡμετερείων.

A Hebrew boy, who rules as god among the blessed,
bids me to leave this house and go to Hades.
Depart in silence, therefore, from our halls.

Greek Anthology Appendix, Oracles Epigram 105

to the Emperor Augustus who asked who will rule after him; cf. Augustus 1

25 Εἴπατε τῷ βασιλεῖ· χαμαὶ πέσε δαίδαλος αὐλά·
οὐκέτι Φοῖβος ἔχει καλύβαν, οὐ μάντιδα δάφνην,
οὐ παγὰν λαλέουσαν· ἀπέσβετο καὶ λάλον ὕδωρ.

Go tell the king: the splendid hall is fallen to the ground;
Apollo has a roof no more, nor prophesying laurel,
nor talking spring; even the chattering water is no more.

Greek Anthology Appendix, Oracles Epigram 122

to Julian the Apostate; interpreted as indicating the end of the Delphic Oracle

26 πάντα λίθον κίνει

Leave no stone unturned.

Translated by W.R. Paton (1916)

Chrysippus, Fragment 800 (von Arnim, *SVF*)

proverbial after a Delphic oracle to one searching a treasure; cf. the identical English phrase

27 ἄρχει γὰρ φύσις ἀκαμάτη κόσμων τε καὶ ἔργων

Tireless Nature rules over worlds and deeds.

Chaldaean Oracles 70 (des Places)

28 ναυηγοὺς οἴκτειρον· ὁ γὰρ πλοῦς ἐστιν ἄδηλος

Pity the shipwrecked sailor; uncertain is a life at sea.

Translated by H.T. Riley (1872)

Sibylline Oracles 2.85

29 ὀψὲ θεῶν ἀλέουσι μύλοι, ἀλέουσι δὲ λεπτά

The mills of the gods are late to grind, but they grind small.

Translated by John Simpson and Jennifer Speake (1982)

Sibylline Oracles 8.14

cf. the English proverb 'the mills of God grind slowly, yet they grind exceeding small'

30 τύφῳ καὶ μανίῃ δὲ βαδίζετε καὶ τρίβον ὀρθὴν
εὐθεῖαν προλιπόντες ἀπήλθετε καὶ δι' ἀκανθῶν
καὶ σκολόπων ἐπλανᾶσθε· βροτοί, παύσασθε, μάταιοι,
καὶ λίπετε σκοτίην νυκτός, φωτὸς δὲ λάβεσθε

You walk in pride and madness,
And leaving the right and straight path, you have gone away
Through thorns and briars. Why do ye wander?
Leave the darkness of night, and lay hold of the light.

Translated by Philip Schaff (1819–1893)

Sibylline Oracles, Fragment 1.23 (Geffcken)

cf. Heraclitus 40

Omens

31 αὐτίκα δ' αἰετὸν ἧκε τελειότατον πετεηνῶν,
νεβρὸν ἔχοντ' ὀνύχεσσι τέκος ἐλάφοιο ταχείης·
πὰρ δὲ Διὸς βωμῷ περικαλλέϊ κάββαλε νεβρόν,
ἔνθα πανομφαίῳ Ζηνὶ ῥέζεσκον Ἀχαιοί

Forthwith he sent an eagle, surest of omens among birds,
holding a fawn in his talons, the young of a swift hind;
beside the altar he let fall the fawn, the altar where
Achaeans sacrifice to Zeus from whom all omens come.

Homer, *Iliad* 8.247

32 κατὰ δ' ὑψόθεν ἧκεν ἐέρσας
αἵματι μυδαλέας ἐξ αἰθέρος, οὕνεκ' ἔμελλε
πολλὰς ἰφθίμους κεφαλὰς Ἄϊδι προϊάψειν

And from air's upper region did bloody vapours rain,
For sad ostent much noble life should ere their times be slain.

Translated by George Chapman (1611)

Homer, *Iliad* 11.53

33 ὄρνις γάρ σφιν ἐπῆλθε περησέμεναι μεμαῶσιν,
αἰετὸς ὑψιπέτης ἐπ' ἀριστερὰ λαὸν ἐέργων,
φοινήεντα δράκοντα φέρων ὀνύχεσσι πέλωρον
ζωὸν ἔτ' ἀσπαίροντα, καὶ οὔ πω λήθετο χάρμης,
κόψε γὰρ αὐτὸν ἔχοντα κατὰ στῆθος παρὰ δειρὴν
ἰδνωθεὶς ὀπίσω· ὃ δ' ἀπὸ ἕθεν ἧκε χαμᾶζε
ἀλγήσας ὀδύνῃσι, μέσῳ δ' ἐνὶ κάββαλ' ὁμίλῳ,
αὐτὸς δὲ κλάγξας πέτετο πνοιῇς ἀνέμοιο·
Τρῶες δ' ἐρρίγησαν ὅπως ἴδον αἰόλον ὄφιν
κείμενον ἐν μέσσοισι Διὸς τέρας αἰγιόχοιο

A bird flew by them
heading to the left across the army,
an eagle beating upward, in its claws
a huge snake, red as blood, live and jerking,
full of fight; it doubled on itself
and struck the captor's chest and throat. At this
the eagle in its agony let go
and veered away screaming downwind. The snake
fell in the mass of troops, and Trojans shuddered
to see the rippling thing lie in their midst,

a portent from Lord Zeus who bears the stormcloud.

Translated by Robert Fitzgerald (1975)

Homer, *Iliad* 12.200

the famous omen to the Trojans on the day Hector was slain; cf. Homer 167–168

34 δ' αἰετὼ ...
πλησίω ἀλλήλοισι τιταινομένω πτερύγεσσιν·
ἀλλ' ὅτε δὴ μέσσην ἀγορὴν πολύφημον ἱκέσθην,
ἔνθ' ἐπιδινηθέντε τιναξάσθην πτερὰ πυκνά,
ἐς δ' ἰδέτην πάντων κεφαλάς, ὄσσοντο δ' ὄλεθρον

Two eagles
side by side with wings outspread;
on reaching o'er the clamorous assembly
they wheeled about, flapping their wings
and looked down on all their heads, presaging death.

Homer, *Odyssey* 2.146

an omen of doom for Penelope's suitors

35 γλαῦξ ἵπταται

An owl in flight.

Zenobius, *Epitome* 2.89

an owl in flight was considered an omen for an Athenian victory

36 Ἁγνὰς χεῖρας ἔχων, καὶ νοῦν καὶ γλῶτταν ἀληθῆ
εἴσιθι μὴ λοετροῖς, ἀλλὰ νόῳ καθαρός.
Ἀρκεῖ γάρ θ' ὁσίοις ῥανὶς ὕδατος· ἄνδρα δὲ φαῦλον
οὐδ' ἂν ὁ πᾶς λούσαι χεύμασιν Ὠκεανός.

Enter with pure hands, with true mind and tongue,
cleansed not by baths but in spirit.
For the pious a sprinkling of water suffices,
but an ocean cannot cleanse a wicked man.

Greek Anthology Appendix, Oracles Epigram 183

entered under the indication 'of Sarapis', the Egyptian deity with a much venerated shrine at Memphis, providing oracles and interpretations of dreams

37 ἔρριπται δ' ὁ βόλος, τὸ δὲ δίκτυον ἐκπεπέτασται,
θύννοι δ' οἰμήσουσι σεληναίης διὰ νυκτός

The cast has been thrown and the net is outspread,
and in the moonlight the tuna come for the taking.

Herodotus, *Histories* 1.62

a prophecy by the diviner Amphilytus, interpreted by Pisistratus as an omen for victory

ORIGEN

*c.*185–*c.*254AD
Alexandrian theologian

1 πάντα γίνεται καθαρὰ τοῖς καθαροῖς

To the pure all things are pure.

Translated by H.T. Riley (1872)

Commentary on the Matthew Gospel 11.12.33

2 συντριβῆς ἡγεῖται ὕβρις

Insolence is a prelude to destruction.

Translated by H.T. Riley (1872)

Fragments in *Lamentations*, 84 (Klostermann)

ORPHICA

Pseudoepigraphical literature ascribed to Orpheus
see also Anonymous 139

1 δεινὴ γὰρ ἀνάγκη πάντα κρατύνει

Dire necessity which nought withstands.

Translated by Thomas Taylor (1787)

Hymn to the Night 3.11

2 ὦ Φύσι, παμμήτειρα θεά, πολυμήχανε μῆτερ,
οὐρανία, πρέσβειρα, πολύκτιτε δαῖμον, πανδαμάτωρ

O goddess Nature, ageless, heavenly mother of all,
endlessly resourceful, all-creating, all-subduing.

Hymn to Nature 10.1

3 γλώσσης δεινὸν ὅπλον τὸ σεβάσμιον ἀνθρώποισι

A fearful weapon is the tongue, held in reverence by men.

Hymn to Hermes 28.10

4 Κικλήσκω μέγαν, ἁγνόν, ἐράσμιον, ἡδὺν Ἔρωτα,

τοξαλκῆ, πτερόεντα, πυρίδρομον, εὔδρομον ὁρμῇ ...
εὐπάλαμον, διφυῆ, πάντων κληῖδας ἔχοντα,
αἰθέρος οὐρανίου, πόντου, χθονός

I call great Cupid, source of sweet delight,
Holy and pure, and lovely to the sight;
Darting, and wing'd, impetuous fierce desire,
Skilful, two-fold, keeper of the keys
Of heav'n and earth, the air, and spreading seas.

Translated by Thomas Taylor (1787)

Hymn to Eros 58.1

5 καὶ Διὸς ὄμμα τέλειον· ἐπεί γ' ὅσα γίγνεται ἡμῖν,
Μοῖρά τε καὶ Διὸς οἶδε νόος διὰ παντὸς ἅπαντα

Fate is Jove's perfect and eternal eye,
For Jove and Fate our ev'ry deed descry.

Translated by Thomas Taylor (1787)

Hymn to the Fates 59.13

6 Μοῖρα γὰρ ἐν βιότῳ καθορᾷ μόνη, οὐδέ τις ἄλλος ἀθανάτων

For Fate alone with vision unconfin'd,
Surveys the conduct of the mortal kind.

Translated by Thomas Taylor (1787)

Hymn to the Fates 59.15

7 ἀνόμοις φέρων κακότητα βαρεῖαν

Foe to the lawless, with avenging ire,
Their steps involving in destruction dire.

Translated by Thomas Taylor (1787)

Hymn to Law 64.8

of celestial law

8 μάκαιρ' Ὑγίεια, φερόλβιε, μῆτερ ἁπάντων

Blessed Health, bringer of happiness, mother of all.

Hymn to Health 68.2

9 πάσης παιδείης ἀρετὴν γεννῶσαι ἄμεμπτον,
θρέπτειραι ψυχῆς, διανοίας ὀρθοδότειραι,
καὶ νόου εὐδυνάτοιο καθηγήτειραι ἄνασσαι

Sources of blameless virtue to mankind,
Who form to excellence the youthful mind;
Who nurse the soul, and give her to descry
The paths of right with Reason's steady eye.
Commanding queens who lead to sacred light
The intellect refin'd from Error's night.

Translated by Thomas Taylor (1787)

Hymn to the Muses 76.4

of the Muses

10 Ὕπνε, ἄναξ μακάρων πάντων θνητῶν τ' ἀνθρώπων ...
λυσιμέριμνε, κόπων ἡδεῖαν ἔχων ἀνάπαυσιν
καὶ πάσης λύπης ἱερὸν παραμύθιον ἔρδων

Sleep, king of gods and mortals all,
Tamer of cares, to weary toil repose,
From whom sweet solace in affliction flows.

Translated by Thomas Taylor (1787)

Hymn to Sleep 85.1

11 θάνατος ... τὸν μακρὸν ζῴοισι φέρων αἰώνιον ὕπνον,
κοινὸς μὲν πάντων, ἄδικος δ' ἐνίοισιν ὑπάρχων,
ἐν ταχυτῆτι βίου παύων νεοήλικας ἀκμάς·
ἐν σοὶ γὰρ μούνῳ πάντων τὸ κριθὲν τελεοῦται

Death, bringing eternal sleep to all the living kind,
common to all, unjust to some,
hastily ending the life of youngsters in their prime;
in you alone all judgement is absolved.

Hymn to Death 87.5

12 ἀλλ' οὐκ ἔσθ' ὑπαλύξαι ἃ δὴ πεπρωμένα κεῖται

There is no way to escape your destined lot.

Argonautica 106

13 εἷς ἔστ', αὐτογενής, ἑνὸς ἔκγονα πάντα τέτυκται·
ἐν δ' αὐτοῖς αὐτὸς περινίσσεται, οὐδέ τις αὐτὸν
εἰσορᾷ θνητῶν, αὐτὸς δέ γε πάντας ὁρᾶται

He is one, self-proceeding; and from

him alone all things proceed,
and in them he himself exerts his activity;
no mortal beholds him, but he beholds all.

Translated by Philip Schaff (1819–1893)

Clement of Alexandria, *Exhortation to the Greeks* 7.74.5

Clement attributes this to Orpheus, cf. Fragment 5 (Abel)

14 τέχναι τε λόγοι τε νόμοι θ', ὅσα τ' ἔργα τέτυκται,
πάντα διὰ μνήμην διασώζεται ἀνθρώποισιν

Art, speech, law, any work achieved,
all are preserved for man by memory.

Joannes Galenus, *Allegory to Hesiod's Theogony* 361.20

P

PALLADAS

4th century AD
Grammarian at Alexandria
see also Anonymous 54

1 Ἀνεστράφησαν, ὡς ὁρῶ, τὰ πράγματα
καὶ τὴν Τύχην νῦν δυστυχοῦσαν εἴδομεν.

Things are turned topsy-turvy as I see,
and we now see Fortune in misfortune.

Translated by W.R. Paton (1917)
Greek Anthology 9.181

2 Γραμματικοῦ θυγάτηρ ἔτεκεν φιλότητι μιγεῖσα
παιδίον ἀρσενικόν, θηλυκόν, οὐδέτερον.

A grammarian's daughter, joined in secret love,
produced a child masculine, feminine, neuter.

Greek Anthology 9.489

3 Ἡ μεγάλη παίδευσις ἐν ἀνθρώποισι σιωπή·
μάρτυρα Πυθαγόραν τὸν σοφὸν αὐτὸν ἔχω,
ὃς λαλέειν εἰδὼς ἑτέρους ἐδίδασκε σιωπᾶν,
φάρμακον ἡσυχίης ἐγκρατὲς εὑρόμενος.

Silence is the greatest thing humankind learns;
Pythagoras the wise serves as my witness.
A gifted speaker himself, he taught others silence,
his strongest potion for serenity.

Translated by Edmund Keeley (2010)
Greek Anthology 10.46

4 Ἂν πάνυ κομπάζῃς προστάγμασι μὴ ὑπακούειν
τῆς γαμετῆς, ληρεῖς· οὐ γὰρ ἀπὸ δρυός εἶ
οὐδ' ἀπὸ πέτρης, φησίν· ὅ θ' οἱ πολλοὶ κατ' ἀνάγκην
πάσχομεν, ἢ πάντες, καὶ σὺ γυναικοκρατῇ.

If you boast that you don't obey your wife's orders
you talk nonsense; for you are not made of wood
or stone, as the saying is; as many or all of us are bound
to suffer, you suffer too; you too are ruled by a woman.

Greek Anthology 10.55

5 Γῆς ἐπέβην γυμνός, γυμνός θ' ὑπὸ γαῖαν ἄπειμι·
καὶ τί μάτην μοχθῶ, γυμνὸν ὁρῶν τὸ τέλος;

Naked I came on earth, and naked I depart;
why do I vainly labour, seeing the naked end?

Translated by J.W. MacKail (1890)
Greek Anthology 10.58

6 Πλοῦς σφαλερὸς τὸ ζῆν· χειμαζόμενοι γὰρ ἐν αὐτῷ
πολλάκι ναυηγῶν πταίομεν οἰκτρότερα·
τὴν δὲ Τύχην βιότοιο κυβερνήτειραν ἔχοντες
ὡς ἐπὶ τοῦ πελάγους ἀμφίβολοι πλέομεν,
οἱ μὲν ἐπ' εὐπλοΐην, οἱ δ' ἔμπαλιν· ἀλλ' ἅμα πάντες
εἰς ἕνα τὸν κατὰ γῆς ὅρμον ἀπερχόμεθα.

Life is a dangerous voyage; tempest-

tossed
we often fare worse than shipwrecked men;
and having Chance as pilot of our life, we sail,
doubtful as on an ocean; some on a fair voyage,
others contrariwise; yet all alike we reach one haven:
earth, our final resting place.

Greek Anthology 10.65

7 Σκηνὴ πᾶς ὁ βίος καὶ παίγνιον· ἢ μάθε παίζειν
τὴν σπουδὴν μεταθεὶς ἢ φέρε τὰς ὀδύνας.

All life is a stage, a play: so learn thy part
All cares removed, or rend with grief thy heart.

Translated by H.T. Riley (1872)

Greek Anthology 10.72

cf. Democritus 66; cf. also: Shakespeare, As You Like It, *2.7.139: 'All the world's a stage'*

8 Νυκτὸς ἀπερχομένης γεννώμεθα ἦμαρ ἐπ' ἦμαρ
τοῦ προτέρου βιότου μηδὲν ἔχοντες ἔτι,
ἀλλοτριωθέντες τῆς ἐχθεσινῆς διαγωγῆς,
τοῦ λοιποῦ δὲ βίου σήμερον ἀρχόμενοι,
μὴ τοίνυν λέγε σαυτὸν ἐτῶν, πρεσβῦτα, περισσῶν·
τῶν γὰρ ἀπελθόντων σήμερον οὐ μετέχεις.

Every morning we are newly born,
Nothing of our former life is left,
For yesterday is gone away.
Daily we begin afresh.
No man is too old to be told:
Forget past years and live the rest.

Greek Anthology 10.79

9 Ἆρα μὴ θανόντες τῷ δοκεῖν ζῶμεν μόνον,
Ἕλληνες ἄνδρες, συμφορᾷ πεπτωκότες,
ὄνειρον εἰκάζοντες εἶναι τὸν βίον;
ἢ ζῶμεν ἡμεῖς τοῦ βίου τεθνηκότος;

Is it not true that we are dead and only seem to live,
we Greeks, fallen into misfortune,
fancying that a dream is life?
Or do we live and life is dead?

Translated by W.R. Paton (1918)

Greek Anthology 10.82

probably refers to the persecution of the pagans by the Christians; Greek here means non-Christian as Palladas was himself

10 Ἂν μὴ γελῶμεν τὸν βίον τὸν δραπέτην
Τύχην τε πόρνην ῥεύμασιν κινουμένην,
ὀδύνην ἑαυτοῖς προξενοῦμεν πάντοτε

If we don't laugh at life, so fugitive,
and harlot Fortune shifting with the current,
we only cause ourselves incessant pain.

Greek Anthology 10.87

11 Αἰνίζειν μὲν ἄριστον, ὁ δὲ ψόγος ἔχθεος ἀρχή,
ἀλλὰ κακῶς εἰπεῖν Ἀττικόν ἐστι μέλι.

Praise, of course, is best; plain speech breeds hate.
But ah, the sweetness, as of Attic honey,
Of telling a man exactly what you think of him!

Greek Anthology 11.341

12 Εἰ μοναχοί, τί τοσοίδε; τοσοίδε δέ, πῶς πάλι μοῦνοι;
ὦ πληθὺς μοναχῶν ψευσαμένη μονάδα.

If monks, why so many? And if so many, how are they solitary?
O crowd of solitaries who give the lie to solitude.

Translated by W.R. Paton (1918)

Greek Anthology 11.384

a play on the double meaning of μοναχός = alone and μοναχός = monk

PALLADIUS

born 364AD
Bishop of Helenopolis

1 βραχὺς ἐκτίσθης καὶ γυμνὸς καὶ εἷς ἄνθρωπος παρῆλθες ἐν τῷ κόσμῳ καὶ αὐξηθεὶς διὰ τί τοὺς πάντας κατασφάττεις; ἵνα τὰ πάντων λάβῃς; καὶ ὅταν νικήσῃς τοὺς πάντας καὶ πᾶσαν κτήσῃ οἰκουμένην, τοσαύτην γῆν καθέξεις μόνην, ὅσην ἐγὼ ἀνακείμενος ἢ σὺ καθήμενος

You were created small of stature and naked, and came into the world alone; what is it that makes you great enough to slaughter all these people? To seize all their possessions? When you have conquered everybody, and taken possession of all the world, you will possess no more land than I have as I lie down.

Translated by Richard Stoneman (2008)

*On the Brahmans** 2.22

Dandamis, a Brahman philosopher, to Alexander

PANYASSIS

5th century BC
Epic poet from Halicarnassus

1 οἶνος ... ἐν μὲν γὰρ θαλίης ἐρατὸν μέρος ἀγλαΐης τε,
ἐν δὲ χοροιτυπίης, ἐν δ' ἱμερτῆς φιλότητος,
ἐν δέ τε μενθήρης καὶ δυσφροσύνης ἀλεωρή

Wine, a delightful element of luxury,
of dancing, of entrancing love,
a refuge from care and depression.

Translated by Martin L. West (2003)

Fragment 16 (Bernabé, *PEG*)

2 ἀλλὰ πέπον, μέτρον γὰρ ἔχεις γλυκεροῖο ποτοῖο,
στεῖχε παρὰ μνηστὴν ἄλοχον ...
ἀλλὰ πιθοῦ καὶ παῦε πολὺν πότον

Now, pal, you've had your ration of the sweet liquor,
so go and join your wedded wife;
do as I say, and stop the excess drinking.

Translated by Martin L. West (2003)

Fragment 17 (Bernabé, *PEG*)

3 φολὶς δ' ἀπέλαμπε φαεινή·
ἄλλοτε μὲν κυάνου, τοτὲ δ' ἄνθεσιν εἴσατο χαλκοῦ

Its shining scales glittered; sometimes it looked like blue enamel, and sometimes like flowers of copper.

Translated by Martin L. West (2003)

Fragment 33 (Bernabé, *PEG*)

probably a description of the serpent that guarded the Golden Apples

PARMENIDES

5th century BC
Pre-Socratic philosopher from Elea
see also Plato 295

1 ὦ κοῦρ' ... χαῖρ' ... χρεὼ δέ σε πάντα πυθέσθαι
ἠμὲν Ἀληθείης εὐκυκλέος ἀτρεμὲς ἦτορ
ἠδὲ βροτῶν δόξας, ταῖς οὐκ ἔνι πίστις ἀληθής

Young man, I greet you. You must learn all things,
both the unwavering heart of persuasive truth
and the opinions of mortals in which there is no true trust.

Translated by Jonathan Barnes (1987)

Fragment 1.47 (D-K)

2 ὁδοὶ μοῦναι διζήσιός εἰσι νοῆσαι·
ἡ μὲν ὅπως ἔστιν τε καὶ ὡς οὐκ ἔστι μὴ εἶναι ...
ἡ δ' ὡς οὐκ ἔστιν τε καὶ ὡς χρεών ἐστι μὴ εἶναι,
τὴν δή τοι φράζω παναπευθέα ἔμμεν ἀταρπόν·
οὔτε γὰρ ἂν γνοίης τό γε μὴ ἐὸν ... οὔτε φράσαις

Note the only two ways of inquiry that can be thought of:
One is the way that *it is*; and that *non-being* cannot be *being*.
Then the path that *it is not*; and that *it* may *not* be *being*.
That path – take it from me! – is a path that just cannot be thought of.
For you can't know what is *not*: it can't be done; nor can you say it.

Translated by Karl Popper (1992)

Fragment 2 (D-K)

this passage has been discussed under the following headings: the Way of Truth, and the Way of Illusion; or, the Way of Conjectures (by Karl Popper); or, the Way of Opinion as a Way of Falsity (Jonathan Barnes); or, der Weg des Irrtums (Hegel); et al.

3 τὸ γὰρ αὐτὸ νοεῖν ἐστίν τε καὶ εἶναι

It is the same thing to think and to be.

Translated by Kathleen Freeman (1948)

Fragment 3 (D-K)

considered by some to be a continuation of the previous fragment

4 χρὴ τὸ λέγειν τε νοεῖν τ' ἐὸν ἔμμεναι· ἔστι γὰρ εἶναι,
μηδὲν δ' οὐκ ἔστιν

Whatever is in word or thought, must *be*; for *to be* is possible,
and nothingness is impossible.

Fragment 6.1 (D-K)

5 βροτοὶ εἰδότες οὐδὲν
πλάττονται, δίκρανοι· ἀμηχανίη γὰρ ἐν αὐτῶν

στήθεσιν ἰθύνει πλακτὸν νόον

Mortals who know nothing
wander about in two minds; for
perplexity in their
breasts steers their intelligence astray.

Fragment 6.4 (D-K)

6 ὡς ἀγένητον ἐὸν καὶ ἀνώλεθρόν ἐστιν, οὖλον μουνογενές τε καὶ ἀτρεμὲς ἠδὲ τέλειον

As uncreated, being is indestructible, whole, unique, unwavering and perfect.

Fragment 8.3 (D-K)

7 κρατερὴ γὰρ Ἀνάγκη
πείρατος ἐν δεσμοῖσιν ἔχει

Mighty necessity holds us within bounds.

Fragment 8.30 (D-K)

8 πρώτιστον μὲν Ἔρωτα θεῶν μητίσατο πάντων

First of all the gods she devised Love.

Translated by Jonathan Barnes (1987)

Fragment 13.11 (D-K)

of a goddess 'who governs all things'; quoted in Plato 295

9 νυκτιφαὲς περὶ γαῖαν ἀλώμενον ἀλλότριον φῶς
αἰεὶ παπταίνουσα πρὸς αὐγὰς ἠελίοιο

Bright in the night with the gift of his light,
Round the Earth she is erring,
Evermore letting her gaze
Turn towards Helios' rays.

Translated by Karl Popper (1992)

Fragments 14 and 15 (D-K)

'his': of the moon

10 τὼς νόος ἀνθρώποισι παρίσταται

It is the mind which is associated with mankind.

Translated by Kathleen Freeman (1948)

Fragment 16 (D-K)

PAUSANIAS (1)

died 467BC

Spartan commander-in-chief at the battle of Plataeae, 479BC

see also Herodotus 175

1 πῶς ἂν οὖν αὕτη πατρὶς ὑμῶν εἴη, ἐν ᾗ οὔτε γέγονέ τις ὑμῶν οὔτ' ἔσται;

How can this be your native land in which no one of you has ever been born nor shall ever be hereafter?

Translated by Frank Cole Babbitt (1931)

Plutarch, *Sayings of Spartans* 230d

to the people of Delos who voiced their right to claim the island, where festivals were held, but where no births or burials were permitted

2 νὴ τοὺς θεούς, λίχνος ἦν ὁ Πέρσης, ὅτι τοσαῦτα ἔχων ἐπὶ τὴν ἡμετέραν ἦλθε μᾶζαν

By Heaven, how greedy the Persian was when, having all this, he came after our barley-cake!

Plutarch, *Sayings of Spartans* 230f

on seeing the sumptuous provisions in the conquered Persian camp; he soon took up a luxurious style of living himself

PAUSANIAS (2)

fl. c.150AD

Periegetic writer from Magnesia in Asia Minor

1 αἰγιαλὸς δὲ ὁ ταύτῃ παρέχεται ψηφῖδας σχῆμα εὐπρεπεστέρας καὶ χρόας παντοδαπῆς

This beach here has the most beautiful pebbles, of every imaginable hue.

Description of Greece 3.23.11

of Minoa, today Monemvasia

2 ἐς Πανοπέας ἐστὶ πόλιν Φωκέων, εἴγε ὀνομάσαι τις πόλιν καὶ τούτους οἷς γε οὐκ ἀρχεῖα οὐ γυμνάσιόν ἐστιν, οὐ θέατρον οὐκ ἀγορὰν ἔχουσιν, οὐχ ὕδωρ κατερχόμενον ἐς κρήνην

Panopeus, a city of Phocis, if city it can be called that has no government offices, no gymnasium, no theatre, no market-place, no water conducted to a fountain.

Translated by J.G. Frazer (1898)

Description of Greece 10.4.1

PERIANDER

*c.*668–587BC

Tyrant of Corinth, *c.*627–587BC, and one of the Seven Sages

see also Herodotus 68, 100–101, Seven Sages 39–40; Solon 68; Thrasybulus 1

1 δημοκρατία κρεῖττον τυραννίδος

Democracy, mightier than tyranny.

Seven Sages, *Apophthegms* 3.7 (D-K)

2 μὴ μόνον τοὺς ἁμαρτάνοντας κόλαζε, ἀλλὰ καὶ τοὺς μέλλοντας κώλυε

Do not only punish wrongdoers, but also hinder those who would do wrong.

Seven Sages, *Apophthegms* 3.10 (D-K)

3 μελέτα τὸ πᾶν

Investigate all things.

Seven Sages, *Apophthegms* 7.2 (D-K)

4 αἱ μὲν ἡδοναὶ θνηταί, αἱ δ' ἀρεταὶ ἀθάνατοι

Pleasures are transient, honours immortal.

Translated by R.D. Hicks (1925)

Seven Sages, *Apophthegms* 7.3 (D-K)

5 εὐτυχῶν μὲν μέτριος ἴσθι, ἀτυχῶν δὲ φρόνιμος

Be moderate in prosperity, prudent in adversity.

Translated by R.D. Hicks (1925)

Seven Sages, *Apophthegms* 7.4 (D-K)

6 φειδόμενον κρεῖττον ἀποθανεῖν ἢ ζῶντα ἐνδεῖσθαι

Better for the miser to die than live in want.

Seven Sages, *Apophthegms* 7.5 (D-K)

7 φίλοις εὐτυχοῦσι καὶ ἀτυχοῦσιν ὁ αὐτὸς ἴσθι

Be the same to your friends in fortune and misfortune.

Seven Sages, *Apophthegms* 7.6 (D-K)

8 ὃ ἂν ἑκὼν ὁμολογήσῃς, διατήρει

Whatever agreement you make, stick to it.

Translated by R.D. Hicks (1925)

Seven Sages, *Apophthegms* 7.7 (D-K)

9 λόγων ἀπορρήτων ἐκφορὰν μὴ ποιοῦ

Betray no secret.

Translated by R.D. Hicks (1925)

Seven Sages, *Apophthegms* 7.8 (D-K)

10 συνετῶν ἀνδρῶν, πρὶν γενέσθαι τὰ δυσχερῆ, προνοῆσαι ὅπως μὴ γένηται, ἀνδρείων δέ, γενόμενα εὖ θέσθαι

It is for prudent men to anticipate difficulties and to provide against their arising; and of courageous men to deal with them when arisen.

Seven Sages, *Apophthegms* 4.8 (Mullach, *FPG*)

11 μηδὲν χρημάτων ἕνεκα πράττειν· δεῖ γὰρ τὰ κερδαντὰ κερδαίνειν

Never do anything for money; leave gain to trades pursued for gain.

Translated by R.D. Hicks (1925)

Seven Sages, *Apophthegms* 7.1 (Mullach, *FPG*)

12 τοὺς μέλλοντας ἀσφαλῶς τυραννήσειν τῇ εὐνοίᾳ δορυφορεῖσθαι δεῖ, καὶ μὴ τοῖς ὅπλοις

In order to be safe, tyrants should make goodwill their bodyguard, not arms.

Seven Sages, *Apophthegms* 7.2 (Mullach, *FPG*)

13 μηδενὶ φθόνει

Be jealous of no one.

Seven Sages, *Apophthegms* 7.3 (Mullach, *FPG*)

14 ἐρωτηθεὶς διὰ τί τυραννεῖ, ἔφη, ὅτι καὶ τὸ ἑκουσίως ἀποστῆναι καὶ τὸ ἀφαιρεθῆναι κίνδυνον φέρει

When someone asked him why he was a tyrant he said that it is as dangerous to retire voluntarily as to be dispossessed.

Translated by R.D. Hicks (1925)

Seven Sages, *Apophthegms* 7.7 (Mullach, *FPG*)

15 ἐρωτηθείς, τί μέγιστον ἐν ἐλαχίστῳ, εἶπε, Φρένες ἀγαθαὶ ἐν σώματι ἀνθρώπου

When asked, what is the greatest within the smallest, he replied, 'An excellent mind within a human body.'

Seven Sages, *Apophthegms* 7.8 (Mullach, *FPG*)

16 ἱκέτας ἐλέει

Spare no alms.

Seven Sages, *Sententiae* 215.12 (Mullach, *FPG*)

17 υἱοὺς παίδευε

Educate your sons.

Seven Sages, *Sententiae* 215.13 (Mullach, *FPG*)

18 ἀγαθοὺς τίμα

Honour the virtuous.

Seven Sages, *Sententiae* 215.14 (Mullach, *FPG*)

19 πρᾶττε ἀμεταμέλητα

Practise only what you will not regret.

Seven Sages, *Sententiae* 215.15 (Mullach, *FPG*)

20 διαβολὴν μίσει

Despise slander.

Seven Sages, *Sententiae* 215.18 (Mullach, *FPG*)

21 ἁμαρτὼν μεταβουλεύου

Repent having erred.

Seven Sages, *Sententiae* 215.19 (Mullach, *FPG*)

22 θνῆσκε ὑπὲρ πατρίδος

Die for your country.

Seven Sages, *Sententiae* 215.23 (Mullach, *FPG*)

23 ἔλπιζε ὡς θνητός· φείδου ὡς ἀθάνατος

Hope as a mortal; be thrifty as if immortal.

Seven Sages, *Sententiae* 215.24 (Mullach, *FPG*)

24 μὴ ἐπαίρου ἐπὶ δόξῃ

Be not elated by honours.

Seven Sages, *Sententiae* 215.25 (Mullach, *FPG*)

cf. Bible, Ecclesiasticus *11.4*

25 Περίανδρος ἐρωτηθεὶς τί ἐστιν ἐλευθερία, εἶπεν ἀγαθὴ συνείδησις

Periander when asked what is freedom answered, 'Consciousness of right.'

Stobaeus, *Anthology* 3.24.12

26 μή ποτε λυπήσῃ σε τὸ μή σε τυχεῖν τινος·
ἀλλὰ
τέρπεο πᾶσιν ὁμῶς οἷσι δίδωσι θεός·
καὶ γὰρ ἀθυμήσας ὁ σοφὸς Περίανδρος ἀπέσβη,
οὕνεκεν οὐκ ἔτυχεν πρήξιος ἧς ἔθελεν

Grieve not because thou hast not gained thine end,
But take with gladness all the gods may send;
Be warned by Periander's fate, who died
Of grief that one desire should be denied.

Translated by R.D. Hicks (1925)

Diogenes Laertius, *Lives of Eminent Philosophers* 1.97

Diogenes Laertius' epitaph on Periander

PERICLES

*c.*495–429BC

Athenian statesman

see also Anaxagoras 14; Aristophanes 8, 118; Plutarch 62–63

1 αἱ δὲ περιουσίαι τοὺς πολέμους μᾶλλον ἢ αἱ βίαιοι ἐσφοραὶ ἀνέχουσιν

It is accumulated wealth, and not taxes levied under stress, that sustains wars.

Translated by Charles Forster Smith (1919)

Thucydides, *History of the Peloponnesian War* 1.141.5

2 τὸ ἐφ' ἑαυτὸν ἕκαστος σπεύδῃ, ἐξ ὧν φιλεῖ μηδὲν ἐπιτελὲς γίγνεσθαι ... ἐν βραχεῖ μὲν μορίῳ σκοποῦσί τι τῶν κοινῶν, τῷ δὲ πλέονι τὰ οἰκεῖα πράσσουσι, καὶ ἕκαστος οὐ παρὰ τὴν ἑαυτοῦ ἀμέλειαν οἴεται βλάψειν, μέλειν δέ τινι καὶ ἄλλῳ ὑπὲρ ἑαυτοῦ τι προϊδεῖν, ὥστε τῷ αὐτῷ ὑπὸ ἁπάντων ἰδίᾳ δοξάσματι λανθάνειν τὸ κοινὸν ἀθρόον φθειρόμενον

Each presses its own ends, which generally results in no action at all; they devote more time to the prosecution of their own purposes than to the consideration of the general welfare; and each supposes that no harm will come of his own neglect, that it is the business of another to do this or that; and so, as each separately entertains the same illusion, the common cause imperceptibly decays.

Translated by John F. Kennedy (1963)

Thucydides, *History of the Peloponnesian War* 1.141.6

as quoted by President John F. Kennedy in a

speech in Frankfurt, 25 June 1963, obviously fitted to his way of speaking

3 καὶ γὰρ οἱ μὲν ὡς μάλιστα τιμωρήσασθαί τινα βούλονται, οἱ δὲ ὡς ἥκιστα τὰ οἰκεῖα φθεῖραι

Some seek to avenge themselves on an enemy, whilst others to suffer least damage in what they possess.

Thucydides, *History of the Peloponnesian War* 1.141.7

4 τοῦ δὲ πολέμου οἱ καιροὶ οὐ μενετοί

In war opportunity waits for no man.

Translated by Rex Warner (1954)

Thucydides, *History of the Peloponnesian War* 1.142.1

5 τὸ δὲ ναυτικὸν τέχνης ἐστίν, ὥσπερ καὶ ἄλλο τι

Seamanship, just like anything else, is an art.

Translated by Rex Warner (1954)

Thucydides, *History of the Peloponnesian War* 1.142.9

6 ἤν τε ἐπὶ τὴν χώραν ἡμῶν πεζῇ ἴωσιν, ἡμεῖς ἐπὶ τὴν ἐκείνων πλευσούμεθα

If they march against our territory, we shall sail against theirs.

Translated by Charles Forster Smith (1919)

Thucydides, *History of the Peloponnesian War* 1.143.4

7 μέγα γὰρ τὸ τῆς θαλάσσης κράτος

A great thing, in truth, is the control of the sea.

Translated by Charles Forster Smith (1919)

Thucydides, *History of the Peloponnesian War* 1.143.5.1

now the motto of the Greek Navy; referred to by Cicero, Letters to Atticus *199.10.8*

8 τήν τε ὀλόφυρσιν μὴ οἰκιῶν καὶ γῆς ποιεῖσθαι, ἀλλὰ τῶν σωμάτων· οὐ γὰρ τάδε τοὺς ἄνδρας, ἀλλ' οἱ ἄνδρες ταῦτα κτῶνται

What we should lament is not the loss of houses or of land, but the loss of men's lives. Men come first; the rest is the fruit of their labour.

Translated by Rex Warner (1954)

Thucydides, *History of the Peloponnesian War* 1.143.5.10

9 εἰδέναι δὲ χρὴ ὅτι ἀνάγκη πολεμεῖν, ἢν δὲ ἑκούσιοι μᾶλλον δεχώμεθα, ἧσσον ἐγκεισομένους τοὺς ἐναντίους ἕξομεν

We must realise that war is inevitable, and that the more willing we show ourselves to accept it, the less eager will our enemies be to attack us.

Translated by Charles Forster Smith (1919)

Thucydides, *History of the Peloponnesian War* 1.144.3

10 οἱ γοῦν πατέρες ἡμῶν ὑποστάντες Μήδους ... γνώμῃ τε πλέονι ἢ τύχῃ καὶ τόλμῃ μείζονι ἢ δυνάμει τόν βάρβαρον ἀπεώσαντο

Our fathers, at any rate, withstood the Persians and by resolve rather than good fortune, and with courage greater than their strength, beat back the foreigners.

Thucydides, *History of the Peloponnesian War* 1.144.4.1

11 οἱ γοῦν πατέρες ἡμῶν ... ὧν οὐ χρὴ λείπεσθαι, ἀλλὰ τούς τε ἐχθροὺς παντὶ τρόπῳ ἀμύνεσθαι καὶ τοῖς ἐπιγιγνομένοις πειρᾶσθαι αὐτὰ μὴ ἐλάσσω παραδοῦναι

We must not fail our forefathers; we shall defend our country in every way and do our best to hand it down undiminished.

Thucydides, *History of the Peloponnesian War* 1.144.4.1–5

Funeral Oration (up to entry no. 41)

12 ἐμοὶ δὲ ἀρκοῦν ἂν ἐδόκει εἶναι ἀνδρῶν ἀγαθῶν ἔργῳ γενομένων ἔργῳ καὶ δηλοῦσθαι τὰς τιμάς

These men have proved themselves valiant in action and by action alone can we make manifest the honours we render them.

Thucydides, *History of the Peloponnesian War* 2.35.1

Funeral Oration, Athens, 430BC

13 τὴν γὰρ χώραν οἱ αὐτοὶ αἰεὶ οἰκοῦντες διαδοχῇ τῶν ἐπιγιγνομένων μέχρι τοῦδε ἐλευθέραν δι' ἀρετὴν παρέδοσαν

This land of ours in which an unbroken line of successive generations has, by their valour, transmitted to our times a free state.

Thucydides, *History of the Peloponnesian War* 2.36.1

14 ὄνομα μὲν διὰ τὸ μὴ ἐς ὀλίγους ἀλλ' ἐς πλείονας οἰκεῖν δημοκρατία κέκληται, μέτεστι δὲ κατὰ μὲν τοὺς νόμους πρὸς τὰ ἴδια διάφορα πᾶσι τὸ ἴσον, κατὰ δὲ τὴν ἀξίωσιν, ὡς ἕκαστος ἔν τῳ εὐδοκιμεῖ, οὐκ ἀπὸ μέρους τὸ πλέον ἐς τὰ κοινὰ ἢ ἀπ' ἀρετῆς προτιμᾶται, οὐδ' αὖ κατὰ πενίαν, ἔχων δέ τι ἀγαθὸν δρᾶσαι τὴν πόλιν, ἀξιώματος ἀφανείᾳ κεκώλυται

Our constitution is called a democracy, because it is in the hands not of the few but of the many; and everyone is equal before the law in their disputes; as to being thought worthy to hold public office, each one is recognized on grounds of excellence alone, not from considerations of rank and family; nor is poverty an obstacle, if he but has the qualities to serve the state.

Thucydides, *History of the Peloponnesian War* 2.37.1

originally included in the Preamble of the proposed European Constitution (June 2003), later removed; the amended Constitution was finally rejected by France and the Netherlands, and thus in its totality

15 οὐ παρανομοῦμεν ... ἀκροάσει καὶ τῶν νόμων, καὶ μάλιστα αὐτῶν ὅσοι τε ἐπ' ὠφελίᾳ τῶν ἀδικουμένων κεῖνται καὶ ὅσοι ἄγραφοι ὄντες αἰσχύνην ὁμολογουμένην φέρουσι

We render obedience to the laws and particularly those offering protection to the oppressed and those which, though unwritten, bring upon the transgressor a disgrace which all men recognize.

Thucydides, *History of the Peloponnesian War* 2.37.3

originally included in the Preamble of the proposed European Constitution (June 2003), later removed; the amended Constitution was finally rejected by France and the Netherlands, and thus in its totality

16 καὶ τῶν πόνων πλείστας ἀναπαύλας τῇ γνώμῃ ἐπορισάμεθα ... ὧν καθ' ἡμέραν ἡ τέρψις τὸ λυπηρὸν ἐκπλήσσει

We are in a position to enjoy all kinds of recreation, the daily delight of which drives away care.

Thucydides, *History of the Peloponnesian War* 2.38.1

17 τήν τε γὰρ πόλιν κοινὴν παρέχομεν, καὶ οὐκ ἔστιν ὅτε ξενηλασίαις ἀπείργομέν τινα

Our city is open to the world and we never by expulsion keep away foreigners.

Thucydides, *History of the Peloponnesian War* 2.39.1.2

as in many instances below, this directly alludes to Spartan practices

18 πιστεύοντες ... ἢ τῷ ἀφ' ἡμῶν αὐτῶν ἐς τὰ ἔργα εὐψύχῳ

We have faith in our courage when we are called to action.

Thucydides, *History of the Peloponnesian War* 2.39.1.5

19 περιγίγνεται ἡμῖν τοῖς τε μέλλουσιν ἀλγεινοῖς μὴ προκάμνειν

We are not distressed by misfortunes which are not yet at hand.

Thucydides, *History of the Peloponnesian War* 2.39.4

20 φιλοκαλοῦμέν τε γὰρ μετ' εὐτελείας καὶ φιλοσοφοῦμεν ἄνευ μαλακίας

Our love of what is beautiful does not lead to extravagance; our love of the things of the mind does not make us soft.

Translated by Rex Warner (1954)

Thucydides, *History of the Peloponnesian War* 2.40.1.1

21 πλούτῳ τε ἔργου μᾶλλον καιρῷ ἢ λόγου κόμπῳ χρώμεθα, καὶ τὸ πένεσθαι οὐχ ὁμολογεῖν τινι αἰσχρόν, ἀλλὰ μὴ διαφεύγειν ἔργῳ αἴσχιον

We use riches rather for opportunities of action than for verbal ostentation: and hold it not a shame to confess poverty, but a shame not to have avoided it.

Translated by Thomas Hobbes (1629)

Thucydides, *History of the Peloponnesian War* 2.40.1.2

22 τόν τε μηδὲν τῶνδε μετέχοντα οὐκ ἀπράγμονα, ἀλλ' ἀχρεῖον νομίζομεν

We regard the man who takes no part in public affairs, not as one who minds his own business, but as good for nothing.

Translated by Charles Forster Smith (1919)

Thucydides, *History of the Peloponnesian War* 2.40.2.3

quoted by Karolos Papoulias, the President of the Greek Republic, when commemorating the fall of the Junta, 24 July 2005

23 οὐ τοὺς λόγους τοῖς ἔργοις βλάβην ἡγούμενοι, ἀλλὰ μὴ προδιδαχθῆναι μᾶλλον λόγῳ πρότερον ἢ ἐπὶ ἃ δεῖ ἔργῳ ἐλθεῖν

We do not consider that debate is a hindrance to action, but believe in using debate to assess beforehand the consequences of the action.

Thucydides, *History of the Peloponnesian War* 2.40.2.6

24 ἀμαθία μὲν θράσος, λογισμὸς δὲ ὄκνον φέρει

Ignorance brings rashness, reflection hesitation.

Thucydides, *History of the Peloponnesian War* 2.40.3.3

25 κράτιστοι δ' ἂν τὴν ψυχὴν δικαίως κριθεῖεν οἱ τά τε δεινὰ καὶ ἡδέα σαφέστατα γιγνώσκοντες καὶ διὰ ταῦτα μὴ ἀποτρεπόμενοι ἐκ τῶν κινδύνων

Those are considered truly brave who are well aware of the perils, and the pleasures of life, and yet go out undeterred to face danger.

Thucydides, *History of the Peloponnesian War* 2.40.3.4

26 οὐ γὰρ πάσχοντες εὖ, ἀλλὰ δρῶντες κτώμεθα τοὺς φίλους

We secure our friends not by accepting benefits but by conferring them.

Thucydides, *History of the Peloponnesian War* 2.40.4

27 ξυνελών τε λέγω τήν τε πᾶσαν πόλιν τῆς Ἑλλάδος παίδευσιν εἶναι

In a word I claim that our city is an education to the whole of Greece.

Thucydides, *History of the Peloponnesian War* 2.41.1

of Athens

28 πᾶσαν μὲν θάλασσαν καὶ γῆν ἐσβατὸν τῇ ἡμετέρᾳ τόλμῃ

Our adventurous spirit has forced an entry into every sea and into every land.

Translated by Rex Warner (1954)

Thucydides, *History of the Peloponnesian War* 2.41.4

29 ἀγαθῷ κακὸν ἀφανίσαντες

They have blotted out evil with good.

Translated by Charles Forster Smith (1919)

Thucydides, *History of the Peloponnesian War* 2.42.3

30 τὸ ἀμύνεσθαι καὶ παθεῖν κάλλιον ἡγησάμενοι ἢ τὸ ἐνδόντες σῴζεσθαι

They thought it more honourable to stand their ground and suffer death than to give in and save their lives.

Translated by Rex Warner (1954)

Thucydides, *History of the Peloponnesian War* 2.42.4

31 τοὺς δὲ λοιποὺς χρὴ ἀσφαλεστέραν μὲν εὔχεσθαι, ἀτολμοτέραν δὲ μηδὲν ἀξιοῦν τὴν ἐς τοὺς πολεμίους διάνοιαν ἔχειν

We who remain behind may hope to be spared their fate, but must resolve to keep the same daring spirit against the foe

Translated by Rex Warner (1954)

Thucydides, *History of the Peloponnesian War* 2.43.1.2

32 τὴν τῆς πόλεως δύναμιν καθ' ἡμέραν ἔργῳ θεωμένους καὶ ἐραστὰς γιγνομένους αὐτῆς, καὶ ὅταν ὑμῖν μεγάλη δόξῃ εἶναι, ἐνθυμουμένους ὅτι τολμῶντες καὶ γιγνώσκοντες τὰ δέοντα καὶ ἐν τοῖς ἔργοις αἰσχυνόμενοι ἄνδρες αὐτὰ ἐκτήσαντο

Behold in wonder, day by day, the greatness of Athens, fall in love with her, and remember that this greatness was won by men with courage, with knowledge of their duty, and with a sense of honour in action.

Thucydides, *History of the Peloponnesian War* 2.43.1.6

33 ἀνδρῶν γὰρ ἐπιφανῶν πᾶσα γῆ τάφος

The whole earth is the sepulchre of famous men.

Translated by Benjamin Jowett (1817–1893)

Thucydides, *History of the Peloponnesian War* 2.43.3

34 ἀνδρῶν γὰρ ἐπιφανῶν πᾶσα γῆ τάφος, καὶ οὐ στηλῶν μόνον ἐν τῇ οἰκείᾳ σημαίνει ἐπιγραφή, ἀλλὰ καὶ ἐν τῇ μὴ προσηκούσῃ ἄγραφος μνήμη παρ' ἑκάστῳ τῆς γνώμης μᾶλλον ἢ τοῦ ἔργου ἐνδιαιτᾶται

To famous men all the earth is a sepulchre: and their virtues shall be testified, not only by the inscription in stone at home, but by an unwritten record of the mind, which more than of any monument will remain with every one for ever.

Translated by Thomas Hobbes (1629)

Thucydides, *History of the Peloponnesian War* 2.43.3

a translation of this full text is inscribed on the memorial to the Royal Scots Fusiliers, Scottish National War Memorial, Edinburgh

35 τὸ εὔδαιμον τὸ ἐλεύθερον, τὸ δ' ἐλεύθερον τὸ εὔψυχον κρίναντες

Happiness depends on being free, and freedom depends on being courageous.

Translated by Rex Warner (1954)

Thucydides, *History of the Peloponnesian War* 2.43.4

36 τὸ δ' εὐτυχές, οἳ ἂν τῆς εὐπρεπεστάτης λάχωσιν, ὥσπερ οἵδε μὲν νῦν, τελευτῆς

This is good fortune, for men to end their lives with honour, as these have done.

Translated by Rex Warner (1954)

Thucydides, *History of the Peloponnesian War* 2.44.1

37 καὶ λύπη οὐχ ὧν ἄν τις μὴ πειρασάμενος ἀγαθῶν στερίσκηται, ἀλλ' οὗ ἂν ἐθὰς γενόμενος ἀφαιρεθῇ

Sorrow is not felt for the loss of blessings never known, but of those we were accustomed to.

Thucydides, *History of the Peloponnesian War* 2.44.2

38 τὸ γὰρ φιλότιμον ἀγήρων μόνον, καὶ οὐκ ἐν τῷ ἀχρείῳ τῆς ἡλικίας τὸ κερδαίνειν, ὥσπερ τινές φασι, μᾶλλον τέρπει, ἀλλὰ τὸ τιμᾶσθαι

The love of honour is ever young; and not riches, as some say, but honour is the delight of men when old.

Translated by Benjamin Jowett (1817–1893)

Thucydides, *History of the Peloponnesian War* 2.44.4

perhaps referring to Simonides 45

39 τῆς τε γὰρ ὑπαρχούσης φύσεως μὴ χείροσι γενέσθαι ὑμῖν μεγάλη ἡ δόξα καὶ ἧς ἂν ἐπ' ἐλάχιστον ἀρετῆς πέρι ἢ ψόγου ἐν τοῖς ἄρσεσι κλέος ᾖ

Your great glory is not to be inferior to what god has made you, and the greatest glory of a woman is to be least talked about by men, whether they are praising you or criticizing you.

Translated by Rex Warner (1954)

Thucydides, *History of the Peloponnesian War* 2.45.2

40 ἆθλα γὰρ οἷς κεῖται ἀρετῆς μέγιστα, τοῖς δὲ καὶ ἄνδρες ἄριστοι πολιτεύουσιν

Where valour is truly recognized, there you will also find the most excellent citizens.

Thucydides, *History of the Peloponnesian War* 2.46.1

Funeral Oration, closing lines

41 τὴν νεότητα ἐκ τῆς πόλεως ἀνῃρῆσθαι ὥσπερ τὸ ἔαρ ἐκ τοῦ ἐνιαυτοῦ εἰ ἐξαιρεθείη

The loss of the youth from this city is like a year being robbed of its spring.

Aristotle, *Rhetoric* 1365a.32

part of the Funeral Oration, quoted by Aristotle but not recorded by Thucydides

42 ἡγοῦμαι πόλιν πλείω ξύμπασαν ὀρθουμένην ὠφελεῖν τοὺς ἰδιώτας ἢ καθ' ἕκαστον τῶν πολιτῶν εὐπραγοῦσαν, ἁθρόαν δὲ σφαλλομένην

A flourishing state benefits all citizens, more so than when individuals prosper but the state is in disarray.

Thucydides, *History of the Peloponnesian War* 2.60.2

43 ὅ τε γὰρ γνοὺς καὶ μὴ σαφῶς διδάξας ἐν ἴσῳ καὶ εἰ μὴ ἐνεθυμήθη

He who knows and never speaks up clearly is as bad as one who has never even faced the problem.

Thucydides, *History of the Peloponnesian War* 2.60.6

44 ὁ φυγὼν τὸν κίνδυνον τοῦ ὑποστάντος μεμπτότερος

Blameworthy is he who shrinks from danger, not he who withstands it.

Thucydides, *History of the Peloponnesian War* 2.61.2

45 καὶ τὴν τόλμαν ἀπὸ τῆς ὁμοίας τύχης ἡ ξύνεσις ἐκ τοῦ ὑπέρφρονος ἐχυρωτέραν

παρέχεται ... γνώμη δὲ ἀπὸ τῶν ὑπαρχόντων, ἧς βεβαιοτέρα ἡ πρόνοια

When the chances on both sides are equal it is intelligence that confirms courage, by estimating what the facts are, and thus obtaining a clearer vision of what to expect.

Translated by Rex Warner (1954)

Thucydides, *History of the Peloponnesian War* 2.62.5

46 τὸ γὰρ ἄπραγμον οὐ σῴζεται μὴ μετὰ τοῦ δραστηρίου τεταγμένον

Men of peace are not safe unless flanked by men of action.

Translated by Charles Forster Smith (1919)

Thucydides, *History of the Peloponnesian War* 2.63.3

47 φέρειν δὲ χρὴ τά τε δαιμόνια ἀναγκαίως τά τε ἀπὸ τῶν πολεμίων ἀνδρείως

Bear with resignation the afflictions sent by heaven and with fortitude the hardships that come from the enemy.

Translated by Charles Forster Smith (1919)

Thucydides, *History of the Peloponnesian War* 2.64.2

48 πάντα γὰρ πέφυκε καὶ ἐλασσοῦσθαι

All things are born to decay.

Translated by Rex Warner (1954)

Thucydides, *History of the Peloponnesian War* 2.64.3

49 τὸ δὲ μισεῖσθαι καὶ λυπηροὺς εἶναι ἐν τῷ παρόντι πᾶσι μὲν ὑπῆρξε δὴ ὅσοι ἕτεροι ἑτέρων ἠξίωσαν ἄρχειν

To be hated and envied is the lot of those who wish to rule over others.

Thucydides, *History of the Peloponnesian War* 2.64.5.1

50 μῖσος μὲν γὰρ οὐκ ἐπὶ πολὺ ἀντέχει, ἡ δὲ παραυτίκα τε λαμπρότης καὶ ἐς τὸ ἔπειτα δόξα αἰείμνηστος καταλείπεται

Hatred does not last long, but the splendour of the moment and the after-glory live on in everlasting remembrance.

Thucydides, *History of the Peloponnesian War* 2.64.5.4

51 ὡς οἵτινες πρὸς τὰς ξυμφορὰς γνώμῃ μὲν ἥκιστα λυποῦνται, ἔργῳ δὲ μάλιστα ἀντέχουσιν, οὗτοι καὶ πόλεων καὶ ἰδιωτῶν κράτιστοί εἰσιν

To face calamity with a mind as unclouded as may be, and quickly to react against it – that, in a city and in an individual, is real strength.

Translated by Rex Warner (1954)

Thucydides, *History of the Peloponnesian War* 2.64.6

52 δυνατὸς ὢν τῷ τε ἀξιώματι καὶ τῇ γνώμῃ χρημάτων τε διαφανῶς ἀδωρότατος γενόμενος κατεῖχε τὸ πλῆθος ἐλευθέρως

Because of his position, his intelligence, and his known integrity, Pericles could respect the liberty of the people and at the same time hold them in check.

Translated by Rex Warner (1954)

Thucydides, *History of the Peloponnesian War* 2.65.8.2

53 καὶ οὐκ ἤγετο μᾶλλον ὑπ᾽ αὐτοῦ ἢ αὐτὸς ἦγε

And led them rather than was led by them.

Translated by Charles Forster Smith (1919)

Thucydides, *History of the Peloponnesian War* 2.65.8.4

54 ἐγίγνετό τε λόγῳ μὲν δημοκρατία, ἔργῳ δὲ ὑπὸ τοῦ πρώτου ἀνδρὸς ἀρχή

And so Athens, though in name a democracy, gradually became in fact a government ruled by its foremost citizen.

Translated by Charles Forster Smith (1919)

Thucydides, *History of the Peloponnesian War* 2.65.9

of Pericles

55 ἁρμόζοντα λόγον ὥσπερ ὄργανον

Tuning his manner of speech like a musical instrument.

Plutarch, *Pericles* 8.1

of Pericles

56 οὐ μόνον τὰς χεῖρας, ὦ Σοφόκλεις, δεῖ καθαρὰς ἔχειν τὸν στρατηγόν, ἀλλὰ καὶ τὰς ὄψεις

It is not his hands only, Sophocles, that a general must keep clean, but his eyes as well.

Translated by Bernadotte Perrin (1916)

Plutarch, *Pericles* 8.8

said to Sophocles who admired a boy when they served together on a naval expedition

57 τρέπεται πρὸς τὴν τῶν δημοσίων διανομήν

He turned to the distribution of public moneys.

Translated by Bernadotte Perrin (1916)

Plutarch, *Pericles* 9.2

58 τόν γε σοφώτατον ... σύμβουλον ἀναμείνας, χρόνον

Wait for the wisest of all counsellors, Time.

Translated by Bernadotte Perrin (1916)

Plutarch, *Pericles* 18.2

59 δένδρα μὲν τμηθέντα καὶ κοπέντα φύεται ταχέως, ἀνδρῶν δὲ διαφθαρέντων αὖθις τυχεῖν οὐ ῥᾴδιόν ἐστι

Trees though cut and lopped will soon recover, but men destroyed are lost forever.

Plutarch, *Pericles* 33.5

cf. Robert Southwell (c.1561–1595) in Times Go by Turns*: 'The lopped tree in time may grow again'; but cf. Herodotus 107*

60 οὐδεὶς γάρ, ἔφη, δι' ἐμὲ τῶν ὄντων Ἀθηναίων μέλαν ἱμάτιον περιεβάλετο

No citizen of Athens wore black because of me.

Plutarch, *Pericles* 38.4

on his death bed

61 πρόσεχε, Περίκλεις· ἐλευθέρων ἄρχεις, Ἑλλήνων ἄρχεις, πολιτῶν Ἀθηναίων

Beware Pericles; you govern free men, you govern Greeks, you govern Athenians.

Plutarch, *Precepts of Statecraft* 813e

to himself

62 Περικλῆς ... δυεῖν αὐτοῦ τὴν θυγατέρα μνηστευομένων, τοῦ μὲν πλουσίου καὶ ἀπαιδεύτου, τοῦ δὲ πένητος καὶ φιλολόγου, τούτῳ αὐτὴν ἐξέδωκεν ... ὅτι ἔφη ἀμείνων ἐστὶ τοῦ ὄντος ὁ δυνάμενος γενέσθαι πλούσιος

Two men were courting for his daughter's hand, one rich and uneducated, the other poor but fond of learning; Pericles chose the second, considering the ability to become wealthy preferable to being wealthy already.

Stobaeus, *Anthology* 4.22d.107

PERICTIONE

4th or 2nd century BC
Pythagorean philosopher

1 σοφία μὲν τὰς τῶν ἐόντων ἁπάντων ἀρχὰς ἀνευρίσκει ... ὅστις ὤν ἀναλῦσαι οἷός τ' ἐστὶ πάντα γένη ὑπὸ μίαν καὶ τὰν αὐτὰν ἀρχάν, καὶ πάλιν ἐκ ταύτας συνθεῖναι καὶ ἀριθμάσασθαι, οὗτος δοκεῖ καὶ σοφώτατος εἶναι καὶ ἀληθέστατος

Wisdom discovers the origins of everything. Whoever can analyze all that is within the same principle, and then synthesize and reckon it up, he is the wisest and truest.

Fragment 146.15 (Thesleff)

from her work On Wisdom, *attributed to her by Stobaeus 3.1.121.12*

PHERECRATES

5th century BC
Athenian Old Comedy poet

1 καὶ μελιλώτινον λαλῶν καὶ ῥόδα προσσεσηρώς·
ὦ φιλῶν μὲν ἀμάρακον, προσκινῶν δὲ σέλινα,
γελῶν δ' ἱπποσέλινα καὶ κοσμοσάνδαλα βαίνων,
ἔγχει κἀπιβόα τρίτον παιῶν'

Thy words are sweet as clover, thy smile is like the rose,
And marjoram thy kisses and parsley thy embrace,
Wild-parsley-like thy laughter, and larkspur-like thy steps:
Pour out the wine, strike up the song.

Fragment 131 (Kock) – 138 (K-A) – *Persians*

PHERECYDES

fl. 544BC
Prose writer from Syros

1 τότε Ζὰς ποιεῖ φᾶρος μέγα τε καὶ καλὸν καὶ ἐν αὐτῷ ποικίλλει Γῆν καὶ Ὠγηνὸν καὶ τὰ Ὠγηνοῦ δώματα

Then Zeus prepared a huge and wondrous cloak in which were wrought the Earth and the Ocean and the sparkling Sky above it.

Fragment 2 (D-K)

as a wedding gift to Gaia or Gē

PHIDIAS

active *c.*465–425BC
Athenian sculptor
see also Philippus of Thessalonica 2

1 ΦΕΙΔΙΟΥ ΕΙΜΙ

I belong to Phidias.

inscription on a cup found in Olympia, where Phidias sculpted the gold-and-ivory statue of Zeus; it is now in the Olympia Archaeological Museum, Inv. no. Π03653

PHIDIPPIDES OR PHILIPPIDES

died 490BC
A long-distance courier

1 χαίρετε, νικῶμεν

Be of good cheer! We won!

Lucian, *A Slip of the Tongue in Greeting* 3

bringing the good news after the battle of Marathon; his run led to the adoption of the Marathon race at the modern Olympic Games; but cf. Herodotus 6.105–106; in Plutarch, Moralia *347c, the name of the Marathon runner is Eucles*

PHILEMON

*c.*361–*c.*263BC
New Comedy poet from Syracuse

1 ὢ πῶς πονηρόν ἐστιν ἀνθρώπου φύσις
τὸ σύνολον· οὐ γὰρ ἄν ποτ' ἐδεήθη νόμου

Oh how wicked is mankind;
if it were not, there'd be no need of laws.

Fragment 2 (Kock) – 2 (K-A) – *Agyrtes – The Beggar*

2 οἴει τι τῶν ἄλλων διαφέρειν θηρίων
ἄνθρωπον; οὐδὲ μικρὸν ἀλλ' ἢ σχήματι

In nothing does man differ from wild animals;
not even a little, except in shape.

Fragment 3 (Kock) – 195 (K-A, Dubia)

3 ὅταν γινώμεθ', εὐθὺς χὴ τύχη
προσγίνεθ' ἡμῖν συγγενής

As we are born, luck fastens herself forthwith.

Fragment 10 (Kock) – 9 (K-A) – *Apokarteron – Suicide by Starvation*

4 κἂν δοῦλος ᾖ τις, οὐδὲν ἧττον, δέσποτα,
ἄνθρωπος οὗτός ἐστιν, ἂν ἄνθρωπος ᾖ

And though he be a slave he is no lesser man,
if indeed he has humanity.

Fragment 22 (Kock) – 22 (K-A) – *Exoikizomenos – The Emigrant*

5 ἥδιον οὐδὲν οὐδὲ μουσικώτερον
ἔστ' ἢ δύνασθαι λοιδορούμενον φέρειν

There's nothing more noble or more elegant
than having the strength to bear abuse.

Fragment 23 (Kock) – 23 (K-A) – *Epidikazomenos – The Claimant*

6 χαλεπὸν τὸ ποιεῖν, τὸ δὲ κελεῦσαι ῥᾴδιον

Achieving is hard, 'tis easier telling others how to.

Fragment 27 (Kock) – 27 (K-A) – *Ephedritae – The Horseback Players*

7 πάντ' ἔστιν ἐξευρεῖν, ἐὰν μὴ τὸν πόνον
φεύγῃ τις

You can achieve everything if you do not shun the toil.

Fragment 37 (Kock) – 37 (K-A) – *Katapseudomenos – The False Accuser*

8 εἰ τὰ παρὰ τοῖς ἄλλοισιν εἰδείης κακά,
ἄσμενος ἔχοις ἄν, Νικοφῶν, ἃ νῦν ἔχεις

If you knew the troubles of others,
gladly, Nicophon, would you keep your own.

Fragment 39 (Kock) – 39 (K-A) – *Korinthia – The Woman from Corinth*

9 πολὺ μεῖζόν ἐστι τοῦ κακῶς ἔχειν κακὸν
τὸ καθ' ἕνα πᾶσι τοῖς ἐπισκοπουμένοις
δεῖν τὸν κακῶς ἔχοντα πῶς ἔχει λέγειν

Worse than the illness itself
is to tell each and every visitor
how the illness is progressing.

Fragment 46 (Kock) – 47 (K-A) – *Mystis – The Woman-Initiate*

10 τοῦ γὰρ δικαίου …
ἀθάνατος ἀεὶ δόξα διατελεῖ μόνου

Only the righteous
live on forever in immortal glory.

Fragment 57 (Kock) – 60 (K-A) – *Palamedes*

11 οἱ φιλόσοφοι ζητοῦσιν, ὡς ἀκήκοα,
περὶ τοῦτό τ' αὐτοῖς πολὺς ἀναλοῦται χρόνος,
τί ἐστιν ἀγαθόν, κοὐδὲ εἷς εὕρηκέ πω
τί ἐστιν. ἀρετὴν καὶ φρόνησίν φασι, καὶ

λέγουσι πάντα μᾶλλον ἢ τί τἀγαθόν.
ἐν ἀγρῷ διατρίβων τήν τε γῆν σκάπτων ἐγὼ
νῦν εὗρον· εἰρήνη 'στίν

Philosophers inquire, I am told,
and spend much time on this investigation:
What is a Blessing?
But none has found an answer.
They discuss Virtue, Wisdom, all but what is a Blessing?
Now I, living in the country, digging up the earth,
have found the answer: It is – Peace.

Fragment 71.1 (Kock) – 74 (K-A) – *Pyrrhus*

12 εἰρήνη 'στίν· ὦ Ζεῦ φίλτατε,
τῆς ἐπαφροδίτου καὶ φιλανθρώπου θεοῦ.
γάμους, ἑορτάς, συγγενεῖς, παῖδας, φίλους,
πλοῦτον, ὑγίειαν, σῖτον, οἶνον, ἡδονὴν
αὕτη δίδωσι

Peace! Oh, dearest Zeus,
how lovely, how benevolent a goddess!
Weddings, feastings, relatives, children, friends,
wealth, health, bread, wine, delight,
all this she gives us.

Fragment 71.7 (Kock) – 74 (K-A) – *Pyrrhus*

13 οὐκ ἔστιν οὔτε ζωγράφος, μὰ τοὺς θεούς,
οὔτ' ἀνδριαντοποιός, ὅστις ἂν πλάσαι
κάλλος τοιοῦτον, οἷον ἀλήθει' ἔχει

By heaven, there is no painter,
nor sculptor, who could mould
such beauty as truth.

Fragment 72 (Kock) – 75 (K-A) – *Pyrphoros – The Fire-Bearer*

14 εἰ τὰ δάκρυ' ἡμῖν τῶν κακῶν ἦν φάρμακον,
ἀεί θ' ὁ κλαύσας τοῦ πονεῖν ἐπαύετο,
ἠλλαττόμεσθ' ἂν δάκρυα δόντες χρυσίον

If only tears were remedy for ills,
And he who weeps obtained relief of woe,
Then we should purchase tears by giving gold.

Translated by Frank Cole Babbitt (1928)

Fragment 73 (Kock) – 77 (K-A) – *Sardios – The Carnelian*

15 ἄλλῳ πονοῦντι ῥᾴδιον παραινέσαι
ἔστιν, ποιῆσαι δ' αὐτὸν οὐχὶ ῥᾴδιον

Easy to give advice to others,
difficult to comply yourself.

Fragment 75.1 (Kock) – 78 (K-A) – *Sicelicos – The Sicilian*

16 τοὺς ἰατροὺς οἶδ' ἐγὼ
ὑπὲρ ἐγκρατείας τοῖς νοσοῦσιν εὖ σφόδρα
πάντας λαλοῦντας, εἶτ' ἐὰν πταίσωσί τι,
αὐτοὺς ποιοῦντας πάνθ' ὅσ' οὐκ εἴων τότε.
ἕτερον τό τ' ἀλγεῖν καὶ θεωρεῖν ἐστ' ἴσως

I know some doctors
preaching to their patients self-restraint;
yet if they fail themselves, they do what they forbade.
It's different to be in pain and different to watch.

Fragment 75.3 (Kock) – 78 (K-A) – *Sicelicos – The Sicilian*

17 ἀεὶ γεωργὸς εἰς νέωτα πλούσιος

Farmers are always rich, next year!

Fragment 82 (Kock) – 85 (K-A) – *Hypobolimaeos – The Changeling*

18 ἡμῶν δ' ὅσα καὶ τὰ σώματ' ἐστὶ τὸν ἀριθμὸν
καθ' ἑνός, τοσούτους ἔστι καὶ τρόπους ἰδεῖν

As many as we are in number,
as many are our ways of thought.

Fragment 89 (Kock) – 93 (K-A)

cf. the Latin 'quot homines tot sententiae'

19 ὦ τρισμακάρια πάντα καὶ τρισόλβια
τὰ θηρί', οἷς οὐκ ἔστι περὶ τούτων λόγος·
οὔτ' εἰς ἔλεγχον οὐδὲν αὐτῶν ἔρχεται,
οὔτ' ἄλλο τοιοῦτ' οὐδέν ἐστ' αὐτοῖς κακὸν
ἐπακτόν, ἣν δ' ἂν εἰσενέγκηται φύσιν
ἕκαστον, εὐθὺς καὶ νόμον ταύτην ἔχει.
ἡμεῖς δ' ἀβίωτον ζῶμεν ἄνθρωποι βίον·
δουλεύομεν δόξαισιν, εὑρόντες νόμους,
προγόνοισιν, ἐγγόνοισιν. οὐκ ἔστ' ἀποτυχεῖν
κακοῦ, πρόφασιν δ' ἀεί τιν' ἐξευρίσκομεν

Thrice blessed, yea, thrice-happy company
Of animals, untroubled by such thoughts!
Not one of them need ever face a test,
Nor have they any other similar ill
Self chosen; but whatever nature each
Has been endowed with, this to him is law.

We men have made our lives unbearable:
We have invented laws, we are the slaves
Of other men's opinions – ancestors,
Posterity. We have invented reasons
For misery, and we cannot fail to find it.

Translated by Kathleen Freeman (1947)

Fragment 93 (Kock) – 96 (K-A)

20 ἀνὴρ δίκαιός ἐστιν οὐχ ὁ μὴ ἀδικῶν,
ἀλλ' ὅστις ἀδικεῖν δυνάμενος μὴ βούλεται

The just man is not he who is not unjust,
but he who, given the opportunity, will not be so.

Fragment 94 (Kock) – 97 (K-A)

21 φύσει γὰρ οὐδεὶς δοῦλος ἐγενήθη ποτέ

No one is born a slave, ever.

Fragment 95.2 (Kock)

22 ἐλευθέρους ἅπαντας ἡ φύσις ποιεῖ,
δούλους δὲ μετεποίησεν ἡ πλεονεξία

Nature creates all men free;
it is greed that turns free men into slaves.

Fragment 95.6 (Kock)

23 τὸν μὴ λέγοντα τῶν δεόντων μηδὲ ἓν
μακρὸν νόμιζε, κἂν δύ' εἴπῃ συλλαβάς,
τὸν δ' εὖ λέγοντα μὴ νόμιζ' εἶναι μακρόν
...
τεκμήριον δὲ τοῦδε τὸν Ὅμηρον λαβέ·
οὗτος γὰρ ἡμῖν μυριάδας ἐπῶν γράφει,
ἀλλ' οὐδὲ εἷς Ὅμηρον εἴρηκεν μακρόν

If one says more than needed,
be it two syllables, he's tedious;
but he is not if they're well said.
Homer is proof of this;
he wrote a myriad words,
yet no one calls him longwinded.

Fragment 97 (Kock) – 99 (K-A)

24 ἂν οἷς ἔχομεν τούτοισι μηδὲ χρώμεθα,
ἃ δ' οὐκ ἔχομεν ζητῶμεν, ὧν μὲν διὰ τύχην,
ὧν δὲ δι' ἑαυτοὺς ἐσόμεθ' ἐστερημένοι

If we don't cherish what we have
but crave for all that we do not,
through fate or fault we lose them.

Fragment 99 (Kock) – 116 (K-A)

25 οὐδὲ φύεται
αὐτόματον ἀνθρώποισιν, ὦ βέλτιστε, νοῦς
ὥσπερ ἐν ἀγρῷ θύμος· ἐκ δὲ τοῦ λέγειν τε καὶ
ἑτέρων ἀκούειν καὶ θεωρῆσαι,
κατὰ μικρὸν ἀεί, φασί, φύονται φρένες

The mind does not automatically grow in humans, my friend,
like thyme grows in the fields; it is through talking
and listening to others and contemplating
that gradually the mind grows.

Fragment 103 (Kock) – 103 (K-A)

26 τί ζῆν ὄφελος ᾧ μὴ 'στι τὸ ζῆν εἰδέναι;

What use is life to him who knows not how to live?

Fragment 104 (Kock) – 104 (K-A)

27 δικαιότατον κτῆμ' ἐστὶν ἀνθρώποις ἀγρός·
ὧν ἡ φύσις δεῖται γὰρ ἐπιμελῶς φέρει,
πυρούς, ἔλαιον, οἶνον, ἰσχάδας, μέλι·
τὰ δ' ἀργυρώματ' ἐστὶν ἥ τε πορφύρα
εἰς τοὺς τραγῳδοὺς εὔθετ', οὐκ εἰς τὸν βίον

The best possession is a plot of land,
supplying naturally all we need,
wheat, oil, wine, figs and honey.
Silver, and purple cloaks,
are fit for tragedies, not real life.

Fragment 105 (Kock) – 105 (K-A)

28 ἂν γνῷς τί ἐστ' ἄνθρωπος, εὐδαίμων ἔσει.
τέθνηκέ τις, μὴ δεινὸν ἔστω τοῦτό σοι.
κεκύηκέ τις, οὐ κεκύηκέ τις· ἠτύχηκέ τις·
βήττει τις· οἰμώζει τις· ἡ φύσις φέρει
ἅπαντα ταῦτα. φεῦγε τὰς λύπας

If you know what is man, you will be truly happy.
If someone dies, do not consider it as fearful.
Someone is pregnant, someone not, someone unlucky,
someone is coughing, some lament. Nature brings
all these things. Do not be grieved.

Fragment 107 (Kock) – 107 (K-A)

29 ἅπαντα νικᾷ καὶ μεταστρέφει τύχη

All is defeated and turned upside down by fortune.

Fragment 111 (Kock)

30 ἆρ' ἐστὶ τοῖς νοσοῦσι χρήσιμος λόγος …
ὡς σπληνίον πρὸς ἕλκος οἰκείως τεθὲν
τὴν φλεγμονὴν ἔπαυσεν, οὕτω καὶ λόγος
εὔκαιρος εἰς τὰ σπλάγχνα κολληθεὶς φίλων
εὐψυχίαν παρέσχε τῷ λυπουμένῳ

A kindly word is ointment for the sick.
As a compress on a wound will help the healing,
thus well-timed words of friends enter the soul,
give courage to the sufferer.

Fragment 112 (Kock)

31 ἂν μὲν πλέωμεν ἡμερῶν πλοῦν τεττάρων,
σκεπτόμεθα τἀναγκαῖ' ἑκάστης ἡμέρας·
ἂν δέῃ δὲ φείσασθαί τι τοῦ γήρως χάριν,
οὐ φειδόμεσθ' ἐφόδια περιποιούμενοι;

If we were to travel for four days by ship,
we would count our needs for every day.
But if we are to keep provisions for old age,
should we not save in order to have something?

Fragment 120 (Kock) – 111 (K-A)

32 εἰ ταῖς ἀληθείαισιν οἱ τεθνηκότες
αἴσθησιν εἶχον, ἄνδρες, ὥς φασίν τινες,
ἀπηγξάμην ἂν ὥστ' ἰδεῖν Εὐριπίδην

If the dead could really see whom they please, as some say,
I'd hang myself to see Euripides.

Translated by Andrew Sinclair (1967)
Fragment 130 (Kock) – 118 (K-A)

33 ἐν δὲ τῇ λύπῃ φρονῶ·
τοῦτό με τὸ τηροῦν ἐστι κἄνθρωπον ποιοῦν

In my sorrows I do not cease to think;
it keeps my wits, it keeps me human.

Fragment 135 (Kock) – 123 (K-A)

34 μὴ νουθέτει γέρονθ' ἁμαρτάνοντά τι·
δένδρον παλαιὸν μεταφυτεύειν δύσκολον

Don't reprimand the aged when they err;
old trees are difficult to transplant.

Fragment 147 (Kock)

35 ἔτεκές με, μῆτερ, καὶ γένοιτό σοι τέκνων
ὄνησις, ὥσπερ καὶ δίκαιόν ἐστί σοι

You have borne me, mother, and it is only right
that delight comes to you from your children.

Fragment 156 (Kock) – 143 (K-A)

36 ὅταν ἐμπέσῃ τις εἰς τὸν νοῦν φόβος,
κἀκ τοῦ καθεύδειν οὗτος οὐκ ἐξέρχεται

When the mind is prey to fear
even sleep will not release it.

Fragment 159 (Kock) – 146 (K-A)

37 ἐνταῦθ' ἀνὴρ γάρ ἐστιν ἀνδρὸς διάφορος,
ἐν τῷ τό τε κακὸν εὖ φέρειν καὶ τἀγαθόν

This is the difference between man and man,
to bear in dignity both good and evil.

Fragment 162 (Kock) – 149 (K-A)

38 αἰτῶ δ' ὑγίειαν πρῶτον, εἶτ' εὐπραξίαν,
τρίτον δὲ χαίρειν, εἶτ' ὀφείλειν μηδενί

Firstly for health I pray,
Then for success;
Thirdly for pleasure,
Lastly, to owe no debts.

Fragment 163 (Kock) – 150 (K-A)

39 τί ἐστιν ὁ θεὸς οὐ θέλει σε μανθάνειν·
ἀσεβεῖς τὸν οὐ θέλοντα μανθάνειν θέλων

What he is, god wishes you not to know;
ungodly he who disrespects this wish.

Fragment 166 (Kock)

40 ἅπαν διδόμενον δῶρον, εἰ καὶ μικρὸν ᾖ,
μέγιστόν ἐστι μετ' εὐνοίας διδόμενον

Every gift which is given, even if it is small,
is very great, if it is given with goodwill

Translated by Gavin Betts and Alan Henry (1989)
Fragment 168 (Kock)

41 ἐὰν γυνὴ γυναικὶ κατ' ἰδίαν ὁμιλεῖ,
μεγάλων κακῶν θησαυρὸς ἐξορύσσεται

When women speak in private to each other,
a great hoard of evil is dug up.

Fragment 169 (Kock)

42 ἐμέθυον· ἱκανὴ πρόφασις εἰς θἀμαρτάνειν

I got drunk; excuse enough for me to

misbehave.

Fragment 193 (Kock) – 162 (K-A)

43 ἄνθρωπος ὢν τοῦτ' ἴσθι καὶ μέμνησ' ἀεί

Always remember, and never forget, that you are human.

Fragment 195 (Kock) – 164 (K-A)

44 κακὸν ἀναγκαῖον γυνή

A wife is a necessary evil.

Fragment 196 (Kock) – 165 (K-A)

45 βούλου γονεῖς πρώτιστον ἐν τιμαῖς ἔχειν

Honour your parents above anything else.

Fragment 199 (Kock) – 168 (K-A)

cf. Menander, One-liners *(Jaekel) 113*

46 πλοῦτον μεταλήψεθ' ἕτερον, οὐχὶ τὸν τρόπον

Wealth can be changed, character cannot.

Fragment 201 (Kock) – 170 (K-A)

47 ψυχῆς πόνος γὰρ ὑπὸ λόγου κουφίζεται

Words can relieve a grieving soul.

Fragment 207 (Kock)

48 ἂν ὀκνῇς τὸ μανθάνειν,
ἀνεπικούρητον σεαυτοῦ τὸν βίον λήσεις ποιῶν

Lazy in learning, helpless for life.

Fragment 213 (Kock) – 178 (K-A)

49 ἐκ τοῦ παθεῖν γίνωσκε καὶ τὸ συμπαθεῖν·
καὶ σοὶ γὰρ ἄλλος συμπαθήσεται παθών

From your own suffering learn compassion;
then others will sympathize with you in time of need.

Fragment 230 (Kock)

50 λύουσιν ἡμῶν συμφοραὶ τὰς συμφοράς,
παρηγοροῦσαι τὰ κακὰ δι' ἑτέρων κακῶν

Misfortunes undo misfortunes,
comforting ills by other ills.

Fragment 234 (Kock)

51 βεβαιοτέραν ἔχε τὴν φιλίαν πρὸς τοὺς γονεῖς

Be steadfast in your affection to your parents.

Fragment 237 (Kock) – 901 (K-A, Adespota)

52 ἐκ τοῦ φιλοπονεῖν γίνεθ' ὧν θέλεις κρατεῖν

All you desire is achieved through love of toil.

Fragment 238 (Kock) – 174 (K-A)

PHILEMON THE YOUNGER

3rd century BC
New Comedy poet, son of Philemon

1 μάγειρός ἐστιν οὐκ ἐὰν ζωμήρυσιν
ἔχων τις ἔλθῃ καὶ μάχαιραν πρός τινα,
οὐδ' ἄν τις εἰς τὰς λοπάδας ἰχθῦς ἐμβάλῃ·
ἀλλ' ἔστι τις φρόνησις ἐν τῷ πράγματι

What makes a man a cook is not his ladle or a carving knife,
Nor if he tosses fish upon the platter:
No, there is skill and science in the art.

Translated by Kathleen Freeman (1947)

Fragment 1 (Kock) – 1 (K-A)

2 ὡς κακῶς ἔχει
ἅπας ἰατρός, ἂν κακῶς μηδεὶς ἔχῃ

How ill fares the doctor if no one's ill!

Translated by Kathleen Freeman (1947)

Fragment 2 (Kock) – 2 (K-A)

3 μόνῳ δ' ἰατρῷ τοῦτο καὶ συνηγόρῳ
ἔξεστ', ἀποκτείνειν μέν, ἀποθνῄσκειν δὲ μή

The doctor and the lawyer alone can kill
And not be killed in turn!

Translated by Kathleen Freeman (1947)

Fragment 3 (Kock) – 3 (K-A)

PHILIP II OF MACEDON

382–336BC
King of Macedon, 359–336BC
see also Alexander the Great 3; Anonymous 85; Demosthenes 32, 42–43; Olympias 1; Plutarch 4; Theopompus (3) 1

1 Φίλιππος ... ᾤετο δεῖν αὐτὸν ὑπομιμνήσκεσθαι ὑπό τινος τῶν παίδων ἕωθεν ὅτι ἄνθρωπός ἐστι

Philip had one of his attendants remind him every morning that he was but human.

Aelian, *Historical Miscellany* 8.15

after his triumph at the battle of Chaeronea

2 εὐήθεις … καὶ ὁμοίους τῷ εἴ τις ἔχων καλὴν γυναῖκα τοὺς ἐπικωμάζοντας ἐρωτῴη διὰ τί ἐπικωμάζουσιν

You are as foolish as a man who has a pretty wife and asks her suitors why they besiege her.

Stobaeus, *Anthology* 3.2.18

when asked by the Byzantines why he besieged their city

3 Φίλιππος ὁ βασιλεὺς ἔλεγε δεῖν τὸν βασιλέα μνημονεύειν ὅτι ἄνθρωπος ὢν ἐξουσίαν εἴληφεν ἰσόθεον, ἵνα προαιρῆται καλὰ μὲν καὶ θεῖα

Philip used to say that a king needs to remember that, though human, he was given godlike power in order to pursue what is good and holy.

Stobaeus, *Anthology* 4.7.21

PHILIPPIDES

4th century BC
Athenian New Comedy poet

1 τὸ Πλάτωνος ἀγαθὸν δ' ἐστὶ τοῦτο …
μὴ λαμβάνειν γυναῖκα, μηδὲ τῇ τύχῃ
διὰ πλειόνων αὑτὸν προβάλλειν πραγμάτων

This is Plato's good fortune: not to marry and not to bring upon oneself
more troubles than the ones put forth by fate.

Fragment 6 (Kock) – 6 (K-A) – *Ananeousa – Rejuvenation or The Rejuvenatrix*

2 ὁ τραχύτατος δὲ συκοφάντης μνᾶς δύο
λαβὼν ἄπεισιν ἀρνίου μαλακώτερος

The toughest slanderer, given two pieces of gold,
will leave as gentle as a lamb.

Fragment 29 (Kock) – 30 (K-A)

one μνᾶ = 100 drachmae, a substantial amount

3 ὁ κοινὸς ἰατρός σε θεραπεύσει χρόνος

The universal doctor will treat you, Time.

Fragment 32 (Kock) – 32 (K-A)

PHILIPPUS OF THESSALONICA

possibly 2nd century AD
Epigrammatist and editor of a Garland of epigrams

1 Οὐρανὸς ἄστρα τάχιον ἀποσβέσει, ἢ τάχα νυκτὸς
ἠέλιος φαιδρὴν ὄψιν ἀπεργάσεται,
καὶ γλυκὺ νᾶμα θάλασσα βροτοῖς ἀρυτήσιμον ἕξει
καὶ νέκυς εἰς ζωῶν χῶρον ἀναδράμεται,
ἤ ποτε Μαιονίδαο βαθυκλεὲς οὔνομ' Ὁμήρου
λήθη γηραλέων ἁρπάσεται σελίδων.

The sky will extinguish its stars, and the sun
will appear shining in the folds of night,
and the sea will be a well of fresh water for men,
and the dead will come back to the land of the living,
before forgetfulness of those ancient lines
can steal from us the far-famed name of Homer.

Translated by Edwin Morgan (1973)

Greek Anthology 9.575

2 Ἢ θεὸς ἦλθ' ἐπὶ γῆν ἐξ οὐρανοῦ εἰκόνα δείξων,
Φειδία, ἢ σύ γ' ἔβης τὸν θεὸν ὀψόμενος.

Either god came to earth to show you his image,
or you, Phidias, went to heaven to see god yourself.

Greek Anthology 16.81

of the statue of Zeus at Olympia

PHILODEMUS

*c.*110–*c.*40/35BC
Poet and philosopher born in Gadara in Syria, lived in Rome

1 Γινώσκω, χαρίεσσα, φιλεῖν πάνυ τὸν φιλέοντα,
καὶ πάλι γινώσκω τόν με δακόντα δακεῖν

I know, fair lady, how to love the lover well,
and I know as well how to bite the biter back.

Translated by William Moebius (1973)

Greek Anthology 5.107

2 Δακρύεις, ἐλεεινὰ λαλεῖς, περίεργα θεωρεῖς,
ζηλοτυπεῖς, ἅπτῃ πολλάκι, πυκνὰ φιλεῖς.
ταῦτα μέν ἐστιν ἐρῶντος· ὅταν δ' εἴπω· παράκειμαι.
καὶ μέλλῃς, ἁπλῶς οὐδὲν ἐρῶντος ἔχεις.

Tears, talk full of pity, curious looks,
jealousy, much touching, deep kisses,
these go with a lover. But when I say,
'I'm going to lie beside you,'
and you hesitate, the lover in you
vanishes into thin air.

Translated by Edmund Keeley (2010)

Greek Anthology 5.306

a woman to a man

3 Ἤδη καὶ ῥόδον ἐστὶ καὶ ἀκμάζων ἐρέβινθος
καὶ καυλοὶ κράμβης, Σωσύλε, πρωτοτόμου
καὶ μαίνη σαλαγεῦσα καὶ ἀρτιπαγὴς ἁλίτυρος
καὶ θριδάκων οὔλων ἀφροφυῆ πέταλα.

Now is rose-time and chick-peas are in season, and the heads of early cabbage, and sprats, and fresh-curdled cheese and the soft spring leaves of curled lettuces.

Greek Anthology 9.412

PHILOLAUS

*c.*470–390BC
Philosopher from Croton in southern Italy

1 ἁρμονία πολυμιγέων ἕνωσις καὶ δίχα φρονεόντων συμφρόνησις

Harmony is union in diversity and agreement among differing opinions.

Fragment 10 (D-K)

his work On the Universe *was considered the first published account of Pythagoreanism*

2 ψεῦδος δὲ οὐδὲν δέχεται ἁ τῶν ἀριθμῶν φύσις

Numbers by their very nature allow no lies.

Fragment 11.25 (D-K)

3 πολέμιον γὰρ καὶ ἐχθρὸν τᾷ φύσει τὸ ψεῦδος

Nature is opposed and hostile to a lie.

Fragment 11.28 (D-K)

PHILON

1st century BC–1st century AD
Jewish Alexandrian philosopher, writer and political leader

1 φύεται γὰρ ἐκ πολυορκίας ψευδορκία καὶ ἀσέβεια

From taking many oaths come perjury and impiety.

Decalogue 92

2 θεῷ δουλεύειν οὐκ ἐλευθερίας μόνον ἀλλὰ καὶ βασιλείας ἄμεινον

To serve god is better not only than liberty but even a kingship.

Special Laws 1.57

3 ἔστι γὰρ ἰσότης ... μήτηρ δικαιοσύνης· ἰσότης δὲ φῶς ἄσκιον, ἥλιος ... νοητός ... πάντα ἰσότης τά τε κατ' οὐρανὸν καὶ τὰ ἐπὶ γῆς εὖ διετάξατο νόμοις καὶ θεσμοῖς ἀκινήτοις

Equality is the mother of justice; equality is light without shadow, sun of the intellect; equality regulates both universe and earth, abiding by laws immovable.

Special Laws 4.231

FLAVIUS PHILOSTRATUS

died 244/249AD
Sophist from Lemnos

1 ἐμοὶ δὲ μόνοις πρόπινε τοῖς ὄμμασιν

Drinke to me onely with thine eyes.

Translated by Ben Jonson (1616)

Epistles and Discourses 1.33

'To Celia', adapted from the Greek by Ben Jonson; this first line is an exact translation; cf. Agathias 1

2 οἱ γὰρ κακοὶ κακίους ἐπαινούμενοι

The bad, when praised, become worse still.

Translated by H.T. Riley (1872)

Life of Apollonius 7.3

PHILOXENUS

435/434–380/379BC
Dithyrambic poet from Cythera

1 γάμε θεῶν λαμπρότατε

Marriage, most radiant of gods!

Translated by David A. Campbell (1993)

PHILYLLIUS

5th–4th century BC
Athenian Old Comedy Poet

1 ἕλκειν τὸ βέδυ σωτήριον προσεύχομαι,
ὅπερ μέγιστόν ἐστιν ὑγιείας μέρος,
τὸ τὸν ἀέρ' ἕλκειν καθαρόν, οὐ τεθολωμένον

I pray that I may draw a lifesaving breath;
this is the most important element of health,
to breathe clean and unpolluted air.

Translated by Ian C. Storey (2011)

Fragment 20 (Kock) – 19 (K-A)

PHOCION

*c.*402–317BC
Athenian statesman and general, pupil of Plato and friend of Xenocrates

1 εἰ σήμερον τέθνηκε, καὶ αὔριον ἔσται καὶ εἰς τρίτην τεθνηκώς

If he is dead today, he also will be dead tomorrow, and the day after.

Translated by Frank Cole Babbitt (1931)

Plutarch, *Phocion* 22.6

to the Athenians pressing for war, on a rumour that Alexander had died

2 οὐ δύναται γὰρ ... μοι καὶ φίλῳ καὶ κόλακι χρῆσθαι

You cannot use me as a friend and flatterer both.

Translated by Frank Cole Babbitt (1931)

Plutarch, *Phocion* 30.3

cf. Plutarch 95

3 μηδὲ ἀποθανεῖν Ἀθήνησι δωρεὰν ἔστιν

You cannot even die in Athens without paying for it.

Plutarch, *Phocion* 36.7

4 σκέπτομαι εἴ τι δύναμαι περιελεῖν ὧν μέλλω λέγειν

I wonder whether there is any part of my speech I can leave out.

Plutarch, *Sayings of Kings and Commanders* 187f

on shortening his speech

5 οὐ δήπου κακόν τι λέγων ἐμαυτὸν λέληθα;

Have I inadvertently said some evil thing?

Translated in *Bartlett's Familiar Quotations* (1980)

Plutarch, *Sayings of Kings and Commanders* 188a.3

when his words seemed to have pleased the people

6 Δημοσθένους δὲ τοῦ ῥήτορος εἰπόντος ἀποκτενοῦσί σε Ἀθηναῖοι ἐὰν μανῶσιν, εἶπεν, σὲ δὲ ἐὰν σωφρονῶσιν

Demosthenes: The Athenians will kill thee should they go mad.
Phocion: But they will kill thee, should they come to their senses.

Translated in *The Oxford Dictionary of Political Quotations* (2006)

Plutarch, *Sayings of Kings and Commanders* 188a.9

7 ὡς πολλοὺς ὁρῶ στρατηγούς, στρατιώτας δ' ὀλίγους

How many generals do I see and how few soldiers!

Translated by Frank Cole Babbitt (1931)

Plutarch, *Sayings of Kings and Commanders* 188e

of several men giving him advice

PHOCYLIDES

fl. 544BC
Philosopher and poet from Miletus

1 Λέριοι κακοί· οὐχ ὁ μέν, ὃς δ' οὔ·
πάντες, πλὴν Προκλέους· καὶ Προκλέης Λέριος

The Lerians are evil. Not one man evil, another not;
but all, except Procles; and Procles too is a Lerian.

Translated by C.A. Trypanis (1971)

Sententiae, Fragment 1 (Diehl)

2 τί πλέον, γένος εὐγενὲς εἶναι,
οἷσ' οὔτ' ἐν μύθοισ' ἕπεται χάρις οὔτ' ἐνὶ βουλῇ;

Of what advantage is high birth to such as have no grace in words or counsel?

Translated by J.M. Edmonds (1931)

Sententiae, Fragment 3 (Diehl)

3 χρηίζων πλούτου μελέτην ἔχε πίονος

ἀγροῦ·
ἀγρὸν γάρ τε λέγουσιν Ἀμαλθείης κέρας εἶναι

If thou desirest riches, see that thou hast a fertile farm;
for a farm, they say, is a horn of Amalthea.

Translated by J.M. Edmonds (1931)

Sententiae, Fragment 7 (Diehl)

4 νυκτὸς βουλεύειν, νυκτὸς δέ τοι ὀξυτέρη φρὴν
ἀνδράσιν· ἡσυχίη δ' ἀρετὴν διζημένῳ ἐσθλή

Take counsel at night, the minds of men are keener at night;
quiet is good for seeking out virtue.

Sententiae, Fragment 8 (Diehl)

5 δίζησθαι βιοτήν, ἀρετὴν δ', ὅταν ᾖ βίος ἤδη

Seek a living, and when thou hast a living, virtue.

Translated by J.M. Edmonds (1931)

Sententiae, Fragment 9 (Diehl)

6 πολλοί τοι δοκέουσι σαόφρονες ἔμμεναι ἄνδρες
σὺν κόσμῳ στείχοντες, ἐλαφρόνοοί περ ἐόντες

Many of little wit seem wise if they bear themselves becomingly.

Sententiae, Fragment 11 (Diehl)

7 πολλὰ μέσοισιν ἄριστα· μέσος θέλω ἐν πόλει εἶναι

Much advantage is theirs who are midmost, and midmost in a city would I be.

Translated by J.M. Edmonds (1931)

Sententiae, Fragment 12 (Diehl)

quoted by Aristotle, Politics *1295b.34, in support of his views on equality among citizens*

8 πόλλ' ἀέκοντα παθεῖν διζήμενον ἔμμεναι ἐσθλόν

Suffering much unwillingly in seeking to be good.

Sententiae, Fragment 13 (Diehl)

9 χρὴ παῖδ' ἔτ' ἐόντα
καλὰ διδάσκειν ἔργα

When still a child
instil the thought of noble deeds.

Sententiae, Fragment 15 (Diehl)

quoted by Plutarch, On the Education of Children *3f, in praise of Phocylides' views*

PSEUDO-PHOCYLIDES

probably 1st–2nd century AD

A moralizing poem in 230 hexameters, probably by an Alexandrian Jew; many of these entries are imitated in *Sibylline Oracles* (see Geffcken 2.26–2.148)

1 μὴ πλουτεῖν ἀδίκως, ἀλλ' ἐξ ὁσίων βιοτεύειν

Gain not wealth unjustly, live by honourable means.

Sententiae 5 (Young)

2 ἀρκεῖσθαι παρ' ἑοῖσι καὶ ἀλλοτρίων ἀπέχεσθαι

Be satisfied with what you have, wish not for what belongs to others.

Sententiae 6 (Young)

3 ψεύδεα μὴ βάζειν, τὰ δ' ἐτήτυμα πάντ' ἀγορεύειν

Shun perjury, speak out for truth.

Sententiae 7 (Young)

4 πάντα δίκαια νέμειν, μὴ δὲ κρίσιν ἐς χάριν ἕλκειν

Dispense justice impartially, stretch not judgement for a favour.

Sententiae 9 (Young)

5 μὴ ῥίψῃς πενίην ἀδίκως, μὴ κρῖνε πρόσωπον

Do not cast out the poor man; never judge by appearance.

Sententiae 10 (Young)

6 μισθὸν μοχθήσαντι δίδου

Render payment according to one's toil.

Sententiae 19 (Young)

7 γλώσσῃ νοῦν ἐχέμεν

Take heed of your tongue.

Translated by P.W. van der Horst (1978)

Sententiae 20 (Young)

8 μήτ' ἀδικεῖν ἐθέλῃς μήτ' οὖν ἀδικοῦντα ἐάσῃς

Never wish to do wrong nor allow wrong-doing by others.

Sententiae 21 (Young)

9 πτωχῷ δ' εὐθὺ δίδου μὴ δ' αὔριον ἐλθέμεν εἴπῃς

Give promptly to the poor man, don't tell him to come back tomorrow.

Sententiae 22 (Young)

10 πληρώσει σέο χεῖρ'· ἔλεον χρῄζοντι παράσχου

When your hands can hold no more, give alms to those in need.

Sententiae 23 (Young)

11 ἄστεγον εἰς οἶκον δέξαι καὶ τυφλὸν ὁδήγει

Receive the homeless in your house, and lead the blind man.

Translated by P.W. van der Horst (1978)

Sententiae 24 (Young)

12 χεῖρα πεσόντι δίδου, σῶσον δ' ἀπερίστατον ἄνδρα

Extend your hand to him who falls, stand by the solitary.

Sententiae 26 (Young)

13 κοινὰ πάθη πάντων· ὁ βίος τροχός· ἄστατος ὄλβος

Misfortunes are common to all; life is a wheel, and prosperity unstable.

Translated by H.T. Riley (1872)

Sententiae 27 (Young)

14 πλοῦτον ἔχων σὴν χεῖρα πενητεύουσιν ὄρεξον

When you have wealth, stretch out your hand to the poor.

Translated by P.W. van der Horst (1978)

Sententiae 28 (Young)

15 ὧν σοι ἔδωκε θεός, τούτων χρῄζουσι παράσχου

From what god has given you give to those who are in need.

Sententiae 29 (Young)

16 τὸ ξίφος ἀμφιβαλοῦ μὴ πρὸς φόνον, ἀλλ' ἐς ἄμυναν

Gird on your sword, not to kill but to defend.

Sententiae 32 (Young)

17 ἀγροῦ γειτονέοντος ἀπόσχεο μὴ δ' ἄρ' ὑπερβῇς

Desist from trespassing your neighbour's field.

Sententiae 35 (Young)

18 μηδέ τιν' αὐξόμενον καρπὸν λωβήσῃ ἀρούρης

Do not destroy the growing produce of the land.

Sententiae 38 (Young)

19 χρυσὸς ἀεὶ δόλος ἐστὶ καὶ ἄργυρος ἀνθρώποισιν

Gold and silver will always be a bait to men.

Sententiae 43 (Young)

20 βουλὴ δ' εὐθύνεθ' ἑκάστου

Each man's opinion is his responsibility.

Sententiae 52 (Young)

21 μὴ προπετὴς ἐς χεῖρα, χαλίνου δ' ἄγριον ὀργήν

Do not rashly raise your hand, bridle a fierce temper.

Sententiae 57 (Young)

22 ὀργὴ δ' ἐστὶν ὄρεξις, ὑπερβαίνουσα δὲ μῆνις

Rage is a desire, but wrath surpasses it.

Translated by P.W. van der Horst (1978)

Sententiae 64 (Young)

23 μέτρῳ ἔδειν, μέτρῳ δὲ πιεῖν καὶ μυθολογεύειν

In moderation eat, in moderation drink
and speak.

Sententiae 69 (Young)

24 μὴ φθονέοις ἀγαθῶν ἑτάροις, μὴ μῶμον ἀνάψῃς.
ἄφθονοι Οὐρανίδαι καὶ ἐν ἀλλήλοις τελέθουσιν.
οὐ φθονέει μήνη πολὺ κρείσσοσιν ἡλίου αὐγαῖς,
οὐ χθὼν οὐρανίοισ' ὑψώμασι νέρθεν ἐοῦσα,
οὐ ποταμοὶ πελάγεσσιν. ἀεὶ δ' ὁμόνοιαν ἔχουσιν

Do not resent another man's good fortune;
many a star shines bright
not begrudging the glorious light of the sun;

the earth does not envy the heights of the universe,
nor do the rivers envy the oceans; all is in harmony.
Sententiae 70 (Young)

25 πειθὼ μὲν γὰρ ὄνειαρ, ἔρις δ' ἔριν ἀντιφυτεύει

Conciliation is profitable, but strife begets strife.
Translated by H.T. Riley (1872)
Sententiae 78 (Young)

26 μὴ πίστευε τάχιστα, πρὶν ἀτρεκέως πέρας ὄψει

Trust not too quickly, not before perceiving the end.
Sententiae 79 (Young)

27 καλὸν ξεινίζειν ταχέως λιταῖσι τραπέζαις
ἢ πλείσταις δολίαισι βραδυνούσαις παρὰ καιρόν

Better a simple meal quickly
than many elaborate courses much delayed.
Sententiae 81 (Young)

28 μηδέποτε χρήστης πικρὸς γένῃ ἀνδρὶ πένητι

Never be a relentless creditor to a poor man.
Translated by P.W. van der Horst (1978)
Sententiae 83 (Young)

29 μηδέποτε κρίνειν ἀδαήμονας ἄνδρας ἐάσῃς

Never allow ignorant men to sit in judgement.
Translated by P.W. van der Horst (1978)
Sententiae 86 (Young)

30 λαῷ μὴ πίστευε, πολύτροπός ἐστιν ὅμιλος

Trust not the populace, the multitude is versatile.
Translated by H.T. Riley (1872)
Sententiae 95 (Young)

31 λαὸς γὰρ καὶ ὕδωρ καὶ πῦρ ἀκατάσχετα πάντα

The multitude, and water, and fire are forever uncontrollable.
Sententiae 96 (Young)

32 μέτρα δὲ τεῦχ' ἔθ' ἑοῖσι· τὸ γὰρ μέτρον ἐστὶν ἄριστον

Be moderate in your grief, for moderation is the best.
Translated by P.W. van der Horst (1978)
Sententiae 98 (Young)

33 ξυνὸς χῶρος ἅπασι, πένησί τε καὶ βασιλεῦσιν·
πάντες ἴσον νέκυες, ψυχῶν δὲ θεὸς βασιλεύει

All take up the same space, be they kings or paupers;
all dead are equal, but it is god that rules our souls.
Sententiae 111 and 113 (Young)

34 ψυχὴ δ' ἀθάνατος καὶ ἀγήρως ζῇ διὰ παντός

The soul is immortal and ageless and lives forever.
Sententiae 115 (Young)

35 οὐδεὶς γινώσκει, τί μετ' αὔριον ἢ τί μεθ' ὥραν·
ἄσκοπός ἐστι βροτῶν θάνατος, τὸ δὲ μέλλον ἄδηλον

Nothing is known of tomorrow or even the next hour;
unknown is the time of death, unknown is the future.
Sententiae 116 (Young)

36 μήτε κακοῖσ' ἄχθου μήτ' οὖν ἐπαγάλλεο χάρμῃ

Let not adversity dismay you, nor exult in success.
Sententiae 118 (Young)

37 ὅπλον τοι λόγος ἀνδρὶ τομώτερόν ἐστι σιδήρου

Speech is a weapon to man, sharper than a sword.
Sententiae 124 (Young)

38 ὅπλον ἑκάστῳ νεῖμε θεός, φύσιν ἠερόφοιτον
ὄρνισιν, πώλοις ταχυτῆτ', ἀλκήν τε λέουσιν,
ταύρους δ' αὐτοχύτως κέρα ἔσσεν, κέντρα μελίσσαις
ἔμφυτον ἄλκαρ ἔδωκε, λόγον δ' ἔρυμ' ἀνθρώποισιν

God has given to each creature some

means of defence: flight to birds, speed to foals, strength to lions, horns to bulls, a sting to bees, speech to man.

Sententiae 125 (Young)

39 ἀμφότεροι κλῶπες, καὶ ὁ δεξάμενος καὶ ὁ κλέψας

Both are thieves, he that steals and he that receives stolen goods.

Sententiae 136 (Young)

40 μοίρας πᾶσι νέμειν, ἰσότης δ' ἐν πᾶσιν ἄριστον

Distribute equal lots between all your children; impartiality is best in everything.

Sententiae 137 (Young)

41 ἐξ ὀλίγου σπινθῆρος ἀθέσφατος αἴθεται ὕλη

From a tiny spark a vast forest is set ablaze.

Sententiae 144 (Young)

42 νηπιάχοις ἀταλοῖς μὴ ἅψῃ χεῖρα βιαίως

Do not apply a forcible hand to tender children.

Sententiae 150 (Young)

43 μὴ κακὸν εὖ ἔρξῃς· σπείρειν ἴσον ἔστ' ἐνὶ πόντῳ

Do no good turn to a bad man; it is like sowing in the sea.

Translated by P.W. van der Horst (1978)

Sententiae 152 (Young)

44 ἐργάζευ μοχθῶν, ὡς ἐξ ἰδίων βιοτεύσῃς

Work hard so that you can live from your own means.

Translated by P.W. van der Horst (1978)

Sententiae 153 (Young)

45 οὐδὲν ἄνευ καμάτου πέλει ἀνδράσιν εὐπετὲς ἔργον

No work is easy, none without toil.

Sententiae 162 (Young)

46 μὴ μείνῃς ἄγαμος, μή πως νώνυμνος ὄληαι

Remain not unmarried, lest you die nameless.

Translated by P.W. van der Horst (1978)

Sententiae 175 (Young)

47 δός τι φύσει καὐτός, τέκε δ' ἔμπαλιν, ὡς ἐλοχεύθης

Give nature her due, beget in your turn as you were begotten.

Translated by P.W. van der Horst (1978)

Sententiae 176 (Young)

48 στέργε τεὴν ἄλοχον· τί γὰρ ἡδύτερον καὶ ἄρειον,
ἢ ὅταν ἀνδρὶ γυνὴ φρονέῃ φίλα γήραος ἄχρις;

Love your wife; for is there anything more wonderful
than when you love each other until deep old age?

Sententiae 195 (Young)

49 μὴ δέ τις ἀμνήστευτα βίῃ κούρῃσι μιγείη

Let no one forcibly have intercourse with maidens without honourable wooing.

Translated by P.W. van der Horst (1978)

Sententiae 198 (Young)

βία is rape under Attic law

50 μηδ' ἀμφὶ κτεάνων συνομαίμοσιν εἰς ἔριν ἔλθῃς

Never quarrel with kin over property.

Sententiae 206 (Young)

51 στέργε φίλους ἄχρις θανάτου· πίστις γὰρ ἀμείνων

Love your friends till death, for faithfulness is best.

Sententiae 218 (Young)

PHRYNICHUS

fl. 511–476BC
Athenian tragic playwright
see also Herodotus 105

1 λάμπει δ' ἐπὶ πορφυρέαις παρῇσι φῶς ἔρωτος

Love's glowing light shines on her rosy cheeks.

Fragment 13 (Snell, *TrGF*)

2 Σχήματα δ' ὄρχησις τόσα μοι πόρεν, ὅσσ' ἐνὶ πόντῳ
κύματα ποιεῖται χείματι νὺξ ὀλοή.

The art of dance has given me as many different steps
as a stormy night brings waves upon the sea.

Greek Anthology Appendix, Epigrammata demonstrativa 18

PILATE

Pontius Pilatus
Prefect of Judaea 26–36AD

1 ἰδὼν δὲ ὁ Πιλᾶτος ὅτι οὐδὲν ὠφελεῖ, ἀλλὰ μᾶλλον θόρυβος γίνεται, λαβὼν ὕδωρ ἀπενίψατο τὰς χεῖρας ἀπέναντι τοῦ ὄχλου λέγων· ἀθῷός εἰμι ἀπὸ τοῦ αἵματος τοῦ δικαίου τούτου· ὑμεῖς ὄψεσθε

When Pilate saw that he could prevail nothing, but that rather a tumult was made, he took water, and washed his hands before the multitude, saying, I am innocent of the blood of this just person: see ye to it.

Matthew 27.24

2 καὶ ἀποκριθεὶς πᾶς ὁ λαὸς εἶπε· τὸ αἷμα αὐτοῦ ἐφ' ἡμᾶς καὶ ἐπὶ τὰ τέκνα ἡμῶν

Then answered all the people, and said, His blood be on us, and on our children.

Matthew 27.25

3 λέγει αὐτῷ ὁ Πιλᾶτος· τί ἐστιν ἀλήθεια;

Pilate saith unto him, What is truth?

John 18.38

cf. Francis Bacon, Essays, *'On Truth' (1625): 'What is truth? Said jesting Pilate; and would not stay for an answer'*

4 ἴδε ὁ ἄνθρωπος

Behold the man!

John 19.5

of Jesus; cf. the Vulgate: 'Ecce homo'

5 ὃ γέγραφα, γέγραφα

What I have written, I have written.

John 19.22

cf. the Vulgate: 'Quod scripsi scripsi'

PINDAR

*c.*518–438BC
Lyric poet from Cynoscephalae, a village on the outskirts of Thebes in Boeotia
see also Proverbial 81

1 εἰ δ' ἀρετᾷ κατάκειται πᾶσαν ὀργάν,
ἀμφότερον δαπάναις τε καὶ πόνοις,
χρή νιν εὑρόντεσσιν ἀγάνορα κόμπον
μὴ φθονεραῖσι φέρειν
γνώμαις

If a man is dedicated to excellence,
employing both expense and effort,
we must with an ungrudging spirit
grant him the praise he deserves.

Isthmian Odes 1.41

2 χρήματα χρήματ' ἀνήρ

It is money, money that makes the man.

Isthmian Odes 2.11

this quotation by Pindar is attributed by his scholiast to Aristodemus the Spartan

3 μήτ' ἀρετάν ποτε σιγάτω πατρῴαν,
μηδὲ τούσδ' ὕμνους· ἐπεί τοι
οὐκ ἐλινύσοντας αὐτοὺς ἐργασάμαν

Let not silence shroud our fathers' glorious deeds,
nor these songs; for, indeed,
I have not composed them to remain unsung.

Isthmian Odes 2.44

4 ἄλλοτε δ' ἀλλοῖος οὖρος
πάντας ἀνθρώπους ἐπαΐσσων ἐλαύνει

Sometimes a fair wind
comes upon men and hurries them along.

Isthmian Odes 4.6

5 ἁμέρᾳ γὰρ ἐν μιᾷ
τραχεῖα νιφὰς πολέμοιο ...
ἐρήμωσεν μάκαιραν ἑστίαν·
νῦν δ' αὖ μετὰ χειμέριον ποικίλα μηνῶν ζόφον
χθὼν ὥτε φοινικέοισιν ἄνθησεν ῥόδοις

In just one day
the storms of war laid waste their happy home;
but now again, after a winter's gloom,
the earth is blossoming with crimson roses.

Isthmian Odes 4.16

6 τοῦτο γὰρ ἀθάνατον φωνᾶεν ἕρπει,
εἴ τις εὖ εἴπῃ τι· καὶ πάγ-
καρπον ἐπὶ χθόνα καὶ διὰ πόντον βέβακεν
ἐργμάτων ἀκτὶς καλῶν ἄσβεστος αἰεί

A thing well said wins immortality;
it carries over land and sea
undying fame of glorious deeds.

Isthmian Odes 4.40

7 τόλμᾳ γὰρ εἰκώς
θυμὸν ἐριβρεμετᾶν θηρῶν λεόντων
ἐν πόνῳ, μῆτιν δ' ἀλώπηξ,
αἰετοῦ ἅ τ' ἀναπιτναμένα ῥόμβον ἴσχει

In daring like a lion, in cunning like the fox
who falls on his back to foil the eagle's swoop.

Isthmian Odes 4.45

of Melissus, a Theban wrestler, twice winner at the pankration, an 'all-in' wrestling contest

8 χρὴ δὲ πᾶν ἔρδοντ' ἀμαυρῶσαι τὸν ἐχθρόν

All means are fair to weaken the enemy.

Isthmian Odes 4.48

9 θνᾴσκομεν γὰρ ὁμῶς ἅπαντες·
δαίμων δ' ἄισος

We die, all of us, alike,
though our fortunes may have been unequal.

Isthmian Odes 7.42

10 τὸ δὲ πὰρ δίκαν
γλυκὺ πικροτάτα μένει τελευτά

A most bitter end awaits the sweetness of unlawful joys.

Translated by Anthony Verity (2007)

Isthmian Odes 7.47

11 τὸ δὲ πρὸ ποδὸς
ἄρειον ἀεὶ βλέπειν
χρῆμα πάν

Rather watch what is before your step.

Isthmian Odes 8.12

12 δόλιος γὰρ αἰ-
ὼν ἐπ' ἀνδράσι κρέμαται,
ἑλίσσων βίου πόρον· ἰ-
ατὰ δ' ἐστὶ βροτοῖς σύν γ' ἐλευθερίᾳ

Deceitful is our age, making crooked our way of life;
but even this can be healed with freedom.

Isthmian Odes 8.14

13 χρὴ δ' ἐν εὐθείαις ὁδοῖς στείχοντα μάρνασθαι φυᾷ

Tread a straight path and strive by all that's in you.

Nemean Odes 1.25

14 πράσσει γὰρ ἔργῳ μὲν σθένος,
βουλαῖσι δὲ φρήν

Action sets strength to work,
And counsel the mind.

Translated by C.M. Bowra (1969)

Nemean Odes 1.26

15 οὐκ ἔραμαι πολὺν ἐν
μεγάρῳ πλοῦτον κατακρύψαις ἔχειν,
ἀλλ' ἐόντων εὖ τε παθεῖν καὶ ἀκοῦσαι φίλοις ἐξαρκέων

To hide away my wealth gives me no pleasure;
I'd rather use it to enjoy my life and to assist my friends.

Nemean Odes 1.31

16 οὐκέτι πρόσω
ἀβάταν ἅλα κιόνων ὕπερ Ἡρακλέος περᾶν εὐμαρές,
ἥρως θεὸς ἃς ἔθηκε ναυτιλίας ἐσχάτας …
οἴκοθεν μάτευε

Never venture further than the intraversable sea beyond the Pillars of Heracles, set by the hero-god as the extreme limit of any voyage; seek nearer home.

Nemean Odes 3.21 and 31

the Latin saying 'non plus ultra', used today for things superlative, extreme bliss etc., originates from this passage; the Pillars of Heracles are the Straits of Gibraltar

17 οὐδ' ἀλλοτρίων ἔρωτες ἀνδρὶ φέρειν κρέσσονες

Passions for things alien are not best for a man to have.

Translated by Richmond Lattimore (1976)

Nemean Odes 3.30

18 ἐν δὲ πείρᾳ τέλος
διαφαίνεται ὧν τις ἐξοχώτερος γένηται,
ἐν παισὶ νέοισι παῖς, ἐν ἀνδράσιν ἀνήρ, τρίτον
ἐν παλαιτέροισι, μέρος ἕκαστον οἷον ἔχομεν
βρότεον ἔθνος

Finally, only by trial will it be shown who is best
as a boy among boys, a man among men, lastly
who among the elders, each part that makes up
our mortal life.

Nemean Odes 3.70

19 Ἄριστος εὐφροσύνα πόνων κεκριμένων
ἰατρός· αἱ δὲ σοφαί
Μοισᾶν θύγατρες ἀοιδαὶ θέλξαν νιν
ἁπτόμεναι

Good cheer is the best healer after the contest is decided; and songs, wise daughters of the Muses, soothe with their magic touch.

Nemean Odes 4.1

20 ῥῆμα δ᾽ ἐργμάτων χρονιώτερον βιοτεύει

The story of things done outlives the act.

Translated by Richmond Lattimore (1976)

Nemean Odes 4.6

21 αἰδέομαι μέγα εἰπεῖν
ἐν δίκᾳ τε μὴ κεκινδυνευμένον

I take shame to speak of a thing done
monstrous, adventured against justice.

Translated by Richmond Lattimore (1976)

Nemean Odes 5.13

22 οὔ τοι ἅπασα κερδίων
φαίνοισα πρόσωπον ἀλάθει᾽ ἀτρεκής·
καὶ τὸ σιγᾶν πολλάκις ἐστὶ σοφώτατον ἀνθρώπῳ νοῆσαι

It is not always best to reveal the whole
truth;
and silence is often the wisest course.

Nemean Odes 5.18

23 Ἓν ἀνδρῶν, ἓν θεῶν γένος· ἐκ μιᾶς δὲ
πνέομεν
ματρὸς ἀμφότεροι

There is one race of men, and one of
gods,
though from one mother we both draw
our breath.

Translated by Anthony Verity (2007)

Nemean Odes 6.1

of Mother Earth

24 παροιχομένων γὰρ ἀνέρων,
ἀοιδαὶ καὶ λόγοι τὰ καλά σφιν ἔργ᾽
ἐκόμισαν

Men pass; but songs
and tales bring back the splendour of
their deeds.

Nemean Odes 6.30

25 τὸ δὲ πὰρ ποδὶ ναὸς ἑλισσόμενον αἰεὶ
κυμάτων
λέγεται παντὶ μάλιστα δονεῖν θυμόν

On a ship, the wave that rolls closest to
the rudder
is said most to alarm every man's heart.

Nemean Odes 6.55

26 ἀναπνέομεν δ᾽ οὐχ ἅπαντες ἐπὶ ἴσα

Not for like ends do we all draw breath.

Translated by C.M. Bowra (1969)

Nemean Odes 7.5

27 ταὶ μεγάλαι γὰρ ἀλκαί
σκότον πολὺν ὕμνων ἔχοντι δεόμεναι

Even the boldest deeds sink into darkness
if not told over again in hymns of
praise.

Nemean Odes 7.12

28 ἐπεὶ ψεύδεσί οἱ ποτανᾷ τε μαχανᾷ
σεμνὸν ἔπεστί τι· σοφία
δὲ κλέπτει παράγοισα μύθοις

Within his lies and cunning stratagems
we yet find something to admire;
genius deceives with persuasive speech.

Nemean Odes 7.22

of Odysseus

29 τυφλὸν δ᾽ ἔχει
ἦτορ ὅμιλος ἀνδρῶν ὁ πλεῖστος

Blind is the heart in almost any man.

Nemean Odes 7.23

30 ἀνάπαυσις ἐν παντὶ γλυκεῖα ἔργῳ

Rest is sweet, after every activity.

Nemean Odes 7.52

31 τυχεῖν δ᾽ ἕν᾽ ἀδύνατον
εὐδαιμονίαν ἅπασαν ἀνελόμενον

It is impossible,
for one man to succeed in winning
complete happiness.

Translated by William H. Race (1997)

Nemean Odes 7.55

32 ἦ τιν᾽ ἄγλωσσον μέν, ἦτορ δ᾽
ἄλκιμον, λάθα κατέχει

Someone lacking eloquence is soon forgotten, be he brave at heart.

Nemean Odes 8.24

33 μέγιστον δ᾽ αἰόλῳ ψεύ-
δει γέρας ἀντέταται

The greatest prize goes to the most

supple liar.

Nemean Odes 8.25

alluding to Odysseus

34 ἐχθρὰ δ' ἄρα πάρφασις ἦν καὶ πάλαι,
αἱμύλων μύθων ὁμόφοι-
τος, δολοφραδής, κακοποιὸν ὄνειδος·
ἃ τὸ μὲν λαμπρὸν βιᾶται,
τῶν δ' ἀφάντων κῦδος ἀντείνει σαθρόν

Hateful deception existed long ago
attended by beguiling words;
a wily-minded, mischievous disgrace,
it ruins brilliant renown,
exalting obscure, unsound fame.

Nemean Odes 8.32

35 κελεύθοις
ἁπλόαις ζωᾶς ἐφαπτοί-
μαν, θανὼν ὡς παισὶ κλέος
μὴ τὸ δύσφαμον προσάψω

May I keep to plain paths of life,
And when I die,
Leave my children a name
Of which no evil is spoken.

Translated by C.M. Bowra (1969)

Nemean Odes 8.35

36 χρυσὸν εὔχονται, πεδίον δ' ἕτεροι
ἀπέραντον, ἐγὼ δ' ἀστοῖς ἁδὼν
καὶ χθονὶ γυῖα καλύψαι,
αἰνέων αἰνητά, μομφὰν δ' ἐπισπείρων
ἀλιτροῖς

Some pray for gold, others for limitless lands,
but I for just enough ground to cover my limbs,
having praised in song who is to be praised
and scattered blame on the wicked.

Nemean Odes 8.37

37 αὔξεται δ' ἀρετά, χλωραῖς ἐέρσαις
ὡς ὅτε δένδρεον ᾄσσει,
ἐν σοφοῖς ἀνδρῶν ἀερθεῖσ'
ἐν δικαίοις τε πρὸς ὑγρὸν
αἰθέρα

Excellence soars upward like a tree fed on fresh dew,
exalted by the wise and just towards liquid heaven.

Nemean Odes 8.40

38 χρεῖαι δὲ παντοῖαι φίλων ἀν-
δρῶν· τὰ μὲν ἀμφὶ πόνοις
ὑπερώτατα, μαστεύει δὲ καὶ
τέρψις ἐν ὄμμασι θέσθαι
πιστόν

The need for friends appears in many forms;
it's valued most in times of trouble,
but in a steady friendship there also is delight.

Nemean Odes 8.42

39 ἐπαοιδαῖς δ' ἀνὴρ
νώδυνον καί τις κάματον
θῆκεν

Many a man has charmed the pain from toil
by chanting songs.

Translated by Anthony Verity (2007)

Nemean Odes 8.49

40 κρέσσων δὲ καππαύει δίκαν τὰν πρόσθεν ἀνήρ

The stronger man beats down the right of old.

Translated by Richmond Lattimore (1976)

Nemean Odes 9.15

41 ἐκ πόνων δ', οἳ σὺν νεότατι γένωνται
σύν τε δίκᾳ, τελέθει πρὸς γῆρας αἰὼν ἡμέρα·
ἴστω λαχὼν πρὸς δαιμόνων θαυμαστὸν ὄλβον

From honest labour, started in early youth,
comes tranquil life as riper age approaches
and with it admirable happiness, a gift of god.

Nemean Odes 9.44

42 Ἄριστον μὲν ὕδωρ, ὁ δὲ χρυσὸς αἰθόμενον πῦρ
ἅτε διαπρέπει νυκτὶ μεγάνορος ἔξοχα πλούτου

Water is best. But gold shines like fire
blazing in the night, supreme of lordly wealth.

Translated in *The Oxford Dictionary of Quotations* (2004)

Olympian Odes 1.1

43 ἁμέραι δ' ἐπίλοιποι
μάρτυρες σοφώτατοι

Days that are still to come
are the wisest witnesses of all.

Olympian Odes 1.33

44 ἀκέρδεια λέλογχεν θαμινὰ κακαγόρους

Many a time disaster has come to the speakers of evil.

Translated by Richmond Lattimore (1976)

Olympian Odes 1.53

45 εἰ δὲ θεὸν ἀνήρ τις ἔλπεταί
τι λαθέμεν ἔρδων, ἁμαρτάνει

Hope not, mortal, e'er to shun
The penetrating eye of Heaven.

Translated by C.A. Wheelwright (1864)

Olympian Odes 1.64

46 ὁ μὰν πλοῦτος ἀρεταῖς δεδαιδαλμένος
φέρει τῶν τε καὶ τῶν
καιρὸν βαθεῖαν ὑπέχων μέριμναν
ἀγροτέραν,
ἀστὴρ ἀρίζηλος, ἐτυμώτατον
ἀνδρὶ φέγγος

Wealth combined with virtue
brings opportunities for great achievement,
prompting desire for high ambition
and marked distinction, man's truest radiance.

Olympian Odes 2.53

47 πολλά μοι ὑπ'
ἀγκῶνος ὠκέα βέλη
ἔνδον ἐντὶ φαρέτρας
φωνάεντα συνετοῖσιν· ἐς δὲ τὸ πὰν
ἑρμανέων
χατίζει. σοφὸς ὁ πολλὰ εἰδὼς φυᾷ·
μαθόντες δὲ λάβροι
παγγλωσσίᾳ κόρακες ὣς ἄκραντα
γαρυέτων
Διὸς πρὸς ὄρνιχα θεῖον

I have many swift arrows in my quiver, vocal to the wise, but for the crowd needing interpreters. A worthy poet is endowed by nature, but those who have been taught their art chatter like ravens, vainly, against the holy bird of Zeus

Olympian Odes 2.83

48 οὐ ψευδεϊ τέγξω
λόγον· διάπειρά τοι βροτῶν ἔλεγχος

I will not steep my speech in lies;
in action lies the test of any man.

Translated by Richmond Lattimore (1976)

Olympian Odes 4.17

49 νυκτὶ θοᾶς ἐκ ναὸς ἀπεσκίμ-
φθαι δύ' ἄγκυραι

In stormy nights 'tis well
that you be doubly anchored.

Olympian Odes 6.101

50 αἱ δὲ φρενῶν ταραχαί
παρέπλαγξαν καὶ σοφόν

Disturbance in the brain has driven
even the wise man out of his course.

Translated by Richmond Lattimore (1976)

Olympian Odes 7.30

51 ἔνθα ποτὲ βρέχε θεῶν βασιλεὺς ὁ μέγας
χρυσέαις νιφάδεσσι πόλιν

Where once the great king of the gods
showered
the city with snows of gold.

Translated by William H. Race (1997)

Olympian Odes 7.34

a legendary statement of the wealth of Rhodes

52 ἐν δὲ μιᾷ μοίρᾳ χρόνου
ἄλλοτ' ἀλλοῖαι διαιθύσσοισιν αὖραι

In a single portion of time
winds quickly shift direction, veering
back and forth.

Translated by Anthony Verity (2007)

Olympian Odes 7.94

53 Μᾶτερ ὦ χρυσοστεφάνων ἀέθλων,
Οὐλυμπία,
δέσποιν' ἀλαθείας ... ἀνθρώπων πέρι
μαιομένων μεγάλαν
ἀρετὰν θυμῷ λαβεῖν

O Mother of gold-crowned games,
Olympia,
queen of truth, where mortals
seek to gain great success.

Olympian Odes 8.1

inscribed on medals used at the 28th Modern Olympic Games, Athens 2004

54 τό γε λοιδορῆσαι θεούς
ἐχθρὰ σοφία

To reproach the gods is wisdom misapplied.

Translated by H.T. Riley (1872)

Olympian Odes 9.37

55 αἴνει δὲ παλαιὸν μὲν οἶνον, ἄνθεα δ'
ὕμνων
νεωτέρων

Praise old wine, but also the blossoms
of poetry

when young.

Olympian Odes 9.48

56 διήρχετο κύκλον ὅσσᾳ βοᾷ
ὡραῖος ἐὼν καὶ καλὸς κάλλιστά τε ῥέξαις

To what acclamation he made his round, in the prime of youth, splendid in the glory of his triumph!

Olympian Odes 9.93

the earliest mention of the 'victory lap' run by a victor at the Olympic Games

57 ἔργων πρὸ πάντων βιότῳ φάος

Work above all brings light into our lives.

Translated by Panos Koronakis-Rohlf and Maria Batzini (2007)

Olympian Odes 10.23

58 ὅ τ' ἐξελέγχων μόνος
ἀλάθειαν ἐτήτυμον
Χρόνος

He alone makes truth apparent, and things as they really are,
Time.

Olympian Odes 10.53

59 τὸ γὰρ ἐμφυὲς οὔτ' αἴθων ἀλώπηξ
οὔτ' ἐρίβρομοι λέοντες διαλλάξαιντο ἦθος

His innate character neither tawny fox
nor roaring lion can forego.

Olympian Odes 11.19

60 σύμβολον δ' οὔ πώ τις ἐπιχθονίων
πιστὸν ἀμφὶ πράξιος ἐσσομένας εὗρεν θεόθεν,
τῶν δὲ μελλόντων τετύφλωνται φραδαί

No man on earth has yet received a sure sign from the gods of things to come; blinded is our perception of the future.

Olympian Odes 12.7

61 ἐν θεῷ γε μὰν τέλος

The outcome lies with god.

Translated by Anthony Verity (2007)

Olympian Odes 13.104

62 κάτα
Ἑλλάδ' εὑρήσεις ἐρευνῶν μάσσον' ἢ ὡς ἰδέμεν

If you search Hellas,
You will find more than the eye can see.

Translated by C.M. Bowra (1969)

Olympian Odes 13.112

63 Ζεῦ τέλει', αἰδῶ δίδοι καὶ τύχαν τερπνῶν γλυκεῖαν

Almighty Jove, preserve our tranquil state,
And may increasing joys our virtuous race await!

Translated by C.A. Wheelwright (1864)

Olympian Odes 13.115

closing line of the ode

64 Φοῖβε ...
ἐθελήσαις ταῦτα νόῳ τιθέμεν εὔανδρόν τε χώραν

Phoebus Apollo,
grant this prayer of mine and make this land a home of noble men.

Pythian Odes 1.39

65 ἐκ θεῶν γὰρ μαχαναὶ πᾶσαι βροτέαις ἀρεταῖς,
καὶ σοφοὶ καὶ χερσὶ βιαταὶ περίγλωσσοί τ' ἔφυν

All human virtues are the gift of god,
wisdom and strength and eloquence.

Pythian Odes 1.41

66 ἀστῶν δ' ἀκοὰ κρύφιον θυμὸν βαρύνει μάλιστ' ἐσλοῖσιν ἐπ' ἀλλοτρίοις

To hear of other men's success
makes others sore of heart.

Pythian Odes 1.84

67 κρέσσον γὰρ οἰκτιρμοῦ φθόνος

Better to be envied than pitied!

Translated in Liddell & Scott

Pythian Odes 1.85

cf. the identical English proverb

68 νώμα δικαίῳ πηδαλίῳ στρατόν

Steer your people with the rudder of justice.

Translated by Anthony Verity (2007)

Pythian Odes 1.86

69 ἀψευδεῖ δὲ πρὸς ἄκμονι χάλκευε γλῶσσαν

Forge your tongue on the anvil of truth.

Translated by C.A. Trypanis (1971)

Pythian Odes 1.86a

70 ἐξίει δ' ὥσπερ κυβερνάτας ἀνήρ
ἱστίον ἀνεμόεν

Like a helmsman, set full sail to the wind.

Translated by C.A. Trypanis (1971)

Pythian Odes 1.91

71 μὴ δολωθῇς,
ὦ φίλε, κέρδεσιν ἐντραπέλοις

Do not be lured, my friend, by deceitful gains.

Translated by C.A. Trypanis (1971)

Pythian Odes 1.92

72 γένοι', οἷος ἐσσὶ μαθών

Learn what you are and be such.

Translated by Richmond Lattimore (1976)

Pythian Odes 2.72

73 ποτὶ κέντρον δέ τοι
λακτιζέμεν τελέθει ὀλισθηρὸς οἶμος

Kicking against the goads is the way of failure.

Translated by Richmond Lattimore (1976)

Pythian Odes 2.94

cf. Aeschylus 39; Bible 190

74 πῦρ ἐξ ἑνός
σπέρματος ἐνθορὸν αἴστωσεν ὕλαν

Fire that starts from one spark can destroy a great forest.

Translated by Anthony Verity (2007)

Pythian Odes 3.36

75 ἀλλὰ κέρδει καὶ σοφία δέδεται

Even wisdom is enchained by gain.

Pythian Odes 3.54

76 μή, φίλα ψυχά, βίον ἀθάνατον
σπεῦδε, τὰν δ' ἔμπρακτον ἄντλει
μαχανάν

Do not, my soul, strive for immortal life,
but make the most of what is in your power.

Pythian Odes 3.61

77 ὄλβος οὐκ ἐς μακρὸν ἀνδρῶν ἔρχεται
σάος, πολὺς εὖτ' ἂν ἐπιβρίσαις ἕπηται

Prosperity does not last for long
when it attends man in its full weight.

Pythian Odes 3.105

78 σμικρὸς ἐν σμικροῖς, μέγας ἐν μεγάλοις ἔσσομαι

I will be small in small things, great in great.

Translated by Richmond Lattimore (1976)

Pythian Odes 3.107

79 ἁ δ' ἀρετὰ κλειναῖς ἀοιδαῖς
χρονία τελέθει

Greatness in noble songs
Endures through time.

Translated by C.M. Bowra (1969)

Pythian Odes 3.114

80 ἤδη με γηραιὸν μέρος ἁλικίας
ἀμφιπολεῖ· σὸν δ' ἄνθος ἥβας ἄρτι κυ-
μαίνει

Old age is hard upon me;
your youth is in its bloom.

Pythian Odes 4.157

81 ῥᾴδιον μὲν γὰρ πόλιν σεῖσαι καὶ ἀφαυροτέροις·
ἀλλ' ἐπὶ χώρας αὖτις ἔσσαι δυσπαλὲς δὴ γίνεται

For easily can even weaklings shake a city;
to set it back again in place is hard indeed.

Pythian Odes 4.272

82 κεῖνος γὰρ ἐν παισὶν νέος,
ἐν δὲ βουλαῖς πρέσβυς ἐγκύρ-
σαις ἑκατονταετεῖ βιοτᾷ

Among youngsters he is young;
giving advice, a centenarian.

Pythian Odes 4.281

83 ὁ γὰρ και-
ρὸς πρὸς ἀνθρώπων βραχὺ μέτρον ἔχει

Time and tide wait for no man.

Translated in Liddell & Scott

Pythian Odes 4.286

84 φαντὶ δ' ἔμμεν
τοῦτ' ἀνιαρότατον, καλὰ γινώσκοντ' ἀνάγκᾳ
ἐκτὸς ἔχειν πόδα

The cruellest thing, they say, is to know the good
but to be forced to stand apart from it.

Translated by Anthony Verity (2007)

Pythian Odes 4.287

85 Ὁ πλοῦτος εὐρυσθενής
ὅταν τις ἀρετᾷ κεκραμένον καθαρᾷ

Wide is the strength of Wealth

when mixed with stainless virtue.

Translated by Richmond Lattimore (1976)

Pythian Odes 5.1

86 σοφοὶ δέ τοι κάλλιον
φέροντι καὶ τὰν θεόσδοτον δύναμιν

The wise are better placed to bear
the power god has given.

Pythian Odes 5.12

87 πόνων δ' οὔ τις ἀπόκλαρός ἐστιν οὔτ' ἔσεται

No one is without his allotted share of toil, nor will be.

Translated by Anthony Verity (2007)

Pythian Odes 5.54

88 κρέσσονα μὲν ἁλικίας
νόον φέρβεται
γλῶσσάν τε· θάρσος δὲ τανύπτερος
ἐν ὄρνιξιν αἰετὸς ἔπλετο·
ἀγωνίας δ', ἕρκος οἷον, σθένος

He has a mind and tongue beyond his years;
in daring, as an eagle above all other birds;
a tower of strength in competition.

Pythian Odes 5.109

89 Κάλλιστον αἱ μεγαλοπόλιες Ἀθᾶναι ...
ἐπεὶ τίνα πάτραν, τίνα οἶκον ναίων ὀνυμάξεαι
ἐπιφανέστερον;

Of all great cities Athens is the loveliest.
What country can you name, what home more glorious?

Pythian Odes 7.1 and 5

90 φυᾷ τὸ γενναῖον ἐπιπρέπει
ἐκ πατέρων παισὶ λῆμα

Their fathers' noble spirit shines in their sons.

Pythian Odes 8.44

91 ὁ δὲ καλόν τι νέον λαχὼν
ἁβρότατος ἔπι μεγάλας
ἐξ ἐλπίδος πέταται
ὑποπτέροις ἀνορέαις, ἔχων
κρέσσονα πλούτου μέριμναν

He who wins, of a sudden, some noble prize
In the rich years of youth
Is raised high with hope; his manhood takes wings;
He has in his heart what is better than wealth.

Translated by H.D.F. Kitto (1951)

Pythian Odes 8.88

to a young winner in wrestling

92 ἐν δ' ὀλίγῳ βροτῶν
τὸ τερπνὸν αὔξεται· οὕτω δὲ καὶ πίτνει χαμαί,
ἀποτρόπῳ γνώμᾳ σεσεισμένον

In a short time the delight
of mortals burgeons; but so too does it fall to the ground
when shaken by a hostile purpose.

Translated by William H. Race (1997)

Pythian Odes 8.92

93 ἐπάμεροι. τί δέ τις; τί δ' οὔ τις; σκιᾶς ὄναρ
ἄνθρωπος. ἀλλ' ὅταν αἴγλα διόσδοτος ἔλθῃ,
λαμπρὸν φέγγος ἔπεστιν ἀνδρῶν καὶ μείλιχος αἰών

Ephemeral man! What is he? What is he not?
He's but a shadow in a dream.
But when god's splendour shines upon him
his is the glory and a gentle life.

Pythian Odes 8.95

94 ὕπνον ἀναλίσκοισα ῥέποντα πρὸς ἀῶ

Wasting time in sleep though dawn drew nigh.

Pythian Odes 9.25

95 μόχθου καθύπερθε νεᾶνις
ἦτορ ἔχοισα· φόβῳ δ' οὐ κεχείμανται φρένες

A girl with a heart that rises above hardship
and a spirit that is untouched by storms of fear.

Translated by Anthony Verity (2007)

Pythian Odes 9.31a

of Cyrene, a lovely girl, with whom Apollo fell in love; at the behest of the centaur Chiron he took her with him to North Africa where he founded the city named after her

96 κύριον ὃς πάντων τέλος
οἶσθα καὶ πάσας κελεύθους·
ὅσσα τε χθὼν ἠρινὰ φύλλ' ἀναπέμπει, χὠπόσαι
ἐν θαλάσσᾳ καὶ ποταμοῖς ψάμαθοι ...

χὤ τι μέλλει

You who know the ordained end of everything,
and all the paths that lead thereto:
how many leaves the earth sends forth in spring,
how many grains of sand in the sea and river;
what will come to pass, and whence it will come.

Translated by Anthony Verity (2007)

Pythian Odes 9.44

of Apollo

97 τὰ δ' εἰς ἐνιαυτὸν ἀτέκμαρτον προνοῆσαι

There is no means of telling what another year may bring.

Translated by Anthony Verity (2007)

Pythian Odes 10.63

98 κακολόγοι δὲ πολῖται

Fellow citizens are given to spreading scandal.

Translated by Anthony Verity (2007)

Pythian Odes 11.28

99 ἴσχει τε γὰρ ὄλβος οὐ μείονα φθόνον

Wealth contains envy in equal measure.

Pythian Odes 11.29

100 θεόθεν ἐραίμαν καλῶν,
δυνατὰ μαιόμενος ἐν ἁλικίᾳ

With god's help may I still love what is beautiful
and strive for what is attainable.

Translated by Paul Shorey (1857–1934)

Pythian Odes 11.50

101 ἀλλοτρίοισιν μὴ προφαίνειν, τίς φέρεται μόχθος ἄμμιν

Do not share your troubles with strangers.

Fragment 42 (Maehler) – *Hymn to Persephone*

102 ἄλλοτ' ἀλλοῖα φρόνει

Face differing situations with a different approach.

Fragment 43 (Maehler) – *Hymn to Persephone*

cf. the English proverbs 'other times, other manners' and 'when in Rome, do as the Romans do'

103 Ἀκτὶς ἀελίου, τί πολύσκοπ' ἐμήσαο,
ὦ μᾶτερ ὀμμάτων, ἄστρον ὑπέρτατον
ἐν ἁμέρᾳ κλεπτόμενον;

All-enlight'ning, all-beholding,
All-transcending star of day!
Why, thy sacred orb enfolding,
Why does darkness veil thy ray?

Translated by Thomas Love Peacock (1806)

Fragment 52k (Maehler)

some scholars believe this to refer to the total eclipse of 463BC

104 οὐ γὰρ ἔσθ' ὅπως τὰ θεῶν
βουλεύματ' ἐρευνάσει βροτέᾳ φρενί

It is not for a mortal mind to search out the will of god.

Fragment 61 (Maehler)

105 τότε βάλλεται, τότ' ἐπ' ἀμβρόταν χθόν' ἐραταί
ἴων φόβαι, ῥόδα τε κόμαισι μείγνυται,
ἀχεῖ τ' ὀμφαὶ μελέων σὺν αὐλοῖς,
οἰχνεῖ τε Σεμέλαν ἑλικάμπυκα χοροί

Now earth, undying, fills with tufts of violets,
now girls mix their hair with roses,
and songs ring to the music of the flute,
songs and dance to honour wreathed Semele.

Fragment 75 (Maehler)

on the coming of spring

106 ὦ ταὶ λιπαραὶ καὶ ἰοστέφανοι καὶ ἀοίδιμοι,
Ἑλλάδος ἔρει-
σμα, κλειναὶ Ἀθᾶναι, δαιμόνιον πτολίεθρον

O glorious Athens! violet-crowned, worthy of song,
bulwark of Greece, city of the gods.

Translated by C.A. Trypanis (1971)

Fragment 76 (Maehler) – *To the Athenians*

107 ὅθι παῖδες Ἀθαναίων ἐβάλοντο φαεννὰν κρηπῖδ' ἐλευθερίας

Where Athens' valiant sons laid the cornerstone of freedom.

Fragment 77 (Maehler) – *To the Athenians*

of the naval battle of Artemisium in 480BC, fought simultaneously with Thermopylae

108 θεῷ δὲ δυνατὸν μελαίνας
ἐκ νυκτὸς ἀμίαντον ὄρσαι φάος,
κελαινεφέι δὲ σκότει

καλύψαι σέλας καθαρόν
ἁμέρας

God can make unsullied light
spring from dark night
and in black-clouded darkness
hide the pure gleam
of day.

Translated by William H. Race (1997)

Fragment 108b (Maehler)

109 γλυκὺ δὲ πόλεμος ἀπείροισιν

War is sweet to those who never tried it.

Translated by D.S. Baker (1998)

Fragment 110 (Maehler) – *To the Thebans later proverbial*

110 θνᾴσκει δὲ σιγαθὲν καλὸν ἔργον

Unsung the noblest deed will die.

Translated in *Bartlett's Familiar Quotations* (1980)

Fragment 121 (Maehler)

111 σὺν δ' ἀνάγκᾳ πὰν καλόν

Under compulsion all is fair.

Translated by William H. Race (1997)

With necessity come many benefits.

Fragment 122 (Maehler)

both translations are valid

112 χρῆν μὲν κατὰ καιρὸν ἐρώτων δρέπεσθαι, θυμέ, σὺν ἁλικίᾳ

Gather the blossoms of love at the right time, my heart – in the prime of life.

Translated by C.A. Trypanis (1971)

Fragment 123 (Maehler)

cf. Robert Herrick (1591–1674), 'To the Virgins, to Make Much of Time': 'Gather ye rosebuds while ye may'

113 τοῖσι λάμπει μὲν μένος ἀελίου
τὰν ἐνθάδε νύκτα κάτω

For them the sun shines at full strength
while we here walk in night.

Translated by Willis Barnstone (1962)

Fragment 129.1 (Maehler)

of the Elysian Fields

114 φοινικορόδοις δ' ἐνὶ λειμώνεσσι
προάστιον αὐτῶν
καὶ λιβάνων σκιαρᾶν
καὶ χρυσοκάρποισιν βέβριθε δενδρέοις
καὶ τοὶ μὲν ἵπποις γυμνασίοισι τε τοὶ δὲ
πεσσοῖς
τοὶ δὲ φορμίγγεσσι τέρπονται, παρὰ δέ
σφισιν
εὐανθὴς ἅπας τέθαλεν ὄλβος

The plains around their city are red
with roses
and shaded by incense trees heavy with
golden fruit.
And some enjoy horses and wrestling,
or table games and the lyre,
and near them blossoms a flower of
perfect joy.

Translated by Willis Barnstone (1962)

Fragment 129.3 (Maehler)

of Hades

115 ὀδμὰ δ' ἐρατὸν κατὰ χῶρον κίδναται
αἰεὶ· θύματα μειγνύντων πυρὶ τηλεφανεῖ
παντοῖα θεῶν ἐπὶ βωμοῖς

Perfumes hover above the land,
from frankincense burning on bright
fires
of the altars of the gods.

Fragment 129.10 (Maehler)

116 ἁλίου δελφῖνος ὑπόκρισιν,
τὸν μὲν ἀκύμονος ἐν πόντου πελάγει
αὐλῶν ἐκίνησ' ἐρατὸν μέλος

Like a dolphin whom the lovely melody of flutes moves on to the surface of the waveless sea.

Translated by William C. Helmbold (1957)

Fragment 140b (Maehler)

quoted by Plutarch, Whether Land or Sea Animals Are Cleverer *984c*

117 τί θεός; τὸ πάν

What is god? Everything.

Translated in *Bartlett's Familiar Quotations* (1980)

Fragment 140d (Maehler)

118 ἀνδρῶν δικαίων Χρόνος σωτὴρ ἄριστος

Time is the best champion to the just.

Fragment 159 (Maehler)

119 Νόμος ὁ πάντων βασιλεὺς
θνατῶν τε καὶ ἀθανάτων
ἄγει δικαιῶν τὸ βιαιότατον
ὑπερτάτᾳ χειρί

Law, the sovereign of all,
Mortals and immortals,
Carries all with highest hand,
Justifying the utmost force.

Translated by W.R.M. Lamb (1925)
Fragment 169a (Maehler)
quoted in full in Plato, Gorgias *484b*

120 ἔσθ' ὅτε πιστόταται σιγᾶς ὁδοί·
κέντρον δὲ μάχας ὁ κρατιστεύων λόγος

Silence is the safest path at times;
an overpowering word may spur to battle.

Fragment 180 (Maehler)

121 ἐλπίς, ἃ μάλιστα θνατῶν πολύστροφον γνώμαν κυβερνᾷ

Hope, most of all, governs the ever-changing mind of men.

Fragment 214 (Maehler)

122 Διὸς παῖς ὁ χρυσός·
κεῖνον οὐ σὴς οὐδὲ κὶς δάπτει

Gold is the child of Zeus;
neither moth nor weevil eats it.

Translated by William H. Race (1997)
Fragment 222 (Maehler)

123 νέων δὲ μέριμναι σὺν πόνοις εἱλισσόμεναι
δόξαν εὑρίσκοντι· λάμπει δὲ χρόνῳ
ἔργα μετ' αἰθέρ' ἀερθέντα

Ambitions of the young, plied with toil, gain fame;
and in good time their deeds shine forth, raised up to heaven.

Fragment 227 (Maehler)

124 τόλμα τέ μιν ζαμενὴς καὶ σύνεσις πρόσκοπος ἐσάωσεν

You have been saved by mighty courage and foreseeing wit.

Fragment 231 (Maehler)

125 τὰς ἐλπίδας εἶναι ἐγρηγορότων ἐνύπνια

Hopes are the dreams of those who do not sleep.

Stobaeus, *Anthology* 4.47.12
attributed to Pindar by Stobaeus

PISANDER

7th or 6th century BC
Epic poet from Camirus in Rhodes

1 οὐ νέμεσις καὶ ψεῦδος ὑπὲρ ψυχῆς ἀγορεύειν

There is no blame in telling a lie to save one's life.

Translated by Martin L. West (2003)
Heraclea Fragment 8 (Bernabé, *PEG*)

2 ταύτας κατατοξεῦσαι τὰς ὄρνιθας Ἡρακλῆς λέγεται· Πείσανδρος δὲ αὐτὸν ὁ Καμιρεὺς ἀποκτεῖναι τὰς ὄρνιθας οὔ φησιν, ἀλλὰ ὡς ψόφῳ κροτάλων ἐκδιώξειεν αὐτάς

It is said that Heracles killed off the Stymphalian birds; but Pisander of Camirus says that he did not kill the birds, only scared them off with the noise of clappers.

Translated by Martin L. West (2003)
Pausanias, *Description of Greece* 8.22.4

PITTACUS

*c.*650–570BC
Statesman of Mytilene, lawgiver and one of the Seven Sages
see also Seven Sages 39–40

1 καιρὸν γνῶθι

Recognize the right instant.

Seven Sages, *Apophthegms* Fragment 5.2 (D-K)

2 τοῖς ἐπιτηδείοις χρῶ

Make use of the competent.

Seven Sages, *Apophthegms* Fragment 5.3 (D-K)

3 ὅσα νεμεσᾷς τῷ πλησίον, αὐτὸς μὴ ποίει

What you resent in others do not do yourself.

Seven Sages, *Apophthegms* Fragment 5.3 (D-K)

4 ἀπραγοῦντα μὴ ὀνείδιζε

Do not upbraid him who fares ill.

Seven Sages, *Apophthegms* Fragment 5.3 (D-K)

5 ἀνέχου ὑπὸ τῶν πλησίον μικρὰ ἐλαττούμενος

Bear your neighbours with patience, even if in small things they try to gain advantage over you.

Seven Sages, *Apophthegms* Fragment 5.5 (D-K)

6 δεινὸν συνιδεῖν τὸ μέλλον, ἀσφαλὲς τὸ γενόμενον

To look into the future is impossible, certain is only what has come to pass.

Seven Sages, *Apophthegms* Fragment 5.6 (D-K)

7 πιστὸν γῆ, ἄπιστον θάλασσα

Land can be relied on, untrustworthy is the sea.

Seven Sages, *Apophthegms* Fragment 5.7 (D-K)

8 θεράπευε εὐσέβειαν, παιδείαν, σωφροσύνην, φρόνησιν, ἀλήθειαν, πίστιν, ἐμπειρίαν, ἐπιδεξιότητα, ἑταιρείαν, ἐπιμέλειαν, οἰκονομίαν, τέχνην

Foster reverence, education, soundness of mind, prudence, truth, faith, experience, tact, friendship, diligence, thrift, art.

Seven Sages, *Apophthegms* Fragment 5.8 (D-K)

9 ἀνάγκῃ δ' οὐδὲ θεοὶ μάχονται

Even the gods do not fight against necessity.

Translated by R.D. Hicks (1925)

Seven Sages, *Apophthegms* 4.4 (Mullach, *FPG*)

10 τῶν μὲν ἀγρίων θηρίων κάκιστον ὁ τύραννος, τῶν δὲ ἡμέρων ὁ κόλαξ

Of all wild beasts a tyrant is the worst; of all the tame ones the flatterer.

Seven Sages, *Apophthegms* 4.10 (Mullach, *FPG*)

also attributed to Bias

11 ἐπύθετό τινος, διότι οὐ βούλεται γῆμαι· τοῦ δὲ φήσαντος· ἐὰν μὲν καλὴν γήμω, ἕξω κοινήν, ἐὰν δὲ αἰσχράν, ἕξω ποινήν· Οὐμενοῦν, ἔφη, ἀλλ' ἐὰν μὲν καλὴν γήμῃς, οὐχ ἕξεις ποινήν, ἐὰν δὲ αἰσχράν, οὐχ ἕξεις κοινήν

He asked someone why he would not marry; and when he said 'If I marry a pretty one all will have her, if an ugly one I will be punished', Pittacus answered 'Yes, but if a pretty one you will not be punished, if an ugly one not all will have her.'

Seven Sages, *Apophthegms* 4.16 (Mullach, *FPG*)

also attributed to Bion by Diogenes Laertius, Lives of Eminent Philosophers *4.48*

12 μὴ ἔριζε γονεῦσι, κἂν δίκαια λέγῃς

Do not quarrel with your parents, even if what you say is right.

Seven Sages, *Sententiae* 216.5 (Mullach, *FPG*)

13 ὃ μέλλεις πράττειν, μὴ πρόλεγε· ἀποτυχὼν γὰρ γελασθήσῃ

Do not announce your plans beforehand; for, if they fail, you will be ridiculed.

Translated by R.D. Hicks (1925)

Diogenes Laertius, *Lives of Eminent Philosophers* 1.78.2

14 ἀτυχίαν μὴ ὀνειδίζειν, νέμεσιν αἰδόμενον

Never scoff at anyone's misfortune, for fear of Nemesis.

Diogenes Laertius, *Lives of Eminent Philosophers* 1.78.3

15 τοὺς ἀγαθοὺς τῶν ἀνθρώπων θεοῦ τι μέρος ἔλεγεν ἔχειν

The virtuous possess a part of god.

Gnomologium Vaticanum, Sententia 560 (Sternbach)

16 τοὺς ὑπηκόους ὁ ἄρχων παρασκευάσειε φοβεῖσθαι μὴ αὐτὸν ἀλλ' ὑπὲρ αὐτοῦ

A ruler should make his subjects fear, not him, but for him.

Translated by Frank Cole Babbitt (1928)

Plutarch, *Dinner of the Seven Wise Men* 152b

17 ἄπληστον τὸ διὰ παντὸς κέρδος

Greedy, those who go to any lengths for profit.

Stobaeus, *Anthology* 3.10.47

18 συγγνώμη τιμωρίας ἀμείνων· τὸ μὲν γὰρ ἡμέρου φύσεώς ἐστι, τὸ δὲ θηριώδους

Better to pardon than punish; pardon belongs to a calm nature, punishment to beasts.

Stobaeus, *Anthology* 3.19.14

PLATO

429–347BC

Athenian philosopher

All quotations from the *Apology* are under Socrates

see also Anonymous 39, 62; Aristotle 84; Callimachus 29; Diogenes Cynic 2; Diogenes Laertius 1; Dionysius II 1; Philippides 1; Plutarch 52, 61; Sappho 45

1 τὸ γὰρ ἐξαπατᾶσθαι αὐτὸν ὑφ' αὑτοῦ πάντων χαλεπώτατον

The worst of all deceptions is self-deception.

Translated by Harold North Fowler (1926)

Cratylus 428d

2 τῷ πάμφορον εὔκαρπόν τε εἶναι ... τότε δὲ πρὸς τῷ κάλλει καὶ παμπλήθη ταῦτα ἔφερε ... τὰ νῦν οἷον νοσήσαντος σώματος ὀστᾶ

In former days all-bearing and blessed with crops, delightful and abundant; by now as but the skeleton of a sick man.

Translated by R.G. Bury (1929)

Critias 110e

of Attica

3 οὐδέποτε ὀρθῶς ἔχοντος οὔτε τοῦ ἀδικεῖν οὔτε τοῦ ἀνταδικεῖν οὔτε κακῶς πάσχοντα ἀμύνεσθαι ἀντιδρῶντα κακῶς

It is never right to do wrong or to requite wrong with wrong, or when we suffer evil to defend ourselves by doing evil in return.

Translated by Harold North Fowler (1914)

Crito 49d

4 πόθεν τοῦτο τὸ ἕρμαιον ηὑρέτην;

Where did you have the luck to pick it up?

Translated by W.R.M. Lamb (1924)

Euthydemus 273e

of Euthydemus, claiming to possess the skill of teaching virtue

5 οὐ μόνον ἄρα εὐτυχίαν ἀλλὰ καὶ εὐπραγίαν ἡ ἐπιστήμη παρέχει τοῖς ἀνθρώποις

Knowledge supplies mankind not only with success, but also with well-being.

Euthydemus 281b

6 οὐδέ γε τῆς ἄλλης ἐπιστήμης ὄφελος γίγνεται οὐδέν, οὔτε χρηματιστικῆς οὔτε ἰατρικῆς οὔτε ἄλλης οὐδεμιᾶς, ἥτις ποιεῖν τι ἐπίσταται, χρῆσθαι δὲ μὴ ᾧ ἂν ποιήσῃ

There is no advantage in the knowledge of money-making or medicine or anything else, without knowing how to use it.

Euthydemus 289a

7 στρατηγοί ... ἐπειδὰν ἢ πόλιν τινὰ θηρεύσωνται ἢ στρατόπεδον, παραδιδόασι τοῖς πολιτικοῖς ἀνδράσιν· αὐτοὶ γὰρ οὐκ ἐπίστανται χρῆσθαι τούτοις ἃ ἐθήρευσαν

Generals, when they have captured either a city or an army, hand it over to the politicians – since they themselves do not know how to use what they have taken.

Euthydemus 290c

8 δεόμενος ... σῶσαι ἡμᾶς ... ἐκ τῆς τρικυμίας τοῦ λόγου

God save us from the turmoil of the discussion!

Euthydemus 293a

9 τὸ γὰρ σπάνιον, ὦ Εὐθύδημε, τίμιον, τὸ δὲ ὕδωρ εὐωνότατον, ἄριστον ὄν, ὡς ἔφη Πίνδαρος

That which is rare is dear, but water is to be had at the cheapest rate, though it is, as Pindar said, the best of all things.

Translated by H.T. Riley (1872)

Euthydemus 304b

quoting Pindar 42

10 πάντα γὰρ ἄνδρα χρὴ ἀγαπᾶν ὅστις καὶ ὁτιοῦν λέγει ἐχόμενον φρονήσεως πρᾶγμα καὶ ἀνδρείως ἐπεξιὼν διαπονεῖται

We should admire anyone who says anything that verges on good sense, and labours steadily in its pursuit.

Euthydemus 306c

11 ἐν παντὶ ἐπιτηδεύματι οἱ μὲν φαῦλοι πολλοὶ καὶ οὐδενὸς ἄξιοι, οἱ δὲ σπουδαῖοι ὀλίγοι καὶ παντὸς ἄξιοι

In every trade the duffers are many and worthless, whereas the good workers are few and worth any price.

Translated by W.R.M. Lamb (1924)

Euthydemus 307a

12 ἆρα τὸ ὅσιον ὅτι ὅσιόν ἐστιν φιλεῖται ὑπὸ τῶν θεῶν, ἢ ὅτι φιλεῖται ὅσιόν ἐστιν;

Is that which is holy loved by the gods because it is holy, or is it holy because it is loved by the gods?

Translated by Harold North Fowler (1914)

Euthyphro 10a

13 τὸ πείθειν ... τοῖς λόγοις ... τῇ ἀληθείᾳ μέγιστον ἀγαθὸν καὶ αἴτιον ἅμα μὲν ἐλευθερίας αὐτοῖς τοῖς ἀνθρώποις, ἅμα δὲ τοῦ ἄλλων ἄρχειν

Persuasion through words is truly the greatest blessing; it is instrumental in giving men freedom and, at the same time, the power to rule over others.

Gorgias 452d–e

14 πειθοῦς δημιουργός ἐστιν ἡ ῥητορική

Rhetoric is a producer of persuasion.

Translated by W.R.M. Lamb (1925)

Gorgias 453a

15 καλῶ τὴν ῥητορικήν ... εἶναί τι ἐπιτήδευμα τεχνικὸν μὲν οὔ, ψυχῆς δὲ στοχαστικῆς καὶ ἀνδρείας καὶ φύσει δεινῆς προσομιλεῖν τοῖς ἀνθρώποις· καλῶ δὲ αὐτοῦ ἐγὼ τὸ κεφάλαιον κολακείαν

Rhetoric doesn't involve expertise; all you need is a mind which is good at guessing, some courage, and a natural talent for interacting with people. The general term I use to refer to it is *flattery*.

Translated by Robin Waterfield (1994)

Gorgias 463a

16 ὑπὸ μὲν οὖν τὴν ἰατρικὴν ἡ ὀψοποιικὴ ὑποδέδυκε, καὶ προσποιεῖται τὰ βέλτιστα σιτία τῷ σώματι εἰδέναι, ὥστ' εἰ δέοι ... διαγωνίζεσθαι ὀψοποιόν τε καὶ ἰατρόν ... περὶ τῶν χρηστῶν σιτίων ... λιμῷ ἂν ἀποθανεῖν τὸν ἰατρόν

Cookery has crept into medicine and professes to know the best foods for the body; yet if the cook and the doctor were to enter a competition as to which are the most beneficial foods – the doctor would starve to death.

Gorgias 464d

17 κακίας ἄρα ψυχῆς ἀπαλλάττεται ὁ δίκην διδούς;

Is he who pays the penalty relieved from evilness of soul?

Translated by W.R.M. Lamb (1925)

Gorgias 477a

18 τὸ δὲ ἀδικοῦντα μὴ διδόναι δίκην πάντων μέγιστόν τε καὶ πρῶτον κακῶν πέφυκεν

To do wrong and not pay the penalty is the greatest among all evils.

Gorgias 479d

19 ἐπεὶ ποίῳ δικαίῳ χρώμενος Ξέρξης ἐπὶ τὴν Ἑλλάδα ἐστράτευσεν ἢ ὁ πατὴρ αὐτοῦ ἐπὶ Σκύθας; ἢ ἄλλα μυρία ... τοιαῦτα

By what right did Xerxes march against Greece, or his father against Scythia? or countless other cases of this sort.

Gorgias 483d

20 εἷς φρονῶν μυρίων μὴ φρονούντων κρείττων

One wise man is better than a multitude of fools.

Gorgias 490a

21 σμικρὰ καὶ ὀλίγου ἄξια ἀνερωτᾷ

He keeps on asking petty, unimportant questions.

Translated by W.R.M. Lamb (1925)

Gorgias 497b

of Socrates

22 ἐὰν ζητῇς καλῶς, εὑρήσεις

Search well, and thou shalt find

Gorgias 503d

23 τοῦ σώματος τάξεσιν ὄνομα εἶναι ὑγιεινόν, ἐξ οὗ ἐν αὐτῷ ἡ ὑγίεια γίγνεται ... της ψυχης τάξεσι καὶ κοσμήσεσιν ... ἔστιν δικαιοσύνη τε καὶ σωφροσύνη

Order of the body leads to health, order and harmony of the soul to lawfulness and prudence.

Gorgias 504c–d

24 ὅτῳ δὲ μὴ ἔνι κοινωνία, φιλία οὐκ ἂν εἴη

Where there is no common understanding there can be no friendship.

Gorgias 507e

25 καὶ οὐρανὸν καὶ γῆν καὶ θεοὺς καὶ ἀνθρώπους τὴν κοινωνίαν συνέχειν καὶ φιλίαν καὶ κοσμιότητα καὶ σωφροσύνην καὶ δικαιότητα, καὶ τὸ ὅλον τοῦτο διὰ ταῦτα κόσμον καλοῦσιν, ὦ ἑταῖρε, οὐκ ἀκοσμίαν οὐδὲ ἀκολασίαν

Heaven and earth and gods and men are held together by communion and friendship, by orderliness, temperance and justice; this is why they call the whole of this world by the name of cosmos, not of disorder or dissoluteness.

Gorgias 508a

the double meaning of κόσμος (world and order), the first name given to the universe by the Pythagoreans

26 τὸν μέλλοντα ὀρθῶς ῥητορικὸν ἔσεσθαι δίκαιον ἄρα δεῖ εἶναι καὶ ἐπιστήμονα τῶν δικαίων

To be a good public speaker, first be well-informed of the ways of justice and, of course, be just yourself.

Gorgias 508c

27 τὴν εἱμαρμένην οὐδ' ἂν εἷς ἐκφύγοι

Not one of us can escape his destiny.

Translated by W.R.M. Lamb (1925)

Gorgias 512e

28 προσήκει δὲ παντὶ τῷ ἐν τιμωρίᾳ ὄντι, ὑπ' ἄλλου ὀρθῶς τιμωρουμένῳ, ἢ βελτίονι γίγνεσθαι καὶ ὀνίνασθαι ἢ παραδείγματι τοῖς ἄλλοις γίγνεσθαι

Punishment rightly inflicted should serve either to improve the culprit and make him profit by it, or serve as an example to the rest.

Gorgias 525b

29 ἀνδρὶ μελετητέον οὐ τὸ δοκεῖν εἶναι ἀγαθὸν ἀλλὰ τὸ εἶναι, καὶ ἰδίᾳ καὶ δημοσίᾳ

A man should train himself not to seem good but to be good both in private and in public.

Gorgias 527b

30 πολὺ γάρ τοι μεῖζόν με ἀγαθὸν ἐργάσει ἀμαθίας παύσας τὴν ψυχὴν ἢ νόσου τὸ σῶμα

You would be doing me more good by curing my soul of ignorance, than my body of disease.

Lesser Hippias 372e

31 κοῦφον γὰρ χρῆμα ποιητής ἐστιν καὶ πτηνὸν καὶ ἱερόν, καὶ οὐ πρότερον οἷός τε ποιεῖν πρὶν ἂν ἔνθεός τε γένηται καὶ ἔκφρων καὶ ὁ νοῦς μηκέτι ἐν αὐτῷ ἐνῇ

A poet is a strange fellow, light-hearted and winged and sacred, unable to create unless inspired by god, out of his wits, beyond reason.

Ion 534b

32 ἐπιστήμῃ γὰρ ... δεῖ κρίνεσθαι, ἀλλ' οὐ πλήθει τὸ μέλλον καλῶς κριθήσεσθαι

Knowledge must decide, not a majority, if there is to be a right decision.

Laches 184e

33 ἐγὼ μὲν γὰρ καὶ ἐπιλανθάνομαι ἤδη τὰ πολλὰ διὰ τὴν ἡλικίαν ὧν ἂν διανοηθῶ ἐρέσθαι καὶ αὖ ἃ ἂν ἀκούσω· ἐὰν δὲ μεταξὺ ἄλλοι λόγοι γένωνται, οὐ πάνυ μέμνημαι

I find that owing to my age I forget the questions I intend to put, and also the answers I receive; and if the discussion changes in the middle, my memory goes all together.

Translated by W.R.M. Lamb (1924)

Laches 189c

34 ἡ μὲν μετὰ φρονήσεως καρτερία καλὴ κἀγαθή

Endurance joined with wisdom is noble and good.

Translated by W.R.M. Lamb (1924)

Laches 192c

35 οὐδὲν λέγει, ἀλλὰ στρέφεται ἄνω καὶ κάτω ἐπικρυπτόμενος τὴν αὑτοῦ ἀπορίαν

He talks no sense, but twists and turns hoping to conceal his own perplexity.

Laches 196b.1

36 μάτην κενοῖς λόγοις αὐτὸς αὑτὸν κοσμοῖ;

Why waste time in adorning oneself with empty words?

Translated by W.R.M. Lamb (1924)

Laches 196b.7

37 τὸ ἄφοβον καὶ τὸ ἀνδρεῖον οὐ ταὐτόν

Fearlessness and courage are not the same thing.

Laches 197b

38 πρέπει μέν που ... τῶν μεγίστων προστατοῦντι μεγίστης φρονήσεως μετέχειν

It is suitable, I presume, for a man in the highest seat of government to be gifted with the highest degree of wisdom.

Translated by W.R.M. Lamb (1924)

Laches 197e

39 ἣν γὰρ καλοῦσιν οἱ πλεῖστοι τῶν ἀνθρώπων εἰρήνην, τοῦτ' εἶναι μόνον ὄνομα, τῷ δ' ἔργῳ πάσαις πρὸς πάσας τὰς πόλεις ἀεὶ πόλεμον ἀκήρυκτον κατὰ φύσιν εἶναι

Peace is but a word; in reality all states are engaged in undeclared wars against all other states.

Laws 626a

40 τὸ νικᾶν αὐτὸν αὑτὸν πασῶν νικῶν πρώτη τε καὶ ἀρίστη

Victory over oneself is of all victories the first and finest.

Laws 626e

41 τό γε μὴν ἄριστον οὔτε ὁ πόλεμος οὔτε ἡ στάσις, ἀπευκτὸν δὲ τὸ δεηθῆναι τούτων, εἰρήνη δὲ πρὸς ἀλλήλους ἅμα καὶ φιλοφροσύνη· καὶ δὴ καὶ τὸ νικᾶν, ὡς ἔοικεν, αὐτὴν αὑτὴν πόλιν οὐκ ἦν τῶν ἀρίστων ἀλλὰ τῶν ἀναγκαίων

Neither war nor civil war is best – both are abominable – but peace and goodwill among men. Thus, for a state to overcome its own shortcomings is not just a great achievement, it is an absolute necessity.

Laws 628c

42 τὸ δὲ τῶν λυπῶν καὶ φόβων ... εἴ τις ἐκ παίδων φευξεῖται διὰ τέλους, ὁπόταν εἰς ἀναγκαίους ἔλθῃ πόνους καὶ φόβους καὶ λύπας, φευξεῖσθαι τοὺς ἐν ἐκείνοις γεγυμνασμένους

If pains and fears are shunned from childhood, when confronted with unavoidable hardships and fears and pains, he will be put to flight by those who are trained to face them.

Laws 635b

43 τὴν πόλιν ἅπαντες ἡμῶν Ἕλληνες ὑπολαμβάνουσιν ὡς φιλόλογός τέ ἐστι καὶ πολύλογος, Λακεδαίμονα δὲ καὶ Κρήτην, τὴν μὲν βραχύλογον, τὴν δὲ πολύνοιαν μᾶλλον ἢ πολυλογίαν ἀσκοῦσαν

Our city, Athens, is, in the general opinion of the Greeks, both fond of talk and full of talk, but Lacedaemon is scant of talk, while Crete is more witty than wordy.

Translated by R.G. Bury (1926)

Laws 641e

a polite way of referring to the proverbial mendacity of the Cretans; cf. Epimenides 1

44 τὸν ὁτιοῦν ἀγαθὸν ἄνδρα μέλλοντα ἔσεσθαι τοῦτο αὐτὸ ἐκ παίδων εὐθὺς μελετᾶν δεῖν

A man who intends to be skilled at a particular occupation must practise it from childhood.

Translated by Trevor J. Saunders (1970)

Laws 643b.4

45 τὸν μέλλοντα ἀγαθὸν ἔσεσθαι ... οἰκοδόμον τῶν παιδείων οἰκοδομημάτων παίζειν χρὴ ... καὶ ὄργανα ἑκατέρῳ σμικρά, τῶν ἀληθινῶν μιμήματα, παρασκευάζειν τὸν τρέφοντα αὐτῶν

To make a good builder a child must play at building toy houses, and those who teach them must provide each child with miniature tools modelled on real ones.

Translated by R.G. Bury (1926)

Laws 643b.7

46 καὶ πειρᾶσθαι διὰ τῶν παιδιῶν ἐκεῖσε τρέπειν τὰς ἡδονὰς καὶ ἐπιθυμίας τῶν παίδων, οἷ ἀφικομένους αὐτοὺς δεῖ τέλος ἔχειν

Use children's games to channel their pleasures and desires towards activities in which they will have to engage when they are adults.

Translated by Trevor J. Saunders (1970)

Laws 643c

47 κεφάλαιον δὴ παιδείας ... ἣ τοῦ παίζοντος τὴν ψυχὴν εἰς ἔρωτα μάλιστα ἄξει τούτου ὃ δεήσει γενόμενον ἄνδρ' αὐτὸν τέλειον εἶναι τῆς τοῦ πράγματος ἀρετῆς

Primarily educate a child by using his playtime to imbue his soul with the greatest possible liking for the occupation which he will have to master when he grows up.

Laws 643d

48 τὴν δὲ πρὸς ἀρετὴν ἐκ παίδων παιδείαν ποιοῦσαν ἐπιθυμητήν τε καὶ ἐραστὴν τοῦ πολίτην γενέσθαι τέλεον

Education from childhood in virtue, a training which produces a keen desire to become a perfect citizen.

Translated by Trevor J. Saunders (1970)

Laws 643e

49 παιδείαν ... τὴν εἰς χρήματα τείνουσαν ἤ τινα πρὸς ἰσχύν, ἢ καὶ πρὸς ἄλλην τινὰ σοφίαν ἄνευ νοῦ καὶ δίκης, βάναυσόν τ' εἶναι καὶ ἀνελεύθερον καὶ οὐκ ἀξίαν τὸ παράπαν παιδείαν καλεῖσθαι

An education which aims only at money-making or physical strength, or even some mental accomplishment devoid of reason and justice, I would term vulgar and illiberal and utterly unworthy of the name.

Translated by R.G. Bury (1926)

Laws 644a

50 δεῖ δὴ τὴν παιδείαν μηδαμοῦ ἀτιμάζειν, ὡς πρῶτον τῶν καλλίστων τοῖς ἀρίστοις ἀνδράσιν παραγιγνόμενον

One should never disparage education; it stands first among the finest gifts that are given to the best men.

Translated by R.G. Bury (1926)

Laws 644b

51 ὡς ἀγαθῶν μὲν ὄντων τῶν δυναμένων ἄρχειν αὑτῶν, κακῶν δὲ τῶν μή

Excellent are those who can control themselves; those who cannot are a nuisance.

Laws 644b

52 δύο δὲ κεκτημένον ἐν αὑτῷ συμβούλω ἐναντίω τε καὶ ἄφρονε ... ἡδονὴν καὶ λύπην

Each possesses within himself two antagonistic and foolish counsellors, pleasure and pain.

Translated by R.G. Bury (1926)

Laws 644c

53 ταῦτα τὰ πάθη ἐν ἡμῖν ... ἀνθέλκουσιν ἐναντίαι οὖσαι ἐπ' ἐναντίας πράξεις, οὗ δὴ διωρισμένη ἀρετὴ καὶ κακία κεῖται

These emotions drag us to opposite actions, towards the dividing line between virtue and vice.

Laws 644e

54 οὔτε γὰρ παρὰ θεάτρου δεῖ τόν γε ἀληθῆ κριτὴν κρίνειν μανθάνοντα καὶ ἐκπληττόμενον ὑπὸ θορύβου τῶν πολλῶν

A true judge must not reach his verdict by listening to the audience, nor be panic-struck by the uproar of the crowd.

Laws 659a

55 τὸ κατὰ φύσιν πηδᾶν εἰθίσθαι πᾶν ζῷον, τὸ δὲ ἀνθρώπινον, ὡς ἔφαμεν, αἴσθησιν λαβὸν τοῦ ῥυθμοῦ ἐγέννησέν τε ὄρχησιν καὶ ἔτεκεν

Every animal has the natural habit of jumping about. The human animal acquired a sense of rhythm, and that led to the birth of dancing.

Translated by Trevor J. Saunders (1970)

Laws 673d

56 ᾗ δ' ἄν ποτε συνοικίᾳ μήτε πλοῦτος συνοικῇ μήτε πενία, σχεδὸν ἐν ταύτῃ γενναιότατα ἤθη γίγνοιτ' ἄν

The community in which neither wealth nor poverty exists will generally produce the finest characters.

Translated by Trevor J. Saunders (1970)

Laws 679b

57 ἐάν τις μείζονα διδῷ τοῖς ἐλάττοσι δύναμιν παρεὶς τὸ μέτριον, πλοίοις τε ἱστία καὶ σώμασι τροφὴν καὶ ψυχαῖς ἀρχάς, ἀνατρέπεταί που πάντα καὶ ἐξυβρίζοντα τὰ μὲν εἰς νόσους θεῖ, τὰ δ' εἰς ἔκγονον ὕβρεως ἀδικίαν

If we provide beyond measure, like fitting large sails to small ships, over-feeding a body or instilling in a soul aspirations that are too high, the result is disastrous: poor health and arrogance.

Laws 691c

58 οὐδείς πω μέγας ἐγγέγονεν ἀληθῶς ... τὸ δ' αἴτιον οὐ τύχης, ἀλλ' ὁ κακὸς βίος ὃν οἱ τῶν διαφερόντως πλουσίων καὶ τυράννων παῖδες τὰ πολλὰ ζῶσιν

No offspring of excessively rich parents, or of tyrants, has really risen to greatness, and the cause of this is not bad luck, but the shocking life that such children almost always lead.

Laws 695e

59 ἡ Περσῶν ἐπίθεσις τοῖς Ἕλλησιν, ἴσως δὲ σχεδὸν ἅπασιν τοῖς τὴν Εὐρώπην οἰκοῦσιν ἐγίγνετο

The Persians made their onslaught upon the Greeks – and indeed one might say on virtually all the nations of Europe.

Translated by R.G. Bury (1926)

Laws 698b

60 οὔτ' ὀρθοὺς νόμους ὅσοι μὴ συμπάσης τῆς

πόλεως ἕνεκα τοῦ κοινοῦ ἐτέθησαν· οἳ δ' ἕνεκά τινων, στασιώτας ἀλλ' οὐ πολίτας τούτους φαμέν

Laws which are not established for the good of the whole state are bogus laws; and when they favour particular sections of the community, their authors are not citizens but party-men.

Translated by Trevor J. Saunders (1970)

Laws 715b

61 τοὺς δ' ἄρχοντας λεγομένους νῦν ὑπηρέτας τοῖς νόμοις ἐκάλεσα οὔτι καινοτομίας ὀνομάτων ἕνεκα, ἀλλ' ἡγοῦμαι παντὸς μᾶλλον εἶναι παρὰ τοῦτο σωτηρίαν τε πόλει καὶ τοὐναντίον. ἐν ᾗ μὲν γὰρ ἂν ἀρχόμενος ᾖ καὶ ἄκυρος νόμος, φθορὰν ὁρῶ τῇ τοιαύτῃ ἑτοίμην οὖσαν

Such people are usually referred to as 'rulers', and if I have called them 'servants of the laws' it's not because I want to mint a new expression but because I believe that the success or failure of a state hinges on this point more than anything else. Where the law is subject to some other authority and has none of its own, the collapse of the state, in my view, is not far off.

Translated by Trevor J. Saunders (1970)

Laws 715c

62 ἐν ᾗ δὲ ἂν δεσπότης τῶν ἀρχόντων, οἱ δὲ ἄρχοντες δοῦλοι τοῦ νόμου, σωτηρίαν καὶ πάντα ὅσα θεοὶ πόλεσιν ἔδοσαν ἀγαθὰ γιγνόμενα καθορῶ

Wherever the law is lord over the magistrates, and the magistrates are servants to the law, there I descry salvation and all the blessings that the gods bestow on States.

Translated by R.G. Bury (1926)

Laws 715d

63 ὁ δὴ θεὸς ἡμῖν πάντων χρημάτων μέτρον ἂν εἴη μάλιστα, καὶ πολὺ μᾶλλον ἤ πού τις, ὥς φασιν, ἄνθρωπος

In our view it is god who is the 'measure of all things', much more so than any 'man', as they say.

Translated by Trevor J. Saunders (1970)

Laws 716c

cf. Protagoras 6

64 ποιητής, ὁπόταν ἐν τῷ τρίποδι τῆς Μούσης καθίζηται, τότε οὐκ ἔμφρων ἐστίν, οἷον δὲ κρήνη τις τὸ ἐπιὸν ῥεῖν ἑτοίμως ἐᾷ

When a poet takes his seat on the tripod of the Muse, he cannot control his thoughts; he's like a fountain where the water is allowed to gush forth unchecked.

Translated by Trevor J. Saunders (1970)

Laws 719c

65 τῷ δὲ νομοθέτῃ τοῦτο οὐκ ἔστι ποιεῖν ἐν τῷ νόμῳ, δύο περὶ ἑνός, ἀλλὰ ἕνα περὶ ἑνὸς ἀεὶ δεῖ λόγον ἀποφαίνεσθαι

The legislator must not let his laws say two different things on the same subject; his rule has to be 'one topic, one doctrine'.

Translated by Trevor J. Saunders (1970)

Laws 719d

unlike the poet

66 τιμὴ δ' ἐστὶν ἡμῖν ... τοῖς μὲν ἀμείνοσιν ἕπεσθαι, τὰ δὲ χείρονα, γενέσθαι δὲ βελτίω δυνατά, τοῦτ' αὐτὸ ὡς ἄριστα ἀποτελεῖν

Honour is to cleave to what is superior and to make as perfect as possible what is deficient.

Translated by Trevor J. Saunders (1970)

Laws 728c

67 μὴ δή τις φιλοχρημονείτω παίδων γ' ἕνεκα, ἵνα ὅτι πλουσιωτάτους καταλίπῃ

No one should seek wealth in order to leave his children as rich as possible.

Laws 729a

68 ἡ γὰρ τῶν νέων ἀκολάκευτος οὐσία, τῶν δ' ἀναγκαίων μὴ ἐνδεὴς ... ἀρίστη

A child's fortune should be modest enough not to attract flatterers, but sufficient to supply all his needs.

Translated by Trevor J. Saunders (1970)

Laws 729a

69 ὅπου ἀναισχυντοῦσι γέροντες, ἀνάγκη καὶ νέους ἐνταῦθα εἶναι ἀναιδεστάτους

Where the old are shameless the young too will inevitably be disrespectful.

Translated by Trevor J. Saunders (1970)

Laws 729c

70 παιδεία γὰρ νέων διαφέρουσά ἐστιν ἅμα καὶ αὐτῶν οὐ τὸ νουθετεῖν, ἀλλ' ἅπερ ἂν ἄλλον νουθετῶν εἴποι τις, φαίνεσθαι ταῦτα αὐτὸν δρῶντα διὰ βίου

The best way to educate the young, as well as yourself, is not by admonition but by practising all your life that which you preach to others.

Laws 729c

71 ἀλήθεια δὴ πάντων μὲν ἀγαθῶν θεοῖς ἡγεῖται, πάντων δὲ ἀνθρώποις

Truth heads the list of all things good, for gods and men alike.

Translated by Trevor J. Saunders (1970)

Laws 730c

72 πᾶς ὁ ἄδικος οὐχ ἑκὼν ἄδικος

Every unjust man is unjust against his will.

Translated by Trevor J. Saunders (1970)

Laws 731c

73 φίλος αὑτῷ πᾶς ἄνθρωπος φύσει τ' ἐστί

Every man is by nature a lover of self.

Translated by R.G. Bury (1926)

Laws 731e

74 τυφλοῦται γὰρ περὶ τὸ φιλούμενον ὁ φιλῶν

Love, which blinds us to the faults of our beloved.

Translated by Trevor J. Saunders (1970)

Laws 731e

75 τὸ τὴν ἀμαθίαν τὴν παρ' αὑτῷ δοκεῖν σοφίαν εἶναι γέγονε πᾶσιν· ὅθεν οὐκ εἰδότες, ὡς ἔπος εἰπεῖν, οὐδέν οἰόμεθα τὰ πάντα εἰδέναι

Stupid people are always convinced of their own shrewdness; which is why we think we know everything when we are almost totally ignorant.

Translated by Trevor J. Saunders (1970)

Laws 732a

76 οὐκ ἐπιτρέποντες δὲ ἄλλοις ἃ μὴ ἐπιστάμεθα πράττειν, ἀναγκαζόμεθα ἁμαρτάνειν αὐτοὶ πράττοντες

Since we will not entrust to others the doing of things we do not understand, we necessarily go wrong in doing them ourselves.

Translated by R.G. Bury (1926)

Laws 732a

77 σώφρονα βίον ... καὶ φρόνιμον ... τὸν ἀνδρεῖον, καὶ τὸν ὑγιεινὸν βίον ταξώμεθα· καὶ τούτοις ... ἐναντίους ... ἄφρονα, δειλόν, ἀκόλαστον, νοσώδη

We shall subscribe to a life of self-control, a life of wisdom, a life of courage, a healthy life; as opposed to a licentious, foolish, cowardly, diseased life

Laws 733e

78 πόνος δ', ὡς ἔοικεν, καὶ κίνδυνός ἐστιν ἐν πάσῃ κατασκευῇ πολιτικῇ

Toil and risk are involved in every exercise of statecraft.

Translated by R.G. Bury (1926)

Laws 736b

79 ἣν νομοθετεῖσθαι ἀναγκασθείσῃ πόλει τῶν ἀρχαίων οὔτε ἐᾶν οἷόν τε ἀκίνητον οὔτ' αὖ κινεῖν δυνατόν ἐστί τινα τρόπον

When an old-established state is forced to resort to legislation, it finds that both leaving things as they are and reforming them are somehow equally impossible.

Translated by Trevor J. Saunders (1970)

Laws 736c

80 ὅπου γὰρ μὴ φῶς ἀλλήλοις ἐστὶν ἀλλήλων ἐν τοῖς τρόποις ἀλλὰ σκότος, οὔτ' ἂν τιμῆς τῆς ἀξίας οὔτ' ἀρχῶν οὔτε δίκης ποτέ τις ἂν τῆς προσηκούσης

Where men conceal their ways one from another in darkness rather than light, there no man will ever rightly gain either his due honour or office, or the justice that is befitting

Translated by R.G. Bury (1926)

Laws 738e

81 πρώτη μὲν τοίνυν πόλις τέ ἐστι ... ὅπου τὸ πάλαι λεγόμενον ἂν γίγνηται ... ὡς ὄντως ἐστὶ κοινὰ τὰ φίλων· τοῦτ' οὖν εἴτε που νῦν ἔστιν εἴτ' ἔσται ποτέ

The ideal state is one where the old saying 'friends' property is genuinely shared' is put into practice; so far there is no such state nor ever shall be.

Laws 739b

cf. Pythagoras 14 and Plato 187; on common property see also Plato, Republic *424a*

82 μηδ' ἐξεῖναι χρυσὸν μηδὲ ἄργυρον κεκτῆσθαι μηδένα μηδενὶ ἰδιώτῃ, νόμισμα δ' ἕνεκα ἀλλαγῆς τῆς καθ' ἡμέραν ... ἀποτίνειν. ὧν ἕνεκά φαμεν τὸ νόμισμα κτητέον αὐτοῖς μὲν ἔντιμον, τοῖς δὲ ἄλλοις ἀνθρώποις ἀδόκιμον

No private person shall be allowed to possess any gold or silver, but only coinage for day-to-day dealings. For these purposes, we agree, they must possess coinage, legal tender for themselves, but valueless to the rest of mankind.

Translated by Trevor J. Saunders (1970)

Laws 742a

advocating a 'valueless' copper coinage

83 μηδὲ δανείζειν ἐπὶ τόκῳ

Never lend at interest.

Laws 742c

84 οὐκ ἂν ἔγωγε ... ποτὲ συγχωροίην τὸν πλούσιον εὐδαίμονα τῇ ἀληθείᾳ γίγνεσθαι μὴ καὶ ἀγαθὸν ὄντα

I'll never concede that the rich man can become really happy without being virtuous as well.

Translated by Trevor J. Saunders (1970)

Laws 743a

85 ὥστε ὁ λόγος ἡμῖν ὀρθός, ὡς οὐκ εἰσὶν οἱ παμπλούσιοι ἀγαθοί· εἰ δὲ μὴ ἀγαθοί, οὐδὲ εὐδαίμονες

Our thesis is therefore correct: the excessively rich cannot be good; and if they are not good, they are not happy either.

Translated by Trevor J. Saunders (1970)

Laws 743c.3

86 ἡμῖν δὲ ἡ τῶν νόμων ὑπόθεσις ἐνταῦθα ἔβλεπεν, ὅπως ὡς εὐδαιμονέστατοι ἔσονται καὶ ὅτι μάλιστα ἀλλήλοις φίλοι

The fundamental purpose of our laws was this, that the citizens should be as happy as possible, and in the highest degree united in mutual friendship.

Translated by R.G. Bury (1926)

Laws 743c.5

87 διὸ δὴ χρημάτων ἐπιμέλειαν οὐχ ἅπαξ εἰρήκαμεν ὡς χρὴ τελευταῖον τιμᾶν

The pursuit of money should come last in our scale of values.

Translated by Trevor J. Saunders (1970)

Laws 743e

88 δεῖ γάρ ἐν πόλει που, φαμέν, τῇ τοῦ μεγίστου νοσήματος οὐ μεθεξούσῃ, ὃ διάστασιν ἢ στάσιν ὀρθότερον ἂν εἴη κεκλῆσθαι, μήτε πενίαν τὴν χαλεπὴν ἐνεῖναι παρά τισιν τῶν πολιτῶν μήτε αὖ πλοῦτον, ὡς ἀμφοτέρων τικτόντων ταῦτα ἀμφότερα

If a state is to avoid the greatest plague of all – I mean civil war, though civil disintegration would be a better term – extreme poverty and wealth must not be allowed to arise in any section of the citizen-body, because both lead to both these disasters.

Translated by Trevor J. Saunders (1970)

Laws 744d

89 σχεδὸν οἷον ὀνείρατα λέγων, ἢ πλάττων καθάπερ ἐκ κηροῦ τινα πόλιν καὶ πολίτας

It is much like recounting dreams, moulding some city and citizens of wax.

Laws 746a

90 τὸ γὰρ ὁμολογούμενον αὐτὸ αὐτῷ δεῖ που πανταχῇ ἀπεργάζεσθαι καὶ τὸν τοῦ φαυλοτάτου δημιουργὸν ἄξιον ἐσόμενον λόγου

The creator of even the most trivial object, if he is to be of any merit, must make it in all points consistent with itself.

Translated by R.G. Bury (1926)

Laws 746c

91 ἓν οὐδὲν οὕτω δύναμιν ἔχει παίδειον μάθημα μεγάλην, ὡς ἡ περὶ τοὺς ἀριθμοὺς διατριβή

No single branch of a child's education has a greater effect than mathematics.

Laws 747b

92 τὸ δὲ μέγιστον, ὅτι τὸν νυστάζοντα καὶ ἀμαθῆ φύσει ἐγείρει καὶ εὐμαθῆ καὶ μνήμονα καὶ ἀγχίνουν ἀπεργάζεται, παρὰ τὴν αὑτοῦ φύσιν ἐπιδιδόντα θείᾳ τέχνῃ

Its greatest advantage is that it wakes up the sleepy ignoramus and makes him quick to understand, retentive and sharp-witted; and thanks to this miraculous science he does better than his natural abilities would have allowed.

Translated by Trevor J. Saunders (1970)

Laws 747b

on the benefits of mathematics

93 ἀνεπιτηδείους ἐπιστῆσαι τοῖς εὖ κειμένοις νόμοις, οὐ μόνον οὐδὲν πλέον εὖ τεθέντων, οὐδ' ὅτι γέλως ἂν πάμπολυς συμβαίνοι

To put incompetent officials in charge of administering the code is a waste of good laws, and the whole business degenerates into farce.

Translated by Trevor J. Saunders (1970)

Laws 751b

94 ἡ δ' ἀρχὴ λέγεται ἥμισυ εἶναι παντός ἐν ταῖς παροιμίαις ἔργου ... τὸ δ' ἔστιν τε, ὡς ἐμοὶ φαίνεται, πλέον ἢ τὸ ἥμισυ

The beginning is said proverbially to be the half of the whole, yet to me it seems more than half.

Laws 753e

cf. Proverbial 66, and the English proverb 'well begun is half done'

95 τὴν δὲ ἀληθεστάτην καὶ ἀρίστην ἰσότητα οὐκέτι ῥᾴδιον παντὶ ἰδεῖν· Διὸς γὰρ δὴ κρίσις ἐστί

The truest and best form of equality is not an easy thing for everyone to discern. It needs the wisdom and judgement of Zeus.

Laws 757b

96 τιμὰς μείζοσι μὲν πρὸς ἀρετὴν ἀεὶ μείζους

Confer high recognition on virtue.

Translated by Trevor J. Saunders (1970)

Laws 757c

97 δή που καὶ τὸ πολιτικὸν ἡμῖν ἀεὶ τοῦτ' αὐτὸ τὸ δίκαιον ... ἀναγκαῖόν γε μὴν καὶ τούτοις παρωνυμίοισί ποτε προσχρήσασθαι πόλιν ἅπασαν

Statesmanship consists of essentially this – strict justice, granting the 'equality' that unequals deserve to get.

Translated by Trevor J. Saunders (1970)

Laws 757c–d

98 τὸ γὰρ ἐπιεικὲς καὶ σύγγνωμον τοῦ τελέου καὶ ἀκριβοῦς παρὰ δίκην τὴν ὀρθήν ἐστι παρατεθραυμένον

Complaisance and toleration, which always wreck complete precision, are the enemies of strict justice.

Translated by Trevor J. Saunders (1970)

Laws 757e

99 ὁ μὴ δουλεύσας οὐδ' ἂν δεσπότης γένοιτο ἄξιος ἐπαίνου

No one will ever make a commendable master without having been a servant first.

Translated by Trevor J. Saunders (1970)

Laws 762e

100 ὁ τῆς παιδείας ἐπιμελητὴς πάσης θηλειῶν τε καὶ ἀρρένων ... ἐτῶν μὲν γεγονὼς μὴ ἔλαττον ἢ πεντήκοντα, παίδων δὲ γνησίων πατήρ ... ταύτην τὴν ἀρχὴν τῶν ἐν τῇ πόλει ἀκροτάτων ἀρχῶν πολὺ μεγίστην

The director of the entire education of the boys and girls must be not younger than fifty years old, and the father of legitimate children. This is by far the most important of all the supreme offices in the state.

Translated by Trevor J. Saunders (1970)

Laws 765d

of the Minister of Education

101 ἄνθρωπος ... ὅμως μὴν παιδείας μὲν ὀρθῆς τυχὸν καὶ φύσεως εὐτυχοῦς, θειότατον ἡμερώτατόν τε ζῷον γίγνεσθαι φιλεῖ, μὴ ἱκανῶς δὲ ἢ μὴ καλῶς τραφὲν ἀγριώτατον ὁπόσα φύει γῆ

A person with a proper education and a happy nature will surely become a most godlike and tame animal; but if his training is deficient or bad, he turns out the wildest of all earth's creatures.

Laws 766a

on education

102 τὸν νομοθέτην ἐᾶν γίγνεσθαι ... τῶν ἐν τῇ πόλει ὃς ἂν ἄριστος εἰς πάντα ᾖ, τοῦτον ... προστάττειν ἐπιμελητήν

The legislators should appoint as their Minister the best all-round citizen in the state.

Translated by Trevor J. Saunders (1970)

Laws 766a

of the Minister of Education

103 μητρὶ καὶ πατρὶ ... γεννῶντάς τε καὶ ἐκτρέφοντας παῖδας, καθάπερ λαμπάδα τὸν βίον παραδιδόντας ἄλλοις ἐξ ἄλλων

The young couple should produce children and bring them up, handing on the torch of life from generation to generation.

Translated by Trevor J. Saunders (1970)

Laws 776a

104 ὅτε οὐδὲ βοὸς ἐτόλμων μὲν γεύεσθαι θύματά τε οὐκ ἦν τοῖς θεοῖσι ζῷα, πέλανοι δὲ καὶ μέλιτι καρποὶ δεδευμένοι καὶ τοιαῦτα ἄλλα ἁγνὰ θύματα

There was a time when we didn't even dare to eat beef, and the sacrifices offered to the gods were not animals, but cakes and meal soaked in honey and other 'pure' offerings like that.

Translated by Trevor J. Saunders (1970)

Laws 782c

on vegetarianism; see also Pythagoras 15 and Diogenes Laertius, Lives of Eminent Philosophers *8.22*

105 σαρκῶν δ' ἀπείχοντο ὡς οὐχ ὅσιον ὂν ἐσθίειν οὐδὲ τοὺς τῶν θεῶν βωμοὺς αἵματι μιαίνειν

They abstained from flesh on the grounds that it was unholy both to eat meat and to pollute the altars of the gods with blood.

Laws 782c

on vegetarianism, an 'Orphic' way of life; cf. Pythagoras 15

106 πάντες δ' ἄνθρωποι κοινωνοὶ πάσης πράξεως, ἡνίκα μὲν ἂν προσέχωσιν αὑτοῖς τε καὶ τῇ πράξει τὸν νοῦν, πάντα καλὰ καὶ ἀγαθὰ ἀπεργάζονται

When human beings co-operate in any project, and give due attention to its planning and execution, the results they achieve are always of the best and finest quality.

Translated by Trevor J. Saunders (1970)

Laws 783e

107 βίου μὲν ἀρχὴ τοῦ παντὸς ἑκάστοις ὁ πρῶτος ἐνιαυτός· ὃν γεγράφθαι χρεὼν ἐν ἱεροῖσι πατρῴοις ζωῆς ἀρχήν

Our first year is the beginning of our whole life, and every boy's and girl's year of birth should be recorded in their family shrines under the heading 'born'.

Translated by Trevor J. Saunders (1970)

Laws 785a

108 τὰ δὲ μαθήματά που διττά, ὥς γ' εἰπεῖν, χρήσασθαι συμβαίνοι ἄν, τὰ μὲν ὅσα περὶ τὸ σῶμα γυμναστικῆς, τὰ δ' εὐψυχίας χάριν μουσικῆς

In practice, formal lessons fall into two categories, physical training for the body, and cultural training to perfect the soul.

Translated by Trevor J. Saunders (1970)

Laws 795d

109 τὰ γὰρ περὶ τὸν πόλεμον ἡγοῦνται ... τῆς εἰρήνης ἕνεκα δεῖν

Some think that it is for the sake of peace that war needs to be conducted.

Translated by R.G. Bury (1926)

Laws 803d

110 παιδεία ... ὃ δή φαμεν ἡμῖν γε εἶναι σπουδαιότατον

Education is in our view the most important activity of all.

Translated by Trevor J. Saunders (1970)

Laws 803d

111 παίζοντά ἐστι διαβιωτέον τινὰς δὴ παιδιάς

A man should spend his whole life at 'play'.

Translated by Trevor J. Saunders (1970)

Laws 803e

on the right use of leisure

112 τὰ αὐτὰ δὲ δὴ καὶ περὶ θηλειῶν ὁ μὲν ἐμὸς νόμος ἂν εἴποι πάντα ὅσαπερ καὶ περὶ τῶν ἀρρένων, ἴσα καὶ τὰς θηλείας ἀσκεῖν δεῖν· καὶ οὐδὲν φοβηθεὶς εἴποιμ' ἂν τοῦτον τὸν λόγον

This law of mine will apply as much to girls as to boys. The girls must be trained in precisely the same way, and I make this proposal without any reservations whatever.

Translated by Trevor J. Saunders (1970)

Laws 804d

the education of girls

113 φημί ... πάντων ἀνοητότατα ... τὸ μὴ πάσῃ ῥώμῃ πάντας ὁμοθυμαδὸν ἐπιτηδεύειν ἄνδρας γυναιξὶν ταὐτά· σχεδὸν γὰρ ὀλίγου πᾶσα ἡμίσεια πόλις ἀντὶ διπλασίας

I maintain that it is ridiculous that men and women are involved in different pursuits, not in all activities with one accord and with all their might; almost every state, under present conditions, is only half a state.

Laws 805a

114 πάρεργον γὰρ οὐδὲν δεῖ τῶν ἄλλων ἔργων διακώλυμα γίγνεσθαι τῶν τῷ σώματι προσηκόντων εἰς ἀπόδοσιν πόνων καὶ τροφῆς, οὐδ᾽ αὖ ψυχῇ μαθημάτων τε καὶ ἐθῶν

Let inessential business never prevent you from allowing the body its proper allotment of exercise and food, nor your soul of its mental and moral training.

Laws 807d

115 καθεύδων γὰρ οὐδεὶς οὐδενὸς ἄξιος, οὐδὲν μᾶλλον τοῦ μὴ ζῶντος

Asleep, a man is useless; he may as well be dead.

Translated by Trevor J. Saunders (1970)

Laws 808b

116 ὁ δὲ παῖς πάντων θηρίων ἐστὶ δυσμεταχειριστότατον

Of all wild animals, children are the most unmanageable.

Laws 808d

117 ἄνευ γὰρ γελοίων τὰ σπουδαῖα καὶ πάντων τῶν ἐναντίων τὰ ἐναντία μαθεῖν μὲν οὐ δυνατόν, εἰ μέλλει τις φρόνιμος ἔσεσθαι

It is impossible to understand the serious without their comic side, nor opposites without their opposites, if a man is really to have intelligence of either.

Laws 816e

118 πᾶσα οὖν ἡμῖν ἡ πολιτεία συνέστηκε μίμησις τοῦ καλλίστου καὶ ἀρίστου βίου

Our entire state has been constructed so as to be a representation of the finest and noblest life.

Translated by Trevor J. Saunders (1970)

Laws 817b

119 τὸν δ᾽ αὖ νέον ... τῶν δὲ περὶ ἕκαστα ἀπειληθέντων μετὰ ζημίας καὶ νομοθετηθέντων, τὰ μετ᾽ ἐπαίνου ῥηθέντα μᾶλλον τιμᾶν

The young man should rather pay attention to what is warmly praised than to threats of the formal law.

Laws 823c

120 μηδ᾽ αὖ πτηνῶν θήρας αἱμύλος ἔρως οὐ σφόδρα ἐλευθέριος ἐπέλθοι τινὶ νέων. πεζῶν δὴ μόνον θήρευσις

Young men should not be seduced into the uncivilized pursuit of trapping birds; only land animals are to be hunted.

Laws 823e

on hunting: written and unwritten rules

121 ἐνυγροθηρευτὴν δέ, πλὴν ἐν λιμέσιν καὶ ἱεροῖς ποταμοῖς τε καὶ ἕλεσι καὶ λίμναις, ἐν τοῖς ἄλλοις δὲ ἐξέστω θηρεύειν, μὴ χρώμενον ὀπῶν ἀναθολώσει μόνον

A fisherman may fish in all waters except in harbours and sacred rivers, pools and lakes, but only on condition that he makes no use of poisonous matter tainting the water.

Laws 824c

122 τὸν μέγιστον τῶν ἀγώνων ... διαμαχούμενον περὶ ψυχῆς καὶ παίδων καὶ χρημάτων καὶ ὅλης τῆς πόλεως

The most important contest of all, to fight for life and children and property and the entire state.

Translated by Trevor J. Saunders (1970)

Laws 830c

123 μὴ κινείτω γῆς ὅρια μηδεὶς ... πολίτου γείτονος

No man shall move the boundary stones of his neighbour.

Translated by Trevor J. Saunders (1970)

Laws 842e

124 ὕδωρ ... εὐδιάφθαρτον ... διὸ δὴ βοηθοῦ δεῖται νόμου ... ἂν τις διαφθείρῃ ἑκὼν ὕδωρ ἀλλότριον ... ὁ βλαπτόμενος δικαζέσθω πρὸς τοὺς ἀστυνόμους, τὴν ἀξίαν τῆς βλάβης ἀπογραφόμενος· ἂν δέ τις ὄφλῃ ... βλάπτων, πρὸς τῷ τιμήματι καθηράτω τὰς πηγὰς ἢ τἀγγεῖον τοῦ ὕδατος, ὅπῃπερ ἂν οἱ τῶν ἐξηγητῶν νόμοι

Water is easily fouled which is why it needs the protection of a law: If any one deliberately spoils someone else's water supply, the injured party shall sue him before the city-stewards, recording the amount of the damage. Anyone convicted of fouling the water shall, in addition to paying the penalty, purify the springs or watercourse, in whatever way the laws prescribe.

Laws 845d–e

PPP, the 'Polluter Pays Principle', was advocated by the United Nations Environment Programme and the European Commission in the 1970s

125 καὶ τὸ παράπαν ᾧτινι τρόπῳ ποιήσει τις μισῆσαι μὲν τὴν ἀδικίαν, στέρξαι δὲ ἢ μὴ μισεῖν τὴν τοῦ δικαίου φύσιν, αὐτό ἐστιν τοῦτο ἔργον τῶν καλλίστων νόμων

By whatsoever means one can employ to make men hate injustice, and love (or at any rate not hate) justice, this is precisely the task of laws most noble.

Translated by R.G. Bury (1926)

Laws 862d

126 περὶ τοῦ πλούτου ... ὡς ἕνεκα σώματός ἐστι, καὶ σῶμα ψυχῆς ἕνεκα

Wealth exists to serve the body, just as the body should be the servant of the soul.

Translated by Trevor J. Saunders (1970)

Laws 870b

127 πολιτικῇ καὶ ἀληθεῖ τέχνῃ οὐ τὸ ἴδιον ἀλλὰ τὸ κοινὸν ἀνάγκη μέλειν – τὸ μὲν γὰρ κοινὸν συνδεῖ, τὸ δὲ ἴδιον διασπᾷ τὰς πόλεις- καὶ ὅτι συμφέρει τῷ κοινῷ τε καὶ ἰδίῳ, τοῖν ἀμφοῖν, ἢν τὸ κοινὸν τιθῆται καλῶς μᾶλλον ἢ τὸ ἴδιον

True political skill is not the interest of private individuals but the common good. This is what knits a state together, whereas private interests make it disintegrate. If the public interest is well served, rather than the private, then the individual and the community alike are benefited.

Translated by Trevor J. Saunders (1970)

Laws 875a

128 πατρὸς γὰρ ἢ μητρὸς ... ὅστις τολμήσει ἅψασθαί ποτε βιαζόμενος αἰκίᾳ τινί ... τούτῳ δεῖ τινος ἀποτροπῆς ἐσχάτης

For whosoever dares to lay hands on father or mother and uses outrageous violence, there is need of some most severe deterrent.

Laws 880e

129 θάνατος μὲν οὖν οὐκ ἔστιν ἔσχατον, οἱ δὲ ... πόνοι ... οὐδὲν ἀνύτουσιν ... ἀποτροπῆς

Death is not an extreme and final penalty, as its distress proves not to have a deterrent effect.

Laws 881a

130 τῶν ἀλλοτρίων μηδένα μηδὲν φέρειν μηδὲ ἄγειν, μηδ' αὖ χρῆσθαι μηδενὶ τῶν τοῦ πέλας, ἐὰν μὴ πείσῃ τὸν κεκτημένον

No one may seize or make off with other people's property, nor use any of his neighbour's possessions without the owner's permission.

Translated by Trevor J. Saunders (1970)

Laws 884a

131 ὦ παῖ, νέος εἶ, προϊὼν δέ σε ὁ χρόνος ποιήσει πολλὰ ὧν νῦν δοξάζεις μεταβαλόντα ἐπὶ τἀναντία τίθεσθαι· περίμεινον οὖν εἰς τότε κριτὴς περὶ τῶν μεγίστων γίγνεσθαι

You are young, my son, and as the years go by, time will change and even reverse many of your present opinions. Refrain therefore awhile from setting yourself up as a judge of the highest matters.

Translated by Benjamin Jowett (1817–1893)

Laws 888a

132 μέγιστον δέ ὃ νῦν οὐδὲν ἡγῇ σύ, τὸ περὶ τοὺς θεοὺς ὀρθῶς διανοηθέντα ζῆν καλῶς ἢ μή

And this which you deem of no moment is the very highest of all: that is whether you have a right idea of the gods, whereby you may live your life well or ill.

Translated by Benjamin Jowett (1817–1893)

Laws 888b

133 τὸ μηδένα πώποτε λαβόντα ἐκ νέου ταύτην τὴν δόξαν περὶ θεῶν, ὡς οὐκ εἰσίν, διατελέσαι πρὸς γῆρας μείναντα ἐν ταύτῃ τῇ διανοήσει

No one who in his youth has doubted the existence of the gods has remained faithful to his conviction into old age.

Laws 888c

134 θεούς ... εἶναι πρῶτόν φασιν οὗτοι τέχνῃ, οὐ φύσει ἀλλά τισιν νόμοις

Some people say about the gods that they are artificial concepts corresponding to nothing in nature, that they are legal fictions.

Translated by Trevor J. Saunders (1970)

Laws 889e

a view ascribed to Critias, cf. Fragment 25 (D-K); this phrase is discussed in endless following pages

135 ὀρθῶς ... ἂν εἶμεν ψυχὴν μὲν προτέραν γεγονέναι σώματος ἡμῖν, σῶμα δὲ δεύτερόν τε καὶ ὕστερον ψυχῆς ἀρχούσης ἀρχόμενον κατὰ φύσιν

We have, then, rightly said that soul is prior to body, and body is secondary and posterior; soul is master and body is naturally subject to soul.

Laws 896c

136 ἄγει μὲν δὴ ψυχὴ πάντα ... βούλεσθαι, σκοπεῖσθαι, ἐπιμελεῖσθαι, βουλεύεσθαι, δοξάζειν ὀρθῶς ἐψευσμένως, χαίρουσαν, λυπουμένην, θαρροῦσαν φοβουμένην, μισοῦσαν, στέργουσαν

Soul drives all things, wish, reflection, forethought, counsel, opinion true and false, joy, grief, confidence, fear, hate, love.

Translated by R.G. Bury (1926)

Laws 896e

137 οὐδὲ γὰρ ἄνευ σμικρῶν τοὺς μεγάλους φασὶν λιθολόγοι λίθους εὖ κεῖσθαι

As masons say, even the largest stones need smaller stones to support them.

Laws 902d

138 ὀρθὸν μὲν δὴ πάλαι τε εἰρημένον ὡς πρὸς δύο μάχεσθαι καὶ ἐναντία χαλεπόν ... καὶ περὶ ταῦτα ἐστὶν πρὸς δύο μάχη, πενίαν καὶ πλοῦτον, τὸν μὲν ψυχὴν διεφθαρκότα τρυφῇ τῶν ἀνθρώπων, τὴν δὲ λύπαις προτετραμμένην εἰς ἀναισχυντίαν

The old saying is quite right, that it is hard to fight against two enemies; our present battle is a case in point: it is a battle against two foes, wealth and poverty – wealth that corrupts our souls by luxury, poverty that drives us by distress into losing all sense of shame.

Translated by Trevor J. Saunders (1970)

Laws 919b

cf. Proverbial 70

139 τὰ περὶ τὴν καπηλείαν ... συνελθεῖν αὖ χρεὼν περὶ ταῦτα τοὺς νομοφύλακας μετὰ τῶν ἐμπείρων ἑκάστης καπηλείας ... ἰδεῖν λῆμμά τε καὶ ἀνάλωμα τί ποτε τῷ καπήλῳ κέρδος ποιεῖ τὸ μέτριον

With respect to retail trading, the law-wardens must meet in consultation with experts in every branch of retail trade to consider what standard of profits and expenses produces a moderate gain for the trader.

Translated by R.G. Bury (1926)

Laws 920b

on price control

140 τὴν τιμὴν τῶν ἔργων ὀφειλέτω ὧν ἂν τὸν ἐκδόντα ... μὴ πλέονος τιμᾶν διαπειρώμενον ἀλλ' ὡς ἁπλούστατα τῆς ἀξίας ... γιγνώσκει γὰρ ὅ γε δημιουργὸς τὴν ἀξίαν

Similarly in construction, the contractor should not take advantage by setting too high a price, but to name the actual value, well knowing what the job is worth.

Laws 921a–b

on price control

141 ἐάν τίς τι κλέπτῃ δημόσιον μέγα ἢ καὶ σμικρόν, τῆς αὐτῆς δίκης δεῖ· μικρόν τι γὰρ ὁ κλέπτων ἔρωτι μὲν ταὐτῷ ... κέκλοφεν

All theft of public property, great or small, should attract the same punishment; for he that steals a small thing steals with equal greed.

Laws 941c

142 μελετητέον εὐθὺς ἐκ τῶν παίδων, ἄρχειν τε ἄλλων ἄρχεσθαί θ' ὑφ' ἑτέρων

Right from childhood we must learn both to be leaders and to submit to the authority of others.

Laws 942c

143 νοῦς ἐστιν τὸ πᾶν διακεκοσμηκώς

It is reason that regulates the order in the universe.

Laws 966e

144 ὁ ἀγαθὸς τῷ ἀγαθῷ μόνος μόνῳ φίλος, ὁ δὲ κακὸς οὔτ' ἀγαθῷ οὔτε κακῷ οὐδέποτε εἰς ἀληθῆ φιλίαν ἔρχεται

The good alone is friend to the good, while the bad never enters into true friendship with either good or bad.

Translated by W.R.M. Lamb (1925)

Lysis 214d

145 οἱ Μαραθῶνι δεξάμενοι τὴν τῶν βαρβάρων δύναμιν καὶ κολασάμενοι τὴν ὑπερηφανίαν ὅλης τῆς Ἀσίας

At Marathon they engaged barbarian power and chastised all Asia's insolent pride.

Menexenus 240d

of the fighters at Marathon

146 πᾶσά τε ἐπιστήμη χωριζομένη δικαιοσύνης καὶ τῆς ἄλλης ἀρετῆς πανουργία, οὐ σοφία φαίνεται

Every form of knowledge when sundered from justice and other virtues is seen to be plain roguery rather than wisdom.

Translated by R.G. Bury (1929)

Menexenus 247a

147 εἶναι μὲν γὰρ τιμὰς γονέων ἐκγόνοις καλὸς θησαυρὸς καὶ μεγαλοπρεπής

The honours bestowed upon parents are a noble and splendid treasure for their children.

Menexenus 247b

148 Ἔχεις μοι εἰπεῖν, ὦ Σώκρατες, ἆρα διδακτὸν ἡ ἀρετή; ἢ οὐ διδακτὸν ἀλλ' ἀσκητόν; ἢ οὔτε ἀσκητὸν οὔτε μαθητόν, ἀλλὰ φύσει παραγίγνεται τοῖς ἀνθρώποις; ... καὶ ἐμαυτὸν καταμέμφομαι ὡς οὐκ εἰδὼς περὶ ἀρετῆς τὸ παράπαν· ὃ δὲ μὴ οἶδα τί ἐστιν, πῶς ἂν ὁποῖόν γέ τι εἰδείην;

Meno: Can you tell me, Socrates, whether virtue can be taught, or is acquired by practice, not teaching? Or, if neither by practice nor by learning, whether it comes to mankind by nature or in some other way?
Socrates: I have to reproach myself with an utter ignorance about virtue; and if I do not know what a thing is, how can I know what its nature may be?

Translated by W.R.M. Lamb (1924)

Meno 70a–71b

opening lines

149 αὐχμός τις τῆς σοφίας γέγονεν, καὶ κινδυνεύει ἐκ τῶνδε τῶν τόπων ... οἴχεσθαι ἡ σοφία

A drought of wisdom is upon us and it seems that wisdom has deserted our borders.

Meno 70c

150 ὅπερ ποιοῦσιν οἱ τρυφῶντες, ἅτε τυραννεύοντες ἕως ἂν ἐν ὥρᾳ ὦσι

The fashion of spoilt beauties, holding as they do a despotic power so long as their bloom is on them.

Translated by W.R.M. Lamb (1924)

Meno 76b

151 φασὶ γὰρ τὴν ψυχὴν τοῦ ἀνθρώπου εἶναι ἀθάνατον, καὶ τοτὲ μὲν τελευτᾶν, ὃ δὴ ἀποθνῄσκειν καλοῦσι, τοτὲ δὲ πάλιν γίγνεσθαι, ἀπόλλυσθαι δ' οὐδέποτε

They say that the soul of man is immortal, and at one time comes to an end, which is called dying, and at another it is reborn, but never perishes.

Translated by W.R.M. Lamb (1924)

Meno 81b

152 οὐδὲν κωλύει ... τἆλλα πάντα αὐτὸν ἀνευρεῖν, ἐάν τις ἀνδρεῖος ᾖ καὶ μὴ ἀποκάμνῃ ζητῶν· τὸ γὰρ ζητεῖν ἄρα καὶ τὸ μανθάνειν ἀνάμνησις ὅλον ἐστίν

There is no reason why we should not discover everything else, if we have courage and tire not in the search; for research and learning are, as a whole, a recollection of something learned.

Meno 81d

153 οἴει οὖν ἂν αὐτὸν πρότερον ἐπιχειρῆσαι ζητεῖν ἢ μανθάνειν τοῦτο, ὃ ᾤετο εἰδέναι οὐκ εἰδώς, πρὶν εἰς ἀπορίαν κατέπεσεν ἡγησάμενος μὴ εἰδέναι, καὶ ἐπόθησεν τὸ εἰδέναι;

Now do you imagine he would have attempted to inquire or learn what he thought he knew, when he did not know it, until he had been reduced to the perplexity of realizing that he did not know, and had felt a craving to know?

Translated by W.R.M. Lamb (1924)

Meno 84c

on learning through enquiry, where the student sets questions and discovers answers on his own

154 πῶς οὖν ἂν εἰδείης περὶ τούτου τοῦ πράγματος, εἴτε τι ἀγαθὸν ἔχει ἐν αὑτῷ εἴτε φλαῦρον, οὗ παντάπασιν ἄπειρος εἴης;

How can you tell whether a thing has any good or evil in it, if you have no experience of it?

Translated by W.R.M. Lamb (1924)

Meno 92c

155 αἱ δόξαι αἱ ἀληθεῖς, ὅσον μὲν ἂν χρόνον παραμένωσιν, καλὸν τὸ χρῆμα καὶ πάντα τἀγαθὰ ἐργάζονται

True opinions, so long as they stay with us, are a fine possession, and effect all that is good.

Translated by W.R.M. Lamb (1924)

Meno 97e

156 ἐὰν οὖν τις τοιαῦτα ἐπιχειρῇ πολλὰ καὶ ἓν ταὐτὰ ἀποφαίνειν, λίθους καὶ ξύλα καὶ τὰ τοιαῦτα, φήσομεν αὐτὸν πολλὰ καὶ ἓν ἀποδεικνύναι, οὐ τὸ ἓν πολλὰ οὐδὲ τὰ πολλὰ ἕν, οὐδέ τι θαυμαστὸν λέγειν, ἀλλ' ἅπερ ἂν πάντες ὁμολογοῖμεν

If anyone then undertakes to show that the same things are both many and one – I mean such things as stones, sticks, and the like – we shall say that he shows that they are many and one, but not the one is many or the many one; he says nothing wonderful, but only what we should all accept.

Translated by Harold North Fowler (1926)

Parmenides 129d

157 γιγνώσκεται δέ γέ που ὑπ' αὐτοῦ τοῦ εἴδους τοῦ τῆς ἐπιστήμης αὐτὰ τὰ γένη ἃ ἔστιν ἕκαστα

The various classes of ideas are known by the absolute idea of knowledge.

Translated by Harold North Fowler (1926)

Parmenides 134b

158 εἴ γέ τις δή αὖ μὴ ἐάσει εἴδη τῶν ὄντων εἶναι, εἰς πάντα τὰ νυν δὴ καὶ ἄλλα τοιαῦτα ἀποβλέψας, μηδέ τι ὁριεῖται εἶδος ἑνὸς ἑκάστου, οὐδὲ ὅπη τρέψει τὴν διάνοιαν ἕξει, μὴ ἐῶν ἰδέαν τῶν ὄντων ἑκάστου τὴν αὐτὴν ἀεὶ εἶναι, καὶ οὕτως τὴν τοῦ διαλέγεσθαι δύναμιν παντάπασι διαφθερεῖ

If a man does away with Forms of things and will not admit that every individual thing has its own determinate Form which is always one and the same, he will have nothing on which his mind can rest; and so he will utterly destroy the power of reasoning.

Translated in *A Dictionary of Philosophical Quotations* (2008)

Parmenides 135b

159 ἄπειρος ἀριθμὸς πλήθει

Numbers infinite in multitude.

Parmenides 144a

160 ἄνευ γὰρ ἑνὸς πολλὰ δοξάσαι ἀδύνατον

Without the one it is impossible to conceive the many.

Parmenides 166b

161 εἰρήσθω τοίνυν τοῦτό τε καὶ ὅτι, ὡς ἔοικεν, ἓν εἴτ' ἔστιν εἴτε μὴ ἔστιν, αὐτό τε καὶ τἆλλα καὶ πρὸς αὑτὰ καὶ πρὸς ἄλληλα πάντα πάντως ἐστί τε καὶ οὐκ ἔστι καὶ φαίνεταί τε καὶ οὐ φαίνεται

Let us affirm what seems to be the truth., that, whether one is or is not, one and the others in relation to themselves and one another, all of them, in every way, are and are not, and appear and appear not to be.

Translated by Benjamin Jowett (1817–1893)

Parmenides 166c

closing lines

162 ὡς ἄτοπον, ἔφη, ὦ ἄνδρες, ἔοικέ τι εἶναι τοῦτο, ὃ καλοῦσιν οἱ ἄνθρωποι ἡδύ· ὡς θαυμασίως πέφυκε πρὸς τὸ δοκοῦν ἐναντίον εἶναι, τὸ λυπηρόν, τῷ ἅμα μὲν αὐτὼ μὴ ἐθέλειν παραγίγνεσθαι τῷ ἀνθρώπῳ, ἐὰν δέ τις διώκῃ τὸ ἕτερον καὶ λαμβάνῃ, σχεδόν τι ἀναγκάζεσθαι ἀεὶ λαμβάνειν καὶ τὸ ἕτερον, ὥσπερ ἐκ μιᾶς κορυφῆς συνημμένω δύ' ὄντε

What a strange thing, my friends, what men call pleasure! And how astonishing its relationship to the opposite, pain! You cannot have both at the same time; but if you pursue and capture the one, you are almost bound to catch the other also, as if they were two creatures with one head!

Phaedo 60b

163 φιλοσοφίας ... μεγίστης μουσικῆς

Philosophy, the highest kind of art.

Translated by G.M.A. Grube (1977), rev. John M. Cooper (1997)

Phaedo 61a

164 ὡς ἔν τινι φρουρᾷ ἐσμεν οἱ ἄνθρωποι καὶ οὐ δεῖ δὴ ἑαυτὸν ἐκ ταύτης λύειν οὐδ' ἀποδιδράσκειν ... μὴ πρότερον αὑτὸν ἀποκτεινύναι δεῖν, πρὶν ἀνάγκην τινὰ θεὸς ἐπιπέμψῃ

We men are in a kind of prison, and one must not free oneself or run away; one should not kill oneself before a god had indicated some necessity to do so.

Translated by G.M.A. Grube (1977), rev. John M. Cooper (1997)

Phaedo 62b–c

165 κινδυνεύουσι γὰρ ὅσοι τυγχάνουσιν ὀρθῶς ἁπτόμενοι φιλοσοφίας λεληθέναι τοὺς ἄλλους ὅτι οὐδὲν ἄλλο αὐτοὶ ἐπιτηδεύουσιν ἢ ἀποθνῄσκειν τε καὶ τεθνάναι

Other people are likely not to be aware that those who pursue philosophy aright study nothing but dying and being dead.

Translated by Harold North Fowler (1914)

Phaedo 64a

166 διὰ γὰρ τὴν τῶν χρημάτων κτῆσιν πάντες οἱ πόλεμοι γίγνονται, τὰ δὲ χρήματα ἀναγκαζόμεθα κτᾶσθαι διὰ τὸ σῶμα, δουλεύοντες τῇ τούτου θεραπείᾳ

All wars arise for the sake of gaining money, and we are compelled to gain money for the sake of the body; we are slaves to its service.

Translated by Harold North Fowler (1914)

Phaedo 66c

167 ἀλλὰ τῷ ὄντι ἡμῖν δέδεικται ὅτι, εἰ μέλλομέν ποτε καθαρῶς τι εἴσεσθαι, ἀπαλλακτέον αὐτοῦ καὶ αὐτῇ τῇ ψυχῇ θεατέον αὐτὰ τὰ πράγματα

We perceive that, if we are ever to know anything absolutely, we must be free from the body and must behold the actual realities with the eye of the soul alone.

Translated by Harold North Fowler (1914)

Phaedo 66d

168 μὴ οὐχὶ πάντα καταναλωθῆναι εἰς τὸ τεθνάναι;

Must not all things be swallowed up by death in the end?

Translated by Benjamin Jowett (1817–1893)

Phaedo 72d

169 ἀνήνυτον ἔργον πράττειν Πηνελόπης

Engage in futile toil like Penelope.

Translated by Harold North Fowler (1914)

Phaedo 84a

of Penelope 'unweaving the web she wove'; cf. Homer 375

170 ἡ μὲν ἁρμονία ἀόρατόν τι καὶ ἀσώματον καὶ πάγκαλόν τι καὶ θεῖόν ἐστιν

Harmony is invisible, incorporeal, delightful, divine.

Phaedo 85e

171 οἱ πάνυ ἀπαίδευτοι ... ὅταν περί του ἀμφισβητῶσιν, ὅπῃ μὲν ἔχει περὶ ὧν ἂν ὁ λόγος ᾖ οὐ φροντίζουσιν, ὅπως δὲ ἃ αὐτοὶ ἔθεντο ταῦτα δόξει τοῖς παροῦσιν, τοῦτο προθυμοῦνται

Uncouth persons, when engaged in a dispute, care nothing about the truth of the matter, but are anxious only to convince their hearers of their own assertions.

Phaedo 91a

172 ὑμεῖς μέντοι, ἂν ἐμοὶ πείθησθε, σμικρὸν φροντίσαντες Σωκράτους, τῆς δὲ ἀληθείας πολὺ μᾶλλον

But you, if you do as I ask, should give little heed to Socrates and much more to the truth.

Phaedo 91c

spoken by Socrates, Phaedo relating the incident

173 χρῆναι εἰς τοὺς λόγους καταφυγόντα ἐν ἐκείνοις σκοπεῖν τῶν ὄντων τὴν ἀλήθειαν

Have recourse to concepts and examine in them the truth of realities.

Translated by Harold North Fowler (1914)

Phaedo 99e

174 ἐπιόντος ἄρα θανάτου ἐπὶ τὸν ἄνθρωπον τὸ μὲν θνητόν, ὡς ἔοικεν, αὐτοῦ ἀποθνῄσκει, τὸ δ' ἀθάνατον σῶν καὶ ἀδιάφθορον οἴχεται ἀπιόν

When death comes to a man, his mortal part dies, it seems, but the immortal part goes away unharmed and undestroyed.

Translated by Harold North Fowler (1914)

Phaedo 106e

175 οὐδὲν γὰρ ἄλλο ἔχουσα εἰς Ἅιδου ἡ ψυχὴ ἔρχεται πλὴν τῆς παιδείας τε καὶ τροφῆς, ἃ δὴ καὶ μέγιστα λέγεται ὠφελεῖν ἢ

βλάπτειν τὸν τελευτήσαντα εὐθὺς ἐν ἀρχῇ τῆς ἐκεῖσε πορείας

The soul takes nothing to the other world but its education and culture, and these are said to greatly benefit or injure the departed from the very beginning of his journey yonder.

Phaedo 107d

176 τὸ μὴ καλῶς λέγειν οὐ μόνον εἰς αὐτὸ τοῦτο πλημμελές, ἀλλὰ καὶ κακόν τι ἐμποιεῖ ταῖς ψυχαῖς

False words are not just evil in themselves, they infect the soul with evil.

Translated by Benjamin Jowett (1817–1893)

Phaedo 115e

177 ταῦτά τε οὖν χρή συννοεῖν, καὶ εἰδέναι τὴν ἐραστοῦ φιλίαν, ὅτι οὐ μετ' εὐνοίας γίγνεται, ἀλλὰ σιτίου τρόπον, χάριν πλησμονῆς, ὡς λύκοι ἄρν' ἀγαπῶσ', ὣς παῖδα φιλοῦσιν ἐρασταί

These are the truths that must be realised, namely that the affection of a lover arises not out of goodwill, but like the need for food, out of a desire for satisfaction: 'As wolves love the lamb, so does the lover love his beloved.'

Translated by Kathleen Freeman (1947)

Phaedrus 241c

178 ψυχὴ πᾶσα ἀθάνατος

Every soul is immortal.

Translated by Harold North Fowler (1914)

Phaedrus 245c

179 τὸ δὲ θεῖον καλόν, σοφόν, ἀγαθόν, καὶ πᾶν ὅ τι τοιοῦτον

The divine is beauty, wisdom, goodness, and all such qualities.

Translated by Harold North Fowler (1914)

Phaedrus 246e

180 τὸν δὲ ὑπερουράνιον τόπον οὔτε τις ὕμνησέ πω τῶν τῇδε ποιητὴς οὔτε ποτὲ ὑμνήσει κατ' ἀξίαν

The place beyond heaven – none of our earthly poets has ever sung or ever will sing its praises enough!

Translated by Alexander Nehamas and Paul Woodruff (1995)

Phaedrus 247c

181 τὸν δ' ἤτοι θνητοὶ μὲν Ἔρωτα καλοῦσι ποτηνόν,
ἀθάνατοι δὲ Πτέρωτα, διὰ πτεροφύτορ' ἀνάγκην

Mortals call him fluttering Love, but the immortals call him
The Winged One, because he must needs grow wings.

Translated by Harold North Fowler (1914)

Phaedrus 252b

supposedly quoting, though some scholars surmise that it is by Plato himself; the pun is on ἔρωτα and πτέρωτα

182 καρπὸν ὧν ἔσπειρε θερίζειν

You reap what you sow.

Phaedrus 260d

cf. Bible 243

183 τοῦ δὲ λέγειν ... ἔτυμος τέχνη ἄνευ τοῦ ἀληθείας ἧφθαι οὔτ' ἔστιν οὔτε μή ποτε ὕστερον γένηται

There is no art in speech nor can there be without a firm hold on truth.

Phaedrus 260e

quoting a Spartan saying

184 ἐὰν μὴ ἱκανῶς φιλοσοφήσῃ, οὐδὲ ἱκανός ποτε λέγειν ἔσται περὶ οὐδενός

Unless he pays proper attention to philosophy he will never be able to speak properly about anything.

Translated by Harold North Fowler (1914)

Phaedrus 261a

185 δεινὸν γάρ που, ὦ Φαῖδρε, τοῦτ' ἔχει γραφή, καὶ ὡς ἀληθῶς ὅμοιον ζωγραφίᾳ· καὶ γὰρ τὰ ἐκείνης ἔκγονα ἕστηκε μὲν ὡς ζῶντα, ἐὰν δ' ἀνέρῃ τι, σεμνῶς πάνυ σιγᾷ. ταὐτὸν δὲ καὶ οἱ λόγοι· δόξαις μὲν ἂν ὥς τι φρονοῦντας αὐτοὺς λέγειν, ἐὰν δέ τι ἔρῃ τῶν λεγομένων βουλόμενος μαθεῖν, ἕν τι σημαίνει μόνον ταὐτὸν ἀεί

Writing, Phaedrus, has this strange quality, and is very like painting; for the creatures of painting stand like living beings, but if one asks them a question, they preserve a solemn silence. And so it is with written words; you might think they spoke as if they had intelligence, but if you question them, wishing to know about their sayings, they always say only one and the same thing.

Translated by Harold North Fowler (1914)

Phaedrus 275d

186 Ὦ φίλε Πάν τε καὶ ἄλλοι ὅσοι τῇδε θεοί, δοίητέ μοι καλῷ γενέσθαι τἄνδοθεν· ἔξωθεν δὲ ὅσα ἔχω, τοῖς ἐντὸς εἶναί μοι φίλια. πλούσιον δὲ νομίζοιμι τὸν σοφόν· τὸ δὲ χρυσοῦ πλῆθος εἴη μοι ὅσον μήτε φέρειν μήτε ἄγειν δύναιτο ἄλλος ἢ ὁ σώφρων.

Beloved Pan, and all ye other gods who haunt this place, give me beauty in the inward soul; and may the outward and inward man be at one. May I reckon the wise to be the wealthy, and may I have such a quantity of gold as none but the temperate can carry.

Translated by Benjamin Jowett (1817–1893)

Phaedrus 279b

sometimes referred to as the 'Prayer of Socrates'

187 κοινὰ γὰρ τὰ τῶν φίλων

Friends have all things in common.

Translated by Harold North Fowler (1914)

Phaedrus 279c

closing lines

188 κρατεῖ δὲ ὁ τῆς ἡδονῆς τὸν τῆς φρονήσεως;

Is the life of pleasure victor over the life of wisdom?

Philebus 11e

cf. Plato 191

189 μὴ κινεῖν εὖ κείμενον

Let sleeping dogs lie.

Translated in Liddell & Scott

Philebus 15c

cf. the Latin 'quieta non movere' and the identical English proverb

190 καθάπερ οἱ παῖδες, ὅτι τῶν ὀρθῶς δοθέντων ἀφαίρεσις οὐκ ἔστι

As with children, there is no taking away what has been rightly given.

Translated by John Simpson and Jennifer Speake (1982)

Philebus 19e

cf. the English proverb 'give a thing, and take a thing, to wear the devil's gold ring'

191 νικῶντα μὲν ἔθεμέν που τὸν μεικτὸν βίον ἡδονῆς τε καὶ φρονήσεως

A life that combines pleasure and wisdom is the best.

Philebus 27d

cf. Plato 188

192 ἀνάπαυλα γάρ ... τῆς σπουδῆς γίγνεται ἐνίοτε ἡ παιδιά

Sometimes a joke is a restful change from serious talk.

Translated by Harold North Fowler (1925)

Philebus 30e

193 ἔστι γὰρ λήθη μνήμης ἔξοδος

Forgetfulness clouds memory.

Philebus 33e

194 ἐπειδὰν μὲν περὶ οἰκοδομίας τι δέῃ πρᾶξαι τὴν πόλιν, τοὺς οἰκοδόμους μεταπεμπομένους συμβούλους περὶ τῶν οἰκοδομημάτων, ὅταν δὲ περὶ ναυπηγίας, τοὺς ναυπηγούς, καὶ τἆλλα πάντα οὕτως, ὅσα ἡγοῦνται μαθητά τε καὶ διδακτὰ εἶναι

If we are to build we summon architects, if to rig a ship, shipwrights; and so in all matters considered learnable and teachable.

Protagoras 319b

195 ἐπειδὰν δέ τι περὶ τῶν τῆς πόλεως διοικήσεως δέῃ βουλεύσασθαι, συμβουλεύει αὐτοῖς ἀνιστάμενος περὶ τούτων ὁμοίως μὲν τέκτων, ὁμοίως δὲ χαλκεύς, σκυτοτόμος, ἔμπορος, ναύκληρος, πλούσιος, πένης, γενναῖος, ἀγεννής, καὶ τούτοις οὐδεὶς τοῦτο ἐπιπλήττει ... δῆλον γὰρ ὅτι οὐχ ἡγοῦνται διδακτὸν εἶναι

In affairs of state, however, advice is equally given by a tinker, tailor, merchant, sailor, rich man, poor man, nobleman and the humbly bred, and no one thinks twice of it; for all accept that matters of state need no prior knowledge.

Protagoras 319c

196 Ζεὺς οὖν δείσας περὶ τῷ γένει ἡμῶν μὴ ἀπόλοιτο πᾶν, Ἑρμῆν πέμπει ἄγοντα εἰς ἀνθρώπους αἰδῶ τε καὶ δίκην

Zeus, fearing that our race was in danger of total extinction, sent Hermes to restore respect and justice among men.

Protagoras 322c

197 ὁ δὲ μετὰ λόγου ἐπιχειρῶν κολάζειν ... οὐ γὰρ ἂν τό γε πραχθὲν ἀγένητον θείη, ἀλλὰ τοῦ μέλλοντος χάριν, ἵνα μὴ αὖθις ἀδικήσῃ μήτε αὐτὸς οὗτος μήτε ἄλλος ὁ

τοῦτον ἰδὼν κολασθέντα

Reasonable punishment is not vengeance for a past wrong – for one cannot undo what has been done – but is undertaken with a view to the future, to deter both the wrongdoer and whoever sees him being punished from repeating the crime.

Translated by Stanley Lombardo and Karen Bell (1992), rev. John M. Cooper (1997)

Protagoras 324b

198 πᾶς ὁ βίος τοῦ ἀνθρώπου εὐρυθμίας τε καὶ εὐαρμοστίας δεῖται

The whole of man's life needs rhythm and harmony.

Protagoras 326b

199 διὰ τί οὖν τῶν ἀγαθῶν πατέρων πολλοὶ ὑεῖς φαῦλοι γίγνονται;

Why is it that so many sons of good fathers turn out so meanly?

Translated by W.R.M. Lamb (1924)

Protagoras 326e

200 εἰ μέλλει πόλις εἶναι, οὐδένα δεῖ ἰδιωτεύειν

If a city is to be a city, no one must remain uninvolved.

Protagoras 327a

201 μὴ ἐφ' ἑκάστῃ ἐρωτήσει μακρὸν λόγον ἀποτείνων, ἐκκρούων τοὺς λόγους καὶ οὐκ ἐθέλων διδόναι λόγον, ἀλλ' ἀπομηκύνων ἕως ἂν ἐπιλάθωνται περὶ ὅτου τὸ ἐρώτημα ἦν οἱ πολλοὶ τῶν ἀκουόντων

Spinning out a lecture on each question, beating off the arguments, refusing to give a reason, and so dilating until most of his hearers have forgotten the point at issue.

Translated by W.R.M. Lamb (1924)

Protagoras 336c

of Protagoras

202 ὁ δὲ νόμος, τύραννος ὢν τῶν ἀνθρώπων, πολλὰ παρὰ τὴν φύσιν βιάζεται

Convention, which tyrannizes the human race, often constrains us contrary to nature.

Translated by Stanley Lombardo and Karen Bell (1992), rev. John M. Cooper (1997)

Protagoras 337d

203 μήτ' αὖ Πρωταγόραν πάντα κάλων ἐκτείναντα, οὐρίᾳ ἐφέντα, φεύγειν εἰς τὸ πέλαγος τῶν λόγων

And you, Protagoras, must not let out full sail, running before the wind, and so escape into the ocean of speech.

Protagoras 338a

204 παιδὸς μηδὲν βελτίω

There's nothing like a child.

Protagoras 342e

205 τὸ λακωνίζειν ... ἐστιν φιλοσοφεῖν

To speak laconically is the pursuit of great philosophers.

Protagoras 342e

206 οὐδεὶς ... ἡγεῖται οὐδένα ἀνθρώπων ἑκόντα ἐξαμαρτάνειν

Nobody ever willingly errs.

Protagoras 345d

207 σοφίαν καὶ ἐπιστήμην ... κράτιστον φάναι εἶναι τῶν ἀνθρωπείων πραγμάτων

Wisdom and knowledge are the most powerful forces in human activity.

Translated by Stanley Lombardo and Karen Bell (1992), rev. John M. Cooper (1997)

Protagoras 352d

208 ἂν μὲν γὰρ κόσμιοι καὶ εὔκολοι ὦσιν, καὶ τὸ γῆρας μετρίως ἐστὶν ἐπίπονον· εἰ δὲ μή, καὶ γῆρας καὶ νεότης χαλεπὴ

If men are sensible and good-tempered, old age is easy enough to bear: if not, youth as well as age is a burden.

Translated by Desmond Lee (1955)

Republic 329d

209 οἱ δὲ κτησάμενοι διπλῇ ἢ οἱ ἄλλοι ἀσπάζονται τὰ χρήματα· ὥσπερ γὰρ οἱ ποιηταὶ τὰ αὑτῶν ποιήματα ... ταύτῃ τε δὴ καὶ οἱ χρηματισάμενοι περὶ τὰ χρήματα σπουδάζουσιν ὡς ἔργον ἑαυτῶν ... χαλεποὶ οὖν καὶ συγγενέσθαι εἰσίν, οὐδὲν ἐθέλοντες ἐπαινεῖν ἀλλ' ἢ τὸν πλοῦτον

Those who have made money for themselves are twice as fond of it as anyone else. For just as poets are fond of their poems, so money-makers become devoted to money because it's their own creation. So they are tiresome company, as they have a good word for nothing but money.

Translated by Desmond Lee (1955)

Republic 330c

210 ὀφειλόμενα ἑκάστῳ ἀποδιδόναι

Render to each his due.

Translated by Paul Shorey (1930)

Republic 331e

attributes this to Simonides; cf. the Latin 'suum cuique tribuere'

211 οὐδὲ ἰατρὸς οὐδείς, καθ' ὅσον ἰατρός, τὸ τῷ ἰατρῷ συμφέρον σκοπεῖ οὐδ' ἐπιτάττει, ἀλλὰ τὸ τῷ κάμνοντι· ὡμολόγηται γὰρ ὁ ἀκριβὴς ἰατρὸς σωμάτων εἶναι ἄρχων ἀλλ' οὐ χρηματιστής

No physician, if a proper physician, will consider his own profit, but the good of his patient; for the true physician is a ruler having the human body as a subject, not a mere money-maker.

Republic 342d

212 ὅταν τέ τινες εἰσφοραὶ ὦσιν, ὁ μὲν δίκαιος ἀπὸ τῶν ἴσων πλέον εἰσφέρει, ὁ δ' ἔλαττον

When there are taxes to be paid, the just man will pay more and the unjust less on the same amount of income.

Republic 343d

213 οὐ γὰρ τὸ ποιεῖν τὰ ἄδικα ἀλλὰ τὸ πάσχειν φοβούμενοι ὀνειδίζουσιν οἱ ὀνειδίζοντες τὴν ἀδικίαν

Those who censure injustice fear that they may be the victims of it, not because they shrink from committing it.

Translated by Benjamin Jowett (1817–1893)

Republic 344c

214 ἰσχυρότερον καὶ ἐλευθεριώτερον καὶ δεσποτικώτερον ἀδικία δικαιοσύνης ἐστὶν ἱκανῶς γιγνομένη

Injustice, given scope, has greater strength and freedom and power than justice.

Translated by Desmond Lee (1955)

Republic 344c

215 οὔτε χρημάτων ἕνεκα ἐθέλουσιν ἄρχειν οἱ ἀγαθοὶ οὔτε τιμῆς

Good men will not consent to govern for cash or honours.

Translated by Desmond Lee (1955)

Republic 347b

216 τῆς δὲ ζημίας μεγίστη τὸ ὑπὸ πονηροτέρου ἄρχεσθαι, ἐὰν μὴ αὐτὸς ἐθέλῃ ἄρχειν

One of the penalties for refusing to participate in politics is that you end up being governed by your inferiors.

Translated in *The Oxford Dictionary of Political Quotations* (2006)

Republic 347c

217 ἀληθινὸς ἄρχων οὐ πέφυκε τὸ αὑτῷ συμφέρον σκοπεῖσθαι ἀλλὰ τὸ τῷ ἀρχομένῳ

The true ruler pursues his subjects' interest and not his own.

Translated by Desmond Lee (1955)

Republic 347d

218 στάσεις γάρ που ... ἥ γε ἀδικία καὶ μίση καὶ μάχας ἐν ἀλλήλοις παρέχει, ἡ δὲ δικαιοσύνη ὁμόνοιαν καὶ φιλίαν

Injustice produces discord and hatred and internal strife, whereas justice brings harmony and friendship.

Republic 351d

219 οὐ γὰρ περὶ τοῦ ἐπιτυχόντος ὁ λόγος, ἀλλὰ περὶ τοῦ ὅντινα τρόπον χρὴ ζῆν

Our discussion is about no ordinary matter, but on the right way to conduct our lives.

Translated in *The Oxford Dictionary of Quotations* (2004)

Republic 352d

220 οὐδεὶς ἑκὼν δίκαιος ἀλλ' ἀναγκαζόμενος, ὡς οὐκ ἀγαθοῦ ἰδίᾳ ὄντος, ἐπεὶ ὅπου γ' ἂν οἴηται ἕκαστος οἷός τε ἔσεσθαι ἀδικεῖν, ἀδικεῖν

No man is just of his own free will, but only under compulsion; and if anyone feels free to act unjustly, he will.

Republic 360c

221 ἐσχάτη γὰρ ἀδικία δοκεῖν δίκαιον εἶναι μὴ ὄντα

The most accomplished form of injustice is to seem just when you are not.

Translated by Desmond Lee (1955)

Republic 361a

222 εἰς Ἅιδου ... ἀρετῆς μισθὸν μέθην αἰώνιον

In Hades the supreme reward of virtue was to be drunk for eternity.

Translated by Desmond Lee (1955)
Republic 363c
taunting the Orpheans

223 οὐ ῥᾴδιον ἀεὶ λανθάνειν κακὸν ὄντα

Not easy for wrongdoers forever to lie hid.

Translated by Paul Shorey (1930)
Republic 365c

224 γίγνεται τοίνυν, ἦν δ' ἐγώ, πόλις, ὡς ἐγῷμαι, ἐπειδὴ τυγχάνει ἡμῶν ἕκαστος οὐκ αὐτάρκης, ἀλλὰ πολλῶν ὢν ἐνδεής

People will live together in towns because no one is totally self-sufficient, having need of many things supplied by others.

Republic 369b

225 ἀγορὰ δὴ ἡμῖν καὶ νόμισμα σύμβολον τῆς ἀλλαγῆς ἕνεκα γενήσεται ἐκ τούτου

We'll need a market, and a currency as the medium of exchange.

Republic 371b
of an imaginary new state

226 τό γε φιλομαθὲς καὶ φιλόσοφον ταὐτόν

Love of learning and philosophy are one and the same.

Republic 376b

227 φιλόσοφος δὴ καὶ θυμοειδὴς καὶ ταχὺς καὶ ἰσχυρὸς ἡμῖν τὴν φύσιν ἔσται ὁ μέλλων καλὸς κἀγαθὸς ἔσεσθαι φύλαξ πόλεως

A philosophic disposition, high spirits, speed and strength are the essential qualities of a truly good future guardian of the state.

Republic 376c

228 ἀρχὴ παντὸς ἔργου μέγιστον

The beginning is what matters most, in any endeavour.

Republic 377a
but cf. Aristotle 87; Hesiod 20; Plato 94

229 ὁ νέος ... ἃ ἂν τηλικοῦτος ὢν λάβῃ ἐν ταῖς δόξαις δυσέκνιπτά τε καὶ ἀμετάστατα φιλεῖ γίγνεσθαι

Children cannot distinguish between what is allegory and what isn't, and opinions formed at that age are usually difficult to eradicate or change.

Translated by Desmond Lee (1955)
Republic 378d

230 περὶ παντὸς ποιητέον ἃ πρῶτα ἀκούουσιν ὅτι κάλλιστα μεμυθολογημένα πρὸς ἀρετὴν ἀκούειν

It is most important that the tales which the young first hear should aim at encouraging the highest excellence of character.

Republic 378e

231 τῶν δὲ κακῶν ἄλλ' ἄττα δεῖ ζητεῖν τὰ αἴτια, ἀλλ' οὐ τὸν θεόν

Look elsewhere for the cause of evil, not to god.

Republic 379c

232 ἀλήθειάν γε περὶ πολλοῦ ποιητέον

Prize truth most highly.

Translated by Paul Shorey (1930)
Republic 389b

233 τοῖς ἄρχουσιν δὴ τῆς πόλεως εἴπερ τισὶν ἄλλοις προσήκει ψεύδεσθαι ἢ πολεμίων ἢ πολιτῶν ἕνεκα ἐπ' ὠφελίᾳ τῆς πόλεως

If anyone at all is to have the privilege of lying, it is the rulers of the state; and they, in dealing either with enemies or their own citizens, may do so if it is in the public interest.

Republic 389b

234 οὐ μὲν δὴ δωροδόκους γε ἐατέον εἶναι τοὺς ἄνδρας οὐδὲ φιλοχρημάτους

No one may be an acceptor of bribes or pursue greedy gain.

Republic 390d

235 εἷς ἕκαστος ἓν μὲν ἂν ἐπιτήδευμα καλῶς ἐπιτηδεύοι, πολλὰ δ' οὔ, ἀλλ' εἰ τοῦτο ἐπιχειροῖ, πολλῶν ἐφαπτόμενος πάντων ἀποτυγχάνοι ἄν, ὥστ' εἶναί που ἐλλόγιμος

One man does only one job well, and if he tries to take on a number of jobs, the division of effort will mean that he will fail to make his mark at any of them.

Translated by Desmond Lee (1955)
Republic 394e

236 τοὺς φύλακας ἡμῖν τῶν ἄλλων πασῶν δημιουργιῶν ἀφειμένους δεῖν εἶναι δημιουργοὺς ἐλευθερίας τῆς πόλεως πάνυ

ἀκριβεῖς καὶ μηδὲν ἄλλο ἐπιτηδεύειν ὅτι μὴ εἰς τοῦτο φέρει

Our guardians, discharged from all other occupations, must be the strict guarantors of civic liberties and make this their sole business.

Translated by Paul Shorey (1930)

Republic 395b

237 οὐ νέον ἀλλὰ γέροντα δεῖ τὸν ἀγαθὸν δικαστὴν εἶναι, ὀψιμαθῆ γεγονότα τῆς ἀδικίας οἷόν ἐστιν, οὐκ οἰκείαν ἐν τῇ αὑτοῦ ψυχῇ ἐνοῦσαν ᾐσθημένον, ἀλλ' ἀλλοτρίαν ἐν ἀλλοτρίαις μεμελετηκότα ἐν πολλῷ χρόνῳ διαισθάνεσθαι, οἷον πέφυκε κακόν, ἐπιστήμῃ, οὐκ ἐμπειρίᾳ οἰκείᾳ κεχρημένον

A judge should not be young; he should have learned to know evil, not from his own soul, but from long observation of the nature of evil in others; knowledge should be his guide, not personal experience.

Translated by Benjamin Jowett (1817–1893)

Republic 409b

238 ἔοικε γάρ ... γοητεύειν πάντα ὅσα ἀπατᾷ

It seems that everything that deceives enchants.

Republic 413c

239 τίς ἂν οὖν ἡμῖν ... μηχανὴ γένοιτο τῶν ψευδῶν τῶν ἐν δέοντι γιγνομένων ... γενναῖόν τι ἓν ψευδομένους πεῖσαι μάλιστα μὲν καὶ αὐτοὺς τοὺς ἄρχοντας, εἰ δὲ μή, τὴν ἄλλην πόλιν;

I wonder, could we not contrive some magnificent lie which would convince the rulers themselves or, failing that, the rest of the city?

Republic 414b

240 πολλὰ καὶ ἀνόσια περὶ τὸ τῶν πολλῶν νόμισμα γέγονεν

Many impious deeds have been done that involve the currency used by ordinary people.

Translated by G.M.A. Grube (1974), rev. C.D.C. Reeve, ed. John M. Cooper (1997)

Republic 416e

241 πλοῦτός τε ... καὶ πενία, ὡς τοῦ μὲν τρυφὴν καὶ ἀργίαν καὶ νεωτερισμὸν ποιοῦντος, τοῦ δὲ ἀνελευθερίαν καὶ κακοεργίαν πρὸς τῷ νεωτερισμῷ

Wealth is the parent of luxury and indolence, poverty of meanness and viciousness, and both of discontent.

Translated by Benjamin Jowett (1817–1893)

Republic 422a

242 ἐκ τῆς παιδείας ὅποι ἄν τις ὁρμήσῃ, τοιαῦτα καὶ τὰ ἑπόμενα εἶναι

The direction in which education starts a man will determine his future life.

Translated by Benjamin Jowett (1817–1893)

Republic 425b

243 χαριέστατοι οἱ τοιοῦτοι, νομοθετοῦντες ... οἰόμενοί τι πέρας εὑρήσειν περὶ τὰ ἐν τοῖς συμβολαίοις κακουργήματα ... ἀγνοοῦντες ὅτι τῷ ὄντι ὥσπερ Ὕδραν τέμνουσιν

Are they not foolish to believe that by enacting laws they could put an end to fraud in business, not realizing that at most they are cutting off a Hydra's head!

Republic 426e

cf. Proverbial 175, of labouring in vain

244 σωφροσύνη ἐστὶν καὶ ἡδονῶν τινων καὶ ἐπιθυμιῶν ἐγκράτεια

Self-control surely includes moderation in sensual desires.

Republic 430e

245 ἀρετὴ ... ὑγίειά τέ τις ἂν εἴη καὶ κάλλος καὶ εὐεξία ψυχῆς, κακία δὲ νόσος τε καὶ αἶσχος καὶ ἀσθένεια

Virtue is beauty, strength and a healthy disposition of the soul, while wickedness is illness, weakness and deformity.

Republic 444d

246 ἓν μὲν εἶναι εἶδος τῆς ἀρετῆς, ἄπειρα δὲ τῆς κακίας

There is one form of virtue, but an infinite variety of vice.

Republic 445c

247 οὐδὲν ἄρα ἐστίν, ὦ φίλε, ἐπιτήδευμα τῶν πόλιν διοικούντων γυναικὸς διότι γυνή, οὐδ' ἀνδρὸς διότι ἀνήρ, ἀλλ' ὁμοίως διεσπαρμέναι αἱ φύσεις ἐν ἀμφοῖν τοῖν ζῴοιν, καὶ πάντων μὲν μετέχει γυνὴ ἐπιτηδευμάτων κατὰ φύσιν, πάντων δὲ ἀνήρ

There is no administrative occupation

which is peculiar to woman as woman or man as man; natural capacities are similarly distributed in each sex, and it is natural for women as well as men to take part in all occupations.

Translated by Desmond Lee (1955)

Republic 455d

248 ἆρ᾽ οὖν σοι συνδοκεῖ μέτριος χρόνος ἀκμῆς τὰ εἴκοσι ἔτη γυναικί, ἀνδρὶ δὲ τὰ τριάκοντα;

What is the prime of life? May it not be defined as a period of about twenty years in a woman's life, and thirty in a man's?

Translated by Benjamin Jowett (1817–1893)

Republic 460e

249 ἔχομεν οὖν τι μεῖζον κακὸν πόλει ἢ ἐκεῖνο ὃ ἂν αὐτὴν διασπᾷ καὶ ποιῇ πολλὰς ἀντὶ μιᾶς;

Is there anything worse for a state than to be split and fragmented?

Translated by Desmond Lee (1955)

Republic 462a

250 ἐὰν μή, ἦν δ᾽ ἐγώ, ἢ οἱ φιλόσοφοι βασιλεύσωσιν ἐν ταῖς πόλεσιν ἢ οἱ βασιλεῖς τε νῦν λεγόμενοι καὶ δυνάσται φιλοσοφήσωσι γνησίως τε καὶ ἱκανῶς, καὶ τοῦτο εἰς ταὐτὸν συμπέσῃ, δύναμίς τε πολιτικὴ καὶ φιλοσοφία, τῶν δὲ νῦν πορευομένων χωρὶς ἐφ᾽ ἑκάτερον αἱ πολλαὶ φύσεις ἐξ ἀνάγκης ἀποκλεισθῶσιν, οὐκ ἔστι κακῶν παῦλα ταῖς πόλεσι, δοκῶ δ᾽ οὐδὲ τῷ ἀνθρωπίνῳ γένει, οὐδὲ αὕτη ἡ πολιτεία μή ποτε πρότερον φυῇ τε εἰς τὸ δυνατὸν καὶ φῶς ἡλίου ἴδῃ

Until philosophers are kings, or the kings and rulers of this world have the spirit and power of philosophy, and political greatness and wisdom meet in one, and those commoner individuals who pursue either to the exclusion of the other are compelled to stand aside, cities will never have rest from their evils – no, nor the human race, as I believe – and then only will this our State have a possibility of life and behold the light of day.

Translated by Benjamin Jowett (1817–1893)

Republic 473c

251 τούτων γὰρ δή ... τῶν πολλῶν καλῶν μῶν τι ἔστιν, ὃ οὐκ αἰσχρὸν φανήσεται; καὶ τῶν δικαίων, ὃ οὐκ ἄδικον; καὶ τῶν ὁσίων, ὃ οὐκ ἀνόσιον;

Is there one beautiful thing, in this welter of beautiful things, which won't turn out to be ugly? Is there one moral deed which won't turn out to be immoral? Is there one just act which won't turn out to be unjust?

Translated by Robin Waterfield (1998)

Republic 479a

252 τῷ γὰρ ἀληθεῖ χαλεπαίνειν οὐ θέμις

They have no right to be annoyed at the truth.

Translated by Desmond Lee (1955)

Republic 480a

253 δειλῇ δὴ καὶ ἀνελευθέρῳ φύσει φιλοσοφίας ἀληθινῆς ... οὐκ ἂν μετείη

A cowardly and illiberal spirit has no place in true philosophy.

Republic 486b

254 πρὸς τὸ ὂν πεφυκὼς εἴη ἁμιλλᾶσθαι ὅ γε ὄντως φιλομαθής, καὶ οὐκ ἐπιμένοι ἐπὶ τοῖς δοξαζομένοις εἶναι πολλοῖς ἑκάστοις, ἀλλ᾽ ἴοι καὶ οὐκ ἀμβλύνοιτο οὐδ᾽ ἀπολήγοι τοῦ ἔρωτος, πρὶν αὐτοῦ ὃ ἔστιν ἑκάστου τῆς φύσεως ἅψασθαι

The true lover of knowledge naturally strives for truth and is not content with common opinion but soars with undimmed and unwearied passion till he grasps the essential nature of things.

Translated in *A Dictionary of Philosophical Quotations* (2008)

Republic 490a

255 ἀλλὰ μήν, ἦν δ᾽ ἐγώ, εἷς ἱκανὸς γενόμενος, πόλιν ἔχων πειθομένην, πάντ᾽ ἐπιτελέσαι τὰ νῦν ἀπιστούμενα

Let there be one capable man – and a city that will be prevailed upon – and he can realize all that now seems so incredible.

Republic 502b

256 καὶ τοῖς γιγνωσκομένοις τοίνυν μὴ μόνον τὸ γιγνώσκεσθαι φάναι ὑπὸ τοῦ ἀγαθοῦ παρεῖναι, ἀλλὰ καὶ τὸ εἶναί τε καὶ τὴν οὐσίαν ὑπ᾽ ἐκείνου αὐτοῖς προσεῖναι, οὐκ οὐσίας ὄντος τοῦ ἀγαθοῦ, ἀλλ᾽ ἔτι ἐπέκεινα τῆς οὐσίας πρεσβείᾳ καὶ δυνάμει ὑπερέχοντος

Objects of knowledge derive from goodness not only their intelligibility, but their very essence and existence; for goodness transcends essence in dignity and power.

Republic 509b

257 ἰδὲ γὰρ ἀνθρώπους οἷον ἐν καταγείῳ οἰκήσει σπηλαιώδει ... ἐν ταύτῃ ἐκ παίδων ὄντας ἐν δεσμοῖς ... ὥστε μένειν τε αὐτοὺς εἴς τε τὸ πρόσθεν μόνον ὁρᾶν ... μὴ ἄλλο πλὴν τὰς σκιὰς ... φῶς δὲ αὐτοῖς πυρὸς ... καόμενον ὄπισθεν αὐτῶν ... ἄτοπον λέγεις ... ὁμοίους ἡμῖν, ἦν δ' ἐγώ ... παντάπασι δή οἱ τοιοῦτοι οὐκ ἂν ἄλλο τι νομίζοιεν τὸ ἀληθὲς ἢ τὰς τῶν σκευαστῶν σκιάς

Imagine men in a subterranean cave, having lived since childhood in fetters allowing them to see only their shadows from a fire burning at their back; strange, you would say; but they are not unlike ourselves, say I; for undoubtedly they would recognize as reality nothing but those shadows.

Republic 514a–515c

The Cave Parable, much shortened; cf. Nietzsche, Die Fröhliche Wissenschaft *3.108: 'there will perhaps be caves, for ages yet, in which man's shadows will be shown'*

258 τὴν παιδείαν ... οὐκ ἐνούσης ἐν τῇ ψυχῇ ἐπιστήμης σφεῖς ἐντιθέναι, οἷον τυφλοῖς ὀφθαλμοῖς ὄψιν ἐντιθέντες ... σημαίνει ταύτην τὴν ἐνοῦσαν ἑκάστου δύναμιν ἐν τῇ ψυχῇ ... οἷον εἰ ὄμμα μὴ δυνατὸν ἦν ἄλλως ἢ σὺν ὅλῳ τῷ σώματι στρέφειν πρὸς τὸ φανὸν ἐκ τοῦ σκοτώδους, οὕτω σὺν ὅλῃ τῇ ψυχῇ ἐκ τοῦ γιγνομένου περιακτέον εἶναι, ἕως ἂν εἰς τὸ ὂν καὶ τοῦ ὄντος τὸ φανότατον δυνατὴ γένηται ἀνασχέσθαι θεωμένη· τοῦτο δ' εἶναί φαμεν τἀγαθόν

Education is not to put into the soul knowledge that was not there before, as if you could put sight into blind eyes. It is a capacity innate in each man's soul; as an eye which cannot be turned from darkness to light unless the whole body is turned, so the entire soul must be turned away from this world of change until its eye can bear to look straight at reality, and at the brightest of realities which is what we call the good.

Republic 518b

259 πόλις εὖ οἰκουμένη ἐν μόνῃ γὰρ αὐτῇ ἄρξουσιν οἱ τῷ ὄντι πλούσιοι, οὐ χρυσίου, ἀλλ' οὗ δεῖ τὸν εὐδαίμονα πλουτεῖν, ζωῆς ἀγαθῆς τε καὶ ἔμφρονος

A well-governed city is one in which those rule who are truly rich, not in gold, but in wealth that brings happiness: a life of kindness and prudence.

Republic 521a

260 περιμάχητον γὰρ τὸ ἄρχειν γιγνόμενον, οἰκεῖος ὢν καὶ ἔνδον ὁ τοιοῦτος πόλεμος αὐτούς τε ἀπόλλυσι καὶ τὴν ἄλλην πόλιν

When office and rule become the prizes of contention, civil and internecine strife destroys the office-seekers themselves and the city as well.

Translated by Paul Shorey (1935)

Republic 521a

261 δεῖ γε μὴ ἐραστὰς τοῦ ἄρχειν ἰέναι ἐπ' αὐτό· εἰ δὲ μή, οἵ γε ἀντερασταὶ μαχοῦνται

Those who take office should not have a passion for rule itself; if not so, rivals will soon contest it.

Republic 521b

262 ἀστρονομία ... γε ἀναγκάζει ψυχὴν εἰς τὸ ἄνω ὁρᾶν καὶ ἀπὸ τῶν ἐνθένδε ἐκεῖσε ἄγει

Astronomy compels the mind to look upwards and leads it from earth to the heavens.

Translated by Desmond Lee (1955)

Republic 529a

263 οὐ γάρ που δοκοῦσί γέ σοι οἱ ταῦτα δεινοὶ διαλεκτικοὶ εἶναι

I have hardly ever known a mathematician who was capable of reasoning.

Translated by Benjamin Jowett (1817–1893)

Republic 531d

264 Σόλωνι γὰρ οὐ πειστέον, ὡς γηράσκων τις πολλὰ δυνατὸς μανθάνειν, ἀλλ' ἧττον ἢ τρέχειν, νέων δὲ πάντες οἱ μεγάλοι καὶ οἱ πολλοὶ πόνοι

Let not Solon persuade us that one can learn a lot as one grows old; for we can no more learn much than run much; youth is the time for all serious effort.

Republic 536d

cf. Solon 24

265 ψυχῇ δὲ βίαιον οὐδὲν ἔμμονον μάθημα

Compulsory learning never sticks in the mind.

Translated by Desmond Lee (1955)

Republic 536e

266 μὴ τοίνυν βίᾳ ... τοὺς παῖδας ἐν τοῖς μαθήμασιν ἀλλὰ παίζοντας τρέφε, ἵνα καὶ μᾶλλον οἷός τ' ᾖς καθορᾶν ἐφ' ὃ ἕκαστος πέφυκεν

Let your children's lessons take the form of play. You will learn more about their natural abilities that way.

Translated by Desmond Lee (1955)

Republic 536e

267 τὸ μὴ μίαν ἀλλὰ δύο ἀνάγκῃ εἶναι τὴν τοιαύτην πόλιν, τὴν μὲν πενήτων, τὴν δὲ πλουσίων, οἰκοῦντας ἐν τῷ αὐτῷ, ἀεὶ ἐπιβουλεύοντας ἀλλήλοις

Oligarchy inevitably splits society into two factions, the rich and the poor, who live in the same place, and are always plotting against each other.

Translated by Desmond Lee (1955)

Republic 551d

268 δημοκρατία ... ἡδεῖα πολιτεία καὶ ἄναρχος καὶ ποικίλη, ἰσότητά τινα ὁμοίως ἴσοις τε καὶ ἀνίσοις διανέμουσα

Democracy is a charming form of government, full of variety and disorder, and dispensing a sort of equality to equals and unequals alike.

Translated by Benjamin Jowett (1817–1893)

Republic 558c

cf. Aristotle 140

269 διαζῇ τὸ καθ' ἡμέραν οὕτω χαριζόμενος τῇ προσπιπτούσῃ ἐπιθυμίᾳ, τοτὲ μὲν μεθύων καὶ καταυλούμενος, αὖθις δὲ ὑδροποτῶν καὶ κατισχναινόμενος, τοτὲ δ' αὖ γυμναζόμενος, ἔστιν δ' ὅτε ἀργῶν καὶ πάντων ἀμελῶν, τοτὲ δ' ὡς ἐν φιλοσοφίᾳ διατρίβων

He lives from day to day, indulging in the pleasure of the moment. One day it's wine, women and song, the next water to drink and a strict diet; one day it's hard physical training, the next indolence and careless ease, and then a period of philosophical study.

Translated by Desmond Lee (1955)

Republic 561c

of the life of a youth living in a democracy

270 οἱ μὲν νέοι πρεσβυτέροις ἀπεικάζονται καὶ διαμιλλῶνται καὶ ἐν λόγοις καὶ ἐν ἔργοις, οἱ δὲ γέροντες συγκαθιέντες τοῖς νέοις εὐτραπελίας τε καὶ χαριεντισμοῦ ἐμπίμπλανται, μιμούμενοι τοὺς νέους, ἵνα δὴ μὴ δοκῶσιν ἀηδεῖς εἶναι μηδὲ δεσποτικοί

The young imitate their elders and compete with them in word and deed, while the old stoop to the level of the young and are full of play and pleasantry, imitating the young for fear of appearing disagreeable and authoritarian.

Translated by G.M.A. Grube (1974), rev. C.D.C. Reeve, ed. John M. Cooper (1997)

Republic 563a

271 ἡ γὰρ ἄγαν ἐλευθερία ἔοικεν οὐκ εἰς ἄλλο τι ἢ εἰς ἄγαν δουλείαν μεταβάλλειν

The probable outcome of too much freedom is only too much slavery.

Translated by Paul Shorey (1935)

Republic 564a

272 οὐκοῦν ἕνα τινὰ ἀεὶ δῆμος εἴωθε διαφερόντως προΐστασθαι ἑαυτοῦ, καὶ τοῦτον τρέφειν τε καὶ αὔξειν μέγαν ... τοῦτο μὲν ἄρα, ἦν δ' ἐγώ, δῆλον, ὅτι, ὅταν περ φύηται τύραννος, ἐκ προστατικῆς ῥίζης καὶ οὐκ ἄλλοθεν ἐκβλαστάνει

The people always have some champion whom they set over them and nurse to greatness. This is the root from which a tyrant springs, whilst he first appears as a protector.

Republic 565c

273 τύραννος ... πρώταις ἡμέραις τε καὶ χρόνῳ προσγελᾷ τε καὶ ἀσπάζεται πάντας, ᾧ ἂν περιτυγχάνῃ

In his early days of power a tyrant is full of smiles and greets everyone he meets.

Republic 566d

274 ὅταν δέ γε, οἶμαι, πρὸς τοὺς ἔξω ἐχθροὺς τοῖς μὲν καταλλαγῇ, τοὺς δὲ καὶ διαφθείρῃ, καὶ ἡσυχία ἐκείνων γένηται, πρῶτον μὲν πολέμους τινὰς ἀεὶ κινεῖ, ἵν' ἐν χρείᾳ ἡγεμόνος ὁ δῆμος ᾖ

When the tyrant has disposed of foreign enemies by conquest or by treaty, and there is nothing to fear from them, then he is always stirring up some war or other, in order that the people may require a leader.

Translated by Benjamin Jowett (1817–1893)

Republic 566e

275 ἐλευθερίας δὲ καὶ φιλίας ἀληθοῦς τυραννικὴ φύσις ἀεὶ ἄγευστος

Tyrants never taste true friendship or freedom.

Republic 576a

276 κάλλιστον ὅτι μάλιστα ἡσυχίαν ἄγειν ἐν ταῖς συμφοραῖς καὶ μὴ ἀγανακτεῖν

It is best, so far as we can, to bear misfortune patiently and without complaint.

Translated by Desmond Lee (1955)

Republic 604b

277 οὔτε τι τῶν ἀνθρωπίνων ἄξιον ὂν μεγάλης σπουδῆς

Nothing in mortal life is worthy of great concern.

Translated by Paul Shorey (1935)

Republic 604c

278 τὴν Ἑλλάδα πεπαίδευκεν οὗτος ὁ ποιητὴς

This poet has been the educator of Greece.

Translated by Paul Shorey (1935)

Republic 606e

of Homer

279 ἀθάνατος ἡμῶν ἡ ψυχὴ καὶ οὐδέποτε ἀπόλλυται

Immortal is the soul of man, and imperishable.

Translated by Benjamin Jowett (1817–1893)

Republic 608d

280 οὐκοῦν ὁπότε μηδ' ὑφ' ἑνὸς ἀπόλλυται κακοῦ, μήτε οἰκείου μήτε ἀλλοτρίου, δῆλον ὅτι ἀνάγκη αὐτὸ ἀεὶ ὂν εἶναι

Since, then, the soul is not destroyed by any evil whatever, either its own or alien, it is evident that it must be immortal.

Republic 610e

281 οὕτως ἄρα ὑποληπτέον περὶ τοῦ δικαίου ἀνδρός, ἐάν τ' ἐν πενίᾳ γίγνηται ἐάν τ' ἐν νόσοις ἤ τινι ἄλλῳ τῶν δοκούντων κακῶν, ὡς τούτῳ ταῦτα εἰς ἀγαθόν τι τελευτήσει ζῶντι ἢ καὶ ἀποθανόντι

We must assume that, if the just man is poor or ill or suffering from any other apparent misfortune, it is for his ultimate good, in this life or in death.

Translated by Desmond Lee (1955)

Republic 613a

282 αἰτία ἑλομένου· θεὸς ἀναίτιος

The blame is his who chooses; god is blameless.

Translated by Paul Shorey (1935)

Republic 617e

283 ἀλλ' ἂν ἐμοὶ πειθώμεθα, νομίζοντες ἀθάνατον ψυχὴν καὶ δυνατὴν πάντα μὲν κακὰ ἀνέχεσθαι, πάντα δὲ ἀγαθά, τῆς ἄνω ὁδοῦ ἀεὶ ἑξόμεθα καὶ δικαιοσύνην μετὰ φρονήσεως παντὶ τρόπῳ ἐπιτηδεύσομεν, ἵνα καὶ ἡμῖν αὐτοῖς φίλοι ὦμεν καὶ τοῖς θεοῖς, αὐτοῦ τε μένοντες ἐνθάδε, καὶ ἐπειδὰν τὰ ἆθλα αὐτῆς κομιζώμεθα

If guided by me we shall believe that the soul is immortal and capable of enduring all extremes of good and evil, and so we shall ever hold to the upward way and pursue righteousness with wisdom always and ever, that we may be dear to ourselves and to the gods both during our sojourn here and when we receive our reward.

Translated by Paul Shorey (1935)

Republic 621c

last paragraph of the Republic

284 διάνοια μὲν καὶ λόγος ταὐτόν· πλὴν ὁ μὲν ἐντὸς τῆς ψυχῆς πρὸς αὑτὴν διάλογος ἄνευ φωνῆς γιγνόμενος

Thought and speech are the same; except that thought is the inward debate of the soul with itself, without the need of voice.

Sophist 263e

285 κατιδόντα δὲ τἀνθρώπινον ἔτι μόνῳ τῷ πτηνῷ συνειληχὸς τὴν δίποδα ἀγέλην πάλιν τῷ ψιλῷ καὶ τῷ πτεροφυεῖ τέμνειν

Seeing that the human race, being biped, shares the same classification as the feathered creatures, we must again divide the biped class into featherless and feathered.

Statesman 266e

cf. Diogenes Cynic 2

286 ἡ τοῦ πλήθους ἀρχή, δημοκρατία τοὔνομα κληθεῖσα

The rule of the multitude is called democracy, is it not?

Translated by Harold North Fowler (1925)

Statesman 291d

287 δοκῶ μοι περὶ ὧν πυνθάνεσθε οὐκ ἀμελέτητος εἶναι

In fact, your question does not find me unprepared.

Translated by Alexander Nehamas and Paul Woodruff (1989)

Symposium 172a

opening lines

288 οἴεσθε τὶ ποιεῖν οὐδὲν ποιοῦντες

You think you are doing a great deal when you really do nothing at all.

Translated by W.R.M. Lamb (1925)

Symposium 173c

289 μὴ οὖν κινεῖτε, ἀλλ' ἐᾶτε

Don't disturb him; let him be.

Translated by Alexander Nehamas and Paul Woodruff (1989)

Symposium 175b

of Socrates, who appeared lost in contemplation

290 εὖ ἂν ἔχοι ... εἰ τοιοῦτον εἴη ἡ σοφία, ὥστ' ἐκ τοῦ πληρεστέρου εἰς τὸν κενώτερον ῥεῖν ἡμῶν

How wonderful it would be if wisdom could simply flow out of the one of us who is fuller into him who is emptier.

Symposium 175d

291 ἡ μὲν γὰρ ἐμὴ σοφία φαύλη τις ἂν εἴη καὶ ἀμφισβητήσιμος ὥσπερ ὄναρ οὖσα

My own wisdom is but meagre, as disputable as a dream.

Translated by W.R.M. Lamb (1925)

Symposium 175e

spoken by Socrates

292 ἐμοὶ γὰρ δὴ τοῦτό γε οἶμαι κατάδηλον γεγονέναι ἐκ τῆς ἰατρικῆς, ὅτι χαλεπὸν τοῖς ἀνθρώποις ἡ μέθη ἐστί

The practice of medicine, I find, has made this clear to me, that drunkenness is harmful to mankind.

Translated by W.R.M. Lamb (1925)

Symposium 176c

293 ταῦτα δὴ ἀκούσαντας συγχωρεῖν πάντας μὴ διὰ μέθης ποιήσασθαι τὴν ἐν τῷ παρόντι συνουσίαν, ἀλλ' οὕτω πίνοντας πρὸς ἡδονήν

At that point they all agreed not to get drunk that evening; they decided to drink only as much as pleased them.

Translated by Alexander Nehamas and Paul Woodruff (1989)

Symposium 176d

294 Ἔρωτα ... ἀλλ' οὕτως ἠμέληται τοσοῦτος θεός

Love! So great a god, and so neglected!

Translated by W.R.M. Lamb (1925)

Symposium 177c

cf. Plato 295

295 Ἔρως θαυμαστὸς ἐν ἀνθρώποις τε καὶ θεοῖς ...
Παρμενίδης δὲ τὴν γένεσιν λέγει
πρώτιστον μὲν Ἔρωτα θεῶν μητίσατο πάντων

Eros, a marvel to gods and men alike; the very first god designed, as Parmenides tells us.

Symposium 178a–b

Phaedrus thus begins his speech, quoting Parmenides 8 (and Hesiod 6)

296 ἐρῶν γὰρ ἀνὴρ ὑπὸ παιδικῶν ὀφθῆναι ἢ λιπὼν τάξιν ἢ ὅπλα ἀποβαλὼν ἧττον ἂν δήπου δέξαιτο

A man in love would never allow his loved one to see him leaving ranks or dropping weapons.

Translated by Alexander Nehamas and Paul Woodruff (1989)

Symposium 179a

297 καὶ ἀτεχνῶς, ὃ ἔφη Ὅμηρος, 'μένος ἐμπνεῦσαι' ἐνίοις τῶν ἡρώων τὸν θεόν, τοῦτο ὁ Ἔρως τοῖς ἐρῶσι παρέχει γιγνόμενον παρ' αὑτοῦ

When Homer says a god 'breathes might' into some of the heroes, this is really Love's gift to every lover.

Translated by Alexander Nehamas and Paul Woodruff (1989)

Symposium 179b

from Phaedrus' speech, with a reference to Iliad *10.482 and 15.262*

298 καὶ μὴν ὑπεραποθνῄσκειν γε μόνοι

ἐθέλουσιν οἱ ἐρῶντες, οὐ μόνον ὅτι ἄνδρες, ἀλλὰ καὶ αἱ γυναῖκες

No one will die for you but a lover, and a lover will do this even if she's a woman.

Translated by Alexander Nehamas and Paul Woodruff (1989)

Symposium 179b

299 οὕτω δὴ ἔγωγέ φημι· Ἔρωτα θεῶν καὶ πρεσβύτατον καὶ τιμιώτατον καὶ κυριώτατον εἶναι εἰς ἀρετῆς καὶ εὐδαιμονίας κτῆσιν ἀνθρώποις

Therefore I say Love is the most ancient of gods, the most honoured, and the most powerful in helping men gain virtue and blessedness.

Translated by Alexander Nehamas and Paul Woodruff (1989)

Symposium 180b

closing words of Phaedrus' speech

300 πᾶσα γὰρ πρᾶξις ὧδ' ἔχει ... καλῶς μὲν γὰρ πραττόμενον καὶ ὀρθῶς καλὸν γίγνεται, μὴ ὀρθῶς δὲ αἰσχρόν. οὕτω δὴ καὶ τὸ ἐρᾶν

Every action done honourably and properly is honourable; if improperly, disgraceful. Thus also it is with love.

Symposium 180e–181a

from Pausanias' speech, the second of six speeches in the Symposium

301 οὐ γὰρ ... συμφέρει τοῖς ἄρχουσι φρονήματα μεγάλα ἐγγίγνεσθαι τῶν ἀρχομένων, οὐδὲ φιλίας ἰσχυρὰς καὶ κοινωνίας, ὃ δὴ μάλιστα φιλεῖ τά τε ἄλλα πάντα καὶ ὁ ἔρως ἐμποιεῖν

It is not in the interest of despots that their subjects entertain lofty notions, nor strong friendships or alliances, all of which Love is pre-eminently apt to create.

Symposium 182c

302 τῶν μὲν ἀρχόντων πλεονεξίᾳ, τῶν δὲ ἀρχομένων ἀνανδρίᾳ· οὗ δὲ καλὸν ἁπλῶς ἐνομίσθη, διὰ τὴν τῶν θεμένων τῆς ψυχῆς ἀργίαν

Lust for power in the rulers and cowardice in the ruled; indiscriminate approval testifies to general dullness and stupidity.

Translated by Alexander Nehamas and Paul Woodruff (1989)

Symposium 182d

303 πονηρὸς δ' ἐστὶν ἐκεῖνος ὁ ἐραστὴς ὁ πάνδημος, ὁ τοῦ σώματος μᾶλλον ἢ τῆς ψυχῆς ἐρῶν ... ἅμα γὰρ τῷ τοῦ σώματος ἄνθει λήγοντι ... οἴχεται ἀποπτάμενος

By wicked we mean that popular lover who craves the body rather than the soul; who, as soon as the bloom of the body begins to fade 'flutters off and is gone'.

Translated by W.R.M. Lamb (1925)

Symposium 183d

from Pausanias' speech; the quotation is from Iliad *2.71*

304 τὸν Ἔρωτα ... καὶ πρὸς ἄλλα πολλὰ καὶ ἐν τοῖς ἄλλοις, τοῖς τε σώμασι τῶν πάντων ζῴων καὶ τοῖς ἐν τῇ γῇ φυομένοις καὶ ὡς ἔπος εἰπεῖν ἐν πᾶσι τοῖς οὖσι

Love is a significantly broader phenomenon; it certainly occurs within the animal kingdom and even in the world of plants; in fact it occurs everywhere in the universe.

Translated by Alexander Nehamas and Paul Woodruff (1989)

Symposium 186a

the beginning of Eryximachus' rather pedantic speech, the third of six speeches in the Symposium

305 Ἔρως ... καὶ παρ' ἡμῖν καὶ παρὰ θεοῖς, οὗτος τὴν μεγίστην δύναμιν ἔχει καὶ πᾶσαν ἡμῖν εὐδαιμονίαν παρασκευάζει

Love, both here on earth and in heaven above, wields the mightiest power of all and provides us with perfect bliss.

Translated by W.R.M. Lamb (1925)

Symposium 188d

the end of Eryximachus' speech

306 πρῶτον μὲν γὰρ τρία ἦν τὰ γένη τὰ τῶν ἀνθρώπων, οὐχ ὥσπερ νῦν δύο, ἄρρεν καὶ θῆλυ, ἀλλὰ καὶ τρίτον προσῆν κοινὸν ὂν ἀμφοτέρων τούτων

In the beginning there were three kinds of human beings, not just two as there are now, male and female; there was a third, with equal shares of the other two.

Symposium 189d

the beginning of Aristophanes' humorous speech, the fourth of six speeches in the Symposium

307 ὁ οὖν Ζεὺς καὶ οἱ ἄλλοι θεοὶ ἐβουλεύοντο … καὶ ἠπόρουν· οὔτε γὰρ ὅπως ἀποκτείναιεν εἶχον … αἱ τιμαὶ γὰρ αὐτοῖς καὶ ἱερὰ τὰ παρὰ τῶν ἀνθρώπων ἠφανίζετο

Then Zeus and the other gods met in council and were sore perplexed. They could not wipe out the human race because that would wipe out the worship they receive, along with the sacrifices we humans give them.

Translated by Alexander Nehamas and Paul Woodruff (1989)

Symposium 190c

from Aristophanes' speech

308 ἔστι δὴ οὖν ἐκ τόσου ὁ ἔρως ἔμφυτος ἀλλήλων τοῖς ἀνθρώποις καὶ τῆς ἀρχαίας φύσεως συναγωγεὺς καὶ ἐπιχειρῶν ποιῆσαι ἓν ἐκ δυοῖν

Love is born into every human being; it calls back our original nature together; it makes one out of two.

Translated by Alexander Nehamas and Paul Woodruff (1989)

Symposium 191c

from Aristophanes' speech

309 συνελθὼν καὶ συντακεὶς τῷ ἐρωμένῳ ἐκ δυοῖν εἷς γενέσθαι … τοῦ ὅλου οὖν τῇ ἐπιθυμίᾳ καὶ διώξει ἔρως ὄνομα

To come together and melt together with the one he loves, so that one person emerged from two. 'Love' is the name for our pursuit of wholeness, for our desire to be complete.

Translated by Alexander Nehamas and Paul Woodruff (1989)

Symposium 192e

the two having been split from a symmetrical whole

310 λέγω δὲ οὖν ἔγωγε καθ' ἁπάντων καὶ ἀνδρῶν καὶ γυναικῶν, ὅτι οὕτως ἂν ἡμῶν τὸ γένος εὔδαιμον γένοιτο, εἰ ἐκτελέσαιμεν τὸν ἔρωτα

I am speaking about everyone, men and women alike, and say there's just one way for the human race to flourish: we must bring love to its perfect conclusion.

Translated by Alexander Nehamas and Paul Woodruff (1989)

Symposium 193c

from Aristophanes' speech

311 νοῦν ἔχοντι ὀλίγοι ἔμφρονες πολλῶν ἀφρόνων φοβερώτεροι

Any intelligent speaker is more alarmed at a few men of wit than at a host of fools.

Translated by W.R.M. Lamb (1925)

Symposium 194b

from Aristophanes' speech

312 ὁ γὰρ παλαιὸς λόγος εὖ ἔχει, ὡς ὅμοιον ὁμοίῳ ἀεὶ πελάζει

The old story holds good that like is always drawn to like.

Translated by Alexander Nehamas and Paul Woodruff (1989)

Symposium 195b

Agathon (in the fifth speech of the Symposium*) quoting from Homer; cf. Homer 360*

313 πᾶς γοῦν ποιητὴς γίγνεται, κἂν ἄμουσος ᾖ τὸ πρίν, οὗ ἂν Ἔρως ἅψηται

Once Love touches him, *anyone* becomes a poet, 'howe'er uncultured he had been before.'

Translated by Alexander Nehamas and Paul Woodruff (1989)

Symposium 196e

Agathon quoting from Euripides' Stheneboea, *a lost play; cf. Euripides 497*

314 οὗτος δὲ ἡμᾶς ἀλλοτριότητος μὲν κενοῖ, οἰκειότητος δὲ πληροῖ, τὰς τοιάσδε συνόδους μετ' ἀλλήλων πάσας τιθεὶς συνιέναι, ἐν ἑορταῖς, ἐν χοροῖς, ἐν θυσίαις γιγνόμενος ἡγεμών· πρᾳότητα μὲν πορίζων, ἀγριότητα δ' ἐξορίζων· φιλόδωρος εὐμενείας, ἄδωρος δυσμενείας· ἵλεως ἀγαθός· θεατὸς σοφοῖς, ἀγαστὸς θεοῖς· ζηλωτὸς ἀμοίροις, κτητὸς εὐμοίροις· τρυφῆς, ἁβρότητος, χλιδῆς, χαρίτων, ἱμέρου, πόθου πατήρ· ἐπιμελὴς ἀγαθῶν, ἀμελὴς κακῶν· ἐν πόνῳ, ἐν φόβῳ, ἐν πόθῳ, ἐν λόγῳ κυβερνήτης, ἐπιβάτης, παραστάτης τε καὶ σωτὴρ ἄριστος, συμπάντων τε θεῶν καὶ ἀνθρώπων κόσμος, ἡγεμὼν κάλλιστος καὶ ἄριστος, ᾧ χρὴ ἕπεσθαι πάντα ἄνδρα ἐφυμνοῦντα καλῶς, ᾠδῆς μετέχοντα ἣν ᾄδει θέλγων πάντων θεῶν τε καὶ ἀνθρώπων νόημα

Love fills us with togetherness and drains all of our divisiveness away. Love calls gatherings like these together. In feasts, in dances, and in ceremonies, he gives the lead. Love moves us to mildness, removes from us wildness. He is giver of kindness, never of meanness.

Gracious, kindly – let wise men see and gods admire! Treasure to lovers, envy to others, father of elegance, luxury, delicacy, grace, yearning, desire. Love cares well for good men, cares not for bad ones. In pain, in fear, in desire, or speech, Love is our best guide and guard; he is our comrade and our savior. Ornament of all gods and men, most beautiful leader and the best! Every man should follow Love, sing beautifully his hymns, and join with him in the song he sings that charms the mind of god or man.

Translated by Alexander Nehamas and Paul Woodruff (1989)

Symposium 197d

closing lines of Agathon's speech, the fifth of the Symposium

315 οὐ μὲν οὖν τῇ ἀληθείᾳ, φάναι, ὦ φιλούμενε Ἀγάθων, δύνασαι ἀντιλέγειν, ἐπεὶ Σωκράτει γε οὐδὲν χαλεπόν

But, my dearest Agathon, it is truth which you cannot contradict; you can without any difficulty contradict Socrates.

Translated in *The Oxford Dictionary of Quotations* (2004)

Symposium 201c

spoken by Socrates

316 κυοῦσι γάρ, ἔφη, ὦ Σώκρατες, πάντες ἄνθρωποι καὶ κατὰ τὸ σῶμα καὶ κατὰ τὴν ψυχήν, καὶ ἐπειδὰν ἔν τινι ἡλικίᾳ γένωνται, τίκτειν ἐπιθυμεῖ ἡμῶν ἡ φύσις

All of us are pregnant, Socrates, both in body and in soul, and, as soon as we come to a certain age, we naturally desire to give birth.

Translated by Alexander Nehamas and Paul Woodruff (1989)

Symposium 206c

from Diotima's speech, the sixth of the Symposium, *as related by Socrates*

317 ἡ γὰρ ἀνδρὸς καὶ γυναικὸς συνουσία τόκος ἐστίν· ἔστι δὲ τοῦτο θεῖον τὸ πρᾶγμα, καὶ τοῦτο ἐν θνητῷ ὄντι τῷ ζῴῳ ἀθάνατον ἔνεστιν

When a man and a woman come together in order to give birth, this is a divine affair, an immortal element in a creature that is mortal.

Symposium 206c

from Diotima's speech

318 τὸ δὲ καλὸν ἁρμόττον τῷ θείῳ

Beauty is in harmony with the divine.

Symposium 206d

from Diotima's speech

319 τὸ ἀπιὸν καὶ παλαιούμενον ἕτερον νέον ἐγκαταλείπειν οἷον αὐτὸ ἦν. ταύτῃ τῇ μηχανῇ ... θνητὸν ἀθανασίας μετέχει

What is departing and aging leaves behind something new, much like the original. In this way, what is mortal shares in immortality.

Symposium 208b

from Diotima's speech

320 οἶμαι ὑπὲρ ἀρετῆς ἀθανάτου καὶ τοιαύτης δόξης εὐκλεοῦς πάντες πάντα ποιοῦσιν ... εἰσὶ γὰρ οὖν οἳ ἐν ταῖς ψυχαῖς κυοῦσιν ἔτι μᾶλλον ἢ ἐν τοῖς σώμασιν

I hold it is for immortal distinction and for illustrious renown that all do all they can, for there are persons who in their souls still more than in their bodies conceive those things.

Translated by W.R.M. Lamb (1925)

Symposium 208d

321 καὶ πᾶς ἂν δέξαιτο ἑαυτῷ τοιούτους παῖδας μᾶλλον γεγονέναι ... καὶ εἰς Ὅμηρον ἀποβλέψας καὶ Ἡσίοδον ... ζηλῶν, οἷα ἔκγονα ἑαυτῶν καταλείπουσιν, ἃ ἐκείνοις ἀθάνατον κλέος καὶ μνήμην παρέχεται

And who would not rather have children as Homer and Hesiod have left us, providing them with immortal glory and remembrance.

Symposium 209c

of their poems

322 τὸ ἐν ταῖς ψυχαῖς κάλλος τιμιώτερον ἡγήσασθαι τοῦ ἐν τῷ σώματι

Set a higher value on the beauty of souls than on that of the body.

Translated by W.R.M. Lamb (1925)

Symposium 210b

323 τοῦτο γὰρ δή ἐστι τὸ ὀρθῶς ἐπὶ τὰ ἐρωτικὰ ἰέναι ... ἀρχόμενον ... ὥσπερ ἐπαναβαθμοῖς χρώμενον, ἀπὸ ἑνὸς ... ἐπὶ πάντα τὰ καλὰ σώματα, καὶ ἀπὸ τῶν καλῶν σωμάτων ἐπὶ τὰ καλὰ ἐπιτηδεύματα, καὶ ἀπὸ τῶν ἐπιτηδευμάτων ἐπὶ τὰ καλὰ μαθήματα,

καὶ ἀπὸ τῶν μαθημάτων ἐπ' ἐκεῖνο τὸ μάθημα τελευτῆσαι, ὅ ἐστιν οὐκ ἄλλου ἢ αὐτοῦ ἐκείνου τοῦ καλοῦ μάθημα, ἵνα γνῷ αὐτὸ τελευτῶν ὃ ἔστι καλόν

This is the true approach to the mystery of Love: upwards step by step, starting from beautiful things, from shapely bodies to noble pursuits, thence to profound knowledge, finally attaining awareness of the very essence of beauty.

Symposium 211b

from the speech of Diotima

324 ὅτι ἐνταῦθα αὐτῷ μοναχοῦ γενήσεται, ὁρῶντι ᾧ ὁρατὸν τὸ καλόν, τίκτειν οὐκ εἴδωλα ἀρετῆς ... ἀλλ' ἀληθῆ ... τεκόντι δὲ ἀρετὴν ἀληθῆ καὶ θρεψαμένῳ ὑπάρχει θεοφιλεῖ γενέσθαι, καὶ εἴπέρ τῳ ἄλλῳ ἀνθρώπων ἀθανάτῳ

Thus only will he recognize Beauty itself, not images of it but as true virtue and, fostering virtue, attain the love of god and touch immortality.

Symposium 212a

from the speech of Diotima

325 Σωκράτης ... αὖ ἀγνοεῖ πάντα καὶ οὐδὲν οἶδεν ... οὔτ' εἴ τις καλός ἐστι μέλει αὐτῷ οὐδέν ... οὔτ' εἴ τις πλούσιος, οὔτ' εἰ ἄλλην τινὰ τιμὴν ἔχων ... ἡγεῖται δὲ πάντα ταῦτα τὰ κτήματα οὐδενὸς ἄξια ... εἰρωνευόμενος δὲ καὶ παίζων πάντα τὸν βίον

Socrates likes to say he's ignorant and knows nothing; little he cares whether a person is beautiful or rich or famous. He considers all these possessions beneath contempt: his whole life is one big game – a game of irony.

Translated by Alexander Nehamas and Paul Woodruff (1989)

Symposium 216d–e

from Alcibiades' eulogy of Socrates

326 τὴν καρδίαν γὰρ ἢ ψυχὴν ἢ ὅ τι δεῖ αὐτὸ ὀνομάσαι πληγείς τε καὶ δηχθεὶς ὑπὸ τῶν ἐν φιλοσοφίᾳ λόγων, οἳ ἔχονται ἐχίδνης ἀγριώτερον, νέου ψυχῆς μὴ ἀφυοῦς

My heart, or my soul, or whatever you want to call it, which has been struck and bitten by philosophy, whose grip on young and eager souls is much more vicious than a viper's.

Translated by Alexander Nehamas and Paul Woodruff (1989)

Symposium 218a

from Alcibiades' eulogy of Socrates

327 ἤ τοι τῆς διανοίας ὄψις ἄρχεται ὀξὺ βλέπειν ὅταν ἡ τῶν ὀμμάτων τῆς ἀκμῆς λήγειν ἐπιχειρῇ

The mind's sight becomes sharp only when the body's eyes go past their prime.

Translated by Alexander Nehamas and Paul Woodruff (1989)

Symposium 219a

spoken by Socrates

328 οἷον ἐλαίου ῥεῦμα ἀψοφητὶ ῥέοντος

Like a stream of oil that flows without sound.

Translated by Harold North Fowler (1921)

Theaetetus 144b

describing how smoothly Theaetetus 'advances toward learning and investigation'

329 τῇ δέ γ' ἐμῇ τέχνῃ τῆς μαιεύσεως τὰ μὲν ἄλλα ὑπάρχει ὅσα ἐκείναις, διαφέρει δὲ τῷ τε ἄνδρας ἀλλὰ μὴ γυναῖκας μαιεύεσθαι καὶ τῷ τὰς ψυχὰς αὐτῶν τικτούσας ἐπισκοπεῖν ἀλλὰ μὴ τὰ σώματα. μέγιστον δὲ τοῦτ' ἔνι τῇ ἡμετέρᾳ τέχνῃ, βασανίζειν δυνατὸν εἶναι παντὶ τρόπῳ, πότερον εἴδωλον καὶ ψεῦδος ἀποτίκτει τοῦ νέου ἡ διάνοια ἢ γόνιμόν τε καὶ ἀληθές

My art of midwifery is just like theirs in most respects. The difference is that I attend men and not women, and that I watch over the labour of their souls, not of their bodies. And the most important thing about my art is the ability to apply all possible tests to the offspring, to determine whether the young mind is being delivered of a phantom, that is, an error, or a fertile truth.

Translated by M.J. Levett, rev. Myles Burnyeat (1997)

Theaetetus 150b

330 τὸ γὰρ θερμόν τε καὶ πῦρ, ὃ δὴ καὶ τἆλλα γεννᾷ καὶ ἐπιτροπεύει

Heat and fire, parent and guardian of all things.

Theaetetus 153a

331 ἡ τῶν σωμάτων ἕξις οὐχ ὑπὸ ἡσυχίας μὲν καὶ ἀργίας διόλλυται, ὑπὸ γυμνασίων δὲ καὶ κινήσεων ἐπὶ τὸ πολὺ σῴζεται;

Is not the body destroyed by idleness and inactivity, whilst it is preserved by exercise?

Theaetetus 153b

332 μάλα γὰρ φιλοσόφου τοῦτο τὸ πάθος, τὸ θαυμάζειν· οὐ γὰρ ἄλλη ἀρχὴ φιλοσοφίας ἢ αὕτη

This is the passion of a philosopher, the desire to know; for philosophy begins in wonder.

Theaetetus 155d

333 ὅτι ἡμεῖς μὲν αὐτὸν ὥσπερ θεὸν ἐθαυμάζομεν ἐπὶ σοφίᾳ, ὁ δ' ἄρα ἐτύγχανεν ὢν εἰς φρόνησιν οὐδὲν βελτίων βατράχου γυρίνου

While we were honouring him like a god for his wisdom, he was after all no better in intellect than any other man, or, for that matter, a tadpole.

Translated by Harold North Fowler (1921)

Theaetetus 161c

of Protagoras

334 αὐτὸς τὰ αὑτοῦ ἕκαστος μόνος δοξάσει, ταῦτα δὲ πάντα ὀρθὰ καὶ ἀληθῆ

Each man is to form his own opinions by himself, and these opinions are always right and true.

Translated by Harold North Fowler (1921)

Theaetetus 161d

commenting on Protagoras' assertions

335 οὐδὲ γὰρ αὐτῶν ἀπέχεται τοῦ εὐδοκιμεῖν χάριν ... ἡ διάνοια αὐτοῦ, ταῦτα πάντα ἡγησαμένη σμικρὰ καὶ οὐδέν, ἀτιμάσασα πανταχῇ πέτεται κατὰ Πίνδαρον τᾶς τε γᾶς ὑπένερθε καὶ τὰ ἐπίπεδα γεωμετροῦσα, οὐρανοῦ θ' ὕπερ ἀστρονομοῦσα, καὶ πᾶσαν πάντῃ φύσιν ἐρευνωμένη τῶν ὄντων ἑκάστου ὅλου

He [the philosopher] does not hold aloof in order to gain a reputation; his mind, disdaining the small and worthless, pursues its winged way throughout the universe, surveying the earth and what is below it, as Pindar says, studying the heavens, investigating the whole nature of each and all in their entirety.

Theaetetus 173e

cf. Pindar, Nemean Odes *10.87; but it may also be possible that Plato is quoting from some lost poem*

336 ἀλλ' οὔτ' ἀπολέσθαι τὰ κακὰ δυνατόν ... ὑπεναντίον γάρ τι τῷ ἀγαθῷ ἀεὶ εἶναι ἀνάγκη· οὔτ' ἐν θεοῖς αὐτὰ ἱδρῦσθαι, τὴν δὲ θνητὴν φύσιν καὶ τόνδε τὸν τόπον περιπολεῖ ἐξ ἀνάγκης. διὸ καὶ πειρᾶσθαι χρὴ ἐνθένδε ἐκεῖσε φεύγειν ὅτι τάχιστα. φυγὴ δὲ ὁμοίωσις θεῷ κατὰ τὸ δυνατόν· ὁμοίωσις δὲ δίκαιον καὶ ὅσιον μετὰ φρονήσεως γενέσθαι

Evils can never pass away, for there must always remain something which is antagonistic to good; having no place among the gods, of necessity evils hover around the mortal nature and this earth. Therefore we ought to leave this earth as quickly as we can; and to escape is to become like god, as far as this is possible; and to become like him is to become holy, just and wise.

Theaetetus 176a

337 ἀγνοοῦσι γὰρ ζημίαν ἀδικίας ... οὐ γάρ ἐστιν ἣν δοκοῦσιν, πληγαί τε καὶ θάνατοι ... ἀλλὰ ἣν ἀδύνατον ἐκφυγεῖν ... ἐνθάδε τὴν αὐτοῖς ὁμοιότητα τῆς διαγωγῆς ἀεὶ ἕξουσι, κακοὶ κακοῖς συνόντες ... καὶ τελευτήσαντας αὐτοὺς ὁ τῶν κακῶν καθαρὸς τόπος οὐ δέξεται

The penalty of unrighteousness is not what some think it is, scourging and death, but a penalty which it is impossible to escape: here on earth the unrighteous will continue to live as evil men associating with evil; and when they die, the blessed place that is pure of evil will never admit them.

Theaetetus 176d–177a

338 ἡ ῥητορικὴ ἐκείνη πως ἀπομαραίνεται, ὥστε παίδων μηδὲν δοκεῖν διαφέρειν

Their brilliant rhetoric withers away, so that they seem no better than children.

Translated by Harold North Fowler (1921)

Theaetetus 177b.6

339 περὶ μὲν οὖν τούτων ... ἀποστῶμεν· εἰ δὲ μή, πλείω ἀεὶ ἐπιρρέοντα καταχώσει ἡμῶν τὸν ἐξ ἀρχῆς λόγον

Let us turn away from these matters; if we do not, they will come on like an ever-rising flood and bury in silt our original argument.

Translated by Harold North Fowler (1921)

Theaetetus 177b.7

340 θὲς δή μοι λόγου ἕνεκα ἐν ταῖς ψυχαῖς ἡμῶν ἐνὸν κήρινον ἐκμαγεῖον, τῷ μὲν μεῖζον, τῷ δ' ἔλαττον, καὶ τῷ μὲν καθαρωτέρου κηροῦ, τῷ δὲ κοπρωδεστέρου, καὶ σκληροτέρου, ἐνίοις δὲ ὑγροτέρου, ἔστι δ' οἷς μετρίως ἔχοντος ... δῶρον τοίνυν αὐτὸ φῶμεν εἶναι τῆς τῶν Μουσῶν μητρὸς Μνημοσύνης, καὶ εἰς τοῦτο, ὅ τι ἂν βουληθῶμεν μνημονεῦσαι ὧν ἂν ἴδωμεν ἢ ἀκούσωμεν ἢ αὐτοὶ ἐννοήσωμεν, ὑπέχοντας αὐτὸ ταῖς αἰσθήσεσι καὶ ἐννοίαις, ἀποτυποῦσθαι, ὥσπερ δακτυλίων σημεῖα ἐνσημαινομένους· καὶ ὃ μὲν ἂν ἐκμαγῇ, μνημονεύειν τε καὶ ἐπίστασθαι ἕως ἂν ἐνῇ τὸ εἴδωλον αὐτοῦ· ὃ δ' ἂν ἐξαλειφθῇ ἢ μὴ οἷόν τε γένηται ἐκμαγῆναι, ἐπιλελῆσθαί τε καὶ μὴ ἐπίστασθαι

Assume, then, that there exists in our mind a block of wax, larger, smaller, purer, dirtier, moister in different men, of middling quality in some. Let us say that this tablet is a gift of Memory, the mother of the Muses, allowing us to remember anything we see or hear or think of, imprinting on it our perceptions and thoughts as if using a signet ring; and whatever is impressed we remember and know as long as the image lasts; but when it is effaced we forget and do not know.

Theaetetus 191c

341 νῦν αὖ ἐν ἑκάστῃ ψυχῇ ποιήσωμεν περιστερεῶνά τινα παντοδαπῶν ὀρνίθων, τὰς μὲν κατ' ἀγέλας οὔσας χωρὶς τῶν ἄλλων, τὰς δὲ κατ' ὀλίγας, ἐνίας δὲ μόνας διὰ πασῶν ὅπῃ ἂν τύχωσι πετομένας ... παιδίων μὲν ὄντων φάναι χρὴ εἶναι τοῦτο τὸ ἀγγεῖον κενόν, ἀντὶ δὲ τῶν ὀρνίθων ἐπιστήμας νοῆσαι· ἣν δ' ἂν ἐπιστήμην κτησάμενος καθείρξῃ εἰς τὸν περίβολον, φάναι αὐτὸν μεμαθηκέναι ἢ ηὑρηκέναι τὸ πρᾶγμα οὗ ἦν αὕτη ἡ ἐπιστήμη, καὶ τὸ ἐπίστασθαι τοῦτ' εἶναι

Let us now assume that in the mind of each of us there is an aviary of all sorts of birds; some in flocks, some solitary, flying hither and thither among them all. We may suppose that the birds are kinds of knowledge, and that when we were children this aviary was empty; whatever kind of knowledge a person acquires and confines in the enclosure, he may be said to have mastered it; and that just this is knowing.

Theaetetus 197d

342 Ἕλληνες ἀεὶ παῖδές ἐστε, γέρων δὲ Ἕλλην οὐκ ἔστιν ... νέοι ἐστέ τὰς ψυχὰς πάντες

You Greeks are always children: there is not such a thing as an old Greek. You are young in soul, every one of you.

Translated by R.G. Bury (1929)

Timaeus 22b

spoken by an exasperated elderly Egyptian priest to Solon who asked him endless questions; Plato thought this a very flattering remark

343 πολλαὶ κατὰ πολλὰ φθοραὶ γεγόνασιν ἀνθρώπων καὶ ἔσονται, πυρὶ μὲν καὶ ὕδατι μέγισται, μυρίοις δὲ ἄλλοις ἕτεραι βραχύτεραι

There have been and there will be many and diverse destructions of mankind, of which the greatest are by fire and water, and lesser ones by countless means.

Translated by R.G. Bury (1929)

Timaeus 22c

344 νῆσον γὰρ πρὸ τοῦ στόματος εἶχεν ὃ καλεῖτε, ὥς φατε, ὑμεῖς Ἡρακλέους στήλας, ἡ δὲ νῆσος ἅμα Λιβύης ἦν καὶ Ἀσίας μείζων ... ἐν δὲ δὴ τῇ Ἀτλαντίδι νήσῳ ταύτῃ μεγάλη συνέστη καὶ θαυμαστὴ δύναμις βασιλέων

There was an island situated in front of the straits called the Pillars of Heracles, larger than Africa and Asia put together; and this island of Atlantis was ruled by kings of great and marvellous power.

Timaeus 24e–25a

told to Solon by an Egyptian priest (as recounted by Critias); the Pillars of Heracles are the Straits of Gibraltar

345 τὰ παίδων μαθήματα θαυμαστὸν ἔχει τι μνημεῖον

Marvellous, indeed, is the way in which the lessons of one's childhood 'grip the mind'.

Translated by R.G. Bury (1929)

Timaeus 26b

346 τὸν μὲν οὖν ποιητὴν καὶ πατέρα τοῦδε τοῦ παντὸς εὑρεῖν τε ἔργον καὶ εὑρόντα εἰς πάντας ἀδύνατον λέγειν

To discover the Maker and Father of this Universe were a task indeed; and having discovered him, to declare him unto all men were a thing impossible.

Translated by R.G. Bury (1929)

Timaeus 28c

347 εἰ μὲν δὴ καλός ἐστιν ὅδε ὁ κόσμος ὅ τε δημιουργὸς ἀγαθός, δῆλον ὡς πρὸς τὸ ἀΐδιον ἔβλεπεν ... ὁ μὲν γὰρ κάλλιστος τῶν γεγονότων, ὁ δ' ἄριστος τῶν αἰτίων

If it be that this Cosmos is beautiful and its Creator good, it is clear that his gaze is fixed on the Eternal; for the Cosmos is the fairest of all that has come into existence, and he the best of all the Causes.

Translated by R.G. Bury (1929)

Timaeus 29a

348 πέρι θεῶν καὶ τῆς τοῦ παντὸς γενέσεως μὴ δυνατοὶ γιγνώμεθα πάντη πάντως αὐτοὺς αὑτοῖς ὁμολογουμένους λόγους καὶ ἀπηκριβωμένους ἀποδοῦναι

Regarding the gods and the generation of the Universe we prove unable to give accounts that are always in all respects self-consistent and perfectly exact.

Translated by R.G. Bury (1929)

Timaeus 29c

349 ἀγαθῷ δὲ οὐδεὶς περὶ οὐδενὸς οὐδέποτε ἐγγίγνεται φθόνος

One who is good will never be afflicted by envy.

Timaeus 29e

350 βουληθεὶς γὰρ ὁ θεὸς ἀγαθὰ μὲν πάντα, φλαῦρον δὲ μηδὲν εἶναι κατὰ δύναμιν

God desired that, as far as possible, all things should be good and nothing evil.

Translated by R.G. Bury (1929)

Timaeus 30a

351 θεὸς ... εἰς τάξιν αὐτὸ ἤγαγεν ἐκ τῆς ἀταξίας

God reduced it to order from disorder.

Translated by Desmond Lee (1956)

Timaeus 30a

of the universe; cf. Plutarch, Table Talk *615f*

352 ὀρθῶς ἕνα οὐρανὸν προσειρήκαμεν, ἢ πολλοὺς καὶ ἀπείρους λέγειν ἦν ὀρθότερον;

Are we right in describing the Heaven as one, or would it be more correct to speak of heavens as many or infinite in number?

Translated by R.G. Bury (1929)

Timaeus 31a

cf. Plotinus 3

353 τόνδε ἕνα ὅλον ὅλων ἐξ ἁπάντων τέλεον καὶ ἀγήρων καὶ ἄνοσον αὐτὸν ἐτεκτήνατο

He fashioned it to be One single Whole, compounded of all wholes, perfect and ageless and unailing.

Translated by R.G. Bury (1929)

Timaeus 33a

of the universe

354 διὸ καὶ σφαιροειδές, ἐκ μέσου πάντῃ πρὸς τὰς τελευτὰς ἴσον ἀπέχον, κυκλοτερὲς αὐτὸ ἐτορνεύσατο, πάντων τελεώτατον ὁμοιότατόν τε αὐτὸ ἑαυτῷ σχημάτων

He wrought it into a round, in the shape of a sphere, equidistant in all directions from the centre to the extremities, which of all shapes is the most perfect and the most self-similar.

Translated by R.G. Bury (1929)

Timaeus 33b

of the universe

355 ὀμμάτων τε γὰρ ἐπεδεῖτο οὐδέν, ὁρατὸν γὰρ οὐδὲν ὑπελείπετο ἔξωθεν, οὐδ' ἀκοῆς, οὐδὲ γὰρ ἀκουστόν· πνεῦμά τε οὐκ ἦν περιεστὸς δεόμενον ἀναπνοῆς

Of eyes it had no need, since outside of it there was nothing visible left; nor yet of hearing, since neither was there anything audible; nor was there any air surrounding it which called for respiration.

Translated by R.G. Bury (1929)

Timaeus 33c

beyond the universe

356 διὸ δὴ κατὰ ταὐτὰ ἐν τῷ αὐτῷ καὶ ἐν ἑαυτῷ περιαγαγὼν αὐτὸ ἐποίησε κύκλῳ κινεῖσθαι στρεφόμενον

He spun it round uniformly in the same spot and within itself and made it move revolving in a circle.

Translated by R.G. Bury (1929)

Timaeus 34a

of the universe

357 ὁ δὲ καὶ γενέσει καὶ ἀρετῇ προτέραν καὶ πρεσβυτέραν ψυχὴν σώματος, ὡς

δεσπότιν καὶ ἄρξουσαν ἀρξομένου

God constructed soul to be older than body and prior in birth and excellence, since soul was to be the mistress and ruler and body the ruled.

Translated by R.G. Bury (1929)

Timaeus 34c

358 ψυχὴ δ' ἐκ μέσου πρὸς τὸν ἔσχατον οὐρανὸν πάντῃ διαπλακεῖσα κύκλῳ τε αὐτὸν ἔξωθεν περικαλύψασα, αὐτὴ τε ἐν αὑτῇ στρεφομένη, θείαν ἀρχὴν ἤρξατο ἀπαύστου καὶ ἔμφρονος βίου πρὸς τὸν σύμπαντα χρόνον

Soul, being woven throughout the universe every way from the centre to the extremity, enveloping it in a circle from without and revolving within itself, initiated a divine beginning of unceasing and intelligent life lasting throughout all time.

Translated by R.G. Bury (1929)

Timaeus 36e

359 συστήσας δὲ τὸ πᾶν διεῖλε ψυχὰς ἰσαρίθμους τοῖς ἄστροις, ἔνειμέ θ' ἑκάστην πρὸς ἕκαστον

When he had created the universe he divided it into stars equal in number to the souls; each soul he assigned to one star.

Timaeus 41d

of the Creator

360 καὶ ὁ μὲν εὖ τὸν προσήκοντα χρόνον βιούς, πάλιν εἰς τὴν τοῦ συννόμου πορευθεὶς οἴκησιν ἄστρου, βίον εὐδαίμονα καὶ συνήθη ἕξοι

He that has lived his appointed time well shall return again to his abode in his native star, and shall gain a life that is blessed and congenial.

Translated by R.G. Bury (1929)

Timaeus 42b

361 νῦν δ' ἡμέρα τε καὶ νὺξ ὀφθεῖσαι ... μεμηχάνηνται μὲν ἀριθμόν, χρόνου δὲ ἔννοιαν περί τε τῆς τοῦ παντὸς φύσεως ζήτησιν ἔδοσαν· ἐξ ὧν ἐπορισάμεθα φιλοσοφίας γένος, οὗ μεῖζον ἀγαθὸν οὔτ' ἦλθεν οὔθ' ἥξει ποτὲ τῷ θνητῷ γένει δωρηθὲν ἐκ θεῶν

Our ability to see the periods of day and night has led to the understanding of number and the notion of time and opened the path of inquiry into the nature of the universe; these pursuits have given us philosophy, a gift from the gods to the mortal race whose value neither has been nor ever will be surpassed.

Translated by Donald J. Zeyl, ed. John M. Cooper (1997)

Timaeus 47a

362 θεὸν ἡμῖν ἀνευρεῖν δωρήσασθαί τε ὄψιν, ἵνα τὰς ἐν οὐρανῷ κατιδόντες τοῦ νοῦ περιόδους χρησαίμεθα ἐπὶ τὰς περιφορὰς τὰς τῆς παρ' ἡμῖν διανοήσεως ... ἀταράκτοις τεταραγμένας

God devised and bestowed upon us vision to behold the revolutions of Reason in the Heaven and use them for the revolvings of the reasoning that is within us, the perturbable to the imperturbable.

Translated by R.G. Bury (1929)

Timaeus 47b

363 ὅσον τ' αὖ μουσικῆς φωνῇ χρήσιμον πρὸς ἀκοὴν ἕνεκα ἁρμονίας ἐστὶ δοθέν· ἡ δὲ ἁρμονία, συγγενεῖς ἔχουσα φορὰς ταῖς ἐν ἡμῖν τῆς ψυχῆς περιόδοις, ... οὐκ ἐφ' ἡδονὴν ἄλογον ... ἀλλ' ἐπὶ τὴν γεγονυῖαν ἐν ἡμῖν ἀνάρμοστον ψυχῆς περίοδον εἰς κατακόσμησιν καὶ συμφωνίαν ἑαυτῇ σύμμαχος ὑπὸ Μουσῶν δέδοται

Music too, in so far as it uses audible sound, was bestowed for the sake of harmony; and harmony, which has motions akin to the revolutions of the soul within us, was given by the Muses not as an aid to irrational pleasure, but as an auxiliary to the inner revolution of the soul, when it has lost its harmony, to assist in restoring it to order and concord with itself.

Translated by R.G. Bury (1929)

Timaeus 47c

364 μεμιγμένη γὰρ οὖν ἡ τοῦδε τοῦ κόσμου γένεσις ἐξ ἀνάγκης τε καὶ νοῦ συστάσεως ἐγεννήθη

In truth, this Cosmos in its origin was generated as a compound, from the combination of Necessity and Reason.

Translated by R.G. Bury (1929)

Timaeus 48a

365 τοῦ μετρίου καὶ ἀναγκαίου διὰ μαργότητα πολλῷ χρησοίμεθα πλέονι

Because of our greed we consume far more than what is moderate and necessary.

Translated by R.G. Bury (1929)

Timaeus 72e

366 νόσον μὲν δὴ ψυχῆς ἄνοιαν συγχωρητέον, δύο δ' ἀνοίας γένη, τὸ μὲν μανίαν, τὸ δὲ ἀμαθίαν

Folly is a disease of the soul; and of folly there are two kinds, the one of which is madness, the other ignorance.

Translated by R.G. Bury (1929)

Timaeus 86b

367 ἡδονὰς δὲ καὶ λύπας ὑπερβαλλούσας τῶν νόσων μεγίστας θετέον τῇ ψυχῇ

We must maintain that pleasures and pains in excess are the greatest of the soul's diseases.

Translated by R.G. Bury (1929)

Timaeus 86b

368 οὔθ' ὁρᾶν οὔτε ἀκούειν ὀρθὸν οὐδὲν δύναται, λυττᾷ δὲ καὶ λογισμοῦ μετασχεῖν ἥκιστα τότε δὴ δυνατός

He is unable either to see or hear; he is distraught and wholly incapable of exercising reason.

Translated by R.G. Bury (1929)

Timaeus 86c

of one in sore distress

369 ἡ περὶ τὰ ἀφροδίσια ἀκολασία ... νόσος ψυχῆς γέγονεν

Sexual incontinence constitutes a disease of the soul.

Translated by R.G. Bury (1929)

Timaeus 86d

370 κακὸς ἑκὼν οὐδείς

No one is voluntarily wicked.

Translated by R.G. Bury (1929)

Timaeus 86d

371 ποικίλλει μὲν εἴδη δυσκολίας καὶ δυσθυμίας παντοδαπά, ποικίλλει δὲ θρασύτητός τε καὶ δειλίας, ἔτι δὲ λήθης ἅμα καὶ δυσμαθίας

They give rise to all varieties of bad temper and bad spirits, and they give rise to all manner of rashness and cowardice, and of forgetfulness also, as well as of stupidity.

Translated by R.G. Bury (1929)

Timaeus 87a

of humours that are confined within

372 αἰτιατέον μὲν τοὺς φυτεύοντας ἀεὶ τῶν φυτευομένων μᾶλλον καὶ τοὺς τρέφοντας τῶν τρεφομένων

We must always blame the begetters more than the begotten, and the nurses more than the nurslings.

Translated by R.G. Bury (1929)

Timaeus 87b

when children are not instructed on forestalling evil

373 μήτε τὴν ψυχὴν ἄνευ σώματος κινεῖν μήτε σῶμα ἄνευ ψυχῆς, ἵνα ἀμυνομένω γίγνησθον ἰσορρόπω καὶ ὑγιῆ

Do not exercise the soul without the body nor the body without the soul, so that they may be evenly matched and sound of health.

Translated by R.G. Bury (1929)

Timaeus 88b

374 Τὴν ψυχὴν Ἀγάθωνα φιλῶν ἐπὶ χείλεσιν ἔσχον·
ἦλθε γὰρ ἡ τλήμων ὡς διαβησομένη.

While kissing Agathon, my soul leapt to my lips,
as if fain, alas! to cross over to him.

Translated by R.D. Hicks (1925)

Epigram 1 (Diehl) – 5.78 (*AG*)

375 Ἀστέρας εἰσαθρεῖς, Ἀστὴρ ἐμός· εἴθε γενοίμην
οὐρανός, ὡς πολλοῖσ' ὄμμασιν εἰς σὲ βλέπω.

You're gazing at the stars, my star; oh, would I were the skies
That I might bend upon your face a million eyes!

Translated by Kathleen Freeman (1947)

Epigram 4 (Diehl) – 7.669 (*AG*)

376 Ἀστὴρ πρὶν μὲν ἔλαμπες ἐνὶ ζωοῖσιν Ἑῷος,
νῦν δὲ θανὼν λάμπεις Ἕσπερος ἐν φθιμένοις.

Thou wert the morning star among the living

Ere thy fair had fled;
Now, having died, thou art as Hesperus, giving
New splendour to the dead.

Translated by Percy Bysshe Shelley (written 1818; printed posthumously 1839)

Epigram 5 (Diehl) – 7.670 (*AG*)

Hesperus, the Evening Star, is the planet Venus

377 Ἀρχεάνασσαν ἔχω τὴν ἐκ Κολοφῶνος ἑταίραν,
ἧς καὶ ἐπὶ ῥυτίδων πικρὸς ἔπεστιν ἔρως.
ἆ δειλοί, νεότητος ἀπαντήσαντες ἐκείνης
πρωτοπλόου, δι' ὅσης ἤλθετε πυρκαϊῆς.

The courtesan of Colophon, Archeanassa 's mine,
And though her face is wrinkled, love burns in every line.
I pity you who met her when she was young and new
To passion – what a furnace she must have led you through!

Translated by Kathleen Freeman (1947)

Epigram 8 (Diehl) – 7.217 (*AG*)

Archeanassa was said to be Plato's mistress

378 Οἵδε ποτ' Αἰγαίοιο βαρύβρομον οἶδμα λιπόντες
Ἐκβατάνων πεδίῳ κείμεθ' ἐνὶ μεσάτῳ.
χαῖρε, κλυτή ποτε πατρὶς Ἐρέτρια, χαίρετ', Ἀθῆναι,
γείτονες Εὐβοίης, χαῖρε, θάλασσα φίλη.

We who left behind the roar of Aegean waves
now lie in the land-locked heart of the Ecbatana plain.
Goodbye to our glorious home, Eretria,
goodbye to Athens, neighbour of our Euboea,
O goodbye to the sea we love.

Translated by Edmund Keeley (2010)

Epigram 10 (Diehl) – 7.256 (*AG*)

speaking of the Eretrian exiles settled in Persia by Darius

379 Αἱ Χάριτες τέμενός τι λαβεῖν ὅπερ οὐχὶ πεσεῖται
ζηλοῦσαι, ψυχὴν ηὗρον Ἀριστοφάνους.

The Graces, seeking for themselves a shrine that would not fall, found the soul of Aristophanes.

Translated by J.M. Edmonds (1931), rev. John M. Cooper (1997)

Epigram 14 (Diehl)

380 Ἡ σοβαρὸν γελάσασα καθ' Ἑλλάδος, ἥ ποτ' ἐραστῶν
ἑσμὸν ἐπὶ προθύροις Λαῒς ἔχουσα νέων,
τῇ Παφίῃ τὸ κάτοπτρον, ἐπεὶ τοίη μὲν ὁρᾶσθαι
οὐκ ἐθέλω, οἵη δ' ἦν πάρος οὐ δύναμαι.

I, Lais, who laughed disdainfully at Greece
and kept my lovers swarming by the door,
to Aphrodite now I dedicate this mirror,
for I do no more wish to see me as I am,
and cannot see me as I was.

Epigram 15 (Diehl) – 6.1 (*AG*)

Lais' Mirror, a dedicatory epigram

381 Ἁ Κύπρις τὰν Κύπριν ἐνὶ Κνίδῳ εἶπεν ἰδοῦσα·
φεῦ, φεῦ, ποῦ γυμνὴν εἶδέ με Πραξιτέλης;

'Shame!' Cypris cries her statue when she sees,
'You saw me naked! When, Praxiteles?'

Translated by Humbert Wolfe (1927)

Epigram 24 (Diehl) – 16.162 (*AG*)

of Praxiteles' famous statue of Aphrodite, the 'Cnidian Venus'

382 Ὑψίκομον παρὰ τάνδε καθίζεο φωνήεσσαν
φρίσσουσαν πυκινοῖς κῶνον ὑπὸ ζεφύροις,
καί σοι καχλάζουσιν ἐμοῖς παρὰ νάμασι σῦριγξ
θελγομένων ἄξει κῶμα κατὰ βλεφάρων.

Sit down by this high-foliaged voiceful pine
that rustles her branches beneath the western breezes,
and beside my chattering waters Pan's pipe
shall bring drowsiness down on thy enchanted eyelids.

Translated by J.W. MacKail (1890)

Epigram 27 (Diehl) – 16.13 (*AG*)

383 Ναυηγοῦ τάφος εἰμί, ὁ δ' ἀντίον ἐστὶ γεωργοῦ·
ὡς ἁλὶ καὶ γαίῃ ξυνὸς ὕπεστ' Ἀίδης.

Mine is a watery grave; opposite, in solid earth, a farmer's;
beneath both sea and land there is a common Hades.

Epigram 28 (Diehl) – 7.265 (*AG*)

384 Αἰὼν πάντα φέρει· δολιχὸς χρόνος οἶδεν ἀμείβειν
οὔνομα καὶ μορφὴν καὶ φύσιν ἠδὲ τύχην.

Time brings everything; length of years can change names, forms, nature, fortune.

Translated by W.R. Paton (1917)

Epigrams 31 (Diehl) – 9.51 (*AG*)

385 οὐκ ἄρα τειχῶν οὐδὲ τριήρων οὐδὲ νεωρίων δέονται αἱ πόλεις ... εἰ μέλλουσιν εὐδαιμονήσειν, οὐδὲ πλήθους οὐδὲ μεγέθους ἄνευ ἀρετῆς

It is not walls, triremes or shipyards that cities need to prosper, nor multitude or size, but virtue.

*Alcibiades I** 134b

386 ἐγὼ μὲν οὖν ἀπορῶ μὴ ὡς ἀληθῶς μάτην θεοὺς ἄνθρωποι αἰτιῶνται, ἐξ ἐκείνων φάμενοι κακά σφισιν εἶναι· οἱ δὲ καὶ αὐτοὶ σφῇσιν εἴτε ἀτασθαλίαισιν εἴτε ἀφροσύναις χρὴ εἰπεῖν, ὑπὲρ μόρον ἄλγε' ἔχουσι

Men falsely blame the gods as authors of their misfortune; it is their own recklessness and folly that cause more than their destined sorrows.

*Alcibiades II** 142d

quoting Homer 245

387 οὐ γὰρ οἶμαι τοιοῦτόν ἐστι τὸ τῶν θεῶν ὥστε ὑπὸ δώρων παράγεσθαι οἷον κακὸν τοκιστήν

It is not, I think, the way of the gods to be seduced with gifts, like evil moneylenders.

*Alcibiades II** 149e.3

388 γὰρ ἂν δεινὸν εἴη εἰ πρὸς τὰ δῶρα καὶ τὰς θυσίας ἀποβλέπουσιν ἡμῶν οἱ θεοὶ ἀλλὰ μὴ πρὸς τὴν ψυχήν, ἄν τις ὅσιος καὶ δίκαιος ὢν τυγχάνῃ

It would be strange and sorry if the gods took more account of our gifts and offerings than of our souls, and whether there is holiness and justice to be found in them.

Translated by D.S. Hutchinson (1997)

*Alcibiades II** 149e.6

389 τοὺς ἀσκοῦντας μὲν τὰ σώματα, τῆς δὲ ψυχῆς ἠμεληκότας ἕτερόν τι πράττειν τοιοῦτον, τοῦ μὲν ἄρξοντος ἀμελεῖν, περὶ δὲ τὸ ἀρξόμενον ἐσπουδακέναι

Those who exercise their bodies and neglect their soul overlook the ruling element and busy themselves with the part to be ruled.

*Cleitophon** 407e

390 χρόνος ἡλίου κίνησις, μέτρον φορᾶς

Time is the movement of the sun, a measure of its motion.

*Definitions** 411b

391 ψυχὴ τὸ αὐτὸ κινοῦν· αἰτία κινήσεως ζωτικῆς ζῴων

Soul is that which moves itself; it is the cause of vital processes in living creatures.

Translated by D.S. Hutchinson (1997)

*Definitions** 411c

392 δικαιοσύνη ὁμόνοια τῆς ψυχῆς πρὸς αὑτήν

Righteousness is the concord of the soul with itself.

*Definitions** 411d

393 αὐτάρκεια τελειότης κτήσεως ἀγαθῶν· ἕξις καθ' ἣν οἱ ἔχοντες αὐτοὶ αὑτῶν ἄρχουσιν

Self-sufficiency is the perfect way of owning possessions; it is a habit by which owners keep full control of themselves.

*Definitions** 412b

394 ἐλευθερία ἡγεμονία βίου· αὐτοκράτεια ἐπὶ παντί· ἐξουσία τοῦ καθ' ἑαυτὸν ἐν βίῳ

Freedom is power over life; power over oneself; control of one's own life.

*Definitions** 412d

395 εὐφροσύνη ἐπὶ τοῖς τοῦ σώφρονος ἔργοις χαρά

Cheerfulness is joy in doing what a temperate man does.

Translated by D.S. Hutchinson (1997)

*Definitions** 413e.2

396 ὁμόνοια ὁμοδοξία ἀρχόντων καὶ ἀρχομένων ὡς δεῖ ἄρχειν καὶ ἄρχεσθαι

Concord is unanimity between governing and governed on how to govern and be governed.

*Definitions** 413e.8

397 μνήμη διάθεσις ψυχῆς φυλακτικὴ τῆς ἐν αὐτῇ ὑπαρχούσης ἀληθείας

Memory is the soul's disposition to safeguard the truth that exists within us.

*Definitions** 414a.8

398 νόησις ἀρχὴ ἐπιστήμης

Understanding is the beginning of knowledge.

*Definitions** 414a.11

399 φιλοσοφία τῆς τῶν ὄντων ἀεὶ ἐπιστήμης ὄρεξις· ἕξις θεωρητικὴ τοῦ ἀληθοῦς, πῶς ἀληθές· ἐπιμέλεια ψυχῆς μετὰ λόγου ὀρθοῦ

Philosophy is the desire for knowledge of what exists; the state which contemplates the truth, what makes it true; cultivation of the soul, based on correct reason.

Translated by D.S. Hutchinson (1997)

*Definitions** 414b

400 φωνὴ ῥεῦμα διὰ στόματος ἀπὸ διανοίας

The voice is the stream that springs from intelligence.

*Definitions** 414d

401 παιδεία δύναμις θεραπευτικὴ ψυχῆς

Education is intent on cultivating the soul.

*Definitions** 416a.27

402 νομοθετικὴ ἐπιστήμη ποιητικὴ πόλεως ἀγαθῆς

Legislative skill is what establishes a serviceable state.

*Definitions** 416a.29

403 εἴπερ ἀριθμὸν ἐκ τῆς ἀνθρωπίνης φύσεως ἐξέλοιμεν, οὐκ ἄν ποτέ τι φρόνιμοι γενοίμεθα

If we deprive human nature of the use of numbers, we will never attain wisdom.

*Epinomis** 977c

404 τὰς μεγάλας οὐσίας καὶ ὑπερόγκους τῶν τε ἰδιωτῶν καὶ τῶν μονάρχων σχεδόν, ὅσῳπερ ἂν μείζους ὦσιν, τοσούτῳ πλείους καὶ μείζους τοὺς διαβάλλοντας καὶ πρὸς ἡδονὴν μετὰ αἰσχρᾶς βλάβης ὁμιλοῦντας τρεφούσας, οὗ κακὸν οὐδὲν μεῖζον γεννᾷ πλοῦτός τε καὶ ἡ τῆς ἄλλης ἐξουσίας δύναμις

Exorbitant wealth, whether in the hands of citizens or monarchs, breeds ever more numerous slanderers and wastrels; this is the worst result of wealth or power of any sort.

*Letters** 317c (Letter III)

405 κακῶν οὖν οὐ λήξειν τὰ ἀνθρώπινα γένη, πρὶν ἂν ἢ τὸ τῶν φιλοσοφούντων ὀρθῶς γε καὶ ἀληθῶς γένος εἰς ἀρχὰς ἔλθῃ τὰς πολιτικὰς ἢ τὸ τῶν δυναστευόντων ἐν ταῖς πόλεσιν ἔκ τινος μοίρας θείας ὄντως φιλοσοφήσῃ

The ills of the human race will never end until either those who are sincerely and truly lovers of wisdom come into political power, or the rulers of our cities, by the grace of god, learn true philosophy.

Translated by Glen R. Morrow (1962)

*Letters** 326a (Letter VII)

406 θεὸς δὲ ἀνθρώποις σώφροσιν νόμος, ἄφροσιν δὲ ἡδονή

God to sound men is Law; to the foolish, Pleasure.

*Letters** 354e (Letter VIII)

407 ἕκαστος ἡμῶν οὐχ αὑτῷ μόνον γέγονεν, ἀλλὰ τῆς γενέσεως ἡμῶν τὸ μέν τι ἡ πατρὶς μερίζεται, τὸ δέ τι οἱ γεννήσαντες, τὸ δὲ οἱ λοιποὶ φίλοι

None of us is born for himself alone; a part of our existence belongs to our country, a part to our parents, a part to our friends.

Translated by Glen R. Morrow (1962)

*Letters** 358a (Letter IX)

408 καὶ ὅτε ὑπὲρ τῆς πατρίδος ἐστρατευόμην, ὑπέμενον τοὺς κινδύνους, καὶ νῦν ὑπὲρ τοῦ καθήκοντος διὰ φίλον ὑπομενῶ

As I faced dangers when serving in the cause of my country, so I will face them now in the cause of duty for a friend.

Translated by R.D. Hicks (1925)

Diogenes Laertius, *Lives of Eminent Philosophers* 3.24

when told that the hemlock awaits him for speaking in favour of the general Chabrias

409 χρόνον τε γενέσθαι εἰκόνα τοῦ ἀϊδίου

Time is the image of eternity.

Translated in *Bartlett's Familiar Quotations* (1980)

Diogenes Laertius, *Lives of Eminent Philosophers* 3.73

410 νόμου διαιρέσεις δύο· ὁ μὲν γὰρ αὐτοῦ γεγραμμένος, ὁ δὲ ἄγραφος. ᾧ μὲν ἐν ταῖς πόλεσι πολιτευόμεθα, γεγραμμένος ἐστίν· ὁ δὲ κατὰ ἔθη γινόμενος οὗτος ἄγραφος καλεῖται

There is a written and an unwritten law. The one by which we regulate our constitutions in our cities is the written law; that which arises from custom is the unwritten law.

Translated in *Bartlett's Familiar Quotations* (1980)

Diogenes Laertius, *Lives of Eminent Philosophers* 3.86

411 Πλάτων ἀπεφήνατ' ἀεὶ γεωμετρεῖν τὸν θεόν

Plato asserted that god is always doing geometry.

Translated by E.L. Minar, F.H. Sandbach and W.C. Helmbold (1961)

Plutarch, *Table Talk* 718c

412 Πλάτων ἔφη τοὺς ἀγαθοὺς ἄνδρας βίου μὴ μακροῦ, ἀλλὰ λαμπροῦ δεῖσθαι

Plato said that a virtuous man has no need of a long life, but of an illustrious one.

Stobaeus, *Anthology* 3.7.26

413 τοῦ λόγου μέτρον ἐστὶν οὐχ ὁ λέγων, ἀλλ' ὁ ἀκούων

Appraise a speech not by the speaker but the listener.

Stobaeus, *Anthology* 3.36.22

414 ἐρωτηθεὶς πόσην δεῖ οὐσίαν ἔχειν, εἶπεν ὅσην ἔχων οὔτ' ἐπιβουλευθήσῃ οὔτε τῶν ἀναγκαίων ἀπορήσεις

When asked how much property a man should have, Plato replied: 'As much as neither to be envied, nor be in want of anything.'

Stobaeus, *Anthology* 4.31d.123

415 ἀγεωμέτρητος μηδεὶς εἰσίτω

No one may enter who knows not geometry.

Elias, *Commentary to Aristotle's 'Categories'* 118

inscribed over the entrance of Plato's Academy

PLATO COMIC

5th–4th century BC
Athenian comic poet

1 προμηθία γάρ ἐστιν ἀνθρώποις ὁ νοῦς

Forethought is what marks the mind of men.

Fragment 1 (Meineke) – 145 (K-A) – *Sophists*

PLOTINUS

205–270AD
Greek/Egyptian/Roman Neoplatonist philosopher

1 ἄναγε ἐπὶ σαυτὸν καὶ ἴδε ... οἷα ποιητὴς ἀγάλματος, ὃ δεῖ καλὸν γενέσθαι, τὸ μὲν ἀφαιρεῖ, τὸ δὲ ἀπέξεσε, τὸ δὲ λεῖον, τὸ δὲ καθαρὸν ἐποίησεν, ἕως ἔδειξε καλὸν ἐπὶ τῷ ἀγάλματι πρόσωπον

Withdraw into yourself and look within; and act as does the creator of a statue that is to be made beautiful; he cuts away here, he smoothes there, he makes this line lighter, this other purer, until a lovely face has grown upon his work.

Translated by Peter Lorie and Manuela Dunn Mascetti (2010)

Ennead 1.6.9.8

on gaining virtue; cf. Marcus Aurelius 38

2 μεστὰ δὲ πάντα σημείων καὶ σοφός τις ὁ μαθὼν ἐξ ἄλλου ἄλλο

All things are filled with signs, and it is a wise man who can learn about one thing from another.

Translated by A.H. Armstrong (1966)

Ennead 2.3.7.12

3 συνηρτῆσθαι δὴ δεῖ ἀλλήλοις τὰ πάντα, καὶ μὴ μόνον ἐν ἑνὶ τῶν καθ' ἕκαστα τοῦ εὖ εἰρημένου σύμπνοια μία, ἀλλὰ πολὺ μᾶλλον καὶ πρότερον ἐν τῷ παντί, καὶ μίαν ἀρχὴν ἓν πολὺ ζῷον ποιῆσαι καὶ ἐκ πάντων ἕν

All things must be joined to one another; not only must there be in each individual part what is well called a single breath of life but before them, and still more, in the All; and one principle must make the universe a single complex living creature, one from all.

Translated by A.H. Armstrong (1966)

Ennead 2.3.7.16

cf. Plato 352

4 ψυχὴ τὸ αὑτῆς ἔργον ποιεῖν ὡρμημένη – ψυχὴ γὰρ πάντα ποιεῖ ἀρχῆς ἔχουσα λόγον – κἂν εὐθυποροῖ καὶ παράγοιτο αὖ

Soul, then, is set upon doing its own work – for soul, since it has the status of a principle, does everything – and it may keep to the straight path and it may also be led astray.

Translated by A.H. Armstrong (1966)

Ennead 2.3.8.1

cf. Plato, Phaedrus *245c ff.*

5 εἰ οὖν χρόνον τις λέγοι ψυχῆς ἐν κινήσει μεταβατικῇ ἐξ ἄλλου εἰς ἄλλον βίον ζωὴν εἶναι, ἆρ' ἂν δοκοῖ τι λέγειν; εἰ γὰρ αἰών ἐστι ζωὴ ἐν στάσει καὶ τῷ αὐτῷ καὶ ὡσαύτως καὶ ἄπειρος ἤδη

To say that in time the life of the soul consists in the movement by which the soul passes from one state of life to another state of life, does this not indicate something to you? Eternity is life in repose and the soul's identity is infinite.

Ennead 3.7.11.43

6 ὁ σπουδαῖος ... πρὸς δὲ αὐτὸν ὄψις· ἤδη γὰρ οὗτος πρὸς τὸ ἓν καὶ πρὸς τὸ ἥσυχον οὐ μόνον τῶν ἔξω, ἀλλὰ καὶ πρὸς αὑτόν, καὶ πάντα εἴσω

A wise man will look unto himself; not only does he tend to unify and isolate himself from exterior matters, but he turns towards himself, and finds everything in himself.

Ennead 3.8.6.38

7 τὸ δὲ ἰδεῖν καὶ τὸ ἑωρακός ἐστιν οὐκέτι λόγος, ἀλλὰ μεῖζον λόγου καὶ πρὸ λόγου

To actually see goes beyond reasoning; it is above reasoning and comes before it.

Translated in Liddell & Scott

Ennead 6.9.10.7

of mystical vision

PLUTARCH

c.46–c.120AD

Biographer and philosopher from Chaeronea

Parallel Lives

1 οὔτε γὰρ ἱστορίας γράφομεν, ἀλλὰ βίους, οὔτε ταῖς ἐπιφανεστάταις πράξεσι πάντως ἔνεστι δήλωσις ἀρετῆς ἢ κακίας, ἀλλὰ πρᾶγμα βραχὺ πολλάκις καὶ ῥῆμα καὶ παιδιά τις ἔμφασιν ἤθους ἐποίησε μᾶλλον ἢ μάχαι μυριόνεκροι καὶ παρατάξεις αἱ μέγισται καὶ πολιορκίαι πόλεων

I am writing biography, not history, and it is not always in the most distinguished achievements that men's virtues or vices may be best discerned; but very often an action of small note, a short saying, or a jest, distinguish a person's real character more than the greatest sieges, or the most important battles.

Translated by John and William Langhorne (1804)

Alexander 1.2

quoted by Boswell in The Life of Samuel Johnson, *Introductory, 1791; cf. Herodotus 1 and Thucydides 1*

2 ἐπεὶ δὲ ληφθέντα τὸν Πῶρον ὁ Ἀλέξανδρος ἠρώτα, πῶς αὐτῷ χρήσηται, βασιλικῶς εἶπε· προσπυθομένου δὲ μή τι καὶ ἄλλο λέγει, πάντα, εἶπεν, ἔνεστιν ἐν τῷ βασιλικῶς. οὐ μόνον οὖν ἀφῆκεν αὐτὸν ἄρχειν ὧν ἐβασίλευε, σατράπην καλούμενον, ἀλλὰ καὶ προσέθηκε χώραν

On taking Porus prisoner, Alexander asked how he wished to be treated. 'Like a king,' answered Porus. Alexander further asked if he had anything to request, 'Everything,' rejoined Porus, 'is included in the words, "like a king".' Alexander then not only reinstated Porus in his kingdom with the title of satrap, but added a large province to it.

Alexander 60.14

Alexander travelled through modern-day Afghanistan and into the Punjab where he defeated Porus in 326BC

3 ὡς ἀνὴρ Ῥωμαῖος ἀπεπέμπετο γυναῖκα, τῶν δὲ φίλων νουθετούντων αὐτόν, οὐχὶ σώφρων; οὐκ εὔμορφος; οὐχὶ παιδοποιός; προτείνας τὸ ὑπόδημα ... εἶπεν, οὐκ εὐπρεπὴς οὗτος; οὐ νεουργής; ἀλλ' οὐκ ἂν εἰδείη τις ὑμῶν, καθ' ὅ τι θλίβεται μέρος οὑμὸς πούς

A Roman divorced from his wife, being highly blamed by his friends, who demanded, 'Was she not chaste? Was she not fair? Was she not fruitful?' holding out his shoe, he asked them whether it was not new and well made. 'Yet,' added he, 'none of you can tell where it pinches me.'

Translated in *Bartlett's Familiar Quotations* (1980)

Aimilius Paulus 5.2

4 τὰς πόλεις αἱρεῖ τῶν Ἑλλήνων οὐ Φίλιππος, ἀλλὰ τὸ Φιλίππου χρυσίον

Not Philip, but Philip's gold, took the cities of Greece.

Translated in *The New Penguin Dictionary of Quotations* (2006)

Aimilius Paulus 12.10

of Philip II of Macedon; cf. Oracles 21

5 λέγεται γὰρ ὡς, ἀμφοτέρους τινὸς ὁμοῦ διαβάλλοντος πρὸς αὐτόν, εἴποι μὴ δεδιέναι τοὺς παχεῖς τούτους καὶ κομήτας, ἀλλὰ τοὺς ὠχροὺς καὶ λεπτοὺς ἐκείνους

For we are told that when a certain man was accusing both of them to him, he [Caesar] said that he had no fear of those fat and long-haired fellows, but rather of those pale and thin ones.

Translated in *The Oxford Dictionary of Quotations* (2004)

Anthony 11.6

cf. Shakespeare, Julius Caesar *1.2.191: 'Let me have men about me that are fat; yond' Cassius has a lean and hungry look … such men are dangerous'*

6 τὴν δ' ἀρετήν, ὃ μόνον ἐστὶ τῶν θείων ἀγαθῶν ἐφ' ἡμῖν, ἐν ὑστέρῳ τίθενται, κακῶς φρονοῦντες, ὡς τὸν ἐν δυνάμει καὶ τύχῃ μεγάλῃ καὶ ἀρχῇ βίον ἡ μὲν δικαιοσύνη ποιεῖ θεῖον, ἡ δ' ἀδικία θηριώδη

As for virtue, the only divine excellence within our reach, they put it at the bottom of the list, unwisely; since a life spent in power and great fortune and authority needs justice to make it divine; by injustice it is made bestial.

Translated by Bernadotte Perrin (1914)

Aristides 6.5

7 νενικήκατε θαλασσίοις ξύλοις χερσαίους ἀνθρώπους, οὐκ ἐπισταμένους κώπην ἐλαύνειν· ἀλλὰ νῦν πλατεῖα μὲν ἡ Θετταλῶν γῆ, καλὸν δὲ τὸ Βοιώτιον πεδίον ἀγαθοῖς ἱππεῦσιν καὶ ὁπλίταις ἐναγωνίσασθαι

Ye have conquered with your maritime timbers landsmen who know not how to ply the oar; but now, broad is the land of Thessaly and fair the plain of Boeotia for brave horseman and men-at-arms to contend in.

Translated by Bernadotte Perrin (1914)

Aristides 10.1

Mardonius to the Greeks, after Salamis and before the battle of Plataeae, 479BC

8 ἐσθῆτος ποικίλματα καὶ χρυσὸς ἐπὶ σώμασι μαλακοῖς καὶ ψυχαῖς ἀνάνδροις

Ornamented garments and gold to cover soft bodies and unmanly spirits.

Aristides 16.4

9 οὐχ οὕτω τοῦ πολέμου διὰ μῆκος καὶ τύχας δαπανηροῦ γενομένου καὶ πολυτελοῦς, ὡς τὸν δῆμον εἰς διανομὰς καὶ θεωρικὰ καὶ κατασκευὰς ἀγαλμάτων καὶ ἱερῶν προαγαγόντες

Not so much because the war became extravagantly expensive by reason of its length and vicissitudes, as because the people were induced to use public moneys for spectacular entertainments and for statues and sanctuaries.

Aristides 24.5

of increased taxes in Athens

10 ἧς φιλανθρωπίας καὶ χρηστότητος ἔτι πολλὰ καὶ καθ' ἡμᾶς ἡ πόλις ἐκφέρουσα δείγματα θαυμάζεται καὶ ζηλοῦται δικαίως

For such humanity and benevolence, of which the city still gives illustrious examples even in my day, she is justly admired and praised.

Translated by Bernadotte Perrin (1914)

Aristides 27.7

of Athens; last lines of Aristides

11 καὶ γὰρ ἡ πόλις, οἴκων τι σύστημα καὶ κεφάλαιον οὖσα ῥώννυται πρὸς τὰ δημόσια τοῖς ἰδίοις βίοις τῶν πολιτῶν εὐθενούντων

The city is but an organised sum total of households, and has public vigour only as its citizens prosper in their private lives.

Translated by Bernadotte Perrin (1914)

Comparison of Aristides and Cato Major 3.1

12 οὐ γὰρ ἔστι πράττειν μεγάλα φροντίζοντα μικρῶν

You'll never tackle greater tasks if you waste your time on trifles.

Comparison of Aristides and Cato Major 4.2

13 μέγα δ' εἰς πολιτείαν ἐφόδιον οὐχὶ πλοῦτος, ἀλλ' αὐτάρκεια, τῷ μηδενὸς ἰδίᾳ τῶν περιττῶν δεῖσθαι πρὸς οὐδεμίαν ἀσχολίαν ἀπάγουσα τῶν δημοσίων

A great equipment for public service is not wealth, but self-sufficiency, with no need for private excess, allowing unswerving attention to the affairs of state.

Comparison of Aristides and Cato Major 4.2

14 δεῖ δὲ τῇ χρείᾳ σύμμετρον ἔχειν τὴν κτῆσιν

A man should make his gains tally with his needs.

Translated by Bernadotte Perrin (1914)

Comparison of Aristides and Cato Major 4.3

15 μέγα γὰρ τὸ εὐτελὲς καὶ αὔταρκες, ὅτι τῆς ἐπιθυμίας ἅμα καὶ τῆς φροντίδος ἀπαλλάττει τῶν περιττῶν

Great is the simple life, and self-sufficiency, for it frees you from the anxious desire of superfluous things.

Comparison of Aristides and Cato Major 4.5

16 τὸ γὰρ ἀφιλότιμον οὐ μικρὸν εἰς πρᾳότητα πολιτικὴν ἐφόδιον, καὶ τοὐναντίον ἡ φιλοτιμία χαλεπὸν καὶ φθόνου γονιμώτατον

Freedom from ambition is no slight requisite for the gentleness which should mark a statesman; and, on the contrary, ambition is harsh, and the greatest fomenter of envy.

Translated by Bernadotte Perrin (1914)

Comparison of Aristides and Cato Major 5.4

17 ὁ γοῦν πρῶτος ὑπιδέσθαι δοκῶν αὐτοῦ καὶ φοβηθῆναι τῆς πολιτείας ὥσπερ θαλάττης τὰ διαγελῶντα καὶ τὴν ἐν τῷ φιλανθρώπῳ καὶ ἱλαρῷ κεκρυμμένην δεινότητα τοῦ ἤθους καταμαθὼν Κικέρων

Cicero was the first to view Caesar's public policy with suspicion and to fear it as one might the smiling surface of the sea, becoming aware of the powerful character hidden beneath his kindly and cheerful exterior.

Caesar 4.8

18 τὸ πιστεύειν σφόδρα καὶ τὸ λίαν ἀπιστεῖν ἐπισφαλές ἐστι διὰ τὴν ἀνθρωπίνην ἀσθένειαν ... ἐκφερομένην ὅπου μὲν εἰς δεισιδαιμονίαν καὶ τῦφον, ὅπου δ' εἰς ὀλιγωρίαν τῶν θεῶν καὶ περιφρόνησιν

Eager credulity and excessive incredulity are alike dangerous because of the weakness of our human nature, carried away now into vain superstition, and now into contemptuous neglect of the gods.

Translated by Bernadotte Perrin (1914)

Camillus 6.6

19 τοὺς πολίτας περισπᾶν βουλόμενος, ὡς ... δημαγωγεῖσθαι καὶ μὴ στασιάζειν ... τὰ ταρακτικὰ πάθη τῆς πολιτείας ἔξω τρέποντες

Wishing to divert the attention of citizens to other matters, he kept them busy with arts and games so that they would not question policy, thereby averting disturbing passions.

Camillus 9.2

20 τοῖς νενικημένοις ὀδύνη

Woe to the vanquished!

Translated by Bernadotte Perrin (1914)

Camillus 28.6

cf. the Latin 'vae victis!' and its translation into Greek 'οὐαὶ τοῖς ἡττημένοις', proverbial after Livy, Ab urbe condita *5.48.9*

21 ἵππων ἀπειρηκότων ὑπὸ χρόνου τροφαὶ καὶ κυνῶν ... τῷ χρηστῷ προσήκουσιν

A kindly man will care for his horses and dogs even when they are worn out with age.

Cato Major 5.2

22 οὐ γὰρ ὡς ὑποδήμασιν ἢ σκεύεσι τοῖς ψυχὴν ἔχουσι χρηστέον, κοπέντα καὶ κατατριβέντα ταῖς ὑπηρεσίαις ἀπορριπτοῦντας

Do not treat living creatures like shoes or pots and pans, casting them aside when bruised and worn out with service.

Translated by Bernadotte Perrin (1914)

Cato Major 5.5

23 πλούτου γὰρ ἀφαίρεσιν οἱ πολλοὶ νομίζουσι τὴν κώλυσιν αὐτοῦ τῆς ἐπιδείξεως, ἐπιδείκνυσθαι δὲ τοῖς περιττοῖς, οὐ τοῖς ἀναγκαίοις

Most men think themselves robbed of their wealth if they are prevented from displaying it; and they display superfluities, not the necessaries of life.

Translated by Bernadotte Perrin (1914)

Cato Major 18.4

24 καὶ μὴν ἐγὼ τούτοις εὐδαίμων καὶ πλούσιός εἰμι, τοῖς ἀχρήστοις καὶ περιττοῖς

And yet my wealth and happiness are based on just such useless and superfluous things.

Translated by Bernadotte Perrin (1914)

Cato Major 18.5

25 ἐν ᾧ … ἡ πόλις ἤρθη μεγίστη, καὶ πρὸς Ἑλληνικὰ μαθήματα καὶ παιδείαν ἅπασαν ἔσχεν οἰκείως

And yet, when the city was at the zenith of its empire, she made every form of Greek learning and culture her own.

Translated by Bernadotte Perrin (1914)

Cato Major 23.3

of Rome; Plutarch's comment when recording that Cato was averse to Greek letters

26 οὐδὲν ἀνθρώπου θηρίον ἐστὶν ἀγριώτερον ἐξουσίαν πάθει προσλαβόντος

No wild beast is more savage than man having grasped authority.

Translated by Bernadotte Perrin (1919)

Cicero 46.6

27 ἡ δὲ φιλοτιμία πάντων ἐπικρατοῦσα τῶν παθῶν τοῖς τῆς πατρίδος ὑπεχώρει καιροῖς

In these critical times for the fatherland even ambition yielded, that master passion.

Cimon 17.9

28 χρηστοτέρα γὰρ ἡ φύσις, ἐν ᾗ γηρᾷ μὲν τὸ χεῖρον, ἐπακμάζει δὲ τὸ ἄμεινον

The better man is he whose evil side diminishes with age, while the good side flourishes.

Comparison of Cimon and Lucullus 1.4

29 ἐν δὲ ταῖς ἀτόποις καὶ παραβόλοις πράξεσι … οὐκ ἀναιροῦντα ποιεῖ τὸν θεόν, ἀλλὰ κινοῦντα τὴν προαίρεσιν … αἷς οὐδὲ ποιεῖ τὴν πρᾶξιν ἀκούσιον, ἀλλὰ τῷ ἑκουσίῳ δίδωσιν ἀρχήν, καὶ τὸ θαρρεῖν καὶ τὸ ἐλπίζειν προστίθησιν

In exploits of a strange and extraordinary nature god is not taking away, but is prompting a man's choice of action, so that the action is not involuntary, but his will is set in motion, while courage and hope are added to sustain him.

Translated by Bernadotte Perrin (1916)

Coriolanus 32.7

cf. Homer 302; of god inspiring elective action

30 ἰατρικῇ τὸ νοσερὸν καὶ ἁρμονικῇ τὸ ἐκμελές, ὅπως ἔχει, σκοπεῖν συμβέβηκε πρὸς τὴν τῶν ἐναντίων ἀπεργασίαν

Medicine, to produce health, has to examine disease; and music, to create harmony, must investigate discord.

Translated in *Bartlett's Familiar Quotations* (1980)

Demetrius 1.3. 5

31 τὴν δ' ἀρετήν, ὥσπερ ἰσχυρὸν καὶ διαρκὲς φυτόν, ἐν ἅπαντι ῥιζοῦσθαι τόπῳ, φύσεώς γε χρηστῆς καὶ φιλοπόνου ψυχῆς ἐπιλαμβανομένην

Virtue, like a strong and hardy plant, will take root wherever she finds a generous nature and an industrious spirit.

Demosthenes 1.3.4

32 πρώτους ἑαυτοὺς οἱ προδόται πωλοῦσιν

Traitors sell themselves first.

Translated by Bernadotte Perrin (1919)

Demosthenes 31.6

33 ὃ δὲ δοκεῖ μάλιστα καὶ λέγεται τρόπον ἀνδρὸς ἐπιδεικνύναι καὶ βασανίζειν, ἐξουσία καὶ ἀρχὴ πᾶν πάθος κινοῦσα καὶ πᾶσαν ἀποκαλύπτουσα κακίαν

Authority and power show and try the character of men, moving every passion and revealing every frailty.

Comparison of Demosthenes and Cicero 3.2

34 τὸ μὲν οὖν εὐτυχεῖν καὶ τοὺς φύσει μικροὺς συνεπικουφίζει τοῖς φρονήμασιν, ὥστε φαίνεσθαί τι μέγεθος περὶ αὐτοὺς καὶ ὄγκον … ὁ δ' ἀληθῶς μεγαλόφρων καὶ βέβαιος ἐν τοῖς σφάλμασι μᾶλλον καὶ ταῖς δυσημερίαις ἀναφέρων γίνεται κατάδηλος

Good fortune will elevate even petty minds, and give them the appearance of a certain greatness and stateliness; but the truly noble and resolved spirit raises itself, and becomes manifest in times of disaster and ill fortune.

Translated in *Bartlett's Familiar Quotations* (1980)

Eumenes 9.1

35 ὡς ἄν τις αἴσχιστα καὶ δυσποτμότατα πεπραχὼς ἐπανίοι, ταπεινοῦ καὶ κατηφοῦς

As one would come back from a most ill-starred and disgraceful experience, in humility and dejection.

Translated by Bernadotte Perrin (1916)

Fabius Maximus 18.4

of Varro's return to Rome after a massive defeat against Hannibal

36 τί κνώσσεις μεγάθυμε λέον; νεβροὶ δέ τοι ἐγγύς

Why dost thou sleep, great lion? the fawns are near for thy taking.

Translated by Bernadotte Perrin (1914)

Lucullus 12.1

37 διάθεσις γὰρ ἦν οὐδενὸς πρὸς οὐδένα πάντων εὐπορούντων

There were no sales for anything to anybody when all had such abundance.

Translated by Bernadotte Perrin (1914)

Lucullus 14.1

38 ἐγγὺς δ' ὁ Καύκασος καὶ ὄρη πολλὰ καὶ βαθέα καὶ μυρίους βασιλεῖς φυγομαχοῦντας ἀρκοῦντα κατακρύψαι

And the Caucasus is near with its endless rugged mountains, sufficient to hide away in safety ten thousand kings shunning battle.

Lucullus 14.6

39 τὴν δ' ὀρεινὴν ὀκνοῦντος προϊέναι, μακρὰν καὶ ὑλώδη καὶ δύσβατον οὖσαν

Hesitated to go into hill country, remote, forested and impassable.

Lucullus 15.3

40 οὕτως ἄρα καὶ τοῖς πράγμασιν ὁ καιρὸς ὥσπερ τοῖς φαρμάκοις καὶ τὴν σῴζουσαν καὶ τὴν ἀναιροῦσαν ῥοπὴν προστίθησιν

So true it is that in life, as in sickness, there is one critical moment which turns the scales towards saving or destruction.

Lucullus 16.7

41 πόρρω δέ που τῆς Ἑλλάδος ἀπῳκισμένη τοῖς ἐλπισθεῖσιν ἀγαθοῖς ὄναρ σύνεστι

Far away from Greece, where the blessings hoped for existed only in her dreams.

Translated by Bernadotte Perrin (1914)

Lucullus 18.4

of a Milesian girl forced into an unhappy marriage abroad

42 ὡς οὐδὲ λεκάνη δελφῖνα χωροίη

A stewpan will not hold a dolphin.

Translated by Bernadotte Perrin (1914)

Lucullus 22.7

cf. the English proverb 'too big for his boots'

43 ἦγον ἐπὶ τιμῇ τοῦ ἀνδρός, καὶ τῆς τιμῆς ἡδίονα τὴν ἀληθινὴν εὔνοιαν αὐτῷ παρεῖχον

They accorded honour to the man and, what is sweeter than honour, their genuine goodwill.

Translated by Bernadotte Perrin (1914)

Lucullus 23.2

44 μηδὲν οὕτως ἀξιόπιστον ἡγεῖσθαι καὶ βέβαιον, ὡς ὅ τι ἂν ἀποσημανθῇ διὰ τῶν ἐνυπνίων

Consider nothing more trustworthy and sure than what is revealed in dreams.

Lucullus 23.6

45 οὔτε διανοίας τῆς τυχούσης ἐν εὐτυχήμασι μεγάλοις μὴ ἐκστῆναι τῶν λογισμῶν

It is natural for a common mind to be confounded in great prosperity.

Lucullus 25.2

46 ἀπληστίᾳ δόξης καὶ ἀρχῆς … εἰς ἔργα δεινὰ καὶ πάθη … ἐξώκειλε

With an insatiate desire for glory and power he drove headlong into terrible deeds and passions.

Translated by Bernadotte Perrin (1914)

Lucullus 38.3

47 εἶναι γάρ τινα καὶ πολιτικῆς περιόδου κατάλυσιν· τῶν γὰρ ἀθλητικῶν ἀγώνων τοὺς πολιτικοὺς οὐδὲν ἧττον ἀκμῆς καὶ ὥρας ἐπιλιπούσης ἐλέγχεσθαι

A political cycle has a natural termination, and political no less than athletic contests are absurd after the full vigour of life has departed.

Translated by Bernadotte Perrin (1914)

Lucullus 38.4

48 νεόπλουτα δ' ἦν τοῦ Λουκούλλου τὰ δεῖπνα ... ὄψων τε παντοδαπῶν καὶ πεμμάτων περιττῶς διαπεπονημένων

The daily repasts of Lucullus were such as the newly rich affect, with an array of all sorts of meats and daintily prepared dishes.

Translated by Bernadotte Perrin (1914)

Lucullus 40.1

49 οὐκ ᾔδεις ὅτι σήμερον παρὰ Λουκούλλῳ δειπνεῖ Λούκουλλος;

As if you did not know that today Lucullus dines with Lucullus!

Lucullus 41.3

reprimanding his servant for preparing a modest meal

50 – Μόναι τῶν ἀνδρῶν ἄρχετε ὑμεῖς αἱ Λάκαιναι
– Μόναι γάρ, ἔφη, τίκτομεν ἄνδρας

To 'You Spartan women are the only ones who rule their men' she answered 'Yes, for we alone give birth to men.'

Translated by Bernadotte Perrin (1914)

Lycurgus 14.4

answer of Gorgo, the wife of Leonidas, to a foreign woman

51 ὁ γὰρ ὅρκῳ παρακρουόμενος τὸν μὲν ἐχθρὸν ὁμολογεῖ δεδιέναι, τοῦ δὲ θεοῦ καταφρονεῖν

A false oath indicates not only fear of one's adversary, but also contempt of god.

Lysander 8.4

52 τοῖς ἀγνοοῦσι κακὸν εἶναι φάμενος τὴν ἄγνοιαν, ὥσπερ τὴν τυφλότητα τοῖς μὴ βλέπουσιν

It is the ignorant who suffer from their ignorance, just as the blind do from their blindness.

Translated by Bernadotte Perrin (1916)

Lysander 18.5

said by Plato

53 ἀλλ' αἱ φιλότιμοι φύσεις ἄλλως μὲν οὐ κακαὶ πρὸς τὰς ἡγεμονίας εἰσί, τὸ δὲ φθονεῖν τοῖς ὁμοίοις διὰ δόξαν οὐ μικρὸν ἐμπόδιον τῶν καλῶν πράξεων ἔχουσι

With ambitious natures, otherwise not ill qualified for command, jealousy of their equals is no slight obstacle to the performance of noble deeds.

Translated by Bernadotte Perrin (1916)

Lysander 23.2

54 οἷον ἐν τραγῳδίαις ... τὸν μὲν ἀγγέλου τινὸς ἐπικείμενον πρόσωπον εὐδοκιμεῖν ... τὸν δὲ διάδημα καὶ σκῆπτρον φοροῦντα μηδὲ ἀκούεσθαι φθεγγόμενον

Just as in tragedies, an actor who takes the part of some messenger may be popular, while the one who bears the crown and sceptre is not even listened to.

Lysander 23.4.1

55 οὕτω περὶ τὸν σύμβουλον ἦν τὸ πᾶν ἀξίωμα τῆς ἀρχῆς, τῷ δὲ βασιλεῖ τοὔνομα τῆς δυνάμεως ἔρημον ἀπελείπετο

Now the whole reputation of the government lay with the counsellor, while the king, in name only, was bereft of all power.

Lysander 23.4.6

56 τοῦ νικᾶν κρεῖττόν ἐστι τὸ καλῶς χρῆσθαι τῇ νίκῃ

Better than the victory itself is the noble use of victory.

Nicias 28.3

57 μειδιάσας, οὐκοῦν εἰς αὔριον, ἔφη, τὰ σπουδαῖα

And with a smile he said, 'Let us leave the serious matters for tomorrow.'

Pelopidas 10.9

spoken by a hierophant

58 κάτθανε Διαγόρα

You may die now, Diagoras!

Pelopidas 34.6

to the famous athlete Diagoras when on the same day his three sons won at the Olympic Games

59 χρὴ διώκειν τὸ βέλτιστον

Pursue what is best.

Translated by Bernadotte Perrin (1916)

Pericles 1.2

60 τοῖς ἀπ' ἀρετῆς ἔργοις ... εἰς μίμησιν ἐμποιεῖ

Virtuous deeds lead to imitation.

Translated by Bernadotte Perrin (1916)

Pericles 1.4

61 κατὰ τὸν Πλάτωνα, καὶ ἄκρατον τοῖς πολίταις ἐλευθερίαν οἰνοχοῶν ... πειθαρχεῖν οὐκέτι τολμᾶν

To use the words of Plato, pouring out too much undiluted freedom, by which the people no longer had the patience to obey the rein.

Translated by Bernadotte Perrin (1916)

Pericles 7.8

cf. Plato, Republic 562c–d

62 δεινὴν ὕβριν ἡ Ἑλλὰς ὑβρίζεσθαι ... τὴν πόλιν καταχρυσοῦντας καὶ καλλωπίζοντας ὥσπερ ἀλαζόνα γυναῖκα

Hellas is insulted with a dire insult when we are gilding and bedizening our city like a wanton woman.

Translated by Bernadotte Perrin (1916)

Pericles 12.2

enemies of Pericles on building the Parthenon

63 οὕτως ἐπανθεῖ καινότης ἀεί τις ἄθικτον ὑπὸ τοῦ χρόνου διατηροῦσα τὴν ὄψιν, ὥσπερ ἀειθαλὲς πνεῦμα καὶ ψυχὴν ἀγήρω καταμεμειγμένην τῶν ἔργων ἐχόντων

A bloom of eternal freshness hovers over these works of his and preserves them from the touch of time, as if some unfading spirit of youth, some ageless vitality had been breathed into them.

Translated by Michael Llewellyn-Smith (2004)

Pericles 13.5

of the Parthenon and Pericles' public works

64 τὸ τῶν θεῶν γένος ἀξιοῦμεν αἴτιον μὲν ἀγαθῶν, ἀναίτιον δὲ κακῶν

We do firmly hold that the gods are capable only of good, and incapable of evil.

Translated by Bernadotte Perrin (1916)

Pericles 39.2

65 χαλεπὸν εἶναι ... δι' εὐτυχίαν ἐπηρμένῳ καὶ σπαργῶντι τῷ δήμῳ χαλινὸν ἐμβαλεῖν

It is a difficult task to bridle a people exalted by prosperity and swollen with insolence and boldness.

Translated by Bernadotte Perrin (1916)

Comparison of Pericles and Fabius Maximus 1.4

66 δεῖ μὴ μόνον χρῆσθαι τοῖς παροῦσιν, ἀλλὰ καὶ τεκμαίρεσθαι περὶ τοῦ μέλλοντος ὀρθῶς τὸν ἀγαθὸν στρατηγόν

It is for a good general not only to deal with the present, but also to correctly assess the future.

Comparison of Pericles and Fabius Maximus 2.3

67 ἀπειρία καὶ θράσος γεννᾷ καὶ θάρσος ἀφαιρεῖται

Inexperience both engenders rashness and robs a man of courage.

Translated by Bernadotte Perrin (1916)

Comparison of Pericles and Fabius Maximus 2.4

68 οὐ δεῖ δ' ἀπιστεῖν τὴν τύχην ὁρῶντας οἵων ποιημάτων δημιουργός ἐστι

Fortune, believe me, is capable of unbelievable deeds.

Romulus 8.9

69 νόμῳ μὲν ὡς καλοῖς ἐχρῶντο, φύσει δ' ὡς ἀναγκαίοις

Sanctioned by custom as good and by nature as necessary.

Translated by Bernadotte Perrin (1914)

Romulus 11.2

70 διαμένει δὲ μέχρι νῦν τὸ τὴν νύμφην αὐτὴν ἀφ' αὑτῆς μὴ ὑπερβαίνειν τὸν οὐδὸν εἰς τὸ δωμάτιον, ἀλλ' αἰρομένην εἰσφέρεσθαι

It continues to be the custom down to the present time that the bride shall not of herself cross the threshold into her new home, but be lifted up and carried in.

Translated by Bernadotte Perrin (1914)

Romulus 15.6

recalling the Sabine women carried off by force; cf. Romulus 6

71 τούτου μὲν οὖν οὐκ ἔστιν ὅ τι μᾶλλον ηὔξησε τὴν Ῥώμην, ἀεὶ προσποιοῦσαν ἑαυτῇ καὶ συννέμουσαν ὧν κρατήσειεν

This more than anything else was what gave increase to Rome: she always united and incorporated into herself those whom she conquered.

Translated by Bernadotte Perrin (1914)

Romulus 16.3

72 τὴν ἐπιμονὴν ἀνυσιμωτέραν τῆς βίας οὖσαν καὶ πολλὰ τῶν ἀθρόως ἀλήπτων ἐνδιδόντα τῷ κατὰ μικρόν

Perseverance is more effective than violence; and many things which cannot be overcome when they stand together yield when taken on little by little.

Sertorius 16.9

spoken by Sertorius Quintus, Roman statesman and general, c.126–72BC

73 ὁ χρόνος ... εὐμενὴς ὢν σύμμαχος τοῖς δεχομένοις λογισμῷ τὸν καιρὸν αὐτοῦ, τοῖς δ' ἀκαίρως ἐπειγομένοις πολεμιώτατος

Time is a kindly ally for attendants on opportunity, but a most bitter enemy for all who urge matters on unseasonably.

Translated by Bernadotte Perrin (1919)

Sertorius 16.10

spoken by Sertorius Quintus, Roman statesman and general, c.126–72BC

74 πολιτικὸν ἀφαιρεῖν τῆς ἔχθρας τὸ ἀΐδιον

It is sound policy to set aside and not perpetuate hatred.

Solon 21.1

75 δεινὸν μὲν εἰπεῖν, μαλακὸν δὲ τῇ ψυχῇ καὶ χρημάτων ἥττονα

Powerful in speech but effeminate in spirit and open to bribes.

Translated by Bernadotte Perrin (1914)

Themistocles 6.1

of Epicydes, a demagogue

76 οὔτε πλήθη νεῶν οὔτε κόσμοι καὶ λαμπρότητες ἐπισήμων οὔτε κραυγαὶ κομπώδεις ἢ βάρβαροι παιᾶνες ἔχουσί τι δεινὸν ἀνδράσιν ἐπισταμένοις εἰς χεῖρας ἰέναι καὶ μάχεσθαι τολμῶσιν

Neither a multitude of ships or a splendid appearance, neither boastful shouts or barbarous battle hymns provoke terror in men prepared to fight.

Themistocles 8.1

77 ἀρχὴ γὰρ ὄντως τοῦ νικᾶν τὸ θαρρεῖν

The foundation of victory is courage.

Translated by Bernadotte Perrin (1914)

Themistocles 8.3

78 κύων Ξανθίππου ... οὐκ ἀνασχόμενος τὴν ἀπ' αὐτοῦ μόνωσιν, ἐναλέσθαι τῇ θαλάττῃ καὶ τῇ τριήρει παρανηχόμενος ἐκπεσεῖν εἰς τὴν Σαλαμῖνα, καὶ λιποθυμήσας ἀποθανεῖν εὐθύς· οὗ καὶ τὸ δεικνύμενον ἄχρι νῦν καὶ καλούμενον Κυνὸς σῆμα τάφον εἶναι λέγουσι

Xanthippus' dog, not bearing separation, sprang into the sea, swam alongside his master's trireme and staggered out on Salamis, only to faint and die straightway; 'Dog Mound', shown to this day, is said to be his tomb.

Themistocles 10.10

on his master leaving for battle at Salamis, 480BC; Xanthippus was the father of Pericles

79 σὺ δ' οὐκ ἔσῃ Ζεὺς ἐὰν λάβῃς κεραυνόν

Thou wilt not be Zeus merely because thou graspest the thunderbolt.

Translated by Bernadotte Perrin (1914)

Themistocles 29.7

80 ὡς ἱππέως ἀρίστου, τἄλλα δ' οὐδενὸς ἀξίου γενομένου

A capital horseman, but good for nothing else.

Translated by Bernadotte Perrin (1914)

Themistocles 32.1

of Themistocles' son; cf. Plato, Meno *93d–e*

81 εἴη μὲν οὖν ἡμῖν ἐκκαθαιρόμενον λόγῳ τὸ μυθῶδες ὑπακοῦσαι καὶ λαβεῖν ἱστορίας ὄψιν

May I succeed in purifying Fable, making her submit to reason and take on the semblance of History.

Translated by Bernadotte Perrin (1914)

Theseus 1.5

opening chapter of Theseus, *the first book of Plutarch's* Lives; *cf. Herodotus 1, Thucydides 6 and Plutarch 83*

82 ὁ γὰρ δὴ χρόνος ἐκεῖνος ἤνεγκεν ἀνθρώπους ... ὑπερφυεῖς καὶ ἀκαμάτους, πρὸς οὐδὲν δὲ τῇ φύσει χρωμένους ἐπιεικὲς οὐδ' ὠφέλιμον

That age produced a breed of men excelling the ordinary, and wholly incapable of fatigue; making use, however, of these gifts of nature to no good or profitable purpose to mankind.

The 'Translation called Dryden's' ed. A.H. Clough (1859)

Theseus 6.4

83 θαυμαστὸν οὐκ ἔστιν ἐπὶ πράγμασιν οὕτω παλαιοῖς πλανᾶσθαι τὴν ἱστορίαν

It is not astonishing that history, when dealing with events of such great antiquity, should wander in uncertainty.

Translated by Bernadotte Perrin (1914)

Theseus 27.6

84 ἔστι δὲ φύξιμον οἰκέταις καὶ πᾶσι τοῖς ταπεινοτέροις ... ὡς καὶ τοῦ Θησέως προστατικοῦ τινος καὶ βοηθητικοῦ γενομένου

His tomb is a place of refuge for runaway slaves and all men of low estate, since Theseus was a champion and helper of such during his life.

Translated by Bernadotte Perrin (1914)

Theseus 36.4

85 ὁ δ' ἐνδιδοὺς ἢ ἐπιτείνων οὐ μένει βασιλεὺς οὐδὲ ἄρχων, ἀλλ' ἢ δημαγωγὸς ἢ δεσπότης γιγνόμενος, ἐμποιεῖ τὸ μισεῖν ἢ καταφρονεῖν τοῖς ἀρχομένοις

He who remits or extends his authority is no longer a king or a ruler; he becomes either a demagogue or a despot, and implants hatred or contempt in the hearts of his subjects.

Translated by Bernadotte Perrin (1914)

Comparison of Theseus and Romulus 2.3

86 ἃ πάμπαν ὀλίγοι τῶν ὄντων διαπεφεύγασιν, ἔρως καὶ ζηλοτυπία καὶ διαβολαὶ γυναικὸς ἔσφηλαν

Love, jealousy, and a woman's slanders, the overmastering power of which very few men have escaped.

Translated by Bernadotte Perrin (1914)

Comparison of Theseus and Romulus 3.2

Moralia

87 τὸ φιλόστοργον ἡ φύσις ... ἐνειργάσατο ταῖς τεκούσαις

It is nature that implanted in mothers tender love for their children.

On Affection for Offspring 496a

88 ἐπιφαίνουσι ... πολλὴν μὲν ἀνδρείαν καὶ δικαιοσύνην πολλὴν δὲ σωφροσύνην καὶ πραότητα μετὰ κόσμου καὶ συνέσεως

Demonstrating fortitude and justice, gentleness and temperance.

On the Fortune or the Virtue of Alexander 332c *of Alexander*

89 οὐκ ἐν τῇ κτήσει τῶν ἀγαθῶν ἀλλ' ἐν τῇ χρήσει τὸ μέγ' ἐστίν

What is important is not to acquire goods but to use them wisely.

On the Fortune or the Virtue of Alexander 337c

90 πολλὰ γάρ ἐστι τοῦ θυμοῦ φοβερά, πολλὰ δὲ καὶ γελοῖα

Many displays of anger are fearful, but many ludicrous as well.

On the Control of Anger 455d–e

91 ἀλλ' ἡμῖν τοῖς ἡμέρως καὶ φιλανθρώπως ζῆν δοκοῦσι ποῖον ἔργον ἀπολείπεται γῆς, ποῖον ἐν θαλάττῃ, τίς ἐναέριος τέχνη, τίς κόσμος διαίτης

We who live in gentleness and love for mankind, it is hard to say what task we have left undone on earth or sea or air, what refinement of living.

Whether Land or Sea Animals Are Cleverer 964a

92 περὶ τἀγαθὸν ἡ φρόνησις πραγματεύεται τετραχῶς, ἢ κτωμένη τἀγαθὰ ἢ φυλάττουσα ἢ αὔξουσα ἢ χρωμένη δεξιῶς

Prudence concerning provisions is fourfold – either acquiring a store of goods, or conserving them, or adding to them, or using them judiciously.

Letter of Condolence to Apollonius 103a

93 ὥσπερ ἐσόπτρου κατεσκευασμένου χρυσῷ καὶ λίθοις ὄφελος οὐδέν ἐστιν, εἰ μὴ δείκνυσι τὴν μορφὴν ὁμοίαν, οὕτως οὐδὲ πλουσίας γαμετῆς ὄνησις, εἰ μὴ παρέχει τὸν βίον ὅμοιον τῷ ἀνδρὶ καὶ σύμφωνον τὸ ἦθος

As a mirror decorated with precious stones is useless if it does not show one's face, so is a rich bride if she does not complement her husband's life and character.

Advice to Bride and Groom 139f

94 τὰ ... μικρὰ καὶ συνεχῆ καὶ καθημερινὰ προσκρούματα γυναικὸς καὶ ἀνδρὸς μᾶλλον διίστησι καὶ λυμαίνεται τὴν συμβίωσιν

It is the petty, continual, daily clashes

between man and wife that disrupt and mar married life.

Translated by Frank Cole Babbitt (1928)

Advice to Bride and Groom 141b

95 οὐ δύνασαί μοι καὶ φίλῳ χρῆσθαι καὶ κόλακι ... οὐ δύναμαι τῇ αὐτῇ καὶ ὡς γαμετῇ καὶ ὡς ἑταίρᾳ συνεῖναι

You cannot use me as a friend and flatterer both; you cannot have the same woman both as wife and as paramour.

Translated by Frank Cole Babbitt (1928)

Advice to Bride and Groom 142c

cf. Phocion 3

96 ὁ Ῥωμαῖος νομοθέτης ἐκώλυσε δῶρα διδόναι καὶ λαμβάνειν παρ' ἀλλήλων τοὺς γεγαμηκότας, οὐχ ἵνα μηδενὸς μεταλαμβάνωσιν, ἀλλ' ἵνα πάντα κοινὰ νομίζωσιν

The Roman legislator forbade couples to exchange presents, not so as not to have something from the other, but in order to consider everything as belonging to both in common.

Advice to Bride and Groom 143a

97 τοῦ λύχνου ἀρθέντος πᾶσα γυνὴ ἡ αὐτή ἐστι

When the candles are out all women are fair.

Translated in *Bartlett's Familiar Quotations* (1980)

Advice to Bride and Groom 144e

98 ἀδελφῶν ὁμοφροσύνη καὶ γένος καὶ οἶκος ὑγιαίνει καὶ τέθηλε

Where brothers are in concord all the family thrives.

On Brotherly Love 479a

99 ἀλλὰ γῆν μὲν οὐδεὶς ὕδατι δεύσας ἀφῆκεν, ὡς ἀπὸ τύχης καὶ αὐτομάτως πλίνθων ἐσομένων

Nobody wets clay with water and leaves it, assuming that by chance and accidentally there will be bricks.

Translated by Frank Cole Babbitt (1928)

Chance 99d

100 τὸ δ' εὖ ζῆν ἐστι κοινωνικῶς ζῆν καὶ φιλικῶς καὶ σωφρόνως καὶ δικαίως

Living well means living sociably and friendlily and moderately and justly.

Reply to Colotes in Defence of Other Philosophers 1108c

101 τὸ μὲν γὰρ ἁμαρτάνειν περὶ δόξαν, εἰ καὶ μὴ σοφῶν, ὅμως ἀνθρώπινόν ἐστι

To be wrong in a belief is a failing, if not of sages, yet of men.

Translated by Benedict Einarson and Phillip H. De Lacy (1967)

Reply to Colotes in Defence of Other Philosophers 1125f

102 τοῦ φιλοσοφεῖν τὸ ζητεῖν ἀρχή, τοῦ δὲ ζητεῖν τὸ θαυμάζειν καὶ ἀπορεῖν, εἰκότως τὰ πολλὰ τῶν περὶ τὸν θεὸν ἔοικεν αἰνίγμασι κατακεκρύφθαι

Since inquiry is the beginning of philosophy, and wonder and uncertainty the beginning of inquiry, it seems only natural that the greater part of what concerns the god should be concealed in riddles.

Translated by Frank Cole Babbitt (1936)

The E at Delphi 385c

103 ἀληθείας φῶς ἀπόδειξις

The light of truth is proof.

Translated by C.W. King (1818–1888)

The E at Delphi 387a

104 οὐδενὸς γὰρ ἀναίτιος ἡ γένεσις

Nothing comes into being without a cause.

The E at Delphi 387b

105 τὰ φρονήματα τῶν ὑπόχαλκον καὶ κίβδηλον ἐχόντων τὸ γένος σφάλλεσθαι καὶ ταπεινοῦσθαι πέφυκε

It so happens that the spirit of those whose parentage is base and false is easily frustrated and humbled.

*The Education of Children** 1b

106 φίλοινοι γὰρ καὶ μεθυστικοὶ γίγνεσθαι φιλοῦσιν ὧν ἂν τὴν ἀρχὴν τῆς σπορᾶς οἱ πατέρες ἐν μέθῃ ποιησάμενοι τύχωσιν

Children whose fathers have chanced to beget them in drunkenness are wont to be fond of wine, and to be given to excessive drinking.

Translated by Frank Cole Babbitt (1927)

*The Education of Children** 1d

107 ὡς εἰς τὴν παντελῆ δικαιοπραγίαν τρία δεῖ συνδραμεῖν, φύσιν καὶ λόγον καὶ ἔθος

There must be three things in order to produce perfectly right action, and these are: nature, reason, and habit.

Translated by Frank Cole Babbitt (1927)

*The Education of Children** 2a

108 εἰσὶ δ' αἱ μὲν ἀρχαὶ τῆς φύσεως, αἱ δὲ προκοπαὶ τῆς μαθήσεως ... ἡ μὲν γὰρ φύσις ἄνευ μαθήσεως τυφλόν

The first beginnings come from nature, advancement from learning; nature without learning is a blind thing.

Translated by Frank Cole Babbitt (1927)

*The Education of Children** 2a–b

109 φύσεως μὲν γὰρ ἀρετὴν διαφθείρει ῥᾳθυμία, φαυλότητα δ' ἐπανορθοῖ διδαχή

Indifference ruins natural talent, instruction amends a poor one.

*The Education of Children** 2c

110 ἀνύσιμον πρᾶγμα καὶ τελεσιουργὸν ἐπιμέλεια καὶ πόνος ἐστίν ... σταγόνες μὲν γὰρ ὕδατος πέτρας κοιλαίνουσι

Diligence and hard work lead to accomplishment and perfection; drops of water hollow out a rock.

*The Education of Children** 2d

111 δηλοῖ δὲ καὶ ἡ φύσις ὅτι δεῖ τὰς μητέρας ἃ γεγεννήκασιν αὐτὰς τιτθεύειν καὶ τρέφειν ... ἡ συντροφία γὰρ ὥσπερ ἐπιτόνιόν ἐστι τῆς εὐνοίας

Nature too dictates that mothers should nurse their babies; and this fellowship in feeding bonds them to each other in kindness.

*The Education of Children** 3c–d

112 εὔπλαστον γὰρ καὶ ὑγρὸν ἡ νεότης

Easy to mould and supple, is youth.

*The Education of Children** 3e

113 πᾶν δὲ τὸ σκληρὸν χαλεπῶς μαλάττεται

What has already hardened is difficult to impress.

*The Education of Children** 3e

114 διδασκάλους γὰρ ζητητέον τοῖς τέκνοις, οἳ καὶ τοῖς βίοις εἰσὶν ἀδιάβλητοι καὶ τοῖς τρόποις ἀνεπίληπτοι καὶ ταῖς ἐμπειρίαις ἄριστοι

Teachers must be sought for the children who are free from scandal in their lives, who are unimpeachable in their manners, and in experience the very best that may be found.

Translated by Frank Cole Babbitt (1927)

*The Education of Children** 4b

115 πηγὴ γὰρ καὶ ῥίζα καλοκαγαθίας τὸ νομίμου τυχεῖν παιδείας

The source and root of honesty and virtue lie in good education.

*The Education of Children** 4c

116 καὶ καθάπερ τὰς χάρακας οἱ γεωργοὶ τοῖς φυτοῖς παρατιθέασιν, οὕτως οἱ νόμιμοι τῶν διδασκάλων ἐμμελεῖς τὰς ὑποθήκας καὶ παραινέσεις παραπηγνύουσι τοῖς νέοις, ἵν' ὀρθὰ τούτων βλαστάνῃ τὰ ἤθη

As farmers support young plants with stakes, thus teachers uphold principles and sound advice for the young so that their characters may grow to be upright.

*The Education of Children** 4c

117 ἓν πρῶτον καὶ μέσον καὶ τελευταῖον ἐν τούτοις κεφάλαιον ἀγωγὴ σπουδαία καὶ παιδεία νόμιμός ἐστι

The beginning, the middle, and the end is good education and proper training.

Translated by Frank Cole Babbitt (1927)

*The Education of Children** 5c

118 ἀγωγὴ σπουδαία καὶ παιδεία νόμιμός ἐστι, καὶ ταῦτα φορὰ καὶ συνεργὰ πρὸς ἀρετὴν καὶ πρὸς εὐδαιμονίαν

Good education and proper training leads towards moral excellence and happiness.

Translated by Frank Cole Babbitt (1927)

*The Education of Children** 5c

119 εὐγένεια καλὸν μέν, ἀλλὰ προγόνων ἀγαθόν

It is indeed desirable to be well descended, but the glory belongs to our ancestors.

Translated in *Bartlett's Familiar Quotations* (1980)

*The Education of Children** 5d

120 κάλλος δὲ περιμάχητον μέν, ἀλλ' ὀλιγοχρόνιον

Beauty is highly prized, but short-lived.

Translated by Frank Cole Babbitt (1927)

*The Education of Children** 5d

121 δύο τὰ πάντων ἐστὶ κυριώτατα ἐν ἀνθρωπίνῃ φύσει, νοῦς καὶ λόγος

Two elements in man's nature are supreme over all, mind and reason.

Translated by Frank Cole Babbitt (1927)

*The Education of Children** 5e

122 ὁ μὲν νοῦς ἀρχικός ἐστι τοῦ λόγου, ὁ δὲ λόγος ὑπηρετικὸς τοῦ νοῦ, τύχῃ μὲν ἀνάλωτος, συκοφαντίᾳ δ' ἀναφαίρετος, νόσῳ δ' ἀδιάφθορος, γήρᾳ δ' ἀλύμαντος

The mind exercises control over reason, and reason is the servant of the mind, unassailable by fortune, impregnable to calumny, uncorrupted by disease, unimpaired by old age.

Translated by Frank Cole Babbitt (1927)

*The Education of Children** 5e

123 μόνος γὰρ ὁ νοῦς παλαιούμενος ἀνηβᾷ

The mind alone grows young with the increase in years.

*The Education of Children** 5e

124 τὸ γὰρ τοῖς πολλοῖς ἀρέσκειν τοῖς σοφοῖς ἐστιν ἀπαρέσκειν

To please the multitude is to displease the wise.

Translated by Frank Cole Babbitt (1927)

*The Education of Children** 6b

125 ἐν ἅπασι γὰρ τὸ τέλειον ἀδύνατον

Perfection in everything is impossible.

Translated by Frank Cole Babbitt (1927)

*The Education of Children** 7c

126 δεῖ τῆς ἄλλης παιδείας ὥσπερ κεφάλαιον ποιεῖν τὴν φιλοσοφίαν

It is necessary to make philosophy the crowning act of all education.

*The Education of Children** 7d

127 περὶ μὲν γὰρ τὴν τοῦ σώματος ἐπιμέλειαν διττὰς εὗρον ἐπιστήμας οἱ ἄνθρωποι, τὴν ἰατρικὴν καὶ τὴν γυμναστικήν ... τῶν δὲ τῆς ψυχῆς ἀρρωστημάτων καὶ παθῶν ἡ φιλοσοφία μόνη φάρμακόν ἐστι

Concerning the care of the body men have discovered two sciences, medicine and gymnastics; but for the sickness and affections of the mind philosophy alone is the remedy.

*The Education of Children** 7d

128 τὸ δὲ μέγιστον, μήτ' ἐν ταῖς εὐπραγίαις περιχαρεῖς μήτ' ἐν ταῖς συμφοραῖς περιλύπους ὑπάρχειν

Most important of all, not to be overjoyed at success or overly distressed by misfortune.

Translated by Frank Cole Babbitt (1927)

*The Education of Children** 7e

cf. Rudyard Kipling: 'If you can meet with triumph and disaster'

129 τὸ μὲν γὰρ εὐγενῶς εὐτυχεῖν ἀνδρός, τὸ δ' ἀνεπιφθόνως εὐηνίου ἀνθρώπου, τὸ δὲ τοῖς λογισμοῖς περιεῖναι τῶν ἡδονῶν σοφοῦ, τὸ δ' ὀργῆς κατακρατεῖν ἀνδρὸς οὐ τοῦ τυχόντος ἐστί

To have a generous heart in prosperity shows a man, to excite no envy shows a disciplined nature; to rule pleasure by reason marks the wise man, and not every man is able to master his passion.

Translated by Frank Cole Babbitt (1927)

*The Education of Children** 7f

130 τελείους δ' ἀνθρώπους ἡγοῦμαι τοὺς δυναμένους τὴν πολιτικὴν δύναμιν μεῖξαι καὶ κεράσαι τῇ φιλοσοφίᾳ, καὶ δυεῖν ὄντοιν μεγίστοιν ἀγαθοῖν ἐπηβόλους ὑπάρχειν ὑπολαμβάνω, τοῦ τε κοινωφελοῦς βίου πολιτευομένους, τοῦ τ' ἀκύμονος καὶ γαληνοῦ διατρίβοντας περὶ φιλοσοφίαν

I regard as perfect those who are able to combine political ability with philosophy, as they have secured two things of the greatest value: a life useful to the world, and calmness in their pursuit of philosophy.

*The Education of Children** 7f

131 τὸν γὰρ αὐτὸν τρόπον ὄργανον τῆς παιδείας ἡ χρῆσις τῶν βιβλίων ἐστί, καὶ ἀπὸ πηγῆς τὴν ἐπιστήμην τηρεῖν συμβέβηκεν

The tool of education is the use of books, and by their means to test knowledge at its source.

*The Education of Children** 8b

132 καλοῦ γὰρ γήρως θεμέλιος ἐν παισὶν ἡ τῶν σωμάτων εὐεξία

Bodily vigour in childhood is the foundation of a healthy old age.

*The Education of Children** 8c

133 ἔπαινοι δὲ καὶ ψόγοι πάσης εἰσὶν αἰκίας ὠφελιμώτεροι

Praise and reproof are better than any physical punishment.

*The Education of Children** 8f

134 ἡ ἀνάπαυσις τῶν πόνων ἐστὶν ἄρτυμα

Rest adds pleasure to labour.

*The Education of Children** 9c

135 οὐδὲν οὕτω πιαίνει τὸν ἵππον ὡς βασιλέως ὀφθαλμός

Nothing cheers the horse as much as the master's eye.

Translated in Liddell & Scott

*The Education of Children** 9d

cf. Xenophon, Oeconomicus *12.20*

136 σοφὸν γὰρ εὔκαιρος σιγὴ καὶ παντὸς λόγου κρεῖττον

Well timed silence is a wise thing, and better than any speech.

Translated by Frank Cole Babbitt (1927)

*The Education of Children** 10e

137 τὸ μὲν σιγηθὲν ἐξειπεῖν ῥᾴδιον, τὸ δὲ ῥηθὲν ἀναλαβεῖν ἀδύνατον

A word unspoken can be said later; the spoken word can never be recalled.

*The Education of Children** 10f

138 ἐθίζειν τοὺς παῖδας τῷ τἀληθῆ λέγειν· τὸ γὰρ ψεύδεσθαι πᾶσιν ἀνθρώποις ἄξιον μισεῖσθαι

Accustom children to speak the truth; lying deserves to be hated by all.

*The Education of Children** 11c

139 στιγμὴ χρόνου πᾶς ἐστιν ὁ βίος·
ζῆν οὐ παραζῆν προσῆκε

All our life is but a moment in time;
live, then, and don't miss out on life.

*The Education of Children** 13b

140 κρονόληρος καὶ σοροδαίμων ἐστί

A silly old fool with one foot already in the grave.

*The Education of Children** 13b

141 πᾶσα φύσις ἀνθρώπου φέρει φιλονεικίαν καὶ ζηλοτυπίαν καὶ φθόνον

All human nature is prone to rivalry, jealousy and envy.

How to Profit by One's Enemies 91e

142 αὐτὸς αὑτοῦ κόλαξ ἕκαστος ὢν πρῶτος καὶ μέγιστος

Everybody is himself his own foremost and greatest flatterer.

Translated by Frank Cole Babbitt (1927)

How to Tell a Flatterer from a Friend 49a

143 ὥσπερ νόμισμα δεῖ τὸν φίλον ἔχειν πρὸ τῆς χρείας δεδοκιμασμένον, μὴ ὑπὸ τῆς χρείας ἐλεγχόμενον

Friends, like a coin, must be tested before the time of need, not proved false when the need arises.

How to Tell a Flatterer from a Friend 49d

144 ὁ μὲν ἀληθὴς φίλος οὔτε μιμητής ἐστι πάντων οὔτ' ἐπαινέτης, ἀλλὰ τῶν ἀρίστων μόνων

A true friend neither imitates nor applauds everything, but only what is best.

How to Tell a Flatterer from a Friend 53c

145 ἄνθρωπον ... ἀπολλύουσιν οἱ ψευδῶς καὶ παρ' ἀξίαν ἐπαινοῦντες

A man is ruined by those who praise him falsely and beyond his worth.

How to Tell a Flatterer from a Friend 59a

146 ὀλίγοι ... οἱ παρρησιάζεσθαι μᾶλλον ἢ χαρίζεσθαι τοῖς φίλοις τολμῶντες

Few dare speak frankly to their friends.

How to Tell a Flatterer from a Friend 66a

147 ἔχει δὲ καὶ κίνδυνον ἡ ἀκαιρία μέγαν

There is much danger in being ill-timed.

Translated by Frank Cole Babbitt (1927)

How to Tell a Flatterer from a Friend 68d

148 δεῖ μάλιστα παρρησιαζομένων φίλων τοῖς εὐτυχοῦσι

In good fortune men have most need of friends to speak frankly.

Translated by Frank Cole Babbitt (1927)

How to Tell a Flatterer from a Friend 68f

cf. Euripides 263

149 τὰ πράγματα τῶν δυστυχούντων οὐ παρρησίαν ἐνδέχεται καὶ γνωμολογίαν, ἀλλ' ἐπιεικείας δεῖται καὶ βοηθείας

What the unfortunate need is understanding and help, not frankness and theorizing.

How to Tell a Flatterer from a Friend 69b

150 ἥκιστα δὲ πρέπει γαμετῆς ἀκουούσης ἄνδρα καὶ παίδων ἐν ὄψει πατέρα … ἀποκαλύπτειν

Least of all is it decent to expose a husband in the hearing of his wife, and a father in the sight of his children.

Translated by Frank Cole Babbitt (1927)

How to Tell a Flatterer from a Friend 71c

151 ἡ ἀληθινὴ φιλία τρία ζητεῖ μάλιστα, τὴν ἀρετὴν ὡς καλόν, καὶ τὴν συνήθειαν ὡς ἡδύ, καὶ τὴν χρείαν ὡς ἀναγκαῖον

True friendship seeks three things, virtue as good, intimacy as pleasant, and usefulness as necessary.

On Having Many Friends 94b

152 δεῖ μὴ ῥᾳδίως προσδέχεσθαι μηδὲ κολλᾶσθαι τοῖς ἐντυγχάνουσι μηδὲ φιλεῖν τοὺς διώκοντας, ἀλλὰ τοὺς ἀξίους φιλίας διώκειν

Do not readily accept or attach to chance acquaintances, nor make suitors your friends, but seek those who are worthy of friendship.

Translated by Frank Cole Babbitt (1928)

On Having Many Friends 94e

153 τὸ ἄρρεν ἀδρανὲς καὶ τὸ θῆλυ χωρὶς ἀλλήλων

Men and women are helpless without one another.

Greek and Roman Questions 263e

154 οὔτε γὰρ φιλοσόφους πωγωνοτροφίαι καὶ τριβωνοφορίαι ποιοῦσιν

Having a beard and wearing a coarse cloak does not make a philosopher.

Translated by Frank Cole Babbitt (1936)

Isis and Osiris 352c

cf. the Latin 'barba non facit philosophum'

155 ἐγώ εἰμι πᾶν τὸ γεγονὸς καὶ ὂν καὶ ἐσόμενον καὶ τὸν ἐμὸν πέπλον οὐδείς πω θνητὸς ἀπεκάλυψεν

I am whatever was, or is, or will be; and no mortal ever lifted up my veil.

Isis and Osiris 354c

inscription on the statue of Isis in a temple at Saïs; cf. Proclus, On Plato's Timaeus *1.98.17*

156 ἐν δὲ Θήβαις εἰκόνες ἦσαν ἀνακείμεναι δικαστῶν ἄχειρες, ἡ δὲ τοῦ ἀρχιδικαστοῦ καταμύουσα τοῖς ὄμμασιν, ὡς ἄδωρον ἅμα τὴν δικαιοσύνην καὶ ἀνέντευκτον οὖσαν

In Thebes there were set up statues of judges without hands, and the statues of the chief of justice had its eyes closed, to indicate that justice is not influenced by gifts or by intercession.

Translated by Frank Cole Babbitt (1936)

Isis and Osiris 355a

Thebes, Egypt

157 ταὐτόν ἐστι τὸ ἕπεσθαι θεῷ καὶ τὸ πείθεσθαι λόγῳ

To follow god and to obey reason are the same thing.

Translated by Frank Cole Babbitt (1927)

On Listening to Lectures 37d

158 δεῖ δὲ τὸν μὲν ἔπαινον ἀφελῶς τοῖς λέγουσι τὴν δὲ πίστιν εὐλαβῶς προΐεσθαι τοῖς λόγοις

In praising a speaker be generous, in believing his words cautious.

Translated by Frank Cole Babbitt (1927)

On Listening to Lectures 41a

159 οἱ δὲ γλίσχροι περὶ τοὺς ἑτέρων ἐπαίνους … πεινῆν ἐοίκασι τῶν ἰδίων

Those who are niggardly in their praise of others give the impression of starving for their own.

Translated by Frank Cole Babbitt (1927)

On Listening to Lectures 44c

160 ἀεὶ δὲ λυπεῖ τοὺς ἀκροωμένους … εἴρων γὰρ ἢ κόλαξ ἢ περὶ λόγους ἀπειρόκαλος

A dissembler, a flatterer, and a boor, a painful affliction to the audience.

Translated by Frank Cole Babbitt (1927)

On Listening to Lectures 44d

of someone who continuously applauds during a lecture

161 ὁ ἔρως ὥσπερ κιττὸς αὑτὸν ἐκ πάσης ἀναδῆσαι προφάσεως

Love, like ivy, is clever in attaching itself to any support.

Translated by Frank Cole Babbitt (1927)

On Listening to Lectures 45a

162 ὁ νοῦς ... ὑπεκκαύματος ὥσπερ ὕλη δεῖται ὁρμὴν ἐμποιοῦντος εὑρετικὴν

The mind, as does fire, requires kindling to create an impulse to think independently.

Translated by Frank Cole Babbitt (1927)

On Listening to Lectures 48c

163 ὡς γὰρ ἐκεῖνοι πρὸς τὴν πρύμναν ἀφορῶντες τῆς νεὼς τῇ κατὰ πρῷραν ὁρμῇ συνεργοῦσιν

Like rowers, who look astern while they row the boat ahead.

Is 'Live Unknown' a Wise Precept? 1128c

164 ὁ γὰρ ἐνθουσιασμὸς ... φῶς ἐν τῇ ψυχῇ ποιεῖ πρὸς τὸ μέλλον

Inspiration creates light in the soul in regard to the future.

The Oracles at Delphi No Longer Given in Verse 397c

165 Πὰν ὁ μέγας τέθνηκε

The great god Pan is dead.

Translated in *Bartlett's Familiar Quotations* (1980)

The Obsolescence of Oracles 419c

echoed by Elizabeth Barrett Browning, 'The Dead Pan': 'Pan is dead! great Pan is dead! Pan, Pan is dead!'

166 ἡ μὲν γὰρ ἀλήθεια ... κἂν ἀτερπὲς ἔχῃ τὸ τέλος, οὐκ ἐξίσταται· τὸ δὲ πλαττόμενον λόγῳ ῥᾷστα περιχωρεῖ καὶ τρέπεται πρὸς τὸ ἥδιον ἐκ τοῦ λυποῦντος

Truth does not deviate from its course, even though the end be unpleasant; whereas fiction very readily follows a roundabout route, and turns from the painful to the pleasant.

How the Young Man Should Study Poetry 16b

167 τὴν πρᾶξιν οὐκ ἐπαινοῦμεν ἧς γέγονεν ἡ μίμησις, ἀλλὰ τὴν τέχνην

It is not the action represented in a poem that we applaud, but the art.

How the Young Man Should Study Poetry 18b

e.g. an act such as Medea killing her children

168 τὸ εὔδαιμον καὶ μακάριον οὐ χρημάτων πλῆθος οὐδὲ πραγμάτων ὄγκος οὐδ' ἀρχαί τινες ἔχουσιν οὐδὲ δυνάμεις, ἀλλ' ἀλυπία καὶ πραότης παθῶν καὶ διάθεσις ψυχῆς τὸ κατὰ φύσιν ὁρίζουσα

Happiness does not consist in vast possessions or authority or power, but in freedom from grief, calmness, and a disposition of the soul as ordained by Nature.

How the Young Man Should Study Poetry 37a

from Epicurus, but now not to be found in just this form; cf. Diogenes Laertius, Lives of Eminent Philosophers *10.139 and 10.144*

169 Λάμπις ὁ ναύκληρος ἐρωτηθεὶς πῶς ἐκτήσατο τὸν πλοῦτον, οὐ χαλεπῶς, ἔφη, τὸν μέγαν, τὸν δὲ βραχὺν ἐπιπόνως καὶ βραδέως

Lampis the shipowner, on being asked how he had made his money, replied, 'Great wealth without difficulty, the lesser slowly and laboriously.'

Whether an Old Man Should Engage in Public Affairs 787a

170 ὅμοιον δ' ἐστὶ τῷ φιλοσοφεῖν τὸ πολιτεύεσθαι

Pursuing public affairs and philosophy is one and the same thing.

Whether an Old Man Should Engage in Public Affairs 796d

171 τίς οὖν ἄρξει τοῦ ἄρχοντος;

Who, then, will rule the ruler?

To an Uneducated Ruler 780c

172 καὶ τῶν φυτῶν τὰ σπέρματα καὶ τῶν ἀνθρώπων οἱ βίοι ταῖς χώραις συνεξομοιοῦνται

As the seeds of plants, so the lives of men assimilate to the land they live in.

Sayings of Kings and Commanders 172f

spoken by Cyrus the Great, founder of the Persian empire

173 μὴ κακούργει τὴν μουσικήν

Do not murder music.

Translated by Frank Cole Babbitt (1931)

Sayings of Spartans 220c

Phrynis, a distinguished musician, on being ordered to cut two of nine strings of his lyre

174 Θεαρίδας ξίφος ἀκονῶν ἠρωτήθη εἰ ὀξύ ἐστιν, καὶ εἶπεν, ὀξύτερον διαβολῆς

Thearidas, as he was whetting his sword, was asked if it was sharp, and he replied, 'Sharper than slander.'

Translated by Frank Cole Babbitt (1931)

Sayings of Spartans 221c

175 τί μοι μικρῶν πέρι μεγάλα φροιμιάζῃ; ὅσον γὰρ εἴη πρᾶγμα, τοσοῦτος καὶ ὁ λόγος, ᾧ χρῆσαι

Why so many words on a small topic? As big as your subject be the words you use.

Sayings of Spartans 224c

176 ὅπου ... μήτε πλείω μήτε ἐλάσσονα κεκτήσονται οἱ ἐνοικοῦντες· καὶ ὅπου τὸ μὲν δίκαιον ἰσχύσει, τὸ δὲ ἄδικον ἀσθενὲς ἔσται

Where inhabitants possess neither too much nor too little, and where right shall be strong and wrong shall be weak.

Translated by Frank Cole Babbitt (1931)

Sayings of Spartans 224f

of a city safe to live in

177 φωνὰ τύ τίς ἐσσι καὶ οὐδὲν ἄλλο

It's all voice ye are, and nought else.

Translated by Frank Cole Babbitt (1931)

Sayings of Spartans 233a

on plucking a nightingale

178 οἴμοι τῶν κακῶν ... ὡς ἅπαντες μὲν οἱ Ἕλληνες ἐπίστανται τὰ καλά, χρῶνται δ' αὐτοῖς μόνοι Λακεδαιμόνιοι

Alas for the evil days! All the Greeks know what is proper, but only the Spartans practise it.

Sayings of Spartans 235c

spoken by an elderly man who could not find a seat at the games; only the Spartans all stood up and offered their seat

179 ἢ τὰν ἢ ἐπὶ τᾶς

Either with it, or upon it.

Sayings of Spartan Women 241f.10

i.e. come back either with your shield or dead upon it; Spartan mother giving her son his shield before going to war; cf. Archilochus 1 and Menander 173

180 βῆμα πρόσθες

Add a step.

Translated by Gavin Betts and Alan Henry (1989)

Sayings of Spartan Women 241f.11

a Spartan woman in answer to her son who complained that his sword was short

181 ἐργώδης γὰρ ἡ μετάθεσις τῶν πολλῶν

It is a difficult task indeed to sway a crowd's opinion.

Precepts of Statecraft 800b.2

182 αὐτὸς δ' ὥσπερ ἐν θεάτρῳ τὸ λοιπὸν ἀναπεπταμένῳ βιωσόμενος, ἐξάσκει καὶ κατακόσμει τὸν τρόπον

Since, then, you are henceforth to live as if on an open stage, take on and practise this way of life accordingly.

Precepts of Statecraft 800b.3

to a an aspirant statesman

183 οὐ γὰρ ὧν λέγουσιν ἐν κοινῷ καὶ πράττουσιν οἱ πολιτευόμενοι μόνον εὐθύνας διδόασιν, ἀλλὰ καὶ δεῖπνον αὐτῶν πολυπραγμονεῖται καὶ κοίτη καὶ γάμος καὶ παιδιὰ καὶ σπουδὴ πᾶσα

Not only are men in public life held responsible for their public words and actions, but people also busy themselves with all their private dealings as well, dinners, love affairs, marriage, amusement, and all their serious travails.

Precepts of Statecraft 800d

184 τὰ μικρὰ φαίνεται μεγάλα τῶν ἁμαρτημάτων ἐν ἡγεμονικοῖς καὶ πολιτικοῖς ὁρώμενα βίοις

Small faults appear great when observed in the lives of leaders and statesmen.

Translated by Harold North Fowler (1936)

Precepts of Statecraft 800e

185 δῆμον δὲ καὶ πόλιν ἐκ τῶν ὤτων ἄγειν δεῖ μάλιστα ... δημαγωγία γὰρ ἡ διὰ λόγου πειθομένων ἐστίν, αἱ δὲ τοιαῦται τιθασεύσεις τῶν ὄχλων οὐδὲν ἀλόγων ζῴων ἄγρας καὶ βουκολήσεως διαφέρουσιν

A people and city are chiefly to be drawn by the ears. For to lead a people is to persuade them by reason and eloquence; but such allurements of the multitude differ nothing from the baits laid for the taking of irrational animals.

Translated by Samuel White (1878)

Precepts of Statecraft 802d

'such allurements' meaning feasts, banquets, money, public shows etc.

186 δίκαιον γὰρ ὑπὸ τῶν μειζόνων κοσμουμένους ἀρχῶν ἀντικοσμεῖν τὰς ἐλάττονας

It is right that men who have adorned the highest offices should not shrink from, in turn, accepting the lesser.

Translated by Harold North Fowler (1936)

Precepts of Statecraft 813d

187 τὸν ἀπὸ δημοσίων χρηματιζόμενον ἡγούμενος ἀφ' ἱερῶν κλέπτειν, ἀπὸ τάφων, ἀπὸ φίλων, ἐκ προδοσίας, ἀπὸ ψευδομαρτυρίας, σύμβουλον ἄπιστον εἶναι, δικαστὴν ἐπίορκον, ἄρχοντα δωροδόκον, οὐδεμιᾶς ἁπλῶς καθαρὸν ἀδικίας

A man who makes money out of public funds is as if stealing from sanctuaries, from tombs, from his friends, through treason and by false testimony, an untrustworthy adviser, a perjured judge, a corrupt magistrate, not free from any kind of iniquity.

Translated by Harold North Fowler (1936)

Precepts of Statecraft 819e

188 ψευδώνυμοι τιμαὶ ... ἑταιρικαῖς ἐοίκασι κολακείαις, ὄχλων ἀεὶ τῷ διδόντι καὶ χαριζομένῳ προσμειδιώντων, ἐφήμερόν τινα καὶ ἀβέβαιον δόξαν

False attested honours are like harlots' flatteries, since the masses always smile upon him who gives to them and does them favours, granting him an ephemeral and uncertain reputation.

Translated by Harold North Fowler (1936)

Precepts of Statecraft 821f.5

189 εὖ μὲν οὖν ὁ πρῶτος εἰπὼν καταλυθῆναι δῆμον ὑπὸ τοῦ πρώτου δεκάσαντος συνεῖδεν, ὅτι τὴν ἰσχὺν ἀποβάλλουσιν οἱ πολλοὶ τοῦ λαμβάνειν ἥττονες γενόμενοι

Whoever first said that democracy was ruined by the first man who was bought by bribes rightly perceived that the many lose most when bribe-taking prevails.

Precepts of Statecraft 821f.9

190 τῷ μεθύειν τὸ ἐρᾶν ὅμοιόν ἐστιν· ποιεῖ γὰρ θερμοὺς καὶ ἱλαροὺς καὶ διακεχυμένους

Love is like drunkenness, for it makes men hot, merry, and distraught.

Translated by Paul A. Clement (1969)

Table Talk 622d

191 εἰς μέσον ... πρόβλημα περὶ τοῦ ᾠοῦ καὶ τῆς ὄρνιθος

The central problem of the egg and the chicken

Table Talk 636a

cf. the English phrase 'what came first, the chicken or the egg?'

192 πᾶσι μὲν οὖν τοῖς καλουμένοις μαθήμασιν, ὥσπερ ... κατόπτροις, ἐμφαίνεται τῆς τῶν νοητῶν ἀληθείας ἴχνη καὶ εἴδωλα

In all of the so-called mathematical sciences, as in mirrors, there appear traces and ghost-images of the truth about objects of intellectual knowledge.

Translated by E.L. Minar, F.H. Sandbach and W.C. Helmbold (1961)

Table Talk 718e

193 ἀπιστοῦνται δ' οἱ λάλοι, κἂν ἀληθεύωσιν

Chatterers are disbelieved, even when telling the truth.

Concerning Talkativeness 503d

194 πολλῶν μὲν δὴ καὶ ἄλλων ἡ πόλις ἥδε μήτηρ καὶ τροφὸς εὐμενὴς τεχνῶν γέγονε, τὰς μὲν εὑραμένη καὶ ἀναφήνασα πρώτη, ταῖς δὲ δύναμιν προσθεῖσα καὶ τιμὴν καὶ αὔξησιν· οὐχ ἥκιστα δ' ὑπ' αὐτῆς ζωγραφία προῆκται καὶ κεκόσμηται

This city has been the mother and kindly nurse of many other arts, some of which she was the first to discover and reveal, while to others she gave added strength and honour and advancement; not least of all, painting was enhanced and embellished by her.

Translated by Frank Cole Babbitt (1936)

Were the Athenians More Famous in War or in Wisdom? 345f

of Athens

195 ὁ δὲ μῦθος εἶναι βούλεται λόγος ψευδὴς ἐοικὼς ἀληθινῷ

A myth wishes to be a false tale but appear a true one.

Were the Athenians More Famous in War or in Wisdom? 348a

196 πυρός ἐστιν ἡ κακία καὶ σιδήρου βιαιοτέρα

Much more violent is vice than either fire or sword.

Translated by William C. Helmbold (1939)

Whether Vice be Sufficient to Cause Unhappiness 498e

197 οὔπω δὲ τῆς ἀρετῆς γεγονὼς θεατής,

οὐδ' ὕπαρ ἀλλ' ὄναρ αὐτῆς ἐν σκιαῖς καὶ εἰδώλοις

He has not yet had a glimpse of virtue, not even a waking vision, but only dreams amid the shadows and phantoms of virtue.

Progress in Virtue 80f

198 οἱ δ' εἰς μελαγχολίαν ἢ φρενῖτιν ἢ παρακοπὴν ἥκοντες οὐδὲ φοιτῶντας ἐνιαχοῦ πρὸς αὐτοὺς ἀνέχονται ... μηδ' ὅτι νοσοῦσιν ὑπὸ τοῦ σφόδρα νοσεῖν αἰσθανόμενοι

Those in melancholia or frenzy or delirium will not even see doctors, not realizing how sick they are.

Progress in Virtue 81f

199 τὸ δ' ἡδέως ζῆν καὶ ἱλαρῶς οὐκ ἔξωθέν ἐστιν, ἀλλὰ τοὐναντίον ὁ ἄνθρωπος τοῖς περὶ αὑτὸν πράγμασιν ἡδονὴν καὶ χάριν ὥσπερ ἐκ πηγῆς τοῦ ἤθους προστίθησιν

A pleasant and happy life comes not from external things; on the contrary, man draws on his own character to add pleasure and joy to the things which surround him.

Virtue and Vice 100c

200 κακία ... σύγκοιτος ὀδυνηρά, φροντίσι καὶ μερίμναις καὶ ζηλοτυπίαις ἐκκόπτουσα τὸν ὕπνον καὶ διαφθείρουσα

Vice is a distressing bedfellow, since by anxieties, cares and jealousies it drives out and destroys sleep.

Translated by Frank Cole Babbitt (1928)

Virtue and Vice 100f

201 τὰ πάθη τῆς ψυχῆς καταστορέσῃς καὶ τὴν ἀπληστίαν παύσῃς καὶ φόβων καὶ φροντίδων ἀπαλλάξῃς σαυτόν

Lay level the emotions of your soul, put a stop to your insatiate desires, and quit yourself of fears and anxieties.

Translated by Frank Cole Babbitt (1928)

Virtue and Vice 101c

202 μὴ παιδὶ μάχαιραν, ἡ παροιμία φησίν· ἐγὼ δὲ φαίην ἄν· μὴ παιδὶ πλοῦτον μηδὲ ἀνδρὶ ἀπαιδεύτῳ δυναστείαν

Don't give a knife to a child, says the proverb; yet I would say, don't give wealth to a child, nor power to an uneducated man.

Fragment 131 (Sandbach) – *A Woman, Too, Should be Educated*

203 ὁ ἔρως οὔτε τὴν γένεσιν ἐξαίφνης λαμβάνει καὶ ἀθρόαν ὡς ὁ θυμός, οὔτε παρέρχεται ταχέως καίπερ εἶναι πτηνὸς λεγόμενος· ἀλλ' ἐξάπτεται μαλακῶς καὶ σχεδὸν οἷον ἐντήκων ἑαυτόν· ἁψάμενός τε τῆς ψυχῆς παραμένει πολὺν χρόνον

Love is not born suddenly and all at once as anger is, nor does it pass away quickly, for all that it is said to have wings. It takes fire gently, almost melting its way in, as it were; and when it has taken hold of the soul it long endures.

Translated by F.H. Sandbach (1969)

Fragment 137.1 (Sandbach) – *On Love*

204 ἀγνοεῖται τί ἦν, πῶς συνέστη, πόθεν εἰς τὴν ψυχὴν ἐνέπεσεν

No one knows what love is, how it came to be, whence it attacked the victim's soul.

Fragment 137.17 (Sandbach) – *On Love*

205 σοφὸν ἔοικε χρῆμα τὸ τῆς ἡσυχίας πρός τ' ἄλλα καὶ εἰς ἐπιστήμης καὶ φρονήσεως μελέτην· λέγω δ' οὐ τὴν καπηλικὴν καὶ ἀγοραίαν, ἀλλὰ τὴν μεγάλην, ἥτις ἐξομοιοῖ θεῷ τὸν αὐτὴν ἀναλαβόντα

How ingenious a thing is quietude, not least for acquiring knowledge and wisdom; not of course the wisdom of the market-place, but that mighty wisdom which makes us like to god.

Fragment 143 (Sandbach) – *On Quietude*

206 τί γάρ; οὐ σύνθετον φύσις ἀνθρώπων ἐκ σώματος καὶ ψυχῆς; ἢ θάτερον ἀρκοῦν ἡμῖν; ... καὶ πῶς οὐ θαυμαστὸν λέγειν τὰ τῆς ψυχῆς καλά, τὰ τοῦ σώματος ὑπερορῶντα;

What? Is not man's nature a thing compounded of body and soul? Or is one enough for us without the other? Surely it would be a strange thing to record the beauties of the soul, but to overlook those of the body.

Translated by F.H. Sandbach (1969)

Fragment 144 (Sandbach) – *On Beauty*

207 ἡ γοῦν τοῦ σώματος εὐμορφία ψυχῆς ἐστιν ἔργον σώματι χαριζομένης δόξαν εὐμορφίας

The most beautiful aspects of the body

are given their appearance by the works of the soul.

Fragment 145 (Sandbach) – *On Beauty*

208 καὶ τὸ παιδείας εὐπρόσωπον κάλλος οἴκου καὶ πόλεως καὶ ἐθνῶν ἀθόρυβος εἰρήνη διατελεῖ γιγνομένη

The beauty of education always leads to undisturbed peace both at home and among nations.

Fragment 146.5 (Sandbach) – *On Beauty*

209 ἡ δὲ γυναικῶν εὐμορφία ἀφορμὴ τοῖς πάθεσι καὶ ταῖς ἐπιθυμίαις

The beauty of women is an incitement to the passions and desires.

Translated by F.H. Sandbach (1969)

Fragment 146.7 (Sandbach) – *On Beauty*

210 ὅσα δ' ὀργῇ χρώμενοι πράττουσιν ἄνθρωποι, ταῦτ' ἀνάγκη τυφλὰ εἶναι καὶ ἀνόητα καὶ τοῦ παντὸς ἁμαρτάνειν· οὐ γὰρ οἷόν τ' ὀργῇ χρώμενον λογισμῷ χρῆσθαι

People in anger are obtuse and silly and entirely miss the mark; for no one in anger can reason rightly.

Fragment 148 (Sandbach) – *On Rage*

211 τὸν φθόνον ἔνιοι τῷ καπνῷ εἰκάζουσι· πολὺς γὰρ ἐν τοῖς ἀρχομένοις ὤν, ὅταν ἐκλάμψωσιν ἀφανίζεται

Some people compare envy to smoke; there is much of it at the start but once the flame is alight it disappears.

Translated by F.H. Sandbach (1969)

Fragment 154 (Sandbach) – *On Calumny*

212 γάμος γὰρ ἀπὸ μὲν φιλίας διττῆς κράσεως βελτίων, ἑτέρως δὲ σφαλερός

Marriage based on mutual affection is best; otherwise it is destined to fail.

Fragment 167 (Sandbach) – *A Letter on Friendliness*

POLEMON

Marcus Antonius Polemon
*c.*88–144AD
Sophist from Laodicea on Lycus, citizen and benefactor of Smyrna

1 δεῖ ἐσθίειν, χεῖρας οὐκ ἔχω· δεῖ βαδίζειν, πόδες οὐκ εἰσί μοι· δεῖ ἀλγεῖν, τότε καὶ πόδες εἰσί μοι καὶ χεῖρες

I must eat, but I have no hands; I must walk, but I have no feet; I must endure pain, and then I find I have both feet and hands.

Translated by Wilmer Cave Wright (1922)

Philostratus Flavius, *Life of the Sophists* 1.543

POLLIANUS

fl. 2nd century AD
Epigrammatist

1 Χαλκὸν ἔχων πῶς οὐδὲν ἔχεις, μάθε· πάντα δανείζεις·
οὕτως οὐδὲν ἔχεις αὐτός, ἵν' ἄλλος ἔχῃ.

Learn why having money you have none: you lend all;
therefore you have nothing and another has it all.

Greek Anthology 11.167

POLYAENUS

2nd century AD
Macedonian rhetorician

1 σπεῦδε βραδέως

Make haste slowly.

Translated by John Simpson and Jennifer Speake (1982)

Stratagems 8.24.4

often quoted in Greek by Augustus according to Suetonius, The Lives of the Caesars, *'Augustus' 25.4; cf. the Latin 'festina lente' and the identical English proverb*

2 καὶ πρόδηλον, ὡς ἀεὶ τὰ πονηρὰ τῶν ἐθῶν ἄρχεται μὲν ἀπὸ μικρῶν, ἀμελούμενα δὲ τὴν ἰσχὺν μείζω λαμβάνει

Bad habits start in a small way, neglected they soon grow powerful.

Fragment 5 (*FGrH*)

POLYAENUS JULIUS

1st century BC
Epigrammatist from Sardis

1 ἤδη μοι ξενίης εἶναι πέρας, ἐν δέ με πάτρῃ
ζώειν, τῶν δολιχῶν παυσάμενον καμάτων

Grant me an end to exile, grant repose
In mine own land from all my weary woes.

Translated by Walter Leaf (1922)

Greek Anthology 9.7

2 Ἐλπὶς ἀεὶ βιότου κλέπτει χρόνον· ἡ πυμάτη δὲ
ἠὼς τὰς πολλὰς ἔφθασεν ἀσχολίας.

Life is the fool of hope, till one last morning
Sweeps all our schemes away, without warning.

Translated by H. Macnaghten (1924)

Greek Anthology 9.8

POLYBIUS

*c.*200–*c.*118BC
Historian from Megalopolis in Arcadia
see also Scipio A. Africanus 1

1 ἀληθινωτάτην μὲν εἶναι παιδείαν καὶ γυμνασίαν πρὸς τὰς πολιτικὰς πράξεις τὴν ἐκ τῆς ἱστορίας μάθησιν

The study of history is in the truest sense an education, and a training for political life

Translated by Evelyn S. Shuckburgh (1889)

The Histories 1.1.2

2 ὥσπερ γὰρ ζῴου τῶν ὄψεων ἀφαιρεθεισῶν ἀχρειοῦται τὸ ὅλον, οὕτως ἐξ ἱστορίας ἀναιρεθείσης τῆς ἀληθείας τὸ καταλειπόμενον αὐτῆς ἀνωφελὲς γίνεται διήγημα

For as a living creature is rendered wholly useless if deprived of its eyes, so if you take truth from history what is left is but an idle unprofitable tale.

Translated by Evelyn S. Shuckburgh (1889)

The Histories 1.14.6

cf. Lucian 18

3 φύεται μὲν ἐκ τῶν τυχόντων πολλάκις τὰ μέγιστα τῶν πραγμάτων

The greatest events often arise from accidents.

Translated by H.T. Riley (1872)

The Histories 3.7.7

4 ὀχλοκόπον μὲν καὶ δημαγωγὸν τέλειον

A mere rabble-rouser and demagogue.

The Histories 3.80.3

of Gaius Flaminius, the Roman general facing Hannibal at Lake Trasimene, 217BC

5 εἰρήνη γὰρ μετὰ μὲν τοῦ δικαίου καὶ πρέποντος κάλλιστόν ἐστι κτῆμα καὶ λυσιτελέστατον, μετὰ δὲ κακίας ἢ δειλίας ἐπονειδίστου πάντων αἴσχιστον καὶ βλαβερώτατον

For peace, with justice and honour, is the fairest and most profitable of possessions, but with disgrace and shameful cowardice it is the most infamous and harmful of all.

Translated in *Bartlett's Familiar Quotations* (1980)

The Histories 4.31.8

6 κακῷ κακὸν ἰώμενος

Curing ill by ill.

Translated by Evelyn S. Shuckburgh (1889)

The Histories 5.11.1

7 τοῖς μὲν καὶ τὰς ἐπιτυχίας βλάβην ἐπιφέρειν, τοῖς δὲ καὶ τὰς περιπετείας ἐπανορθώσεως γίνεσθαι παραιτίας

Good fortune may damage some, misfortune can be a means of improvement for others.

The Histories 5.88.3

8 τρία γένη λέγειν πολιτειῶν, ὧν τὸ μὲν καλοῦσι βασιλείαν, τὸ δ' ἀριστοκρατίαν, τὸ δὲ τρίτον δημοκρατίαν. δοκεῖ δέ μοι πάνυ τις εἰκότως ἂν ἐπαπορῆσαι πρὸς αὐτούς, πότερον ὡς μόνας ταύτας ἢ καὶ νὴ Δί' ὡς ἀρίστας ἡμῖν εἰσηγοῦνται τῶν πολιτειῶν. κατ' ἀμφότερα γὰρ ἀγνοεῖν μοι δοκοῦσι. δῆλον γὰρ ὡς ἀρίστην μὲν ἡγητέον πολιτείαν τὴν ἐκ πάντων τῶν προειρημένων ἰδιωμάτων συνεστῶσαν

They distinguish three kinds of constitutions, which they designate kingship, aristocracy, democracy. But in my opinion the question might fairly be put to them, whether they name these as being the 'only' ones, or as the 'best'. In either case I think they are wrong. For it is plain that we must regard as the 'best' constitution that which partakes of all these three elements.

Translated by Evelyn S. Shuckburgh (1889)

The Histories 6.3.5

this theory of a tripartite constitution influenced political thinking for the next two thousand years (Peter Sidney Derow in OCD*); cf. Aeschines 1*

9 τοῦ κατορθοῦν ἐν πράγμασι καὶ περιγίνεσθαι τῶν ἐχθρῶν ἐν ταῖς ἐπιβολαῖς, πολλῷ μείζονος ἐμπειρίας προσδεῖται καὶ φυλακῆς τὸ καλῶς χρήσασθαι τοῖς κατορθώμασι

Those who know how to win are much more numerous than those who know how to make proper use of their victories.

Translated in *Bartlett's Familiar Quotations* (1980)

The Histories 10.36.1

10 ἐπεὶ ψιλῶς λεγόμενον αὐτὸ τὸ γεγονὸς ψυχαγωγεῖ μέν, ὠφελεῖ δ' οὐδέν· προστεθείσης δὲ τῆς αἰτίας ἔγκαρπος ἡ τῆς ἱστορίας γίνεται χρῆσις. ἐκ γὰρ τῶν ὁμοίων ἐπὶ τοὺς οἰκείους μεταφερομένων καιροὺς ἀφορμαὶ γίνονται καὶ προλήψεις εἰς τὸ προϊδέσθαι τὸ μέλλον

The mere statement of a fact may interest us, but it is when reason is added that the study of history becomes fruitful: it is the mental transference of similar circumstances to our own that gives us the means of forming presentiments about what is going to happen.

Translated by Peter Sidney Derow (2003)

The Histories 12.25b.2

11 ἐγὼ δὲ διότι μὲν δεῖ ῥοπὰς διδόναι ταῖς αὑτῶν πατρίσι τοὺς συγγραφέας, συγχωρήσαιμ' ἄν, οὐ μὴν τὰς ἐναντίας τοῖς συμβεβηκόσιν ἀποφάσεις ποιεῖσθαι περὶ αὐτῶν. ἱκανὰ γὰρ τὰ κατ' ἄγνοιαν γινόμενα τοῖς γράφουσιν, ἃ διαφυγεῖν ἄνθρωπον δυσχερές· ἐὰν δὲ κατὰ προαίρεσιν ψευδογραφῶμεν ἢ πατρίδος ἕνεκεν ἢ φίλων ἢ χάριτος, τί διοίσομεν τῶν ἀπὸ τούτου τὸν βίον ποριζομένων;

That historians should give their own country a break, I grant you; but not so far as to state things contrary to fact. For there are plenty of mistakes made by writers out of ignorance, and which any man finds it difficult to avoid. But if we knowingly write what is false, whether for the sake of our country or our friends or just to be pleasant, what difference is there between us and hack writers?

Translated by Samuel Eliot Morison (1949)

The Histories 16.14.6

12 οὐδεὶς γὰρ οὕτως οὔτε μάρτυς ἐστὶ φοβερὸς οὔτε κατήγορος δεινὸς ὡς ἡ σύνεσις ἡ κατοικοῦσ' ἐν ταῖς ἑκάστων ψυχαῖς

There is no witness so dreadful, no accuser so terrible as the conscience that dwells in the heart of every man.

Translated in *Bartlett's Familiar Quotations* (1980)

The Histories 18.43.13

13 ἔφη γὰρ αὐτοὺς τοὺς Ῥωμαίους αἰτίους εἶναι τοῦ μὴ πειθαρχεῖν αὐτοῖς τοὺς Ἕλληνας, ἀλλὰ παρακούειν καὶ τῶν γραφομένων καὶ τῶν παραγγελλομένων

He said that the Romans themselves were responsible for Greeks being disobedient, taking no heed of either written or oral orders.

The Histories 24.9.1

spoken by Callicrates, a Greek envoy, to the Roman Senate

14 καὶ τὴν γεῦσιν εὕροι τις ἂν οὐδὲ τοῖς πολυτελεστάτοις βρώμασιν ἐπιμένειν δυναμένην, ἀλλὰ σικχαίνουσαν καὶ χαίρουσαν ταῖς μεταβολαῖς καὶ προσηνεστέρως ἀποδεχομένην πολλάκις καὶ τὰ λιτὰ τῶν ἐδεσμάτων ἢ τὰ πολυτελῆ διὰ τὸν ξενισμόν

One will also notice that the palate can not remain gratified by the same meats, however costly, but grows to feel a loathing for them, and delights in changes of diet, and often prefers plain to rich food merely for the sake of variety.

Translated by Evelyn S. Shuckburgh (1889)

The Histories 38.5.7

15 μάλιστα δὲ περὶ τὴν ψυχὴν τοῦτό τις ἂν ἴδοι συμβαῖνον· αἱ γὰρ μεταλήψεις τῶν ἀτενισμῶν καὶ τῶν ἐπιστάσεων οἷον ἀναπαύσεις εἰσὶ τοῖς φιλοπόνοις τῶν ἀνδρῶν

Above all, even the mind enjoys change; for a man of action change means relaxation, be it in his field of attention or the objects in his care.

The Histories 38.5.9

POMPEIUS MACER

1st century BC–1st century AD
Tragedian

1 παίζετ' ὦ νέαι φρένες·
ὡς ἔστιν ἡμῖν τοῦτ' ἔαρ παντὸς βίου,

ἥβη δὲ λῦπαι φροντίδες θ' ἡβῶσ' ὁμοῦ

Play now, young spirits,
for now is your life's springtide;
worries grow as you grow.

Fragment 1 (Snell, *TrGF*)

POMPEY

Gnaeus Pompeius Magnus
106–48BC
Roman general and statesman

1 τὸν ἥλιον ἀνατέλλοντα πλείονες ἢ δυόμενον προσκυνοῦσιν

More worship the rising than the setting sun.

Translated in *Bartlett's Familiar Quotations* (1980)

Plutarch, *Pompey* 14.3

to Sulla on not allowing him to celebrate his African triumph, 81BC; later used proverbially

2 πλεῖν ἀνάγκη, ζῆν οὐκ ἀνάγκη

To sail is necessary; to live is not.

Translated by Bernadotte Perrin (1917)

Plutarch, *Pompey* 50.2

insisting on setting sail during a storm

POSIDIPPUS

3rd century BC
New Comedy poet of Macedonia

1 ὧν τοῖς θεοῖς ἄνθρωπος εὔχεται τυχεῖν
τῆς εὐθανασίας κρεῖττον οὐδὲν εὔχεται

Of all that men ask of the gods,
most wished for is an easy, happy death.

Fragment 18 (Kock) – 19 (K-A) – *Myrmix – The Ant*

an early mention of the word 'euthanasia'; cf. Cicero, Letters to Atticus *16.7.3, quoting the word in Greek*

2 ἔργον γε λύπην ἐκφυγεῖν, ἡ δ' ἡμέρα
ἀεί τι καινὸν εἰς τὸ φροντίζειν φέρει

'Tis hard to flee away from grief, and every day
brings ever some new worry.

Fragment 20 (Kock) – 21 (K-A) – *Omoioi – People who Resemble Each Other*

3 διὰ τὴν τέχνην μὲν γνωρίμους ἐκτησάμην
πολλούς, διὰ τὸν τρόπον δὲ τοὺς πλείστους φίλους

Through art I have acquired many an acquaintance;
and my character has brought me many a friend.

Fragment 32 (Kock) – 34 (K-A)

POSIDONIUS

*c.*135–*c.*51BC
Syrian Greek Stoic philosopher from Apamea on the Orontes

1 ζῴῳ μᾶλλον εἰκάζειν ἠξίου τὴν φιλοσοφίαν, αἵματι μὲν καὶ σαρξὶ τὸ φυσικόν, ὀστέοις δὲ καὶ νεύροις τὸ λογικόν, ψυχῇ δὲ τὸ ἠθικόν

He substituted the image of philosophy as a living creature where natural philosophy was the blood and flesh, logic the bones and sinews, and ethics the soul.

Translated by I.G. Kidd (1999)

Fragment 252b (Theiler)

PRAXILLA

5th century BC
Lyric poet from Sicyon

1 κάλλιστον μὲν ἐγὼ λείπω φάος ἠελίοιο,
δεύτερον ἄστρα φαεινὰ σεληναίης τε πρόσωπον
ἠδὲ καὶ ὡραίους σικύους καὶ μῆλα καὶ ὄγχνας

Fairest of all that I leave is the light of the sun
and the shining stars and the face of the moon,
and fresh cucumbers, and apples, and pears.

Fragment 1 (Page, *PMG*)

of Adonis being asked what he would miss most in the Underworld; the name of Praxilla's city Sicyon means 'cucumber-bed'

2 ὑπὸ παντὶ λίθῳ σκορπίον ὦ ἑταῖρε φυλάσσεο

Beware of the scorpion, my friend, that lurks under every stone.

Fragment 4 (Page, *PMG*)

PROCLUS

*c.*410–485AD

Athenian Neoplatonist philosopher, born in Lycia

1 Κλῦθι, πυρὸς νοεροῦ βασιλεῦ, χρυσήνιε Τιτάν,
κλῦθι, φάους ταμία, ζωαρκέος, ὦ ἄνα, πηγῆς
αὐτὸς ἔχων κληῖδα καὶ ὑλαίοις ἐνὶ κόσμοις
ὑψόθεν ἁρμονίης ῥύμα πλούσιον ἐξοχετεύων

Hear, golden Titan, king of intellectual fire,
hear, light-provider, keyholder of the fount,
who from on high pours life-supporting streams
harmoniously to the material world below.

Hymn to the Sun 1.1

2 ζωσάμενοι δὲ πλάνητες ἀειθαλέας σέο πυρσοὺς
αἰὲν ὑπ' ἀλλήκτοισι καὶ ἀκαμάτοισι χορείαις
ζωογόνους πέμπουσιν ἐπιχθονίοις ῥαθάμιγγας

The planets surround your ever-burning torches,
forever dancing, ceaseless and untiring
send life-producing dew-drops down to earth.

Hymn to the Sun 1.8

3 πᾶσα δ' ὑφ' ὑμετέρῃσι παλιννόστοισι διφρείαις
Ὡράων κατὰ θεσμὸν ἀνεβλάστησε γενέθλη

Under your chariot's returning courses
the hours and seasons in succession rise.

Hymn to the Sun 1.11

4 δίκης, ἣ πάντα δέδορκεν

Justice sees all.

Hymn to the Sun 1.38

5 δὸς βιότῳ πλώοντι γαληνιόωντας ἀήτας,
τέκνα, λέχος, κλέος, ὄλβον, εὐφροσύνην ἐρατεινήν,
πειθώ, στωμυλίην φιλίης, νόον ἀγκυλομήτην,
κάρτος ἐπ' ἀντιβίοισι, προεδρίην ἐνὶ λαοῖς

Grant me a voyage sailing with calm breezes,
children, wife, fame, wealth, merry festivities,
persuasion, friendly conversation, a shrewd mind,
strength against enemies, and the respect of men.

Hymn to Athena 7.47

6 οὐδὲν ... κακὸν ἀμιγὲς καὶ τοῦ ἀγαθοῦ

There's no evil without some admixture of good.

Translated by W.H.S. Jones (1956)

Platonic Theology 1.84.16

cf. Pliny, Natural History *27.3.9: 'malum quidem nullum esse sine aliquo bono'; today usually quoted as 'οὐδὲν κακὸν ἀμιγὲς καλοῦ'*

PROCOPIUS

*c.*500–*c.*562AD

Greek historian born in Caesarea, Palestine

1 οὐκ ἀνθρώπων βουλαῖς, ἀλλὰ τῇ ἐκ θεοῦ ῥοπῇ πρυτανεύεται τὰ ἀνθρώπεια

Not the wishes of man, but the will of god prevails.

Anecdota 4.44

usually quoted as 'ἄλλαι μὲν βουλαὶ ἀνθρώπων, ἄλλα δὲ θεὸς κελεύει', perhaps a translation from the Latin; cf. the English expression 'man proposes, god disposes'

PRODICUS

5th–4th century BC

Sophist philosopher from Ceos, contemporary of Socrates

1 ἐπιθυμίαν μὲν διπλασιασθεῖσαν ἔρωτα εἶναι, ἔρωτα δὲ διπλασιασθέντα μανίαν γίγνεσθαι

Desire when doubled is love, love when doubled is madness.

Translated by Kathleen Freeman (1948)

Fragment 7 (D-K)

PROTAGORAS

*c.*490–410BC

Sophist philosopher from Abdera

see also Plato 201, 203, 333

1 δύο λόγους εἶναι περὶ παντὸς πράγματος ἀντικειμένους ἀλλήλοις

There are two sides to every question, the one opposing the other.

Testimonies, Fragment 1 (D-K)

2 ἀπὸ νεότητος δὲ ἀρξαμένους δεῖ μανθάνειν

Learning must begin in youth.

Translated by Kathleen Freeman (1948)

Fragment 3 (D-K)

3 περὶ μὲν θεῶν οὐκ ἔχω εἰδέναι, οὔθ' ὡς εἰσὶν οὔθ' ὡς οὐκ εἰσὶν οὔθ' ὁποῖοί τινες ἰδέαν· πολλὰ γὰρ τὰ κωλύοντα εἰδέναι ἥ τ' ἀδηλότης καὶ βραχὺς ὢν ὁ βίος τοῦ ἀνθρώπου

About the gods, I am not able to know whether they exist or do not exist, nor what they are like in form; for the factors preventing knowledge are many: the obscurity of the subject, and the shortness of human life.

Translated by Kathleen Freeman (1948)

Fragment 4 (D-K)

4 τὸν ἥττω λόγον κρείττω ποιεῖν

Making the worse appear the better argument.

Translated by J.H. Freese (1926)

Fragment 6b (D-K)

5 μηδὲν εἶναι μήτε τέχνην ἄνευ μελέτης μήτε μελέτην ἄνευ τέχνης

Art is worth nothing without practice, practice nothing without art.

Fragment 10 (D-K)

for 'art' read also 'skill'; cf. Hippocrates 9

6 πάντων χρημάτων μέτρον ἄνθρωπος

Man is the measure of all things.

Translated by Karl Popper (1989)

Testimonies, Fragment 13 (D-K)

but cf. Plato 63: 'in our eyes god is the measure of all things'

PROVERBIAL

see also Alcaeus 21; Apelles 1, 2; Aristophanes 138; Athenaeus 2; Euripides 467; Hesiod 20, 47, 68; Homer 87, 213; Oracles 26; Timotheus (1) 2

1 ἐξέστω Κλαζομενίοις ἀσχημονεῖν

It is usual for the Clazomenians to behave unseemly; let them be.

Aelian, *Historical Miscellany* 2.15

usually quoted as 'ἔξεστι Κλαζομενίοις ἀσχημονεῖν'

2 ἐπ' ἀμφότερα τὰ ὦτα καθεύδειν

Asleep on both his ears.

Aeschines Socraticus, Fragment 54 (Dittmar)

3 ἄνω ποταμῶν ἱερῶν χωροῦσι παγαί

Backward to their sources flow the streams of holy rivers.

Translated by David Kovacs (1994)

Aeschylus, Fragment 655 (Mette) Tetralogy 44 Play A

ἄνω ποταμῶν is used to to this day for an impossible statement, or a preposterous allegation; cf. Euripides 232

4 δράσαντα παθεῖν

As you do, so you shall be done by.

Aeschylus, *Libation Bearers* 313

5 ἐκ λύκου στόματος

Saved from the wolf's mouth.

Aesop, The Wolf and the Heron, Fable 225 (Chambry, *Fabulae dodecasyllabi*) – Perry 156

6 χωλῷ παροικήσας ὑποσκάζειν μάθοις

If you live with the lame you'll soon come to limp a little.

Aesop, Proverb 2 (Perry)

7 κύων ἀναπεσὼν εἰς φάτνην αὐτός τε οὐκ ἐσθίει τῷ τε ὄνῳ ἐμποδίζει

A dog lying in the manger does not eat the straw, but will not allow the donkey to eat either.

Aesop, Proverb 74 (Perry)

8 τὸν λύκον τῶν ὤτων ἔχω, ὃν οὔτε κατέχειν ἐπὶ πολὺ δυνατόν, οὔτε μὴν ἀκίνδυνον ἀφεῖνα

I have the wolf by the ears; I can neither hold him nor let him go.

Aristaenetus, *Epistles* 2.3

9 ἐγώ τε καὶ σὺ ταὐτὸν ἕλκομεν ζυγόν

Both you and I bear the same yoke.

Translated by Denis L. Drysdall (2005)

Aristaenetus, *Epistles* 2.7

cf. the Latin 'ego ac tu idem trahimus iugum' (Erasmus, Adages *3.4.48) and the English expression 'we're all in the same boat'*

10 οἱ διψῶντες σιωπῇ πίνουσιν

The thirsty drink in silence.

Aristides Aelius, *Πρὸς Πλάτωνα περὶ ῥητορικῆς* 77.12

11 τὸν ξύοντα ἀντιξύειν

Scratch him who scratches you.

Translated by D.S. Baker (1998)

Aristides Aelius, *Πρὸς Πλάτωνα περὶ ῥητορικῆς* 84.10

cf. the English proverb 'you scratch my back and I'll scratch yours'

12 τίς γλαῦκ' Ἀθήναζ' ἤγαγεν;

Who would bring an owl to Athens?

Aristophanes, *Birds* 301

cf. the English proverb 'bringing coals to Newcastle'

13 βάλλ' εἰς κόρακας

Go and be hanged!

Translated in Liddell & Scott

Aristophanes, *Clouds* 133

14 ἐγὼ γὰρ οὐδ' ἂν ὀρνίθων γάλα ἀντὶ τοῦ βίου λάβοιμ' ἂν

I wouldn't trade my way of life even for bird's milk.

Aristophanes, *Wasps* 508

of rare and dainty things; an utmost luxury

15 ἱερὸν συμβουλή

Good counsel is a divine thing.

Translated by H.T. Riley (1872)

Aristophanes, Fragment 33 (Kock) – 32 (K-A) – *Amphiaraus*

16 τὴν αὑτοῦ σκιὰν δέδοικεν

He's afraid of his own shadow.

Translated by Jeffrey Henderson (2007)

Aristophanes, Fragment 77 (Kock) – *Babylonians*

cf. the English phrase 'afraid of your own shadow'

17 ἔνεστι κἀν μύρμηκι κἀν σέρφῳ χολή

Even the ant and the gnat have a sting.

Comments to Aristophanes' Wasps 352

18 ἀεὶ Λιβύη φέρει τι καινόν

There's always something new out of Africa.

Aristotle, *History of Animals* 606b.19

19 ἀεὶ κολοιὸς πὰρ κολοιὸν ἱζάνει

A jackdaw always perches near a jackdaw

Translated by H.T. Riley (1872)

Aristotle, *Magna Moralia* 1208b.8

cf. the English proverb 'birds of a feather flock together'

20 πολλὰ ψεύδονται ἀοιδοί

Many the lies the poets tell.

Translated by Frank Cole Babbitt (1927)

Aristotle, *Metaphysics* 983a.3

21 μία γὰρ χελιδὼν ἔαρ οὐ ποιεῖ

One swallow does not make spring.

Translated by H. Rackham (1926)

Aristotle, *Nicomachean Ethics* 1098a.18

cf. the English proverb 'one swallow does not make a summer'; cf. Aristotle 86

22 ἐν δὲ δικαιοσύνῃ συλλήβδην πᾶσ' ἀρετὴ ἔνι

All virtue is condensed in justice.

Aristotle, *Nicomachean Ethics* 1129b.29

variously attributed to Theognis and Phocylides

23 οὐκ ἔστιν εἰδῆσαι ἀλλήλους πρὶν τοὺς λεγομένους ἅλας συναναλῶσαι

Men cannot know each other till they have 'eaten salt together'.

Translated by W.D. Ross (1925)

Aristotle, *Nicomachean Ethics* 1156b.26

24 τὰ κακὰ συνάγει τοὺς ἀνθρώπους

Evils draw men together.

Translated by W. Rhys Roberts (1858–1929), rev. Jonathan Barnes (1984)

Aristotle, *Rhetoric* 1363a.1

25 μὴ τὸ πῦρ τῇ μαχαίρᾳ σκαλεύειν

Don't poke the fire with a sword.

Translated by Kathleen Freeman (1947)

Aristotle, Fragment 197 (Rose)

referring to a saying of the Pythagoreans on provoking an angry man, cf. Plutarch, Numa *14.3 et al.*

26 ὤδινεν ὄρος, Ζεὺς δ' ἐφοβεῖτο, τὸ δ' ἔτεκεν μῦν

The mountain was in labour – and Zeus was in dread – but it was delivered of a mouse.

Translated by H.T. Riley (1872)

Athenaeus, *Deipnosophists* 14.616d

27 δὶς κράμβη θάνατος

Cabbage, twice over, is death.

Translated by H.T. Riley (1872)

St Basil, *Epistles* 187.1

of stale repetition

28 πέτρην κοιλαίνει ῥανὶς ὕδατος ἐνδελεχείῃ

Constant dropping hollows out a rock.

Translated by Kathleen Freeman (1947)

Choerilus, Fragment 11 (Bernabé, *PEG*) – *Persica*

later proverbial; cf. the English proverb 'constant dropping wears away a stone'

29 πατὴρ ἀνουθέτητος παῖδα νουθετεῖ

The father who took no admonition admonishes his son.

Translated by Philip Schaff (1819–1893)

Comica Adespota, Fragment 1257 (Kock)

30 αὐτὸς ἔφα

The Master himself has said it.

Clement of Alexandria, *Stromateis* 2.5.24.3

of Pythagoras, in Latin 'ipse dixit'; countering any differing views

31 πολλοὶ στρατηγοὶ Καρίαν ἀπώλεσαν

Too many generals lost Caria.

Comica Adespota, Fragment 556 (Kock) – *469 (K-A)

cf. the English proverb 'too many cooks spoil the broth'

32 ξενίων δέ τε θυμὸς ἄριστος

It is the spirit of hospitality that matters most.

Lucius Annaeus Cornutus, *De natura deorum* 19.14

33 νεκρὸν ἰατρεύειν καὶ γέροντα νουθετεῖν ταὐτόν

You might as well physic the dead as give advice to an old man.

Translated by H.T. Riley (1872)

Democritus, Fragment 302 (D-K)

quoted in Sententiae Pythagoreorum *199a*

34 καὶ ἄρρητ' ὀνομάζων, ὥσπερ ἐξ ἁμάξης

You pelt obscene words at me, as if from a wagon.

Demosthenes, *On the Crown* 18.122

returning on a wagon from the Dionysiac festival it was customary to use coarse raillery; 'τὰ ἐξ ἁμάξης' is used in Modern Greek to this day

35 ἔφυγον κακόν, εὗρον ἄμεινον

I have escaped the bad, I have found the better.

Translated by David A. Campbell (1993)

Demosthenes, *On the Crown* 18.259

a proverbial expression said to have been spoken at Athenian weddings

36 μέτριον ὕδωρ πίνοντες, ἀμετρὶ δὲ μᾶζαν ἔδοντες

They drink their water by measure, but eat their cake without.

Translated by H.T. Riley (1872)

Diodorus Siculus, *Library of History* 12.10.5

of people who are 'penny-wise and pound-foolish'

37 Ἰλιὰς κακῶν

An Iliad of woes.

Translated by H.T. Riley (1872)

Diodorus Siculus, *Library of History* 36.6.1

38 ἐν δὲ διχοστασίῃ καὶ ὁ πάγκακος ἔλλαχε τιμῆς

In times of dissension even the utterly bad will rise to authority.

Elegiaca Adespota, Fragment 12 (West, *IEG*)

39 οὐ γὰρ ἀπὸ δρυός ἐσσι παλαιφάτου οὐδ' ἀπὸ πέτρης

For thou art not born from an oak, as the saying goes, nor from stone.

Homer, *Odyssey* 19.163

quoted by Socrates in his Apology (Plato 34d); probably a quotation from older folk-poetry, meaning 'you have not a casual origin'

40 ἅμ' ἔπος τε καὶ ἔργον

No sooner said than done.

Homeric Hymns, *Hymn to Hermes* 4.46

a common expression to this day; cf. Homer 222 and the Latin 'dictum factum'

41 ἐν τυφλῶν πόλει γλάμυρος βασιλεύει

In the country of the blind the one-eyed man is king.

Translated by Kathleen Freeman (1947)

Scholia in Iliadem, 24.192

cf. the Latin 'inter caecos regnat strabus' (Erasmus, Adages *3.4.96)*

42 ἐς θυμὸν ὦν βάλευ καὶ τὸ παλαιὸν ἔπος ὡς εὖ εἴρηται, τὸ μὴ ἅμα ἀρχῇ πᾶν τέλος καταφαίνεσθαι

Bear in mind the truth of the old saying that the end is not obvious at the beginning.

Translated by Robin Waterfield (1998)

Herodotus, *Histories* 7.51

recorded by Herodotus as a Persian proverb

43 μὴ κινεῖν κακὸν εὖ κείμενον

Do not arouse an evil at rest.

Hyperides, Fragment 30 (Jensen)

cf. the English proverb 'let sleeping dogs lie'; now often quoted as 'μὴ θίγεις τὰ κακῶς κείμενα' (do not touch what is already in a bad state)

44 παχεῖα γαστὴρ λεπτὸν οὐ τίκτει νόον

A fat belly breeds no subtle wit.

Iambica Adespota, Fragment 16 (Diehl)

quoted by St Gregory of Nazianzus, MPG 37.723.2

45 πομφόλυξ ὁ ἄνθρωπος

Man is but a bubble.

Translated by H.T. Riley (1872)

St John Chrysostom, *In illud: Verumtamen frustra conturbatur** 55.559.26

46 εἰς … τὸ πῦρ ἐκ τοῦ καπνοῦ

Out of the smoke, into the fire.

Translated by D.S. Baker (1998)

Lucian, *Menippus or The Descent Into Hades* 4.7

cf. the English expression 'out of the frying pan into the fire'

47 πίθηκος γὰρ ὁ πίθηκος … κἂν χρύσεα ἔχῃ σύμβολα

An ape is an ape even with golden spangles.

Lucian, *The Ignorant Book-Collector* 4.12

cf. the English proverb 'an ape's an ape, a varlet's a varlet, though they be clad in silk or scarlet'

48 ὄνος λύρας ἀκούεις κινῶν τὰ ὦτα

As a donkey that listens to the lyre and wags his ears.

Translated by A.M. Harmon (1921)

Lucian, *The Ignorant Book-Collector* 4.15

49 τὰ σῦκα σῦκα, τὴν σκάφην δὲ σκάφην ὀνομάσων

Call a fig a fig, a trough a trough.

Translated by K. Kilburn (1959)

Lucian, *How to Write History* 41

cf. the English phrase 'to call a spade a spade'

50 δρυὸς πεσούσης πᾶς ἀνὴρ ξυλεύεται

Once the oak is fallen, everyone is out for wood.

Menander, *Sententiae* 185 (Jaekel)

by now proverbial for someone fallen from office

51 φοβοῦ τὸ γῆρας· οὐ γὰρ ἔρχεται μόνον

Fear old age; for it does not come alone.

Translated by Gavin Betts and Alan Henry (1989)

Menander, *Sententiae* 802 (Jaekel)

often quoted as 'οὐ γὰρ ἔρχεται μόνον τὸ γῆρας'

52 ὡς οὐδὲν ἡ μάθησις, ἂν μὴ νοῦς παρῇ

Learning is worth nothing if there is no understanding.

Menander, *Sententiae* 865 (Jaekel)

53 τρυγόνος λαλίστερος

More garrulous than a turtle dove.

Menander, Fragment 346 (Körte and Thierfelder)

54 ὕπνος τὰ μικρὰ τοῦ θανάτου μυστήρια

Sleep is the lesser mystery of death.

Mnesimachus, Fragment 11 (Kock) – 11 (K-A)

55 συνειδὸς ἀγαθὸν φιλεῖ παρρησιάζεσθαι

A clear conscience can afford to speak openly.

Pausanias, *Description of Greece* 7.10.10

56 ἀγαθοὶ δ' ἀριδάκρυες ἄνδρες

Gentle are men of ready tears.

Pausanias Lexicographer, *Ἀττικῶν Ὀνομάτων Συναγωγή* Letter Alpha 5

of men that are easily moved to pity

57 οὐδὲ τὰ τρία Στησιχόρου

You don't even know the Stesichorus three.

Pausanias Lexicographer, *Ἀττικῶν Ὀνομάτων Συναγωγή* Letter Tau 45

of unpardonable ignorance; Stesichorus completed the choral ode by adding the epode to the strophe and antistrophe

58 ᾠὸν τίλλειν

To shave an egg.

Phrynichus Arabius, *Sophistic Preparations* 121

of a labour in vain, an exercise in futility

59 καὶ παρέλκει πραγμάτων ὀρθὰν ὁδόν
ἔξω φρενῶν

He draws aside from the straight path
of things,
quite out of his senses.

Pindar, *Olympian Odes* 7.46

'ἔξω φρενῶν' is proverbial to this day with the meaning 'I am mad at him, at the way he acts'

60 λέοντος ... μοῖραν αἱρεῖσθαι

Taking for himself the lion's share.

Plato, *Charmides* 155d

quoting Cydias, Fragment 1 (Page, PMG*); cf. Aesop, Chambry 207 – Perry 339, on the lion keeping all the shares for himself*

61 χαλεπὰ τὰ καλά ἐστιν ὅπῃ ἔχει μαθεῖν

Whatever is good to know is difficult to learn.

Translated by D.S. Baker (1998)

Plato, *Cratylus* 384b

62 ἀθυμοῦντες ἄνδρες οὔπω τρόπαιον ἔστησαν

Men without spirit never erected a trophy.

Translated by H.T. Riley (1872)

Plato, *Critias* 108c

cf. the English proverb 'faint heart never won fair lady'

63 κατόπιν ἑορτῆς ἥκομεν;

Have we come after the feast?

Plato, *Gorgias* 447a

still used verbatim in Modern Greek

64 μὴ κινεῖν τὰ ἀκίνητα

Thou shalt not move the immovable.

Translated by R.G. Bury (1926)

Plato, *Laws* 684e

65 μήτε γράμματα μήτε νεῖν ἐπίστωνται

They can neither read nor swim.

Plato, *Laws* 689d

of the stupid – whereas in Athens all were supposed to be literate and able to swim

66 ἀρχὴ ἥμισυ παντός

Well begun is half done.

Plato, *Laws* 753e

cf. the identical English proverb; mentioned as proverbial in both Plato and Aristotle; but see Plato 94 and Aristotle 87

67 ἰσότης φιλότητα ἀπεργάζεται

Equality leads to friendship.

Translated by Trevor J. Saunders (1970)

Plato, *Laws* 757a

68 τὸ ὅμοιον τῷ ὁμοίῳ φίλον

Like is friend to like.

Translated by W.R.M. Lamb (1925)

Plato, *Lysis* 214d and elsewhere

cf. Homer 360 and the English proverb 'like will to like'

69 ναρθηκοφόροι μὲν πολλοί, βάκχοι δέ τε παῦροι

Many the Bacchi that brandish the rod:
Few that be filled with the fire of god.

Translated by Richard Garnett (1927)

Plato, *Phaedo* 69c

i.e. there are many officials but few inspired

70 πρὸς δύο ... οὐδ' ὁ Ἡρακλῆς

Even Heracles is not a match for two.

Translated by Harold North Fowler (1914)

Plato, *Phaedo* 89c

71 κοινὰ γὰρ τὰ τῶν φίλων

Common are the possessions of friends.

Plato, *Phaedrus* 279c

variously attributed to Pittacus, and Pythagoras who wished his followers to share common goods; cf. Plato 187 and Euripides, Orestes *735*

72 ξυρεῖν ἐπιχειρεῖν λέοντα

Shave the lion.

Translated by Kathleen Freeman (1947)

Plato, *Republic* 341c

today also 'beard the lion': of a dangerous undertaking

73 δῶρα θεοὺς πείθει, δῶρ' αἰδοίους βασιλῆας

The gods can be won with gifts, and so can the king's majesty.

Translated by Desmond Lee (1955)

Plato, *Republic* 390e

Plato refutes this; some attribute it to Hesiod

74 αἵ τε κύνες ... οἷαίπερ αἱ δέσποιναι γίγνονται

The dog comes to resemble its mistress.

Translated by Desmond Lee (1955)

Plato, *Republic* 563c

quoted in Greek by Cicero, Letters to Atticus *104.5.11*

75 φεύγων καπνὸν ... εἰς πῦρ ἐμπεπτωκὼς

Out of the frying pan into the fire.

Translated in Liddell & Scott

Plato, *Republic* 569b

76 νεκρὸς οὐ δάκνει

A dead man does not bite.

Translated by John Simpson and Jennifer Speake (1982)

Plutarch, *Pompey* 77.4

cf. the English proverb 'dead men don't bite'

77 ὄνῳ τις ἔλεγε μῦθον, ὁ δὲ τὰ ὦτα ἐκίνει

Someone related a fable to an ass, and he wagged his ears.

Translated by H.T. Riley (1872)

Plutarch, Fragment 32 (Crusius) – *On Proverbs in Use among the Alexandrians**

78 ἄλλην δρῦν βαλάνιζε

Shake acorns from another oak.

Translated in Liddell & Scott

Plutarch, Fragment 40 (Crusius) – *On Proverbs in Use among the Alexandrians**

proverbial answer to beggars

79 πρὸς στάθμη
πέτρον τίθεσθαι, μή τι πρὸς πέτρῳ στάθμην

Adjust the stone to fit
The line, and not the line to fit the stone.

Translated by Frank Cole Babbitt (1927)

Plutarch, *Progress in Virtue* 75f

a building line indicated by a horizontal thread, a level

80 οὐκ ἂν ... τετρημένου χαλκοῦ πριάμενοι

I would not buy this for a brass farthing.

Translated by H.T. Riley (1872)

Plutarch, *Reply to Colotes in Defence of Other Philosophers* 1108c

as an expression of contempt

81 τῇ χειρὶ δεῖν σπείρειν, ἀλλὰ μὴ ὅλῳ τῷ θυλάκῳ

Sow by the hand, not by the whole sack!

Plutarch, *Were the Athenians More Famous in War or in Wisdom?* 348a

Corinna to young Pindar when he produced a song comprising far too many tales (Pindar, Fragment 29 (Maehler)); it has become proverbial

82 μὴ παιδὶ μάχαιραν

Don't give a knife to a child.

Translated by Kathleen Freeman (1947)

Posidonius, Fragment 247.101 (Theiler)

83 σοφίᾳ γὰρ ἔκ του
κλεινὸν ἔπος πέφανται,
τὸ κακὸν δοκεῖν ποτ' ἐσθλὸν
τῷδ' ἔμμεν ὅτῳ φρένας
θεὸς ἄγει πρὸς ἄταν

There's wisdom in the famous saying 'foul is fair, fair is foul to the man a god wishes to ruin.'

Sophocles, *Antigone* 620

84 ὀξηρὸν ἄγγος οὐ μελισσοῦσθαι πρέπει

Don't put honey in a vinegar vat.

Sophocles, Fragment 306 (Radt, *TrGF*) – *Iphigenia*

85 ἐξ ὄνυχος τὸν λέοντα

Recognizing the lion from his claw.

Sophron, Fragment 110 (Kaibel, *CGF*) – 105 (K-A)

also attributed to Alcaeus (by Plutarch, Oracles *410c)*

86 τηλοῦ φίλοι ναίοντες οὐκ εἰσὶν φίλοι

Distant friends are no friends.

Tragica Adespota, Fragment 94 (Nauck, *TGF*)

cf. the proverb 'seldom seen, soon forgotten'

87 ἢν μὴ καθάρῃς κἀλέσῃς, οὐ μὴ φάγῃς

Unless you winnow and grind you will not eat.

Tragica Adespota, Fragment 134 (Nauck, *TGF*)

88 οἴμοι, τὸ κακὸν τῆς εὐτυχίας
ὡς μᾶλλον ἐς οὖς φέρεται θνητῶν

Alas!
How much more readily than glad events
Is mischance carried to the ears of men!

Translated by William C. Helmbold (1939)

Tragica Adespota, Fragment 386 (Nauck, *TGF*)

cf. the English proverb 'bad news travels fast'

89 γλυκεῖ' ὀπώρα φύλακος ἐκλελοιπότος

Fruit is sweet when the watchman is away.

Tragica Adespota, Fragment 403 (Nauck, *TGF*)

Collections of Proverbs – Paroemiographers

90 ἀετὸς μυίας οὐ θηρεύει

An eagle will not chase flies.

Apostolius Michael, *Collection of Proverbs* 1.44

91 ἀνὴρ ἀτεχνὴς τοῖς πᾶσιν ἐστὶ δοῦλος

An unskilled person is slave to all.

Apostolius Michael, *Collection of Proverbs* 2.97

92 ἀπορία ψάλτου, βήξ

The musician coughs to hide his blunder.

Translated by D.S. Baker (1998)

Apostolius Michael, *Collection of Proverbs* 3.33

of people covering up a deficiency

93 ἐδίδαξά σε κυβισᾷν καὶ σὺ βυθίσαι με ζητεῖς

I taught you to dive, and now you wish to drown me.

Translated by D.S. Baker (1998)

Apostolius Michael, *Collection of Proverbs* 6.49

94 ἔμπροσθεν κρημνός, ὄπισθεν λύκοι

An abyss in front, and wolves behind.

Translated by Denis L. Drysdall (2005)

Apostolius Michael, *Collection of Proverbs* 7.15

cf. the Latin 'a fronte praecipitium, a tergo lupi' (Erasmus, Adages *3.4.94)*

95 εὐτυχία πολύφιλος

Success has many friends.

Translated by H.T. Riley (1872)

Apostolius Michael, *Collection of Proverbs* 8.7

96 ἰχθὺς ἐκ τῆς κεφαλῆς ὄζειν ἄρχεται

A fish begins to stink from the head downwards.

Translated by John Simpson and Jennifer Speake (1982)

Apostolius Michael, *Collection of Proverbs* 9.18

when the leader is rotten, the rest will soon follow; cf. the identical English proverb

97 κακὸς ἀνὴρ μακρόβιος

The wicked never die.

Apostolius Michael, *Collection of Proverbs* 9.36

98 λίθος κυλιόμενος φῦκος οὐ ποιεῖ

A rolling stone gathers no seaweed.

Translated by Kathleen Freeman (1947)

Apostolius Michael, *Collection of Proverbs* 10.72

cf. the English proverb 'a rolling stone gathers no moss'; originally for seashore pebbles

99 μῦς εἰς τρώγλην οὐ χωρῶν, κολοκύνταν ἔφερεν

A mouse, not fitting in his hole, brought a pumpkin.

Apostolius Michael, *Collection of Proverbs* 11.90

100 ὄπισθεν κεφαλῆς ὄμματ' ἔχει

He has eyes in the back of his head.

Translated by Kathleen Freeman (1947)

Apostolius Michael, *Collection of Proverbs* 12.94

of someone very clever; cf. the identical English phrase

101 ὁ πηλὸς ἢν μὴ δαρῇ κέραμος οὐ γίνεται

If you don't work the clay, you won't have the pot.

Apostolius Michael, *Collection of Proverbs* 12.97

102 ὄρος ὄρει οὐ μίγνυται

Mountain will not mingle with mountain.

Translated by H.T. Riley (1872)

Apostolius Michael, *Collection of Proverbs* 13.2

103 ὁ φεύγων μύλον ἄλφιτα φεύγει

He who shuns the millstone shuns the meal.

Translated by H.T. Riley (1872)

Apostolius Michael, *Collection of Proverbs* 13.78

cf. the expression 'no mill no meal'

104 στρατηγοῦ παρόντος πᾶσα ἀρχὴ παυσάσθω

When the general is present all authority ends.

Apostolius Michael, *Collection of Proverbs* 15.63

now usually quoted as 'αρχηγοῦ παρόντος πᾶσα ἀρχὴ παυσάσθω'

105 τέττιγος εὐφωνότερος

Sweeter voiced than a cicada.

Apostolius Michael, *Collection of Proverbs* 16.37

106 τὴν Χάρυβδιν ἐκφυγών, τῇ Σκύλῃ περιέπεσον

Having escaped Charybdis I fell to Scylla.

Apostolius Michael, *Collection of Proverbs* 16.49

cf. Shakespeare, Merchant of Venice *3.5.[17]: 'when I shun Scylla, your father, I fall into Charybdis, your mother'; also the English expression 'fall from the frying pan into the fire'*

107 ψεκάδες ὄμβρον γεννῶσαι

Many drops make up the rain.

Translated by D.S. Baker (1998)

Apostolius Michael, *Collection of Proverbs* 18.52

108 γλυκὺ μέλι καὶ πνιξάτω

Sweet is honey, even if it chokes you.

Appendix Proverbiorum 1.77

109 γλῶσσα γὰρ οἰκεῖ ὅπου ὁ κουρεύς

Gossip resides wherever the barber is.

Appendix Proverbiorum 1.78

110 λίθῳ λαλεῖς

Talking to a rock.

Appendix Proverbiorum 3.68

111 μία ἡμέρα σοφὸν οὐ ποιεῖ

One day does not make you wise.

Appendix Proverbiorum 3.96

112 ὄνος ἐν μύροις

A perfumed ass.

Appendix Proverbiorum 4.23

113 οὐδὲ τῶν τὰ Πυθαγόρου μυθολογούντων ἤκουσας

You didn't even listen to the teachings of Pythagoras.

Appendix Proverbiorum 4.40

of someone who knows nothing

114 τὰ πολλὰ πράττειν οὐκ ἐν ἀσφαλεῖ βίῳ

Many activities do not lead to a steadfast life.

Appendix Proverbiorum, Appendix 4.83

115 ἀδικεῖ τοὺς ἀγαθοὺς ὁ φειδόμενος τῶν κακῶν

By sparing the bad you do injustice to the good.

Arsenius, *Apophthegms* 1.34b

116 ἐξ ἁπαλῶν ὀνύχων

From when his nails were soft.

Arsenius, *Apophthegms* 7.51a

i.e. known from childhood

117 μακραὶ τυράννων χεῖρες

Long are the arms of tyrants.

Translated by Kathleen Freeman (1947)

Arsenius, *Apophthegms* 11.7a

cf. the English proverb 'kings have long arms'

118 ἀετὸν ἵπτασθαι διδάσκεις

You are teaching an eagle to fly.

Translated by H.T. Riley (1872)

Diogenianus, *Proverbs* 1.65

119 πολλαῖσι πληγαῖς δρῦς δαμάζεται

Little strokes fell great oaks.

Translated by D.S. Baker (1998)

Diogenianus, *Proverbs* 1.70

120 ἀεὶ τὰ πέρυσι βελτίω

The things of yesteryear are always better.

Translated by Laura Gibbs (2008)

Diogenianus, *Proverbs* 2.54

121 ἄκουε τἀπὸ καρδίας

Listen to words that come from the heart.

Diogenianus, *Proverbs* 2.59

cf. Lucian, Jupiter tragoedus *19.6*

122 ἄλλοι μὲν σπείρουσιν, ἄλλοι δὲ ἀμήσονται

Others sow, others reap.

Diogenianus, *Proverbs* 2.62

123 μία λόχμη οὐ τρέφει δύο ἐριθάκους

One bush will not hold two robins.

Diogenianus, *Proverbs* 3.15

cf. Aristophanes 141

124 ἅμαξα τὸν βοῦν ἕλκει

The cart is pulling the ox.

Translated by Kathleen Freeman (1947)

Diogenianus, *Proverbs* 3.30

of things happening the wrong way round; cf. the English proverb 'putting the cart before the horse'

125 γέρων ἀλώπηξ οὐχ ἁλίσκεται

No old fox is caught in a trap.

Diogenianus, *Proverbs* 4.7

126 ἐν ἀμούσοις καὶ κόρυδος φθέγγεται

With those who know no melody even the sparrow is musical.

Translated by H.T. Riley (1872)

Diogenianus, *Proverbs* 4.56

127 εὕρηκα ὃ οὐκ ἐζήτουν

I have found what I did not seek.

Translated by H.T. Riley (1872)

Diogenianus, *Proverbs* 4.90

cf. the expression 'getting more than bargained for'

128 ζεῖ χύτρα, ζῇ φιλία

When the pot boils, friendship thrives.

Diogenianus, *Proverbs* 4.96

129 ἐκ τοῦ καρποῦ τὸ δένδρον

Know the tree by its seed.

Diogenianus, *Proverbs* 5.15

130 ἵππος με φέρει, βασιλεύς με τρέφει

The horse carries me, the king feeds me.

Diogenianus, *Proverbs* 5.31

of living well on foreign goods

131 κάμηλος καὶ ψωριῶσα πολλῶν ὄνων ἀνατίθεται φορτία

One mangy camel can carry the loads of many donkeys.

Diogenianus, *Proverbs* 5.81

132 κενὰ κενοὶ βουλεύονται

Empty people, empty thoughts.

Diogenianus, *Proverbs* 5.100

133 λαγὼς καθεύδων

A sleeping hare.

Translated by H.T. Riley (1872)

Diogenianus, *Proverbs* 6.1

cf. 'one who sleeps with his eyes open'; similar to the saying 'catch a weasel asleep'

134 λύχνον ἐν μεσημβρίᾳ ἅπτειν

Lighting a lamp at midday.

Diogenianus, *Proverbs* 6.27

cf. Diogenes 4

135 μικρὸν κακὸν, μέγα ἀγαθόν

A small evil could turn out to be a great good.

Diogenianus, *Proverbs* 6.62

136 Μίδας ὄνου ὦτα

King Midas has donkey's ears.

Diogenianus, *Proverbs* 6.73

sometimes interpreted as 'having many informers'

137 ξύλον ἀγκύλον οὐδέποτ' ὀρθόν

A crooked log will never be straight.

Diogenianus, *Proverbs* 6.92

of those who will not be bettered

138 πρὸ τῆς νίκης τὸ ἐγκώμιον ᾄδει

Chanting triumph before the victory.

Diogenianus, *Proverbs* 7.56

139 πρὶν τοὺς ἰχθῦς ἑλεῖν, τὴν ἅλμην κυκᾷς

You stir the brine before you catch the fish.

Diogenianus, *Proverbs* 7.93

cf. the English proverb 'first catch your hare, then cook it'

140 ῥαχίας λαλίστερος

Chattering more than the waves do.

Diogenianus, *Proverbs* 7.99

141 ῥόδον παρελθὼν μηκέτι ζήτει πάλιν

Ask not for past roses.

Diogenianus, *Proverbs* 8.2

142 τυφλότερος ἀσπάλακος

As blind as a mole.

Diogenianus, *Proverbs* 8.25

cf. the English phrase 'as blind as a bat'

143 ὑπὸ παντὶ λίθῳ σκόρπιος εὕδει

Beneath every stone a scorpion lurks.

Diogenianus, *Proverbs* 8.59

cf. Sophocles 305 and Aristophanes 132

144 ἐλέφας μυὸς οὐκ ἀλεγίζει

The elephant heedeth not the fly.

Translated by H.T. Riley (1872)

Gregorius, *Proverbs* 2.48

cf. Epistles of Phalaris* *86.1*

145 λίθοις τὸν ἥλιον βάλλει

Throwing stones at the sun.

Translated by Gavin Betts and Alan Henry (1989)

Mantissa Proverbiorum 1.99

146 ἥλῳ τὸν ἧλον, παττάλῳ τὸν πάτταλον

Drive out one nail with another, one peg with another.

Iulius Pollux, *Onomasticon* 9.120

cf. the English proverb 'one nail knocks out another'; cf. Aristotle, Politics *1314a.5*

147 ἀπὸ λεπτοῦ φασὶ μίτου τὸ ζῆν ἠρτῆσθαι

Life hangs from the thin thread of destiny.

Suda, Lexicon Alpha.3388

148 δὶς πρὸς τὸν αὐτὸν αἰσχρὸν προσκρούειν λίθον

It is silly to stumble on the same stone twice.

Suda, Lexicon Delta.1267

149 ὁδοῦ παρούσης τὴν ἀτραπὸν ζητεῖς

When the high road is before you, don't look for a footpath.

Suda, Lexicon Omikron.48

cf. Aristophanes, Fragment 47 (K-A)

150 ῥήματα ἀντ' ἀλφίτων

Offering fine words rather than barley biscuits.

Suda, Lexicon Rho.131

cf. the expression 'fine words butter no parsnips'

151 εἰς τὸν τετρημένον πίθον ἀντλεῖν

Draw water in a leaky jar.

Translated by E.C. Marchant (1923)

Xenophon, *Oeconomicus* 7.40

of the task of the Danaids, i.e. of labour in vain

152 ἀνέμῳ διαλέγῃ

Talking to the wind.

Zenobius, *Epitome* 1.38

153 αἶξ οὔπω τέτοκεν, ἔριφος δ' ἐπὶ δώματος παίζει

The kid hasn't been born yet and you imagine it playing in the yard.

Zenobius, *Epitome* 1.42

cf. the English proverb 'don't count your chickens before they're hatched'

154 ἄκαιρος εὔνοι' οὐδὲν ἔχθρας διαφέρει

Untimely benevolence is no different to hostility.

Zenobius, *Epitome* 1.50

referring to Hippolytus, cf. Scholia in Euripidem *597*

155 ἀλλ' οὐκ αὖθις ἀλώπηξ

A fox is not caught twice in the same snare.

Translated by H.T. Riley (1872)

Zenobius, *Epitome* 1.67

156 ἀλωπεκίζειν πρὸς ἑτέραν ἀλώπεκα

Playing sly to another fox.

Zenobius, *Epitome* 1.70

157 ἀντὶ πέρκης σκορπίον

Instead of the perch, the scorpion fish.

Zenobius, Epitome 1.88

of those who, not content with what they have, receive worse

158 ἀνεῳγμέναι Μουσῶν θύραι

The gates of the Muses are open.

Zenobius, *Epitome* 1.89

of education; of poetry (cf. Plato, Phaedrus *245a)*

159 ἄνθρακες ὁ θησαυρὸς πέφηνεν

The treasure turned out to be charcoal.

Zenobius, *Epitome* 2.1

of illusions destroyed

160 ἁλιεὺς πληγεὶς νοῦν οἴσει

A stung fisherman will never forget.

Zenobius, *Epitome* 2.15

stung by the venomous spines of a scorpion fish; cf. the English proverb 'once bitten, twice shy'

161 ἀγὼν πρόφασιν οὐκ ἐπιδέχεται, οὔτε φιλία

War and friendship admit of no excuses.

Translated by H.T. Riley (1872)

Zenobius, *Epitome* 2.45

attributed to Ibycus; cf. Aristophanes, Fragment 331 (Kock) – 349 (K-A)

162 ἀετὸς ἐν νεφέλαις

An eagle in the clouds.

Zenobius, *Epitome* 2.50

of something quite out of reach

163 βατράχῳ ὕδωρ

Water to a frog.

Zenobius, *Epitome* 2.79

giving someone something he adores

164 γλῶσσα ποῖ πορεύῃ; πόλιν ἀνορθώσασα καὶ πόλιν καταστρέψουσα;

Tongue, where goest thou? To save a city or to destroy a city?

Zenobius, *Epitome* 2.99

165 δίκη δίκην ἔτικτε καὶ βλάβη βλάβην

Justice brings justice and evil brings evil.

Zenobius, *Epitome* 3.28

166 ἐκ τριχὸς κρέμαται

Hanging by a thread.

Zenobius, *Epitome* 3.47

cf. the identical English expression

167 εἰς θεῶν ὦτα ἦλθεν

This did reach the ears of the gods.

Zenobius, *Epitome* 3.49

of not avoiding punishment

168 εἰς ἀρχαίας φάτνας

Back to my old ways.

Zenobius, *Epitome* 3.50

169 εἷς ἀνήρ, οὐδεὶς ἀνήρ

One man doesn't make humankind.

Zenobius, *Epitome* 3.51

170 εἰ μὴ δύναιο βοῦν ἐλᾶν ἔλαυν' ὄνον

If you cannot carry off a bull, run off with a donkey

Zenobius, *Epitome* 3.54

171 ἔξω βελῶν καθῆσθαι

Keeping out of shot.

Translated by H.T. Riley (1872)

Zenobius, *Epitome* 3.89

172 οὐκ ἐπαινεθείης οὐδ' ἐν περιδείπνῳ

No good words will be spoken of you, even at your funeral.

Zenobius, *Epitome* 5.28

173 ὁ Κρὴς τὴν θάλατταν
ὁ Κρὴς δὴ τὸν πόντον ἀγνοεῖ

The Cretan and the sea.

Translated by D.A. Campbell (1982)

Like a Cretan feigning ignorance of the sea.

Translated in Liddell & Scott

Zenobius, *Epitome* 5.30

variously attributed to Sappho, Alcaeus or Alcman; of those who feign ignorance (as the Cretans were excellent seamen); cf. Epimenides 1

174 πτωχοῦ πήρα οὐ πίμπλαται

A beggar's pouch is never filled.

Translated by H.T. Riley (1872)

Zenobius, *Epitome* 5.66

175 Ὕδραν τέμνεις

Wounding Hydra.

Zenobius, *Epitome* 6.26

of labour in vain, because two heads sprang up for every one which was cut off; cf. Plato 243

Paradoxa and Nonsensical

see also Epimenides 1; Eubulides 1–3

176 δικτύῳ ἄνεμον θηρᾷς

Hunting the wind with a net.

Plutarch, *Collection of Impossibilities* 3

177 εἰς ὕδωρ γράφεις

Writing on water.

Plutarch, *Collection of Impossibilities* 5

178 εἰς ψάμμον οἰκοδομεῖς

You are building your house on sand.

Plutarch, *Collection of Impossibilities* 10

179 σίδηρον πλεῖν διδάσκεις

Teaching iron to float.

Plutarch, *Collection of Impossibilities* 14

180 κύματα μετρεῖς

Counting the waves.

Plutarch, *Collection of Impossibilities* 17

181 ὑπὲρ τὰ ἐσκαμμένα πηδᾷς

You leap beyond the trench.

Plutarch, *Collection of Impossibilities* 18

on going too far; cf. Plato, Cratylus *413a; a trench was the limit of the leap for the pentathletes*

182 τράγον ἀμέλγεις

Milking a billy goat.

Plutarch, *Collection of Impossibilities* 20

183 ἄμμον θαλάσσης κοφίνῳ ζητεῖς μετρεῖν

Trying to measure the sand of the sea with a basket.

Plutarch, *Collection of Impossibilities* 21

184 ἐλαίῳ πῦρ σβεννύεις

Extinguishing a fire with oil.

Plutarch, *Collection of Impossibilities* 22

185 ἄνευ πτερῶν ζητεῖς ἵπτασθαι

Trying to fly without wings.

Plutarch, *Collection of Impossibilities* 25

186 φαλακρῷ κτένας δανείζεις

Lending combs to a bald man.

Plutarch, *Collection of Impossibilities* 26

187 τυφλῷ κάτοπτρον χαρίζῃ

Giving a mirror to a blind man.

Plutarch, *Collection of Impossibilities* 27

188 ἄνεμον διώκεις

Chasing the wind.

Plutarch, *Collection of Impossibilities* 30

189 ἀνδριάντα γαργαλίζεις

Tickling a statue.

Plutarch, *Collection of Impossibilities* 45

190 ἄστρα τοξεύεις

Shooting arrows at the stars.

Plutarch, *Collection of Impossibilities* 47

191 κοσκίνῳ φέρεις ὕδωρ

Carrying water in a sieve.

Plutarch, *Collection of Impossibilities* 50

PROVERBIAL EXPRESSIONS

1 κέρας Ἀμαλθίης

The horn of Amalthea, a horn of plenty.

Translated in Liddell & Scott

Anacreon, Fragment 16 (Page, *PMG*)

2 σολοικισμὸς

A solecism.

Translated by E.S. Forster (1955)

Aristotle, *Sophistical Refutations* 165b.14

referring to the way of speaking of the people of Soloi, often at variance with accepted grammar and syntax

3 Τενέδιος πέλεκυς

A Tenedian double-edged axe.

Aristotle, Fragment 253 (Rose)

of impartial and over-harsh justice, referring to a Tenedian law by which both adulterers were executed; Tenedos is an island in the Aegean

4 Λερναία ὕδρα

The Lernaean hydra.

Diodorus Siculus, *Library of History* 4.11.5

a many-headed snake whose heads regrew when cut off; cf. Plato 243; Proverbial 175

5 τὴν αὐλὴν τὴν Αὐγέου καθᾶραι

To clean the Augean stables.

Diodorus Siculus, *Library of History* 4.13.3

one of the labours of Heracles was to clean the Augean stables where an enormous amount of dung had accumulated

6 κλίνη Προκρούστου

The bed of Procrustes.

Diodorus Siculus, *Library of History* 4.59.5

'Procrustean' is now used an adjective for enforcing conformity; Procrustes was a brigand who would stretch or cut his victims to fit his bed

7 κύκνειον ᾆσμα

Swan song.

Diodorus Siculus, *Library of History* 31.5.1

a swan's dying song is first mentioned in Aeschylus, Agamemnon *1444*

8 Κυλώνειον ἄγος

The Cylonian pollution.

Translated by Bernadotte Perrin (1914)

Epimenides, *Testimonies*, Fragment 1 (D-K)

the pollution brought about by the Athenians who murdered the followers of Cylon though they had taken refuge in the temples; the Cylonian guilt was expiated by Epimenides

9 Καδμείη τις νίκη

A Cadmean victory.

Herodotus, *Histories* 1.166

where victor and vanquished suffer alike; originally of the two sons of Cadmus killing each other for the possession of Thebes

10 Στέντορι εἰσαμένη μεγαλήτορι χαλκεοφώνῳ,
ὃς τόσον αὐδήσασχ' ὅσον ἄλλοι πεντήκοντα

Stentor
whose brazen lungs could give a battle shout
as loud as fifty soldiers.

Translated by Robert Fitzgerald (1975)

Homer, *Iliad* 5.785

a 'stentorian voice' is now an expression in both Greek and English

11 ἐπὶ ξυροῦ ἀκμῆς

On razor's edge.

Translated by A.T. Murray (1924)

Homer, *Iliad* 10.171

12 μυίης θάρσος

The reckless persistence of a fly.

Translated in Liddell & Scott

Homer, *Iliad* 17.570

13 σαρδάνιος γέλως
... (μείδησε δὲ θυμῷ σαρδάνιον)

A sardonic smile.

Translated by E.V. Rieu (1946)

Homer, *Odyssey* 20.301

cf. the Latin 'risus sardonicus'; the common explanation given of this laugh was that it resembled the grinning effect produced by the Sardinian crowfoot, or hairy buttercup (Ranunculus sardous)*; cf. Apostolius 15.35*

14 Ἡρακλέους ἆθλοι

The labours of Heracles.

Translated in Liddell & Scott

Isocrates, *To Demonicus* 1.8

a Herculean task is a common expression in many modern languages

15 συκίνη μάχαιρα

A sword made of the wood of a fig tree.

Pausanias Lexicographer, *Αττικών Ονομάτων Συναγωγή* Letter Sigma 25

a dry branch from a fig tree is notoriously brittle

16 Πολυγνώτου λαγώς

The hare of Polygnotus.

Suda Lexicon Pi.440

of a perfectly naturalistic painting

17 Γόρδιος δεσμός

The Gordian knot.

Plutarch, *Alexander* 18.1–4

according to tradition, whoever solved the Gordian knot would become ruler of Asia; Alexander just cut through it with his sword; of a problem solved in a forceful way

18 Πάρθων τοξεύματα

Parthian shots.

Plutarch, *Antony* 49.1

of some last arrows shot by a retreating army

19 ἄπληστος πίθος

A jar that will never fill.

Plutarch, *On the Proverbs in Use among the Alexandrians** Fragment 7 (Crusius)

a reference to the pierced vessel of the Danaids; also of Hades, never to fill with souls

20 εἰς μακάρων νήσους

To the Islands of the Blest.

Translated in Liddell & Scott

Plato, *Republic* 540b

cf. Hesiod, Works and Days *171; used to signify someone's decease; cf. Tennyson, 'Ulysses' (1842) 70: 'It may be we shall touch the Happy Isles, And see the great Achilles'*

21 Δρακόντειος νόμος

A draconian law.

Xenarchus, Fragment 4.22 (Kock) – 4 (K-A)

– Pentathlos

of an excessively harsh and severe law

22 ἀκέφαλος μῦθος

A story without a head.

Translated by H.T. Riley (1872)

Apostolius Michael, *Collection of Proverbs* 2.2

telling only part of the story

23 Θεσσαλὸν νόμισμα

A Thessalian coin.

Translated in Liddell & Scott

Hesychius, *Lexicon* Theta.406

of false money

24 Πύρρειος νίκη

A Pyrrhic victory.

Anonymous

a victory won at too great a cost to have been worthwhile for the victor; cf. Pyrrhus 1

PTOLEMAEUS

Uncertain which as there are many with the same name

1 Οἶδ', ὅτι θνατὸς ἐγὼ καὶ ἐφάμερος· ἀλλ' ὅταν ἄστρων
μαστεύω πυκινὰς ἀμφιδρόμους ἕλικας,
οὐκέτ' ἐπιψαύω γαίης ποσίν, ἀλλὰ παρ' αὐτῷ
Ζανὶ θεοτρεφέος πίμπλαμαι ἀμβροσίης.

Mortal though I be, yea ephemeral, if but a moment
I gaze up to the night's starry domain of heaven,
Then no longer on earth I stand; I touch the Creator,
And my lively spirit drinketh immortality.

Translated by Robert Bridges (1916)

Greek Anthology 9.577

PTOLEMY

Claudius Ptolemaeus

*c.*100–178AD

Alexandrian mathematician, astronomer and geographer

1 τῶν δὲ μετὰ τὴν γένεσιν συμπτωμάτων ἡγεῖται μὲν ὁ περὶ χρόνων ζωῆς λόγος

The length of life takes the leading place among inquiries about events following birth.

Translated by F.E. Robbins (1940)

Tetrabiblos 3.10.1

2 συνῆπται δ' ὥσπερ ἡ μὲν κτητικὴ τύχη ταῖς τοῦ σώματος οἰκειώσεσιν, ἡ δὲ ἀξιωματικὴ ταῖς τῆς ψυχῆς

As material fortune is associated with the properties of the body, so honour belongs to those of the soul.

Translated by F.E. Robbins (1940)

Tetrabiblos 4.1.1

3 οὐκ εἰσὶ πλείονες τῶν τριῶν διαστάσεις ... δύο μέν, καθ' ἃς τὸ ἐπίπεδον ὁρίζεται, τρίτην δὲ τὴν τὸ βάθος μετροῦσαν· ὥστε, εἴ τις εἴη μετὰ τὴν τριχῇ διάστασιν ἄλλη, ἄμετρος ἂν εἴη παντελῶς καὶ ἀόριστος

There are no more than three dimensions: two by which a plane is defined, a third giving depth; thus, if there is another after the third, it can only be beyond measure and indeterminate.

Fragment 6 (Heiberg)

PYRRHON

*c.*365–275BC

Philosopher and founder of Greek Scepticism from Elis

1 τό τε πεῖθον οὐχ ὑποληπτέον ἀληθὲς ὑπάρχειν

We must not assume that what convinces us is actually true.

Translated by R.D. Hicks (1925)

Diogenes Laertius, *Lives of Eminent Philosophers* 9.94

2 τὸ πείθειν ... γίνεται δὲ καὶ παρὰ τὰ ἐκτὸς ἡ πιθανότης, παρὰ τὸ ἔνδοξον τοῦ λέγοντος ἢ παρὰ τὸ φροντιστικὸν ἢ παρὰ τὸ αἱμύλον ἢ παρὰ τὸ σύνηθες ἢ παρὰ τὸ κεχαρισμένον

Persuasiveness may depend on external circumstances, on the reputation of the speaker, on his ability as a thinker or his artfulness, on the familiarity or the pleasantness of the topic.

Translated by R.D. Hicks (1925)

Diogenes Laertius, *Lives of Eminent Philosophers* 9.94

PYRRHUS

319–272BC
King of Epirus, 306–272BC

1 ἂν ἔτι μίαν μάχην νικήσωμεν, ἀπολούμεθα παντελῶς

If we have such another victory, we are undone.

Translated by Francis Bacon (1625)

Plutarch, *Pyrrhus* 21.14

on defeating the Romans at Ausculum, 279BC; cf. Proverbial Expressions 24

2 Πύρρος δ' ὁ βασιλεὺς ὁδεύων ἐνέτυχε κυνὶ φρουροῦντι σῶμα πεφονευμένου, καὶ πυθόμενος τρίτην ἡμέραν ἐκείνην ἄσιτον παραμένειν καὶ μὴ ἀπολέιπειν τὸν μὲν νεκρὸν ἐκέλευσε θάψαι, τὸν δὲ κύνα μεθ' ἑαυτοῦ κομίζειν ἐπιμελομένους

King Pyrrhus on a journey chanced upon a dog guarding the body of a murdered man; in answer to his questions he was told that the dog had remained there without eating for three days and refused to leave. Pyrrhus gave orders for the corpse to be buried and the dog cared for and brought along in his train.

Translated by William C. Helmbold (1957)

Plutarch, *Whether Land or Sea Animals Are Cleverer* 969C

PYTHAGORAS

*c.*580–*c.*500BC
Philosopher and mathematician from Samos
see also Aelian 2; Anonymous 149; Euclid 6; Heraclitus 52; Herodotus 87; Palladas 3; Proverbial 30, 113

1 Ἀθανάτους μὲν πρῶτα θεούς, νόμῳ ὡς διάκειται, τίμα

First of all, honour the immortal gods, as by law enjoined.

Translated by H.T. Riley (1872)

Carmen Aureum 1

Pythagoras, as Socrates after him, never set his teachings in writing; what is available to us are testimonies written by his disciples, some of whom were active long after his death

2 κρατεῖν δ' εἰθίζεο
τῶνδε, γαστρὸς μὲν πρώτιστα καὶ ὕπνου
λαγνείης τε καὶ θυμοῦ

Control the following: primarily your belly, then sleep and lust and anger.

Carmen Aureum 9

3 πάντων δὲ μάλιστ' αἰσχύνεο σαυτόν

But most of all respect thyself.

Translated by H.T. Riley (1872)

Carmen Aureum 12

4 δικαιοσύνην ἀσκεῖν ἔργῳ τε λόγῳ τε

Practise righteousness in both word and deed.

Carmen Aureum 13

5 ἀλλὰ γνῶθι μέν, ὡς θανέειν πέπρωται ἅπασιν

Know this well, that death is in store for all.

Carmen Aureum 15

6 χρήματα δ' ἄλλοτε μὲν κτᾶσθαι φιλεῖ, ἄλλοτ' ὀλέσθαι

Money is wont now to be won, now to be lost.

Carmen Aureum 16

7 οὐ δ' ὑγιείας τῆς περὶ σῶμ' ἀμέλειαν ἔχειν χρή,
ἀλλὰ ποτοῦ τε μέτρον καὶ σίτου γυμνασίων τε
ποιεῖσθαι

Be not neglectful of your health; keep due measure of drink and food and exercise.

Carmen Aureum 32

8 εἰθίζου δὲ δίαιταν ἔχειν καθάρειον ἄθρυπτον

Accustom yourself to a clean and simple diet.

Carmen Aureum 35

9 μέτρον δ' ἐπὶ πᾶσιν ἄριστον

Moderation in all things is best.

Carmen Aureum 38

10 πῆ παρέβην; τί δ' ἔρεξα; τί μοι δέον οὐκ ἐτελέσθη;

Where did I overstep? What did I do to him? What duty did I leave undone?

Carmen Aureum 42

11 χρηστὰ δὲ τέρπευ·
ταῦτα πόνει, ταῦτ' ἐκμελέτα, τούτων χρὴ ἐρᾶν σε·
ταῦτά σε τῆς θείης ἀρετῆς εἰς ἴχνια θήσει

Delight in righteousness; this be your effort, this your practice, this your desire; this will make you achieve divine virtue.

Carmen Aureum 44

12 ναὶ μὰ τὸν ἁμετέρᾳ ψυχᾷ παραδόντα τετρακτύν,
παγὰν ἀενάου φύσεως

I call to witness him who to our souls expressed The Tetractys, eternal Nature's fountain-spring.

Translated by Kenneth Sylvan Guthrie (1920)

Carmen Aureum 47

the oath of the Pythagoreans; the tetractys was the Pythagorean symbol of an isosceles triangle made up of four rows of one, two, three and four points, a sum of ten

13 μηδένα γὰρ εἶναι σοφὸν ἄνθρωπον ἀλλ' ἢ θεόν

No man is wise, but god alone.

Translated by R.D. Hicks (1925)

Diogenes Laertius, *Lives of Eminent Philosophers* 1.12

14 κοινὰ τὰ φίλων

Friends share all things.

Translated by R.D. Hicks (1925)

Diogenes Laertius, *Lives of Eminent Philosophers* 8.10

15 τοῦτον γὰρ καὶ τὸ φονεύειν ἀπαγορεύειν, μὴ ὅτι γε ἅπτεσθαι τῶν ζῴων κοινὸν δίκαιον ἡμῖν ἐχόντων ψυχῆς

Pythagoras forbade even the killing, let alone the eating, of animals which share with us the privilege of having a soul.

Translated by R.D. Hicks (1925)

Diogenes Laertius, *Lives of Eminent Philosophers* 8.13

16 ὑπελάμβανε δὲ καὶ τὴν μουσικὴν μεγάλα συμβάλλεσθαι πρὸς ὑγείαν

Pythagoras was likewise of the opinion that music, if properly used, greatly contributed to health.

Iamblichus, *Life of Pythagoras* 25.110

17 τοὺς Πυθαγορικούς ... εἴ ποτε προαχθεῖεν εἰς λοιδορίαν ὑπ' ὀργῆς, πρὶν ἢ τὸν ἥλιον δῦναι τὰς δεξιὰς ἐμβαλόντες ἀλλήλοις καὶ ἀσπασάμενοι διελύοντο

Pythagoreans, if ever they were led by anger into recrimination, never let the sun go down before they joined right hands, embraced each other, and were reconciled.

Translated by William C. Helmbold (1939)

Plutarch, *On Brotherly Love* 488c

cf. Bible 245 and the English proverb 'never let the sun go down on your anger'

18 ὁ μὲν γὰρ λόγος τροφὴ διανοίας ἐστί

Speech is the food of thought.

Translated by Frank Cole Babbitt (1927)

Plutarch, *Education of Children** 12f

19 ἑλοῦ βίον ἄριστον, ἡδὺν δ' αὐτὸν ἡ συνήθεια ποιήσει

Choose the life that is best, and constant habit will make it pleasant.

Translated by Frank Cole Babbitt (1928)

Plutarch, *On Exile* 602c

20 μηδὲν θαυμάζειν

Wonder at nothing.

Translated by Frank Cole Babbitt (1927)

Plutarch, *On Listening to Lectures* 44b

21 ὅ τε Πυθαγόρας, ἐρωτηθεὶς τί χρόνος ἐστί, τὴν τοὐρανοῦ ψυχὴν εἰπεῖν

Pythagoras, when asked what time was, answered that it was the soul of the heavens.

Translated by Harold Cherniss (1957)

Plutarch, *Platonic Essays* 1007b

22 εἱμαρμένην τε τῶν ὅλων καὶ κατὰ μέρος αἰτίαν εἶναι

Fate is the cause of things, both separately and in their entirety.

Pythagoristae, Fragment b1a.21 (D-K)

23 τὸ μὲν φρόνιμον ἀθάνατον, τὰ δὲ λοιπὰ θνητά

Reason is immortal, all else mortal.

Translated by R.D. Hicks (1925)

Pythagoristae, Fragment b1a.47 (D-K)

24 μέγιστον δέ φησι τῶν ἐν ἀνθρώποις εἶναι τὴν ψυχὴν πεῖσαι ἐπὶ τὸ ἀγαθὸν ἢ ἐπὶ τὸ κακόν

The most momentous thing in life is the art of winning the soul to good or to evil.

Translated by R.D. Hicks (1925)

Pythagoristae, Fragment b1a.61 (D-K)

25 τήν τε ἀρετὴν ἁρμονίαν εἶναι καὶ τὴν ὑγίειαν καὶ τὸ ἀγαθὸν ἅπαν καὶ τὸν θεόν

Virtue is harmony; and so is health, and all things of value; and god.

Pythagoristae, Fragment b1a.65 (D-K)

26 τάς λεωφόρους μὴ βαδίζειν

Do not pursue the well-trod avenues.

Pythagoristae, Fragment c6 (D-K)

i.e. do not follow common views, ways of thinking etc.

27 φείδεο τῆς ζωῆς, μή μιν καταθυμοβορήσῃς

Spare your life, let not sorrows vex your heart.

Fragment 159.23 (Thesleff)

28 φυτὸν ἥμερον μήτε φθίνειν μήτε σίνεσθαι, ἀλλὰ μηδὲ ζῷον ὃ μὴ βλάπτει ἀνθρώπους

Never destroy or injure trees, nor any animal that does no harm to man.

Translated by R.D. Hicks (1925)

Fragment 162.29 (Thesleff)

29 ἐν ὀργῇ μήτε τι λέγειν μήτε πράσσειν

In anger restrain hand and tongue.

Translated by R.D. Hicks (1925)

Fragment 163.3 (Thesleff)

30 κυάμων ἄπο χεῖρας ἔχειν

Keep your hands off beans!

Translated by Kathleen Freeman (1948)

Testimonies, Fragment 9 (D-K)

various interpretations, including undisturbed sleep and politics (as beans were then used for counting votes)

31 τίνες οὖν ἄγκυραι δυναταί; φρόνησις, μεγαλοψυχία, ἀνδρεία· ταύτας οὐδεὶς χειμὼν σαλεύει

Which anchors are indeed powerful? Wisdom, greatness of soul, courage; these no storm can shake.

Stobaeus, *Anthology* 3.1.29

32 τὰ ἁμαρτήματά σου πειρῶ μὴ λόγοις ἐπικαλύπτειν, ἀλλὰ θεραπεύειν ἐλέγχοις

Do not cover up your mistakes with words, but by correcting redress them.

Stobaeus, *Anthology* 3.13.53

33 Πυθαγόρας ἐρωτηθεὶς πῶς ἂν οἰνόφλυξ τοῦ μεθύειν παύσαιτο, εἰ συνεχῶς ἔφη θεωροίη τὰ ὑπ' αὐτοῦ πρασσόμενα

When Pythagoras was asked by a drunkard how to stop drinking, he answered, 'By continuously observing what drunkards do.'

Stobaeus, *Anthology* 3.18.33

34 ἔλεγεν ὁ Πυθαγόρας χρὴ σιγᾶν ἢ κρείσσονα σιγῆς λέγειν

Be silent or, when you speak, say something better than silence.

Stobaeus, *Anthology* 3.34.7

later proverbial

35 μὴ ἐν πολλοῖς ὀλίγα λέγε, ἀλλ' ἐν ὀλίγοις πολλά

Say not little with a lot, but a lot with little.

Stobaeus, *Anthology* 3.35.8

36 Πυθαγόρας ἐρωτηθεὶς πῶς δεῖ ἀγνωμονούσῃ πατρίδι προσφέρεσθαι, εἶπεν ὡς μητρί

Pythagoras, on being asked how one should behave to an inconsiderate fatherland, replied, 'As to a mother.'

Stobaeus, *Anthology* 3.39.25

37 Πυθαγόρας εἶπεν εἰσιέναι εἰς τὰς πόλεις πρῶτον τρυφήν, ἔπειτα κόρον, εἶτα ὕβριν, μετὰ δὲ ταῦτα ὄλεθρον

First to enter a city is luxury, then satiety, insolence next, and finally total ruin.

Stobaeus, *Anthology* 4.1.80

38 ἀπαιδευσία πάντων τῶν παθῶν μήτηρ ... τὸ δὲ πεπαιδεῦσθαι οὐκ ἐν πολυμαθείας λόγων ἀναλήψει, ἐν ἀπαλλάξει δὲ τῶν φύσει παθῶν θεωρεῖται

Lack of education is the mother of all passions; and being educated does not consist in much learning, but in being delivered from natural passions.

Sententiae Pythagoreorum, 2 (Chadwick)

39 πᾶν δὲ πάθος ψυχῆς εἰς σωτηρίαν πολεμιώτατον

Every passion of the soul is the greatest enemy of salvation.

Sententiae Pythagoreorum, 2 (Chadwick)

40 ἄγρυπνος ἔσο κατὰ νοῦν· συγγενὴς γὰρ τοῦ ἀληθινοῦ θανάτου ὁ περὶ τὸν νοῦν ὕπνος

Keep your mind wide awake; a mind asleep is kindred to true death.

Sententiae Pythagoreorum, 5 (Chadwick)

41 ἐλεύθερον ἀδύνατον εἶναι τὸν πάθεσι δουλεύοντα καὶ ὑπὸ παθῶν κρατούμενον

It is impossible to be free if ruled by passions.

Sententiae Pythagoreorum, 23 (Chadwick)

42 θέλε τοὺς συνόντας σοι αἰδεῖσθαί σε μᾶλλον ἢ φοβεῖσθαι· αἰδοῖ μὲν γὰρ πρόσεστι σέβας, φόβῳ δὲ μῖσος

Wish that your companions respect rather than fear you, for respect is associated with esteem, fear with hatred.

Sententiae Pythagoreorum, 42 (Chadwick)

43 ἰσχύειν τῇ ψυχῇ αἱροῦ μᾶλλον ἢ τῷ σώματι

Prefer strength of soul to strength of body.

Sententiae Pythagoreorum, 45 (Chadwick)

44 ἰσχὺς καὶ τεῖχος καὶ ὅπλον τοῦ σοφοῦ ἡ φρόνησις

Prudence is strength and bulwark and weapon to the wise.

Sententiae Pythagoreorum, 46 (Chadwick)

45 ὥσπερ γὰρ ἰατρικῆς μηδὲν ὄφελος μὴ τὰς νόσους ἐκβαλλούσης ἀπὸ τῶν σωμάτων, οὕτως οὐδὲ φιλοσοφίας εἰ μὴ τὸ τῆς ψυχῆς κακὸν ἐκβάλοι

There is no point in medicine if it cannot expel disease from the body; this also applies to philosophy, if it cannot expel evil from the soul.

Sententiae Pythagoreorum, 50 (Chadwick)

46 οὐδεὶς ἐλεύθερος ἑαυτοῦ μὴ κρατῶν

No one is free if not master of his own self.

Sententiae Pythagoreorum, 77 (Chadwick)

cf. Lao Tse: He who controls others may be powerful, but he who has mastered himself is mightier still

47 παντὸς καλοῦ κτήματος πόνος προηγεῖται ὁ κατ' ἐγκράτειαν

Every achievement comes from hard work and self-restraint.

Sententiae Pythagoreorum, 78 (Chadwick)

48 ποίει ἃ κρίνεις εἶναι καλά, κἂν ποιῶν μέλλῃς ἀδοξήσειν

Act as you deem right, even in fear of being criticized.

Sententiae Pythagoreorum, 82 (Chadwick)

49 πολλῷ ἄμεινον μὴ ἁμαρτάνειν, ἁμαρτάνοντα δὲ ἄμεινον γινώσκειν ἢ ἀγνοεῖν

Best is not to do wrong; but having erred it is better to be conscious of it than to ignore it.

Sententiae Pythagoreorum, 84 (Chadwick)

50 πρᾶττε μεγάλα, μὴ ὑπισχνούμενος μεγάλα

Do great things without having promised them.

Sententiae Pythagoreorum, 86 (Chadwick)

51 συγγενεῖ καὶ ἄρχοντι καὶ φίλῳ πάντα εἶκε πλὴν ἐλευθερίας

To kin and ruler and friend give everything except your freedom.

Sententiae Pythagoreorum, 97 (Chadwick)

52 τέκνα μάθε τίκτειν οὐ τὰ γηροβοσκήσοντα τὸ σῶμα, τὰ δὲ τὴν ψυχὴν θρέψοντα τῇ ἀϊδίῳ τροφῇ

Do not rear children who will support your body in old age, but who will give everlasting satisfaction to your soul.

Sententiae Pythagoreorum, 99 (Chadwick)

53 χαλεπὸν πολλὰς ὁδοὺς ἅμα τοῦ βίου βαδίζειν

It is difficult in life to proceed along many roads at the same time.

Sententiae Pythagoreorum, 114 (Chadwick)

54 Οὔτε οἱ ἄμουσοι τοῖς ὀργάνοις, οὔτε οἱ ἀπαίδευτοι ταῖς τύχαις δύνανται συναρμόσασθαι

As the unmusical with instruments, so the uneducated cannot adapt himself to sorrow.

Sententiae Pythagoreorum, 12 (Elter)

also attributed to Socrates

55 ἐν μὲν τοῖς ἐσόπτροις ὁ τῆς ὄψεως, ἐν δὲ ταῖς ὁμιλίαις ὁ τῆς ψυχῆς χαρακτὴρ βλέπεται

In mirrors one can see the face, in speech the character of the soul.

Sententiae Pythagoreorum, 119a (Elter)

attributed to Democritus, probably erroneously

PYTHEAS

4th century BC
Athenian orator

1 ἐλλυχνίων ἔφησεν ὄζειν αὐτοῦ τὰ ἐνθυμήματα

His arguments smell of the lamp.

Plutarch, *Demosthenes* 8.4

of the orations of Demosthenes, who worked late into the night preparing them; cf. Demosthenes 105

PYTHEAS OF MASSALIA

4th century BC
Navigator

1 Πυθέαν ... ὅλην μὲν τὴν Βρεττανικὴν ἐμβαδὸν ἐπελθεῖν φάσκοντος ... προσιστορήσαντος δὲ καὶ τὰ περὶ τῆς Θούλης

Pytheas states that he travelled all over Britain on foot; it is likewise he who describes Thule.

Translated by H.C. Hamilton and W. Falconer (1854)

Fragment 7a (Mette)

Pytheas presented the first account of a visit to Britain in his book Περὶ τοῦ Ὠκεανοῦ (About the Ocean), *now lost*

Q

QUINTUS
probably 3rd century AD
Epic poet from Smyrna

1 ὦ φίλαι …
οὐ γὰρ ἀπόπροθέν εἰμεν ἐυσθενέων αἰζηῶν,
ἀλλ' οἷον κείνοισι πέλει μένος, ἔστι καὶ ἡμῖν

Women are not far from able men, my friends,
whatever resolve they have we have as well.

Posthomerica 1.409–419

2 γλῶσσαν ἀναιδέα τίνυται Ἄτη

A bridleless tongue is sure to bring ruin.

Posthomerica 1.753

3 τάρβος ἀσφαλὲς αἰὲν ἔχοιμι

May I always have fear enough to keep me from danger.

Posthomerica 2.91

4 πολὺ λώιον ἄνδρες
ἔργῳ ἐποίχονται, ὁπότ' εἰσορόωσιν ἄνακτες

Men toil much harder at their work, when the master is in sight.

Posthomerica 12.342

cf. the English proverb 'the eye of a master does more work than both his hands'

5 μέγα θάρσος ἀνάγκη ὤπασεν

Necessity produces mighty courage.

Posthomerica 13.121

6 ἀνδρῶν γὰρ γένος ἐστὶν ὁμοίιον ἄνθεσι ποίης,
ἄνθεσιν εἰαρινοῖσι· τὰ μὲν φθινύθει, τὰ δ' ἀέξει

The race of men is like flowers in spring;
others blossom and others wither away.

Posthomerica 14.207

7 οὐδέ τις ἐλπωρὴ βιότου πέλεν, οὕνεκ' ἐρεμνὴ
νὺξ ἅμα καὶ μέγα χεῖμα καὶ ἀθανάτων χόλος αἰνὸς ὦρτο

There was no hope of life as the night came on dark, and, with it, a great storm and the terrible anger of the gods.

Translated by C.A. Trypanis (1971)

Posthomerica 14.505

8 ἔβραχε δ' ἅλμη
βυσσόθεν, ὥς τε θάλασσαν ἰδ' οὐρανὸν ἠδὲ καὶ αἶαν
φαίνεσθ' ἀλλήλοισιν ὁμῶς συναρηρότα πάντα

The ocean roared from its depth, so that the water, sky and earth all seemed to be joined together.

Translated by C.A. Trypanis (1971)

Posthomerica 14.527

R

ROMULUS

Legendary founder of Rome
see also Dionysius of Halicarnassus 5, 7–8

1 ὁ δὲ Ῥωμύλος ... ἕνα νόμον ... καταστησάμενος εἰς σωφροσύνην καὶ πολλὴν εὐκοσμίαν ἤγαγε τὰς γυναῖκας. ἦν δὲ τοιός δε ὁ νόμος· γυναῖκα γαμετὴν τὴν κατὰ γάμους ἱεροὺς συνελθοῦσαν ἀνδρὶ κοινωνὸν ἁπάντων εἶναι χρημάτων τε καὶ ἱερῶν

By instituting a single law, Romulus led women towards modesty and good behaviour. The law was this, that a woman joined to her husband by holy marriage should share in all his possessions and sacred rites.

Translated by Dan Hogg (2006)

Dionysius of Halicarnassus, *Roman Antiquities* 2.25.1

2 φθορὰ σώματος καί ... εἴ τις οἶνον εὑρεθείη πιοῦσα γυνή. ἀμφότερα γὰρ ταῦτα θανάτῳ ζημιοῦν συνεχώρησεν ὁ Ῥωμύλος, ὡς ἁμαρτημάτων γυναικείων αἴσχιστα, φθορὰν μὲν ἀπονοίας ἀρχὴν νομίσας, μέθην δὲ φθορᾶς

Romulus allowed them to punish adultery and drunkenness in women with death, considering them to be the gravest offences they could be guilty of, looking upon adultery as the source of reckless folly, and drunkenness as the source of adultery.

Dionysius of Halicarnassus, *Roman Antiquities* 2.25.6

cf. Dionysius of Halicarnassus 8

3 ὁ δὲ τῶν Ῥωμαίων νομοθέτης ἅπασαν ὡς εἰπεῖν ἔδωκεν ἐξουσίαν πατρὶ καθ᾽ υἱοῦ καὶ παρὰ πάντα τὸν τοῦ βίου χρόνον ... ἐάν τε ἀποκτιννύναι προαιρῆται, ... κἂν διὰ τὴν εἰς τὰ κοινὰ φιλοτιμίαν ἐπαινούμενος

The lawgiver of the Romans gave virtually full power to the father over the son, even during his whole life, even to put him to death, even if he already be celebrated for public service rendered.

Dionysius of Halicarnassus, *Roman Antiquities* 2.26.4

4 καὶ τοῦτο συνεχώρησε τῷ πατρί, μέχρι τρίτης πράσεως ἀφ᾽ υἱοῦ χρηματίσασθαι, μείζονα δοὺς ἐξουσίαν πατρὶ κατὰ παιδὸς ἢ δεσπότῃ κατὰ δούλων

And he even gave leave to the father to make a profit by selling his son as often as three times, thereby giving greater power to the father over his son than to the master over his slaves.

Translated by Earnest Cary (1937)

Dionysius of Halicarnassus, *Roman Antiquities* 2.27.1

5 Ῥωμύλος ... δύο μόνα τοῖς ἐλευθέροις ἐπιτηδεύματα κατέλιπε τά τε κατὰ γεωργίαν καὶ τὰ κατὰ πολέμους

Romulus permitted free men but two occupations: agriculture and warfare.

Translated by Dan Hogg (2006)

Dionysius of Halicarnassus, *Roman Antiquities* 2.28.2

6 τῆς ἁρπαγῆς ... καὶ τρόπων συμπάντων καθ᾽ οὓς συνάπτονται γάμοι ταῖς γυναιξὶν ἐπιφανέστατον

Of all methods of contracting marriage,
this way – kidnapping – was the best.

Translated by Dan Hogg (2006)

Dionysius of Halicarnassus, *Roman Antiquities* 2.30.5

cf. Plutarch 70

7 ἡγεμονικοῦ μᾶλλον ἢ πειθαρχικοῦ φύσει γεγονότος

Born to command rather than to obey.

Translated by Bernadotte Perrin (1914)

Plutarch, *Romulus* 6.3

RUFINUS

uncertain, perhaps 2nd or 3rd century AD
Epigrammatist

1 Μήτ' ἰσχνὴν λίην περιλάμβανε μήτε παχεῖαν,
τούτων δ' ἀμφοτέρων τὴν μεσότητα θέλε.

Choose the middle term between
The two extremes of fat and lean.

Translated by R.A. Furness (1931)

Greek Anthology 5.37

2 Ὄμματα μὲν χρύσεια καὶ ὑαλόεσσα παρειὴ
καὶ στόμα πορφυρέης τερπνότερον κάλυκος,
δειρὴ λυγδινέη καὶ στήθεα μαρμαίροντα
καὶ πόδες ἀργυρέης λευκότεροι Θέτιδος·
εἰ δέ τι καὶ πλοκαμῖσι διαστίλβουσιν ἄκανθαι,
τῆς λευκῆς καλάμης οὐδὲν ἐπιστρέφομαι.

Her eyes are gold, her cheek is hyalite,
Her mouth delicious as a dark red rose;
Her bosom gleams, her neck is marbly bright,
And white as silvery Thetis' are her toes:
In those dark locks some thistle-down she hath?
I take no heed of that white aftermath!

Translated by William Sinclair Marris (1938)

Greek Anthology 5.48

of grey hair

3 Πέμπω σοι τόδε στέφος, ἄνθεσι καλοῖς
αὐτὸς ὑφ' ἡμετέραις πλεξάμενος παλάμαις.
ἔστι κρίνον, ῥοδέη τε κάλυξ, νοτερή τ' ἀνεμώνη,
καὶ νάρκισσος ὑγρὸς, καὶ κυαναυγὲς ἴον.
ταῦτα στεψαμένη, λῆξον μεγάλαυχος ἐοῦσα·
ἀνθεῖς καὶ λήγεις καὶ σὺ καὶ ὁ στέφανος.

I send thee this garland that with my own hands
I wove out of beautiful flowers.
There are lilies and roses and fresh anemones,
and tender narcissus and purple violets.
Wear it but stop being vain.
Both thou and the garland flower and fade.

Translated by W.R. Paton (1916)

Greek Anthology 5.74

4 Αὔτη μοι προσέπαιζε καί, εἴ ποτε καιρός, ἐτόλμων·
ἠρυθρία. τί πλέον; τὸν πόνον ἠσθάνετο·
ἤνυσα πολλὰ καμών. παρακήκοα νῦν, ὅτι τίκτει·
ὥστε τί ποιοῦμεν; φεύγομεν ἢ μένομεν;

She'd jest with me and I took heart;
she'd blush – what then? – she'd suffer for it.
I hastened to, and now she is with child!
What shall I do? I stay or run away?

Greek Anthology 5.75

5 Ὥπλισμαι πρὸς Ἔρωτα περὶ στέρνοισι λογισμόν,
οὐδέ με νικήσει, μοῦνος ἐὼν πρὸς ἕνα·
θνατὸς δ' ἀθανάτῳ συστήσομαι· ἢν δὲ βοηθὸν
Βάκχον ἔχῃ, τί μόνος πρὸς δύ' ἐγὼ δύναμαι;

I am armed against Love with a breast-plate of Reason,
neither shall he conquer me, one against one;
yes, I a mortal will contend with him the immortal:
but if he have Bacchus to second him,
what can I do alone against the two?

Translated by J.W. MacKail (1890)

Greek Anthology 5.93

6 Πάντα σέθεν φιλέω· μοῦνον δὲ σὸν ἄκριτον ὄμμα
ἐχθαίρω, στυγεροῖς ἀνδράσι τερπόμενον.

All else I love, but this abhor:
  Your eye, so fondly turning
On men I have no stomach for
  A look so undiscerning.

Translated by T.F. Higham (1938)

Greek Anthology 5.284

S

SAPPHO

*c.*630–*c.*560BC (?)
Lyric poet from Lesbos
see also Solon 47

1 ποικιλόθρον' ἀθανάτἈφρόδιτα …
μή μ' ἄσαισι μηδ' ὀνίαισι δάμνα,
πότνια, θῦμον

Immortal Aphrodite on your rich-
wrought throne,
do not overpower my heart
with ache and anguish.

Fragment 1 (Lobel and Page, *PLF*)
opening lines of a prayer to Aphrodite

2 καὶ γὰρ αἰ φεύγει, ταχέως διώξει,
αἰ δὲ δῶρα μὴ δέκετ', ἀλλὰ δώσει,
αἰ δὲ μὴ φίλει, ταχέως φιλήσει
κωὐκ ἐθέλοισα

For if she flees, soon she'll pursue;
if she takes not your gifts, others she'll
give;
if she loves not, soon she'll love,
even unwillingly.

Translated by Anne L. Klinck (2008)
Fragment 1.21 (Lobel and Page, *PLF*)

3 ἔλθε μοι καὶ νῦν, χαλέπαν δὲ λῦσον
ἐκ μερίμναν, ὄσσα δέ μοι τέλεσσαι
θῦμος ἰμέρρει, τέλεσον· σὺ δ' αὔτα
σύμμαχος ἔσσο

Come to me now too, and set me free
from grievous cares; fulfil for me
those things my heart desires. It's you I
need.
Fight on my side!

Translated by Anne L. Klinck (2008)
Fragment 1.25 (Lobel and Page, *PLF*)
closing lines of the prayer to Aphrodite

4 ἐν δ' ὔδωρ ψῦχρον κελάδει δι' ὔσδων
μαλίνων, βρόδοισι δὲ παῖς ὀ χῶρος
ἐσκίαστ', αἰθυσσομένων δὲ φύλλων
κῶμα κατέρρει

Cool water murmurs through apple
boughs,
and the whole place is shadowed by
roses,
and from the quivering leaves
deep sleep flows down upon me.

Fragment 2.5 (Lobel and Page, *PLF*)

5 ἐν δὲ λείμων ἰππόβοτος τέθαλεν
ἠρίνοισιν ἄνθεσιν, αἰ δ' ἄηται
μέλλιχα πνέοισιν

A horse-pasturing meadow blooms
with spring flowers, and the winds
breathe gently.

Translated by Marguerite Johnson (2007)
Fragment 2.9 (Lobel and Page, *PLF*)

6 κάλλιστον ἔγω δὲ κῆν' ὄτ-
τω τις ἔραται

The most beautiful thing, I say, is whatever you love.

Fragment 16.3 (Lobel and Page, *PLF*)

7 τᾶς κε βολλοίμαν ἔρατόν τε βᾶμα
κἀμάρυχμα λάμπρον ἴδην προσώπω

I'd rather see her lovely step,
her face so full of brightness.

Fragment 16.17 (Lobel and Page, *PLF*)
of Helen of Troy, reminding her of absent Anactoria, one of Sappho's favourites

8 κέλομαι σ' ἀείδην
Γογγύλαν Ἄβανθι λάβοισαν ἀ …
πᾶκτιν, ἇς σε δηὖτε πόθος τ …
ἀμφιπόταται

I bid you to sing of Gongyla,
Abanthis, taking up your strings,
of her for whom desire once more
whirls over you.

Translated by Anne L. Klinck (2008)

Fragment 22 (Lobel and Page, *PLF*)

9 ὄττινας γὰρ
εὖ θέω, κῆνοί με μάλιστα πάντων
σίνονται

Those
whom I treat well, they most of all
harm me.

Fragment 26 (Lobel and Page, *PLF*)

10 φαίνεταί μοι κῆνος ἴσος θέοισιν
ἔμμεν' ὤνηρ, ὄττις ἐνάντιός τοι
ἰσδάνει καὶ πλάσιον ἆδυ φωνεί-
σας ὐπακούει

καὶ γελαίσας ἰμέροεν, τό μ' ἦ μὰν
καρδίαν ἐν στήθεσιν ἐπτόαισεν·
ὠς γὰρ ἔς σ' ἴδω βρόχε', ὤς με φώναι-
σ' οὐδ' ἒν ἔτ' εἴκει,

ἀλλὰ κὰμ μὲν γλῶσσά μ' ἔαγε, λέπτον
δ' αὔτικα χρῷ πῦρ ὐπαδεδρόμηκεν,
ὀππάτεσσι δ' οὐδ' ἒν ὄρημμ', ἐπιρρόμ-
βεισι δ' ἄκουαι,

κὰδ δέ μ' ἴδρως κακχέεται, τρόμος δὲ
παῖσαν ἄγρει, χλωροτέρα δὲ ποίας
ἔμμι, τεθνάκην δ' ὀλίγω 'πιδεύης
φαίνομ' ἔμ' αὔτᾳ

Equal of the gods seems to me
that man who sits opposite you
and, close to you,
listens to your sweet words

And lovely laugh, which
passionately excites my heart in my
breast;
whenever I look at you, even for a
moment,
no voice comes to me.

But my tongue is frozen,
at once a delicate fire flickers under my
skin.
I no longer see anything with my eyes
and my ears are full of strange sounds.

Sweat pours down me,
and trembling seizes me all over.
I am paler than grass
and seem little short of death.

Translated by C.A. Trypanis (1971)

Fragment 31 (Lobel and Page, *PLF*)

'Is it not wonderful how she summons at the same time, soul, body, hearing, tongue, sight, skin; contradictory sensations, freezes, burns, raves, reasons!' ('Longinus', On the Sublime *10, tr. W. Hamilton Fyfe)*

11 ἄστερες μὲν ἀμφὶ κάλαν σελάνναν
ἂψ ἀπυκρύπτοισι φάεννον εἶδος,
ὄπποτα πλήθοισα μάλιστα λάμπη
γᾶν

The stars around the lovely moon
hide away their radiant form
when at her full most brilliantly
she lights the earth.

Translated by Anne L. Klinck (2008)

Fragment 34 (Lobel and Page, *PLF*)

12 καὶ ποθήω καὶ μάομαι

And I long and yearn.

Translated by D.A. Campbell (1982)

Fragment 36 (Lobel and Page, *PLF*)

13 ταῖσι δὲ ψῦχρος μὲν ἔγεντ' ὀ θῦμος,
πὰρ δ' ἴεισι τὰ πτέρα

Their hearts have grown cold,
and their wings droop.

Translated by Anne L. Klinck (2008)

Fragment 42 (Lobel and Page, *PLF*)

of pigeons

14 ἀλλ' ἄγιτ', ὦ φίλαι,
ἄγχι γὰρ ἀμέρα

But come, my friends,
for day is near.

Translated by D.A. Campbell (1982)

Fragment 43 (Lobel and Page, *PLF*)

15 αὖλος δ' ἀδυμέλης κίθαρίς τ' ὀνεμίγνυτο
καὶ ψόφος κροτάλων λιγέως δ' ἄρα
πάρθενοι
ἄειδον μέλος ἄγνον, ἴκανε δ' ἐς αἴθερα
ἄχω θεσπεσία

The sweet pipe and cithara mingled
with the sound of castanets; the maidens
were singing a pure strain, and into the
air
rose the wondrous echo.

Fragment 44 (Lobel and Page, *PLF*)

16 Ἔρος δ' ἐτίναξέ μοι
φρένας, ὠς ἄνεμος κὰτ ὄρος δρύσιν ἐμπέτων

Love shook my heart,
like a mountain-wind that falls upon the oak trees.

Translated by C.A. Trypanis (1971)

Fragment 47 (Lobel and Page, *PLF*)

17 ἤλθες, καὶ ἐπόησας, ἔγω δέ σ' ἐμαιόμαν,
ὂν δ' ἔψυξας ἔμαν φρένα καιομέναν πόθῳ

You came, and I was longing for you;
you cooled my heart burning with desire.

Translated by D.A. Campbell (1982)

Fragment 48 (Lobel and Page, *PLF*)

18 ἠράμαν μὲν ἔγω σέθεν, Ἄτθι, πάλαι ποτά ...
σμίκρα μοι πάις ἔμμεν' ἐφαίνεο κἄχαρις

Atthis, I loved you
long ago while you
still seemed to me a
small ungracious child.

Translated by Mary Barnard (1958)

Fragment 49 (Lobel and Page, *PLF*)

19 ὀ μὲν γὰρ κάλος ὄσσον ἴδην πέλεται κάλος,
ὀ δὲ κἄγαθος αὔτικα καὶ κάλος ἔσσεται

One who is lovely is only so to look upon,
but one who is good is instantly lovely too.

Translated by Anne L. Klinck (2008)

Fragment 50 (Lobel and Page, *PLF*)

20 οὐκ οἶδ' ὄττι θέω· δύο μοι τὰ νοήμματα

I do not know
what to do: I
am of two minds.

Translated by Mary Barnard (1958)

Fragment 51 (Lobel and Page, *PLF*)

21 κατθάνοισα δὲ κείση οὐδέ ποτα μναμοσύνα σέθεν
ἔσσετ' οὐδὲ ποτ' ὔστερον· οὐ γὰρ πεδέχης βρόδων
τὼν ἐκ Πιερίας· ἀλλ' ἀφάνης κὰν Ἀίδα δόμῳ
φοιτάσης πεδ' ἀμαύρων νεκύων ἐκπεποταμένα

Dead shalt thou lie; and nought
Be told of thee or thought,
For thou hast plucked not of the Muses' tree:
And even in Hades' halls
Amidst thy fellow-thralls
No friendly shade thy shade shall company!

Translated by Thomas Hardy (1901)

Fragment 55 (Lobel and Page, *PLF*)

22 τίς δ' ἀγροΐωτις θέλγει νόον ...
ἀγροΐωτιν ἐπεμμένα στόλαν ...
οὐκ ἐπισταμένα τὰ βράκε' ἔλκην ἐπὶ τὼν σφύρων;

What country girl has bewitched your senses
wearing country clothes,
not even trained to hold her dress above her ankles?

Translated by Anne L. Klinck (2008)

Fragment 57 (Lobel and Page, *PLF*)

23 ὔμμες πεδὰ Μοΐσαν ἰοκόλπων κάλα δῶρα παῖδες,
σπουδάσδετε καὶ τὰν φιλάοιδον λιγύραν χελύνναν·

ἔμοι δ' ἄπαλον πρίν ποτ' ἔοντα χρόα γῆρας ἤδη
ἐπέλλαβε, λεῦκαι δ' ἐγένοντο τρίχες ἐκ μελαίναν·

βάρυς δε μ' ὀ θῦμος πεπόηται, γόνα δ' οὐ φέροισι,
τὰ δή ποτα λαίψηρ' ἔον ὄρχησθ' ἴσα νεβρίοισιν·

τὰ μὲν στεναχίσδω θαμέως· ἀλλὰ τί κεν ποείην;
ἀγήραον ἄνθρωπον ἔοντ' οὐ δύνατον γένεσθαι.

καὶ γάρ ποτα Τίθωνον ἔφαντο βροδόπαχυν Αὔων
ἔρωι φ ... αθεισαν βάμεν' εἰς ἔσχατα γᾶς φέροισαν,

ἔοντα κάλον καὶ νέον, ἀλλ' αὖτον ὔμως ἔμαρψε
χρόνωι πόλιον γῆρας, ἔχοντ' ἀθανάταν ἄκοιτιν

Be passsionate for the beautiful gifts of the fragrant-breasted Muses,
o children, and for the clear, sweet-singing lyre.

Old age has now seized my once-tender body;
my hair has become light instead of dark;

my heart has grown heavy; my knees refuse to support me,
which once upon a time were as lithe for the dance as fawns.

I often mourn this state; but what am I so to do?
There is no way, being human, not to grow old.

They say that rosy-armed Dawn, mad with love,
once carried Tithonus to the end of the world;

beautiful and youthful then, but in time grey age
engulfed him, he the husband of a goddess.

Translated by Marguerite Johnson (2007)

Fragment 58.11 (Lobel and Page, *PLF*)

half (vertically) of this poem was known from an Oxyrhynchus papyrus since 1922; the other half was retrieved some eighty years later from another papyrus at Cologne, giving us the full poem (Martin West in 'The Times Literary Supplement', *24 June 2005)*

24 τοῦτο καί μοι τὸ λάμπρον ἔρος τὠελίω καὶ τὸ κάλον λέλογχε

Love for me has acquired the brightness and beauty of the sun.

Translated by D.A. Campbell (1982)

Fragment 58.25 (Lobel and Page, *PLF*)

25 νῦν δὲ Λύδαισιν ἐμπρέπεται γυναί-
κεσσιν ὤς ποτ' ἀελίω
δύντος ἀ βροδοδάκτυλος σελάννα

πάντα περρέχοισ' ἄστρα· φάος δ' ἐπίσχει θάλασσαν ἐπ' ἀλμύραν
ἴσως καὶ πολυανθέμοις ἀρούραις·

ἀ δ' ἐέρσα κάλα κέχυται, τεθά-
λαισι δὲ βρόδα κἄπαλ' ἄν-
θρυσκα καὶ μελίλωτος ἀνθεμώδης

Now among Lydian women she in her
turn stands first as the red-
fingered moon rising at sunset takes

precedence over stars around her;
her light spreads equally
on the salt sea and fields thick with bloom.

Delicious dew pours down to freshen
roses, delicate thyme
and blossoming sweet clover.

Translated by Mary Barnard (1958)

Fragment 96 (Lobel and Page, *PLF*)

26 γλύκηα μᾶτερ, οὔτοι δύναμαι κρέκην τὸν ἴστον
πόθῳ δάμεισα παῖδος βραδίναν δι' Ἀφροδίταν

Darling mother, I can no longer ply my loom:
I'm overcome with longing for a slender lad.

Translated by M.L. West (1994)

Fragment 102 (Lobel and Page, *PLF*)

27 Ἔσπερε πάντα φέρων ὄσα φαίνολις ἐσκέδασ' Αὔως,
φέρεις ὄιν, φέρεις αἶγα, φέρεις ἄπυ μάτερι παῖδα

Hesperus, you herd
homeward whatever
Dawn's light dispersed

You herd sheep – herd
goats – herd children
home to their mothers.

Translated by Mary Barnard (1958)

Fragment 104a (Lobel and Page, *PLF*)

Hesperus is the Evening Star

28 οἶον τὸ γλυκύμαλον ἐρεύθεται ἄκρῳ ἐπ' ὔσδῳ,
ἄκρον ἐπ' ἀκροτάτῳ, λελάθοντο δὲ μαλοδρόπηες·
οὐ μὰν ἐκλελάθοντ', ἀλλ' οὐκ ἐδύναντ' ἐπίκεσθαι

Like the sweet apple which reddens upon the topmost bough,
A-top on the top-most twig, – which the pluckers forgot, somehow, –
Forgot it not, nay, but got it not, for none could get it till now.

Translated by Dante Gabriel Rossetti (1861)

Fragment 105a (Lobel and Page, *PLF*)

of a young bride

29 οἴαν τὰν ὐάκινθον ἐν ὤρεσι ποίμενες ἄνδρες
πόσσι καταστείβοισι, χάμαι δέ τε πόρφυρον ἄνθος

Like a hyacinth in
the mountains, trampled
by shepherds until
only a purple stain
remains on the ground.

Translated by Mary Barnard (1958)

Fragment 105c (Lobel and Page, *PLF*)

30 σοὶ χάριεν μὲν εἶδος, ὄππατα δ' ...
μέλλιχ', ἔρος δ' ἐπ' ἰμέρτῳ κέχυται προσώπῳ

Your form is graceful, your eyes
Gentle, and love flows over your beautiful face.

Translated by D.A. Campbell (1982)

Fragment 112 (Lobel and Page, *PLF*)

31 – παρθενία, παρθενία, ποῖ με λίποισα ἀποίχῃ;
– οὐκέτι ἤξω πρὸς σέ, οὐκέτι ἤξω

– Virginity, virginity, where have you gone, deserting me?
– Never again shall I come to you: never again shall I come.

Translated by D.A. Campbell (1982)

Fragment 114 (Lobel and Page, *PLF*)

32 Ἔρος δηὖτέ μ' ὁ λυσιμέλης δόνει,
γλυκύπικρον ἀμάχανον ὄρπετον

Desire shakes me once again,
here is that melting of my limbs.
It is a creeping thing, and bittersweet.
I can do nothing to resist.

Translated by Suzy Q. Groden (1964)

Fragment 130 (Lobel and Page, *PLF*)

33 ἔστι μοι κάλα πάις χρυσίοισιν ἀνθέμοισιν
ἐμφέρην ἔχοισα μόρφαν

I have a lovely daughter who looks like golden flowers.

Translated by Denys Page (1955)

Fragment 132 (Lobel and Page, *PLF*)

of her daughter Cleis

34 ἦρος ἄγγελος ἰμερόφωνος ἀήδων

The nightingale, lovely voiced messenger of spring.

Translated by Anne L. Klinck (2008)

Fragment 136 (Lobel and Page, *PLF*)

35 αἰ δ' ἦχες ἔσλων ἵμερον ἢ κάλων
καὶ μή τί τ' εἴπην γλῶσσ' ἐκύκα κάκον,
αἴδως κέν σε οὐκ ἦχεν ὄππατ',
ἀλλ' ἔλεγες περὶ τὼ δικαίω

If you truly desired something honest or good
and you tongue were not concocting some new evil,
there would be no shame in your eyes
and you would plead your cause outright.

Translated by Josephine Balmer (1992)

Fragment 137 (Lobel and Page, *PLF*)

36 στᾶθι κἄντα φίλος
καὶ τὰν ἐπ' ὄσσοισ' ὀμπέτασον χάριν

Stand facing me, my friend,
display to me the beauty of your eyes.

Fragment 138 (Lobel and Page, *PLF*)

37 μήτε μοι μέλι μήτε μέλισσα

I desire neither the bees nor yet the honey.

Translated by Beram Saklatvala (1968)

Fragment 146 (Lobel and Page, *PLF*)

38 μνάσασθαί τινά φαιμι καὶ ἕτερον ἀμμέων

Let me tell you
this: someone in
some future time
will think of us.

Translated by Mary Barnard (1958)

Fragment 147 (Lobel and Page, *PLF*)

39 ὁ πλοῦτος ἄνευ ἀρέτας οὐκ ἀσίνης πάροικος,
ἀ δ' ἀμφοτέρων κρᾶσις εὐδαιμονίας ἔχει τὸ ἄκρον

Wealth without virtue is a harmful neighbour;
Their blending is the height of happiness.

Fragment 148 (Lobel and Page, *PLF*)

the second line may not be by Sappho

40 οὐ γὰρ θέμις ἐν μοισοπόλων οἰκίᾳ
θρῆνον ἔμμεν'· οὔ κ' ἄμμι πρέποι τάδε

There is no place for grief,
in a house which serves the Muses;
our own is no exception.

Translated by Josephine Balmer (1992)

Fragment 150 (Lobel and Page, *PLF*)

to her daughter – sometimes described as her dying words

41 σκιδναμένας ἐν στήθεσιν ὄργας
μαψυλάκαν γλῶσσαν πεφύλαχθαι

When anger swells within the breast,
Restrain the idly barking tongue.

Translated by William C. Helmbold (1939)

Fragment 158 (Lobel and Page, *PLF*)

42 δέδυκε μὲν ἀ σελάννα
καὶ Πληΐαδε· μέσαι δὲ

νύκτες, παρὰ δ' ἔρχετ' ὤρα·
ἔγω δὲ μόνα κατεύδω

The moon has set and the Pleiades;
it is midnight, and time goes by,
and I lie alone.

Translated by D.A. Campbell (1982)

Fragment 168b (Voigt)

43 ποικίλλεται μὲν γαῖα πολυστέφανος

Much decorated earth, continuously changing.

Fragment 168c (Voigt)

attributed by Wilamowitz to Sappho; Lobel and Page, PLF, dissent; cf. Fragment 46a (Page, PMG)

44 τὸ ἀποθνήσκειν κακόν·
οἱ θεοὶ γὰρ οὕτω κεκρίκασιν·
ἀπέθνησκον γὰρ ἄν

Death is an evil;
we have the gods'
word for it; they too
would die if death
were a good thing.

Translated by Mary Barnard (1958)

Aristotle, *Rhetoric* 1398b.29

45 Ἐννέα τὰς Μούσας φασίν τινες. ὡς ὀλιγώρως·
ἠνίδε· καὶ Σαπφὼ Λεσβόθεν ἡ δεκάτη.

Some say there are nine Muses. How imprudent!
Note well: Sappho of Lesbos is the tenth!

Translated by Marguerite Johnson (2007)

Plato, *Epigram* 16 (Diehl)

46 οὐχ ὁρᾷς ... ὅσην χάριν ἔχει τὰ Σαπφικὰ μέλη κηλοῦντα καὶ
καταθέλγοντα τοὺς ἀκροωμένους;

Do you not see what grace the songs of Sappho have, charming and bewitching all who listen to them?

Translated by Frank Cole Babbitt (1936)

Plutarch, *The Oracles at Delphi no Longer Given in Verse* 397a

47 εὐδίαι γὰρ ἐκ μεγάλον ἀήταν
αἶψα πέλονται

Periods of calm quickly follow after
Great squalls.

Translated by Tim Whitmarsh (2014)

from a newly discovered papyrus (owner anonymous) with a fragment believed to be by Sappho; cf. the article 'Two New Poems by Sappho', Dirk Obbink, ZPE 189 (2014)

48 αἴ κε ...
Λάριχος καὶ δήποτ' ἄνηρ γένηται,
καὶ μάλ' ἐκ πόλλην 'αν' βαρυθύμιάν κεν
αἶψα λύθειμεν

If Larichus should ...
at some point become a man,
then from full many a despair
would we be swiftly freed.

Translated by Tim Whitmarsh (2014)

from a newly discovered fragment that many believe to be by Sappho; Larichus was one of Sappho's brothers

SAPPHO OR ALCAEUS

7th–6th century BC

Fragments by the lyric poets Sappho or Alcaeus

1 Κρῆσσαί νύ ποτ' ὦδ' ἐμμελέως πόδεσσιν
ὤρχηντ' ἀπάλοισ' ἀμφ' ἐρόεντα βῶμον,
πόας τέρεν ἄνθος μάλακον μάτεισαι

The Cretan girls, keeping the rhythm,
dancing softly around the altar,
treading gently on the delicate flowers.

Fragment 16 (Lobel and Page, *PLF*)

2 ὡς δὲ πάις πεδὰ μάτερα πεπτερύγωμαι

As a child to its mother, on wings I fly to you.

Fragment 25 (Lobel and Page, *PLF*)

SATYRUS

dates unknown

Unknown, also named Satyrius, Thyilus and Thyillus

1 Ποιμενίαν ἄγλωσσος ἀν' ὀργάδα μέλπεται Ἀχὼ
ἀντίθρουν πτανοῖς ὑστερόφωνον ὄπα.

Tongueless Echo sings in the shepherd's meadow,
her voice responding to the voices of the birds.

Greek Anthology 16.153

on a statue of Echo

SCIPIO A. AFRICANUS

Publius Cornelius Scipio Aemilianus Africanus (Numantinus)
185/184–129BC
Conqueror of Carthage in 147–146BC
see also Homer 92

1 τὸ Πολυβίου παράγγελμα διαφυλάττων ἐπειρᾶτο μὴ πρότερον ἐξ ἀγορᾶς ἀπελθεῖν ἢ ποιήσασθαί τινα συνήθη καὶ φίλον ἁμωσγέπως τῶν ἐντυγχανόντων

He observed the precept of Polybius, and tried never to leave the Forum before he had in some way made an acquaintance and friend of somebody among those who spoke with him.

Translated by Frank Cole Babbitt (1931)
Plutarch, *Sayings of Romans* 199f

SCLERIAS

dates uncertain
Tragic playwright – details unknown

1 πολλοῖσι θνητῶν ἡ μὲν ὄψις εὐγενής,
ὁ νοῦς δ' ἐν αὐτοῖς δυσγενὴς εὑρίσκεται

Of many mortals the countenance is fair,
the mind behind it mean.

Fragment 1 (Snell, *TrGF*)

2 ὡς οὐκ ἀνεκτός, ὅστις ἢ πάροινος ὢν
ἢ καὶ μεμηνὼς εἰς μὲν αὑτὸν ἀσφαλὴς
ἀεί ποτ' ἐστίν, εἰς δὲ τοὺς πέλας νοσεῖ

Intolerable he who, either drunk
or mad, thinks himself safe
but to all nearby is ailing.

Fragment 2 (Snell, *TrGF*)

SEMONIDES

mid 7th century BC
Iambic poet from Amorgos and contemporary of Archilochus

1 ἐλπὶς δὲ πάντας κἀπιπειθείη τρέφει
ἄπρηκτον ὁρμαίνοντας

Yet hope and confidence urge us on
to more exercises in futility.

Fragment 1.6 (West, *IEG*)

2 νέωτα δ' οὐδεὶς ὅστις οὐ δοκεῖ βροτῶν
πλούτῳ τε κἀγαθοῖσιν ἵξεσθαι φίλος

Next year will bring, all mortals think,
an abundance of wealth and good
fortune.

Fragment 1.9 (West, *IEG*)

3 πολλὸς γὰρ ἥμιν ἐστι τεθνάναι χρόνος,
ζῶμεν δ' ἀριθμῷ παῦρα κακῶς ἔτεα

We will be dead for many years,
yet we live our short lives wrongly.

Fragment 3 (West, *IEG*)

4 πάμπαν δ' ἄμωμος οὔ τις οὐδ' ἀκήριος

No one is utterly blameless, nor utterly harmless.

Fragment 4 (West, *IEG*)

5 γυναικὸς οὐδὲν χρῆμ' ἀνὴρ ληΐζεται
ἐσθλῆς ἄμεινον οὐδὲ ῥίγιον κακῆς

Nothing is better than a good wife,
nothing worse than a bad one.

Fragment 6 (West, *IEG*)

6 χωρὶς γυναικὸς θεὸς ἐποίησεν νόον

From the start, the gods made women different.

Translated by Diane Arnson Svarlien (1995)
Fragment 7.1 (West, *IEG*)

7 ἴσην δ' ἔχοντες μοῖραν οὐ γινώσκομεν

We all have an equal lot – and do not know it.

Fragment 7.114 (West, *IEG*)

8 καὶ μήτ' ἄλουτος γαυρία σύ, μήτ' ὕδωρ
θαύμαζε, μηδὲ κουρία γενειάδα,
μηδὲ ῥύπῳ χιτῶνος ἔντυε χρόα

Don't take pride in being unwashed, don't stand in
awe of water, don't let your beard need trimming,
and don't deck out your body in a filthy tunic.

Translated by Douglas E. Gerber (1999)
Fragment 10a (West, *IEG*)

SEVEN SAGES

7th–6th century BC
All the following entries are diversely attributed to two or more of the Seven Sages: Thales, Solon, Periander, Cleobulus, Chilon, Bias, Pittacus

1 ἐγγύα, πάρα δ' ἄτα

Give a pledge, and suffer for it.

Translated by R.D. Hicks (1925)
Apophthegms Fragment 4 (D-K)

2 νόμῳ πείθου

Obey the law.

Precepts 217.3 (Mullach, *FPG*)

3 θεοὺς σέβου

Honour the gods.

Precepts 217.3 (Mullach, *FPG*)

4 ἡττῶ ὑπὸ δικαίου

Give way to justice.

Precepts 217.4 (Mullach, *FPG*)

5 ἄρχε σαυτοῦ

Govern yourself.

Translated by George Norlin (1928)

Precepts 217.7 (Mullach, *FPG*)

6 ὅρκῳ μὴ χρῶ

Do not use oaths.

Precepts 217.9 (Mullach, *FPG*)

7 καλὸν εὖ λέγε

Praise what is good.

Precepts 217.11 (Mullach, *FPG*)

8 εὐγένειαν ἄσκει

Exercise nobility of character.

Precepts 217.13 (Mullach, *FPG*)

9 ἄκουε πάντα

Listen to all.

Precepts 217.15 (Mullach, *FPG*)

10 ἱκέτας αἰδοῦ

Respect a suppliant's misfortune.

Precepts 217.17 (Mullach, *FPG*)

11 γνοὺς πρᾶττε

Judge and then act.

Precepts 217.20 (Mullach, *FPG*)

12 λαβὼν ἀπόδος

Give back what you have received.

Precepts 217.22 (Mullach, *FPG*)

13 τέχνῃ χρῶ

Use your skills.

Precepts 217.23 (Mullach, *FPG*)

14 ὁμοίοις χρῶ

Associate with your peers.

Precepts 217.28 (Mullach, *FPG*)

15 δαπανῶν ἄρχου

Govern your expenses.

Precepts 217.28 (Mullach, *FPG*)

16 τύχην στέργε

Be content with your fortune.

Precepts 217.30 (Mullach, *FPG*)

17 ἀκούων ὅρα

Listen, take heed.

Precepts 217.30 (Mullach, *FPG*)

18 γλῶσσαν ἴσχε

Restrain your tongue.

Precepts 217.32 (Mullach, *FPG*)

19 κρῖνε δίκαια

Judge fairly.

Precepts 217.33 (Mullach, *FPG*)

20 ἀδωροδόκητος δοκίμαζε

Be incorruptible in judgement.

Precepts 217.33 (Mullach, *FPG*)

21 αἰτιῶ παρόντα

Accuse only when the accused is present.

Precepts 217.34 (Mullach, *FPG*)

22 λέγε εἰδώς

Speak only of what you know.

Precepts 217.34 (Mullach, *FPG*)

23 βίας μὴ ἔχου

Do not depend on force.

Precepts 217.34 (Mullach, *FPG*)

24 ὁμίλει πρᾴως

Be gentle in your ways.

Precepts 217.35 (Mullach, *FPG*)

25 πέρας ἐπιτέλει μὴ ἀποδειλιῶν

Finish the job without flinching.

Precepts 217.36 (Mullach, *FPG*)

26 φιλίαν φύλασσε

Cherish friendship.

Precepts 217.41 (Mullach, *FPG*)

27 γῆρας προσδέχου

Accept old age.

Precepts 217.45 (Mullach, *FPG*)

28 ἐπὶ ῥώμῃ μὴ καυχῶ

Boast not of your strength.

Precepts 217.45 (Mullach, *FPG*)

29 πλούτει δικαίως

Acquire wealth justly.

Precepts 217.46 (Mullach, *FPG*)

30 μανθάνων μὴ κάμνε

Never tire of learning.

Precepts 217.48 (Mullach, *FPG*)

31 κινδύνευε φρονίμως

Take only calculated risks.

Precepts 217.48 (Mullach, *FPG*)

32 σεαυτὸν αἰδοῦ

Respect your own self.

Precepts 218.3 (Mullach, *FPG*)

33 ἀτυχοῦντι συνάχθου

Share the burden of the unfortunate.

Precepts 218.5 (Mullach, *FPG*)

34 φθιμένους μὴ ἀδίκει

Do not wrong the dead.

Precepts 218.8 (Mullach, *FPG*)

35 τύχῃ μὴ πίστευε

Trust not in fortune.

Precepts 218.9 (Mullach, *FPG*)

36 παῖς ὢν κόσμιος ἴσθι, ἡβῶν ἐγκρατής, μέσος δίκαιος, πρεσβύτερος εὔλογος· τελεύτα ἀλύπως

As a child be well-behaved, as an adult self-disciplined, in middle age just, as an elder sensible; die without grief.

Precepts 218.9 (Mullach, *FPG*)

inscribed with another 150 'Delphic maxims' on a stele in honour of Cineas, founder of Ai Khanoum, a Greek-Bactrian city (in modern Afghanistan) at the instance of Clearchus of Soloi in Cyprus

37 μηδὲν ἄγαν

Nothing in excess.

Translated in *The Oxford Dictionary of Quotations* (2004)

Testimonies, Fragment 1 (D-K)

inscribed on the temple of Apollo at Delphi – ascribed to several of the seven sages, but Plato, Protagoras *343a, says it was devised by all Seven Sages conferring together*

38 ἀρχὴ ἄνδρα δείκνυσι

Rule shows forth the man.

Demosthenes, *Preambles* 48.2

this form used by Demosthenes is quoted verbatim to this day; variously attributed to Pittacus, Bias and Solon, in varying forms; cf. Epaminondas 5

39 Ἑπτὰ σοφῶν ἐρέω κατ' ἔπος πόλιν, οὔνομα, φωνήν.
Μέτρον μὲν Κλεόβουλος ὁ Λίνδιος εἶπεν ἄριστον·
Χίλων δ' ἐν κοίλῃ Λακεδαίμονι· Γνῶθι σεαυτόν·
ὃς δὲ Κόρινθον ἔναιε Χόλου κρατέειν Περίανδρος·
Πιττακὸς Οὐδὲν ἄγαν, ὃς ἔην γένος ἐκ Μυτιλήνης·
Τέρμα δ' ὁρᾶν βιότοιο Σόλων ἱεραῖς ἐν Ἀθήναις.
Τοὺς πλέονας κακίους δὲ Βίας ἀπέφηνε Πριηνεύς.
Ἐγγύην φεύγειν δὲ Θαλῆς Μιλήσιος ηὔδα.

I'll tell you in verse the names and sayings of the seven sages.
Cleobulus of Lindos said that measure was best;
Chilon in hollow Lacedaemon said 'Know thyself;'
and Periander, who dwelt in Corinth, 'Master anger;'
Pittacus, who was from Mytilene, said 'Naught in excess;'
and Solon, in holy Athens, 'Look to the end of life';
Bias of Priene declared that most men are evil,
and Thales of Miletus said 'Never be sure.'

Translated by W.R. Paton (1917)

Greek Anthology 9.366

40 Θαλῆς ὁ Μιλήσιος καὶ Πιττακὸς ὁ Μυτιληναῖος καὶ Βίας ὁ Πριηνεὺς καὶ Σόλων ὁ ἡμέτερος καὶ Κλεόβουλος ὁ Λίνδιος καὶ Μύσων ὁ Χηνεύς, καὶ Λακεδαιμόνιος Χίλων … καὶ καταμάθοι ἂν τις αὐτῶν τὴν σοφίαν τοιαύτην οὖσαν, ῥήματα βραχέα ἀξιομνημόνευτα ἑκάστῳ εἰρημένα

Thales of Miletus, Pittacus of Mytilene, Bias of Priene, our Solon (of Athens), Cleobulus of Lindos, Myson of Chen, and Chilon of Sparta ... You can recognize their wisdom by their short, quotable sayings.

Plato, *Protagoras* 343a

mentioning that all of them were admirers of the Spartan culture of laconic expression. Plato did not recognize Periander (considered a ruthless tyrant in his days) as one of the Seven Sages and counted Myson in his stead

SEXTUS EMPIRICUS

2nd–3rd century AD
Pyrrhonist sceptic and medical doctor

1 ἐκ κακοῦ κόρακος κακὸν ᾠόν

From a bad crow, a bad egg.

Against the Professors 2.99

SIMONIDES

*c.*556–468BC
Poet from Iulis on Ceos
see also Plato 210; Xenophon 44

1 Ὦ ξεῖν', ἀγγέλλειν Λακεδαιμονίοις, ὅτι τῇδε
κείμεθα τοῖς κείνων ῥήμασι πειθόμενοι.

Go tell the Spartans, thou who passest by,
That here, obedient to their laws, we lie.

Translated by W.L. Bowles (1762–1850)

Greek Anthology Epigram 7.249

epitaph for the Spartans at Thermopylae

2 Ἀκμᾶς ἑστακυῖαν ἐπὶ ξυροῦ Ἑλλάδα πᾶσαν
ταῖς αὑτῶν ψυχαῖς κείμεθα ῥυσάμενοι.

When Hellas stood on razor's edge
we saved her, giving up our souls.

Greek Anthology Epigram 7.250

on the tomb of the Corinthians who fell at Salamis; the stone has been found and is now in the Epigraphical Museum in Athens (Inv. no. EM 22 I2 927)

3 Ἄσβεστον κλέος οἵδε φίλῃ περὶ πατρίδι θέντες

These men bestowed ever-shining glory upon their fatherland.

Translated by C.A. Trypanis (1971)

Greek Anthology Epigram 7.251

probably of the Spartan dead at Plataeae

4 Εἰ τὸ καλῶς θνήσκειν ἀρετῆς μέρος ἐστὶ μέγιστον,
ἡμῖν ἐκ πάντων τοῦτ' ἀπένειμε Τύχη·
Ἑλλάδι γὰρ σπεύδοντες ἐλευθερίην περιθεῖναι
κείμεθ' ἀγηράντῳ χρώμενοι εὐλογίῃ.

If to die honourably is the greatest
Part of virtue, for us fate's done her best.
Because we fought to crown Greece with freedom
We lie here enjoying timeless fame.

Translated by Peter Jay (1973)

Greek Anthology Epigram 7.253

for the Athenian dead at Plataeae

5 Χαίρετ' ἀριστῆες πολέμου μέγα κῦδος ἔχοντες,
κοῦροι Ἀθηναίων ἔξοχοι ἱπποσύνῃ,
οἵ ποτε καλλιχόρου περὶ πατρίδος ὠλέσαθ' ἥβην
πλείστοις Ἑλλάνων ἀντία μαρνάμενοι.

Farewell noble and glorious sons of Athens, outstanding horsemen, who sacrificed your youth for your country, fighting against the greater part of Greeks.

Greek Anthology Epigram 7.254

6 Πολλὰ πιὼν καὶ πολλὰ φαγὼν καὶ πολλὰ κάκ' εἰπὼν
ἀνθρώπους κεῖμαι Τιμοκρέων Ῥόδιος.

Having drunk much and eaten much and gossiped much
of men, here I lie, Timocreon of Rhodes

Greek Anthology Epigram 7.348

7 Σπάρτᾳ δ' οὐ τὸ θανεῖν, ἀλλὰ φυγεῖν θάνατος

For Sparta it is fleeing, not dying, that is death.

Greek Anthology Epigram 7.431

8 οἳ βούλοντο πόλιν μὲν ἐλευθερίᾳ τεθαλυῖαν
παισὶ λιπεῖν, αὐτοὶ δ' ἐν προμάχοισι θανεῖν

They wished to leave to their children a city blossoming with freedom, and to die themselves in the forefront of the battle.

Translated by C.A. Trypanis (1971)

Greek Anthology Epigram 7.512

of the defenders of Tegea (but it is uncertain for which occasion the epigram was written)

9 Μνῆμα τόδε κλεινοῖο Μεγιστία, ὅν ποτε Μῆδοι
Σπερχειὸν ποταμὸν κτεῖναν ἀμειψάμενοι,
μάντιος, ὃς τότε Κῆρας ἐπερχομένας σάφα εἰδὼς
οὐκ ἔτλη Σπάρτης ἡγεμόνας προλιπεῖν.

Here fought and fell Megistias, hero brave,
Slain by the Medes, who crossed Sper-cheius' wave;
Well knew the seer his doom, but scorned to fly,
And rather chose with Sparta's king to die.

Translated by A.D. Godley (1922)

Greek Anthology Epigram 7.677

epitaph for Megistias, the seer who forewarned the deaths at Thermopylae; despite being told by Leonidas to leave he stayed, sending away his only son in his place; Spercheios is the river just north of Thermopylae

10 Μίλωνος τόδ' ἄγαλμα καλοῦ καλόν, ὅς ποτε Πίσῃ
ἑπτάκι νικήσας ἐς γόνατ' οὐκ ἔπεσεν.

This is the beautiful statue of handsome Milon,
victorious seven times by the water of Pisa,
never once falling to his knees.

Greek Anthology Epigram 16.24

Milon won six wrestling victories, and a seventh when no opponent appeared

11 Ὑγιαίνειν μὲν ἄριστον ἀνδρὶ θνητῷ,
δεύτερον δὲ φυὰν καλὸν γενέσθαι,
τὸ δὲ τρίτον πλουτεῖν ἀδόλως,
τέταρτον δὲ ἡβᾶν μετὰ τῶν φίλων.

Health is best for mortal man,
and second comes good looks,
third is wealth honestly obtained,
last not least, youth spent with friends.

Greek Anthology Appendix, Epigrammata exhortatoria et supplicatoria 6 (Cougny)

also attributed to Epicharmus

12 πῖνε πῖν' ἐπὶ συμφοραῖς

Drink, drink for good fortune!

Translated by David A. Campbell (1991)

Drink, drink on misadventures!

Fragment 7 (Page, *PMG*)

both translations are valid

13 χαίρετ' ἀελλοπόδων θύγατρες ἵππων

Hail to you, daughters of storm-footed steeds.

Translated by W. Rhys Roberts (1858–1929), rev. Jonathan Barnes, 1984

Fragment 10 (Page, *PMG*)

written for the victor of a mule race (after he had exchanged his small fee to Simonides for a larger one); quoted by Aristotle, Rhetoric *1405b.27*

14 ἄνθρωπος ἐὼν μή ποτε φάσῃς ὅ τι γίνεται αὔριον,
μηδ' ἄνδρα ἰδὼν ὄλβιον ὅσσον χρόνον ἔσσεται·
ὠκεῖα γὰρ οὐδὲ τανυπτερύγου μυίας
οὕτως ἁ μετάστασις

If you are a simple mortal, do not speak of tomorrow
or how long this man may be among the happy;
like the shining flight of the dragonfly,
change comes suddenly.

Fragment 16 (Page, *PMG*)

15 πάντα γὰρ μίαν ἱκνεῖται δασπλῆτα Χάρυβδιν,
αἱ μεγάλαι τ' ἀρεταὶ καὶ ὁ πλοῦτος

For all things arrive at one single horrible Charybdis,
great excellence and wealth alike.

Translated by David A. Campbell (1991)

Fragment 17 (Page, *PMG*)

16 ὁ δ' αὖ θάνατος κίχε καὶ τὸν φυγόμαχον

Death reaches even him who shuns battle.

Fragment 19 (Page, *PMG*)

17 ῥεῖα θεοὶ κλέπτουσιν ἀνθρώπων νόον

Gods easily deceive the minds of mortals.

Translated by Douglas E. Gerber (1999)

Fragment 20 (Page, *PMG*)

18 οὐκ ἔστιν κακὸν
ἀνεπιδόκητον ἀνθρώποις· ὀλίγῳ δὲ χρόνῳ
πάντα μεταρρίπτει θεός

There is no evil
which men cannot expect; and within a brief time
god turns everything upside down.

Translated by David A. Campbell (1991)

Fragment 22 (Page, *PMG*)

19 τῶν ἐν Θερμοπύλαις θανόντων
εὐκλεὴς μὲν ἁ τύχα, καλὸς δ' ὁ πότμος,
βωμὸς δ' ὁ τάφος, πρὸ γόων δὲ μνᾶστις, ὁ
δ' οἶκτος ἔπαινος

Of those who died at Thermopylae
glorious is the fate and beautiful their death;
their tomb is an altar;
for lamentation they have remembrance,
for sorrow praise.

Translated by C.A. Trypanis (1971)

Fragment 26.1 (Page, *PMG*)

20 ἐντάφιον δὲ τοιοῦτον οὔτ' εὐρὼς
οὔθ' ὁ πανδαμάτωρ ἀμαυρώσει χρόνος·
ἀνδρῶν ἀγαθῶν ὅδε σηκὸς οἰκέταν
εὐδοξίαν
Ἑλλάδος εἵλετο

Such a burial-place for the brave
neither mould shall obscure nor all-subduing time;
it enshrines the glory that is Greece.

Fragment 26.4 (Page, *PMG*)

of the Spartan dead at Thermopylae

21 χρὴ κορυδαλλίσι
πάσῃσιν ἐμφῦναι λόφον

Every lark must have its crest.

Translated by David A. Campbell (1991)

Fragment 33 (Page, *PMG*)

22 ἄνδρ' ἀγαθὸν μὲν ἀλαθέως γενέσθαι
χαλεπὸν χερσίν τε καὶ ποσὶ καὶ νόῳ
τετράγωνον ἄνευ ψόγου τετυγμένον

It is hard to be truly excellent,
four-square in hand and foot and mind,
formed without blemish.

Translated in *Bartlett's Familiar Quotations* (1980)

Fragment 37.1 (Page, *PMG*)

cf. Aristotle 108

23 τῶν γὰρ ἠλιθίων ἀπείρων γενέθλα

Infinite is the race of fools.

Translated by W.R.M. Lamb (1924)

Fragment 37.37 (Page, *PMG*)

quoted by Plato, Protagoras *346c*

24 ὦ τέκος οἷον ἔχω πόνον, σὺ δ' ἀωτεῖς

Child, how much I suffer, but you sleep.

Translated by C.A. Trypanis (1971)

Fragment 38 (Page, *PMG*)

25 τοῦ καὶ ἀπειρέσιοι
πωτῶντ' ὄρνιθες ὑπὲρ κεφαλᾶς,
ἀνὰ δ' ἰχθύες ὀρθοὶ
κυανέου 'ξ ὕδατος ἅλ-
λοντο καλᾷ σὺν ἀοιδᾷ

Over his head flew numberless birds,
and fish leaped straight up from the dark blue water
at his beautiful song.

Translated by David A. Campbell (1991)

Fragment 62 (Page, *PMG*)

26 ἴσχει δέ με πορφυρέας ἁλὸς
ἀμφιταρασσομένας ὀρυμαγδός

I am held fast by the crash of the surging sea seething all around.

Translated by David A. Campbell (1991)

Fragment 66 (Page, *PMG*)

27 ἀεναοῖς ποταμοῖς ἄνθεσί τ' εἰαρινοῖς
ἀελίου τε φλογὶ χρυσέας τε σελάνας
καὶ θαλασσαίαισι δίναις ἀντιθέντα μένος
στάλας

Ever-flowing rivers, the flowers of spring,
the flame of the sun, and the golden moon
and the eddies of the sea.

Translated by R.D. Hicks (1925)

Fragment 76 (Page, *PMG*)

28 τίς γὰρ ἁδονᾶς ἄτερ θνατῶν βίος
ποθεινὸς; ...
τᾶς ἄτερ οὐδὲ θεῶν ζηλωτὸς αἰών

What human life is desirable without pleasure? ...
Without it not even the life of the gods is enviable.

Translated by David A. Campbell (1991)

Fragment 79 (Page, *PMG*)

29 ἄγγελε κλυτὰ
ἔαρος ἁδυόδμου
κυανέα χελιδοῖ

Noble messenger
of sweet-scented spring,
blue-black swallow!

Translated by David A. Campbell (1991)

Fragment 92 (Page, *PMG*)

30 τὸ δοκεῖν καὶ τὰν ἀλάθειαν βιᾶται

Appearance does violence even to the truth.

Translated by David A. Campbell (1991)
Fragment 93 (Page, *PMG*)

31 τὸ γὰρ γεγενημένον οὐκέτ' ἄρεκτον ἔσται

What has been done can never be undone.

Fragment 98 (Page, *PMG*)

32 ἓν δὲ τὸ κάλλιστον Χῖος ἔειπεν ἀνήρ·
οἵη περ φύλλων γενεή, τοίη δὲ καὶ ἀνδρῶν· ...
ἀλλὰ σὺ ταῦτα μαθὼν βιότου ποτὶ τέρμα
ψυχῇ τῶν ἀγαθῶν τλῆθι χαριζόμενος

The man from Chios called Homer said a beautiful thing:
'The generations of men are like the leaves of a tree.'
But since you know this now that your end is near,
treat yourself entirely to what good things there are.

Translated by Edmund Keeley (2010)
Fragment 8.1–13 (West, *IEG*)
cf. Homer 84

33 πάρεστι γὰρ ἐλπὶς ἑκάστῳ
ἀνδρῶν, ἥ τε νέων στήθεσιν ἐμφύεται

Hope, present in every man,
clings closely to the hearts of the young.

Fragment 8.4 (West, *IEG*)

34 θνητῶν δ' ὄφρά τις ἄνθος ἔχῃ πολυήρατον ἥβης,
κοῦφον ἔχων θυμὸν πόλλ' ἀτέλεστα νοεῖ

A mortal, while he has the lovely bloom of youth,
has many empty-headed, vain ideas.

Translated by M.L. West (1994)
Fragment 8.6 (West, *IEG*)

35 οὐδὲ ἴσασιν
ὡς χρόνος ἔσθ' ἥβης καὶ βιότου ὀλίγος

Nor do they know
how short youth and life are.

Fragment 8.10 (West, *IEG*)

36 εἰ δ' ἄρα τιμῆσαι, θύγατερ Διός, ὅστις ἄριστος,
δῆμος Ἀθηναίων ἐξετέλεσσε μόνος

But if it is right, daughter of Zeus, to honour the best,
it was the people of Athens that performed it alone.

Translated by David A. Campbell (1991)
Fragment 9 (West, *IEG*)
perhaps referring to Marathon

37 ὅ τοι Χρόνος ὀξὺς ὀδόντας,
καὶ πάντα ψήχει καὶ τὰ βιαιότατα

Time is sharp-toothed, and he grinds up all things, even the mightiest.

Translated by David A. Campbell (1991)
Fragment 13 (West, *IEG*)

38 μνήμην δ' οὔτινά φημι Σιμωνίδῃ ἰσοφαρίζειν
ὀγδωκονταέτει

I declare that in power of memory no one rivals Simonides,
now eighty years old.

Translated by David A. Campbell (1991)
Fragment 14 (West, *IEG*)
written by himself according to Aelius Aristides 379.22; Simonides was well known for his excellent memory and his method of mnemonics

39 πόλις ἄνδρα διδάσκει

The city is the teacher of men.

Fragment 15 (West, *IEG*)

40 ἔστι καὶ σιγῆς ἀκίνδυνον γέρας

Silence too can be a prerogative, free from danger.

Fragment 66 (Bergk, *PLG*)
much quoted in antiquity, cf. Caesar Augustus in Plutarch 207c; Horace, Odes *3.2.25: 'est et fideli tuta silentio merces'; et al.*

41 Σιμωνίδης τὸν Ἡσίοδον κηπουρὸν ἔλεγε, τὸν δὲ Ὅμηρον στεφανηπλόκον, τὸν μὲν ὡς φυτεύσαντα τὰς περὶ θεῶν καὶ ἡρώων μυθολογίας, τὸν δὲ ὡς ἐξ αὐτῶν συμπλέξαντα τὸν Ἰλιάδος καὶ Ὀδυσσείας στέφανον

Simonides said Hesiod was a gardener, Homer a garland-maker: Hesiod planted the mythologies of gods and heroes, Homer plaited them from the garland of the *Iliad* and *Odyssey*.

Translated by David A. Campbell (1991)
Fragment 6 (*FGrH*)

42 ὅθεν καὶ τὸ Σιμωνίδου εἴρηται περὶ τῶν σοφῶν καὶ πλουσίων πρὸς τὴν γυναῖκα τὴν Ἱέρωνος ἐρομένην πότερον γενέσθαι κρεῖττον πλούσιον ἢ σοφόν· πλούσιον εἰπεῖν· τοὺς σοφοὺς γὰρ ἔφη ὁρᾶν ἐπὶ ταῖς

τῶν πλουσίων θύραις διατρίβοντας

Simonides, when asked by Hieron's wife, which was preferable, to be born wise or wealthy, replied, 'Wealthy; for it seems that the wise wait at the doors of the rich.'

Aristotle, *Rhetoric* 1391a.8

43 Σιμωνίδης ἔλεγε μηδέποτ' αὐτῷ μεταμελῆσαι σιγήσαντι, φθεγξαμένῳ δὲ πολλάκις

Simonides said he had never regretted remaining silent, but had many times, having spoken.

Plutarch, *Advice About Keeping Well* 125d

44 τὴν μὲν ζωγραφίαν ποίησιν σιωπῶσαν προσαγορεύει, τὴν δὲ ποίησιν ζωγραφίαν λαλοῦσαν

Painting is silent poetry, poetry is eloquent painting.

Translated in *The Oxford Dictionary of Quotations* (2004)

Plutarch, *Were the Athenians More Famous in War or in Wisdom?* 346f

45 τῶν ἄλλων ἀπεστερημένος διὰ τὸ γῆρας ἡδονῶν ὑπὸ μιᾶς ἔτι γηροβοσκεῖται τῆς ἀπὸ τοῦ κερδαίνειν

Deprived by old age of other pleasures, he is still comforted by one, that of gain.

Translated by Charles Forster Smith (1919)

Plutarch, *Whether an Old Man Should Engage in Public Affairs* 786b

Simonides' reply to those who accused him of love of money; cf. Pericles 38

46 Σιμωνίδης ἐρωτηθεὶς διὰ τί ἐσχατογήρως ὢν φιλάργυρος εἴη, ὅτι εἶπε βουλοίμην ἂν ἀποθανὼν τοῖς ἐχθροῖς μᾶλλον ἀπολιπεῖν ἢ ζῶν δεῖσθαι τῶν φίλων

When asked why he was so money-minded even in old age, Simonides replied that he'd rather leave something for his enemies when he died than depend on his friends while alive.

Stobaeus, *Anthology* 3.10.61

47 Σιμωνίδης ἐρωτηθεὶς πόσον χρόνον βιῴη χρόνον εἶπεν ὀλίγον, ἔτη δὲ πολλά

When Simonides was asked the length of life, he answered, 'A little time, but many years.'

Stobaeus, *Anthology* 4.34.59

48 παίζειν ἐν τῷ βίῳ καὶ περὶ μηδὲν ἁπλῶς σπουδάζειν

Play throughout our lives and take nothing quite seriously.

Translated by David A. Campbell (1991)

Theon Aelius, *Preliminary Exercises in Rhetoric* 105

SOCRATES

469–399BC

Athenian philosopher

see also Aeschines Socraticus 1; Aristophanes 44–50; Cato the Elder 12; Epictetus 16, 60; Oracles 17; Proverbial 39

1 ὡς ἔστιν τις Σωκράτης σοφὸς ἀνήρ, τά τε μετέωρα φροντιστὴς καὶ τὰ ὑπὸ γῆς πάντα ἀνεζητηκὼς

There is a certain Socrates, a wise fellow, who meditates on supra-terrestrial things and has investigated all that lies below the earth.

Plato, *Apology* 18b.6

quoting accusations against him

2 τὸν ἥττω λόγον κρείττω ποιῶν

He makes the worse appear the better cause.

Translated by Benjamin Jowett (1817–1893)

Plato, *Apology* 18b.8

quoting accusations against him

3 ἃ μὴ οἶδα οὐδὲ οἴομαι εἰδέναι

What I do not know I do not think I know either.

Translated by Harold North Fowler (1914)

Plato, *Apology* 21d

4 τῷ ὄντι ὁ θεὸς σοφὸς εἶναι ... ἡ ἀνθρωπίνη σοφία ὀλίγου τινὸς ἀξία ἐστὶν καὶ οὐδενός

Only god is truly wise. Human wisdom is of little or no value.

Plato, *Apology* 23a

5 Σωκράτη φησὶν ἀδικεῖν τούς τε νέους διαφθείροντα καὶ θεοὺς οὓς ἡ πόλις νομίζει οὐ νομίζοντα, ἕτερα δὲ δαιμόνια καινά

Socrates, he says, breaks the law by corrupting young men and not recognizing the gods that the city recognizes, but some other new deities.

Translated in *The Oxford Dictionary of Quotations* (2004)

Plato, *Apology* 24b

quoting accusations against him

6 τίθημι γάρ σε ὁμολογοῦντα, ἐπειδὴ οὐκ ἀποκρίνῃ

I assume that you agree, since you do not answer.

Translated by Harold North Fowler (1914)

Plato, *Apology* 27c

7 φιλοσοφοῦντά με δεῖν ζῆν καὶ ἐξετάζοντα ἐμαυτὸν καὶ τοὺς ἄλλους

I was bent on spending my life in philosophy and in examining myself and others.

Plato, *Apology* 28e

8 τὸ γάρ τοι θάνατον δεδιέναι, ὦ ἄνδρες, οὐδὲν ἄλλο ἐστὶν ἢ δοκεῖν σοφὸν εἶναι μὴ ὄντα· δοκεῖν γὰρ εἰδέναι ἐστὶν ἃ οὐκ οἶδεν. οἶδε μὲν γὰρ οὐδεὶς τὸν θάνατον οὐδ' εἰ τυγχάνει τῷ ἀνθρώπῳ πάντων μέγιστον ὂν τῶν ἀγαθῶν, δεδίασι δ' ὡς εὖ εἰδότες ὅτι μέγιστον τῶν κακῶν ἐστι

To fear death is to think one is wise when one is not, since it is presuming one knows what one does not know. Death may even be the greatest of all blessings to man, but some fear it as if they knew that it is the greatest of evils.

Plato, *Apology* 29a

9 ἕωσπερ ἂν ἐμπνέω καὶ οἷός τε ὦ, οὐ μὴ παύσωμαι φιλοσοφῶν

As long as I live and am able to continue I shall never give up philosophy.

Translated by Harold North Fowler (1914)

Plato, *Apology* 29d

10 ὦ ἄριστε ἀνδρῶν, Ἀθηναῖος ὤν, πόλεως τῆς μεγίστης καὶ εὐδοκιμωτάτης εἰς σοφίαν καὶ ἰσχύν, χρημάτων μὲν οὐκ αἰσχύνῃ ἐπιμελούμενος ὅπως σοι ἔσται ὡς πλεῖστα, καὶ δόξης καὶ τιμῆς, φρονήσεως δὲ καὶ ἀληθείας καὶ τῆς ψυχῆς ὅπως ὡς βελτίστη ἔσται οὐκ ἐπιμελῇ οὐδὲ φροντίζεις;

My good man, you, a citizen of Athens, greatest of cities, most famous for wisdom and power, are you not ashamed to strive for wealth, reputation and honour, and care not for wisdom and truth and the perfection of your soul?

Plato, *Apology* 29d

11 οὐκ ἐκ χρημάτων ἀρετὴ γίγνεται, ἀλλ' ἐξ ἀρετῆς χρήματα καὶ τὰ ἄλλα ἀγαθὰ τοῖς ἀνθρώποις ἅπαντα καὶ ἰδίᾳ καὶ δημοσίᾳ

Virtue does not come from money, but from virtue comes money and all other good things to man, both to the individual and to the state.

Translated by Harold North Fowler (1914)

Plato, *Apology* 30b

12 τότε μέντοι ἐγὼ οὐ λόγῳ ἀλλ' ἔργῳ αὖ ἐνεδειξάμην ὅτι ἐμοὶ θανάτου μὲν μέλει ... οὐδ' ὁτιοῦν, τοῦ δὲ μηδὲν ἄδικον μηδ' ἀνόσιον ἐργάζεσθαι, τούτου δὲ τὸ πᾶν μέλει

I showed, not in words only, but in deed, that I care not a straw for death, but that my great and only care is lest I should do anything unjust or unholy.

Translated by Benjamin Jowett (1817–1893)

Plato, *Apology* 32d

13 ἐνταῦθα ᾖα, ἐπιχειρῶν ἕκαστον ὑμῶν πείθειν μὴ πρότερον μήτε τῶν ἑαυτοῦ μηδενὸς ἐπιμελεῖσθαι πρὶν ἑαυτοῦ ἐπιμεληθείη ὅπως ὡς βέλτιστος καὶ φρονιμώτατος ἔσοιτο, μήτε τῶν τῆς πόλεως, πρὶν αὐτῆς τῆς πόλεως, τῶν τε ἄλλων οὕτω κατὰ τὸν αὐτὸν τρόπον ἐπιμελεῖσθαι· τί οὖν εἰμι ἄξιος παθεῖν τοιοῦτος ὤν;

I tried to persuade you to seek perfection in virtue and wisdom rather than in wealth – for yourself and equally for the state. What then does such a man as I deserve?

Plato, *Apology* 36c

14 ὁ δὲ ἀνεξέταστος βίος οὐ βιωτὸς ἀνθρώπῳ

An uninvestigated life is not worth living.

Plato, *Apology* 38a

15 ὁρᾶτε γὰρ δὴ τὴν ἡλικίαν ὅτι πόρρω ἤδη ἐστὶ τοῦ βίου θανάτου δὲ ἐγγύς

You see how old I am, how far advanced in life and how near death.

Translated by Harold North Fowler (1914)

Plato, *Apology* 38c

16 δυοῖν γὰρ θάτερόν ἐστιν τὸ τεθνάναι· ἢ γὰρ οἷον μηδὲν εἶναι μηδὲ αἴσθησιν μηδεμίαν μηδενὸς ἔχειν τὸν τεθνεῶτα, ἢ κατὰ τὰ λεγόμενα μεταβολή τις τυγχάνει οὖσα καὶ μετοίκησις τῇ ψυχῇ τοῦ τόπου τοῦ ἐνθένδε εἰς ἄλλον τόπον ... εἰ οὖν τοιοῦτον ὁ θάνατός ἐστιν, κέρδος ἔγωγε λέγω· καὶ γὰρ οὐδὲν πλείων ὁ πᾶς χρόνος φαίνεται οὕτω δὴ εἶναι ἢ μία νύξ

Either death is a state of nothingness and utter unconsciousness, or, as men say, there is a change and migration of the soul from this world to another. Now if death be of such a nature, I say that to die is to gain; for eternity is then only a single night.

Translated by Benjamin Jowett (1817–1893)

Plato, *Apology* 40c–e

17 ἔστιν ἀνδρὶ ἀγαθῷ κακὸν οὐδὲν οὔτε ζῶντι οὔτε τελευτήσαντι

To a good man no evil can come, either in life or after death.

Plato, *Apology* 41d

18 ἀλλὰ γὰρ ἤδη ὥρα ἀπιέναι, ἐμοὶ μὲν ἀποθανουμένῳ, ὑμῖν δὲ βιωσομένοις· ὁπότεροι δὲ ἡμῶν ἔρχονται ἐπὶ ἄμεινον πρᾶγμα, ἄδηλον παντὶ πλὴν ἢ τῷ θεῷ

The hour of departure has arrived, and we go our ways – I to die, and you to live; which is the better, god only knows.

Translated by Benjamin Jowett (1817–1893)

Plato, *Apology* 42a

last lines, spoken to the judges who convicted him

19 καὶ σοῦ πάλαι θαυμάζω αἰσθανόμενος ὡς ἡδέως καθεύδεις

I have been wondering at you for some time, seeing how sweetly you sleep.

Translated by Harold North Fowler (1914)

Plato, *Crito* 43b.5

of Socrates on the day of his execution

20 πολλάκις μὲν δή σε καὶ πρότερον ἐν παντὶ τῷ βίῳ εὐδαιμόνισα τοῦ τρόπου, πολὺ δὲ μάλιστα ἐν τῇ νῦν παρεστώσῃ συμφορᾷ, ὡς ῥᾳδίως αὐτὴν καὶ πρᾴως φέρεις

I have often thought that throughout your life you were of a happy disposition, and I think so more than ever in this present misfortune, since you bear it so easily and calmly.

Translated by Harold North Fowler (1914)

Plato, *Crito* 43b.6

of Socrates

21 πλημμελὲς εἴη ἀγανακτεῖν τηλικοῦτον ὄντα εἰ δεῖ ἤδη τελευτᾶν

It would be absurd if at my age I were disturbed because I must die now.

Translated by Harold North Fowler (1914)

Plato, *Crito* 43b.10

just before he was given the hemlock

22 τί ἡμῖν ... οὕτω τῆς τῶν πολλῶν δόξης μέλει;

Why do we care so much for what most people think?

Translated by Harold North Fowler (1914)

Plato, *Crito* 44c

23 εἰ γὰρ ὤφελον ... οἷοί τ' εἶναι οἱ πολλοὶ τὰ μέγιστα κακὰ ἐργάζεσθαι, ἵνα οἷοί τ' ἦσαν καὶ ἀγαθὰ τὰ μέγιστα

I only wish that as people are able to accomplish the greatest evils, they were also able to accomplish the greatest good.

Plato, *Crito* 44d

24 ἢ γὰρ οὐ χρὴ ποιεῖσθαι παῖδας ἢ συνδιαταλαιπωρεῖν καὶ τρέφοντα καὶ παιδεύοντα

Either don't have children, or endure hardship with them, raise them and educate them.

Plato, *Crito* 45d

25 οὐκ ἄρα, ὦ βέλτιστε, πάνυ ἡμῖν οὕτω φροντιστέον τί ἐροῦσιν οἱ πολλοὶ ἡμᾶς, ἀλλ' ὅτι ὁ ἐπαΐων περὶ τῶν δικαίων καὶ ἀδίκων, ὁ εἷς καὶ αὐτὴ ἡ ἀλήθεια

Then, most excellent friend, we must not consider at all what the many will say of us, but only he who knows what is just and what unjust; only he, and his will be the truth.

Plato, *Crito* 48a

26 οὐ τὸ ζῆν περὶ πλείστου ποιητέον ἀλλὰ τὸ εὖ ζῆν

It is not living, but living well which we ought to consider most important.

Translated by Harold North Fowler (1914)

Plato, *Crito* 48b

27 τό γε ἀδικεῖν τῷ ἀδικοῦντι καὶ κακὸν καὶ αἰσχρὸν τυγχάνει ὂν παντὶ τρόπῳ;

Is not wrongdoing inevitably an evil and a disgrace to the wrongdoer?

Translated by Harold North Fowler (1914)

Plato, *Crito* 49b

28 δοκεῖ σοι οἷόν τε ἔτι ἐκείνην τὴν πόλιν εἶναι καὶ μὴ ἀνατετράφθαι, ἐν ᾗ ἂν αἱ γενόμεναι δίκαι μηδὲν ἰσχύωσιν ἀλλὰ ὑπὸ ἰδιωτῶν ἄκυροί τε γίγνωνται καὶ διαφθείρωνται;

Do you think that a state can exist and not be overturned, in which the decisions reached by the courts have no force but are made invalid and annulled by private persons?

Translated by Harold North Fowler (1914)

Plato, *Crito* 50b

29 μητρός τε καὶ πατρὸς καὶ τῶν ἄλλων προγόνων ἁπάντων τιμιώτερόν ἐστιν πατρὶς καὶ σεμνότερον καὶ ἁγιώτερον καὶ ἐν μείζονι μοίρᾳ καὶ παρὰ θεοῖς καὶ παρ' ἀνθρώποις τοῖς νοῦν ἔχουσι

More than mother and father and all ancestors, your country is more precious and nobler and holier and in higher esteem both among gods and among men of understanding.

Plato, *Crito* 51a

30 μήτε παῖδας περὶ πλείονος ποιοῦ μήτε τὸ ζῆν μήτε ἄλλο μηδὲν πρὸ τοῦ δικαίου

Regard neither children nor life nor anything else more highly than justice.

Translated by Gavin Betts and Alan Henry (1989)

Plato, *Crito* 54b

31 εἰ δ' ἀναγκαῖον εἴη ἀδικεῖν ἢ ἀδικεῖσθαι, ἑλοίμην ἂν μᾶλλον ἀδικεῖσθαι ἢ ἀδικεῖν

If it were necessary either to do wrong or to suffer it, I should choose to suffer rather than do it.

Translated by W.R.M. Lamb (1925)

Plato, *Gorgias* 469c

cf. Plato 3

32 ἔδεισα μὴ παντάπασι τὴν ψυχὴν τυφλωθείην βλέπων πρὸς τὰ πράγματα τοῖς ὄμμασι καὶ ἑκάστῃ τῶν αἰσθήσεων ἐπιχειρῶν ἅπτεσθαι αὐτῶν

I was afraid my soul would be blinded if I looked at things with my eyes and tried to grasp them with any of my senses.

Translated by Harold North Fowler (1914)

Plato, *Phaedo* 99e

33 παντὸς μᾶλλον ἄρα, ἔφη, ὦ Κέβης, ψυχὴ ἀθάνατον καὶ ἀνώλεθρον, καὶ τῷ ὄντι ἔσονται ἡμῶν αἱ ψυχαὶ ἐν Ἅιδου

It is perfectly certain that the soul is immortal and imperishable, and our souls will actually exist in another world.

Translated by Harold North Fowler (1914)

Plato, *Phaedo* 106e

34 θαρρεῖν χρὴ περὶ τῇ ἑαυτοῦ ψυχῇ ἄνδρα ὅστις ἐν τῷ βίῳ τὰς μὲν ἄλλας ἡδονὰς τὰς περὶ τὸ σῶμα καὶ τοὺς κόσμους εἴασε χαίρειν … τὰς δὲ περὶ τὸ μανθάνειν ἐσπούδασέ τε καὶ κοσμήσας τὴν ψυχὴν … τῷ αὐτῆς κόσμῳ, σωφροσύνῃ τε καὶ δικαιοσύνῃ καὶ ἀνδρείᾳ καὶ ἐλευθερίᾳ καὶ ἀληθείᾳ, οὕτω περιμένει τὴν εἰς Ἅιδου πορείαν

Be of good cheer about your soul; he who has rejected bodily pleasures and has sought for those of learning, he who has adorned his soul with its proper ornaments of self-restraint and justice and courage and freedom and truth – he thus is ready for the journey to the world below.

Translated by Harold North Fowler (1914)

Plato, *Phaedo* 114d

35 θάπτωμεν δέ σε τίνα τρόπον; ὅπως ἂν βούλησθε, ἐάνπερ γε λάβητέ με καὶ μὴ ἐκφύγω ὑμᾶς

'How shall we bury you?'
'However you wish, only keep hold of me so I do not run away.'

Plato, *Phaedo* 115c

36 ὦ Σώκρατες, ἔφη, οὐ καταγνώσομαί γε σοῦ ὅπερ ἄλλων καταγιγνώσκω, ὅτι μοι χαλεπαίνουσι καὶ καταρῶνται ἐπειδὰν αὐτοῖς παραγγείλω πίνειν τὸ φάρμακον … σὲ δὲ ἐγὼ καὶ ἄλλως ἔγνωκα ἐν τούτῳ τῷ χρόνῳ γενναιότατον καὶ πρᾳότατον καὶ ἄριστον ἄνδρα ὄντα τῶν πώποτε δεῦρο ἀφικομένων, καὶ δὴ καὶ νῦν εὖ οἶδ' ὅτι οὐκ ἐμοὶ χαλεπαίνεις … καὶ ἅμα δακρύσας μεταστρεφόμενος ἀπῄει

'Socrates, I shall not find fault with you, as I do with others, for being angry and cursing me when I tell them to drink the poison. All this time I have found you the noblest and gentlest and best man who has ever come here, and I know your anger is not directed against me.' And with a tear he went his way.

Plato, *Phaedo* 116c

Socrates' jailor handing him the hemlock

37 τί λέγεις, ἔφη, περὶ τοῦδε τοῦ πώματος πρὸς τὸ ἀποσπεῖσαί τινι; ἔξεστιν ἢ οὔ; τοσοῦτον, ἔφη, ὦ Σώκρατες, τρίβομεν ὅσον οἰόμεθα μέτριον εἶναι πιεῖν. μανθάνω, ἦ δ' ὅς· ἀλλ' εὔχεσθαί γέ που τοῖς θεοῖς ἔξεστί τε καὶ χρή, τὴν μετοίκησιν τὴν ἐνθένδε ἐκεῖσε εὐτυχῆ γενέσθαι· ἃ δὴ καὶ ἐγὼ εὔχομαί τε καὶ γένοιτο ταύτῃ. καὶ ἅμ' εἰπὼν ταῦτα ἐπισχόμενος καὶ μάλα εὐχερῶς καὶ εὐκόλως ἐξέπιεν

'What do you say about pouring a libation to some god from this cup? Is it allowed or not?' 'We only prepare just the right amount to drink, Socrates,' the jailor said. 'I understand,' he went on; 'but it is allowed and necessary to pray to the gods, that my moving from hence to there may be blessed; thus I pray, and so be it.'

Translated in *The Oxford Dictionary of Quotations* (2004)

Plato, *Phaedo* 117b

of the cup containing his hemlock

38 ὦ Κρίτων, ἔφη, τῷ Ἀσκληπιῷ ὀφείλομεν ἀλεκτρυόνα· ἀλλὰ ἀπόδοτε καὶ μὴ ἀμελήσητε

Crito, we owe a cock to Asclepius; render to him what is due and do not neglect it.

Plato, *Phaedo* 118a.7

Socrates' last words

39 ἥδε ἡ τελευτή, ὦ Ἐχέκρατες, τοῦ ἑταίρου ἡμῖν ἐγένετο, ἀνδρός, ὡς ἡμεῖς φαῖμεν ἄν, τῶν τότε ὧν ἐπειράθημεν ἀρίστου καὶ ἄλλως φρονιμωτάτου καὶ δικαιοτάτου

Such was the end, Echecrates, of our friend, who was, as we may say, of all those of his time whom we have known, the best and wisest and most righteous of men.

Translated by Harold North Fowler (1914)

Plato, *Phaedo* 118a.15

of Socrates – last lines of Phaedo

40 κρεῖττον γάρ που σμικρὸν εὖ ἢ πολὺ μὴ ἱκανῶς περᾶναι

It is better to finish a small task well than many imperfectly.

Translated by Harold North Fowler (1914)

Plato, *Theaetetus* 187e

41 μᾶλλον ἂν ἐβούλου με ὁρᾶν δικαίως ἢ ἀδίκως ἀποθνῄσκοντα;

Would you prefer to see me put to death justly or unjustly?

Xenophon, *Apology* 28

on a comment that he was condemned unjustly; cf. Diogenes Laertius, Lives of Eminent Philosophers *2.35*

42 ἀδικεῖ Σωκράτης οὓς μὲν ἡ πόλις νομίζει θεοὺς οὐ νομίζων, ἕτερα δὲ καινὰ δαιμόνια εἰσφέρων· ἀδικεῖ δὲ καὶ τοὺς νέους διαφθείρων

Socrates is guilty of rejecting the gods acknowledged by the state and of bringing in strange deities; he is also guilty of corrupting the youth.

Translated by E.C. Marchant (1923)

Xenophon, *Memorabilia* 1.1.1

the indictment against Socrates

43 Σωκράτης δὲ πάντα μὲν ἡγεῖτο θεοὺς εἰδέναι, τά τε λεγόμενα καὶ πραττόμενα καὶ τὰ σιγῇ βουλευόμενα, πανταχοῦ δὲ παρεῖναι καὶ σημαίνειν τοῖς ἀνθρώποις περὶ τῶν ἀνθρωπείων πάντων

Socrates thought that the gods know all things, our words and deeds and secret purposes; that they are present everywhere, and grant signs to men of all that concerns man.

Translated by E.C. Marchant (1923)

Xenophon, *Memorabilia* 1.1.19

44 Σωκράτης ... συνεβούλευε φυλάττεσθαι τὰ πείθοντα μὴ πεινῶντας ἐσθίειν μηδὲ διψῶντας πίνειν

Socrates advised the avoidance of appetizers that encourage you to eat when not hungry and drink when not thirsty.

Xenophon, *Memorabilia* 1.3.6

45 μὴ ἀμέλει τῶν τῆς πόλεως, εἴ τι δυνατόν ἐστι διὰ σὲ βέλτιον ἔχειν

Don't neglect public affairs, if you have the power to improve them.

Translated by E.C. Marchant (1923)

Xenophon, *Memorabilia* 3.7.9

46 ποτὲ ἔργῳ ἄνθρωπος ὀψοφάγος καλεῖται;

What makes a man a gourmet?

Xenophon, *Memorabilia* 3.14.2

47 τῷ γὰρ ὄντι ὁ οἶνος ἄρδων τὰς ψυχὰς τὰς μὲν λύπας ὥσπερ ὁ μανδραγόρας τοὺς ἀνθρώπους κοιμίζει, τὰς δὲ φιλοφροσύνας ὥσπερ ἔλαιον φλόγα ἐγείρει

Wine fosters the soul and lulls our griefs to sleep, just as mandrake does with men, and awakens kindly feelings as oil quickens a flame.

Xenophon, *Symposium* 2.24

48 οὐκ Ἀθηναῖος οὐδ' Ἕλλην ἀλλὰ κόσμιος εἶναι

I am not Athenian or Greek but a citizen of the world.

Translated in *The Oxford Dictionary of Political Quotations* (2006)

Plutarch, *On Exile* 600f

49 Ξενοφῶντα ἰδὼν κείμενον τὸν Γρύλλου Σωκράτης ὁ φιλόσοφος στρατεύων πεζὸς τοῦ ἵππου γεγονότος ἐκποδὼν ἀνέλαβε τοῖς ὤμοις αὐτόν, καὶ ἔσωσεν ἐπὶ πολλοὺς σταδίους ἕως ἐπαύσατο ἡ φυγή

Socrates the philosopher, seeing Xenophon lying wounded in battle, dismounted from his horse, took him on his shoulders and carried him for several furlongs to safety.

Strabo, *Geography* 9.2.8

50 ὁρᾷς ὡς οὐ θεωρήσουσα θεωρησομένη δὲ μᾶλλον βαδίζεις;

Do you not perceive that you goe not to see, but rather to be seen?

Translated by Thomas Stanley (1665)

Aelian, *Historical Miscellany* 7.10

to his notoriously disagreeable wife Xanthippe who would not go out in Socrates' old coat

51 τὸν δὲ φάναι, ἃ μὲν συνῆκα, γενναῖα· οἶμαι δὲ καὶ ἃ μὴ συνῆκα· πλὴν Δηλίου γέ τινος δεῖται κολυμβητοῦ

The part I understand is excellent, and so too is, I dare say, the part I do not understand; but it needs a Delian diver to get to the bottom of it.

Translated by R.D. Hicks (1925)

Diogenes Laertius, *Lives of Eminent Philosophers* 2.22

on Heraclitus' book

52 πόσων ἐγὼ χρείαν οὐκ ἔχω

How many things I can do without!

Translated by R.D. Hicks (1925)

Diogenes Laertius, *Lives of Eminent Philosophers* 2.25

on looking at a multitude of goods exposed for sale

53 ἔλεγεν ... ἐλαχίστων δεόμενος ἔγγιστα εἶναι θεῶν

Having fewest wants I am nearest to the gods.

Translated in *Bartlett's Familiar Quotations* (1980)

Diogenes Laertius, *Lives of Eminent Philosophers* 2.27

54 ἓν μόνον ἀγαθὸν εἶναι, τὴν ἐπιστήμην, καὶ ἓν μόνον κακόν, τὴν ἀμαθίαν

There is only one good, knowledge, and one evil, ignorance.

Translated in *Bartlett's Familiar Quotations* (1980)

Diogenes Laertius, *Lives of Eminent Philosophers* 2.31

55 προσημαίνειν τὸ δαιμόνιον τὰ μέλλοντα αὐτῷ

My divine sign indicates the future to me.

Translated in *Bartlett's Familiar Quotations* (1980)

Diogenes Laertius, *Lives of Eminent Philosophers* 2.32.5

56 ἔλεγε δὲ ... καὶ εἰδέναι μὲν μηδὲν πλὴν αὐτὸ τοῦτο εἰδέναι

I know nothing except the fact of my ignorance.

Translated in *Bartlett's Familiar Quotations* (1980)

Diogenes Laertius, *Lives of Eminent Philosophers* 2.32.6

often quoted as 'ἓν οἶδα ὅτι οὐδὲν οἶδα'; cf. Milton, Paradise Regained *4.293 (1671): 'The first and wisest of them all professed / To know this only, that he nothing knew.'*

57 πότερον γῆμαι ἢ μή, ἔφη, ὃ ἂν αὐτῶν ποιήσῃς, μεταγνώσῃ

To marry or not to marry, whichever you

do you will repent it.

Diogenes Laertius, *Lives of Eminent Philosophers* 2.33

when someone asked whether he should marry or not

58 ἔλεγέ τε τοὺς μὲν ἄλλους ἀνθρώπους ζῆν ἵν' ἐσθίοιεν· αὐτὸν δὲ ἐσθίειν ἵνα ζῴη

He said that other men live to eat, but he eats to live.

Translated by John Simpson and Jennifer Speake (1982)

Diogenes Laertius, *Lives of Eminent Philosophers* 2.34

cf. the English proverb 'eat to live, not live to eat'; cf. Alexis 12; and Molière, L'avare *3.1: 'il faut manger pour vivre, et non pas vivre pour manger'*

59 ὥσπερ ἄλλος τις χαίρει τὸν ἀγρὸν τὸν αὑτοῦ ποιῶν κρείσσονα, ἄλλος τὸν ἵππον, οὕτως ἐγὼ καθ' ἡμέραν χαίρω παρακολουθῶν ἐμαυτῷ βελτίονι γινομένῳ

As one man rejoices in improving his own farm, and another his own horse, so I rejoice day by day in following the course of my own improvement.

Translated by W.A. Oldfather (1928)

Epictetus, *Discourses* 3.5.14

60 ἐπαινεῖν χρὴ τὸ κατὰ τέχνην γινόμενον

Let us praise whatever is done with artistry.

Translated by Panos Koronakis-Rohlf and Maria Batzini (2007)

Stobaeus, *Anthology* 3.1.190

61 ταὐτὸν ἐξ ἀσθενοῦς ἀγκυρίου σκάφος ὁρμίζειν καὶ ἐκ φαύλης γνώμης ἐλπίδα

A hope based on false premises is like a boat moored to a weak anchor.

Stobaeus, *Anthology* 3.2.45

62 Σωκράτης πρὸς τὸν πυθόμενον τίς πλουσιώτατος εἶπεν ὁ ἐλαχίστοις ἀρκούμενος· αὐτάρκεια γὰρ φύσεώς ἐστι πλοῦτος

Socrates, when asked who is the richest man, replied, 'He who is satisfied with the least'; for self-sufficiency is wealth by its very nature.

Stobaeus, *Anthology* 3.5.31

63 Σωκράτης ἐρωτηθεὶς τί ῥώμη, εἶπε κίνησις ψυχῆς μετὰ σώματος

Socrates when asked what is strength, answered, 'Harmony of body and soul.'

Stobaeus, *Anthology* 3.7.15

cf. Socrates 69

64 Σωκράτης ἐρωτηθεὶς διὰ τί οὐ συγγράφει, ὅτι εἶπεν ὁρῶ τὰ χαρτία πολὺ τῶν γραφησομένων τιμιώτερα

Socrates, when asked why he did not write, replied, 'Because, I believe paper is of greater value than what could be written on it.'

Stobaeus, *Anthology* 3.21.9

65 τοὺς μὲν κενοὺς ἀσκοὺς τὸ πνεῦμα διίστησι, τοὺς δὲ ἀνοήτους ἀνθρώπους τὸ οἴημα

Empty wine skins are blown up by air, fools by self-conceit.

Stobaeus, *Anthology* 3.22.37

66 κρεῖττον ὀψιμαθῆ εἶναι ἢ ἀμαθῆ

Better to learn late than not at all.

Stobaeus, *Anthology* 3.29.68

on learning to play the cithara late in life

67 Σωκράτης τὸν φθόνον εἶπεν ἕλκος εἶναι τῆς ψυχῆς

Socrates said that envy was an ulcer of the soul.

Stobaeus, *Anthology* 3.38.48

68 ῥᾷον ἄν τις διάπυρον ἄνθρακα ἐπὶ τῆς γλώττης κατάσχοι ἢ λόγον ἀπόρρητον

It is easier to have charcoal burning on one's tongue than to keep a secret.

Stobaeus, *Anthology* 3.41.5

69 Σωκράτης ἐρωτηθεὶς τί εὐγένεια, εὐκρασία ἔφη ψυχῆς καὶ σώματος

When Socrates was asked what is nobility, he answered, 'Temperance of mind and body.'

Stobaeus, *Anthology* 4.29a.20

70 Σωκράτης εἶπε πολλοῦ ἂν ἄξιον ἦν τὸ πλουτεῖν, εἰ καὶ τὸ χαίρειν αὐτῷ συνῆν· νῦν δὲ ἄμφω ταῦτα κεχώρισται· ἐάν τε γὰρ θέλωσι χρῆσθαι τῷ πλούτῳ, τῇ ἡδυπαθείᾳ διαφθείρονται· ἐάν τε τὸ πλουτεῖν φυλάττειν, τῇ φροντίδι· ἐάν τε κτήσασθαι, τῇ ἐπιθυμίᾳ

Socrates said that wealth would be a blessing if one could also enjoy it; for in the spending of wealth the rich are destroyed by excess, in its hoarding by anxiety, and in its acquisition by desire.

Stobaeus, *Anthology* 4.31c.90

71 Σωκράτης ἐρωτηθεὶς τί εὐδαιμονία ἡδονὴ ἀμεταμέλητος ἔφη

Socrates when asked what is happiness, replied, 'Pleasures that you do not regret.'

Stobaeus, *Anthology* 4.39.18

SOLON

c.639–*c*.559BC

Athenian statesman, poet and one of the Seven Sages

see also Anacharsis 6; Aristotle 1–2; Herodotus 61; Oracles 3; Plato 342; Seven Sages 39–40

1 ἴομεν ἐς Σαλαμῖνα μαχησόμενοι περὶ νήσου
ἱμερτῆς χαλεπόν τ' αἶσχος ἀπωσόμενοι

Let us to Salamis, to fight for the lovely isle,
spurning dishonour hard to bear.

Fragment 3 (West, *IEG*)

entreating the Athenians not to abandon Salamis

2 κακὰ πλεῖστα πόλει δυσνομίη παρέχει

Bad laws create no end of problems in a state.

Fragment 4.31 (West, *IEG*)

3 εὐνομίη δ' εὔκοσμα καὶ ἄρτια πάντ' ἀποφαίνει ...
τραχέα λειαίνει, παύει κόρον, ὕβριν ἀμαυροῖ

Good rule makes all things orderly and perfect,
smoothes the rough, checks excess, dims hubris.

Fragment 4.32 (West, *IEG*)

4 γιγνώσκω, καί μοι φρενὸς ἔνδοθεν ἄλγεα κεῖται,
πρεσβυτάτην ἐσορῶν γαῖαν Ἰαονίης κλινομένην

I mark, and sorrow fills my heart to see,
the eldest country of Ionia listing.

Translated by M.L. West (1994)

Fragment 4a (West, *IEG*)

of Athens under aristocratic rule

5 ὑμεῖς δ' ἡσυχάσαντες ἐνὶ φρεσὶ καρτερὸν ἦτορ,
οἳ πολλῶν ἀγαθῶν ἐς κόρον ἠλάσατε,
ἐν μετρίοισι τίθεσθε μέγαν νόον· οὔτε γὰρ ἡμεῖς
πεισόμεθ', οὔθ' ὑμῖν ἄρτια ταῦτ' ἔσεται

Refrain ye in your hearts those stubborn moods,
Plunged in a surfeit of abundant goods,
And moderate your pride! We'll not submit,
Nor even you yourselves will this befit.

Translated by H. Rackham (1935)

Fragment 4c (West, *IEG*)

6 δήμῳ μὲν γὰρ ἔδωκα τόσον γέρας ὅσσον ἐπαρκεῖν,
τιμῆς οὔτ' ἀφελὼν οὔτ' ἐπορεξάμενος·
οἳ δ' εἶχον δύναμιν καὶ χρήμασιν ἦσαν ἀγητοί,
καὶ τοῖς ἐφρασάμην μηδὲν ἀεικὲς ἔχειν·
ἔστην δ' ἀμφιβαλὼν κρατερὸν σάκος ἀμφοτέροισι,
νικᾶν δ' οὐκ εἴασ' οὐδετέρους ἀδίκως

I gave the people as much privilege as they have a right to:
I neither degraded them from rank nor gave them free hand;
and for those who already held the power and were envied for money,
I worked it out that they also should have no cause for complaint.
I stood there holding my sturdy shield over both parties;
I would not let either side win a victory that was wrong.

Translated by Richmond Lattimore (1960)

Fragment 5 (West, *IEG*)

7 δῆμος δ' ὧδ' ἂν ἄριστα σὺν ἡγεμόνεσσιν ἕποιτο,
μήτε λίην ἀνεθεὶς μήτε βιαζόμενος

So will the people follow their leaders best,
neither too little restrained nor yet constrained.

Translated by J.M. Edmonds (1931)

Fragment 6 (West, *IEG*)

8 ἔργμασι ἐν μεγάλοις πᾶσιν ἁδεῖν χαλεπόν

In great matters it is hard to please all.

Translated by J.M. Edmonds (1931)
Fragment 7 (West, *IEG*)

9 λίην δ' ἐξάραντ' οὐ ῥᾴδιόν ἐστι κατασχεῖν
ὕστερον, ἀλλ' ἤδη χρὴ καλὰ πάντα νοεῖν

Once too far from land 'tis not easy to make haven;
consider such things ere it be too late.

Fragment 9 (West, *IEG*)

10 εἰ δὲ πεπόνθατε λυγρὰ δι' ὑμετέρην κακότητα,
μὴ θεοῖσιν τούτων μοῖραν ἐπαμφέρετε

If by your own wickedness you suffer,
do not blame the gods.

Fragment 11.1 (West, *IEG*)

11 ὑμέων δ' εἷς μὲν ἕκαστος ἀλώπεκος ἴχνεσι βαίνει,
σύμπασιν δ' ὑμῖν χαῦνος ἔνεστι νόος

Separately, each of you treads as cautious as the fox,
when all in concert, empty is your mind.

Fragment 11.5 (West, *IEG*)

12 ἐς γὰρ γλῶσσαν ὁρᾶτε καὶ εἰς ἔπη αἱμύλου ἀνδρός,
εἰς ἔργον δ' οὐδὲν γιγνόμενον βλέπετε

You pay heed to the words of a wily man
and look to none of his deeds.

Fragment 11.7 (West, *IEG*)

13 ταχέως δ' ἀναμίσγεται ἄτη·
ἀρχῆς δ' ἐξ ὀλίγης γίγνεται ὥστε πυρός,
φλαύρη μὲν τὸ πρῶτον, ἀνιηρὴ δὲ τελευτᾷ

Ruin is not slow to come;
from a small beginning it runs wild like fire,
trivial at first, grievous in the end.

Fragment 13.14 (West, *IEG*)

14 Ζεὺς πάντων ἐφορᾷ τέλος

Zeus surveyeth the end of every matter.

Translated by J.M. Edmonds (1931)
Fragment 13.17 (West, *IEG*)

15 οἳ δὲ φύγωσιν
αὐτοί, μηδὲ θεῶν μοῖρ' ἐπιοῦσα κίχῃ,
ἤλυθε πάντως αὖτις· ἀναίτιοι ἔργα τίνουσιν
ἢ παῖδες τούτων ἢ γένος ἐξοπίσω

And if they escape pursuing destiny,
vengeance comes always; for their deeds are paid
by their innocent children or their offspring after them.

Translated by J.M. Edmonds (1931)
Fragment 13.29 (West, *IEG*)

16 θνητοὶ ... χάσκοντες κούφαις ἐλπίσι τερπόμεθα

We mortal men delight in vain hopes, gaping.

Fragment 13.36 (West, *IEG*)

17 σπεύδει δ' ἄλλοθεν ἄλλος· ὁ μὲν κατὰ πόντον ἀλᾶται
ἐν νηυσὶν χρῄζων οἴκαδε κέρδος ἄγειν
ἰχθυόεντ' ἀνέμοισι φορεόμενος ἀργαλέοισιν,
φειδωλὴν ψυχῆς οὐδεμίαν θέμενος

They hurry here and there; one man roams
in ships hoping to bring home some profit,
tossed by grievous winds over the fishy deep,
quite careless of his life.

Fragment 13.43 (West, *IEG*)

18 ἄλλος γῆν τέμνων πολυδένδρεον εἰς ἐνιαυτὸν
λατρεύει, τοῖσιν καμπύλ' ἄροτρα μέλει·
ἄλλος Ἀθηναίης τε καὶ Ἡφαίστου πολυτέχνεω
ἔργα δαεὶς χειροῖν ξυλλέγεται βίοτον,
ἄλλος Ὀλυμπιάδων Μουσέων πάρα δῶρα διδαχθείς,
ἱμερτῆς σοφίης μέτρον ἐπιστάμενος

Another with curved ploughshares tills the land,
cultivating, year in, year out, the fertile soil;
another, trained in Athena's and Hephaestus' skills,
secures a living by the labour of his hands;
another yet, having received the Olympian Muses' gifts,
generates art and wisdom yearned for by mankind.

Fragment 13.47 (West, *IEG*)

19 ἃ δὲ μόρσιμα πάντως
οὔτε τις οἰωνὸς ῥύσεται οὔθ' ἱερά

What is destined to be
no augury or offering can avert.

Fragment 13.55 (West, *IEG*)

20 πολλάκι δ' ἐξ ὀλίγης ὀδύνης μέγα γίγνεται ἄλγος

From small sufferings often comes much pain.

Fragment 13.59 (West, *IEG*)

21 πᾶσι δέ τοι κίνδυνος ἐπ' ἔργμασιν

There's risk in every sort of business.

Translated by J.M. Edmonds (1931)

Fragment 13.65 (West, *IEG*)

22 πολλοὶ γὰρ πλουτέουσι κακοί, ἀγαθοὶ δὲ πένονται·
ἀλλ' ἡμεῖς τούτοις οὐ διαμειψόμεθα

Many evil men are rich and good men poor,
but we shall not exchange excellence for riches.

Fragment 15 (West, *IEG*)

23 πάντη δ' ἀθανάτων ἀφανὴς νόος ἀνθρώποισιν

The mind of the immortal gods is all unseen to man.

Translated by J.M. Edmonds (1931)

Fragment 17 (West, *IEG*)

24 γηράσκω δ' αἰεὶ πολλὰ διδασκόμενος

I grow old ever learning many things.

Translated in *The Oxford Dictionary of Quotations* (2004)

Fragment 18 (West, *IEG*)

cf. Plato 264

25 ὄλβιος, ᾧ παῖδές τε φίλοι καὶ μώνυχες ἵπποι
καὶ κύνες ἀγρευταὶ καὶ ξένος ἀλλοδαπός

Happy he who hath dear children, whole-hoovèd steeds
and hunting hounds and friends in foreign parts.

Translated by J.M. Edmonds (1931)

Fragment 23 (West, *IEG*)

26 ἶσόν τοι πλουτέουσιν, ὅτῳ πολὺς ἄργυρός ἐστι
καὶ χρυσὸς καὶ γῆς πυροφόρου πεδία
ἵπποι θ' ἡμίονοί τε, καὶ ᾧ μόνα ταῦτα πάρεστι,
γαστρί τε καὶ πλευραῖς καὶ ποσὶν ἁβρὰ παθεῖν

Surely equal is the wealth of him that hath much silver
and gold and fields of wheatland and mules and horses;
to that of him that hath but this:
a comfortable life, his food and clothes and shoes.

Fragment 24.1 (West, *IEG*)

27 χρήματ' ἔχων οὐδεὶς ἔρχεται εἰς Ἀΐδεω

No one goes to Hades carrying his possessions.

Fragment 24.8 (West, *IEG*)

28 εἰ δὲ γῆς ἐφεισάμην
πατρίδος, τυραννίδος δὲ καὶ βίης ἀμειλίχου
οὐ καθηψάμην μιάνας καὶ καταισχύνας κλέος,
οὐδὲν αἰδέομαι· πλέον γὰρ ὧδε νικήσειν δοκέω
πάντας ἀνθρώπους

And if I spared my country
Refrained from ruthless violence and tyranny
And chose to keep my name free from all taint
I feel no shame at this; instead, I think
It will be my greatest glory.

Translated by Ian Scott-Kilvert (1960)

Fragment 32 (West, *IEG*)

from a letter to his friend Phocus

29 ἐσθλὰ γὰρ θεοῦ διδόντος αὐτὸς οὐκ ἐδέξατο·
περιβαλὼν δ' ἄγρην ... οὐκ ἐπέσπασεν μέγα δίκτυον

Of his own will he refused god's blessings;
though his net was full he did not haul it to.

Fragment 33 (West, *IEG*)

on being ridiculed for refusing the rule of Athens

30 συμμαρτυροίη ταῦτ' ἂν ἐν δίκῃ Χρόνου
...
Γῆ μέλαινα, τῆς ἐγώ ποτε
ὅρους ἀνεῖλον πολλαχῇ πεπηγότας,
πρόσθεν δὲ δουλεύουσα, νῦν ἐλευθέρη

Before the judgement-seat of Time
Black Earth will best bear witness, for 'twas I

Removed her many boundary-posts implanted;
Ere then she was a slave, but now is free.

Translated by H. Rackham (1935)

Fragment 36.3 (West, *IEG*)

of boundary-posts marking mortgaged estates; seisachtheia, the shaking off of land burdens, was the revolutionary legislation introduced by Solon returning property to its indebted owners

31 ὁμοῦ βίην τε καὶ δίκην ξυναρμόσας ἔρεξα

This I achieved combining force and justice.

Fragment 36.15 (West, *IEG*)

32 θεσμοὺς δ' ὁμοίως τῷ κακῷ τε κἀγαθῷ

And rules of law alike for base and noble.

Translated by H. Rackham (1935)

Fragment 36.18 (West, *IEG*)

33 οὐδ' ἐπαύσατο
πρὶν ἀνταράξας πῖαρ ἐξεῖλεν γάλα

Nor refrained
Ere he had churned and skimmed the milk of cream.

Translated by H. Rackham (1935)

Fragment 37 (West, *IEG*)

34 ἡδονὴν φεῦγε, ἥτις λύπην τίκτει

Avoid pleasures; they only beget sorrow.

Seven Sages, *Apophthegms* Fragment 2.3 (D-K)

35 φίλους μὴ ταχὺ κτῶ, οὓς δ' ἂν κτήσῃ, μὴ ταχὺ ἀποδοκίμαζε

Be not rash to make friends; but once you have, keep them.

Seven Sages, *Apophthegms* Fragment 2.5 (D-K)

36 ἄρχεσθαι μαθὼν ἄρχειν ἐπιστήσῃ

Learn to obey before you command.

Translated by R.D. Hicks (1925)

Seven Sages, *Apophthegms* Fragment 2.6 (D-K)

37 εὔθυναν ἑτέρους ἀξιῶν διδόναι καὶ αὐτὸς ὕπεχε

When you call others to account apply it also to yourself.

Seven Sages, *Apophthegms* Fragment 2.7 (D-K)

38 ὃ ἂν μὴ ἴδῃς, μὴ λέγε

If you don't know, don't speak.

Seven Sages, *Apophthegms* Fragment 2.9 (D-K)

39 εἰδὼς σίγα

Be silent even though thou knowest well.

Seven Sages, *Apophthegms* Fragment 2.10a (D-K)

40 τὰ ἀφανῆ τοῖς φανεροῖς τεκμαίρου

Surmise the unseen from what is manifest.

Seven Sages, *Apophthegms* Fragment 2.10b (D-K)

41 τέλος ὁρᾶν μακροῦ βίου

Keep in view the end of a long life.

Seven Sages, *Apophthegms* 2.1 (Mullach, *FPG*)

Solon's words to Croesus

42 λόγος εἴδωλον τῶν ἔργων

Speech is the image of actions.

Translated in *Bartlett's Familiar Quotations* (1980)

Seven Sages, *Apophthegms* 2.7 (Mullach, *FPG*)

43 ἐκείνη ἡ πόλις ἄριστα οἰκεῖται, ἐν ᾗ τοὺς ἀγαθοὺς ἄνδρας συμβαίνει τιμᾶσθαι, καὶ τὸ ἐναντίον, ἐν ᾗ τοὺς κακοὺς ἀμύνεσθαι

This city is best, where the good are honoured, the bad warded off.

Seven Sages, *Apophthegms* 2.10 (Mullach, *FPG*)

44 καλὸν μέν ἐστιν ἡ τυραννὶς χωρίον, οὐκ ἔχει δὲ ἀπόβασιν

Tyranny may look good, but there is no way of escape.

Seven Sages, *Apophthegms* 2.11 (Mullach, *FPG*)

45 τὸ θεῖον καὶ οἱ νόμοι εὖ μὲν ἀγόντων εἰσὶν ὠφέλιμοι, κακῶς δὲ ἀγόντων οὐδὲν ὠφελοῦσιν

If things go well, religion and legislation are beneficial; if not, they are of no avail.

Translated by R.D. Hicks (1925)

Seven Sages, *Apophthegms* 2.14 (Mullach, *FPG*)

46 ὁ πολλοῖς φοβερὸς ὢν πολλοὺς φοβείσθω

Who is feared by many has also much to fear.

Seven Sages, *Apophthegms* 2.19 (Mullach, *FPG*)

47 ὃ δὲ ἔφη ἵνα μαθὼν αὐτὸ ἀποθάνω

That I may learn the song and die.

Seven Sages, *Apophthegms* 2.36 (Mullach, *FPG*)

when asked why he wanted to be taught one of Sappho's songs

48 τοῦτον ἄριστον ... δοκεῖν οἶκον, ὅπου τὰ χρήματα μήτε κτωμένοις ἀδικία, μήτε φυλάττουσιν ἀπιστία, μήτε δαπανῶσι μετάνοια πρόσεστιν

The best household is where wealth was not obtained by wrongdoings nor kept unjustly nor spent regretfully.

Seven Sages, *Apophthegms* 8.1 (Mullach, *FPG*)

49 πόλις ἄριστα πράττειν καὶ μάλιστα σώζειν δημοκρατίαν, ἐν ᾗ τὸν ἀδικήσαντα τοῦ ἀδικηθέντος οὐδὲν ἧττον οἱ μὴ ἀδικηθέντες προβάλλονται καὶ κολάζουσιν

A city flourishes and democracy is upheld when those, who have not been wronged, equally expose and chastise the wrongdoer as those who have been wronged.

Seven Sages, *Apophthegms* 9.1 (Mullach, *FPG*)

50 φίλοις βοήθει

Stand by your friends.

Seven Sages, *Sententiae* 216.36 (Mullach, *FPG*)

51 γονεῖς αἰδοῦ

Honour your parents.

Seven Sages, *Sententiae* 216.36 (Mullach, *FPG*)

52 τὸν μὲν κόρον ὑπὸ τοῦ πλούτου γεννᾶσθαι, τὴν δὲ ὕβριν ὑπὸ τοῦ κόρου

Wealth breeds satiety, satiety outrage.

Translated by R.D. Hicks (1925)

Diogenes Laertius, *Lives of Eminent Philosophers* 1.59

53 συμβούλευε μὴ τὰ ἥδιστα, ἀλλὰ τὰ ἄριστα

When giving advice propose not what is pleasant but what is best.

Diogenes Laertius, *Lives of Eminent Philosophers* 1.60.6

54 νοῦν ἡγεμόνα ποιοῦ

Let your intellect show the way.

Diogenes Laertius, *Lives of Eminent Philosophers* 1.60.7

55 οὐδ' ἐγὼ προλέγων πιστὸς ἦν· ἐκεῖνος δὲ πιστότερος κολακεύων Ἀθηναίους ἐμοῦ ἀληθεύοντος

Nor did they believe me when warned; he found more credence flattering the Athenians than I telling the truth.

Diogenes Laertius, *Lives of Eminent Philosophers* 1.65

extract of a letter to Epimenides on warning that Pisistratus would start a tyranny

56 ἀλλὰ καὶ ἡδίων ἡμῖν ἡ βιοτὴ ἔνθα πᾶσι τὰ δίκαια καὶ ἴσα

To live in a place where all have equal rights is more to my liking.

Translated by R.D. Hicks (1925)

Diogenes Laertius, *Lives of Eminent Philosophers* 1.67

extract of a letter, attributed to Solon, written to Croesus

57 Πεφυλαγμένος ἄνδρα ἕκαστον,
ὅρα μὴ κρυπτὸν ἔγχος ἔχων
κραδίῃ, φαιδρῷ
προσεννέπῃ προσώπῳ,
γλῶσσα δέ οἱ διχόμυθος
ἐκ μελαίνης φρενὸς γεγωνῇ.

Watch every man
to discern whether, hiding hatred in his heart,
he speaks with friendly countenance,
while his tongue rings with double speech
emanating from a dark soul.

Translated by R.D. Hicks (1925)

Greek Anthology Appendix, Epigrammata exhortatoria et supplicatoria 1 (Cougny)

58 ὡς ἄμεινον εἴη ἀνθρώπῳ τεθνάναι μᾶλλον ἢ ζώειν

Yet sometimes it is better for a man to die than to live.

Herodotus, *Histories* 1.31

Solon to Croesus, recounting instances of blessed lives

59 πᾶν ἐστὶ ἄνθρωπος συμφορή

Human life is entirely a matter of chance.

Translated by Robin Waterfield (1998)

Herodotus, *Histories* 1.32.20

to Croesus

60 πολλοὶ μὲν γὰρ ζάπλουτοι ἀνθρώπων ἀνόλβιοι εἰσί, πολλοὶ δὲ μετρίως ἔχοντες βίου εὐτυχέες

Many are unblest although immensely rich, and many live a happy life on moderate means.

Herodotus, *Histories* 1.32.27

to Croesus

61 πρὶν δ' ἂν τελευτήσῃ μηδὲ καλέειν κω ὄλβιον, ἀλλ' εὐτυχέα

Call no man happy till he dies, he is at best but fortunate.

Herodotus, *Histories* 1.32.37

to Croesus; cf. Bible 369

62 χώρη οὐδεμία καταρκέει πάντα ἑωυτῇ παρέχουσα, ἀλλὰ ἄλλο μὲν ἔχει ἑτέρου δὲ ἐπιδέεται· ἣ δὲ ἂν τὰ πλεῖστα ἔχῃ, αὕτη ἀρίστη· ὣς δὲ καὶ ἀνθρώπου σῶμα ἓν οὐδὲν αὔταρκες ἐστί· τὸ μὲν γὰρ ἔχει, ἄλλου δὲ ἐνδεές ἐστι

No country is entirely self-sufficient; any given country has some things, but lacks others, and the best country is the one which has the most. By the same token, no one person is self-sufficient: he has some things, but lacks others.

Translated by Robin Waterfield (1998)

Herodotus, *Histories* 1.32.40

63 σκοπέειν δὲ χρὴ παντὸς χρήματος τὴν τελευτὴν κῇ ἀποβήσεται

We must look to the conclusion of every matter, and see how it shall end.

Translated by A.D. Godley (1920)

Herodotus, *Histories* 1.32.46

to Croesus

64 γνῶθι σαυτόν

Know thyself.

Plato, *Protagoras* 343e

motto inscribed on the 6th century BC *temple of Apollo at Delphi; some references attribute it to Solon, but Plato says it was devised by all Seven Sages conferring together; cf. Philemon, Fragment 152 (Kock) – 139 (K-A); cf. the identical English expression*

65 τῶν δ' ἄλλων αὐτοῦ νόμων ἴδιος ... ὁ κελεύων ἄτιμον εἶναι τὸν ... μηδετέρας μερίδος γενόμενον· βούλεται δ', ὡς ἔοικε, μὴ ἀπαθῶς μηδ' ἀναισθήτως ἔχειν πρὸς τὸ κοινόν... ἀλλ' αὐτόθεν τοῖς τὰ βελτίω καὶ δικαιότερα πράττουσι

Among his other laws there is one which ordains that he shall be considered dishonourable who takes neither side, wishing that a man should not be insensible or indifferent to the common weal, but should rather espouse promptly the better and more righteous cause.

Translated by Bernadotte Perrin (1914)

Plutarch, *Solon* 20.1

66 Σόλων δὲ τοῖς πράγμασι τοὺς νόμους μᾶλλον ἢ τὰ πράγματα τοῖς νόμοις προσαρμόζων

Solon adapted his laws to the situation, rather than the situation to his laws.

Translated by Bernadotte Perrin (1914)

Plutarch, *Solon* 22.3

67 ἰσότης στάσιν οὐ ποιεῖ

Where there is equality of citizenship sedition is absent.

Plutarch, *On Brotherly Love* 484b

68 Σόλων ἐρωτηθεὶς ὑπὸ Περιάνδρου ... ἐπεὶ σιωπῶν ἐτύγχανε, πότερα διὰ λόγων σπάνιν ἢ διὰ μωρίαν σιωπᾷ, ἀλλ' οὐδεὶς ἂν εἶπε μωρὸς σιωπᾶν ἐν συμποσίῳ δύναιτο

Periander asked Solon if his silence was due to lack of words or foolishness, to which Solon replied, 'A fool would be unable to remain silent during a symposium.'

Stobaeus, *Anthology* 3.34.15

also attributed to Demaratus by Plutarch, Sayings of Spartans *220a; cf. Plutarch,* Concerning Talkativeness *503f*

69 Σόλων ἐρωτηθεὶς πῶς ἂν μὴ γίγνοιτο ἀδίκημα ἐν πόλει, εἶπεν εἰ ὁμοίως ἀγανακτοῖεν οἱ μὴ ἀδικούμενοι τοῖς ἀδικουμένοις

Wrongdoing can only be avoided if those who are not wronged feel the same indignation as those who are.

Translated in *Great Quotations that Shaped the Western World* (2008)

Stobaeus, *Anthology* 4.1.77

70 Σόλων ὁ νομοθέτης ἐρωτηθεὶς ὑπό τινος, πῶς ἄριστα αἱ πόλεις οἰκοῖντο, ἔφη ἐὰν οἱ μὲν πολῖται τοῖς ἄρχουσι πείθωνται, οἱ δὲ ἄρχοντες τοῖς νόμοις

The best way for a state to be governed is when the people obey the rulers, and the rulers obey the law.

Stobaeus, *Anthology* 4.1.89

71 χαλεπόν φορτίον ἡ γυνή

An irksome burden is a wife.

Stobaeus, *Anthology* 4.22b.64

SONGS

Various popular, folk and drinking songs
see also Bacchylides 27–28

1 ἦλθ' ἦλθε χελιδὼν
καλὰς ὥρας ἄγουσα
καλοὺς ἐνιαυτούς

The swallow is here, is here,
Bringing the lovely weather,
Bringing the best of the year!

Translated by Kathleen Freeman (1947)

Anonymous, *Popular Songs (Carmina Popularia)* Fragment 2 (Page, *PMG*)

a Rhodian song

2 ὗσον ὗσον ὦ φίλε
Ζεῦ κατὰ τῆς ἀρούρας
τῆς Ἀθηναίων καὶ τῶν πεδίων

Rain, rain, please, dear Zeus, send rain,
Over the fields of Athens
And over the fields of the plain.

Translated by Kathleen Freeman (1947)

Anonymous, *Popular Songs (Carmina Popularia)* Fragment 8 (Page, *PMG*)

quoted in Marcus Aurelius, Τὰ εἰς ἑαυτόν *5.7 as a simple way of addressing the gods; the children would chant for sun and their elders for rain*

3 ἄγετ', ὦ Σπάρτας εὐάνδρου
κοῦροι πατέρων πολιητᾶν,
λαιᾷ μὲν ἴτυν προβάλεσθε,
δόρυ δ' εὐτόλμως πάλλοντες,
μὴ φειδόμενοι τᾶς ζωᾶς

Onward, youths of Sparta,
sons of famous fathers,
proudly hold your shields
brandishing your spears,
not afraid to lose your life.

Anonymous, *Popular Songs (Carmina Popularia)* Fragment 10 (Page, *PMG*)

some scholiasts attribute this to Tyrtaeus

4 ἁμὲς δέ γ' ἐσσόμεσθα πολλῷ κάρρονες

And we shall be better by far.

Translated by David A. Campbell (1993)

Anonymous, *Popular Songs (Carmina Popularia)* Fragment 24 (Page, *PMG*)

sung at Spartan festivals: the elders first, the young men next of their current strength, and the children would chant that they would be better than both

5 Παλλὰς Τριτογένει' ἄνασσ' Ἀθηνᾶ,
ὄρθου τήνδε πόλιν καὶ πολίτας
ἄτερ ἀλγέων καὶ στάσεων
καὶ θανάτων ἀώρων

Pallas Athena, our goddess,
keep this city and its citizens
free from sorrows and rebellions
and untimely deaths.

Anonymous, *Drinking Songs (Carmina Convivialia)* Fragment 1 (Page, *PMG*)

6 εἴθ' ἐξῆν ὁποῖός τις ἦν ἕκαστος
τὸ στῆθος διελόντ', ἔπειτα τὸν νοῦν
ἐσιδόντα

If only it were possible to see what
everyone is like
by opening his breast and reading his
resolve!

Anonymous, *Drinking Songs (Carmina Convivialia)* Fragment 6 (Page, *PMG*)

7 ὁ δὲ καρκίνος ὧδ' ἔφα
χαλᾷ τὸν ὄφιν λαβών·
εὐθὺν χρὴ τὸν ἑταῖρον ἔμ-
μεν καὶ μὴ σκολιὰ φρονεῖν

The crab spoke thus,
catching the snake in its claw:
'A comrade ought to be straight,
and not have crooked thoughts.'

Translated by Dimitrios Yatromanolakis (2009)

Anonymous, *Drinking Songs (Carmina Convivialia)* Fragment 9 (Page, *PMG*)

cf. the saying 'the only straight snake is a dead snake'; in this drinking song, referring to Aesop's fable 211 (H-H) – Perry 196, the emphasis is on drinking companions hiding secret thoughts

8 σύν μοι πῖνε συνήβα συνέρα
συστεφανηφόρει,
σύν μοι μαινομένῳ μαίνεο, σὺν σώφρονι
σωφρόνει

When I am drinking, drink with me,
With me spend youth's gay hours:
My lover equal-hearted be,
Go crowned, like me, with flowers.
When I am merry and mad,
Merry and mad be you:
When I am sober and sad,
Be sad and sober too.

Translated after H.H. Milman (1865)

Anonymous, *Drinking Songs (Carmina Convivialia)* Fragment 19 (Page, *PMG*)

9 οὐκ ἔστιν ἀλωπεκίζειν
οὐδ' ἀμφοτέροισι γίγνεσθαι φίλον

It is not possible to play the fox
or to be a friend to both sides.

Translated by David C. Campbell (1993)

Anonymous, *Drinking Songs (Carmina Convivialia)* Fragment 29a (Page, *PMG*)

quoted by Aristophanes, Wasps *1241*

10 ἀγαθούς τε καὶ εὐπατρίδας,
οἳ τότ' ἔδειξαν οἵων πατέρων ἔσαν

True patriots and fighters,
proving to be their valiant fathers' offspring.

Aristotle, *Athenian Constitution* 19.3

a song of Athenian exiles during tyranny (6th century BC)

11 κρήνας αὐτορύτους μέλιτος τρεῖς ἤθελον ἔχειν,
πέντε γαλακτορύτους, οἴνου δέκα, δώδεκα μύρου,
καὶ δύο πηγαίων ὑδάτων, καὶ τρεῖς χιονέων

I wish I had three natural springs of honey,
five of milk, ten of wine, of scent a dozen,
two of fountains, and three of snow.

Translated by D.L. Page (1941)

Lyrica Adespota, Fragment 37 (Powell, *Coll. Alex*)

SOPHILUS

*fl. c.*340BC
Middle comedy poet

1 ἡδύ γε μετ' ἀνδρῶν ἐστιν Ἑλλήνων ἀεὶ συνάγειν

It is of course a pleasure to be always among Greeks.

Fragment 4 (Kock) – 5 (K-A) – *Parakatathike – The Deposit*

2 γαστρισμὸς ἔσται δαψιλής· τὰ προοίμια
ὁρῶ ... χορτασθήσομαι
... ὀψοφάγος καὶ κνισολοιχός

There is going to be gluttony at large expense; I can see it coming.
And I, connoisseur of good and rich food, shall feed myself to the full.

Fragments 6 and 7 (Kock) – 7 and 8 (K-A) – *Phylarchos – The Leader of the Tribe*

SOPHOCLES

*c.*496–406BC
Athenian tragic playwright
see also Aristophanes 77; Aristotle 188; Hieronymus of Rhodes 1; Pericles 56

1 οὔκουν γέλως ἥδιστος εἰς ἐχθροὺς γελᾶν;

Is not laughing at one's enemies the most delightful kind of laughter?

Translated by Hugh Lloyd-Jones (1994)

Ajax 79

2 ὡς εὖ παρέστης

I greet you!

Translated by E.F. Watling (1953)

Ajax 92

a greeting used well into the 20th century

3 οὐδὲν τὸ τούτου μᾶλλον ἢ τοὐμὸν σκοπῶν·
ὁρῶ γὰρ ἡμᾶς οὐδὲν ὄντας ἄλλο πλὴν
εἴδωλ' ὅσοιπερ ζῶμεν ἢ κούφην σκιάν

Not him alone I pity, but Mankind,
Myself, and all that live, mere empty Nothings,
Appearances of Things, unbody'd shadows.

Translated by Nicholas Rowe (1714)

Ajax 125

4 μηδέν ποτ' εἴπῃς αὐτὸς ἐς θεοὺς ἔπος,
μηδ' ὄγκον ἄρῃ μηδέν', εἴ τινος πλέον
ἢ χειρὶ βρίθεις ἢ μακροῦ πλούτου βάθει

Utter no boastful word against the gods,
Nor swell with pride if haply might of arm
Exalt thee o'er thy fellows, or vast wealth.

Translated by F. Storr (1913)

Ajax 128

spoken by Athena

5 τοιούσδε λόγους ψιθύρους πλάσσων
εἰς ὦτα φέρει

Whispering secret scandal
to credulous ears.

Translated by E.F. Watling (1953)

Ajax 148

6 γυναιξὶ κόσμον ἡ σιγὴ φέρει

Silence is a woman's ornament.

Translated by John Simpson and Jennifer Speake (1982)

Ajax 293

cf. the English proverb 'silence is a woman's best garment'

7 οὐ γὰρ γένοιτ' ἂν ταῦθ' ὅπως οὐχ ὧδ' ἔχοι

What's done is done and naught can alter it.

Translated by F. Storr (1913)

Ajax 378

cf. the English proverb 'what's done cannot be undone' and Shakespeare, Macbeth *3.2.12: 'what's done, is done'*

8 ξὺν τῷ θεῷ πᾶς καὶ γελᾷ κὠδύρεται

Laughter or tears, 'tis god that sends them both.

Translated by E.F. Watling (1953)

Ajax 383

9 μηδὲν μέγ' εἴπῃς

Speak no proud word!

Translated by Hugh Lloyd-Jones (1994)

Ajax 386

10 ἰὼ
σκότος, ἐμὸν φάος,
ἔρεβος ὦ φαεννότατον, ὡς ἐμοί,
ἕλεσθ' ἕλεσθέ μ' οἰκήτορα,
ἕλεσθέ μ'

O darkness that is my light,
O night of death, my only day,
Take me, take me, I pray,
Into your house for ever.

Translated by E.F. Watling (1953)

Ajax 394

Ajax about to kill himself

11 οὐκ ἂν πριαίμην οὐδενὸς λόγου βροτὸν
ὅστις κεναῖσιν ἐλπίσιν θερμαίνεται

I wouldn't count a person of any worth
Who likes to warm himself on empty hope.

Translated by David Raeburn (2008)

Ajax 477

12 ἢ καλῶς ζῆν ἢ καλῶς τεθνηκέναι
τὸν εὐγενῆ χρή

Nobly to live, or else nobly to die,
Befits proud birth.

Translated in *Bartlett's Familiar Quotations* (1980)

Ajax 479

spoken by Ajax

13 τῆς ἀναγκαίας τύχης
οὐκ ἔστιν οὐδὲν μεῖζον ἀνθρώποις κακόν

Of all human ills, greatest is fortune's wayward tyranny.

Translated by R.C. Trevelyan (1919)

Ajax 485

14 ἀνδρί τοι χρεὼν
μνήμην προσεῖναι, τερπνὸν εἴ τί που πάθοι

How can any man forget the happiness that once was his!

Ajax 520

15 χάρις χάριν γάρ ἐστιν ἡ τίκτουσ' ἀεί·
ὅτου δ' ἀπορρεῖ μνῆστις εὖ πεπονθότος,
οὐκ ἂν λέγοιτ' ἔθ' οὗτος εὐγενὴς ἀνήρ

For kindness breeds new kindness.
If recollection of the good received
evaporates, that man should lose
the title of a noble man.

Translated by Oliver Taplin (2015)

Ajax 522

cf. the English expression 'one good turn deserves another'

16 ὦ παῖ, γένοιο πατρὸς εὐτυχέστερος

My son, may you be happier than your father.

Translated by R.C. Jebb (1841–1905)

Ajax 550

17 ἐν τῷ φρονεῖν γὰρ μηδὲν ἥδιστος βίος

Ignorance is life's extremest bliss.

Translated by F. Storr (1913)

Ajax 554

18 οὐ πρὸς ἰατροῦ σοφοῦ
θρηνεῖν ἐπῳδὰς πρὸς τομῶντι πήματι

A well-skilled doctor doesn't warble incantations

for an abcess calling for the knife.

Translated by Oliver Taplin (2015)

Ajax 581

19 οὐ γάρ μ' ἀρέσκει γλῶσσά σου τεθηγμένη

I am not much pleased with the sharpness of your tongue.

Ajax 584

spoken by the Chorus to Ajax

20 μὴ κρῖνε, μὴ 'ξέταζε· σωφρονεῖν καλόν

Don't judge, don't question, possess yourself in patience.

Ajax 586

21 ὦ κλεινὰ Σαλαμίς, σὺ μέν που
ναίεις ἁλίπλακτος εὐδαίμων,
πᾶσιν περίφαντος αἰεί.
ἐγὼ δ' ὁ τλάμων παλαιὸς ἀφ' οὗ χρόνος
Ἰδαῖα μίμνων λειμωνίᾳ ποίᾳ μηνῶν ἀνήριθμος αἰὲν εὐνῶμαι
χρόνῳ τρυχόμενος,
κακὰν ἐλπίδ' ἔχων
ἔτι μέ ποτ' ἀνύσειν τὸν ἀπότροπον
ἀΐδηλον Ἅιδαν

Fair Salamis, the billow's roar,
Wander around thee yet,
And sailors gaze upon thy shore
Firm in the Ocean set.
Thy son is in a foreign clime
Where Ida feeds her countless flocks,
Far from thy dear, remembered rocks,
Worn by the waste of time –
Comfortless, nameless, hopeless save
In the dark prospect of the yawning grave.

Translated by Winthrop Mackworth Praed (1802–1839)

Ajax 596

these were the last words written by US Secretary of Defence James Forrestal (1892–1949), interpreted to have been an implied suicide note

22 ἅπανθ' ὁ μακρὸς κἀναρίθμητος χρόνος
φύει τ' ἄδηλα καὶ φανέντα κρύπτεται

Unmeasured, ageless time reveals all hidden things
and hides again what has been seen.

Ajax 646

23 κοὐκ ἔστ' ἄελπτον οὐδέν, ἀλλ' ἁλίσκεται
χὠ δεινὸς ὅρκος χαὶ περισκελεῖς φρένες

Nothing should be beyond our expectation;
the sternest oath is overruled, the firmest will.

Ajax 648

24 ἐχθρῶν ἄδωρα δῶρα κοὐκ ὀνήσιμα

Enemies' gifts are no gifts; profit bring they none.

Translated by R.C. Trevelyan (1919)

Ajax 665

even today quoted as 'δῶρον ἄδωρον' (a useless gift); cf. Virgil's 'timeo Danaos et dona ferentes'

25 καὶ γὰρ τὰ δεινὰ καὶ τὰ καρτερώτατα
τιμαῖς ὑπείκει· τοῦτο μὲν νιφοστιβεῖς
χειμῶνες ἐκχωροῦσιν εὐκάρπῳ θέρει·
ἐξίσταται δὲ νυκτὸς αἰανὴς κύκλος
τῇ λευκοπώλῳ φέγγος ἡμέρᾳ φλέγειν·
δεινῶν δ' ἄημα πνευμάτων ἐκοίμισε
στένοντα πόντον· ἐν δ' ὁ παγκρατὴς Ὕπνος
λύει πεδήσας

Even the wildest and the strongest
yield to eternal law; just as snow-bearing
wintry storms give way to fruitful summer,
the everlasting circle of the night
gives way to blazing daylight;
fearful winds subside and lull to rest
the groaning sea; even all-powerful sleep
loosens its shackles.

Ajax 669

26 ἔγωγ'· ἐπίσταμαι γὰρ ἀρτίως ὅτι
ὅ τ' ἐχθρὸς ἡμῖν ἐς τοσόνδ' ἐχθαρτέος,
ὡς καὶ φιλήσων αὖθις, ἔς τε τὸν φίλον
τοσαῦθ' ὑπουργῶν ὠφελεῖν βουλήσομαι,
ὡς αἰὲν οὐ μενοῦντα. τοῖς πολλοῖσι γὰρ
βροτῶν ἄπιστός ἐσθ' ἑταιρείας λιμήν

I now know this, that while I hate my enemy
I must remember that the time may come
When he will be my friend; as, loving my friend
And doing him service, I shall not forget
That he one day may be my enemy.
Friendship is but a treacherous anchorage.

Translated by E.F. Watling (1953)

Ajax 678

27 ὦ Πάν, Πὰν ἁλίπλαγκτε, Κυλ-
λανίας χιονοκτύπου
πετραίας ἀπὸ δειράδος φάνηθ', ὦ
θεῶν χοροποί', ἄναξ ...
νῦν γὰρ ἐμοὶ μέλει χορεῦσαι

Pan, O Pan, come, sea-rover,
down from the snow-beaten mountain crag.
Lord of the dance the gods delight in,
come, for now I, too, would dance. O joy!

Translated by Edith Hamilton (1964)

Ajax 695

cf. Elizabeth Barrett Browning, 'A Musical Instrument', 'What was he doing, the great god Pan?' (1862)

28 οἱ γὰρ κακοὶ γνώμαισι τἀγάθ' ἐν χεροῖν
ἔχοντες οὐκ ἴσασι πρίν τις ἐκβάλῃ

For those who have bad judgement never know
The good they hold until it's thrown away.

Translated by Oliver Taplin (2015)

Ajax 964

29 θεοῖς τέθνηκεν οὗτος, οὐ κείνοισιν, οὔ

'Tis the gods
Must answer for his death, not these men, no.

Translated by R.C. Trevelyan (1919)

Ajax 970

of Ajax' suicide

30 ἀνὴρ δύσοργος, ἐν γήρᾳ βαρύς

A man, heavy with age, is quick to anger.

Ajax 1017

31 οὔτ' ἂν στρατός γε σωφρόνως ἄρχοιτ' ἔτι,
μηδὲν φόβου πρόβλημα μηδ' αἰδοῦς ἔχων

Nor can an army be held sensibly in sway
without the barrier of respect and dread.

Ajax 1075

32 ἀλλ' ἄνδρα χρή, κἂν σῶμα γεννήσῃ μέγα,
δοκεῖν πεσεῖν ἂν κἂν ἀπὸ σμικροῦ κακοῦ

A man of mighty frame
may yet fall at a small mischance.

Ajax 1077

33 ὅπου δ' ὑβρίζειν δρᾶν θ' ἃ βούλεται παρῇ,
ταύτην νόμιζε τὴν πόλιν χρόνῳ ποτὲ
ἐξ οὐρίων δραμοῦσαν εἰς βυθὸν πεσεῖν

Where licence reigns,
And insolence, the ship of state is doomed,
However fair her course at first, to plunge
To bottomless disaster.

Translated by E.F. Watling (1953)

Ajax 1081

34 ξὺν τῷ δικαίῳ γὰρ μέγ' ἔξεστιν φρονεῖν

There's nothing wrong in being proud
with justice on your side.

Translated by Oliver Taplin (2015)

Ajax 1125

35 τίς ἄρα νέατος, ἐς πότε λή-
ξει πολυπλάγκτων ἐτέων ἀριθμός;

What will be the final number
of my wandering years?

Translated by Hugh Lloyd-Jones (1994)

Ajax 1185

36 ὄφελε πρότερον αἰθέρα δῦναι μέγαν ἢ τὸν πολύκοινον Ἅιδαν
κεῖνος ἀνήρ, ὃς στυγερῶν ἔδειξεν ὅ-
πλων Ἕλλασιν κοινὸν Ἄρη ...
κεῖνος γὰρ ἔπερσεν ἀνθρώπους

That man should be dissolved into thin air,
or else condemned to Hades,
whoever it was that first revealed hateful arms
to the Hellenes to use in deadly war;
it was he who was the ruin of mankind.

Ajax 1192

37 ἀλλ' οἱ φρονοῦντες εὖ κρατοῦσι πανταχοῦ

The wise and prudent everywhere prevail.

Translated by F. Storr (1913)

Ajax 1252

38 μέγας δὲ πλευρὰ βοῦς ὑπὸ σμικρᾶς ὅμως
μάστιγος ὀρθὸς εἰς ὁδὸν πορεύεται

A hulking ox can still be kept on straight along the road
by means of a small whip.

Translated by Oliver Taplin (2015)

Ajax 1253

39 φεῦ, τοῦ θανόντος ὡς ταχεῖά τις βροτοῖς χάρις διαρρεῖ

How quickly gratitude towards the dead
can slip away.

Translated by Oliver Taplin (2015)

Ajax 1266

40 μηδ' ἡ βία σε μηδαμῶς νικησάτω
τοσόνδε μισεῖν ὥστε τὴν δίκην πατεῖν

Let not your violent temper lead you into
such hatred as would tread down justice.

Ajax 1334

41 ἄνδρα δ' οὐ δίκαιον, εἰ θάνοι,
βλάπτειν τὸν ἐσθλόν, οὐδ' ἐὰν μισῶν κυρῇς

It is unjust to injure a good man dead,
however much you hate him.

Ajax 1344

42 σκληρὰν ἐπαινεῖν οὐ φιλῶ ψυχὴν ἐγώ

It is not my way to approve of a stubborn mind.

Translated by Hugh Lloyd-Jones (1994)

Ajax 1361

43 ἢ πάνθ' ὅμοια· πᾶς ἀνὴρ αὑτῷ πονεῖ

It is always the same: each man works for himself.

Translated by Oliver Taplin (2015)

Ajax 1366

44 ἦ πολλὰ βροτοῖς ἔστιν ἰδοῦσιν
γνῶναι· πρὶν ἰδεῖν δ' οὐδεὶς μάντις
τῶν μελλόντων ὅ τι πράξει

We all can judge of many things that we have seen;
not having seen, what prophet can foretell the future?

Ajax 1418

closing lines, spoken by the Chorus

45 Ὦ κοινὸν αὐτάδελφον Ἰσμήνης κάρα,
ἆρ' οἶσθ' ὅ τι Ζεὺς τῶν ἀπ' Οἰδίπου κακῶν
ὁ, ποῖον οὐχὶ νῷν ἔτι ζώσαιν τελεῖ;

Ismene, sister of my blood and heart,
See'st thou how Zeus would in our lives fulfil
The destiny of Oedipus, a world of woes!

Translated by F. Storr (1912)

Antigone 1

opening lines

46 οὐδὲν γὰρ οὔτ' ἀλγεινὸν οὔτ' ἄτης ἄτερ
οὔτ' αἰσχρὸν οὔτ' ἄτιμόν ἐσθ', ὁποῖον οὐ
τῶν σῶν τε κἀμῶν οὐκ ὄπωπ' ἐγὼ κακῶν

There is no pain, affliction, outrage, shame,
lacking in our fortunes, thine and mine.

Antigone 4

47 ἐᾶν δ' ἄκλαυτον, ἄταφον, οἰωνοῖς γλυκὺν
θησαυρὸν εἰσορῶσι πρὸς χάριν βορᾶς

He's to be left unwept, unburied,
a feast for vultures.

Antigone 29

Antigone of her slain brother Polynices

48 καὶ δείξεις τάχα
εἴτ' εὐγενὴς πέφυκας εἴτ' ἐσθλῶν κακή

Now 'tis thine to show
If thou art worthy of thy blood, or base.

Translated by F. Storr (1912)

Antigone 37

Antigone to Ismene

49 ἀλλ' ἐννοεῖν χρὴ τοῦτο μὲν γυναῖχ' ὅτι
ἔφυμεν, ὡς πρὸς ἄνδρας οὐ μαχουμένα

Remember that we are but women,
not made by nature to contend with men.

Antigone 61

spoken by Ismene – throughout the play Ismene questions Antigone's strong views

50 τὸ γὰρ
περισσὰ πράσσειν οὐκ ἔχει νοῦν οὐδένα

There is no sense in actions that exceed
our powers.

Translated by Hugh Lloyd-Jones (1994)

Antigone 67

spoken by Ismene

51 τὸ δὲ
βίᾳ πολιτῶν δρᾶν ἔφυν ἀμήχανος

I do not possess the strength to defy the state.

Antigone 78

spoken by Ismene

52 θερμὴν ἐπὶ ψυχροῖσι καρδίαν ἔχεις

Thou hast a fiery heart for chilling deeds.

Antigone 88

spoken by Ismene

53 ἀμηχάνων ἐρᾷς

You are in love with the impossible.

Translated by David Grene (1991)
Antigone 90
spoken by Ismene

54 ὅταν δὴ μὴ σθένω πεπαύσομαι

Only when my powers fail me will I be done.

Antigone 91
Antigone's immediate reply to Ismene

55 πείσομαι γὰρ οὖν
τοσοῦτον οὐδὲν ὥστε μὴ οὐ καλῶς θανεῖν

The worst that can befall
Is not to die an honourable death.

Translated by F. Storr (1912)
Antigone 96
a quadruple negation

56 ἀκτὶς ἀελίου, τὸ κάλ-
λιστον ἑπταπύλῳ φανὲν
Θήβᾳ τῶν πρότερων φάος,
ἐφάνθης ποτ', ὦ χρυσέας
ἁμέρας βλέφαρον

Sunbeam, fairest to shine on seven-gated Thebes,
finally you came forth, eye of a golden day.

Antigone 100

57 Ζεὺς γὰρ μεγάλης γλώσσης κόμπους ὑπερεχθαίρει

Zeus detests the boasts of a proud tongue.

Translated by Hugh Lloyd-Jones (1994)
Antigone 127

58 ἐπέπνει
ῥιπαῖς ἐχθίστων ἀνέμων

He breathed upon us a blast of raging winds.

Antigone 136

59 ἐκ μὲν δὴ πολέμων
τῶν νῦν θέσθε λησμοσύναν,
θεῶν δὲ ναοὺς χοροῖς
παννύχοις πάντας ἐπέλθωμεν

Now let us win oblivion from the wars,
thronging the temples of the gods
in singing, dancing choirs through the night!

Translated by Robert Fagles (1982)
Antigone 150

60 τὰ μὲν δὴ πόλεος ἀσφαλῶς θεοὶ
πολλῷ σάλῳ σείσαντες ὤρθωσαν πάλιν

Our city's fortunes, storm-tossed by the gods,
have now been set aright in safety.

Antigone 162

61 ἀμήχανον δὲ παντὸς ἀνδρὸς ἐκμαθεῖν
ψυχήν τε καὶ φρόνημα καὶ γνώμην, πρὶν ἂν
ἀρχαῖς τε καὶ νόμοισιν ἐντριβὴς φανῇ

It is no easy matter to discern
The temper of a man, his mind and will,
Till he be proved by exercise of power.

Translated by F. Storr (1912)
Antigone 175

62 ἐμοὶ γὰρ ὅστις πᾶσαν εὐθύνων πόλιν
μὴ τῶν ἀρίστων ἅπτεται βουλευμάτων …
κάκιστος εἶναι νῦν τε καὶ πάλαι δοκεῖ·
καὶ μείζον' ὅστις ἀντὶ τῆς αὑτοῦ πάτρας
φίλον νομίζει, τοῦτον οὐδαμοῦ λέγω

I have nothing but contempt for the kind of governor who is afraid, for whatever reason, to follow the course that he knows is best for the State; and as for the man who sets private friendship above the public welfare – I have no use for him, either.

Translated by Dudley Fitts and Robert Fitzgerald (1939)
Antigone 178

63 ὑπ' ἐλπίδων
ἄνδρας τὸ κέρδος πολλάκις διώλεσεν

Hope of gain
Hath lured men to their ruin oftentimes.

Translated by F. Storr (1912)
Antigone 221

64 τοιαῦθ' ἑλίσσων ἤνυτον σχολῇ βραδύς,
χοὔτως ὁδὸς βραχεῖα γίγνεται μακρά

Thus leisurely I hastened on my road;
Much thought extends a furlong to a league.

Translated by F. Storr (1912)
Antigone 231

65 στέργει γὰρ οὐδεὶς ἄγγελον κακῶν ἐπῶν

Nobody likes the messenger who brings bad news.

Antigone 277

66 ἄναξ, ἐμοί τοι μή τι καὶ θεήλατον
τοὔργον τόδ' ἡ ξύννοια βουλεύει πάλαι

I had misgivings from the first, my liege,
Of something supernatural at work.

Translated by F. Storr (1912)

Antigone 278

i.e. something caused by the gods, not by man

67 οὐδὲν γὰρ ἀνθρώποισιν οἷον ἄργυρος
κακὸν νόμισμ' ἔβλαστε

There is no institution so ruinous for men as money.

Translated by Hugh Lloyd-Jones (1994)

Antigone 295

68 τοῦτο καὶ πόλεις
πορθεῖ, τόδ' ἄνδρας ἐξανίστησιν δόμων·
τόδ' ἐκδιδάσκει καὶ παραλλάσσει φρένας
χρηστὰς πρὸς αἰσχρὰ πράγμαθ' ἵστασθαι βροτῶν·
πανουργίας δ' ἔδειξεν ἀνθρώποις ἔχειν
καὶ παντὸς ἔργου δυσσέβειαν εἰδέναι

Money 'tis that sacks
Cities, and drives men forth from hearth and home;
Warps and seduces native innocence,
And breeds a habit of dishonesty.

Translated by F. Storr (1912)

Antigone 296

69 οὐκ ἐξ ἅπαντος δεῖ τὸ κερδαίνειν φιλεῖν

Seek not to make a profit from all things.

Antigone 312

70 ἐκ τῶν γὰρ αἰσχρῶν λημμάτων τοὺς πλείονας
ἀτωμένους ἴδοις ἂν ἢ σεσωσμένους

You will see more ruined than saved by wealth ill gotten.

Translated by H.T. Riley (1872)

Antigone 313

71 φεῦ·
ἦ δεινόν, ᾧ δοκεῖ γε, καὶ ψευδῆ δοκεῖν

Oh! How terrible to guess, and guess at lies!

Translated by Elizabeth Wyckoff (1954)

Antigone 323

72 πολλὰ τὰ δεινὰ κοὐδὲν ἀνθρώπου δεινότερον πέλει

Many wonders there are,
but none more wondrous than man.

Translated by F. Storr (1912)

Antigone 332

73 Γᾶν
ἄφθιτον, ἀκαμάταν, ἀποτρύεται,
ἰλλομένων ἀρότρων ἔτος εἰς ἔτος,
ἱππείῳ γένει πολεύων

Earth,
immortal, inexhaustible, tilled
year after year, to and fro,
with horse-drawn ploughs.

Antigone 338

74 κουφονόων τε φῦλον ὀρ-
νίθων ἀμφιβαλὼν ἄγει
καὶ θηρῶν ἀγρίων ἔθνη
πόντου τ' εἰναλίαν φύσιν
σπείραισι δικτυοκλώστοις,
περιφραδὴς ἀνήρ

With woven nets he snares the race of thoughtless birds,
the tribes of savage beasts, the sea-brood of the deep,
man of subtle wit.

Translated by C.A. Trypanis (1971)

Antigone 342

75 καὶ φθέγμα καὶ ἀνεμόεν
φρόνημα καὶ ἀστυνόμους
ὀργὰς ἐδιδάξατο καὶ δυσαύλων
πάγων ὑπαίθρεια καὶ
δύσομβρα φεύγειν βέλη
παντοπόρος· ἄπορος ἐπ' οὐδὲν ἔρχεται
τὸ μέλλον· Ἅιδα μόνον
φεῦξιν οὐκ ἐπάξεται·
νόσων δ' ἀμηχάνων φυγὰς
ξυμπέφρασται

And speech and thought, quick as the wind
and the mood and mind for law that rules the city –
all these he has taught himself
and shelter from the arrows of the frost
when there's rough lodging under the cold clear sky
and the shafts of lashing rain –
ready, resourceful man!
Never without resources
never an impasse as he marches on the future –
only Death, from Death alone he will find no rescue
but from desperate sickness he has plotted his escapes.

Translated by Robert Fagles (1982)
Antigone 353

76 σοφόν τι τὸ μηχανόεν
τέχνας ὑπὲρ ἐλπίδ᾽ ἔχων,
τοτὲ μὲν κακόν, ἄλλοτ᾽ ἐπ᾽ ἐσθλὸν ἕρπει

Man the master, ingenious past all measure
past all dreams, the skills within his grasp –
he forges on, now to destruction
now again to greatness.

Translated by Robert Fagles (1982)
Antigone 365

77 βροτοῖσιν οὐδέν ἐστ᾽ ἀπώμοτον.
ψεύδει γὰρ ἡ ᾽πίνοια τὴν γνώμην

There's nothing you can swear you'll never do;
second thoughts make liars of us all.

Translated by Robert Fagles (1982)
Antigone 388

78 ἀλλ᾽ ἡ γὰρ εὐκτὸς καὶ παρ᾽ ἐλπίδας χαρὰ
ἔοικεν ἄλλῃ μῆκος οὐδὲν ἡδονῇ

But the wild rapture of a glad surprise
is like no other pleasure.

Antigone 392

79 ἡ παῖς ὁρᾶται κἀνακωκύει πικρῶς
ὄρνιθος ὀξὺν φθόγγον, ὡς ὅταν κενῆς
εὐνῆς νεοσσῶν ὀρφανὸν βλέψῃ λέχος

A piercing cry she uttered, sad and shrill,
As when the mother bird beholds her nest
Robbed of its nestlings

Translated by F. Storr (1912)
Antigone 423

80 τὸ μὲν γὰρ αὐτὸν ἐκ κακῶν πεφευγέναι
ἥδιστον, ἐς κακὸν δὲ τοὺς φίλους ἄγειν
ἀλγεινόν

It is good to escape from trouble oneself,
but grievous to lead your friends into it.

Antigone 437

81 οὐδὲ σθένειν τοσοῦτον ᾠόμην τὰ σὰ
κηρύγμαθ᾽ ὥστ᾽ ἄγραπτα κἀσφαλῆ θεῶν
νόμιμα δύνασθαι θνητά γ᾽ ὄνθ᾽ ὑπερδραμεῖν.
οὐ γάρ τι νῦν γε κἀχθές, ἀλλ᾽ ἀεί ποτε
ζῇ ταῦτα

Nor did I think your proclamations
strong enough
to have power to overrule, mortal as they were,
the unwritten and unfailing ordinances of the gods.
For these have life, not simply today and yesterday,
but for ever.

Translated by Hugh Lloyd-Jones (1994)
Antigone 453

82 θανουμένη γὰρ ἐξῄδη, τί δ᾽ οὔ;
κεἰ μὴ σὺ προὐκήρυξας. εἰ δὲ τοῦ χρόνου
πρόσθεν θανοῦμαι, κέρδος αὔτ᾽ ἐγὼ λέγω.
ὅστις γὰρ ἐν πολλοῖσιν ὡς ἐγὼ κακοῖς
ζῇ, πῶς ὅδ᾽ οὐχὶ κατθανὼν κέρδος φέρει;

I know that I must die,
E'en hadst thou not proclaimed it; and if death
Is thereby hastened, I shall count it gain.
For death is gain to him whose life, like mine,
Is full of misery.

Translated by F. Storr (1912)
Antigone 460

83 ἀλλ᾽ ἴσθι τοι τὰ σκλήρ᾽ ἄγαν φρονήματα
πίπτειν μάλιστα

Well, let her know the stubbornest of wills
Are soonest bended.

Translated by F. Storr (1912)
Antigone 473

84 σμικρῷ χαλινῷ δ᾽ οἶδα τοὺς θυμουμένους
ἵππους καταρτυθέντας

A small bit will control the fiercest horse.

Antigone 477

85 τοῦτ᾽ ἔχων ἅπαντ᾽ ἔχω

Possessing this I've everything.

Antigone 498

86 τούτοις τοῦτο πᾶσιν ἁνδάνειν
λέγοιμ᾽ ἄν, εἰ μὴ γλῶσσαν ἐγκλῄοι φόβος

To this all my townsmen would agree,
were they not gagged by terror.

Antigone 504

87 ἀλλ᾽ ἡ τυραννὶς πολλά τ᾽ ἄλλ᾽ εὐδαιμονεῖ
κἄξεστιν αὐτῇ δρᾶν λέγειν θ᾽ ἃ βούλεται

Tyrants are fortunate in many ways,

but most to act and speak whichever way they please.

Antigone 506

88 οὐδὲν γὰρ αἰσχρὸν τοὺς ὁμοσπλάγχνους σέβειν

There is nothing shameful in worshiping one's kin.

Antigone 511

89 οὔτοι ποθ' οὐχθρός, οὐδ' ὅταν θάνῃ, φίλος

An enemy can never be a friend, not even after death.

Antigone 522

Creon speaking

90 οὔτοι συνέχθειν, ἀλλὰ συμφιλεῖν ἔφυν

I have been born for mutual love, not hate.

Antigone 523

Antigone's reply

91 κάτω νυν ἐλθοῦσ', εἰ φιλητέον, φίλει
κείνους· ἐμοῦ δὲ ζῶντος οὐκ ἄρξει γυνή

Die then, and love the dead if love thou must,
No woman shall be master while I live.

Translated by F. Storr (1912)

Antigone 524

Creon's counter answer

92 ὡς ἔχιδν' ὑφειμένη

Like a viper unperceived.

Translated by F. Storr (1912)

Antigone 531

93 λόγοις δ' ἐγὼ φιλοῦσαν οὐ στέργω φίλην

A friend in word is never friend of mine.

Translated by F. Storr (1912)

Antigone 543

94 σὺ μὲν γὰρ εἵλου ζῆν, ἐγὼ δὲ κατθανεῖν

You chose to live, I chose to die.

Translated by Robert Fagles (1982)

Antigone 555

95 οὐ γάρ ποτ' … οὐδ' ὃς ἂν βλάστῃ μένει
νοῦς τοῖς κακῶς πράσσουσιν, ἀλλ' ἐξίσταται

Misfortune causes the steadiest minds to waver.

Antigone 563

96 ἀρώσιμοι γὰρ χἀτέρων εἰσὶν γύαι

There are more lands from which to raise his seed.

Antigone 569

97 φεύγουσι γάρ τοι χοἰ θρασεῖς, ὅταν πέλας
ἤδη τὸν Ἅιδην εἰσορῶσι τοῦ βίου

For e'en the bravest spirits run away
When they perceive death pressing on life's heels.

Translated by F. Storr (1912)

Antigone 580

98 εὐδαίμονες οἷσι κακῶν ἄγευστος αἰών

Thrice blest are they who never tasted pain!

Translated by F. Storr (1912)

Antigone 582

99 οἷς γὰρ ἂν σεισθῇ θεόθεν δόμος, ἄτας
οὐδὲν ἐλλείπει γενεᾶς ἐπὶ πλῆθος ἕρπον

But for those whose house has been shaken by god
there is never cessation of ruin;
it steals on generation after generation.

Translated by David Grene (1991)

Antigone 583

100 τό τ' ἔπειτα καὶ τὸ μέλλον
καὶ τὸ πρὶν ἐπαρκέσει
νόμος ὅδ'

Throughout the future, now and always,
as in the past, this law shall stand.

Antigone 611

101 ἁ γὰρ δὴ πολύπλαγκτος ἐλπὶς πολλοῖς μὲν ὄνησις ἀνδρῶν,
πολλοῖς δ' ἀπάτα κουφονόων ἐρώτων

Hope, deceitful hope, to many brings advantage,
to many, though, a host of unfulfilled desires.

Antigone 615

102 τὸ κακὸν δοκεῖν ποτ' ἐσθλὸν
τῷδ' ἔμμεν ὅτῳ φρένας
θεὸς ἄγει πρὸς ἄταν

When evil appears expedient
it is a god that leads you to disaster.

Antigone 622

103 ψυχρὸν παραγκάλισμα τοῦτο γίγνεται,
γυνὴ κακὴ ξύνευνος ἐν δόμοις· τί γὰρ
γένοιτ' ἂν ἕλκος μεῖζον ἢ φίλος κακός;

Ill fares the husband mated with a shrew,
And her embraces very soon wax cold.
For what can wound so surely to the quick
As a false friend?

Translated by F. Storr (1912)
Antigone 650

104 ἐν τοῖς γὰρ οἰκείοισιν ὅστις ἔστ' ἀνὴρ
χρηστός, φανεῖται κἀν πόλει δίκαιος ὤν

Show me the man who rules his household well:
I'll show you someone fit to rule the state.

Translated by Robert Fagles (1982)
Antigone 661

105 ἀναρχίας δὲ μεῖζον οὐκ ἔστιν κακόν·
αὕτη πόλεις ὄλλυσιν, ἥδ' ἀναστάτους
οἴκους τίθησιν, ἥδε συμμάχου δορὸς
τροπὰς καταρρήγνυσι

Anarchy! There is no greater evil!
This is what ruins states and tears down houses,
this is what breaks up armies, turning them to flight.

Antigone 672

106 κρεῖσσον γάρ, εἴπερ δεῖ, πρὸς ἀνδρὸς ἐκπεσεῖν,
κοὐκ ἂν γυναικῶν ἥσσονες καλοίμεθ' ἄν

Better to fall from power, if fall we must,
at the hands of a man – never be rated
inferior to a woman, never.

Translated by Robert Fagles (1982)
Antigone 679

107 θεοὶ φύουσιν ἀνθρώποις φρένας
πάντων ὅσ' ἐστὶ κτημάτων ὑπέρτατον

Reason is god's crowning gift to man.

Translated by Dudley Fitts and Robert Fitzgerald (1939)
Antigone 683

108 τί γὰρ πατρὸς θάλλοντος εὐκλείᾳ τέκνοις
ἄγαλμα μεῖζον, ἢ τί πρὸς παίδων πατρί;

What higher good
Can children covet than their fathers' fame,
As fathers too take pride in glorious sons?

Translated by F. Storr (1912)
Antigone 703

109 ὅστις γὰρ αὐτὸς ἢ φρονεῖν μόνος δοκεῖ,
ἢ γλῶσσαν, ἣν οὐκ ἄλλος, ἢ ψυχὴν ἔχειν,
οὗτοι διαπτυχθέντες ὤφθησαν κενοί.
ἀλλ' ἄνδρα, κεἴ τις ᾖ σοφός, τὸ μανθάνειν
πόλλ' αἰσχρὸν οὐδὲν

For whoso thinks that wisdom dwells with him,
That he alone can speak or think aright,
Such oracles are empty breath when tried.
The wisest man will let himself be swayed
By others' wisdom.

Translated by F. Storr (1912)
Antigone 707

110 ὁρᾷς παρὰ ῥείθροισι χειμάρροις ὅσα
δένδρων ὑπείκει, κλῶνας ὡς ἐκσῴζεται,
τὰ δ' ἀντιτείνοντ' αὐτόπρεμν' ἀπόλλυται

You notice how by streams in wintertime
the trees that yield preserve their branches safely,
but those that fight the tempest perish utterly.

Translated by David Grene (1991)
Antigone 712

111 φήμ' ἔγωγε πρεσβεύειν πολὺ
φῦναι τὸν ἄνδρα πάντ' ἐπιστήμης πλέων·
εἰ δ' οὖν, φιλεῖ γὰρ τοῦτο μὴ ταύτῃ ῥέπειν,
καὶ τῶν λεγόντων εὖ καλὸν τὸ μανθάνειν

It would be best by far, I admit,
if a man were born infallible, right by nature.
If not – and things don't often go that way,
it's best to learn from those with good advice.

Translated by Robert Fagles (1982)
Antigone 720

112 οὐ τὸν χρόνον χρὴ μᾶλλον ἢ τἄργα σκοπεῖν

Weigh me upon my merit, not my years.

Translated by F. Storr (1912)
Antigone 729

113 καλῶς ἐρήμης γ' ἂν σὺ γῆς ἄρχοις μόνος

You would be a fine ruler over a deserted city!

Translated by Hugh Lloyd-Jones (1994)

Antigone 739

114 Ἔρως ἀνίκατε μάχαν

Love, unconquered in battle.

Translated by C.A. Trypanis (1971)

Antigone 781

cf. Virgil, Eclogues *10.69 'omnia vincit amor'*

115 Ἔρως ἀνίκατε μάχαν,
Ἔρως, ὃς ἐν κτήμασι πίπτεις,
ὃς ἐν μαλακαῖς παρειαῖς
νεάνιδος ἐννυχεύεις,
φοιτᾷς δ' ὑπερπόντιος ἔν τ'
ἀγρονόμοις αὐλαῖς·
καί σ' οὔτ' ἀθανάτων φύξιμος οὐδεὶς
οὔθ' ἀμερίων σέ γ' ἀν-
θρώπων, ὁ δ' ἔχων μέμηνεν

Love, unconquered in battle, Love, ravager of wealth,
who sleeps all night on the soft cheeks of maidens,
voyager over the seas, visitor of dwellers in the wilds;
from thee none has the power to escape, neither gods
nor mortal men; who touches thee holds madness.

Antigone 781

116 νικᾷ δ' ἐναργὴς βλεφάρων
ἵμερος εὐλέκτρου
νύμφας, τῶν μεγάλων πάρεδρος ἐν ἀρχαῖς
θεσμῶν· ἄμαχος γὰρ ἐμ-
παίζει θεὸς Ἀφροδίτα

Sharp desire, kindled by the eyes of the lovely bride is the conqueror: desire sits enthroned and rules together with the great laws; and Aphrodite playfully mocks, the goddess none can defeat.

Translated by C.A. Trypanis (1971)

Antigone 795

117 Ἀχέροντι νυμφεύσω

'Tis death I wed.

Translated by F. Storr (1912)

Antigone 816

118 ἰὼ δύστανος, βροτοῖς
οὔτε νεκρὸς νεκροῖσιν
μέτοικος, οὐ ζῶσιν, οὐ θανοῦσιν

Ah, unhappy one, living neither among mortals
nor as a shade among the shades,
an alien midst the living and the dead!

Antigone 850

119 ἄκλαυτος, ἄφιλος, ἀνυμέναιος
ταλαίφρων ἄγομαι

Unwept, unwed, unfriended, hence I go.

Translated by F. Storr (1912)

Antigone 876

120 οὐκέτι μοι τόδε λαμπάδος ἱερὸν
ὄμμα θέμις ὁρᾶν

No longer may I see the day's bright eye.

Translated by F. Storr (1912)

Antigone 879

of the sun

121 ἔτι τῶν αὐτῶν ἀνέμων αὑταὶ
ψυχῆς ῥιπαὶ τήνδε γ' ἔχουσιν

Like blasts of wind
her will still drives her on.

Antigone 929

of Antigone

122 οἷα πρὸς οἵων ἀνδρῶν πάσχω,
τὴν εὐσεβίαν σεβίσασα

See what I suffer at the hands of men
for honouring what is sacred.

Antigone 942

123 ἀλλ' ἁ μοιριδία τις δύνασις δεινά·
οὔτ' ἄν νιν ὄλβος οὔτ' Ἄρης,
οὐ πύργος, οὐχ ἁλίκτυποι
κελαιναὶ νᾶες ἐκφύγοιεν

Terrible is the power of Fate;
neither by wealth or war can you escape it,
no fort will keep it out,
no ships outrun it.

Antigone 951

124 φρόνει βεβὼς αὖ νῦν ἐπὶ ξυροῦ τύχης

Then reflect, my son; you are poised,
once more, on the razor-edge of fate.

Translated by Robert Fagles (1982)

Antigone 996

125 ἀνθρώποισι γὰρ
τοῖς πᾶσι κοινόν ἐστι τοὐξαμαρτάνειν·
ἐπεὶ δ' ἁμάρτῃ, κεῖνος οὐκέτ' ἔστ' ἀνὴρ

ἄβουλος οὐδ' ἄνολβος, ὅστις ἐς κακὸν
πεσὼν ἀκεῖται μηδ' ἀκίνητος πέλει·
αὐθαδία τοι σκαιότητ' ὀφλισκάνει

To err is common to all men;
but he who, having erred,
tries to repair the damage
is neither fool nor worthless;
obstinacy is the hallmark of a fool.

Antigone 1023

cf. the Latin 'errare humanum est'

126 τίς ἀλκὴ τὸν θανόντ' ἐπικτανεῖν;

What use to kill the dead a second time?

Translated by Elizabeth Wyckoff (1954)

Antigone 1030

127 βροτῶν
χοἰ πολλὰ δεινοὶ πτώματ' αἴσχρ', ὅταν λόγους
αἰσχροὺς καλῶς λέγωσι τοῦ κέρδους χάριν

Exceptionally clever people fall hardest in disgrace
when they hide ugly schemes in pretty speeches
in the pursuit of gain.

Antigone 1045

128 τὸ μαντικὸν γὰρ πᾶν φιλάργυρον γένος

Prophets are all a money-seeking breed.

Antigone 1055

129 τὸ δ' αὖ τυράννων αἰσχροκερδείαν φιλεῖ

The whole race of tyrants lust for filthy gain.

Translated by Robert Fagles (1982)

Antigone 1056

130 καὶ γὰρ ἡδοναὶ
ὅταν προδῶσιν ἀνδρός, οὐ τίθημ' ἐγὼ
ζῆν τοῦτον, ἀλλ' ἔμψυχον ἡγοῦμαι νεκρόν·
πλούτει τε γὰρ κατ' οἶκον, εἰ βούλῃ, μέγα,
καὶ ζῆ τύραννον σχῆμ' ἔχων, ἐὰν δ' ἀπῇ
τούτων τὸ χαίρειν, τἄλλ' ἐγὼ καπνοῦ σκιᾶς
οὐκ ἂν πριαίμην ἀνδρὶ πρὸς τὴν ἡδονήν

A life without life's joys I count a living death,
The pomp and circumstance of kings; but if
These give no pleasure, all the rest I count
The shadow of a shade, nor would I weigh
His wealth and power 'gainst a dram of joy.

Translated by F. Storr (1912)

Antigone 1165

131 ἐν ἀνθρώποισι τὴν ἀβουλίαν
ὅσῳ μέγιστον ἀνδρὶ πρόσκειται κακόν

Of all the ills
afflicting men the worst is lack of judgement.

Translated by Robert Fagles (1982)

Antigone 1242

132 μεγάλοι δὲ λόγοι
μεγάλας πληγὰς τῶν ὑπεραύχων ἀποτείσαντες
γήρᾳ τὸ φρονεῖν ἐδίδαξαν

Big words are punished by big blows which teach proud men in old age to be wise.

Antigone 1350

closing lines

133 ἡμὶν ἤδη λαμπρὸν ἡλίου σέλας
ἑῷα κινεῖ φθέγματ' ὀρνίθων σαφῆ
μέλαινά τ' ἄστρων ἐκλέλοιπεν εὐφρόνη

The brilliance of the rising sun arouses birds to song,
the starry curtain of the night is drawn away.

Electra 17

134 ὡς ἐνταῦθ' ἐμὲν
ἵν' οὐκέτ' ὀκνεῖν καιρός, ἀλλ' ἔργων ἀκμή

This is no time to hesitate, it is a time to act.

Electra 21

135 καιρὸς γάρ, ὅσπερ ἀνδράσιν
μέγιστος ἔργου παντός ἐστ' ἐπιστάτης

Now's the time, and time is the umpire in all human business.

Translated by E.F. Watling (1953)

Electra 75

136 ὦ φάος ἁγνὸν
καὶ γῆς ἰσόμοιρ' ἀὴρ

O hallowed light,
that sharest earth equally with air!

Translated in Liddell & Scott

Electra 86

137 μούνη γὰρ ἄγειν οὐκέτι σωκῶ
λύπης ἀντίρροπον ἄχθος

I can no longer bear alone
the burden of my grief.

Electra 118

138 ἀλλ' ἀπὸ τῶν μετρίων ἐπ' ἀμήχανον
ἄλγος ἀεὶ στενάχουσα διόλλυσαι

If past the bounds of sense you dwell
in cureless grief you just destroy yourself.

Electra 140

139 τί μοι τῶν δυσφόρων ἐφίῃ;

Why are you set on misery?

Translated by Hugh Lloyd-Jones (1994)

Electra 143

140 οὔτοι σοὶ μούνᾳ ...
ἄχος ἐφάνη βροτῶν

You are not alone in sorrow, the lot of mortals.

Electra 153

141 χρόνος γὰρ εὐμαρὴς θεός

Time is the sacred healer.

Translated by E.F. Watling (1953)

Electra 179

142 δόλος ἦν ὁ φράσας, ἔρος ὁ κτείνας,
δεινὰν δεινῶς προφυτεύσαντες
μορφάν

Cunning was the teacher, passion the killer;
they were the horrid parents of this horrendous act.

Electra 197

of the killing of Agamemnon

143 τάδε τοῖς δυνατοῖς
οὐκ ἐριστὰ τλᾶθι

You cannot struggle against those in power!

Translated by Hugh Lloyd-Jones (1994)

Electra 219

144 ἄνετέ μ' ἄνετε παράγοροι

Leave me alone, leave me alone, you would-be comforters.

Electra 229

Electra asks the Chorus to leave her to her grief

145 μὴ τίκτειν σ' ἄταν ἄταις

You must not make
Evil more evil still.

Translated by E.F. Watling (1953)

Electra 235

146 καὶ τί μέτρον κακότατος ἔφυ;

Is there no limit to my misery?

Electra 236

147 εἰ γὰρ ὁ μὲν θανὼν γᾶ τε καὶ οὐδὲν ὢν
κείσεται τάλας, οἱ δὲ μὴ πάλιν
δώσουσ' ἀντιφόνους δίκας,
ἔρροι τ' ἂν αἰδὼς
ἁπάντων τ' εὐσέβεια θνατῶν

If he that is dead is earth and nothing,
and if they never in their turn
pay death for death in justice,
then shall all shame be dead
and all men's piety.

Translated by David Grene (1957)

Electra 245

148 φιλεῖ γὰρ ὀκνεῖν πρᾶγμ' ἀνὴρ πράσσων μέγα

Any man will hesitate on the verge of a great undertaking.

Translated by R.C. Jebb (1841–1905)

Electra 320

149 ἐν κακοῖς μοι πλεῖν ὑφειμένῃ δοκεῖ

In times of trouble run with lowered sails.

Electra 335

150 νῦν γὰρ ἐν καλῷ φρονεῖν

Now you have the chance to show good sense!

Translated by Hugh Lloyd-Jones (1994)

Electra 384

151 καλόν γε μέντοι μὴ 'ξ ἀβουλίας πεσεῖν

No one would wish you to fall by your own folly.

Translated by E.F. Watling (1953)

Electra 398

152 εἰ δὲ σοὶ δοκῶ φρονεῖν κακῶς,
γνώμην δικαίαν σχοῦσα τοὺς πέλας ψέγε

If you want to sling abuse
try slinging it at somebody else in the family
get on the right track, put the blame

where it belongs.

Translated by Ezra Pound (tr. 1949, published 1989)

Electra 550

153 αἰσχροῖς γὰρ αἰσχρὰ πράγματ' ἐκδιδάσκεται

Villainy is taught by vile example.

Translated by E.F. Watling (1953)

Electra 621

154 ὅταν δέ τις θεῶν
βλάπτῃ, δύναιτ' ἂν οὐδ' ἂν ἰσχύων φυγεῖν

When the gods set out to do harm, not even the strong can escape.

Translated by C.A. Trypanis (1971)

Electra 696

155 δεινὸν τὸ τίκτειν ἐστίν· οὐδὲ γὰρ κακῶς
πάσχοντι μῖσος ὧν τέκῃ προσγίγνεται

Strange it is to bear children: even if wronged
a mother will never hate her child.

Electra 770

156 ὅρα, πόνου τοι χωρὶς οὐδὲν εὐτυχεῖ

Remember, there is no success without hard work.

Translated by Hugh Lloyd-Jones (1994)

Electra 945

157 φιλεῖ γὰρ πρὸς τὰ χρηστὰ πᾶς ὁρᾶν

Excellence draws the eyes of all.

Electra 972

158 τιμᾶν ἅπαντας οὕνεκ' ἀνδρείας χρεὼν …
ζώσαιν θανούσαιν θ' ὥστε μὴ 'κλιπεῖν κλέος

All will honour our valour,
so that in life and death our fame will never die.

Electra 983

159 οὐκ εἰσορᾷς; γυνὴ μὲν οὐδ' ἀνὴρ ἔφυς,
σθένεις δ' ἔλασσον τῶν ἐναντίων χερί

Don't you see? You're but a woman, not a man,
your strength is less than those you are up against.

Electra 997

160 οὐ γὰρ θανεῖν ἔχθιστον, ἀλλ' ὅταν θανεῖν
χρῄζων τις εἶτα μηδὲ τοῦτ' ἔχῃ λαβεῖν

Death is not the worst; rather
to wish for death, and not be able to attain it.

Electra 1007

cf. Hippocrates 18 and 51

161 προνοίας οὐδὲν ἀνθρώποις ἔφυ
κέρδος λαβεῖν ἄμεινον οὐδὲ νοῦ σοφοῦ

There's nothing more useful
to a human being than forethought, and a prudent mind.

Translated by Ezra Pound (tr. 1949, published 1989)

Electra 1015

162 ἀπροσδόκητον οὐδὲν εἴρηκας· καλῶς δ'
ᾔδη σ' ἀπορρίψουσαν ἁπηγγελλόμην

You have said nothing unexpected. Well
I knew you would reject what I proposed.

Translated by David Grene (1957)

Electra 1017

163 ἀλλ' ἦ φύσιν γε, τὸν δὲ νοῦν ἥσσων τότε

The will indeed was there, but the wit was weaker.

Translated by E.F. Watling (1953)

Electra 1023

164 ἦ δεινὸν εὖ λέγουσαν ἐξαμαρτάνειν

How terrible it is to speak so well and be so wrong!

Electra 1039

165 ἀλλ' ἔστιν ἔνθα χἡ δίκη βλάβην φέρει

But there are times when being right brings harm.

Translated by Hugh Lloyd-Jones (1994)

Electra 1042

166 τούτοις ἐγὼ ζῆν τοῖς νόμοις οὐ βούλομαι

By such laws I do not wish to live.

Electra 1043

167 βουλῆς γὰρ οὐδέν ἐστιν ἔχθιον κακῆς

No enemy is worse than bad advice.

Translated by David Grene (1957)

Electra 1047

168 οὔτε γὰρ σὺ τἄμ' ἔπη
τολμᾷς ἐπαινεῖν οὔτ' ἐγὼ τοὺς σοὺς τρόπους

You cannot bring yourself

to approve my words, nor I your temper.

Electra 1050

169 πολλῆς ἀνοίας καὶ τὸ θηρᾶσθαι κενά

It's useless chasing after shadows,
such a lot of them,
all of them void.

Translated by Ezra Pound (tr. 1949, published 1989)

Electra 1054

170 οὔτε τι τοῦ θανεῖν προμηθὴς
τό τε μὴ βλέπειν ἑτοίμα,
διδύμαν ἑλοῦσ᾽ Ἐρινύν.
τίς ἂν εὔπατρις ὧδε βλάστοι;

For life
She cares no longer, she would fain
Die to rid her house of the tyranny
Of the coupled fiends. So rare
A pattern of breed we shall not see
again.

Translated by E.F. Watling (1953)

Electra 1078

of Electra

171 τοιγὰρ σὺ δέξαι μ᾽ ἐς τὸ σὸν τόδε στέγος,
τὴν μηδὲν ἐς τὸ μηδέν

I am now nothing, make place beside
thee
naught unto naught, zero to zero.

Translated by Ezra Pound (tr. 1949, published 1989)

Electra 1165

172 ὅρα γε μὲν δὴ κἀν γυναιξὶν ὡς Ἄρης
ἔνεστιν

Consider that in women too
there lives a warlike spirit.

Translated by David Grene (1957)

Electra 1243

173 ὁ πᾶς ἂν πρέποι παρὼν ἐννέπειν
τάδε δίκᾳ χρόνος

Any time is the proper time for saying what is just.

Translated by H.T. Riley (1872)

Electra 1254

174 τὰ μέν σ᾽ ὀκνῶ χαίρουσαν εἰργαθεῖν, τὰ
δὲ
δέδοικα λίαν ἡδονῇ νικωμένην

I would not curb your joy; but there is
danger
In too much happiness.

Translated by E.F. Watling (1953)

Electra 1271

175 τὰ … περισσεύοντα τῶν λόγων ἄφες

Spare me all superfluous words!

Electra 1288

176 ὅταν γὰρ εὐτυχήσωμεν, τότε
χαίρειν παρέσται καὶ γελᾶν ἐλευθέρως

When the victory's won
We shall have time and liberty to laugh.

Translated by F. Storr (1913)

Electra 1299

177 ἴσθι δ᾽ ὡς μάλιστά σ᾽ ἀνθρώπων ἐγὼ
ἤχθηρα κἀφίλησ᾽ ἐν ἡμέρᾳ μιᾷ

I have hated you,
And loved you, more than any man
alive,
All in one day.

Translated by E.F. Watling (1953)

Electra 1362

178 τόδ᾽ εἰ καλὸν
τοὔργον, σκότου δεῖ;

If what you do is right
Why do you have to do it in the dark?

Translated by David Raeburn (2008)

Electra 1493

Aegisthus to Orestes

179 χρῆν δ᾽ εὐθὺς εἶναι τήνδε τοῖς πᾶσιν
δίκην,
ὅστις πέρα πράσσειν γε τῶν νόμων
θέλοι,
κτείνειν· τὸ γὰρ πανοῦργον οὐκ ἂν ἦν
πολύ

If swift justice were to come to all
who step outside the law,
crime would not abound.

Electra 1505

closing lines

180 πόλις γάρ, ὥσπερ καὐτὸς εἰσορᾷς, ἄγαν
ἤδη σαλεύει κἀνακουφίσαι κάρα
βυθῶν ἔτ᾽ οὐχ οἵα τε φοινίου σάλου

King, you yourself
have seen our city reeling like a wreck
already; it can scarcely lift its prow
out of the depths, out of the bloody surf.

Translated by David Grene (1991)

Oedipus the King 22

181 ὡς οὐδέν ἐστιν οὔτε πύργος οὔτε ναῦς
ἔρημος ἀνδρῶν

Ramparts are nothing, ships are nothing
when destitute of men.

Oedipus the King 56

182 ἴστε πολλὰ μέν με δακρύσαντα δή,
πολλὰς δ' ὁδοὺς ἐλθόντα φροντίδος πλάνοις

Many, my children, are the tears I've wept,
and many roads I've travelled in roaming thought.

Oedipus the King 66

183 ἐς πάντας αὔδα

Speak out, speak to us all.

Translated by Robert Fagles (1982)

Oedipus the King 93

184 οἱ δ' εἰσὶ ποῦ γῆς; ποῦ τόδ' εὑρεθήσεται
ἴχνος παλαιᾶς δυστέκμαρτον αἰτίας;

Where in the wide world to find
The far, faint traces of a bygone crime?

Translated by F. Storr (1912)

Oedipus the King 108

185 ἐν τῇδ' ἔφασκε γῇ. τὸ δὲ ζητούμενον
ἁλωτόν, ἐκφεύγει δὲ τἀμελούμενον

The killers are still here in Thebes;
pursue a thing and you may catch it;
ignored, it slips away.

Translated by Stephen Berg and Diskin Clay (1978)

Oedipus the King 110

186 ἄνδρα δ' ὠφελεῖν ἀφ' ὧν
ἔχοι τε καὶ δύναιτο κάλλιστος πόνων

No work is more nobly human than helping others,
helping with all the strength and skill we possess.

Translated by Stephen Berg and Diskin Clay (1978)

Oedipus the King 314

187 φρονεῖν ὡς δεινὸν ἔνθα μὴ τέλη
λύῃ φρονοῦντι

How terrible – to see the truth
when the truth is only pain to him who sees!

Translated by Robert Fagles (1982)

Oedipus the King 316

spoken by the blind seer Tiresias

188 τυφλὸς τά τ' ὦτα τόν τε νοῦν τά τ'
ὄμματ' εἶ

You're blind.
Blind in your eyes. Blind in your ears.
Blind in your mind.

Translated by Stephen Berg and Diskin Clay (1978)

Oedipus the King 371

a classic example of assonance (παρήχησις): observe the nine-fold use of 't'

189 μιᾶς τρέφῃ πρὸς νυκτός, ὥστε μήτ' ἐμὲ
μήτ' ἄλλον, ὅστις φῶς ὁρᾷ, βλάψαι ποτ' ἄν

Offspring of endless Night, thou hast no power
O'er me or any man who sees the sun.

Translated by F. Storr (1912)

Oedipus the King 374

Oedipus to the blind seer Tiresias

190 ὦ πλοῦτε καὶ τυραννὶ καὶ τέχνη τέχνης
ὑπερφέρουσα τῷ πολυζήλῳ βίῳ,
ὅσος παρ' ὑμῖν ὁ φθόνος φυλάσσεται

O wealth and kingship and skill surpassing skill
in the endless rivalries of life,
what spite and envy follow in your train!

Oedipus the King 380

191 οὐκ οἶδ'· ἐφ' οἷς γὰρ μὴ φρονῶ σιγᾶν φιλῶ

I know not, and not knowing hold my tongue.

Translated by F. Storr (1912)

Oedipus the King 569

192 εἴ τιν' ἂν δοκεῖς
ἄρχειν ἑλέσθαι ξὺν φόβοισι μᾶλλον ἢ
ἄτρεστον εὕδοντ', εἰ τά γ' αὔθ' ἕξει κράτη

What man, what sane man, would prefer a king's power
with all its dangers and anxieties,
when he could enjoy that same power, without its cares,
and sleep in peace each night?

Translated by Stephen Berg and Diskin Clay (1978)

Oedipus the King 584

193 οὐκ ἂν γένοιτο νοῦς κακὸς καλῶς φρονῶν

A mind that thinks sensibly cannot become evil.

Translated by Hugh Lloyd-Jones (1994)

Oedipus the King 600

194 φίλον γὰρ ἐσθλὸν ἐκβαλεῖν ἴσον λέγω
καὶ τὸν παρ' αὑτῷ βίοτον, ὃν πλεῖστον φιλεῖ

To throw away a good and loyal friend
is to destroy what you love most –
your own life, and what makes life worth living.

Translated by Stephen Berg and Diskin Clay (1978)

Oedipus the King 611

195 χρόνος δίκαιον ἄνδρα δείκνυσιν μόνος,
κακὸν δὲ κἂν ἐν ἡμέρᾳ γνοίης μιᾷ

For time alone reveals the just;
A villain is detected in a day.

Translated by F. Storr (1912)

Oedipus the King 614

196 φρονεῖν γὰρ οἱ ταχεῖς οὐκ ἀσφαλεῖς

Swift counsels are not safe.

Translated by F. Storr (1912)

Oedipus the King 617

197 οἷόν μ' ἀκούσαντ' ἀρτίως ἔχει, γύναι,
ψυχῆς πλάνημα κἀνακίνησις φρενῶν

What memories, what wild tumult of the soul
Came o'er me, lady, as I heard thee speak!

Translated by F. Storr (1912)

Oedipus the King 726

cf. next entry

198 ἔδοξ' ἀκοῦσαι σοῦ τόδ', ὡς ὁ Λάϊος
κατασφαγείη πρὸς τριπλαῖς ἁμαξιτοῖς

I thought I heard you say that Laius
Was murdered at a place where three ways meet.

Translated by H.D.F. Kitto (1962)

Oedipus the King 729

on hearing of his father's murder at the triple crossroads, the first indication that he himself might have slain him; cf. Oracles 1

199 ὕβρις φυτεύει τύραννον· ὕβρις, εἰ
πολλῶν ὑπερπλησθῇ μάταν …
ἀκρότατα γεῖσ' ἀναβᾶσ'
ἀπότομον ὤρουσεν εἰς ἀνάγκαν
ἔνθ' οὐ ποδὶ χρησίμῳ
χρῆται

Pride breeds the tyrant,
vain, insatiable pride;
mounting the highest precipice
it suddenly comes to the edge of the cliff
with no foothold there to avert its doom.

Oedipus the King 873

200 ἔννους τὰ καινὰ τοῖς πάλαι τεκμαίρεται

A wise man deduces from the past what is to come.

Translated by H.T. Riley (1872)

Oedipus the King 916

201 εἰκῇ κράτιστον ζῆν, ὅπως δύναιτό τις.
σὺ δ' ἐς τὰ μητρὸς μὴ φοβοῦ νυμφεύματα·
πολλοὶ γὰρ ἤδη κἀν ὀνείρασιν βροτῶν
μητρὶ ξυνηυνάσθησαν

Best live a careless life from hand to mouth.
This wedlock with thy mother fear thou not.
How oft it chances that in dreams a man
Has wed his mother!

Translated by F. Storr (1912)

Oedipus the King 979

spoken by his mother; cf. Freud's deliberations leading to his 'Oedipus complex'

202 τὰ τῶν τεκόντων ὄμμαθ' ἥδιστον βλέπειν

How sweet it is to look into one's parents eyes.

Translated by Oliver Taplin (2015)

Oedipus the King 999

203 δέδοιχ' ὅπως
μὴ 'κ τῆς σιωπῆς τῆσδ' ἀναρρήξει κακά

I am afraid that from
this silence will break out some storm of ill.

Translated by Oliver Taplin (1978)

Oedipus the King 1074

204 ὦ φῶς, τελευταῖόν σε προσβλέψαιμι νῦν,
ὅστις πέφασμαι φύς τ' ἀφ' ὧν οὐ χρῆν, ξὺν οἷς τ'
οὐ χρῆν ὁμιλῶν, οὕς τέ μ' οὐκ ἔδει κτανών

O light, I shall behold thee nevermore!
I stand a wretch, in birth, in wedlock cursed,

A parricide, incestuous, triply cursed.

Translated by F. Storr (1912)

Oedipus the King 1183

Oedipus, before blinding himself

205 ἰὼ γενεαὶ βροτῶν,
ὡς ὑμᾶς ἴσα καὶ τὸ μη-
δὲν ζώσας ἐναριθμῶ

Ah, generations of men,
how close to nothingness
I count your life to be!

Translated by F. Storr (1912)

Oedipus the King 1186

206 εἴθε σ' εἴθε σε
μήποτ' εἰδόμαν

Would I had never beheld thy face!

Translated by F. Storr (1912)

Oedipus the King 1217

207 τῶν δὲ πημονῶν
μάλιστα λυποῦσ' αἳ φανῶσ' αὐθαίρετοι

And self-inflicted wounds are those
that give us sharpest pain.

Translated by Oliver Taplin (2015)

Oedipus the King 1230

208 κάλλος κακῶν ὕπουλον ἐξεθρέψατε.
νῦν γὰρ κακός τ' ὢν κὰκ κακῶν εὑρίσκομαι

You have reared evil well disguised in beauty;
and now I am unmasked as evil sprung from evil.

Oedipus the King 1396

209 προσβλέπειν γὰρ οὐ σθένω·
νοούμενος τὰ πικρὰ τοῦ λοιποῦ βίου,
οἷον βιῶναι σφὼ πρὸς ἀνθρώπων χρεών

I weep for you, although I cannot look on you,
as I reflect how bitter your whole life will be,
the kind of life that people will impose upon you.

Translated by Oliver Taplin (2015)

Oedipus the King 1486

Oedipus to his daughters

210 πάντα γὰρ καιρῷ καλά

All things are good that are in season.

Translated by Hugh Lloyd-Jones (1994)

Oedipus the King 1516

211 ἃ μὴ φρονῶ γὰρ οὐ φιλῶ λέγειν μάτην

I do not like to vainly speak on what I do not know full well.

Oedipus the King 1520

212 πάντα μὴ βούλου κρατεῖν·
καὶ γὰρ ἁκράτησας οὔ σοι τῷ βίῳ ξυνέσπετο

Do not desire to be master of all things.
Your past mastery has not stayed with you to the end of life.

Translated by Oliver Taplin (1978)

Oedipus the King 1522

213 λεύσσετ', Οἰδίπους ὅδε,
ὃς τὰ κλείν' αἰνίγματ' ᾔδει καὶ κράτιστος ἦν ἀνήρ

Look now on Oedipus,
who solved the Sphinx's riddle, the mighty king that was.

Oedipus the King 1524

cf. Enigmata and Riddles 1

214 ὥστε θνητὸν ὄντ' ἐκείνην τὴν τελευταίαν ἔδει
ἡμέραν ἐπισκοποῦντα μηδέν' ὀλβίζειν, πρὶν ἂν
τέρμα τοῦ βίου περάσῃ μηδὲν ἀλγεινὸν παθών

Therefore wait to see life's ending ere thou count a mortal blest;
Wait till free from pain and sorrow he has gained his final rest.

Translated by F. Storr (1912)

Oedipus the King 1528

closing lines

215 ἐν γὰρ τῷ μαθεῖν
ἔνεστιν ηὑλάβεια τῶν ποιουμένων

A prudent man will ever shape his course by what he learns.

Translated by F. Storr (1912)

Oedipus at Colonus 115

Oedipus at Colonus, *a posthumous victory, was Sophocles' last play, produced by his grandson in 401BC*

216 ξεῖνος ἐπὶ ξένας

A stranger in a strange land.

Translated by Hugh Lloyd-Jones (1994)

Oedipus at Colonus 184

217 ἆρ' ἔστιν; ἆρ' οὐκ ἔστιν; ἢ γνώμη πλανᾷ;
καὶ φημὶ κἀπόφημι

Is it, or is it not? Are my thoughts wandering?
Now I say yes and now I say no.

Translated by Hugh Lloyd-Jones (1994)

Oedipus at Colonus 316

218 δὶς γὰρ οὐχὶ βούλομαι
πονοῦσά τ' ἀλγεῖν καὶ λέγουσ' αὖθις πάλιν

Surely 'twere a double pain
To suffer, first in act and then in telling.

Translated by F. Storr (1912)

Oedipus at Colonus 363

219 τοῖς τεκοῦσι γὰρ
οὐδ' εἰ πονῇ τις, δεῖ πόνου μνήμην ἔχειν

For with parents
even if there be suffering, suffering must be forgot.

Oedipus at Colonus 508

220 δεινὸν μὲν τὸ πάλαι κείμενον ἤδη κακόν, ὦ ξεῖν', ἐπεγείρειν

It is dreadful, stranger, to reawaken evil
long laid to rest.

Translated by Hugh Lloyd-Jones (1994)

Oedipus at Colonus 510

221 θυμὸς δ' ἐν κακοῖς οὐ ξύμφορον

In misfortune, anger brings no advantage

Oedipus at Colonus 592

222 μόνοις οὐ γίγνεται
θεοῖσι γῆρας οὐδὲ κατθανεῖν ποτε,
τὰ δ' ἄλλα συγχεῖ πάνθ' ὁ παγκρατὴς χρόνος

Gods alone are free
from aging and from death.
All other things are put in flux by all-controlling Time.

Translated by Oliver Taplin (2015)

Oedipus at Colonus 607

223 συγχεῖ πάνθ' ὁ παγκρατὴς χρόνος·
φθίνει μὲν ἰσχὺς γῆς, φθίνει δὲ σώματος,
θνῄσκει δὲ πίστις, βλαστάνει δ' ἀπιστία,
καὶ πνεῦμα ταὐτὸν οὔποτ' οὔτ' ἐν ἀνδράσιν
φίλοις βέβηκεν οὔτε πρὸς πόλιν πόλει

Nothing escapes all-ruinous time.
Earth's might decays, the might of men decays,
Honour grows cold, dishonour flourishes,
There is no constancy 'twixt friend and friend,
Or city and city.

Translated by F. Storr (1912)

Oedipus at Colonus 609

224 θαμίζουσα μάλιστ' ἀη-
δὼν χλωραῖς ὑπὸ βάσσαις,
τὸν οἰνωπὸν ἔχουσα κισσὸν

Where the clear-singing nightingale
warbles her song in the green glens,
clinging to the wine-dark ivy.

Translated by C.A. Trypanis (1971)

Oedipus at Colonus 672

of Colonos, a small Athenian deme near Plato's Academy, birthplace of Sophocles

225 τὰν ἄβατον θεοῦ
φυλλάδα μυριόκαρπον ἀνήλιον
ἀνήνεμόν τε πάντων
χειμώνων

The untrodden grove of god,
thick with leaves and berry-clusters, without sun
and without the blast of storms.

Translated by C.A. Trypanis (1971)

Oedipus at Colonus 675

of Colonos, a small Athenian deme near Plato's Academy, birthplace of Sophocles

226 ὃ τᾷδε θάλλει μέγιστα χώρᾳ,
γλαυκᾶς παιδοτρόφου φύλλον ἐλαίας.
τὸ μέν τις οὐ νεαρὸς οὔτε γήρᾳ
συνναίων ἁλιώσει χερὶ πέρσας·
ὁ δ' αἰὲν ὁρῶν κύκλος
λεύσσει νιν Μορίου Διὸς
χὰ γλαυκῶπις Ἀθάνα

The self-sown, self-begotten shape that gives
Athenian intellect its mastery,
Even the grey-leaved olive-tree
Miracle-bred out of the living stone;
Nor accident of peace nor war
Shall wither that old marvel, for
The great grey-eyed Athena stares thereon.

Translation adapted by W.B. Yeats in 'The Tower: Colonus' Praise' (1928)

Oedipus at Colonus 700

of the olive

227 κἀπὸ παντὸς ἂν φέρων
λόγου δικαίου μηχάνημα ποικίλον

Thy subtle tongue would twist
To thy advantage every plea of right.

Translated by F. Storr (1912)
Oedipus at Colonus 761

228 σκληρὰ μαλθακῶς λέγων

Wrapping hard thoughts in soft words.

Translated by F. Storr (1912)
Oedipus at Colonus 774

229 δωροῖθ', ὅτ' οὐδὲν ἡ χάρις χάριν φέροι·
ἆρ' ἂν ματαίου τῆσδ' ἂν ἡδονῆς τύχοις;
...
λόγῳ μὲν ἐσθλά, τοῖσι δ' ἔργοισιν κακά

Granting a kindness from which all grace had fled,
Would not such favour seem an empty boon?
Fair in appearance, but when tested false.

Translated by F. Storr (1912)
Oedipus at Colonus 779

230 χώρας ἀλάστωρ οὑμὸς ἐνναίων ἀεί

May my ghost haunt thy country without end.

Oedipus at Colonus 788

231 τὸ σὸν ... στόμα,
πολλὴν ἔχον στόμωσιν· ἐν δὲ τῷ λέγειν
κάκ' ἂν λάβοις τὰ πλείον' ἢ σωτήρια

Thy tongue is sharper than a sword; yet thy speech
Will bring thee more defeats than victories.

Translated by F. Storr (1912)
Oedipus at Colonus 794

232 οὐδὲ τῷ χρόνῳ φύσας φανῇ
φρένας ποτ', ἀλλὰ λῦμα τῷ γήρᾳ τρέφῃ;

Will years ne'er make thee wise?
Must thou live on to cast a slur on age?

Translated by F. Storr (1912)
Oedipus at Colonus 804

233 χωρὶς τό τ' εἰπεῖν πολλὰ καὶ τὸ καίρια

It is one thing to speak much, another to speak to the point.

Oedipus at Colonus 808

234 μὴ 'πίτασσ' ἃ μὴ κρατεῖς

Withhold your orders where you hold no sway.

Oedipus at Colonus 839

235 τοῖς τοι δικαίοις χὼ βραχὺς νικᾷ μέγαν

If the cause be just, even the humble will prevail over the mighty.

Oedipus at Colonus 880

236 θυμοῦ γὰρ οὐδέν γῆράς ἐστιν

Anger knows no old age.

Translated by Hugh Lloyd-Jones (1994)
Oedipus at Colonus 954

237 πῶς ἂν τό γ' ἆκον πρᾶγμ' ἂν εἰκότως ψέγοις;

How can you justly blame actions unwittingly performed?

Oedipus at Colonus 977

238 ἔχω γὰρ ἅχω διὰ σὲ κοὐκ ἄλλον βροτῶν

I have all that I have through you and no one else.

Translated by David Grene (1991)
Oedipus at Colonus 1129

239 οὐ γὰρ λόγοισι τὸν βίον σπουδάζομεν
λαμπρὸν ποιεῖσθαι μᾶλλον ἢ τοῖς δρωμένοις

It is not by words I would attain distinction,
rather by deeds achieved.

Oedipus at Colonus 1143

240 πρᾶγος δ' ἀτίζειν οὐδὲν ἄνθρωπον χρεών

A wise man heeds all matters great or small.

Translated by F. Storr (1912)
Oedipus at Colonus 1153

241 κακοῦ
θυμοῦ τελευτὴν ὡς κακὴ προσγίγνεται

Of evil passion evil is the end.

Translated by F. Storr (1912)
Oedipus at Colonus 1197

242 ὅστις τοῦ πλέονος μέρους
χρῄζει τοῦ μετρίου παρεὶς
ζώειν, σκαιοσύναν φυλάσ-
σων ἐν ἐμοὶ κατάδηλος ἔσται

Whoever longs for life
beyond the measured lot

is clearly in my eyes
an idiot.

Translated by Oliver Taplin (2015)

Oedipus at Colonus 1211

243 ἐπεὶ πολλὰ μὲν αἱ μακραὶ
ἁμέραι κατέθεντο δὴ
λύπας ἐγγυτέρω, τὰ τέρ-
ποντα δ' οὐκ ἂν ἴδοις ὅπου,
ὅταν τις ἐς πλέον πέσῃ
τοῦ δέοντος

For the long, looming days lay up a thousand things
closer to pain than pleasure, and the pleasures disappear,
you look and know not where.

Translated by Robert Fagles (1982)

Oedipus at Colonus 1215

244 ὁ δ' ἐπίκουρος ἰσοτέλεστος,
Ἄϊδος ὅτε μοῖρ' ἀνυμέναιος
ἄλυρος ἄχορος ἀναπέφηνε,
θάνατος ἐς τελευτάν

And come it slow or fast.
One doom of fate
Doth all await,
For dance and marriage bell
The dirge and funeral knell.
Death the deliverer freeth all at last.

Translated by F. Storr (1912)

Oedipus at Colonus 1220

245 μὴ φῦναι τὸν ἅπαντα νικᾷ λόγον

Not to be born is, past all prizing, best.

Translated by R.C. Jebb (1841–1905)

Oedipus at Colonus 1224

cf. W.B. Yeats, 'Oedipus at Colonus' (1928): 'Never to have lived is best, ancient writers say; Never to have drawn the breath of life, never to have looked into the eye of day ...'

246 τὸ δ', ἐπεὶ φανῇ,
βῆναι κεῖθεν ὅθεν περ ἥ-
κει πολὺ δεύτερον ὡς τάχιστα

Next best by far for one who has been born
is to go swiftly back from where he came.

Oedipus at Colonus 1225

cf. W.B. Yeats, 'Oedipus at Colonus' (1928): '... The second best's a gay goodnight and quickly turn away'

247 τίς οὐ καμάτων ἔνι;
φόνοι, στάσεις, ἔρις, μάχαι
καὶ φθόνος· τό τε κατάμεμπτον
ἐπιλέλογχε
πύματον ἀκρατὲς ἀπροσόμιλον
γῆρας ἄφιλον, ἵνα πρόπαντα
κακὰ κακῶν ξυνοικεῖ

What suffering will not be his? Envy, disputes, strife, battles and bloodshed; and, last of all, old age falls to his lot, hated by all, infirm, friendless, lonely old age, home of the worst of ills.

Translated by C.A. Trypanis (1971)

Oedipus at Colonus 1234

248 ἐν ᾧ τλάμων ὅδ' ...
πάντοθεν βόρειος ὥς τις ἀκτὰ
κυματοπλὴξ χειμερία κλονεῖται,
ὣς καὶ τόνδε κατ' ἄκρας
δειναὶ κυματοαγεῖς
ἆται κλονέουσιν ἀεὶ ξυνοῦσαι

Thus the unhappy man, like a wave-beaten coast battered by storms, battered by violent troubles that break over him like waves.

Oedipus at Colonus 1239

249 αἱ μὲν ἀπ' ἀελίου δυσμᾶν,
αἱ δ' ἀνατέλλοντος,
αἱ δ' ἀνὰ μέσσαν ἀκτῖν',
αἱ δ' ἐννυχιᾶν ἀπὸ Ῥιπᾶν

Now from the west, the dying sun
now from the first light rising
now from the blazing beams of noon
now from the north engulfed in endless night.

Translated by Robert Fagles (1982)

Oedipus at Colonus 1245

250 ὄλωλε γὰρ δὴ πάντα τἀμά, κοὐκέτι
τὴν δυσπόνητον ἕξετ' ἀμφ' ἐμοὶ τροφήν

For all that was mine is gone; no longer will you bear the heavy burden of looking after me.

Translated by C.A. Trypanis (1971)

Oedipus at Colonus 1613

251 ἀλλ' ἓν γὰρ μόνον
τὰ πάντα λύει ταῦτ' ἔπος μοχθήματα.
τὸ γὰρ φιλεῖν

One word
Frees us of all the weight and pain of life:
That word is love.

Translated by Robert Fitzgerald (1939)

Oedipus at Colonus 1615

252 πόθος τοι καὶ κακῶν ἄρ' ἦν τις.
καὶ γὰρ ὃ μηδαμὰ δὴ φίλον ἦν φίλον

Love can turn past pain to bliss;
What seemed bitter now is sweet.

Translated by F. Storr (1912)

Oedipus at Colonus 1697

253 ἐν οἷς γὰρ
χάρις ἡ χθονία νὺξ ἀπόκειται,
πενθεῖν οὐ χρή

For whom, in death, the gods have shown their grace grieve not.

Oedipus at Colonus 1751

254 Ἀκτὴ μὲν ἥδε τῆς περιρρύτου χθονὸς
Λήμνου, βροτοῖς ἄστιπτος οὐδ' οἰκουμένη

This is the shore of Lemnos isle, encircled by the sea,
not trodden or inhabited by men.

Translated by Oliver Taplin (2015)

Philoctetes 1

opening lines

255 ἡδὺ γάρ τι κτῆμα τῆς νίκης λαβεῖν

'Tis sweet to snatch a victory.

Translated by F. Storr (1913)

Philoctetes 81

256 βούλομαι ... καλῶς
δρῶν ἐξαμαρτεῖν μᾶλλον ἢ νικᾶν κακῶς

I'd rather lose by fair means than win by foul.

Translated by E.F. Watling (1953)

Philoctetes 94

257 ὁρῶ βροτοῖς
τὴν γλῶσσαν, οὐχὶ τἄργα, πάνθ' ἡγουμένην

Words count more than deeds in this world of men.

Translated by E.F. Watling (1953)

Philoctetes 98

Odysseus on telling lies to Philoctetes

258 τί χρή τί χρή με ... στέγειν, ἢ τί λέγειν

Tell me, master, what to hide,
tell me what to say out loud.

Translated by Oliver Taplin (2015)

Philoctetes 135

Chorus

259 ἁ δ' ἀθυρόστομος
Ἀχὼ τηλεφανὴς πικραῖς
οἰμωγαῖς ὑπακούει

And none to answer his cries
But the echo in far-off hills.

Translated by E.F. Watling (1953)

Philoctetes 188

260 τίς σ', ὦ τέκνον, κατέσχε ...
τίς ἀνέμων ὁ φίλτατος;

Oh my lad, my son, what brings you here?
What blessed wind?

Translated by E.F. Watling (1953)

Philoctetes 236

261 πόλεμος οὐδέν' ἄνδρ' ἑκὼν
αἱρεῖ πονηρόν, ἀλλὰ τοὺς χρηστοὺς ἀεί

War never willingly destroys a villain,
but always noble men.

Translated by Hugh Lloyd-Jones (1994)

Philoctetes 436

262 ἐπεὶ οὐδέν πω κακόν γ' ἀπώλετο,
ἀλλ' εὖ περιστέλλουσιν αὐτὰ δαίμονες

Does nothing evil ever die? It seems
A special providence protects all such.

Translated by E.F. Watling (1953)

Philoctetes 446

263 ὅπου δ' ὁ χείρων τἀγαθοῦ μεῖζον σθένει
κἀποφθίνει τὰ χρηστὰ χὠ δειλὸς κρατεῖ

Where the worse man has more power than the better,
where the good are always on the wane and cowards rule.

Translated by David Grene (1957)

Philoctetes 456

264 ὡς πάντα δεινὰ κἀπικινδύνως βροτοῖς
κεῖται παθεῖν μὲν εὖ, παθεῖν δὲ θἄτερα

All our mortal lives
Are set in danger and perplexity:
One day to prosper, and the next – who knows?

Translated by E.F. Watling (1953)

Philoctetes 502

265 οὐκ ἔστι λησταῖς πνεῦμ' ἐναντιούμενον,
ὅταν παρῇ κλέψαι τε χἀρπάσαι βίᾳ

The wind is never against pirates,
when there's a chance to rob and seize by force.

Translated by Carl Phillips (2003)

Philoctetes 643

266 ὅστις γὰρ εὖ δρᾶν εὖ παθὼν ἐπίσταται,
παντὸς γένοιτ' ἂν κτήματος κρείσσων
φίλος

Whoever knows how to return a kindness is a friend more precious than any possession.

Translated by Hugh Lloyd-Jones (1994)

Philoctetes 672

267 ἵν' αὐτὸς ἦν, πρόσουρον οὐκ ἔχων βάσιν,
οὐδέ τιν' ἐγχώρων κακογείτονα,
παρ' ᾧ στόνον ἀντίτυπον νόσον
βαρυβρῶτ' ἀποκλαύσειεν αἱματηρόν

All by himself, no other footfall near,
no local people, no one by to share
his agony, or join with him to weep
his blood-drunk, hungry sore.

Translated by Oliver Taplin (2015)

Philoctetes 691

268 παῖς ἄτερ ὡς φίλας τιθήνας

Just as a child without a loving nurse.

Philoctetes 703

269 οὐ φορβὰν ἱερᾶς γᾶς σπόρον ...
ὃς μηδ' οἰνοχύτου πώματος ἥσθη δεκέτει
χρόνῳ,
λεύσσων δ' ὅπου γνοίη

No fruit of the earth
For him might grow;
Never a taste,
These ten long years,
Of gladdening wine
To quench his thirst.

Translated by E.F. Watling (1953)

Philoctetes 707 and 715

270 ὦ θάνατε θάνατε, πῶς ἀεὶ καλούμενος
οὕτω κατ' ἦμαρ οὐ δύνῃ μολεῖν ποτε;

O death, death, why can you never
come
though daily I call for you?

Translated by E.F. Watling (1953)

Philoctetes 797

271 Ὕπν' ὀδύνας ἀδαής, Ὕπνε δ' ἀλγέων,
εὐαὴς ἡμῖν ἔλθοις, εὐαίων,
εὐαίων, ὦναξ

Come sleep, sleep ignorant of pain,
come like a gentle breeze,
come, happy, happy sleep.

Philoctetes 827

272 καιρός τοι πάντων γνώμαν ἴσχων
πολύ τι πολὺ παρὰ πόδα κράτος ἄρνυται

The right moment decides all things;
take it and win!

Philoctetes 837

273 τό τ' ἔνδικόν με καὶ τὸ συμφέρον

Both just and to my own advantage.

Philoctetes 926

274 ὦ λιμένες, ὦ προβλῆτες, ὦ ξυνουσίαι
θηρῶν ὀρείων, ὦ καταρρῶγες πέτραι,
ὑμῖν τάδ', οὐ γὰρ ἄλλον οἶδ' ὅτῳ λέγω

Caverns and headlands, dens of wild
creatures,
you jutting broken crags, to you I raise
my cry,
there is no one else that I can speak to.

Translated by David Grene (1957)

Philoctetes 936

275 κοὐκ οἶδ' ἐναίρων νεκρόν, ἢ καπνοῦ σκιάν

Does he not see
He fights a ghost, a shadow with no
substance?

Translated by E.F. Watling (1953)

Philoctetes 946

276 ἀνδρός τοι τὸ μὲν ὂν δίκαιον εἰπεῖν,
εἰπόντος δὲ μὴ φθονερὰν
ἐξῶσαι γλώσσας ὀδύναν

A man should speak up for the right,
but not unleash his tongue to spiteful
insults.

Translated by E.F. Watling (1953)

Philoctetes 1140

277 πόθεν γὰρ ἔσται βιοτά;
τίς ὧδ' ἐν αὔραις τρέφεται;

How shall I live?
Who can live on thin air?

Philoctetes 1159

278 οὔτοι νεμεσητὸν
ἀλύοντα χειμερίῳ
λύπᾳ καὶ παρὰ νοῦν θροεῖν

You cannot blame a man distraught by
pain
if he speaks words that don't make
sense.

Philoctetes 1193

279 ἴσθι τόδ' ἔμπεδον,
οὐδ' εἰ πυρφόρος ἀστεροπητὴς
βροντᾶς αὐγαῖς μ' εἶσι φλογίζων.

ἐρρέτω Ἴλιον

I will not go
Though thunder and lightning burn me up.
Cursed be Troy.

Translated by E.F. Watling (1953)

Philoctetes 1197

280 ξὺν τῷ δικαίῳ τὸν σὸν οὐ ταρβῶ στρατόν

With justice on my side, I don't fear anything.

Translated by E.F. Watling (1953)

Philoctetes 1251

281 νὺξ γὰρ εἰσάγει
καὶ νὺξ ἀπωθεῖ διαδεδεγμένη πόνον

Each night's new terror drives away
The terror of the night before.

Translated by E.F. Watling (1953)

Women of Trachis 29

282 κἀφύσαμεν δὴ παῖδας, οὓς κεῖνός ποτε,
γήτης ὅπως ἄρουραν ἔκτοπον λαβών,
σπείρων μόνον προσεῖδε κἀξαμῶν ἅπαξ

Children were born to us, but them he hardly sees,
E'en as the tiller of a distant field
Sees it at seedtime, sees it once again
At harvest, and no more.

Translated by F. Storr (1913)

Women of Trachis 31

Deianeira of her husband

283 κἀξ ἀγεννήτων ἄρα μῦθοι καλῶς πίπτουσιν

Even from humble lips may come words of wisdom.

Women of Trachis 61

284 ὃν αἰόλα νὺξ ἐναριζομένα
τίκτει κατευνάζει τε φλογιζόμενον,
Ἅλιον Ἅλιον αἰτῶ

Sun, born of star-spangled night when she yields to day,
and then again she lulls to sleep as you still blaze with fire,
you, Helios, Helios I call!

Women of Trachis 94

Helios is the sun-god

285 πολλὰ γὰρ ὥστ' ἀκάμαντος
ἢ νότου ἢ βορέα τις
κύματ' ἂν εὐρέι πόντῳ
βάντ' ἐπιόντα τ' ἴδοι

Under the sway of the south wind
under the lash of the north wind,
crests of the waves on a vast main
rear and then vanish from sight.

Translated by William Mullen (2010)

Women of Trachis 112

286 φαμὶ γὰρ οὐκ ἀποτρύειν
ἐλπίδα τὰν ἀγαθὰν
χρῆναί σ'

We cannot think it prudent
To kill the root of hope.

Translated by E.F. Watling (1953)

Women of Trachis 124

287 ἀλλ' ἐπὶ πῆμα καὶ χαρὰν
πᾶσι κυκλοῦσιν οἷον ἄρ-
κτου στροφάδες κέλευθοι

In a cycle of joy and pain
Fortune revolves from day to day,
Orbiting like the Great Bear.

Translated by David Raeburn (2008)

Women of Trachis 129

288 μένει γὰρ οὔτ' αἰόλα
νὺξ βροτοῖσιν οὔτε κῆ-
ρες οὔτε πλοῦτος, ἀλλ' ἄφαρ
βέβακε, τῷ δ' ἐπέρχεται
χαίρειν τε καὶ στέρεσθαι

Nothing abides; the starry night,
Our wealth, our sorrows, pass away.
Tomorrow another has his day
Of happiness, of disappointment.

Translated by E.F. Watling (1953)

Women of Trachis 132

289 ὕβριν γὰρ οὐ στέργουσιν οὐδὲ δαίμονες

The gods hate insolence as much as we.

Translated by E.F. Watling (1953)

Women of Trachis 280

290 τὸ μὴ πυθέσθαι, τοῦτό μ' ἀλγύνειεν ἄν·
τὸ δ' εἰδέναι τί δεινόν;

To be kept in ignorance – that alone can hurt me.
To know the truth – what is terrible in that?

Translated by Kathleen Freeman (1947)

Women of Trachis 458

291 ἀλλὰ ταῦτα μὲν
ῥείτω κατ' οὖρον

Let the stream run on,
And the wind blow where it will.

Translated by E.F. Watling (1953)
Women of Trachis 467

292 ἐπεί σε μανθάνω
θνητὴν φρονοῦσαν θνητὰ κοὐκ ἀγνώμονα,
πᾶν σοι φράσω τἀληθὲς οὐδὲ κρύψομαι

Now that I see you
look with human eyes on human weakness, not without charity,
I will tell the whole truth and keep nothing back.

Translated by E.F. Watling (1953)
Women of Trachis 472

293 κόρην γάρ ...
παρεισδέδεγμαι, φόρτον ὥστε ναυτίλος,
λωβητὸν ἐμπόλημα τῆς ἐμῆς φρενός

I have to welcome into my house a girl,
a baggage thrust on me like a cargo on a ship,
to wreck my peace of mind!

Translated by E.F. Watling (1953)
Women of Trachis 536

294 νοσοῦντι κείνῳ πολλὰ τῇδε τῇ νόσῳ

His nature is too much prone to this disorder.

Translated by E.F. Watling (1953)
Women of Trachis 544
of Heracles' adultery

295 τὸ μὴ 'πιθυμεῖν πομπὸς ὢν περισσὰ δρᾶν

Messengers
Should never try to better their instructions.

Translated by E.F. Watling (1953)
Women of Trachis 617

296 ὁ καλλιβόας τάχ' ὑμῖν αὐλὸς οὐκ ἀναρσίαν
ἀχῶν καναχὰν ἐπάνεισιν, ἀλλὰ θείας
ἀντίλυρον μούσας

For you sweet flutes shall sing,
Not sorrow's woeful tune,
But lyric melodies
Of heavenly joy.

Translated by E.F. Watling (1953)
Women of Trachis 640

297 τί σῖγ' ἀφέρπεις; οὐ κάτοισθ' ὁθούνεκα
ξυνηγορεῖς σιγῶσα τῷ κατηγόρῳ;

Why do you depart in silence? Do you not know
that your silence seconds the accuser?

Translated by Hugh Lloyd-Jones (1994)
Women of Trachis 813

298 ὥστ' εἴ τις δύο
ἢ κἀπὶ πλείους ἡμέρας λογίζεται,
μάταιός ἐστιν· οὐ γὰρ ἔσθ' ἥ γ' αὔριον
πρὶν εὖ πάθῃ τις τὴν παροῦσαν ἡμέραν

Only a foolish man
Would reckon on the future – one day, two,
Or more to come. Tomorrow – what is tomorrow?
'Tis nothing, until today is safely past.

Translated by E.F. Watling (1953)
Women of Trachis 943

299 γυνὴ δέ, θῆλυς οὖσα κἄνανδρος φύσιν,
μόνη με δὴ καθεῖλε φασγάνου δίχα

A woman, weak as all her sex,
hath quelled me, single-handed and unarmed.

Translated by F. Storr (1913)
Women of Trachis 1062

300 τοῖς γὰρ θανοῦσι μόχθος οὐ προσγίγνεται

For the dead there's no more toil.

Translated by Michael Jameson (1957)
Women of Trachis 1173

301 ὡς ἐπίχαρτον
τελεοῦσ' ἀεκούσιον ἔργον

Accomplish this unwelcome task as though it were a pleasure.

Translated by Hugh Lloyd-Jones (1994)
Women of Trachis 1262
Heracles' final words

302 ἄνθρωπός ἐστι πνεῦμα καὶ σκιὰ μόνον

Man is but breath and shadow.

Fragment 13 (Radt, *TrGF*) – *Aias Locros – Ajax the Locrian*

303 σοφοὶ τύραννοι τῶν σοφῶν ξυνουσίᾳ

Rulers are wise if they keep company with the wise.

Fragment 14 (Radt, *TrGF*) – *Aias Locros – Ajax the Locrian*
widely quoted in antiquity, sometimes attributed to Euripides who seems to have written

a similar line: 'αγαθὸν τυράννοις αἱ σοφῶν ξυνουσίαι'

304 ὥσπερ γὰρ ἐν φύλλοισιν αἰγείρου μακρᾶς,
κἂν ἄλλο μηδέν, ἀλλὰ τοὐκείνης κάρα
κινεῖ τις αὔρα

As with the leaves of poplars,
while all are quite still
the breeze will move the top.

Fragment 23 (Radt, *TrGF*) – *Aegeus*

305 ἐν παντὶ γάρ τοι σκορπίος φρουρεῖ λίθῳ

For under every stone a scorpion is on guard.

Translated by Hugh Lloyd-Jones (1996)

Fragment 37 (Radt, *TrGF*) – *Aechmalotides – Captive Women*

cf. Proverbial 143

306 καὶ νησιώτας καὶ μακρᾶς Εὐρωπίας οἰκήτορας

Islanders and inhabitants of wide Europe.

Fragment 39 (Radt, *TrGF*) – *Aechmalotides – Captive Women*

307 ἅπαντα γάρ τοι τῷ φοβουμένῳ ψοφεῖ

For the fearful every rustle is a threat.

Fragment 61 (Radt, *TrGF*) – *Acrisius*

308 οὐδὲν ἕρπει ψεῦδος εἰς γῆρας χρόνου

No falsehood lasts into old age.

Translated by Hugh Lloyd-Jones (1996)

Fragment 62 (Radt, *TrGF*) – *Acrisius*

309 τὰ πολλὰ τῶν δεινῶν, ὄναρ
πνεύσαντα νυκτός, ἡμέρας μαλάσσεται

Many a fearful sight that blows our way in dreams
grows mild when daylight comes.

Fragment 65 (Radt, *TrGF*) – *Acrisius*

310 τοῦ ζῆν γὰρ οὐδεὶς ὡς ὁ γηράσκων ἐρᾷ

No one loves life so much as he who is growing old.

Translated by Hugh Lloyd-Jones (1996)

Fragment 66 (Radt, *TrGF*) – *Acrisius*

311 τὸ ζῆν γάρ, ὦ παῖ, παντὸς ἥδιον γέρας·
θανεῖν γὰρ οὐκ ἔξεστι τοῖς αὐτοῖσι δίς

Life, my child, is sweetest, for we have only one.

Fragment 67 (Radt, *TrGF*) – *Acrisius*

312 ἐνταῦθα μέντοι πάντα τἀνθρώπων νοσεῖ,
κακοῖς ὅταν θέλωσιν ἰᾶσθαι κακά

All the concerns of men go wrong,
when they wish to cure evil with evil.

Translated by Hugh Lloyd-Jones (1996)

Fragment 77 (Radt, *TrGF*) – *Aleadai – Sons of Aleus*

313 τοῖς γὰρ δικαίοις ἀντέχειν οὐ ῥᾴδιον

It is not easy to resist those who are in the right.

Translated by Hugh Lloyd-Jones (1996)

Fragment 78 (Radt, *TrGF*) – *Aleadai – Sons of Aleus*

314 κακὸν τὸ κεύθειν κοὐ πρὸς ἀνδρὸς εὐγενοῦς

Concealment is wrong and not the trait of a noble man.

Fragment 79 (Radt, *TrGF*) – *Aleadai – Sons of Aleus*

315 δικαία γλῶσσ' ἔχει κράτος μέγα

Righteous speech possesses great power.

Fragment 80 (Radt, *TrGF*) – *Aleadai – Sons of Aleus*

316 τὰ γὰρ περισσὰ πανταχοῦ λυπήρ' ἔπη

Excess is painful in all circumstances.

Fragment 82 (Radt, *TrGF*) – *Aleadai – Sons of Aleus*

317 μὴ πάντ' ἐρεύνα· πολλὰ καὶ λαθεῖν καλόν

Do not investigate everything – let some things remain unknown.

Fragment 83 (Radt, *TrGF*) – *Aleadai – Sons of Aleus*

318 τό τοι νομισθὲν τῆς ἀληθείας κρατεῖ

What people believe prevails over the truth.

Translated by Hugh Lloyd-Jones (1996)

Fragment 86 (Radt, *TrGF*) – *Aleadai – Sons of Aleus*

319 – ὁ δὴ νόθος τις γνησίοις ἴσον σθενεῖ;
– ἅπαν τὸ χρηστὸν γνησίαν ἔχει φύσιν

– Is a bastard as capable as those who are legitimate?
– Nobility is always legitimate by nature.

Fragment 87 (Radt, *TrGF*) – *Aleadai – Sons of Aleus*

320 δεινὸς γὰρ ἕρπειν πλοῦτος ἔς τε τἄβατα
καὶ πρὸς τὰ βατά

Wealth has a strange power to get to places sacred and profane.

Translated by Hugh Lloyd-Jones (1996)

Fragment 88 (Radt, *TrGF*) – *Aleadai – Sons of Aleus*

321 ζῆ, πῖνε, φέρβου

Live, drink and be merry!

Fragment 167 (Radt, *TrGF*) – *Danae*

322 ὅπου δὲ μὴ τἄριστ' ἐλευθέρως λέγειν
ἔξεστι, νικᾷ δ' ἐν πόλει τὰ χείρονα

Where it is not possible to freely say what is best
the worst will prevail in the city.

Fragment 201b (Radt, *TrGF*) – *Eriphyle*

323 ἀρετῆς βέβαιαι δ' εἰσὶν αἱ κτήσεις μόνης

The possessions of virtue alone are secure.

Fragment 201d (Radt, *TrGF*) – *Eriphyle*

324 ἀνδρῶν γὰρ ἐσθλῶν στέρνον οὐ μαλάσσεται

The hearts of noble men never go soft.

Fragment 201e (Radt, *TrGF*) – *Eriphyle*

325 τὸν Ἅιδαν γὰρ οὐδὲ
γῆρας οἶδε φιλεῖν

Even the old cannot come to terms with death.

Fragment 298 (Radt, *TrGF*) – *Iobates*

326 κρύπτε μηδέν· ὡς ὁ πάνθ' ὁρῶν
καὶ πάντ' ἀκούων πάντ' ἀναπτύσσει χρόνος

Conceal nothing; for all is revealed
by all-seeing, all-hearing time.

Fragment 301 (Radt, *TrGF*) – *Hipponous*

327 τίκτει γὰρ οὐδὲν ἐσθλὸν εἰκαία σχολή

Nothing good comes of purposeless idleness.

Fragment 308 (Radt, *TrGF*) – *Iphigeneia*

328 τοῖς μὲν λόγοις τοῖς σοῖσιν οὐ τεκμαίρομαι,
οὐ μᾶλλον ἢ λευκῷ 'ν λίθῳ λευκῆ στάθμη

I deduce nothing from your words, any more
than a white measuring line is apparent on a white stone.

Fragment 330 (Radt, *TrGF*) – *Cedalion*

later used proverbially

329 ὅστις δὲ τόλμῃ πρὸς τὸ δεινὸν ἔρχεται,
ὀρθὴ μὲν ἡ γλῶσσ' ἐστίν, ἀσφαλὴς δ' ὁ νοῦς

Whoever approaches danger boldly
talks straight and is not shaken in his purpose.

Fragment 351 (Radt, *TrGF*) – *Creusa*

330 καλὸν μὲν οὖν οὐκ ἔστι τὰ ψευδῆ λέγειν·
ὅτῳ δ' ὄλεθρον δεινὸν ἀλήθει' ἄγει,
συγγνωστὸν εἰπεῖν ἐστι καὶ τὸ μὴ καλόν

Best not to tell lies;
but if the truth means ruin
even an untruth is forgiven.

Fragment 352 (Radt, *TrGF*) – *Creusa*

331 ἄπλατον ἀξύμβλητον ἐξεθρεψάμην

I reared a creature unapproachable, inexplicable.

Translated by Hugh Lloyd-Jones (1996)

Fragment 387 (Radt, *TrGF*) – *Lemniai – Women of Lemnos*

332 οὐκ ἔστι τοῖς μὴ δρῶσι σύμμαχος τύχη

To those who act not, fortune is no ally.

Translated by Philip Schaff (1819–1893)

Fragment 407 (Radt, *TrGF*) – *Minos*

cf. the English proverb 'God helps them that help themselves'

333 ἄμοχθος γὰρ οὐδείς

No one is free from toil and trouble.

Translated in Liddell & Scott

Fragment 410 (Radt, *TrGF*) – *Mysoi – The Mysians*

334 τῷ γὰρ κακῶς πράσσοντι μυρία μία
νύξ ἐστιν, εὖ παθόντα δ' ἡμέρα φθάνει

For the unhappy one night is equal to ten thousand;
the fortunate are taken by surprise by day.

Fragment 434 (Radt, *TrGF*) – *Nauplius*

335 γενοίμαν αἰετὸς ὑψιπέτας,
ὡς ἀμποταθείην ὑπὲρ ἀτρυγέτου
γλαυκᾶς ἐπ' οἶδμα λίμνας

O to become a high-flying eagle,
to soar beyond the barren sky
over the waves of the gleaming sea.

Fragment 476 (Radt, *TrGF*) – *Oenomaus*

quoted verbatim by Aristophanes, Birds *1337*

336 πεσσοὺς κύβους τε, τερπνὸν ἀργίας ἄκος

Draughts and dice, delightful remedy for idleness.

Fragment 479 (Radt, *TrGF*) – *Palamedes*

337 τούτοις γὰρ ὄντες δεσπόται δουλεύομεν,
καὶ τῶνδ' ἀνάγκη καὶ σιωπώντων κλύειν

For though we are their masters, we are slaves to them,
and we must listen to them even though they do not speak.

Translated by Hugh Lloyd-Jones (1996)

Fragment 505 (Radt, *TrGF*) – *Poimenes – The Shepherds*

a shepherd of his flock

338 φιλεῖ γὰρ ἄνδρας πόλεμος ἀγρεύειν νέους

War likes to hunt down men who are young.

Translated by Hugh Lloyd-Jones (1996)

Fragment 554 (Radt, *TrGF*) – *Scyrioi – Men of Scyros*

339 οὐδὲν γὰρ ἄλγος οἷον ἡ πολλὴ ζόη

There is no pain like long life.

Translated by Hugh Lloyd-Jones (1996)

Fragment 556 (Radt, *TrGF*) – *Scyrioi – Men of Scyros*

340 φορεῖτε, μασσέτω τις, ἐγχείτω βαθὺν
κρατῆρ'· ὅδ' ἀνὴρ οὐ πρὶν ἂν φάγῃ καλῶς
ὅμοια καὶ βοῦς ἐργάτης ἐργάζεται

Bring the stuff, let someone knead cakes, fill a deep mixing bowl! This man, like a working ox, does not work well till he has eaten!

Translated by Hugh Lloyd-Jones (1996)

Fragment 563 (Radt, *TrGF*) – *Syndeipnoi – Companions at Table*

341 ὢ δύνασις
θνατοῖς εὐποτμοτάτα μελέων,
ἀνέχουσα βίου βραχὺν ἰσθμόν

O what power there is in songs!
What greater happiness
can make bearable
our narrow course of life!

Fragment 568 (Radt, *TrGF*) – *Syndeipnoi – Companions at Table*

342 θάρσει· λέγων τἀληθὲς οὐ σφαλῇ ποτε

Have courage; speaking the truth you'll never go wrong.

Fragment 588 (Radt, *TrGF*) – *Tereus*

343 ὅστις γὰρ ἐν κακοῖσι θυμωθεὶς βροτῶν
μεῖζον προσάπτει τῆς νόσου τὸ φάρμακον,
ἰατρός ἐστιν οὐκ ἐπιστήμων κακῶν

Any mortal who, annoyed by his wrongs,
applies a remedy too strong for the disease
is like a doctor unable to determine the illness.

Fragment 589 (Radt, *TrGF*) – *Tereus*

344 οὐδεὶς ἔξοχος ἄλλος ἔβλαστεν ἄλλου

No one was born superior to any other.

Translated by Hugh Lloyd-Jones (1996)

Fragment 591 (Radt, *TrGF*) – *Tereus*

345 ζώοι τις ἀνθρώπων τὸ κατ' ἦμαρ ὅπως
ἥδιστα πορσύνων· τὸ δ' ἐς αὔριον αἰεὶ
τυφλὸν ἕρπει

Let men derive all pleasure they can in their daily life;
for the morrow is always obscure.

Fragment 593 (Radt, *TrGF*) – *Tereus*

346 φεῦ φεῦ, τί τούτου χάρμα μεῖζον ἂν λάβοις,
τοῦ γῆς ἐπιψαύσαντα κᾆθ' ὑπὸ στέγῃ
πυκνῆς ἀκοῦσαι ψακάδος εὑδούσῃ φρενί;

What greater joy can you have than to reach land and to hear the rain on the roof as you sleep?

Fragment 636 (Radt, *TrGF*) – *Tympanistae – The Drummers*

347 μὴ σπεῖρε πολλοῖς τὸν παρόντα δαίμονα·
σιγώμενος γάρ ἐστι θρηνεῖσθαι πρέπων

Do not proclaim your misfortune abroad;
it is fitter to lament in silence.

Fragment 653 (Radt, *TrGF*) – *Tyro*

348 πόλλ' ἐν κακοῖσι θυμὸς εὐνηθεὶς ὁρᾷ

When in trouble you will see more clearly if you restrain your anger.

Fragment 661 (Radt, *TrGF*) – *Tyro*

349 τίκτουσι γάρ τοι καὶ νόσους δυσθυμίαι

Sicknesses too are caused by depressions.

Translated by Hugh Lloyd-Jones (1996)

Fragment 663 (Radt, *TrGF*) – *Tyro*

350 γῆρας διδάσκει πάντα καὶ χρόνου τριβή

Old age and time, as it passes, teach all things.

Fragment 664 (Radt, *TrGF*) – *Tyro*

351 οὐ γὰρ δίκαιον ἄνδρα γενναῖον φρένας
τέρπειν, ὅπου γε μὴ δίκαια τέρψεται

It is not right that a noble man should take pleasure when the pleasure is not right.

Translated by Hugh Lloyd-Jones (1996)

Fragment 677 (Radt, *TrGF*) – *Phaedra*

352 οὕτω γυναικὸς οὐδὲν ἂν μεῖζον κακὸν
κακῆς ἀνὴρ κτήσαιτ' ἂν οὐδὲ σώφρονος
κρεῖσσον

A man could acquire no plague worse
than a bad wife
nor any treasure better than a right-
minded one.

Translated by Hugh Lloyd-Jones (1996)

Fragment 682 (Radt, *TrGF*) – *Phaedra*

cf. the Latin: 'nihil melius muliere bone'

353 οὐ γάρ ποτ' ἂν γένοιτ' ἂν ἀσφαλὴς πόλις
ἐν ᾗ τὰ μὲν δίκαια καὶ τὰ σώφρονα
λάγδην πατεῖται

No city can be safe in which justice and good sense are trampled under foot.

Translated by Hugh Lloyd-Jones (1996)

Fragment 683 (Radt, *TrGF*) – *Phaedra*

354 Ἔρως γὰρ ἄνδρας οὐ μόνους ἐπέρχεται
οὐδ' αὖ γυναῖκας, ἀλλὰ καὶ θεῶν ἄνω
ψυχὰς ταράσσει κἀπὶ πόντον ἔρχεται·
καὶ τόνδ' ἀπείργειν οὐδ' ὁ παγκρατὴς
σθένει
Ζεύς, ἀλλ' ὑπείκει καὶ θέλων ἐγκλίνεται

For Love comes not only upon men and women, but troubles the minds of the gods in the sky, and moves over the sea. And not even the all-powerful Zeus can keep him off, but he too yields and willingly gives way.

Translated by Hugh Lloyd-Jones (1996)

Fragment 684 (Radt, *TrGF*) – *Phaedra*

355 εἰσὶ μητρὶ παῖδες ἄγκυραι βίου

Children are the anchors of a mother's life.

Fragment 685 (Radt, *TrGF*) – *Phaedra*

356 νέος πέφυκας· πολλὰ καὶ μαθεῖν σε δεῖ
καὶ πόλλ' ἀκοῦσαι καὶ διδάσκεσθαι
μακρά

You are young; you have much to learn
and much to listen to, and need long
schooling.

Translated by Hugh Lloyd-Jones (1996)

Fragment 694 (Radt, *TrGF*) – *Phthiotides – Women of Phthia*

357 ἀλλ' ἔσθ' ὁ θάνατος λοῖσθος ἰατρὸς νόσων

Death, the final healer of all illnesses.

Fragment 698 (Radt, *TrGF*) – *Philoctetes at Troy*

358 τοὺς εὐγενεῖς γὰρ κἀγαθούς ... φιλεῖ
Ἄρης ἐναίρειν

Ares loves to kill the noble and the valiant.

Translated by Hugh Lloyd-Jones (1996)

Fragment 724.1 (Radt, *TrGF*) – *Phryges – The Phrygians*

359 οἱ δὲ τῇ γλώσσῃ θρασεῖς
φεύγοντες ἄτας ἐκτός εἰσι τῶν κακῶν

The arrogant in speech
escape both penalty and trouble.

Fragment 724.2 (Radt, *TrGF*) – *Phryges – The Phrygians*

360 τὸ πρὸς βίαν
πίνειν ἴσον πέφυκε τῷ διψῆν κακόν

To be forced
To drink is as bad as being thirsty.

Translated by Reginald Gibbons (2008)

Fragment 735 (Radt, *TrGF*)

361 τὸ μεθύειν πημονῆς λυτήριον

Drunkenness, relief from misery.

Fragment 758 (Radt, *TrGF*)

362 διψῶντι γάρ τοι πάντα προσφέρων σοφὰ
οὐκ ἂν πλέον τέρψειας ἢ πιεῖν διδούς

Offering a thirsty man wise sayings
will not please him more than a drink.

Fragment 763 (Radt, *TrGF*)

363 πρὸς δ' οἷον ἥξεις δαίμον' ὡς ἔρωτα

ὃς οὔτε τοὐπιεικὲς οὔτε τὴν χάριν
οἶδεν, μόνην δ' ἔστερξε τὴν ἁπλῶς δίκην

To what deity shall you appeal
who knows no fairness, no kindness,
but is content with plain justice only!

Fragment 770 (Radt, *TrGF*)

364 τὸν θεὸν τοιοῦτον ἐξεπίσταμαι,
σοφοῖς μὲν αἰνικτῆρα θεσφάτων ἀεί,
σκαιοῖς δὲ φαῦλον κἀν βραχεῖ
διδάσκαλον

God, I know,
will tell clever men the truth in riddles,
but he'll not favour fools with many
words.

Fragment 771 (Radt, *TrGF*)

365 ὅρκους ἐγὼ γυναικὸς εἰς ὕδωρ γράφω

A woman's vows are writ on water.

Fragment 811 (Radt, *TrGF*)

366 ἔργου δὲ παντὸς ἤν τις ἄρχηται καλῶς,
καὶ τὰς τελευτὰς εἰκός ἐσθ' οὕτως ἔχειν

If a man begins a task well,
it is natural that he will finish it well.

Translated by Panos Koronakis-Rohlf and Maria Batzini (2007)

Fragment 831 (Radt, *TrGF*)

367 οὐκ ἐξάγουσι καρπὸν οἱ ψευδεῖς λόγοι

False words bear no fruit.

Translated by Hugh Lloyd-Jones (1996)

Fragment 834 (Radt, *TrGF*)

368 τὰ μὲν διδακτὰ μανθάνω, τὰ δ' εὑρετὰ
ζητῶ, τὰ δ' εὐκτὰ παρὰ θεῶν ᾐτησάμην

What can be taught, I learn; what can be
found, I seek;
what can be prayed for I beg the gods.

Translated by Hugh Lloyd-Jones (1996)

Fragment 843 (Radt, *TrGF*)

369 βραδεῖα μὲν γὰρ ἐν λόγοισι προσβολὴ
μόλις δι' ὠτὸς ἔρχεται ῥυπωμένου

The impact of the words comes slowly,
and has difficulty in getting through an
ear that is blocked.

Translated by Hugh Lloyd-Jones (1996)

Fragment 858.1 (Radt, *TrGF*)

370 πρόσω δὲ λεύσσων ἐγγύθεν γε πᾶς τυφλός

A far-sighted man may not see clearly close up.

Fragment 858.3 (Radt, *TrGF*)

cf. 'can't see the wood for the trees'

371 φίλων τοιούτων οἱ μὲν ἐστερημένοι
χαίρουσιν, οἱ δ' ἔχοντες εὔχονται φυγεῖν

Glad to be deprived of such friends
and praying to see the last of them.

Fragment 863 (Radt, *TrGF*)

372 χρόνῳ δ' ἀργῆσαν ἤμυσε στέγος

A house neglected will collapse in time.

Fragment 864 (Radt, *TrGF*)

373 δεινὸν τὸ τᾶς Πειθοῦς πρόσωπον

Marvellously strong is the face of
Persuasion.

Fragment 865 (Radt, *TrGF*)

374 ἤρθη χαρᾷ
γραίας ἀκάνθης πάππος ὣς φυσώμενος

Joy raised him up like thistle-seed blown
about by the wind.

Fragment 868 (Radt, *TrGF*)

375 ταχεῖα πειθὼ τῶν κακῶν ὁδοιπορεῖ

Persuasion moves fast when it is driving
men to evil.

Translated by Hugh Lloyd-Jones (1996)

Fragment 870 (Radt, *TrGF*)

376 ὅστις γὰρ ὡς τύραννον ἐμπορεύεται
κείνου 'στι δοῦλος, κἂν ἐλεύθερος μόλῃ

Whoever traffics with a king
becomes his slave though freely born.

Fragment 873 (Radt, *TrGF*)

quoted by Pompey before being killed; cf. Plutarch, Pompey *78.4*

377 Ζεὺς νόστον ἄγοι τὸν νικόμαχον
καὶ παυσανίαν καὶ ἀτρείδαν

May god grant a return with victory
and an end to pain and fear!

Fragment 887 (Radt, *TrGF*)

the three adjectives are also proper names

378 ἀεὶ γὰρ εὖ πίπτουσιν οἱ Διὸς κύβοι

Zeus' dice fall always right.

Fragment 895 (Radt, *TrGF*)

also used proverbially with various meanings; cf. Albert Einstein, The Born-Einstein Letters: *'I, at any rate, am convinced that "He" is not playing dice'*

379 εἴθ' ἦσθα σώφρων ἔργα τοῖς λόγοις ἴσα

I wish you were as sensible in your actions as in your words.

Translated by Hugh Lloyd-Jones (1996)

Fragment 896 (Radt, *TrGF*)

380 χῶρος γὰρ αὐτός ἐστιν ἀνθρώπου φρενῶν
ὅπου τὸ τερπνὸν καὶ τὸ πημαῖνον φέρει·
δακρυρροεῖ γοῦν καὶ τὰ χαρτὰ τυγχάνων

Delight and pain may both bring tears;
they dwell not far apart.

Fragment 910 (Radt, *TrGF*)

381 πάντ' ἐκκαλύπτων ὁ χρόνος εἰς τὸ φῶς ἄγει

Time uncovers all things and brings them to the light.

Translated by Hugh Lloyd-Jones (1996)

Fragment 918 (Radt, *TrGF*)

382 σκαιοῖσι πολλοῖς εἷς σοφὸς διόλλυται

One wise man is ruined by many blunderers.

Translated by Hugh Lloyd-Jones (1996)

Fragment 921 (Radt, *TrGF*)

383 ἐσθλοῦ γὰρ ἀνδρὸς τοὺς πονοῦντας ὠφελεῖν

It is the way of a good man to help those in trouble.

Translated by Hugh Lloyd-Jones (1996)

Fragment 922 (Radt, *TrGF*)

384 ὡς δυσπάλαιστόν ἐστιν ἀμαθία κακόν

How hard it is to wrestle against stupidity!

Translated by Hugh Lloyd-Jones (1996)

Fragment 924 (Radt, *TrGF*)

cf. Schiller, Die Jungfrau von Orleans *3.6.28: 'Mit der Dummheit kämpfen die Götter selbst vergebens' (against stupidity the gods themselves contend in vain)*

385 οὐ τοῖς ἀθύμοις ἡ τύχη ξυλλαμβάνει

Fortune does not side with the faint-hearted.

Fragment 927 (Radt, *TrGF*)

386 Ἐλευθερία Διὸς ὄλβιον τέκος

Freedom, blessed child of Zeus!

Fragment 927b (Radt, *TrGF*)

387 αἰδὼς γὰρ ἐν κακοῖσιν οὐδὲν ὠφελεῖ·
ἡ γὰρ σιωπὴ τῳγκαλοῦντι σύμμαχος

Shamefastness is of no use when in trouble;
for silence is on the side of the accuser.

Translated by Hugh Lloyd-Jones (1996)

Fragment 928 (Radt, *TrGF*)

388 οἴκοι μένειν δεῖ τὸν καλῶς εὐδαίμονα

The man who is truly fortunate should stay at home.

Translated by Hugh Lloyd-Jones (1996)

Fragment 934 (Radt, *TrGF*)

389 οὐκ ἔστιν αὕτη σωφρόνων ἀνδρῶν πόλις

This is not a city of prudent men.

Fragment 936 (Radt, *TrGF*)

cf. Voltaire, La Pucelle d'Orléans, *chant III, line 63: 'de ce pays la reine est la sottise' (in this country foolishness is queen)*

390 σμικροῦ δ' ἀγῶνος οὐ μέγ' ἔρχεται κλέος

No great fame comes from a petty contest.

Translated by Hugh Lloyd-Jones (1996)

Fragment 938 (Radt, *TrGF*)

391 γνῶμαι πλέον κρατοῦσιν ἢ σθένος χερῶν

Right judgement has more power than strength of arm.

Translated by Hugh Lloyd-Jones (1996)

Fragment 939 (Radt, *TrGF*)

392 Κύπρις …
ἔστιν μὲν Ἅιδης, ἔστι δ' ἄφθιτος βίος,
ἔστιν δὲ λύσσα μανιάς, ἔστι δ' ἵμερος
ἄκρατος, ἔστ' οἰμωγμός. ἐν κείνῃ τὸ πᾶν
σπουδαῖον, ἡσυχαῖον, ἐς βίαν ἄγον

Cypris:
she is Hades, she is immortal life,
she is raving madness, she is desire
untempered, she is lamentation;
in her is all activity, all tranquillity,
all that leads to violence.

Translated by Hugh Lloyd-Jones (1996)

Fragment 941.2 (Radt, *TrGF*)

Cypris, a name for Aphrodite, personifying Love/Passion

393 νωμᾷ δ' ἐν οἰωνοῖσι …
ἐν θηρσίν, ἐν βροτοῖσιν, ἐν θεοῖς ἄνω

She rules among birds,
among beasts, among mortals, among the gods above.

Fragment 941.11 (Radt, *TrGF*)

of Aphrodite, the goddess of love

394 τίς δ' οἶκος ἐν βροτοῖσιν ὠλβίσθη ποτὲ
γυναικὸς ἐσθλῆς χωρὶς ὀγκωθεὶς χλιδῇ;

What home, however luxurious, was ever thought happy without a good wife?

Fragment 942 (Radt, *TrGF*)

395 ἐλπὶς γὰρ ἡ βόσκουσα τοὺς πολλοὺς βροτῶν

It is hope that maintains most of mankind.

Fragment 948 (Radt, *TrGF*)

396 θανόντι κείνῳ συνθανεῖν ἔρως μ' ἔχει

He being dead, I long to die with him.

Translated by Hugh Lloyd-Jones (1996)

Fragment 953 (Radt, *TrGF*)

397 χρόνος δ' ἀμαυροῖ πάντα κεἰς λήθην ἄγει

Time obscures all things and leads them to oblivion.

Translated by Reginald Gibbons (2008)

Fragment 954 (Radt, *TrGF*)

398 Σοφοκλῆς ... ὑπὸ Ἰοφῶντος τοῦ υἱέος ἐπὶ τέλει τοῦ βίου παρανοίας κρινόμενος ἀνέγνω τοῖς δικασταῖς Οἰδίπουν τὸν ἐπὶ Κολωνῷ, ἐπιδεικνύμενος διὰ τοῦ δράματος ὅπως τὸν νοῦν ὑγιαίνει, ὡς τοὺς δικαστὰς τὸν μὲν ὑπερθαυμάσαι, καταψηφίσασθαι δὲ τοῦ υἱοῦ αὐτοῦ μανίαν

Sophocles when old, accused by his son of feeble-mindedness, read the jurors his *Oedipus at Colonus*, proving that he was sound of mind; the jury applauded and convicted the son himself of insanity.

Lucian, *Octogenarians* 24

Oedipus at Colonus *was produced posthumously by his grandson in 401*

399 δὴ καὶ Σοφοκλεῖ ποτε τῷ ποιητῇ παρεγενόμην ἐρωτωμένῳ ὑπό τινος Πῶς, ἔφη, ὦ Σοφόκλεις, ἔχεις πρὸς τἀφροδίσια; ἔτι οἷός τε εἶ γυναικὶ συγγίγνεσθαι; καὶ ὅς, Εὐφήμει, ἔφη, ὦ ἄνθρωπε· ἀσμεναίτατα μέντοι αὐτὸ ἀπέφυγον, ὥσπερ λυττῶντα τινα καὶ ἄγριον δεσπότην ἀποφυγών

Someone asked Sophocles, 'How is your sex-life now? Are you still able to have a woman?' He replied, 'Hush, man; most gladly indeed am I rid of it all, as though I had escaped from a mad and savage master.'

Translated in *The Oxford Dictionary of Quotations* (2004)

Plato, *Republic* 329b

400 βραχεῖ λόγῳ δὲ πολλὰ πρόσκειται σοφά

There is much wisdom to be found in few words.

Stobaeus, *Anthology* 3.35.4

401 ἀνὴρ γὰρ ὅστις ἥδεται λέγων ἀεί,
λέληθεν αὑτὸν τοῖς ξυνοῦσιν ὢν βαρύς

Someone who loves to speak endlessly knows not how much he bores his listeners.

Stobaeus, *Anthology* 3.36.16

402 ἡλίου φαεινότερον

Brighter than the sun.

Scholia in Sophoclem (scholia vetera) Ajax Verse 395

i.e. so evident that it needs no further proof; cf. Bible Apocrypha, Ecclesiasticus *17.31: 'τί φωτεινότερον ἡλίου;'*

SOSICRATES

3rd century BC
Comic poet

1 ἀγαθοὶ δὲ τὸ κακόν ἐσμεν ἐφ' ἑτέρων ἰδεῖν,
αὐτοὶ δ' ὅταν ποιῶμεν οὐ γινώσκομεν

We are able to recognize the errors of others;
but not when we commit them ourselves.

Fragment 3 (Kock) – 3 (K-A)

SOSIPATER

3rd century BC
New Comedy poet

1 τὰ γὰρ ὄψα, φασί, καὶ τὰ βρώματα σχεδὸν
ἐν τῇ περιφορᾷ τῆς ὅλης συντάξεως
ἑτέραν ἐν αὑτοῖς λαμβάνει τὴν ἡδονήν

All delicacies and dishes
as they are served and carried round
provoke a pleasure all their own.

Fragment 1 (Kock) – 1 (K-A) – *Katapseudomenos – The False Accuser*

a cook boasting about his profession

SOSIPHANES

4th century BC
Tragic playwright from Syracuse

1 ὦ δυστυχεῖς μὲν πολλά, παῦρα δ' ὄλβιοι
βροτοί, τί σεμνύνεσθε ταῖς ἐξουσίαις,
ἃς ἕν τ' ἔδωκε φέγγος ἕν τ' ἀφείλετο;

You mortals, with so many griefs and so little joy,
do not boast of your authority,
one day gives to you, the other takes away.

Fragment 3 (Snell, *TrGF*)

SOSTRATUS

3rd century BC
Flute player who lived around the time of Antiochus I

1 Σώστρατος ὁ αὐλητὴς ὀνειδιζόμενος ὑπό τινος ἐπὶ τῷ γονέων ἀσήμων εἶναι εἶπε καὶ μὴν διὰ τοῦτο ὤφειλον μᾶλλον θαυμάζεσθαι, ὅτι ἀπ' ἐμοῦ τὸ γένος ἄρχεται

When someone reproached Sostratus the piper because of his lowly birth, he said, 'You should admire me for this, for my family begins with me.'

Stobaeus, *Anthology* 4.29a.14

SOTION

dates unknown
not known which Sotion Stobaeus refers to

1 κύνα μὲν χαλεπὸν ὄντα ἐπιχειρεῖς πραΰνειν, ὅπως σοι πρᾶος ᾖ, τὸν ἀδελφὸν δὲ οὔ;

You try to calm a savage dog; why not an irksome brother?

Stobaeus, *Anthology* 4.27.18

STESICHORUS

active *c.*600–550BC
Lyric Poet, lived most of his life in Himera in Sicily
see also Proverbial 57

1 Ἀέλιος δ' Ὑπεριονίδας δέπας ἐσκατέβαινε
χρύσεον, ὄφρα δι' Ὠκεανοῖο περάσας
ἀφίκοιθ' ἱαρᾶς ποτὶ βένθεα νυκτὸς ἐρεμνᾶς

The sun descended into the Ocean's golden bowl, reaching the darkest depths of hallowed night.

Fragment 8 (Page, *PMG*)

Stesichorus, known as 'Himeraean'; probably died in Catana, where they erected his statue mentioned by Cicero, Verrine Oration II, *2.35.87*

2 οὐκ ἔστ' ἔτυμος λόγος οὗτος,
οὐδ' ἔβας ἐν νηυσὶν ἐϋσσέλμοις
οὐδ' ἵκεο πέργαμα Τροίας

This story is not true:
you neither boarded the well-benched ships,
nor reached the citadel of Troy.

Fragment 15 (Page, *PMG*)

blaming Homer for the story of the Trojan war

3 ἀτέλεστά τε γὰρ καὶ ἀμάχανα τοὺς θανόντας κλαίειν

It is futile and pointless to weep for the dead.

Translated by David A. Campbell (1991)

Fragment 67 (Page, *PMG*)

4 θανόντος ἀνδρὸς πᾶσα πολιὰ ποτ' ἀνθρώπων χάρις

When a man dies, all men's goodwill perishes with him.

Fragment 68 (Page, *PMG*)

STRATTIS

5th century BC
Athenian Old Comedy poet

1 οὐ λίνον λίνῳ συνάπτεις

You are not comparing like with like.

Translated in Liddell & Scott

Fragment 38 (Kock) – 39 (K-A) – *Potamii – Potamians*

i.e. join like with like, deal with matters of like kind; later proverbial, cf. Plato, Euthydemus *298c and Aristotle,* Physics *207a.17*

2 οἶνον γὰρ πιεῖν
οὐδ' ἂν εἷς δέξαιτο θερμόν, ἀλλὰ πολὺ τοὐναντίον
ψυχόμενον ἐν τῷ φρέατι καὶ χιόνι μεμιγμένον

No one would drink warm wine, but cooled in a well or mixed with snow.

Fragment 57 (Kock) – 60 (K-A) – *Psychastae – Chill-Seekers*

SULLA

Lucius Cornelius Sulla Felix
*c.*138–78BC
Roman general and politician

1 χαρίζεσθαι πολλοῖς μὲν ὀλίγους, ζῶντας δὲ τεθνηκόσιν

I forgive the few for the sake of the many, the living for the sake of the dead.

Translated by Rex Warner (1958)

Plutarch, *Sulla* 14.5

of the Athenians, after taking Athens

SUSARION

6th/5th century BC
Old Comedy poet

1 οὐκ ἔστιν οἰκεῖν οἰκίαν ἄνευ κακοῦ·
καὶ γὰρ τὸ γῆμαι καὶ τὸ μὴ γῆμαι κακόν

It is impossible not to have problems at home
since it is bad to marry and equally bad to remain unwed.

Fragment 3 (Kock) – 1 (K-A)

Susarion may have been a fictitious person according to some scholars; by some he is considered a 'forerunner of comedy'

SYNESIUS

*c.*370–413AD
Christian Neoplatonist from Cyrene; bishop of Ptolemais 410–413AD

1 ἀφοβία μεγίστη τὸ φοβεῖσθαι τοὺς νόμους

It is the greatest security from fear to fear the laws.

Translated by H.T. Riley (1872)

Epistles 2

2 χειρῶν δεῖ τῷ πολέμῳ, καὶ οὐκ ὀνομάτων πολλῶν

We want hands in war, not many names.

Translated by H.T. Riley (1872)

Epistles 78

3 τύχη δὲ ἀρετῆς ἀναίτιος

Fortune is not the cause of worth.

Translated by H.T. Riley (1872)

Oration on Kingship 4.39

4 ὡς οὐ φιλεῖ συγγίνεσθαι φαντασία τε καὶ ἀλήθεια

Appearances and reality do not always agree.

Translated by H.T. Riley (1872)

Oration on Kingship 14.10

T

THALES

*c.*624BC–*c.*546BC

Philosopher from Miletus and one of the Seven Sages

see also Chilon 7; Herodotus 18; Seven Sages 39–40

1 ἐρωτηθεὶς διὰ τίνα αἰτίαν οὐ παιδοποιεῖ, ἔφη διὰ φιλοτεκνίαν

When asked why he had no children, he answered 'because of my love for children'.

Testimonies, Fragment 1.38 (D-K)

also attributed to Anacharsis

2 καὶ λέγουσιν ὅτι τῆς μητρὸς ἀναγκαζούσης αὐτὸν γῆμαι ἔλεγεν οὐδέπω καιρός, εἶτα ἐπειδὴ παρήβησεν ἐγκειμένης εἰπεῖν οὐκέτι καιρός

When his mother tried to force him to marry, he said it was too soon, and when she pressed him again later in life, he replied it was too late.

Translated by R.D. Hicks (1925)

Testimonies, Fragment 1.38 (D-K)

3 ἀρχὴ δὲ τῶν πάντων ὕδωρ

Everything has its beginning in water.

Testimonies, Fragment 1.44 (D-K)

4 σὺ γάρ, ὦ Θαλῆ, τὰ ἐν ποσὶν οὐ δυνάμενος ἰδεῖν τὰ ἐπὶ τοῦ οὐρανοῦ οἴει γνώσεσθαι;

How can you expect to understand the heavens, Thales, when you cannot even see what is just before your feet?

Translated by R.D. Hicks (1925)

Testimonies, Fragment 1.114 (D-K)

5 πρεσβύτατον τῶν ὄντων θεός· ἀγένητον γάρ

Of all things, the most ancient is god, for he is uncreated.

Translated by R.D. Hicks (1925)

Testimonies, Fragment 1.127 (D-K)

6 κάλλιστον κόσμος· ποίημα γὰρ θεοῦ

The most beautiful is the universe, for it is god's handiwork.

Testimonies, Fragment 1.128 (D-K)

7 μέγιστον τόπος· ἅπαντα γὰρ χωρεῖ

The greatest is space, for it holds all things.

Translated by R.D. Hicks (1925)

Testimonies, Fragment 1.128 (D-K)

8 τάχιστον νοῦς· διὰ παντὸς γὰρ τρέχει

Mind is the swiftest – for it runs through everything.

Translated by Jonathan Barnes (1987)

Testimonies, Fragment 1.129 (D-K)

9 ἰσχυρότατον ἀνάγκη· κρατεῖ γὰρ πάντων

The strongest is necessity, for it masters all.

Translated by R.D. Hicks (1925)

Testimonies, Fragment 1.129 (D-K)

10 σοφώτατον χρόνος· ἀνευρίσκει γὰρ πάντα

Time is the wisest, for it brings everything to the light.

Translated by R.D. Hicks (1925)

Testimonies, Fragment 1.130 (D-K)

11 ἐρωτηθεὶς τί δύσκολον, ἔφη 'τὸ ἑαυτὸν γνῶναι'
τί δὲ εὔκολον, 'τὸ ἄλλῳ ὑποθέσθαι'

Being asked what is difficult, he replied, 'To know oneself.'
'What is easy?' 'To give advice to another.'

Translated by R.D. Hicks (1925)

Testimonies, Fragment 1.135 (D-K)

12 τί ἥδιστον, 'τὸ ἐπιτυγχάνειν'

What is most pleasant? 'Success.'

Translated by R.D. Hicks (1925)

Testimonies, Fragment 1.136 (D-K)

13 τί τὸ θεῖον, 'τὸ μήτε ἀρχὴν ἔχον μήτε τελευτήν'

'What is the divine?' 'That which has neither beginning or end.'

Translated by R.D. Hicks (1925)

Testimonies, Fragment 1.137 (D-K)

14 φίλων παρόντων καὶ ἀπόντων μεμνῆσθαί φησι

Remember friends, be they present or absent.

Translated by R.D. Hicks (1925)

Testimonies, Fragment 1.141 (D-K)

15 μὴ τὴν ὄψιν καλλωπίζεσθαι, ἀλλὰ τοῖς ἐπιτηδεύμασιν εἶναι καλόν

Do not beautify your face, be beautiful in your way of life.

Testimonies, Fragment 1.142 (D-K)

16 μὴ πλούτει φησί κακῶς

Shun ill-gotten gains.

Translated by R.D. Hicks (1925)

Testimonies, Fragment 1.143 (D-K)

17 μηδὲ διαβαλλέτω σε λόγος πρὸς τοὺς πίστεως κεκοινωνηκότας

Let not idle words prejudice you against those who have shared your confidence.

Translated by R.D. Hicks (1925)

Testimonies, Fragment 1.143 (D-K)

18 ἥδιστον οὗ ἐπιθυμεῖς τυχεῖν

Most pleasant it is to realize your desires.

Seven Sages, *Apophthegms* Fragment 4.7 (D-K)

19 δίδασκε καὶ μάνθανε τὸ ἄμεινον

Teach and learn what is best.

Seven Sages, *Apophthegms* Fragment 4.8 (D-K)

20 ἀργὸς μὴ ἴσθι, μηδ' ἂν πλουτῇς

Be not idle, even if you are rich.

Seven Sages, *Apophthegms* Fragment 4.8 (D-K)

21 μέτρῳ χρῶ

Keep due measure.

Seven Sages, *Apophthegms* Fragment 4.10 (D-K)

22 μὴ πᾶσι πίστευε

Do not trust everyone.

Seven Sages, *Apophthegms* Fragment 5.10 (D-K)

23 τί κάλλιστον; κόσμος· πᾶν γὰρ τὸ κατὰ τάξιν τούτου μέρος ἐστί

What is most beautiful? Our Universe! All that is orderly is part of it.

Seven Sages, *Apophthegms* 5.3 (Mullach, *FPG*)

24 ἐρωτηθεὶς ὑπό τινος, πόσον ἀπέχει τὸ ψεῦδος τοῦ ἀληθοῦς· ὅσον, ἔφη, ὀφθαλμοὶ τῶν ὤτων

Asked what distance there is between lies and truth, 'As distant as your eyes from your ears,' he said.

Seven Sages, *Apophthegms* 5.15 (Mullach, *FPG*)

25 κρατίστην εἶναι δημοκρατίαν ... τὴν μήτε πλουσίους ἄγαν, μήτε πένητας ἔχουσαν πολίτας

The best democracy is one where there are neither very rich nor very poor citizens.

Seven Sages, *Apophthegms* 9.1 (Mullach, *FPG*)

26 καὶ Θαλῆς πρῶτος σοφὸς ὠνομάσθη ... καθ' ὃν καὶ οἱ ἑπτὰ σοφοὶ ἐκλήθησαν

Thales was the first to receive the name of Sage when the term was applied to all the Seven Sages.

Translated by R.D. Hicks (1925)

Diogenes Laertius, *Lives of Eminent Philosophers* 1.22

27 οὐδὲν ἔφη τὸν θάνατον διαφέρειν τοῦ ζῆν. σὺ οὖν, ἔφη τις, διὰ τί οὐκ ἀποθνήσκεις;

ὅτι, ἔφη, οὐδὲν διαφέρει

Thales said once that there is no difference between life and death. 'So why don't you die?' a bystander asked. 'Because it will make no difference,' he replied.

Translated by R.D. Hicks (1925)

Diogenes Laertius, *Lives of Eminent Philosophers* 1.35

THAMUS

Legendary king of Egypt

1 τοῦτο δέ, ὦ βασιλεῦ, τὸ μάθημα, ἔφη ὁ Θεύθ, σοφωτέρους Αἰγυπτίους καὶ μνημονικωτέρους παρέξει· μνήμης τε γὰρ καὶ σοφίας φάρμακον ηὑρέθη. ὁ δ' εἶπεν· ὦ τεχνικώτατε Θεύθ ... τοῦτο γὰρ τῶν μαθόντων λήθην μὲν ἐν ψυχαῖς παρέξει μνήμης ἀμελετησίᾳ ... οὔκουν μνήμης ἀλλ' ὑπομνήσεως φάρμακον ηὗρες

'This invention, O king,' said Theuth, 'will make the Egyptians wiser and will improve their memories; for it is an elixir of memory and wisdom that I have discovered.' But Thamus replied, 'Most ingenious Theuth, this invention will produce forgetfulness in the minds of those who learn to use it, because they will not practise their memory. You have invented an elixir not of memory, but of reminding.'

Translated by Harold North Fowler (1914)

Plato, *Phaedrus* 274e

on the invention of writing; today sometimes quoted to counter criticism on the use of computers

THEANO

4th century BC (?)

Probably the wife of Pythagoras, possibly a daughter or disciple

1 τὰ σπαταλῶντα τῶν παιδίων, ὅταν ἀκμάσῃ πρὸς ἄνδρας, ἀνδράποδα γίνεται

Children brought up in luxury will become slaves to their desires when men.

Fragment 196.24 (Thesleff) – *Letter to Eubule*

2 συμφέρον δὲ κακοῖς κακὰ μὴ μίσγειν, μηδὲ παρανοίᾳ παράνοιαν ἐπάγειν

It is of advantage not to mix bad with bad, nor to add madness to madness.

Fragment 199.2 (Thesleff) – *Letter to Nikostrate*

3 Θεανὼ ἐρωτηθεῖσα τί πρέπον εἴη γυναικί, τὸ τῷ ἰδίῳ ἔφη ἀρέσκειν ἀνδρί

Theano, when asked what is fitting for a woman, replied, 'To please her husband.'

Stobaeus, *Anthology* 4.23.55

THEMISTIUS

*c.*317–388AD

Philosopher and rhetorician from Paphlagonia in Asia Minor

1 οὐδεμία γὰρ μοχθηρία μᾶλλον δυσκοινώνητος ἀπιστίας

Nothing causes lack of communication more than mistrust.

Βασανιστὴς ἢ Φιλόσοφος 258b

2 καὶ μνήμονα εἶναι τὸν βασιλέα καὶ ἐπιλήσμονα·
μνήμονα μὲν τῶν ἀγαθῶν, ἐπιλήσμονα δὲ τῶν ἐναντίων

A ruler should both remember and be ready to forget;
remember the good and forget the bad.

Πενταετηρικός 109c

THEMISTOCLES

*c.*528–*c.*462BC

Athenian general and statesman

see also Aristides 16; Herodotus 157, 160; Timocreon 1

1 Θεμιστοκλεῖ δὲ τὰ μὲν ἐκ γένους ἀμαυρότερα πρὸς δόξαν ὑπῆρχε

In the case of Themistocles, his family was too obscure to be of advantage in his ambitions.

Plutarch, *Themistocles* 1.1

2 ἔτι δὲ παῖς ὢν ὁμολογεῖται φορᾶς μεστὸς εἶναι, καὶ τῇ μὲν φύσει συνετός, τῇ δὲ προαιρέσει μεγαλοπράγμων καὶ πολιτικός

However lowly his birth, it is agreed on all hands that while yet a boy he was impetuous, by nature sagacious, and by election enterprising and prone to public life.

Translated by Bernadotte Perrin (1914)

Plutarch, *Themistocles* 2.1

3 οὐδὲν ἔσει, παῖ, σὺ μικρόν, ἀλλὰ μέγα πάντως ἀγαθὸν ἢ κακόν

My boy, thou wilt be nothing insignificant, but surely something great, either for good or evil.

Translated by Bernadotte Perrin (1914)

Plutarch, *Themistocles* 2.2

spoken by Themistocles' teacher

4 ὅτι λύραν μὲν ἁρμόσασθαι καὶ μεταχειρίσασθαι ψαλτήριον οὐκ ἐπίσταιτο, πόλιν δὲ μικρὰν καὶ ἄδοξον παραλαβὼν ἔνδοξον καὶ μεγάλην ἀπεργάσασθαι

Tuning the lyre and handling the harp are no accomplishments of mine, but rather taking charge of a city that was small and inglorious and making it glorious and great.

Translated by Bernadotte Perrin (1914)

Plutarch, *Themistocles* 2.4

5 καὶ τοὺς τραχυτάτους πώλους ἀρίστους ἵππους γίνεσθαι φάσκων, ὅταν ἧς προσήκει τύχωσι παιδείας καὶ καταρτύσεως

Even the wildest colts make very good horses, if only they got the proper breaking and training.

Translated by Bernadotte Perrin (1914)

Plutarch, *Themistocles* 2.7

6 ὡς οὔτ' ἐκεῖνος ἂν γένοιτο ποιητὴς ἀγαθὸς ᾄδων παρὰ μέλος οὔτ' αὐτὸς ἀστεῖος ἄρχων παρὰ νόμον χαριζόμενος

You would not be a good poet if you sing out of tune, nor I a good magistrate if I grant favours contrary to the law.

Plutarch, *Themistocles* 5.6

to Simonides of Ceos asking for an 'improper favour'

7 ξύλινον τεῖχος ἢ τὰς ναῦς

The wooden wall is your ships.

Translated in *Bartlett's Familiar Quotations* (1980)

Plutarch, *Themistocles* 10.3

interpreting the words of the second Delphic oracle to the Athenians, before the battle of Salamis in 480BC; cf. Oracles 14

8 τοῦ γὰρ Εὐρυβιάδου πρὸς αὐτὸν εἰπόντος· 'ὦ Θεμιστόκλεις, ἐν τοῖς ἀγῶσι τοὺς προεξανισταμένους ῥαπίζουσι', 'ναί' εἶπεν ὁ Θεμιστοκλῆς, 'ἀλλὰ τοὺς ἀπολειφθέντας οὐ στεφανοῦσιν'

When Eurybiades said to him, 'Themistocles, at the games those who start too soon get a caning,' 'Yes,' said Themistocles, 'but those who lag behind get no crown.'

Translated by Bernadotte Perrin (1914)

Plutarch, *Themistocles* 11.3

9 πάταξον μέν, ἄκουσον δέ

Strike me if you wish, but listen to me first.

Plutarch, *Themistocles* 11.4

to Eurybiades, commander of the Spartan fleet, on his raising his staff as though to strike

10 οἳ καθάπερ αἱ τευθίδες μάχαιραν μὲν ἔχετε, καρδίαν δ' οὐκ ἔχετε;'

Like the cuttlefish, you have a long pouch in the place where your heart ought to be.

Translated by Bernadotte Perrin (1914)

Plutarch, *Themistocles* 11.6

11 οὔτ' ἂν ἐγὼ Σερίφιος ὢν ἐγενόμην ἔνδοξος, οὔτε σὺ Ἀθηναῖος

If I were from Seriphus, I should not have become famous, nor would you if you were from Athens.

Translated by Frank Cole Babbitt (1931)

Plutarch, *Themistocles* 18.5

to a Seriphian who said that Themistocles' fame was due to the city, not to himself

12 τὸν δ' υἱὸν ... ἔλεγε πλεῖστον τῶν Ἑλλήνων δύνασθαι· τοῖς μὲν γὰρ Ἕλλησιν ἐπιτάττειν Ἀθηναίους, Ἀθηναίοις δ' αὐτόν, αὐτῷ δὲ τὴν ἐκείνου μητέρα, τῇ μητρὶ δ' ἐκεῖνον

The boy is the most powerful of all the Hellenes; for the Hellenes are commanded by the Athenians, the Athenians by myself, myself by the boy's mother, and the mother by her boy.

Translated in *Bartlett's Familiar Quotations* (1980)

Plutarch, *Themistocles* 18.7

of his son (who was pert towards his mother)

13 χωρίον μὲν πιπράσκων ἐκέλευε κηρύττειν ὅτι καὶ γείτονα χρηστὸν ἔχει

When he put up a plot of land for sale he stressed that it also had a good neighbour.

Plutarch, *Themistocles* 18.8

14 τὸν ἐπιεικῆ τοῦ πλουσίου προκρίνας, ἔφη ζητεῖν ἄνδρα χρημάτων δεόμενον μᾶλλον ἢ χρήματα ἀνδρός

I prefer an able man to a rich man; I prefer a man without money rather than money without a man.

Plutarch, *Themistocles* 18.9

of two suitors for his daughter's hand

15 δύο γὰρ ἥκειν ἔφη θεοὺς κομίζων, Πειθὼ καὶ Βίαν

I have with me two gods, Persuasion and Compulsion.

Translated in *Bartlett's Familiar Quotations* (1980)

Plutarch, *Themistocles* 21.2

said to the Andrians, demanding money; to which they replied that they already had two great gods, Penury and Powerlessness, who hindered them from giving

16 οὐδὲ τριῶν ἄξια ταλάντων κεκτημένου τοῦ Θεμιστοκλέους πρὶν ἅπτεσθαι τῆς πολιτείας

And yet Themistocles did not possess the worth of three talents before he entered political life.

Translated by Bernadotte Perrin (1914)

Plutarch, *Themistocles* 25.3

as compared to eighty or a hundred talents after

17 τὸν λόγον ἐοικέναι τοῦ ἀνθρώπου τοῖς ποικίλοις στρώμασιν· ὡς γὰρ ἐκεῖνα καὶ τοῦτον ἐκτεινόμενον μὲν ἐπιδείκνυσθαι τὰ εἴδη, συστελλόμενον δὲ κρύπτειν καὶ διαφθείρειν

The speech of man is like embroidered tapestries, since like them this too has to be extended in order to display its patterns, but when it is rolled up it conceals and distorts them.

Translated by Bernadotte Perrin (1914)

Plutarch, *Themistocles* 29.4

18 οὐκ ἐᾷ με καθεύδειν ... τὸ Μιλτιάδου τρόπαιον

The laurels of Miltiades will not let me sleep.

Plutarch, *Sayings of Kings and Commanders* 185a.2

Miltiades was the Athenian general at Marathon

19 πότερον ἤθελες ὁ νικῶν Ὀλυμπίασιν ἢ ὁ κηρύττων τοὺς νικῶντας εἶναι;

Would you rather be the victor at the Olympic games or the announcer of the victor?

Translated by Frank Cole Babbitt (1931)

Plutarch, *Sayings of Kings and Commanders* 185a.5

on being asked who he would like to be, Achilles or Homer

20 τῶν τε παραχρῆμα δι' ἐλαχίστης βουλῆς κράτιστος γνώμων καὶ τῶν μελλόντων ἐπὶ πλεῖστον τοῦ γενησομένου ἄριστος εἰκαστής

He was beyond other men, with the briefest deliberation, both a shrewd judge of the immediate present and wise in forecasting what would happen in the most distant future.

Translated by Charles Forster Smith (1919)

Thucydides, *History of the Peloponnesian War* 1.138.3

of Themistocles

THEOCRITUS

c.300–260BC

Bucolic poet from Syracuse

see also Anaximenes (2) 4

1 Ἀδύ τι τὸ ψιθύρισμα καὶ ἁ πίτυς αἰπόλε τήνα
ἁ ποτὶ ταῖς παγαῖσι μελίσδεται

There is sweet music in that pine-tree's whisper, goatherd,
There by the spring.

Translated by Anthony Verity (2002)

Idylls 1.1

2 οὐ θέμις, ὦ ποιμήν, τὸ μεσαμβρινὸν οὐ θέμις ἄμμιν
συρίσδεν. τὸν Πᾶνα δεδοίκαμες· ἦ γὰρ ἀπ' ἄγρας
τανίκα κεκμακὼς ἀμπαύεται· ἔστι δὲ πικρός,
καί οἱ ἀεὶ δριμεῖα χολὰ ποτὶ ῥινὶ κάθηται

I dare not, faith, I dare not pipe at *Noon*,
Afraid of *Pan*, for when his Hunting's done,
And He lyes down to sleep by purling streams,
He's very touchy if we break his dreams.

Translated by Thomas Creech (1684)

Idylls 1.15

3 τὰ δ' οὐ φρενὸς ἅπτεται αὐτᾶς
ἀλλ' ὀκὰ μὲν τῆνον ποτιδέρκεται ἄνδρα γελᾶσα,
ἄλλοκα δ' αὖ ποτὶ τὸν ῥιπτεῖ νόον

Yet these things do not touch her heart, but she glances for a time at the one and smiles, and then she shifts her thoughts to the other.

Translated by C.A. Trypanis (1971)

Idylls 1.35

of a lady being courted by two suitors

4 ἠνίδε σιγῇ μὲν πόντος, σιγῶντι δ' ἀῆται·
ἁ δ' ἐμὰ οὐ σιγῇ στέρνων ἔντοσθεν ἀνία,
ἀλλ' ἐπὶ τήνῳ πᾶσα καταίθομαι, ὅς με τάλαιναν
ἀντὶ γυναικὸς ἔθηκε κακὰν καὶ ἀπάρθενον ἦμεν

Behold, the sea is silent, and silent are the winds;
But never silent is the anguish here within my breast,
Since I am all on fire for him who has made me, unhappy me,
Not a wife, but a worthless woman, a maiden now no more.

Translated by R.C. Trevelyan (1947)

Idylls 2.38

5 φράζεό μευ τὸν ἔρωθ' ὅθεν ἵκετο, πότνα Σελάνα

Consider, lady Moon, whence came my love.

Translated by C.A. Trypanis (1971)

Idylls 2.69 (repeated several times)

6 Ἔρως δ' ἄρα καὶ Λιπαραίω
πολλάκις Ἀφαίστοιο σέλας φλογερώτερον αἴθει

Truly, Love often kindles a blaze hotter than Hephaestus' fire.

Idylls 2.133

7 Ἀῶ τὰν ῥοδόπαχυν ἀπ' Ὠκεανοῖο φέροισαι,
κεῖπέ μοι ἄλλα τε πολλὰ καὶ ὡς ἄρα Δέλφις ἔραται.
κεἴτε νιν αὖτε γυναικὸς ἔχει πόθος εἴτε καὶ ἀνδρός

When the horses of rosy Dawn were bringing her swiftly from the Ocean to the sky, she told me many other things, and also that Delphis was in love. She did not say for certain if it was a woman he desired or a man.

Translated by C.A. Trypanis (1971)

Idylls 2.148

8 χαῖρε, Σελαναία λιπαρόθρονε, χαίρετε δ' ἄλλοι
ἀστέρες, εὐκάλοιο κατ' ἄντυγα Νυκτὸς ὀπαδοί

Farewell, Moon, on your gleaming throne, and farewell you other stars that follow the chariot of quiet Night.

Translated by C.A. Trypanis (1971)

Idylls 2.165

9 θαρσεῖν χρή, τάχ' αὔριον ἔσσετ' ἄμεινον

Have courage! Tomorrow is another day.

Idylls 4.41

'θαρσεῖν χρή' is still used today as a proverbial expression

10 ἐλπίδες ἐν ζωοῖσιν, ἀνέλπιστοι δὲ θανόντες

While there is life there is hope, when we are dead there is none.

Translated by H.T. Riley (1872)

Idylls 4.42

cf. the English proverb 'while there's life there's hope'

11 Ζεὺς ἄλλοκα μὲν πέλει αἴθριος, ἄλλοκα δ' ὕει

Zeus gives rain one day, shine the next.

Translated by J.M. Edmonds (1912)

Idylls 4.43

12 λέγ', εἴ τι λέγεις

Say it now, if you have something to say.

Idylls 5.78

13 οὐ θεμιτὸν Λάκων ποτ' ἀηδόνα κίσσας ἐρίσδειν,
οὐδ' ἔποπας κύκνοισι

It is against nature for the jay to vie with the nightingale, the hoopoe with the swan.

Idylls 5.136

14 ἦ γὰρ ἔρωτι
πολλάκις τὰ μὴ καλὰ καλὰ πέφανται

In the eyes of love what is not beautiful

often seems beautiful.

Translated by John Simpson and Jennifer Speake (1982)

Idylls 6.18

cf. the English proverb 'beauty is in the eye of the beholder'

15 ὡς μὴ βασκανθῶ δέ, τρὶς εἰς ἐμὸν ἔπτυσα κόλπον

To avert the bad omen I spat thrice in my bosom.

Idylls 6.39

a practice continued to this day – but 'spitting' is purely symbolical …

16 πᾷ δὴ τὸ μεσαμέριον πόδας ἕλκεις,
ἁνίκα δὴ καὶ σαῦρος ἐν αἱμασιαῖσι καθεύδει;

Whither go you in the noonday heat,
when even the lizard dozes in his nook?

Idylls 7.21

cf. Noël Coward: 'Mad dogs and Englishmen go out in the midday sun' (1931 song)

17 χἀλκυόνες στορεσεῦντι τὰ κύματα τάν τε θάλασσαν
τόν τε νότον τόν τ' εὗρον, ὃς ἔσχατα φυκία κινεῖ,
ἁλκυόνες, γλαυκαῖς Νηρηΐσι ταὶ τὰ μάλιστα
ὀρνίχων ἐφίληθεν, ὅσαις τέ περ ἐξ ἁλὸς ἄγρα

Halcyons shall soothe the sea's waves, and shall calm
The south wind and the east, which churns the wrack
In the sea's lowest depths – halcyons, most loved birds by the
Grey-green Nereids, and those who seek their catch in the sea.

Translated by Anthony Verity (2002)

Idylls 7.57

18 ἐν κνίδαισι καθεύδοις

May you sleep in nettles.

Translated by C.A. Trypanis (1971)

Idylls 7.110

19 ἄμμιν δ' ἁσυχία τε μέλοι, γραία τε παρείη,
ἅτις ἐπιφθύζοισα τὰ μὴ καλὰ νόσφιν ἐρύκοι

Our concern be peace of mind, and may an old crone come and spit for luck and keep all ill at bay.

Idylls 7.126

20 πολλαὶ δ' ἄμμιν ὕπερθε κατὰ κρατὸς δονέοντο
αἴγειροι πτελέαι τε· τὸ δ' ἐγγύθεν ἱερὸν ὕδωρ
Νυμφᾶν ἐξ ἄντροιο κατειβόμενον κελάρυζε

Above us was the constant quiet movement of elm
And poplar, and from the cave of the Nymphs nearby
The sacred water ran with a bubbling sound.

Translated by Anthony Verity (2002)

Idylls 7.135

21 τοὶ δὲ ποτὶ σκιαραῖς ὀροδαμνίσιν αἰθαλίωνες
τέττιγες λαλαγεῦντες ἔχον πόνον· ἁ δ' ὀλολυγὼν
τηλόθεν ἐν πυκιναῖσι βάτων τρύζεσκεν ἀκάνθαις·
ἄειδον κορύδοι καὶ ἀκανθίδες, ἔστενε τρυγών,
πωτῶντο ξουθαὶ περὶ πίδακας ἀμφὶ μέλισσαι

On the shady boughs the dark cicadas were chattering busily, and the tree-frog cried far off in the thick thornbrake. Larks and finches sang, the dove sighed, and the yellow bees flitted about the springs.

Translated by C.A. Trypanis (1971)

Idylls 7.138

22 πάντ' ὦσδεν θέρεος μάλα πίονος, ὦσδε δ' ὀπώρας
ὄχναι μὲν πὰρ ποσσί, περὶ πλευραῖσι δὲ μᾶλα
δαψιλέως ἁμῖν ἐκυλίνδετο· τοὶ δ' ἐκέχυντο
ὄρπακες βραβίλοισι καταβρίθοντες ἔραζε·
τετράενες δὲ πίθων ἀπελύετο κρατὸς ἄλειφαρ

All things smelt of a very rich harvest and of fruit time. Pears were rolling in abundance at our feet and apples at our side, and the branches heavy with sloes, drooped down to the ground. And the four-year seal was loosened from the head of the wine jar.

Translated by C.A. Trypanis (1971)

Idylls 7.143

23 τέττιξ μὲν τέττιγι φίλος, μύρμακι δὲ μύρμαξ,
ἴρηκες δ' ἴρηξιν, ἐμὶν δ' ἁ Μοῖσα καὶ ᾠδά

Cicada is to cicada dear, and ant to ant,
And kestrels dear to kestrels, but to me the Muse and song.

Translated by R.C. Trevelyan (1947)

Idylls 9.31

24 ἁ αἲξ τὰν κύτισον, ὁ λύκος τὰν αἶγα διώκει,
ἁ γέρανος τὤροτρον, ἐγὼ δ' ἐπὶ τὶν μεμάνημαι

The goat goes after the clover, the wolf the goat,
the crane the plough, and I am mad for you.

Idylls 10.30

25 εὐκτὸς ὁ τῶ βατράχω, παῖδες, βίος· οὐ μελεδαίνει
τὸν τὸ πιεῖν ἐγχεῦντα· πάρεστι γὰρ ἄφθονον αὐτῷ

O to be a frog, my lads, and live aloof from care!
He needs no drawer to his drink; 'tis plenty everywhere.

Translated by J.M. Edmonds (1912)

Idylls 10.52

26 φοιτῇς δαῦθ' οὕτως, ὄκκα γλυκὺς ὕπνος ἔχῃ με,
οἴχῃ δ' εὐθὺς ἰοῖσ', ὄκκα γλυκὺς ὕπνος ἀνῇ με;

Why do you only come just as sleep claims me,
Why do you leave me just as sweet sleep lets me go?

Translated by Anthony Verity (2002)

Idylls 11.22

27 τὰν παρεοῖσαν ἄμελγε· τί τὸν φεύγοντα διώκεις;

Milk the ewe at hand;
why chase the one who runs away?

Translated by Anthony Verity (2002)

Idylls 11.75

cf. the English proverb 'a bird in the hand is worth two in the bush'

28 χὤτι τὸ φάρμακόν ἐστιν ἀμηχανέοντος ἔρωτος,
οὐκ οἶδα

What be the medicine for helpless love,
'faith, I know not.

Idylls 14.52

29 μόλις ὔμμιν ἐσώθην,
Πραξινόα, πολλῶ μὲν ὄχλω, πολλῶν δὲ τεθρίππων·
παντᾷ κρηπῖδες, παντᾷ χλαμυδηφόροι ἄνδρες

I scarcely got here alive,
Such a huge crowd, racing chariots everywhere, and the
Military all over the place, with their big boots and uniforms.

Translated by Anthony Verity (2002)

Idylls 15.4

30 ἀεργοῖς αἰὲν ἑορτά

It's always a holiday for the idle.

Translated by C.A. Trypanis (1971)

Idylls 15.26

31 αἱ γαλέαι μαλακῶς χρῄζοντι καθεύδειν

Cats like soft beds to sleep on.

Translated by C.A. Trypanis (1971)

Idylls 15.28

32 ἐς Τροίαν πειρώμενοι ἦνθον Ἀχαιοί,
καλλίστα παίδων· πείρᾳ θην πάντα τελεῖται

'Persistence got the Greeks inside of Troy,'
My dears. Persistence is everything.

Translated by John Talbot (2010)

Idylls 15.61

33 πάντα γυναῖκες ἴσαντι

Women know everything about everything.

Translated by D.S. Baker (1998)

Idylls 15.64

34 βάρδισται μακάρων Ὧραι φίλαι, ἀλλὰ ποθειναὶ
ἔρχονται πάντεσσι βροτοῖς αἰεί τι φορεῦσαι

The Seasons, the Seasons, full slow they go and come,
But some sweet thing they bring for all.

Translated by J.M. Edmonds (1912)

Idylls 15.104

35 ἅλις πάντεσσιν Ὅμηρος

Homer is enough for everybody.

Translated by C.A. Trypanis (1971)
Idylls 16.20

36 Τὸν κλέπταν ποτ' Ἔρωτα κακὰ κέντασε μέλισσα …
τυτθὸν θηρίον ἐστὶ μέλισσα καὶ ἁλίκα τραύματα ποιεῖ.
χἀ μάτηρ γελάσασα· τὶ δ'; οὐκ ἴσος ἐσσὶ μελίσσαις,
ὃς τυτθὸς μὲν ἔεις, τὰ δὲ τραύματα ταλίκα ποιεῖς;

Eros, stealing honey, was stung badly by a bee.
'What beast is this, so little, and makes so big a wound?'
'Are you not, Eros, equal to a bee' his smiling mother said,
'So little, and yet able to cause wounds so great!'
Idylls 19.1
of Aphrodite and her son Eros

37 καὶ πολὺ τᾷ μορφᾷ θηλύνετο, καί τι σεσαρὸς
καὶ σοβαρόν μ' ἐγέλαξεν. ἐμοὶ δ' ἄφαρ ἔζεσεν αἷμα,
καὶ χρόα φοινίχθην ὑπὸ τὤλγεος ὡς ῥόδον ἕρσᾳ

And of her beutie wondrous coy she was; her mouth she wride,
And proudly mockt me to my face; my blud boild in each vaine,
And red I woxe for griefe as doth the rose with dewye rain.
Translated by Anonymous (Sixe Idillia 1588)
Idylls 20.14

38 Ἁ πενία μόνα τὰς τέχνας ἐγείρει

Poverty is the mother of invention.
Idylls 21.1
cf. 'necessity is the mother of invention'

39 οὐδὲ γὰρ εὕδειν
ἀνδράσιν ἐργατίναισι κακαὶ παρέχοντι μέριμναι·
κἂν ὀλίγον νυκτός τις ἐπιβρίσσησι, τὸν ὕπνον
αἰφνίδιον θορυβεῦσιν ἐφιστάμεναι μελεδῶναι

A man of toil barely sleeps for the anxieties in his heart; and if he sleeps just a little at night, his slumber is broken by the cares that plague him.
Idylls 21.2

40 οὐ κλεῖδ', οὐχὶ θύραν ἔχον, οὐ κύνα· πάντα περισσά
ταῦτ' ἐδόκει τήνοις· ἁ γὰρ πενία σφας ἐτήρει·
οὐδεὶς δ' ἐν μέσσῳ γείτων πέλεν, ἁ δὲ παρ' αὐτὰν
θλιβομένα καλύβαν τρυφερὸν προσέναχε θάλασσα

Key, door, watchdog they have none,
for all are useless in their poverty;
they have no neighbours either, for the sea surrounds their humble hut.
Idylls 21.15
of fishermen

41 χαλεπὸν δ' ἑτέρου νόον ἴδμεναι ἀνδρός

'Tis hard to know the mind of another man.
Idylls 25.67

42 τάχα γάρ σε παρέρχεται ὡς ὄναρ ἥβη

Youth passes by as swiftly as a dream.
Idylls 27.8

43 οὐκ ὀδύνην, οὐκ ἄλγος ἔχει γάμος, ἀλλὰ χορείην

A marriage is a thing neither of pain nor grief but rather of dancing.
Translated by J.M. Edmonds (1912)
Idylls 27.26

44 ἦ μεγάλα χάρις
δώρῳ σὺν ὀλίγῳ· πάντα δὲ τίματα τὰ πὰρ φίλων

Truly great goodwill goes with a small gift; yet all that comes from friends is precious.
Translated by C.A. Trypanis (1971)
Idylls 28.24

45 νεότατα δ' ἔχην παλινάγρετον
οὐκ ἔστι· πτέρυγας γὰρ ἐπωμμαδίαις φόρη

Youth, once fled, cannot be brought back;
it is as if she has wings on her shoulders.
Idylls 29.28

46 θράσει μὲν οὐδεὶς οὐδέπω πόνῳ δὲ καὶ γενναιότητι καὶ ἐπιεικείᾳ ἀρετὴν ἐπεκτήσατο

Nobody ever acquired virtue through insolence, but only through toil and courage and kindness.

Arsenius, *Apophthegms* 8.91k

47 Θεόκριτος ἐρωτηθεὶς ποῖα τῶν θηρίων ἐστὶ τὰ χαλεπώτατα, εἶπεν ἐν μὲν τοῖς ὄρεσιν ἄρκοι καὶ λέοντες, ἐν δὲ ταῖς πόλεσι τελῶναι καὶ συκοφάνται

Theocritus was asked which beast he considered the most dangerous; he replied, 'In the mountains, bears and lions, in the cities tax collectors and informers.'

Stobaeus, *Anthology* 3.2.33

48 Θεόκριτος τοὺς πολλοὺς τῶν πλουσίων ἔλεγεν ἐπι τρόπους εἶναι, ἀλλὰ μὴ δεσπότας τῶν χρημάτων

Theocritus said that most of the wealthy were guardians, not masters of their wealth.

Stobaeus, *Anthology* 3.16.24

49 Θεόκριτος ἐρωτηθεὶς διὰ τί οὐ συγγράφει, ὅτι εἶπεν ὡς μὲν βούλομαι, οὐ δύναμαι· ὡς δὲ δύναμαι, οὐ βούλομαι

Theocritus, when asked why he didn't write, answered: 'As I want to, I cannot, and as I can, I do not want to.'

Stobaeus, *Anthology* 3.21.10

THEODECTES

4th century BC
Tragic playwright and orator from Phaselis in Lycia

1 ἅπαντ' ἐν ἀνθρώποισι γηράσκειν ἔφυ
καὶ πρὸς τελευτὴν ἔρχεται τακτοῦ χρόνου,
πλὴν ὡς ἔοικε τῆς ἀναιδείας μόνον·
αὕτη δ' ὅσωπερ αὔξεται θνητῶν γένος,
τοσῷδε μείζων γίγνεται καθ' ἡμέραν

All in mankind is bound to mellow
and in good time the end draws near.
All except insolence: as humankind expands
impudence grows stronger every day.

Fragment 12 (Snell, *TrGF*)

2 ὅταν γὰρ ἄλοχον εἰς δόμους ἄγῃ πόσις,
οὐχ ὡς δοκεῖ γυναῖκα λαμβάνει μόνον,
ὁμοῦ δὲ τῇδ' ἔτ' εἰσκομίζεται λαβὼν
καὶ δαίμον' ἤτοι χρηστὸν ἢ τοὐναντίον

When a man brings home a wife
it is not a woman only as he thinks;
with her he carries to his house
his good or evil destiny.

Fragment 13 (Snell, *TrGF*)

THEOGNIS

fl. c.550–540BC
Elegiac poet from Megara
a number of couplets, not always identifiable, may not be by Theognis himself and the collection is better referred to as *Theognidea*

1 ἀστοῖσιν δ' οὔπω πᾶσιν ἁδεῖν δύναμαι·
... οὐδὲ γὰρ ὁ Ζεὺς
οὔθ' ὕων πάντεσσ' ἁνδάνει οὔτ' ἀνέχων

Of course there is no way to please everyone; not even Zeus pleases all,
either when he sends rain or when he doesn't.

Elegies 24

cf. the English proverb 'you can't please everyone'

2 κακοῖσι δὲ μὴ προσομίλει
ἀνδράσιν, ἀλλ' αἰεὶ τῶν ἀγαθῶν ἔχεο
καὶ παρὰ τοῖσιν πῖνε καὶ ἔσθιε

Do not consort with evil men, but dine at the tables of those who are good.

Elegies 31

3 πιστὸς ἀνὴρ χρυσοῦ τε καὶ ἀργύρου ἀντερύσασθαι
ἄξιος ἐν χαλεπῇ, Κύρνε, διχοστασίῃ

In a sore dissension, Cyrnus, a trusty man is to be reckoned against gold and silver.

Translated by J.M. Edmonds (1931)
Elegies 77

4 μή μ' ἔπεσιν μὲν στέργε, νόον δ' ἔχε καὶ φρένας ἄλλῃ,
εἴ με φιλεῖς ... φίλει καθαρὸν θέμενος νόον

Love me not with words alone, with heart and mind elsewhere;
if you love me, do so with all your heart.

Elegies 87

5 ὃς δὲ μιῇ γλώσσῃ δίχ' ἔχει νόον, οὗτος ...
ἐχθρὸς βέλτερος ἢ φίλος ὤν

He of one tongue but a mind asunder
better be foe than friend.

Elegies 91

6 τί δ' ἔστ' ὄφελος δειλὸς ἀνὴρ φίλος ὤν;

What worth is a cowardly friend?

Elegies 102

7 πολλοί τοι πόσιος καὶ βρώσιός εἰσιν ἑταῖροι,
ἐν δὲ σπουδαίῳ πρήγματι παυρότεροι

Many, for sure, are companions for food and drink,
but in grave matters you will find but few.

Elegies 115

8 πολλάκι γὰρ γνώμην ἐξαπατῶσ' ἰδέαι

All too often outward appearances deceive understanding.

Elegies 127

cf. Dante, Purgatory *22.28: 'più volte appaion cose, che danno a dubitar falsa matera' (it often happens that appearances give mistaken occasion for suspicions, tr. C.H. Sisson)*

9 χρήματα μὲν δαίμων καὶ παγκάκῳ ἀνδρὶ δίδωσιν,
ἀρετῆς δ' ὀλίγοις ἀνδράσι μοῖρ' ἕπεται

Heaven gives possessions even to the wicked,
but the gift of virtue comes to but a few.

Elegies 149

10 τίκτει τοι κόρος ὕβριν, ὅταν κακῷ ὄλβος ἕπηται
ἀνθρώπῳ

Surfeit breeds hubris when wealth comes to a wicked man.

Elegies 153

11 μήποτε ἀγοράσθαι ἔπος μέγα· οἶδε γὰρ οὐδείς
ἀνθρώπων ὅτι νὺξ χἠμέρη ἀνδρὶ τελεῖ

Never boast; for no one knows
what a night and day may bring.

Elegies 159

12 ἄλλ' ἄλλῳ κακόν ἐστι, τὸ δ' ἀτρεκὲς ὄλβιος οὐδείς
ἀνθρώπων ὁπόσους ἠέλιος καθορᾷ

One man hath this ill, another that; and no man under the sun is truly happy.

Elegies 167

13 πᾶς γὰρ ἀνὴρ πενίῃ δεδμημένος οὔτε τι εἰπεῖν
οὔθ' ἔρξαι δύναται, γλῶσσα δέ οἱ δέδεται

Any man that is subject to poverty never is able
Either to speak or act; nay, but his tongue is tied.

Translated by Frank Cole Babbitt (1927)

Elegies 177

14 οὐδείς τοι φεύγοντι φίλος καὶ πιστὸς ἑταῖρος·
τῆς δὲ φυγῆς ἐστιν τοῦτ' ἀνιηρότερον

Surely no man is friend and faithful comrade to one who is in exile; and this is more grievous than the exile itself.

Translated by J.M. Edmonds (1931)

Elegies 209

15 οἶνόν τοι πίνειν πουλὺν κακόν· ἢν δέ τις αὐτὸν
πίνῃ ἐπισταμένως, οὐ κακὸς, ἀλλ' ἀγαθός

Surely to drink much wine is an ill; yet if one drink it with knowledge, wine is not bad but good.

Translated by J.M. Edmonds (1931)

Elegies 211

16 πουλύπου ὀργὴν ἴσχε πολυπλόκου, ὃς ποτὶ πέτρῃ,
τῇ προσομιλήσῃ, τοῖος ἰδεῖν ἐφάνη·
νῦν μὲν τῇδ' ἐφέπου, τοτὲ δ' ἀλλοῖος χρόα γίνου.
κρέσσων τοι σοφίη γίνεται ἀτροπίης

Be crafty as the octopus which adopts the colour of the stone;
now follow this track, now take on a different hue;
better, surely, is cunning than inflexibility.

Elegies 215

17 ὅστις τοι δοκέει τὸν πλησίον ἴδμεναι οὐδέν,
ἀλλ' αὐτὸς μοῦνος ποικίλα δήνε' ἔχειν,
κεῖνός γ' ἄφρων ἐστὶ νόου βεβλαμμένος ἐσθλοῦ

Whoever thinks his neighbour knows nothing,
but he alone possesses wily arts,
surely is a fool and his mind perverted.

Elegies 221

18 ἀκρόπολις καὶ πύργος ἐὼν κενεόφρονι δήμῳ,
Κύρν', ὀλίγης τιμῆς ἔμμορεν ἐσθλὸς ἀνήρ

Being tower and castle to an empty-minded people
brings little credit even to the best.

Elegies 233

19 σοὶ μὲν ἐγὼ πτέρ' ἔδωκα, σὺν οἷσ' ἐπ' ἀπείρονα πόντον
πωτήσει, καὶ γῆν πᾶσαν ἀειρόμενος ῥηϊδίως

I have given thee wings to fly with ease
aloft the boundless sea and all the land.

Translated by J.M. Edmonds (1931)

Elegies 237

20 ὀλίγης παρὰ σεῦ οὐ τυγχάνω αἰδοῦς,
ἀλλ' ὥσπερ μικρὸν παῖδα λόγοις μ' ἀπατᾷς

You have no respect for me,
you lie to me as if I were a little child.

Elegies 253

21 κάλλιστον τὸ δικαιότατον· λῷστον δ' ὑγιαίνειν·
πρᾶγμα δὲ τερπνότατον, τοῦ τις ἐρᾷ, τὸ τυχεῖν

Righteousness is fairest, health is best,
but sweetest to win what your heart desires.

Elegies 255

inscribed at Delphi according to Aristotle (who does not mention Theognis as the author), Nicomachean Ethics *1099a.27; but see Aristotle 14*

22 ἵππος ἐγὼ καλὴ καὶ ἀεθλίη, ἀλλὰ κάκιστον
ἄνδρα φέρω, καί μοι τοῦτ' ἀνιηρότατον·
πολλάκι δ' ἠμέλλησα διαρρήξασα χαλινόν
φεύγεν ἀπωσαμένη τὸν κακὸν ἡνίοχον

I am a fair and champion steed, but my rider is a knave, and this grieveth me much; often have I almost broken my bridle, cast my evil rider, and run away.

Translated by J.M. Edmonds (1931)

Elegies 257

the horse may signify a city ruled by a bad man

23 τοὶ κακοὶ οὐ πάντες κακοὶ ἐκ γαστρὸς γεγόνασιν,
ἀλλ' ἄνδρεσσι κακοῖς συνθέμενοι φιλίην
ἔργα τε δείλ' ἔμαθον καὶ ἔπη δύσφημα καὶ ὕβριν
ἐλπόμενοι κείνους πάντα λέγειν ἔτυμα

Not all the bad are bad from womb,
but from association with bad men
have learnt base deeds and words and insolence
believing all they said was true.

Elegies 305

24 μήποτ' ἐπὶ σμικρῇ προφάσει φίλον ἄνδρ' ἀπολέσσαι
πειθόμενος χαλεπῇ, Κύρνε, διαβολίῃ

Never destroy a friendship on some trivial ground,
believing wicked slanderous tongues.

Translated by M.L. West (1994)

Elegies 323

25 ἥσυχος ὥσπερ ἐγὼ μέσσην ὁδὸν ἔρχεο ποσσίν

Walk quietly, as I, choosing the middle way.

Elegies 331

26 μήποτε φεύγοντ' ἄνδρα ἐπ' ἐλπίδι, Κύρνε, φιλήσῃς·
οὐδὲ γὰρ οἴκαδε βὰς γίνεται αὐτὸς ἔτι

Never befriend a man in exile with hopes of future benefit;
when he comes back he'll never be the same.

Elegies 333

27 πενίην
μητέρ' ἀμηχανίης ἔλαβον τὰ δίκαια φιλεῦντες
ἥτ' ἀνδρὸς παράγει θυμὸν ἐς ἀμπλακίην

Penury the mother of perplexity, Penury that misleadeth a man's heart to evil-doing.

Translated by J.M. Edmonds (1931)

Elegies 384

28 ἐν πενίῃ δ' ὅ τε δειλὸς ἀνὴρ ὅ τε πολλὸν ἀμείνων
φαίνεται

In poverty both the good and the bad
are seen for what they are.

Elegies 393

29 μηδὲν ἄγαν σπεύδειν· καιρὸς δ' ἐπὶ πᾶσιν ἄριστος

Never press on in haste; there is a best time for everything.

Elegies 401

30 πολλάκι γὰρ τὸ κακὸν κατακείμενον ἔνδον ἄμεινον

What is bad is often better to remain within.

Elegies 423

31 πάντων μὲν μὴ φῦναι ἐπιχθονίοισιν ἄριστον
μηδ' ἐσιδεῖν αὐγὰς ὀξέος ἠελίου·
φύντα δ' ὅπως ὤκιστα πύλας Ἀίδαο περῆσαι
καὶ κεῖσθαι πολλὴν γῆν ἐπαμησάμενον

Not to be born into the world is best,
nor to see the beams of the keen sun;
but being born, as swiftly as may be to pass the
gates of Hades, and lie under a heap of earth.

Translated by J.W. MacKail (1890)

Elegies 425

32 διδάσκων
οὔποτε ποιήσεις τὸν κακὸν ἄνδρ' ἀγαθόν

Not by teaching will you ever make the bad man good.

Translated by W.R.M. Lamb (1924)

Elegies 437

33 οὐδεὶς γὰρ πάντ' ἐστὶ πανόλβιος

No one is totally happy in all things.

Elegies 441

34 οὔ τοι σύμφορόν ἐστι γυνὴ νέα ἀνδρὶ γέροντι·
οὐ γὰρ πηδαλίῳ πείθεται ὡς ἄκατος,
οὐδ' ἄγκυραι ἔχουσιν· ἀπορρήξασα δὲ δεσμά
πολλάκις ἐκ νυκτῶν ἄλλον ἔχει λιμένα

A young wife is not proper to an old man; she is a boat that answers not the helm, nor do her anchors hold, but she slips her moorings often overnight to make another haven.

Translated by J.M. Edmonds (1931)

Elegies 457

35 ῥήϊον ἐξ ἀγαθοῦ θεῖναι κακὸν ἢ 'κ κακοῦ ἐσθλόν

'Tis easier to make bad of good than good of bad.

Translated by J.M. Edmonds (1931)

Elegies 577

36 μήτε κακοῖσιν ἀσῶ τι λίην φρένα μήτ' ἀγαθοῖσιν
τερφθῇς ἐξαπίνης, πρὶν τέλος ἄκρον ἰδεῖν

Do not grieve too much with ill fortune,
nor rejoice too quickly with good fortune,
before the end is in sight.

Elegies 593

37 οἱ δ' ἀγαθοὶ πάντων μέτρον ἴσασιν ἔχειν

The good know how to keep due measure in every matter.

Translated by J.M. Edmonds (1931)

Elegies 614

38 πᾶς τις πλούσιον ἄνδρα τίει, ἀτίει δὲ πενιχρόν

All respect the rich and slight the poor.

Elegies 621

39 ἀργαλέον φρονέοντα παρ' ἄφροσι πόλλ' ἀγορεύειν

It's hard for a man of sense to talk at length with fools.

Translated by M.L. West (1994)

Elegies 625

40 βουλεύου δὶς καὶ τρίς, ὅ τοί κ' ἐπὶ τὸν νόον ἔλθῃ·
ἀτηρὸς γάρ τοι λάβρος ἀνὴρ τελέθει

Take counsel twice and thrice before you act;
a hasty man hurries to his ruin.

Elegies 633

41 ἐλπὶς καὶ κίνδυνος ἐν ἀνθρώποισιν ὁμοῖα·
οὗτοι γὰρ χαλεποὶ δαίμονες ἀμφότεροι

Hope and risk are alike to men;
both are demons dangerous to deal with.

Elegies 637

42 πολλοὶ πὰρ κρητῆρι φίλοι γίνονται ἑταῖροι,
ἐν δὲ σπουδαίῳ πράγματι παυρότεροι

Many are comrades by the wine-jug,
but few in graver matters.

Elegies 643

43 ἤδη νῦν αἰδὼς μὲν ἐν ἀνθρώποισιν ὄλωλεν,
αὐτὰρ ἀναιδείη γαῖαν ἐπιστρέφεται

Respect for what is right has perished among men;
now shamelessness walks freely upon

the earth.

Elegies 647

44 ἀλλότριον κῆδος ἐφημέριον

Pain for another is pain for a day.

Translated by J.M. Edmonds (1931)

Elegies 656

45 καί τε πενιχρὸς ἀνὴρ
αἶψα μάλ' ἐπλούτησε· καὶ ὃς μάλα πολλὰ πέπαται
ἐξαπίνης πάντ' οὖν ὤλεσε νυκτὶ μιῇ

A poor man
may quickly become rich; and he that owns a lot
may suddenly lose all in but a single night.

Elegies 662

46 καὶ σώφρων ἥμαρτε, καὶ ἄφρονι πολλάκι δόξα
ἔσπετο, καὶ τιμῆς καὶ κακὸς ὢν ἔλαχεν

The wise man may err, and fame often cometh to the fool and honour to the wicked.

Translated by J.M. Edmonds (1931)

Elegies 665

47 πολλούς τοι κόρος ἄνδρας ἀπώλεσεν ἀφραίνοντας·
γνῶναι γὰρ χαλεπὸν μέτρον, ὅτ' ἐσθλὰ παρῇ

Surfeit, 'tis sure, destroyeth many a fool; because it is hard to know due measure when good things are to thy hand.

Translated by J.M. Edmonds (1931)

Elegies 693

48 δικαίως χρήματα ποιοῦ,
σώφρονα θυμὸν ἔχων ἐκτὸς ἀτασθαλίης

Earn money righteously,
keeping a sound mind, far from wickedness.

Elegies 753

49 τὰ μὲν μῶσθαι, τὰ δὲ δεικνύναι, ἄλλα δὲ ποιεῖν·
τί σφιν χρήσηται μοῦνος ἐπιστάμενος;

Inquire into this, explain that, create the other;
what use can it be if only you know of it?

Elegies 769

50 οὕτως οὐδὲν ἄρ' ἦν φίλτερον ἄλλο πάτρης

How true is it after all that there's no place like home.

Translated by J.M. Edmonds (1931)

Elegies 788

51 τοὺς ἀγαθοὺς ἄλλος μάλα μέμφεται, ἄλλος ἐπαινεῖ·
τῶν δὲ κακῶν μνήμη γίνεται οὐδεμία

Of the good, one man is loud in blame, another in praise;
men worth nothing nobody remembers.

Elegies 797

52 ἀνθρώπων δ' ἄψεκτος ἐπὶ χθονὶ γίνεται οὐδείς·
ἀλλ' ὡς λώϊον, εἰ μὴ πλεόνεσσι μέλοι

No man on earth is without blame; yet even so 'tis better not to be too much spoken of.

Translated by J.M. Edmonds (1931)

Elegies 799

53 βοῦς μοι ἐπὶ γλώσσῃ κρατερῷ ποδὶ λὰξ ἐπιβαίνων
ἴσχει κωτίλλειν καίπερ ἐπιστάμενον

An ox that setteth his strong hoof upon my tongue restraineth me from blabbing albeit I know.

Translated by J.M. Edmonds (1931)

Elegies 815

of people who keep silence for some weighty reason; later proverbial; cf. Aeschylus 3

54 πίστει χρήματ' ὄλεσσα, ἀπιστίῃ δ' ἐσάωσα

By trusting I lost money, and by distrusting saved it.

Translated by H.T. Riley (1872)

Elegies 831

55 εὖ μὲν κείμενον ἄστυ κακῶς θέμεν εὐμαρές ἐστιν,
εὖ δὲ θέμεν τὸ κακῶς κείμενον ἀργαλέον

'Tis easy to make a city's good plight ill,
but hard to make a city's ill plight good.

Translated by J.M. Edmonds (1931)

Elegies 845

56 ἔστιν ὁ μὲν χείρων ὁ δ' ἀμείνων ἔργον ἕκαστον·
οὐδεὶς δ' ἀνθρώπων αὐτὸς ἅπαντα σοφός

In everything one man is better and another worse; no man can possibly be skilled in all things.

Translated by J.M. Edmonds (1931)

Elegies 901

57 οὐ δύναμαι φωνῇ λίγ' ἀειδέμεν ὥσπερ ἀηδών …
ἀλλά με γῆρυς
ἐκλείπει σοφίης οὐκ ἐπιδευόμενον

I cannot sing sweet and clear like the nightingale, but 'tis that my voice, not without skill, has left me.

Translated by J.M. Edmonds (1931)

Elegies 939

58 εἶμι παρὰ στάθμην ὀρθὴν ὁδόν, οὐδετέρωσε
κλινόμενος· χρὴ γάρ μ' ἄρτια πάντα νοεῖν

I'll walk a path straight as a line, bending to neither side; for all my thoughts are right and true.

Translated by J.M. Edmonds (1931)

Elegies 945

59 πρήξας δ' οὐκ ἔπρηξα, καὶ οὐκ ἐτέλεσσα τελέσσας·
δρήσας δ' οὐκ ἔδρησ', ἤνυσα δ' οὐκ ἀνύσας

Acting, I did not act. Completing, I did not complete.
Achieving, I did not achieve.
Doing, I didn't.

Translated by Barbara Hughes Fowler (1992)

Elegies 953

60 ἄλλης δὴ κρήνης πίομαι ἡδυπότου

I drink from another and a purer spring.

Translated by J.M. Edmonds (1931)

Elegies 962

61 μήποτ' ἐπαινήσῃς, πρὶν ἂν εἰδῇς ἄνδρα σαφηνέως,
ὀργὴν καὶ ῥυθμὸν καὶ τρόπον ὄντιν' ἔχει

Don't ever praise a man until you know for sure
his temperament, his style, his turn of mind.

Translated by M.L. West (1994)

Elegies 963

62 αἶψα γὰρ ὥστε νόημα παρέρχεται ἀγλαὸς ἥβη

Glorious youth passes as swiftly as a thought.

Elegies 985

63 οἱ μὲν γὰρ κακότητα κατακρύψαντες ἔχουσι
πλούτῳ, τοὶ δ' ἀρετὴν οὐλομένῃ πενίῃ

Some keep wickedness concealed by wealth
and some their worth by poverty.

Elegies 1061

64 κρεῖσσόν τοι σοφίη καὶ μεγάλης ἀρετῆς

Wisdom is better even than great valour.

Translated by H.T. Riley (1872)

Elegies 1074

65 ἐλπὶς ἐν ἀνθρώποισι μόνη θεὸς ἐσθλὴ ἔτ' εστίν

Hope is the one good god yet left among mankind.

Translated by J.M. Edmonds (1931)

Elegies 1135

66 νοῦς ἀγαθὸν καὶ γλῶσσ'· ἀτὰρ ἐν παύροισι πέφυκεν
ἀνδράσιν, οἳ τούτων ἀμφοτέρων ταμίαι

Mind is a good thing and so is speech, but few there are who can control them both.

Elegies 1185

67 ἀργαλέος παρεὼν καὶ φίλος εὖτ' ἂν ἀπῇς

Troublesome you are when present and missed when absent.

Elegies 1207

68 οὔποθ' ὕδωρ καὶ πῦρ συμμείξεται, οὐδέ ποθ' ἡμεῖς
πιστοὶ ἐπ' ἀλλήλοις καὶ φίλοι ἐσσόμεθα

We shall never be true friends to one another any more than fire and water will mingle together.

Translated by J.M. Edmonds (1931)

Elegies 1245

69 δαμνᾷς ἀνθρώπων πυκινὰς φρένας, οὐδέ τίς ἐστιν
οὕτως ἴφθιμος καὶ σοφὸς ὥστε φυγεῖν

You overwhelm the sharpest wits of men, and there is not one as strong or wise enough to take flight from you.

Elegies 1386

of Aphrodite, goddess of love

70 οὐδέν, Κύρν', ἀγαθῆς γλυκερώτερόν ἐστι γυναικός

Nothing, dear Cyrnus, is sweeter than a good wife.

Fragment 1225 (Young)

THEOPHILUS

4th century BC
Athenian comic poet

1 μέγας
θησαυρός ἐστι καὶ βέβαιος μουσικὴ
ἅπασι τοῖς μαθοῦσι παιδευθεῖσί τε

A great
treasure, and durable, is music
to all who learn and all who teach it.

Fragment 5 (Kock) – 5 (K-A) – *Citharodos – The Lyre Player*

THEOPHRASTUS

*c.*371–*c.*287BC
Philosopher from Eresus in Lesbos, associate and successor of Aristotle

1 οὐκ ἂν σιωπήσειεν, οὐδ' εἰ τῶν χελιδόνων δόξειεν εἶναι λαλίστερος

Never to be silenced, a greater chatterer than a swallow!

Characters 7.7

2 ἡ δεισιδαιμονία δόξειεν ἂν εἶναι δειλία πρὸς τὸ δαιμόνιον

Superstition is but cowardice before the supernatural.

Characters 16.16

3 ἔστι δὲ ἡ μεμψιμοιρία ἐπιτίμησις παρὰ τὸ προσῆκον τῶν δεδομένων

Grumbling is undue censure of one's assigned lot.

Translated by R.C. Jebb (1841–1905)
Characters 17.1

4 τοὺς ἀλλοτρίους οὐ φιλοῦντα δεῖ κρίνειν ἀλλὰ κρίναντα φιλεῖν

Judge strangers first, then love them.

Fragment 74 (Wimmer)

5 ἐρωτηθεὶς ὑπό τινος, τί συνέχει τὸν ἀνθρώπων βίον, ἔφη, εὐεργεσία καὶ τιμὴ καὶ τιμωρία

When asked what holds mankind together, he answered, 'Kindness, honour and punishment.'

Fragment 86e (Wimmer)

6 μουσικῆς ἀρχὰς τρεῖς εἶναι ... λύπην ἡδονὴν ἐνθουσιασμὸν

Music has three sources, sorrow, joy, and enthusiasm.

Fragment 90 (Wimmer)

7 ὀλίγων οἱ ἀγαθοὶ νόμων δέονται· οὐ γὰρ τὰ πράγματα πρὸς τοὺς νόμους ἀλλ' οἱ νόμοι πρὸς τὰ πράγματα τίθενται

Good people need few laws; situations will not adapt to laws, but laws are enacted to fit the situation.

Fragment 106 (Wimmer)
cf. Solon 66

8 ἐρωτηθεὶς τί ἐστιν ἔρως, πάθος, ἔφη, ψυχῆς σχολαζούσης

When asked what Love is Theophrastus said, 'the passion of an idle soul'.

Fragment 114 (Wimmer)

9 ἔρως δέ ἐστιν ἀλογίστου τινὸς ἐπιθυμίας ὑπερβολὴ ταχεῖαν μὲν ἔχουσα τὴν πρόσοδον βραδεῖαν δὲ τὴν ἀπόλυσιν

Love is the excess of an irrational desire whose onset is swift but its deliverance slow.

Fragment 115 (Wimmer)

10 οἱ δὲ φθονοῦντες πρὸς τοῖς ἑαυτῶν κακοῖς καὶ ἐπὶ τοῖς τῶν ἄλλων ἀγαθοῖς λυπούμενοι διατελοῦσιν

Besides begrudging their own misfortunes they also resent the good fortune of others.

Fragment 156 (Wimmer)

11 οὐ χρὴ δὲ τὴν γυναῖκα δεινὴν ἐν τοῖς πολιτικοῖς ἀλλ' ἐν τοῖς οἰκονομικοῖς εἶναι

A woman should be knowledgeable in housekeeping, not in politics.

Fragment 158 (Wimmer)

12 θᾶττον ἔφη πιστεύειν δεῖν ἵππῳ ἀχαλίνῳ ἢ λόγῳ ἀσυντάκτῳ

Rather have confidence in an unbridled horse than an ill-composed discourse.

Diogenes Laertius, *Lives of Eminent Philosophers* 5.39

13 πρὸς σιωπῶντα ἔφη, εἰ μὲν ἀμαθὴς εἶ, φρονίμως ποιεῖς, εἰ δὲ πεπαίδευσαι, ἀφρόνως

If ignorant it is wise to keep silent, if educated it is foolish.

Diogenes Laertius, *Lives of Eminent Philosophers* 5.40.2

14 συνεχές τε ἔλεγε πολυτελὲς ἀνάλωμα εἶναι τὸν χρόνον

Time is the most valuable thing a man can spend.

Translated in *Bartlett's Familiar Quotations* (1980)

Diogenes Laertius, *Lives of Eminent Philosophers* 5.40.3

15 ῥήγνυσθαι σοφίης τόξον ἀνιέμενον

Slacken the bow of wisdom and it breaks.

Translated by R.D. Hicks (1925)

Diogenes Laertius, *Lives of Eminent Philosophers* 5.40.9

from the epigram on Theophrastus by Diogenes Laertius

16 πολλὰ τῶν ἡδέων ὁ βίος διὰ τὴν δόξαν καταλαζονεύεται

Many of the pleasures which life boasts are but in the seeming.

Translated by R.D. Hicks (1925)

Diogenes Laertius, *Lives of Eminent Philosophers* 5.40.13

17 ἡμεῖς γὰρ ὁπότ' ἀρχόμεθα ζῆν, τότ' ἀποθνήσκομεν

For when we are just beginning to live, lo! we die.

Translated by R.D. Hicks (1925)

Diogenes Laertius, *Lives of Eminent Philosophers* 5.41.1

one of the final messages to his disciples before he died

18 οὐδὲν οὖν ἀλυσιτελέστερόν ἐστι φιλοδοξίας

Nothing is so unprofitable as the love of glory.

Translated by R.D. Hicks (1925)

Diogenes Laertius, *Lives of Eminent Philosophers* 5.41.2

one of the final messages to his disciples before he died

19 χαλεπὸν καταμαντεύεσθαι περὶ τῶν νέων· ἀστόχαστος γὰρ ἡλικία καὶ πολλὰς ἔχουσα μεταβολὰς ἄλλοτε ἐπ' ἄλλο φερομένη

It is hard to predict the behaviour of the young, for they are without reflection, with many fluctuations, turning hither and thither.

Stobaeus, *Anthology* 4.11.16

20 ἰδὼν νεανίσκον τινὰ εὐχόμενον τοῖς θεοῖς νοῦν καὶ φρένας ἀγαθὰς αὐτῷ περιποιεῖν, ὦ νεανίσκε, εἶπεν, οὐ τοῖς εὐχομένοις νοῦς καὶ φρένες περιγίνονται, ἀλλὰ τοῖς μανθάνουσιν

Seeing a young man praying to the gods that he may be granted sense and a sound mind, 'Young man,' he said, 'these will come to you not by prayer but by study.'

Gnomologium Vaticanum Sententia 323 (Sternbach)

THEOPOMPUS (1)

King of Sparta, 720–675BC

1 ἀσφαλέστατα τηροίη τις τὴν βασιλείαν, εἰ τοῖς μὲν φίλοις μεταδιδοίη παρρησίας δικαίας, τοὺς δ' ἀρχομένους κατὰ δύναμιν μὴ περιορῴη ἀδικουμένους

To most securely keep a kingdom allow friends freedom of speech and suffer no subject to be wronged.

Translated by Frank Cole Babbitt (1931)

Plutarch, *Sayings of Spartans* 221d

THEOPOMPUS (2)

active *c.*410–*c.*370BC
Athenian Old Comedy poet

1 ὁ μὲν ἄρτος ἡδύ, τὸ δὲ φενακίζειν προσὸν ἔμβαμμα τοῖς ἄρτοις πονηρὸν γίγνεται

Bread is surely sweet; but if you cheat, adding sauces of the baser sort, the sweetness is all gone.

Fragment 8 (Kock) – 9 (A-K) – *Irini – Peace*

THEOPOMPUS (3)

377–c.320BC
Historian of Chios

1 ἀνδροφόνοι δὲ τὴν φύσιν ὄντες ἀνδρόπορνοι τὸν τρόπον ἦσαν ἐκαλοῦντο μὲν ἑταῖροι, ἦσαν δὲ ἑταῖραι

Men-slayers by nature, they were men-harlots in behaviour; they were called companions but were concubines.

Translated by Doreen C. Innes (1995, based on W. Rhys Roberts)

Fragment 225c (*FGrH*)

on the friends of Philip; quoted by Demetrius, On Style *27*

THRASYBULUS

beginning of 6th century BC
Tyrant of Miletus
see also Herodotus 100–101

1 σὺ δὲ ποίει οὕτως, ἤν γ' ἐθέλῃς καρτύνασθαι τὴν αἰσυμνητίην· τοὺς ἐξόχους τῶν πολιτέων ἐξαίρειν, ἤν τέ τις ἐχθρός τοι φαίνηται, ἤν τε μή. ὕποπτος γὰρ ἀνδρὶ αἰσυμνήτῃ καὶ τῶν τις ἑτάρων

This is what you must do if you want to strengthen your absolute rule: put to death those among the citizens who are pre-eminent, whether they are hostile to you or not. For to an absolute ruler even a friend is an object of suspicion.

Translated by R.D. Hicks (1925)

Diogenes Laertius, *Lives of Eminent Philosophers* 1.100

letter written to Periander, Tyrant of Corinth; cf. Herodotus 100

THRASYMACHUS

fl. c.430–400BC
Orator and sophist from Chalcedon

1 φημὶ γὰρ ἐγὼ εἶναι τὸ δίκαιον οὐκ ἄλλο τι ἢ τὸ τοῦ κρείττονος ξυμφέρον

Justice is nothing else than the interest of the stronger.

Translated by Benjamin Jowett (1817–1893)

Fragment 6a (D-K)

cf. the English proverb 'might is right'; and Plato, Republic *338c*

2 οἱ θεοὶ οὐχ ὁρῶσι τὰ ἀνθρώπινα· οὐ γὰρ ἂν τὸ μέγιστον τῶν ἐν ἀνθρώποις ἀγαθῶν παρεῖδον τὴν δικαιοσύνην· ὁρῶμεν γὰρ τοὺς ἀνθρώπους ταύτῃ μὴ χρωμένους

The gods do not see human affairs; otherwise they would not have overlooked the greatest of all blessings among mankind, Justice; for we see mankind not using this virtue.

Translated by Kathleen Freeman (1948)

Fragment 8 (D-K)

3 ἡ δὲ τέχνη σοφίη

My art is wisdom.

Testimonies, Fragment 8 (D-K)

his epitaph

THUCYDIDES

c.472–c.396BC
Athenian historian
Some of the finest passages of Thucydides are attributed by him to well-known personalities and are entered under their respective headings, e.g. Archidamus, Hermocrates, Nicias, Pericles, Themistocles
see also Anonymous 46

1 Θουκυδίδης Ἀθηναῖος ξυνέγραψε τὸν πόλεμον τῶν Πελοποννησίων καὶ Ἀθηναίων ὡς ἐπολέμησαν πρὸς ἀλλήλους, ἀρξάμενος εὐθὺς καθισταμένου καὶ ἐλπίσας μέγαν τε ἔσεσθαι καὶ ἀξιολογώτατον τῶν προγεγενημένων

Thucydides, an Athenian, wrote the history of the war between the Peloponnesians and the Athenians; he began at the moment that it broke out, believing that it would be a great war, and more memorable than any that had preceded it.

Translated by Richard Livingston (1968)

History of the Peloponnesian War 1.1.1

2 Λακεδαιμονίων γὰρ εἰ ἡ πόλις ἐρημωθείη, λειφθείη δὲ τά τε ἱερὰ καὶ τῆς κατασκευῆς τὰ ἐδάφη, πολλὴν ἂν οἶμαι ἀπιστίαν τῆς δυνάμεως προελθόντος πολλοῦ χρόνου τοῖς ἔπειτα πρὸς τὸ κλέος αὐτῶν εἶναι

If Sparta were laid waste and nothing be left but its temples and foundations of buildings, posterity would be hesitant to believe that its power was as great as its renown.

History of the Peloponnesian War 1.10.2

public buildings being much inferior to those in Athens

3 αἴτιον δ' ἦν οὐχ ἡ ὀλιγανθρωπία τοσοῦτον ὅσον ἡ ἀχρηματία

The cause was not so much lack of men as lack of money.

Translated by Charles Forster Smith (1919)

History of the Peloponnesian War 1.11.1

4 οἱ γὰρ ἄνθρωποι τὰς ἀκοὰς τῶν προγεγενημένων, καὶ ἢν ἐπιχώρια σφίσιν ᾖ, ὁμοίως ἀβασανίστως παρ' ἀλλήλων δέχονται

Men accept hearsay reports of former events, neglecting to test them, even though these events belong to the history of their own country.

History of the Peloponnesian War 1.20.1

5 οὕτως ἀταλαίπωρος τοῖς πολλοῖς ἡ ζήτησις τῆς ἀληθείας καὶ ἐπὶ τὰ ἑτοῖμα μᾶλλον τρέπονται

Most people will not take the trouble in finding out the truth, but are much more inclined to accept the first story they hear.

Translated by Rex Warner (1954)

History of the Peloponnesian War 1.20.3

6 τὰ δ' ἔργα τῶν πραχθέντων ἐν τῷ πολέμῳ οὐκ ἐκ τοῦ παρατυχόντος πυνθανόμενος ἠξίωσα γράφειν, οὐδ' ὡς ἐμοὶ ἐδόκει, ἀλλ' οἷς τε αὐτὸς παρῆν καὶ παρὰ τῶν ἄλλων ὅσον δυνατὸν ἀκριβείᾳ περὶ ἑκάστου ἐπεξελθών. ἐπιπόνως δὲ ηὑρίσκετο, διότι οἱ παρόντες τοῖς ἔργοις ἑκάστοις οὐ ταὐτὰ περὶ τῶν αὐτῶν ἔλεγον, ἀλλ' ὡς ἑκατέρων τις εὐνοίας ἢ μνήμης ἔχοι. καὶ ἐς μὲν ἀκρόασιν ἴσως τὸ μὴ μυθῶδες αὐτῶν ἀτερπέστερον φανεῖται· ὅσοι δὲ βουλήσονται τῶν τε γενομένων τὸ σαφὲς σκοπεῖν καὶ τῶν μελλόντων ποτὲ αὖθις κατὰ τὸ ἀνθρώπινον τοιούτων καὶ παραπλησίων ἔσεσθαι, ὠφέλιμα κρίνειν αὐτὰ ἀρκούντως ἕξει. κτῆμά τε ἐς αἰεὶ μᾶλλον ἢ ἀγώνισμα ἐς τὸ παραχρῆμα ἀκούειν ξύγκειται

As to the events of the war I have thought it my duty to describe them, not as ascertained from any chance informant nor as seemed to me probable, but only after investigating each detail with the greatest possible accuracy, both if present myself or hearing reports of others. This was a laborious task, because eyewitnesses gave differing reports arising sometimes from imperfect memory, sometimes from undue partiality for one side. The absence of fabled detail may seem to detract somewhat from the interest of my story; but whoever wishes to have a clear view of events and to use them as an aid to the interpretation of the future which, human nature being what it is, may well repeat itself in the same or a similar way, for these to adjudge my history profitable will be enough for me. And, indeed, it has been composed, not as a showpiece to be heard for the moment, but as a possession for all time.

History of the Peloponnesian War 1.22.2

cf. Herodotus 1, Plutarch 81

7 κτῆμά ἐς αἰεὶ

A possession for all time.

Translated by Charles Forster Smith (1919)

History of the Peloponnesian War 1.22.4

8 οὐ γὰρ ὁ δουλωσάμενος, ἀλλ' ὁ δυνάμενος μὲν παῦσαι περιορῶν δὲ ἀληθέστερον αὐτὸ δρᾷ

It is not he who enslaves others, but he who could prevent it yet looks on carelessly who in reality reduces others to slavery.

History of the Peloponnesian War 1.69.1

9 νεωτεροποιοὶ καὶ ἐπινοῆσαι ὀξεῖς καὶ ἐπιτελέσαι ἔργῳ ἃ ἂν γνῶσιν

Given to innovation, quick to form plans, quick to carry out their decisions.

History of the Peloponnesian War 1.70.2

of the Athenians

10 παρὰ δύναμιν τολμηταὶ καὶ παρὰ γνώμην κινδυνευταὶ καὶ ἐν τοῖς δεινοῖς εὐέλπιδες

Bold beyond their strength, venturesome beyond their better judgement, and cheerful in the face of dangers.

Translated by Charles Forster Smith (1919)

History of the Peloponnesian War 1.70.3

of the Athenians

11 μήτε αὐτοὺς ἔχειν ἡσυχίαν μήτε τοὺς ἄλλους ἀνθρώπους ἐᾶν

They are neither capable of living in peace nor will they allow others to do so.

History of the Peloponnesian War 1.70.9
of the Athenians

12 ἀνάγκη δὲ ὥσπερ τέχνης αἰεὶ τὰ ἐπιγιγνόμενα κρατεῖν

In politics, as in the arts, the new must always prevail over the old.

Translated by Charles Forster Smith (1919)
History of the Peloponnesian War 1.71.3

13 ἀλλ' αἰεὶ καθεστῶτος τὸν ἥσσω ὑπὸ τοῦ δυνατωτέρου κατείργεσθαι

It has ever been an established fact that the weaker is subdued by the stronger.

History of the Peloponnesian War 1.76.2.5

14 ὃν οὐδείς πω παρατυχὸν ἰσχύι τι κτήσασθαι προθεὶς τοῦ μὴ πλέον ἔχειν ἀπετράπετο

No one resists taking advantage of an opportunity to acquire power.

History of the Peloponnesian War 1.76.2.8

15 τοῦ δὲ πολέμου τὸν παράλογον ὅσος ἐστί, πρὶν ἐν αὐτῷ γενέσθαι προδιάγνωτε· μηκυνόμενος γὰρ φιλεῖ ἐς τύχας τὰ πολλὰ περιίστασθαι, ὧν ἴσον τε ἀπέχομεν καὶ ὁποτέρως ἔσται ἐν ἀδήλῳ κινδυνεύεται

Ponder the incalculable element of war before entering upon it; the longer it lasts, the more things tend to depend on accidents, and the outcome is unknown and precarious.

History of the Peloponnesian War 1.78.1

16 αἰδὼς σωφροσύνης πλεῖστον μετέχει

Self-control is the chief element in self-respect.

Translated by Charles Forster Smith (1919)
History of the Peloponnesian War 1.84.3
spoken by Archidamus, King of Sparta

17 καὶ μάχης γενομένης ἰσορρόπου ... ἐνόμισαν αὐτοὶ ἑκάτεροι οὐκ ἔλασσον ἔχειν ἐν τῷ ἔργῳ

An indecisive battle was fought, each side thinking they had not got the worst of it in the action.

Translated by Charles Forster Smith (1919)
History of the Peloponnesian War 1.105.5
a battle between Athenians and Corinthians at Megara, each side proceeding to set up a trophy of victory

18 ὅ τε γὰρ διὰ τὴν ἡδονὴν ὀκνῶν τάχιστ' ἂν ἀφαιρεθείη τῆς ῥᾳστώνης τὸ τερπνὸν δι' ὅπερ ὀκνεῖ, εἰ ἡσυχάζοι, ὅ τε ἐν πολέμῳ εὐτυχίᾳ πλεονάζων οὐκ ἐντεθύμηται θράσει ἀπίστῳ ἐπαιρόμενος

He who for the sake of comfort shrinks from war is likely, if tranquil, to soon forfeit the delights which made him shrink; and he who presumes upon success in war has failed to reflect how treacherous is the confidence which elates him.

Translated by Charles Forster Smith (1919)
History of the Peloponnesian War 1.120.4

19 πολλὰ γὰρ κακῶς γνωσθέντα ἀβουλοτέρων τῶν ἐναντίων τυχόντα κατωρθώθη, καὶ ἔτι πλείω καλῶς δοκοῦντα βουλευθῆναι ἐς τοὐναντίον αἰσχρῶς περιέστη

For though many things ill advised come to good effect against enemies worse advised, yet more, though well advised, have fallen but badly out against well advised enemies.

Translated by Thomas Hobbes (1629)
History of the Peloponnesian War 1.120.5.1

20 ἐνθυμεῖται γὰρ οὐδεὶς ὁμοίᾳ τῇ πίστει καὶ ἔργῳ ἐπεξέρχεται, ἀλλὰ μετ' ἀσφαλείας μὲν δοξάζομεν, μετὰ δέους δὲ ἐν τῷ ἔργῳ ἐλλείπομεν

For no man comes to execute a thing with the same confidence he premeditates it; for we deliver opinions in safety, whereas in the action itself we fail through fear.

Translated by Thomas Hobbes (1629)
History of the Peloponnesian War 1.120.5.4

21 ὃ γὰρ ἡμεῖς ἔχομεν φύσει ἀγαθόν, ἐκείνοις οὐκ ἂν γένοιτο διδαχῇ, ὃ δ' ἐκεῖνοι ἐπιστήμῃ προύχουσι, καθαιρετὸν ἡμῖν ἐστὶ μελέτῃ

They cannot acquire our natural qualities through instruction, whereas we can match their skill through practice.

History of the Peloponnesian War 1.121.4

22 ἥκιστα γὰρ πόλεμος ἐπὶ ῥητοῖς χωρεῖ

War least of all conforms to fixed rules.

Translated by Charles Forster Smith (1919)
History of the Peloponnesian War 1.122.1.5

23 ὁ μὲν εὐοργήτως αὐτῷ προσομιλήσας βεβαιότερος, ὁ δ' ὀργισθεὶς περὶ αὐτὸν οὐκ ἐλάσσω πταίει

He who keeps his temper is likely to succeed, he who loses it is sure to falter.

History of the Peloponnesian War 1.122.1.6

24 πάτριον γὰρ ὑμῖν ἐκ τῶν πόνων τὰς ἀρετὰς κτᾶσθαι

It is our heritage to win the rewards of virtue by toil.

Translated by Charles Forster Smith (1919)

History of the Peloponnesian War 1.123.1

25 εἴπερ βεβαιότατον τὸ ταὐτὰ ξυμφέροντα καὶ πόλεσι καὶ ἰδιώταις εἶναι

Identity of interest both among cities and among individuals is the surest of all guarantees.

Translated by Charles Forster Smith (1919)

History of the Peloponnesian War 1.124.1

26 ἐκ πολέμου μὲν γὰρ εἰρήνη μᾶλλον βεβαιοῦται, ἀφ' ἡσυχίας δὲ μὴ πολεμῆσαι οὐχ ὁμοίως ἀκίνδυνον

War gives peace its security, but one is still not safe from danger if, for the sake of quiet, one refuses to fight.

Translated by Rex Warner (1954)

History of the Peloponnesian War 1.124.2

cf. the Latin 'si vis pacem, para bellum', i.e. if you wish for peace, prepare for war

27 ἢ εἰ πολεμήσομεν ... καὶ ἐπὶ μεγάλῃ καὶ ἐπὶ βραχείᾳ ὁμοίως προφάσει μὴ εἴξοντες

If we mean to go to war, let us do so with the determination not to yield on any pretext, great or small.

Translated by Charles Forster Smith (1919)

History of the Peloponnesian War 1.141.1

28 Ἄρχεται δὲ ὁ πόλεμος ἐνθένδε ἤδη Ἀθηναίων καὶ Πελοποννησίων καὶ τῶν ἑκατέροις ξυμμάχων

Here then begins the war between Athenians and Peloponnesians and their respective allies.

History of the Peloponnesian War 2.1.1

29 περὶ πρῶτον ὕπνον

Just when they had fallen asleep – in the first hours of the night.

History of the Peloponnesian War 2.2.1

of the Thebans entering Plataeae, the first episode of the war; an expression still used today; cf. Aristophanes, Wasps *31; et al.*

30 ἔπειτα πολλῷ θορύβῳ αὐτῶν τε προσβαλόντων καὶ τῶν γυναικῶν καὶ τῶν οἰκετῶν ἅμα ἀπὸ τῶν οἰκιῶν κραυγῇ τε καὶ ὀλολυγῇ χρωμένων λίθοις τε καὶ κεράμῳ βαλλόντων

Then they charged upon them with a great uproar, while women and slaves on the house-tops, uttering screams and yells, kept pelting them with stones and tiles.

Translated by Charles Forster Smith (1919)

History of the Peloponnesian War 2.4.2

of the Plataeans

31 γεγενημένου δὲ τοῦ ἐν Πλαταιαῖς ἔργου καὶ λελυμένων λαμπρῶς τῶν σπονδῶν οἱ Ἀθηναῖοι παρεσκευάζοντο ὡς πολεμήσοντες, παρεσκευάζοντο δὲ καὶ Λακεδαιμόνιοι καὶ οἱ ξύμμαχοι

Now that the affair at Plataeae had occurred and the treaty had been glaringly violated, the Athenians began preparing for war, and the Lacedaemonians and their allies also began.

Translated by Charles Forster Smith (1919)

History of the Peloponnesian War 2.7.1

32 ἀρχόμενοι γὰρ πάντες ὀξύτερον ἀντιλαμβάνονται

There is always greater enthusiasm at the start.

History of the Peloponnesian War 2.8.1.2

33 νεότης ... οὐκ ἀκουσίως ὑπὸ ἀπειρίας ἥπτετο τοῦ πολέμου

The young men were unfamiliar enough with war and consequently far from unwilling to join in this one.

History of the Peloponnesian War 2.8.1.3

34 ἥδε ἡ ἡμέρα τοῖς Ἕλλησι μεγάλων κακῶν ἄρξει

This day will be the beginning of great misfortunes for all Hellenes.

History of the Peloponnesian War 2.12.3

Melesippus, a Spartan envoy, on being escorted out of Athenian borders

35 τὰ δὲ πολλὰ τοῦ πολέμου γνώμῃ καὶ χρημάτων περιουσίᾳ κρατεῖσθαι

Most things in war depend on abundance of money and wise policy.

History of the Peloponnesian War 2.13.2

36 χρησμολόγοι τε ᾖδον χρησμοὺς παντοίους, ὧν ἀκροᾶσθαι ὡς ἕκαστος ὥρμητο

Oracle-mongers came forward with prophecies of all kinds, eagerly listened to as each was eager to hear.

History of the Peloponnesian War 2.21.3

37 σχόντες δ' ἐν τῷ παράπλῳ ἐς Κεφαλληνίαν καὶ ἀπόβασιν ποιησάμενοι ἐς τὴν Κρανίων γῆν, ἀπατηθέντες ὑπ' αὐτῶν ἐξ ὁμολογίας τινὸς ... ἐπιθεμένων ἀπροσδοκήτοις τῶν Κρανίων

On their way down the coast they put in at Cephallenia, invading the territory of the Cranians; but the Cranians deceitfully pretended to come to terms and then suddenly set upon them.

History of the Peloponnesian War 2.33.3

Crane is one of the four districts of Cephallenia

38 μία δὲ κλίνη κενὴ φέρεται ἐστρωμένη τῶν ἀφανῶν, οἳ ἂν μὴ εὑρεθῶσιν ἐς ἀναίρεσιν

One empty bier, covered with a pall, is carried in the procession for the missing whose bodies could not be found for burial.

Translated by Charles Forster Smith (1919)

History of the Peloponnesian War 2.34.3

first known tribute to the 'Unknown Soldier' fallen in battle; inscribed on the present Unknown Soldier Cenotaph in Athens

39 τιθέασιν οὖν ἐς τὸ δημόσιον σῆμα, ὅ ἐστιν ἐπὶ τοῦ καλλίστου προαστείου τῆς πόλεως καὶ αἰεὶ ἐν αὐτῷ θάπτουσι τοὺς ἐκ τῶν πολέμων

Those fallen in war were always laid in the public cemetery, in the most beautiful suburb of Athens.

History of the Peloponnesian War 2.34.5

the Outer Ceramicus, just outside the Dipylon gate

40 τὸν γὰρ οὐκ ὄντα ἅπας εἴωθεν ἐπαινεῖν

It is customary that all praise the dead.

History of the Peloponnesian War 2.45.1

41 ὅσα τε πρὸς ἱεροῖς ἱκέτευσαν ἢ μαντείοις καὶ τοῖς τοιούτοις ἐχρήσαντο, πάντα ἀνωφελῆ ἦν, τελευτῶντές τε αὐτῶν ἀπέστησαν ὑπὸ τοῦ κακοῦ νικώμενοι

The supplications made at sanctuaries, or appeals to oracles and the like, were all futile, and at last men desisted from them, overcome by calamity.

Translated by Charles Forster Smith (1919)

History of the Peloponnesian War 2.47.4

of the plague that struck Athens in 430BC

42 ὑπερβιαζομένου γὰρ τοῦ κακοῦ οἱ ἄνθρωποι ... ἐς ὀλιγωρίαν ἐτράποντο καὶ ἱερῶν καὶ ὁσίων ὁμοίως

The catastrophe was so overpowering that men became indifferent to every rule of religion or of law.

Translated by Rex Warner (1954)

History of the Peloponnesian War 2.52.3

of the plague that struck Athens in 430BC

43 ὥστε ταχείας τὰς ἐπαυρέσεις καὶ πρὸς τὸ τερπνὸν ἠξίουν ποιεῖσθαι, ἐφήμερα τά τε σώματα καὶ τὰ χρήματα ὁμοίως ἡγούμενοι

They resolved to spend their money quickly and to spend it on pleasure, since money and life alike seemed equally ephemeral.

Translated by Rex Warner (1954)

History of the Peloponnesian War 2.53.2

of the plague that struck Athens in 430BC

44 θεῶν δὲ φόβος ἢ ἀνθρώπων νόμος οὐδεὶς ἀπεῖργε

No fear of god or law of man had a restraining influence.

Translated by Rex Warner (1954)

History of the Peloponnesian War 2.53.4

of the plague that struck Athens in 430BC

45 οἱ γὰρ ἄνθρωποι πρὸς ἃ ἔπασχον τὴν μνήμην ἐποιοῦντο

It was a case of people adapting their memories to suit their sufferings.

Translated by Rex Warner (1954)

History of the Peloponnesian War 2.54.3

46 πᾶσαν γὰρ δὴ ἰδέαν ἐπενόουν

There was no possible scheme that they did not examine.

History of the Peloponnesian War 2.77.2

47 εἰ μὴ λόγοις πείθοιεν, ἔργῳ πειρῷντο

If words don't prevail, try action.

History of the Peloponnesian War 2.81.2

48 οὐκ ἀντιτιθέντες τὴν ... ἐκ πολλοῦ ἐμπειρίαν τῆς σφετέρας δι' ὀλίγου μελέτης

Failing to take into account the difference between long experience and short practice.

History of the Peloponnesian War 2.85.2

49 φοβουμένους καὶ οὐ προθύμους

Downhearted and by no means eager for action.

Translated by Rex Warner (1954)

History of the Peloponnesian War 2.86.6

50 ταῖς μὲν τύχαις ἐνδέχεσθαι σφάλλεσθαι τοὺς ἀνθρώπους, ταῖς δὲ γνώμαις τοὺς αὐτοὺς αἰεὶ ὀρθῶς ἀνδρείους εἶναι

Men may fall from high fortunes, but brave men are rightly always considered brave.

History of the Peloponnesian War 2.87.3

51 ὑμῶν δὲ οὐδ' ἡ ἀπειρία τοσοῦτον λείπεται ὅσον τόλμῃ προύχετε

Your inexperience is more than counterbalanced by your superior daring.

Translated by Charles Forster Smith (1919)

History of the Peloponnesian War 2.87.4.1

52 ἄνευ δὲ εὐψυχίας οὐδεμία τέχνη πρὸς τοὺς κινδύνους ἰσχύει· φόβος γὰρ μνήμην ἐκπλήσσει, τέχνη δὲ ἄνευ ἀλκῆς οὐδὲν ὠφελεῖ

If a stout heart is lacking, all the skill in the world will not avail in the face of peril. Fear drives out all memory of previous instruction, and without the will to resist, skill is useless.

Translated by Rex Warner (1954)

History of the Peloponnesian War 2.87.4.4

53 τὰ δὲ πολλὰ τῶν πλεόνων καὶ ἄμεινον παρεσκευασμένων τὸ κράτος ἐστίν

Victory is generally on the side of those who are the more numerous and better prepared.

Translated by Charles Forster Smith (1919)

History of the Peloponnesian War 2.87.6

cf. the English proverb 'providence is always on the side of the big battalions'

54 καὶ ὅσα ἡμάρτομεν πρότερον, νῦν αὐτὰ ταῦτα προσγενόμενα διδασκαλίαν παρέξει

As to our earlier mistakes, the very fact that they were made will teach us a lesson.

Translated by Charles Forster Smith (1919)

History of the Peloponnesian War 2.87.7

55 ἐπαιάνιζόν τε ἅμα πλέοντες ὡς νενικηκότες

Singing a paean as they rowed, as if victorious already.

History of the Peloponnesian War 2.91.2

56 κατὰ σπουδὴν καὶ πολλῷ θορύβῳ

In haste and with much confusion.

Translated by Charles Forster Smith (1919)

History of the Peloponnesian War 2.94.2

57 τὰ ξυντομώτατα, ἢν αἰεὶ κατὰ πρύμναν ἵστηται τὸ πνεῦμα

By the shortest route, with a fair wind all the way.

History of the Peloponnesian War 2.97.1

58 λαμβάνειν μᾶλλον ἢ διδόναι

To receive rather than to give.

Translated by Rex Warner (1954)

History of the Peloponnesian War 2.97.4.3

of the Odrysians, contrary to Persian custom

59 οὐ γὰρ ἦν πρᾶξαι οὐδὲν μὴ διδόντα δῶρα

It was quite impossible to accomplish anything without giving gifts.

Translated by Charles Forster Smith (1919)

History of the Peloponnesian War 2.97.4.5

of the Odrysians

60 μεῖζον μέρος νέμοντες τῷ μὴ βούλεσθαι ἀληθῆ εἶναι

Giving weight to the hope that it may not be true.

History of the Peloponnesian War 3.3.1

61 εἰδότες οὔτε φιλίαν ἰδιώταις βέβαιον γιγνομένην οὔτε κοινωνίαν πόλεσιν ἐς οὐδέν, εἰ μὴ μετ' ἀρετῆς δοκούσης ἐς ἀλλήλους γίγνοιντο

Friendship between men will not last, nor a league between states, unless there is honesty of purpose on both sides.

History of the Peloponnesian War 3.10.1.2

62 ἐν γὰρ τῷ διαλλάσσοντι τῆς γνώμης καὶ αἱ διαφοραὶ τῶν ἔργων καθίστανται

Differences in men's actions arise from the diversity of their convictions.

Translated by Charles Forster Smith (1920)

History of the Peloponnesian War 3.10.1.5

63 τὸ δὲ ἀντίπαλον δέος μόνον πιστὸν ἐς ξυμμαχίαν

Only the fear of equal strength is a firm basis of alliance.

History of the Peloponnesian War 3.11.2

'ἀντίπαλον δέος' has become a Modern Greek proverbial expression

64 τηρήσαντες νύκτα χειμέριον ὕδατι καὶ ἀνέμῳ καὶ ἅμ' ἀσέληνον ἐξῆσαν

They waited for a stormy moonless night, with wind and rain.

History of the Peloponnesian War 3.22.1

65 εἴ τε μὴ παύσεται, ὀλίγους μὲν αὐτὸν τῶν ἐχθρῶν ἐς φιλίαν προσάξεσθαι, πολὺ δὲ πλείους τῶν φίλων πολεμίους ἕξειν

Unless he changes his ways he will make few enemies his friends and many friends his enemies.

History of the Peloponnesian War 3.32.2

66 ἐλπίδα οὐδὲ τὴν ἐλαχίστην εἶχον μή ποτε Ἀθηναίων τῆς θαλάσσης κρατούντων

They did not have the slightest expectation while the Athenians dominated the sea.

Translated by Charles Forster Smith (1920)

History of the Peloponnesian War 3.32.3

67 ὅτι χείροσι νόμοις ἀκινήτοις χρωμένη πόλις κρείσσων ἐστὶν ἢ καλῶς ἔχουσιν ἀκύροις

Imperfect laws kept valid give greater strength to a city than good laws unenforced.

Translated by Martin Hammond (2009)

History of the Peloponnesian War 3.37.3

68 εἰώθατε θεαταὶ μὲν τῶν λόγων ... ἀκροαταὶ δὲ τῶν ἔργων

You have come to be spectators of words and hearers of deeds!

Translated by Charles Forster Smith (1920)

History of the Peloponnesian War 3.38.4

69 ἁπλῶς τε ἀκοῆς ἡδονῇ ἡσσώμενοι καὶ σοφιστῶν θεαταῖς ἐοικότες καθημένοις μᾶλλον ἢ περὶ πόλεως βουλευομένοις

You would rather sit as spectators, enthralled by a sophist's oratory, than discuss the welfare of the state.

History of the Peloponnesian War 3.38.7

70 ἐλπίσαντες μακρότερα μὲν τῆς δυνάμεως, ἐλάσσω δὲ τῆς βουλήσεως, πόλεμον ἤραντο, ἰσχὺν ἀξιώσαντες τοῦ δικαίου προθεῖναι

Conceiving hopes which, though greater than their powers, were less than their ambition, they took up arms, presuming to put might before right.

Translated by Charles Forster Smith (1920)

History of the Peloponnesian War 3.39.3

71 εἴωθε δὲ τῶν πόλεων αἷς ἂν μάλιστα ἀπροσδόκητος καὶ δι' ἐλαχίστου εὐπραγία ἔλθῃ, ἐς ὕβριν τρέπειν

It is a fact that states, which suddenly and unexpectedly become prosperous, turn to arrogance.

History of the Peloponnesian War 3.39.4

72 πέφυκε γὰρ καὶ ἄλλως ἄνθρωπος τὸ μὲν θεραπεῦον ὑπερφρονεῖν, τὸ δὲ μὴ ὑπεῖκον θαυμάζειν

It is human nature to be contemptuous of those who pay court but to admire those who will not yield.

Translated by Charles Forster Smith (1920)

History of the Peloponnesian War 3.39.5

73 ξύγγνωμον δ' ἐστὶ τὸ ἀκούσιον

That which is unintentional is excusable.

Translated by Charles Forster Smith (1920)

History of the Peloponnesian War 3.40.2.1

74 τρισὶ τοῖς ἀξυμφορωτάτοις τῇ ἀρχῇ, οἴκτῳ καὶ ἡδονῇ λόγων καὶ ἐπιεικείᾳ, ἁμαρτάνειν

Error by pity, delight in eloquence, and clemency, the three influences most prejudicial to a ruling state.

Translated by Charles Forster Smith (1920)

History of the Peloponnesian War 3.40.2.3

spoken by Cleon

75 βραχέα ἡσθεῖσα μεγάλα ζημιώσεται

Paying a heavy penalty for a brief pleasure.

Translated by Charles Forster Smith (1920)
History of the Peloponnesian War 3.40.3

76 νομίζω δὲ δύο τὰ ἐναντιώτατα εὐβουλίᾳ εἶναι, τάχος τε καὶ ὀργήν

The two things most opposed to good counsel are haste and anger.

Translated by Charles Forster Smith (1920)
History of the Peloponnesian War 3.42.1

77 τούς τε λόγους ὅστις διαμάχεται μὴ διδασκάλους τῶν πραγμάτων γίγνεσθαι, ἢ ἀξύνετός ἐστιν ἢ ἰδίᾳ τι αὐτῷ διαφέρει

As for words, whoever contends that they are not to be guides of our actions is either dull of wit or has some private interest at stake.

Translated by Charles Forster Smith (1920)
History of the Peloponnesian War 3.42.2

78 πεφύκασί τε ἅπαντες καὶ ἰδίᾳ καὶ δημοσίᾳ ἁμαρτάνειν, καὶ οὐκ ἔστι νόμος ὅστις ἀπείρξει τούτου

All men are by nature prone to err, both in private and in public life, and there is no law which will prevent this.

Translated by Charles Forster Smith (1920)
History of the Peloponnesian War 3.45.3.1

79 ἐπεὶ διεξεληλύθασί γε διὰ πασῶν τῶν ζημιῶν οἱ ἄνθρωποι προστιθέντες, εἴ πως ἧσσον ἀδικοῖντο ὑπὸ τῶν κακούργων

Mankind has gone through the complete range of penalties, making them ever more severe, hoping that the offences of evil-doers might be abated.

History of the Peloponnesian War 3.45.3.3

80 ἢ τοίνυν δεινότερόν τι θανάτου δέος εὑρετέον ἐστὶν ἢ τόδε γε οὐδὲν ἐπίσχει

Some penalty more terrible than death must be invented; for we must concede that death is no deterrent.

History of the Peloponnesian War 3.45.4.1

81 ἀλλ᾽ ἡ μὲν πενία ἀνάγκῃ τὴν τόλμαν παρέχουσα, ἡ δ᾽ ἐξουσία ὕβρει τὴν πλεονεξίαν καὶ φρονήματι, αἱ δ᾽ ἄλλαι ξυντυχίαι ὀργῇ τῶν ἀνθρώπων, ὡς ἑκάστη τις κατέχεται ὑπ᾽ ἀνηκέστου τινὸς κρείσσονος ἐξάγουσιν ἐς τοὺς κινδύνους

Men are lured into hazardous enterprises by the constraint of poverty which makes them bold, by the insolence and pride of affluence which makes them greedy, and by the various passions engendered in the other conditions of human life as these are severally mastered by some mighty and irresistible impulse.

Translated by Charles Forster Smith (1920)
History of the Peloponnesian War 3.45.4.3

82 ἥ τε ἐλπὶς καὶ ὁ ἔρως ἐπὶ παντί, ὁ μὲν ἡγούμενος, ἡ δ᾽ ἐφεπομένη, καὶ ὁ μὲν τὴν ἐπιβουλὴν ἐκφροντίζων, ἡ δὲ τὴν εὐπορίαν τῆς τύχης ὑποτιθεῖσα πλεῖστα βλάπτουσι, καὶ ὄντα ἀφανῆ κρείσσω ἐστὶ τῶν ὁρωμένων δεινῶν

Hope and desire are everywhere; desire leads, hope attends; desire contrives the plan, hope suggests the facility of fortune; the two passions are most ruinous and, being unseen, prevail over seen dangers.

Translated by Charles Forster Smith (1920)
History of the Peloponnesian War 3.45.5

83 ἁπλῶς τε ἀδύνατον καὶ πολλῆς εὐηθείας, ὅστις οἴεται, τῆς ἀνθρωπείας φύσεως ὁρμωμένης προθύμως τι πρᾶξαι, ἀποτροπήν τινα ἔχειν νόμων ἰσχύι

It is impossible and simply absurd that human nature when bent upon some favourite project can be restrained by the strength of law.

Translated by Benjamin Jowett (1817–1893)
History of the Peloponnesian War 3.45.7

84 χρὴ δὲ τοὺς ἐλευθέρους οὐκ ἀφισταμένους σφόδρα κολάζειν, ἀλλὰ πρὶν ἀποστῆναι σφόδρα φυλάσσειν καὶ προκαταλαμβάνειν

Instead of severely punishing free peoples when they revolt, we ought to watch them carefully before and thus forestall their even thinking of such a thing.

History of the Peloponnesian War 3.46.6

85 ὅστις γὰρ εὖ βουλεύεται πρὸς τοὺς ἐναντίους κρείσσων ἐστὶν ἢ μετ᾽ ἔργων ἰσχύος ἀνοίᾳ ἐπιών

He who is wise in counsel is stronger against the foe than he who recklessly rushes on with brute force.

Translated by Charles Forster Smith (1920)
History of the Peloponnesian War 3.48.2

86 ᾧ τὰ μὲν ἀληθῆ ἀποκρίνασθαι ἐναντία γίγνεται, τὰ δὲ ψευδῆ ἔλεγχον ἔχει

A truthful answer is against our interests and a false one will be exposed at once.

Translated by Charles Forster Smith (1920)
History of the Peloponnesian War 3.53.2

87 οὐκ εἰκὸς ἀμνημονεῖν

It is not to your advantage to forget.

History of the Peloponnesian War 3.54.5

88 τοῦ μὲν ὀρθοῦ φανεῖσθε οὐκ ἀληθεῖς κριταὶ ὄντες, τὸ δὲ ξυμφέρον μᾶλλον θεραπεύοντες

You will show yourselves not true judges of what is right, but rather fostering your own advantage.

History of the Peloponnesian War 3.56.3

89 οἱ γὰρ ἄγοντες παρανομοῦσι μᾶλλον τῶν ἑπομένων

It is those who lead that break the law rather than those who follow.

History of the Peloponnesian War 3.65.2

90 ἔργων ἀγαθῶν ὄντων βραχεῖα ἡ ἀπαγγελία ἀρκεῖ

Honourable actions need only a brief report.

Translated by Martin Hammond (2009)
History of the Peloponnesian War 3.67.6

91 ἐπ' ἀδίκοις ἔργοις λόγους καλοὺς ζητήσει

Seeking fair words after foul deeds.

Translated by Charles Forster Smith (1920)
History of the Peloponnesian War 3.67.7

92 αἵ τε γυναῖκες αὐτοῖς τολμηρῶς ξυνεπελάβοντο βάλλουσαι ἀπὸ τῶν οἰκιῶν τῷ κεράμῳ καὶ παρὰ φύσιν ὑπομένουσαι τὸν θόρυβον

The women boldly joined in the fight, hurling tiles from the houses and enduring the uproar with a courage beyond their sex.

History of the Peloponnesian War 3.74.1
of the women of Corcyra (Corfu)

93 πᾶσά τε ἰδέα κατέστη θανάτου, καὶ οἷον φιλεῖ ἐν τῷ τοιούτῳ γίγνεσθαι, οὐδὲν ὅ τι οὐ ξυνέβη καὶ ἔτι περαιτέρω. καὶ γὰρ πατὴρ παῖδα ἀπέκτεινε καὶ ἀπὸ τῶν ἱερῶν ἀπεσπῶντο καὶ πρὸς αὐτοῖς ἐκτείνοντο, οἱ δέ τινες καὶ περιοικοδομηθέντες ἐν τοῦ Διονύσου τῷ ἱερῷ ἀπέθανον

Death in every form ensued, and whatever horrors are wont to be perpetrated at such times all happened then – aye, and even worse. For father slew son, men were dragged from the temples and slain near them, and some were even walled up in the temple of Dionysus and perished there.

Translated by Charles Forster Smith (1920)
History of the Peloponnesian War 3.81.5
among Corcyraean factions

94 ἐπέπεσε πολλὰ καὶ χαλεπὰ κατὰ στάσιν ταῖς πόλεσι, γιγνόμενα μὲν καὶ αἰεὶ ἐσόμενα, ἕως ἂν ἡ αὐτὴ φύσις ἀνθρώπων ᾖ

The sufferings which civil strife entailed were many and terrible, such as have occurred and always will occur as long as the nature of mankind remains the same.

Translated by Richard Crawley (1874)
History of the Peloponnesian War 3.82.2.1

95 ἐν μὲν γὰρ εἰρήνῃ καὶ ἀγαθοῖς πράγμασιν αἵ τε πόλεις καὶ οἱ ἰδιῶται ἀμείνους τὰς γνώμας ἔχουσι διὰ τὸ μὴ ἐς ἀκουσίους ἀνάγκας πίπτειν

In peace and prosperity both states and individuals have gentler feelings, because men are not then forced to face dire necessity.

Translated by Charles Forster Smith (1920)
History of the Peloponnesian War 3.82.2.5

96 ὁ δὲ πόλεμος ὑφελὼν τὴν εὐπορίαν τοῦ καθ' ἡμέραν βίαιος διδάσκαλος

War, which robs men of their daily needs, is a rough schoolmaster.

Translated by Charles Forster Smith (1920)
History of the Peloponnesian War 3.82.2.7

97 καὶ τὴν εἰωθυῖαν ἀξίωσιν τῶν ὀνομάτων ἐς τὰ ἔργα ἀντήλλαξαν τῇ δικαιώσει

Even the meaning of words was changed as men considered expedient.

History of the Peloponnesian War 3.82.4.1

98 τόλμα μὲν γὰρ ἀλόγιστος ἀνδρεία φιλέταιρος ἐνομίσθη, μέλλησις δὲ προμηθὴς δειλία εὐπρεπής, τὸ δὲ σῶφρον τοῦ ἀνάνδρου πρόσχημα, καὶ τὸ πρὸς

ἅπαν ξυνετὸν ἐπὶ πᾶν ἀργόν

Reckless audacity came to be regarded as courageous loyalty to party, prudent hesitation as specious cowardice, moderation as a cloak for unmanly weakness, and to be clever in everything was to do naught in anything.

Translated by Charles Forster Smith (1920)

History of the Peloponnesian War 3.82.4.2

99 καὶ τὰς ἐς σφᾶς αὐτοὺς πίστεις οὐ τῷ θείῳ νόμῳ μᾶλλον ἐκρατύνοντο ἢ τῷ κοινῇ τι παρανομῆσαι

Their pledges to one another were confirmed not so much by divine law as by common transgression of the law.

Translated by Charles Forster Smith (1920)

History of the Peloponnesian War 3.82.6

100 ῥᾷον δ' οἱ πολλοὶ κακοῦργοι δεξιοὶ κέκληνται ἢ ἀμαθεῖς ἀγαθοί

Men are more willing to be called clever rogues than honest simpletons.

History of the Peloponnesian War 3.82.7

101 πάντων δ' αὐτῶν αἴτιον ἀρχὴ ἡ διὰ πλεονεξίαν καὶ φιλοτιμίαν

The desire for power, inspired by greed and ambition, was the cause of all these evils.

History of the Peloponnesian War 3.82.8

102 τὸ εὔηθες, οὗ τὸ γενναῖον πλεῖστον μετέχει, καταγελασθὲν ἠφανίσθη, τὸ δὲ ἀντιτετάχθαι ἀλλήλοις τῇ γνώμῃ ἀπίστως ἐπὶ πολὺ διήνεγκεν

Kind-heartedness, the chief element of a noble mind, was ridiculed and disappeared, while antagonism, combined with mistrust, prevailed.

History of the Peloponnesian War 3.83.1

103 καὶ οἱ φαυλότεροι γνώμην ὡς τὰ πλείω περιεγίγνοντο

It was generally those of meaner intellect who won the day.

Translated by Charles Forster Smith (1920)

History of the Peloponnesian War 3.83.3

104 ἐπὶ πολὺ γὰρ ἐποίει τῆς δόξης ἐν τῷ τότε τοῖς μὲν ἠπειρώταις μάλιστα εἶναι καὶ τὰ πεζὰ κρατίστοις, τοῖς δὲ θαλασσίοις τε καὶ ταῖς ναυσὶ πλεῖστον προύχειν

At this time the Lacedaemonians were renowned as a land power, and invincible with their army, and the Athenians as seamen, and vastly superior with their fleet.

History of the Peloponnesian War 4.12.3

105 οἱ ἀήθως τι ἀγαθὸν λαμβάνοντες τῶν ἀνθρώπων αἰεὶ τοῦ πλέονος ἐλπίδι ὀρέγονται

Those who achieve some unwonted success are always led on by hope to grasp at more.

Translated by Charles Forster Smith (1920)

History of the Peloponnesian War 4.17.4

106 ὥστε οὐκ εἰκὸς ὑμᾶς ... τὸ τῆς τύχης οἴεσθαι αἰεὶ μεθ' ὑμῶν ἔσεσθαι

It is unreasonable for you to expect that fortune will always be on your side.

History of the Peloponnesian War 4.18.3

107 πεφύκασί τε τοῖς μὲν ἑκουσίως ἐνδοῦσιν ἀνθησσᾶσθαι μεθ' ἡδονῆς, πρὸς δὲ τὰ ὑπεραυχοῦντα καὶ παρὰ γνώμην διακινδυνεύειν

It is natural for men joyfully to give way to those who give way themselves, but to fight to the bitter end, even contrary to their better judgement, against an overbearing foe.

History of the Peloponnesian War 4.19.4

108 τὰς μὲν σπονδάς ... ἤδη σφίσιν ἐνόμιζον ἑτοίμους εἶναι, ὁπόταν βούλωνται ποιεῖσθαι πρὸς αὐτούς, τοῦ δὲ πλέονος ὠρέγοντο

They could have made peace at any time, but they were greedy for more.

History of the Peloponnesian War 4.21.2

of the Athenians

109 οἱ δέ, οἷον ὄχλος φιλεῖ ποιεῖν, ὅσῳ μᾶλλον ὁ Κλέων ... ἐξανεχώρει τὰ εἰρημένα τόσῳ ... ἐκείνῳ ἐπεβόων πλεῖν

And, as is the way with a crowd, the more Cleon tried to back out of his own proposal the more insistently they urged him to sail.

Translated by Charles Forster Smith (1920)

History of the Peloponnesian War 4.28.3

110 εἰ δ' αὖ ἐς δασὺ χωρίον βιάζοιτο ὁμόσε ἰέναι, τοὺς ἐλάσσους, ἐμπείρους δὲ τῆς χώρας, κρείσσους ἐνόμιζε τῶν πλεόνων ἀπείρων

If he should force his way into the thicket and there close with the enemy, the smaller force which was acquainted with the ground would, he thought, be stronger than the larger number who were unacquainted with it.

Translated by Charles Forster Smith (1920)
History of the Peloponnesian War 4.29.4

111 τοὺς γὰρ Λακεδαιμονίους οὔτε λιμῷ οὔτ' ἀνάγκῃ οὐδεμιᾷ ἠξίουν τὰ ὅπλα παραδοῦναι, ἀλλὰ ἔχοντας καὶ μαχομένους ὡς ἐδύναντο ἀποθνήσκειν

The Lacedaemonians were known to never surrender their arms, even in famine or under duress, but to fight to the last and die sword in hand.

History of the Peloponnesian War 4.40.1

112 πολλοῦ ἂν ἄξιον εἶναι τὸν ἄτρακτον ... εἰ τοὺς ἀγαθοὺς διεγίγνωσκε

The arrow would indeed be a valuable weapon if it could pick out the brave.

Translated by Benjamin Jowett (1817–1893)
History of the Peloponnesian War 4.40.2

113 τὸ μὴ ἐπιχειρούμενον αἰεὶ ἐλλιπὲς ἦν τῆς δοκήσεώς τι πράξειν

To miss an opportunity is to lose a victory.

Translated by Benjamin Jowett (1817–1893)
History of the Peloponnesian War 4.55.2

114 πλεῖστον δὴ χρόνον αὕτη ὑπ' ἐλαχίστων γενομένη ἐκ στάσεως μετάστασις ξυνέμεινεν

No government based on revolution effected by so few ever lasted so long a time.

Translated by Charles Forster Smith (1920)
History of the Peloponnesian War 4.74.4

115 ὧν χρὴ μνησθέντας ἡμᾶς τούς τε πρεσβυτέρους ὁμοιωθῆναι τοῖς πρὶν ἔργοις, τούς τε νεωτέρους ... πειρᾶσθαι μὴ αἰσχῦναι τὰς προσηκούσας ἀρετάς

Remembering these things, let the older men among us emulate their former deeds, and the younger try not to disgrace the virtues which are their heritage.

Translated by Charles Forster Smith (1920)
History of the Peloponnesian War 4.92.7

116 εἰωθότες οἱ ἄνθρωποι οὗ μὲν ἐπιθυμοῦσιν ἐλπίδι ἀπερισκέπτῳ διδόναι, ὃ δὲ μὴ προσίενται λογισμῷ αὐτοκράτορι διωθεῖσθαι

When they desire something, men are inclined to trust in mindless hope and to reject unwisely whatever they do not care for.

History of the Peloponnesian War 4.108.4

117 ὅπερ φιλεῖ μεγάλα στρατόπεδα ἀσαφῶς ἐκπλήγνυσθαι

Large armies are wont to be smitten with unaccountable panic.

Translated by Charles Forster Smith (1920)
History of the Peloponnesian War 4.125.1

118 πολέμου δὲ καθεστῶτος αἰεὶ ἀνάγκην εἶναι τοὺς προύχοντας ἀπὸ τῶν ξυμφορῶν διαβάλλεσθαι

As long as there is war it must always be that the leaders are accused in the event of any misfortunes.

History of the Peloponnesian War 5.17.1

119 αὐτονόμους εἶναι καὶ αὐτοτελεῖς καὶ αὐτοδίκους

Governed by their own laws, taxed by their own state, and judged by their own judges.

Translated by Rex Warner (1954)
History of the Peloponnesian War 5.18.2

120 εἰδότες ἔργων ἐκ πολλου μελέτην πλείω σῴζουσαν ἢ λόγων δι' ὀλίγου καλῶς ῥηθεῖσαν παραίνεσιν

Long and continued training is more important for survival than any admonition just before going into action, however well spoken.

History of the Peloponnesian War 5.69.2

121 ἐπισταμένους ... ὅτι δίκαια μὲν ἐν τῷ ἀνθρωπείῳ λόγῳ ἀπὸ τῆς ἴσης ἀνάγκης κρίνεται, δυνατὰ δὲ οἱ προύχοντες πράσσουσι καὶ οἱ ἀσθενεῖς ξυγχωροῦσιν

We all know that justice is arrived at in human arguments only when the necessity on both sides is equal, and that the powerful exact what they can, while the weak yield what they must.

Translated by Charles Forster Smith (1921)
History of the Peloponnesian War 5.89.1

quoted by Margaret Thatcher in her speech on the 40th Anniversary of the United Nations, 24 October 1985: 'The strong do what they will and the weak suffer what they must'; this and the following passages (to Thucydides 132) are from 'The Melian Controversy' after which the Athenians, based on a hasty decision (repealed the next day), ignominiously annihilated the Melians

122 τοὺς μὲν ὑπάρχοντας πολεμίους μεγαλύνετε, τοὺς δὲ μηδὲ μελλήσαντας γενέσθαι ἄκοντας ἐπάγεσθε

You are strengthening your enemies and provoking those who would be your friends

History of the Peloponnesian War 5.98.1

123 τὰ τῶν πολέμων ἔστιν ὅτε κοινοτέρας τὰς τύχας λαμβάνοντα ἢ κατὰ τὸ διαφέρον ἑκατέρων πλῆθος

The fortunes of war are sometimes impartial and not always on the side of numbers.

Translated by Benjamin Jowett (1817–1893)

History of the Peloponnesian War 5.102.1.1

124 καὶ ἡμῖν τὸ μὲν εἶξαι εὐθὺς ἀνέλπιστον, μετὰ δὲ τοῦ δρωμένου ἔτι καὶ στῆναι ἐλπὶς ὀρθῶς

For us, to yield is at once to give up hope; but if we make an effort, there is still hope that we may stand erect.

Translated by Charles Forster Smith (1921)

History of the Peloponnesian War 5.102.1.3

125 ἐπειδὰν … ἐπιλίπωσιν αἱ φανεραὶ ἐλπίδες, ἐπὶ τὰς ἀφανεῖς καθίστανται, μαντικήν τε καὶ χρησμοὺς καὶ ὅσα τοιαῦτα μετ' ἐλπίδων λυμαίνεται

When visible hopes fail we turn to the invisible, to prophecies and oracles and the like which, with the hopes they inspire, bring men to ruin.

History of the Peloponnesian War 5.103.2

126 ἡγούμεθα γὰρ τό τε θεῖον δόξῃ, τὸ ἀνθρώπειόν τε σαφῶς διὰ παντὸς ὑπὸ φύσεως ἀναγκαίας, οὗ ἂν κρατῇ, ἄρχειν

Of the gods we hold the belief, and of men we know, that by their nature whenever they can rule, rule they will.

History of the Peloponnesian War 5.105.2

127 μακαρίσαντες ὑμῶν τὸ ἀπειρόκακον οὐ ζηλοῦμεν τὸ ἄφρον

While we admire your simplicity, we do not envy your folly.

Translated by Charles Forster Smith (1921)

History of the Peloponnesian War 5.105.3

128 τὰ μὲν ἡδέα καλὰ νομίζουσι, τὰ δὲ ξυμφέροντα δίκαια

They consider what is agreeable to be honourable, and what is expedient just.

Translated by Charles Forster Smith (1921)

History of the Peloponnesian War 5.105.4

129 οὐδὲν ἐν τοσούτῳ λόγῳ εἰρήκατε

You have not in this long discussion advanced a single argument.

Translated by Charles Forster Smith (1921)

History of the Peloponnesian War 5.111.2

130 τὴν ἐν τοῖς αἰσχροῖς καὶ προύπτοις κινδύνοις πλεῖστα διαφθείρουσαν ἀνθρώπους αἰσχύνην τρέψεσθε

The fear of disgrace often ruins those who are confronted by foreseeable and possibly shameful dangers.

History of the Peloponnesian War 5.111.3

131 ἐνθυμεῖσθε … ὅτι περὶ πατρίδος βουλεύεσθε, ἧς μιᾶς πέρι καὶ ἐς μίαν βουλὴν τυχοῦσάν τε καὶ μὴ κατορθώσασαν ἔσται

Remember that your fatherland is at stake, your one and only fatherland, and that upon one decision only will depend her fate for weal or woe.

Translated by Charles Forster Smith (1921)

History of the Peloponnesian War 5.111.5

132 ἀλλ' οὖν μόνοι γε ἀπὸ τούτων τῶν βουλευμάτων, ὡς ἡμῖν δοκεῖτε, τὰ μὲν μέλλοντα τῶν ὁρωμένων σαφέστερα κρίνετε, τὰ δὲ ἀφανῆ τῷ βούλεσθαι ὡς γιγνόμενα ἤδη θεᾶσθε

Judging by your decision, it seems that you regard what is unknown as more certain than what is obvious – only because you wish it so.

History of the Peloponnesian War 5.113.1

The Melian Dialogue – the passage is spoken by the Athenians after the Melians decide to protect their liberty

133 νομίζων ὁμοίως ἀγαθὸν πολίτην εἶναι ὃς ἂν καὶ τοῦ σώματός τι καὶ τῆς οὐσίας

προνοῆται· μάλιστα γὰρ ἂν ὁ τοιοῦτος καὶ τὰ τῆς πόλεως δι' ἑαυτὸν βούλοιτο ὀρθοῦσθαι

I esteem the citizen who protects his life and property; for he will uphold the affairs of the state, even if for his own advantage.

History of the Peloponnesian War 6.9.2

Nicias' speech against the expedition to Sicily

134 ἀνόητον δ' ἐπὶ τοιούτους ἰέναι ὧν κρατήσας τε μὴ κατασχήσει τις καὶ μὴ κατορθώσας μὴ ἐν τῷ ὁμοίῳ καὶ πρὶν ἐπιχειρῆσαι ἔσται

It is folly to go to war if victory will not lead to control, and defeat will render the situation worse than before.

History of the Peloponnesian War 6.11.1

Nicias' speech against the expedition to Sicily

135 τὰ γὰρ διὰ πλείστου πάντες ἴσμεν θαυμαζόμενα καὶ τὰ πεῖραν ἥκιστα τῆς δόξης δόντα

It is things that are farthest off and least allow a test of their reputation which excite wonder.

Translated by Charles Forster Smith (1921)

History of the Peloponnesian War 6.11.4

Nicias' speech against the expedition to Sicily

136 τὸ πρᾶγμα μέγα εἶναι καὶ μὴ οἷον νεωτέρῳ βουλεύσασθαί τε καὶ ὀξέως μεταχειρίσαι

The matter is one of great seriousness, and not such as a youth may decide and rashly take in hand.

Translated by Charles Forster Smith (1921)

History of the Peloponnesian War 6.12.2

Nicias' speech against the expedition to Sicily

137 ἐπιθυμίᾳ μὲν ἐλάχιστα κατορθοῦνται, προνοίᾳ δὲ πλεῖστα

Few successes are won by greed, but very many by foresight.

Translated by Charles Forster Smith (1921)

History of the Peloponnesian War 6.13.1

Nicias' speech against the expedition to Sicily

138 προύχοντα οὐ μόνον ἐπιόντα τις ἀμύνεται, ἀλλὰ καὶ ὅπως μὴ ἔπεισι προκαταλαμβάνει

Do not wait for the attack of a superior power to go on the defence, rather take precaution not to be attacked.

History of the Peloponnesian War 6.18.2

from Alcibiades' speech to the Athenians

139 ἐλάχιστα τῇ τύχῃ παραδοὺς ἐμαυτὸν βούλομαι ἐκπλεῖν, παρασκευῇ δὲ ἀπὸ τῶν εἰκότων ἀσφαλής

I wish, when I set sail, to have committed myself as little as possible to chance, but so far as preparation is concerned to be, in all human probability, safe.

Translated by Charles Forster Smith (1921)

History of the Peloponnesian War 6.23.3

Nicias' warning to the Athenians after they are clearly in support of war upon hearing Alcibiades' speech

140 ὥστε διὰ τὴν ἄγαν τῶν πλειόνων ἐπιθυμίαν, εἴ τῳ ἄρα καὶ μὴ ἤρεσκε, δεδιὼς μὴ ἀντιχειροτονῶν κακόνους δόξειεν εἶναι τῇ πόλει ἡσυχίαν ἦγεν

In view of the exceeding eagerness of the majority those opposed kept silent, so as not to seem disloyal to the state.

History of the Peloponnesian War 6.24.4

on the silencing power of democracy

141 καὶ ἐν τῷ παρόντι καιρῷ, ὡς ἤδη ἔμελλον μετὰ κινδύνων ἀλλήλους ἀπολιπεῖν, μᾶλλον αὐτοὺς ἐσῄει τὰ δεινὰ ἢ ὅτε ἐψηφίζοντο πλεῖν

But now, when the time had come to bid farewell, they realized the dangers much more than when they had voted to set sail.

History of the Peloponnesian War 6.30.2

on the day the Athenians were manning the expedition to Sicily – one of the few passages in Thucydides with a personal touch

142 οἱ γὰρ δεδιότες ἰδίᾳ τι βούλονται τὴν πόλιν ἐς ἔκπληξιν καθιστάναι, ὅπως τῷ κοινῷ φόβῳ τὸ σφέτερον ἐπηλυγάζωνται

Being afraid themselves they wish to plunge the city into a state of alarm, so that in the general panic their own be overshadowed.

History of the Peloponnesian War 6.36.2

143 τὸν γὰρ ἐχθρὸν οὐχ ὧν δρᾷ μόνον, ἀλλὰ καὶ τῆς διανοίας προαμύνεσθαι χρή, εἴπερ καὶ μὴ προφυλαξάμενός τις προπείσεται

Forestall not only the actions of the enemy but his intentions also; he who does not act first will suffer first.

History of the Peloponnesian War 6.38.4

144 ἐγὼ δέ φημι πρῶτα μὲν δῆμον ξύμπαν ὠνομάσθαι, ὀλιγαρχίαν δὲ μέρος, ἔπειτα φύλακας μὲν ἀρίστους εἶναι χρημάτων τοὺς πλουσίους, βουλεῦσαι δ' ἂν βέλτιστα τοὺς ξυνετούς, κρῖναι δ' ἂν ἀκούσαντας ἄριστα τοὺς πολλούς

I say, first, that democracy is a name for all, oligarchy for only a part; next, while the wealthy are the best guardians of property, the wise are the best counsellors, and the people, after hearing matters discussed, the best judges.

Translated by Charles Forster Smith (1921)

History of the Peloponnesian War 6.39.1

145 ὀλιγαρχία δὲ τῶν μὲν κινδύνων τοῖς πολλοῖς μεταδίδωσι, τῶν δ' ὠφελίμων οὐ πλεονεκτεῖ μόνον, ἀλλὰ καὶ ξύμπαντ' ἀφελομένη ἔχει

An oligarchy gives the many a share of the dangers, but of advantages it not merely claims the lion's share, but even takes and keeps it all.

Translated by Charles Forster Smith (1921)

History of the Peloponnesian War 6.39.2

146 διαβολὰς μὲν οὐ σῶφρον οὔτε λέγειν τινὰς ἐς ἀλλήλους οὔτε τοὺς ἀκούοντας ἀποδέχεσθαι

There is little wisdom in exchanging abuse or in sitting by and accepting it.

Translated by Benjamin Jowett (1817–1893)

History of the Peloponnesian War 6.41.2

147 ἀδήλως τῇ ὄψει πλασάμενος πρὸς τὴν ξυμφορὰν

Disguising his looks so as to betray nothing in regard to the calamity.

Translated by Charles Forster Smith (1921)

History of the Peloponnesian War 6.58.1

Hippias on learning of his brother's assassination

148 οἰόμεθα τοῦ ἄπωθεν ξυνοίκου προαπολλυμένου οὐ καὶ ἐς αὐτόν τινα ἥξειν τὸ δεινόν;

Do we not think that, when a distant compatriot perishes before us, the same danger will not also befall ourselves?

Translated by Charles Forster Smith (1921)

History of the Peloponnesian War 6.77.2

149 οὐ γὰρ οἷόν τε ἅμα τῆς τε ἐπιθυμίας καὶ τῆς τύχης τὸν αὐτὸν ὁμοίως ταμίαν γενέσθαι

It is not possible for the same person to be in like measure the controller of his own desires and his fate.

Translated by Charles Forster Smith (1921)

History of the Peloponnesian War 6.78.2

150 οἱ ξένοι ... οἰόμενοι χρηματιεῖσθαι μᾶλλον ἢ μαχεῖσθαι

The mercenaries thought they were going to make money rather than fight.

Translated by Charles Forster Smith (1923)

History of the Peloponnesian War 7.13.2

extract of a letter from Nicias to the Athenians

151 τὰς φύσεις ἐπιστάμενος ὑμῶν, βουλομένων μὲν τὰ ἥδιστα ἀκούειν, αἰτιωμένων δὲ ὕστερον, ἤν τι ὑμῖν ἀπ' αὐτῶν μὴ ὁμοῖον ἐκβῇ

I know your nature; you wish to hear pleasant news, but then find fault when things turn out differently.

History of the Peloponnesian War 7.14.4

extract of a letter from Nicias to the Athenians

152 ἡ μεγίστη ἐλπὶς μεγίστην καὶ τὴν προθυμίαν παρέχεται

The greatest hope inspires in men the greatest zeal.

Translated by Charles Forster Smith (1923)

History of the Peloponnesian War 7.67.1

153 καὶ κινδύνων οὗτοι σπανιώτατοι οἳ ἂν ἐλάχιστα ἐκ τοῦ σφαλῆναι βλάπτοντες πλεῖστα διὰ τὸ εὐτυχῆσαι ὠφελῶσιν

Those dangers are rarest which bring least harm from failure yet most benefit from success.

Translated by Dan Hogg (2006)

History of the Peloponnesian War 7.68.3

154 ἔργον τοῦτο τῶν κατὰ τὸν πόλεμον τόνδε μέγιστον γενέσθαι ... τοῖς τε κρατήσασι λαμπρότατον καὶ τοῖς διαφθαρεῖσι δυστυχέστατον ... καὶ πεζὸς καὶ νῆες καὶ οὐδὲν ὅ τι οὐκ ἀπώλετο, καὶ ὀλίγοι ἀπὸ πολλῶν ἐπ' οἴκου ἀπενόστησαν. ταῦτα μὲν τὰ περὶ Σικελίαν γενόμενα

This was the greatest event in the war, most glorious to the victors, most ruinous to the vanquished, army, navy, everything destroyed, and, out of many, only few returned. Thus ended the

Sicilian expedition.

History of the Peloponnesian War 7.87.5

155 ἀλλ' ἡσυχίαν εἶχεν ὁ δῆμος καὶ κατάπληξιν τοιαύτην ὥστε κέρδος ὁ μὴ πάσχων τι βίαιον, εἰ καὶ σιγῴη, ἐνόμιζεν

The people were so depressed and afraid to move that he who escaped violence thought himself fortunate, even though he never said a word.

Translated by Benjamin Jowett (1817–1893)

History of the Peloponnesian War 8.66.2

of the end of democracy in Athens and the beginning of oligarchy in 411 BC

156 τῶν ἱστορικῶν κράτιστος ὁ τὴν διήγησιν ὥσπερ γραφὴν πάθεσι καὶ προσώποις εἰδωλοποιήσας. ὁ γοῦν Θουκυδίδης ἀεὶ τῷ λόγῳ πρὸς ταύτην ἁμιλλᾶται τὴν ἐνάργειαν, οἷον θεατὴν ποιῆσαι τὸν ἀκροατὴν

The most effective historian is he who, by vivid representation of emotions and characters, makes his narration like a painting. Assuredly Thucydides is always striving for vividness in his writing, since it is his desire to make the reader a spectator.

Translated by Frank Cole Babbitt (1936)

Plutarch, *Were the Athenians More Famous in War or in Wisdom?* 347a

THYILLUS

dates unknown

1 Ἤδη πηλοδομεῦσι χελιδόνες, ἤδη ἀν' οἶδμα
κολποῦται μαλακὰς εἰς ὀθόνας ζέφυρος·
ἤδη καὶ λειμῶνες ὑπὲρ πετάλων ἐχέαντο
ἄνθεα, καὶ τρηχὺς σῖγα μέμυκε πόρος.
σχοίνους μηρύεσθε, ἐφ' ὁλκάδα φορτίζεσθε
ἀγκύρας, καὶ πᾶν λαῖφος ἔφεσθε κάλοις.
ταῦτ' ὔμμιν πλώουσιν ἐπ' ἐμπορίην ὁ Πρίηπος
ὁ λιμενορμίτης ναυτιλίην γράφομαι.

Already swallows build their homes of mud,
and clinging sails cup the Zephyr's
infancy; already flowers have gilded
the meadow's leaf of green, and now
the sea has stopped his savage muttering.
Cast off your moorings, mariners,
and stow your anchors; give the wind full sail:
the harbour god gives this advice.

Translated by Adrian Wright (1947–)

Greek Anthology 10.5

TIMOCLES

4th century BC
Middle Comedy poet

1 τἀργύριόν ἐστιν αἷμα καὶ ψυχὴ βροτοῖς·
ὅστις δὲ μὴ ἔχει τοῦτο μηδ' ἐκτήσατο,
οὗτος μετὰ ζώντων τεθνηκὼς περιπατεῖ

Money is the very blood and life of mortals;
not having any, or not making any,
is to walk dead among the living.

Fragment 35 (Kock) – 37 (K-A)

TIMOCREON

late 6th/early 5th century BC
Lyric and elegiac poet from Rhodes, known for his feud with Themistocles

1 Μοῦσα τοῦδε τοῦ μέλεος
κλέος ἀν' Ἕλλανας τίθει,
ὡς ἐοικὸς καὶ δίκαιον

Muse, spread the fame of this song among the Greeks, as is fitting and just.

Translated by David A. Campbell (1992)

Fragment 2 (Page, *PMG*)

beginning of a song slandering Themistocles

2 ὤφελέν σ' ὦ τυφλὲ Πλοῦτε
μήτε γῇ μήτ' ἐν θαλάσσῃ
μήτ' ἐν ἠπείρῳ φανῆμεν,
ἀλλὰ Τάρταρόν τε ναίειν
κ' Ἀχέροντα· διὰ σὲ γὰρ πάντ'
αἰὲν ἀνθρώποις κακά

You should, blind Wealth,
neither on land or sea
nor on this continent appear,
but live in Tartarus
and Acheron; for thanks to you
men have all evils always.

Fragment 5 (Page, *PMG*)

Plutus as the god of wealth; Tartarus and Acheron, symbolically of the nether world

TIMON

*c.*320–230BC

Sceptic philosopher from Phlius, disciple of Pyrrhon

see also Zeno of Elea 3

1 λιχνόγραυν σκιερῷ ἐνὶ τύφῳ
πάντων ἱμείρουσαν ... νοῦν δ' εἶχεν
ἐλάσσονα κινδαψοῖο

A pampered old woman ensconced in gloomy pride; she had no more intelligence than a banjo!

Translated by R.D. Hicks (1925)

Fragment 812 (Lloyd-Jones and Parsons, *SH*) – *Silloi – Lampoons*

most of Timon's surviving fragments come from the Silloi where he ridicules all philosophers past and present; the above extract refers to Zeno of Citium

TIMOTHEUS (1)

*c.*450–360BC

Famous lyre player, singer, and dithyrambic poet from Miletus

1 θυιάδα φοιβάδα μαινάδα λυσσάδα

Ecstatic, bacchic, frantic, fanatic.

Translated by Frank Cole Babbitt (1927)

Fragment 2b (Page, *PMG*)

when Timotheus was singing his Artemis *in Athens, and called the goddess as above, Cinesias (the lyric poet) stood up in the audience and said, 'May you have a daughter like that!'*

2 Ἄρης τύραννος· χρυσὸν Ἑλλὰς οὐ δέδοικε

Ares is lord; Greece has no fear of gold.

Translated by D.A. Campbell (1993)

Fragment 14 (Page, *PMG*)

'Ares is lord' became proverbial

TIMOTHEUS (2)

4th century BC (died *c.*356BC)

Athenian statesman and general with a reputation for luck

1 εἰ τηλικαύτας πόλεις λαμβάνω καθεύδων,
τί με οἴεσθε ποιήσειν ἐγρηγορότα;

If I can capture such cities in my sleep, what do you think I shall do when I am awake?

Translated by Frank Cole Babbitt (1931)

Plutarch, *Sayings of Kings and Commanders* 187c

of a painting of cities captured whilst he was asleep

TRIPHIODORUS

3rd or 4th century AD

Epic poet native of Egypt

1 τὴν γὰρ Ἀπόλλων
ἀμφότερον μάντιν τ' ἀγαθὴν καὶ ἄπιστον
ἔθηκεν

Apollo had made her a true prophetess, and yet not to be believed.

Translated by H.T. Riley (1872)

The Capture of Troy 417

of Cassandra

2 ἡσυχίη δὲ πόλιν κατεβόσκετο, νυκτὸς ἑταίρη,
οὐδ' ὑλακὴ σκυλάκων ἠκούετο, πᾶσα δὲ σιγὴ
εἱστήκει καλέουσα φόνον πνείουσαν ἀυτήν

Stillness, night's cohort, swoops ravenously down on Troy. No dogs bark.
Silence, reigning unassailed, summons death-breathing battle.

Translated by Peter Constantine (2010)

The Capture of Troy 503

TRYPHON

1st century AD (?)

Epigrammatist

1 προφάσεων οὐκ ἀπορεῖ θάνατος

Death is never at a loss for a pretext.

Greek Anthology 9.488

TYRTAEUS

mid 7th century BC

Spartan elegiac poet

see also Songs 3

1 μυθεῖσθαί τε τὰ καλὰ καὶ ἔρδειν πάντα δίκαια

Speak honourably, do what is right.

Fragment 4 (West, *IEG*)

2 ταλασίφρονα θυμὸν ἔχοντες
αἰχμηταὶ πατέρων ἡμετέρων πατέρες

They had an unfaltering heart,
the warrior fathers of our fathers!

Fragment 5 (West, *IEG*)

3 ὥσπερ ὄνοι μεγάλοις ἄχθεσι τειρόμενοι

As donkeys crushed under mighty loads.

Translated by Kathleen Freeman (1947)

Fragment 6 (West, *IEG*)

of the Messenians, oppressed by the Spartans

4 τεθνάμεναι γὰρ καλὸν ἐνὶ προμάχοισι πεσόντα
ἄνδρ' ἀγαθὸν περὶ ᾗ πατρίδι μαρνάμενον

It is noble for a brave man to fall in the front line of battle, fighting for his country.

Translated by C.A. Trypanis (1971)

Fragment 10.1 (West, *IEG*)

5 γῆς πέρι τῆσδε μαχώμεθα καὶ περὶ παίδων

For this land let us fight bravely, and for our children too.

Fragment 10.13 (West, *IEG*)

6 τοὺς δὲ παλαιοτέρους, ὧν οὐκέτι γούνατ' ἐλαφρά,
μὴ καταλείποντες φεύγετε, τοὺς γεραιούς

Do not run and abandon the older men, who no longer have agile knees; do not abandon the old.

Translated by C.A. Trypanis (1971)

Fragment 10.19 (West, *IEG*)

7 νέοισι δὲ πάντ' ἐπέοικεν,
ὄφρ' ἐρατῆς ἥβης ἀγλαὸν ἄνθος ἔχῃ

Nothing is improper for the young, nothing as long as a man has the bright flower of lovely youth.

Translated by C.A. Trypanis (1971)

Fragment 10.27 (West, *IEG*)

8 μηδ' ἀνδρῶν πληθὺν δειμαίνετε, μηδὲ φοβεῖσθε

Fear ye not a multitude of men, nor flinch.

Translated by J.M. Edmonds (1931)

Fragment 11 (West, *IEG*)

9 ἥδ' ἀρετή, τόδ' ἄεθλον ἐν ἀνθρώποισιν ἄριστον
κάλλιστόν τε φέρειν γίνεται ἀνδρὶ νέῳ

This is prowess, this is the noblest prize and the fairest for a lad to win.

Translated by J.M. Edmonds (1931)

Fragment 12.13 (West, *IEG*)

10 οὐδέποτε κλέος ἐσθλὸν ἀπόλλυται οὐδ' ὄνομ' αὐτοῦ,
ἀλλ' ὑπὸ γῆς περ ἐὼν γίνεται ἀθάνατος,
ὅντιν' ἀριστεύοντα μένοντά τε μαρνάμενόν τε
γῆς πέρι καὶ παίδων θοῦρος Ἄρης ὀλέσῃ

His name and glorious reputation never die;
he is immortal even in his grave,
that man the furious War-god kills as he defends
his soil and children with heroic stand.

Translated by M.L. West (1994)

Fragment 12.31 (West, *IEG*)

X

XENO

3rd century BC
Comic poet

1 πάντες τελῶναι, πάντες εἰσὶν ἅρπαγες

All tax collectors, all of them, are thieves.

Fragment 1 (Kock) – 1 (K-A)

XENOCRATES

4th century BC
Philosopher from Chalcedon, head of the Academy 339–314BC

1 καὶ πότε χρήσεται αὐτῇ, ἐὰν ἄρτι ζητῇ;

When will he use it, if he is only now seeking for it?

Translated by Frank Cole Babbitt (1931)

Testimonies, Fragment 55 (Parente)

spoken by Eudamidas of Xenocrates who, at a great age, was discussing philosophy and seeking virtue

2 Ξενοκράτης εἴ ποτε σταμνίον οἴνου ἀνοίξειεν, ἔφθανεν ὁ οἶνος τρεπόμενος πρὶν ἀναλωθῆναι· καὶ τὰ ὄψα δὲ πολλάκις ἔωλα ἐξέρριπτεν· ἔνθεν καὶ ἡ παροιμία, τὸ Ξενοκράτους τυρίον

Out of stinginess Xenocrates allowed wine to grow sour and food to moulder without consuming it; hence the saying 'Xenocrates' cheese.'

Stobaeus, *Anthology* 3.17.24

XENOPHANES

*c.*580–*c.*484BC
Poet, theologian and natural philosopher from Colophon

1 οὐδὲ δίκαιον
προκρίνειν ῥώμην τῆς ἀγαθῆς σοφίης

It is not right to prefer physical strength to noble Wisdom.

Translated by Kathleen Freeman (1948)

Fragment 2 (D-K)

2 ἐξ ἀρχῆς καθ' Ὅμηρον ἐπεὶ μεμαθήκασι πάντες

From the beginning everybody learned from Homer.

Translated by Barbara Graziosi and Johannes Haubold (2009)

Fragment 10 (D-K)

3 πάντα θεοῖσ' ἀνέθηκαν Ὅμηρός θ' Ἡσίοδός τε, ὅσσα παρ' ἀνθρώποισιν ὀνείδεα καὶ ψόγος ἐστίν

Homer and Hesiod attributed to the gods everything that is shameful and reproachful among men.

Fragment 11 (D-K)

4 ἀλλ' εἰ χεῖρας ἔχον βόες ἵπποι τ' ἠὲ λέοντες
ἢ γράψαι χείρεσσι καὶ ἔργα τελεῖν ἅπερ ἄνδρες,
ἵπποι μέν θ' ἵπποισι, βόες δέ τε βουσὶν ὁμοίας …
Αἰθίοπές τε θεοὺς σφετέρους σιμοὺς μέλανάς τε

If horses had hands they would fashion their gods as horses, and oxen theirs as oxen; Ethiopians would rather have their gods stub-nosed and black. If lions could think, their gods would have a mane and roar.

The last part of the translation is by Irvin Yalom (2001)

Fragment 15 and 16 (D-K)

cf. Montesquieu, Lettres Persanes *(1721) 59: 'Si les triangles faisaient un dieu,ils lui donneraient trois côtés' (If triangles were to make a god he would have three sides)*

5 οὔ τοι ἀπ' ἀρχῆς πάντα θεοὶ θνητοῖσ' ὑπέδειξαν,
ἀλλὰ χρόνῳ ζητοῦντες ἐφευρίσκουσιν ἄμεινον

Not from the beginning did the gods grant man the knowledge of all things but, with time, by seeking he discovers.

Fragment 18 (D-K)

6 εἷς θεὸς ἔν τε θεοῖσι καὶ ἀνθρώποισι μέγιστος,
οὔ τι δέμας θνητοῖσιν ὁμοίιος οὐδὲ νόημα.
οὖλος ὁρᾷ, οὖλος δὲ νοεῖ, οὖλος δέ τ' ἀκούει

There is One God only, greatest among gods and men,
similar to mortals neither in shape nor in thought.
He sees all, hears all, knows everything.

Fragment 23 and 24 (D-K)

7 ἐκ γαίης γὰρ πάντα καὶ εἰς γην πάντα τελευτᾷ

For all things come of earth and in earth all things end.

Translated by J.M. Edmonds (1931)

Fragment 27 (D-K)

8 γῆ καὶ ὕδωρ πάντ' ἐσθ' ὅσα γίνονται ἠδὲ φύονται

All things that come into being and grow are earth and water.

Translated by Kathleen Freeman (1948)

Fragment 29 (D-K)

9 μέγας πόντος γενέτωρ νεφέων ἀνέμων τε καὶ ποταμῶν

The great ocean is generator of clouds and winds and rivers.

Translated by Jonathan Barnes (1987)

Fragment 30 (D-K)

10 πάντες γὰρ γαίης τε καὶ ὕδατος ἐκγενόμεσθα

We all have our origin from earth and water.

Translated by Kathleen Freeman (1948)

Fragment 33 (D-K)

11 τὸ μὲν οὖν σαφὲς οὔ τις ἀνὴρ ἴδεν οὐδέ τις ἔσται εἰδὼς ἀμφὶ θεῶν

The absolute truth concerning the gods no man has seen nor will ever know.

Fragment 34.1 (D-K)

12 δόκος δ' ἐπὶ πᾶσι τέτυκται

Of all things there can only be a vague suspicion.

Fragment 34.5 (D-K)

13 οὐσίαν θεοῦ σφαιροειδῆ, μηδὲν ὅμοιον ἔχουσαν ἀνθρώπῳ· ὅλον δὲ ὁρᾶν καὶ ὅλον ἀκούειν, μὴ μέντοι ἀναπνεῖν· σύμπαντά τε εἶναι νοῦν καὶ φρόνησιν καὶ ἀίδιον

The substance of god is spherical, in no way resembling man. He is all eye and ear, but does not breathe; he is the totality of mind and thought, and is eternal.

Translated by R.D. Hicks (1925)

Testimonies, Fragment 1.15 (D-K)

the sphere being considered the perfect shape

14 τὰ πολλὰ ἥσσω νοῦ εἶναι

The intellect is mightier than everything.

Testimonies, Fragment 1.19 (D-K)

15 σοφὸν γὰρ εἶναι δεῖ τὸν ἐπιγνωσόμενον τὸν σοφόν

It takes a wise man to recognize a wise man.

Translated by R.D. Hicks (1925)

Testimonies, Fragment 1.21 (D-K)

to Empedocles who stated that it is impossible to find a wise man

16 τοῖς τυράννοις ἐντυγχάνειν ὡς ἥκιστα

The less one associates with tyrants the better.

Testimonies, Fragment 19 (D-K)

17 Ξενοφάνης ... ἀποφαίνεται δὲ καὶ τὰς αἰσθήσεις ψευδεῖς

Xenophanes proclaimed that even the senses lie.

Testimonies, Fragment 32 (D-K)

18 τὸν θεὸν εἶναι ἀίδιον καὶ ἕνα καὶ ὅμοιον πάντῃ

God is Eternal, One, Uniform in every way.

Testimonies, Fragment 33 (D-K)

XENOPHON

c.428–*c*.354BC
Historian and general from Athens

1 πρᾳότατός γε μὴν φίλοις ὢν ἐχθροῖς φοβερώτατος ἦν

Most gentle with his friends, but formidable with his enemies.

Agesilaus 11.10
of Agesilaus, King of Sparta

2 ἡ μὲν τοῦ σώματος ἰσχὺς γηράσκει, ἡ δὲ τῆς ψυχῆς ῥώμη τῶν ἀγαθῶν ἀνδρῶν ἀγήρατός ἐστιν

Though the bodily strength decays, the vigour of good men's souls is ageless.

Translated by E.C. Marchant (1925)
Agesilaus 11.14

3 ποίας οὐ νεότητος κρεῖττον τὸ ἐκείνου γῆρας ἐφάνη;

What man's youth did not seem weaker than his old age?

Translated by E.C. Marchant (1925)
Agesilaus 11.15
of Agesilaus

4 ἔσεσθε ἄνδρες ἄξιοι τῆς ἐλευθερίας ἧς κέκτησθε

Be sure to be men worthy of the freedom you possess.

Translated by Carleton L. Brownson (1921)
Anabasis 1.7.3

5 ἡ δὲ τύχη ἐστρατήγησε κάλλιον

But fortune made better plans.

Anabasis 2.2.13

6 πᾶς δὲ ὄχλος φοβερός

Every crowd excites our fears.

Translated by Carleton L. Brownson (1921)
Anabasis 2.5.9.5a

7 φοβερώτατον δ' ἐρημία

But most fearful of all is solitude.

Translated by Carleton L. Brownson (1921)
Anabasis 2.5.9.5b

8 ἡ μὲν γὰρ εὐταξία σῴζειν δοκεῖ, ἡ δὲ ἀταξία πολλοὺς ἤδη ἀπολώλεκεν

As discipline preserves armies, so the want of it has already been fatal to many.

Translated by Edward Spelman (1776)
Anabasis 3.1.38

9 ὑμᾶς τοὺς Ἀθηναίους ἀκούω δεινοὺς εἶναι κλέπτειν τὰ δημόσια ... καὶ τοὺς κρατίστους μέντοι μάλιστα, εἴπερ ὑμῖν οἱ κράτιστοι ἄρχειν ἀξιοῦνται

I am informed, that you Athenians are very expert in stealing the public money, and that your best men are most expert at it, indeed if you choose your best men for your magistrates.

Translated by Edward Spelman (1776)
Anabasis 4.6.16
the reply of a Spartan to an Athenian who commented on the Spartan way of learning to steal from a young age

10 θάλαττα θάλαττα

The sea! the sea!

Translated by Carleton L. Brownson (1922)
Anabasis 4.7.24
Xenophon's army on finally reaching the sea after their long march through inhospitable Asia Minor

11 ἀλλὰ πάντα μὲν ἄρα ἄνθρωπον ὄντα προσδοκᾶν δεῖ

There is nothing a man ought not to expect.

Translated by Edward Spelman (1776)
Anabasis 7.6.11

12 φοβεῖν γε μὴν τοὺς πολεμίους καὶ ψευδενέδρας οἷόν τε καὶ ψευδοβοηθείας καὶ ψευδαγγελίας ποιοῦντα

The means to employ for scaring the enemy are false ambushes, false reliefs and false information.

Translated by E.C. Marchant (1925)
The Cavalry Commander 5.8

13 ὄντως γὰρ οὐδὲν κερδαλεώτερον ἐν πολέμῳ ἀπάτης

Nothing is more profitable in war than deception.

Translated by E.C. Marchant (1925)
The Cavalry Commander 5.10.1

14 καὶ οἱ παῖδες ὅταν παίζωσι ποσίνδα, δύνανται ἀπατᾶν προΐσχοντες ὥστε ὀλίγους τ᾽ ἔχοντες πολλοὺς δοκεῖν ἔχειν … πῶς οὐκ ἄνδρες … δύναιντ᾽ ἂν τοιαῦτα μηχανᾶσθαι;

Even children are successful deceivers when playing 'Guess the number', having few pretending they have many: surely men can play similar tricks.

The Cavalry Commander 5.10.2

15 τῶν μὲν γυμνικῶν ἀσκημάτων τὰ πολλὰ σὺν ἱδρῶτι ἐκπονοῦνται, τῆς δὲ ἱππικῆς τὰ πλεῖστα μεθ᾽ ἡδονῆς

Most gymnastic exercises are carried out with sweat and drudgery, but nearly all equestrian exercises are pleasant work.

Translated by E.C. Marchant (1925)

The Cavalry Commander 8.6.1

16 ὅπερ γὰρ εὔξαιτ᾽ ἄν τις πτηνὸς γενέσθαι, οὐκ ἔστιν ὅ τι μᾶλλον τῶν ἀνθρωπίνων ἔργων ἔοικεν αὐτῷ

It is true that any man would like to fly, and no action of man bears a closer resemblance to flying.

Translated by E.C. Marchant (1925)

The Cavalry Commander 8.6.3

of equestrianism

17 ἐννοεῖν δὲ τὸ παρατυγχάνον αὐτῷ ἀεὶ δεῖ καὶ πρὸς τὸ παριστάμενον σκοποῦντα τὸ συμφέρον ἐκπονεῖν

Decide what is right at the right moment, assess what is at hand and implement what is expedient.

The Cavalry Commander 9.1

18 Λυκούργου … τὸ κατεργάσασθαι ἐν τῇ πόλει αἱρετώτερον εἶναι τὸν καλὸν θάνατον ἀντὶ τοῦ αἰσχροῦ βίου

Lycurgus caused his people to choose an honourable death in preference to a disgraceful life.

Translated by E.C. Marchant (1925)

Constitution of the Lacedaemonians 9.1

19 εἶδος μὲν κάλλιστος, ψυχὴν δὲ φιλανθρωπότατος καὶ φιλομαθέστατος καὶ φιλοτιμότατος

Handsome to look at, benevolent in spirit, fond of learning, with high ambitions.

Cyropaedia 1.2.1

of Cyrus the Great, King of Persia

20 οὐδὲ θέμις εἴη αἰτεῖσθαι παρὰ τῶν θεῶν οὔτε ἱππεύειν μὴ μαθόντας ἱππομαχοῦντας νικᾶν

If you haven't learnt to ride a horse do not hope to win in a cavalry battle, even by the grace of god.

Cyropaedia 1.6.6

21 μηδέποτε ἀναμένειν τὸ πορίζεσθαι τὰ ἐπιτήδεια ἔστ᾽ ἂν ἡ χρεία σε ἀναγκάσῃ· ἀλλ᾽ ὅταν μάλιστα εὐπορῇς, τότε πρὸ τῆς ἀπορίας μηχανῶ

Never postpone procuring supplies until want compels you to it; but when you have the greatest abundance, then take measures against want.

Translated by Walter Miller (1914)

Cyropaedia 1.6.10

22 καὶ οἱ ἰατροί, ὅταν τινὲς νοσήσωσι, τότε ἰῶνται τούτους· σοὶ δὲ τούτου μεγαλοπρεπεστέρα ἔσται ἡ τῆς ὑγιείας ἐπιμέλεια· τὸ γὰρ ἀρχὴν μὴ κάμνειν τὸ στράτευμα, τούτου σοι δεῖ μέλειν

These physicians heal us when we fall sick. But your responsibility is greater than that: to prevent the army from falling sick at all.

Cyropaedia 1.6.16

spoken to Cyrus by his father

23 οὐκ ἔστιν ἔφη, ὦ παῖ, συντομωτέρα ὁδὸς ἐπὶ τό περὶ ὧν βούλει, δοκεῖν φρόνιμος εἶναι ἢ τὸ γενέσθαι περὶ τούτων φρόνιμον

There is no shorter road, my son, than really to be wise in those things in which you wish to seem to be wise.

Translated by Walter Miller (1914)

Cyropaedia 1.6.22

24 ὁπόσους ἂν ἀξιοῖς σοι πείθεσθαι, καὶ ἐκεῖνοι πάντες ἀξιώσουσι σὲ πρὸ ἑαυτῶν βουλεύεσθαι

All those from whom you expect obedience will, on their part, expect you to take thought for them.

Translated by Walter Miller (1914)

Cyropaedia 1.6.42

25 ἔκ γε σοῦ πῦρ ῥᾷον ἄν τις ἐκτρίψειεν ἢ γέλωτα

It would be easier to strike a spark from

you than laughter.

Translated by Doreen C. Innes (1995, based on W. Rhys Roberts)

Cyropaedia 2.2.15

quoted by Demetrius, On Style *134 (on how to draw laughter in a sullen case)*

26 τὸν πλεῖστα καὶ πονοῦντα καὶ ὠφελοῦντα τὸ κοινὸν τοῦτον καὶ μεγίστων ἀξιοῦσθαι ... καὶ τοῖς κακίστοις συμφέρον φανεῖσθαι τοὺς ἀγαθοὺς πλεονεκτεῖν

The one who suffers most and does most for the state should also receive the highest rewards; even to the worst it will seem proper that the good should have the largest share.

Translated by Walter Miller (1914)

Cyropaedia 2.2.20

27 οὐ γὰρ ἔστι διδάσκαλος οὐδεὶς τούτων κρείττων τῆς ἀνάγκης

There is no better teacher than necessity.

Cyropaedia 2.3.13

28 οὕτω πάντων τῶν δεινῶν ὁ φόβος μάλιστα καταπλήττει τὰς ψυχάς

Fear crushes men's spirits more than all other terrors.

Cyropaedia 3.1.25

29 τὸ μὲν γὰρ νῦν πλεονεκτῆσαι ὀλιγοχρόνιον ἂν τὸν πλοῦτον ἡμῖν παράσχοι· τὸ δὲ ταῦτα προεμένους ἐκεῖνα κτήσασθαι ὅθεν ὁ πλοῦτος φύεται, τοῦτο, ὡς ἐγὼ δοκῶ, ἀεναώτερον ἡμῖν δύναιτ' ἂν τὸν ὄλβον καὶ πᾶσι τοῖς ἡμετέροις παρέχειν

To secure a present advantage would give us but short-lived riches; but to sacrifice this and procure the means from which riches are acquired, that, as I see it, would provide us all with everlasting wealth.

Cyropaedia 4.2.44

30 ὡς τὸ μὲν πῦρ τοὺς ἁπτομένους καίει, οἱ δὲ καλοὶ καὶ τοὺς ἄπωθεν θεωμένους ὑφάπτουσιν, ὥστε αἴθεσθαι τῷ ἔρωτι

Fire burns those that touch it, beautiful persons inflame those that look at them even from afar, so that they are set on fire with love.

Translated by J.S. Watson and Henry Dale (1855)

Cyropaedia 5.1.16

31 τὸ γὰρ ἁμαρτάνειν ἀνθρώπους ὄντας οὐδὲν οἴομαι θαυμαστόν· ἄξιοί γε μέντοι ἐσμὲν τοῦ γεγενημένου πράγματος τούτου ἀπολαῦσαί τι ἀγαθόν, τὸ μαθεῖν μήποτε

It is not strange for mortal man to err; but we may still profit if we learn from our mistakes.

Cyropaedia 5.4.19

32 τήν τε γὰρ πόλιν νομίζω ἂν διαφθαρῆναι, ἔν τε τῇ ἁρπαγῇ εὖ οἶδ' ὅτι οἱ πονηρότατοι πλεονεκτήσειαν ἄν

If a city is corrupt, the worst men get the largest booty.

Cyropaedia 7.2.11

33 οὐ γὰρ τὸ μὴ λαβεῖν τἀγαθὰ οὕτω χαλεπὸν ὥσπερ τὸ λαβόντα στερηθῆναι

Not to obtain good things is less painful than losing what we have.

Cyropaedia 7.5.82

34 ἄρχων ἀγαθὸς οὐδὲν διαφέρει πατρὸς ἀγαθοῦ· οἵ τε γὰρ πατέρες προνοοῦσι τῶν παίδων ὅπως μήποτε αὐτοὺς τἀγαθὰ ἐπιλείψει

A good ruler is not at all different from a good father who provides for his children that they may never be in want.

Cyropaedia 8.1.1

35 εἰ τοίνυν μέγιστον ἀγαθὸν τὸ πειθαρχεῖν φαίνεται εἰς τὸ καταπράττειν τἀγαθά, οὕτως εὖ ἴστε ὅτι τὸ αὐτὸ τοῦτο καὶ εἰς τὸ διασῴζειν ἃ δεῖ μέγιστον ἀγαθόν ἐστι

If discipline is the first essential to achieving success, I can assure you that it is also the first essential for maintaining it.

Cyropaedia 8.1.3

36 ἀδύνατον οὖν πολλὰ τεχνώμενον ἄνθρωπον πάντα καλῶς ποιεῖν

It is impossible for a man of many trades to be proficient in all of them.

Translated by Walter Miller (1914)

Cyropaedia 8.2.5

37 πολλοὺς ἐποίησεν ἀνθρώπους καὶ ὠτακουστεῖν καὶ διοπτεύειν τί ἂν ἀγγείλαντες ὠφελήσειαν βασιλέα

He prompted many men to make it their business to use their eyes and ears to spy out what they could report to the king to his advantage.

Translated by Walter Miller (1914)

Cyropaedia 8.2.10

of the Persian king

38 χαλεπώτερον εἶναι εὑρεῖν ἄνδρα τἀγαθὰ καλῶς φέροντα ἢ τὰ κακά

It is more difficult to find a man who bears prosperity well than one who bears misfortune well.

Translated by H.T. Riley (1872)

Cyropaedia 8.4.14

39 ἔρρει τὰ κᾶλα. Μίνδαρος ἀπεσσύα. πεινῶντι τὤνδρες. ἀπορίομες τί χρὴ δρᾶν

Ships lost. Mindarus dead. Men starving. Don't know what to do.

Translated by Rex Warner (1966)

Hellenica 1.1.23

a laconic message sent to Sparta after the Cyzicus disaster in 411

40 Λακεδαιμόνιοι δὲ οὐκ ἔφασαν πόλιν Ἑλληνίδα ἀνδραποδιεῖν μέγα ἀγαθὸν εἰργασμένην ἐν τοῖς μεγίστοις κινδύνοις γενομένοις τῇ Ἑλλάδι

The Lacedaemonians, however, said that they would not enslave a Greek city which had done great service amid the greatest perils that had befallen Greece.

Translated by J.S. Watson and Henry Dale (1855)

Hellenica 2.2.20

of Athens

41 οὕτω χρὴ ποιεῖν ὅπως ἕκαστός τις ἑαυτῷ συνείσεται τῆς νίκης αἰτιώτατος ὤν

We must exert ourselves so that each may consider himself the chief contributor to the victory.

Translated by H.T. Riley (1872)

Hellenica 2.4.17

42 ὁρῶ γὰρ τῶν ἀνθρώπων οὐδένα ἀναμάρτητον διατελοῦντα

I find no man free from error.

Translated by H.T. Riley (1872)

Hellenica 6.3.10

43 ἐμοὶ μὲν δὴ μέχρι τούτου γραφέσθω· τὰ δὲ μετὰ ταῦτα ἴσως ἄλλῳ μελήσει

Let this, then, be the end of my narrative. Someone else, perhaps, will deal with what happened later.

Translated by Rex Warner (1966)

Hellenica 7.5.27

last lines

44 οὐδεὶς γὰρ ἐθέλει τυράννου κατ' ὀφθαλμοὺς κατηγορεῖν

No one would speak against a despot to his face.

Hiero 1.14

said by Simonides to Hieron of Syracuse

45 ὅσῳ ἂν πλείω τις παραθῆται τὰ περιττὰ τῶν ἱκανῶν, τοσούτῳ καὶ θᾶττον κόρος ἐμπίπτει τῆς ἐδωδῆς

The more superfluous dishes there are, the sooner you feel surfeited.

Hiero 1.19

46 τὸν ἑκάστῳ ἡδόμενον μάλιστα, τοῦτον οἴει καὶ ἐρωτικώτατα ἔχειν τοῦ ἔργου τούτου

The more a man derives pleasure from an occupation, the stronger will be his devotion to it.

Hiero 1.21

47 ὁ δὲ σπανίσας τινός οὗτός ἐστιν ὁ μετὰ χαρᾶς πιμπλάμενος, ὅταν αὐτῷ προφανῇ τι

Offer a man a dish he seldom tastes and he eats a bellyful.

Translated by E.C. Marchant (1925)

Hiero 1.25

48 ὅστις εὔπους μὲν εἴη, πρᾶος δέ, ἀρκούντως δὲ ποδώκης, ἐθέλοι δὲ καὶ δύναιτο πόνους ὑποφέρειν, πείθοιτο δὲ μάλιστα, οὗτος ἂν εἰκότως ἀλυπότατός τ' εἴη καὶ σωτηριώτατος τῷ ἀναβάτῃ ἐν τοῖς πολεμικοῖς

A gentle and speedy horse, ready to work and, above all, tractable, is a pleasure to the rider and his best guarantee of safety in wartime.

The Art of Horsemanship 3.12

49 ἔστι δὲ ὥσπερ ἀνθρώπῳ οὕτω καὶ ἵππῳ ἀρχόμενα πάντα εὐιατότερα ἢ ἐπειδὰν ἐνσκιρρωθῇ τε καὶ ἐξαμαρτηθῇ τὰ νοσήματα

It is the same with horses as with men: all distempers in the early stage are more easily cured than when they have become chronic and have been wrongly treated.

Translated by E.C. Marchant (1925)

The Art of Horsemanship 4.2

50 τὸ δὲ μήποτε σὺν ὀργῇ τῷ ἵππῳ προσφέρεσθαι ... ἀπρονόητον γὰρ ἡ ὀργή, ὥστε πολλάκις ἐξεργάζεται ὧν μεταμέλειν ἀνάγκη

Never approach a horse in anger; for anger is a reckless thing that often makes a man do what he will regret.

Translated by E.C. Marchant (1925)

The Art of Horsemanship 6.13

51 πρῶτον τοίνυν χρὴ τοῦτο γνῶναι, ὅτι ἐστὶ θυμὸς ἵππῳ ὅπερ ὀργὴ ἀνθρώπῳ· ὥσπερ οὖν καὶ ἄνθρωπον ἥκιστ᾽ ἂν ὀργίζοι τις ... οὕτω καὶ ἵππον θυμοειδῆ ὁ μὴ ἀνιῶν ἥκιστ᾽ ἂν ἐξοργίζοι

Spirit in a horse is what anger is in a man. As you would not provoke an angry man, equally abstain from irritating a spirited horse.

The Art of Horsemanship 9.2

52 ἃ μὲν γὰρ ὁ ἵππος ἀναγκαζόμενος ποιεῖ ... οὔτ᾽ ἐπίσταται οὔτε καλά ἐστιν, οὐδὲν μᾶλλον ἢ εἴ τις ὀρχηστὴν μαστιγοίη καὶ κεντρίζοι ... ἀλλὰ δεῖ ἑκόντα πάντα τὰ κάλλιστα καὶ λαμπρότατα ἐπιδείκνυσθαι

What a horse does under constraint he does without understanding, and with no more grace than a dancer would show if he was whipped and goaded. No, a horse must make the most graceful and brilliant appearance of his own will.

Translated by E.C. Marchant (1925)

The Art of Horsemanship 11.6

53 οὕτω δὲ καὶ ἔστιν ὁ μετεωρίζων ἑαυτὸν ἵππος σφόδρα ἀγαστὸν, ὡς πάντων τῶν ὁρώντων καὶ νέων καὶ γεραιτέρων τὰ ὄμματα κατέχει· οὐδεὶς γοῦν ... ἀπαγορεύει θεώμενος, ἔστ᾽ ἂν περ ἐπιδεικνύηται τὴν λαμπρότητα

A prancing horse is a thing so graceful and admirable that it rivets the gaze of all beholders, young and old alike; no one is tired of looking at him when he shows off his brilliance.

The Art of Horsemanship 11.9

54 οὐδὲν γὰρ τῶν ὄντων ἰσομέγεθες τούτῳ ὅμοιόν ἐστι πρὸς ἁρμόν

There is nothing in the world of equal size to match the hare as a piece of mechanism.

Translated by E.C. Marchant (1925)

On Hunting 5.29

55 ἀστράπτουσαι τοῖς ὄμμασιν

Eyes flashing like lightning.

On Hunting 6.15

of hunting dogs sensing game

56 ἀεὶ γὰρ ἔστι τοῖς τὰ σώματα καὶ τὰς ψυχὰς εὖ ἔχουσιν ἐγγὺς εἶναι τοῦ εὐτυχῆσαι

Men who are sound in body and mind will always stand on the threshold of success.

On Hunting 12.5

cf. the Latin 'mens sana in corpore sano' for which there is no direct equivalent in Greek (except as translated from the Latin: 'νοῦς ὑγιὴς ἐν σώματι ὑγιεῖ')

57 θαυμάζω δὲ τῶν σοφιστῶν καλουμένων ὅτι φασὶ μὲν ἐπ᾽ ἀρετὴν ἄγειν οἱ πολλοὶ τοὺς νέους, ἄγουσι δ᾽ ἐπὶ τοὐναντίον ... ὅτι ἐν τοῖς ὀνόμασι σοφίζονται καὶ οὐκ ἐν τοῖς νοήμασιν ... οἱ σοφισταὶ δ᾽ ἐπὶ τῷ ἐξαπατᾶν λέγουσι καὶ γράφουσιν ἐπὶ τῷ ἑαυτῶν κέρδει

I am surprised at the sophists who profess to lead the young to virtue and do the very opposite; their wisdom consists of words and not of ideas; they talk to deceive and pocket the profit.

On Hunting 13.1

58 οὐ γὰρ δοκεῖν αὐτὰ βούλομαι μᾶλλον ἢ εἶναι χρήσιμα, ἵνα ἀνεξέλεγκτα ᾖ εἰς ἀεί

I wish my work not to seem, but to be useful, so that it may stand for ever unrefuted.

On Hunting 13.7

59 τὸ θεῖον ὅτι τοσοῦτον καὶ τοιοῦτόν ἐστιν ὥσθ᾽ ἅμα πάντα ὁρᾶν καὶ πάντα ἀκούειν καὶ πανταχοῦ παρεῖναι καὶ ἅμα πάντων ἐπιμελεῖσθαι

Such is the greatness and such the nature of god that he sees all things, hears all things, is present in all places and attends to all things.

Memorabilia 1.4.18

spoken by Socrates

60 πάντων ἡδίστου ἀκούσματος, ἐπαίνου

The sweetest of all sounds is praise.

Translated by H.T. Riley (1872)

Memorabilia 2.1.31

61 πάντων κτημάτων κράτιστον ... φίλος σαφὴς καὶ ἀγαθός

Of all possessions the best is a true and noble friend.

Memorabilia 2.4.1

62 χαλεπὸν γὰρ οὕτω τι ποιῆσαι, ὥστε μηδὲν ἁμαρτεῖν, χαλεπὸν δὲ καὶ ἀναμαρτήτως τι ποιήσαντα μὴ ἀγνώμονι κριτῇ περιτυχεῖν

Whatever ones does, it is difficult to avoid mistakes, and it is difficult to escape unfair criticism even if one makes no mistakes.

Translated by E.C. Marchant (1923)

Memorabilia 2.8.5

63 λίθοι τε καὶ πλίνθοι καὶ ξύλα καὶ κέραμος ἀτάκτως ἐρριμμένα

Stones, bricks, timber and tiles, all flung together.

Translated by E.C. Marchant (1923)

Memorabilia 3.1.7

64 εὑρήσεις ἐν πᾶσιν ἔργοις τοὺς μὲν εὐδοκιμοῦντάς τε καὶ θαυμαζομένους ἐκ τῶν μάλιστα ἐπισταμένων ὄντας, τοὺς δὲ κακοδοξοῦντάς τε καὶ καταφρονουμένους ἐκ τῶν ἀμαθεστάτων

Men who are famous and admired always come from those who have the widest knowledge, the infamous and despised from the most ignorant.

Translated by E.C. Marchant (1923)

Memorabilia 3.6.17

65 βασιλεῖς δὲ καὶ ἄρχοντας οὐ τοὺς τὰ σκῆπτρα ἔχοντας ἔφη εἶναι οὐδὲ τοὺς ὑπὸ τῶν τυχόντων αἱρεθέντας οὐδὲ τοὺς κλήρῳ λαχόντας οὐδὲ τοὺς βιασαμένους οὐδὲ τοὺς ἐξαπατήσαντας, ἀλλὰ τοὺς ἐπισταμένους ἄρχειν

Kings and rulers are not those who hold the sceptre, nor those who are chosen by the multitude, nor those on whom the lot falls, nor those who owe their power to force or deception; but those who know how to rule.

Translated by E.C. Marchant (1923)

Memorabilia 3.9.10

66 μὴ γίγνεσθαι σπουδαίους ἄνευ διδασκάλων ἱκανῶν

You cannot achieve excellence without competent teachers.

Memorabilia 4.2.2

67 δίκαια μὲν γὰρ λέγοντες πολλοὶ ἄδικα ποιοῦσι

Many say what is just and do what is unjust.

Translated by E.C. Marchant (1923)

Memorabilia 4.4.10

68 ἄνευ δὲ ὁμονοίας οὔτ᾽ ἂν πόλις εὖ πολιτευθείη οὔτ᾽ οἶκος καλῶς οἰκηθείη

Without concord neither a city can be well administered nor a family made to prosper.

Memorabilia 4.4.16

69 τοῦ γὰρ οὕτω προσέχοντος ἑαυτῷ ἔργον ἔφη εἶναι εὑρεῖν ἰατρὸν τὰ πρὸς ὑγίειαν συμφέροντα αὐτῷ μᾶλλον διαγιγνώσκοντα

By such attention to yourself you can judge, better than any doctor, what suits your constitution.

Memorabilia 4.7.9

70 ἡ οἰκονομία ἐπιστήμη ... εἶναι εὖ οἰκεῖν τὸν ἑαυτοῦ οἶκον ... τελεῖν τε ὅσα δεῖ καὶ περιουσίαν ποιῶν αὔξειν τὸν οἶκον

Economy is a branch of knowledge concerned with the management of one's own estate and doing whatever is necessary to increase its value.

Oeconomicus 1.1.2–1.4.5

an early reference to economics as a separate science; all pronouncements in this dialogue are presented as having been made by Socrates

71 ταὐτὰ ἄρα ὄντα τῷ μὲν ἐπισταμένῳ χρῆσθαι αὐτῶν ἑκάστοις χρήματά ἐστι, τῷ δὲ μὴ ἐπισταμένῳ οὐ χρήματα ... αὐλοὶ τῷ μὲν ἐπισταμένῳ ἀξίως λόγου αὐλεῖν χρήματά εἰσι, τῷ δὲ μὴ ἐπισταμένῳ οὐδὲν μᾶλλον ἢ ἄχρηστοι λίθοι

The same thing can be wealth or non-wealth, depending on if one knows, or does not know, how to use it; a flute is wealth to one who knows how to use it, if not it is no better than useless stones.

Oeconomicus 1.10

72 ἀφ' ὧν τις ὠφελεῖσθαι δύναται χρήματα εἶναι

Wealth is that from which a man can derive profit.

Translated by E.C. Marchant (1923)

Oeconomicus 1.13

73 καταμαθὼν γάρ ποτε ἀπὸ τῶν αὐτῶν ἔργων τοὺς μὲν πάνυ ἀπόρους ὄντας, τοὺς δὲ πάνυ πλουσίους ἀπεθαύμασα … καὶ εὗρον ἐπισκοπῶν πάνυ οἰκείως ταῦτα γιγνόμενα· τοὺς μὲν γὰρ εἰκῇ ταῦτα πράττοντας ζημιουμένους ἑώρων, τοὺς δὲ γνώμῃ συντεταμένῃ ἐπιμελουμένους καὶ θᾶττον καὶ ῥᾷον καὶ κερδαλεώτερον κατέγνων πράττοντας

Observing once that the same pursuits lead in one case to great poverty and in another to great riches, I was filled with amazement; and on consideration I saw that those who follow these pursuits carelessly suffer loss, while those who devote themselves diligently accomplish them more quickly, more easily and with more profit.

Translated by E.C. Marchant (1923)

Oeconomicus 2.17

74 νομίζω δὲ γυναῖκα κοινωνὸν ἀγαθὴν οἴκου οὖσαν πάνυ ἀντίρροπον εἶναι τῷ ἀνδρὶ ἐπὶ τὸ ἀγαθόν

I think that the wife who is a good partner in the household contributes just as much as her husband to its welfare.

Translated by E.C. Marchant (1923)

Oeconomicus 3.15

75 ἐγὼ δὲ καὶ τοῦτο ἡγοῦμαι μέγα τεκμήριον ἄρχοντος ἀρετῆς εἶναι, ᾧ ἂν ἑκόντες πείθωνται καὶ ἐν τοῖς δεινοῖς παραμένειν ἐθέλωσιν

I think you have one clear proof of a ruler's excellence, when men obey him willingly and choose to stand by him in moments of danger.

Translated by E.C. Marchant (1923)

Oeconomicus 4.19

76 ἐθαύμαζεν … ὡς καλὰ μὲν τὰ δένδρα εἴη, δι' ἴσου δὲ τὰ πεφυτευμένα, ὀρθοὶ δὲ οἱ στίχοι … εὐγώνια δὲ πάντα καλῶς εἴη, ὀσμαὶ δὲ πολλαὶ καὶ ἡδεῖαι

He admired the beauty of the trees, the accuracy of the spacing, the straightness of the rows, the regularity of the angles and the multitude of sweet scents.

Translated by E.C. Marchant (1923)

Oeconomicus 4.21

Lysander on the beauty of Cyrus' gardens

77 ἐγὼ πάντα καὶ διεμέτρησα καὶ διέταξα, ἔστι δ' αὐτῶν … ἃ καὶ ἐφύτευσα αὐτός

All the measurement and arrangement is my own work, and I did some of the planting myself.

Translated by E.C. Marchant (1923)

Oeconomicus 4.22

Cyrus on designing his garden

78 τῆς γεωργίας οὐδ' οἱ πάνυ μακάριοι δύνανται ἀπέχεσθαι

Even the wealthiest cannot hold aloof from husbandry.

Translated by E.C. Marchant (1923)

Oeconomicus 5.1

79 συμπαιδεύει δὲ καὶ εἰς τὸ ἐπαρκεῖν ἀλλήλοις ἡ γεωργία

Husbandry helps to train men for corporate effort.

Translated by E.C. Marchant (1923)

Oeconomicus 5.14

80 τὴν γεωργίαν τῶν ἄλλων τεχνῶν μητέρα καὶ τροφὸν εἶναι

Agriculture is the mother and nurse of the other arts.

Oeconomicus 5.17

81 φυλακτέον ὅπως μὴ ἡ εἰς τὸν ἐνιαυτὸν κειμένη δαπάνη εἰς τὸν μῆνα δαπανᾶται

Take care not to spend a year's income in a month.

Oeconomicus 7.36

82 ἡδεῖαί σοι γίγνονται, ὁπόταν ἀνεπιστήμονα … ἐπιστήμονα ποιήσῃς καὶ διπλασίου σοι ἀξία γένηται

How wonderful to teach an unskilled person into becoming a professional!

Oeconomicus 7.41

83 ἀπειλεῖ γὰρ ὁ θεὸς καὶ κολάζει τοὺς βλᾶκας

God threatens and punishes careless fools.

Translated by E.C. Marchant (1923)

Oeconomicus 8.16

84 κερδαλέον ἐστὶν ἡ ἐπιμέλεια

Diligence pays.

Oeconomicus 12.16.1

85 ὅταν μὲν γὰρ ἐπιμελουμένους ἴδω, καὶ ἐπαινῶ καὶ τιμᾶν πειρῶμαι αὐτούς, ὅταν δὲ ἀμελοῦντας, λέγειν τε πειρῶμαι καὶ ποιεῖν ὁποῖα δήξεται αὐτούς

Commend good work and honour it; nettle the negligent.

Oeconomicus 12.16.5

86 τὴν φιλανθρωπίαν ταύτης τῆς τέχνης ἀκούσῃ· τὸ γὰρ ὠφελιμωτάτην οὖσαν καὶ ἡδίστην ἐργάζεσθαι καὶ καλλίστην καὶ προσφιλεστάτην θεοῖς τε καὶ ἀνθρώποις

How kindly a thing is this art; helpful, pleasant, honourable, dear to the gods and men in the highest degree.

Translated by E.C. Marchant (1923)

Oeconomicus 15.4

of agriculture

87 διὰ πυρὸς ἰοίην

I would go through fire and water.

Translated in Liddell & Scott

Symposium 4.16

88 τοὺς ἀνθρώπους οὐκ ἐν τῷ οἴκῳ τὸν πλοῦτον καὶ τὴν πενίαν ἔχειν ἀλλ' ἐν ταῖς ψυχαῖς

People's wealth and poverty are to be found not in their real estate but in their hearts.

Translated by O.J. Todd (1923)

Symposium 4.34

89 ὁποῖοί τινες ἂν οἱ προστάται ὦσι, τοιαύτας καὶ τὰς πολιτείας γίγνεσθαι

Whatever the rulers are, such is also the body of citizens.

Ways and Means 1.1

90 ὅσῳ γε μὴν πλείονες εἰσοικίζοιντό τε καὶ ἀφικνοῖντο, δῆλον ὅτι τοσούτῳ ἂν πλεῖον καὶ εἰσάγοιτο καὶ ἐκπέμποιτο καὶ πωλοῖτο καὶ μισθοφοροῖτο καὶ τελεσφοροίη

The more residents and visitors arrive, the more there will be an increase of our imports and exports, of sales, rents and customs.

Ways and Means 3.5

91 οἷόν τε δὴ οὕτως καὶ ἰδιώτας συνισταμένους καὶ κοινουμένους τὴν τύχην ἀσφαλέστερον κινδυνεύειν. μηδὲ μέντοι τοῦτο φοβεῖσθε, ὡς ἢ τὸ δημόσιον οὕτω κατασκευαζόμενον παραλυπήσει τοὺς ἰδιώτας ἢ οἱ ἰδιῶται τὸ δημόσιον

Private persons can of course share in their enterprises and minimize their risks. There is no reason, however, to fear that a public company formed on such a plan will conflict with the interests of the private owner, or the private owner prove injurious to the state.

Ways and Means 4.32

92 εὐδαιμονέσταται μὲν γὰρ δήπου πόλεις λέγονται, αἳ ἂν πλεῖστον χρόνον ἐν εἰρήνῃ διατελῶσι

Those states are reckoned the happiest that enjoy the longest period of unbroken peace.

Translated by E.C. Marchant (1925)

Ways and Means 5.2

93 ἐν εἰρήνῃ μὲν πάνυ πολλὰ χρήματα εἰς τὴν πόλιν ἀνενεχθέντα, ἐν πολέμῳ δὲ ταῦτα πάντα καταδαπανηθέντα

In times of peace a very great amount of money was paid into the treasury, and the whole of it was spent in times of war.

Translated by E.C. Marchant (1925)

Ways and Means 5.12

94 θεοῖς ηὐξάμην οὐκ ἀθάνατον οὐδὲ πολυχρόνιον γενέσθαι μοι τὸν υἱόν … ἀγαθὸν δὲ καὶ φιλόπατριν, ὃ δὴ καὶ γέγονεν

I did not pray to the gods that my son should be immortal or even long of life, but that he should be brave and patriotic; and so it has come to pass.

Translated by Frank Cole Babbitt (1928)

Plutarch, *Letter of Condolence to Apollonius** 119a

speaking of his son Gryllus who died in battle at Mantinea in 362BC

PSEUDO-XENOPHON

possibly 420–430BC
unknown

1 ὁπόσαι δ' εἰσὶν ἀρχαὶ μισθοφορίας ἕνεκα καὶ ὠφελίας εἰς τὸν οἶκον, ταύτας ζητεῖ ὁ δῆμος ἄρχειν

Offices which involve receipt of pay and domestic benefit are the ones which the people are eager to uphold.

Constitution of the Athenians 1.3

otherwise known as The Old Oligarch, *a short pamphlet on 5th-century Athens*

2 μισεῖσθαι μὲν ἀνάγκη τὸν ἄρχοντα ὑπὸ τοῦ ἀρχομένου

The ruler is necessarily hated by the ruled.

Translated by G.W. Bowersock (1925)

Constitution of the Athenians 1.14

3 ἀπὸ χρημάτων πολλὰ διαπράττεσθαι Ἀθήνησι, καὶ ἔτι ἂν πλείω διαπράττεσθαι, εἰ πλείους ἔτι ἐδίδοσαν ἀργύριον

Many things are accomplished at Athens for money and still more would be accomplished if still more gave money.

Translated by G.W. Bowersock (1925)

Constitution of the Athenians 3.3

XERXES I

King of Persia, 486–465BC, son of Darius and Atossa

For more quotations by Xerxes *see* Herodotus 115, 122, 123, 127, 130, 134

see also Aeschylus 65, 68, 77; Alexander the Great 5; Aristides 16; Herodotus 116, 158, 161; Leonidas 2

1 ἐσῆλθε γάρ με λογισάμενον κατοικτῖραι ὡς βραχὺς εἴη ὁ πᾶς ἀνθρώπινος βίος

I was moved to compassion when I considered the shortness of all human life.

Translated by A.D. Godley (1922)

Herodotus, *Histories* 7.46

Xerxes on looking upon his huge army

2 οἱ μὲν ἄνδρες γεγόνασί μοι γυναῖκες, αἱ δὲ γυναῖκες ἄνδρες

My men have turned into women and my women into men!

Translated by Robin Waterfield (1998)

Herodotus, *Histories* 8.88

on being told that Artemisia sunk an enemy ship (according to Herodotus 8.87 it was in fact one of their own ships)

Z

ZALEUCUS

*c.*650BC (?)

Possibly the earliest Greek lawgiver, of the town Locri Epizephyrii in Magna Grecia

1 ἕκαστον οὖν ἔχειν καὶ παρασκευάζειν δεῖ τὴν αὑτοῦ ψυχὴν πάντων τῶν κακῶν καθαράν

Everybody must prepare and keep his soul clean of all evil.

Stobaeus, *Anthology* 4.2.19

2 τοὺς νόμους ἔφησε τοῖς ἀραχνίοις ὁμοίους εἶναι· ὥσπερ γὰρ εἰς ἐκεῖνα ἐὰν μὲν ἐμπέσῃ μυῖα ἢ κώνωψ, κατέχεται· ἐὰν δὲ σφὴξ ἢ μέλιττα, διαρρήξασα ἀφίπταται· οὕτω καὶ εἰς τοὺς νόμους ἐὰν μὲν ἐμπέσῃ πένης, συνέχεται· ἐὰν δὲ πλούσιος ἢ δυνατὸς λέγειν, διαρρήξας ἀποτρέχει

Laws are like spider webs; a fly or mosquito is trapped, a bee or wasp tears them apart and escapes; so with laws, the poor man is trapped, the rich or powerful tear them up and get away.

Stobaeus, *Anthology* 4.4.25

ZENO OF CITIUM

*c.*335–*c.*263BC

Philosopher, founder of Stoicism, loved to speak in riddles

see also Antigonus (2) 1; Timon 1

1 περὶ Ζήνωνος, χρηστηριασαμένου αὐτοῦ, τί πράττων ἄριστα βιώσεται, ἀποκρίνασθαι τὸν θεόν, εἰ συγχρωτίζοιτο τοῖς νεκροῖς· ὅθεν ξυνέντα τὰ τῶν ἀρχαίων ἀναγινώσκειν

Zeno consulted the oracle to know how he could attain the best life, and the god's response was that he should take up contact with the dead; whereupon, perceiving what this meant, he studied ancient authors.

Testimonies, Fragment 1 (von Arnim, *SVF*)

Diogenes Laertius, Lives of Eminent Philosophers *7.2, quotes extracts from Apollonius of Tyre's first book on Zeno*

2 νῦν εὐπλόηκα, ὅτε νεναυάγηκα

This was a happy voyage when I suffered shipwreck.

Testimonies, Fragment 2 (von Arnim, *SVF*)

Zeno arrived in Athens and studied philosophy after being shipwrecked; also used proverbially

3 τῇ φύσει ζῆν, ὅπερ ἐστὶ κατ' ἀρετὴν ζῆν· ἄγει γὰρ πρὸς ταύτην ἡμᾶς ἡ φύσις

To live in agreement with nature is to live in virtue; for it is to virtue that nature leads us.

Testimonies, Fragment 179 (von Arnim, *SVF*)

4 οὐκ ἔστι δοῦλος, ἢν ἐλεύθερος μόλῃ

No one is a slave, if a free man he come.

Testimonies, Fragment 219 (von Arnim, *SVF*)

cf. Aristippus in Diogenes Laertius 2.82

5 δύο ὦτα ἔχομεν, στόμα δὲ ἕν, ἵνα πλείω μὲν ἀκούωμεν, ἥττονα δὲ λέγωμεν

The reason why we have two ears and only one mouth is that we may listen the more and talk the less.

Translated by R.D. Hicks (1925)

Testimonies, Fragment 310 (von Arnim, *SVF*)

to a youth who was talking nonsense

6 τὰ ὦτά σου εἰς τὴν γλῶτταν συνερρύηκεν

Your ears have slid down and merged with your tongue.

Translated by R.D. Hicks (1925)

Testimonies, Fragment 311 (von Arnim, *SVF*)

to a young man who was talking a lot

7 Ζήνων ἔλεγεν οὐδενὸς ἡμᾶς οὕτω πένεσθαι ὡς χρόνου· βραχὺς γὰρ ὄντως ὁ βίος, ἡ δὲ τέχνη μακρή, καὶ μᾶλλον ἡ τὰς τῆς ψυχῆς νόσους ἰάσασθαι δυναμένη

Zeno said that, more than in any other thing, we are poor in time; for life is short, and the art is long and few are they who heal the diseases of the soul.

Testimonies, Fragment 323 (von Arnim, *SVF*)

cf. the translation in Hippocrates 9

8 ἐρωτηθεὶς τίς ἐστι φίλος, ἄλλος, ἔφη, ἐγώ

When asked, 'What is a friend?' – 'Another I,' he said

Translated in *Bartlett's Familiar Quotations* (1980)

Testimonies, Fragment 324 (von Arnim, *SVF*)

ZENO OF ELEA

5th century BC

Philosopher, most famous for his four paradoxes

1 τὸ κινούμενον ἤτοι ἐν ᾧ ἐστι τόπῳ κινεῖται ἢ ἐν ᾧ οὐκ ἔστι· καὶ οὔτε ἐν ᾧ ἐστι τόπῳ κινεῖται οὔτε ἐν ᾧ οὐκ ἔστιν· οὐκ ἄρα τι κινεῖται

The moving object either moves in the place where it is, or where it is not; and neither where it is does it move, nor where it is not; ergo, it does not move.

Epiphanius, *Panarion* 3.505.30

The Arrow Paradox, cf. Aristotle, Physics *239a–b and Zeno, Fragment 4 (D-K)*

2 μεγέθους γὰρ μηδενὸς ὄντος, προσγενομένου δέ, οὐδὲν οἷόν τε εἰς μέγεθος ἐπιδοῦναι ... εἰ δὲ ... μηδὲ αὖ προσγινομένου αὐξήσεται, δῆλον ὅτι τὸ προσγενόμενον οὐδὲν ἦν

If a unit without magnitude were added to anything else, it would not make it larger. For if it is of no magnitude but is added, the other thing cannot increase at all in magnitude. Thus what is added will therefore be nothing.

Translated by Jonathan Barnes (1987)

Fragment 2 (D-K)

3 ἀμφοτερογλώσσου τε μέγα σθένος οὐκ ἀλαπαδνὸν
Ζήνωνος πάντων ἐπιλήπτορος

He could argue both ways with resistless fury,
Zeno, assailer of all things.

Translated by Bernadotte Perrin (1916)

Testimonies, Fragment 1 (D-K)

of Zeno the inventor of dialectic, ready to argue in favour of either side; written by Timon, Fragment 819 (Lloyd-Jones and Parsons, SH*)*

ZENODOTUS

3rd century BC (?)

1 Τίς γλύψας τὸν Ἔρωτα παρὰ κρήνησιν ἔθηκεν
οἰόμενος παύσειν τοῦτο τὸ πῦρ ὕδατι;

Who carved Eros and placed him by the fountain,
thinking to quench the fire of love with water?

Greek Anthology 16.14

ZONAS

dates unknown

presumed to be the Diodorus Zonas of Sardis, *fl.* 80BC

1 Ἀρτιχανῆ ῥοιάν τε καὶ ἀρτίχνουν τόδε μῆλον
καὶ ῥυτιδόφλοιον σῦκον ἐπομφάλιον
πορφύρεόν τε βότρυν μεθυπίδακα, πυκνορρᾶγα,
καὶ κάρυον χλωρῆς ἀντίδορον λεπίδος

A newly split pomegranate, this quince covered with fresh down, a navelled fig with wrinkled skin, a purple cluster of grapes, fountain of wine, and a walnut just out of its rind.

Translated by W.R. Paton (1916)

Greek Anthology 6.22

a dedication to Priapus, the Orchard God

ZOPYRUS

possibly 3rd century BC
Tragic playwright

1 μηδεὶς ἄπειρος τῶν ἐμῶν εἴη φίλων
ἔρωτος, εὐτυχῶν δὲ τὸν θεὸν λάβοι

May no one of my friends be ignorant
of love;
attaining love he will take hold of god.

Fragment 1 (Snell, *TrGF*)

APPENDIX 1

QUOTATIONS ON GREECE AND GREEKS

Joseph Addison
1672–1719
English poet, dramatist, and essayist; co-founder of *The Spectator*

> It must be so – Plato, thou reason'st well! –
> Else hence this pleasing hope, this fond desire,
> This longing after immortality ...?
>
> *Cato* (1713), Act 5, Scene 1

Jean Le Rond d'Alembert
1717–1783
French mathematician and philosopher

> *Chaque siècle, et le nôtre surtout, auraient besoin d'un Diogène; mais la difficulté est de trouver des hommes qui aient le courage de l'être, et des hommes qui aient le courage de le souffrir.*
>
> Every century, ours above all, have need of a Diogenes; but the difficulty is to find men who have the courage to be Diogenes, and men who have the courage to tolerate one.
>
> *Essais sur la sociéte des gens de lettres* (1759)

Anonymous

> Ah! You Greeks are forever children – not one of you is a grown-up! ... All of you are young at heart!
>
> *an Egyptian priest to Solon (c.640 – after 556BC); cf. Plato 342*

> Some talk of Alexander, and some of Hercules;
> Of Hector and Lysander, and such great names as these;
> But of all the world's brave heroes, there's none that can compare
> With a tow, row, row, row, row, row, for the British Grenadiers.
>
> *'The British Grenadiers' (traditional song)*

> This story of Homer is like our own: It tells of a war-torn country in which mad gods mix with men and women who never know exactly what the fighting is about, or when they will be happy, or why they will be killed.
>
> from an article 'Mucho más que libros' in *Semana*, 4 June 2001, Bogotá, quoted by Alberto Manguel in *The Iliad and the Odyssey*, Books that Shook the World (2007), p.6
>
> *villagers of a Colombian village who refused to return the Spanish translation of the* Iliad, *the only book ever not to be returned to this itinerant library.*

> The Acropolis is the she-wolf who gave milk to Romeo and Juliet.
>
> *some schoolchild, somewhere, in a history test*

> Who is he callin'?
>
> quoted by Kouka Anjou guiding foreigners in the Olympia Archaeological Museum
>
> *a good lady on seeing a sculpture of a philosopher holding his head in contemplation, as if using a telephone*

St Thomas Aquinas
c.1225–1274
Italian Dominican friar and doctor of the Church

> *Et tamen minimum quod potest haberi de cognitione rerum altissimum desiderabilius est quam certissima cognito quae habetur de minimis rebus, ut dicitur in De Animal.*
>
> As Aristotle also points out, the slenderest acquaintance we can form with heavenly things is more desirable than a thorough grasp of mundane matters.
>
> *Summa Theologiae* (1266–1273), pt. Ia, qu. I, art. 5

Mathew Arnold
1822–1888
English poet and essayist

> Hebraism and Hellenism – between these two points of influence moves our World.
>
> *Culture and Anarchy* (1869), ch. 4

> The governing idea of Hellenism is spontaneity of consciousness; that of Hebraism strictness of conscience.
>
> *Culture and Anarchy* (1869), ch. 4

> The translator of Homer should above all be penetrated by a sense of four qualities of his author: – that he is eminently rapid … eminently plain … eminently direct … and eminently noble.
>
> *On Translating Homer* (1861), Lecture I

> The power of the Latin classic is in *character*, that of the Greek is in *beauty*. Now character is capable of being taught, learnt, and assimilated: beauty hardly.
>
> *Schools and Universities on the Continent* (1868)

Augustus
63BC–14AD
First Roman emperor

> That they would pay at the Greek Kalends.
>
> Suetonius, *Lives of the Caesars*, 'Divus Augustus', sect. 87
>
> *meaning never; the Greeks did not use calends in reckoning time.*

Joachim du Bellay
c.1522–1560
French poet and critic

> *Heureux qui comme Ulysse a fait un beau voyage.*
>
> Happy the wanderer who, like Ulysses, has made a lovely voyage.
>
> *Sonnets*

Richard Bentley
1662–1742
English classical scholar

> It is a pretty poem, Mr. Pope, but you must not call it Homer.
>
> John Hawkins (ed.), *The Works of Samuel Johnson* (1787), vol. 4, 'The Life of Pope'
>
> *when pressed by Pope to comment on 'My Homer' (i.e. his translation of Homer's* Iliad*)*

Henry St John, 1st Viscount Bolingbroke
1678–1751
English politician

> I have read somewhere or other – in Dionysius of Halicarnassus, I think – that History is Philosophy teaching by examples.
>
> *On the Study of History* (1809), letter 2
>
> *cf. Dionysius of Halicarnassus 33*

Sir Thomas Browne
1605–1682
English writer and physician

> I have often admired the mystical way of Pythagoras, and the secret magic of numbers.
>
> *Religio Medici* (1643), pt. I, sect. 12
>
> *cf. Pythagoras 12*

Elizabeth Barrett Browning
1806–1861
English poet; wife of Robert Browning

> … Pan is dead! Pan is dead!
> Pan, Pan is dead!
>
> 'The Dead Pan'
>
> *cf. Plutarch 165*

> What was he doing, the great god Pan,
> Down in the reeds by the river …?

'A Musical Instrument' (1862)

cf. Sophocles 27

Edmund Burke
1729–1797
Irish-born Whig politician and man of letters

Nobility is a graceful ornament to the civil order. It is the Corinthian capital of polished society

Reflections on the Revolution in France (1790)

Robert Burns
1759–1796
Scottish poet

But tell me whiskey's name in Greek,
I'll tell the reason.

'The Author's Earnest Cry and Prayer' (1786)

Myles Fredric Burnyeat
(1939–)
English classicist and philosopher

Always, someone somewhere is reading the *Republic*.

'Plato as Educator of 19th century Britain', in *Philosophers on Education*, ed. Amélie Oskenberg Rorty (1998); quoted in Simon Blackburn, *Plato's Republic: A Biography* (2006), p.9

Robert Burton
1577–1640
English clergyman and scholar

We can say nothing, but what has been said …
Our poets steal from Homer …

The Anatomy of Melancholy (1621–1651), 'Democritus to the Reader'

And this is that Homer's golden chain, which reacheth
Down from Heaven to earth, by which every creature is annexed, and depends on his Creator.

The Anatomy of Melancholy (1621–1651), pt. 3, sect. 1, member 1, subsect. 2

cf. Homer 102

Diogenes struck the father when the son swore.

The Anatomy of Melancholy (1621–1651), pt. 3, sect. 2, member 5, subsect. 5

Samuel Butler
1612–1680
English poet

Beside, 'tis known he could speak Greek,
As naturally as pigs squeak.

Hudibras, pt. I, canto I

George Gordon, Lord Byron
1788–1824
English poet

Dull is the eye that will not weep to see
Thy walls defaced, thy mouldering shrines removed
By British hands.

Childe Harold's Pilgrimage (1812–1818), canto 2, st. 15

of the Elgin marbles

Dark Sappho! could not verse immortal save
That breast imbued with such immortal fire?
Could she not live who life eternal gave?

Childe Harold's Pilgrimage (1812–1818), canto 2, st. 39

Fair Greece! sad relic of departed worth!
Immortal, though no more; though fallen, great!

Childe Harold's Pilgrimage (1812–1818), canto 2, st. 73

The isles of Greece, the isles of Greece!
Where burning Sappho loved and sung,
Where grew the arts of war and peace,
Where Delos rose, and Phoebus sprung!

Don Juan (1819–1824), canto 3, st. 86

The mountains look on Marathon –
And Marathon looks on the sea;
And musing there an hour alone,
I dreamed that Greece might still be free.

Don Juan (1819–1824), canto 3, st. 86

Place me on Sunium's marble steep,
Where nothing save the waves and I
May hear our mutual murmurs sweep;
There, swanlike, let me sing and die.
A land of slaves shall ne'er be mine –
Dash down yon cup of Samian wine!

Don Juan (1819–1824), canto 4, st. 16

I've stood upon Achilles' tomb,
And heard Troy doubted; time will
doubt of Rome.

Don Juan (1819–1824), canto 4, st. 101

Cato the Elder
234–149BC
Roman statesman, orator and writer

On the whole he thought the words of the Greeks were born on their lips, but those of the Romans in their hearts.

Plutarch, *Lives Cato Major* 12.7

cf. Cato 6

There is nothing else to admire in Socrates of old except that he was kind and gentle to his shrewish wife and his stupid sons.

Plutarch, *Lives Cato Major*, 20.3

cf. Cato 12

Winston Spencer Churchill
1874–1965
British author, historian, politician and statesman, served as prime minister 1940–1945 and 1951–1955

I am biased in favour of boys learning English; I would make them all learn English: and then I would let the clever ones learn Latin as an honour, and Greek as a treat.

Roving Commission: My Early Life (1930)

And we will not say that Greeks fight like heroes, but we will say that heroes fight like Greeks.

BBC broadcast, shortly after 28 October 1940 when Greece was invaded by the Italians, who were defeated and pushed back into Albania

Cicero
Marcus Tullius Cicero
106–43BC
Roman orator and statesman

For if anyone thinks that the glory won by the writing of Greek verse is naturally less than that accorded to the poet who writes in Latin, he is entirely in the wrong. Greek literature is read in nearly every nation under heaven, while the vogue of Latin is confined to its own boundaries, and they are, we must grant, narrow.

Translated by N.H. Watts in *Cicero, The Speeches*, The Loeb Classical Library (1923)

Pro Archia Poeta 23

Socrates was the first to call philosophy down from the heavens and to place it in cities, and even to introduce it into homes and compel it to inquire about life and standards and goods and evils.

Tusculanae Disputationes v. 4

S. Marc Cohen, Patricia Curd, and C.D.C. Reeve
Professors of Philosophy, University of Washington, Purdue University and University of North Carolina, Chapel Hill, respectively

Every university and college, every intellectual discipline and scientific advance, every step toward freedom and away from ignorance, superstition, and enslavement to repressive dogma is eloquent testimony to the power of their invention. If they had not existed, our world would not exist

Readings in Ancient Greek Philosophy, 3rd edn, Indianapolis (2005), Introduction

of Greek philosophers

Dante Alighieri
1265–1321
Italian poet

Onorate l'altissimo poeta.
Honour the greatest poet.

Divina Commedia, 'Inferno' (1300), canto 4

of Homer

Il maestro di color che sanno.
The master of those who know.

Translated by Mark Musa (1984)

Divina Commedia, 'Inferno' (1300), canto 4

of Aristotle

Charles Darwin
1809–1882
English natural historian

From quotations which I had seen, I had a high notion of Aristotle's merits, but I had not the most remote notion what a wonderful man he was. Linnaeus and

Cuvier have been my two gods, though in very different ways, but they were mere schoolboys of old Aristotle.

to William Ogle, on the publication of his translation of The Parts of Animals (1882)

Johann Gustav Droysen
1808–1884
German historian

Nicht die abgestorbenen Vergangenheiten sollen uns wiederkehren; aber was in ihnen Grosses und Unvergänliches … kein Babel toter Trümmerstücke, sondern ein Pantheon der Vergangenheit sei unsere Gegenwart.

Not that the dead past should return; but whatever in it is Great and Everlasting … not a Babel of ruins, but a pantheon of the Past be our Present.

Kleine Schriften zur Alten Geschichte II, Leipzig (1894), S.146–152

Gerald Durrell
1925–1995
English writer of books on animals

The tiny ship throbbed away from the heel of Italy out into the twilit sea, and as we slept in our stuffy cabins, somewhere in that tract of moon-polished water we passed the invisible dividing-line and entered the bright, looking-glass world of Greece.

My Family and Other Animals (1956), pt. 1, 'The Migration'

Albert Einstein
1879–1955
German-born American theoretical physicist

How can an educated person stay away from the Greeks? I have always been far more interested in them than in Science.

from an interview by Niccolo Tucci in The New Yorker, *22 November 1947*

Ralph Waldo Emerson
1803–1882
American essayist, philosopher and poet

Plato is philosophy, and philosophy, Plato … his broad humanity transcends all sectional lines.

Representative Men, London, John Chapman (1850), 'Plato'; quoted in Simon Blackburn, *Plato's Republic: A Biography* (2006), Introduction, p.3

Olympian bards who sung
Divine ideas below,
Which always find us young,
And always keep us so.

'Ode to Beauty' (1847)

Earth proudly wears the Parthenon
As the best gem upon her zone.

'The Problem' (1847), st. 3

Robert Fitzgerald
1910–1985
Poet, critic and translator

The Odyssey, considered strictly as an aesthetic object, is to be appreciated only in Greek. It can no more be translated into English than rhododendron can be translated into dogwood. You must learn Greek if you want to experience Homer.

Robert Fitzgerald, *The Odyssey* (1963), postscript, p.505

Kathleen Freeman
1897–1959
British classical scholar

The advice is: learn Greek. Why? Because there is nothing which will give you so much entertainment in return for an initial effort … and its literature is a veritable Aladdin's Cave.

The Greek Way, Introduction (1947)

Henry Fuseli
Johann Heinrich Füssli
1741–1825
Swiss-born British painter and art critic

The Greeks were gods! The Greeks were gods!

J. Mordaunt Crook, *The Greek Revival* (1995)
on first seeing the Elgin marbles

Thomas Gaisford
1779–1855
English classicist; Dean of Christ Church, Oxford, from 1831

Nor can I do better, in conclusion, than impress upon you the study of Greek literature, which not only elevates above the vulgar herd, but leads not infrequently to positions of considerable emolument.

Christmas Day Sermon in the Cathedral, Oxford, in W. Tuckwell, *Reminiscences of Oxford* (2nd edn, 1907)

Valéry Giscard d'Estaing
1926–
French politician, President of France 1974–1981

Une Europe sans la Grèce aurait été comme un enfant sans certificat de naissance.

Europe without Greece would be like a child without a birth certificate.

Article by Philippe Gumy in *Le Temps*, 30 April 2010

Johann Wolfgang von Goethe
1749–1832
German poet, novelist, playwright, courtier and natural philosopher

Gieb mir wo ich stehe!
Archimedes ...
Behaupte wo du stehst!

Tell me where I stand, Archimedes!
Assert where you stand!

In *Goethe's Werke, Herausgegeben von Heinrich Kurz*, Leipzig, Verlag des Bibliographischen Instituts, 'Maximen und Reflexionen', Dritte Abtheilung, vol. 12, p.691

Allen andern Künsten muss man Etwas vorgeben, der Griechischen allein bleibt man ewig Schuldner.

In all art we must pretend, somehow; only to Greek art we always remain debtors.

'Maximen und Reflexionen', Dritte Abtheilung, vol. 12, p.701

Your letter found me, as you would wish, in the *Iliad*, to which I return with ever greater pleasure, for one is always raised up above everything earthly, just as in an air balloon, and one finds oneself truly in the intermediate zone where the gods glide to and fro.

quoted in R.L. Fox, *Travelling Heroes*, London (2008), title page

Goethe writing to Schiller, 12 May 1798

W.K.C. Guthrie
1906–1981
Scottish classical scholar

The Hellenic mind has its romantic as well as its classical aspect, and both reach their climax without incongruity in the genius of that remarkable Sicilian Empedocles, who sums up and personifies the spirit of his age and race.

A History of Greek Philosophy, vol. II: The Presocratic Tradition from Parmenides to *Democritus*, p.126

Edith Hamilton
1867–1963
American educationist, classicist and author

The Greeks were the first Westerners; the spirit of the West, the modern spirit, is a Greek discovery and the place of the Greeks is in the modern world.

The Greek Way (1930), ch. 1, p.16, Norton paperback (1993)

The Greeks were the first intellectualists. In a world where the irrational had played the chief role, they came forward as the protagonists of the mind.

The Greek Way (1930), ch. 1, p.16, Norton paperback (1993)

To rejoice in life, to find the world beautiful and delightful to live in, was a mark of the Greek spirit which distinguished it from all that had gone before.

The Greek Way (1930), ch. 2, p.25, Norton paperback (1993)

The Greeks knew to the full how bitter life is as well as how sweet. Joy and sorrow, exultation and tragedy, stand hand in hand in Greek literature ... The Greeks were keenly aware, terribly aware, of life's uncertainty and the imminence of death.

The Greek Way (1930), ch. 2, pp.25–26, Norton paperback (1993)

Horace
Quintus Horatius Flaccus
65–8BC
Roman poet

Vos exemplaria Graeca
Nocturna versate manu, versate diurnu.

You should turn the pages of your Greek models by night and by day.

Ars Poetica 1.268

Grais ingenium, Grais dedit ore rotundo Musa loqui

It was the Greeks who had at the Muse's hand the native gift, the Greeks who had the utterance of finished grace.

Ars Poetica 1.323

Indignor quandoque bonus dormitat Homerus

I'm aggrieved when sometimes even excellent Homer nods.

Ars Poetica 1.359

Quidquid delirant reges plectuntur Achivi.

For every folly their leaders commit the Greeks themselves are punished.

Epistles bk. 1, no. 2, 1.14

Principibus placuisse viris non ultima laus est.
Non ciuvis homini contingit adire Corinthum.

It is not the least praise to have pleased leading men.
Not everyone is lucky enough to get to Corinth.

Epistles bk. 1, no. 17, 1.35

cf. Aristophanes 169, Demosthenes 102 and George Orwell (below)

Graecia capta ferum victorem cepit et artis intulit agresti Latio.

Captured Greece enslaved her victor bringing arts to uncouth Latium.

Epistles bk. 2, no. 1, 1.156

James Howell
*c.*1594–1666
British historian and writer

Plato, Aristotle, and Socrates are secretaries of Nature.

Letters 2.2

Ted Hughes
1930–1998
English poet

Fourteen centuries have learned,
From charred remains, that what took place
When Alexandria's library burned
Brain-damaged the human race.

'Hear it Again' (1997)

Thomas Hughes
1822–1896
English lawyer, politician, and writer

'I don't give a straw for Greek particles, or the digamma, no more does his mother. What is he sent to school for ...?'

Tom Brown's Schooldays (1857), pt. I, ch. 4

William Ralph Inge
1860–1954
English writer; Dean of St Paul's, 1911–1934

The nations which have put mankind and posterity most in their debt have been small states – Israel, Athens, Florence, Elizabethan England.

Outspoken Essays: Second Series (1922), 'State, visible and invisible'

Thomas Jefferson
1743–1826
American statesman, third President of the United States, 1801–1809

Greece was the first of civilized nations which presented an example of what man should be.

to Adamantios Koraes, 1823

Samuel Johnson
1709–1784
English poet, critic, and lexicographer

My old friend, Mrs. Carter, could make a pudding as well as translate Epictetus.

Boswell, *Life of Johnson*; L.F. Powell's revision of G.B. Hill's edition, vol. i, p.123, n. 1738

All our religion, all our arts, almost all that sets us above savages, has come from the shores of the Mediterranean.

Life of Johnson, vol. ii, pp.25–26 (1776),

Everyman edition, Dutton (1906, repr. 1973)

Classical quotation is the *parole* of literary men all over the world.

James Boswell, *Life of Johnson* (1791), 8 May (1781, ed. G.B. Hill, rev. L.F. Powell 1934)

A man is in general better pleased when he has a good dinner upon his table, than when his wife talks Greek.

John Hawkins (ed.), *The Works of Samuel Johnson* (1787), 'Apophthegms, Sentiments, Opinion, etc.', vol. II

Ben Jonson
*c.*1572–1637
English dramatist and poet

Greek was free from rhyme's infection,
Happy Greek, by this protection,
Was not spoiled.

Underwoods: Poems of Devotion, xlviii, 'A Fit of Rhyme against Rhyme'

Juvenal
*c.*55–*c.*140AD
Roman satirist

Grammaticus, rhetor, geometres, pictor, aliptes,
Augur, schoenobates, medicus, magnus, omnia novit
Graeculus esuriens: in caelum iusseris ibit.

Scholar, public speaker, geometrician, painter,
Physical training instructor, diviner of the future,
Rope-dancer, doctor, magician, the hungry little
Greek can do everything: send him to – heaven
(and he'll go there).

Satires, no. 3, I.76

John Keats
1795–1821
English poet

O Attic shape! Fair attitude!

'Ode on a Grecian Urn' (1820), st. 5

Much have I travell'd in the realms of gold,
And many goodly states and kingdoms seen;
Round many western islands have I been
Which bards in fealty to Apollo hold.
Oft of one wide expanse had I been told
That deep-brow'd Homer ruled as his demesne;
Yet did I never breathe its pure serene
Till I heard Chapman speak out loud and bold:
Then felt I like some watcher of the skies
When a new planet swims into his ken;
Or like stout Cortez when with eagle eyes
He star'd at the Pacific – and all his men
Look'd at each other with a wild surmise –
Silent, upon a peak in Darien.

'On First Looking into Chapman's Homer' (1817)

Helen Keller
1880–1968
American writer and social reformer, blind and deaf from the age of 19 months

If it is true that the violin is the most perfect of musical instruments, then Greek is the violin of human thought.

Letter to Mrs Laurence Hutton, 20 February 1898, in *The Story of My Life* (1903)

Rudyard Kipling
1865–1936
English writer and poet

When 'Omer smote 'is bloomin' lyre,
He'd 'eard men sing by land an' sea;
An' what he thought e'might require,
'E went an' took – the same as me!

'When 'Omer Smote 'is bloomin' lyre' (1896)

H.D.F. Kitto
1897–1982
British classical scholar

Talk was the breath of life to the Greek – as indeed it still is, though somewhat spoiled by a serious addiction to newspapers.

The Greeks (1958), p.36

Nathaniel Lee
*c.*1653–1692
English dramatist

When Greeks joined Greeks, then was the tug of war!

The Rival Queens (1677), Act 4, Scene 2

F.L. Lucas
1894–1967
English literary critic, poet and novelist

A public tends to get the literature it deserves: a literature, to get the public it deserves ... Only a fine society could have bred Homer: and he left it finer for hearing him.

Critical Thoughts in Critical Days (1942)

Not Ibsen, not Voltaire, not Tolstoy ever forged a keener weapon in defence of womanhood, in defiance of superstition, in denunciation of war, than the *Medea*, the *Ion*, the *Trojan Women*.

Euripides and His Influence, 15 (1923)

Lucretius
Titus Lucretius Carus
*c.*99–55BC
Roman poet

Ergo vivida vis animi pervicit, et extra
Processit longe flammantia moenia mundi
Atque omne immensum peragravit, mente animoque.

So the vital strength of his spirit won through, and he made his way far outside the flaming walls of the world and ranged over the measureless whole, both in mind and spirit.

De Rerum Natura I.72
on Epicurus

Thomas Babington Macaulay
1800–1859
English politician and historian

With the dead there is no rivalry. In the dead there is no change. Plato is never sullen. Demosthenes never comes unseasonably.

Essays Contributed to the Edinburgh Review (1843), vol. 2, 'Lord Bacon'

Harold Macmillan
1894–1986
British conservative statesman; prime minister 1957–1963

We ... are Greeks in this American empire ... We must run the Allied Forces HQ as the Greeks ran the operations of the Emperor Claudius.

Sunday Telegraph, 9 February 1964
to Richard Crossman in 1944

Henry Maine
1822–1888
English jurist

Except blind forces of Nature, nothing moves in this world which is not Greek in its origin.

Village Communities (3rd edn, 1876)

Nelson Mandela
1918–2013
South African politician; president 1994–1999

Greece is the Mother of Democracy and South Africa its youngest daughter.

quoted by George Bizos, friend and lawyer to Nelson Mandela, in *Odyssey to Freedom* (2007), p.587

Christopher Marlowe
1564–1593
English dramatist and poet

Live and die in Aristotle's works.

Doctor Faustus (1604), Act 1, Scene 33

Was this the face that launched a thousand ships,
And burnt the topless towers of Ilium?
Sweet Helen, make me immortal with a kiss!

Doctor Faustus (1604), Act 5, Scene 1

John Stuart Mill
1806–1873
English philosopher and economist

The battle of Marathon was more important an event for British history than the battle of Hastings.

quoted in Vivi Vassilopoulou, *Marathon 2,500 Years*, Athens (2010), p.92

Edna St Vincent Millay
1892–1950
American poet

Euclid alone
Has looked on Beauty bare.

The Harp-Weaver and Other Poems (1923), sonnet 22

Henry Miller
1891–1980
American novelist and painter

Marvellous things happen to one in Greece – marvellous *good* things which can happen to one nowhere else on earth. Somehow, almost as if He were nodding, Greece still remains under the protection of the Creator.

The Colossus of Maroussi (1941), pt. I

Greece is the home of the gods; they may have died but their presence still makes itself felt. The gods were of human proportion: they were created out of the human spirit.

The Colossus of Maroussi (1941), pt. III

Until he [man] has become fully human, until he learns to conduct himself as a member of the earth, he will continue to create gods who will destroy him. The tragedy of Greece lies not in the destruction of a great culture but in the abortion of a great vision.

The Colossus of Maroussi (1941), pt. III

John Milton
1608–1674
English poet

How charming is divine philosophy!
Not harsh and crabbèd, as dull fools
suppose,
But musical as is Apollo's lute.

Comus (1637), 1.516

Athens, the eye of Greece, mother of
arts
And eloquence.

Paradise Regained (1671), bk. 4, 1.240

Socrates …
Whom well inspired the oracle
pronounced
Wisest of men.

Paradise Regained (1671), bk. 4, 1.274

cf. Oracles 17

The first and wisest of them all
professed
To know this only, that he nothing
knew.

Paradise Regained (1671), bk. 4, 1.293

Alfonso E. Moreno
Tutorial fellow at Magdalen College, Oxford

Thucydides is a writer who may tell the truth and nothing but the truth, but often (and especially in matters of politics) not the *whole* truth.

Feeding the Democracy: The Athenian Grain Supply in the Fifth and Fourth Centuries BC, Oxford (2007), p.126, n.231

M. Morgan
Translator and editor of Plutarch's *Morals*

Plutarch was the wisest man of his age, and if he had been a Christian, one of the best too.

Morgan's dedication to the Archbishop of Canterbury, William Wake, in 1718; quoted by Ralph Waldo Emerson, introduction to *Plutarch's Morals* (1878)

Friedrich Nietzsche
1844–1900
German philosopher and writer

How could even Plato have endured life – a Greek life which he repudiated – without an Aristophanes?

Beyond Good and Evil, ed. Walter Kaufmann (1966); quoted in Simon Blackburn, *Plato's Republic: A Biography* (2006), p.18

Nietzsche on learning that on his deathbed Plato was reading Aristophanes

Und nun würdige man die Grösse jener Ausnahme-Griechen, welche die Wissenschaft schufen! Wer von ihnen erzählt, erzählt die heldenhafteste Geschichte des menschlichen Geistes!

And now let us acknowledge the greatness of those Exceptional Greeks who created science! Whoever tells of them, tells the most heroic story of the human mind!

Menschliches, Allzumenschliches II, Meinungen und Sprüche 221, tr. Oscar Levy

A great value of antiquity lies in the fact that its writings are the only ones that modern men still read with exactness.

We Philologists, no. 17, tr. J.M. Kennedy (1911)

What we can obtain from the Greeks only begins to dawn upon us in later years: only after we have undergone many experiences, and thought a great deal.

We Philologists, no. 23, tr. J.M. Kennedy (1911)

The Greeks have created the greatest number of individuals, and thus they give us so much insight into men,—a Greek cook is more of a cook than any other.

We Philologists, no. 44, tr. J.M. Kennedy (1911)

One is no longer at home anywhere, so in the end one longs to be back where one can somehow be at home because it is the only place where one would wish to be at home: and that is the world of Greece.

Quoted by Gregory Nagy, *Onassis International Prizes*, Athens, 18 October 2006

Charles Eliot Norton
1827–1908
American author, social critic and professor of art

A knowledge of Greek thought and life, and of the arts in which the Greeks expressed their thought and sentiment, is essential to high culture. A man may know everything else, but without this knowledge he remains ignorant of the best intellectual and moral achievements of his own race.

Letter to F.A. Tupper (1885)

Omar
c.581–644
Arab caliph, conqueror of Syria, Palestine and Egypt

If these writings of the Greeks agree with the book of God, they are useless and need not be preserved; if they disagree, they are pernicious and ought to be destroyed.

Edward Gibbon, *The Decline and Fall of the Roman Empire* (1776–1788), ch. 51

on burning the library of Alexandria, c.641AD

George Orwell
1903–1950
English novelist

The other day I picked up a copy of Lemprière's *Classical Dictionary*, the *Who's Who* of the ancients. Opening it at random, I came upon the biography of Laïs, the famous courtesan. ... She first began to sell her favours at Corinth for 10,000 drachmas. Demosthenes visited Corinth for the sake of Laïs, but informed by the courtesan that admittance to her bed was to be bought at this enormous sum the orator departed, and observed that he would not buy repentance at so dear a price. That was 2,283 years ago. I wonder how many of the present denizens of *Who's Who* will seem worth reading about in A.D. 4226?

'As I Please', *Tribune*, 17 December 1943

cf. Demosthenes 102

Thomas Love Peacock
1785–1866
English novelist and poet

Ancient sculpture is the true school of modesty. But where the Greeks had modesty, we have cant; where they had poetry, we have cant; where they had patriotism, we have cant; where they had anything that exalts, delights, or adorns humanity, we have nothing but cant, cant, cant.

Crotchet Castle (1831), ch. 7

Charles Péguy
1873–1914
French poet, essayist and editor

Homère est nouveau ce matin, et rien n'est peut-être aussi vieux que le journal d'aujourd-hui.

Homer is new and fresh this morning, and nothing, perhaps is as old and tired as today's newspaper.

Note sur M. Bergson et la Philosophie Bergsonienne (1914)

Žarko Petan

1929–2014

Slovenian writer, essayist, screenwriter, and theatre and film director

'All flows' said the modern day Heraclitus, and we cannot find a plumber!

Aphorisms (Greek edn, 1998)

cf. Heraclitus 56

Edgar Allan Poe

1809–1849

American writer

The glory that was Greece
And the grandeur that was Rome.

'To Helen' (1831)

Alexander Pope

1688–1744

English poet

For I, who hold sage Homer's rule the best,
Welcome the coming, speed the going guest.

Imitations of Horace, bk. 2, Satire 2 (1734), 1.159

cf. Homer 345

Cole Porter

1891–1964

American songwriter

The girls today in society
Go for classical poetry,
So to win their hearts one must quote with ease
Aeschylus and Euripides.

'Brush up your Shakespeare', *Kiss Me Kate* (1948), Act 2

Ezra Pound

1885–1972

American poet

Shades of Callimachus, Coan ghosts of Philetus,
It is in your groves I would walk.

Homage to Sextus Propertius (1934)

Bertrand Russell

1872–1970

British philosopher, logician, essayist and social critic

A man must not write on Plato unless he has spent so much of his youth on Greek as to have had no time for the things Plato thought important.

Platonism Ancient and Modern, Berkeley, Calif., University of California Press (1938), p.146

Heinrich Schliemann

1822–1890

German archaeologist

I have gazed upon the face of Agamemnon.

W.M. Calder and D.A. Traill, *Myth, Scandal, and History* (1986)

on discovering a gold mask at Mycenae, 1876; traditional version of his telegram to the minister at Athens: 'This one is very like the picture which my imagination formed of Agamemnon long ago.'

C.P. Scott

1846–1932

British journalist; editor of the *Manchester Guardian*, 1872–1929

Television? The word is half Greek, half Latin. No good can come of it.

Asa Briggs, *The BBC: The First Fifty Years* (1985)

William Shakespeare

1564–1616

English dramatist

Cassius: Did Cicero say any thing?
Casca: Ay, he spoke Greek.
Cassius: To what effect?
Casca: Nay, an I tell you that, I'll ne'er look you i'
the face again; but those that understood him
smiled at one another and shook their heads;
but, for mine own part, it was Greek to me.

Julius Caesar (1599), Act 1, Scene 2, 1

Clown: What is the opinion of
Pythagoras concerning wild fowl?
Malvolio: That the soul of our grandam
might haply inhabit a bird.
Clown: What thinkest thou of his
opinion?
Malvolio: I think nobly of the soul, and
no way approve his opinion.

Twelfth Night, Act 4, Scene 2, 55

cf. Pythagoras 15

George Bernard Shaw
1856–1950
Irish dramatist

Nobody can say a word against Greek: it stamps a man at once as an educated gentleman.

Major Barbara (1907), Act 1

John Sheffield, 1st Duke of Buckingham and Normanby
1648–1721
English poet and politician

Read Homer once, and you can read no
more,
For all books else appear so mean, so
poor,
Verse will seem prose; but still persist
to read,
And Homer will be all the books you
need.

An Essay on Poetry (1682)

Percy Bysshe Shelley
1792–1822
English poet

We are all Greeks: our laws, our literature, our religion, our arts, have their roots in Greece.

Hellas (1822), preface

Let there be light! said Liberty,
And like sunrise from the sea,
Athens arose!

Hellas (1822), 1.682

A brighter Hellas rears its mountains
From waves serener far;
A new Peneus rolls his fountains
Against the morning star.
Where fairer Tempes bloom, there sleep
Young Cyclads on a sunnier deep.

Hellas (1822), 1.1066

Another Orpheus sings again,
And loves, and weeps, and dies.
A new Ulysses leaves once more
Calypso for his native shore.

Hellas (1822), 1.1072

Riddles of death Thebes never knew.

Hellas (1822), 1.1083

cf. Oracles 1, Riddles 1 and Sophocles 213

Another Athens shall arise
And to remoter time
Bequeath, like sunset to the skies,
The splendour of its prime.

Hellas (1822), 1.1090

William Shenstone
1714–1763
English poet and essayist

Laws are generally found to be nets of such a texture, as the little creep through, the great break through, and the middle-sized are alone entangled.

Works in Verse and Prose (1764), vol. 2, 'On Politics'

cf. Anacharsis 6 and Jonathan Swift (below)

Robert South
1634–1716
English court preacher

An Aristotle was but the rubbish of an Adam, and Athens but the rudiments of Paradise.

Twelve Sermons (1692), vol. I, no. 2

Edmund Spenser
c.1552–1599
English poet

Of such deep learning little had he need,
Ne yet of Latin, ne of Greek that breed
Doubts 'mongst Divines, and difference
of texts,
From whence arise diversity of sects,
And hateful heresies.

Prosopopoia or *Mother Hubbard's Tale* (1591), 1.385

Adlai Ewing Stevenson
1900–1965
American politician

The art of government has grown from its seeds in the tiny city-states of Greece to become the political mode of half the world.

Speech at Harvard University, 17 June 1965
of democracy

Jonathan Swift
1667–1745
Irish poet and satirist

Laws are like cobwebs, which may catch small flies, but let wasps and hornets break through.

A Critical Essay upon the Faculties of the Mind (1709)
cf. Anacharsis 6 and William Shenstone (above)

As learned commentators view
In Homer more than Homer knew.

On Poetry (1733), 1.103

Algernon Charles Swinburne
1837–1909
English poet

In the fair days when God
By man as godlike trod,
And each alike was Greek, alike was free.

'To Victor Hugo' (1866)

Alfred, Lord Tennyson
1809–1892
English poet

Nor at all can tell
Whether I mean this day to end myself,
Or lend an ear to Plato where he says,
That men like soldiers may not quit the post
Allotted by the Gods.

'Lucretius' (1868)

For my purpose holds
To sail beyond the sunset, and the baths
Of all the western stars, until I die.
It may be that the gulfs will wash us down:
It may be we shall touch the Happy Isles,
And see the great Achilles, whom we knew.

'Ulysses' (1842)

Leo Tolstoy
1828–1910
Russian novelist

Without knowledge of Greek there is no education.

Letter to A.A. Fet, 10 June 1871, in A.A. Fet, *My Recollections*
Tolstoy learned Greek very quickly; at some point his wife complained that he was muttering Greek in his sleep

Virgil
Publius Vergilius Maro
70–19BC
Roman poet

Equo ne credite, Teucri.
Quidquid id est, timeo Danaos et dona ferentes.

Do not trust the horse, Trojans. Whatever it is, I
Fear the Greeks even when they bring gifts.

Aeneid, bk. 2, i.48

Horace Walpole, Lord Orford
1717–1797
English writer and connoisseur

Alexander at the head of the world never tasted the true pleasure that boys of his own age have enjoyed at the head of a school.

Letter to George Montagu, 6 May 1736

The next Augustan age will dawn on the other side of the Atlantic. There will, perhaps, be a Thucydides at Boston, a Xenophon at New York, and, in time, a Virgil at Mexico, and a Newton at Peru. At last, some curious traveller from Lima will visit England and give a description of the ruins of St Paul's, like the editions of Balbec and Palmyra.

Letter to Horace Mann, 24 November 1774, in *Correspondence* (Yale edn), vol. 24

Isaac Watts
1674–1748
English hymn-writer

Alexander the Great … when he had conquered what was called the Eastern World … wept for want of more Worlds to conquer.

The Improvement of the Mind (1741)

cf. Alexander the Great 12

Alfred North Whitehead
1861–1947
English philosopher and mathematician

The safest general characterization of the European philosophical tradition is that it consists of a series of footnotes to Plato.

Process and Reality (1929), pt. 2, ch. 1, sect. 1

Oscar Wilde
1854–1900
Irish dramatist and poet

When one returns to the Greek it is like going into a garden of lilies out of some narrow and dark house. And to me, the pleasure is doubled by the reflection that it is extremely probable that we have the actual terms, the *ipsissima verba*, used by Christ.

De Profundis (1905)

of the New Testament in its original Greek

William Butler Yeats
1865–1939
Irish poet

What were all the world's alarms
To mighty Paris when he found
Sleep upon a golden bed,
That first dawn in Helen's arms.

'Lullaby' (1929)

Why, what could she have done, being what she is?
Was there a second Troy for her to burn?

'No Second Troy' (1910)

Never to have lived is best, ancient writers say;
Never to have drawn the breath of life, never to
have looked into the eye of day.
The second best 's a gay goodnight and quickly
turn away.

Oedipus at Colonus (1928)

cf. Sophocles 245

Homer is my example and his unchristened heart.

'Vacillation' (1932), VIII

APPENDIX 2

ABBREVIATIONS

*	an asterisk denotes that this treatise has been considered uncertain, spurious or dubious as a work by the author indicated
AAA	*Ἀρχαιολογικὰ Ἀνάλεκτα ἐξ Ἀθηνῶν*
ACO	*Acta conciliorum oecumenicorum*, ed. E. Schwartz, vol. 1.1.1–1.1.3, 1927; vol. 2.1.1–2.1.2, 1933. Berlin: De Gruyter
AG	*Anthologia Graeca, The Greek Anthology* (Liddell & Scott uses *AP* = *Anthologia Palatina*)
ALCLA	*Ancient Letters: Classical & Late Antique Epistolography*, ed. Ruth Morello and A.D. Morrison. Oxford: Oxford University Press, 2007
von Arnim	*Dionis Prusaensis quem vocant Chrysostomum quae exstant omnia*, ed. J. von Arnim, vol. 2. Berlin: Weidmann, 1896 (repr. 1962)
Arrighetti	*Epicuro. Opere*, ed. G. Arrighetti, 2nd edn. Turin: Einaudi, 1973
Austin	*Menander: Eleven Plays*, ed. Colin Austin, *Cambridge Classical Journal Supplement*, vol. 37. Cambridge Philological Society, 2013
Barigazzi	*Favorino di Arelate. Opere*, ed. A. Barigazzi. Florence: Monnier, 1966
Baudry	*Atticos. Fragments de son oeuvre*, ed. J. Baudry. Paris: Les Belles Lettres, 1931
BCH	*Bulletin de correspondance Hellénique, 1877–*
BFQ	*Bartlett's Familiar Quotations*, 15th edn, ed. Emily Morison Beck and the staff of Little, Brown and Company. Little Brown and Company, 1980; originally compiled by John Bartlett, 1855
c.	circa, approximately
CAF	T. Kock, *Comicorum Atticorum fragmenta*, 3 vols. Leipzig, 1880–1888
Caizzi	*Antisthenis fragmenta*, ed. F. Caizzi. Milan: Istituto Editoriale Cisalpino, 1966
Carey	*Lysiae orationes cum fragmentis*, ed. C. Carey. Oxford: Oxford University Press, 2007
CCGL	*The Cambridge Companion to Greek Lyric*, ed. Felix Budelmann. Cambridge: Cambridge University Press, 2009

CEG	1: *Carmina epigraphica graeca saeculorum viii-v a. Chr. n.*, P.A. Hansen. Berlin, 1983 2: *Carmina epigraphica graeca saeculi iv a. Chr. n. Accedunt addenda et corrigenda ad CEG* 1. Berlin, 1989
cf.	compare, see also
CGD	*The Complete Greek Drama*, ed. Whitney J. Oates and Eugene O'Neill, Jr, in 2 vols. New York: Random House, 1938
CGF	*Comicorum Graecorum fragmenta*, ed. G. Kaibel. Berlin: Weidmann, 1899
CGFPR	*Comicorum Graecorum fragmenta in papyris reperta*, ed. C. Austin. Berlin: De Gruyter, 1973
CGT	*The Complete Greek Tragedies*, ed. David Grene and Richmond Lattimore. Chicago: The University of Chicago Press, 1954 and 1991
CH	*Corpus Hermeticum*, ed. A.D. Nock and A.-J. Festugière, vols 3 and 4. Paris: Les Belles Lettres, 1954 (repr. 1972)
Chadwick	*The Sentences of Sextus*, ed. H. Chadwick. Cambridge: Cambridge University Press, 1959
Chambry	*Fabulae (dodecasyllabi)*, ed. E. Chambry, *Aesopi fabulae*. Paris: Les Belles Lettres, vol. 1, 1925; vol. 2, 1926
CMAL	*The Cynics: The Cynic Movement in Antiquity and its Legacy*, ed. R. Bracht Branham and Marie-Odile Goulet-Cazé. California University Press, 1996
Coll.Alex	*Collectanea Alexandrina*, ed. J.U. Powell. Oxford: Clarendon Press, 1925 (repr. 1970)
Conomis	*Lycurgi oratio in Leocratem*, ed. N.C. Conomis (post C. Scheibe and F. Blass). Leipzig: Teubner, 1970
Cougny	*Epigrammatum anthologia Palatina cum Planudeis et appendice nova*, ed. E. Cougny, vol. 3. Paris: Didot, 1890
CPG	*Corpus paroemiographorum Graecorum*, ed. E.L. von Leutsch, vol. 2. Göttingen: Vandenhoeck & Ruprecht, 1851 (repr. Hildesheim: Olms, 1958)
Crusius	*Plutarchi de proverbiis Alexandrinorum libellus ineditus*, ed. O. Crusius. Tübingen: Fues & Kostenbader, 1887
Cunningham	*Herodas. Mimiambi*, ed. I.C. Cunningham. Oxford: Clarendon Press, 1971
CWA	*The Complete Works of Aristotle: The Revised Oxford Translation*, ed. Jonathan Barnes, Bollingen Series LXXI. Princeton University Press, 1984. © 1984 by The Jowett Copyright Trustees
D-K	*Die Fragmente der Vorsokratiker*, ed. H. Diels and W. Kranz, 6th edn. Berlin: Weidmann, vol. 1. 1951; vol. 2. 1952 (repr. Dublin/Zurich: 1966)
Demiańczuk	*Supplementum comicum*, ed. J. Demiańczuk. Krakau: Nakladem Akademii, 1912 (repr. Hildesheim: Olms, 1967)
Denis	*Fragmenta pseudepigraphorum quae supersunt Graeca*, ed. A.-M. Denis. Leiden: Brill, 1970
Diehl	*Anthologia lyrica Graeca*, ed. E. Diehl, Leipzig: Teubner, 1949–1952
Dittmar	Aischines von Sphettos, *Studien zur Literaturgeschichte der Sokratiker*, ed. H. Dittmar, Philologische Untersuchungen, vol. 21. Berlin: Weidmann, 1912
Eberhard	*Fabulae romanenses Graece conscriptae*, ed. A. Eberhard. Leipzig: Teubner, 1872
ed.	edited by, editor

ELTE	*Encyclopedia of Literary Translation into English*, ed. Olive Classe. London: Fitzroy Dearborn, 2000
Elter	*Gnomica homoeomata*, ed. A. Elter, pt. 5. Bonn: Georg, 1905
ESFP I	Euripides, *Selected Fragmentary Plays Volume I*, with Translations and Commentaries by C. Collard, M.J. Cropp and K.H. Lee. Aris & Phillips Ltd, 1997
ESFP II	Euripides, *Selected Fragmentary Plays Volume II*, with Translations and Commentaries by C. Collard, M.J. Cropp and J. Gibert, Aris & Phillips Classical Texts. Oxbow Books, 2004
et al.	and others (*et alii, et alia*)
de Falco	*Demade oratore. Testimonianze e frammenti*, ed. V. de Falco, 2nd edn. Naples: Libreria Scientifica Editrice, 1955
FGrH	*Fragmente der griechischen Historiker*, ed. F. Jacoby. Berlin, 1923–1929; Leiden, 1926–1958 [1954–60] (3 parts in 17 vols)
FHG	*Fragmenta historicorum Graecorum*, ed. K. Müller. Paris: Didot, 1841–1870
fl.	flourished; prolific or active (*floruit*)
FPG	*Fragmenta philosophorum Graecorum*, ed. F.W.A. Mullach. Paris: Didot, 1860 (repr. Aalen: Scientia, 1968)
GAPC	*The Greek Anthology and Other Ancient Greek Epigrams*, ed. Peter Jay. Penguin Classics, 1973
Garofalo	*Erasistrati fragmenta*, ed. I. Garofalo. Pisa: Giardini, 1988
Geffcken	*Die Oracula Sibyllina*, ed. J. Geffcken. Leipzig: Hinrichs, 1902
GLAA	*Greek Literature: An Anthology*, chosen by Michael Grant. Penguin Classics, 1973
Gow	*Bucolici Graeci*, ed. A.S.F. Gow. Oxford: Clarendon Press, 1952 (repr. 1969)
GPHP	*The Greek Poets: Homer to the Present*, ed. Peter Constantine, Rachel Hadas, Edmund Keeley and Karen Van Dyck. New York: W.W. Norton & Co, 2010
Guarducci	*L'epigrafia greca dalle origini al tardo impero*, ed. Margherita Guarducci, Instituto Poligrafico e Zecca dello Stato. Rome: Libreria dello Stato, 1987. References are from the Greek translation, *Ἡ Ἑλληνικὴ Ἐπιγραφική*, tr. Κώστας Κουρεμένος, Μορφωτικὸ Ἵδρυμα Ἐθνικῆς Τραπέζης, Athens, 2008
H-H	A. Hausrath and H. Hunger, *Corpus fabularum Aesopicarum*, 2nd edn. Leipzig: Teubner, vol. 1.1, 1970; vol. 1.2, 1959
HBM	*Hesiod, Bion and Moschus, Sappho, Musaeus and Lycophron*, Family Classical Library no. XXX, with translations by C.E. Elton, F. Fawkes and Viscount Royston. London: A.J. Valpy, 1832
Heiberg	*Claudii Ptolemaei opera*, ed. J.L. Heiberg. Leipzig: Teubner, 1907
Heiberg and Stamatis	*Archimedis opera omnia*, ed. J.L. Heiberg and E. Stamatis. Leipzig: Teubner, 1913 (repr. Stuttgart: 1972)
HEPC	*Homer in English*, ed. George Steiner. Penguin Classics, 1996
Hercher	*Claudii Aeliani de natura animalium*, ed. R. Hercher. Leipzig: Teubner, 1866
IC	*Inscriptiones Creticae*, ed. M. Guarducci, IV. *Tituli Gortynii*. Rome, 1950
IEG	*Iambi et elegi Graeci*, ed. M.L. West. Oxford: Clarendon Press, vol. 1, 1971; vol. 2, 1972

IG	*Inscriptiones Graecae*, several volumes, various dates (see Liddell & Scott, II. *Epigraphical Publications*)
IGASMG	*Iscrizioni greche archaiche di Sicilia e Magna Grecia*, ed. R. Arena. Pisa, 1994
inv. no.	inventory number
Jaekel	*Menandri sententiae*, ed. S. Jaekel. Leipzig: Teubner, 1964
Jensen	*Hyperidis orationes*, ed. C. Jensen. Leipzig: Teubner, 1917 (repr. Stuttgart: 1963)
K-A	*Poetae comici Graeci*, ed. Rudolph Kassel and Colin Austin. Berlin and New York, several volumes, various dates
Kaibel	*Epigrammata Graeca ex lapidibus conlecta*, G. Kaibel. Berlin: Reimer, 1878
Kindstrand	*Bion of Borysthenes*, ed. J.F. Kindstrand. Uppsala: Uppsala University Press, 1976
Kinkel	*Epicorum Graecorum fragmenta*, ed. G. Kinkel. Leipzig: Teubner, 1877
Klostermann	*Origenes Werke*, ed. E. Klostermann, vol. 3. Leipzig: Hinrichs, 1901
Kock	*Comicorum Atticorum fragmenta*, ed. T. Kock. Leipzig: Teubner, vol. 1, 1880; vol. 2, 1884; vol. 3, 1888
Körte and Thierfelder	*Menandri quae supersunt*, ed. A. Körte and A. Thierfelder, 2nd edn. Leipzig: Teubner, vol. 2, 1959
lit.	literally, literal
Liddell & Scott	*A Greek–English Lexicon*, compiled by Henry George Liddell and Robert Scott, revised and augmented throughout by Sir Henry Stuart Jones with the assistance of Roderick McKenzie and with the cooperation of many scholars. With a revised Supplement 1996. 1st edn 1843, New (9th) edn completed 1940, New Supplement added 1996. Oxford: Oxford University Press
Loeb	The Loeb Classical Library ®, a registered trademark of and © by the President and Fellows of Harvard University
Lutz	*Musonius Rufus: The Roman Socrates*, ed. C.E. Lutz. New Haven: Yale University Press, 1947
Maehler	*Pindari carmina cum fragmentis*, ed. H. Maehler (post B. Snell), pt. 2, 4th edn. Leipzig: Teubner, 1975
Mathieu and Brémond	Isocrat, *Discours*, ed. G. Mathieu and É. Brémond, vol. 4. Paris: Les Belles Lettres, 1962
Meineke	*Fragmenta comicorum Graecorum*, ed. A. Meineke. Berlin: Reimer, 1841 (repr. De Gruyter, 1970)
Merkelbach and West	*Fragmenta Hesiodea*, ed. R. Merkelbach and M.L. West. Oxford: Clarendon Press, 1967
Mette	*Pytheas von Massalia*, ed. H.J. Mette. Berlin: De Gruyter, 1952 *Die Fragmente der Tragödien des Aischylos*, ed. H.J. Mette. Berlin: Akademie-Verlag, 1959
MPG	*Patrologia Graeca*, ed. J.-P. Migne, 162 vols. Paris, 1857–1868
Nauck	*Aristophanis Byzantii grammatici Alexandrini fragmenta*, ed. A. Nauck, 2nd edn. Halle: Lippert & Schmid, 1848 (repr. Hildesheim: Olms, 1963)
OBCV	*The Oxford Book of Classical Verse*, ed. Adrian Poole and Jeremy Maule. Oxford: Oxford University Press, 1995

OBGVT	*The Oxford Book of Greek Verse in Translation*, ed. T.F. Higham and C.M. Bowra. Oxford: Oxford University Press, 1938
OBVET	*The Oxford Book of Verse in English Translation*, ed. Charles Tomlinson. Oxford: Oxford University Press, 1980
OCD	*The Oxford Classical Dictionary*, 3rd edn revised, ed. Simon Hornblower and Antony Spawforth. Oxford: Oxford University Press, 2003
ODPQ	*The Oxford Dictionary of Political Quotations*, 3rd edn, ed. Antony Jay. Oxford: Oxford University Press, 2006
ODQ	*The Oxford Dictionary of Quotations*, 2nd edn. London: Oxford University Press, 1953 (reprinted with revisions, 1975); 6th edn, ed. Elizabeth Knowles. Oxford: Oxford University Press, 2004
Orat.Att	*Oratores Attici*, ed. J. Baiter and H. Sauppe. Zurich: Hoehr, 1850 (repr. Hildesheim: Olms, 1967)
Parente	*Senocrate-Ermodoro. Frammenti*, ed. M.I. Parente. Naples: Bibliopolis, 1982
PCW	*Plato: Complete Works*, ed. John M. Cooper, associate ed. D.S. Hutchinson. Hackett Publishing Company, Inc., 1997
PDQ	*The New Penguin Dictionary of Quotations*, ed. Robert Andrews. Penguin Books, 2006
PEG	*Poetarum epicorum Graecorum testimonia et fragmenta*, ed. A. Bernabé. Leipzig: Teubner, 1987
Perry	*Babrius and Phaedrus*, Section 1: *Mythiambi*, ed. B.E. Perry. Harvard University Press, 1965 *Aesopica*, ed. B.E. Perry. Urbana: University of Illinois Press, 1952 (repr. 2007)
Pfeiffer	*Callimachus*, ed. R. Pfeiffer. Oxford: Clarendon Press, 1949
des Places	*Oracles chaldaïques*, ed. É. des Places. Paris: Les Belles Lettres, 1971
PGM	*Papyri Graecae magicae. Die griechischen Zauberpapyri*, ed. K. Preisendanz and A. Henrichs, 2nd edn. Stuttgart: Teubner, 1973–1974
PGR	*The Portable Greek Reader*, ed. W.H. Auden. Viking Penguin, 1948
PLF	*Poetarum Lesbiorum fragmenta*, ed. E. Lobel and D.L. Page. Oxford: Clarendon Press, 1955 (repr. 1968 (1st edn corr.))
PLG	*Poetae lyrici Graeci*, ed. T. Bergk, 4th edn. Leipzig: Teubner, 1882
PM	*Plutarch's Morals*. Translated from the Greek by Several Hands. Corrected and Revised by William W. Goodwin, with an Introduction by Ralph Waldo Emerson, 5 vols. Boston: Little Brown & Company, 1878
PMG	*Poetae melici Graeci*, ed. D.L. Page. Oxford: Clarendon Press, 1962 (repr. 1967 (1st edn corr.))
publ.	published, published by
RAGP	*Readings in Ancient Greek Philosophy from Thales to Aristotle*, ed. S. Marc Cohen, Patricia Curd and C.D.C. Reeve, 3rd edn. Hackett Publishing Company, Inc., 2005
repr.	reprinted
rev.	revised, revised by
Rose	*Aristotelis qui ferebantur librorum fragmenta*, ed. V. Rose. Leipzig: Teubner, 1886 (repr. Stuttgart, 1967)

Roussel	*Isée. Discours*, ed. P. Roussel, 2nd edn. Paris: Les Belles Lettres, 1960
Sandbach	*Plutarchi moralia*, ed. F.H. Sandbach. Leipzig: Teubner, 1967
Schenkl	*Epicteti dissertationes ab Arriano digestae*, ed. H. Schenkl. Leipzig: Teubner, 1916 (repr. Stuttgart: 1965)
SEG	*Supplementum Epigraphicum Graecum*, vols 42–44, eds Henry W. Pleket, Ronald S. Stroud and Johan H.M. Strubbe. Amsterdam, 1995–1997; vol. 52, eds A. Chaniotis, T. Corsten, R.A. Tybout, R.S. Stroud. Amsterdam, 2002
SH	*Supplementum Hellenisticum*, ed. H. Lloyd-Jones and P. Parsons. Berlin: De Gruyter, 1983
SIG	*Sylloge inscriptionum Graecarum*, ed. W. Dittenberger, editio tertia, Leipzig, 1915–1924; Hildesheim, 1960
Smith	*Diogenes of Oenoanda: The Epicurean Inscription*, ed. M.F. Smith. Naples: Bibliopolis, 1993
Stählin	*Clemens Alexandrinus*, ed. O. Stählin, L. Früchtel and U. Treu. Berlin: Akademie-Verlag, 1970
Sternbach	*Gnomologium Vaticanum*, ed. L. Sternbach. Repr. Berlin: De Gruyter, 1963
SVF	*Stoicorum veterum fragmenta*, ed. J. von Arnim. Leipzig: Teubner, 1903 (repr. Stuttgart, 1968)
TGF	*Tragicorum Graecorum fragmenta*, ed. A. Nauck. Leipzig: Teubner, 1889 (repr. Hildesheim: Olms, 1964)
Theiler	*Posidonios. Die Fragmente*, ed. W. Theiler. Berlin: De Gruyter, 1982
Thesleff	*The Pythagorean Texts of the Hellenistic Period*, ed. H. Thesleff. Abo: Abo Akademi, 1965
TLG	Thesaurus Linguae Graecae, CD-ROM, version E, as available in the years 2005–2011, Compilation © 1999, Property of the Regents of the University of California, or newer versions now available on 'Online TLG'
tr.	translation(s), translated, translated by, translator
TrGF	*Tragicorum Graecorum fragmenta*; vol. 1 ed. B. Snell 1971; vol. 2 ed. B.R. Kannicht, B. Snell 1981; vol. 3 ed. S. Radt 1985; vol. 4 ed. S. Radt 1977. Göttingen: Vandenhoeck & Ruprecht
UP	University Press
Voigt	*Sappho et Alcaeus*, ed. Eva-Maria Voigt. Amsterdam: Polak & van Gennep, 1971
vol.	volume
Walters	H.B. Walters, *Catalogue of the Engraved Gems and Cameos: Greek, Etruscan and Roman in the British Museum*. London, 1926
Wehrli	*Die Schule des Aristoteles, Fragmenta*, ed. F. Wehrli, 2nd edn. Basel: Schwabe, 1967–1969
West	*Carmina Anacreontea*, ed. M.L. West. Leipzig: Teubner, 1984
Wimmer	*Theophrasti Eresii opera*, ed. F. Wimmer. Paris: Didot, 1866 (repr. Frankfurt am Main: Minerva, 1964)
YBQ	*The Yale Book of Quotations*, ed. Fred R. Shapiro. New Haven: Yale University Press, 2006
Young	*Theognis*, ed. D. Young (post E. Diehl). Leipzig: Teubner, 1971
ZPE	*Zeitschrift für Papyrologie und Epigraphik*. Bonn

APPENDIX 3

LIST OF TRANSLATORS

The earliest date of translation of the book used is given in this list. Where the translation date is not known, life dates are given in brackets.

Adams, Charles Darwin (1919)	*The Speeches of Aeschines*. Loeb
Adams, Francis (1749)	*The Genuine Works of Hippocrates* vol. II, *On the Articulation*. London: printed for the Sydenham Society
Adcock, Fleur (1934–)	in *GAPC*
Allinson, Francis G. (1921)	Menander, *Principal Fragments*. Loeb
Andrew, S.O. (1948)	*Homer's Odyssey*. London, in *HEPC*
Anonymous (1588)	*Sixe Idillia*. Oxford: printed by Joseph Barnes
Armstrong, A.H. (1966)	Plotinus, *Enneads*. Loeb vols I–II
Armstrong, G. Cyril (1935)	Aristotle, *Oeconomica & Magna Moralia*. Loeb vol. XVIII
Arnold, Matthew (1861)	*On Translating Homer*. London, in *HEPC*
Arnott, W.G. (1979)	Menander, *Aspis – Epitrepontes*. Loeb vol. I
Ascham, Roger (1568)	*The Scholemaster*, ed. D.C. Whimster (1934)
Athanassakis, A.N. (1976)	*The Homeric Hymns*, 2nd edn. Johns Hopkins University Press
Authorized Version (1611)	*The Bible*. The Authorized (King James) Version
Babbitt, Frank Cole (1927)	Plutarch, *Moralia*. Loeb vol. I
Babbitt, Frank Cole (1928)	Plutarch, *Moralia*. Loeb vol. II
Babbitt, Frank Cole (1931)	Plutarch, *Moralia*. Loeb vol. III
Babbitt, Frank Cole (1936)	Plutarch, *Moralia*. Loeb vol. IV
Babbitt, Frank C. (1936)	Plutarch, *Moralia*. Loeb vol. V
Bacon, Francis (1625)	*Apophthegms*. London: printed for Hanna Barret
Baker, D.S. (1998)	*Greek Proverbs*. Belfast: Appletree Press
Balme, Maurice (2002)	Menander, *The Plays and Fragments*. Oxford World's Classics, Oxford University Press
Balmer, Josephine (1992)	*Sappho: Poems & Fragments*. Newcastle upon Tyne: Bloodaxe Books

Balmer, Josephine (1996)	*Classical Women Poets*. Newcastle upon Tyne: Bloodaxe Books
Barnard, Mary (1958)	*Sappho: A New Translation*. University of California Press
Barnes, Jonathan (1979)	*The Presocratic Philosophers*. Routledge
Barnes, Jonathan (1984)	co-translator of Aristotle, *Fragments*, in *CWA*, with Gavin Lawrence
Barnes, Jonathan (1987)	*Early Greek Philosophy*. Penguin Classics
Barnstone, Willis (1962)	*Greek Lyric Poetry*. New York: Bantam Books Inc.
Barrett, David (1964)	Aristophanes, *Wasps, The Poet and the Women, Frogs*, Penguin Classics
Barrett, David (1978)	Aristophanes, *The Birds, The Assemblywomen*, tr. David Barrett; *The Knights, Peace, Wealth*, tr. Alan H. Sommerstein. Penguin Classics
Basore, John W. (1932)	Seneca, *Moral Essays*. Loeb vol. II
Batzini, Maria (2007)	co-translator of *Ancient Greece and the Modern Manager: An Anthology of Quotations*. Athens: Kalendis, with Panos Koronakis-Rohlf
Beare, J.I. (d. 1918)	Aristotle, *On Sense and the Sensible*, in *CWA*
Bell, Karen (1992)	co-translator of Plato, *Protagoras*, in *PCW*, with Stanley Lombardo
Berg, Stephen (1978)	co-translator of Sophocles, *Oedipus the King*. Oxford University Press, with Diskin Clay
Betts, Gavin (1989)	co-author of *Teach Yourself Ancient Greek: A Complete Course*. London: Hodder Headline plc., with Alan Henry
Bevan, Edwyn (1931)	*The Poems of Leonidas of Tarentum*, Clarendon Press, in *OBGVT*
Bland, Robert (1813)	*Collections from the Greek Anthology*. London: John Murray
Bourne, Thomas (1864)	*Anacreon (Anacreontea)*. Michigan Historical Reprint Series
Bowersock, G.W. (1925)	Xenophon, *Pseudo-Xenophon, Constitution of the Athenians*. Loeb vol. VII
Bowles, William Lisle (1762–1850)	in *BFQ*
Bowra, C.M. (1938)	co-editor of *OBGVT*, with T.F. Higham – many translations are his
Bowra, C.M. (1957)	*The Greek Experience*. London: Weidenfeld & Nicholson, in *GLAA*
Bowra, C.M. (1969)	*The Odes of Pindar*. Penguin Classics
Bradshaw, Claire	Assistant editor of *A Dictionary of Classical Greek Quotations*
Branham, R. Bracht (1994)	'Diogenes' Rhetoric', in *CMAL*
Branham, R. Bracht (1996)	co-editor of *CMAL*, with Marie-Odile Goulet-Cazé
Brenton, Lancelot C.L. (1851)	*The Septuagint Version of the Old Testament*, with an English Translation. London: S. Bagster (no date given, repr. 1884)
Bridges, Robert (1916)	*The Spirit of Man*. Longmans, Green & Co., in *OBGVT*
Brock, Arthur J. (1916)	Galen, *On the Natural Faculties*. Loeb
Broome, William (1720)	Homer, *Odyssey*, with Pope and Elijah Fenton

Browning, Elizabeth Barrett (1833)	*Prometheus Bound and other Poems*, ed. Alice Meynell. Ward, Lock & Co. (1896)
Browning, Elizabeth Barrett (1850)	*Prometheus Bound*, revised version, in *Poems*. London: Chapman and Hall, in *ELTE*
Brownson, Carleton L. (1921)	Xenophon, *Hellenica* Books VI–VII; *Anabasis* Books I–VI. Loeb
Brownson, Carleton L. (1922)	Xenophon, *Anabasis*, Books IV–VII, *Symposium*, *Apology*. Loeb
Brunt, P.A. (1976)	Arrian, *Anabasis of Alexander*, Books I–IV (revised edn, 1st edn by E. Iliff Robson, 1929). Loeb vol. I
Brunt, P.A. (1983)	Arrian, *Anabasis of Alexander*, Books V–VII, *Indica* (revised edn, 1st edn by E. Iliff Robson, 1929). Loeb vol. II
Buckley, T.A. (1850)	*The Tragedies of Euripides*. London: Henry G. Bohn
Burtt, J.O. (1954)	*Minor Attic Orators, Lycurgus, Dinarchus, Demades, Hyperides*. Loeb vol. II
Bury, R.G. (1926)	Plato, *Laws*. Loeb vols X–XI
Bury, R.G. (1929)	Plato, *Timeaus, Critias, Cleitophon, Menexenus, Epistles*. Loeb vol. IX
Butler, A.J. (1881)	*Amaranth and Asphodel: Poems from the Greek Anthology*. Oxford: Blackwell
Butterworth, G.W. (1919)	*Clement of Alexandria*. Loeb
Bywater, Ingram (1840–1914)	Aristotle, *Poetics*, in *CWA*
Caine-Suarez, Helena (1996)	translated into English: *Religion and the Early Cynics* by Marie-Odile Goulet-Cazé, in *CMAL*
Campbell, D.A. (1982)	*Greek Lyric, Sappho & Alcaeus*. Loeb vol. I
Campbell, D.A. (1988)	*Greek Lyric, Anacreon, Anacreontea, Choral Lyric from Olympus to Alcman*. Loeb vol. II
Campbell, D.A. (1991)	*Greek Lyric, Stesichorus, Ibycus, Simonides, and Others*. Loeb vol. III
Campbell, D.A. (1992)	*Greek Lyric, Bacchylides, Corinna, and Others*. Loeb vol. IV
Campbell, D.A. (1993)	*Greek Lyric, The New School of Poetry & Anonymous Songs & Hymns*. Loeb vol. V
Carter, Elizabeth (1758)	*All the works of Epictetus, which are now extant; consisting of his Discourses, preserved by Arrian, in four books, the Enchiridion, and fragments*. London: printed by S. Richardson, in *PDQ*
Cary, Ernest (1937)	Dionysius of Halicarnassus, *Roman Antiquities*, Books I–II. Loeb vol. I
Cary, Ernest (1939)	Dionysius of Halicarnassus, *Roman Antiquities*, Books III–IV. Loeb vol. II
Cashford, Jules (2003)	*The Homeric Hymns*. Penguin Books
Caxton, William (1484)	*The Subtyl Historyes and Fables of Esope*. Westminster: William Caxton
Chapman, George (1598)	*Seven Bookes of the Iliades of Homere, Prince of Poets*. London: John Windet

Chapman, George (1609)	*Homer Prince of Poets … Twelve Books of his Iliads*
Chapman, George (1611)	*The Iliads of Homer, Prince of Poets*, 'neuer before in any language truely translated'. London: Nathaniell Butter
Chapman, George (1615)	*Homer's Odysses* (sic), in *HEPC*
Charles, R.H. (1913)	'The Letter of Aristeas', *The Apocrypha and Pseudepigrapha of the Old Testament in English*, vol. 2. Oxford University Press, 1913
Chaucer, Geoffrey (*c*.1343–1400)	*The Parliament of Fowls* (*c*.1380)
Cheesman, Clive (2004)	co-translator of *Classical Love Poetry*. The British Museum Press, with Jonathan Williams
Cherniss, Harold (1957)	Plutarch, *Moralia, Face on the Moon*. Loeb vol. XII
Clay, Diskin (1978)	co-translator of Sophocles, *Oedipus the King*. Oxford University Press, with Stephen Berg
Clement, Paul A. (1969)	Plutarch, *Moralia, Table-Talk*, Books I–III. Loeb vol. VIII
Cohen, S. Marc (2005)	in *RAGP*
Cohoon, J.W. (1932)	Dio Chrysostom. Loeb vols I–II; vol. III, with H. Lamar Crosby
Coleridge, E.P. (1891)	*The Plays of Euripides*, vols I–II. London: George Bell and Sons
Coleridge, E.P. (1938)	Euripides, in *CGD*
Collard, Christopher (1997)	in *ESFP I*
Collard, Christopher (2004)	in *ESFP II*
Collard, Christopher (2008)	co-translator of Euripides, *Fragments*. Loeb vols VII–VIII, with Martin Cropp
Collard, Christopher (2009)	Aeschylus, *Persians and Other Plays*. Oxford World's Classics, Oxford University Press
Constantine, Peter (2010)	in *GPHP*
Constantinidi, Maria	Μαρία Κωνσταντινίδη
Cooper, John M. (1997)	revised several translations in *PCW*
Cornford, Francis (1929)	co-translator of Aristotle, *Physics*. Loeb vols IV–V, with Philip H. Wicksteed
Cory, William (1858)	*Ionica*. Smith, Elder & Co., in *OBGVT*
Cowper, William (1791)	*The Iliad and Odyssey of Homer*. London, in *HEPC*
Cowper, William (1791)	*Homer's Iliad*, 1st edn 1791; 2nd edn 1802; the 2nd edition had considerable alterations, in *OBGVT*
Cowper, William (1791)	*Homer's Iliad and Odyssey*, 2 vols (3rd edn 1809), in *OBVET*
Crawley, Richard (1874)	Thucydides, *The History of the Peloponnesian War*, in *GLAA*
Creech, Thomas (1684)	*The Idylliums of Theocritus*. Oxford, in *OBCV*
Cropp, Martin J. (1997)	in *ESFP I*
Cropp, Martin J. (2004)	in *ESFP II*
Cropp, Martin J. (2008)	co-translator of Euripides, *Fragments*. Loeb vols VII–VIII, with Christopher Collard
Cruttwell, Patrick (1986)	in Samuel Johnson, *Selected Writings*. Penguin Classics

Curd, Patricia (2005)	in *RAGP*
Dale, Henry (1855)	co-translator of *The Cyropaedia, and The Hellenics*. Bohn's Classical Library, London: Henry G. Bohn, with J.S. Watson
Davenport, Guy (1976)	*Herakleitos and Diogenes*. San Francisco: Grey Fox Press
Davie, John (2002)	Euripides, *Heracles and Other Plays*. Penguin Classics
De Lacy, Phillip H. (1967)	co-translator of Plutarch, *Moralia*. Loeb vol. XIV, with Benedict Einarson
de Sélincourt, Aubrey (1954)	Herodotus, *The Histories*. Penguin Classics
Derby, Edward, Earl of (1864)	*The Iliad of Homer*. John Murray, in *OBGVT* and *HEPC*
Derow, Peter Sidney (2003)	entry 'Polybius' in *OCD*
DeWitt, Norman J. (1949)	co-translator of Demosthenes, *Funeral Oration*. Loeb vol. VII, with Norman W. DeWitt
DeWitt, Norman W. (1949)	co-translator of Demosthenes, *Funeral Oration*. Loeb vol. VII, with Norman J. DeWitt
Dorsch, T.S. (1965)	*Classical Literary Criticism*. Penguin Books
Dryden, John (1679)	co-translator of *Oedipus: A Tragedy*, an adaptation of Sophocles' *Oedipus the King*. London: R. Bentley and M. Magnes, with Nathaniel Lee
Dryden, John (1700)	*The First Book of Homer's Ilias*, in *Fables Ancient and Modern*. London: Jacob Tonson
Dryden, John (1631–1700)	*Plutarch's Lives*. The Translation called Dryden's, revised by A.H. Clough, 1859. Boston: Little Brown and Company
Drysdall, Denis L. (2005)	*Collected Works of Erasmus*. Adages III iv.1–IV.ii 100, ed. John N. Grant, University of Toronto Press
Dunn Mascetti, Manuela (2010)	co-editor of *The Quotable Spirit*. Sterling Publishing Co., Inc., with Peter Lorie
Economou, Daphne	Δάφνη Οικονόμου
Edmonds, J.M. (1912)	*The Greek Bucolic Poets, Theocritus, Bion, Moschus*. Loeb
Edmonds, J.M. (1931)	*Greek Elegy and Iambus*. Loeb vol. I
Edmonds, J.M. (1931)	*Elegy and Iambus with Anacreontea*. Loeb vol. II
Einarson, Benedict and (1967)	co-translator of Plutarch, *Moralia*. Loeb vol. XIV, with Phillip H. De Lacy
Elton, Charles Abraham (1812)	*The Remains of Hesiod*, rev. 1825. London: Lackington Allen, cf. *HBM*
Evelyn-White, Hugh G. (1914)	Hesiod, *The Homeric Hymns & Homerica*. Loeb
Fagles, Robert (1975)	Aeschylus, *The Oresteia, Agamemnon, The Libation Bearers, The Eumenides*. Penguin Classics
Fagles, Robert (1982)	Sophocles, *The Three Theban Plays: Antigone, Oedipus the King, Oedipus at Colonus*. Penguin Classics
Fagles, Robert (1996)	Homer, *The Odyssey*. Penguin Classics
Falconer, W. (1854)	co-translator of Strabo, *Geographica*, repr. London: G. Bell, 1903 with H.C. Hamilton

Fawkes, Francis (1789)	Bion and Moschus, Sappho and Musaeus, in *HBM*
Fenton, Elijah (1720)	Homer, *Odyssey*, with Alexander Pope and William Broome
Fisher, R. Swainson (1838)	*Select Translations from the Greek Minor Poets*. London: Simpkin, Marshall & Co.
Fitts, Dudley (1936)	*The Alcestis of Euripides*. New York: Harcourt, Brace and Company, with Robert Fitzgerald, in *BFQ*
Fitts, Dudley (1939)	Sophocles, *The Oedipus Cycle: Oedipus Rex, Oedipus at Colonus, Antigone*. Harcourt, Inc., with Robert Fitzgerald, in *BFQ*
Fitts, Dudley (1954)	Aristophanes, *Four Comedies: Lysistrata, The Frogs, The Birds, Ladies' Day*. Harcourt, in *GLAA*
Fitzgerald, Robert (1936)	*The Alcestis of Euripides*. New York: Harcourt, Brace and Company, with Dudley Fitts, in *BFQ*
Fitzgerald, Robert (1939)	Sophocles, *The Oedipus Cycle: Oedipus Rex, Oedipus at Colonus, Antigone*. Harcourt, Inc., with Dudley Fitts, in *BFQ*
Fitzgerald, Robert (1961)	Homer, *The Odyssey*. Anchor Books
Fitzgerald, Robert (1975)	Homer, *The Iliad*. Anchor Books
Fletcher, Phineas (1623)	in Giles Fletcher, *The Reward of the Faithfull* (sic), in *OBCV*
Forster, E.S. (1955)	Aristotle, *On the Sophistical Refutations, On Coming-To Be and Passing-Away*. Loeb vol. III
Forster, E.S. (1879–1950)	Aristotle, *Problems*, in *CWA*
Fowler, F.G. (1905)	co-translator of *The Works of Lucian of Samosata*, vol. II. Oxford: The Clarendon Press, with H.W. Fowler
Fowler, Harold North (1914)	Plato, *Euthyphro, Apology, Crito, Phaedo, Phaedrus*. Loeb vol. I
Fowler, Harold North (1921)	Plato, *Theaetetus, Sophist*. Loeb vol. VII
Fowler, Harold North (1925)	Plato, *Statesman, Philebus*. Loeb vol. VIII
Fowler, Harold North (1926)	Plato, *Cratylus, Parmenides, Greater Hippias, Lesser Hippias*. Loeb vol. IV
Fowler, Harold North (1936)	Plutarch, *Moralia*. Loeb vol. X
Fowler, H.W. (1905)	co-translator of *The Works of Lucian of Samosata*, vol. II. Oxford: The Clarendon Press, with F.G. Fowler
Frazer, J.G. (1898)	Pausanias, *Description of Greece*. London: Macmillan
Freeman, Kathleen (1947)	*The Greek Way: An Anthology*. London: MacDonald
Freeman, Kathleen (1948)	*Ancilla to The Pre-Socratic Philosophers*. Blackwell
Freese, John Henry (1926)	Aristotle, *The Art of Rhetoric*. Loeb vol. XXII
Furley, D.J. (1955)	Aristotle, *On the Cosmos*. Loeb vol. III
Furness, Robert Allason (1931)	*Poems of Callimachus*. Jonathan Cape, in *OBGVT*
Furness, Robert Allason (1931)	*Translations from the Greek Anthology*. Jonathan Cape, in *OBGVT* and *GLAA*
Fyfe, W.H. (1878–1965)	Longinus, *On the Sublime*, rev. Donald Russell (in the same volume as Aristotle XXIII, *Poetics*). Loeb
Garnett, Richard (1927)	*The Twilight of the Gods*. John Lane – The Bodley Head Ltd, in *OBGVT*
Gasper, Giles E.M. (2004)	*Anselm of Canterbury and his Theological Inheritance*. Ashgate

Gaye, R.K. (1877–1909)	co-translator of Aristotle, *Physics*, in *CWA*, with R.P. Hardie
Gelzer, Thomas (1958)	co-translator of Musaeus, *Hero & Leander* (in same volume as Callimachus, *Aetia*). Loeb, with Cedric H. Whitman
Gerber, Douglas E. (1999)	*Greek Iambic Poetry*. Loeb
Gibbs, Laura (2002)	*Aesop's Fables*. Oxford World's Classics, Oxford University Press
Gibert, John (2004)	in *ESFP II*
Gibbons, Reginald (2008)	Sophocles, *Selected Poems, Odes and Fragments*. Princeton University Press
Godley, A.D. (1920)	Herodotus. Loeb vol. I
Godley, A.D. (1921)	Herodotus. Loeb vol. II
Godley, A.D. (1922)	Herodotus. Loeb vol. III
Godley, A.D. (1925)	Herodotus. Loeb vol. IV
Goulet-Cazé, Marie-Odile (1996)	co-editor of *CMAL*, with R. Bracht Branham
Goulet-Cazé, Marie-Odile (1996)	'Religion and the Early Cynics', in *CMAL*, translated into English by Helena Caine-Suarez
Graziosi, Barbara (2009)	co-author of 'Greek Lyric and Early Greek Literary history', in *CCGL*, with Johannes Haubold
Grene, David (1942)	Euripides I, *Hippolytus*, in *CGT*
Grene, David (1957)	Sophocles II, *Electra, Philoctetes*, in *CGT*
Grene, David (1991)	Sophocles I, *Oedipus the King, Oedipus at Colonus, Antigone*, in *CGT*
Groden, Suzy Q. (1964)	Sappho translated in 'Arion' vol. III, no. 3. University of Texas, in *GLAA*
Grube, G.M.A. (1974)	Plato, *Republic*, rev. C.D.C. Reeve, in *PCW*
Grube, G.M.A. (1977)	Plato, *Phaedo*, in *PCW*
Gulick, Charles Burton (1927)	Athenaeus, *The Deipnosophists*, Books I–III. Loeb vol. I
Guthrie, Kenneth Sylvan (1920)	*The Complete Pythagoras: The Life of Pythagoras*, ed. Patrick Roussel
Hadas, Rachel (2010)	in *GPHP*
Haines, C.R. (1916)	Marcus Aurelius. Loeb
Halliwell, Stephen (1995)	Aristotle, *Poetics*. Loeb vol. XXIII
Hamilton, Edith (1958)	Aeschylus, *Prometheus Bound*, in *BFQ*
Hamilton, Edith (1964)	*The Greek Way*. London: Norton
Hamilton, H.C. (1854)	co-translator of Strabo, *Geographica*, repr. London: G. Bell, 1903, with W. Falconer
Hammond, Martin (2009)	Thucydides, *The Peloponnesian War*, Oxford World's Classics, Oxford University Press
Hardie, R.P. (1864–1942)	co-translator of Aristotle, *Physics*, in *CWA*, with R.K. Gaye
Hardy, Thomas (1901)	*Poems of the Past and Present*, from *London Magazine*, Jan. 1956, in *OBCV*

Harmon, A.M. (1913)	Lucian. Loeb vol. I
Harmon, A.M. (1915)	Lucian. Loeb vol. II
Harmon, A.M. (1921)	Lucian. Loeb vol. III
Harrison, Nonna Verna (2008)	Saint Gregory of Nazianzus, *Festal Orations*. Crestwood, New York: St Vladimir's Seminary Press
Haubold, Johannes (2009)	co-author of 'Greek lyric and early Greek literary history', in *CCGL*, with Barbara Graziosi
Heath, Thomas Little (1908)	*Euclid: The Thirteen Books of Euclid's Elements*. New York: Dover
Helmbold, William C. (1939)	Plutarch, *Moralia*. Loeb vol. VI
Helmbold, William C. (1957)	Plutarch, *Moralia*. Loeb vol. XII (except *The Face on the Moon*, tr. Harold Cherniss)
Helmbold, William C. (1961)	co-translator of Plutarch, *Moralia, Table-Talk*, Books VII–IX. Loeb vol. IX, with Edwin L. Minar, Jr and F.H. Sandbach
Henderson, Jeffrey (1998)	Aristophanes, *Acharnians, Knights*. Loeb vol. I
Henderson, Jeffrey (1998)	Aristophanes, *Clouds, Wasps, Peace*. Loeb vol. II
Henderson, Jeffrey (2000)	Aristophanes, *Birds, Lysistrata, Thesmophoriazusae*. Loeb vol. III
Henderson, Jeffrey (2002)	Aristophanes, *Frogs, Assemblywomen, Wealth*. Loeb vol. IV
Henderson, Jeffrey (2007)	Aristophanes, *Fragments*. Loeb vol. V
Henry, Alan (1989)	co-author of *Teach Yourself Ancient Greek*: A *Complete Course*. London: Hodder Headline Plc., with Gavin Betts
Hewlett, Maurice (1928)	*The Iliad of Homer*. Cresset Press, in *OBGVT*
Hickie, William James (1853?)	*The Comedies of Aristophanes*. London: John Bohn
Hicks, R.D. (1925)	Diogenes Laertius. Loeb vol. I
Hicks, R.D. (1925)	Diogenes Laertius. Loeb vol. II
Higginson, Thomas Wentworth (1865)	*The Works of Epictetus*. A Translation based on that of Elizabeth Carter. Boston: Little, Brown
Higham, T.F. (1938)	co-editor of *OBGVT*, with C.M. Bowra – many translations are his
Hobbes, Thomas (1629)	*The English Works*, vols VII & IX (*The Peloponnesian War*). London: John Bohn
Hodkinson, Owen (2007)	'Some Advantages of the Letter', in *ALCLA*
Hogg, Dan (2006)	translated selections from Thucydides and Dionysius of Halicarnassus
Holland, Philemon (1603)	*The Philosphie, commonlie called The Morals* (Plutarch)
Holland, Tom (2013)	Herodotus, *The Histories*. Penguin Classics
Horst, P.W. van der (1978)	*The Sentences of Pseudo-Phocylides*. Leiden: E.J. Brill
Hughes, Ted (1999)	Aeschylus, *The Oresteia*. London: Faber and Faber
Hunt, Leigh (1816)	in A.S.F. Gow, *Bucolici Graeci*, in *GLAA*
Hutchinson, D.S. (1997)	Plato, *Alcibiades II*, first translated in *PCW*
Hutchinson, D.S. (1997)	Plato, *Definitions*, first translated in *PCW*

Innes, Doreen C. (1995)	Demetrius, *On Style*, based on W. Rhys Roberts (in the same volume as Aristotle XXIII, *Poetics*). Loeb vol. XXIII
Jameson, Michael (1957)	Sophocles II, *The Women of Trachis*, in *CGT*
Jay, Peter (1973)	editor of *The Greek Anthology* (*GAPC*) – many translations are his
Jebb, R.C. (1870)	*Theophrastou Charactēres: The Characters of Theophrastus*. London and Cambridge: Macmillan and Co.
Jebb, R.C. (1893)	*The Ajax of Sophocles*. Cambridge University Press
Jebb, R.C. (1894)	*The Electra of Sophocles*. Cambridge University Press
Jenkinson, A.J. (1878?–1928)	Aristotle, *Prior Analytics*, in *The Works of Aristotle*, vol. I, Encyclopaedia Britannica
Joachim, H.H. (1868–1938)	Aristotle, *On Generation and Corruption*, in *CWA*
Johnson, Marguerite (2007)	*Sappho*. Ancients in Action Series. Bristol Classical Press
Johnson, Samuel (1709–1784)	in Charles Burney, *General History of Music*, in *OBCV*
Johnston, Ian (2003)	Euripides, *Bacchae*. Malaspina University-College, Nanaimo, BC (Vancouver Island University)
Jones, W.H.S. (1923)	Hippocrates. Loeb vols I–II
Jones, W.H.S. (1931)	Hippocrates. Heraclitus, *On the Universe*. Loeb vol. IV
Jonson, Ben (1616)	in *OBVET*
Jowett, Benjamin (1817–1893)	Aristotle, *Politics*, in *CWA*
Jowett, Benjamin (1817–1893)	Plato, in *BFQ*, *ODQ* and *PDQ*
Jowett, Benjamin (1817–1893)	Thucydides, *History of the Peloponnesian War*. Oxford: Clarendon Press, 1900
Keeley, Edmund (2010)	in *GPHP*
Kendall, Timothe (sic) (1577)	*Flowers of Epigrammes*, in *OBGVT*
Kennedy, John Fitzgerald (1963)	Speech at the Paulskirche in Frankfurt, 25 June 1963
Kidd, I.G. (1999)	Posidonius: *The Translation of the Fragments*, vol. III. Cambridge University Press
Kilburn, K. (1959)	Lucian. Loeb vol. VI
King, C.W. (1882)	*Plutarch's Morals: Theosophical Essays*. London: George Bell and Sons
Kitto, H.D.F. (1951)	*The Greeks*. Pelican Books
Kitto, H.D.F. (1962)	Sophocles, *Three Tragedies: Antigone, Oedipus the King, Electra*. Oxford University Press
Klinck, Anne L. (2008)	*Woman's Songs in Ancient Greece*. McGill-Queen's University Press
König, Jason (2007)	'Alciphron's Epistolarity', in *ALCLA*
Koronakis-Rohlf, Panos (2007)	co-translator of *Ancient Greece and the Modern Manager: An Anthology of Quotations*. Athens: Kalendis, with Maria Batzini

Kosmopoulou, Angeliki (2009)	*Eros: From Hesiod's Theogony to Late Antiquity*. Exhibition catalogue. Museum of Cycladic Art, Athens, ed. Nicholas Chr. Stampolidis and Yorgos Tassoulas
Kovacs, David (1994)	Euripides, *Cyclops, Alcestis, Medea*. Loeb vol. I
Kovacs, David (1995)	Euripides, *Children of Heracles, Hippolytus, Andromache, Hecuba*. Loeb vol. II
Kovacs, David (1998)	Euripides, *Suppliant Women, Electra, Heracles*. Loeb vol. III
Kovacs, David (1999)	Euripides, *Trojan Women, Iphigenia Among the Taurians, Ion*. Loeb vol. IV
Kovacs, David (2002)	Euripides, *Helen, Phoenician Women, Orestes*. Loeb vol. V
Kovacs, David (2002)	Euripides, *Bacchae, Iphigenia at Aulis, Rhesus*. Loeb vol. VI
Lacy, Phillip H. De (1967)	see De Lacy, Philip H.
Lamar Crosby, H. (1951)	co-translator of Dio Chrysostom. Loeb vols III–V; vol. III, with J.W. Cohoon
Lamb, W.R.M. (1924)	Plato, *Laches, Protagoras, Meno, Euthydemus*. Loeb vol. II
Lamb, W.R.M. (1925)	Plato, *Lysis, Symposium, Gorgias*. Loeb vol. III
Lamb, W.R.M. (1927)	Plato, *Alcibiades II*. Loeb vol. XII
Lamb, W.R.M. (1930)	Lysias. *Against Eratosthenes, Subverting the Democracy*. Loeb
Landor, Walter Savage (1842)	'Writings of Catullus', *The Foreign Quarterly Review*, 29 (July 1842), in *OBCV*
Lane Fox, Robin (2008)	*Travelling Heroes: Greeks and their Myths in the Epic Age of Homer*. Penguin
Langhorne, John (1804)	co-translator of Plutarch, *Lives*, vol. 4, 1st Worcester edn (Massachusetts), with William Langhorne
Langhorne, William (1804)	co-translator of Plutarch, *Lives*, vol. 4, 1st Worcester edn (Massachusetts), with John Langhorne
Lattimore, Richmond (1953)	Aeschylus I, *Oresteia*, in *CGT*
Lattimore, Richmond (1959)	Hesiod, *Works and Days*. Ann Arbor: University of Michigan Press, in *ODQ*
Lattimore, Richmond (1960)	Solon, *Greek Lyrics*. University of Chicago Press
Lattimore, Richmond (1976)	*The Odes of Pindar*, 2nd edn. University of Chicago Press
Lawrence, Gavin (1984)	co-translator of Aristotle, *Fragments*, in *CWA*, with Jonathan Barnes
Lawrence, T.E. (Shaw, T.E.) (1932)	*The Odyssey of Homer*, newly translated into English Prose by T.E. Shaw. Oxford University Press, in *OBGVT*
Leaf, Walter (1922)	*Little Poems from the Greek*. Richards Press, in *OBGVT*
Lee, Desmond (1955)	Plato, *The Republic*. Penguin Classics
Lee, Desmond (H.D.P.) (1956)	Plato, *Timaeus*. Penguin Books, in *GLAA*
Lee, Nathaniel (1679)	co-translator of *Oedipus: A Tragedy*, an adaptation of Sophocles' *Oedipus the King*. London: R. Bentley and M. Magnes, with John Dryden
Levett, M.J. (1997)	Plato, *Theaetetus*, rev. Myles Burnyeat, in *PCW*

Liddell & Scott	*A Greek–English Lexicon*, compiled by Henry George Liddell and Robert Scott. 1st edn 1843, New (9th) edn completed 1940, New Supplement 1996. Oxford University Press
Livingston, Richard (1968)	Thucydides, *The History of the Peloponnesian War*, Oxford University Press, in *BFQ*
Llewellyn-Smith, Michael (2004)	*Athens: A Cultural and Literary History*. Oxford: Signal Books
Lloyd-Jones, Hugh (1994)	Sophocles, *Ajax, Electra, Oedipus the King*. Loeb vol. I
Lloyd-Jones, Hugh (1994)	Sophocles, *Antigone, Women of Trachis, Philoctetes, Oedipus at Colonus*. Loeb vol. II
Lloyd-Jones, Hugh (1996)	Sophocles, *Fragments*. Loeb vol. III
Lombardo, Stanley (1993)	Hesiod, *The Theogony*, quoted in *RAGP*
Lombardo, Stanley (1992)	co-translator of Plato, *Protagoras*, in *PCW*, with Karen Bell
Lombardo, Stanley (1988)	co-translator of *Callimachus: Hymns, Epigrams, Select Fragments*. Johns Hopkins University Press, with Diane Rayor
Long, George (1800–1879)	Marcus Aurelius, *Meditations (Τὰ εἰς ἑαυτόν)*
Long, George (1890)	*The Discourses of Epictetus, with the Enchiridion and Fragments*. London: George Bell
Lorie, Peter (2010)	co-editor of *The Quotable Spirit*. Sterling Publishing Co., Inc., with Manuela Dunn Mascetti
Lucas, F.L. (1950)	Homer, *The Iliad*. The Folio Society, London, in *HEPC*
Lucie-Smith, Edward (1933–)	in *GAPC*
McGuckin, John (1986)	Saint Gregory Nazianzen, *Selected Poems*. Fairacres, Oxford: SLG Press, Convent of the Incarnation
MacKail, J.W. (1890)	*Select Epigrams from The Greek Anthology*. London: Longmans, Green, and Co.
MacKail, J.W. (1903)	*The Odyssey*. London: John Murray, 1903–1910, in *HEPC*
McKirahan, Jr, Richard D. (1995)	Antiphon, *A Presocratics Reader*, in *RAGP*
Macleod, M.D. (1961)	Lucian. Loeb vol. VII
Macnaghten, H. (1924)	*Little Masterpieces from the Greek Anthology*. Glasgow: Gowans and Gray Ltd, in *OBGVT*
Mair, A.W. (1921)	Callimachus, *Hymns & Epigrams*, Lycophron, *Alexandria*. Loeb
Mair, G.R. (1921)	Aratus, *Phaenomena*. Loeb (in Callimachus)
Marchant, E.C. (1923)	Xenophon, *Memorabilia/Oeconomicus*. Loeb vol. IV
Marchant, E.C. (1925)	Xenophon, *Scripta Minora*. Loeb vol. VII
Maritain, Jacques (2005)	*An Introduction to Philosophy* by Jacques Maritain, tr. E.I. Watkin. New York: Sheed & Ward
Marris, William Sinclair (1938)	in *OBGVT*, in which he also revised some translations from *Translations from the Greek Anthology*, privately printed at the Bharat Bandhu Press, Aligarh, University Press, India, 1919
Merwin, W.S. (1973)	in *GAPC*
Miller, Walter (1914)	Xenophon, *Cyropaedia*. Loeb vols V–VI

Milman, Henry Hart (1865)	*The Agamemnon of Aeschylus and the Bacchanals of Euripides, with passages from the lyric and later poets of Greece*, in *OBGVT*
Minar Jr, Edwin L. (1961)	co-translator of Plutarch *Moralia, Table Talk*, Books VII–IX. Loeb vol. IX, with F.H. Sandbach and William C. Helmbold
Moebius, William (1973)	in *GAPC*
Moir, David Macbeth (1824)	*Mansie Wauch* (sic), in *OBGVT*
Morgan, Edwin (1973)	in *GAPC*
Morgan, Morris Hicky (1859–1910)	Marcus Aurelius, Euripides, in *BFQ*
Morison, Samuel Eliot (1949)	*History of United States Naval Operations in World War II: The Struggle for Guadalcanal* (vol. 5: Aug. 1942–Feb. 1943). Little, Brown and Company
Morrow, Glen R. (1962)	*Plato's Epistles*. Indianapolis: Bobbs-Merrill, 1962
Morwood, James (2001)	Euripides, *The Trojan Women and Other Plays*. Oxford World's Classics
Most, Glenn W. (2007)	Hesiod, *The Shield, Catalogue of Women, Other Fragments*. Loeb vol. II
Mullen, William (2010)	in *GPHP*
Murray, A.T. (1919)	Homer, *The Odyssey*. Loeb vols I–II
Murray, A.T. (1924)	Homer, *The Iliad*. Loeb vol. I
Murray, A.T. (1925)	Homer, *The Iliad*. Loeb vol. II
Murray, A.T. (1939)	Demosthenes, *Orations XLI–XLIX*. Loeb vol. V
Murray, A.T. (1939)	Demosthenes, *Private Orations L–LVIII, In Nearam LIX*. Loeb vol. VI
Murray, Gilbert (1902)	Euripides, *Hippolytus*, translated into English rhyming verse. London: George Allen & Company Ltd, in *PDQ*
Murray, Gilbert (1906)	Euripides, *The Electra of Euripides*. London: George Allen, in *BFQ*
Murray, Gilbert (1906)	Euripides, *The Medea of Euripides*. Oxford University Press, in *The Greek Way*, by Edith Hamilton
Murray, Gilbert (1913)	Euripides, *The Rhesus of Euripides*. London: George Allen & Company Ltd
Murray, Gilbert (1913)	Euripides (*Fragments*), *Euripides and His Age*. London: George Allen & Unwin Ltd, in *GLAA*
Nehamas, Alexander (1989)	co-translator of Plato, *Symposium*. Hackett Publishing Company, and in *PCW*, with Paul Woodruff
Nehamas, Alexander (1995)	co-translator of Plato, *Phaedrus*. Hackett Publishing Company, and in *PCW*, with Paul Woodruff
New English Bible (1970)	*The New English Bible with the Apocrypha*. Oxford University Press
Norlin, George (1928)	Isocrates. Loeb vol. I
Norlin, George (1929)	Isocrates. Loeb vol. II
North, Thomas (1579)	*Plutarks Lyves* (sic), in *ODQ*
Ogilby, John (1665)	*Homer's Odysses* (sic), in *HEPC*

Ogle, William (1827–1912)	Aristotle, *Parts of Animals*, in *CWA*
Oldfather, W.A. (1925)	Epictetus. Loeb vol. I
Oldfather, W.A. (1928)	Epictetus. Loeb vol. II
Oldfather, C.H. (1933)	Diodorus Siculus, *Library of History*. Loeb vol. I
Oldfather, C.H. (1946)	Diodorus Siculus, *Library of History*. Loeb vol. IV
O'Neill, Jr, Eugene (1938)	Aristophanes, *Women at the Thesmophoria, Birds, Wasps, Knights, Wealth, Peace, Ecclesiazusae*, in *CGD*
Page, D.L. (1941)	*Select Papyri, Poetry*. Loeb vol. III
Page, Denys (1955)	*Sappho & Alcaeus: An Introduction to the Study of Ancient Lesbian Poetry*. Oxford: Clarendon Press
Paton, W.R. (1916)	*The Greek Anthology*, Books I–VI. Loeb vol. I
Paton, W.R. (1917)	*The Greek Anthology*, Books VII–IX. Loeb vols II–III
Paton, W.R. (1918)	*The Greek Anthology*, Books X–XVI. Loeb vols IV–V
Peacock, Thomas Love (1806)	*Palmyra, and Other Poems*, in *OBCV*
Perrin, Bernadotte (1914)	Plutarch, *Lives*. Loeb vols I–II
Perrin, Bernadotte (1916)	Plutarch, *Lives*. Loeb vols III–IV
Perrin, Bernadotte (1917)	Plutarch, *Lives*. Loeb vol. V
Perrin, Bernadotte (1919)	Plutarch, *Lives*. Loeb vol. VII
Perry, Ben Edwin (1965)	Babrius and Phaedrus. Loeb
Philips (sic), John (1878)	*Concerning the Fortune or Virtue of Alexander*, in *PM*
Phillips, Carl (2003)	Sophocles, *Philoctetes*. Oxford University Press
Platt, Arthur (1860–1925)	Aristotle, *Generation of Animals*, in *CWA*
Podlecki, Anthony J. (1991)	Aeschylus, *The Persians*. Bristol Classical Press
Pope, Alexander (1715)	Homer, *Iliad*
Pope, Alexander (1725)	Homer, *Odyssey*, with William Broome and Elijah Fenton
Popper, Karl (1958 et al.)	*The World of Parmenides: Essays on the Presocratic Enlightenment*, ed. Arne F. Petersen. Routledge (various articles with various dates)
Pott, John Arthur (1911)	*Greek Love Songs and Epigrams: from the Anthology*. Kegan Paul, Trench, Trübner & Company, Ltd (1st series 1911, 2nd series 1913)
Potter, Paul (1988)	Hippocrates. Loeb vols V–VI
Potter, Paul (1995)	Hippocrates. Loeb vol. VIII
Potter, Robert (1781)	*The Tragedies of Euripides* in two volumes. London: J. Dodsley; and in *CGD*
Pound, Ezra (1933)	'Canto I', *A Draft of XXX Cantos*. Faber & Faber, in *OBCV*
Pound, Ezra (1989)	Sophocles, *Elektra*. Princeton University Press
Praed, Winthrop Mackworth (1802–1839)	in *Odes From The Greek Dramatists*, ed. Alfred W. Pollard. London: David Scott
Race, William H. (1997)	Pindar. Loeb vols I–II
Rackham, H. (1926)	Aristotle, *The Nicomachean Ethics*. Loeb vol. XIX

Rackham, H. (1932)	Aristotle, *Politics*. Loeb vol. XXI
Rackham, H. (1935)	Aristotle, *Athenian Constitution, Eudemian Ethics, Virtues & Vices*. Loeb vol. XX
Raeburn, David (2008)	Sophocles, *Electra and other Plays*. Penguin Classics
Rayor, Diane (1988)	co-translator of *Callimachus: Hymns, Epigrams, Select Fragments*. Johns Hopkins University Press, with Stanley Lombardo
Reeve, C.D.C. (2005)	in *RAGP*
Rieu, E.V. (1946)	Homer, *The Odyssey*. Penguin Classics
Rieu, E.V. (1950)	Homer, *The Iliad*. Penguin Classics
Riley, H.T. (1872)	*A Dictionary of Latin and Greek Quotations, Proverbs and Mottos*. London: Bell and Daldy
Robbins, F.E. (1940)	Ptolemy, *Tetrabiblos*. Loeb
Roberts, W. Rhys (1858–1929)	Aristotle, *Rhetoric*, in *CWA*
Rogers, Benjamin B. (1897)	*The Wasps* of Aristophanes, a verse translation, as performed at Cambridge, 19–24 November 1897
Rogers, Benjamin B. (1924)	Aristophanes. Loeb vols I–II
Rolfe, John C. (1927)	Aulus Gellius, *Attic Nights*. Loeb vol. I
Ross, David (W.D.) (1925)	Aristotle, *Nicomachean Ethics*, rev. J.L. Ackrill and J.O. Urmson.
Ross, W.D. (1877–1971)	Aristotle, *Nicomachean Ethics*, in *CWA*
Ross, W.D. (1877–1971)	Aristotle, *Metaphysics*, in *CWA*
Rossetti, Dante Gabriel (1861)	'Beauty: A Combination from Sappho', in *ODQ*
Rowe, Nicholas (1714)	*Ajax of Sophocles*. London: Lintott, in *ELTE*
Rutherford, R.B. (2003)	entry 'Marcus Aurelius' in *OCD*
Saklatvala, Beram (1968)	*Sappho of Lesbos*. London: Charles Skilton, in *PDQ*
Sandbach, F.H. (1961)	co-translator of Plutarch, *Moralia, Table-Talk*, Books VII–IX. Loeb vol. IX, with Edwin L. Minar and William C. Helmbold
Sandbach, F.H. (1969)	Plutarch, *Moralia, Fragments*. Loeb vol. XV
Saunders, Trevor J. (1970)	Plato, *The Laws*. Penguin Classics
Schaff, Philip (1819–1893)	*Fathers of the Second Century*
Scott-Kilvert, Ian (1960)	Plutarch, *The Rise and Fall of Athens: Nine Greek Lives*. Penguin, in *GLAA*
Sélincourt, Aubrey de (1952)	see de Sélincourt, Aubrey
Shaw, T.E. (Lawrence, T.E.) (1932)	*The Odyssey of Homer*, newly translated into English Prose. Oxford University Press, in *OBGVT*
Shelley, Percy Bysshe (1816)	*Alastor, or The Spirit of Solitude: And Other Poems, in OBCV*
Shelley, Percy Bysshe (wr. 1820, pbl. 1824)	*Posthumous Poems*, first published by Mrs Shelley, in *OBGVT*
Shelley, Percy Bysshe (wr. 1818, pbl. 1839)	*Poetical Works*, written 1818, published by Mrs Shelley, in *OBGVT*

Shelley, Percy Bysshe (wr. 1818, pbl. 1839)	*Posthumous Poems*, first published by Mrs Shelley, 2nd edn, in *OBGVT*
Shepherd, W.G. (1973)	in *GAPC*
Shewring, Walter (1980)	Homer, *The Odyssey*, Oxford, in *HEPC*
Shorey, Paul (1930)	Plato, *Republic*, Books I–V. Loeb vol. V
Shorey, Paul (1935)	Plato, *Republic*, Books VII–X. Loeb vol. VI
Shorey, Paul (1857–1934)	in Edith Hamilton, *The Greek Way*. Norton
Shuckburgh, Evelyn S. (1889)	Polybius, *Histories*. Macmillan
Silk, M.S. (2000)	*Aristophanes and the Definition of Comedy*. Oxford University Press
Simpson, John (1982)	co-editor of *The Concise Oxford Dictionary of Proverbs*. Oxford University Press, with Jennifer Speake
Simpson, R.S. (1996)	*Demotic Grammar in the Ptolemaic Sacerdotal Decrees*. Oxford, Griffith Institute
Sinclair, Andrew (1967)	*The Greek Anthology: The Wisdom and Wit of the Sons of Hellas*. New York: Macmillan
Smith, Charles Forster (1919)	Thucydides, Books I–II. Loeb vol. I
Smith, Charles Forster (1920)	Thucydides, Books III–IV. Loeb vol. II
Smith, Charles Forster (1921)	Thucydides, Books V–VI. Loeb vol. III
Smith, Charles Forster (1923)	Thucydides, Books VII–VIII. Loeb vol. IV
Smith, J.A. (1863–1939)	Aristotle, *On the Soul*, in *CWA*
Smith, Martin Ferguson (1993)	*Diogenes of Oinoanda: The Epicurean Inscription*. Naples: Bibliopolis
Smith, Wesley D. (1994)	Hippocrates. Loeb vol. VII
Smyth, Herbert Weir (1922)	Aeschylus. Loeb vol. I
Smyth, Herbert Weir (1926)	Aeschylus. Loeb vol. II
Solomon, J. (1984)	Aristotle, *Eudemian Ethics*, in *CWA*
Sommerstein, Alan H. (1973)	Aristophanes, *Lysistrata, Acharnians, Clouds*. Penguin Classics
Sommerstein, Alan H. (1978)	Aristophanes, *The Knights, Peace, Wealth* (*The Birds, Assembly-women* tr. David Barrett). Penguin Classics
Sommerstein, Alan H. (2002)	Aristophanes, *Lysistrata, Acharnians, Clouds*. Penguin Classics
Sommerstein, Alan H. (2008)	Aeschylus, *Oresteia*: *Agamemnon, Libation-Bearers, Eumenides*. Loeb vol. I
Sommerstein, Alan H. (2008)	Aeschylus, *Persians, Seven Against Thebes, Suppliants, Prometheus Bound*. Loeb vol. II
Sommerstein, Alan H. (2008)	Aeschylus, *Fragments*. Loeb vol. III

Sotheby, William (1834)	*The Odyssey of Homer*, London, in *HEPC*
Speake, Jennifer (1982)	co-editor of *The Concise Oxford Dictionary of Proverbs*. Oxford University Press, with John Simpson
Spelman, Edward (1776)	Xenophon, *The Expedition of Cyrus into Persia; and the Retreat of the Ten Thousand Greeks*. London
Staniforth, Maxwell (1964)	Marcus Aurelius, *Meditations*. Penguin Books
Stanley, Thomas (1665)	Claudius Aelianus, *His Various History*. London: Thomas Dring
Stephens, W.R.W. (1886)	St. Chrysostom: *Homilies on the Statutes, To the People of Antioch*. Oxford
Stocks, J.L. (1882–1937)	Aristotle, *On the Heavens*, in *CWA*
Stoneman, Richard (2008)	*Alexander the Great: A Life in Legend*. Yale University Press
Storey, Ian C. (2011)	*Fragments of Old Comedy*. Loeb vols I–III
Storr, F. (1912)	Sophocles. Loeb vol. I
Storr, F. (1913)	Sophocles. Loeb vol. II
Svarlien, Diane Arnson (1995)	in *GPHP*
Symonds, John Addington (1876)	*The Greek Poets*, 2nd series (1876), in *OBCV*
Talbot, John (2010?)	in *GPHP*
Taplin, Oliver (1978)	*Greek Tragedy in Action*. London: Methuen & Co Ltd
Taplin, Oliver (2015)	*Sophocles: Four Tragedies*. Oxford University Press
Taylor, Jennifer (1989)	*The Wine Quotation Book: A Literary Celebration*, ed. Jennifer Taylor. London: Robert Hale
Taylor, Thomas (1787)	*The Mystical Hymns of Orpheus*. London.
Tennyson, Alfred, Lord (1863–1864?, pr. 1969)	*The Poems of Tennyson*, ed. Christopher Ricks, London and Harlow
Tennyson, Alfred, Lord (1877)	*The Nineteenth Century*. Reprinted in *Ballads and other Poems*. London: Macmillan, in *OBCV*
Thomas, Ivor (1939)	*Greek Mathematical Works, From Thales to Euclid*. Loeb vol. I
Thompson, d'Arcy Wentworth (1860–1948)	*History of Animals*, in *CWA*
Thomson, J.A.K. (1953)	*The Ethics of Aristotle*. Penguin Classics
Todd, O.J. (1923)	Xenophon, *Symposium, Apology*. Loeb vol. IV
Todd, Stephen Charles (2000)	Lysias, from the series 'The Oratory of Classical Greece', ed. M. Gagarin. University of Texas Press
Toomer, G.J. (2003)	entry 'Archimedes' in *OCD*
Tredennick, Hugh (1933)	Aristotle, *Metaphysics*. Loeb vol. XVII
Tredennick, Hugh (1935)	Aristotle, *Metaphysics*. Loeb vol. XVIII
Trevelyan, R.C. (1919)	*The Ajax of Sophocles*. London: Allen & Unwin, in *PDQ* and *BFQ*
Trevelyan, R.C. (1947)	*A Translation of the Idylls of Theocritus*. Cambridge University Press, in *BFQ* and *PGR*

Trypanis, Constantine A. (1958)	Callimachus, *Aetia, Iambi, Hecale & Other Fragments*. Loeb
Trypanis, Constantine A. (1971)	*The Penguin Book of Greek Verse*. Penguin
Urmson, J.O. (1984)	revised Aristotle, *Nicomachean Ethics* by W.D. Ross, in *CWA*
van der Horst, P.W. (1978)	see Horst, P.W. van der
Van Hook, LaRue (1945)	Isocrates. Loeb vol. III
Vellacott, Philip (1953)	Euripides, *Alcestis, Hippolytus, Iphigenia in Tauris*. Penguin Classics
Vellacott, Philip (1960)	Menander, *Dyscolus, The Bad-Tempered Man* first published by Oxford University Press (in *Plays & Fragments*, Penguin Classics)
Vellacott, Philip (1961)	Aeschylus, *Prometheus, Suppliants, Seven Against Thebes, Persians*. Penguin Classics
Vellacott, Philip (1967)	Menander, *Plays & Fragments*. Penguin Classics
Vellacott, Philip (1972)	Euripides, *Children of Heracles, Andromache, Suppliant Women, Orestes, Iphigenia in Aulis*. Penguin Classics
Verity, Anthony (2002)	Theocritus, *Idylls*. Oxford World's Classics, Oxford University Press
Verity, Anthony (2007)	*Pindar, The Complete Odes*. Oxford World's Classics, Oxford University Press
Vince, C.A. (1926)	co-translator of Demosthenes, *Orations XVIII–XIX*. Loeb vol. II, with J.H. Vince
Vince, J.H. (1926)	co-translator of Demosthenes, *Orations XVIII–XIX*. Loeb vol. II, with C.A. Vince
Vince, J.H. (1930)	Demosthenes, *Orations I–XVII, XX*. Loeb vol. I
Vince, J.H. (1935)	Demosthenes, *Orations XXI–XXVI*. Loeb vol. III
Waller, Edmund (1606–1687)	Poem 'To a Lady singing a Song of his own Composing', footnote in Aeschylus, *Fragments*. Loeb vol. II
Warner, Rex (1944)	Euripides I, *Medea*, in *CGT*
Warner, Rex (1954)	Thucydides, *The Peloponnesian War*. Penguin Classics
Warner, Rex (1958)	*Life of Sulla* from Plutarch, *The Fall of the Roman Empire*. Penguin Classics
Warner, Rex (1966)	Xenophon, *A History of My Time*. Penguin Classics
Waterfield, Robin (1994)	Plato, *Gorgias*. Oxford World's Classics, Oxford University Press
Waterfield, Robin (1998)	Herodotus, *The Histories*. Oxford World's Classics, Oxford University Press
Waterfield, Robin (1998)	Plato, *Republic*. Oxford World's Classics, Oxford University Press
Waterfield, Robin (2000)	*The First Philosophers, The Presocratics and Sophists*. Oxford World's Classics, Oxford University Press
Waterfield, Robin (2003)	Euripides, *Heracles and Other Plays*. Oxford World's Classics, Oxford University Press

Watkin, E.I. (2005) — *An Introduction to Philosophy*, by Jacques Maritain, tr. E.I. Watkin. Rowman & Littlefield

Watling, E.F. (1953) — Sophocles, *Electra & Other Plays*. Penguin Classics

Watson, J.S. (1855) — co-translator of *The Cyropaedia, and The Hellenics*. Bohn's Classical Library, London: Henry G. Bohn, with Henry Dale

Watts, N.S. (1931) — Cicero, *Orations, Pro Milone, Pro Marcello et al.* Loeb vol. XIV

Way, A.S. (1912) — Euripides, *The Phoenician Maidens*. Loeb

West, M.L. (1988) — Hesiod, *Theogony and Works and Days*. Oxford World's Classics, Oxford University Press

West, M.L. (1994) — *Greek Lyric Poetry*. Oxford World's Classics, Oxford University Press

West, Martin L. (2003) — *Greek Epic Fragments*. Loeb

West, Stephanie Roberta (2003) — entry 'Hecataeus' in *OCD*

Wheelwright, C.A. (1864) — Pindar, in *HBM*

Whimster, D.C. (1934) — editor and translator of passages in Roger Ascham, *The Scholemaster (1568)*

White, Samuel (1878) — Plutarch, *Political Precepts*, in *PM*

Whitman, Cedric H. (1958) — co-translator of Musaeus, *Hero & Leander* (in the same volume as Callimachus, *Aetia*). Loeb, with Thomas Gelzer

Whitmarsh, Tim (2014) — 'Sappho: two previously unknown poems indubitably hers', article by Charlotte Higgins, theguardian.com, 29.01.2014

Wicksteed, Philip H. (1929) — co-translator of Aristotle, *Physics*. Loeb vols IV–V, with Francis Cornford

Williams, Jonathan (2004) — co-translator of *Classical Love Poetry*. The British Museum Press, with Clive Cheesman

Wilson, N.G. (1997) — Aelian, *Historical Miscellany*. Loeb

Winstedt, E.O. (1913) — Cicero, *Letters to Atticus*. Loeb vol. II

Withington, E.T. (1928) — Hippocrates. Loeb vol. III

Wolfe, Humbert (1927) — *Others Abide*. Ernest Benn Ltd, in *OBGVT*

Wood, Michael (2003) — *The Road to Delphi: The Life and Afterlife of Oracles*. London: Pimlico (first published by Chatto & Windus)

Woodruff, Paul (1989) — co-translator of Plato, *Symposium*. Hackett Publishing Company, and in *PCW*, with Alexander Nehamas

Woodruff, Paul (1995) — co-translator of Plato, *Phaedrus*. Hackett Publishing Company, with Alexander Nehamas

Wordsworth, Christopher (1836) — *Athens and Attica: Journal of a Residence There*. London: John Murray

Wright, Adrian (1947–) — in *GAPC*

Wright, Wilmer Cave (1922) — Philostratus, *The Lives of the Sophists*. Loeb

Wyckoff, Elizabeth (1954) — Sophocles I, *Antigone*, in *CGT*

Yalom, Irvin (2001) — speech on being awarded the 2000 Oscar Pfister Award, 6 May 2001

Yeats, William Butler (1928) — *Collected Poems*. Macmillan, in *OBVET*

Yatromanolakis, Dimitrios (2009)	'Ancient Greek Popular Song', in *CCGL*
Yeroulanos, Marinos	Μαρίνος Γερουλάνος
Yonge, Charles Duke (1854)	Athenaeus, *The Deipnosophists, or, Banquet of the Learned,* vol. II. London: Henry G. Bohn
Zeyl, Donald J. (1997)	Plato, *Timaeus,* first published in *PCW*

APPENDIX 4

USEFUL WEBSITES

For the Greek text

http://stephanus.tlg.uci.edu/
Thesaurus Linguae Graecae – A Digital Library of Greek Literature
Used for all Greek texts, references and word searches.

For translations and/or original Greek text

http://www.perseus.tufts.edu/hopper/
The Perseus Digital Library of Tufts University
A large collection of translations and in many cases the original Greek text.

https://archive.org/index.php
The Internet Archive
Digital copies of various books, used for finding alternative translations and for checking publishing dates of books that are no longer in print.

http://books.google.com/
Google Books
Used for finding alternative translations, checking publishing dates of books that are no longer in print, and specific references and spelling.

http://classics.mit.edu/
The Internet Classics Archive
Many translations of Greek texts.

http://www.ccel.org/
Christian Classics Ethereal Library
Used for translations of Christian texts such as those by Clement of Alexandria and St John Chrysostom.

http://ebooks.adelaide.edu.au/
ebooks@Adelaide of the University of Adelaide
Downloadable digital copies of translations for many out-of-print books; useful when searching for alternative translations as well as checking references, spelling and publishing dates.

http://www.gutenberg.org/wiki/Main_Page
Project Gutenberg
Downloadable digital copies of translations for many out-of-print books; useful when searching for alternative translations as well as checking references, spelling and publishing dates.

http://penelope.uchicago.edu/Thayer/E/Roman/home.html
Translations of Greek and Latin texts.

http://mythfolklore.net/aesopica/
Laura Gibbs's website, Aesopica: Aesop's Fables in English, Latin and Greek.
An invaluable resource for Aesop's fables with extremely helpful cross references to other fable versions.

www.thestoiclife.org/
The Stoic Life. A great resource for Musonius Rufus.

Inscriptions

http://epigraphy.packhum.org/inscriptions/main
Packard Humanities Institute
A record of all inscriptions with their references and texts (but no translations).

https://www.atticinscriptions.com/
Attic Inscriptions Online (AIO)
The inscriptions of ancient Athens and Attica in English translation with many useful notes.

APPENDIX 5

COPYRIGHT ACKNOWLEDGEMENTS

We are grateful for permission to include translations from the Loeb Classical Library, ® registered trademark of and copyright © by the President and Fellows of Harvard College. All Loeb volumes used are listed against each translator in Appendix 3: List of Translators.

Furthermore, we are grateful for permission to include translations under copyright by other publishers and authors. These are listed in alphabetical order of translator:

Leonidas of Tarentum, poem 189 in *The Greek Anthology and Other Ancient Greek Epigrams*, a selection in modern verse translations ed. with an introduction by Peter Jay (first publ. by Allen Lane 1973, rev. edn publ. by Penguin Books, 1981), copyright © Peter Jay, 1973, 1981, tr. Fleur Adcock, by permission of the translator. *The Homeric Hymns*, 2nd edn, tr. Apostolos N. Athanassakis, copyright © 1976, 2004 The Johns Hopkins University Press, pp.8, 27, by permission of Johns Hopkins University Press. Menander, *The Plays and Fragments*, tr. Maurice Balme, Oxford World's Classics (first publ. 2001, reissued 2008), p.28, by permission of Oxford University Press. *Classical Women Poets*, by Josephine Balmer (Bloodaxe Books, 1996); and *Sappho: Poems & Fragments*, by Josephine Balmer (Bloodaxe Books, 1992), by permission of Bloodaxe Books on behalf of the translator. *Sappho: A New Translation*, tr. Mary Barnard, copyright © 1958, by The Regents of the University of California, renewed 1986, by Mary Barnard, by permission of the University of California Press. 'Fragments', tr. Jonathan Barnes and Gavin Lawrence, in *The Complete Works of Aristotle*, The Revised Oxford Translation, ed. Jonathan Barnes, 1984, Bollingen Series LXXI: 1 & 2, Princeton University Press, copyright © 1984 by The Jowett Copyright Trustees, by permission of Princeton University Press. *Early Greek Philosophy*, tr. and ed. with an introduction by Jonathan Barnes (Penguin Classics, 1987), copyright © Jonathan Barnes, 1987, pp.68, 82, 98, 102–104, 109, 111, 113, 119, 125–126, 131, 137, 149, 153, 166, 174, 182, 190–191, 200–201, 228, 232, 252, 256–257, 265, 267–269, 270–272, 274, 276–277, 279, 281, 283, 285–288, by permission of Penguin Books Ltd. *The Presocratic Philosophers*, by Jonathan Barnes (Routledge, 1979, rev. 1982), copyright © Jonathan Barnes, 1979, 1982, by permission of Taylor & Francis Books UK. *Greek Lyric Poetry*, tr. Willis Barnstone (Bantam Books Inc., 1962), by permission of the translator. Aristophanes, *The Wasps, The Poet and The Women, The Frogs*, tr. with an introduction by David Barrett (Penguin Classics, 1964), copyright © David Barrett, 1964, pp.107, 182–183, 211; and Aristophanes, *The Birds and Other Plays*, tr. David Barrett and Alan H. Sommerstein (Penguin Books, 1978, repr. with a Select Bibliography 2003) copyright © David Barrett and Alan H. Sommerstein, 1978, pp.159, 165, 170, 191, 229, by permission of Penguin Books Ltd. 'On Sense and the Sensible', tr. J.I. Beare, in *The Complete Works of Aristotle*, The Revised Oxford Translation, ed. Jonathan Barnes, 1984, Bollingen Series LXXI: 1 & 2, Princeton University Press, copyright © 1984 by The Jowett Copyright Trustees, by permission of Princeton University Press. Sophocles, *Oedipus the King*, tr. Stephen Berg and Diskin Clay (Oxford University Press, 1988), pp.28, 37, 40, 49, 50, by permission of Oxford University Press. *Greek Anthology*, an epigram of Leonidas of

Tarentum, in *The Poems of Leonidas of Tarentum*, tr. Edwyn Bevan (The Clarendon Press, 1931), by permission of Oxford University Press. *The New English Bible* (no translator indicated), copyright © Cambridge University Press and Oxford University Press, 1961, 1970, by permission of Cambridge University Press. *The Greek Experience*, by C.M. Bowra (Weidenfeld & Nicholson, 1957), copyright © by C.M. Bowra, by permission of The Orion Publishing Group, London. Erinna, 'A Distaff', p.522, tr. C.M. Bowra, in *The Oxford Book of Greek Verse in Translation*, ed. T.F. Higham and C.M. Bowra (Oxford University Press, 1938), by permission of Oxford University Press. *The Odes of Pindar*, tr. with an introduction by C.M. Bowra (Penguin Classics, 1969), copyright © The Estate of C.M. Bowra, 1969, pp.72, 99, 158, 175, 217, by permission of Penguin Books Ltd. *The Cynics: The Cynic Movement in Antiquity and Its Legacy*, ed. R. Bracht Branham and Marie-Odile Goulet-Cazé, copyright © 1996 by The Regents of the University of California, by permission of the University of California Press. 'Poetics', tr. Ingram Bywater, in *The Complete Works of Aristotle*, The Revised Oxford Translation, ed. Jonathan Barnes, 1984, Bollingen Series LXXI: 1 & 2, Princeton University Press, copyright © 1984 by The Jowett Copyright Trustees, by permission of Princeton University Press. *The Homeric Hymns*, tr. Jules Cashford with an introduction and notes by Nicholas Richardson (Penguin Books, 2003), tr. copyright © Jules Cashford, 2003, introduction and notes copyright © Nicholas Richardson, 2003, by permission of David Higham Associates Ltd on behalf of the translator. 'The Letter of Aristeas' in *The Apocrypha and Pseudepigrapha of the Old Testament in English*, vol. 2, by R.H. Charles (Oxford University Press, 1913), p.117, by permission of Oxford University Press. *Readings in Ancient Greek Philosophy from Thales to Aristotle*, ed. S. Marc Cohen, Patricia Curd and C.D.C. Reeve, 3rd edn, copyright © 2005 by Hackett Publishing Company, Inc., by permission of Hackett Publishing Company, Inc. Aeschylus, *Persians and Other Plays*, tr. Christopher Collard (Oxford World's Classics, 2009), pp.24, 50, 102, 104, 115, by permission of Oxford University Press. Euripides, *Selected Fragmentary Plays*, vol. I, with Translations and Commentaries by C. Collard, M.J. Cropp and K.H. Lee (Aris & Phillips Ltd, 1997); and Euripides, *Selected Fragmentary Plays*, vol. II, with Translations and Commentaries by C. Collard, M.J. Cropp and J. Gibert (Aris & Phillips Classical Texts, 2004), by permission of Oxbow books. *Herakleitos and Diogenes*, tr. Guy Davenport (Greyfox Press), republished in *7 Greeks*, tr. Guy Davenport, copyright ©1995 by Guy Davenport, by permission of New Directions Publishing Corp. Euripides, *Heracles and Other Plays*, tr. John Davie, with an introduction by Richard Rutherford (Penguin Classics, 2002), tr. copyright © John Davie, 2002, introduction and notes copyright © Richard Rutherford 2002, pp.65, 113, 133, 170, by permission of Penguin Books Ltd. 'Polybius', by Peter Sidney Derow, in *The Oxford Classical Dictionary*, ed. Simon Hornblower and Antony Spawforth (Oxford University Press, 3rd rev. edn, 2003), p.1210, by permission of Oxford University Press. Herodotus, *The Histories*, tr. Aubrey de Sélincourt, rev. with introductory matter and notes by John Marincola (Penguin Classics, 1954; 2nd rev. edn, 1996), tr. copyright © 1954 by Aubrey de Sélincourt, rev. edn copyright © John Marincola, 1996, p.483, by permission of Penguin Books Ltd. *Classical Literary Criticism*, by T.S. Dorsch and Penelope Murray with an introduction and notes by Penelope Murray (Penguin Books, 1965, 2000, 2004), original tr. copyright © by T.S. Dorsch, 1965, introduction, rev. translations, new material and notes copyright © by Penelope Murray, 2000, 2004, pp.120, by permission of Penguin Books Ltd. *Adages III iv 1–IV ii 100: Collected Works of Erasmus*, tr. Denis L. Drysdall, ed. John N. Grant (University of Toronto Press, 2005), by permission of University of Toronto Press. Aeschylus, *The Oresteia*, tr. Robert Fagles, copyright © 1966, 1967, 1975, 1977 by Robert Fagles, pp.125, 134, 137, 140, 155, 198, 244, 265, 269, by permission of Viking Penguin, a division of Penguin Group (USA) LLC and Georges Borchardt, Inc., on behalf of Robert Fagles; Homer, *The Odyssey*, tr. Robert Fagles, copyright © 1996 by Robert Fagles, pp.77, 84, 107, 174, 209, 210, 212, 223, 224, 381, 401, 402, 408, 411, 459; and Sophocles, *The Three Theban Plays*, tr. Robert Fagles, copyright © 1982 by Robert Fagles, pp.66, 77, 79, 88, 94, 96, 110, 114, 123, 163, 176, 216, 322, 358, 359, by permission of Viking Penguin, a division of Penguin Group (USA) LLC. Excerpt from 'Ladies Day', in *Aristophanes: Four Comedies*, tr. Dudley Fitts, copyright © by Houghton Mifflin Harcourt Publishing Company, 1954, copyright © renewed by Cornelia Fitts, Daniel H. Fitts and Deborah W. Fitts, 1982, by permission of Houghton Mifflin Harcourt Publishing Company; excerpts from *The Alcestis of Euripides*, an English Version by Dudley Fitts and Robert Fitzgerald, copyright © by Houghton Mifflin Harcourt Publishing Company, 1936, copyright © renewed by Dudley Fitts and Robert Fitzgerald, 1964; and excerpts from 'Antigone', 'Oedpius Rex', and 'Oedipus at Colonus', in Sophocles, *The Oedipus Cycle*, an English Version by Dudley Fitts and Robert Fitzgerald, copyright © by Houghton Mifflin Harcourt Publishing Company, 1939, copyright © renewed by Dudley Fitts and Robert Fitzgerald, 1967, by permissions of Houghton Mifflin Harcourt Publishing Company. Homer, *The Odyssey*, tr. Robert Fitzgerald, copyright © 1961, 1963 by Robert Fitzgerald, copyright renewed 1989 by Benedict R.C. Fitzgerald, on behalf of the Fitzgerald children, by permission of Farrar, Straus and Giroux, LLC. 'Problems', tr. E.S. Forster, in *The Complete Works of Aristotle*, The Revised Oxford Translation, ed. Jonathan Barnes, 1984, Bollingen Series LXXI: 1 & 2, Princeton University Press, copyright © 1984 by The Jowett Copyright Trustees, by permission of Princeton University Press. *The Works of Lucian of Samosata*, vol. II, tr. H.W. Fowler and F.G. Fowler (The Clarendon Press, 1905), by permission of Oxford University Press. *Anselm of Canterbury and his Theological Inheritance*, by Giles E.M. Gasper (Ashgate Publishing, 2004), by permission of Ashgate Publishing. *Aesop's Fables*, tr. Laura Gibbs (Oxford World's Classics, 2002), pp.29, 54, 78, 98, 196, 201, 222, 228, 253, by permission of Oxford University Press. Sophocles, *Selected Poems: Odes and Fragments*, tr. Reginald Gibbons, copyright © 2008 by Princeton University Press, by permission of Princeton University Press. 'Greek lyric and early Greek literary history', by Barbara Graziosi and Johannes Haubold, in *The Cambridge Companion to Greek Lyric*, ed. Felix Budelmann (2009), by permission of Cambridge University Press. 'Hippolytus', tr. David Grene, in Euripides I, *Four Tragedies*, ed. David Grene and Richmond Lattimore, The Complete Greek Tragedies, copyright © 1955 by The University of Chicago; Sophocles I, *Three Tragedies: Oedipus the King, Oedipus at Colonus, Antigone*, tr. David Grene, ed. David Grene and Richmond Lattimore, The Complete Greek Tragedies, 2nd edn, copyright © 1991 by The University of Chicago; and 'Electra' and 'Philoctetes', tr. David Grene, in Sophocles II, *Four Tragedies*, ed. David Grene and Richmond Lattimore, The Complete Greek Tragedies, copyright © 1957, 1969 by The University of Chicago, by permission of Chicago University Press. 'Phaedo' and 'Republic', tr. G.M.A. Grube ('Republic', rev. C.D.C. Reeve), in *Plato, Complete Works*, ed. with introduction and notes by John M. Cooper, associate ed. D.S. Hutchinson, copyright © 1977 by Hackett Publishing Company, Inc., by permission of Hackett Publishing Company, Inc. An epigram of Asclepiades, tr. Rachel Hadas, *in The Greek Poets, Homer to the Present*, ed. Peter Constantine, Rachel Hadas, Edmund Keeley and Karen Van Dyck (W.W. Norton & Company, 2010), by permission of the translator. Thucydides, *The Peloponnesian War*, tr. Martin Hammond (Oxford World's Classics, 2009), pp.41, 146, 164, 218, by permission of Oxford University Press. 'Physics', tr. R.P. Hardie and R.K. Gaye, in *The Complete Works of Aristotle*, The Revised Oxford Translation, ed. Jonathan Barnes, 1984, Bollingen Series LXXI: 1 & 2, Princeton University Press, copyright © 1984 by The Jowett Copyright Trustees, by permission of Princeton University Press. Anoymous, 'A Mountain Glen', p.615, Callimachus, 'The Battle of the Books', p.587, Rufinus, 'Her only Flaw', p.661, tr. T.F. Higham, in *The Oxford Book of Greek Verse in Translation*, ed. T.F. Higham and C.M. Bowra (Oxford University Press, 1938), by permission of Oxford University Press. 'Some Advantages of the Letter', by Owen Hodkinson, in *Ancient Letters, Classical & Late Antique Epistolography*, ed. Ruth Morello and A.D. Morrison (Oxford University Press, 2007), pp.289, 299, by permission of Oxford University Press. Herodotus, *The Histories*, tr. Tom Holland, copyright © 2013 by Tom Holland, pp.205, 454–455, 482, 612, by permission of Viking Penguin, a division of Penguin Group (USA) LLC and Penguin Books Ltd. *The Sentences of Pseudo-Phocylides*, by P.W. van der Horst (Leiden: E.J. Brill, 1978), by permission of Koninklijke Brill. Aeschylus, *The Oresteia*, tr. Ted Hughes (Faber and Faber Ltd, 1999), p.99, by permission of Faber and Faber Ltd and Farrar, Strauss, Giroux. 'Alcibiades II' and 'Definitions', tr. D.S. Hutchinson, in *Plato, Complete Works*, ed. with introduction and notes by John M. Cooper, associate ed. D.S. Hutchinson, copyright © 1977 by Hackett Publishing Company, Inc., by permission of Hackett Publishing Company, Inc. 'Women of Trachis', tr. Michael Jameson, in Sophocles II, *Four Tragedies*, ed. David Grene and Richmond Lattimore, The Complete Greek Tragedies, copyright © 1957, 1969 by The University of Chicago, by permission of Chicago University Press. Simonides, 'For the Athenian Dead at Plataia', p.40, Callimachus, p.89 and 'On Himself', p.92, tr. Peter Jay, *The Greek Anthology and*

Other Ancient Epigrams, a selection in modern verse translations ed. with an introduction by Peter Jay (first publ. by Allen Lane 1973, rev. edn publ. by Penguin Books, 1981), copyright © Peter Jay, 1973, 1981, by permission of Penguin Books Ltd. 'On Generation and Corruption', tr. H.H. Joachim, in *The Complete Works of Aristotle*, The Revised Oxford Translation, ed. Jonathan Barnes, 1984, Bollingen Series LXXI: 1 & 2, Princeton University Press, copyright © 1984 by The Jowett Copyright Trustees, by permission of Princeton University Press. *Sappho*, by Marguerite Johnson, Ancients in Action Series (Bristol Classical Press, an imprint of Bloomsbury Publishing plc, 2007), copyright © 2007 by Marguerite Johnson, by permission of Bloomsbury Publishing plc. Euripides, *Bacchae* (e-text), tr. Ian Johnston, Malaspina University-College, Nanaimo, by permission of the translator. 'Politics', tr. Benjamin Jowett, in *The Complete Works of Aristotle*, The Revised Oxford Translation, ed. Jonathan Barnes, 1984, Bollingen Series LXXI: 1 & 2, Princeton University Press, copyright © 1984 by The Jowett Copyright Trustees, by permission of Princeton University Press. Thucydides, *History of the Peloponnesian War*, tr. Benjamin Jowett (The Clarendon Press, 1900), books 2.43.3, 2.44.4, 3.45.7, 4.40.2, 4.55.2, 5.102.1, 6.41.2, 8.66.2, by permission of Oxford University Press. Several excerpts, tr. Edmund Keeley, in *The Greek Poets, Homer to the Present*, ed. Peter Constantine, Rachel Hadas, Edmund Keeley and Karen Van Dyck (W.W. Norton & Company, 2010), by permission of the translator. *Posidonius: The Translation of the Fragments*, ed. I.G. Kidd, vol. 3 (1999), by permission of Cambridge University Press. *The Greeks*, by H.D.F. Kitto (Pelican Books, 1951, 1957; Penguin Books, 1991), copyright © 1951, 1957 by H.D.F. Kitto, p.174, by permission of Penguin Books Ltd. 'Oedipus the King' lines 729–730, in Sophocles, *Three Tragedies*, tr. H.D.F. Kitto (Oxford University Press, 1962), by permission of Oxford University Press. *Woman's Songs in Ancient Greece*, by Anne L. Klinck (McGill-Queen's University Press, 2008), pp.77, 87, 91, 93, 97, 99, 127, by permission of McGill-Queen's University Press. 'Alciphron's Epistolarity', by Jason König, in *Ancient Letters, Classical & Late Antique Epistolography*, ed. Ruth Morello and A.D. Morrison (Oxford University Press, 2007), pp.273, 275, 277, by permission of Oxford University Press. *Ancient Greece and the Modern Manager: An Anthology of Quotations*, by Panos Koronakis-Rohlf and Maria Batzini (Kalendis, 2000), by permission of Kalendis Publishing. *Eros, From Hesiod's Theogony To Late Antiquity*, Exhibition Catalogue, tr. into English by Angeliki Kosmopoulou, ed. Nicholas Chr. Stampolidis and Yorgos Tassoulas, copyright © Museum of Cycladic Art, 2009, pp.55–56, by permission of The Museum of Cycladic Art. *Travelling Heroes: Greeks and their Myths in The Epic Age* by Robin Lane Fox (Penguin Books, 2008), copyright © Robin Lane Fox 2008, p.217, by permission of Penguin Books Ltd and Random House (USA) LLC. 'Agamemnon', tr. Richmond Lattimore, in Aeschylus I, *Oresteia*, ed. David Greene and Richmond Lattimore, The Complete Greek Tragedies, copyright © 1953 by The University of Chicago; *Greek Lyrics*, tr. Richmond Lattimore (first publ. 1955, 2nd edn 1960), copyright © 1949, 1955 and 1960 by Richmond Lattimore; and *The Odes of Pindar*, tr. Richmond Lattimore, 2nd edn, copyright © 1947, 1976 by The University of Chicago, by permission of Chicago University Press. Hesiod, *Works and Days*, tr. Richmond Lattimore (Ann Arbor: University of Michigan Press, 1991), by permission of the University of Michigan Press. *The Odyssey of Homer*, tr. T.E. Lawrence (Oxford University Press, 1932, 1991), lines 17.291, 17.300, by permission of Oxford University Press, USA. Plato, *The Republic*, tr. with an introduction by Desmond Lee (Penguin Classics, 1955; 4th rev. edn, 2002), copyright © H.D.P. Lee, 1953, 1974, 1987, 2002, pp.5, 6, 26, 29, 44, 47, 70, 83, 165, 176, 204, 260, 269, 270, 286, 298, 300, 348, 359–360; and Plato, *Timaeus and Critias*, tr. with an introduction and appendix on 'Atlantis' by Desmond Lee (Penguin Classics, 1965; 2nd rev. edn 1977), copyright © H.D.P. Lee, 1965, 1971, 1977, p.42, by permission of Penguin Books Ltd. 'Theaetetus' (rev. Myles Burnyeat), tr. M.J. Levett, in *Plato, Complete Works*, ed. with introduction and notes by John M. Cooper, associate ed. D.S. Hutchinson, copyright © 1977 by Hackett Publishing Company, Inc., by permission of Hackett Publishing Company, Inc. Thucydides, *The History of the Peloponnesian War*, tr. Sir Richard Livingston (Oxford University Press, 1968), line 1.1.1, by permission of Oxford University Press, USA. *Athens: A Cultural and Literary History*, by Michael Llewellyn-Smith (Signal Books, 2004), copyright © Michael Llewellyn-Smith, 2004, by permission of the author and Signal Books Ltd. *Hesiod, Works and Days, The Theogony*, tr. Stanley Lombardo with an introduction, notes and glossary by Robert Lamberton, copyright © 1993 by Hackett Publishing Company, Inc., by permission of Hackett

Publishing Company, Inc. 'Protagoras', tr. Stanley Lombardo and Karen Bell, in *Plato, Complete Works,* ed. with introduction and notes by John M. Cooper, associate ed. D.S. Hutchinson, copyright © 1977 by Hackett Publishing Company, Inc., by permission of Hackett Publishing Company, Inc. *Callimachus: Hymns, Epigrams, Select Fragments,* tr. with an introduction and notes by Stanley Lombardo and Diane Rayor, copyright © 1988 The Johns Hopkins University Press, pp.xv, 5, 6, 40, 49, 55, 57, by permission of Johns Hopkins University Press. Homer, *The Iliad: Translated in Selection,* by F.L. Lucas (The Folio Society, 1950), by permission of The Folio Society. Diophanes of Myrina, poem 729 in *The Greek Anthology and Other Ancient Greek Epigrams,* a selection in modern verse translations ed. with an introduction by Peter Jay (first publ. by Allen Lane 1973; rev. edn publ. by Penguin Books, 1981), copyright © Peter Jay, 1973, 1981, tr. Edward Lucie-Smith, Book 5 Epigram 309 in *The Well-Wishers,* copyright © Edward Lucie-Smith 1981, reproduced by permission of the author, c/o Rogers, Coleridge & White Ltd. *Saint Gregory Nazianzen: Selected Poems,* translated with an introduction by John McGuckin (Oxford: SLG Press, 1986), FP094, © Sisters of the Love of God, by permission of SLG Press. *A Presocratics Reader,* by Richard D. McKirahan, ed. with an introduction by Patricia Curd, copyright © 1995, 1996 by Hackett Publishing Company, Inc., quoted in *Readings in Ancient Greek Philosophy from Thales to Aristotle,* by permission of Hackett Publishing Company, Inc. *An Introduction to Philosophy,* by Jacques Maritain, tr. from French into English by E.I. Watkin, A Sheed & Ward Book (Rowman & Littlefield Publishers, 2005), by permission of Rowman & Littlefield Publishers, Inc. Archias 'A Tomb by the Sea' rev. from *Translations from the Greek Anthology,* tr. William Sinclair Marris, privately printed at the Bharat Bandhu Press (1919); and Archias 'Echo' and Rufinus 'Grey Hair', tr. William Sinclair Marris, in *The Oxford Book of Greek Verse in Translation,* ed. T.F. Higham and C.M. Bowra (Oxford University Press, 1938), by permission of Oxford University Press. Philodemus, poem 332 in *The Greek Anthology and Other Ancient Greek Epigrams,* a selection in modern verse translations ed. with an introduction by Peter Jay (first publ. by Allen Lane 1973; rev. edn publ. by Penguin Books, 1981), copyright © Peter Jay, 1973, 1981, tr. William Moebius, by permission of the translator. *Collected Translations,* by Edwin Morgan (Carcanet Press, 1996), by permission of Carcanet Press Ltd. Euripides, *The Trojan Women and Other Plays,* tr. James Morwood (Oxford World's Classics, first publ. 2001; reissued 2008), pp.39, 56, 88, by permission of Oxford University Press. Sophocles, *Women of Trachis* 112, tr. William Mullen, *in The Greek Poets, Homer to the Present,* ed. Peter Constantine, Rachel Hadas, Edmund Keeley and Karen Van Dyck (W.W. Norton & Company, 2010), by permission of the translator. *The Medea of Euripides,* tr. Gilbert Murray (Oxford University Press, 1906), lines 248, 384, by permission of Oxford University Press. Plato, *Symposium,* tr. with an introduction and notes by Alexander Nehamas and Paul Woodruff, copyright © 1989 by Alexander Nehamas and Paul Woodruff; and Plato, *Phaedrus,* tr. with an introduction and notes by Alexander Nehamas and Paul Woodruff, copyright © 1995 by Alexander Nehamas and Paul Woodruff, by permission of Hackett Publishing Company, Inc. 'Parts of Animals', tr. William Ogle, in *The Complete Works of Aristotle,* The Revised Oxford Translation, ed. Jonathan Barnes, 1984, Bollingen Series LXXI: 1 & 2, Princeton University Press, copyright © 1984 by The Jowett Copyright Trustees, by permission of Princeton University Press. *Sappho & Alcaeus: an Introduction to the Study of Ancient Lesbian Poetry,* by Denys Page (The Clarendon Press, first publ. 1955; repr. 1975), pp.132, 312, by permission of Oxford University Press. Sophocles, *Philoctetes,* tr. Carl Phillips (Oxford University Press, 2003), p.60, by permission of Oxford University Press, USA. 'Generation of Animals', tr. Arthur Platt, in *The Complete Works of Aristotle,* The Revised Oxford Translation, ed. Jonathan Barnes, 1984, Bollingen Series LXXI: 1 & 2, Princeton University Press, copyright © 1984 by The Jowett Copyright Trustees, by permission of Princeton University Press. Aeschylus, *The Persians,* tr. Anthony J. Podlecki (Bristol Classical Press, an imprint of Bloomsbury Publishing plc, first publ. 1970; rev. edn 1991), copyright © 1991 by Anthony J. Podlecki, by permission of Bloomsbury Publishing plc. *The World of Parmenides: Essays on the Presocratic Enlightenment,* by Karl Popper, ed. Arne F. Petersen with the assistance of Jørgen Mejer (Routledge, first publ. 1998; repr., 2002), © 1998, 2001 The Estate of Karl Popper, by permission of Manfred Lube on behalf of the University of Klagenfurt/Karl Popper Library, with the consent of Arne F. Petersen. 'Canto I', *A Draft of XXX Cantos,* by Ezra Pound (Faber and Faber Ltd, 1933), by permission of

(1973 edn), pp.50, 79, 117 (2002 edn), by permission of the translator. Marcus Aurelius, *Meditations,* tr. with an introduction by Maxwell Staniforth (Penguin Classics, 1964), copyright © Maxwell Staniforth, 1964, entries 4.3, 9.21, by permission of Penguin Books Ltd. 'On the Heavens', tr. J.L. Stocks, in *The Complete Works of Aristotle,* The Revised Oxford Translation, ed. Jonathan Barnes, 1984, Bollingen Series LXXI: 1 & 2, Princeton University Press, copyright © 1984 by The Jowett Copyright Trustees, by permission of Princeton University Press. *Alexander the Great, A Life in Legend,* by Richard Stoneman (Yale University Press, 2010) copyright © 2008 Richard Stoneman, by permission of Yale University Press. An epigram of Semonides, tr. Diane Arnson Svarlien, *in The Greek Poets, Homer to the Present,* ed. Peter Constantine, Rachel Hadas, Edmund Keeley and Karen Van Dyck (W.W. Norton & Company, 2010), by permission of the translator. Theocritus, Idyll 15, tr. John Talbot, *in The Greek Poets, Homer to the Present,* ed. Peter Constantine, Rachel Hadas, Edmund Keeley and Karen Van Dyck (W.W. Norton & Company, 2010), by permission of the translator. *Greek Tragedy in Action,* by Oliver Taplin (Methuen & Co Ltd, 1978), copyright © 1978 Oliver Taplin, by permission of the author. *Sophocles, Four Tragedies: Oedipus the King; Aias; Philoctetes; Oedipus at Colonus,* a new verse translation by Oliver Taplin (Oxford University Press, 2015), copyright © 2015 Oliver Taplin, lines: Oedipus the King 999, 1230, 1486, 1522, Aias 522, 581, 964, 1125, 1253, 1266, 1366, Philoctetes 1, 135, 691, Oedipus at Colonus 607, 1211, by permission of the author and Oxford University Press. *The Wine Quotation Book: A Literary Celebration,* ed. Jennifer Taylor (Robert Hale Ltd, 1989), by permission of Robert Hale Ltd. 'History of Animals', tr. D'Arcy Wentworth Thompson, in *The Complete Works of Aristotle,* The Revised Oxford Translation, ed. Jonathan Barnes, 1984, Bollingen Series LXXI: 1 & 2, Princeton University Press, copyright © 1984 by The Jowett Copyright Trustees, by permission of Princeton University Press. *The Ethics of Aristotle,* tr. J.A.K. Thomson, rev. with notes and appendices by Hugh Tredennick, introduction and bibliography by Jonathan Barnes (Penguin Classics, 1955; rev. edn 1976), tr. copyright © 1953 by J.A.K. Thomson, rev. tr. copyright © Hugh Tredennick, 1976, introduction and bibliography copyright © Jonathan Barnes, 1976, pp.91, 101, 129, 199, 215, 220, 223, 257, 299, 304, 317–318, 320, by permission of Penguin Books Ltd. *Lysias,* tr. S.C. Todd, from the series 'The Oratory of Classical Greece', ed. M. Gagarin, copyright © 2000 by the University of Texas Press, by permission of the University of Texas Press. 'Archimedes', by G.J. Toomer, in *The Oxford Classical Dictionary,* ed. Simon Hornblower & Antony Spawforth (Oxford University Press, 3rd rev. edn 2003), p.146, by permission of Oxford University Press. *A Translation of the Idylls of Theocritus,* ed. and tr. R.C. Trevelyan (first publ. 1947, first paperback edn 2014), by permission of Cambridge University Press. *The Penguin Book of Greek Verse* introduced and ed. Constantine A. Trypanis (Penguin Books, first publ. 1971; repr. 1979), copyright © Constantine A. Trypanis, 1971, by permission of Marilena Trypanis. Aeschylus, *Prometheus Bound and Other Plays,* tr. with an introduction by Philip Vellacott (Penguin Books, first publ. 1961; repr. 1970), copyright © Philip Vellacott, 1961, pp.20–22, 24–25, 28–29, 32, 34–35, 37, 41–47, 49–50, 52, 60, 65, 67–68, 85, 89, 124, 126, 128–129, 134, 139, 141, 143; Euripides, *Orestes and Other Plays,* tr. Philip Vellacott (Penguin Books, 1972), copyright © Philip Vellacott, 1972, pp.108, 112, 124, 128, 133–134, 151–152, 160, 203–204, 207–209, 227, 242–243, 248–254, 261, 271, 286–287, 301, 308, 311, 313, 317, 321, 323–324, 342, 379, 382–383, 386–387, 401–402, 419; Euripides, *Three Plays: Alcestis; Hippolytus; Iphigenia In Tauris,* tr. Philip Vellacott (Penguin Books, 1953; reissued 1974), copyright © Philip Vellacott, 1953, 1974, pp.53–56, 64, 66, 77, 88–90, 96–99, 104, 111, 143, 165; and Menander, *Plays and Fragments,* Theophrastus, *The Characters,* tr. Phillip Vellacott (Penguin Classics, 1967), copyright © The Estate of Phillip Vellacott, 1967, pp.209, 241, 246, by permission of Penguin Books Ltd. and The Society of Authors as the Literary Representative of the Estate of Philip Vellacott. Menander, *The Bad-Tempered Man,* tr. Philip Vellacott (Oxford University Press, 1960), lines 6–8, 62–63, by permission of Oxford University Press. Pindar, *The Complete Odes,* tr. Anthony Verity (Oxford World's Classics, 2007), pp.23–24, 39, 44, 51, 64, 67, 77, 82, 84, 102, 110, 136; and Theocritus, *Idylls,* tr. Anthony Verity (Oxford World's Classics, 2003), pp.1, 26, 28, 33, 35, 44, by permission of Oxford University Press. 'The Medea', tr. Rex Warner, in Euripides I, *Four Tragedies* (first publ. 1944, repr. 1946 by John Lane), ed. David Grene and Richmond Lattimore, The Complete Greek Tragedies, copyright © 1955 by The University of Chicago, by permission of Chicago University Press. Plutarch, *The Fall of the Roman Republic,* tr. Rex Warner, rev. Robin Seager (Penguin Classics, 1958, 1972, 2005), copyright © Rex Warner, 1958, notes copyright © Robin Seager, 1972, corrections to text, preface and comparisons copyright © Robin Seager, 2005, Penguin Plutarch copyright © Christopher Pelling, 2005, p.75; Thucydides, *The History Of The Peloponnesian War*, tr. Rex Warner, with an introduction and notes by M.I. Finley (Penguin Classics, 1954; rev. edn 1972), tr. copyright © Rex Warner, 1954, introduction and appendices copyright © M.I. Finley, 1972, extracts from books 1, 2, 5, 6; and Xenophon, *A History Of My Times*, tr. Rex Warner, introduction and notes George Cawkwell, 1979 (Penguin Classics, 1966, repr. edn 1978), tr. copyright © Rex Warner, 1966, introduction and notes copyright © George Cawkwell, 1979, pp.56, 403, by permission of Penguin Books Ltd. Euripides, *Heracles and Other Plays*, tr. Robin Waterfield (Oxford World's Classics, 2003), p.33; Herodotus, *The Histories*, tr. Robin Waterfield (Oxford World's Classics, first publ. 1998; reissued 2008), pp.15–16, 26, 39–40, 73, 165, 288, 322, 356, 426, 457, 517, 529, 570; Plato, *Gorgias*, tr. Robin Waterfield (Oxford World's Classics, first publ. 1994; reissued 2008), p.30; Plato, *Republic*, tr. Robin Waterfield (Oxford World's Classics, 1998), p.201; and *The First Philosophers, The Presocratics and Sophists*, tr. Robin Waterfield (Oxford World's Classics, 2000), p.18, by permission of Oxford University Press. Sophocles, *Electra and other Plays*, tr. E.F. Watling (Penguin Classics, 1953), copyright © E.F. Watling, 1953, pp.21, 23, 31, 41, 55, 71, 74–75, 80, 87, 99, 101, 108, 111, 120, 123, 128, 135, 137, 139–140, 150, 164, 166, 170–171, 178–179, 186–187, 190, 195, 201–202, 204, by permission of Penguin Books Ltd. *Greek Lyric Poetry*, tr. M.L. West (Oxford World's Classics, 2008), pp.27, 45, 63, 69, 75, 136, 145, 170; and Hesiod, *Theogony and Works and Days*, tr. M.L. West (Oxford World's Classics, 2008), pp.10, 47, 58, by permission of Oxford University Press. 'Hecataeus', by Stephanie Roberta West, in *The Oxford Classical Dictionary*, ed. Simon Hornblower a Antony Spawforth (Oxford University Press, 3rd rev. edn 2003), p.671, by permission of Oxford University Press. Two new Sappho poems, tr. Tim Whitmarsh, in 'Sappho: two previously unknown poems indubitably hers' (theguardian.com, 29.01.2014), by Charlotte Higgins, by permission of the translator. *Classical Love Poetry*, by Jonathan Williams and Clive Cheesman (The British Museum Press, 2004), by permission of The British Museum Press. *The Road to Delphi: The Life and Afterlife of Oracles*, by Michael Wood (Chatto and Windus, 2003), by permission of The Random House Group Ltd. 'Antigone', tr. Elizabeth Wyckoff, in Sophocles I, *Three Tragedies*, ed. David Grene and Richmond Lattimore, The Complete Greek Tragedies, 2nd edn, copyright © 1991 by The University of Chicago, by permission of Chicago University Press. *The Yale Book of Quotations*, ed. Fred R. Shapiro with a foreword by Joseph Epstein (Yale University Press, 2006), copyright © 2006 Fred R. Shapiro, foreword copyright © 2006 Joseph Epstein, by permission of Yale University Press. *Carmina Convivialia* extract from 'Ancient Greek Popular Song', by Dimitrios Yatromanolakis, in *The Cambridge Companion to Greek Lyric*, ed. Felix Budelmann (2009), by permission of the translator. 'Timaeus', tr. Donald J. Zeyl, in *Plato, Complete Works*, ed. with introduction and notes by John M. Cooper, associate ed. D.S. Hutchinson, copyright © 1977 by Hackett Publishing Company, Inc., by permission of Hackett Publishing Company, Inc.

Every effort has been made to trace and contact all copyright holders. We will be glad to make good any omissions brought to our attention.

APPENDIX 6

MAPS

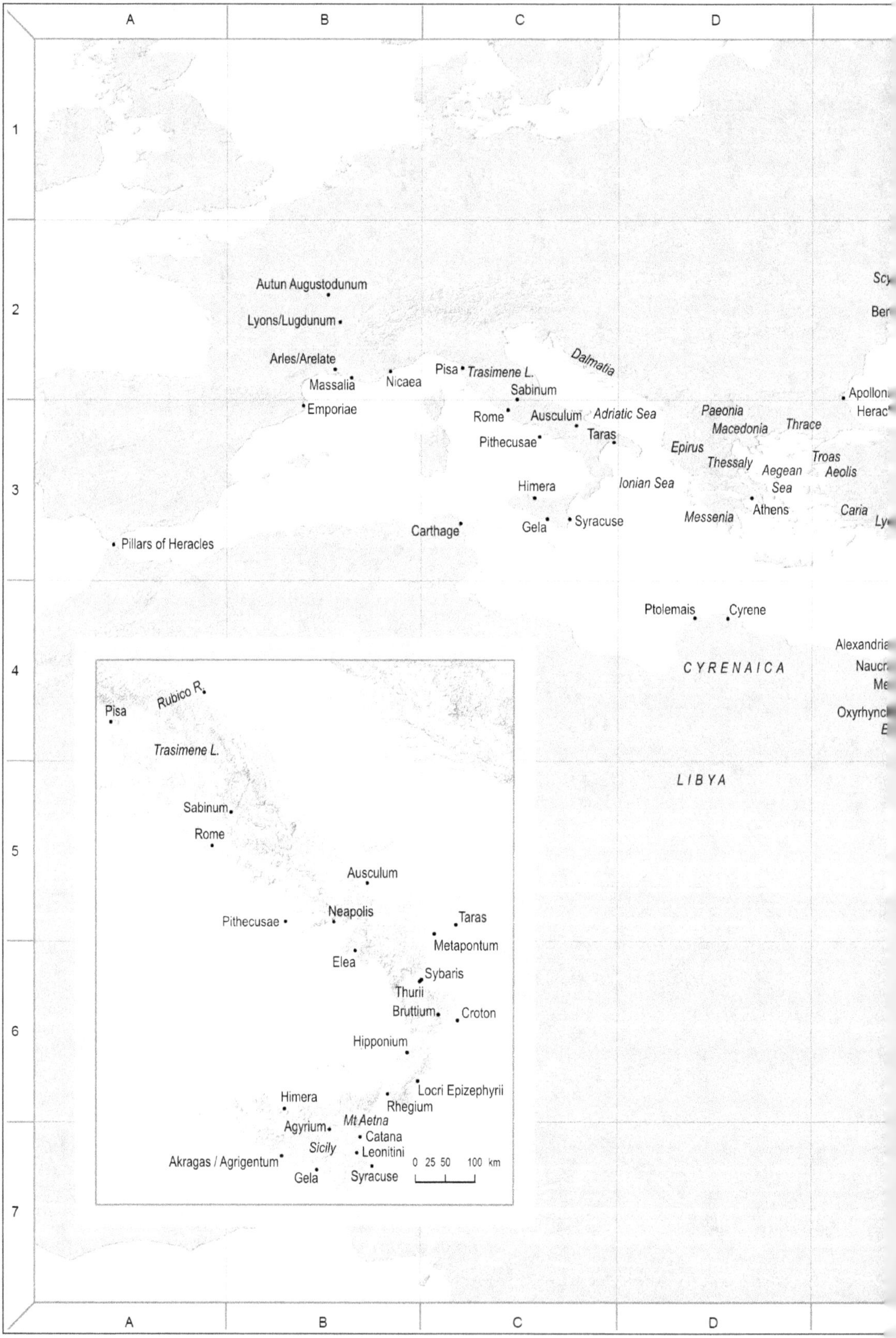

A B C D

1
2
3
4
5
6
7

Autun Augustodunum
Lyons/Lugdunum
Arles/Arelate
Massalia
Nicaea
Pisa
Trasimene L.
Dalmatia
Sabinum
Emporiae
Rome
Ausculum
Adriatic Sea
Paeonia
Macedonia
Thrace
Pithecusae
Taras
Epirus
Thessaly
Troas
Aegean Sea
Aeolis
Himera
Ionian Sea
Athens
Messenia
Caria
Carthage
Gela
Syracuse
Pillars of Heracles
Scy
Ber
Apollon
Herac
Ly
Ptolemais
Cyrene
Alexandria
CYRENAICA
Naucr
Me
Oxyrhync
E
LIBYA

Pisa
Rubico R.
Trasimene L.
Sabinum
Rome
Ausculum
Pithecusae
Neapolis
Taras
Metapontum
Elea
Sybaris
Thurii
Bruttium
Croton
Hipponium
Locri Epizephyrii
Himera
Rhegium
Mt Aetna
Agyrium
Catana
Sicily
Leonitini
Akragas / Agrigentum
Gela
Syracuse
0 25 50 100 km

A B C D

F G H I

1 2 3 4 5 6 7

Olbia
Borysthenes R.
Tauri
Pontus
Caucasus
Sinope
Parthia
Paphlagonia
Alexandria Eschate
Galatia
Caesarea
Oxus R.
Nazianzus
Tyana
Samosata
Ai Khanoum
Soli/Soloi
Antioch
Orontes R.
Chalcis in Coele
Gaugamela
Tamassos
Apamea
Bactria
Ecbatana
Sidon
Tyre
Damascus
Tigris R.
Galilee
SYRIA
Caesarea
Gadara
Babylon
Susa
PERSIA
Judaea
Euphrates R.
Indus R.
INDIA
Thebes
Erythrean Sea
Meroe
Indian Ocean
ETHIOPIA
N
0 250 500 1.000 km

F G H I

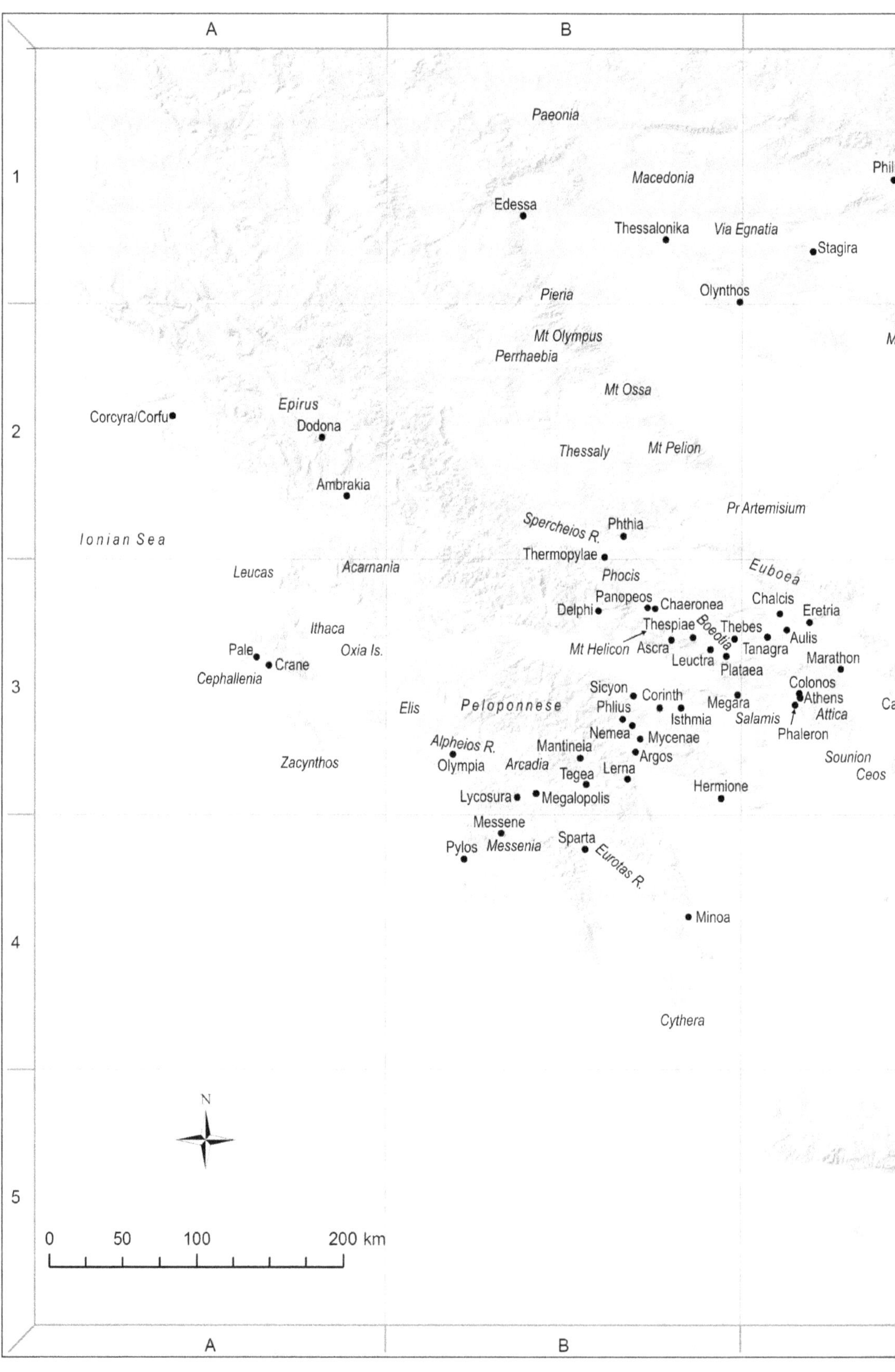
A
B
1
2
3
4
5
Paeonia
Macedonia
Philip
Edessa
Thessalonika
Via Egnatia
Stagira
Olynthos
Pieria
Mt Olympus
Perrhaebia
Mt
Mt Ossa
Epirus
Corcyra/Corfu
Dodona
Thessaly
Mt Pelion
Ambrakia
Pr Artemisium
Spercheios R.
Phthia
Ionian Sea
Thermopylae
Leucas
Acarnania
Phocis
Euboea
Panopeos
Chaeronea
Chalcis
Delphi
Eretria
Thespiae
Boeotia
Thebes
Ithaca
Aulis
Pale
Mt Helicon
Ascra
Tanagra
Oxia Is.
Leuctra
Marathon
Crane
Plataea
Cephallenia
Colonos
Sicyon
Corinth
Athens
Elis
Peloponnese
Phlius
Megara
Isthmia
Salamis
Attica
Ca
Nemea
Mycenae
Phaleron
Alpheios R.
Mantineia
Argos
Sounion
Zacynthos
Olympia
Arcadia
Ceos
Tegea
Lerna
Hermione
Lycosura
Megalopolis
Messene
Sparta
Pylos
Messenia
Eurotas R.
Minoa
Cythera
N
0
50
100
200 km

D E

Black Sea
(Pontus Euxinus)
Bosporus
Constantinople / Byzantium
Chalcedon
Thrace
Via Egnatia
Perinthus
Abdera
1
Nicaea in Bythinia
Hellespont
Lampsacos
Cyzicus
Prusa
Abydos
Troy/Ilion
Troas
Scamender R.
Myrina
Lemnos
Tenedos
ASIA MINOR
Assos
2
Maeonia
Pergamon
Eresos
Mytilene
Elaea in Aeolis
Lydia
Scyros
Lesbos
Pitane
Aeolis
Myrina
Sardis
Clazomenae
Ionia
Aegean Sea
Chios
Smyrna
Phrygia
Teos
Colophon
3
Andros
Ephesus
Hierapolis
Samos
Magnesia
Laodicea
Colossae
Priene
Syros
Miletus
Caria
Delos
Cyclades
os
Leros
Myndos
Halicarnassus
Paros
Calymnos
Oenoanda
Amorgos
Cos/Kos
Cnidos
Pholegandros
4
Rhodos
Lycia
Camirus
Lindos
Crete
Gortyna
5

D E

INDEX OF NAMES AND PLACES

This index includes authors and also people and places mentioned within quotations, comments and maps.
The provenance of quotations are not indexed (e.g. Plato *Gorgias* is not entered under 'Gorgias'), except in specific cases.
All references are to page numbers, not entry numbers.
Numbers in **bold** refer to the full entry of the author in question.
Numbers in *italics* are references to plays (e.g. Agamemnon, *5–7*, a play by Aeschylus).
A semicolon separates page numbers of Quotations, Quotations on Greece and Greeks, and Maps. A semicolon also separates cross-references from page references.
Special categories of entries (Inscriptions, Oracles, Proverbs etc.) are appended to the index.

Special categories (*see also* relevant entries in Keyword Index)

KEYWORD INDEX

Life – Death

see also Dead – Living, Death, Life, Live – Living etc.

Naught – Nought

Near – Far

Necessary

Necessity

Need(s)

Neglect

www.ingramcontent.com/pod-product-compliance
Lightning Source LLC
Chambersburg PA
CBHW081128300726
48982CB00005B/892

* 9 7 8 1 7 8 4 5 3 4 9 2 9 *